POMEROY'S

EQUITY JURISPRUDENCE

AND

EQUITABLE REMEDIES

SIX VOLUMES.

POMEROY'S

EQUITY JURISPRUDENCE,

IN FOUR VOLUMES.

BY JOHN NORTON POMEROY, LL.D.

THIRD EDITION, ANNOTATED AND MUCH ENLARGED,

AND SUPPLEMENTED BY

A TREATISE ON EQUITABLE REMEDIES,

IN TWO VOLUMES

BY JOHN NORTON POMEROY, JR.

SAN FRANCISCO:
BANCROFT-WHITNEY COMPANY,
LAW PUBLISHERS AND LAW BOOKSELLERS.
1905.

A TREATISE

ON

EQUITABLE REMEDIES;

SUPPLEMENTARY TO

POMEROY'S EQUITY JURISPRUDENCE.

(INTERPLEADER, RECEIVERS; INJUNCTIONS; REFORMATION AND CANCELLATION, PARTITION; QUIETING TITLE; SPECIFIC PERFORMANCE; CREDITORS' SUITS; SUBROGATION; ACCOUNTING; ETC.)

BY

JOHN NORTON POMEROY, JR., A.M., LL.B.

IN TWO VOLUMES.

VOLUME ONE.

SAN FRANCISCO

BANCROFT-WHITNEY COMPANY,

LAW PUBLISHERS AND LAW BOOKSELLERS.

1905.

SAN FRANCISCO
THE FILMER BROTHERS ELECTROTYPE COMPANY,
TYPOGRAPHERS AND STEREOTYPERS.

TO THE MEMORY OF

MY FATHER.

PREFACE.

The present treatise is the outgrowth of a desire to annotate the brief Part Fourth of Pomeroy's Equity Jurisprudence in a way that should secure to the important topics therein contained a treatment as ample as is accorded, in that work, to other parts of Equity. It was my father's purpose—prevented by his untimely death—to supplement his work by the addition of one or more volumes on Equitable Remedies. In choosing the present form of carrying out this design, rather than that of extensive annotation of a brief text, I have had in mind, solely, the consideration of the reader's convenience. It is hardly necessary to state. that no pretension is made to those high qualities, both of style and of original thought, which have given to my father's book its important place in our legal literature. My point of view has been that of the annotator. Thus, I have used to a rather unusual degree, at some sacrifice of brevity, the exact language of the courts, rather than my own; and have retained nearly all the language of my father's brief text pertinent to the subjects treated. All the authorities cited in his Part Fourth have been re-examined; but, as is appropriate to the newness of many of the subjects, the great bulk of the citations is made up of very recent cases.

In the arrangement of the chapters, the order of chapters and sections of the older book has been followed, with but few variations. The paragraphs relating to the division of the equitable remedies into logical groups have been brought together, in the introductory chapter; I have also attempted, in that chapter, to present some of the more striking results of the great mass of confused and conflicting *dicta* on the subject of Laches. The two remedies of Receivers and Injunctions have allotted to them more than half the space at my command, as is due to the vast importance which they have assumed in very recent years. In the chapters on Receivers, the grounds of the receiver's appointment, and the general principles relating to his possession, etc., have been treated with some fullness; while only an outline is attempted of the more technical matters concerning his duties in the management of the estate. In the chapters on Injunctions it has been the constant aim to discriminate between questions of the propriety of the equitable remedy, and questions of substantive or primary rights,—an effort, at times, by no means easy; indeed, as many of these substantive rights are, in practice, secured by the remedy of injunction only, and are comparatively novel as subjects for judicial discussion, it has sometimes been found necessary to examine and state them at considerable length; see, *e. g.,* Chapter XXVIII, as to injunctions in labor controversies.

The freshness of most of the material relied upon has prevented much assistance from existing text-books; indeed, the collection of this material has been an enormous labor, involving the study of at least twice the number of cases finally selected for citation. I am greatly indebted to my assistant, Mr. E. S. Page, of Oakland, Cal., without whose help the task of surveying so wide a field would have been impossible.

In conclusion, I cannot refrain, as a student of modern Equity, from adding my testimony of admiration to the great ability of many of our contemporary American judges in dealing with the momentous and novel questions which form much of the subject-matter of these volumes. That nearly sixty independent jurisdictions, largely within the life of one generation, should have built up a legal structure so sound, so original, and, in the main, so harmonious in all its parts, as that of our distinctively American Equity, is surely one of the greatest achievements in all legal history. The author may be pardoned if he here repeats the conviction, that his father's labors, and the true spirit of equity and liberality with which they were animated, have become a chief source of inspiration to the builders of this splendid structure.

J. N. P., JR.

SAN FRANCISCO, September, 1905.

TABLE OF CONTENTS.

CONTENTS OF VOLUME I.

CHAPTER I.

INTRODUCTION.

ANALYSIS.

I.

II.

III.

CHAPTER II.

INTERPLEADER.

ANALYSIS.

CHAPTER III.

APPOINTMENT OF RECEIVERS.

ANALYSIS.

CHAPTER IV.

THE RECEIVER'S POSSESSION; AND CONFLICTING APPOINTMENTS.

ANALYSIS.

CHAPTER V.

ACTIONS AGAINST THE RECEIVER.

ANALYSIS.

CHAPTER VI.

SUITS BY THE RECEIVER.

ANALYSIS.

CHAPTER VII.

RECEIVER'S RELATION TO PENDING SUITS; AND WHEN IS HE A NECESSARY PARTY.

ANALYSIS.

CHAPTER VIII.

RECEIVERS—MANAGEMENT AND DISPOSITION OF PROPERTY.

ANALYSIS.

CHAPTER IX.

RECEIVERS; CLAIMS AND ALLOWANCES.

ANALYSIS.

CHAPTER X.

REMOVAL AND DISCHARGE OF RECEIVERS.

ANALYSIS.

CHAPTER XI.

FOREIGN RECEIVERS; ANCILLARY RECEIVERS.

ANALYSIS.

CHAPTER XII.

INJUNCTIONS; GENERAL PRINCIPLES—INJUNCTION TO PROTECT EQUITABLE ESTATES AND INTERESTS.

ANALYSIS.

CHAPTER XIII.

INJUNCTIONS TO PREVENT THE VIOLATION OF CONTRACTS.

ANALYSIS.

CHAPTER XIV.

INJUNCTIONS AGAINST CORPORATIONS AND THEIR OFFICERS.

ANALYSIS.

CHAPTER XV.

INJUNCTIONS RELATING TO VOLUNTARY ASSOCIATIONS AND NON-STOCK CORPORATIONS.

ANALYSIS.

CHAPTER XVI.

INJUNCTIONS BETWEEN MORTGAGOR AND MORTGAGEE.

ANALYSIS.

CHAPTER XVII.

INJUNCTIONS AGAINST PUBLIC OFFICERS.

ANALYSIS.

CHAPTER XVIII.

INJUNCTIONS AGAINST MUNICIPAL CORPORATIONS AND THEIR OFFICERS.

ANALYSIS.

CHAPTER XIX.

INJUNCTION AGAINST TAXATION; AND AGAINST SPECIAL OR LOCAL ASSESSMENTS.

ANALYSIS.

CHAPTER XX.

INJUNCTION AGAINST EXERCISE OF THE POWER OF EMINENT DOMAIN.

ANALYSIS.

CHAPTER XXI.

INJUNCTIONS TO PREVENT OR RESTRAIN THE COMMISSION OF TORTS IN GENERAL: TO RESTRAIN CRIMINAL ACTS.

ANALYSIS.

CHAPTER XXII.

INJUNCTION AGAINST WASTE.

ANALYSIS.

CHAPTER XXIII.

INJUNCTIONS AGAINST TRESPASS.

ANALYSIS.

CHAPTER XXIV.

INJUNCTION AGAINST NUISANCE.

ANALYSIS.

A TREATISE

ON

EQUITABLE REMEDIES.

EQUITABLE REMEDIES

CHAPTER I.

INTRODUCTION.

ANALYSIS.

I.

§§ 1–11. Classification and definitions of equitable remedies.
§ 2. (1) First group: Ancillary and provisional remedies.
§ 3. (2) Second group: Preventive remedies.
§ 4. (3) Third group: Reformation and cancellation.
§§ 5–8. (4) Fourth group: Remedies by which estates, interests, and primary rights, either legal or equitable, are directly declared, established or recovered, or the enjoyment thereof fully restored.
§ 6. Fourth group: First class.
§ 7. Fourth group: Second class.
§ 8. Fourth group: Third class.
§ 9. (5) Fifth group. Remedies by which equitable obligations are specifically and directly enforced.
§ 10. (6) Sixth group: Remedies in which the final relief is pecuniary, but is obtained by the enforcement of a lien or charge upon some specific property or fund.
§ 11. (7) Seventh group: Remedies in which the final relief is wholly pecuniary, and is obtained in the form of a general pecuniary recovery.

II.

§ 12. Equitable remedies acted *in personam*.
§ 13. Same—Modern legislation—Decree may transfer title—Abstract of statutes.

I.

§ 1. Classification and Definitions of Equitable Remedies. It is the chief purpose of this introductory chapter to treat, somewhat briefly, of the maxim, "Equity acts *in personam,*" and of the effect of decrees in equity; and to present the more important results of the recent cases on the doctrine of Laches. Other general principles and maxims which affect the whole range of equitable remedies have either been sufficiently treated in the work to which the present volumes are a supplement, or may be more appropriately taken up in their application to the individual remedies. But before taking up these matters, the author conceives that it may serve the convenience of many readers to collect and compare Professor Pomeroy's classification and definitions of the various equitable remedies, as set forth in Part IV of his work, with the several tentative classifications of the same subject-matter made in the earlier chapters of that work.[1]

§ 2. **(1) First Group: Ancillary and Provisional Remedies.**—"The first class embraces those remedies which are wholly ancillary and provisional." "The distinguishing characteristic of the remedies belonging to this group is, that they determine no primary rights, and grant no final reliefs, either directly or indirectly. They are, in fact, instruments and means by which the court is enabled more conveniently and perfectly to adjudicate upon the *ultimate* rights and interests of the parties, and to award the *final* reliefs, in the further judicial proceedings to which they are auxiliary, and of which they are really the preliminary stage." This class includes interpleader and receivers.[2]

§ 3. **(2) Second Group: Preventive Remedies.**—"Preventive remedies, or those by which a violation of a primary right is prevented before the threatened injury is done, or by which the further violation is prevented after the injury has been partially effected, so that some other relief for the wrong actually accomplished can be granted. The ordinary injunction, whether final or pre-

1 Pom. Eq. Jur., §§ 110, 112, 171, 185-189.

2 Pom. Eq. Jur., §§ 171, 1316, 1319. Section 171 includes in this group, also, "the ordinary preventive injunction."

liminary, is the familiar example of this class; the mandatory injunction is essentially a restorative remedy."[3]

§ 4. (3) **Third Group: Reformation and Cancellation.**—"The ultimate object of the remedies belonging to this group is the establishment or protection of interests, estates, and primary rights; but this object is accomplished *indirectly*. While these remedies are not so completely ancillary as interpleader and receivership, yet they are to a certain extent auxiliary. They do not, like a specific performance, or the execution of a trust, or an assignment of dower, or partition of land, operate directly and immediately to establish the plaintiff's title, and to confer upon him the complete dominion over his estate—the ultimate relief which he seeks. Their effect in establishing his ultimate dominion is indirect. They are often used as the preparatory step which enables him to obtain, sometimes in the same action, and sometimes in a subsequent suit, the ultimate remedy which finally establishes his rights or obligations, or restores him to the full enjoyment of his estate. The reformation of a policy of insurance is not a final remedy; but it establishes the real contract, and thus enables the assured to recover the amount actually due according to the terms of that contract. The reformation of a deed does not directly restore the grantee to the dominion and possession of the land which had been omitted; but it places him in a position which enables him, if necessary, to assert his dominion and recover the possession. The cancellation of a deed does not of itself *directly* establish the plaintiff's title and put him in possession of the land, but it enables him, if necessary, to assert his title and obtain the possession. These remedies may be obtained on behalf of either a legal or

3 Pom. Eq. Jur., §§ 112, 1316.

an equitable interest, by either a legal or an equitable owner. The remedies constituting this group are the two following: Reformation or re-execution of instruments, and rescission, cancellation, surrender up, or discharge of instruments."[4]

§ 5. (4) Fourth Group: Remedies by Which Estates, Interests, and Primary Rights, Either Legal or Equitable, are Directly Declared, Established, or Recovered, or the Enjoyment Thereof Fully Restored.—"All the remedies belonging to

[4] 4 Pom. Eq. Jur., § 1375. To the same effect, 1 Pom. Eq. Jur., § 171 ("second class"), 4 Pom. Eq. Jur., § 1316. The classification, Ibid, § 112, contains these definitions: "5. *Remedies of Reformation, Correction, or Re-execution,* by means of which a written instrument, contract, deed, or other muniment of title, which for some reason does not conform to the actual rights and duties of the parties thereto, is reformed, corrected, or re-executed. Sometimes this remedy is asked for and obtained simply on its own account, merely for purpose of correcting the instrument; but it is often, and perhaps generally, obtained as a necessary step to the granting of a further and more substantial relief needed by the plaintiff, such as a restoration to full rights of property, or the specific performance of the contract after it has been corrected. 6. *Remedies of Rescission or Cancellation,* or those by which an instrument, contract, deed, judgment, and even sometimes a legal relation itself subsisting between two parties, is, for some cause, set aside, avoided, rescinded, or annulled. This remedy, like the preceding, is sometimes conferred as the sole and final relief needed by the plaintiff, but is often the preliminary step to a more effective remedy by which his primary right is declared or restored." In Professor Pomeroy's arrangement of equitable remedies in *three* classes (Pom. Eq. Jur., § 110), viz., "those which are entirely different from any kind of reliefs known and granted by the law" (*e. g.,* injunction, reformation, specific performance, etc.), "those which are substantially the same both in equity and at the law" (*e. g.,* partition of land, admeasurement of dower, accounting, etc.), and "those which the legal procedure recognizes, but does not *directly* confer, and the beneficial results of which it obtains in an indirect manner," the remedy of rescission or cancellation is given as typical of this last class, and the distinction pointed out between this equitable relief and the analogous legal method, an action for the recovery of chattels, land or damages,

this group have one most important distinctive feature in common, which is apparent upon even a slight examination. In all of them the estate or interest of the complaining party, whether it be legal or equitable, is *directly* established or recovered, or the enjoyment thereof is *directly* restored. These remedies are not, therefore, provisional or auxiliary, but they are, for the purposes of the complaining party, as truly final or ultimate reliefs as is the judgment in an action of ejectment or of replevin.[5] The estate, interest, or primary right to be established or recovered, or fully enjoyed by their means, may be either legal or equitable; and when it is equitable, the establishment may consist in cloth-

based on the assumption of a rescission by the act of a party to the contract or conveyance; for further explanation and illustration of this distinction, and observations on the frequent confusion as to the requisites of legal and of equitable rescission, see *post*, chapter on Cancellation.

5 4 Pom. Eq. Jur., § 1378. "This is manifestly so in 'assignment of dower,' 'settlement of disputed boundaries,' and 'partition of land,' since in each of these instances the plaintiff establishes his individual right to and obtains sole possession of a specific tract of land, and in 'partition of personal property,' he procures the same with respect to specific chattels. The statement is no less true of the other suits included within this group. In a suit to construe a will, estates in specific property are directly established; in suits to quiet title, the very object of the judgment is to declare and establish the plaintiff's legal or equitable estate in some specific property, and perhaps to convert his equitable estate into a legal one. Even in suits to remove a cloud from title, although the relief is often obtained by means of a cancellation, yet, from the nature of the whole proceeding, the plaintiff's estate is thereby established, and he is left in its full enjoyment. In strict foreclosures of mortgages or pledges, and in redemptions of mortgages or pledges, the plaintiff plainly establishes his estate in, and secures his possession of, the specific land or chattels, free from any claim of the defendant. However much these remedies may differ in appearance, they all have this same *essential* element which brings them within the same group": Pom. Eq. Jur., § 1378, note.

ing the plaintiff with the legal estate.[6] The remedies composing this group are separated, by a natural line of division, into *three* general classes, namely: 1. Suits by which purely legal estates are established, and the enjoyment thereof recovered; 2. Suits by which some

6 "As in some statutory suits to quiet title, and some suits to remove a cloud from title": Pom. Eq. Jur., § 1378, and note.

This group corresponds, in the main, with classes "1. *Declarative Remedies,*" and "2. *Restorative Remedies,*" of Pom. Eq. Jur., § 112, and with the "third class" of Pom. Eq. Jur., § 171 (which, however, is made to embrace remedies of *specific performance* also); compare the following description in § 171: "3. The third class embraces those remedies by which a primary right of property, estate, or interest is *directly* declared, established, acquired, or enforced; and they often consist in the conveyance by defendant of a *legal* estate, corresponding to the complainant's equitable title. These remedies deal directly with the plaintiff's right of property, and grant to him the *final* relief which he needs, by establishing and enforcing such right. The particular remedies properly belonging to this class may assume an almost unlimited variety of forms, since form depends upon and corresponds to the nature of the primary right to be established, and of the subject-matter over which that right extends; it is chiefly in its relation with this class that the peculiarly *elastic* quality of the equity remedial system is found. The remedies belonging to this class may, for purposes of clearer description, be again subdivided into three principal groups. Some are simply *declarative,* that is, their main and direct object is to declare, confirm, and establish the right, title, interest, or estate of the plaintiff, whether legal or equitable; they are usually granted in combination with others, and often need other kinds of relief as a preliminary step to making them efficient; as, for example, a preliminary reformation, re-execution, or cancellation. Others are *restorative,* or those by which the plaintiff is restored to the full enjoyment of the right, interest, or estate to which he is entitled, but the use and enjoyment of which has been hindered, interfered with, prevented, or withheld by the wrong-doer. These also are often granted in combination with other kinds of relief, and frequently need some other preliminary equitable remedy, such as cancellation or reformation, to remove a legal obstacle to the full enjoyment of the plaintiff's right, and to render them efficient in restoring him to that enjoyment. Others are remedies of *specific performance,*" etc., enumerating examples of remedies belonging to this class.

general right, either legal or equitable, is established; and 3. Suits by which some particular estate or interest, either legal or equitable, is established."[7]

§ 6. **Fourth Group: First Class.**—"Since the particular cases belonging to this class are primarily adapted to purely legal interests, the common law gives similar relief by means of appropriate legal actions. The jurisdiction of equity was based wholly upon the superiority of the equitable methods and procedure; and while the equitable jurisdiction in cases of dower and partition has become so established that it has almost displaced the legal remedies, that of settling disputed boundaries still requires the presence of some special equitable incident or circumstance."[8] These remedies all belong to the "concurrent jurisdiction," in the strict definition of that term.

§ 7. **Fourth Group: Second Class.**—"In all the remedies belonging to this class, some *general* right, which may be either legal or equitable, is declared and established. The class includes suits to establish a will, suits to construe a will, and the bills of peace and bills *quia timet* for the purpose of quieting title, which belong to the original general jurisdiction of equity." "Some of the

7 Pom. Eq Jur, § 1378.

8 Pom. Eq. Jur., § 1379. See, also, § 185, relating to the "ordinary and well-settled instances" of the "concurrent" jurisdiction: "1. Under the first of these classes, where the final relief is substantially a recovery or obtaining possession of specific portions of land, the concurrent jurisdiction is clearly established, and its exercise is a matter of ordinary occurrence, in suits for the partition of land among joint owners or owners in common; in suits for the assignment or admeasurement of dower; and in suits for the adjustment of disputed boundaries, where some equitable incident or feature is involved, and the dispute is not wholly confined to an assertion of mere conflicting legal titles or possessory rights."

remedies of this class undoubtedly depend upon what the early chancellors called the 'jurisdiction *quia timet.*' Since the conception of a *quia timet* jurisdiction is so broad, and runs through so many different branches of the remedial jurisprudence, I have not adopted it as a basis of classification. The object of suits to establish and to construe wills is plainly the establishment of a general right; and the same is no less true of those suits to quiet title, bills of peace, and the like, which belong to the original jurisdiction of equity."[9]

§ 8. **Fourth Group: Third Class.**—"In all the instances of this class, as distinguished from those of the preceding one, the direct object of the remedy is to declare and establish some particular estate, interest, or right, either legal or equitable, in the property which is the subject-matter. The class as a whole embraces suits for the strict foreclosure of a mortgage or a pledge, suits for the redemption of a mortgage, suits for the redemption of a pledge, statutory suits to quiet title, and suits to remove a cloud from title." "Some of these remedies, also, have been said to depend upon the *quia timet* jurisdiction."[10]

§ 9. **(5) Fifth Group: Remedies by Which Equitable Obligations are Specifically and Directly Enforced.**—"The remedies embraced in this group are all purely equitable, and the rights of the complainant and obligations of the defendant which are enforced by their means are also equitable.[11] They belong, therefore, to the exclusive

9 Pom. Eq. Jur., § 1393, and note. For suits to construe a will, see 3 Pom. Eq. Jur., §§ 1155-1157; for suits to establish a will, see 3 Pom. Eq. Jur., § 1158.

10 Pom. Eq. Jur., § 1395, and note.

11 "Although contracts may also give rise to a legal right, yet when equity compels their specific performance, it enforces the

jurisdiction of equity. Their distinctive object is to specifically enforce the complainant's equitable right, and to compel the defendant to specifically perform the actual equitable obligation which rests upon him. This group, as a whole, contains the specific performance of contracts, including the performance of verbal contracts for the sale of land which have been part performed, and the delivery up of specific chattels; the specific enforcement of trusts, express and implied; and the specific enforcement of obligations arising from fiduciary relations analogous to trusts,"[12] the last-named class including the important sub-classes, "suits against administrators or executors, and suits against corporations and their managing officers."[13] The broad scope of this class of remedies, perhaps the most characteristic of the whole equity system, is thus described in another place: "4. *Remedies of Specific Performance,* or those by which the party violating his primary duty is compelled to do the very acts which his duty and the plaintiff's primary right[14] require from him. The remedies of this class are very numerous in their special forms and in respect to the juridical relations in which they are applicable. 'Specific performance' is often spoken of as though it was confined to the case of executory contracts; but in reality it is constantly employed in

equitable obligation arising from them, and not the legal duty. In most cases, it turns the vendee's equitable *estate* into a legal one". Pom. Eq Jur., § 1400, note.

12 Pom. Eq. Jur, § 1400. As to suits for the delivery of specific chattels, written instruments, etc. (an instance of the "concurrent" jurisdiction), see 1 Pom. Eq. Jur., § 185.

13 Pom. Eq. Jur., § 1411.

14 For definitions of the terms "primary right" and "remedial right," see 1 Pom. Eq. Jur., §§ 90, 91. The remedial right, or right to a remedy, is that which arises on the breach of a "primary" or (as it is perhaps more frequently and familiarly called) "substantive" right.

the enforcement of rights and duties arising from relations between specific persons which do not result from contracts, as, for example, between *cestuis que trustent* and their trustees, wards and their guardians, legatees, distributees, or creditors and executors or administrators, and the like. In these latter cases, however, as well as in that of the specific performance of an executory contract at the suit of a vendor, the form and nature of the final relief is often the same as that of accounting, pecuniary compensation, or restoration."[15]

§ 10. (6) **Sixth Group: Remedies in Which the Final Relief is Pecuniary, but is Obtained by the Enforcement of a Lien or Charge upon Some Specific Property or Fund.**—"The title of this group plainly indicates the nature and object of the remedies composing it. They are all purely equitable, and therefore belong to the exclusive jurisdiction; because, although the *final* relief is pecuniary, and so resembles the ordinary relief at law, it is obtained through preliminary proceedings, forming a part of the judgment, which belong solely to the procedure and jurisdiction of equity."[16] This group is elsewhere described as follows: "Those remedies which establish and enforce liens and charges *on* property, rather than rights and interests *in* property, either by means of a judicial sale of the property itself which is affected by the lien and a distribution of its proceeds, or by means of a sequestration of the property, and an appropriation of its rents, profits, and income, until they satisfy the claim secured by the lien."[17] "Those cases in which the relief is not a *general* pecuniary judgment, but is a decree of money to be obtained and paid out of some

15 1 Pom. Eq. Jur., § 112.

16 4 Pom. Eq. Jur., § 1413.

17 1 Pom. Eq. Jur., § 171.

particular fund or funds. The equitable remedies of this species are many in number and various in their external forms and incidents. They assume that the creditor has, either by operation of law, or from contract, or from some acts or omissions of the debtor, a lien, charge, or encumbrance upon some fund or funds belonging to the latter, either land, chattels, things in action, or even money; and the *form* of the remedy requires that this lien or charge should be established, and then enforced, and the amount due obtained by a sale total or partial of the fund, or by a sequestration of its rents, profits, and proceeds. These preliminary steps may, on a casual view, be misleading as to the nature of the remedy, and may cause it to appear to be something more than compensatory; but a closer view shows that all these steps are merely auxiliary, and that the *real* remedy, the final object of the proceeding, is the pecuniary recovery. . . . . There is also another species of pecuniary remedies, closely analogous to the last, and differing from it only in the additional element of a distribution of the final pecuniary awards among two or more parties having claims either upon one common fund or upon several funds. The final relief in all these cases is simply pecuniary; the amounts to which the different parties are entitled are ascertained, and are obtained by a distribution of the fund or funds upon which they are chargeable."[18] "The group contains the following species of remedies: Suits for the foreclosure by judicial sale of mortgages of real property; suits for the similar foreclosure of mortgages of

[18] 1 Pom. Eq. Jur., § 112. "Of this species are suits to wind up partnerships and distribute partnership assets; to settle and distribute the personal estate of decedents; to marshal assets; and the statutory proceeding to wind up the affairs of insolvent corporations": Id. Probably some of these last-named remedies are preferably classed in the next group.

personal property; suits for the similar foreclosure of pledges; suits to enforce the various equitable liens; suits to enforce the equitable contracts of married women upon their separate property;[19] suits to marshal securities; and creditors' suits."[20]

§ 11. (7) Seventh Group: Remedies in Which the Final Relief is Wholly Pecuniary, and is Obtained in the Form of a General Pecuniary Recovery.—"The remedies composing this group belong to the concurrent jurisdiction of equity, since the final reliefs are the same in form and substance as that granted under like circumstances by a judgment at law,—a general pecuniary recovery,—and since the primary rights and interests of the parties are generally recognized and protected by the law."[21] "This group contains the following particular suits: By assignees of things in action, equitable assignees of a fund, etc.; by persons entitled to participate in a common fund; for contribution in general; suits growing out of suretyship, for exoneration, contribution, or subrogation; suits growing out of partnership; suits for an accounting in general; recovery of damages, etc."[22] Elsewhere, the following are enumerated as the most im-

19 "Although the late English cases hold that these contracts of married women do *not* create any lien, yet the whole remedy in form and substance is exactly the same as though there *was* a lien, and as though its object was to enforce that lien. Furthermore, the American courts generally hold that a lien *is* created": Pom. Eq. Jur., § 1413, note.

20 Pom. Eq. Jur., § 1413. "'Creditors' suits' belong to this group, because they are based upon the conception that an equitable lien is created upon the judgment debtor's property by means of the judgment and execution returned unsatisfied; and this lien is in reality enforced, although the enforcement may, perhaps, require the ancillary remedies of cancellation, a receiver, etc.": Pom. Eq. Jur., § 1413, note.

21 Pom. Eq. Jur., § 1416.

22 Pom. Eq. Jur., § 1316, note.

portant and frequent instances of the "concurrent" jurisdiction, when the relief is pecuniary:[23] Suits growing out of the contract of suretyship; suits growing out of the contract of partnership; contribution, in general; accounting, especially as between principal and agent, and other persons standing in fiduciary relations to each other; "the ascertaining and adjustment of the respective amounts of persons entitled to participate in the same fund, and of the respective shares of persons subjected to some common liability; the ascertaining and adjustment of the shares of persons liable to contribute to a general average; the ascertaining and adjustment of the shares of persons liable to contribute with respect to charges of any kind upon land or other property; the appropriation of payments; the apportionment of rents; and numerous other instances where a number of persons are differently interested in the same subject-matter, or are differently liable with respect to some common object." Other important instances are suits for the recovery of legacies and of gifts *causa mortis*, and other suits connected with the administration of the estates of decedents; pecuniary relief occasioned by or growing out of fraud, mistake, or accident (rarely an independent ground of jurisdiction in this country); the recovery of damages by way of compensation in addition to or (occasionally) in place of other equitable relief; and certain suits—as, to compel a set-off—depending on imperfections of the legal procedure.[24]

23 Pom. Eq. Jur., §§ 186-189.

24 See 1 Pom. Eq Jur, § 189. Suits for specific performance brought by the vendor, where the recovery is pecuniary, seem, in strict logic, to belong in this group: See 1 Pom. Eq. Jur., § 112, note 1.

II.

§ 12. **Equitable Remedies Acted in Personam.**—"In the infancy of the court of chancery while the chancellors were developing their system in the face of a strong opposition, in order to avoid a direct collision with the law and with the judgments of law courts, they adopted the principle that their own remedies and decrees should operate *in personam* upon defendants, and not *in rem*. The meaning of this simply is, that a decree of a court of equity, while declaring the equitable estate, interest, or right of the plaintiff to exist, did not operate by its own intrinsic force to vest the plaintiff with the legal estate, interest or right to which he was pronounced entitled; it was not itself a legal title, nor could it either directly or indirectly transfer the title from the defendant to the plaintiff. A decree of chancery spoke in terms of personal command to the defendant, but its directions could only be carried into effect by his personal act. It declared, for example, that the plaintiff was equitable owner of certain land, the legal title of which was held by the defendant, and ordered the defendant to execute a conveyance of the estate; his own voluntary act was necessary to carry the decree into execution; if he refused to convey, the court could endeavor to compel his obedience by fine and imprisonment. The decree never stood as a title in the place of an actual conveyance by the defendant; nor was it ever carried into effect by any officer acting in the defendant's name."[25] Thus, on a bill for the removal of a

[25] 1 Pom. Eq. Jur., § 428. See, also, Id., §§ 134, 135, 170. 1317; Penn v. Lord Baltimore, 1 Ves. Sr. 444, 2 Lead Cas Eq., 4th Am ed., 1806, and notes; Proctor v. Ferebee, 1 Ired. Eq. (36 N. C.) 143, 36 Am. Dec. 34, and note. Pom. Eq. Jur., § 1317, is cited, as to the effect of decrees, in Powell v. Campbell, 20 Nev. 232, 19 Am. St. Rep. 350, 20 Pac. 156, 2 L. R. A. 615.

cloud upon title, the decree operated *in personam* only, by restraining the defendant from asserting his claim, and directing him to deliver up his deed to be canceled, or to execute a release to the plaintiff.[26] When the chancellor directed the sale of property, "it was by his control over the person of the owner that he made the sale effective, *i. e.,* when the sale had been made he compelled the owner to execute a deed, pursuant to the sale; and hence when the owner was out of the jurisdiction the chancellor was powerless."[27] And a decree in partition "did not transfer or convey title even after the allotment of the respective shares of each of the parties to the proceeding, but the legal title remained as it was before. . . . . This difficulty was remedied by a decree that the parties should make the necessary conveyances to each other, which, if they refused, they could be compelled to do by attachment, imprisonment and other powers of the court over them in person."[28]

§ 13. **Same—Modern Legislation—Decree may Transfer Title.**—"This original doctrine has been abrogated, for all classes of remedies to which it could apply, by statutory legislation in a large number of the states. This legislation may be reduced to two general types: (1) That by which the decree itself without any act of the defendant or of an officer on his behalf becomes a

26 Hart v. Sansom, 110 U. S. 151, 3 Sup. Ct. 586, 28 L. ed. 101 (citing Langdell Eq. Pl. (2d ed), §§ 43, 184; Massie v. Watts, 6 Cranch, 148, 3 L. ed. 181; Orton v Smith, 18 How. 263, 15 L. ed. 263; Vandever v. Freeman, 20 Tex. 334, 70 Am. Dec. 391).

27 McCann v. Randall, 147 Mass. 81, 99, 9 Am. St. Rep. 666, 17 N. E. 75, 88 (citing Langdell's Eq. Pl. (2d ed.), § 43, note 4; Pom. Eq Jur., § 1317; Hart v. Sansom, *supra*).

28 Gay v. Parpart, 106 U. S. 679, 690, 1 Sup. Ct. 456, 465, 27 L. ed. 256, per Miller, J. (quoting from Waley v. Dawson, 2 Schoales & L. 366, per Lord Redesdale; Mitford's Eq. Pl. (Jeremy's ed.), 120; Adams' Eq. 231).

title, and vests a legal estate in the subject-matter in the plaintiff; (2) That by which a commissioner, master, or other officer of the court executes the decree, and through his conveyance or other official act transfers the legal estate from the defendant to the plaintiff, or otherwise vests the plaintiff with title. Both these types are often found in the statutes of the same state. In all cases where an instrument is directed to be executed by an officer, the statutes provide that it shall have exactly the same effect as if executed by the party himself."[29] "In some statutes of the first type the lan-

29 Pom. Eq. Jur., § 1317. As illustrations of the first type of statute, where the decree itself operates as a title, see King v. Bill, 28 Conn. 593; Hoffman v. Stigers, 28 Iowa, 302 (partition); Young v. Frost, 1 Md. 377, 403 (partition); Gitt v. Watson, 18 Mo. 274; Sensenderfer v. Kemp, 83 Mo. 581 (decree divesting title of constructive trustee, a purchaser with notice of equitable title); Bohart v. Chamberlain, 99 Mo. 622, 13 S. W. 85 (re-execution of a lost instrument; instead of ordering its re-execution court may make a declaratory decree, establishing the existence of the deed in question; citing Pom. Eq. Jur., §§ 171, 429, 827; Garrett v. Lynch, 45 Ala. 204); Macklin v. Allenberg, 100 Mo. 337, 13 S. W. 350 (setting aside deed as fraud on creditors); Price v. Sisson, 13 N. J. Eq. 168 (reformation of deed); Skinner v. Terry, 134 N. C. 305, 46 S. E. 517; Taylor v. Boyd, 3 Ohio, 337, 17 Am. Dec. 603, Jelke v. Goldsmith, 52 Ohio St. 499, 49 Am. St. Rep. 730, 40 N. E. 167 (statute of Ohio does not apply to decrees concerning *personal* property); Griffiths v. Phillips, 3 Grant Cas. (Pa.) 331 (partition).

It has been held that "the rights of the parties in case of a variance between the terms of the decree and of the conveyance, must depend upon the former rather than upon the latter": Price v. Sisson, 13 N. J. Eq. 168, 172, *supra;* and that "the terms of the decree must be construed precisely as the conveyance itself would be if executed within the time appointed for its execution": Id.; Hoffman v. Stigers, 28 Iowa, 302, *supra.*

"Whenever the decree itself thus operates to transfer title, a reversal of the decree upon appeal necessarily destroys this effect *as between the parties themselves,* divests the title from the party to whom it had been transferred, and revests it in the party from whom it had passed. But if the decree had been executed by means of a

guage is positive and peremptory, that the decree shall operate to transfer the title, etc.; in others it is permissive,—the court may provide in the decree that it shall operate to transfer the title in case the defendant neglects or refuses to obey its mandates. Similar variations are found in the statutes of the second type."[30]

conveyance, and the title had thus passed to a *bona fide* purchaser, before the appeal, a reversal may not divest him of the title or compel him to reconvey: See Stats. of Delaware; Taylor v. Boyd, 3 Ohio, 337, 17 Am. Dec. 603"; Pom. Eq. Jur., § 1317, note; see, also, McCormick v. McClure, 6 Blackf. (Ind.) 466, 39 Am. Dec. 441; Macklin v. Allenberg, 100 Mo. 337, 13 S. W. 350 (*bona fide* purchaser not affected by reversal on a *writ of error*, that being in effect a new suit). The question in such cases is largely one of the continuance of the *lis pendens* of the original suit: See 2 Pom. Eq. Jur. (3d ed.), § 634, and notes.

As to the time when title passes under these statutes, there is some dispute. Compare Shotwell v. Lawson, 30 Miss. 27, 64 Am. Dec. 145 (deed executed by commissioner under decree vacating title to real estate relates back to commencement of suit, as against defendant in such suit and those subsequently claiming title under him), with King v. Bill, 28 Conn. 593 (third person to whom defendant conveyed after filing of the bill but before decree not divested of his title by the decree).

30 Pom. Eq Jur., § 1317, note 2. The following are the most important of these statutes:

Alabama.—Civ. Code, 1896, § 849: "When a decree is made for a conveyance, release, or acquittance, and the party against whom the decree is made does not execute the same by the time specified in the decree, such decree operates in all respects as fully as if the conveyance, release or acquittance was made; or the court may decree, in default of the execution of such conveyance, release or acquittance, the same to be executed by the register or a commissioner in the name of the party; and the conveyance, release or acquittance, when so executed, is as valid in all respects as if executed by the party; or the court may directly divest title out of one party and vest it in another"

Arizona.—Rev. Stats. 1901, § 1430 "When the judgment is for the conveyance of real estate, or for the delivery of personal property, the decree may pass the title to such property without any act to be done on the part of the party against whom the judgment is rendered."

Arkansas.—Sandel & Hill's Dig. of Stat, § 4241: "In all cases where the court may decree the conveyance of real estate, or the delivery of personal property, they may, by decree, pass the title of such property without any act to be done on the part of the defendant, where it shall be proper, and may issue a writ of possession if necessary, to put the party in possession of such real or personal property, or may proceed by attachment or sequestration."

§ 4242 "When an unconditional decree shall be made for a conveyance, release or acquittance, and the party required to execute the same shall not comply therewith, the decree shall be considered and taken to have the same operation and effect, and be as available as if the conveyance, release or acquittance had been executed conformably to the decree."

Connecticut.—Gen. Stats. 1902, § 555: "Courts of equitable jurisdiction may pass the title to real estate by decree, without any act on the part of the defendant, when, in their judgment, it shall be the proper mode to carry the decree into effect; and such decree, having been recorded in the records of lands in the town where such real estate is situated, shall, while in force, be as effectual to transfer the same as the deed of the defendant."

Delaware.—Rev. Stats, c. 95, § 12: "All real estate, within this state, shall be liable to be sold, by order of the chancellor, on such terms and in such manner as he shall direct, by the sheriff, or by any party to a suit in chancery, when such sale shall be necessary to give effect to, and carry into execution a decree of the court of chancery. And when any such real estate shall be so sold, and there shall be a surplus of money, arising from the sale, above what is sufficient for the purposes of the sale, such surplus shall be paid over, or applied as the chancellor shall order. Such sales shall be as available in law to the vendees as sales of land seized and sold upon judgment and execution are by virtue of any law of this state, *provided*, that if any such decree, under which any real estate shall be so sold, shall be reversed by the court of errors and appeals, none of the real estate, so sold, shall be restored, nor shall the sale thereof be avoided, but restitution shall be made, in such cases, of the money for which such real estate was sold; *and provided also*, that no sale shall be valid until return thereof shall be made to the court of chancery, and it shall be approved and confirmed by the chancellor."

Florida.—Rev. Stats. 1892, § 1451: "Where a decree in chancery shall be made for a conveyance, release or acquittance of land, or any interest therein, and the party against whom the said decree shall pass shall not comply therewith by the time appointed, then such decree shall be considered and taken in all courts of law and equity to have the same operation and effect and to be as available as if the conveyance and release or acquittance had been executed conformably to such decree, and this, notwithstanding any disability of such parties by infancy, lunacy, coverture or otherwise."

Georgia.—Code 1895, § 4852: "A decree for specific performance shall operate as a deed to convey land or other property without any conveyance being executed by the vendor. Such decree certified by the clerk shall be recorded in the registry of deeds in the county where the land lies, and shall stand in the place of a deed."

Illinois.—Hurd's Rev. Stats 1899, p. 225, § 46: "Whenever a decree shall be made in a suit in equity, directing the execution of any deed or other writing, it shall be lawful for the court to appoint a commissioner, or direct the master in chancery to execute the same, in case the parties under no disability fail to execute the same, in a time to be named in the decree, or on behalf of minors or persons having conservators." Such conveyance shall have the same effect "as if executed by the right party in proper person, and he or she were under no disability."

Indiana.—Burns' Ann. Stats. 1901, § 1027: "Real property may be conveyed by a commissioner appointed by the court:

"First, where, by the judgment in an action, a party is ordered to convey real property to another or any interest therein."

Iowa.—Code 1897, § 3805: Same as Indiana, but omitting "or any interest therein."

Kansas.—Rev. Stats. 1901, § 4849; Code, § 400: Similar to Alabama, except that conveyance may be executed by the sheriff instead of by a register or commissioner, and that the provision that the court may directly divest title is omitted.

Kentucky.—Codes 1900, § 394: Same as Iowa.

Maine.—Rev. Stats. 1903, p. 873, c. 114, § 10: In certain actions for specific performance of contracts to convey land, "if the defendant neglects or refuses to convey according to the decree, the court may render judgment for the plaintiff for possession of the land, to hold according to the terms of the intended conveyance, and may issue a writ of seizin as in a real action, under which the plaintiff, having obtained possession, shall hold the premises as effectually as if conveyed in pursuance of the decree; or the court may enforce its decree by any other process according to chancery proceedings."

Maryland.—Pub. Gen. Laws, § 91: "In all cases where the court shall decree that a deed of any kind shall be executed, a trustee to execute such deed may be appointed, and until such trustee shall execute a deed, the decree itself, if passed in the county where the land lies, shall have the same effect that the deed would if executed; but if passed in another county, the decree shall have that effect if recorded in the county where the land lies within six months from the date thereof."

Michigan.—Howell's Ann. Stats., § 6650: "And if such decree shall direct the execution of a conveyance or other instrument affecting the title to real estate, the record of such certified copy shall have the same effect as the record of such conveyance or other instrument affecting the title to real estate would have if duly executed pursuant to said decree."

Minnesota.—Gen. Stats. 1894, c. 75, § 14: "The district court has power to pass the title to real estate by a judgment, without any other act to be done on the part of the defendant, when such appears to be the proper mode to carry its judgments into effect; and such judgment, being recorded in the registry of deeds of the county where such real estate is situated, shall, while in force, be as effectual to transfer the same as the deed of the defendant."

Mississippi.—Annotated Code 1892, § 594: "The decree of a court of chancery shall have the force, operation and effect of a judgment at law in the circuit court."

§ 595. "When a decree shall be made for a conveyance, release, or acquittance, or other writing, and the party against whom the decree is made shall not comply therewith, then such decree shall be considered and taken in all courts of law and equity to have the same operation and effect, and shall be as available, as if the conveyance, release, or acquittance, or other writing had been executed in conformity to the decree; or the court may appoint a commissioner to execute such writing, which shall have the same effect as if executed by the party."

Missouri.—Rev. Stats. 1889, § 6041: "In all cases where any court of record shall judge or decree a conveyance of real estate, or that any real estate shall pass, the party in whose favor the judgment or decree is rendered shall cause a copy thereof to be recorded in the office of the recorder of the county wherein the lands passed or to be conveyed lie, within eight months after such judgment or decree is entered."

Nebraska.—Cobbey's Statutes 1903, § 1416: "That when any judgment or decree shall be rendered for a conveyance, release, or acquittance, in any court of this state, and the party or parties against whom the judgment or decree shall be rendered do not comply therewith within the time mentioned in said judgment or decree, such judgment or decree shall have the same operation and effect, and be as available as if the conveyance, release, or acquittance had been executed conformable to such judgment or decree."

§ 1441: "Real property may be conveyed by master commissioners as hereinafter provided: *First* When by an order or judgment in an action or proceeding, a party is ordered to convey such property to another, and he shall neglect or refuse to comply with such order or judgment. *Second.* When specific real property is required to be sold under an order or judgment of the court."

New Jersey.—Gen. Stats. 1895, p. 383: "That where a decree of the court of chancery shall be made for a conveyance, release, or acquittance of lands or any interest therein, and the party against whom the said decree shall pass shall not comply therewith by the time appointed, then such decree shall be considered and taken, in all courts of law and equity, to have the same operation and effect, and be as available as if the conveyance, release, or acquittance had been executed conformably to such decree, and this, notwithstanding any disability of such party by infancy, lunacy, coverture, or otherwise."

New York.—Code Civ. Proc. 1896, § 718: "Where a judgment directs a party to . . . convey real property; if the direction is disobeyed, the courts, besides punishing the disobedience as a contempt, may, by order, require the sheriff . . . . to convey the real property, in conformity with the direction of the court."

North Carolina.—Clark's Code of Civ. Proc., § 426: "In any action, wherein the court shall declare that a party is entitled to the possession of property, real or personal, the legal title whereof may be in another or others, parties to the suit, and the court shall order a conveyance of such legal title to him so declared to be entitled, or where, for any cause, the court shall order that one of the parties holding property in trust shall convey the legal title therein to be held in trust to another person, although not a party, the court, after declaring the right and ordering the conveyance, shall have power, also, to be used in its discretion, to declare in the order then made, or in any made in the progress of the cause, that the effect thereof shall be to transfer to the party to whom the conveyance is directed to be made the legal title of the said property, to be held in the same plight, condition and estate as though the conveyance ordered was in fact executed."

§ 427: "Every judgment, in which the transfer of title shall be so declared, shall be regarded as a deed of conveyance, executed in due form and by capable persons, notwithstanding the want of capacity in any person ordered to convey."

North Dakota.—Revised Code 1899, § 5486: "In all actions arising under chapter 30 of this code and in actions commenced for the satisfaction of record of mortgages or other liens upon real property or for the specific performance of contracts relating to real property, the court may by its judgment without any act on the part of the defendant transfer the title to real property and remove or discharge a cloud or encumbrance thereon, and a certified copy of such judgment may be recorded in the office of the register of deeds of the county in which the property affected is situated."

Ohio.—Bates' Ann. Code, 4th ed., § 5318: "When the party against whom a judgment for a conveyance, release, or acquittance is rendered, does not comply therewith by the time appointed, such judgment shall have the same operation and effect, and be as available, as if the conveyance, release, or acquittance had been executed conformably to such judgment."

Oklahoma.—Rev. Stats. 1903, § 4589: Similar to Kansas.

Oregon.—Bellinger & Cotton's Codes and Stats., § 415. "A decree requiring a party to make a conveyance, transfer, release, acquittance, or other like act within a period therein specified shall, if such party do not comply therewith, be deemed and taken to be equivalent thereto."

Tennessee.—Code, 1896: "The decree may divest the title to property, real or personal, out of any of the parties, and vest it in others, and such decree shall have all the force and effect of a conveyance by such parties, executed in due form of law."

Texas.—Sayles' Stats., art 1338: "Where the judgment is for the conveyance of real estate, or for the delivery of personal property, the decree may pass title to such property without any act to be done on the part of the party against whom the judgment is rendered."

Utah.—Rev. Stats. 1898, § 3279: "When the judgment requires the person against whom it is rendered to execute and deliver to any other person a conveyance of any specific real property, and the person against whom it is rendered shall refuse or neglect to execute and deliver said conveyance for five days after the service upon him of a certified copy of such judgment, or if he is absent or concealed, so that service of such certified copy cannot be had, upon proof satisfactory to the court that such service has been made, or that it cannot be made by reason of such absence or concealment, the person entitled to the conveyance may obtain from the court an order that the certified copy of the judgment, together with the order, be recorded by the recorder of deeds of the county where the real property is situated, and when recorded, it shall give to the person entitled to such conveyance a right to the possession of the real property described in the judgment, and to hold the same according to the terms of the conveyance ordered, in like manner as if it had been conveyed in pursuance of the judgment. The recording of any judg-

§ 14. **Same—Limitations on Effect of this Legislation.**— "These statutes do not generally interfere with the original power of courts of equity to enforce obedience to their decrees by the parties themselves, and to punish such parties for their disobedience by attachment, fine, imprisonment, or sequestration.[31] The operation of

ment as above provided shall not prevent the court rendering the judgment from enforcing the same by any proper process, according to the course of proceedings therein."

Vermont.—Stats. 1894, § 980: "When a decree is made by a court of chancery for a conveyance, release, or acquittance, and the party against whom the decree is made does not comply therewith by the time appointed, the decree shall be held to have the same effect as if the conveyance, release, or acquittance had been executed agreeably to such decree. But such decree shall not be deemed a conveyance of real estate, unless a copy of the same, certified by the clerk of the court, is recorded in the office in which a deed of such real estate is required by law to be recorded."

Virginia.—Pollard's Ann Code 1904, § 3418: "A court of equity, in a suit wherein it is proper to decree or order the execution of any deed or writing, may appoint a commissioner to execute the same; and the execution thereof shall be as valid to pass, release, or extinguish the right, title, and interest of the party on whose behalf it is executed, as if such party had been at the time capable in law of executing the same, and had executed it."

West Virginia.—Code 1899, c. 132: "A court of law or equity, in a suit in which it is proper to decree or order the execution of any deed or writing, may appoint a commissioner to execute the same; and the execution thereof shall be as valid to pass, release or extinguish the right, title, and interest of the party on whose behalf it is executed, as if such party had been at the time capable in law of executing the same and had executed it."

Wisconsin.—Stats. 1898, § 2236: "All judgments, decrees and orders rendered or made by any court in cases where the title to land shall have been in controversy may be recorded in the office of the register of deeds of every county where any part of the lands are situate, in the same manner and with like effect as conveyances. Such recording may be done from a duly certified copy thereof."

Wyoming.—Rev. Stats. 1899, § 3759: Same as Ohio.

31 Pom. Eq. Jur., § 1317; so held in Randall v. Pryor, 4 Ohio, 424; Penn v. Hayward, 14 Ohio St. 302. It seems, however, that under

these statutes is confined to the territorial limits and jurisdiction of the states in which they are respectively enacted."[32] It is impossible for a decree of a court of one state to directly affect property in another. No state has power to interfere with the sovereign rights of a sister state. This legislation, it has been said, "does not extend to decrees of the United States courts. The effect of equitable remedies granted and decrees rendered by the United States courts, in the absence of legislation by Congress, is governed by the original doctrine of equity; their decrees do not transfer title; they must be executed by the parties, and obedience is compelled by proceedings in the nature of punishment for contempt, attachment, or sequestration.[33] There are,

the statutes of Georgia relating to execution for enforcement of pecuniary judgments, a decree for the payment of money cannot be enforced by attachment of the person: Clement v. Tullman, 79 Ga. 451, 11 Am. St Rep. 441, 5 S. E. 194.

32 Pom. Eq. Jur., § 1317. See, also, Watkins v. Holman, 16 Pet 25, 10 L. ed. 873 ("neither the decree itself, nor any conveyance under it, can operate beyond the jurisdiction of the court"); Corbett v. Nutt, 10 Wall. 464, 19 L. ed. 976, Carpenter v Strange, 141 U. S. 87, 106, 11 Sup. Ct. 960, 35 L. ed. 640; Dull v. Blackman, 169 U S. 243, 18 Sup Ct. 333, 42 L. ed. 733; Guarantee Trust etc. Co. v. Delta etc. Co, 104 Fed. 5, and cases cited; Lindley v. O'Reilly, 50 N J. L. 636, 15 Atl. 379; Bullock v Bullock, 52 N. J. Eq 561, 46 Am St. Rep. 528, 27 L. R. A. 213, 30 Atl. 676.

33 Pom. Eq. Jur, § 1317. See, also, Shepherd v. Commissioners of Ross Co., 7 Ohio, 271.

But Professor Pomeroy's statement, above quoted, does not accurately describe the present practice of the United States courts The act of Congress (March 3, 1875; 18 Stats. 470; Rev. Stats, § 738) providing for "substituted" service upon absent defendants in suits to enforce any legal or equitable lien upon, or claim to, or to remove any encumbrance or lien or cloud upon the title to real or personal property within the district where the suit is brought, would, it is pointed out, be idle legislation unless the court possessed the power, in this class of cases, to transfer title by means of its decree, without the agency of the defendant: See Deck v. Whitman, 96 Fed. 873, 890, and cases cited; Single v. Scott Paper Mfg. Co, 55 Fed. 553. See, also, authorities mentioned in the next section fol of course, classes of remedies to which this legislation cannot apply—as, for example, decrees prohibiting any act, general pecuniary recoveries, analogous to money judgments at law, and many purely ancillary or provisional reliefs."[34]

§ 15. Validity of Decree Based upon Service by Publication.—Equity decrees ordinarily act only *in personam*, and can therefore, in general, have effect only as against parties duly served with process within the territorial jurisdiction of the court.[35] It is competent, however, for a state to provide methods for the determination of title to land within its borders, and in the exercise of such power, it may give to equity decrees relating to or affecting the title to land, the effect of judgments *in rem*, which, therefore, may be based upon service of process by publication. "It is true that, in a strict sense, a proceeding *in rem* is one taken directly against property, and has for its object the disposition of the

lowing. But apart from the effect of this act of Congress, the weight of recent authority appears to be in favor of the view that the state legislation in question does not deal merely with a matter of procedure, but establishes a substantive right, and that it is therefore within the power, if it is not the duty, of a United States court to conform to the same, in an appropriate case. Single v. Scott Paper Mfg. Co., 55 Fed. 553; Deck v. Whitman, 96 Fed. 873, 891; Langdon v. Sherwood, 124 U. S. 74, 8 Sup. Ct. 429, 31 L. ed 344. In the last case Mr. Justice Miller remarks, in speaking of this legislation: "The validity of these statutes has never been questioned, so far as we know, though long in existence in nearly all the states of the Union. There can be no doubt of their efficacy in transferring the title, in the courts of the states which have enacted them; nor do we see any reason why the courts of the United States may not use this mode of effecting that which is clearly within their power."

34 Pom. Eq. Jur., § 1317. See, also, Merrill v. Beckwith, 163 Mass 503, 10 N. E. 855; Adams v. Heckscher, 80 Fed. 742, 83 Fed. 281. These are cases in which there was no personal service of summons.

35 Hart v. Sansom, 110 U S. 151, 3 Sup. Ct. 586, 28 L. ed. 101, Ames' Cas. in Eq. Jur., 11.

property, without reference to the title of individual claimants; but, in a larger and more general sense, the terms are applied to actions between parties, where the direct object is to reach and dispose of property owned by them, or of some interest therein. Such are cases commenced by attachment against the property of debtors, or instituted to partition real estate, foreclose a mortgage, or enforce a lien. So far as they affect property in the state, they are substantially proceedings *in rem*, in the broader sense which we have mentioned."[36] Statutes in many of the states make an equity decree the equivalent of a conveyance. As a result of statute, it is held in many states that a decree removing a cloud from or quieting title to land within the jurisdiction may be based upon publication of summons.[37] Likewise, a decree for specific performance,

36 Pennoyer v. Neff, 95 U. S. 714, 24 L. ed. 565, per Field, J.

37 "If a state has no power to bring a nonresident into its courts for any purposes by publication, it is impotent to perfect the titles of real estate within its limits held by its own citizens; and a cloud cast upon such title by a claim of a nonresident will remain for all time a cloud, unless such nonresident shall voluntarily come into its courts for the purpose of having it adjudicated. But no such imperfections attend the sovereignty of the state. It has control over property within its limits; and the condition of ownership of real estate therein, whether the owner be stranger or citizen, is subjection to its rules concerning the holding, the transfer, liability to obligations, private or public, and the modes of establishing titles thereto. It cannot bring the person of a nonresident within its limits—its process goes not out beyond its borders—but it may determine the extent of his title to real estate within its limits, and, for the purpose of such determination, may provide any reasonable methods of imparting notice": Arndt v. Griggs, 134 U. S. 316, 10 Sup. Ct. 557, 33 L. ed. 918, per Brewer, J. See, also, Bryan v. Kennett, 113 U. S. 179, 5 Sup. Ct. 407, 28 L. ed. 908; Ormsby v. Ottman, 85 Fed. 492, 29 C. C. A. 295; Morrison v. Marker, 93 Fed. 692; Perkins v. Wakeham, 86 Cal. 580, 21 Am. St. Rep. 67, 25 Pac. 51; Knudson v. Litchfield, 87 Iowa, 111, 54 N. W 199; Dillon v. Heller, 39 Kan. 599, 18 Pac. 693; Oldham v. Stephens, 45 Kan. 369, 25 Pac. 863; Short v. Caldwell, 155 Mass. 57, 28 N. E. 1124; Scarborough v. Myrick, 47 Neb. 794, 66 N. W. 867; Robinson v. Kind, 23 Nev. 330, 47 Pac. 1,

acting upon the land itself, may issue upon such service.[38] Proceedings for the partition of real estate, the foreclosure of mortgages and the enforcement of liens upon land within the state, are also within the class.[39] In all of these cases the title is directly affected by the decree.

§ 16. **Remedies in Personam Beyond the Territorial Jurisdiction.**—"Where the subject-matter is situated within another state or country, but the parties are within the jurisdiction of the court, any suit may be maintained and remedy granted which *directly* affect and operate upon the person of the defendant and not upon the subject-matter, although the subject-matter is referred to in the decree, and the defendant is ordered to do or to refrain from certain acts toward it, and it is thus ultimately but *indirectly* affected by the relief granted.[40] This rule applies to the United States courts[41] as well

977; American B. & L. Assn. v. Mathews, 13 Tex. Civ. App. 425, 35 S. W. 690.

38 Bostwell v. Otis, 9 How. 336, 13 L. ed. 164 (*semble*). In general, see Robinson v. Kind, 23 Nev. 330, 47 Pac. 1, 977 (action to cancel deed); Corson v. Shoemaker, 55 Minn 386, 57 N. W. 134 (reformation); Seculovich v. Martin, 101 Cal. 673, 36 Pac. 387 (suit to compel conveyance by absent trustee); but compare Adams v. Hecksher, 80 Fed. 742, 83 Fed. 281 (statute does not apply, when complaint requires a personal act of the defendant)

39 Martin v. Pond, 30 Fed. 15 (foreclosure); Palmer v. McCormick, 28 Fed. 541 (same); Roller v. Holly, 176 U. S. 398, 20 Sup. Ct. 410, 44 L. ed. 520 (action to enforce vendor's lien); Wilson v. Martin-Wilson etc. Co., 151 Mass. 515, 24 N. E. 784 (creditor's bill to reach patent right of absent defendant). See, also, Pennoyer v. Neff, 95 U. S. 714, 24 L. ed. 565.

40 Pom. Eq. Jur., § 1318. This portion of Pom. Eq. Jur is quoted in Schmaltz v. York Mfg. Co., 204 Pa. St. 1, 93 Am. St. Rep. 782, 59 L. R. A. 957, 53 Atl. 522; Allen v. Buchanan, 97 Ala. 399, 38 Am. St. Rep. 187, 11 South. 777; Butterfield v. Nogales Copper Co. (Ariz.), 80 Pac. 345

41 Pom. Eq. Jur, § 298.

as to the state courts, and is also well settled in England."[42]

[42] "The courts of England are, and always have been, courts of conscience, operating *in personam* and not *in rem;* and in the exercise of this personal jurisdiction they have always been accustomed to compel the performance of contracts and trusts as to subjects which were not locally or *ratione domicilii* within their jurisdiction": Ewing v. Orr Ewing, L. R. 9 App Cas. 34, 40, per Lord Selborne.

The leading English case is Penn v. Lord Baltimore, 1 Ves. Sr. 444, 2 Lead. Cas Eq, 4th Am. ed, 1806, where the subject is fully discussed and conclusions are reached in accordance with the statements of the text. See, also, Toller v. Carteret, 2 Vern. 494. The leading American case on this subject is Massie v. Watts, 6 Cranch, 148, 3 L ed. 181, where Marshall, C. J., laid down the rule as follows: "When the defendant is liable, either in consequence of a contract, or as trustee, or as holder of a legal title acquired by a species of *mala fides* practiced on the plaintiff, the principles of equity give a court jurisdiction wherever the person may be found, and the circumstance that a question of title may be involved in the inquiry, and may even constitute the essential point on which the case depends, does not seem sufficient to arrest the jurisdiction. . . . In case of fraud, of trust, or of contract, the jurisdiction of a court of chancery is sustainable wherever the person may be found, although lands not within the jurisdiction may be affected by the decree." See similar expressions in Lindley v. O'Reilly, 50 N. J. L. 636, 7 Am. St Rep. 802, 15 Atl. 379, 1 L. R. A. 79; Lynde v. Columbus C. & I. Ry. Co., 57 Fed. 993; Smith v. Davis, 90 Cal. 25, 25 Am. St. Rep. 94, 27 Pac. 27; Johnson v. Gibson, 116 Ill. 302, 6 N. E. 205; De Klyn v. Watkins, 3 Sandf. Ch. 185; Davis v. Morris, 76 Va. 21.

In Pomeroy's Equity Jurisprudence, § 1318, "suits for specific performance of contracts, for the enforcement of express or implied trusts, for relief on the ground of fraud, actual or constructive, for the final accounting and settlement of a partnership, and the like" are given as examples of the rule. The following cases are given as illustrations:

Specific Performance.—Municipal Inv. Co. v. Gardiner, 62 Fed. 954; Montgomery v United States, 36 Fed. 4, 13 Saw. 383 (citing Pom. Eq. Jur, § 1317); Penn v. Hayward, 14 Ohio St 302; Epperly v. Ferguson, 118 Iowa, 47, 91 N. W. 816 (dictum); Brown v. Desmond, 100 Mass. 267; Pingree v. Coffin, 12 Gray, 288 (specific performance of contract to assign bond for conveyance of land in another state); Newton v. Bronson, 13 N. Y. 587, 67 Am. Dec. 89, Cleveland v. Burrill, 25 Barb. 532; Ward v. Arredondo, Hopk. Ch.

§ 17. Same: Limitations of the Doctrine.—"On the other hand, where the suit is strictly local, the subject-matter is specific property, and the relief when granted is such

213, 14 Am. Dec. 543; Mitchell v. Bunch, 2 Paige, 606, 22 Am. Dec. 669, Sutphen v. Fowler, 9 Paige, 280; Burnley v. Stevenson, 24 Ohio St. 474, 15 Am. Rep. 621; Western Union Tel. Co. v. Pittsburg, C. C. & St. L. R. Co., 137 Fed. 435.

Partnership Affairs.—Dunlap v. Byers, 110 Mich. 109, 67 N. W. 1067.

Enforcement of Trust.—Smith v. Davis, 90 Cal. 25, 25 Am St. Rep. 94, 27 Pac. 27, Gilliland v. Inabuit, 92 Iowa, 46, 60 N. W. 211; Hawley v. James, 7 Paige, 213, 32 Am. Dec. 623; Dickinson v. Hoomes' Admr., 8 Gratt. 353.

Fraud.—Muller v. Dows, 94 U. S. 444, 24 L. ed. 207; Johnson v. Gibson, 116 Ill. 302, 6 N. E. 205; Clark v. Seagraves, 186 Mass. 430, 71 N. E. 813; Noble v. Grandin, 125 Mich 383, 84 N. W. 465; United States v. Maxwell Land Grant Co., 5 N. Mex. 304, 21 Pac. 153; De Klyn v. Watkins, 3 Sand. Ch. 185.

Suit to Remove Cloud on Title.—Remer v. McKay, 54 Fed. 432; Kirklin v. Atlas S. & L. Assn. (Tenn. Ch. App.), 60 S. W. 149.

Suit to Reform a Deed—Bethell v. Bethell, 92 Ind. 318.

Foreclosure of Mortgages.—It is within the jurisdiction of an equity court to order the sale of mortgaged property without the jurisdiction. Such decrees do not act against the property itself, but must be enforced by process against the defendant: Muller v. Dows, 94 U. S. 444, 24 L. ed. 207; International B. & T. Co. v. Holland Trust Co., 26 C. C A. 469, 81 Fed. 422, Woodbury v. Allegheny & K R R Co, 72 Fed. 371; Craft v. Indianapolis, D. & W. Ry. Co., 166 Ill. 580, 46 N. E. 1132 (quoting Pom. Eq. Jur., § 1318); Eaton v. McCall, 86 Me. 346, 41 Am. St. Rep. 561, 29 Atl. 1103; Union Trust Co. v. Olmsted, 102 N. Y. 729, 7 N. E. 822; Toller v Carteret (1705), 2 Vern. 494. This jurisdiction will not be exercised, however, except under unusual or extraordinary conditions. "Wherever it is necessary in order to prevent loss or to protect the rights of a mortgagee, it may be done; for instance, in the case of a mortgage upon property situated both within and without the state, where unless a sale of the entire property could be made at one time, great loss might ensue, or in other cases where an equally good reason existed. But ordinarily we think that the holder of a mortgage should be required to resort to the remedies of the courts of jurisdiction in which the land is situated": Eaton v. McCall, 86 Me 346, 41 Am. St. Rep 561, 29 Atl. 1103. To the effect that a sale of land in another state by a that it must act directly upon the subject-matter and not merely upon the person of the defendant, the jurisdiction must be exercised in the state where the subject-matter is situated."[43] A decree may have extra-territorial effect where the imprisonment of the person is the most proper means to effect that which is decreed to be done, viz., the payment of money, making a conveyance, or the like. "But where no obedience of the person imprisoned, or any act of his, can sufficiently execute such a decree, there it is in vain to hold such a plea."[44] Accordingly, it is generally held that a bill to partition realty must be brought in the state in which

referee under foreclosure is nugatory, see Farmers' L. & T. Co. v. Postal Tel. Co., 55 Conn. 334, 3 Am. St. Rep. 53, 11 Atl. 184.

In general, to the effect that a court of equity may compel a conveyance of property outside its jurisdiction, see Muller v. Dows, 94 U. S. 444, 24 L. ed. 207; Guarantee Trust & S. D. Co. v. Delta & Pine Land Co., 43 C. C. A. 396, 104 Fed. 5; Butterfield v. Nogales Copper Co. (Ariz.), 80 Pac. 345; McGee v. Sweeney, 84 Cal. 100, 23 Pac 1117; Winn v. Strickland, 34 Fla 630, 16 South. 606; Hayes v. O'Brien, 149 Ill. 403, 37 N. E. 73, 23 L. R. A. 555 (land in another county); Johnson v. Gibson, 116 Ill. 294, 6 N. E. 205 (suit by creditors to set aside fraudulent conveyance); Barringer v. Ryder, 119 Iowa, 121, 93 N. W. 56; McQuerry v. Gilliland, 89 Ky. 434, 12 S. W. 1037, 7 L. R. A. 454; Carver v. Peck, 131 Mass. 292 (suit to restrain the transfer of property outside the jurisdiction of the court); Noble v. Grandin, 125 Mich. 383, 84 N. W. 465; Vreeland v. Vreeland, 49 N. J. Eq. 322, 24 Atl. 551; Gardner v. Ogden, 22 N. Y. 327, 332-339, 78 Am. Dec. 192; Bailey v. Ryder, 10 N. Y. 363; Vaught v. Meador, 99 Va. 569, 86 Am. St. Rep. 908, 39 S. E. 225; Poindexter v. Burwell, 82 Va. 507; Gates v. Paul, 117 Wis. 170, 94 N. W. 55. See, also, Wood v. Warner, 15 N. J. Eq. 81 ("the power of the court to decree the settlement of the accounts between the parties, and the payment of the balance, if any found due, and to enforce such decree *in personam* cannot be qestioned").

43 Pom. Eq. Jur., §§ 1318, 298. For illustration, see Cooley v. Scarlett, 38 Ill. 316, 87 Am. Dec. 298 (cancellation of deed recorded in another state refused).

44 Carteret v. Petty, 2 Swans. 323. This was a bill for account and partition.

the land is situated.[45] Likewise, it would seem that an action to abate a nuisance must be maintained in the state in which the land is.[46]

§ 18. **Injunctions Against Acts in Foreign States.**—The courts are not in entire harmony as to when an injunction will issue to restrain acts in another state. It is well settled that bills to enjoin the prosecution of suits or the enforcement of judgments in other jurisdictions may, upon proper showing, be sustained.[47] As to torts in general, however, there is a conflict of authority. It is sometimes held that suits to enjoin a trespass or nuisance are purely local and consequently come within the limitation stated in the preceding paragraph.[48] On the other hand, it is held by other courts that such suits are maintainable if jurisdiction of the person is obtained.[49]

45 Carteret v. Petty, 2 Swans. 323; Schick v. Whitcomb (Neb.), 94 N. W. 1023, Poindexter v. Burwell, 82 Va. 507; Wimer v. Wimer, 82 Va. 890, 3 Am. St. Rep. 126, 5 S. E 536, Pillow v. Southwest Va. Imp. Co., 92 Va. 144, 53 Am. St. Rep. 804, 23 S. E. 32; but see Vreeland v. Vreeland, 49 N. J. Eq. 322, 24 Atl. 551, affirming 48 N. J Eq. 56, 21 Atl. 627.

46 People v. Central R. R. Co., 42 N. Y. 283; Morris v. Remington, 1 Pars Eq. Cas. 389.

47 This subject is discussed at length, *post*, Vol. II. See, also, Cole v. Cunningham, 133 U. S. 107, 10 Sup. Ct. 269, 33 L. ed. 538; Pickett v. Ferguson, 45 Ark. 177, 55 Am. Rep. 545; Hawkins v. Ireland, 64 Minn. 339, 58 Am. St. Rep. 534, 67 N. W. 73; Kendall v. McClure Coke Co., 182 Pa. St. 1, 61 Am. St. Rep 688, 37 Atl 823; Allen v. Buchanan, 97 Ala. 399, 38 Am. St. Rep 187, 11 South. 777, and cases cited (injunction against foreign garnishment suit brought to evade the laws of plaintiff's and defendant's domicile); Mead v. Merritt, 2 Paige, 402.

48 Northern Indiana R. Co. v Michigan Central R. Co., 15 How. 233, 14 L. ed. 674; Miss. & Mo. R. R. v. Ward, 2 Black, 485, 17 L. ed. 311.

49 Great Falls Mfg. Co. v. Worster, 23 N. H. 462; Alexander v. Tolleston Club, 110 Ill. 65. See the following miscellaneous cases in

III.

§ 19. **Laches: In General.**—Probably no principles of equity have been the subject of more contradictory judicial statements than those relating to the effect of *laches* or delay. The resulting confusion is the more deplorable owing to the frequency with which the defense is asserted, and the favor with which it appears to be regarded by many courts.[50] Apart from the element of uncertainty shared by it in common with other equitable defenses, the application of which must necessarily rest in judicial discretion, there appears to be a fundamental difference of opinion as to the ultimate reasons in ethics or in public policy upon which the defense of *laches* should be based.[51] The subject is further complicated by a hopeless confusion in nomenclature. The term "acquiescence," in one of its two legal significations, is often used interchangeably with the term "laches";[52] while in the innumerable cases re-

which injunctions were issued: Schmaltz v. York Mfg. Co., 204 Pa. St. 1, 93 Am. St. Rep. 782, 53 Atl. 522, 59 L. R. A. 907 (injunction against removing fixtures from property in another state); Frank v. Peyton, 82 Ky. 150 (injunction against disposing of property pending suit). The same principle has been held to apply to suits for injunction against trespass in another county: Jennings v. Beale, 158 Pa. St. 283, 27 Atl. 948; Clad v. Paist, 181 Pa. St. 148, 37 Atl. 194. It is said in Western Union Tel. Co. v. Western & Atlantic R., 8 Baxt. 54, that equity will not make a decree which it cannot enforce by its own authority.

50 See *post*, § 23, note 66.

51 Compare the passages quoted in §§ 21, 23, *post*.

52 The two significations of "acquiescence" are clearly stated in De Bussche v. Alt, L. R. 8 Ch. Div. 286, 314; see the passage quoted in full, 2 Pom. Eq. Jur., § 965, note 1; and particularly, the following portion: "The term 'acquiescence,' . . . . if used at all, must have attached to it a very different signification, according to whether the acquiescence alleged occurs while the act acquiesced in is in progress or only after it has been completed. . . . . But when once the act is completed, without any knowledge or assent upon the part

lating to relief from fraud, actual or constructive, the courts have seldom been at pains to distinguish the general doctrines relating to *laches* from the particular doctrine as to "confirmation" of the fraudulent act, and the necessity of prompt election to rescind by the defrauded party.[53] These topics have been sufficiently treated elsewhere;[54] the following paragraphs merely

of the person whose right is infringed, the matter is to be determined upon very different legal considerations. A right of action has then vested in him which, at all events as a general rule, cannot be divested without accord and satisfaction, or release under seal. *Mere submission* to the injury for any time short of the period limited by statute for the enforcement of the right of action, cannot take away such right, although under the name of *laches* it may afford a ground for refusing relief under some peculiar circumstances," etc. For other definitions of "acquiescence," see Hall v. Otterson, 52 N. J. Eq 522, 28 Atl. 907; Babb v. Sullivan, 43 S. C. 436, 21 S. E. 277. The following paragraphs concern the effect of delay by the injured party, after the commission of the injury, whether or not that delay is termed by the courts "acquiescence" or something else.

53 Cases involving the doctrine as to "ratification," "confirmation" or "election to rescind" are excluded from the following discussion. For instances see, in addition to those cited in the paragraphs of Pom Eq. Jur., mentioned below, and *post,* in chapter on Cancellation, Baker v. Cummings, 169 U. S. 189, 18 Sup. Ct. 367, 42 L. ed. 711 (enjoying profits of transaction with knowledge of fraud); Rugan v. Sabin, 53 Fed. 415, 418, 3 C. C. A. 578, 580, 10 U. S. App. 519, 530 (necessity of prompt election); Kinne v. Webb, 54 Fed. 34, 4 C. C. A. 170, 12 U. S. App. 137, affirming 49 Fed. 512 (same); Scheftel v. Hays, 58 Fed. 457, 7 C. C. A. 308, 19 U. S. App. 220; Mudsill Mining Co v. Watrous, 61 Fed. 163, 9 C. C. A. 415 (delay for purpose of securing evidence of the fraud does not show ratification); Brown v. Brown, 142 Ill. 409, 32 N. E. 500; Provident Loan Trust Co. v. McIntosh, 68 Kan. 452, 75 Pac. 498; Norfolk & N. B. Hosiery Co v. Arnold, 49 N. J. Eq 390, 23 Atl. 514; Hilliard v. Allegheny Geometrical Wood Carving Co., 173 Pa. St. 1, 34 Atl. 231; Dunn v. Columbia Nat. Bank, 204 Pa. St. 53, 53 Atl. 519.

54 See 2 Pom. Eq. Jur., § 817 (acquiescence as a *quasi* estoppel upon rights of remedy), §§ 818-820 (acquiescence as a true estoppel upon rights of property or of contract); § 897 (necessity of prompt disaffirmance of fraudulent transaction); §§ 916, 917 (ratification of,

attempt to set forth the more important statements in the recent cases defining: (1) The attitude of courts of equity to statutes of limitations, in the cases where those statutes are not, by their terms, binding upon such courts; (2) the general view, that the doctrine of laches is an application of the general principles of estoppel; (3) a broader view, chiefly expressed in a series of important decisions by the United States supreme court; (4) circumstances which operate as an excuse for delay, or tend to minimize its effect in equity.

§ 20. **Following the Analogy of Statutes of Limitations.**— The following language of an able federal judge has been frequently referred to as defining the attitude of courts of equity to the statutes of limitations, in those cases, where, from the nature of the relief sought, such statutes are capable of affording guidance.[55] "In the application of the doctrine of laches, the settled rule is that courts of equity are not bound by, but that they usually act or refuse to act in analogy to, the statute of limitations relating to actions at law of like character[56] The meaning of this rule is that, under ordinary circumstances, a suit in equity will not be stayed for laches before, and will be stayed after the time fixed by the analogous statute of limitations at law; but if

and acquiescence in, fraudulent transaction); § 964 (confirmation or ratification in cases of fraud, actual or constructive); § 965 (acquiescence and lapse of time in cases of fraud, actual or constructive).

55 Kelley v. Boettcher, 85 Fed. 55, 62, 29 C. C. A 14, 21, 56 U. S. App. 363, 383, per Sanborn, C. J. (suit to rescind sale of one-sixth of a mining claim, and to obtain an accounting and recovery of the proceeds thereof).

56 Citing Rugan v. Sabin, 10 U. S. App. 519, 534, 3 C. C. A. 578, 582, 53 Fed. 415, 420; Billings v. Smelting Co., 10 U. S App. 1, 62, 2 C. C. A. 252, 262, 263, 51 Fed. 338, 349; Bogan v Mortgage Co, 27 U. S. App. 346, 357, 11 C. C. A. 128, 135, 63 Fed 192, 199, Kinne v. Webb, 12 U. S. App. 137, 148, 4 C. C. A. 170, 177, 54 Fed. 34, 40;

unusual conditions or extraordinary circumstances make it inequitable to allow the prosecution of a suit after a briefer, or to forbid its maintenance after a longer, period than that fixed by the statute, the chancellor will not be bound by the statute, but will determine the extraordinary case in accordance with the equities which condition it. . . . . When a suit is brought within the time fixed by the analogous statute,

Scheftel v. Hays, 19 U. S. App. 220, 226, 7 C. C. A 308, 312, 58 Fed. 457, 460; Wagner v. Baird, 7 How. 234, 258, 12 L. ed. 681; Godden v. Kimmell, 99 U. S 201, 210, 25 L. ed. 431; Wood v. Carpenter, 101 U S. 135, 139, 25 L. ed. 807

See, in general, Baker v Cummings, 169 U. S. 189, 18 Sup. Ct 367, 42 L. ed. 711 (no jurisdiction when an adequate remedy at law has been barred by limitation); Church of Christ v. Reorganized Church etc., 70 Fed. 179, 17 C. C. A. 387, 36 U. S. App. 110; Kelley v Boettcher, 85 Fed. 55, 62, 56 U. S. App 363, 383, 29 C. C. A 14, 21; Continental Nat. Bank v. Heilman, 86 Fed. 514, 30 C. C. A. 232; Williamson v. Monroe, 101 Fed 322; Nash v. Ingalls, 101 Fed 645, 41 C. C. A. 545 (affirming 79 Fed. 510); Stevens v Grand Central Min Co (C. C. A.), 133 Fed. 28; Moore v. Moore, 103 Ga. 517, 30 S. E 535; Sherwood v. Baker, 105 Mo. 472, 24 Am St. Rep. 399, 16 S. W 938 (one having equitable title to realty, although there is no right to recover possession at law, can lose his right only by adverse possession for the time required to extinguish a legal title), Colton v Depew, 60 N J Eq. 454, 83 Am. St. Rep. 650, 46 Atl. 728 (foreclosure of mortgage); Church v. Winton, 196 Pa. St. 107, 46 Atl. 363, Maxwell v. Wilson, 54 W. Va. 495, 46 S. E. 349; Newberger v. Wells, 51 W. Va. 624, 42 S. E. 625; Waldron v. Harvey, 54 W. Va. 608, 102 Am. St. Rep 959, 46 S. E. 603.

In the following cases relief was refused because the corresponding legal remedy was barred by the statute of limitations: Kansas City Southern R. Co. v. Stevenson, 135 Fed. 553; Kinne v. Webb, 54 Fed. 34, 4 C. C. A. 170, 12 U. S. App. 137 (bill to set aside transfer of personal property); Southern Pac. R. Co. v. Groeck, 68 Fed. 609; Hale v. Coffin, 120 Fed. 470 (bill to follow properties of a deceased stockholder and to charge legatee, based on a legal demand); Ela v. Ela, 158 Mass. 54, 32 N. E. 957 (action for accounting by guardian, when plaintiff might have brought trover); St. John v. Coates, 63 Hun, 460, 18 N. Y. Supp. 419, Drake v. Wild, 70 Vt. 52, 39 Atl. 248. An instructive instance of the granting of relief by a federal court, though the period prescribed by the statute of limitations of the

the burden is on the defendant to show, either from the face of the bill or by his answer, that extraordinary circumstances exist which require the application of the doctrine of laches; and, when such a suit is brought after the statutory time has elapsed, the burden is on the complainant to show, by suitable averments in his bill; that it would be inequitable to apply it to his case."[57] It should be noticed that the courts of the

state had run, is found in the very recent case of Stevens v. Grand Central Min. Co. (C. C. A.), 133 Fed. 28, relying on Kelley v. Boettcher.

In the following cases the period of the statute had not run, and the delay was not fatal: Fowle v Park, 48 Fed. 789; Jonathan Mills Mfg. Co. v. Whitehurst, 60 Fed. 81 (suit for infringement of patent); Ritchie v. Sayers, 100 Fed. 520; Williamson v. Monroe, 101 Fed. 322; Ide v. Trorlicht, Duncker & Renard Carpet Co., 115 Fed. 137, 148, Brown v. Arnold (C. C. A.), 131 Fed. 723; Davis v. Williams, 121 Ala. 542, 25 South. 704; First Nat. Bank v. Nelson, 106 Ala. 535, 18 South. 154; Gordon v. Johnson, 186 Ill. 18, 57 N. E. 790; Ross v. Payson, 160 Ill. 358, 43 N. E. 399; Moore v Dick (Mass.), 72 N. E. 967; Oliver v. Lansing, 48 Neb 338, 67 N. W. 195; Michigan Trust Co. v. City of Red Cloud (Neb.), 92 N. W. 900; Condit v. Bigalow, 64 N. J. Eq. 504, 54 Atl. 160; Renshaw v. First Nat. Bank (Tenn. Ch. App.), 63 S. W 194; Watson v. Texas & P. Ry. Co. (Tex. Civ. App.), 73 S. W. 830; Ludington v. Patton, 111 Wis. 208, 86 N. W. 571.

57 Sanborn, Cir. J., continues: "The cases of Wagner v. Baird, 7 How. 234, 12 L. ed 681; Godden v. Kimmell, 99 U. S. 201, 25 L. ed. 431; Wood v. Carpenter, 101 U. S. 135, 139, 25 L. ed. 807, and Rugan v. Sabin, 10 U. S. App. 519, 534, 3 C. C. A. 578, 582, 53 Fed. 415, 420, belong to the class of cases in which the doctrine of laches was applied after the statute of limitations had run. The cases of Billings v. Smelting Co., 10 U. S. App. 1, 62, 2 C. C. A. 252, 262, 263, 51 Fed 338, 349, and Bogan v. Mortgage Co., 27 U. S. App. 347, 357, 11 C. C. A. 128, 135, 63 Fed. 192, 199, belong to the class of cases in which the court refused to apply the doctrine of laches within the time fixed by the statute." See, also, Boynton v. Haggart, 120 Fed. 819; Kansas City Southern R. Co. v. Stevenson, 135 Fed. 553.

The effect of statutes which are by their very terms applicable to suits in equity is well described in a very recent judgment of the supreme court of the United States: Patterson v. Hewitt, 195 U. S. 309, 25 Sup Ct 35, 49 L. ed. ——, by Mr Justice Brown· "When the

United States are not bound, by way of analogy or otherwise, by the statutes of limitations of the several states, in cases where to apply such statutes would be to im-

statute is in terms applicable to suits in equity, as well as at law, it is ordinarily construed, in cases demanding equitable relief, as fixing a time beyond which the suit will not, under any circumstances, lie; but not as precluding the defense of laches, provided there has been unreasonable delay within the time limited by the statute. In an action at law, courts are bound by the literalism of the statute; but in equity the question of unreasonable delay within the statutory limitation is still open: Alsop v. Riker, 155 U. S. 448-460, 39 L. ed. 218-222, 15 Sup. Ct. 162. . . . . If this were not so, it would seem to follow that in the code states, where there is but one form of action applicable both to proceedings of a legal and equitable nature, a statute of limitations, general in its terms, would apply to suits of both descriptions, and the doctrine of laches become practically obsolete. This, however, is far from being the case, as questions of laches are as often arising and being discussed in the code states as in the others. In a few cases where the statute of limitations is made applicable in terms to suits in equity, it has been construed as allowing a suit to be begun at any time within the period limited by the statute, notwithstanding the intermediate laches of the complainant, although in those cases it will usually be found that the language of the statute is explicit and imperative: Hill v. Nash, 73 Miss. 849, 19 South. 709; Washington v. Soria, 73 Miss. 665, 55 Am. St. Rep. 555, 19 South. 485. But the weight of authority is the other way, and we consider the better rule to be that, even if the statute of limitations be made applicable, in general terms, to suits in equity, and not to any particular defense, the defendant may avail himself of the laches of the complainant, notwithstanding the time fixed by the statute has not expired. This has been expressly held in Alabama (Scruggs v. Decatur Mineral & Land Co., 86 Ala. 173, 5 South. 440), in Missouri (Bliss v. Prichard, 67 Mo. 181; Kline v. Vogel, 90 Mo. 239, 1 S. W. 733, 2 S. W. 408), and in New York (Calhoun v. Millard, 121 N. Y. 69, 8 L. R. A. 248, 24 N. E. 27). In the last case the question is discussed at considerable length by Chief Judge Andrews, and the conclusion reached that 'the period of limitations of equitable actions fixed by the statute is not, where a purely equitable remedy is invoked, equivalent to a legislative direction that no period short of that time shall be a bar to relief in any case, or precludes the court from denying relief in accordance with equitable principles for unreasonable delay, although the full period of ten years has not elapsed since the cause of action accrued.' "

pair or abridge the equity jurisdiction of such courts;[58] as for example, statutes which alter the settled rule of equity that a cause of action for fraud accrues at the time when the fraud was or should have been discovered.[59]

§ 21. General Doctrine: Laches is Prejudicial Delay.— The true doctrine concerning laches has never been more concisely and accurately stated than in the following language of an able living judge: "Laches, in legal significance, is not mere delay, but delay that works a disadvantage to another. So long as parties are in the same condition, it matters little whether one presses a right promptly or slowly, within limits allowed by law; but when, knowing his rights, he takes no step to enforce them until the condition of the other party has, in good faith, become so changed that he cannot be restored to his former state, if the right be then enforced, delay becomes inequitable, and operates as estoppel against the assertion of the right. The disadvantage

58 Kirby v. Lake Shore & M S. R Co., 120 U. S. 137, 7 Sup. Ct. 430, 30 L. ed. 571; Stevens v. Grand Central Min. Co. (C. C. A.), 133 Fed. 28, Johnston v. Roe, 1 McCrary, 165, 1 Fed. 692, 695; Tice v. School District, 5 McCrary, 362, 17 Fed. 283, 285. But "although the ordinary chancery jurisdiction of the courts of the United States cannot be abridged by state statutes, they recognize those of the state in which the court is sitting, limiting the time for bringing suits, and adopt them, if they do not act in obedience to them. Accordingly, they will adjudge, in cases over which there is a concurrent jurisdiction by courts of law and equity, that lapse of time to be a bar in equity which would have constituted a bar if the action had been at law": Per Wallace, Cir. J., in Miles v. Vivian, 79 Fed. 848, 25 C. C. A. 208; and see Pulliam v. Pulliam, 10 Fed. 30; Percy v. Cockrill, 53 Fed. 872, 4 C. C. A. 73, 10 U. S. App. 574; Hale v. Coffin, 120 Fed. 470; Higgins Oil & Fuel Co. v. Snow, 113 Fed. 433, 51 C. C. A. 267.

59 Kirby v. Lake Shore & M. S. Ry. Co., 120 U. S. 137, 7 Sup. Ct. 430, 30 L. ed. 571.

may come from loss of evidence, change of title, intervention of equities, and other causes; but when a court sees negligence on one side and injury therefrom on the other it is a ground for denial of relief."[60] The follow-

60 Chase v. Chase, 20 R. I. 202, 37 Atl. 804, by Stinness, C. J. See, also, Abraham v. Ordway, 158 U. S 416, 15 Sup. Ct. 894, 39 L. ed. 1036, Willard v. Wood, 164 U. S. 502, 524, 17 Sup. Ct. 176, 41 L. ed. 531; Penn Mutual Life Ins. Co. v. City of Austin, 168 U. S. 685, 18 Sup. Ct. 223, 42 L. ed. 627 (no injunction against enforcement of ordinance for municipal waterworks, where there has been a delay of five years, during which bonds had been issued and a large part of the proceeds expended); O'Brien v. Wheelock, 184 U. S. 450, 22 Sup. Ct. 354, 46 L ed. 636, affirming 95 Fed. 883, 37 C. C. A. 309 ("it is not a mere matter of lapse of time, but of change of situation during neglectful repose, rendering it inequitable to afford relief"); McIntire v. Pryor, 173 U. S. 38, 19 Sup. Ct. 352, 43 L. ed. 606 (affirming 10 App. D. C. 432); Hammond v Hopkins, 143 U. S. 224, 250, 12 Sup. Ct. 418, 36 L. ed. 134; Wilson v. Smith, 117 Fed. 707; State Trust Co. v. Kansas City P. & G. R. Co., 120 Fed. 398; London & S. F. Bank, Ltd., v. Dexter Horton & Co., 126 Fed. 593, Jonathan Mills Mfg. Co v. Whitehurst, 60 Fed. 81; Lasher v. McCreery, 66 Fed. 834, O'Brien v. Wheelock, 78 Fed. 673, Bartlett v. Ambrose, 78 Fed. 839, 24 C. C A. 397, Wheeling Bridge & Terminal Ry. Co. v. Reymann Brewing Co., 90 Fed. 189, 32 C. C. A. 571 (delay of seven years not laches when no change in condition); Hanchett v. Blair, 100 Fed. 817, 41 C. C. A. 76; Williamson v. Monroe, 101 Fed. 322; Bissell Chilled Plow Works v. T. M Bissell Plow Co., 121 Fed. 357 (mere delay of six years no bar to injunction against unfair competition), Shea v. Nilima (C. C. A.), 133 Fed 209 (delay of two years in suing to recover interest in mining claim, no laches when defendants have not been prejudiced), Haney v. Legg, 129 Ala 619, 87 Am. St. Rep. 81, 30 South. 34; Pratt Land & Imp. Co. v. McClain, 135 Ala 452, 93 Am. St. Rep. 35, 33 South. 185; Duke v. State, 56 Ark 485, 20 S. W. 600 (foreclosure of mortgage made in 1837 allowed in 1876, when no prejudice); Bryan v. Hobbs (Ark), 83 S. W. 340; Hovey v. Bradbury, 112 Cal. 620, 44 Pac. 1077; Ex-Mission Land & Water Co. v. Flash, 97 Cal. 610, 32 Pac. 600; Earl v. Van Natta, 29 Ind. App. 532, 64 N E. 901; Brake v. Payne, 137 Ind. 479, 37 N. E 140, Citizens' Nat. Bank v. Judy, 146 Ind. 322, 43 N. E. 259 (delay of eleven months in asking reformation is not such laches as will bar relief when there is no change in the relative positions of the parties), Dunbar v. Green (Kan), 72 Pac 243 ("the mere extent of the delay is one item to be considered. Among others

ing definition has probably been more often relied on by recent cases than any other proceeding from an English judge: "The doctrine of laches in courts of equity is not an arbitrary or technical doctrine. Where it would be practically unjust to give a remedy, either because the party has, by his conduct, done that which might fairly be regarded as equivalent to a waiver of it, or where, by his conduct and neglect, he has, perhaps, not

are any change of conditions, the intervention of the rights of third parties, the likelihood of other interests being affected by the delay, the presence of fraud and its character, the diligence required to discover it, and so on"); Spalding v. St. Joseph's Industrial School, 107 Ky. 382, 54 S. W. 200 (delay of twenty-five years without knowledge of facts not laches when relative positions of parties not changed); Cooke v. Barrett, 155 Mass 413, 29 N. E. 625 (delay of four months after distribution is fatal to objection to composition with creditors, because of change of position of parties); Ripley v. Seligman, 88 Mich. 177, 50 N. W. 143; Washington Lodge v. Frelinghuysen (Mich.), 101 N. W. 569 (delay of twelve years, during which rights had accrued); Sherwood v. Baker, 105 Mo. 472, 24 Am. St. Rep. 399, 16 S. W. 938; Dunklin County v. Choteau, 120 Mo. 577, 25 S. W. 553; Lindell Real Estate Co. v Lindell, 142 Mo. 61, 43 S. W. 368 (delay of eleven years not laches when no change in condition); Wolf v. Great Falls etc. Co., 15 Mont. 49, 38 Pac. 115, Mantle v. Speculator Min. Co., 27 Mont. 473, 71 Pac 665; Fitzgerald v. Fitzgerald & Mallory Const. Co, 44 Neb. 463, 62 N W. 899; Daggers v. Van Dyck, 37 N J. Eq. 130; Tynan v. Warren, 53 N. J Eq 313, 31 Atl. 596, Lundy v. Seymour, 55 N. J. Eq. 1, 35 Atl 893 (mere delay of fourteen years is not laches); Law v. Smith (N. J. Eq.), 59 Atl. 327 (four years; no change in position); Spencer v. Seaboard Air Line Ry. Co. (N. C.), 49 S. E. 96, Wilson v. Wilson, 69 Pac. 923, 41 Or. 459; Gorham v. Sayles, 23 R. I. 449, 50 Atl. 848; Parker v. Bethel Hotel Co., 96 Tenn 252, 31 L. R. A. 706, 34 S. W. 209; Renshaw v. First Nat. Bank (Tenn. Ch. App.), 63 S. W. 194; Robinson v. Kampmann, 5 Tex. Civ. App. 605, 24 S. W. 529, Hamilton v. Dooly, 15 Utah, 280, 49 Pac. 769; Tidball's Exrs. v. Shenandoah Nat. Bank (W. Va.), 42 S. E. 867 (good statement), Ludington v. Patton, 111 Wis. 208, 86 N W. 571; Northern Trust Co. v. Snyder, 113 Wis. 516, 90 Am. St. Rep. 867, 89 N. W. 460 (mere delay not sufficient to bar taxpayers' suit against municipal corporation); Farr v. Hauenstein (N. J. Eq.), 61 Atl. 147; Wollaston v. Tribe, L. R. 9 Eq. Cas. 44, per Romily, M. R.

waiving that remedy, yet put the other party in a situation in which it would not be reasonable to place him if the remedy were afterward to be asserted in either of these cases, lapse of time is most material."[61] The language of an able western court in a very recent case describes the general doctrine with notable accuracy: "Several conditions may combine to render a claim or demand stale in equity. If by the laches and delay of the complainant it has become doubtful whether adverse parties can command the evidence necessary to a fair presentation of the case on their part, or if it appears that they have been deprived of any such advantages they might have had if the claim had been seasonably insisted upon, or before it became antiquated, or if they be subjected to any hardship that might have been avoided by reasonably prompt proceedings, a court of equity will not interfere to give relief, but will remain passive; and this although the full time may not have elapsed which would be required to bar a remedy at law. If, however, upon the other hand, it clearly appears that lapse of time has not in fact changed the conditions and relative positions of the parties, and that they are not materially impaired, and there are peculiar circumstances entitled to consideration as excusing the delay, the court will not deny the appropriate relief, although a strict and unqualified application of the rule of limitations would seem to require it. Every case is gov-

61 Lindsay Petroleum Co. v. Hurd, L. R. 5 P. C. 221, per Lord Selborne, who continues: "But in every case, if an argument against relief which otherwise would be just is founded upon mere delay, that delay, of course, not amounting to a bar by any statute of limitations, the validity of that defense must be tried upon principles substantially equitable. Two circumstances, always important in such cases, are the length of the delay and the nature of the acts done during the interval, which might affect either party and cause a balance of justice or injustice in taking one course or the other." See Ryason v. Dunten (Ind.), 73 N. E. 74.

erned chiefly by its own circumstances."[62] Dicta to substantially the same effect from nearly all the American courts may be readily accumulated, all tending to show that the doctrine of laches is, for the most part, merely an application of the broader maxims of equity, "He who seeks equity must do equity," and "He who comes into equity must come with clean hands." It exacts of the plaintiff no more than fair dealing with his adversary. It is in no way dependent on those general considerations of public utility, and the "repose of society," which are, in legal theory, the legislative motive for statutes of limitations.

§ 22. **Illustrations: Improvements or Sales by Defendant —Loss or Obscuring of Defendant's Evidence.**—"A delay of a party holding an equitable right to property which has permitted another, who holds the legal title, to expend large sums of money in the improvement of the property, and thereby greatly enhance it in value, which he would not have done had the right been properly asserted, has usually been considered such laches as will preclude the party guilty of it from relief. If the party holding the equitable right would avail himself of it, he must assert it in a reasonable time. Equity will not permit him to stand by and permit the other party, who holds the legal title, to improve and develop the property until it has become valuable, or greatly increased in value, and then assert his right."[63]

62 Wilson v. Wilson, 41 Or. 459, 69 Pac. 923, per Woolverton, J.

63 Gibson v. Herriott, 55 Ark. 85, 29 Am. St. Rep. 17, 17 S. W. 589. See, also, Gildersleeve v. New Mexico Min Co., 161 U. S. 573, 582, 16 Sup. Ct. 663, 40 L. ed. 812 (delay of thirty years); O'Brien v. Wheelock, 184 U. S. 450, 22 Sup. Ct. 354, 46 L. ed. 636 (delay of nine years), Halstead v. Grinnan, 152 U. S. 412, 14 Sup. Ct. 641, 38 L. ed. 495; Schlawig v. Purslow, 59 Fed. 848, 8 C. C. A. 315, 19 U. S. App. 501 (delay of ten years); Wetzel v. Minnesota Ry. Transfer Co., 65 Fed. 23, 12 C. C. A. 490, 27 U. S. App. 594 (delay of forty-two

Again, when the property in dispute has been sold by the party at fault to innocent parties, a delay by the complainant may amount to laches.[64]

Where important evidence in behalf of the defendant has been lost during the delay of the complainant, he will generally be barred from relief. The loss may result from the death or incapacity of some of the witnesses. Again, the delay may be so long that under the circumstances many of the important facts have become obscured. To allow a complainant relief in such cases would frequently risk a great hardship to innocent parties. Consequently, the courts decline to interfere.[65]

years); Dickman v. Dryden, 90 Minn. 244, 95 N. W. 1120; Loomis v. Rosenthal, 34 Or. 585, 57 Pac. 55; Chezum v. McBride, 21 Wash. 558, 58 Pac 1067; Melms v. Pabst Brewing Co., 93 Wis. 153, 57 Am. St. Rep. 899, 66 N. W. 518.

64 Wetzel v. Minnesota Ry. Transfer Co, 65 Fed. 23, 12 C. C. A. 490, 27 U. S App. 594; Nantahala Marble & Talc Co v. Thomas, 76 Fed. 59 (delay of twelve years); Helfenstein v. Reed, 62 Fed. 214, 10 C. C. A. 327, 27 U. S. App 103 (delay of twenty-five years); St Paul, S. & T. F. R. Co. v. Sage, 49 Fed 315, 1 C. C. A. 256, 4 U. S. App. 160 (reversing 32 Fed. 821, 44 Fed. 817); Bateman v. Butler, 19 Colo. 547, 36 Pac. 548, Converse v. Brown, 200 Ill. 166, 65 N. E. 644; Dunbar v. Green, 66 Kan. 557, 72 Pac. 243 (delay of twenty-one years); Snow v. Mfg. Co., 158 Mass. 325, 33 N. E. 588 (delay of one year in suing to set aside sale of corporate property to directors, during which time property had been sold to others), Berkey v. St. Paul Nat. Bank, 54 Minn. 448, 56 N. W. 53 (plaintiff barred by delay of seven years although purchaser had constructive notice); North v. Platte County, 29 Neb 447, 26 Am St. Rep. 395, 45 N. W. 692 (delay of nine years); Commonwealth v. Reading Traction Co., 204 Pa. 151, 53 Atl. 755.

65 In the following cases, the death of witnesses, coupled with delay by complainant, was held sufficient to bar relief: Foster v. Mansfield etc. Co, 146 U. S. 88, 13 Sup. Ct. 28, 36 L. ed. 899; Hinchman v. Kelley, 54 Fed. 63, 4 C. C. A. 189, 7 U. S. App. 481; Eiffert v. Craps, 58 Fed. 470, 7 C. C. A. 319, 8 U. S. App 436 (delay of forty years); Socrates Quicksilver Mines v. Carr Realty Co., 64 C. C. A 539, 130 Fed. 293 (delay of twenty-eight years); Rives v. Morris,

§ 23. **Defense of Laches Favored by United States Courts—Increase in Value of the Property Fatal to Plaintiff's Claim.**—This fair degree of unanimity as to the theoretical basis

108 Ala. 527, 18 South. 743; Street v. Henry, 124 Ala. 153, 27 South. 411 (delay of twenty-six years); Ryan v. Woodin (Idaho), 75 Pac. 261 (delay of five years); Thomas v. Van Meter, 164 Ill. 304, 45 N. E. 405 (delay of sixteen years); New York Life Ins. Co. v. Weaver's Admr., 24 Ky. Law Rep. 1086, 70 S. W. 628; Ripple v. Kuehne (Md.), 60 Atl. 464 (delay of eight years after fraud, and almost a year after death of party charged with fraud, and of attorney who transacted the business); Hadaway v. Hynson, 89 Md. 305, 43 Atl. 806; Preston v. Horwitz, 85 Md. 164, 36 Atl. 710; Eames v. Manley, 121 Mich. 300, 80 N. W. 15; Baker v. Cunningham, 162 Mo 134, 85 Am. St. Rep 490, 62 S. W. 445; McKechnie v. McKechnie, 39 N. Y. Supp. 402, 3 App Div. 91; Taylor v. Slater, 21 R. I. 104, 41 Atl. 1001; Garland's Admr. v. Garland's Admr. (Va.), 24 S. E. 505; Snipes v. Kelleher, 31 Wash. 386, 72 Pac 67. See, however, Ball v. Ball, 20 R. I 520, 40 Atl. 234; Young v. Young, 51 N. J. Eq. 491, 27 Atl 627 (death of witnesses not sufficient when it causes no serious disadvantage); Holsberry v. Harris (W. Va.), 49 S. E. 404.

In the following cases witnesses became incapacitated during the time of complainant's delay, and relief was denied Whitney v. Fox, 166 U. S. 637, 17 Sup. Ct. 713, 41 L. ed. 1145 (defendant became mentally impaired); Dispeau v. First Nat. Bank, 24 R. I. 508, 53 Atl. 868.

Illustrations of refusal of relief on account of the evidence becoming obscure are found in the following cases: In Doane v. Preston, 183 Mass 569, 67 N. E. 867, a bill founded upon neglect of corporation officers to act upon an offer to convey the right to manufacture patented machines was filed after a delay of six years. Relief was refused because it would rquire an investigation of an alleged offer made six years before suit, as well as conduct and motives of parties, and of the state and condition at that time of a branch of manufacture in which new inventions play an important part. In Lutjen v. Lutjen (N. J. Eq.), 53 Atl. 625, the court says: "Lapse of time alone is deemed by the authorities to be a sufficient ground of estoppel in cases like the present, when the court cannot feel confident of its ability to ascertain the truth now, as well as it could when the subject for investigation was recent, and before the memories of those who had knowledge of the material facts have become faded and weakened by time. To constitute estoppel of this description, it is not essential that any actual loss of testimony, through death or otherwise, or means of proof, or changed of the doctrine is shaken by a series of decisions by the supreme court of the United States, followed, of course, by recent cases in the lower federal and the territorial courts, and to a limited extent by state courts. The decisive feature in these cases has been that the property which is the subject-matter of the litigation has greatly risen in value since the complainant's cause of action accrued. The courts profess to find in the plaintiff's delay under such circumstances an element of injury to the defendant, consisting, apparently, in the latter's uncertainty whether suit will or will not be brought; and base the doctrine of laches not on the unfairness of the plaintiff's conduct, but rather on motives of public policy against the disturbance of possessory titles, however acquired. The "growing favor" with which the defense is recognized by the federal courts has not escaped judicial comment.[66]

relations, to the prejudice of the other party, should have occurred. But the estoppel arises because the court cannot, after so great a lapse of time, rely upon the memory of witnesses to reproduce the details that entered into the final execution of the instrument of settlement."

In general, see the following cases, where the questions were considered. Abraham v Ordway, 158 U. S. 416, 15 Sup. Ct. 894, 39 L. ed. 1036; Lemoine v. Dunklin County, 51 Fed. 487, 2 C C. A. 343, 10 U. S App 227 (affirming 46 Fed. 219); Wood v. Perkins, 64 Fed 817; Jones v. Perkins, 76 Fed. 82, Anderson v. Northrop, 30 Fla. 612, 12 South. 318; Patterson v. Hewitt (N. Mex.), 66 Pac. 552, 55 L. R. A. 658; Lockwood v. White, 65 Vt. 466, 26 Atl. 639; Nelson v Triplett, 99 Va. 421, 39 S. E. 150; Jameson v. Rixey, 94 Va. 342, 64 Am. St. Rep. 726, 26 S. E. 861; Pethtel v. McCullough, 49 W. Va. 520, 39 S E. 199; Seymour v. Alkire, 47 W. Va. 302, 34 S. E. 953.

66 As in Lasher v. McCreery, 66 Fed. 834, 840 (1895), by Jackson, D. J., speaking from the vantage ground of over thirty years' experience as federal judge. "This is an equitable defense, and is often resorted to when the party who sets it up has no defense in law, and for this reason courts should be very cautious in applying this doctrine to defeat a rightful owner of the land who, from neglect, which may be the result of the want of proper information,

This view of the federal courts is well presented in the following excerpts: "In cases of actual fraud, or of want of knowledge of the facts, the law is very tolerant of delay; but where the circumstances of the case negative this idea, and the transaction is sought to be impeached only by reason of the confidential relations between the parties, and the *cestuis que trustent* have ample notice of the facts, they ought not to wait and make their action in setting aside the sale dependent upon the question whether it is likely to prove a profitable speculation. As the question whether the sale should be vacated or not depends upon the facts as they existed at the time of the sale, so, in taking proceedings to avoid such sale, the plaintiff should act upon his information as to such facts, and not delay for the purpose of ascertaining whether he is likely to be benefited by a rise in the property, since that would practically amount to throwing upon the purchaser any losses he might sustain by a fall, and denying him the benefit of a possible rise."[67] "No doctrine is so wholesome,

refrains from an assertion of his rights until the presumption of abandonment arises from his course of conduct. I am aware of the tendency in the courts of this day to recognize the defense with growing favor as both meritorious and valid."

67 Hoyt v. Latham, 143 U. S. 553, 12 Sup. Ct. 568, 36 L. ed 259. See in general, as to change in value proving fatal to complainant's case, Oil Co. v. Marbury, 91 U. S. 592, 23 L. ed 331, Galliher v. Cadwell, 145 U. S 368, 12 Sup. Ct. 873, 36 L. ed. 738 (affirming 3 Wash T. 501, 18 Pac. 68); McIntire v. Pryor, 173 U. S 38, 19 Sup Ct. 352, 43 L. ed. 606 (affirming 10 App. D C. 432), Felix v. Patrick, 145 U. S 317, 12 Sup. Ct 862, 36 L. ed. 719 (affirming 36 Fed 457), Johnston v Standard Min. Co, 148 U. S. 360, 13 Sup. Ct. 585, 37 L. ed. 480; Patterson v. Hewitt, 195 U. S. 309, 25 Sup. Ct. 35, 49 L ed ——; Sagadahoc Land Co. v. Ewing, 65 Fed. 702, 13 C. C. A. 83, 31 U. S. App. 102; Continental Nat. Bank v. Heilman, 81 Fed 36 (affirmed 86 Fed. 514, 30 C. C. A. 232); Old Colony Trust Co. v Dubuque L. & T. Co, 89 Fed. 794; Kinne v. Webb, 49 Fed. 512, Lemoine v. Dunklin County, 51 Fed. 487, 2 C. C. A. 343, 10 U. S. App. 227 (af-

when wisely administered, as that of laches. It prevents the resurrection of stale titles, and forbids the spying out from the records of ancient and abandoned rights. It requires of every owner that he take care of his property, and of every claimant that he make known his claims. It gives to the actual and longer possessor security, and induces and justifies him in all efforts to improve and make valuable the property he holds. It is a doctrine received with favor, because its proper application works out justice and equity, and often bars the holder of a mere technical right, which he has abandoned for years, from enforcing it when its enforcement will work large injury to many."[68] "The equitable rule that one who is negligent shall not have relief, and the barring of proceedings after the lapse of stated periods of time by statutory enactments, are alike based upon public policy, as well as upon considerations affecting only individual rights. It is to the public interest that stability in the title to property should exist, and that all uncertainties and disputes as to the ownership of land should be speedily put at rest. . . . . Hence, there lies at the foundation of the principle that the lapse of time will become a defense to the title of the one in possession of prop-

firming 46 Fed. 219); Church of Jesus Christ v. Reorganized Church etc., 70 Fed. 179, 17 C. C. A. 387, 36 U. S. App. 110; Curtis v. Lakin, 94 Fed. 251, 36 C. C. A. 222 (delay of two years only); Meyer v Johnson, 60 Ark. 50, 28 S. W. 797; Bateman v. Reitler, 19 Colo. 547, 36 Pac. 548; Graff v. Portland Town & Mineral Co., 12 Colo. App. 106, 54 Pac. 854; Burke v Backus, 51 Minn. 174, 53 N. W. 458; Patterson v. Hewitt (N. Mex.), 66 Pac. 552, 55 L. R. A. 658 (eight years' delay in enforcing resulting trust); affirmed, 195 U. S. 309, 25 Sup. Ct. 35; Loomis v. Rosenthal, 34 Or. 585, 57 Pac. 55; Bryant v. Groves, 42 W. Va 10, 24 S. E. 605; Melms v. Pabst Brewing Co, 93 Wis. 153, 57 Am. St. Rep. 899, 66 N. W. 518.

68 Naddo v. Bardon, 51 Fed. 493, 2 C. C. A. 335, 4 U. S. App. 642, per Brewer, J.

erty not only consideration for his personal rights and equities, but also a recognition of the higher public interests which can only be subserved by putting at rest, as speedily as possible, all doubts and uncertainties touching the title of realty, to which end it is the duty of courts to discourage delays in the assertion of conflicting claims thereto."[69]

69 St Paul etc. R. Co. v. Sage, 49 Fed. 315, 326, 1 C. C. A. 256, 4 U. S App 160, per Shiras, J., reversing 32 Fed. 821, 44 Fed 817. See, also, Halstead v. Grinnan, 152 U. S. 412, 14 Sup. Ct. 641, 38 L. ed 495.

It appears to the writer far from easy to adjust the principle announced in these decisions, if worked out to its logical conclusion, with those ordinary ideas of fair dealing whch usually guide the chancellor's discretion. It practically amounts to saying, that if the defendant's wrong has turned out to be an enormously profitable one to him, that affords a reason, either alone or in connection with other reasons, why he should be protected in the enjoyment of his profit by a court of equity; and the greater the profit, the stronger the protection The fact that the plaintiff, in the exercise of ordinary business prudence, has delayed until it has become apparent that his success in the litigation will not be a fruitless victory is, in this view, conduct more inequitable than any of which the defendant can possibly have been guilty, and excuses the court from investigation of the defendant's wrong. The delay may be far less than that allowed by the most stringent statute of limitations; and the circumstance which most strongly operates upon the conscience of the court—viz., the rise in value of the property—is a purely accidental one, unconnected with any fault of the plaintiff or merit of the defendant. The motives of public policy and the repose of society by which this favoritism shown to the defense of laches has been justified seem rather appropriate for the consideration of a legislature than of a court, and hardly warrant the court's overruling a legislative policy already expressed in statutes of limitation.

Laches from Long Delay Alone.—For the sake of completeness, it should be noticed that in a considerable number of cases no element of laches save the long delay alone is mentioned by the court; but it is not impossible that some of the additional elements heretofore described may have existed to influence these decisions. See, for examples, De Martin v. Phelan, 51 Fed. 865, 2 C. C. A. 523, 7 U. S. App. 233, affirming 47 Fed. 761 (action to declare deed a mortgage); Reed v. Dingess, 56 Fed. 171 (bill to redeem); Streight v. Junk, 59

§ 24. Limitation of the General Doctrine in Case of Injunction in Support of Strict Legal Right.—An important limitation upon the general rule as to the effect of delay has been established by a considerable preponderance of authority. "Where an injunction is asked in support of a strict *legal* right, the party is entitled to it if his legal right is established; mere delay and acquiescence will not, therefore, defeat the remedy unless it has continued so long as to defeat the right itself."[70] This rule has had frequent application where injunction has been sought against the pollution[71] or diversion[72] of water; or against the infringement of a patent[73] or a trade-mark.[74]

Fed. 321, 8 C. C. A. 137, 16 U. S. App. 608 (delay of two years by stockholder in suing to enforce the rights of a corporation against a director); Kemp v. Nickerson, 66 Fed. 682, Halsey v. Cheney, 68 Fed. 763, 15 C. C. A. 656, 34 U. S. App. 50; Guarantee Trust & S. D. Co. v. Delta & Pine Land Co., 104 Fed. 5, 43 C. C. A. 396 (delay of twenty-five years, unexcused); Jones v. Perkins, 76 Fed. 82; Tetrault v. Fournier (Mass.), 72 N. E. 350; Fennyery v. Ransom, 170 Mass. 303, 49 N. E. 620; Wiggin v. Swamscot Mach. Co., 68 N. H. 14, 38 Atl. 727; Shields v. Tarleton, 48 W. Va. 343, 37 S. E. 589.

70 2 Pom. Eq. Jur., § 817. See, also, Galway v. Metropolitan Elev. R. Co., 128 N. Y. 132, 28 N. E. 479, 13 L. R. A. 788, citing Pom. Eq. Jur., § 817, and many cases (nuisance); Higgins Oil & Fuel Co. v. Snow, 113 Fed. 433, 51 C. C. A. 267, and cases cited (in Texas, laches not imputable to one whose title is capable of being established at law).

71 Goldsmid v. Tunbridge Wells Imp. Commrs., L. R. 1 Eq. 161; State of Missouri v. State of Illinois, 180 U. S. 208, 21 Sup. Ct. 331, 45 L. ed. 497; Chapman v. Rochester, 110 N. Y. 273, 6 Am. St. Rep. 366, 18 N. E. 88, 1 L. R. A. 296.

72 Lonsdale Co. v. City of Woonsocket, 21 R. I. 498, 44 Atl. 929 (sixteen years' delay); Rigney v. Tacoma L. & W. Co., 9 Wash. 576, 38 Pac. 147, 26 L. R. A. 425 (relying on Pom. Eq. Jur., § 817).

73 Taylor v. Sawyer Spindle Co., 75 Fed. 301, 304, 22 C. C. A. 203, 206, and cases cited, Ide v. Thorlicht etc. Carpet Co., 115 Fed. 137, 148, and cases cited.

74 Fullwood v. Fullwood, L. R. 9 Ch. Div. 176; Menendez v. Holt, 128 U. S. 514, 9 Sup. Ct. 143, 32 L. ed. 526. Compare Grand Lodge A. O. U. W. v. Graham, 96 Iowa, 592, 65 N. W. 837, 31 L. R. A. 133.

§ 25. **Whether Laches is Imputable to the Government.**—Laches is not imputable to the government of the United States when it has a direct pecuniary interest in the subject of the litigation.[75] This rule is based on public policy. Where, however, "the government is a mere formal complainant in a suit, not for the purpose of asserting any public right, or protecting any public interest, title, or property, but merely to form a conduit through which one private person can conduct litigation against another private person," laches may be imputed.[76] It has been held that it is imputable to a state,[77] and also to a municipal corporation, but the doctrine should be applied cautiously.[78]

§ 26. **Excuses for Laches—(1) Party's Ignorance of His Rights.**—"A person cannot be deprived of his remedy in equity on the ground of laches, unless it appears that he had knowledge of his rights. As one cannot acquiesce in the performance of an act of which he is ignorant, so one cannot be said to neglect the prosecution

75 San Pedro & Canon del Agua Co v. United States, 146 U S. 120, 13 Sup Ct. 94, 36 L. ed. 912; United States v. State of Michigan, 190 U. S. 379, 23 Sup Ct. 742, 47 L. ed. 1103; Southern Pac. R. Co. v. Stanley, 49 Fed. 263, United States v. Dastervignes, 118 Fed. 199; United States v Willamette Val. & C. M. Wagon Road Co, 54 Fed 807. In this last case the court said· "It is held that laches is not imputable to the government upon grounds of public policy. The common-law rule that no lapse of time can bar the right of the king is not only recognized in the United States, but is deemed to be applicable with added reason, from the fact that here property is held, not as by a monarch for personal or private purposes, but in trust for the common welfare; and, where the agencies of the people are so numerous and scattered, the utmost vigilance would not save the public from loss."

76 United States v. Beebe, 127 U. S. 338, 8 Sup. Ct. 1083, 32 L. ed. 121; United States v. Chicago, M. & St. P. R. Co., 54 C. C. A. 545, 116 Fed. 969.

77 Attorney-General v. Central R. Co. (N. J. Eq.), 59 Atl. 348.

78 Dunklin County v. Chouteau, 120 Mo. 577, 25 S. W. 553.

of a remedy when he has no knowledge that his rights have been invaded, excepting, always, that his want of knowledge is not the result of his own culpable negligence. It is not a little difficult to determine what knowledge is necessary to place the party in the position of negligently delaying his action."[79]

79 Hall v. Otterson, 52 N. J. Eq. 522, 28 Atl. 907, per Green, V. C. See, also, Hodge v. Palms, 68 Fed. 61, 15 C. C. A. 220, 37 U. S. App. 61; Kansas City Southern R. Co. v. Stevenson, 135 Fed. 553; Spalding v. St. Joseph's Industrial School, 107 Ky. 382, 54 S. W. 200; Whitridge v. Whitridge, 76 Md. 54, 24 Atl. 645 (delay of twelve years); Moorman v Arthur, 90 Va 455, 18 S. E. 869; Jameson v. Rixey, 94 Va 342, 64 Am. St. Rep. 726, 26 S. E. 861 (delay of twenty years); Craufurd's Admr. v. Smith's Exr., 93 Va. 623, 23 S. E. 235, 25 S. E. 657.

Where there is no fraud in the case, plaintiff's ignorance may be no excuse after a great lapse of time. "The interests of public order and tranquility demand that parties shall acquaint themselves with their rights within a reasonable time, and, although this time may be extended by their actual ignorance, or want of means, it is by no means illimitable": Wetzel v. Minn. Ry. Transfer Co, 169 U. S. 237, 18 Sup. Ct 307, 2 L. ed 730 (affirming 65 Fed. 23, 12 C. C. A. 490). The delay in this case was thirty years. Ignorance is not an excuse when the plaintiff has notice of facts which should put him on inquiry: Loomis v. Rosenthal, 34 Or. 585, 57 Pac. 55. It has been held that one who knows that another is selling an article in violation of contract cannot justify delay on the ground that he did not have enough evidence, since he could bring suit and have a discovery of details by means of interrogatories: Fowler v. Park, 48 Fed. 789

See, also, *post*, at note 109.

Ignorance of Law.—Though a party may be fully apprised of the facts from which his equitable right arises, his ignorance of that right has sometimes been held to excuse a long delay in its enforcement: See Lasher v. McCreery, 66 Fed. 834, where the law was generally supposed to be settled adversely to the plaintiff during the period of the plaintiff's inaction, Dinwiddie v. Self, 145 Ill. 290, 33 N. E 892, where delay of twenty years in suing to reform a deed for mistake of law was due to the advice of a reputable attorney that the deed correctly expressed the grantor's intention. But see Wetzel v. Minnesota Ry. Transfer Co., 65 Fed. 23, 12 C. C. A. 490, 27 U. S. App. 594; affirmed, 169 U. S. 237, 241, 18 Sup. Ct. 307, 42 L. ed. 730.

§ 27. Ignorance of Fraud.—"The right of the party defrauded is not affected by the lapse of time, or generally speaking, by anything done or omitted to be done, so long as he remains, without any fault of his own, in ignorance of the fraud that has been committed."[80] What is culpable negligence on the part of the defrauded party in acquainting himself with the fraud is incapable of exact definition. Such negligence is not imputed where the relation between the parties is one of trust and confidence;[81] and a considerable degree of inaction is excused by active measures taken by the fraudulent party for the concealment of the fraud.[82] "The defense of want of knowledge on the part of one charged with laches is one easily made, easy to prove by his own oath, and hard to disprove; and hence the tendency of courts in recent years has been to hold the plaintiff to a rigid compliance with the law which demands, not only that he should have been ignorant of the fraud, but that he should have used reasonable dili-

80 Rolfe v. Gregory, 4 De Gex, J. & S. 576, per Lord Westbury; 2 Pom. Eq. Jur., § 917 and note. See, also, Alger v. Anderson, 78 Fed. 729; Wilson v. Augur, 176 Ill. 561, 52 N. E. 289; Butler v. Prentiss, 158 N. Y. 49, 52 N. E. 652 (reversing 36 N. Y. Supp. 301, 91 Hun, 643), Simpkins v. Taylor, 81 Hun, 467, 31 N. Y. Supp. 169.

81 Bitzeman v. Bitzeman, [1895] 2 Ch. 474 (no duty of inquiry); Reavis v. Reavis, 103 Fed. 813 (reliance upon a relative); Penn v. Folger, 182 Ill. 76, 55 N. E. 192 (reversing 77 Ill. App. 365); Stanwood v. Wishard, 134 Fed. 959 (fraud of attorney; client a nonresident).

82 "The perpetrator of a fraud can hardly be permitted to successfully plead in a court of equity that he so completely secured and betrayed the confidence of his victim that the latter believed his false statement that no inquiry or examination would avail him aught so long that, when his faith faltered, it was too late for him to recover": Kelley v. Boettcher, 85 Fed. 55, 62, 29 C. C. A. 14, 56 U. S. App. 363. See, also, Salsbury v. Ware, 183 Ill. 505, 56 N. E. 149 (reversing 80 Ill. App. 485). Compare Townsend v. Vanderwerker, 160 U. S. 171, 16 Sup. Ct. 258, 40 L. ed. 383.

gence to have informed himself of all the facts."[83] Knowledge of facts which would put a person of ordinary prudence and diligence on inquiry is, in the eyes of the law, equivalent to a knowledge of all the facts which a reasonably diligent inquiry would disclose.[84]

[83] Foster v. Mansfield C. & L M R. Co, 146 U. S. 88, 99, 13 Sup. Ct 28, 36 L ed 899, affirming 36 Fed. 627; Wetzel v. Minnesota Ry. Tr. Co., 65 Fed 23, 12 C. C. A 490, 27 U. S. App. 594, affirmed, 169 U S. 237, 18 Sup Ct. 309. See, also, Felix v Patrick, 145 U. S. 317, 36 L. ed 719, 12 Sup. Ct. 862 (affirming 36 Fed. 457); Eiffert v. Craps, 58 Fed. 470, 7 C. C A. 319, 8 U. S. App. 436 (chargeable when fraud might have been discovered by inspection of one recorded deed), Scheftel v. Hays, 58 Fed. 457, 7 C. C. A. 308, 19 U. S. App. 220 (inquiry of the chief perpetrator of the fraud is not sufficient), Lant v. Manley, 71 Fed. 7, 19 (fraud evidenced by a public record); McMonagle v. McGlinn, 85 Fed. 88; Reynolds & Hamby etc. Co. v. Martin, 116 Ga. 495, 42 S E. 796; Fitch v. Miller, 200 Ill. 170, 65 N. E. 650; Donaldson v. Jacobitz, 67 Kan. 244, 72 Pac. 846; Cole v. Boyd (Neb.), 93 N. W. 1003. The bill must show with particularity how and when the plaintiffs' knowledge was obtained, in order that the court may determine whether reasonable effort was made by him to ascertain the facts· Hardt v. Heidweyer, 152 U S 547, 558, 14 Sup. Ct. 671, 38 L. ed. 548 and cases cited; Stearns v. Page, 1 Story, 204 215, 217, Fed. Cas. No. 13,339, by Story, J ; Stearns v. Page, 7 How 819, 829, 12 L. ed. 928, by Grier, J.; Badger v. Badger, 2 Wall. 87, 95, 17 L. ed 836; Wood v. Carpenter, 101 U. S. 135, 140, 25 L. ed. 807; Bangs v. Loveridge, 60 Fed. 963 ("a party seeking to avoid the bar of the statute on the ground of fraud must aver and show that he used due diligence to detect the fraud, and if he had the means of discovering it, he will be held in equity to have known it"); Hubbard v. Manhattan Trust Co, 87 Fed 51, 30 C. C. A. 520; Cutter v. Iowa Water Co, 128 Fed. 505 ("there must be allegations and evidence showing what he did to discover the fraud, and a showing why he did not discover it"); Melms v. Pabst Brewing Co, 93 Wis. 153, 57 Am. St. Rep. 899, 66 N. W. 518. See, also, Felix v. Patrick, 145 U. S. 317, 12 Sup. Ct. 862, 36 L. ed 719 (affirming 36 Fed. 457).

[84] Swift v. Smith, 79 Fed. 709, 713, 25 C. C. A. 154, 49 U. S. App 188 (citing many cases); Melms v. Pabst Brewing Co., 93 Wis. 153, 174, 57 Am. St Rep. 899, 66 N. W. 518, and cases cited; Johnston v. Standard Min. Co, 148 U. S. 360, 13 Sup. Ct. 585, 37 L. ed. 480, affirming 39 Fed. 304 (plaintiff is "chargeable with such knowledge as he might have obtained upon inquiry, provided the facts already

§ 28. **Breach of Express Continuing Trust.**—In cases of express continuing trusts, "so long as the relation of trustee and *cestui que trust* continues to exist, no length of time will bar the *cestui que trust* of his rights in the subject of the trust as against the trustee, unless circumstances exist to raise a presumption from lapse of time of an extinguishment of the trust, or unless there has been an open denial or repudiation of the trust brought home to the knowledge of the *cestui que trust* which requires him to act as upon an asserted adverse title."[85] But where the repudiation or breach of the trust has been brought home to the actual knowledge of the *cestui que trust,* the ordinary rules as to laches apply. the same degree of diligence is required of him as in cases of the rescission of a contract for fraud or mistake.[86]

known to him were such as to put upon a man of ordinary intelligence the duty of inquiry''), Edwards v. Mercantile Trust Co, 124 Fed. 381. See, also, Rugan v. Sabin, 53 Fed. 415, 418, 3 C. C. A. 578, 580, 10 U. S. App. 519, 530.

85 Anderson v. Northrop, 30 Fla. 612, 12 South. 318, 324, and cases cited; Hoyt v. Latham, 143 U. S. 553, 12 Sup. Ct. 568, 36 L ed. 259; New Orleans v. Warner, 175 U. S. 120, 130, 20 Sup Ct. 44, 44 L. ed. 96; Wood v. Perkins, 64 Fed. 817, 57 Fed. 258, Haney v. Legg, 129 Ala 619, 87 Am. St. Rep. 81, 30 South. 34; Hovey v. Bradbury, 112 Cal 620, 44 Pac. 1077 (delay of eight years not laches when no notice of repudiation); White v. Costigan, 138 Cal. 564, 72 Pac. 178; French v. Woodruff, 25 Colo. 339, 54 Pac. 1015; Stanley's Estate v. Pence, 160 Ind. 636, 66 N. E. 51, 67 N. E. 441; Raymond v. Flavel, 27 Or. 219, 40 Pac. 158; Joy v Ft Worth Compress Co., 24 Tex. Civ. App. 94, 58 S. W. 173. See, however, Preston v. Horwitz, 85 Md. 164, 36 Atl. 710, citing Maryland cases, *contra.*

86 In states where the statutes of limitations apply to equitable actions, the rules as to the time when the statute begins to run are generally analogous to those which apply to the running of time considered as an element of laches. Consequently both classes of cases may be cited as authority for the text: See Naddo v. Bardon, 51 Fed. 493, 2 C. C. A. 335, 4 U. S. App. 642, 681 (affirming 47 Fed. 782); Church of Christ v. Reorganized Church of Jesus Christ of

Constructive and resulting trusts are also governed by the ordinary rules as to laches;[87] but in cases of resulting trust, where the trustee constantly acknowledges the right of the one in whose favor the trust is raised by virtue of his payment of the purchase-money,

Latter-Day Saints, 70 Fed. 179, 17 C. C. A. 387, 36 U. S. App. 110; Curtis v. Lakin, 94 Fed 251, 36 C. C. A. 222; Nash v. Ingalls, 101 Fed. 645, 41 C. C. A. 545 (affirming 79 Fed. 510); Swift v. Smith, 79 Fed 709, 714, 25 C. C. A. 154, 159, 49 U. S. App. 188; Hitchcock v. Cosper (Ind.), 73 N E. 264, Mantle v. Speculator Min. Co., 27 Mont. 473, 71 Pac. 665, Church v. Winton, 196 Pa. St. 107, 46 Atl 363; Snipes v. Kelleher, 31 Wash. 386, 72 Pac. 67.

87 The rules in this respect as to laches and the statute of limitations are identical; cases of both kinds are therefore cited: See Lemoine v. Dunklin County, 51 Fed. 487, 2 C C. A. 343, 10 U. S. App 227 (affirming 46 Fed. 219), McMonagle v. McGlinn, 85 Fed. 88; Nouges v. Newlands, 118 Cal. 102, 50 Pac. 386; Schofield v. Wooley, 98 Ga. 548, 58 Am. St. Rep. 315, 25 S. E. 769, McLaflin v. Jones, 155 Ill 539, 40 N. E. 330, affirming 55 Ill. App. 518 (delay of thirteen years); Blackledge v. Blackledge (Iowa), 91 N. W. 818; Wilson v. Louisville Trust Co., 102 Ky. 522, 44 S. W. 121; Patterson v. Hewitt (N. Mex.), 66 Pac. 552, 55 L R. A. 658; Southall v. Southall, 6 Tex. Civ. App. 694, 26 S. W. 150; Redford v. Clark, 100 Va. 115, 40 S. E. 630; Merton v. O'Brien, 117 Wis. 437, 94 N. W. 340; Boyd v Mutual Fire Assn., 116 Wis. 155, 96 Am. St. Rep. 948, 90 N. W. 1086, 61 L. R. A. 918, 94 N. W. 171 (officers and directors of corporations are not express trustees and are not precluded from setting up limitations). In Landis v. Saxton, 105 Mo. 486, 24 Am. St. Rep. 406, 16 S. W 912, the rule is stated as follows: "The trusts against which the statute will not run are those technical and continuing trusts which are not at all cognizable at law, but fall within the proper, peculiar, and exclusive jurisdiction of a court of equity; but other trusts which are the ground of an action at law are open to the operation of the statute."

The United States supreme court has drawn a distinction between cases involving actual fraud and cases of constructive fraud merely—such as the purchase by the trustee of the trust property for a price which was fair at the time of the transaction—holding the *cestui que trust* to a more stringent obligation of diligence in the latter class of cases: See Hammond v. Hopkins, 143 U. S. 224, 250, 12 Sup. Ct. 418, 36 L. ed. 134.

the trust is properly treated as express, so far as the operation of the doctrine of laches is concerned.[88]

§ 29. **Excuses: (2) Infancy.**—Infancy is a defense for delay both at law and in equity.[89] An infant, having no capacity to sue, cannot be held blameworthy for delaying to sue. After becoming of age, however, he must act promptly.[90] Following the analogy of the statute of limitations, it has been held that where time has commenced to run against the ancestor, it still continues to run against the minor heir.[91]

§ 30. **Excuses: (3) Mental Unsoundness.**—Laches cannot be imputed to one of unsound mind;[92] and this rule holds, although the next friend who brings the suit is clearly guilty of laches.[93]

§ 31. **Excuses: (4) Coverture.**—Whether the common-law rule that a married woman cannot be guilty of laches[94] has been changed by the modern statutes permitting a married woman to sue in her own name, is a question on which there appears to be some disagree-

88 Fawcett v. Fawcett, 85 Wis. 332, 39 Am. St Rep. 844, 55 N. W 405, Haney v. Legg, 129 Ala. 619, 87 Am St. Rep 81, 30 South. 34.

89 Robinson v. Kampmann, 5 Tex. Civ. App. 605, 24 S. W. 529; Cole v. Grigsby (Tex. Civ. App.), 35 S W. 680; Robinett v Robinett's Heirs (Va.), 19 S. E 845; Melms v. Pabst Brewing Co., 93 Wis. 153, 57 Am. St. Rep. 899, 66 N. W 518.

90 Melms v. Pabst Brewing Co., 93 Wis. 153, 57 Am. St. Rep. 899, 66 N. W. 518.

91 Gibson v. Herriott, 55 Ark. 85, 29 Am. St. Rep. 17, 17 S. W. 589.

92 Van Buskirk v. Van Buskirk, 148 Ill 9, 35 N. E. 383 (delay of forty-two years); Kidder v. Houston (N. J Eq.), 47 Atl. 336; Trowbridge v. Stone's Admr., 42 W. Va. 454, 26 S. E. 363.

93 Kidder v. Houston (N. J. Eq.), 47 Atl. 336

94 Gibson v. Herriott, 55 Ark. 85, 29 Am. St. Rep. 17, 17 S W. 589; Lindell Real Estate Co. v. Lindell, 142 Mo. 61, 43 S. W. 368; Cole v. Grigsby (Tex. Civ. App.), 35 S. W. 680.

ment.[95] The marital relation may, so long as cohabitation continues, afford the wife a partial or total excuse for delay in commencing litigation to which the husband is a party defendant.[96]

§ 32. (5) **When Laches not Imputed to Reversioners.**—It is generally held "that no laches can be imputed to reversioners in a contest between them and the tenant for life over the reversionary property until after the termination of the life estate, unless it be shown clearly and unequivocally that before that time they had actual knowledge of an abandonment by the life tenant of her *status* as such, and of a holding of the property by her under a different and adverse right."[97] And it is further held "that the *onus* of showing such notice or knowledge as, when coupled with long acquiescence, would amount to laches, is on the party urging laches as a defense."[98]

§ 33. (6) **When Party in Possession not Chargeable with Laches.**—A party in possession of land who resorts

95 Compare Lindell Real Estate Co. v. Lindell, 142 Mo. 61, 43 S. W. 368 (no laches), with Gibson v Herriott, 55 Ark. 85, 29 Am. St. Rep. 17, 17 S. W. 589 (guilty of laches with respect to her separate property). See, also, Phillips v. Pinney Coal & Coke Co, 53 W. Va. 543, 97 Am. St. Rep. 1040, 44 S. E. 774, where a married woman was held guilty of laches; McPeck's Heirs v. Graham's Heirs (W. Va.), 49 S. E. 125 (same); Waldron v. Harvey, 54 W. Va 608, 102 Am. St. Rep. 959, 46 S. E. 603 (laches cannot be imputed to a married woman to defeat her right to land not her separate estate).

96 Fawcett v. Fawcett, 85 Wis. 332, 39 Am. St. Rep. 844, 55 N. W. 405; Conner v. Leach, 84 Md. 571, 36 Atl. 591.

97 Anderson v. Northrop, 30 Fla. 612, 12 South. 318, and cases cited, Howell v Jump, 140 Mo. 441, 41 S. W. 976. And see Gibson v. Herriott, 55 Ark. 85, 29 Am. St Rep. 17, 17 S. W. 589

98 Anderson v. Northrop, 30 Fla. 612, 12 South. 318, and cases cited. "And it is for the party urging laches to show when his adversary acquired a knowledge of the truth, and to prove that he knowingly forebore to assert his right."

to a court of equity to settle a question of title is not chargeable with laches, no matter how long his delay.[99] Such a party is at liberty to wait until his title is attacked before he is obliged to act. The most frequent illustrations of this principle are found in suits by parties in possession to remove a cloud on title or to quiet title. Where, however, statutes permit such suits by parties out of possession, the doctrine of laches does apply, if the plaintiff is not in possession.[100]

§ 34. **(7) Pendency of Another Suit as Excuse for Delay.** The pendency in the same or in another jurisdiction of a suit relating to the subject-matter is generally regarded as an excuse for delay until its termination; provided, however, this other suit is prosecuted with due diligence. Such a condition may arise when the

99 Simmons Creek Coal Co. v. Doran, 142 U. S. 417, 12 Sup. Ct. 239, 35 L. ed. 1063 (delay of forty years); Thompson v. Dumas, 85 Fed. 517, 29 C. C. A. 312, Massenburg v. Denison, 71 Fed. 618, 18 C. C. A. 280, 30 U. S. App. 612; Gunnison Gas & Water Co. v. Whitaker, 91 Fed. 191; Shaw v. Allen, 184 Ill. 77, 56 N. E. 403 (affirming 85 Ill. App. 23); Gordon v. Johnson, 186 Ill. 18, 57 N. E. 790 (reversing 79 Ill. App. 423), Brumback v. Brumback, 198 Ill. 66, 64 N. E. 740 (owner in common in possession cannot be precluded by laches from asserting a right to partition or to assignment of dower); Sheldon v. Dunbar, 200 Ill. 490, 65 N. E. 1095 (delay of eleven years in asserting right to specific performance not laches); Hayes v. Carroll, 74 Minn. 134, 76 N. W. 1017 (delay of twenty-three years). In Cook v. Lasher, 73 Fed. 701, 19 C. C. A. 654, 42 U. S. App. 42, it was held that a delay of twenty-one years in suing to annul a void tax deed to the state was not laches. It has been held that "so long as a defendant can assert an equitable title without invoking any affirmative relief," the doctrine of stale demand does not apply: Hensel v. Kegans (Tex. Civ. App), 28 S. W. 705. In Jackson v. Boyd (Ark.), 87 S. W. 126, neither party was in possession, and a delay of thirteen years was held not to be laches. See, also, Weir v. Cordy-Fisher Lumber Co. (Mo.), 85 S. W. 341; Waldron v. Harvey, 54 W. Va. 608, 102 Am. St. Rep 959, 46 S. E. 603

100 Sage v. Winona & St. P. R. Co., 58 Fed. 297, 7 C. C. A. 237, 19 U. S. App. 1.

complainant seeks the wrong jurisdiction or the wrong remedy in the first instance; and it may also occur when the decision in one case depends largely upon that in another.[101] As already intimated, however, the mere institution of a suit does not relieve a person from the charge of laches. If he fails in the diligent prosecution of the action the consequences are the same as though no action had been begun.[102]

§ 35. (8) **Miscellaneous Excuses.**—As what amounts to laches depends largely upon the circumstances of each particular case, so, also, the excuses which may be satisfactory to the court are many and various. A few additional ones may here be mentioned. It has been held that where the party interposing the defense of laches has contributed to or caused the delay, he cannot take advantage of it.[103] Likewise, a constant recognition of the right by all the parties has been held a sufficient excuse.[104] In some instances, prompt action looking toward the enforcement of the claim has

101 Thus, a failure to sue pending the decision of the federal Land Department has been held not to be laches. Hodge v. Palms, 117 Fed. 396. Likewise, the pendency of one suit to test the validity of a patent has excused delay in bringing other suits: United States Mitis Co v. Detroit Steel & Spring Co., 122 Fed. 863. The pendency of a suit in the federal court which has finally been dismissed for want of jurisdiction has excused delay in suing in a state court: Russell v. Dayton Coal & Iron Co., 109 Tenn. 43, 70 S W. 1. Delay in suing to set aside an agreement has been excused pending an unsuccessful suit for reformation: Russell v. Russsell, 129 Fed. 434. In general, see, also, McAfee v. Reynolds, 130 Ind. 33, 30 Am. St. Rep. 194, 28 N. E. 423.

102 Johnston v. Standard Min. Co, 148 U. S. 360, 13 Sup. Ct. 585, 37 L. ed. 480.

103 Richards v. Hatfield, 40 Neb. 879, 59 N. W. 777; Hellams v. Prior, 64 S. C. 296, 42 S. E. 106 (delay due to defendant's requests for time).

104 Riggs v. Polk, 3 Tex. Civ. App. 179, 21 S. W. 1013.

excused delay in suing.[105] It is sometimes said that the same diligence is not required between members of the same family as between strangers.[106] A few other miscellaneous cases will be found in the note.[107]

It has been distinctly held that the plaintiff's poverty is not a sufficient excuse for laches;[108] but the reason assigned for this ruling is not so convincing as to preclude the hope that it may sometimes be a circumstance to be considered in his favor, at least in connection with other disabilities or excuses. The mere fact that the complainant resides in a remote region, and therefore remains in ignorance of facts which are notorious at the place where the property is situated, is not an ex-

105 Billings v. Aspen Min & S. Co., 51 Fed. 338, 2 C. C. A. 252, 10 U. S. App. 1; Ulman v. Clark, 75 Fed. 868 (claimants not guilty of laches "when they do everything that is necessary to protect their rights, except the commencement of a legal action"); Dunning v. Bates, 186 Mass. 123, 71 N. E. 309.

106 Hall v. Otterson, 52 N. J. Eq. 522, 28 Atl. 907. See, also, *ante*, note 96

107 Southern Pac. R. Co. v. Stanley, 49 Fed 263; West Arlington Imp. Co. v. Mt. Hope Retreat, 97 Md. 191, 54 Atl. 982 (plaintiff's delay in suing to enjoin pollution of stream until convinced that water was rendered unfit for use is not laches); Kinkead v. Ryan, 64 N. J. Eq. 454, 53 Atl. 1053 (failure of life tenant to insist upon his rights against the remainderman while the latter is an infant is not laches).

108 Leggett v. Standard Oil Co., 149 U. S. 287, 13 Sup. Ct. 902, 37 L. ed. 737; Hayward v. National Bank, 96 U. S. 611, 24 L. ed. 855; Naddo v. Bardon, 51 Fed. 493, 2 C. C. A. 335, 4 U. S. App. 642 (affirming 47 Fed. 782); Wolf v Great Falls etc. Co., 15 Mont. 49, 38 Pac. 115; Patterson v. Hewitt (N. Mex.), 66 Pac. 552, 55 L. R. A. 658. In Naddo v. Bardon, *supra*, Brewer, J., says, with apparent seriousness: "It is to the glory of our profession in this country that it is ever ready to champion the cause of the poor; and no man who has a just claim, and makes an effort to assert it, will ever fail of securing the needed professional assistance. The courts are always open, and the lawyers are always willing and at hand; and if he fails to establish his rights it is because he does not make an effort to assert them."

cuse.[109] And the fact that the complainant delays because he fears that action may interfere with his employment or with contractual rights is not sufficient.[110]

§ 36. **Pleading Excuses for Laches.**—"The party who appeals to the conscience of the chancellor in support of a claim, when there has been laches in prosecuting it, or long acquiescence in the assertion of adverse rights, should set forth in his bill, specifically, what were the impediments to an earlier prosecution of his claim, how he came to be so long ignorant of his rights, and the means used by the respondents to fraudulently keep him in ignorance; and how and when he first came to a knowledge of the matters alleged in his bill; otherwise the chancellor must refuse to consider his case, on his own showing, without inquiring whether there is a demurrer or formal plea of the statute of limitations contained in the answer."[111]

109 Broderick's Will, 21 Wall. 503, 22 L. ed. 599, Rudland v. Mastic, 77 Fed. 688; Naddo v. Bardon, 51 Fed. 493, 2 C. C. A. 335, 4 U. S. App. 642 (affirming 47 Fed. 782).

110 Lane & Bodley Co. v. Locke, 150 U. S 193, 14 Sup. Ct. 78, 37 L. ed 1049 (fear of dismissal from employment is no excuse); Thorn Wire Hedge Co. v. Washburn & Moen Mfg. Co., 159 U. S. 423, 16 Sup. Ct. 94, 40 L ed 205 (fear that litigation might imperil receipt of future royalties under contract is no excuse).

111 Badger v. Badger, 2 Wall. 95, 17 L. ed. 836; Potts v. Alexander, 118 Fed. 885; Gibson v. Herriott, 55 Ark. 85, 29 Am. St. Rep. 17, 17 S. W. 589, Wetzel v. Minn Ry. Transfer Co., 65 Fed. 23, 12 C. C. A. 490, 27 U. S. App 594; Lant v. Manley, 71 Fed. 7; Wilcoxon v. Wilcoxon, 199 Ill. 244, 65 N. E. 229. It is not necessary for the defendant to set up laches. "To let in the defense that the claim is stale, and that the bill cannot, therefore, be supported, it is not necessary that a foundation shall be laid by any averment in the answer of the defendants. If the case, as it appears at the hearing, is liable to the objection by reason of the laches of the complainants, the court will, upon that ground, be passive and refuse relief": Sullivan v. Railroad Co., 94 U. S. 806, 24 L. ed. 324; Moore v. Nickley (C. C. A.), 133 Fed. 289.

CHAPTER II.

INTERPLEADER.

ANALYSIS.

§ 37. **Common-law Interpleader.**—"Under the ancient common law, the relief of interpleader was allowed in two special cases in a legal action by a court of law: when two or more persons had made a joint bailment and then brought separate actions of detinue against the depositary for the thing bailed; and when the thing came into the holder's possession by finding, and two or more persons claiming to be owners sued him in separate actions of detinue. Modern statutes, English and American, have enabled courts of law to grant a similar relief, in a summary manner, in certain legal actions, but this legislation has no connection with the ancient common-law jurisdiction above mentioned."[1]

§ 38. **Interpleader—General Nature and Object.**—"I purpose in this chapter to describe the general equitable jurisdiction to grant the remedy of interpleader independent of statute; and afterwards to notice briefly the modern statutes, some of which may perhaps have enlarged that jurisdiction, but most of which have simply conferred a similar jurisdiction upon courts of law, to be exercised in certain kinds of legal actions. Where two or more persons, whose titles are connected by reason of one being derived from the other, or of both being derived from a common source, claim the same thing, debt, or duty by different or separate interests, from a third person, and he, not knowing to which of the claimants he ought of right to render the debt or duty, or to deliver the thing, fears he may be hurt by some of them, he may maintain a suit and obtain against them the remedy of interpleader. In his bill of complaint he must state his own rights and their several claims, and pray that they may interplead, so that the court may adjudge to whom the thing, debt, or duty belongs, and he may be indemnified. If any suits at law have been brought against him, he may also pray that such proceedings be restrained until the

1 "For a more full account of this common-law relief, see Mitford's Eq. Pl, Jeremy's ed., 141, 142; Crawshay v. Thornton, 2 Mylne & C. 1": Pom. Eq Jur., § 1320, note. As to interpleader in common-law actions under the practice in Pennsylvania, see Brownfield v. Canon, 25 Pa. St. 299; Pennypacker's Appeal, 57 Pa. St. 114.

right be determined.[2] The object of the suit is, that the conflicting claimants shall litigate the matter among themselves, without involving the stake-holder in their controversy, with which he has no interest. It is plain, therefore, that the plaintiff can obtain no *specific* relief. So far as he is concerned, upon his filing the bill, and surrendering up the thing or money into the custody of the court, *his* remedy is exhausted by the decree that the defendants do interplead with each other, and that he be freed from or indemnified

2 This description is taken, with some additions and alterations, to conform to later decisions, from Mitford's Equity Pleading, 58, 59 As to the general nature of the remedy, see Crawshay v. Thornton, 2 Mylne & C 1; Sieveking v. Behrens, 2 Mylne & C. 581, Glyn v. Duesbury, 11 Sim. 139, 147; Langston v. Boylston, 2 Ves. 101, 103, 109; Jones v. Thomas, 2 Smale & G. 186; Prudential Assur. Co. v. Thomas, L R 3 Ch. 74; Farley v. Blood, 30 N H. 354, Lincoln v. Rutland etc R. R., 24 Vt. 639, Crane v. McDonald, 118 N. Y. 648, 23 N. E. 991; Bassett v. Leslie, 123 N. Y 396, 25 N. E 386; Dorn v. Fox, 61 N. Y. 264; Shaw v. Coster, 8 Paige, 339, 35 Am. Dec. 690; Mohawk etc. R. R. v. Clute, 4 Paige, 384; Bedell v. Hoffman, 2 Paige, 199, Badeau v. Rogers, 2 Paige, 209; Bell v. Hunt, 3 Barb. Ch. 391; Richards v. Salter, 6 Johns. Ch. 445; Atkinson v. Manks, 1 Cow. 691; Cady v. Potter, 55 Barb. 463; Delaware, L. & W. R. Co. v. Corwith, 5 N. Y. Supp. 792, 16 Civ. Proc. Rep. 312; Packard v. Stevens, 58 N. J. Eq. 489, 46 Atl. 250; Wakeman v. Kingsland, 46 N. J. Eq 113, 18 Atl. 680; Mount Holly etc. Tp. Co v. Ferree, 17 N. J. Eq. 117; Coates v. Roberts, 4 Rawle (Pa.), 100, National Park Bk. v. Lanahan, 60 Md. 477; Dickeshied v. Exchange Bank, 28 W. Va. 340, Strange v. Bell, 11 Ga. 103, Burton v. Black, 32 Ga 53; Hayes v. Johnson, 4 Ala. 267; Morris v. Cain's Exrs., 34 La. Ann. 657, 35 La. Ann. 759; Michigan etc Co v. White, 44 Mich 25, 5 N W. 1086; Cogswell v. Armstrong, 77 Ill. 139; Hinckley v. Pfister, 83 Wis. 64, 53 N. W. 21; Roselle v. Farmers' Bank, 119 Mo. 84, 24 S. W. 744; Hathaway v. Foy, 40 Mo. 540; Orr Water Ditch Co. v. Larcombe, 14 Nev. 53, Pope v. Ames, 20 Or. 199, 25 Pac. 393; North Pacific Lumber Co. v. Lang, 28 Or. 246, 52 Am. St Rep. 780, 42 Pac. 799; Pfister v. Wade, 56 Cal. 43; McWhirter v. Halstead, 24 Fed. 828; Louisiana State Lottery Co. v. Clark, 16 Fed. 20, 4 Woods, 169.

against their demands, and that he recover his costs; with the result of their dispute he has no concern."[3]

§ 39. **Rationale of the Remedy.**—"The ground of the jurisdiction is plain. The party seeking the remedy is exposed to the hazard, vexation and expense of several actions at law for the same demand, while he is ready and willing to satisfy that demand in favor of the claimant who establishes his right thereto. For this liability the law furnishes no adequate remedy, and in most instances no remedy whatever."[4] "It is sometimes supposed that the remedy of interpleader is allowed to avoid the risk of two recoveries. This is entirely a mistaken view. . If a party has in any way made him-

3 Pom. Eq. Jur., § 1320. This section of Pom. Eq. Jur. is cited in Crass v. Memphis & C. R. Co., 96 Ala. 447, 11 South. 480. That the decree of interpleader is interlocutory and does not determine the validity of the claims in controversy, see Heald v. Rhind, 86 Md. 320, 38 Atl. 43; Owings v. Rhodes, 65 Md. 408, 9 Atl. 903. In general, as to the practice upon a decree of interpleader see Penn Mutual Life Ins. Co. v. Union Trust Co., 83 Fed. 891 (after interpleader the parties occupy the position of plaintiff and defendant); Willson v. Salmon, 45 N. J. Eq. 257, 17 Atl. 815; Lamon v. McKee, 18 D. C. (7 Mackey) 446, 479; State v. Kumpff, 62 Mo. App. 332 (result of decree upon plaintiff's rights); McMurray v. Sisters of Charity, 68 N. J. L. 312, 53 Atl. 389.

That an ordinary interpleader suit is not an action *in rem* so as to dispense with personal service of process, see Cross v. Armstrong, 44 Ohio St. 613, 10 N. E. 160; Gary v. Northwestern M. A. Assn. (Iowa), 50 N. W. 27; Washington Life Ins. Co. v. Gooding, 19 Tex. Civ. App 490, 49 S W. 123; Expressman's Mut. Benef. Assn. v. Hurlock, 91 Md. 585, 80 Am. St. Rep. 470, 46 Atl. 957.

In addition to the summary remedy by motion in a legal action, the statutes of some states contain provisions relating to the action of interpleader: See National Sav. Bank v. Cable, 73 Conn. 568, 48 Atl. 428 (Pub. Acts of Conn., 1893, c. 42); Barnes v. Bamberger, 196 Pa. St. 123, 46 Atl. 303 (act of June 13, 1836); Mosher v. Bruhn, 15 Wash. 332, 46 Pac. 397 (2 Hill's Code, Wash, § 153); City of Atlanta v McDaniel, 96 Ga. 190, 22 S. E. 896 (Georgia Code, § 3234).

4 Pom. Eq Jur., § 1320, end. Quoted in Atkinson v. Carter, 101 Mo. App. 477, 74 S. W. 502.

self liable, even for the same demand, to two claimants, he is not entitled to an interpleader. It is the essential fact that he should actually be liable to only one of the claimants. The true *rationale* of interpleader is, that the party thereby avoids the risk of being vexed by two or more suits. Even though there is no danger of his being compelled to pay the same demand twice, the danger of two suits against him, with the consequent trouble and expense, is the sufficient ground for the remedy.[5] The supreme object of an interpleader is to protect the plaintiff,—the stake-holder.—and not the claimants against him; to protect him from the danger and vexation of two opposing suits for the same demand by those claimants, while he is ready and willing to pay the demand to the one who is judicially ascertained to be entitled to it."[6]

§ 40. Nature of the Risk to Which Plaintiff is Exposed. The danger of a double vexation must be real; a mere

5 Pom. Eq Jur., § 1320, note; Crawford v. Fisher, 1 Hare, 436, 441; East and West India Dock Co. v. Littledale, 7 Hare, 57, 60, Langston v. Boylston, 2 Ves. 101; Sablicich v. Russell, L. R. 2 Eq. 441; Greene v. Mumford, 4 R. I. 313; School District v Weston, 31 Mich 85; Pfister v. Wade, 56 Cal. 43; Hechmer v. Gilligan, 28 W. Va. 750, 757; Livingstone v. Bank of Montreal, 50 Ill. App. 562; Yarborough v. Thompson, 3 Smedes & M. (Miss.) 291, 41 Am. Dec. 626 In Crawford v. Fisher, Wigram, V. C., said. "The office of an interpleading suit is, not to protect a party against a *double liability*, but against double vexation in respect of *one* liability. If the circumstances of a case show that the plaintiff is liable to both claimants, that is no case for interpleader. It is of the essence of an interpleading suit that the plaintiff shall be liable to one only of the claimants; and the relief which the court affords him is against the vexation of two proceedings on a matter which may be settled in a single suit."

6 Pom. Eq. Jur, § 1320, note; Trigg v. Hitz, 17 Abb. Pr. 436; Farley v. Blood, 30 N. H. 354; Michigan etc Co v. White, 44 Mich. 25, 5 N W. 1086; Newhall v Kastens, 70 Ill 156; Nelson v. Barter, 2 Hem. & M. 334, 33 L. J. Ch. 705, 10 Jur., N. S., 832.

suspicion of risk will not be sufficient to support a bill.[7] It is settled, by a long series of cases in New York, that it is not enough for the party seeking interpleader to show that a claim has been presented against a fund already claimed by another, but he must prove that such claim is plausible, and has some reasonable foundation, so that he cannot, without hazard, determine to which of the claimants he should pay the fund.[8] The plain-

7 Pom Eq. Jur, § 1320, note; Blair v. Porter, 13 N. J. Eq 267; Baltimore and Ohio R. R. Co. v Arthur, 90 N. Y 234; Partlow v. Moore, 184 Ill. 119, 56 N E. 317, affirming Moore v. Partlow, 84 Ill. App. 119, Fitch v. Brower, 42 N. J. Eq. 300, 11 Atl. 330 (reasonable doubt arises from the claim); National Bank of Augusta v. Augusta etc. Co., 99 Ga. 286, 25 S. E 686 (claims should be sufficiently set forth to enable the court to determine whether it is doubtful or dangerous for plaintiff to act).

8 Dorn v. Fox, 61 N Y. 264; Crane v McDonald, 118 N. Y. 648; Pustet v. Flannelly, 60 How. Pr. 67; Nassau Bank v Yandes, 44 Hun, 55; Pratt v. Myers, 63 Hun, 634, 28 Abb. N. C. 460, 18 N. Y. Supp. 466; Mars v. Albany Savings Bank, 64 Hun, 429, 19 N. Y. Supp. 791, affirmed 69 Hun, 398, 23 N. Y. Supp. 658; Stevenson v New York L. I. Co., 10 App Div. 233, 41 N. Y. Supp. 964, Lennon v. Metropolitan L. I. Co., 20 Misc. Rep. 403, 45 N. Y. Supp 1033, Roberts v. Van Horne, 21 App. Div. 369, 47 N Y. Supp. 448; Cosgriff v. Hudson City Sav. Inst., 24 Misc. Rep. 4, 52 N. Y. Supp. 189; Sexton v. Home Fire Ins. Co., 35 App. Div. 170, 54 N. Y. Supp. 862, Southwark Nat. Bank v. Childs, 39 App. Div. 560, 57 N. Y. Supp. 789, Wells v. National City Bank, 40 App. Div. 498, 29 Civ. Proc. Rep. 158, 58 N. Y. Supp. 125; Post v. Emmett, 40 App. Div 477, 58 N. Y. Supp. 129; Kreiser v. City of New York, 46 App. Div. 16, 61 N. Y. Supp. 329; Merchant v. Northwestern M. L. I. Co., 57 App. Div 375, 68 N. Y. Supp. 406. Many of these cases concerned the showing required to be made by affidavits in the statutory interpleader by motion in an action at law; but it has been repeatedly held that there is no difference between the rule in statutory interpleader and that in interpleader by suit. The moving party is merely required to show that the claim interposed renders his position hazardous to the extent of creating a reasonable doubt; he need not show that the claim would probably be successful: Burritt v Press Pub. Co, 19 App. Div. 609, 46 N. Y. Supp 295; Dreyfus v. Casey, 52 Hun, 95, 5 N. Y. Supp. 65; and his affidavit need not allege that he himself is in doubt as to who has the just claim, if it gives facts which

tiff's risk may depend upon a doubtful and disputed question of law, instead of a question of fact. "So long as a principle is still under discussion . . . . it would seem fair to hold that there was sufficient doubt and hazard to justify the protection which is afforded by the beneficent action of interpleader."[9]

§ 41. **At What Stage Interpleader may be Brought.**—"Such being the theory of the remedy, it is not essential that any suit should have been actually commenced by either claimant against the plaintiffs.[10] It is enough that the conflicting claimants make their respective claims and threaten suit.[11] The plaintiff must, however, positively allege an actual claim made by each defendant."[12] It is held that the plaintiff cannot interplead claimants who have reduced their claims to judgment, as this would be to increase instead of diminish

may raise a reasonable doubt in the mind of the court: Schell v. Lowe, 75 Hun, 43, 23 Civ. Proc. Rep. 300, 26 N. Y. Supp. 991. The rule, as applied in statutory interpleader by motion in a pending action, is designed for the protection of the plaintiff in that action, and cannot be invoked by the adverse claimant; it is the latter's duty either to take position squarely with respect to the nature of his claim or to withdraw the same: Butler v. Atlantic Trust Co., 28 Misc Rep. 42, 59 N Y. Supp. 814.

9 Dorn v. Fox, 61 N. Y. 270; Crane v. McDonald, 118 N Y. 648, 654, 23 N. E. 991; Sovereign Camp, Woodmen of the World v. Wood, 100 Mo. App. 655, 75 S. W. 377.

10 Angell v. Hadden, 15 Ves. 244; Morgan v. Marsack, 2 Mer. 107; Farley v. Blood, 30 N. H. 354; Richards v. Salter, 6 Johns. Ch. 445; Yates v. Tisdale, 3 Edw. Ch. 71; Schuyler v. Pelissier, 3 Edw. Ch. 191; Strange v. Bell, 11 Ga. 103; Gibson v. Goldthwaite, 7 Ala. 281, 42 Am. Dec. 592; Pom. Eq. Jur, § 1320, note

11 Langston v. Boylston, 2 Ves. 101; Providence Bank v. Wilkinson, 4 R. I 507, 70 Am. Dec. 160; Briant v. Reed, 14 N. J. Eq. 271, Yarborough v Thompson, 3 Smedes & M. (Miss.) 291, 41 Am. Dec. 626; Pom. Eq. Jur., § 1320, note.

12 State Ins Co. v. Gennett, 2 Tenn. Ch. 82; Pom. Eq. Jur., § 1320, note.

the number of suits, and because of the familiar rule that a court of equity cannot give relief when the party might have made defense at law.[13]

§ 42. **The Claims, Legal or Equitable.**—"The equitable jurisdiction exists, although both or all the conflicting claims against the stake-holder are legal,[14] since it depends upon the fact that distinct claims are made, rather than upon their intrinsic nature as being legal or equitable. It is not necessary, however, that all the claims should be legal; the remedy is granted when one of them is legal and the other equitable.[15] Indeed, if

13 Yarborough v. Thompson, *supra;* McKinney v. Kuhn, 59 Miss. 186. See, also, Larabrie v. Brown, 26 L. J. Rep., Eq., N. S., 605; Bank v. Kerr, 2 Md. Ch. 460; Hichmer v. Gilligan, 28 W. Va. 757; Wabash R. Co. v. Flannigan, 95 Mo. App. 477, 75 S. W. 691. In Yarborough v. Thompson it was said: "There is no evidence that anything unconscientious was done by either of the defendants in this case, in obtaining their judgments. Each proceeded upon a legal claim. The complainant defended each, but for some cause was unsuccessful in both. One of the judgments is no doubt wrong; but, from the bill, the error was induced by the complainant's answer to the garnishment. . . . . If a case of fraud or surprise in obtaining either of the judgments were made out against either of the parties, that might entitle the complainant to relief against such party; but that would be done upon an original bill, not a bill of interpleader."

14 Lowndes v. Cornford, 18 Ves. 299.

15 Quoted in Atkinson v. Carter, 101 Mo. App. 477, 74 S. W. 502. See, also, Lowndes v. Cornford, *supra;* Morgan v. Marsack, 2 Mer. 107; Wright v. Ward, 4 Russ. 215; Paris v. Gilham, Coop. 56; Martinius v. Helmuth, 2 Ves. & B. 412; Smith v. Hammond, 6 Sim. 10; Crawford v. Fisher, 10 Sim. 479; Hamilton v. Marks, 5 De Gex & S. 638; Prudential Assur. Co v. Thomas, L. R. 3 Ch. 74; Duke of Bolton v. Williams, 4 Brown Ch. 297, 309; Farley v. Blood, 30 N. H. 354; Fairbanks v. Belknap, 135 Mass. 179; Richards v. Salter, 6 Johns. Ch. 445, Yates v. Tisdale, 3 Edw. Ch. 71; Schuyler v. Pelissier, 3 Edw Ch. 191; Lozier's Exrs. v. Van Saun's Admrs., 3 N. J. Eq. 325; Ireland v. Kelly, 60 N J Eq 308, 47 Atl. 51; Oil Run Petroleum Co. v. Gale, 6 W. Va. 525; Strange v. Bell, 11 Ga. 103, Burton v. Black, 32 Ga. 53; Gibson v. Goldthwaite, 7 Ala. 281, 42 Am. Dec. 592; Whitney v. Cowan, 55 Miss 626, 647, Newhall v. Kastens, 70

one or more of the conflicting claims are purely equitable, there is the stronger reason for a resort to the equity jurisdiction; and prior to recent legislation in England and in the United States, such a resort was indispensable under those circumstances."[16]

§ 43. **Essential Elements.**—"From the description given in a previous paragraph, and from the whole course of authorities, it is clear that the equitable remedy of interpleader, independent of recent statutory regulations, depends upon and requires the existence of the four following elements, which may be regarded as its essential conditions: 1. The same thing, debt, or duty must be claimed by both or all the parties against whom the relief is demanded; 2. All their adverse titles or claims must be dependent, or be derived from a common source; 3. The person asking the relief—the plaintiff—must not have nor claim any interest in the subject-matter; 4. He must have incurred no independ-

Ill. 156; People's Sav. Bank v. Look, 95 Mich. 7, 54 N. W. 629. In England the necessity of a resort to equity is removed, although the equity jurisdiction is not at all affected, by the statute of 1 & 2 Wm. IV, c. 58, § 1, as amended and enlarged by the common-law procedure act (23 & 24 Vict., c. 126, § 12), which enabled a court of law, on motion, to direct what amounts to an interpleader in actions of debt, assumpsit, trover and detinue. Under the present system of procedure, equitable claims may be adjudicated upon in an interpleader issue connected with a legal action: Rusden v. Pope, L R. 3 Ex. 269; Engleback v. Nixon, L. R. 10 Com. P. 645; Duncan v. Cashin, L. R 10 Com P. 554; Attenborough v. London and St. Katherine's Dock Co., L. R. 3 C. P. D. 450; see Langton v. Horton, 3 Beav. 464. Analogous statutes have been passed in many American states, *post*, § 61. For illustrations of relief against equitable claims in interpleader proceedings under these statutes, see Underwood v Boston etc. Bank, 141 Mass. 305, 4 N. E. 822; Dixon v. National L. I. Co, 168 Mass. 48, 46 N. E. 430; Brierly v. Equitable Aid Union, 170 Mass. 218, 64 Am. St. Rep 297, 48 N. E. 1090, Windecker v. Mut. L. Ins Co., 12 App. Div. (N. Y.) 73, 43 N. Y. Supp. 358.

16 Pom. Eq Jur., § 1321.

ent liability to either of the claimants; that is, he must stand perfectly indifferent between them, in the position merely of a stake-holder. As the original equitable jurisdiction is founded, to a great extent, upon these four propositions, I shall examine them separately."[17]

§ 44. **First: The Same Thing, Debt, or Duty.**—"The same thing, debt, or duty must be claimed by both the parties against whom the interpleader is demanded.[18] This requisite results from the very nature and object of the remedy. If the subject in dispute has a bodily existence,—is a *thing,*—there can be no doubt nor question as to the identity. The difficulty in applying the rule arises where the subject is a chose in action; and then the identity must be determined in each particular case, not by any general rules, but by the nature, constitu-

17 Pom Eq. Jur., § 1322. This analysis was quoted and approved in Wells, Fargo & Co. v. Miner, 25 Fed. 533, 537, by Sawyer, J.; in Morrill v. Manhattan Life Ins. Co., 82 Ill. App. 410, affirmed and opinion adopted 183 Ill. 260, 55 N. E. 656, in Kile v. Goodrum, 87 Ill App. 462; in Platte Valley State Bank v. National Livestock Bank, 54 Ill. App. 483, affirmed and opinion adopted, 155 Ill. 250, 40 N. E. 621; in Newman v. Commercial Nat. Bank, 156 Ill. 530, 41 N E. 156 (affirming 55 Ill. App. 534); in Northwestern Mut. Life Ins. Co. v. Kidder, 162 Ind. 382, 70 N. E. 489, and other cases; and cited in Northwestern Mut. Life Ins. Co. v Kidder (Ind. App.), 69 N. E. 204.

18 Desborough v. Harris, 5 De Gex, M. & G. 439, 455. See, also, Standley v Roberts, 59 Fed. 836, 19 U. S. App. 407, 8 C. C. A 305; Ryan v. Lamson, 44 Ill. App 204, affirmed in 153 Ill. 520, 39 N. E. 979; Taylor v. Satterthwaite, 22 N. Y. Supp. 187, 2 Misc. Rep 441; Heyman v. Smadbeck, 27 N. Y. Supp. 141, 6 Misc. Rep. 527; Travelers' Insurance Co. v Healey, 86 Hun, 524, 33 N. Y. Supp. 911, Du Bois v. Union Dime Sav. Inst., 89 Hun, 382, 35 N. Y. Supp. 397, 25 Civ Proc. R. 288, 2 N. Y. Ann. Cas. 221; Freda v Montauk Co., 55 N. Y. Supp. 748, 26 Misc. Rep. 199, Johnston v. Oliver, 51 Ohio St. 6, 36 N. E. 458; and additional cases cited in the notes to this and the following paragraphs.

tion, and incidents of the debt, demand, or duty itself."[19]

§ 45. **Same; Claims of Different Amounts.**—"In Glyn v. Duesbury, 11 Sim. 139, 148, Shadwell, V. C., said: '*Where the claims made by the defendants are of different amounts, they can never be identical;* but where they are the same in amount, that circumstance goes far to determine their identity. The amount, however, may not be sufficient of itself to determine the identity; for the amount may be the same and the debt may be different.' This *dictum* was approved in Pfister v. Wade, 56 Cal. 43. In my opinion, however, that portion of the *dictum* which is italicized—the statement that claims of different amounts can never be identical —is incorrect; it seems alike opposed to principle and to authority. Where both defendants claim one, single, undivided *debt,* technically so called, the statement is undoubtedly true; a difference in their amounts would be fatal to their identity. But it is clearly not necessarily so where the claims are for unliquidated damages. Where, for example, a chattel is in the plaintiff's hands, to which both defendants claim title, they do not sue to recover the article itself, but allege a *technical* conversion, and seek to recover damages—the value of the chattel. Here the claim of the defendants would not be for a 'thing,' nor for a 'debt,' but it would be for a 'duty'—a *chose in action.* If each defendant alleged a different value, and claimed a different

19 Pom. Eq. Jur., § 1323. This section of Pom. Eq. Jur is cited in Northwestern Mut. Life Ins. Co. v. Kidder, 162 Ind. 382, 70 N. E. 489. See City Bank v. Bangs, 2 Paige, 570; Briant v. Reed, 14 N. J. Eq. 271; Dodd v. Bellows, 29 N. J. Eq. 127; Leddel's Exr. v. Starr, 20 N J. Eq. 274; Salisbury Mills v. Townsend, 109 Mass. 115; Oil Run Petroleum Co. v. Gale, 6 W. Va. 525; Pfister v. Wade, 56 Cal. 43; Blue v. Watson, 59 Miss. 619.

amount of damages, the *duty* asserted would still be identically the same in each demand.[20] Another instance of difference in the amounts claimed by the different defendants, where the debt or duty may still be the same, occurs in cases where a fund being in plaintiff's hands, the whole of it is claimed by one defendant, and parts of it are claimed by the others. With regard to such cases, Christiancy, J., said, in School District v. Weston, 31 Mich. 85: 'Upon the great weight of authority, both English and American, a much more liberal and reasonable rule has been established, and bills of interpleader have been frequently maintained, where the several claimants, instead of claiming the whole fund or matter in dispute, have claimed different portions of the fund, when the aggregate of all the claims exceeded the full amount of the fund; and the complainant being, as in the present case, virtually a stake-holder, and unable to determine to whom or in what proportions the payments should be made.' In this case the plaintiff had let a contract for building a school-house for a specified sum to a contractor, and portions of this contract price were claimed by subcontractors and material-men, the total amount of their claims exceeding the whole contract price."[21]

20 See, to the same effect, Packard v. Stevens, 58 N. J. Eq. 489, 46 Atl. 255, criticising Glyn v. Duesbury.

21 Pom. Eq. Jur., § 1323, note. See, also, as examples of such partial claims, Yates v. Tisdale, 3 Edw. Ch. 71; Fargo v. Arthur, 43 How. Pr. 193; Newhall v. Kastens, 70 Ill. 156; Board of Education v. Scoville, 13 Kan. 17; Barnes v. City of New York, 27 Hun, 236; Van Zandt v. Van Zandt, 7 N Y. Supp 706, 17 Civ. Proc R. 448; Koenig v. New York Life Ins. Co., 14 N Y St. R. 250, 14 Civ. Proc R. 269. "Additional cases may be found in the many interpleader suits in this court, under the mechanics' lien act, when the contract is filed, and noticing creditors and holders of equitable assignments are brought in because their claims upon the contract price conflict. In these cases the claims often vary widely in amount, and sometimes involve little other dispute than a settlement of the order of

§ 46. **Same; Illustrations.**—"Where the same property had been taxed to the owner in two counties, in some cases for different amounts, in others for the same amount, a bill of interpleader by the owner to determine which of the counties was entitled to the tax has been maintained. It is difficult to perceive how the tax levied by two different counties, even though the amount of each tax is the same, is one and the same debt or duty, so as to sustain a bill of interpleader."[22]

The question whether the plaintiff is liable for the same debt, or has incurred a double liability, has frequently arisen where a vendor seeks to interplead two rival brokers, both claiming commissions by reason of the same sale to the same purchaser;[23] and where an insurance company has issued a policy or certificate on the surrender of a previous policy or certificate, and

their priority; yet, if the situation be such that the contract price is not enough to pay all, and the owner may be compelled to determine the order of priority of payment, it is common practice in this state to settle the rights of all the claimants under an interpleader bill'''. Packard v. Stevens, 58 N. J. Eq. 489, 46 Atl. 250, citing Trenton Schools v. Heath, 15 N. J. Eq. 22; Wakeman v. Kingsland, 46 N. J. Eq. 113, 18 Atl. 680; Lanigan's Admr. v. Bradley & Currier Co., 50 N. J. Eq. 202, 24 Atl 505; Board etc. v. Duparquet, 50 N. J. Eq 234, 24 Atl. 922. But it is to be observed, in such cases, that the claims must be *conflicting;* if there is no doubt as to the order of their priority, there is no ground for interpleader: Ter Knile v. Reddick (N. J. Eq.), 39 Atl. 1062.

22 Pom. Eq. Jur., § 1323, note. See Thompson v. Ebbets, Hopk Ch. (N. Y) 272; Mohawk etc R. R. Co. v. Clute, 4 Paige (N. Y), 384, 391; Redfield v. Supervisors, Clarke Ch. (N. Y.) 42; Dorn v. Fox, 61 N. Y. 264; but, *per contra,* see Greene v. Mumford, 4 R. I. 313. In Massachusetts, it seems that such a bill is demurrable, but has been sustained, neither party objecting: See Macy v. Nantucket, 121 Mass 351; Forest River Land Co. v. City of Salem, 165 Mass. 193, 42 N. E. 802.

23 See Shipman v. Scott, 12 Civ. Proc. Rep. (N. Y.) 109, 14 Daly, 233, and Brooke v. Smith, 13 Pa Co. Ct. R. 557, 2 Pa. Dist R. 767, 33 Wkly. Not. Cas. 74, holding that the debt was the same, and

seeks to interplead rival beneficiaries.[24] In a recent case of much interest it was held that interpleader was proper "when the complainant employs two or more persons to do work upon a common object, under an agreement that each shall be paid according to the amount of the work he may separately do, to be ascertained by measurement when the work shall be completed, and without fault of the complainant a confusion of the work done arises, which prevents an ascertainment of the amount separately done by each, so that the complainant cannot safely pay either."[25]

"In other cases, one defendant claiming rent for certain premises, and the other claiming damages for their use and occupation, the demands were held not to be the same.[26] If the conflicting claims relate to a specific 'thing' in the plaintiff's possession, the identity is clear, and the value alleged is immaterial."[27]

awarding interpleader; and McCreery v. Inge, 63 N. Y. Supp. 158, 49 App Div. 133, and Sachsel v. Farrer, 35 Ill. App. 277, holding that there was a double liability.

24 See National Life Ins. Co v. Pingrey, 141 Mass 411, holding that the company could not have an order that the defendants interplead, where one important question to be tried was whether, by reason of its own act, it is under a liability to each of them, and compare Supreme Commandery U. O. G. C. v. Merrick, 163 Mass. 374, 40 N E. 183 (distinguishing the last case as one where the contracts of insurance were independent), and McCormick v. Supreme Council, 39 N. Y. Supp 1010, 6 App. Div. 175, where there were two outstanding mutual benefit insurance certificates, but only one insurance effected and one set of premiums paid, and interpleader was, therefore, awarded.

25 Packard v. Stevens, 58 N. J. Eq. 489, 46 Atl. 250.

26 Pom. Eq. Jur, § 1323, note, Dodd v. Bellows, 29 N. J. Eq. 127; Johnson v. Atkinson, 2 Anstr. 798.

27 Pom. Eq. Jur, § 1323, note; Cady v. Potter, 55 Barb 463 In Lozier's Exrs. v Van Saun's Admrs., 3 N. J. Eq. 325, a bill of interpleader was sustained, where the controversy was as to which of the defendants was entitled to receive payment of certain notes made by plaintiff's testator, although the amount to be paid was not ascertained; the amount, it was held, could not vary the rights of the

§ 47. Second: Privity Between the Opposing Claimants.—"A second requisite is, that the adverse title of the claimants must be connected, or dependent, or one derived from the other, or both derived from a common source. It is not every instance of conflicting claims against a person for the same thing, debt, or duty which will entitle him to the remedy of an interpleader. Where there is no privity between the claimants, where their titles are independent, not derived from a common source, but each asserted as wholly paramount to the other, the stake-holder is obliged, in the language of the authorities, to defend himself as well as he can against each separate demand; a court of equity will not grant him an interpleader."[28] "This doctrine, which was left

claimants. In Bassett v. Leslie, 123 N. Y. 396, 25 N. E. 386, the plaintiff sought to interplead two defendants, both claiming the same amount, but one claiming for goods sold to the plaintiff, and the other claiming upon a draft accepted by the plaintiff on the understanding that its proceeds should be used in payment of the debt for the goods sold; it was held, under the circumstances of the case, that the claims were not identical. Where A's claim against B is for the price of goods sold, and C's claim is that these goods were converted by A, the demands are not so identical as to warrant interpleader on B's petition: Coleman v. Chambers, 127 Ala 615, 29 South. 58; Sherman v. Partridge, 11 How. Pr. (N. Y.) 154. It was held that where one claimant included in his suit a cause of action with which the other claimant had nothing to do, interpleader was not proper, in Carroll v. Demarest, 58 N. Y. Supp. 1028, 42 App. Div. 155. That it is incorrect for a plaintiff to unite in one suit three different issues of interpleader between three different groups of parties merely because of the similarity of the questions involved, see Wallace v. Sortor, 52 Mich. 159, 17 N. W. 794, distinguishing School District v. Weston (for which case see last paragraph.)

28 Pom. Eq. Jur., § 1324. This section of Pom. Eq. Jur. is cited with approval in Northwestern Mut. Life Ins. Co. v. Kidder, 162 Ind 382, 70 N. E. 489. See, also, Pearson v. Cardon, 2 Russ & M. 606, 609-612; Crawshay v. Thornton, 2 Mylne & C. 1, 19-24; Nickolson v. Knowles, 5 Madd. 47; Cooper v. De Tastet, Tam. 177; Pfister v. Wade, 56 Cal. 43; Third Nat. Bank v. Lumber Co., 132 Mass. 410; Kyle v. Mary Lee Coal & R. Co., 112 Ala. 606, 20 South. 851; North

somewhat doubtful by the previous cases, was finally settled by the decision of Lord Brougham in Pearson v. Cardon, and of Lord Cottenham in Crawshay v. Thornton. It finds its most frequent application in cases of a tenant interpleading his landlord and a third person claiming under paramount title, of a bailee interpleading his bailor and an adverse claimant asserting a paramount title, and of an agent interpleading his principal and an adverse paramount claimant. Examples of these cases are given in subsequent paragraphs.[29]

"Such being the doctrine, it is a manifest imperfection of the equity jurisdiction that it should be so limited. A person may be, and is, exposed to danger, vexation, and loss from conflicting *independent* claims to the same thing, as well as from claims which are dependent; and there is certainly nothing in the nature of the remedy which need prevent it from being extended to both classes of demands."[30]

Pacific Lumber Co. v. Lang, 28 Or. 246, 52 Am. St. Rep. 780, 42 Pac. 799; Hoyt v Gouge (Iowa), 101 N. W. 464; City of Montpelier v. Capital Sav. Bank, 75 Vt. 433, 98 Am. St. Rep. 834, 56 Atl. 89, *Contra,* see Boyle v. Manion, 74 Miss. 572, 21 South. 530. For a case where privity between the claimants was held to exist, see Fairbanks v. Belknap, 135 Mass 179, a bill of interpleader by trustees for the benefit of creditors against, on the one hand, certain creditors whose claims were subsequent in time to the conveyance to the plaintiffs, and who assert rights in the property of the debtor as beneficiaries of the trust, and ask its appropriation to the payment of their debts; and, on the other hand, against the assignees in insolvency of the debtor, who claim the debtor's property, discharged from any supposed trust, by virtue of the assignment in insolvency. In Packard v. Stevens, 58 N. J. Eq. 489, 46 Atl. 255, it was held that the objection of lack of privity cannot be maintained where each claimant, with the knowledge or assent of the other, contracted to take employment on the same undertaking, and for payment on the basis of the total work done, and they are in dispute as to the amount of work which each contributed toward the total; though their contracts are several, they are not independent

29 Pom. Eq. Jur., § 1324, note See *post,* §§ 54, 55.

30 Pom. Eq Jur., § 1324, note, quoted with approval in Crane v.

§ 48. **Third: Plaintiff a Mere Stake-holder.**—"The person seeking the relief must not have nor claim any interest in the subject-matter. He must occupy the posi-

McDonald, 118 N. Y. 648, 657, 23 N. E. 991. The court in this case declined to decide whether the doctrine exists in New York, holding that the case under consideration fully met the requirements of the rule, and remarking that "our statutory interpleader by order apparently does not recognize the doctrine." Professor Pomeroy continues: "It is not surprising, therefore, that courts have sometimes ignored this doctrine in their decisions, or have been ready to admit exceptions to its operation. In the common-law procedure act of 1860, which provides for a summary interpleader by motion in legal actions, it was enacted that the order of interpleader may be made 'though the titles of the claimants have not a common origin, but are adverse to and independent of each other' In Attenborough v. London etc. Dock Co., L. R. 3 C. P. D. 450, which was an interpleader proceeding in a legal action, the court of appeal held that the statute above quoted had abrogated this doctrine as laid down in Crawshay v. Thornton, at all events in the proceedings authorized by the statute. Bramwell, L. J., who was one of the commissioners who drew up the statute, said (p. 456): 'From my own knowledge as one of the common-law commissioners, I can say that it was intended to do away with the effect of that decision.' Baggallay, L. J., a very eminent equity lawyer, said (p. 458): 'I may go further, and say that, in my opinion, if, after the common-law procedure act of 1860, a bill of interpleader had been filed, raising facts like those in Crawshay v. Thornton, any judge of the court of chancery would have felt himself no longer bound by the somewhat narrow principle laid down by Lord Cottenham, but would have acted upon the fuller powers contained in that statute.' The Code of Civil Procedure of California, as lately amended, in section 386, goes even further, and provides for an interpleader, 'although the titles or claims have not a common origin, *or are not identical*' [See this section applied in Wells, Fargo & Co. v Miner, 25 Fed 533.] This last provision, that the claims need not be identical, is certainly unnecessary and most unreasonable; it violates the whole ground and reason upon which the remedy is based; if interpreted literally by the courts, it would remove almost every limitation upon this kind of suit, and render it a means of vexation and annoyance. There is no valid objection to the requisite that the opposing claims should be identical; the only question has been, What *is* such identity? Experience shows the danger of legislative intermeddling with doctrines long settled and approved by the consenting judgments of able courts."

tion of a stake-holder. He must stand entirely indifferent between the conflicting claimants, and be ready and willing to surrender the entire thing in dispute, or to pay the entire debt, or render the entire duty, without any charge, deduction, or commission as against the one rightfully entitled. He cannot mingle up a demand of his own upon the property or fund, with the demand that the other persons shall interplead. As soon as the decree is made that the defendants do interplead, and that he be indemnified, the plaintiff must be wholly without the controversy. . . . . To sum up the doctrine, the plaintiff can only obtain the remedy of an interpleader; and the circumstances must be such that the entire rights of both defendants to the thing, fund, debt, or duty can be fully adjusted and determined in the one suit."[31]

31 Pom. Eq. Jur, § 1325; Mitchell v Hayne, 2 Sim. & St. 63; Langston v. Boylston, 2 Ves 101; Moore v Usher, 7 Sim. 383; Bignold v. Audland, 11 Sim. 23; Hoggart v. Cutts, Craig & P. 197; Lincoln v. Rutland etc. R. R., 24 Vt. 639; Atkinson v. Manks, 1 Cow. 691; Shaw v Coster, 8 Paige, 339, 35 Am. Dec. 690; Lozier's Exrs. v. Van Saun's Admrs, 3 N. J. Eq. 325; Kerr v. Union Bank, 18 Md. 396; Burton v. Black, 32 Ga. 53; Adams v. Dixon, 19 Ga. 513, 65 Am. Dec. 608; Anderson v. Wilkinson, 10 Smedes & M. 601; Cullen v. Dawson, 24 Minn. 66; Baltimore etc. R. R. v. Arthur, 90 N. Y. 234; Stone v. Reed, 152 Mass. 179, 25 N. E. 49, Blue v. Watson, 59 Miss. 19; Appeal of Bridesburg Mfg. Co., 106 Pa. St. 275. See, also, Statham v. Hall, 1 Turn. & R. 30; Groves v. Sentell, 153 U. S. 465, 14 Sup. Ct. 898, 38 L. ed. 785; Crass v. Memphis & Charleston R. R Co., 96 Ala. 447, 11 South. 480, quoting and approving the above text National Park Bank v. Lanahan, 60 Md. 477; Chase v. Ladd, 155 Mass 417, 29 N. E. 637; Atkinson v. Flannigan, 70 Mich. 639, 38 N. W. 655; Swan v. Bartlett, 82 Mo. App. 642. See, also, Supreme Council of Legion of Honor v. Palmer, 107 Mo. App. 157, 80 S. W. 699, citing Pom. Eq. Jur.; Holland Trust Co. v. Sutherland, 177 N. Y. 327, 69 N. E. 647; Dodge v. Lawson, 19 N. Y. Supp. 904, 22 Civ. Proc. R. 112; Barnstein v. Hamilton, 49 N. Y. Supp. 932, 26 App. Div. 206; Dohnert's Appeal, 64 Pa. St. 311, Wing v. Spaulding, 64 Vt. 83, 23 Atl. 615; and see cases cited in the following notes

Illustrations.—A frequent application of the principle is furnished

§ 49. Same; Admission or Waiver of Plaintiff's Claim; Dispute as to His Liability.—"While the plaintiff cannot set up a claim, charge, or lien upon the fund, which shall enter into the litigation, and form a part of the controversy,[32] it seems this rule is not without exceptions. It does not apply where the claim is admitted

by cases where the plaintiff claims the right to retain a portion of the fund in controversy as commission or charge for his services rendered in connection with the fund: See, for example, Mitchell v. Hayne, 2 Sim. & St. 63, where the plaintiff, an auctioneer, seeking to interplead a vendor and a purchaser who both laid claim to a deposit made by the latter, asserted a right to retain a portion of the sum as his commission, Baltimore & Ohio R. R. Co. v Arthur, 90 N. Y. 234, where the plaintiff, a vendee of merchandise, seeking an interpleader of the claims of his vendor and the latter's receiver, attempted to reserve less than one per cent of the sum in controversy as freight charges.

The plaintiff, trustee of a disputed trust, is not an indifferent stake-holder if he is entitled to a large commission in case the validity of the trust is sustained: National Park Bank v. Lanahan, 60 Md. 477; compare Chase v. Ladd, 155 Mass 417, 29 N. E. 637 (executor cannot maintain interpleader to ascertain the respective rights of defendants to property belonging to the estate of the testator, because of his interest in the property; but the bill may be treated as a petition for instructions in the management of the trust). The plaintiff is not an indifferent stake-holder if he has taken an indemnity from some of the defendants: Statham v. Hall, 1 Turn. & R. 30; or if one of the claims is made against him by his own procurement: Swain v. Bartlett, 82 Mo. App. 642. He must, of course, admit a liability to some one: Bernstein v. Hamilton, 49 N. Y. Supp. 932, 26 App. Div 206. In a strict bill of interpleader, he can claim no further *equitable* relief Dohnert's Appeal, 64 Pa. St. 311; and see *post*, § 60, *Bills in the Nature of Bills of Interpleader.*

Since the plaintiff's interest or want of interest is not a mere formal matter, but goes to the very right of maintaining the bill, the objection on this score may be taken at the hearing: Wing v. Spaulding, 64 Vt. 83, 23 Atl. 615, relying on Toulmin v. Reid, 14 Beav. 499, Statham v. Hall, 1 Turn. & R. 30, Yates v. Tisdale, 3 Edw. Ch. 71, and Mount Holly etc. Turnpike Co. v. Ferree, 17 N. J. Eq. 117.

32 Pom. Eq. Jur., § 1325, note; Wakeman v. Dickey, 19 Abb. Pr. (N. Y.) 124; Crass v. Memphis & C. R. Co., 96 Ala. 447, 11 South. 480,

by both defendants.[33] If the plaintiff has a claim or charge on the fund, he may waive it, and maintain the suit.[34] It necessarily follows from the general doctrine that if the plaintiff expressly denies his liability in whole or in part to one of the defendants, he strikes at the very foundation of the remedy, and shows that he is not indifferent."[35]

§ 50. Same; Stake-holder Must be Plaintiff; Fund Must be in His Custody.—"The stake-holder—the person in possession of the thing or fund, or from whom the debt or duty

holding that a carrier's lien for freight, the correctness of which is not assented to, cannot be litigated in a suit to interplead the consignee's vendor and attaching creditors of the consignee. See, also, cases in the last note and the following notes.

33 Pom. Eq. Jur., § 1325, note; Cotter v. Bank of England, 2 Dowl. Pr. 728, and see Attenborough v. London etc. Co., L. R. 3 C. P. D 450; Gibson v. Goldthwaite, 7 Ala. 281, 42 Am. Dec. 592; Webster v. McDaniel, 2 Del. Ch. 297. In McFadden v. Swinerton, 36 Or. 336, 59 Pac. 816, 62 Pac. 12, the claim of the plaintiff, an attorney, on the fund for his fees did not prevent the interpleader.

34 Pom. Eq. Jur., § 1325, note; Jacobson v. Blackhurst, 2 Johns. & H 486; and see Orient Ins. Co. v. Reed, 81 Cal. 145, 22 Pac. 484

35 Pom. Eq Jur., § 1325, note; Moore v. Usher, 7 Sim. 383; Greene v. Mumford, 4 R. I. 313, Patterson v. Perry, 14 How. Pr. 505; Cogswell v. Armstrong, 77 Ill. 139; Williams v. Matthews, 47 N. J. Eq. 196, 20 Atl. 261; Du Bois v. Union Dime Sav. Inst., 89 Hun, 382, 35 N. Y. Supp 397, 25 Civ. Proc. Rep. 288, 2 N. Y. Ann. Cas. 221. A denial not in the complaint but made on some previous occasion, is not within this rule: Orient Ins. Co. v. Reed, 81 Cal. 145, 22 Pac. 484. As to the effect of a dispute or uncertainty with respect to the amount of the fund or debt for which plaintiff is liable, see City Bank v. Bangs, 2 Paige, 570; Consociated Pres Soc. v Staples, 23 Conn. 544; Chamberlain v. O'Connor, 1 E. D. Smith, 665; Bender v. Sherwood, 15 How. Pr. 258; Patterson v. Perry, 14 How. Pr 505, Williams v. Matthews, 47 N J. Eq. 196, 20 Atl. 261; Appeal of Bridesburg Mfg. Co, 106 Pa. St. 275; Diplock v. Hammond, 2 Smale & G. 141, Southwestern Tel & T. Co. v. Benson, 63 Ark. 283, 38 S. W. 341; New England Mut. L. Ins. Co. v. Odell, 50 Hun, 279, 2 N. Y. Supp. 873; Sibley v. Society, 3 N. Y Supp. 8, 15 Civ. Proc. Rep. 316, 56 N. Y. Super. Ct. (24 J. & S.) 274; Jackson v. Knickerbocker Athletic

is owing, and against whom two or more conflicting claimants assert their demands—must necessarily be the plaintiff. No interpleader suit can be maintained by one of the contestants against the other contestant and the stake-holder.[36] Furthermore, the plaintiff must be in possession of the fund, or have it in his custody, so that he can deliver or pay it in pursuance of the decree. If he has already delivered the thing or paid the fund to one of the contestants, no suit for interpleader can be maintained."[37]

§ 51. Same; Plaintiff may have Interest in the Legal Question.—"The interest, however, which shall defeat the relief must be in the very *thing or fund* itself which is the subject-matter of the controversy and of the suit. An interest in the legal question at issue to be determined by the result of the litigation will not prejudice the plaintiff's right to the relief. If, therefore, the plaintiff has, with respect to other property not the subject-matter of the present suit, an interest that one of the defendants shall succeed, because the decision thus made will be favorable to his own future litigation

Club, 49 App. Div. 107, 62 N. Y. Supp. 1109; Dodge v. Lawson, 19 N. Y. Supp. 904, 22 Civ. Proc. Rep. 112. That the defendants are entitled to show that the amount offered by the complainant is not the amount due, see Williams v. Matthews, 47 N. J. Eq. 196, 20 Atl. 261.

36 See Sprague v. West, 127 Mass. 471; Hyman v. Cameron, 46 Miss. 725; Hathaway v. Foy, 40 Mo. 540; Boyce v. Hamilton, 21 Mo. App. 520, 525; Kontjohn v. Seimers, 29 Mo. App. 271; Arn v. Arn, 81 Mo App. 133; Wenstrom Electric Co. v. Bloomer, 85 Hun, 389, 32 N. Y. Supp 903.

37 Pom. Eq Jur, § 1325, note; Mount Holly etc Co. v. Ferree, 17 N. J. Eq. 117; Tiernan v. Rescaniere's Admrs., 10 Gill & J. 217; Vosburg v. Huntington, 15 Abb Pr. 254; Martin v. Maberry, 1 Dev. Eq. 169; Burnet v. Anderson, 1 Mer. 405; Hechmer v. Gilligan, 28 W. Va. 750, 758.

concerning that other property,—this is no objection to his maintaining a suit for an interpleader."[38]

§ 52. Fourth: No Independent Liability to One Claimant.—"The party seeking the relief must have incurred no independent liability to either of the claimants. Such an independent liability may be incurred in two classes of cases: 1. In the first place, the agent, depositary, bailee, or other party demanding an interpleader, in his dealings with one of the claimants, may have expressly acknowledged the latter's title, or may have bound himself by contract, so as to render himself liable upon such independent undertaking, without reference to his possible liability to the rival claimant upon the general nature of the entire transaction. Under these circumstances, as the plaintiff is liable at all events to one of the defendants, whatever may be their own respective claims upon the subject-matter as between themselves, he cannot call upon these defendants to interplead. He does not stand indifferent between the claimants, since one of them has a valid legal demand against him at all events.[39] Even if the ac-

38 Pom. Eq. Jur., § 1325, and note; Oppenheim v. Leo Wolf, 3 Sandf. Ch. 571; McHenry v. Hazard, 45 Barb. 657; Gibson v. Goldthwaite, 7 Ala 281, 42 Am. Dec. 592.

39 Pom. Eq. Jur, § 1326. Quoted in Atkinson v. Carter, 101 Mo. App. 477, 74 S. W. 502; Newman v. Commercial Nat. Bank, 156 Ill. 530, 41 N. E. 156 (affirming 55 Ill. App. 534). Cited to this effect in Northwestern Mut. Life Ins. Co. v. Kidder (Ind. App.), 69 N. E. 204; S. C., 162 Ind. 382, 70 N. E. 489, Pratt v. Worrell (N. J. Eq), 57 Atl. 450. See, also, Crawshay v. Thornton, 2 Mylne & C. 1, 19-24; Suart v. Welch, 4 Mylne & C. 305; Jew v. Wood, Craig & P. 185; Lindsay v. Barron, 60 E. C. L. 291; Patorni v. Campbell, 12 Mees. & W. 277; Standley v. Roberts, 59 Fed. 836, 8 C. C. A. 305, 19 U. S. App. 407; Pfister v. Wade, 56 Cal. 43; Tyus v. Rust, 37 Ga. 574, 95 Am. Dec. 365; Hatfield v. McWhorter, 40 Ga. 269; Cullen v. Dawson, 24 Minn. 66; Wakeman v. Kingsland, 46 N. J. Eq. 113;

knowledgment or promise has been obtained by fraud or mistake, the right of the party thus deceived to be

McKinney v. Kuhn, 59 Miss. 186 (claimants have reduced their demands to judgment); Ter Knile v. Reddick (N, J. Eq), 39 Atl. 1062; Johnston v. Oliver, 51 Ohio St. 6, 36 N. E. 458; Connecticut Mut. L. Ins. Co. v Tucker, 23 R. I 1, 91 Am. St Rep. 590, 49 Atl. 26, and see cases cited below, and in the following notes. As to the effect produced by the English statute of 1860, interpreted by the decision in Attenborough v London etc. Co, L. R 3 C. P. D. 450, and the amendment of section 386 of the California Code of Civil Procedure (applied in Wells, Fargo & Co. v. Miner, 25 Fed. 533) see *ante*, in note under § 47.

Illustrations.—It is held the plaintiff cannot interplead the claimants after one of them has obtained judgment upon his claim. Home Ins. Co. v. Caulk, 86 Md. 385, 38 Atl 901; Baker v. Brown, 64 Hun, 627, 19 N. Y. Supp. 258; Wabash R. Co. v. Flannigan, 95 Mo. App. 477, 75 S W. 691. Where the complainant, a bailee, became surety on the bond of one of the claimants for delivery of the chattels, his right to interpleader was defeated: Kyle v. Mary Lee Coal & R. Co., 112 Ala. 606, 20 South. 851, quoting the above text. Where money was deposited in the N. bank (the plaintiff and appellant) to the credit of the P. bank, a mere notification by the former to the latter of the deposit and credit, before receiving information of a rival claim to deposit, does not constitute an express acknowledgment of the P. bank's title, or an independent undertaking, within the meaning of the text. "The liability of [the plaintiff], whatever and to whosoever it was, arose from the act of deposit and acceptance of the fund. It did not spring from the telegram and letter of notification. Such papers did not constitute the contract, but were mere evidences of it; neither did they increase appellant's liability or affect it in any way" Platte Valley State Bank v. National Livestock Assn., 54 Ill. App. 483; opinion affirmed and adopted, 155 Ill. 250, 40 N. E. 621. A written receipt by the plaintiff, an insurance company, of an assignment of the policy is not an acknowledgment of liability to the assignee: Morrill v. Manhattan L. I. Co., 82 Ill. App. 410; opinion affirmed and adopted, 183 Ill. 260, 55 N. E. 656 In a case of rival sets of beneficiaries, claiming under a benefit insurance certificate, no independent liability on the part of the company to one set of beneficiaries resulted from assessments and dues paid by them, as the payments were made on behalf of the member, and under his contract with the company Supreme Commandery, U. O. G. C. v. Merrick, 163 Mass. 374, 40 N. E. 183.

relieved in equity from his liability cannot be considered and sustained in an interpleader suit."[40]

"Another instance of the doctrine is, where the plaintiff, in stating the case in his bill, is obliged to admit himself to be a wrong-doer to either one of the defendants; he thus shows an independent liability to that defendant, and is not entitled to an interpleader.[41] If the liability has been occasioned by some act of the plaintiff himself, he is not entitled to the remedy."[42]

§ 53. **Same; 2. Independent Liability Arising from Nature of Original Relation.**—"In the second class of cases, the independent liability of the plaintiff to one of the defendants arises from the very nature of the original relation subsisting between them, without reference to any collateral acknowledgment of title, or promise to be bound. The most important examples of such relations are those subsisting between a bailee and his bailor, an agent or attorney and his principal, a tenant and his landlord, and the like. In pursuance of the doctrine above stated, if a bailee is sued by his bailor, or an agent by his principal, or a tenant by his landlord, and at the same time a third person asserts a claim of title adverse and paramount to that of the bailor, principal, or landlord, a suit of interpleader

40 Pom. Eq Jur., § 1326. See Mitchell v. Northwestern Mfg. & C. Co., 26 Ill. App. 295 (acknowledgment obtained by mistake).

41 Pom. Eq. Jur., § 1326, note; Slingsby v. Boulton, 1 Ves. & B. 334; Morgan v. Fillmore, 18 Abb. Pr. 217; United States v. Vietor, 16 Abb. Pr. 153; Mount Holly etc. Co. v. Ferree, 17 N. J. Eq. 117; Dewey v. White, 65 N. C. 225; Hatfield v. McWhorter, 40 Ga. 269; Tyus v. Rust, 37 Ga 574, 95 Am. Dec. 365; Coleman v. Chambers, 127 Ala. 615, 29 South. 58; Dodge v. Lawson, 19 N. Y. Supp. 904, 22 Civ. Proc. Rep. 112. See, also, Stephenson v. Burdett (W. Va.), 48 S. E 846.

42 Pom. Eq. Jur., § 1326, note. See Desborough v. Harris, 5 De Gex, M & G. 439, 455; Cochrane v. O'Brien, 2 Jones & L. 380, 8 Ir. Eq. Rep. 241; Conley v. Alabama Gold Life Ins. Co., 67 Ala. 472.

cannot, in general, be maintained against the two conflicting claimants, since, from the very nature of the relation, there is an independent personal liability, with respect to the subject-matter, of the bailee to his bailor, of the agent to his principal, and of the tenant to his landlord.[43]

"The rule is not, however, of universal application. There are cases in which a bailee, agent, or tenant may interplead his bailor, principal, or landlord, and a third person setting up an opposing claim to the thing, fund, or duty. These cases may be described by one general formula, as those in which the title of the opposing claimant is *derivative* under, and not antagonistic and paramount to, that of the bailor, principal, or landlord. An interpleader is allowed wherever the adverse claim originates from some act of the bailor, principal, or landlord, done or suffered after the commencement of the bailment, agency, or tenancy, and causing a dispute as to which of the parties is entitled to the thing, fund, or duty. The claim of the third person, instead of being under an independent, antagonistic, paramount title, must be made under a title *derived* from that of the bailor, principal, or landlord; it must acknowledge, and not deny, such original title."[44]

§ 54. **Same; Bailees and Agents.**[45]—"A bailee or agent cannot maintain an interpleader suit against the bailor or the principal and a third person who asserts an independent, antagonistic, and paramount title to the funds.[46] Nor can an attorney maintain such a suit

43 Pom. Eq. Jur., § 1326.

44 Pom. Eq. Jur., § 1327.

45 Pom. Eq. Jur., § 1327, note.

46 Nickolson v. Knowles, 5 Madd. 47; Dixon v. Hammond, 2 Barn. & Ald. 310, 313; Cooper v. De Tastet, Tam. 177, 181, 182; Smith v. Hammond, 6 Sim. 10; Pearson v. Cardon, 2 Russ. & M.

against his client and a third person who claims the money which he has collected, by an independent and antagonistic title.[47] For the same reason, where A claims as legatee under a will, and B claims the property by a title paramount to that of the testator, the executor cannot compel them to interplead; he is under a direct liability to the legatee.[48] On the other hand, there are cases in which a bailee or an agent may interplead his bailor or his principal with third persons claiming adversely. Wherever the third person claims the thing, fund, debt, or duty from the bailee or agent under a title *derived from* the bailor or the principal, created by the latter's own act subsequently to the bailment or agency,—such as his assignment, agreement, sale, mortgage, trust, or lien given by him,—the bailee or agent may compel the parties to interplead. There

606, 609, 610, 612; Crawshay v. Thornton, 2 Mylne & C. 1, 19-24; Cook v. Earl of Rosslyn, 1 Giff. 167; Atkinson v. Manks, 1 Cow. 691, 703-706; United States Trust Co. v. Wiley, 41 Barb. 477; Lund v. Seamen's Bank, 37 Barb. 129; United States v. Vietor, 16 Abb. Pr. 153; Vosburgh v. Huntington, 15 Abb. Pr. 254; First Nat. Bank v. Bininger, 26 N. J. Eq. 345; Tyus v. Rust, 37 Ga. 574, 95 Am. Dec. 365; Hatfield v. McWhorter, 40 Ga. 269; Crane v. Burntrager, 1 Ind. 165; White Water etc. Co. v. Comegys, 2 Ind. 469; Bartlett v. The Sultan, 23 Fed. 257; De Zouche v. Garrison, 140 Pa. St. 430, 21 Atl. 450; Whitbeck v. Whiting, 59 Ill. App. 520; Cromwell v. American L. & T. Co., 57 Hun, 149, 11 N. Y. Supp. 144; Pacific Express Co. v. Williams, 2 Willson (Tex.) Civ. Cas. Ct. App., § 810.

Lord Brougham declares, in Pearson v. Cardon, 2 Russ. & M. 606, "That an agent should have the power of filing a bill of interpleader, when his principal demands the redelivery of his goods bailed with him, appeared to me so monstrous a proposition, and to involve such frightful consequence in mercantile transactions, that I could not suppose it was meant to contend for any such doctrine. For, in fact, it amounts to this: that an agent may, at any moment, treat his principal to a chancery suit," etc.

47 Marvin v. Ellwood, 11 Paige, 365; but see, *per contra*, Goddard v. Leech, Wright, 476.

48 Adams v. Dixon, 19 Ga. 513, 65 Am. Dec. 608.

is in such a case no denial of the original title; the only dispute is concerning the effect of the subsequent act, and as to which of the claimants is thereby entitled to the thing or fund. On this general ground an attorney may interplead his client and a person who sets up a derivative claim from such client.[49] And where money is in the hands of an agent, and the principal has created a lien or charge on the fund, in favor of a third person, in respect to which a controversy has arisen, the agent may compel his principal and the other claimant to interplead;[50] and where the principal has assigned the fund in the agent's hands, or the bailor has transferred his interest in the thing bailed.[51] For a like reason an interpleader is permitted where a bailor or principal has given orders for the property to two different persons who set up conflicting claims, since their titles are derivative, and not antagonistic.[52] An interpleader by the bailee is also allowed where a joint bailment has been made, or a transaction in the nature of a joint bailment, to await the happening of some event or the determination of some dispute.[53] It should be remembered that in all such cases if the bailee or agent has recognized the title of the assignee or other holder of a

49 Gibson v. Goldthwaite, 7 Ala 281, 42 Am. Dec 592, McFadden v. Swinerton, 36 Or. 336, 59 Pac. 816, 62 Pac. 12, Sammis v. L'Engle, 19 Fla 800.

50 Smith v. Hammond, 6 Sim. 10; Wright v. Ward, 4 Russ 215-220.

51 Crawford v. Fisher, 1 Hare, 436, 440; Smith v. Hammond, 6 Sim. 10; Wright v. Ward, 4 Russ. 215-220; Tanner v. European Bank, L. R. 1 Ex 261; Gibson v. Goldthwaite, 7 Ala. 281, 42 Am. Dec. 592

52 Pearson v. Cardon, 2 Russ. & M. 606, 4 Sim 218; Atkinson v Manks, 1 Cow. 691. The decision in Schuyler v. Pelissier, 3 Edw. Ch. 191, goes too far.

53 Suart v. Welch, 4 Mylne & C. 305; City Bank v. Skelton, 2 Blatchf. 14, Fed. Cas No. 2739; First Nat. Bank v. West River R. R., 46 Vt. 633; Perkins v. Trippe, 40 Ga. 225. For special cases, see Mason v. Hamilton, 5 Sim. 19, Crellin v Levland, 6 Jur. 733.

derivative title, and has stipulated to hold the property at his disposal, the independent liability thus assumed will prevent the bailee or agent from compelling the assignee to interplead with the bailor or principal who repudiates the transaction."[54]

§ 55. **Same; Tenant and Landlord.**[55]—"The general doctrine is familiar, that a tenant cannot deny his landlord's title; he cannot therefore maintain a suit for interpleader against his landlord and a stranger who claims under a title antagonistic and paramount to that of the lessor.[56] But the tenant is entitled to interplead his landlord and an opposing claimant whenever there is some privity between the two,—when the title of the other claimant is derivative from that of the lessor,—as, for example, when the relation of mortgagor and mortgagee, trustee and *cestui que trust,* assignor and assignee, etc., has been created between the two. In such a case the tenant does not dispute his landlord's title.[57] So, when both contestants claim under the lessor by differ-

54 See *ante,* § 52; Tyus v. Rust, 37 Ga. 574, 95 Am. Dec. 365; Hatfield v. McWhorter, 40 Ga. 269; Horton v. Earl of Devon, 4 Welsb. H. & G. 496.

55 Pom Eq Jur., § 1327, note.

56 Dungey v. Angove, 2 Ves. 304, 310; Woolaston v. Wright, 3 Anstr. 801; Smith v. Target, 2 Anstr. 529; Johnson v. Atkinson, 3 Anstr. 798; Cook v. Earl of Rosslyn, 1 Giff. 137; Crawshay v. Thornton, *supra;* Seaman v. Wright, 12 Abb. Pr 304; Crane v. Burntrager, 1 Ind 165; Snodgrass v. Butler, 54 Miss 45; Standley v. Roberts, 59 Fed. 836, 8 C. C. A 305, 19 U. S. App. 407; Whitewater Valley etc. Co v. Comegys, 2 Ind. 469.

57 Dungey v. Angove, 2 Ves. 304, 310, 312; Metcalf v. Hervey, 1 Ves. Sr. 248; Cowtan v. Williams, 9 Ves. 107; Clarke v. Byne, 13 Ves. 383; Johnson v. Atkinson, 3 Anstr. 798; Seaman v. Wright, 12 Abb. Pr. 304, Snodgrass v. Butler, 54 Miss. 45; Oil Run Petro. Co. v. Gale, 6 W. Va. 525; Ketcham v. Brazil Block Coal Co, 88 Ind. 515; Van Zandt v Van Zandt, 7 N. Y. Supp. 706, 17 Civ. Proc. Rep. 448, McCoy v. McMurtrie, 12 Phila. 180 (mortgagor and mortgagees).

ent titles; for example, one as heir and the other as devisee."[58]

§ 56. **Same; Parties to Contracts.**[59]—"As a general rule, where A and B are bound by express contract, A cannot maintain an interpleader suit against B or a person holding or claiming under him, and a stranger who asserts and claims under an antagonistic and paramount title. A is under an independent liability to B.[60] For example, a vendee of real or personal property, with respect to his liability to pay the purchase price, cannot interplead his vendor and a third person claiming to own the property by an independent antagonistic title.[61] On the other hand, as in cases of bailees, agents, and tenants, a party to a contract may interplead his co-contractor and other persons in privity with him, or distinct claimants all of whom are in privity with his co-contractor,—that is, may interplead his co-contractor and persons who derive their title under him, or several claimants all of whom thus hold by derivative title.[62] As example: A vendee may interplead his vendor and an attaching creditor of A, alleged to be the real owner, the sale being alleged to have been really made by the vendor as A's agent.[63] One owing a sum of money un-

58 Jew v. Wood, 3 Beav. 579; Badeau v. Tylee, 1 Sandf. Ch. 270; Glaser v. Priest, 29 Mo. App. 1.

59 Pom. Eq. Jur., § 1327, note.

60 *Ante*, § 52.

61 Quoted in Northwestern Mut. Life Ins. Co. v. Kidder, 162 Ind. 382, 70 N. E. 489. See, also, James v Pritchard, 7 Mees. & W. 216; Trigg v. Hitz, 17 Abb. Pr. 436; Shehan's Heirs v. Barnett's Heirs, 6 T. B. Mon. 592; Tynan v. Cadenas, 7 Civ. Proc. Rep. (N. Y.) 305 (no interpleader by vendee of goods against persons each of whom claim to have sold him the goods).

62 Bechtel v. Sheafer, 117 Pa. St. 555, 562, 11 Atl. 889.

63 Richards v. Salter, 6 Johns. Ch. 445; Johnston v. Lewis, 4 Abb. Pr., N. S., 150.

der a contract may interplead the legal assignee of his co-contractor, and one claiming the fund either by equitable assignment from the co-contractor or by attachment levied upon the fund.[64] A vendor of land may interplead the husband of the deceased vendee and her heirs, where both claimed to be entitled to a conveyance.[65] Insurance companies may compel opposing claimants of the insurance money to interplead when they claim by assignment from the assured, or by mortgage, or by attachment, etc.—that is, when they claim *derivatively*.[66] On like ground, corporations may interplead opposing claimants of stock or dividends, whose titles are derivative from a stockholder, by assignment, execution, attachment, trust, etc.[67] A maker of a note may compel claimants holding under the payee by derivative title to interplead; for example, an attaching creditor of payee and an assignee;[68] the administrator of a deceased guardian to whom the note was made payable, and a new guardian appointed in place

64 Crane v. McDonald, 118 N. Y. 648, 23 N. E. 991. The titles of both defendants were plainly derivative.

65 Farley v. Blood, 30 N. H. 354.

66 Nelson v. Barter, 2 Hem. & M. 334; Hamilton v. Marks, 5 De Gex & S. 638; Spring v. South Carolina Ins. Co., 8 Wheat. 268, 5 L. ed. 614; Prudential Assur. Co. v. Thomas, L. R. 3 Ch. 74; Aetna Nat. Bank v. United States L. Ins. Co., 25 Fed. 531; Heusner v. Mutual Life Ins. Co, 47 Mo. App. 336; Supreme Conclave I. O. H. v. Dailey, 61 N. J. Eq. 145, 47 Atl. 277 (interpleader by a benefit society); Grill v. Globe & R. F. I. Co., 67 N. Y. Supp. 253, 55 App. Div. 612, citing Bacon v. Surety Co, 65 N. Y. Supp. 738, 53 App. Div. 150, and Woolworth v. Insurance Co., 49 N. Y. Supp. 512, 25 App. Div. 629.

67 Salisbury Mills v. Townsend, 109 Mass. 115; Providence Bank v Wilkinson, 4 R. I. 507, 70 Am. Dec. 160; Cady v. Potter, 55 Barb. 463; American Press Association v. Brantingham, 68 N. Y. Supp. 285, 57 App. Div. 399. See Cheever v. Hodgson, 9 Mo. App. 565; Bruggeman v. Bank, 1 City Ct. R. (N. Y.) 86 (rival claimants to a certified check).

68 Briant v Reed, 14 N. J. Eq. 271; Bryan v. Salterstall, 3 J. J. Marsh. 672; Fabie v. Lindsay, 8 Or. 474.

of the one deceased."[69] A very common class of interpleader suits is that where a bank, holding the relation of debtor to its depositor, interpleads the depositor and one claiming under him, or two opposing claimants under the same depositor.[70]

§ 57. **Same; by Receiver; by Master of a Vessel; by Sheriff.**[71]—"A receiver has been held entitled to interplead opposing claimants of the fund in his hands.[72] *(Quaere, would not the court direct the proper distribution of the fund by the receiver?)* Where suits by persons claiming to be owners of the cargo are instituted in admiralty against a ship, causing her arrest, the master cannot maintain interpleader against these claimants, because —1. The claims are not against him, but against the ship; and 2. The court of admiralty has full jurisdiction to settle all the questions.[73] Independently of statute, it has generally been held that a sheriff levying on goods by execution against A, which are claimed by B to be his property, cannot compel the execution cred-

69 Van Buskirk v. Roy, 8 How. Pr. 425

70 See Platte Valley State Bank v. National Livestock Bank, 54 Ill App. 483, affirmed and opinion adopted, 155 Ill. 250, 40 N. E. 621; People's Savings Bank v Look, 95 Mich. 7, 54 N. W. 629, German Exchange Bank v. Commissioners, 6 Abb. N. C. (N. Y.) 394; Smith v. Emigrant Industrial Sav. Bank, 17 N. Y. St. Rep. 852, 2 N. Y. Supp. 617. See Masten v. Bowery Sav. Bank, 63 N. Y. Supp. 964, 31 Misc. Rep. 178 (no interpleader when, by statute, a draft does not constitute an equitable assignment). If one of the claimants asserts a title superior to that of the depositor, interpleader is not allowed: Third National Bank v. Skillings Lumber Co., 132 Mass. 410 (claimant asserts that depositor was its agent, and that the draft deposited was its property); German Sav. Bank v. Friend, 61 N. Y. Super. Ct. (29 J. & S.) 400, 20 N. Y. Supp. 434.

71 Pom. Eq. Jur., § 1327, note.

72 Winfield v Bacon, 24 Barb. 154.

73 Sablicich v. Russell, L. R. 2 Eq. 441.

itor and B to interplead.[74] Nor can the sheriff compel the opposing claimants of a surplus in his hands after satisfying an execution to interplead; such claims can be adjusted by the courts.[75] Statutes in England and in many of the states have authorized the sheriff to interplead the claimants of property seized by him under process."

§ 58. Requisites of the Bill or Complaint.[76]—"The bill of complaint must contain allegations which show that all of the requisites entitling the plaintiff to the remedy exist in the case. It must allege positively that conflicting claims to substantially the same thing, fund, debt, or duty are set up by the defendants; that plaintiff claims no interest in the subject-matter; that he is indifferent between the claimants, and is ready and willing to deliver the thing or fund, or pay the debt, or render the duty to the rightful claimant, but that he is ignorant or in doubt which is the rightful one, and is in a real danger or hazard by means of such doubt, from their conflicting demands.[77] The bill need not show

74 Slingsby v. Boulton, 1 Ves. & B. 334; Shaw v. Coster, 8 Paige, 339, 35 Am. Dec 690; S. C., *sub nom.* Shaw v. Chester, 2 Edw. Ch. 405, Quinn v. Green, 1 Ired. Eq. 229, 36 Am. Dec. 46, Quinn v. Patton, 2 Ired. Eq 48, Dewey v. White, 65 N. C. 225.

75 Parker v. Barker, 42 N. H. 78, 77 Am. Dec. 789; McDonald v. Allen, 37 Wis. 108, 19 Am. Rep. 754. But see Kring v. Green's Exrs, 10 Mo. 195; Lawson v. Jordan, 19 Ark. 297, 70 Am. Dec. 596, Child v. Mann, L. R. 3 Eq 806.

76 Pom. Eq. Jur., § 1328, and notes.

77 Farley v. Blood, 30 N. H. 354; Parker v. Barker, 42 N. H. 78, 77 Am Dec 789; Atkinson v. Manks, 1 Cow. 691; Wilson v. Duncan, 11 Abb. Pr. 3; Lozier's Exrs. v. Van Saun's Admrs, 3 N. J. Eq. 325; Briant v. Reed, 14 N. J. Eq. 271, Snodgrass v. Butler, 54 Miss. 45, Starling v. Brown, 7 Bush, 164; State Ins. Co. v. Gennett, 2 Tenn. Ch. 82; Pfister v. Wade, 56 Cal. 43; Killian v. Ebbinghaus, 110 U. S. 568, 4 Sup. Ct. Rep. 232, 28 L. ed. 246; Crane v. McDonald, 118 N. Y. 648, 654, 23 N. E. 991; Stone v. Reed, 152 Mass. 179, 25 N. E.

an apparent title in either of the defendants.[78] On the contrary, if the bill should show that plaintiff was fully informed of the defendants' rights and of his own liability, or if it should show that one of the defendants was certainly entitled, on the facts alleged, to the thing, debt, or duty, in either case it would be demurrable; there would be no ground for an interpleader."[79]

49; Sullivan v. Knights of F. M., 73 Mo. App. 43; Funk v. Thomasson, 84 Mo. App. 490; North Pacific Lumber Co. v. Lang, 28 Or. 246, 52 Am. St. Rep. 780, 42 Pac. 799. "The material allegations in a bill of interpleader . . . . are: (1) That two or more persons have preferred a claim against the complainant; (2) that they claim the same thing; (3) that the complainant has no beneficial interest in the thing claimed; and (4) that he cannot determine without hazard to himself, to which of the defendants the thing belongs": Crane v. McDonald, 118 N. Y. 648, 654, 23 N. E. 991; Atkinson v. Manks, 1 Cow. (N. Y.) 691, 703. The claims should be sufficiently set forth to enable the court to determine whether it is doubtful or dangerous for the plaintiff to act: National Bank of Augusta v. Augusta etc. Co., 99 Ga. 286, 25 S. E. 686; sufficiently to give a color of right to each of the defendants. Robards v. Clayton, 48 Mo. App. 608; specifically, so that they may appear to be of the same nature and character, and the fit subject for a bill of interpleader Varrien v. Berrien, 42 N. J. Eq. 1, 10 Atl. 875; Connecticut Mut. Life Ins. Co. v. Lea, 7 Ohio N. P. 399, 10 Ohio S & C. P. Dec. 39. As to what is a sufficiently specific description of the claims, see, also, Crane v. McDonald, 118 N. Y 648, 23 N. E 991. As to *proof* of the claims, it is held that the answers of the defendants may be read against each other to establish the fact that each makes claim to the fund, and further proof of that fact is not necessary: Morrill v. Manhattan L. I. Co., 183 Ill. 260, 55 N E. 656, affirming and adopting opinion in 82 Ill. App 410, Balchen v Crawford, 1 Sandf. Ch (N. Y.) 380. That the bill must contain averments showing privity between the claimants, see Kyle v. Mary Lee Coal & R. Co., 112 Ala. 606, 20 South 851.

78 East & W. Ind. Dock Co. v Littledale, 7 Hare, 57, Pfister v. Wade, 56 Cal. 43; Supreme Lodge O. M. P. v. Raddatz, 57 Ill. App. 119, Stewart v. Fallon (N. J. Eq.), 58 Atl. 96

79 Parker v. Barker, 42 N. H. 78, 77 Am. Dec 789; Mohawk etc. R. R. v. Clute, 4 Paige, 384, Morgan v. Fillmore, 18 Abb. Pr. 217; Wilson v. Duncan, 11 Abb. Pr. 3; Briant v. Reed, 14 N. J Eq. 271, Barker v. Swain, 4 Jones Eq. 220; Bassett v. Leslie, 123 N. Y. 396, 25 N. E. 386; Pusey & Jones Co. v. Miller, 61 Fed. 401; Sugar Co. v.

§ 59. Affidavit of Non-collusion; Payment into Court; Costs.—"It is the settled practice that the bill of complaint must be accompanied by an affidavit of the plaintiff, stating that the suit is not brought in collusion with either of the defendants; and the omission of such affidavit may generally be taken advantage of by demurrer.[80] The plaintiff must also bring or pay, or offer

Alberger, 22 Hun, 349, 353; Shaw v. Coster, 8 Paige, 339, 35 Am. Dec. 690 (both defendants may demur). "When, from complainant's own showing, there can be no doubt in the case, the party entitled to the debt or duty claimed is not to be subjected to the delay and expense of a chancery suit": Crass v. Memphis & C. R. Co., 96 Ala 447, 11 South 480. "If the plaintiff denies his liability to either of the defendants, he is not entitled to the remedy; he destroys the very foundation on which it rests. McHenry v. Hazard, 45 Barb. 657, 45 N. Y. 580 [Southwark Nat. Bank v. Childs, 57 N. Y. Supp. 789, 39 App. Div. 560; *ante*, § 49]. If the bill is taken as confessed by one of the conflicting defendants, the fund indisputably belongs to the other. And where in such a case a stranger was afterwards admitted by the lower court, on petition, to contest the interest of the remaining defendant, it was held on appeal that there was no practice allowing a third person thus to come into the cause by petition; that the bill could not be amended to reach him, as it was filed to guard against *known* claims; the order that the remaining defendant and the third person should interplead was irregular: Michigan etc. Co. v. White, 44 Mich. 25, 5 N. W. 1086. (*Quaere*, would such a proceeding be allowed under the provisions of the Iowa and California codes permitting *Intervention*?)" Pom. Eq. Jur., § 1328, note.

80 Hamilton v. Marks, 5 De Gex & S. 638; Farley v. Blood, 30 N. H. 354; Atkinson v. Manks, 1 Cow. 691; Beck v. Stephani, 9 How. Pr. 193; Mount Holly etc. Co. v. Ferree, 17 N. J. Eq. 117; Tyus v. Rust, 37 Ga 574, 95 Am. Dec. 365; Snodgrass v. Butler, 54 Miss. 45; Starling v Brown, 7 Bush, 164; Biggs v. Kouns, 7 Dana, 405, 411; Blue v. Watson, 59 Miss. 619; Ammendale Norm. Inst. v. Anderson, 71 Md. 128, 17 Atl. 1030, Home Ins. Co. v. Caulk, 86 Md. 385, 38 Atl. 901; Bliss v. French, 117 Mich. 538, 76 N. W. 73; but a contrary practice seems to prevail in Connecticut. Consociated Pres. Soc. v. Staples, 23 Conn 544, 555; Nash v. Smith, 6 Conn. 421; and in Indiana the absence of the affidavit is not a ground of demurrer under the code, since demurrers under the code can be sustained for specified causes only, and the want of verification of a pleading is not one of them· Nofsinger v Reynolds, 52 Ind. 218, 224; while in Oregon

to bring or pay, the entire thing, fund, or money in controversy into court; an omission to do so renders the bill demurrable.[81] If the bill was properly filed, and if the plaintiff has acted in good faith, he is generally entitled to his costs out of the fund in controversy, which costs, as between the defendants, must ultimately be paid by the unsuccessful party."[82]

it is "perhaps sufficient under code practice that the fact [of non-collusion] appear by appropriate allegations in the complaint" North Pacific Lumber Co. v Lang, 28 Or 246, 52 Am. St Rep. 780, 42 Pac. 799 The plaintiff's affidavit is conclusive; defendants cannot contradict it, even though the plaintiff has filed supplemental affidavits Manby v Robinson, L R 4 Ch 347; Langston v. Boylston, 2 Ves. 101, Stevenson v. Anderson, 2 Ves & B. 407; and see Fahie v. Lindsay, 8 Or. 474. If collusion appears on the face of the bill, relief will, of course, be denied Marvin v. Ellwood, 11 Paige, 365; Kerr v. Union Bank, 18 Md. 396, Williams v. Halbert, 7 B. Mon. 184. Pom. Eq. Jur., § 1328, and note.

81 The whole fund must be put at the disposal of the court; an offer to bring in what may be found due is not sufficient: Mohawk etc. R. R. v. Clute, 4 Paige, 384, Atkinson v. Manks, 1 Cow. 691; Williams v Walker, 2 Rich. Eq. 291, 46 Am. Dec. 58; Snodgrass v. Butler, 54 Miss 45; McGarrah v. Prather, 1 Blackf. 299; Starling v. Brown, 7 Bush, 164, Ammendale Norm. Inst. v. Anderson, 71 Md. 128, 17 Atl. 1030, Home Ins. Co. v. Caulk, 86 Md. 385, 38 Atl. 901; Barroll v. Foreman, 86 Md. 675, 39 Atl. 273 ("this offer is required to prevent an abuse of this proceeding, just as the affidavit that there is no collusion"); Bliss v. French, 117 Mich. 538, 76 N. W. 73. *Contra*, as to the omission being a ground for demurrer, Blue v. Watson, 59 Miss. 619; Manx v Bell, 6 Sim. 175. It seems that if the petition contains such offer, actual payment of the fund into court is not a condition precedent to an order of interpleader: Barnes v. Bamberger, 196 Pa. St 123, 46 Atl. 303. It was held in Farley v. Blood, 30 N. H. 354, that in a suit concerning the defendants' rights to a conveyance under a land contract, the plaintiff must offer to convey, and must have the deeds executed ready for delivery. Pom. Eq. Jur., § 1328, and note.

82 See Laing v. Zeden, L. R. 9 Ch. 736; Aldridge v. Thompson, 2 Brown Ch. 149; Cowtan v. Williams, 9 Ves. 107; Farley v. Blood, 30 N. H. 354; Manchester Print Works v. Stimson, 2 R. I. 415; Atkinson v. Manks, 1 Cow. 691; Canfield v Morgan, Hopk. Ch. 224; Aymer v. Gault, 2 Paige, 284, Badeau v. Rogers, 2 Paige, 209; Spring v.

§ 60. Bill in the Nature of a Bill of Interpleader.—A bill in the nature of a bill of interpleader is one in which the complainant seeks some relief of an equitable nature concerning the fund or other subject-matter in dispute, in addition to the interpleader of conflicting claimants. The complainant is not required, as in strict interpleader, to be an indifferent stake-holder, without interest in the subject-matter.[83] It is essential, however, that the facts on which he relies entitle him to equitable, as distinguished from legal, relief; he is not permitted, under the guise of a bill in equity, to litigate a purely legal claim or interest in the subject-matter.[84] The additional relief most frequently granted is the redemption of a mortgage or other encumbrance on prop-

South Carolina Ins. Co., 8 Wheat. 268, 5 L. ed. 614; Long v. Superior Court, 127 Cal. 686, 60 Pac. 464; Glaser v. Priest, 29 Mo. App. 1. That the complainant is entitled to reasonable attorney's fees, see Louisiana State Lottery Co. v. Clark, 16 Fed. 20, 4 Woods, 169; Franco-American L. & B. Assn. v. Joy, 56 Mo. App. 433; Christian v. National L. I. Co., 62 Mo. App. 35; Supreme Council Legion of Honor v. Palmer, 107 Mo. App. 157, 80 S. W. 699; but see *contra,* Helmken v. Meyer (Ga.), 45 S. E. 450. If the decree is irregular in not directing payment into court and plaintiff's discharge, the plaintiff should not have costs out of the fund: Gardiner Sav. Inst. v. Emerson, 91 Me. 535, 40 Atl. 551. As in all equity suits, costs are within the discretion of the court, and depend somewhat upon the circumstances of each case. Pom. Eq. Jur., § 1328, and note.

83 Nofsinger v. Reynolds, 52 Ind. 218; Van Winkle v. Owen, 54 N. J. Eq. 253, 34 Atl. 400, and cases cited in following notes. That, aside from the plaintiff's interest in the subject-matter, the bill is governed by the same principles as the strict bill of interpleader, see Stephenson v. Burdett (W. Va.), 48 S. E. 846 (reviewing many cases); but that the affidavit of non-collusion is not required, see Koppinger v. O'Donnell, 16 R. I. 417, 16 Atl. 714; Van Winkle v. Owen, 56 N. J. Eq. 253, 34 Atl. 400.

84 Killian v. Ebbinghaus, 110 U. S. 568, 4 Sup. Ct. 232, 28 L. ed. 246 (relief demanded amounts to ejectment); Aleck v. Jackson, 49 N. J. Eq. 507, 23 Atl. 760; Parks v. Jackson, 11 Wend. 442; Mohawk etc. R. Co. v. Clute, 4 Paige, 384; Bedell v. Hoffman, 2 Paige, 199.

erty, when there are conflicting claimants to the debt secured.[85]

§ 61. Interpleader in Legal Actions.[86]—"In England and in many of the American states a summary mode of interpleader by motion and order in certain legal actions is authorized.[87] These statutes substantially pro-

85 See Vyvyan v. Vyvyan, 30 Beav. 65; Crass v. Memphis etc R. Co., 96 Ala. 447, 11 South. 480; Robson v. Du Bose, 79 Ga. 72, 4 S. E. 329 (taxes); Newhall v. Kastens, 70 Ill. 156 (mechanics' liens); Curtis v. Williams, 35 Ill. App. 518; Nofsinger v. Reynolds, 52 Ind. 218; Board v. Scoville, 13 Kan. 17 (mechanics' liens); Illingworth v. Rowe, 52 N. J. Eq 360, 28 Atl. 456 (same); Van Winkle v. Owen, 54 N. J. Eq. 253, 34 Atl. 400 (judgment); Bedell v. Hoffman, 2 Paige, 199; Badeau v. Rogers, 2 Paige, 209; Parks v. Jackson, 11 Wend 442; Mohawk etc. R. Co. v. Clute, 4 Paige, 384 (taxes); Van Loan v. Squires, 23 Abb. N Cas. (N. Y.) 230; Dohnert's Appeal, 64 Pa. St 311; Koppinger v. O'Donnell, 16 R. I. 417, 16 Atl. 714. See, also, Union Trust Co. v. Stamford Trust Co., 72 Conn. 86, 43 Atl. 555, for a bill of this character authorized by statute.

86 Pom. Eq Jur., § 1329, and notes. This section of Pom. Eq. Jur. is cited in Northwestern Mut. Life Ins. Co. v. Kidder, 162 Ind 382, 70 N. E. 489.

87 The English statute of 1 & 2 Wm. IV, c. 58, § 1, allowed this proceeding in actions of assumpsit, debt, trover, and detinue. For cases under this statute see Frost v. Heywood, 2 Dowl., N. S., 801; Dalton v. Railway Co., 74 E. C. L. (12 Com. B.) 458; Baker v. Bank of Australasia, 1 Com. B., N. S, 515; Turner v. Kendal, 13 Mees. & W. 171. For the amendment made by the common-law procedure act of 1860, see *ante*, note 30, § 47. The American statutes mainly differ with respect to the kinds of actions in which the proceeding is allowed. In a few states it is confined to actions on contract for money: *Alabama:* Code 1876, §§ 2906, 2907; Code 1886, §§ 2610, 2611; Code 1896, § 2633; Jackson v. Jackson, 84 Ala. 343, 4 South 174; Coleman v. Chambers, 127 Ala. 615, 29 South. 58; or to actions for the recovery of personal property: *Arkansas:* Code 1874, §§ 4483, 4484; *Iowa:* 2 McClain's Stats. 1880, § 2572; *Oregon:* Gen Laws, 1872, p. 111, § 39. In several states the proceeding is allowed in actions on contract, and in those for the recovery of specific personal property: *California:* Code Civ. Proc., § 336 (for recent amendment, see *ante*, note under § 47), *Idaho;* Gen. Laws 1880-81, § 201; *Kansas:* Dassler's Comp. Laws 1881, §§ 3564, 3565; *Nebraska:* Brown's Comp. Stats. 1881, pp. 535, 536, § 48; *Ohio:* 2 Rev. Stats.

vide that in actions specified the defendant may show by affidavit that the same thing or money is claimed by another person besides the plaintiff; that he has sued or threatens to sue; that defendant is not in collusion with him; and that defendant is ready and willing to bring the thing or money into court. The court on motion may order such claimant to be substituted as defendant in the action in place of the original defendant. It is universally held that these statutes do not at all limit nor affect the equitable jurisdiction by suit; they merely furnish another special, cumulative, and concurrent remedy. The ordinary type of these statutes does not alter the settled doctrines concerning interpleader. The statutory remedy is a mere substitute for the equitable remedy by suit, in the kinds of actions to which it applies, and is governed by the same rules.[88] Of

1880, §§ 5016, 5017; *Mississippi:* Rev. Code, 1880, § 1578, interpleader by garnishee; Code 1880, § 2449; Dodds v. Gregory, 61 Miss. 351. In others it embraces actions on contract, and actions for the recovery of real or of personal property: *Dakota:* Rev. Codes 1877, p. 491, § 91; *Indiana:* Rev. Stats. 1881, § 273; Mansfield v. Shipp, 128 Ind. 55, 27 N. E. 427; *Minnesota:* Stats. 1878, p 725, § 131; *New York:* Code Civ. Proc. (new code), § 820; Sickles v. Wilmerding, 59 Hun, 375, 13 N. Y. Supp. 43 (what is an "action upon contract" within this section); Laws 1882, c. 409, § 259, Laws 1892, c. 689, § 115, interpleader in action against savings bank; see as to this act, Progressive Handlanger Union v. German Sav. Bank, 23 Abb. N. C. 42, 7 N. Y. Supp. 3; affirmed, 57 N. Y. Super. Ct. (25 J. &. S) 594, 8 N. Y Supp. 545; Faivre v. Union Dime Sav. Inst., 59 N. Y. Super. Ct. (27 J & S.) 558, 13 N. Y. Supp. 423; Mahro v. Greenwich Sav. Bank, 16 Misc. Rep. 275, 38 N. Y. Supp. 126, reversed in 16 Misc Rep. 537, 40 N Y. Supp. 29, *North Carolina:* Battle's Rev. 1873, p. 156, § 65; *South Carolina;* Rev. Stats. 1873, p. 597, § 145. In two states it is authorized "in any action": *Virginia.* Code 1873, c. 149, p 1019; *West Virginia* · 1 Kelly's Rev. Stats. 1879, c. 7, p. 238; Dickeshied v. Exchange Bank, 28 W Va. 340. In some other states a similar proceeding is authorized by statute in certain special cases: *Colorado:* King's Code Civ. Proc. 1880, p. 151, § 404.

88 Oriental Bank v Nicholson, 3 Jur., N. S , 857; Slaney v. Sidney, 14 Mees. & W. 800; Tauton v. Groh, 4 Abb. App. 358, Vosburgh

course, the statutes may change the equitable doctrines; may enlarge their scope of operation; and a few of them have doubtless produced this effect, as in the clauses introduced by amendment into the statutes of England and California, already noticed."[89]

v. Huntington, 15 Abb Pr. 254; Johnson v. Maxey, 43 Ala. 521; Nelson v. Goree's Admr., 34 Ala 565; Starling v Brown, 7 Bush, 164; Board of Education v. Scoville, 13 Kan 17; Pfister v. Wade, 56 Cal. 43; Coleman v. Chambers, 127 Ala 615, 29 South. 58; Fox v. Sutton, 127 Cal. 515, 59 Pac. 939; Hartford Life Ann. Co. v. Cummings, 50 Neb. 236, 69 N. W. 782, American Trust & S. Bank v Thalheimer, 51 N. Y. Supp. 813, 29 App. Div. 170; Brock v. Southern Ry. Co., 44 S. C. 444, 22 S. E. 601 (approving above text); Kinney v Hynds, 7 Wyo. 22, 49 Pac. 403, 52 Pac. 1081. That the statutory remedy is concurrent, and has not done away with interpleader by suit in equity, see, also, New England Mut. L. I. Co. v Keller, 7 Civ. Proc. Rep. (N. Y.) 109; Cronin v Cronin, 9 Civ. Proc Rep. (N. Y.) 137, 3 How. Pr., N S, 184; Lane v. New York L. Ins. Co., 56 Hun, 92, 9 N Y Supp. 52; Dubois v. Union Dime Sav. Inst., 89 Hun, 382, 35 N. Y. Supp. 397; First Nat. Bank v. Beebe, 62 Ohio St. 41, 56 N. E. 485. That the statutory remedy is governed by the same principles as the remedy in equity, see Pustet v. Flannelly, 60 How Pr. 67; Lawrence v. Watson, 8 Hun, 593, Schell v. Lowe, 75 Hun, 43, 23 Civ. Proc. Rep. 300, 26 N. Y. Supp. 991; Dinley v McCullagh, 92 Hun, 454, 36 N. Y. Supp 1007; Windecker v. Mut L. Ins. Co., 43 N. Y. Supp 358, 12 App. Div. 73; Burritt v. Press Pub. Co, 19 App Div. 609, 25 App. Div. 141, 46 N. Y. Supp. 95, 49 N. Y. Supp. 201. As to the discretionary nature of the order, see Burritt v. Press Pub. Co., 25 App Div. 141, 49 N. Y. Supp. 201.

89 See *ante*, § 47, note 30; Tanner v. European Bank, L. R. 1 Ex. 261, Wells, Fargo & Co. v. Miner, 25 Fed. 533; Dickeshied v. Exchange Bank, 28 W. Va. 340. As to actions under codes of procedure adopting the reformed procedure, see Cady v. Potter, 55 Barb. 463; Washington etc. Ins. Co. v. Lawrence, 28 How. Pr. 435, St. Louis Life Ins. Co. v. Alliance Mut. L. Ins. Co., 23 Minn. 7; Board of Education v. Scôville, 13 Kan. 17; Pfister v. Wade, 56 Cal. 43.

CHAPTER III.

APPOINTMENT OF RECEIVERS.

ANALYSIS.

§ 62. Definition of Receiver; a Provisional Remedy.— "A receiver is a person standing indifferent between the parties, appointed by the court as a *quasi* officer or representative of the court, to hold, manage, control, and deal with the property which is the subject-matter of or involved in the controversy, under the direction of the court, during the continuance of the litigation."[1]

1 Pom. Eq. Jur., § 1330, continuing: "either where there is no person entitled competent to thus hold it—as, for example, in the case of an infant, or in the interval before an executor or administrator of a deceased owner is appointed; or where two or more litigants are equally entitled, but it is not just and proper that either of them should retain it under his control—as, for example, in some suits between partners; or where a person is legally entitled, but there is danger of his misapplying or misusing it—as, for example, in some suits against an executor or administrator, or, under some particular circumstances, in suits for the enforcement of a mortgage; or he is appointed in like manner and under like circumstances for the purpose of carrying into effect a decree of the court concerning the property—as, for example, a decree for the winding up and settlement of a corporation, or the decree in a creditor's suit." This classification of the objects for which a receiver may be appointed has been adopted in the present work. "A receiver is an indifferent person between parties, appointed by the court to receive the rents, issues or profits of land or other thing in question in this court, pending the suit, where it does not seem reasonable to the court that either party should do it. He is an officer of the court; his appointment is provisional. He is appointed in behalf of all parties, and not of the complainant or of the defendant only. He is appointed for the benefit of all parties who may establish rights in the cause. The money in his hands is *in custodia legis* for whoever can make out a title to it. It is the court itself which has the care of the property in dispute. The receiver is but the creature of the court, he has no powers except such as are conferred upon him by the order of his appointment and the course and practice of the court": Booth v. Clark, 17 How. 322, 331, 15 L. ed. 164. See the following cases, among others, for definitions of the nature and purpose of the receiver's office and general statements as to the motives that influence the court in making or refusing the appointment: Gayle v. Johnson, 80 Ala 388; Ashurst v. Lehman, Durr & Co., 86 Ala. 370, 5 South. 731, and cases cited; Baker v. Backus's Admr., 32 Ill 79, 96; Jackson v. King, 9 Kan. App. 160, 58 Pac. 1013; Corey v. Long, 12 Abb. Pr.,

As is said in a leading case, "By means of the appointment of a receiver, a court of Equity takes possession of the property which is the subject of the suit, preserves it from waste or destruction, secures and collects the proceeds or profits, and ultimately disposes of them according to the rights and priorities of those entitled.[2]

"The receiver appointed is the officer and representative of the court, subject to its orders, accountable in such manner and to such persons as the court may direct, and having in his character of receiver no personal interest, but that arising out of his responsibility for the correct and faithful discharge of his duties. It is of no consequence to him how, or when, or to whom, the court may dispose of the funds in his hands, provided the order or decree of the court furnishes to him a sufficient protection."[3]

"The order of appointment is in the nature, not of an attachment, but of a sequestration; it gives in itself no advantage to the party applying for it over other claimants; and operates prospectively upon rents and profits which may come to the hands of the receiver, as a lien in favor of those interested, according to their rights and priorities in or to the principal subject out of which those rents and profits issue."[4]

N S 427; Skinner v. Maxwell, 66 N. C. 45; Battle v. Davis, 66 N. C. 252.

2 Beverley v. Brooke, 4 Gratt. (Va.) 187, 208.

3 Beverley v Brooke, 4 Gratt. (Va.) 187, 208.

4 Beverley v. Brooke, 4 Gratt (Va) 187, 208 "A receiver derives his authority from the act of the court appointing him, and not from the act of the parties at whose suggestion or by whose consent he is appointed; and the utmost effect of his appointment is to put the property from that time into his custody, as an officer of the court, for the benefit of the party ultimately proved to be entitled, but not to change the title, or even the right of possession, in the property": Union Nat. Bank of Chicago v. Kansas City Bank, 136 U. S. 223, 10 Sup. Ct 1013, 34 L. ed. 341, per Gray, J. For further statements

§ 63. The Appointment Discretionary.—"The appointment of a receiver is, as a general rule, discretionary.[5] The discretion is not arbitrary or absolute; it is a sound and judicial discretion, taking into account all the circumstances of the case,[6] exercised for the purpose of promoting the ends of justice, and of protect-

of the doctrine that the appointment of the receiver *does not affect the title* of either party, see Howell v. Hough, 46 Kan. 152, 26 Pac. 436; Jackson v King, 9 Kan. App. 160, 58 Pac. 1013; Chase's Case, 1 Bland (Md), 206, 17 Am. Dec. 277, Ellicott v. Warford, 4 Md. 85; Ellis v. Boston H. & E. R. R. Co., 107 Mass. 1, 28; Mays v. Rose, Freem. Ch. (Miss) 718, Bank of Mississippi v. Duncan, 52 Miss. 740, 743; Battle v. Davis, 66 N. C. 252, 256, Harman v. McMullin, 85 Va. 187, 7 S. E. 349; Krohn v. Weinberger, 47 W. Va. 127, 34 S. E. 746; Mead v. Burk, 156 Ind. 577, 60 N. E 338; Bitting v. Ten Eyck, 85 Ind. 357; Ex parte Walker, 25 Ala. 81, 104.

5 The passage quoted is from Pom. Eq. Jur., § 1331; its language has been frequently adopted by the courts. See, also, Pennsylvania Co. v. Jacksonville T. & K. W. R. Co., 55 Fed. 131, 2 U. S. App. 606; Moore v. Bank of British Columbia, 106 Fed. 574 (citing Pom. Eq. Jur., § 1331); Crane v. McCoy, 1 Bond, 422, Fed Cas. No. 3354; Forsaith Mach. Co. v. Hope Mill Lumber Co., 109 N. C. 576, 13 S. E. 869; Warren v Pitts, 114 Ala. 65, 21 South. 494; Provident Life Ins. Co. v. Keniston, 53 Neb. 86, 73 N. W. 216; Woodward v. Woodward, 17 Ky. Law Rep. 464, 31 S. W. 734 (though the appointing power was given by statute); Fluker v. Emporia R. R. Co., 48 Kan. 587, 30 Pac. 18; Simmons Hardware Co. v. Waibel, 1 S. D. 488, 36 Am. St. Rep. 755, 47 N. W. 418, 814, 11 L. R. A. 267 (citing Pom. Eq. Jur., § 1331); Pullan v. Cincinnati etc. R. R. Co., 4 Biss. 47, Fed. Cas. No. 11,461; Chicago etc. Oil & Min. Co. v United States Petroleum Co., 57 Pa. St. 83 (possession under lease not disturbed).

6 Owen v. Homan, 4 H. L. Cas. 997; Norris v. Lake, 89 Va. 513, 16 S. E. 663; Meyer v. Thomas et al., 131 Ala. 111, 30 South. 89; Vose v. Reed, 1 Woods, 647, Fed. Cas. No. 17,011; Hanna v. Hanna, 89 N. C. 68 (allowing receiver for necessary part); May v. Rase, (Miss.), Freem. Ch. 703 (sale in fraud of creditors). In Vose v. Reed, 1 Wood, 650, Fed. Cas. No. 17,011, the court said: "But all the circumstances of the case are to be taken into consideration, and if the case be such that a greater injury would ensue from the appointment of a receiver than from leaving the property in the hands now holding it, or if any consideration of propriety or convenience render the appointment of a receiver improper or inexpedient, none will be appointed."

ing the rights of *all* the parties interested in the controversy and the subject-matter,[7] and based upon the fact that there is no other adequate remedy or means of accomplishing the desired objects of the judicial proceeding." Therefore, the discretion of the court in appointing a receiver will not be interfered with by an appellate court, unless it is clear that it has been abused or exercised in a manner inconsistent with well-established rules governing such application.[8]

§ 64. Principles Governing the Court's Discretion; Imminent Danger.—The general principles which should

7 American Biscuit & Mfg. Co. v. Klatz, 44 Fed. 721 (will not aid improper or illegal scheme); McGeorge v. Big Stone Gap Imp. Co., 57 Fed. 262 (probability of injury to defendant); Fort Payne Furnace Co. v. Fort Payne Coal Co., 96 Ala. 472, 38 Am. St. Rep. 109, 11 South. 439 (corporation not divested of lands it intended selling, in commenting on the exercise of the court's discretion in appointing receivers, the court quotes Pom. Eq Jur., § 1331, with approval); Sales v. Lusk, 60 Wis. 490, 19 N. W. 362 (subsequent mortgagees protected).

8 Mead v. Burke, 156 Ind. 577, 60 N. E. 338 ("there must be a plain abuse, to the prejudice of the complaining party"); Rider v. Bagley, 84 N. Y. 461 (fraud on lower court); Bagley v. Scudder, 66 Mich. 97, 33 N. W. 47 (approved in Dutton v. Thomas, 97 Mich. 93, 56 N. W. 229), Fluker v. Emporia R. R. Co., 48 Kan. 587, 30 Pac. 18 (discretion not abused); Naylor v. Sidener, 106 Ind. 179, 6 N. E. 345 (weight of evidence insufficient); Crawford v. Ross, 39 Ga. 44 (not unless illegal); Heinze v. Butte & Boston Consolidated Min. Co., 126 Fed. 1, 11, 61 C. C. A. 63 (citing Beaumont v. Beaumont, 166 Pa. St 615, 31 Atl. 336; Nimocks v. Shingle Co., 110 N. C. 230, 14 S E. 684, Sanders v. Slaughter, 89 Ga. 34, 14 S. E. 903); Woods v. Grayson, 16 App. D. C. 174. But see *contra*, Meyer v. Thomas, 131 Ala 111, 30 South 89; Pelzer v. Hughes, 27 S. C. 408, 3 S. E. 781; De Walt v. Kinard, 19 S. C. 286; Simmons Hardware Co. v. Waibel, 1 S. D 488, 36 Am. St. Rep. 755, 47 N. W. 814, 11 L. R. A. 267 (lower court refused to take possession of copy of secret code); Perrin v. Lepper, 56 Mich. 351, 23 N. W. 39. "The discretion is not so absolute that it may not be reviewed, and its exercise, if improper, reversed": 4 Pom Eq. Jur, § 1331, note 1, citing La Société Francaise v. District Court, 53 Cal. 495; Milwaukee R. R. v. Soutter, 2 Wall 521, 17 L. ed. 860.

govern the court in the exercise of its discretion have been thus formulated in a leading case: The plaintiff must show, first, either that he has a clear right to the property itself, or that he has some lien upon it; or that the property constitutes a special fund to which he has a right to resort for the satisfaction of his claim; and secondly, that the possession of the property by the defendant was obtained by fraud; or that the property itself, or the income arising from it, is in danger of loss from the neglect, waste, misconduct or insolvency of the defendant.[9] The element of danger is an important

9 May v. Rose, Freem. Ch. (Miss.) 703, 718; Steele v. Aspy, 128 Ind. 367, 27 N E. 739; State v. Union Nat. Bank, 145 Ind. 537, 57 Am St. Rep. 209, 44 N. E. 585. "As a general rule, a receiver will be appointed for the purpose of protecting the fund when the complainant has an equitable interest in the subject, and the defendant having possession of the property is wasting it, or removing it out of the jurisdiction of the court": Vose v. Reed, 1 Woods, 647, Fed. Cas. No. 17,011, per Bradley, J. See, also, Lancaster v. Asheville St. Ry. Co., 90 Fed. 129, 133; Ryder v. Bateman, 93 Fed. 16. "The power to appoint a receiver is most usually called into action either to prevent fraud, save the subject of litigation from material injury, or rescue it from threatened destruction": Baker v. Backus's Admr., 32 Ill. 79, 96. That the plaintiff cannot have a receiver when he has parted with his entire interest in the property, see Steele v. Aspy, *supra;* Smith v. Wells, 20 How. Pr. 158.

In Pom. Eq Jur., § 1331, note, are the following quotations and comment: "In Bainbrigge v. Baddeley, 3 Macn. & G. 413, 419, the court, speaking of the general grounds for the appointment of a receiver, said: 'There are, I apprehend, two grounds, and two only. 1. That there is a reasonable probability of success on the part of the plaintiff; and 2. That the property, the subject of the suit, is in danger.' In Blondheim v. Moore, 11 Md. 365, the following rules controlling the exercise of the discretion were laid down, which have been frequently quoted as a correct generalization: '1. That the power of appointment is a delicate one, and is to be exercised with great circumspection; 2. That it must appear the claimant has a title to the property, and the court must be satisfied by affidavit that a receiver is necessary to preserve the property; 3. That there is no case in which the court appoints a receiver merely because the measure can do no harm; 4. That fraud or imminent danger, if the intermediate consideration; a remote or past danger will not suffice as a ground for the relief, but there must be a well-grounded apprehension of immediate injury. Nor will the court act upon a possible danger only; the danger must be great and imminent, and demanding immediate relief.[10]

It has been truly said that a court will never appoint a receiver merely on the ground that it will do no harm.[11] This would seem to follow naturally from the rule that the appointment is primarily to prevent imminent injury.[12]

possession should not be taken by the court, must be clearly proved; and 5. That unless the necessity be of the most stringent character, the court will not appoint a receiver until the defendant is first heard in response to the application.' These rules, however, must be taken with some reservations; they are certainly too strong to be of universal application, especially the fourth. There are classes of cases in which a receiver is appointed almost as a matter of course, although no fraud nor *imminent* danger is proved."

10 Lancaster v. Asheville St. Ry. Co., 90 Fed. 129, 133. See, also, Mead v. Burk, 156 Ind. 577, 60 N. E. 338; Kean v. Colt, 5 N. J. Eq 365; Orphan Asylum v. McCartee, Hopk. Ch. (N. Y.) 429; Pelzer v. Hughes, 27 S. C. 408, 3 S E. 781; City Nat Bank v. Dunham, 18 Tex. Civ. App. 184, 44 S. W. 605; Morris v. Lake, 89 Va. 513, 16 S. E 663; Beecher v Bininger, 7 Blatchf. 170, Fed. Cas. No. 1222; Kelley v. Boettcher, 89 Fed. 125; Ft. Payne Furnace Co v. Fort Payne Coal etc. Co., 96 Ala. 473, 38 Am. St. Rep. 109, 11 South. 439, and cases cited. "It is well settled that when there is reasonable ground to apprehend that pending litigation the property may be so disposed of as to deprive the complaining party of the fruit of his victory when had, a court of equity will secure the property, or in a proper case have it sold and secure the fund arising from it by the appointment of a receiver, or by an injunction, and when need be, by both": Ellett v. Newman, 92 N. C. 519, 523. That the requirement of imminent danger is not universal, see end of last note.

11 Orphan Asylum Society v. McCartee et al, 1 Hopk. Ch. 429; approved in Clark v. Ridgely, 1 Md. Ch. 70; Blondheim v. Moore, 11 Md. 365; Owen v. Homan, 4 H. L. Cas. 997 (unless the property is not in the enjoyment of either party).

12 Yet, the assurance that no harm will follow tends to aid the appointment, where there are other proper grounds. Nimocks v.

§ 65. **Same; Insolvency of Defendant.**—While insolvency, alone, is not a ground for the appointment of a receiver, unless it has been so declared by statute,[13] "the solvency or insolvency of the party to be affected is an important consideration with a court of equity, in all cases guiding, if it does not govern, its discretion, in the appointment of receivers."[14] "The insolvency of a defendant in possession of property involved in litigation in any case necessarily intensifies the probability of loss to the complainant, and will serve, at least, to show that his remedy at law, for any loss or injury that may be sustained, would be inadequate."[15]

§ 66. **Same; Probability of Plaintiff's Success in the Suit.** While it is true, as a general rule, that in making or refusing the appointment of a receiver, the court will

Grimm, 110 N. C. 230, 14 S. E. 684 (refusing to discharge receiver); American Biscuit & Mfg. Co. v. Klotz, 44 Fed. 721 (appointing receiver of "trust monopoly").

13 Lawrence Iron-Works Co. v. Rockbridge Co, 47 Fed 755, McCreery v. Berney Nat Bank, 116 Ala. 224, 67 Am. St. Rep 105, 22 South. 577.

14 Warren v. Pitts, 114 Ala. 65, 21 South. 494; Thompson v. Tower Mfg. Co., 87 Ala. 733, 6 South. 928; Irwin v. Everson, 95 Ala. 64, 10 South. 320; Stillwell v. Savannah Grocery Co, 88 Ga 100, 13 S. E. 963, Chase's Case, 1 Bland (Md), 206, 213, 17 Am. Dec 277

15 Mead v. Burk, 156 Ind. 577, 60 N. E. 338 In this case the court holds that "insolvency of a person in the possession or enjoyment of the use of property for which a receiver is sought is not, as a general rule, indispensable to a successful prosecution of the application. . . . . The probability of a fierce and long-continued litigation in respect to the rights of property will sometimes justify a court in withdrawing it from the operation of such prolonged contest by placing it for preservation or security in charge of a receiver for the benefit of all parties concerned therein, until there can be a full and final adjudication of their rights"; citing Crane v. McCoy, 1 Bond, 422, Fed. Cas. No. 3354. To the effect that the insolvency of the debtor is necessary to justify the appointment, when the collection of a debt is the sole purpose of the suit, see Joseph Dry Goods Co. v. Hecht, 120 Fed. 760, 57 C. C. A. 64.

not forestall or anticipate the decision which may be made on final hearing, yet the primary inquiry is whether there is shown a reasonable probability that the plaintiff asking the appointment will ultimately succeed in obtaining the general relief sought by the suit. If ultimate success is a matter of grave doubt, or if it be clear that the general relief sought cannot be obtained, the appointment ought not to be made.[16] This principle, however, does not involve the necessity that the pleadings be drawn with technical accuracy. The bill may be subject to demurrer for the want of proper parties, or because of defects of form or the absence of substantial allegations,—insufficiencies curable by amendment. These insufficiencies, of themselves, do not form an impediment to the appointment of a receiver, if a case be made by a party having interests to be protected and preserved entitling him to the general relief which is prayed.[17]

§ 67. **Caution Observed in Making the Appointment.**— The appointment of a receiver is one of the most responsible duties which a court of equity is called upon to perform; and while resting within the sound, judicial discretion of the court, the power is, or should be, exer-

16 Pom. Eq. Jur, § 1331; Bank of Florence v. United States Savings & Loan Co., 104 Ala. 297, 16 South. 110; Randle v. Carter, 62 Ala. 95. See, to the same effect, Owen v. Homan, 3 Macn. & G 378, 412, affirmed 4 H. L. Cas. 997, quoted in 4 Pom. Eq. Jur., § 1331, note 2; Bainbrigge v. Baddeley, 3 Macn. & G. 413; Kelley v. Boettcher, 89 Fed. 125, 129; People v. Weigley, 155 Ill. 491, 40 N. E. 300; Mead v. Burk, 156 Ind. 577, 60 N. E. 338; Sheridan Brick Works v. Marion Trust Co., 157 Ind. 292, 87 Am. St Rep. 207, 61 N. E. 666; Pelzer v. Hughes, 27 S. C. 408, 3 S. E. 781; Norris v. Lake, 89 Va. 513, 16 S. E. 663; Beecher v. Beninger, 7 Blatchf 170, Fed. Cas. No. 1222; Chase's Case, 1 Bland (Md.), 206, 213, 17 Am. Dec. 277.

17 Bank of Florence v. United States Savings and Loan Co., 104 Ala. 297, 16 South 110; Ex parte Walker, 25 Ala. 81.

cised with great caution and circumspection.[18] It is well said by the supreme court of Alabama:[19] "Property is not taken from a party in possession, claiming in good faith[20] the right to it, before judgment in actions at law, without first exacting from him at whose suit it is done ample security for the protection of his adversary against injury. In courts of equity, writs of injunction and equitable attachment are allowed only upon like conditions. And whenever the plaintiff's rights are disputed, the court should rarely appoint a receiver to take the property from the defendant; receivers being ordinarily appointed without bonds of indemnity from those procuring the appointment to be made, and only upon the bond of the receiver for his fidelity as such. There has been, indeed, too much facility on the part of chancellors and registers in the exercise of this authority." The rea-

18 Ashurst v. Lehman, 86 Ala. 370, 5 South. 731 (receiver allowed in case of mortgaged crops); note to Cameron v. Groveland Imp Co., 72 Am. St. Rep. 34; Corbin v. Thompson, 141 Ind. 128, 40 N. E. 533 ("the power is one of the highest vested in a court of chancery and is only exercised where justice would in all probability be defeated by withholding it"); Rollins v. Henry, 77 N. C. 469 (same); Gilbert v. Block, 51 Ill. App 516; Williamson v. Wilson, 1 Bland (Md), 418; Holmes v. Stix, 104 Ky. 351, 47 S. W. 243 (this applies in the extreme when the property is held jointly).

19 Briarfield Iron Works v. Foster, 54 Ala. 622. This is quoted approvingly in Fort Payne Furnace Co. v. Fort Payne Coal & Iron Co., 96 Ala. 472, 38 Am. St. Rep. 109, 11 South. 439 (refusing to take possession of lands of a corporation). To same effect, Moritz v. Miller, 87 Ala. 331, 6 South. 269 (refusing a receiver on information and belief); approved in Lindsay v. American Mtg. Co., 97 Ala. 412, 11 South 770.

20 Where the one against whom the remedy is sought is *acting fraudulently*, it is a common ground of equitable interference: Brundage v. Home Savings etc. Assn., 11 Wash. 277, 39 Pac. 666 (mortgaged property); Mays v. Rose, Freem Ch. (Miss.) 703; Furlong v. Edwards, 3 Md. 99 (fraud must be clearly proved); Williamson v. Wilson, 1 Bland (Md.), 418.

son for the necessity of exercising such great caution is clearly stated by Baldwin, J., in Beverly v. Brooke:[21] "In the exercise of this summary jurisdiction, a court of equity reverses, in a great measure, its ordinary course of administering justice; beginning at the end, and levying upon the property a kind of equitable execution, by which it makes a general, instead of a specific, appropriation of the issues and profits, and afterwards determining who is entitled to the benefit of its *quasi*-process. But, acting, as it often must of necessity, before the merits of the cause have been fully developed, and not infrequently, where the proper parties in interest are not all before the court, it proceeds with much caution and circumspection, in order to avoid disturbing, unnecessarily or injuriously, legal rights and equitable priorities." McKay, J., in Crawford v. Ross and Ross, 39 Ga. 44, said: "The exercise of the extraordinary powers granted to the Chancellor of the appointment of receivers is a very delicate and responsible duty. It is a serious interference, without the verdict of a jury and without a regular hearing, with the *prima facie* rights of the citizen, and should only be granted to prevent manifest wrong."[22]

21 Beverley v. Brooke, 4 Gratt. (Va) 187.

22 Crawford v Ross, 39 Ga. 44. See, also, Blondheim et al v. Moore, 11 Md 365 (information and belief insufficient); Mays v Rose et al (Miss), Freem. Ch. 703 (rights of both parties considered); Furlong v. Edwards, 3 Md. 99 (mortgage); Fox v. Curtis, 34 Atl. 952, 176 Pa. St. 52 (partnership creditors); State v. Ross, 122 Mo 435, 25 S. W. 947, 23 L. R. A. 534 (rights in the insolvency of railroad corporation). Atkinson, J., in Dozier v. Logan, 101 Ga. 173, 28 S. E. 612, says: "The appointment of a receiver is recognized as one of the harshest remedies which the law provides for the enforcement of rights, and is allowable only in extreme cases, and under circumstances where the interest of the creditors is exposed to manifest peril The courts, of late years, are drifting away from the landmark which in former years marked the line of division between the power of chancery courts to seize the property

§ 68. Applicant Must Come with "Clean Hands" and Without Laches.—The rule that one who comes into equity must come with clean hands applies to an applicant for a receiver.[23] An applicant for a receiver must not be guilty of laches before bringing[24] his bill, or pending the application.[25]

of an individual through the instrumentality of a receiver, and the right of the individual himself to retain possession until, by the judgment of the court, his property could be judicially appropriated to purposes inconsistent with his individual possession. In the exercise of the great discretionary power conferred upon our brethren of the circuit bench, with respect to such matters, they cannot be too cautious, and unless there is immediate and present necessity for such action, the appointment of a receiver should be refused.'' See, also, American Investment Co. v. Ferrar, 87 Iowa, 437, 54 N. W. 361 (receiver of mortgaged property refused); Clark v. Raymond, 86 Iowa, 61, 53 N. W. 354 (same); Roberts v. Washington Nat. Bank, 9 Wash. 12, 37 Pac. 26 (''the court should restrict, rather than extend, the growing tendency'' to appoint receivers); Whitehead v. Hale, 118 N. C. 601, 24 S. E. 360.

The rights of both parties should be carefully considered: Vose v. Reed, 1 Woods, 650, Fed. Cas No. 17,011; Provident Life & T. Co. v. Keniston, 53 Neb. 86, 73 N. W. 216 (mortgaged premises); Lancaster v. Asheville St. Ry. Co., 90 Fed. 129 (railroad corporation; apprehension of danger to plaintiff must be well grounded, and of ''immediate'' injury); Pullan v. Cincinnati etc. R. R. Co, 4 Biss. 47, Fed. Cas. No. 11,461 (a receiver should never be appointed in case of mortgage foreclosure, where the property is certain to produce the amount on sale). The statement set forth in the text has been repeatedly quoted as expressing the proper view. See Latham v. Chaffee, 7 Fed. 525; note to Cameron v. Groveland Imp Co., 72 Am St. Rep. 34.

23 Thus, failure, on the part of executors, to have a sale recorded, allowing the vendee in the meantime to expend money in improvements, will defeat their right to a receiver: Bennallack v. Richards, 125 Cal. 427, 58 Pac. 651. Where the object of the applicant is illegal: American Biscuit & Mfg. Co. v. Klotz, 44 Fed. 721; Cameron v. Havemeyer, 12 N. Y. Supp 126, 25 Abb. N. C. 438 (trust adjudged illegal, the stockholders have a right to a receiver).

24 Thus, where the injury occurred two years before suit brought, appointment was refused: Kean v. Colt, 5 N. J. Eq. 365.

25 An application having been allowed to sleep for six years, was dismissed, though evidence had been taken in the meantime: Hood

§ 69. **Inadequacy of Legal Remedy.**—It is one of the fundamental principles on which receivers are granted that the applicant shall have no plain, adequate, and complete remedy at law.[26] Therefore, as "equity will not help those who have power to help themselves,"[27] he must, as a usual thing, have exhausted his legal remedies prior to his application for equitable relief.[28] This applies both to the original chancery practice and to the reformed procedure.[29] The objection to the appointment being made on these grounds should be taken before the appointment.[30]

§ 70. **Bill Fully Denied by Answer.**—It is a well-established rule that where the equities of the bill have been fully met and denied in every material part by the defendant's sworn answer, the plaintiff is not entitled to the appointment of a receiver, unless he overcomes the

v. First Nat. Bank of Fremont, 29 Fed. 55; Brown v. Lake Superior Iron Co., 134 U. S. 530, 10 Sup. Ct. 604, 33 L. ed. 1021 (not allowed to contest receiver's right to appointment after nine months); Tibbals v. Sargeant, 14 N. J. Eq. 449 (delay of two years after notice).

26 Fort Payne Furnace Co. v. Ft. Payne Coal & Iron Co., 96 Ala. 472, 38 Am. St. Rep. 109, 11 South. 439; approved, Etowah Min. Co. v. Wills Valley Min. & Mfg. Co., 106 Ala. 492, 17 South. 522 (corporation creditors); Bennallack v. Richards et al., 125 Cal. 427, 58 Pac. 65 ("a departure from the rule can only be justified upon strong grounds of judicial necessity"); Spooner v. Bay St. Louis Syndicate, 44 Minn. 401, 46 N W. 848 (corporation creditors); Rice v. St. Paul etc. R. R. Co. 24 Minn. 467 (receiver of railroad); Cahn v. Johnson, 12 Tex. Civ. App 304, 33 S. W. 1000.

27 Sollory v. Learer, L. R. 9 Eq. Cas. 22; Importers' Nat. Bank v. Quackenbush, 143 N. Y. 567, 38 N. E. 728.

28 Importers' etc. Nat. Bank v. Quackenbush, 143 N. Y. 567, 38 N. E. 728.

29 Spooner v. Bay St. Louis Syndicate, 44 Minn. 401, 46 N. W. 848 (corporation creditors).

30 Brown v. Lake Superior Iron Co., 134 U. S. 530, 10 Sup. Ct. 604, 33 L. ed. 1021 (where a bill was suffered to be taken *pro confesso*, defendant could not object nine months later).

denials by such further proof as will tend to establish his bill.[31] The usual weight allowed to answers in chancery is due the defendant in this class of cases,[32] and they are conclusive until overcome by testimony.[33]

§ 71. Must be a Suit Pending.—The appointment of a receiver being made merely to assist in the ultimate disposition of the property in controversy, a receiver will not ordinarily[34] be appointed unless there is a suit pending, concerning the subject-matter in regard to which the receiver is sought.[35] Thus an application by

31 Sweeny v. Mayhew, 6 Idaho, 455, 56 Pac. 85; Crombie v. Order of Solon, 157 Pa. St. 588, 27 Atl. 710 (bill alleging illegality of corporation election); Henn v. Walsh, 2 Edw. Ch. (N Y.) 129 (partnership); Whitehouse v. Point Defiance T. & E. Ry. Co, 9 Wash. 558, 38 Pac. 152 (stating the reason to be that "the plaintiff, having addressed himself to the conscience of the defendant, has made him a witness, and must take his answer as true, unless he can overcome it"), Wilson v. Maddox, 46 W. Va. 641, 33 S E. 775.

32 Thompson v. Diffenderfer, 1 Md. Ch 489 (though the truth of the answer is attacked by the plaintiff).

33 Voshell & Heaton v. Hyman & Gross, 26 Ala. 83. It has been said that in such a case "the question is no longer addressed to the discretion of the court; but it is a judicial error to appoint a receiver when the charges are thus met": Wilson v. Maddox, 46 W. Va. 641, 33 S. E. 775; Sweeny v. Mayhew, 6 Idaho, 455, 56 Pac. 85.

34 The case of receivers appointed over the estates of lunatics and infants is an exception.

35 The suit must be one of equitable cognizance: Miller v. Perkins, 154 Mo. 629, 55 S. W. 874("jurisdiction to appoint a receiver cannot be acquired simply by a petition therefor, nor by the appointment of one"). In American Loan & Trust Co. v. Toledo etc. Co, 29 Fed. 416, it is said: "Whatever may be the powers of a court of equity to construct railroads or manage them through receivers, in form, at least, these powers must be exercised as an adjunct to the jurisdiction of enforcing some of the well-understood equitable rights of the parties in relation to these contracts" See Barber v. International Co. of Mexico, 73 Conn. 587, 48 Atl. 758; Guy v. Doak, 47 Kan. 236, 27 Pac. 968; Burnes v. City of Atchison, 48 Kan. 507, 29 Pac. 579 (a receiver will not be appointed merely to bring suit); State v. Union Nat. Bank, 145 Ind. 537, 57 Am. St. Rep.

"a debtor for the appointment of a receiver to manage and carry on its business, so that the creditors cannot enforce their legal rights in the courts of the country, and not a petition stating a cause of action, either in law or equity, in which, as incident thereto, a receiver be appointed," was dismissed.[36]

209, 44 N. E. 585; In re Hancock, 27 Hun, 575 (the suit must be pending in the court where the application is made); Popp v. Daisy Gold Min. Co., 27 Utah, 83, 74 Pac. 426 (no suit pending); Grand Island Electric L., I. & C. S. Co. (Neb.), 94 N. W. 136 (not in suit brought merely for appointment); Hay v. McDaniel, 26 Ind. App 683, 60 N. E. 729 (same). What constitutes the pendency of an action is largely a question of practice; but see Hellebush v. Blake, 119 Ind. 349, 21 N. E. 976, where the right to a receiver in a legal proceeding being given by statute, it was held that though the notice or service was defective, and the defendant had entered only a special appearance, the action was pending. As to service generally, where the property is within the jurisdiction of the chancery court, see Quarl v. Abbett, 102 Ind. 233, 52 Am. Rep. 662, 1 N. E 476; Pennoyer v. Neff, 95 U. S. 729, 24 L. ed. 565. See Hardy v. McClellan, 53 Miss. 507 (in case of *ex parte* application); Merchants' & Mfg Nat. Bank of Detroit v. Kent Circuit Judge, 43 Mich. 292, 5 N. W. 627 (suit must concern the property); approved in Jones v. Schall, 45 Mich. 379, 4 N. W. 68 (criticising the appointment of receivers on *ex parte* application); Arnold v. Bright, 41 Mich. 210, 2 N. W. 16 (same); note to Cortelyou v. Hathaway, 64 Am. Dec. at 482; Pressley v. Harrison, 102 Ind. 19, 1 N. E. 188; approved in Sullivan Election etc. Co. v. Blue, 142 Ind. 407, 41 N. E. 805; Winchester etc. Co. v. Gordon, 143 Ind 681, 42 N. E. 914. That subsequent filing of the bill, and giving of the requisite bond by the receiver, cannot impart validity to the void act of his appointment before the bill was filed, see Harwell v. Potts, 80 Ala. 70. Clearly, a receiver should not be appointed after the action is dismissed: Dale v. Kant, 58 Ind. 584.

36 State v. Ross, 122 Mo. 435, 25 S. W. 947; approved in Miller v. Perkins, 154 Mo. 629, 55 S. W. 874. See Jones v. Bank of Leadville, 10 Colo. 464, 17 Pac. 272: "To hold that courts of equity can entertain jurisdiction to appoint a receiver of property, as the substantive ground, and ultimate object of the suit, on the petition of the owner of the property to be controlled and protected, would be to make them the administrators of every estate, the owners of which were either incapable or unwilling of administering themselves." The necessary implication from the cases seems to be

§ 72. **The Supreme Court of Judicature Act, in England.**—In England, since 1873, the appointment of receivers is regulated by § 25, par. 8, of this act: "A *mandamus* or an injunction may be granted, or a receiver appointed by an interlocutory order of the court in all cases in which it shall appear to the court to be just or convenient that such order should be made; and any such order may be made either unconditionally or upon such terms and conditions as the court shall think just." The liberal terms of this statutory provision render the recent English decisions on the appointment of receivers of little value as precedents to the American practitioner. A few of them are cited in the note, by way of illustration merely.[37]

§ 73. **Statutory Provisions in the United States.**—"In the states adopting the reformed procedure, the codes of procedure generally contain provisions regulating the appointment of receivers." As these general provisions

that, "a receiver being appointed for all the parties, he whose property is to be taken from him and placed in the power of a receiver, should be a party to the pending suit". Baker v. Backus's Admrs, 32 Ill. 79.

37 Cummins v. Perkins, [1899] 1 Ch. 16; Smith v. Port Dover etc. R. Co, 12 Ont. App. 288; Mason v. Westoby, L. R 32 Ch. Div 206; but see 42 Ch Div. 590 (receiver of mortgaged property); Bryant v. Bull, L. R. 10 Ch Div. 153 (married women's contracts); Taylor v. Eckersley, L. R. 2 Ch. Div. 302 (specific performance of agreement to execute bill of sale of chattels; receiver appointed on evidence of immediate danger of the chattels being disposed of). Receivers in aid of judgment creditors, by way of "equitable execution," etc.: Anglo-Italian Bank v. Davies, L. R. 9 Ch. Div 275 (to reach rents and profits of mortgaged lands), Salt v. Cooper, L. R. 16 Ch Div. 544 (appointment by motion in the original action); Westhead v. Riley, L. R. 25 Ch. Div. 413 (to collect debts payable to judgment debtor); In re Coney, L. R. 29 Ch. Div. 993 (to reach equitable interest of judgment debtor who is out of the jurisdiction); Manchester etc. Banking Co. v. Parkinson, L. R. 22 Q B. Div. 173 (no receiver when no impediment to execution in the ordi-

vary somewhat in detail, and as a knowledge of the precise terms of the statute is frequently necessary to an estimate of the value as a precedent of the decisions based thereon, they are given in full in the note. Reference is also made to many of the statutes authorizing the appointment in special cases, as on the dissolution or insolvency of corporations. In a few of the states, however, these statutes are so detailed and elaborate that a statement of them would transcend the limits of this treatise. Several of the states have general legislation, briefly referred to below, on matters other than the appointment; as, declaring who is ineligible (see, *e. g.,* Arizona, Arkansas, North Dakota, Ohio, Oklahoma, South Dakota, Utah, Wyoming); describing his powers in general terms (Arizona, Arkansas, California, Indiana, Iowa, Kansas, Kentucky, New York, North Dakota, Ohio, Oklahoma, South Dakota, Texas, Utah, Washington, Wyoming); authorizing suits against him without leave of court (see Alabama, Texas, Virginia); authorizing suits by him in his own name (Arkansas, California, and, generally, the states in which the statute defines his powers); providing for the investment of funds (California, Kansas, North Dakota, Ohio, Oklahoma, South Dakota, Texas, Utah, Wyoming); regulating the priority of certain claims (Indiana, New Jersey, Oregon, Texas, Utah, Washington, Wisconsin); regulating his compensation (Mississippi, New York, North Carolina, West Virginia).[38]

nary way); Holmes v. Millage, [1893] 1 Q. B 551 (ordinarily, no receiver of future earnings of the judgment debtor); Harris v. Beauchamp, [1894] 1 Q. B. 801 (receiver only where impediment to execution); Cadogan v. Lyric Theatre, [1894] 3 Ch. 338; Tyrrell v. Painton, [1895] 1 Q. B. 202 (reversionary interest in personalty).

38 See 4 Pom. Eq. Jur., § 1335.

Alabama.—Civ. Code, 1896.

§ 429: An appeal may be taken from an order appointing or refusing a receiver.

§ 799: May be appointed by chancellor in term time or in vacation, and by register in vacation. In vacation reasonable notice must be given of application, or good cause shown for failure to give notice.

§ 801: Complainant must give bond before appointment.

§ 803: Receiver "may be sued in respect to any act or transaction of his, in carrying on the business connected with such property in this state," without previous leave of court

§ 1294: "Upon decree of dissolution [of a corporation], the chancellor shall appoint a receiver of all the property and assets of the corporation. The chancellor shall direct the receiver to collect, by suit or otherwise, all the debts due the corporation, and sell property, real or personal, belonging to the corporation, and how he shall make title thereto to the purchaser; the chancellor may, in his discretion, authorize the receiver to proceed, without suit, to sell any or all of the debts and assets of the corporation at public sale for cash, or on such terms as in his judgment the interests of the parties may require."

§ 1295: How selected on dissolution; bond.

§ 1296: Receiver must pay debts in full or ratably. If contested, determined as other contested claims in chancery. Residue must be paid to stockholders.

§ 821: In creditors' bill, if answer shows that defendant has any property, court may appoint a receiver "with authority to demand, sue for and recover, or otherwise to reduce to possession such property, moneys, effects, or choses in action; and may require the debtor to make to such receiver all conveyances, assignments, or transfers, which may be necessary and proper to enable him to receive, or to sue for and recover such property."

§ 2580: Court may appoint a receiver for an insolvent domestic insurance company.

Arizona.—Rev. Stats. 1901, §§ 1532-1541.

§ 1532: "Judges of the district courts, in term time or in vacation, may appoint a receiver in suits pending in said courts, when no other adequate remedy is given by law for the protection and preservation of property, or the rights of parties therein pending litigation in respect thereto."

§ 1533: Application must be in writing, supported by affidavit.

§ 1534: Notice must be given to adverse party.

§ 1535: Receiver's bond.

§ 1536: "No party, attorney or other person interested in a suit shall be appointed receiver therein."

§ 1537: Oath and bond.

§ 1539: "The receiver shall have power, subject to the control of the court, to bring and defend suits, to take and keep possession of the property, to receive rents, to collect debts and generally to do such acts respecting the property as may be authorized by the court."

§ 1540: May be removed at any time and another appointed.

§ 1541· Rules of equity govern when not inconsistent with statutory provisions.

Arkansas.—Sandel's & Hill's Digest of Statutes (1894), §§ 5964-5979. The important provisions relating to the appointment are:

§ 5964: "Whenever it shall not be forbidden by law, and shall be deemed fair and proper in any case in equity, the court, judge or chancellor shall appoint," etc.

§ 5965· "Such receiver may be appointed either before or after answer or after a decree"

§ 5975· "In an action by a vendor to vacate a fraudulent purchase of property, or by a creditor to subject any property or fund to his claim, or between partners or others jointly owning or interested in any property or fund, on the application of plaintiff or of any party whose right to or interest in the property or fund or the proceeds thereof is probable, and where it is shown that the property or fund is in danger of being lost, removed or materially injured, the court may appoint a receiver to take charge thereof during the pendency of the action, and may order and coerce the delivery of it to him."

§ 5976: "In an action by a mortgagee for the foreclosure of his mortgage and the sale of the mortgaged property, a receiver may, in like manner, be appointed where it appears that the mortgaged property is in danger of being lost, removed or materially injured, or that the condition of the mortgage has not been performed, and that the property is probably insufficient to discharge the mortgage debt."

§ 5977: "No party or attorney, or person interested in an action, shall be appointed receiver therein."

§ 5968· Receiver may sue in his own name, shall have power to employ attorneys and make to them a reasonable allowance for services.

§ 5970· Receiver of corporation, partnership, or joint stock company, when the order places in his hands all the rights and interests, etc., of the same, shall, until further order of the court, etc., "have full possession, custody and control thereof, and shall be vested with the title, so far as it shall be necessary to collect debts, preserve the assets and property for the benefit of creditors and all persons interested, and may and shall bring and prosecute and defend all suits in his own name that may be necessary for that purpose."

§ 5971. Receiver mentioned in last section may be substituted in pending suits by or against the corporation, etc.

§ 5973: May be removed for failure to discharge any duty incumbent upon them, or for other sufficient cause.

§ 5974: Must report every six months, or oftener, if required by court. Confirmation of accounts—conclusive as against all persons, except in case of actual fraud.

§ 5979: Powers.—Same as in California, except no provisions as to suing or defending in his own name, or as to compounding for and compromising debts.

California.—Code Civ. Proc., § 564: "A receiver may be appointed by the court in which an action is pending, or by the judge thereof:

"1. In an action by a vendor to vacate a fraudulent purchase of property, or by a creditor to subject any property or fund to his claim, or between partners or others jointly owning or interested in any property or fund, on the application of the plaintiff, or of any party whose right to or interest in the property or fund, or the proceeds thereof, is probable, and where it is shown that the property or fund is in danger of being lost, removed, or materially injured;

"2. In an action by a mortgagee for the foreclosure of his mortgage and sale of the mortgaged property, where it appears that the mortgaged property is in danger of being lost, removed, or materially injured, or that the condition of the mortgage has not been performed, and that the property is probably insufficient to discharge the mortgage debt;

"3. After judgment, to carry the judgment into effect;

"4. After judgment, to dispose of the property according to the judgment, or to preserve it during the pendency of an appeal, or in proceedings in aid of execution, when an execution has been returned unsatisfied, or when the judgment debtor refuses to apply his property in satisfaction of the judgment;

"5. In the cases when a corporation has been dissolved, or is insolvent, or in imminent danger of insolvency, or has forfeited its corporate rights;

"6. In all other cases where receivers have heretofore been appointed by the usages of courts of equity."

§ 565: Appointment of receivers on dissolution of corporations.

§ 566 authorizes the court to require on an *ex parte* application, an undertaking from the applicant to pay all damages the defendant may sustain by reason of the appointment of the receiver in case the applicant shall have procured the appointment wrongfully, maliciously or without sufficient cause.

§ 567: Oath and bond by receiver.

§ 568: *Powers of receiver.*—"The receiver has, under the control of the court, power to bring and defend actions in his own name, as receiver; to take and keep possession of the property, to receive rents, collect debts, to compound for and compromise the same, to make transfers, and generally to do such acts respecting the property as the court may authorize ''

§ 569. Funds in the hands of a receiver may be invested upon interest, by order of the court; but no such order can be made, except upon the consent of all the parties to the action.

§ 963: An appeal lies from an order appointing a receiver.

§ 1270: May be appointed for escheated estates.

§ 1348: Corporation may be appointed receiver.

Colorado.—Mills' Statutes (1891), § 497, receiver in dissolution of corporation (like Illinois); § 3387 (to prevent waste by surviving partner).

Code of Procedure (1890), §§ 163, 164, 165 —§ 163· ''A receiver may be appointed by the court in which the action is pending, or by a judge thereof, or, pending proceedings in the supreme court upon an appeal or writ of error, by the court from whose final judgment such appellate proceedings are prosecuted or by the judge of such court: First, before judgment, provisionally, on application of either party, when he establishes a *prima facie* right to the property, or to an interest in the property, which is the subject of the action, and which is in the possession of an adverse party, and the property, or its rents and profits, are in danger of being lost, or materially injured and impaired. Second, after judgment to dispose of the property according to the judgment, or to preserve it during the pending of an appeal; and, third, in such other cases as are in accordance with the practice of courts of equity jurisdiction.''

Connecticut.—Gen. Stats. 1888, § 1322: ''Receivers of a corporation, appointed by judicial authority, shall have the right to the possession of all its books, papers and property, and power in their own names, or in its name, to commence and prosecute suits for and on behalf of said corporation, to defend all suits brought against it or them; to demand and receive all evidences of debt and property belonging to it, and to do and execute in its name, or in their names, as such receivers, all other acts and things which shall be necessary or proper in the execution of their trust; and shall have all the power for any of said purposes possessed by said corporation.'' § 1942 (receivers in winding up of corporations on petition of stockholders); §§ 1313-1317 (receivers of dissolved partnerships); § 1313 (appointment); § 1314 (orders of court as to the partnership property); § 1315 (all the property of the partnership vests in the receiver on his appointment); §§ 1316, 1317 (proceedings when property is attached for claim against individual partner); §§ 1833-1852 (receivers of banks, savings banks, and trust companies), §§ 2869-2879 (receivers of life insurance companies); §§ 1172-1177 (receivers of turnpike and toll bridge companies).

Delaware.—Rev Stats. 1852, as Am. 1893, p 686, c. 90, § 3: Receiver may be appointed when surviving member of partnership fails to file the certificate required by law.

Page 718, c. 96, § 21· "If a minor have real, or personal property, and no guardian, the court may appoint a receiver to take charge of such property during its pleasure; and may make such regulations touching this matter, as shall be deemed proper.

"It may enforce any order made upon a receiver. Such receiver shall be required to account annually, or oftener, and shall deposit any balance, appearing in his hands, to be invested, or otherwise disposed of, for the minor's benefit."

Florida.—Rev. Stats. 1892.

§ 1211: May be appointed on application of judgment creditor, for corporation, when execution returned unsatisfied in whole or in part.

§ 2107: May be appointed for estate of infant when property has been managed by one not a guardian, and there is no legal guardian.

§ 2157: May be appointed on voluntary dissolution of insolvent corporation, at suit of three creditors.

§ 2192: May be appointed at suit of comptroller when bank insolvent, or officers violate law.

Georgia.—Code 1895, §§ 1970, 1971 (receivers of banks); §§ 2324, 2325 (liability of railroad receivers for injury to employees; see 91 Ga 731), § 2333 (duties of railroad receivers); §§ 2716-2722 (receivers for insolvent traders), §§ 4900-4912 (receivers in general)

The general provisions relating to the appointment are.

§ 4900 "When any fund or property may be in litigation, and the rights of either or both parties cannot otherwise be fully protected, or when there may be a fund or property having no one to manage it, a receiver of the same may be appointed (on a proper case made) by the judge," etc.

§ 4901: "Courts of equity shall have authority to appoint receivers to take possession of and protect trust or joint property and funds, whenever the danger of destruction and loss shall require such interference."

§ 4904: "A court of equity may appoint a receiver to take possession of, and hold subject to the direction of the court, any assets charged with the payment of debts, where there is manifest danger of loss, or destruction or material injury to those interested. Under extraordinary circumstances, a receiver may be appointed before and without notice to the trustee or other person having charge of the assets. The terms on which a receiver is appointed shall be in the discretion of the chancellor."

See, also, § 2855 (receiver of excess of homestead applicant's real estate); § 1886 (receivers on dissolution of corporations).

Idaho.—See Code of Civil Procedure (1901), §§ 3318-3323 (general provisions); § 3947 (receivers in insolvency proceedings).

The grounds of appointment are the same as in the California Code.

Illinois.—Hurd's Revised Statutes (1899), c. 32, § 25 (receivers of corporations); c. 73, § 15 (receiver on dissolution of insurance companies); c. 62, § 24 (receiver in garnishments); c. 32, § 127 (of co-operative associations).

Indiana.—Horner's Rev. Stats. (1896), §§ 1222-1231 (general provisions); § 3012 (on expiration of charter of corporation); § 3736 (of insurance company); § 1270 (receiver, in replevin, of property having a peculiar value); §§ 6049, 6050 (receiver of partnership on death of partner); § 5134 (receiver in wife's suit for support).

The provisions relating to grounds of appointment are somewhat fuller than those usually found in the codes, and the interpretation put upon them by the courts is liberal; in fact, such an effect is given to subdivision seventh of § 1222 as frequently to render the Indiana cases unsafe authority in other jurisdictions.

§ 1222: "A receiver may be appointed by the court, or the judge thereof in vacation in the following cases:

"*First.* In an action by a vendor to vacate a fraudulent purchase of property, or by a creditor to subject any property or fund to his claim.

"*Second.* In actions between partners, or persons jointly interested in any property or fund.

"*Third.* In all actions, when it is shown that the property, fund, or rents and profits in controversy is in danger of being lost, removed, or materially injured.

"*Fourth.* In actions by a mortgagee for the foreclosure of a mortgage and the sale of the mortgaged property, when it appears that such property is in danger of being lost, removed, or materially injured; or when such property is not sufficient to discharge the mortgaged debt—to secure the application of the rents and profits accruing before a sale can be had.

"*Fifth.* When a corporation has been dissolved, or is insolvent, or is in imminent danger of insolvency, or has forfeited its corporate rights.

"*Sixth.* To protect or preserve, during the time allowed for redemption, any real estate or interest therein sold on execution or order of sale, and to secure to the person entitled thereto the rents and profits thereof.

"*Seventh.* And in such other cases as may be provided by law; or where, in the discretion of the court, or the judge thereof in vacation, it may be necessary to secure ample justice to the parties."

§ 1228. Powers of receiver.—Like Arkansas, except that after "debts" is added, "in his own name."

§ 5206: Debts owing laborers or employees are preferred debts.

Iowa.—Annotated Code (1897), §§ 3822-3825 (general provisions); § 3904 (for joint or partnership property taken under attachment); § 3978 (for same, taken under execution); § 3988 (for mortgaged personal property taken under execution); § 4077 (in proceedings, auxiliary to execution); § 1640 (receiver on dissolution of corporations); § 1731 (on dissolution of insurance companies); §§ 1777-1795 (on dissolution of life insurance companies); § 1877 (of insolvent bank).

The general provision relating to the appointment is:

§ 3822. "On petition of either party to a civil action or proceeding, wherein he shows that he has a probable right to, or interest in, any property which is the subject of the controversy, and that such property, or its rents or profits, are in danger of being lost or materially injured or impaired, and on such notice to the adverse party as the court or judge shall prescribe, the court, or, in vacation, the judge thereof, if satisfied that the interests of one or both parties will be thereby promoted, and the substantial rights of neither unduly infringed, may appoint a receiver to take charge of and control such property under its direction during the pendency of the action, and may order and coerce the delivery of it to him. Upon the hearing of the application, affidavits, and such other proof as the court or judge permits, may be introduced, and upon the whole case such order made as will be for the best interest of all parties concerned."

§ 3824: Powers of receivers.—Similar to Arkansas.

§ 3825: Priority of liens.—Persons having liens upon the property placed in the hands of a receiver shall, if there is a contest as to their priority, submit them to the court for determination.

Kansas.—Rev. Stats. 1901, §§ 4701-4707; Code, §§ 254-260.

§ 254: *Appointment of receivers.*—Similar to California provision, with following exceptions. The fifth subdivision reads as follows: "In the cases provided in this code, or by special statutes, when a corporation has been dissolved, or is insolvent or in imminent danger of insolvency, or has forfeited its corporate rights." An additional subdivision, numbered 7, providing for the appointment of a receiver at suit of the state or of an officer for the collection of a tax from a toll-bridge company, is added.

§ 255· Oath and bond.

§ 257: Powers.—Same as in California.

§ 258. Investment of funds.—Same as in California (Cal. Code Civ. Proc., § 569).

§ 207: Receiver may be appointed to take charge of attached property in custody of the sheriff.

Kentucky.—Carroll's Code (1888), §§ 298-302 (general provisions); § 218 (to take charge of attached property); Bullitt & Feland's General Statutes (1887), p. 675 (receiver of property conveyed in contemplation of insolvency); p. 852 (receiver where waste is committed pending an action to recover or charge land); p. 719 (receiver of estate of female under sixteen years of age, who marries without consent of parent, etc.).

The general provisions relating to the appointment are:

§ 298: "On the motion of any party to an action who shows that he has, or probably has, a right to, a lien upon, or an interest in, any property or fund, the right to which is involved in the action, and that the property or fund is in danger of being lost, removed, or materially injured, the court, or the judge thereof during vacation, may appoint a receiver to take charge of the property or fund during the pendency of the action, and may order and coerce the delivery of it to him"

§ 299 Receiver in mortgage foreclosure; similar provision to that of California.

§ 302 Powers of receiver —Like Arkansas.

Maine—Rev. Stats. 1903, p. 447 (receivers on dissolution of corporation); pp. 497, 498 (receivers for casualty companies); pp. 485, 506 (receivers for insurance company); pp. 529, 530, (receivers for railroads); p. 460 (receivers for savings banks); p. 468 (receivers for loan and building associations).

Maryland.—Pub. Gen. Laws, 1904, p. 226, art. 5, § 27 (order appointing or refusing receiver is appealable); pp. 697-699, art. 23, § 381 ff (receivers upon dissolution of corporations).

Massachusetts.—Rev. Laws, 1902, c. 144, p 1304 ff (receivers may be appointed to take charge of property of absentees); c. 167, § 126, p. 1517 (appointment of receiver dissolves attachment); c. 109, §§ 54 ff, p. 957 (receivers upon dissolution of corporations); c. 118, § 7, p. 1123 (receivers for insolvent insurance corporations); c. 113, § 6, p. 1066 (receivers for insolvent savings banks); c. 116, § 18, p. 1112 (trust companies may act as receivers).

Michigan.—Comp. Laws, 1897, §§ 7091, 7249, 7282-7283, 7301, 7316, 7331, 7396, 7518, 7600, 9552, 9765-9770, 9963, 10859-10888 (receivers for various corporations).

Minnesota.—Kelly's Stats. (1891), § 5044: "A receiver may be appointed:

"*First.* Before judgment, on the application of either party, when he establishes an apparent right to property which is the subject of the action, and which is in the possession of an adverse party, and the property or its rents and profits are in danger of being lost, or materially injured or impaired, except in cases where judgment upon failure to answer may be had without application to the court;

"*Second.* After judgment, to carry the judgment into effect;

"*Third.* After judgment, to dispose of the property according to the judgment, or to preserve it during the pendency of an appeal, or when an execution has been returned unsatisfied, and the judgment debtor refuses to apply his property in satisfaction of the judgment;

"*Fourth.* In the cases provided by law, when a corporation has been dissolved, or is insolvent, or in imminent danger of insolvency, or has forfeited its corporate rights, and, in like cases, of the property, within this state, of foreign corporations,

"*Fifth.* In such other cases as are now provided by law, or may be in accordance with the existing practice, except as otherwise provided herein."

See, also, § 4263 (act 1881, c. 148, § 2), (receiver of insolvent debtor), § 4966 (receiver in proceedings supplementary to execution); § 4968 (action by such receiver against an adverse claimant); § 5341 (receiver on judgment of exclusion from corporate rights); § 3138 (receiver on dissolution of corporation); § 5575 (on forfeiture of charter of banking and insurance companies); § 5572 (on application of judgment creditors of corporation).

Mississippi.—Annotated Code, 1892.

§ 574: Receiver not appointed without notice, "unless it shall appear that an immediate appointment is necessary, or good cause be shown for not giving notice."

§ 575 Bond upon appointment of *ex parte* receiver.

§ 576: Removal.

§ 577: "Receivers shall be subject to the orders, instructions and decrees of the court, and of the chancellor in vacation, and they, or any party in interest, may apply therefor in term time, or to the chancellor in vacation, or for modifications of previous orders or instructions; and obedience thereto may be enforced by attachment."

§ 578: Bond in lieu of receiver.

§ 579: Bond of receiver.

§ 581: "In all cases in which it may be thought to be necessary for the protection of estates of decedents, minors and persons of unsound mind, a receiver may be appointed, either by the court or by the chancellor in vacation, subject to the foregoing conditions."

§ 582: "Receivers shall be entitled to have such compensation for their services as the court shall allow, and shall have a lien upon the property in their hands for the payment thereof, and of their necessary expenses. The court shall make such order to compel the payment thereof as may be just and necessary, and may decree the payment thereof by any of the parties as a portion of the costs of suit."

Missouri.—Rev. Stats. (1899), §§ 753-755. Power is given to appoint "whenever such appointment shall be deemed necessary."

§ 754: "Such receiver shall give bond, and have the same powers and be subject to all the provisions, as far as they may be applicable, enjoined upon a receiver appointed by virtue of the law providing for suits by attachment."

Montana.—Code of Civil Procedure (1895), §§ 950, 956, same as California; Civil Code (1895), § 727 (receiver of accident insurance company); §§ 830, 832 (for building, loan and savings company).

Nebraska.—Code of Civil Procedure (1899), §§ 266-276.

§ 266: Like Montana, omitting (party) "whose right to, or interest in, the property or fund, is probable." Also, omitting "in proceedings in aid of execution," etc.; and "in cases where a corporation has been dissolved," etc.

§§ 267, 268. Suit must be pending; notice of the application required; sheriff to take possession of the property when delay is hazardous.

§ 269: Applicant required to give bond.

§ 272: The order of appointment to contain special directions as to his powers and duties.

§ 273: "Every receiver shall be considered the receiver of any party to the suit, and no others."

§ 274: Appointment without notice is void.

§ 275: Effect of decree not finally determining the rights of the parties; and appeal.

See, also, §§ 213-217 (receiver in attachment); §§ 542, 543 (in proceedings supplementary to execution); Compiled Statutes (1899), c. 8, §§ 34, 35 (receivers of banks); c. 28, § 16a (compensation of receivers).

New Jersey.—Gen. Stats. 1895.

Page 918: Receivers may be appointed to wind up corporation.

Pages 2688, 2689: May be appointed for railroad which fails to run its trains for ten days.

Page 974: Receiver of railroad may operate the road; "and all expenses incident to the operation of said railroad shall be a first lien on the receipts, to be paid before any other incumbrance whatever."

Page 974: Leases by railroad receivers.

Page 2688: "That whenever the chancellor shall appoint a receiver of any railroad company, said receiver shall apply all unincumbered personal effects and all moneys which may be transferred to him at the time of entering upon his duties as such receiver, toward the payment of wages at that time due the employees of said company, and the chancellor may, from time to time, make such orders as he may deem proper to equitably carry out the provisions of this section; *provided*, that no such payments shall be made for more than two months' wages."

Page 353. Receivers for cemetery associations.

Page 1755: Receivers for life insurance corporations.

Page 3011: Receivers for savings banks.

New York.—Stover's Annotated Code of Civil Procedure, 1902.

§ 713: "In addition to the cases, where the appointment of a receiver is specially provided for by law, a receiver of property, which is the subject of an action, in the supreme court or a county court, may be appointed by the court, in either of the following cases:

"1. Before final judgment, on the application of a party who establishes an apparent right to, or interest in, the property, where it is in the possession of an adverse party, and there is danger that it will be removed beyond the jurisdiction of the court or lost, materially injured or destroyed.

"2. By or after the final judgment, to carry the judgment into effect, or to dispose of the property, according to its directions.

"3 After final judgment, to preserve the property, during the pendency of an appeal. The word 'property,' as used in this section, includes the rents, profits, or other income, and the increase, of real or personal property."

§ 714: Notice of application must be given, unless defendant has failed to appear or service of summons is by publication.

§ 715: Bond of receiver.

§ 716: "A receiver, appointed by or pursuant to an order or a judgment, in an action in the supreme court, or a county court, or in a special proceeding for the voluntary dissolution of a corporation, may take and hold real property, upon such trusts and for such purposes as the court directs, subject to the direction of the court, from time to time, respecting the disposition thereof."

§ 1772: May be appointed in action for divorce to enforce payment of alimony.

§ 1788: May be appointed in action to dissolve corporation.

§ 1789: Powers of such receiver.

§ 1810: "A receiver of the property of a corporation can be appointed only by the court, and in one of the following cases:

"1. An action, brought as prescribed in article second, third, or fourth of this title. [Actions against directors, etc., for misconduct; actions to dissolve; actions by the people to annul.]

"2. An action brought for the foreclosure of a mortgage upon the property, of which the receiver is appointed, where the mortgage debt, or the interest thereupon, has remained unpaid, at least thirty days after it was payable, and after payment thereof was duly demanded of the proper officer of the corporation; and where either the income of the property is specifically mortgaged, or the property itself is probably insufficient to pay the mortgage debt.

"3. An action brought by the attorney-general, or by a stockholder, to preserve the assets of a corporation, having no officer empowered to hold the same.

"4. A special proceeding for the voluntary dissolution of a corporation.

"Where the receiver is appointed in an action, otherwise than by or pursuant to a final judgment, notice of the application for his appointment, must be given to the proper officer of the corporation."

§ 1877. May be appointed in judgment creditor's action.

§§ 2464-2471: Receivers in supplementary proceedings.

§ 3320: "A receiver, except as otherwise specially prescribed by statute, is entitled, in addition to his lawful expenses, to such commissions, not exceeding five per centum upon the sums received and disbursed by him, as the court by which, or the judge by whom he is appointed, allows."

North Carolina.—Clark's Code of Civil Proc.

§ 379: "A receiver may be appointed.

"(1) Before judgment, on the application of either party, when he establishes an apparent right to property which is the subject of the action and which is in the possession of an adverse party, and the property or its rents and profits are in danger of being lost or materially injured and impaired, except in cases where judgment upon failure to answer may be had on application to the court.

"(2) After judgment, to carry the judgment into effect.

"(3) After judgment, to dispose of the property according to the judgment, or to preserve it during the pendency of an appeal, or when an execution has been returned unsatisfied, and the judgment debtor refuses to apply his property in satisfaction of the judgment

"(4) In cases . . . . when a corporation has been dissolved, or is insolvent, or in imminent danger of insolvency, or has forfeited its corporate rights, and in like cases of the property within this state of foreign corporations Receivers of the property within this state of foreign or other corporations shall be allowed such commissions as may be fixed by the judge appointing them, not exceeding five per cent. on the amount received and disbursed by them."

Appointment of receiver may be refused when the subject of the action is the recovery of a money demand and a bond is tendered.

§ 383: Bond of receiver.

§ 494: Appointment in proceedings supplementary to execution

North Dakota.—Revised Code, 1899.

§ 5403: *Appointment of receivers.*—Same as Cal. Code Civ. Proc., § 564, but adding to subdivision 5, "and in like cases within this state, of foreign corporations."

§ 5404: "No party or person interested in an action can be appointed receiver therein without the written consent of the party filed with the clerk.'' If appointed upon *ex parte* application court may require a bond of the party seeking its aid.

§ 5405: Oath and bond of receiver.

§ 5406: Powers.—Same as Cal. Code Civ. Proc., § 568.

§ 5407: Investment of funds.—Same as Cal. Code Civ. Proc., § 569.

§§ 5765, 5770, 5779, 5780: Receivers for corporations.

§§ 5568-5570: Receivers in supplemental proceedings.

Ohio.—Bates Ann. Stats. (4th ed.)

§ 5587: Appointment of receivers.—Same as Cal. Code Civ. Proc., § 564.

§ 5588: "No party, attorney, or person, interested in an action, shall be appointed receiver therein, except by consent of the parties.''

§ 5589: Oath and undertaking by receiver.

§ 5590· Powers.—Same as Cal. Code Civ. Proc, § 568

§ 5591· Investment of funds—Same as Cal. Code Civ. Proc., § 569.

§§ 5539 ff. Receivers for attached property.

§§ 5656 ff. Receivers on dissolution of corporations

§ 5705: Receiver of husband's property in action for divorce.

§§ 3821, c, f: Trust company may act as receiver

Oklahoma.—Rev. Stats. 1903.

§ 4441: Appointment of receivers—Same as Cal. Code Civ. Proc., § 564.

§ 4442: "No party or attorney, or person interested in an action, shall be appointed receiver therein.''

§ 4443: Oath and bond of receiver.

§ 4444: Powers of receiver.—Same as Cal. Code. Civ. Proc., § 568.

§ 4445· Investment of funds—Same as Cal. Code Civ. Proc., § 569.

§§ 4398-4402: Receivers for attached property.

§§ 4683 ff: Appointment in proceedings in aid of execution

Oregon.—Bellinger & Cotton's Codes & Stats.

§ 1080. Definition of receiver.

§ 1081: "A receiver may be appointed in any civil action, suit, or proceeding, other than an action for the recovery of specific personal property,

"1. Provisionally, before judgment or decree, on the application of either party, when his right to the property, which is the subject of the action, suit, or proceeding, and which is in the possession of an adverse party, is probable, and the property or its rents or profits are in danger of being lost or materially injured or impaired;

"2. After judgment, or decree, to carry the same into effect;

"3. To dispose of the property according to the judgment or decree, or to preserve it during the pendency of an appeal, or when an execution has been returned unsatisfied, and the debtor refuses to apply his property in satisfaction of the judgment or decree;

"4. In cases provided in this code, or by other statutes, when a corporation has been dissolved, or is insolvent, or in imminent danger of insolvency, or has forfeited its rights;

"5. In the cases provided in this code when a debtor has been declared insolvent."

§ 1082: Oath and undertaking of receiver.

§ 1083: Claims for wages for services performed within six months before receivership are preferred claims. Employees of receiver must be paid at least once in every thirty days.

Rhode Island.—Gen. Laws, 1896.

Pages 536, 537: Appointment of receivers on dissolution of corporations.

Page 937: May be appointed to receive rents and profits of estates owned by joint tenants and tenants in common, upon application of any party interested.

South Carolina.—Code of Laws, 1902.

Code Civ. Proc., § 265: Appointment.—Similar to Oregon. Not appointed without notice. Bond required when application made before judgment.

§ 318: Appointment in supplementary proceedings.

Civil Code, § 1869: Appointment on dissolution of corporation.

South Dakota.—Revised Codes, 1903.

Code Civ. Proc., § 227: Appointment.—Same as California.

§ 228: Receivers on dissolution of corporations.

§ 229: No party or person interested can be appointed, without written consent. Applicant for *ex parte* receiver must give an undertaking.

§ 230. Oath and bond of receiver.

§ 231: Powers —Same as Cal. Code Civ. Proc., § 568.

§ 232: Investments.—Same as Cal. Code Civ. Proc., § 569.

§ 404: Appointment in supplementary proceedings.

Tennessee.—Code, 1896.

§ 5182: Appointment of receiver on dissolution of corporation.

Texas.—Sayles' Stats.

Art. 1469: Appointment.—Same as California, but omitting the third and fourth subdivisions of the California provision.

Art. 1469: Oath and bond of receiver.

Art. 1470: Powers.—Same as Cal. Code Civ. Proc., § 568.

Art. 1471. Investments —Same as Cal. Code Civ. Proc., § 569. Claims are entitled to priority as follows: (1) Court costs; (2) Wages of employees of receiver; (3) Debts for materials and supplies furnished during receivership, (4) Debts for betterments and improvements made during receivership; (5) Personal injury and damage claims accruing during the receivership; (6) Judgments recovered before receivership.

Art 1477: "The discharge of a receiver does not work an abatement of the suit against a receiver, nor shall it in any way affect the right of the party to sue the receiver if he sees proper."

Art. 1483: Receiver may sue and be sued without leave.

Art. 1490: "All judgments, claims, or causes of action when determined, existing against any corporation at the time of the appointment of a receiver, shall be paid out of the net earnings of such corporation while in the hands of the receiver, to the exclusion of mortgage action; and the same shall be a lien on such earnings."

Art. 1491: Receivership of corporations is limited to three years.

Art. 2595: May be appointed for estate of minor, person of unsound mind, or habitual drunkard, when there is no guardian.

Utah.—Rev. Stats. 1898.

§ 3114: Appointment.—Same as California.

§ 3115: Appointment on dissolution of corporation.

§ 3116: Party in interest appointed only on consent. Undertaking on *ex parte* application.

§ 3117: Oath and undertaking of receiver.

§ 3118: Powers.—Same as Cal Code Civ. Proc., § 568.

§ 3119: Investments.—Same as Cal. Code Civ. Proc., § 569.

§ 424: Certain corporations may act as receivers

§ 1344: Wages of employees for labor performed within one year before receivership are entitled to preference.

Vermont.—Stats. 1894.

§§ 3700-3703: Appointment of receivers on dissolution of corporations.

§§ 4057-4059: Receivers for insolvent banks.

Virginia.—Pollard's Ann. Code, 1904.

§ 1105e: Receivers on dissolution of corporations.

§ 1169: Bank receivers.

§ 2291: Appointment for estate of married woman who is a minor.

§ 3415a: Suits against corporation receivers in respect of acts done by them in carrying on business may be maintained without leave of court. No execution shall issue, but the court in which the receivers were appointed shall order the payment of judgments.

Washington.—Pierce's Code.

§ 574: "A receiver is a person appointed by a court or judicial officer to take charge of property during the pending of a civil action or proceeding, or upon a judgment, decree or order therein, and to manage, and dispose of it as the court or officer may direct."

§ 575: "A receiver may be appointed by the court in the following cases:

"1. In an action by a vendor to vacate a fraudulent purchase of property, or by a creditor to subject any property or fund to his claim;

"2. In an action between partners, or other persons jointly interested in any property or fund;

"3. In all actions where it is shown that the property, fund or rents and profits in controversy are in danger of being lost, removed or materially injured;

"4. In an action by a mortgagee for the foreclosure of a mortgage and the sale of the mortgaged property, when it appears that such property is in danger of being lost, removed, or materially injured, or when such property is insufficient to discharge the debt, to secure the application of the rents and profits accruing, before a sale can be had;

"5. When a corporation has been dissolved, or is insolvent, or is in imminent danger of insolvency, or has forfeited its corporate rights;

"6. And in such other cases as may be provided for by law, or when, in the discretion of the court it may be necessary to secure ample justice to the parties, provided that no party or attorney or other person interested in an action shall be appointed receiver therein."

§ 576: Oath and bond of receiver.

§ 580 "The receiver shall have power, under control of the court, to bring and defend actions, to take and keep possession of the property, to receive rents, collect debts and generally to do such acts respecting the property as the court may authorize."

§ 524: Receiver may be appointed for property under attachment.

§§ 904 ff: Receivers in proceedings supplementary to execution

§ 925: Notice of application in supplementary proceedings must be given to other creditors.

§§ 927-930: Powers and duties of receivers appointed in supplementary proceedings.

§ 6137. "Whenever a receiver or assignee is appointed for any person, company or corporation, the court shall require such receiver or assignee to pay all claims for which a lien could be filed under this act [laborers' claims], before the payment of any other debts or claims, other than operating expenses."

West Virginia.—Code, 1899, c. cxxxiii.

Pages 892 ff: A general receiver may be appointed by the court, to receive, take charge of and invest moneys paid into court.

Page 893: Bond of receiver.

Page 893: "He shall receive as compensation for his services such per centum of the amount received and invested or paid out by him in each case as the court may direct, for receiving, investing or paying out the same."

Page 895: "A court of equity may in any proper case pending therein, in which the property of a corporation, firm or person is involved, and there is danger of the loss or misappropriation of the same or a material part thereof, appoint a special receiver of such property or the rents, issues and profits thereof, or both, who shall give bond. . . . . But no such receiver shall be appointed of any real estate, or of the rents, issues or profits thereof until reasonable notice of the application therefor has been given to the owner or tenant thereof."

Page 808: Appointment of receivers upon dissolution of corporation.

Wisconsin.—Stats. 1898.

§ 2787. "A receiver may be appointed:

"1. Before judgment, on the application of either party, when he establishes an apparent right to or interest in property which is the subject of the action and which is in the possession of an adverse party, and the property or its rents and profits are in danger of being lost or materially impaired;

"2. By the judgment, or after judgment, to carry the judgment into effect or to dispose of the property according to the judgment;

"3. After judgment, to preserve the property during the pendency of an appeal; or when an execution has been returned unsatisfied and the judgment debtor refuses to apply his property in satisfaction of the judgment, or in an action by a creditor under section 3029;

"4. In cases provided by any statute when a corporation has been dissolved or is insolvent or in imminent danger of insolvency, or has forfeited its corporate rights,

"5. In such cases as are now provided by law or may be in accordance with the existing practice except as otherwise provided in this chapter."

§ 2787a: Wages of employees accruing within three months of receivership are preferred claims.

§ 1769: Wages of railroad employees accruing within six months before receivership are preferred claims

§ 3036: Notice of application must be given to plaintiff in supplementary proceedings.

§§ 3216 ff Receivers for insolvent corporations.

§ 1791g: Trust company may act as receiver.

Wyoming.—Rev. Stats. 1899.

§ 4054: Appointment of receivers.—Practically the same as Cal. Code Civ. Proc., § 564.

§ 4055· "No party, attorney, or person interested in an action shall be appointed receiver therein except by consent of the parties."

§ 4056: Oath and undertaking of receiver.

§ 74. Class I: (1) Infants' Estates.—"The cases in which a receiver may be appointed, subject to the general rules regulating the exercise of the judicial discretion, may be reduced to four general classes. The first class contains those cases where there is no person entitled to the property who is at the same time competent to hold and manage it during the judicial proceeding. In instances of this class a receiver is appointed more readily and without proof of imminent danger, perhaps, than in any other."[39]

"A court of equity exercises control over the property of its infant ward, where there is no trustee, by means of a receiver, even though there is a guardian. The main reason for appointing a receiver, in the absence of a trustee, was that the guardian at common law had not full power of control and management. The necessity of a receiver in such cases may have been obviated in many states by statutes enlarging the powers of guardians."[40]

§ 4057. Powers of receiver.—Practically the same as Cal. Code Civ. Proc., § 568.

§ 4058 Investment of funds.—Same as Cal. Code Civ. Proc., § 569.

§ 3952: Appointment in aid of execution.

§§ 4006 ff: Receivers for attached property.

39 4 Pom. Eq. Jur., § 1332.

40 Pom. Eq. Jur., § 1332, and note, citing Gardner v. Blane, 1 Hare, 381; Butler v. Freeman, Amb. 301, 303; Duke of Beaufort v. Berty, 1 P. Wms. 703. See, also, Ex parte Whitfield, 2 Atk. 315, per Lord Hardwicke. A statute in North Carolina provides for a receiver in case of the removal of a guardian for certain specified causes. See Temple v. Williams, 91 N. C. 82.

The recent case of Keister v. Cubine, 101 Va. 768, 45 S. E 285, is of considerable interest. A mother, M. C., deeded a house to her daughter, R. C., in consideration of a "proper and comfortable home" for life. On the death of the daughter the property descended to her infant children. M. C. was compelled by the widower of R. C. to abandon the home. Rescission of the deed as against the infant owners was refused, since they were not at fault; but a receiver was appointed to administer and, if necessary, sell, the

§ 75. **(2) Lunatics' Estates.**—"The control of the court over the property of a lunatic is ordinarily exercised by means of a committee; but instead of a committee, and especially where no person will act as a committee, the court may appoint a receiver."[41] "Where a suit was brought by the committee of a lunatic to set aside a conveyance of land alleged to have been obtained by defendant from the lunatic by fraud and undue influence, and defendant was in possession receiving the rents and profits, and was alleged to be insolvent, the appointment of a receiver during the litigation was held proper."[42]

§ 76. **(3) Estates of Decedents.**—"During the litigation concerning the admission of a will to probate, and during the interval before an executor or administrator is appointed, a court of equity has power to appoint a receiver of the personal property and of the rents and profits of the real estate, while there is any danger of their loss, misuse, or misapplication.[43] The necessity

property, primarily for the support of the grantor, M. C., and after that to hold the property or its proceeds for the infant owners.

41 Pom. Eq. Jur., § 1332. The appointment of a receiver pending an inquisition of lunacy, or a statutory inquiry into insanity, to prevent mismanagement or waste, rests in the sound discretion of the court. In re Misselwitz, 177 Pa. St. 359, 35 Atl. 722; In re Pountain, L. R. 37 Ch. D. 609. See, also, Beall v. Stokes, 95 Ga. 357, 22 S. E. 637 (lunatic committed to asylum in another state, but having an estate in Georgia, receiver appointed at suit of wife); In re Hybart, 119 N. C. 359, 25 S. E. 963 (practice in appointing receiver of lunatic's estate, under statutes of North Carolina).

42 Pom. Eq. Jur., § 1332, note; Mitchell v. Barnes, 22 Hun, 194. For the appointment of a receiver in a suit under the inherent jurisdiction of equity to protect the property of a person of weak or unsound mind, who cannot be adjudged to be *non compos mentis* (Pom. Eq Jur., § 1314), see Edwards v. Edwards, 14 Tex. Civ. App. 87, 36 S. W. 1080.

43 Pom. Eq. Jur., § 1332 See Whitworth v. Whyddon, 2 Macn. & G. 52, 55; King v. King, 6 Ves. 172; Atkinson v. Henshaw, 2 Ves.

of such a receiver has been greatly lessened by modern statutes authorizing the probate court to appoint an administrator *ad litem*, and enlarging his powers."[44] "The recent English decisions hold that the jurisdiction will not be exercised if the probate court has already appointed an administrator *ad litem*;[45] but if no such temporary administrator has been appointed, the court of equity will still appoint a receiver" in a proper case.[46] The death of one of two executors and the refusal of the other to act has also been considered a good reason for the appointment of a receiver of the estate;[47] and the appointment might be made, on a case of strong presumption, pending a suit in the ecclesiastical court to recall probate.[48]

& B. 85, Ball v. Oliver, 2 Ves. & B. 96; Watkins v. Brent, 1 Mylne & C. 97, 102; Anderson v. Guichard, 9 Hare, 245; Rendall v. Rendall, 1 Hare, 152; Wood v. Hitchings, 2 Beav. 289; Reed v. Harris, 7 Sim. 639; Robinson v. Taylor, 42 Fed. 803; Flagler v. Blunt, 32 N J. Eq. 518, 523 (property liable to be removed from the state); Long v. Richardson, 26 Tex. Civ. App. 197, 62 S. W. 964. For cases where the court refused to exercise the power, see Whitworth v. Whyddon, 2 Macn. & G 52 (property of small value); Richards v. Chave, 12 Ves. 462 (no danger shown); Jones v. Goodrich, 10 Sim. 327. A receiver may be appointed of the estate of a lunatic after his death, since the functions of the lunatic's committee cease with the death of the lunatic; but such receivership should be discontinued on the appointment of an administrator *in litem:* In re Colvin's Estate, 3 Md Ch. 278.

44 4 Pom. Eq. Jur., § 1332. See Goodman v. Kopperl, 169 Ill. 136, 48 N. E 172 (receiver not appointed on application of a creditor of decedent, as he has a right to take out administration of the estate); Colvin's Case, 3 Md. Ch. 278 (receiver must surrender the property when an administrator *pendente lite* is appointed).

45 Veret v. Duprez, L. R. 6 Eq. 329; Hitchen v. Birks, L. R. 10 Eq. 471.

46 4 Pom. Eq. Jur., § 1332, note; Parkin v. Siddons, L. R. 15 Eq. 34.

47 Palmer v. Wright, 10 Beav. 234.

48 Rutherford v. Douglas, 1 Sim. & St. 111, note.

§ 77. **Class II: In General.**—"The second class of cases is based upon the fact that all of the parties are equally entitled to the possession of the property which is the subject-matter of the controversy, but it is not just and proper, from the nature of the dispute and of their relations with each other, that either one of them should be allowed to retain possession and control during the litigation. While the foundation of the remedy is, of course, the danger, yet it is not always essential that there should be any element of actual fraud or breach of trust."[49] The most important instances which do or may belong to this class are: 1. Suits between partners; 2. Suits for partition between co-owners. 3. Suits between conflicting claimants of land, so far as they afford occasion for the appointment of a receiver, may conveniently be discussed in connection with this class, though not strictly falling within its definition.

§ 78. **(1) Receivers in Settlement of Partnership Affairs: In General.**—The power of a court of equity to appoint receivers in the settlement of partnership affairs, where a dissolution is sought or has occurred, is well established.[50] The power is, however, always exercised with great carefulness and caution.[51] The appointment is

49 4 Pom. Eq. Jur., § 1333.

50 Pom. Eq. Jur., § 1333. See notes, Slemmer's Appeal, 98 Am. Dec. 269-271; Cameron v. Groveland Imp. Co., 72 Am. St. Rep. 80-85. The power is inherent in the court, and is not dependent upon any statute: Cox v. Volkert, 86 Mo. 505, 511.

51 Pom. Eq Jur., § 1333. "It is a high power, never exercised where it is likely to produce irreparable injustice or injury to private rights, or where there exists any other safe or expedient remedy": Speights v. Peters, 9 Gill (Md.), 475. Where the time limited for the partnership has not expired, it is a familiar rule that the court will not interfere by the extreme measure of a receiver, except for the purpose of preservation of the assets in the face of a real danger of loss: Warwick v. Stockton, 55 N. J. Eq. 61, 36 Atl. 488 See, also, Heflebower v. Buck, 64 Md. 15, 20 Atl. 991; Bard v. Bingham, 54 Ala. 463.

only made in connection with a pending suit.[52] Upon a preliminary application for a receiver, the court does not determine the questions arising between the partners, the only question for consideration being whether, upon the facts disclosed, there is an apparent necessity for a receiver to protect the assets of the partnership until the rights of the partners can be definitely determined upon full hearing of the case.[53] As a general rule, the court will not order the business to be continued by the receiver; the object of the court in appointing a receiver is the care of the partnership property until the cause shall be decided, not the conducting of the business of the partnership.[54] In some exceptional cases, however, the management of the business may be continued by the receiver, during the pendency of the action for dissolution, for the purpose of preserving the good-will of the business, or when the property is liable to injury from remaining idle.[55]

52 Jones v. Schall, 45 Mich. 379, 8 N. W. 68, Webb v. Allen, 15 Tex. Civ. App. 605, 40 S. W. 342.

53 Blakeney v. Dufour, 15 Beav. 40; Heflebower v. Buck, 64 Md. 15, 20 Atl. 991. But where the case is ready for final hearing upon the proofs, it is error to appoint a receiver without adjudging the merits upon which the right or the propriety of the appointment necessarily depends: Morey v. Grant, 48 Mich. 326, 12 N. W. 202, per Cooley, J.

54 Wolbert v. Harris, 7 N. J. Eq 621; Martin v. Van Schaick, 4 Paige (N. Y.), 479; Allen v. Hawley, 6 Fla. 142, 63 Am. Dec. 198, and see Waters v. Taylor, 15 Ves 10; Taylor v. Neate, 39 Ch. D. 538.

55 Marten v. Van Schaick, 4 Paige (N. Y.), 479 (a newspaper); Allen v. Hawley, 6 Fla. 164, 63 Am. Dec. 198 (a steamboat); Jackson v. De Forest, 14 How. Pr. 81 (a livery-stable). Under the present English practice, on a dissolution by notice pursuant to the articles of partnership, where a sale of the business as a "going concern" is directed as being the most beneficial mode of realization, the court will appoint a receiver and manager for the purpose, in the meantime, of preserving the assets by carrying into effect existing contracts, and entering into such new contracts as are necessary

§ 79. **Existence of Partnership Must be Proved; and Necessity for Dissolution Must be Shown.**—In a suit for dissolution and appointment of a receiver, the court should not intervene if the existence of the partnership is denied by the defendant, and there is a substantial doubt involving that issue;[56] especially where the party in possession of the property is solvent, and able to respond fully to any measure of relief that can be decreed to the complainant.[57] If the partnership is still in existence, the showing made on application for a receiver must be such as to leave no doubt that the complainant will be entitled to a dissolution, if the facts shown are proved at the hearing.[58]

§ 80. **Mere Right to Dissolution not Sufficient.**—But the mere right to a dissolution of the partnership is not

for the purpose of carrying on the business in the ordinary way, but so as not to impose, by speculative dealing or otherwise, onerous liabilities on the partners Taylor v. Neate, 39 Ch. D. 538.

56 Irwin v. Everson, 95 Ala. 64, 10 South. 320, Goulding v. Bain, 4 Sandf. 716; Popper v. Scheider, 7 Abb. Pr., N. S., 56, McCarty v. Stanwix, 16 Misc. Rep. 132, 38 N. Y. Supp. 820, Guild v. Meyer, 56 N. J. Eq 183, 38 Atl. 959; Hobart v. Ballard, 31 Iowa, 521 (right to participate in profits the test of existence of a partnership) See, also, Taylor v. Bliley, 86 Ga. 154, 12 S. E. 210; Leeds v. Townsend, 74 Ill App. 444; Davis v. Niswonger, 145 Ind. 426, 44 N. E 542. The burden of proof rests on the plaintiff: Hobart v. Ballard, 31 Iowa, 521. That an issue may be directed to a jury to determine whether a partnership exists, or whether the plaintiff has an interest in the profits, see Peacock v. Peacock, 16 Ves. 49, Fairburn v. Pearson, 2 Macn. & G. 144. That the same equitable principles apply, whether the relation between the parties is that of *joint adventurers*, or of partners, see Wilcox v. Pratt, 125 N. Y. 688, 25 N. E. 1091, Warwick v. Stockton, 55 N. J. Eq. 61, 36 Atl. 488.

57 Irwin v Everson, 95 Ala. 64, 10 South. 320; Goulding v. Bain, 4 Sandf. 716.

58 Goodman v. Whitcomb, 1 Jacob & W. 589; Smith v Jeyes, 4 Beav. 503; Roberts v. Eberhardt, Kay, 148, Hall v. Hall, 3 Macn & G. 79; Const v. Harris, Turn. & R. 517, Garretson v. Weaver, 3 Edw Ch. (N. Y.) 385. A receiver cannot be appointed where the bill contains no prayer for a dissolution: Pirtle v. Fenn, 3 Dana (Ky), 247, 28 Am. Dec. 70.

sufficient to warrant the appointment of a receiver; there must be some breach of the duty of a partner, or of the contract of partnership, and a necessity of preservation of the assets in the face of a real danger of loss.[59] Such facts as the unprofitable nature of the business,[60] or the refusal of the defendant partner to co-operate in its management,[61] furnish no grounds for a receiver. But if the conduct of the defendant partner has been such as justly to destroy all confidence in him, this is an important fact to be considered by the court;[62] and where the firm is admitted to be insolvent,

59 Harding v. Glover, 18 Ves 281, per Lord Eldon; Warwick v. Stockton, 55 N. J. Eq 61, 36 Atl. 488; Weissenborn v. Sieghortner, 21 N. J. Eq. 483, reversing 20 N. J. Eq. 172; Randall v. Morrell, 17 N. J. Eq. 343, Cox v Peters, 13 N. J. Eq. 39; Wilson v. Fitchter, 11 N. J. Eq 71; Birdsall v. Colie, 10 N. J Eq. 63; Renton v. Chaplain, 9 N. J. Eq 62 (the relief refused to a purchaser of one partner's interest at a sheriff's sale). This is true of partnerships determinable at the will of one partner: Birdsall v. Colie, and Cox v. Peters, *supra;* though Chancellor Walworth is credited with the statement that in such cases a receiver is a matter of course, if the articles of partnership have made no provision for closing up the concern, see Law v. Ford, 2 Paige, 310.

60 Shoemaker v. Smith, 74 Ind. 71.

61 Roberts v. Eberhardt, Kay, 148. See the frequently quoted remarks of Lord Eldon on the subject of disagreement among the partners as a ground of dissolution: "Where partners differ, as they sometimes do, when they enter into another kind of partnership, they should recollect that they enter it for better and worse, and this court has no jurisdiction to make a separation between them because one is more sullen or less good-tempered than the other. Another court, in the partnership to which I have alluded, cannot, nor can this court in this kind of partnership, interfere, unless there is a cause of separation which, in the one case, must amount to downright cruelty, and in the other must be conduct amounting to an entire exclusion of the partner from his interest in the partnership. Whether a dissolution may ultimately be decreed I will not say, but trifling circumstances of conduct are not sufficient to authorize the court to award a dissolution": Goodman v. Whitcomb, 1 Jacob & W. 589.

62 Smith v. Jeyes, 4 Beav 503; Todd v. Rich, 2 Tenn. Ch. 107; Williamson v. Wilson, 1 Bland (Md), 418.

and each partner charges the other with threatened waste of the partnership property and an intent to give an unlawful preference to certain creditors;[63] or where willful acts of fraud by the defendants are shown, and application of the partnership funds to their own use;[64] or when the petition shows insolvency, dissension between the partners, probability of waste, and a necessity for an accounting and dissolution—in such cases sufficient grounds are presented for a receiver.[65]

§ 81. **Exclusion from Management as Ground.**—The exclusion of one partner from his full share of participation in the business of the partnership is considered one of the strongest grounds for the appointment of a receiver.[66] When the application is made on this ground, it is not always a necessary condition of the action of

63 Williamson v. Wilson, *supra*.

64 Barns v. Jones, 91 Ind. 161; Shannon v. Wright, 60 Md 520.

65 Veith v. Ress, 60 Neb. 52, 82 N. W. 116.

66 Const v. Harris, Turn & R. 517, 24 Rev Rep. 108, per Lord Eldon; Wilson v. Greenwood, 1 Swanst. 471 (exclusion of assignees of bankrupt partner); Butchart v. Dresser, 4 De Gex, M. & G. 542; Einstein v. Schnebly, 89 Fed. 540, 552; Katz v. Brewington, 71 Md. 79, 20 Atl. 139 (although the plaintiff may have an interest only in the profits, and not in the capital); Speights v. Peters, 9 Gill (Md.), 475; Wolbert v. Harris, 7 N. J. Eq. 621; Wilcox v. Pratt, 125 N. Y. 688, 25 N. E. 1091, affirming 52 Hun, 340, 5 N. Y. Supp. 361; Cole v. Price, 22 Wash 18, 60 Pac. 153; Redding v. Anderson (Wash.), 79 Pac. 628. Otherwise, if, by agreement, the business was to be conducted by the defendant alone: Warwick v. Stockton, 55 N. J. Eq. 61, 36 Atl. 488; and a receiver in behalf of an excluded partner was refused, in a case where the partner in possession, prior to the formation of the partnership, had owned all the property and conducted the business, and the complainant purchased a half interest in the property and business on long credit, mortgaging it back to secure the debt; the complainant did not aver or show that the partner in possession was insolvent, or that the property was endangered in his custody; nor did he aver or show any willingness or ability to make the payments as they fell due, or that his interest was equal to the amount due: Bard v. Bingham, 54 Ala. 463.

the court that the property should be in imminent peril;[67] but if there is in addition to the exclusion, a showing of fraudulent conduct on the defendant's part, and a dissolution is inevitable, the court will unhesitatingly appoint a receiver.[68]

§ 82. After Dissolution; Partner Liquidating Under Agreement.—Where dissolution of the partnership has already occurred, and an agreement has been made that one or more of the partners shall have charge of its properties and wind up the concern, "their possession is not to be interfered with on slight grounds. There must be some palpable breach of conduct or of duty, or some misconduct amounting to fraud, or such as will endanger the property and the rights of the partner who has withdrawn, in order to justify the court's interference. It does not follow that the complainant has a right to intercept their proceeding, under a mere apprehension of such loss, or because he may think the defendants have not acted discreetly or judiciously in some particulars."[69] But where such an agreement gives the con-

67 Speights v. Peters, *supra*.

68 See Cole v. Price, 22 Wash. 18, 60 Pac. 153; Haight v. Burr, 19 Md 130, Shannon v. Wright, 60 Md. 520; Barnes v. Jones, 91 Ind. 161. Thus, in the last case, the complaint showed willful acts of fraud by the defendants, the application by them of the partnership funds to their own use, the making by them of false entries upon the books, the preventing of the plaintiff from having access to such books, and the willful concealment from him of the condition of the partnership business.

69 Walker v. Trott, 4 Edw. Ch. 38. To the same effect, see Waters v. Taylor, 15 Ves. 10, 19; Bufkin v. Boyce, 104 Ind. 53, 3 N. E. 615; Heflebower v. Buck, 64 Md. 15, 20 Atl. 991; Simon v. Schloss, 48 Mich 233, 12 N. W. 196; Weston v. Watts, 1 N. Y. St. Rep. 763; Alcott v Vulter, 33 App. Div. 245, 53 N. Y. Supp. 474; Meyer v. Reimers, 30 Misc Rep. 307, 63 N. Y. Supp. 681, affirmed 49 App. Div. 638, 63 N. Y. Supp. 1112. See, however, Bennett v. Smith, 108 Ga. 466, 34 S. E. 156.

tinuing partners the exclusive right to the possession of the partnership property, and holds the retiring partner harmless, a receiver may be appointed for the preservation of the assets, on a showing that the continuing partners are wasting or misapplying them, or that by reason of their insolvency the retiring partner is in danger of being sued for the debts of the firm;[70] and a receiver is also warranted by the fact that after dissolution the remaining partners continue to carry on the business on their own account with the partnership effects.[71]

§ 83. **After Dissolution; No Agreement for Liquidation.**— In the absence of any provision or agreement by the partners as to the division of the property or the manner of closing its affairs, a receiver will readily be appointed, after dissolution, in case of a disagreement between the partners. This rule is based on the principle that each partner has an equal right to the possession and control of the partnership effects.[72]

70 Allen v. Cooley, 53 S. C. 414, 31 S E 634; West v. Chasten, 12 Fla. 315; Drury v. Roberts, 2 Md. Ch. 157.

71 Harding v. Glover, 18 Ves 281. See, also, Joselove v. Bohrman, 119 Ga 204, 45 S. E. 982 (insolvent continuing partner contracts new liabilities in firm name; injunction and receiver).

72 McElvey v. Lewis, 76 N. Y. 373; Law v. Ford, 2 Paige, 310; Marten v. Van Schaick, 4 Paige, 479; Whitman v. Robinson, 21 Md. 43; Sloan v. Moore, 37 Pa. St. 217; Fleming v. Carson, 37 Or. 252, 62 Pac. 374; Martin v. Hurley, 84 Mo. App. 670; Mitchell v. Lister, 21 Ont. 22; and see McIntosh v. Perkins, 13 Mont. 143, 32 Pac. 653. Some of the cases speak of the receivership being almost a matter of course under such circumstances. See the New York cases above cited; and Pini v. Roncoroni, [1892] 1 Ch. 633; but compare the New Jersey cases cited *ante*, in note to § 80. By the rule in New Jersey, a receiver, after dissolution, is appointed only when necessary to protect the interests of the parties; but the circumstance of the insolvency of one of the partners, in addition to the fact of the dissolution of the firm, would, under ordinary circumstances, induce the court to assume the administration of the partnership affairs: Randall v. Morrell, 17 N. J. Eq. 343, 346.

§ 84. **Receiver on Death of Partner.**—The surviving partner being the one in whom the deceased himself reposed confidence, and being in law entitled to the possession and control of the firm assets, control should not be wrested from him, by the appointment of a receiver, without a clear showing of mismanagement or improper conduct, and of danger of ultimate loss to the estate of the deceased partner.[73] But where the surviving partner is acting negligently or faithlessly—as, by failing to take an account of stock, and to keep an account of sales;[74] or by refusing to close up the firm

While in cases of this character a receiver is not a matter of absolute right, one will be appointed where the defendant partner "has withdrawn from the partnership funds a very large sum, and has so brought about its insolvency. That is a good ground for saying that the plaintiff can no longer trust him": Pini v. Roncoroni, [1892] 1 Ch. 633. In this case, the jurisdiction to appoint a receiver was not ousted by a very broad arbitration clause, requiring the submission of all differences; so, too, where the articles provide that on dissolution the partners should appoint a person to collect the accounts and settle the partnership affairs, on their failure to agree on any person the court will appoint a receiver: Mitchell v. Lister, 21 Ont. 22.

Dissolution by Bankruptcy of Partner.—In England, "the usual course where disputes as to the management of partnership affairs arise between the trustees of a bankrupt partner and the solvent partners, and there is no reason for distrusting the latter, is that the court will appoint one of them receiver of the partnership property, directing him to give security, to pass his accounts, and to furnish the trustee with proper accounts, and to allow him at all reasonable times to inspect the partnership books": Lindley, Partn. (5th ed.), p. 670, quoted in Collins v. Barker, [1893] 1 Ch. 578.

73 Painter v. Painter (Cal.), 36 Pac. 865, 875; Huggins v. Huggins, 117 Ga. 151, 43 S. E. 759 (not appointed when survivor solvent, and no special circumstances); Walker v. House, 4 Md. Ch. 39, 44; Comstock v. McDonald, 113 Mich. 626, 71 N. W. 1087; Mason v. Dawson, 15 Misc. Rep. 595, 37 N. Y. Supp. 90 (survivors entitled to wind up the affairs of the partnership by virtue of an express provision in the articles; mere delay, slightly in excess of that permitted by the articles, not sufficient ground for receiver).

74 Word v. Word, 90 Ala. 81, 7 South. 412.

business within a reasonable time, and by continuing to manage it in his own name and for his own benefit;[75] or by conducting the firm business for the purpose of continuing and enlarging it, and not to close it[76]—if there is danger that the estate of the deceased co-partner will suffer, a receiver may be appointed on the application of the legal representatives of the latter.[77] On the death of both partners, it has been held that a receiver should be appointed on the ground that no relation of confidence exists between their representatives.[78]

§ 85. **Miscellaneous.**—Where both partners have assigned their respective interests in the firm, the jurisdiction may be exercised between the assignees upon the same principles which govern the jurisdiction as between partners themselves.[79] Where each partner has attempted separately to make an assignment of the partnership assets for the benefit of creditors, a receiver is proper.[80]

There can be no ground for a receiver in behalf of a partner who is himself in possession.[81]

The fact that a motion for a receiver was denied in a former suit for the settlement of the partnership affairs, which suit was dismissed without prejudice, constitutes no bar to the relief in another action.[82]

A receiver will generally be refused where the equities of the plaintiff in the bill are fully met and denied by

75 Holden's Admrs. v. McMakin, Par. Eq. Cas. (Pa.) 270.

76 Dawson v. Parsons, 66 Hun, 628, 21 N. Y. Supp. 212.

77 Clegg v. Fishwick, 1 Macn. & G. 294.

78 In the early case of Phillips v. Atkinson, 2 Bro. C. C. 272; but see Perrin v. Lepper, 56 Mich. 351, 23 N. W. 39.

79 Maynard v. Railey, 2 Nev. 133.

80 Fox v. Curtis, 176 Pa. St. 52, 34 Atl. 952, 38 Wkly. Not. Cas. 321.

81 Smith v. Lowe, 1 Edw. Ch. 33.

82 Anderson v. Powell, 44 Iowa, 20.

the answer;[83] and where the appointment would destroy the value of the business without benefit to either party.[84] In some cases, the necessity of a receiver has been obviated by a bond executed by the defendant for the satisfaction of any decree that might be rendered in favor of the plaintiff.[85]

It is said that the receiver should be directed to take charge of all the partnership property, not of a portion merely, where the suit is for a final accounting; and where the ownership of some of the property is in dispute, that the order should furnish the means of distinguishing the private property of the defendant from the partnership property.[86]

§ 86. (2) In Partition and Other Suits Between Co-owners.—"In suits between co-owners of mines and collieries the English courts grant a receiver upon the same grounds and under the same circumstances as in those between partners," since "the working of a mine by co-owners is necessarily a business analogous to a partnership."[87]

83 Williamson v. Monroe, 3 Cal. 383; Coddington v. Tappan, 26 N. J. Eq. 141.

84 Slemmer's Appeal, 58 Pa. St. 168, 98 Am. Dec. 255.

85 See Popper v. Scheider, 7 Abb. Pr., N. S., 56; Saverios v. Levy, 1 N. Y. St. Rep. 758, Buchanan v. Comstock, 57 Barb. 568; Philipp v. Von Raven, 26 Misc. Rep. 552, 57 N. Y. Supp. 701 (under Code Civ. Proc., § 1947); Word v. Word, 90 Ala. 81, 7 South. 412; Devereux v. Fleming, 47 Fed. 177; Cary Bros. v. Dalhoff Const. Co., 126 Fed. 584, and see Fleming v. Carson, 37 Or. 252, 62 Pac. 374 (bond refused).

86 Morey v. Grant, 48 Mich. 326, 12 N. W. 202, per Cooley, J.

87 4 Pom. Eq. Jur, § 1333, and note 2; Jefferys v. Smith, 1 Jacob & W. 298, per Lord Eldon. In this case there was a dispute as to the management of the property among a large number of owners of a colliery. "Here there are twenty shares; and if each owner may employ a manager and a set of workmen, you destroy the subject altogether; it renders it impossible to carry it on." In Parker v. Parker, 82 N. C. 165, where co-tenants in possession of a gold mine were of doubtful responsibility to respond in damages for gold ap-

In all ordinary suits, including suits for partition, between legal co-owners of land, a receiver is not usually appointed unless some of the parties are in sole possession, to the exclusion of the others.[88] Beyond this statement it is difficult to formulate any rule that will be supported by authority.[89] In a well-considered

propriated by them, a receiver was held to be proper *pendente lite*, instead of an injunction, as the public had an interest in the continued working of the mine. But mere colorable ouster on the part of a tenant in common who is in possession of a mining claim by the consent of a co-tenant who has brought a suit for partition, and the mere fact that the care of the property involves considerable expense, will not authorize the appointment of a receiver. Heinze v. Kleinschmidt, 25 Mont. 89, 63 Pac. 927. In Heinze v. Butte & Boston Consolidated Min. Co, 61 C. C. A. 63, 126 Fed. 1, 7-11, a receiver was appointed, in a partition suit, to receive the share of ore pertaining to an interest the ownership of which was in dispute, and the subsequent extension of the receivership to the entire property, under directions to operate the mine, on a showing of fraud by the co-tenants in possession in withholding such share from the receiver, was held not to be an abuse of discretion on the part of the trial court. This decision was based in part, however, upon conduct of the co-tenant in possession showing acquiescence in the order extending the receivership; and Ross, Cir. J., dissented (at pp. 28, 29) both as respects the appointment and the extension. In general, as to receivers of mining property, see next section.

88 Pom. Eq Jur, § 1333; Milbank v. Revett, 2 Mer. 405; Cassetty v. Capps, 3 Tenn. Ch. 524; Vaughan v. Vincent, 88 N. C. 116; Kill v. Murdock, 4 Ohio N. P. 244; Lamaster v. Elliott, 53 Neb. 424, 73 N. W. 925 (mere ill-will and hostility between joint owners does not warrant the appointment of receiver). The appointment will not be made solely because one of the co-tenants is occupying all of the common property without paying rent; he has a right so to occupy it, unless his occupation is a virtual ouster of the complainant: Varnum v. Leek, 65 Iowa, 751, 23 N. W. 151. That a notice to undertenants not to pay rent to co-tenants entitled thereto by agreement does not amount to an exclusion, see Tyson v. Fairclough, 2 Sim. & St. 142.

89 Freeman on Co-tenancy and Partition, § 327. "In most of the early cases, the circumstances inducing the action of the court cannot be ascertained from the reports. No conclusion can, therefore, be drawn from these cases as to the grounds which warrant the interposition of the court. Most of the recent cases were so curtly

case in Georgia it was held "that a court of equity has jurisdiction to appoint a receiver, at the instance of one tenant in common against his co-tenants, who are in possession of undivided valuable property, receiving the whole of the rents and profits and excluding their companion from the receipt of any portion thereof,

disposed of as to leave us without any knowledge of the reasons which, in their own minds, justified the action of the judges We therefore find it impossible to state with precision the general principles upon which the action of courts of equity have been or will be predicated in disposing of applications for the appointment of receivers of undivided estates. It is certain, however, that the application will be denied, except in extreme cases.'' In New York it has been held that a receiver may be appointed to preserve the property during the pendency of an action for partition, where it is shown that a portion of the property cannot be rented, and that the rents of the remaining portions cannot be collected, because of the refusal of one of the co-tenants to unite with the others· Pignolet v Bushe, 28 How. Pr. 9; or where there was a strong feeling of hostility between the co-tenants, and a probability of future injury to the interests of both parties: Goldberg v. Richards, 26 N. Y. Supp 335, 5 Misc. Rep. 419. In Bender v. Van Allen, 28 Misc Rep. 304, 59 N Y. Supp. 885, a receiver was refused where one defendant in an action of partition claimed as tenant by the curtesy, since none of the heirs were entitled to possession during the life of such tenant, if his claim should be established; and in Darcin v. Wells, 61 How. Pr, 259, and Bathmann v. Bathmann, 79 Hun, 447, 29 N. Y. Supp. 959, also actions of partition, no grounds existed for the appointment In Illinois, it was held that the appointment on a bill for partition by infants of a receiver for a long term of years, on the application of adult co-tenants, without the consent of the infants or their guardians, was unauthorized: Ames v. Ames, 148 Ill. 321, 340, 36 N. E. 110. The court has no power to appoint a receiver over other lands of the co-tenant not involved in the suit, in order to collect a judgment for rents: Branner v. Webb, 10 Kan. App. 217, 63 Pac. 274.

Under the broad power to appoint receivers conferred by the Supreme Court of Judicature (see *ante*, § 72), the English courts now hold that a receiver may be appointed until the hearing although the co-owner is not in exclusive possession: Porter v. Lopes, L. R. 7 Ch D. 358, per Jessel, M. R. And in Indiana, under § 1222 of Revised Statutes of 1881, the appointment is a matter solely within the discretion of the court or judge, and the defendant cannot defeat the when such tenants are insolvent."[90] Courts are averse to appointing a receiver over *personal* property at the suit of one co-owner against the other; and in a suit for the partition of such property will refuse a receiver if the defendant in exclusive possession will give adequate security against the deterioration or destruction of the property and to compensate the plaintiff for its use.[91]

§ 87. (3) "**In Suits Between Conflicting Claimants of Land**, especially between parties claiming under legal titles, a receiver will not ordinarily be appointed. The remedy, however, may be granted under special circumstances, in cases of gross fraud or great danger, or where possession is maintained by violence, and the like. In such cases the court acts with great caution, only where the plaintiff's rights are reasonably certain, and the danger is apparent."[92] The insolvency of a

appointment by showing the collector of the rents to be amply responsible or by offering to indemnify and secure the plaintiff against loss: Rapp v. Reehling, 122 Ind 255, 23 N. E. 68.

90 Williams v. Jenkins, 11 Ga. 595, citing Street v. Anderton, 4 Bro. C. C. 415, and Milbank v Revett, 2 Mer. 405.

91 Low v. Holmes, 17 N. J. Eq. 148. But in California it was held that where a tenant in common of a growing crop was in sole possession thereof, and denied the right of his co-tenant to any part thereof, and threatened to sell the entire crop and appropriate the proceeds to his own use, the co-tenant might maintain an action for the partition of the crop, and that in such an action a receiver *pendente lite* was authorized by Code of Civil Procedure, § 564: Baughman v. Reed, 75 Cal. 319, 7 Am. St. Rep. 170, 17 Pac 222. For a case where a receiver was appointed at the suit of certain part owners of a vessel, where the defendant part owners had been acting in fraud of the plaintiff's rights, see Brenan v. Preston, 2 De Gex, M. & G. 813.

92 Pom. Eq Jur., § 1333. See Owen v. Homan, 4 H. L. Cas. 997, 3 Macn. & G 378; Bainbrigge v. Baddeley, 3 Macn. & G. 413; Earl Talbot v. Hope Scott, 4 Kay & J. 96; Lloyd v. Passingham, 16 Ves. 68; Clark v. Dew, 1 Russ. & M. 103 (suit by devisee against heir at

defendant in possession does not of itself warrant the court in appointing a receiver, but, in addition, it must appear that the plaintiff has a probable right to recover

law); Ryder v. Bateman, 93 Fed. 16; St. Louis etc. R. R. Co. v. Dewees, 23 Fed. 519; Bateman v. Superior Court, 54 Cal. 285, Scott v. Sierra Lumber Co., 67 Cal. 71, 76, 7 Pac. 131; San Jose Safe Deposit Bank v. Bank of Madera, 121 Cal. 543, 54 Pac. 85; Bennallack v. Richards, 125 Cal. 427, 58 Pac 65; Kelly v. Steele (Idaho), 72 Pac. 887; Mapes v. Scott, 4 Ill. App. 268; Cofer v. Echerson, 6 Iowa. 502; Tarvin v. Walker's Creek etc. Co., 109 Ky. 579, 60 S. W. 185; Squire v. Hewlett, 141 Mass. 597, 6 N. E. 779; State v. Second Judicial Dist. Ct., 13 Mont. 416, 34 Pac 609; Smith v. White, 62 Neb. 56, 86 N. W 930; Corey v. Long, 12 Abb. Pr., N. S., 427; Thompson v Sherrard, 35 Barb. 593, 22 How. Pr. 155; Gregory v. Grgeory, 1 Jones & S. (33 N. Y. Super. Ct) 1; McCool v. McNamara, 19 Abb. N. C 344; Guernsey v. Powers, 9 Hun, 78; Willis v. Corlies, 2 Edw. Ch. 281; Rollins v. Henry, 77 N. C. 467; Twitty v. Logan, 80 N. C. 69; Bryan v. Moring, 94 N. C. 694; Emerson's Appeal, 95 Pa. St. 258, De Walt v. Kinard, 19 S. C. 286; Pearson v. Gillenwaters, 99 Tenn. 446, 63 Am. St. Rep. 844, 42 S. W. 9, Davis v. Reaves, 2 Lea (Tenn.), 649; Sengfelder v. Hill, 16 Wash. 355, 58 Am. St Rep 36, 47 Pac. 757; Spokane v. Amsterdamsch Trustees Kantoor, 18 Wash. 81, 50 Pac. 1088; Union Boom Co v. Samish River Boom Co, 33 Wash. 144, 74 Pac 53; Freer v. Davis, 52 W. Va. 35, 94 Am. St. Rep. 910, 43 S E 172.

In Talbot v. Hope Scott, *supra*, Vice-Chancellor Woods says· "That there may be a possible case in which this court would interfere to prevent absolute destructive waste, where the value of the property would be destroyed if no steps were taken, I can understand, but I have found nothing that bears any resemblance to the doctrine contended for, that at the instance of a person alleging a mere legal title, this court will interfere against another who is in possession, to deprive him of that possession. . . . . The ground of the rule adopted by the court, in this respect, I conceive to be extremely sound; the general ground being that the court cannot interfere with a legal title of any description, unless there be some equity by which it can affect the conscience of the defendant. Where there is an entire want of privity between the plaintiff and the defendant, and the defendant is simply a wrong-doer at law, this court does not take upon itself to interpose, unless in very exceptional cases." In Carrow v. Ferrior, L. R. 3 Ch. App 719, the same judge points out the distinction between the interference of the court to protect real property, and its interference to protect personal estate pending a litigation as to probate. "It may be true, on the highest general prinin the end.[93] If the object of the receiver is to preserve the rents and profits, there must be danger that they will be squandered and lost by reason of the insolvency

ciples, that there ought to be no difference in this respect between real and personal property, but our law clearly regards them very differently, and looks upon the person in possession of real estate as entitled to keep it till some one else shows a better title. Unless the person in possession of real estate is affected by some equity, this court will not interfere. The consideration is not unimportant that personal estate may be made way with altogether, if this court does not interfere, but only the rents of real estate can be lost. But, in my opinion, the leading principle governing the case is that this court does not interfere unless there is an equity."

Under the provision of the Judicature Act of 1873, § 25, paragraph 8, permitting the appointment of a receiver "in all cases where it shall appear to the court to be just or convenient," Talbot v. Hope Scott and Carrow v. Ferrior are no longer law in England, but the court has power to appoint a receiver, pending an action to recover possession of land, although the plaintiff's title is legal and the defendant is in possession: Berry v. Keen, [1882] 51 L. J. (Ch.) 912; Foxwell v. Van Greetten, [1897] 1 Ch 64 (insufficient grounds); John v. John, [1898] 2 Ch. 573. In the last case it was said that the discretion of the court must be exercised with a view to all the circumstances of the case, that it is important to bear in mind the position of the tenants, who, if the defendant is not a person of undoubted solvency, and remains in receipt of the rents, may be called upon to pay twice over if the plaintiff succeeds; and that the court has also to consider the probability of the plaintiff's succeeding, and the length of the defendant's possession, and whether he has any *prima facie* title.

93 Ryder v. Bateman, 93 Fed 16; Gregory v. Gregory, 33 N. Y. Super. Ct. (1 Jones & S.) 1; Cofer v. Echerson, 6 Iowa, 502. See, also, as to probability of plaintiff's recovery, *ante*, § 66; Owen v. Homan, 3 Macn. & G. 378, 412, 4 H L. Cas. 997; Bainbrigge v. Baddeley, 3 Macn. & G. 413, 419. In the latter case the contest was as to the validity of a will, under which the defendant in possession of the property claimed title. The chancellor, Lord Truro, says. "When the parties are litigating the right to property, and the litigation depends upon questions then to be decided at law, what are the circumstances in which the jurisdiction is to be exercised and is properly applicable in granting a receiver? There are, I apprehend, two grounds, and two only: First, that there is a reasonable probability of success on the part of the plaintiff; and second, that the property, the subject of the suit, is in danger. . . . . I apprehend I ought to presume, until I have the case so before me as to enable

of the party in possession, who will be unable to respond to a final decree.[94]

In accordance with the rule as above stated, receivers have been appointed in suits to cancel conveyances obtained by fraud or undue influence, where there was a strong probability of the plaintiff's success in the suit;[95] or where the plaintiff shows a right to the immediate possession of the land, together with the insolvency of the defendant in possession and imminent danger to the property;[96] or where the land is claimed by both parties, and both claim to be in possession, interfering with each other in harvesting the crops grown by each respectively and threatening each other with assaults and forcible resistance.[97]

The relief has sometimes been granted to the plaintiff after a judgment in his favor, pending a motion for

me judicially to form an opinion upon the subject, that the will is good. This court ought not, in any case, to disturb the possession of a party who stands upon his legal title, without a reasonable probability that the plaintiff will ultimately succeed. . . . . I do not see any such reasonable probability here; not at all using that expression to prejudice the plaintiff's title, or to express any opinion of it. His case may be the strongest that ever was presented; it may, when it comes to be laid before the proper tribunal, entitle him to a verdict without any doubt or hesitation; but I have not the materials before me to warrant me in coming to that conclusion."

94 Vause v. Woods, 46 Miss. 120; Bryan v Moring, 94 N. C. 694. See, also, Vizard v. Moody, 117 Ga. 67, 43 S. E. 426, where a receiver was appointed. But even in such a case, a bond to account for the rents in a sum to be designated by the court, may obviate the necessity of a receiver: Spokane v. Amsterdamsch Trustees Kantoor, 18 Wash. 81, 50 Pac. 1088.

95 Huguenin v. Basely, 13 Ves. 105; Stilwell v. Wilkins, Jacob, 280.

96 Smith v. Lusk, 119 Ala. 394, 24 South. 256; Nesbitt v. Turrentine, 83 N. C. 535 (action by lessor against lessee); and see Mayo v. McPhaul, 71 Ga. 758; Davis v. Taylor, 86 Ga. 506, 12 S. E. 881 (right lost by laches); Troughber v. Akin, 109 Tenn. 451, 73 S. W. 118 (see this opinion for a careful review of the Tennessee cases on the question of appointment).

97 Hlawacek v. Bohman, 51 Wis. 92, 8 N. W. 102.

a new trial, or the like, where it was necessary to protect the proceeds of the land from loss at the hands of an insolvent defendant.[98]

In North Carolina the relief is granted with some freedom, although the statute authorizing the relief seems to be merely declaratory of the general rule of equity;[99] and it is held, in several instances, that a re-

[98] See Whitney v. Buckman, 26 Cal. 447; Collier v. Sapp, 49 Ga. 93; Atlas Sav. etc. Assn. v. Kirklin, 110 Ga. 572, 35 S. E. 772 (one in whose favor it has been finally adjudged that, as against an insolvent person, the former has the title to, and the right to the possession of, given realty, but who is under an injunction, sued out at the instance of others, preventing him from taking possession, is entitled to have a receiver appointed to collect and hold rents which such insolvent is seeking by judicial process to collect from the tenants to whom he had undertaken to rent the premises); Stephens v. Kaga, 142 Ind. 523, 41 N. E. 930 (receiver to take charge of crops rendered unnecessary by a statutory bond, given by defendant on motion for a new trial, to pay all costs and damages which shall be recovered against him). Of course, a receiver will not be granted, pending appeal, in favor of a party against whom judgment in an ejectment suit has been rendered: Corbin v. Thompson, 141 Ind. 128, 40 N. E. 533 ("to have entertained the appellant's petition was to deny the force and effect of a judgment adverse to the very claim which his petition asserted").

[99] Code N. C., § 379: "A receiver may be appointed, before judgment, on the application of either party, when he establishes an apparent right to property which is the subject of the action, and which is in the possession of an adverse party, and the property, or its rents and profits, are in danger of being lost, or materially injured or impaired." Under this statute, "where a party to an action asks, as affirmative relief, the possession of land, and alleges that his adversary, who wrongfully withholds it, is insolvent, and the latter directly admits or fails to deny the allegation, it only remains for the plaintiff, in order to establish his right to the appointment of a receiver to take charge of the rents and profits, to show that he has set up in an affidavit filed under the sanction of the court, or in a verified pleading in the cause, used as an affidavit, an apparently good title, either not controverted at all, or not unequivocally and sufficiently denied by the affidavits of the claimant in posession": Lovett v. Slocumb, 109 N. C. 110, 13 S. E. 893. And a statute requiring the defendant in ejectment to give a bond for costs and damages before putting in a defense to the action does not abridge the

ceiver may be awarded against an insolvent plaintiff in possession, in a proper case.[100]

A receiver of mining property, the title to which is in litigation, is rarely appointed, and still more rarely is such receiver directed to extract the ore, since that is of the very substance of the estate.[101] Exceptional cases are those where there are timbers to be repaired, or water to be controlled; or, in the case of oil-wells, when it is necessary for the preservation of the claim that the work be continued to prevent the oil from being drawn off by the operation of wells on adjoining ground; or where a receiver is necessary in order that the annual work required by law may be performed for the benefit of the party who may ultimately be adjudged entitled to the ground.[102]

power of the court to appoint a receiver to secure the rents and profits: Kron v. Dennis, 90 N. C. 327. And where the plaintiff was charged with cutting and carrying away timber of peculiar value, he was compelled to give a bond to answer possible damages, and a receiver was appointed to take and state accounts of the timber so cut until the cause should be heard on its merits, although the plaintiff was solvent: John L. Roper Lumber Co. v. Wallace, 93 N. C 23. See, further, Stith v. Jones, 101 N. C. 360, 8 S. E. 151 (receiver appointed on conflicting evidence).

100 Horton v. White, 84 N. C. 297 (against plaintiff suing *in forma pauperis*); McNair v. Pope, 96 N. C. 502, 2 S. E. 54; John L Roper Lumber Co. v. Wallace, 93 N. C. 23 (receiver, for a special purpose, against a solvent plaintiff).

101 Tornanses v. Melsing, 106 Fed. 775, 784, 45 C. C. A. 615; approved in Heinze v Butte & Boston Consol. Min. Co., 61 C. C. A. 63, 126 Fed. 1, 11. See, also, Thomas v. Nantahala Marble etc. Co., 58 Fed. 485, 7 C. C. A. 330 (injunction proper, but not receiver), Bigbee v. Summerour, 101 Ga. 201, 28 S. E. 642 (a most vigorous and convincing opinion); Hickey v. Parrot Silver etc. Min. Co., 25 Mont. 164, 64 Pac. 330; Stith v. Jones, 101 N. C. 360, 8 S E. 151 (receiver not to operate the mine, but to receive the proceeds); Chicago & Allegheny Oil etc Co. v. U. S. Petroleum Co., 57 Pa. St. 83.

102 Tornanses v. Melsing, 106 Fed. 775, 784, 45 C. C. A. 615, by Ross, Cir. J.; Nevada Sierra v. Home Oil Co., 98 Fed. 673 (receiver denied). For other instances where receivers were appointed, under special circumstances, see, in addition to the partition cases men-

§ 88. **Class III: In General.**—"The third class embraces those cases in which the person holding title to the property is in a position of trust or of *quasi* trust, and is violating his fiduciary duties by misusing, misapplying, or wasting the property, and is thereby endangering the rights of other persons beneficially interested. In many, but not in all, the instances falling within this class, the plaintiff has, and is seeking to enforce, some equitable estate or interest; but whatever be the nature of his right, the ground of the remedy is always the misconduct of the party holding the title, and the consequent danger of loss."[103]

§ 89. **(1) Receivers in Suits Against Trustees, for Breach of Trust.**—Courts will not interfere with trustees' possession by a receiver unless there is real danger from their misconduct.[104] Instances of such misconduct,

tioned in the last section, Ulman v. Clark, 75 Fed. 868 (coal mine; receiver's appointment did not disturb defendants' operations, but merely secured the rents and profits, which were in danger of being scattered among many persons, thus imposing on the plaintiff the necessity of bringing many suits); Stith v. Jones, 101 N. C. 360, 8 S. E. 151.

103 4 Pom. Eq. Jur. § 1334.

104 4 Pom. Eq. Jur., § 1334, note; 72 Am. St. Rep. 95; Barkley v. Reay, 2 Hare, 306; Browell v. Reed, 1 Hare, 434, Latham v. Chafee, 7 Fed. 525, Vose v. Reed, 1 Woods, 647, 651, Fed. Cas. No. 17,011; Orphan Asylum v. McCartee, Hopk. Ch. (N. Y.) 429, Poythress v. Poythress, 16 Ga. 406. "The court would not, at the instance of one of several parties interested in an estate, displace a competent trustee, or take the possession from him, unless he willfully or ignorantly permitted the property to be placed in a state of insecurity, which due care or conduct would have prevented". Barkley v. Reay, *supra*. Where the defendant had been in possession of the property and administering the trust for a period of over seven years, the court would not, on a bill for his removal, appoint a receiver, before answer and a hearing on the merits, if there was not great danger that the complainant would suffer irreparable loss by any delay: Latham v. Chafee, *supra*. Even the mingling of the trust funds with his own, by one of the trustees, does not render a receiver necessary, when it is not alleged that the fund is in danger. Orphan Asylum v. Mc-

fraudulent or negligent, resulting in danger to the trust property and justifying the appointment of a receiver,[105] are as follows: Where there was an abuse of trust by an insolvent party in possession of real property, whereby the rents and profits were exposed to imminent danger of loss;[106] where a trustee of lands is insolvent, has sold parts of the trust property and misapplied the proceeds, has never accounted to the plaintiff for the rents and profits, but has applied the same to his own use, and has proposed to sell other parts of the trust property within a short time before the plaintiff's application for an injunction and receiver;[107] where the trustee has conveyed lands in fraud of the equitable interest of the *cestui que trust;*[108] where the trustee, in violation of the condition of his trust, loaned trust funds to a firm of which he was a member, which afterwards became insolvent;[109] where trustees of leasehold property had failed to keep the premises in proper

Cartee, *supra.* The court is extremely reluctant to interfere where the trust is vested by the legislature in state officers: Vose v. Reed, *supra.*

The refusal of one of several trustees to act does not necessitate the appointment of a receiver: Browell v. Reed, 1 Hare, 434; compare Tait v. Jenkins, 1 Younge & C. Ch. 492; otherwise where some of the trustees refuse to act, and all the parties in interest are before the court and consent to the appointment· Brodie v. Barry, 3 Mer. 695.

105 "It is the impending danger to the trust fund which induces the court to interpose with these extraordinary remedies in the case of an express trust, where a trustee has failed to take possession of the trust property, and has allowed it to remain in the hands of the debtor, who may dispose of it at any moment, or where he is about to part with it in a fraudulent manner, so that it will be lost to the trust estate, or where the trustee is clearly proven to have been guilty of acts of fraud, so that the fund is not safe in his hands for any length of time": Latham v. Chafee, 7 Fed. 525

106 Chase's Case, 1 Bland Ch. 206, 17 Am. Dec. 277.

107 Albright v Albright, 91 N C. 220.

108 Gunn v Blair, 9 Wis 352

109 North Carolina R. R. Co. v. Wilson, 81 N. C. 223.

repair, so as to prevent a forfeiture of the leasehold;[110] where the rents of the property had not been collected, and encumbrancers were threatening to take possession of the estate.[111] A receiver has been appointed in an action to compel an accounting, where the trustee wrongfully withheld the fund because of an alleged claim for damages against the beneficiary arising from a breach of contract.[112] For further instances, see the next two sections.

§ 90. **Same; Assignees for Benefit of Creditors.**—In the following cases the validity of the assignment was not attacked, but a receiver was sought on the ground of some incapacity or misconduct of the assignee, whereby the interests of the creditors were supposed to be imperiled.[113] Such receiver was not appointed, on the allegation of the insolvency of one of the sureties of the assignee, where there was no allegation of misfeasance or misappropriation on the latter's part, since the creditors had a perfect security in the statutory bond given by the assignee.[114] Upon general allegations of benefits to be derived from the appointment, the court has no authority to place an estate, assigned for the benefit of creditors, in the hands of a receiver to be sold, upon the application of a preferred creditor, though

110 In re Fowler, 16 Ch. D. 723.

111 Hart v. Tulk, 6 Hare, 611; and where rents have fallen in arrears, owing to dissensions among the trustees. Wilson v. Wilson, 2 Kean, 249.

112 Hagenback v. Hagenback etc. Co, 59 Fed. 14

In England, under the provisions of the Judicature Act, where the defaulting trustee is out of the jurisdiction, so that service of a writ of attachment could not be effected, a judgment against him for the payment of money into court may be enforced by the appointment of a receiver of his equitable interest in property: In re Coney, L. R. 29 Ch. D. 993.

113 See 72 Am. St. Rep. 43-45, note.

114 Dozier v. Logan, 101 Ga. 173, 28 S. E. 612.

the assignor and assignee consent to the appointment.[115] Nor are the youth and inexperience of an assignee, and the fact that he is not required to give a bond, and that his property is inconsiderable when compared with the value of the property conveyed by the assignment, sufficient to justify his removal and the appointment of a receiver in his stead.[116] If a trustee with power to continue the assignor's business is unfaithful or incompetent, the remedy is to require that he furnish ample security for the protection of those interested, or that he be removed, and another who is suitable be substituted. It would be an extreme case, if such could exist, which would call for the appointment of a receiver to execute an express trust continuous in its nature, and not merely to hold *pendente lite* for the removal of the trustee.[117]

The cases seem to indicate that receivers are commonly appointed with somewhat greater freedom than in other classes of trusts. Thus, insolvency of the assignee has been held to be a good cause for a receiver of his trust.[118] Refusal of the assignee to proceed with the execution of the trust,[119] or his resignation,[120] presents a proper ground for a reçeiver to protect the assets for the benefit of the creditors. The violation of his duty to keep the trust fund separate and distinct from his individual funds, and a separate bank account,

115 Penzel Grocer Co. v. Williams, 53 Ark. 81, 13 S. W. 736.

116 Jones v. McPhillips, 77 Ala. 314.

117 Etowah Min. Co. v. Wills Val. Min. etc. Co., 106 Ala. 492, 17 South. 522.

118 Haggarty v. Pittman, 1 Paige, 298, 19 Am. Dec. 434; City Nat. Bank v. Bridges, 114 N. C. 381, 19 S. E. 642 (insolvent trustee fails to give a bond when required by the court); Connah v. Sedgwick, 1 Barb. 210; Reed v. Emery, 8 Paige, 417, 35 Am. Dec. 720.

119 Suydam v. Dequindre, Harr. Ch (Mich.) 347.

120 McFerran v. Davis, 70 Ga. 661; or upon any vacancy: Andrews v. Wilson's Assignee, 114 Ky. 671, 71 S. W. 890.

to the injury, or great risk of injury, of those who may be ultimately entitled to the fund, requires the substitution of a receiver.[121] Gross mismanagement, with failure to comply with the terms of the assignment, resulting in danger of waste of the assets, clearly justifies the interposition of the court.[122]

§ 91. (2) In Suits Against Executors and Administrators. A strong case is required to induce the appointment of a receiver to take assets from the custody of an executor or administrator, displacing his authority. There must be actual misconduct or fraud, and immediate danger of loss, or the appointment of a receiver cannot be justified.[123] Such a case is not presented by charges

121 Wagner v. Coen, 41 W. Va. 351, 23 S. E. 735; or continuing to carry on the business of the assignor, and keeping no account of the sales of the assigned property: Connah v. Sedgwick, 1 Barb. 210; Hart v. Crane, 7 Paige, 37.

122 Jones v. Dougherty, 10 Ga. 273; Cohen & Co. v. Morris & Co, 70 Ga. 313, Goldsmith v. Fletcheimer, 16 Ky. Law Rep. 433, 28 S. W. 211. See, also, Robinson v. Worley, 19 Ky. Law Rep. 791, 42 S. W. 95.

123 Randle v. Carter, 62 Ala. 95, 102, where it is further said: "The executor is appointed by the testator, who has the right to declare in whom the management of his estate after his death shall be reposed. The administrator derives his authority from, and is, in a qualified sense, the officer of another court of exclusive jurisdiction, compelled to give and keep a bond, with sufficient sureties, for the prompt and faithful discharge of the trusts of the administration. The court is, therefore, reluctant to interfere with them by the appointment of a receiver. . . . . A different rule obtains, and should obtain, than in the case of trustees. The court of probate has, by the constitution, a general jurisdiction over the grant of letters testamentary, and of administration, in which is involved the power of revocation. The grant may be revoked whenever gross misconduct is shown, or, whenever a necessity exists, additional security may be required. Protection against loss to creditors, legatees, or next of kin, and security for a faithful administration, are within the power of the parties and the competency of that court. There can but seldom be a necessity for the exercise of any other preventive or protective remedy than such as that court can afford, and hence, though a court

stated on information and belief,[124] or otherwise lacking in certainty.[125] The mere poverty of the executor does not justify his removal, in the absence of proof of danger of loss to the estate.[126] Disagreement between executors as to the management of the estate does not warrant the interposition of the court by means of a receiver.[127] Where the application is based on the executor's incompetency and misconduct, his resignation and the appointment of an administrator *de bonis non* remove the ground for a receiver.[128] The relief is said to be designed to prevent future injury, and not to redress past grievances.[129]

Notwithstanding the emphatic expressions of reluctance to interfere noted above, it has been observed that the "strong" or "extraordinary" cases in which a receiver may be appointed seem to be quite common in chancery practice.[130] Any serious misconduct, gross

of equity has the jurisdiction to appoint a receiver of the assets, practically taking the administration into its hands, the jurisdiction is not exercised, unless there is manifest danger of loss which may be irreparable.'' See, also, substantially to the same effect, Werborn v. Kahn, 93 Ala. 201, 9 South. 729; Haines v. Carpenter, 1 Woods, 262, Fed. Cas. No. 5905, affirmed in 91 U. S. 254, 23 L. ed 345; Dougherty v. McDougald, 10 Ga. 121; Harrup v. Winslet, 37 Ga. 655; Powell v. Quinn, 49 Ga. 523; Pom. Eq. Jur., § 1334, note; 72 Am. St. Rep. 63-66, note.

124 Haines v. Carpenter, 1 Woods, 262, Fed. Cas. No. 5905.

125 Powell v. Quinn, 49 Ga. 523.

126 Knight v. Duplessis, 1 Ves. 324; Anonymous, 12 Ves. 4; Howard v. Papera, 1 Madd (86) 141; Johns v. Johns, 23 Ga. 31; Fairbairn v. Fisher, 4 Jones Eq. 390.

127 Wanneker v. Hitchcock, 38 Fed. 383; Fairbairn v. Fisher, 4 Jones Eq. 390.

128 Lunsford v. Lunsford, 122 Ala. 242, 25 South. 171.

129 Dougherty v. McDougald, 10 Ga. 121.

130 See note, 72 Am. St. Rep. 651. In *Ex parte* Walker, 25 Ala. 81, it was said: ''Nothing is more common in chancery practice than the appointment of receivers in suits against executors, when there is danger to the fund without such appointment; so, also, if he has wasted the effects, or in other respects has misconducted himself.

mismanagement, misuse, or misappropriation of funds by an irresponsible executor or administrator which imperils the estate justifies the appointment of a receiver.[131] While mere insolvency of the executor is not sufficient, an actual adjudication of bankruptcy, it has been held, presents a strong ground;[132] and his removal from the state, leaving both his *cestui que trust* and the trust estate within the state, amounts to an abandonment of his trust, and, it seems, renders it the duty of the court to appoint a receiver.[133]

§ 92. **(3) Receivers in Suits to Enforce Mortgages—English Rule.**—In England, by the rule that prevailed prior to the year 1860, an equitable mortgagee was, in general, alone entitled to a receiver, because a legal mortgagee could at any time gain possession after a default, and thus secure the rents and profits.[134] Yet where,

Although mere poverty, of itself, may not furnish sufficient ground for the appointment of a receiver, as against an executor, yet where it is coupled with other facts or circumstances, showing that he has proceeded not in accordance with law (as where he has made private sales of the property of the estate, or is dealing with it on his private account), especially where it is doubtful whether he is, in fact, the legal representative, or is not shorn of his authority by removal, the court, in all such cases, should promptly secure the effects by placing them in the hands of a receiver.''

131 Middleton v. Dodswell, 13 Ves. 266 (appointment may be made before answer), *Ex parte* Walker, 25 Ala. 81; Calhoun v. King, 5 Ala. 523; Werborn v. Kahn, 93 Ala. 201, 9 South. 729; Chappell v. Akin, 39 Ga. 177; Ware v Ware, 42 Ga. 408; Thompson v. Orser, 105 Ga. 482, 30 S. E. 626; Jenkins v. Jenkins, 1 Paige, 243, Stairley v. Rabe, McMull. Eq. (S. C.) 22; Price v. Price, 23 N. J. Eq. 428

132 For the reason that there is no person to protect the assets· Steele v. Cobham, L. R. 1 Ch. App. 325; and see Gladdon v. Stoneman, 1 Madd. (86) 141, note.

133 *Ex parte* Galluchat, 1 Hill Eq. (S. C.) 148; Elting v. First Nat. Bk., 173 Ill. 368, 50 N. E. 1095. For further instances, see Marvine v. Drexel, 68 Pa. St. 362; Du Val v. Marshall, 30 Ark. 230.

134 4 Pom. Eq. Jur, § 1334, note 3; 27 Am. St. Rep. 794, Berney v. Sewell, 1 Jacob & W. 647, per Lord Eldon; Sturch v. Young, 5 Beav.

under peculiar circumstances, the legal mortgagee could not obtain possession, a receiver might be appointed;[135] and the jurisdiction was freely exercised in behalf of equitable, as distinguished from legal, mortgagees.[136]

§ 93. General Rule in United States; Receiver Appointed When Security Inadequate and Mortgagor Insolvent.—The rule is well settled in a strong majority of the states where the question has been passed upon, that a receiver of the rents and profits will generally be appointed, at the application of the mortgagee, upon the commencement of a suit to foreclose the mortgage, upon a sufficient showing of two things: First, that the property covered by the mortgage is an inadequate security for the payment of the debt, with the accrued interest and

557; Ackland v. Gravener, 31 Beav. 482, per Romilly, M. R. By the statute 23 & 24 Vict., c. 145, §§ 11-32, it is provided that the mortgagee, in all cases where the payment of the principal is in arrear one year, or the interest six months, or after any omission to pay any insurance premium which, by the terms of the deed, ought to be paid, may obtain the appointment of a receiver of the rents and profits of the estate mortgaged. As to the effect of authority given to the mortgagee to appoint a receiver, previous to this statute, see Jolly v. Arbuthnot, 4 De Gex & J. 224; and as to the appointment of a receiver and manager under the liberal provisions of the Judicature Act, see Peek v. Trinsmaran Iron Co., L. R. 2 Ch. D. 115; Makins v. Percy, Ibotson & Sons, [1891] 1 Ch. 133; Campbell v. Lloyd's etc Bank, 1 Ch. 136, note, Edwards v. Standard etc Stock Syndicate, [1893] 1 Ch. 574; County etc. Bank v. Colliery Co., [1895] 1 Ch. 629; Whitley v. Challis, [1892] 1 Ch. 64.

135 Ackland v. Gravener, 31 Beav. 482; Shakel v. Duke of Marlborough, 4 Madd. 463; Truman v. Redgrave, L. R. 18 Ch D. 547 See, also, Warner v. Rising Fawn Iron Co., 3 Woods, 514, Fed. Cas. No. 17,188, where a receiver was granted to enforce the right to immediate possession of the mortgaged premises conferred on a trustee for bondholders by the deed of trust, which right the trustee refused to exercise at the request of the bond-holders.

136 Pom Eq. Jur., § 1334, note; Meaden v. Sealey, 6 Hare, 620; Holmes v. Bell, 2 Beav. 290 (equitable mortgage by deposit of title deeds).

costs of suit; and second, that the mortgagor, or other person who is personally liable for the payment of the debt, is insolvent, or beyond the jurisdiction, or in such doubtful financial standing that an execution against him for any deficiency would be unavailing.[137] This

137 **United States.**—Kountze v. Omaha Hotel Co., 107 U. S. 378, 2 Sup. Ct. 911, 27 L. ed. 609; Grant v. Phoenix Mut. L. Ins. Co, 121 U S. 105, 7 Sup. Ct. 841, 30 L. ed. 905; Shepherd v. Pepper, 133 U. S. 626, 10 Sup. Ct. 438, 33 L. ed. 706, American Nat. Bank v. Northwestern Mut. L. Ins. Co., 89 Fed. 610, 32 C. C. A. 275; Boyce v. Continental Wire Co, 125 Fed. 741.

Alabama.—Hughes v. Hatchett, 55 Ala. 631; Lehman v. Tallassee Mfg Co, 64 Ala. 567; Scott v. Ware, 65 Ala. 174; Lindsay v. American Mtg. Co., 97 Ala. 412, 11 South. 470; Jackson v. Hooper, 107 Ala. 634, 18 South. 254; Warren v. Pitts, 114 Ala. 65, 21 South. 494.

Arkansas.—Price v Dowdy, 34 Ark. 285.

California.—La Societe Francaise v. Salheimer, 57 Cal 623; Montgomery v. Merrill, 65 Cal. 432, 4 Pac. 414; Simpson v. Ferguson, 112 Cal. 180, 53 Am. St. Rep. 201, 40 Pac. 104, 44 Pac. 484.

Florida.—Pasco v. Gamble, 15 Fla. 562 (a valuable case).

Georgia.—The rule appears to be recognized in Hart v. Respeas, 89 Ga. 87, 14 S. E. 910.

Illinois.—Haas v. Chicago Bldg. Soc., 89 Ill. 498.

Indiana.—Main v. Ginthert, 92 Ind. 180; Storm v. Ermantrout, 89 Ind. 214.

Kentucky.—Douglass v. Cline, 12 Bush, 608, Wooley v. Holt, 14 Bush, 788.

Mississippi.—Hill v. Robertson, 24 Miss. 368, Whitehead v. Wooten, 43 Miss. 523; Myers v. Estell, 48 Miss. 372; Phillips v. Eiland, 52 Miss 721.

Nevada—Hyman v. Kelly, 1 Nev. 179.

New York.—Sea Insurance Co. v. Stebbins, 8 Paige, 565; Astor v. Turner, 11 Paige, 436, 43 Am. Dec. 766; Shotwell v. Smith, 3 Edw. Ch. 588; Post v. Dorr, 4 Edw. Ch. 412; Quincy v. Cheeseman, 4 Sandf. Ch. 405; Hollenbeck v Donnell, 94 N. Y. 342, 29 Hun, 94; Warner v. Gouverneur, 1 Barb. 36; Syracuse City Bank v. Tallman, 31 Barb. 201; Smith v. Tiffany, 13 Hun, 671.

North Carolina.—Kerchner v. Fairley, 80 N. C. 24; Oldham v. First Nat. Bank, 84 N. C. 304; Durant v. Crowell, 97 N. C. 367, 2 S. E. 541 (alternative of a receiver or a bond to secure to plaintiff the rents, profits and damages to which he may be adjudged entitled).

relief does not grow directly out of the relations of the parties or the stipulations contained in the mortgage, but out of equitable considerations alone. It is not, therefore, a matter of strict right, but is addressed to the sound discretion of the court.[138] The relief, not being a matter of strict legal right, is held, in many of the states which have adopted the "lien theory" of mortgages,[139] not to be affected by statutes entitling the

South Carolina.—Greenwood Loan & G. Co. v. Childs, 67 S. C. 251, 45 S. E. 167.

Tennessee.—Henshaw v. Wells, 9 Humph. 568.

Texas—Rogers v. Southern Pine Co., 21 Tex Civ App. 48, 51 S. W. 26; De Berrera v. Frost (Tex. Civ. App), 77 S. W. 637.

Virginia.—Bristow v. Home Bldg. Co, 91 Va. 18, 20 S. E. 946.

Wisconsin.—Finch v. Houghton, 19 Wis. 150; Schreiber v. Carey, 48 Wis. 208, 4 N. W. 124, Morris v. Branchaud, 52 Wis. 187, 8 N. W. 883; Sales v. Lusk, 60 Wis. 490, 19 N. W. 362.

In Indiana, Nebraska and South Dakota, the statutes are interpreted as permitting the appointment of a receiver on the ground of insufficiency of the mortgaged property to discharge the mortgage debt, without averment or proof of the mortgagor's insolvency: Ponder v. Tate, 96 Ind. 330; Hursh v. Hursh, 99 Ind. 500; Sellers v. Stoffel, 139 Ind. 468, 39 N. E. 52; Jacobs v. Gibson, 9 Neb. 380, 2 N W. 893; Philadelphia Mtg. etc. Co. v. Goos, 47 Neb. 804, 66 N. W. 843, Waldron v. First Nat. Bank, 60 Neb. 245, 82 N. W. 856; Philadelphia Mortgage & T. Co. v. Oyler, 61 Neb. 702, 85 N. W. 899; Roberts v. Parker, 14 S. Dak. 323, 85 N. W. 591. The statutes of several states contain a provision that a receiver may be appointed "in an action by a mortgagee for the foreclosure of his mortgage and sale of the mortgaged property, where it appears that the mortgaged property is in danger of being lost, removed, or materially injured, or that the condition of the mortgage has not been performed, and that the property is probably insufficient to discharge the mortgage debt." These states are Arkansas, California, Code Civ Proc, § 564; Idaho; Kentucky; Montana, Nebraska, Civ. Code, § 266; New York, North Dakota, Ohio; South Dakota, Comp. Laws, § 5015; Washington, Wyoming.

138 Syracuse City Bank v. Tallman, 31 Barb. 201; Hollenbeck v. Donnell, 94 N. Y. 342, 346. "The mortgagor holds the estate in some respects as a trustee for the benefit of the mortgagee": Schreiber v. Carey, 48 Wis. 208, 4 N. W. 124.

139 See Pom. Eq. Jur., § 1188.

mortgagor to possession upon default and until sale under the decree of foreclosure.[140]

Both of the conditions mentioned must co-exist,[141] and be alleged and satisfactorily proved; if either the inadequacy of the security[142] or the financial irresponsibility[143] of the person liable for the debt is not shown, the application for a receiver of rents and profits must be denied.

§ 94. **Same; Rule not Followed in Certain States.**—On the other hand, the courts of a number of states hold that they are prohibited by their statutes, which entitle the mortgagor to the possession of the mortgaged property until sale under the foreclosure decree, from assisting the mortgagee to obtain indirectly, through the agency of a receiver, the benefit of the rents and profits incidental to ownership and possession.[144] It is said,

140 See the cases above from Florida, Indiana, Nebraska, Nevada, New York, Texas and Wisconsin; especially Schreiber v. Carey, 48 Wis. 208, 4 N. W. 124.

141 Except in Indiana, Nebraska and South Dakota; see note 137, *supra.*

142 Shotwell v. Smith, 3 Edw. Ch. (N. Y.) 621; Whitehead v. Wooten, 43 Miss. 523; Rogers v. Southern Pine Co., 21 Tex. Civ. App. 48, 51 S. W. 26; Lindsay v. American Mortgage Co., 97 Ala. 412, 11 South. 770. In the last case it was said: "It is clear that when lands are the subject of a mortgage security the mortgagee is not entitled to a receiver unless it is made to appear that the preservation of the rents and profits is necessary to the mortgagee's security. If the lands are of sufficient value to secure the debt, the possession of the mortgagee should not be disturbed by the appointment of a receiver. It is incumbent on the mortgagee to show that such necessity exists." But that the appellate court is reluctant to disturb a finding as to the inadequacy of the security, see Ponder v. Tate, 96 Ind. 330.

143 Myers v. Estell, 48 Miss 372, Warren v. Pitts, 114 Ala. 65, 21 South. 494. In the latter case the property had been sold under a judgment against the mortgagor, and the purchaser was in possession and solvent.

144 California.—Guy v. Ide, 6 Cal. 99, 65 Am. Dec. 490, but the rule is now changed; see note to last section.

however, that the fact that the premises are inadequate security, or that the mortgagor is insolvent, or both combined, might be a very material consideration in passing upon the propriety or necessity of appointing

Iowa.—White v. Griggs, 54 Iowa, 650, 7 N. W. 125; American Invest. Co. v. Farrar, 87 Iowa, 437, 54 N. W. 361. See, also, Callanan v. Shaw, 19 Iowa, 183.

Michigan.—Wagar v. Stone, 36 Mich. 364; Beecher v. Marquette etc. Co., 40 Mich 307; Hazeltine v. Granger, 44 Mich. 503, 7 N. W. 74; Fifth Nat. Bank v. Pierce, 117 Mich. 376, 75 N. W. 1058; Union Mut. L. Ins. Co. v. Union Mills Plaster Co, 37 Fed. 286, 3 L. R. A. 90 (Michigan decisions held binding on the federal courts sitting in Michigan, since the right of the mortgagor to the rents and profits is a substantial right, and the appointment of a receiver is not a mere question of practice).

Minnesota.—Marshall etc. Bank v. Cady, 76 Minn. 112, 78 N. W. 978; National Fire Ins. Co. v. Broadbent, 77 Minn. 175, 79 N. W. 676.

South Carolina.—Hardin v. Hardin, 34 S C. 77, 27 Am. St. Rep. 786, 12 S E. 936.

Washington.—Norfor v. Busby, 19 Wash. 450, 53 Pac. 715.

In Wagar v. Stone, 36 Mich. 367, Marston, J., said: "Since the passage of this act, which prevents the mortgagee from obtaining possession until he has acquired an absolute title to the mortgaged premises, the mortgage binds only the lands. The rents and profits of the land do not enter into or form any part of the security. At the time of giving the security both parties understand that the mortgagor will, and that the mortgagee will not, be entitled to the rents, issues or profits of the mortgaged premises, until the title shall have become absolute upon a foreclosure of the mortgage. Until the happening of this event, the mortgagor has a clear right to the possession and to the income which he may derive therefrom, and the legislature, by the passage of this statute, contemplated that he should have such possession and income to aid him in paying the debt It would be a novel doctrine to hold that the mortgagee had a right to the profits incident to ownership, and yet that he had neither a legal title or right to possession. The legislature, in depriving him of the means of enforcing possession, intended thereby also to cut off and deprive him of all rights which he could have acquired in case he obtained possession before acquiring an absolute title. To deprive him of this particular remedy, and yet allow him in some other proceeding to, in effect, arrive at the same result, would be but a meaningless proceeding, and would not be securing to the mortgagor those substantial rights which it was the evident intent he should have. We do not overlook the fact that a contrary a receiver in order to prevent waste, or for the purpose of preserving the premises.[145]

In New Jersey, a similar result is reached by adherence to the former English doctrine, that the legal mortgagee must appropriate the property to the payment of his debt by means of his legal remedy of ejectment. Inadequacy of the security and insolvency of the mortgagor are not in themselves regarded as sufficient grounds to warrant the appointment of a receiver in that state.[146]

§ 95. **Other Grounds.**—The mortgagee's case may be strengthened by other circumstances in addition to the essential conditions for relief above mentioned. Such circumstances are, the mortgagor's neglect to pay taxes, or to comply with his agreement to keep the premises insured;[147] and where such neglect is shown, the court will not closely scrutinize conflicting evidence as to the value of the mortgaged property, but will be satisfied with less convincing proof than usual of the inadequacy of the security.[148]

doctrine has been held elsewhere under a similar statute. We cannot avoid thinking, however, that for us to so hold would be a mere evasion of our statute."

145 Marshall etc. Bank v. Cady, 76 Minn. 112, 78 N. W. 978; National Fire Ins. Co. v. Broadbent, 77 Minn. 175, 79 N. W. 676.

146 Cortleyou v. Hatheway, 11 N. J Eq 39, 64 Am. Dec. 478; Best v. Schermier, 6 N. J. Eq. 154, Frisbie v. Bateman, 24 N. J. Eq. 28; Horner v. Dey, 61 N. J. Eq. 554, 49 Atl. 154.

147 Shepherd v. Pepper, 133 U. S. 626, 10 Sup. Ct. 438, 33 L. ed. 706; American Nat. Bank v. Northwestern Mut. L. Ins. Co., 89 Fed. 610, 32 C. C. A. 275; Eslava v. Crampton, 61 Ala. 507; Jackson v. Hooper, 107 Ala. 634, 18 South. 254; Harris v. United States etc. Inv. Co., 146 Ind. 265, 45 N. E. 328; Philadelphia Mortgage & T. Co. v. Oyler, 61 Neb. 702, 85 N. W. 899; Finch v. Houghton, 19 Wis. 150; Schreiber v. Carey, 48 Wis. 208, 4 N. W. 124; Winkler v. Magdeburg, 100 Wis. 421, 76 N. W. 332.

148 Eslava v. Crampton, 61 Ala. 507; Jackson v. Hooper, 107 Ala 634, 18 South. 254; Winkler v. Magdeburg, 100 Wis. 421, 76 N. W. 332.

In the group of states mentioned in the last section it is held that the statutes abrogating the common-law theory of the mortgage have not abrogated the power to afford such remedies for the protection of the mortgagee's equitable rights as do not rest upon the doctrine of the legal title or right of possession being in the mortgagee.[149]

§ 96. General Considerations Governing the Appointment. A court should not appoint a receiver in a foreclosure action unless the facts establish a case which clearly invokes the exercise of the equitable power of the court to grant that relief; for the right to the rents and profits—in those states at least which have discarded the common-law theory of the mortgage—does not grow directly out of the relation of the parties as a matter of strict right, but is founded upon equitable considerations which address themselves to the sound discretion of the court.[150]

149 Lowell v. Doe, 44 Minn. 144, 46 N. W. 297; Union Mut. Life Ins. Co. v. Union Mills Plaster Co., 37 Fed. 286, 3 L. R. A. 90 In the former case the grounds for the appointment were, in addition to the inadequacy of the security and the insolvency of the mortgagor, non-payment of taxes, probable cancellation of the insurance, and permanent impairment of the value of the property by the cessation of its use for hotel purposes. In the latter case it was held that the mere disuse of a manufacturing plant was not such serious waste as to justify the appointment of a receiver. In South Carolina, the mere non-payment of taxes is not a sufficient ground, where it is not alleged that the security is inadequate, and where the statute provides that the mortgagee may pay the taxes and include the amount in the mortgage debt: Nathans v. Steinmeyer, 57 S. C. 386, 35 S. E. 733

As to the grounds of appointment in New Jersey, see Cortleyou v Hatheway, 11 N. J. Eq. 39, 64 Am. Dec. 478, Mahon v. Crothers, 28 N. J. Eq. 567, Stockman v. Wallis, 30 N. J. Eq. 449; Chetwood v. Coffin, 30 N. J. Eq. 450, Brasted v. Sutton, 30 N. J. Eq. 462.

150 Sales v. Lusk, 60 Wis. 490, 19 N. W 362, citing Syracuse City Bank v. Tallman, 31 Barb. 201, 208; Rider v. Bagley, 84 N Y. 461; Schreiber v. Carey, 48 Wis. 208, 4 N. W. 124.

In an often cited case the rule is laid down in a negative form, that "a receiver in mortgage cases will never be appointed unless it is clearly shown that the security is inadequate, or that the rents and profits have been expressly pledged for the debt, or that there is imminent danger of waste, removal, or destruction of the property. There must be some strong special reason for it."[151] The substance of this rule has been embodied in the statutes of many of the states in a positive form.[152]

Receivers should not be appointed simply because an occasion for their appointment is anticipated or may in the future arise. The occasion must exist when the appointment is made.[153] The insufficiency of the security on which the appointment is grounded must be an insufficiency existing at the time when the application is made or acted on, not merely one that may arise at some future date.[154]

§ 97. **Effect of Stipulations in the Mortgage.**—That a mortgage contains a clause mortgaging the rents and profits as an additional security for the debt does not require the court to appoint a receiver in an action to foreclose the mortgage. Unless the land is inadequate security the appointment of a receiver is an unnecessary annoyance and hardship.[155] It seems, however, that such a clause may cause the court to dispense with proof of the mortgagor's insolvency.[156] In Iowa a difference between the right to the appointment of a receiver under a mortgage which pledges rents and profits,

151 Morrison v. Buckner, Hempst. 442, Fed. Cas. No. 9844.

152 See ante, § 93, note 137.

153 Chaldron Banking Co. v. Mahoney, 43 Neb. 214, 61 N. W. 594.

154 Laune v. Hauser, 58 Neb. 663, 79 N. W. 555.

155 Brick v. Hornbeck, 19 Misc. Rep. (N. Y.) 218, 43 N. Y. Supp. 301.

156 Butler v. Frazer (Sup. Ct.), 57 N. Y. Supp. 900.

and under one that does not, is recognized, and the appointment of a receiver in the former case, on proof of the mortgagor's insolvency and the inadequacy of the security, is said to be a matter of course;[157] but in a later case, where the mortgage gave the mortgagee the right of possession in case of default on the part of the mortgagor, and pledged the rents and profits, such pledge was construed to take effect only in case possession should be taken by the mortgagee, and the appointment of a receiver was held to be unauthorized.[158]

Stipulations in the mortgage providing that the mortgagee may have a receiver of rents and profits on default by the mortgagor have been frequently considered by the inferior courts of New York. It is there held that such a stipulation gives the mortgagee no absolute right to the appointment of a receiver, and will not be enforced when, under all the circumstances, it is inequitable to take the property out of the owner's hands pending the action of foreclosure; but, at the same time, such a clause is entitled to weight, and is to be considered, among other features of the case, in determining the propriety of making such appointment.[159] It will not be enforced when the security is ample.[160]

157 Des Moines Gas Co. v. West, 44 Iowa, 25.

158 Swan v. Mitchell, 82 Iowa, 307, 47 N. W 1042, explained in American Investment Co. v. Farrar, 87 Iowa, 437, 54 N. W. 361.

159 C. B. Keogh Mfg. Co. v. Whiston, 14 N. Y. Supp. 344 (approved in Bagley v. Illinois Trust & Sav. Bank, 199 Ill. 76, 64 N. E. 1085); Eidlitz v. Lancaster, 40 App. Div. 446, 59 N. Y. Supp. 54; Fletcher v. Krupp, 35 App. Div. 586, 55 N. Y. Supp. 146.

160 Degener v. Stiles, 53 Hun, 637, 6 N. Y. Supp. 474; and see Jarvis v. McQuaide, 24 Misc Rep. 17, 53 N. Y. Supp. 97; United States Life Ins. Co. v. Ettinger, 32 Misc. Rep. 378, 66 N. Y. Supp 1. Where the plaintiff's affidavit showed that default had been made in the payment of insurance, taxes, and interest, and stated that he did not believe that the premises afforded adequate security, the stipulation for the appointment of a receiver was properly enforced: Fletcher v. Krupp, 35 App. Div. 586, 55 N. Y. Supp. 146.

In Iowa, it is held that the stipulation is a controlling fact in the case, and will be enforced as the parties intended, even when there is no showing of the insolvency of the party personally liable for the mortgage debt, and the inadequacy of the security is in dispute;[161] but the mortgagee is not entitled to a receiver on an application made at the time of taking judgment, if the agreement therefor contemplated such appointment at the commencement of the action.[162] In Illinois, too, a pledge of the rents and profits, and a stipulation for a receiver to collect and apply them to the payment of the debt and costs, authorizes the appointment of a receiver, without regard to the solvency of the mortgagor; the authority arises from the contract, the express words giving a lien on the rents and profits.[163]

In California, on the other hand, it is held that where a court has no authority under the law to appoint a receiver, such authority cannot be conferred by consent or stipulation of the parties; in such case consent of parties cannot confer jurisdiction upon a court, or impose upon it the duty of taking care of and disposing

161 "We think it is not to be seriously questioned that the court could, by a stipulation of the parties, place the property in the hands of a receiver, to be held under its direction And it seems to us equally clear that the parties could, by contract, when the property was pledged on security, settle the conditions on which it should be preserved and applied. The parties, in making the contract, seem to have been in such doubt, as to the sufficiency of the property as security, as to provide that if proceedings to foreclose should be commenced, a receiver should take the rents and profits, and apply them, and otherwise preserve the property, under the direction of the court. We see nothing in such a contract that is unconscionable or against public policy; nor do we see why it should not be enforced as the parties intended". Hubbell v. Avenue Investment Co, 97 Iowa, 135, 66 N. W. 85.

162 Paine v. McElroy, 73 Iowa, 81, 34 N. W. 615.

163 First Nat. Bank v. Illinois Steel Co., 174 Ill. 140, 51 N. E. 200; Bagley v. Illinois Trust & Sav. Bank, 199 Ill. 76, 64 N. E. 1085.

of the property.[164] In Michigan, also, and in Oregon, such stipulations are held to be contrary to the public policy of those states as expressed in the statutes which secure a mortgagor in his possession until a foreclosure has become absolute.[165]

§ 98. **Time of the Appointment.**—A receiver will not generally be appointed when the mortgage debt is not yet due.[166] When the mortgage debt is only partly due, and the usual grounds for the appointment of a receiver on foreclosure proceedings exist, a receiver of the whole premises may be appointed, provided that the premises are indivisible, or so circumstanced that they must inevitably be sold in one parcel;[167] but where the mortgaged premises are divided into two parcels nearly equal, which can be sold separately without injury to the parties interested, and there is no pledge or specific lien by which the accruing rents of that portion of the premises not yet liable to be sold are constituted a security to the mortgagee for that portion

164 "It might as well be said that in a suit upon a promissory note, or upon any simple contract for the payment of money, a stipulation in the instrument by which the debt was evidenced that the court might appoint a receiver upon suit brought would give jurisdiction to the court to appoint such receiver; or that there could be a specific performance of a contract in any kind of a case because the parties had stipulated for a decree of specific performance": Baker v. Varney, 129 Cal. 564, 79 Am. St. Rep. 140, 62 Pac. 100. The order appointing the receiver in this case, based solely upon the stipulation of the parties in the mortgage, was held to be void and subject to collateral attack. See, also, Scott v. Hotchkiss, 115 Cal. 94, 47 Pac. 45.

165 Hazeltine v. Granger, 44 Mich. 503, 7 N. W. 74; Couper v. Shirley, 75 Fed. 168, 21 C. C. A. 288, affirming s. c., *sub nom.* Thompson v. Shirley, 69 Fed. 484.

166 Bank of Ogdensburgh v. Arnold, 5 Paige, 38; Mayfield v. Wright (Ky.), 54 S. W. 864.

167 Quincy v. Cheeseman, 4 Sandf. Ch. (N. Y.) 405; Hollenbeck v. Donnell, 94 N. Y. 342; Buchanan v. Berkshire etc. Ins. Co., 96 Ind. 510, 527 et seq.

of the mortgage not due, the latter is not entitled to a receivership for the protection of the unmatured portion of the debt, or of that portion of the premises as to which his right to sell has not yet accrued, but only as to one of the parcels.[168]

The question of the appointment of a receiver after the decree of foreclosure, or after the sale under the decree and during the statutory period of redemption, has arisen in a number of the states, and has received very diverse answers. It may be stated as a general rule, that a receiver may be appointed, after judgment and before sale, especially when the sale is delayed for some considerable length of time thereafter;[169] and the denial of a receiver in foreclosure before judgment is

168 Hollenbeck v. Donnell, 94 N. Y. 342.

169 Schreiber v. Carey, 48 Wis. 208, 219, 4 N W. 124, citing Bank v. Tallman, 31 Barb. 201; Smith v. Tiffany, 13 Hun, 671; Astor v. Turner, 11 Paige, 436, 43 Am Dec. 766; Hackett v. Snow, 10 Irish Eq. 220; Cooke v. Gwyn, 3 Atk 690; Thomas v. Davies, 11 Beav. 29. See, also, Brinkman v. Ritzinger, 82 Ind. 358. In the first case the court say: "We think there would be great propriety in many cases in delaying the appointment until after the rights of the parties are fixed by the judgment, and especially so where there is a dispute as to the amount actually due upon the mortgage, or where there is a question as to what real estate the mortgage covers In cases of this kind great injustice might be done by the appointment of a receiver before judgment, whereas after judgment, when the amount of the mortgage claim is fixed, and the property subjected to the payment of the same ascertained, the court is in a much more advantageous position for determining whether equity requires the appointment of a receiver or not." The plaintiff's laches may influence the court to deny his application. Cone v. Combs, 18 Fed. 576, 5 McCrary, 651. When the right to a receiver depended on a stipulation for appointment on commencement of foreclosure, the mortgagee is not entitled to a receiver at the time of taking judgment: Paine v. McElroy, 73 Iowa, 81, 34 N. W. 615. In England, the mortgagee cannot have a receiver after a judgment for foreclosure absolute, the action being at an end; "the plaintiff is, in fact, asking for a receiver order against himself, in respect of the interest which is all vested in him"; Wills v. Luff, L. R. 38 Ch. D. 197.

not a bar to an application for a receiver after judgment.[170] In Nebraska, however, it is held that a receiver is unnecessary, unless an appeal is taken, as the mortgagee may proceed to sell the property in twenty days after the final decree in foreclosure[171]

In several states the owner of the equity of redemption has a right to the possession of the premises until the expiration of a specified time—usually a year—from the date of the foreclosure sale. It is held in Iowa and in California that this right to the possession forbids the appointment of a receiver on the application of the mortgagee who has purchased the premises at the foreclosure sale.[172] In Illinois and Indiana, on the other hand, the question of appointment after sale appears to be governed by much the same considerations as if the application were made at the commencement of the suit. If the property is bid in at the sale for the full amount of the debt, interest and costs, there is no occasion for the appointment or continuance of a

170 Nash v. Meggett, 89 Wis. 486, 61 N. W. 283

171 Chadron Banking Co v. Mahoney, 43 Neb. 214, 61 N W 594. That a receiver is proper after the taking of an appeal, see Eastman v. Cain, 45 Neb 48, 63 N W 127, Philadelphia Mortgage etc. Co v. Goos, 47 Neb. 804, 66 N. W. 843.

172 White v. Griggs, 54 Iowa, 650, 7 N. W. 125, West v. Conant, 100 Cal 231, 34 Pac 705 In the latter case it is held that a statute which entitles the purchaser to receive from the tenant in possession the rents of the property sold on execution, or the value of the use and occupation, during the period for redemption, does not warrant the appointment of a receiver to oust the judgment debtor. Compare the case of Hill v. Taylor, 22 Cal 191, where a receiver was appointed on behalf of the purchaser on foreclosure of the mortgagor's part interest in a gold mine, the mortgagor being insolvent, working the mine and refusing to pay the purchaser his share of the dividends, with a likelihood that the mine would be exhausted before the expiration of the redemption period. In Iowa, a stipulation in the mortgage for the appointment of a receiver during the period for redemption is controlling upon the court Hubbell v. Avenue Inv. Co., 97 Iowa, 135, 66 N W. 85.

receiver.[173] In Illinois, where there is a deficiency decree, the appointment is made on the same grounds as before the decree—viz., the insufficiency of the security and the insolvency of the mortgagor,[174] or a stipulation in the mortgage for such appointment during the period of redemption.[175] In Indiana, similarly, it is held that the redemption statute postpones the time for the ending of the equity of redemption, and gives a year's additional existence to the mortgage lien; and, notwithstanding that the redemption statute is silent as to the judgment debtor's liability for the rents and profits during the year of his occupancy, the mortgage creditor, who has purchased at the foreclosure sale, may, in case of the inadequacy of the security and the insolvency

173 Bogardus v. Moses, 181 Ill 554, 54 N E. 984; Davis v. Dale, 150 Ill. 239, 37 N. E. 215, World Bldg. etc. Co v. Marlin, 151 Ind. 630, 52 N E 198, except where he is appointed or continued for the benefit of a second mortgagee, who is a party to the suit, the amount of the bid being insufficient to satisfy both mortgages: Roach v. Glos, 181 Ill. 440, 54 N. E 1022.

174 First Nat. Bank v. Illinois Steel Co, 174 Ill. 140, 51 N. E. 200; Roach v. Glos, 181 Ill 440, 54 N. E 1022; Christie v Burns, 83 Ill. App. 514; Haas v. Chicago Building Society, 89 Ill. 498, 506. In the last case it was said: "The necessity for the appropriation of the rents to the payment of the mortgage debt may frequently not appear until after both decree and sale. The amount due is often matter of dispute, and can only be determined by the decree, and what the property will sell for can only be ascertained with certainty from the result of the judicial sale. If an appropriation of the rents on the indebtedness is justified by the surrounding facts before sale, we see no good reason why the same and more weighty facts existing after sale may not warrant a similar procedure. The security, plainly, is not exhausted by the sale, for there is a fund included in it which is secondarily liable It is true, the mortgagee has elected to foreclose and sell, but then he has pursued that remedy to the end, and without getting satisfaction of his debt, and he may avail himself of any just and equitable means of collecting the residue."

175 First Nat. Bank v. Illinois Steel Co, 174 Ill 140, 51 N. E. 200; Oakford v. Robinson, 48 Ill. App. 270.

of the debtor, have a receiver to collect and hold the rents and profits, during the year allowed for redemption, of such parts of the land as are in the possession of the mortgagor's tenants.[176]

§ 99. Effect of Assignment of the Mortgaged Premises; of Administration Thereof; and of Homestead Right Therein.— It has been held that if the mortgagee is entitled to a receiver, his right thereto is not affected by the fact that the mortgagor has made an assignment of the property for the benefit of creditors.[177]

It has been held that the administrator of a deceased mortgagor is entitled to no exception in his favor;[178] but in Missouri, where an administrator has taken possession of the intestate's land under an order of the probate court, and his bond secures the faithful application of the rents, the necessity for the appointment of a receiver does not exist, since the property is already *in custodia legis*.[179]

Whether a homestead may ever be placed in the possession of a receiver at the commencement of a suit to foreclose a mortgage thereon is also a question on which

176 Merritt v. Gibson, 129 Ind. 155, 27 N. E. 136, 15 L. R. A. 277, examining Connelly v. Dickson, 76 Ind. 444; Travelers' Ins. Co. v. Brouse, 83 Ind. 62; Sheeks v. Klotz, 84 Ind. 471, and other Indiana cases decided under previous statutes. The principal case contains an interesting and very able discussion of the distinction between an execution sale, and a sale based on a decree foreclosing a mortgage, of the purpose of the redemption statutes, and of their effect upon the right to a receiver.

177 Sweet & Clark Co. v. Union Nat. Bank, 149 Ind. 305, 49 N. E. 159; Bristow v. Home Bldg. Co., 91 Va. 18, 20 S. E. 947; and see Post v. Dorr, 4 Edw. Ch. 412. *Contra*, Seignious v. Pate, 32 S. C. 134, 17 Am. St. Rep. 846, 10 S. E. 880; but the grounds alleged for the appointment in the last case were soon after declared by the same court to be insufficient. Hardin v. Hardin, 34 S. C. 77, 27 Am. St. Rep. 794, 12 S. E. 936.

178 Jacobs v. Gibson, 9 Neb. 380, 2 N. W. 893.

179 St. Louis Nat. Bank v. Field, 156 Mo. 306, 56 S. W. 1095.

the courts are at variance. The question has received a negative answer in Nebraska;[180] while in Minnesota, although in such a case the court should ordinarily require a somewhat stronger showing, yet, when the debtor mortgages his homestead it is held that he subjects the property to all the legal and equitable rights of a mortgagee, among which is the right to have a receiver appointed when necessary to prevent waste or preserve the property.[181]

§ 100. To What the Receiver's Title Extends.—The receiver's title to the rents extends to those, and those only, which accrue after his appointment, or such as have theretofore accrued but have not yet come to the hands of the owner of the equity of redemption or his assignee.[182] He has no title to crops sold on execution

180 "We cannot read into the law the incidental remedies which accompany mortgage liens ordinarily or in general. Any invasion of the homestead right will not be extended beyond the fair, direct import of the enactment by which it may be sought to make it less absolute": Chadron L. & B. Assn. v. Smith, 58 Neb. 469, 78 N. W. 938; Laune v. Hauser, 58 Neb. 663, 79 N W. 555. See, also, Hoge v. Hollister, 8 Baxt. (Tenn.) 533; Nash v. Meggett, 89 Wis. 486, 61 N. W 283 (an order excepting the homestead is proper) It has been held in Nebraska, however, that where the homestead right does not extend to the whole property, and there is no difficulty in separating it, a receiver may be appointed to take charge of the excess: Sanford v. Anderson (Neb.), 95 N W. 632

181 Marshall etc Bank v. Cady, 75 Minn 241, 77 N. W. 831; Lowell v. Doe, 44 Minn. 144, 46 N. W. 297.

182 Lofsky v. Manjer, 3 Sandf Ch (N. Y.) 69, Rider v. Bagley, 84 N. Y. 461; Wyckoff v. Scofield, 98 N. Y. 475, Lawrence v. Conlon, 26 Misc. Rep. 44, 56 N. Y. Supp. 345; Alabama Nat. Bank v. Mary Lee Coal etc. Co, 108 Ala. 288, 19 South. 404; but see Bank of Woodland v. Heron, 120 Cal. 614, 54 Pac. 1006. The mortgagor cannot evade the rule by leasing the premises *pendente lite* for one or more years, and taking payment of the rent in advance; the lessee, in such case, must either surrender or attorn to the receiver, or pay him a reasonable rent for the use of the premises from the date of the appointment: Gaynor v. Blewett, 82 Wis 313, 33 Am. St. Rep 47, 52 N. W. 313. His lien on the rents is superior to the rights of the mortgagor's assignee in bankruptcy Post v. Dorr, 4 Edw. Ch.

against the mortgagor before his appointment.[183] In California it is held that he cannot be directed before the decree of foreclosure to take possession of the crops of the mortgagor upon which the mortgagee has no lien previous to the appointment.[184]

In an action to foreclose a mortgage which covers only the interests of a lessee, it is not competent for the court to appoint a receiver who should represent not only that interest, but also that of the lessor.[185]

§ 101. **Receiver on Application of Junior Mortgagee.**— Where a prior mortgagee is in possession of the mortgaged premises, the court will not, upon the application of a subsequent mortgagee, appoint a receiver, to the prejudice of such prior mortgagee, while anything remains due on his mortgage;[186] but to justify the court's refusal on the ground of the prior mortgagee's possession it must clearly appear that his mortgage has not been fully paid.[187] In case the prior mortgagee has not taken possession, it is well settled that, on a proper showing, the court may appoint a receiver on behalf of a junior mortgagee, without the consent of the prior encumbrancer.[188]

(N. Y.) 412. The propriety of the appointment of the receiver cannot be questioned, in an action by him to recover rents, by one who was a party to the suit in which the receiver was appointed. Goodhue v. Daniels, 54 Iowa, 19, 6 N. W 129.

183 Favorite v. Deardoff, 84 Ind. 555.

184 Locke v. Klunker, 123 Cal. 231, 55 Pac. 993; Bank of Woodland v. Heron, 120 Cal. 614, 52 Pac. 1006; Simpson v. Ferguson, 112 Cal 180, 53 Am. St. Rep. 201, 40 Pac. 104, 44 Pac. 484.

185 Woodward v. Winehill, 14 Wash. 394, 44 Pac. 860.

186 See 27 Am. St. Rep 798; Berney v. Sewell, 1 Jacob & W 647, per Lord Eldon, Rowe v Wood, 2 Jacob & W 553, Codrington v. Parker, 16 Ves. 469; Hiles v. Moore, 15 Beav. 175; Trenton Banking Co. v. Woodruff, 3 N J. Eq. 210.

187 Codrington v. Parker, 16 Ves. 469, Hiles v. Moore, 15 Beav 175.

188 Bryan v Cormick, 1 Cox, 422; Dalmer v. Dashwood, 2 Cox, 378; and cases in the following notes.

The usual grounds for the appointment are, the insolvency of the person liable for the debt, and the insufficiency of the property to secure the plaintiff's mortgage and those prior to it;[189] or in jurisdictions where these are not recognized as sufficient grounds, the additional fact that the owner, who is in possession, refuses to keep down the interest on the first mortgage;[190] or, in New Jersey, the facts that the buildings upon the mortgaged premises have been burned down, and the property generally has been permitted to go to waste, through the fault of the person in possession, or that fraud or bad faith is shown by the misappropriation of the rents and profits.[191]

§ 102. **Same; Right to Rents as Between Prior and Junior Mortgagees.**—It is an established rule that a junior mortgagee, who succeeds in getting a receiver ap-

189 Roach v Glos, 181 Ill. 440, 54 N. E. 1022; Buchanan v. Berkshire etc. Ins. Co., 96 Ind. 510, Pearson v. Kendrick, 74 Miss 235, 21 South 37 (the application of a junior encumbrancer said to staud upon much more favorable grounds than that of first mortgagee), Ecklund v. Willis, 42 Neb. 737, 60 N. W. 1026, Browning v. Stacey, 52 App. Div. 626, 65 N. Y. Supp 203, Fletcher v. Krupp, 35 App Div. 586, 55 N. Y. Supp. 146 In the first case cited, a receiver appointed at the instance of a first mortgagee, after a sale which realized only enough to satisfy the first mortgage, was continued for the collection of rents and profits during the year of redemption, for the benefit of the second mortgagee, and against a purchaser of the equity of redemption.

190 Haugan v. Netland, 51 Minn. 552, 53 N. W. 873, cf. Myton v. Davenport, 51 Iowa, 583, 2 N. W 462. In Wisconsin, it was held, in Sales v. Lusk, 60 Wis. 490, 19 N. W. 362, where the security had not decreased since the mortgage was given, and there was no evidence that the property was being mismanaged by the mortgagor's assignees in possession, that although the mortgagors were non-resident and insolvent, a receiver should not have been appointed upon the application of a plaintiff who sought thereby to intercept the rents and profits and divert them to his own use to the prejudice of the prior mortgagees.

191 Cortelyou v. Hatheway, 11 N. J. Eq. 39, 64 Am. Dec. 478.

pointed, becomes thereby entitled, as against a prior mortgagee, to the rents collected during the appointment, until such prior mortgagee obtains the appointment of a receiver, or the extension of the existing receivership, for his own benefit. This is on the principle that a mortgagee acquires a specific lien upon the rents by obtaining the appointment of a receiver of them, and if he be a second or third encumbrancer, the court will give him the benefit of his superior diligence over his senior in respect to the rents which accrued during the time that the elder mortgagee took no measures to have the receivership extended to his suit and for his benefit.[192] But this exclusive right of a junior mortgagee to the income of a receivership created upon his application is limited to the cases in which either (1) the senior mortgagee was not a party to the action, or, (2) the senior mortgagee being a party, the receiver was appointed for the benefit of the junior mortgagee and the receivership was not extended to the other liens. If (3) the senior mortgagee was a party to the action, and the appointment was general in its nature,

192 Howell v. Ripley, 10 Paige, 43; Post v. Dorr, 4 Edw Ch 412; Ranney v. Peyser, 83 N. Y. 1; Washington Life Ins. Co. v. Fleischauer, 10 Hun, 117, Sanders v. Lord Lisle, 4 Irish Eq. 43; Bank v. Barry, 3 Irish Eq. 443; Lanauze v. Railway Co, 3 Irish Eq. 454; Nesbit v. Wood, 22 Ky. Law Rep. 127, 56 S. W. 714. The prior mortgagee may either have an additional receiver appointed for his own benefit, thus displacing the rights of the receiver previously appointed to the further receipt of rents. Holland Trust Co v. Con. Gas etc. Co, 85 Hun, 455, 32 N. Y. Supp. 830; Hennessy v. Sweeney, 57 N. Y. Supp. 901; or the existing receivership may be extended, on the application of the prior mortgagee: Putnam v. McAllister (Sup. Ct.), 57 N. Y. Supp. 404; Anderson v. Matthews, 8 Wyo. 513, 58 Pac. 898.

In Virginia, the general rule is not followed, but the receiver is regarded as appointed in behalf of all the parties, and must account according to the priorities of the different encumbrances: Beverley v. Brooke, 4 Gratt. 187.

the respective rights to the rents are controlled by the priority of the liens.[193]

§ 103. Receivers in Behalf of Others than Mortgagees.— A receiver will not be appointed, on the application of a mortgagor, against a mortgagee who is in possession by virtue of an agreement with a mortgagor, where the mortgagee practiced no fraud in obtaining possession, and it is undisputed that the mortgagor is indebted to the mortgagee. Waste, alone, by the mortgagee in possession is not a sufficient ground for a receiver in such a case.[194]

The right to have a receiver appointed, in aid of proceedings to foreclose a mortgage, does not rest exclusively with the mortgagee, or his assignee, but may be exercised by any other party to the proceeding, when necessary to protect his interest in the subject-matter of the litigation.[195]

193 Miltenberger v. Railroad Co., 106 U S 286, 307, 1 Sup. Ct. 140, 158, Williamson v. Gerlach, 41 Ohio St. 682; Bank v. Tilden, 66 Hun, 635, 22 N. Y Supp. 11; Cross v. Will Co. Nat Bank, 177 Ill 33, 52 N. E. 322. See, also, New Jersey Title G. & T. Co. v. Cone, 64 N. J. Eq. 45, 53 Atl. 97. *Contra,* that it is immaterial whether the appointment was general: Nesbit v. Wood, 22 Ky. Law Rep. 127, 56 S. W 714.

194 Brundage v Home etc. Loan Assn, 11 Wash 277, 39 Pac 666 For receivers in behalf of judgment creditors of the mortgagor, see *post,* § 107.

195 Main v. Ginthert, 92 Ind. 180 In this case a wife joined her husband in the execution of a mortgage of his lands to secure his debt; and her inchoate interest afterward becoming absolute by reason of a sheriff's sale, according to a statute of the state, it was her right, upon foreclosure of the mortgage, to have the other two-thirds of the land exhausted before resort should be had to her interest. Held, if the two-thirds were insufficient in value to satisfy the mortgage, and her husband was insolvent, she was entitled, pending the suit, to have a receiver appointed of the rents and profits of the two-thirds, so that, if necessary, they might be applied upon the debt. In Philadelphia Mortgage & T. Co. v. Oyler, 61 Neb. 702, 85

§ 104. **Chattel Mortgages.**—A receiver cannot be appointed in behalf of a chattel mortgagee except in a suit to foreclose the mortgage.[196] A receiver was refused on foreclosure of a chattel mortgage where it appeared *prima facie* that the mortgagor was solvent;[197] and where it appeared that, although the mortgagor was insolvent, the security was not being impaired, whether any amount was due was controverted, and the appointment of a receiver would absolutely destroy the value of the property as a newspaper.[198] Danger of the loss or impairment of the mortgaged property is a common ground for a receiver.[199] Attachment and sale thereunder by the unsecured creditors of the mortgaged personalty does not defeat the right of the mortgagee to a receiver of the property;[200] and where a chattel mortgagee filed his bill to foreclose, and an attaching creditor of a person not the mortgagor seized upon the same chattels, and by an auditor offered them for sale, the court not only restrained the attaching creditor from selling, but also appointed a receiver with authority to make a sale, in order to avoid a multiplicity of suits and to preserve the value of the property until the rights of the parties could be determined.[201]

N. W. 899, it was held that a receiver might be appointed on the application of a defendant who was liable for a deficiency judgment, on proper grounds being shown.

196 State v. Union Nat. Bank, 145 Ind. 537, 57 Am. St. Rep. 209, 44 N. E. 585.

197 Stillwell-Bierce etc. Co. v. Williamston etc. Co., 80 Fed. 68.

198 Whitehead v. Hale, 118 N. C. 601, 24 S. E. 360.

199 Valley Nat. Bank v. H. B. Claflin Co, 108 Iowa, 504, 79 N. W. 279 (under the Iowa statute concerning receivers); Maish v. Bird, 59 Iowa, 307, 13 N. W. 298 (same); Logan v. Slade, 28 Fla. 699. 10 South 25.

200 Cooper v. Berney Nat. Bank, 99 Ala. 119, 11 South. 760.

201 Wiedemann v Sann (N. J. Eq), 31 Atl. 211. See, also, Crow v. Red River County Bank, 52 Tex 362.

§ 105. **(4) Suits to Enforce Equitable Liens; Statutory Liens.**—Receivers may be appointed in suits to enforce equitable liens under circumstances similar to those in which they may be appointed in foreclosing mortgages.[202] It has been held, however, that the plaintiff in an action to foreclose a mechanic's lien has no interest in the property, like that of a mortgagee, which entitles him to a receiver of the rents and profits *pendente lite,* in the absence of statutory authority for the appointment.[203] On the other hand, it has been decided that in an action to enforce a statutory lien for machinery furnished to a steamboat, in the absence of special provisions regulating the proceedings, the full equity powers of the court may be invoked, and a receiver appointed to take charge of the property pending the proceedings;[204] and the same is true of an action to enforce a statutory lien of a laborer on an oil-well.[205]

§ 106. **Judgment Creditors' Suits: In General.**—It has been held, in many cases, that in a judgment creditor's suit, on the return of the execution unsatisfied, it is almost a matter of course to appoint a receiver to col-

202 Pom. Eq. Jur., § 1334; Price v. Dowdy, 34 Ark. 285 (inadequacy of the security and insolvency of the mortgagor). Receiver to protect rent charge: Pritchard v. Fleetwood, 1 Mer. 54 Pending a suit to subject a debtor's real estate to the payment of liens upon it, the court may sequester the rents and profits of such real estate, and appoint a receiver for that purpose, whenever it appears that the debtor is insolvent: Ogden v. Chalfant, 32 W. Va. 559, 9 S. E. 879; and see Dunlap v. Hedges, 35 W. Va. 287, 13 S. E. 656.

203 Meyer v Seebald, 11 Abb. Pr., N S., 326, note; Stone v Tyler, 173 Ill. 147, 50 N. E. 688; *contra,* Webb v. Van Zandt, 16 Abb. Pr. 314. By the amendments of 1895 to the mechanic's lien law of Illinois, § 12 (Laws 1895, p 231), a receiver is allowed in such cases, "for the same causes, and for the same purposes, as in cases of foreclosure of mortgages."

204 Washington Iron Works Co. v. Jensen, 3 Wash. 584, 28 Pac. 1019.

205 Gallagher v. Kearns, 27 Hun, 375.

lect and preserve the judgment debtor's property pending the litigation.[206] If the debtor has property, the return of the execution unsatisfied yields the inference that the property will be misapplied; while if there is nothing for the receiver to take, the defendant cannot be injured by the appointment, and the complainant proceeds at the peril of costs.[207] Indeed, it is declared to be the duty of a complainant who has obtained an injunction upon such a bill, restraining the defendant from collecting his debts or disposing of property which might be liable to waste or deterioration, to apply to the court and have a receiver appointed without any unreasonable delay.[208]

It is usually a prerequisite to the filing of a creditor's bill that execution must have been returned unsatisfied upon the plaintiff's judgment; unless the purpose of the suit is merely to set aside a fraudulent conveyance or transfer and thus remove an obstacle which may render the execution inefficient. In the latter case it is usually held sufficient if the plaintiff has proceeded

206 Bloodgood v. Clark, 4 Paige (N. Y.), 574, Osborn v. Heyer, 2 Paige, 343; Fitzburgh v. Everingham, 6 Paige, 29; Bank of Monroe v. Schermerhorn, Clarke Ch. (N. Y.) 214, Lent v McQueen, 15 How. Pr. 313, Gage v. Smith, 79 Ill 219; Lutt v. Grimont, 17 Ill. App. 308, Hirsch v. Israel, 106 Iowa, 498, 76 N. W. 811; Turnbull v. Prentiss Lumber Co., 55 Mich. 587, 21 N. W. 345, Johnson v. Tucker, 2 Tenn. Ch. 398. The court has a broad discretion in the appointment of a receiver in a creditor's suit where an execution has been returned unsatisfied: Bagley & Co. v. Scudden, 66 Mich. 97, 33 N. W. 47; Dutton v. Thomas, 97 Mich. 93, 56 N. W. 229. That the court has authority to appoint a receiver in all cases where it entertains jurisdiction of a creditor's bill, see Livingston v. Swafford Bros. etc Co., 12 Colo. App 331, 56 Pac. 351 That on application for a receiver it cannot go behind the judgment and execution, see Lent v. McQueen, 15 How Pr. (N. Y) 313.

207 Bloodgood v. Clark, 4 Paige, 474; Fitzburgh v. Everingham, 6 Paige, 29, Fuller v. Taylor, 6 N. J. Eq. (2 Halst. Ch.) 301.

208 Osborn v Heyer, 2 Paige, 342; Bloodgood v Clark, 4 Paige, 474; Bank of Monroe v. Schermerhorn, Clarke Ch. 214.

so far in pursuit of his legal remedies as to obtain a lien upon the property.[209] The assertion frequently made, that the creditor must have exhausted his legal remedy before applying for a receiver, must, therefore, be considered in the light of this distinction, and with reference to the facts of the particular case.[210]

Fraudulent assignments by a judgment debtor often afford a ground for the appointment of a receiver in favor of judgment creditors.[211]

The question whether a creditor's suit may be maintained and a receiver appointed against the estate of a decedent in the process of administration is one that has received different answers, varying with the view

209 See *post*, vol. II, chapter on "Creditors' Bills."

210 That a receiver should not be appointed when the plaintiff and the sheriff know of the existence of property subject to execution, and that there was no impediment to the sale, see Congdon v. Lee, 3 Edw. Ch. 304; or when no necessity existed, and no copy of the bill was served upon the defendant. Hart v. Sims, 3 Edw Ch 266; or when execution was not issued to the county of the defendant's residence: Minkler v United States Sheep Co, 4 N. D 507, 62 N. W. 594, 33 L. R. A. 546; Williams v. Hogeboom, 8 Paige, 469. As to receiver of joint property of two defendants on a judgment rendered against one, see Austin v. Figueira, 4 Paige, 56. As to the appointment on return of the execution unsatisfied made before the proper return day, see Williams v. Hubbard, Walk Ch. (Mich) 28.

That a return of the execution unsatisfied is not necessary where the purpose of the suit is to set aside a fraudulent conveyance, see Chautauqua County Bank v. White, 6 N Y 236, 57 Am. Dec 442 For an interpretation, in such cases, of the Iowa statute requiring the applicant to show that "he has a probable right to or interest in the property which is in controversy," see Clark v. Raymond, 86 Iowa, 661, 53 N. W. 354; Hirsch v. Israel, 106 Iowa, 498, 76 N. W. 811.

211 Connah v. Sedgwick, 1 Barb. 210 (insolvency of the assignee a good cause for the appointment of a receiver); Shainwald v. Lewis, 7 Saw. 148, 6 Fed. 766 (an instructive case); Strong v Goldman, 8 Biss. 552, Fed. Cas. No. 13,542, Nat. Bank of the Republic v Hobbs, 118 Fed. 627. That a state of facts which would warrant a receiver in aid of a judgment creditor whose debtor has made a fraudulent conveyance, authorizes the appointment in behalf of a purchaser at sheriff's sale under the judgment, see Mays v. Rose, Freem. Ch. (Miss.) 718.

held in regard to the jurisdiction of equity in matters of administration.[212]

§ 107. **Same; Receiver of Debtor's Property Subject to Prior Mortgage.**—With respect to a receiver of the rents and profits of mortgaged premises belonging to the judgment debtor, the plaintiff in a creditor's suit stands in much the same position as a junior mortgagee. Thus, such a receiver will not be appointed as against a mortgagee in possession, if anything remains due upon his mortgage.[213] But a receiver of the rents and profits of an equity of redemption fraudulently conveyed is proper, where the debtor and his grantee are insolvent;[214] and such a receiver may be appointed where the debtor's property is encumbered by numerous mortgages and judgments whose priorities are to be ascertained, and the real estate is insufficient to pay the indebtedness.[215]

A receiver may be appointed and an injunction granted, in a proper case, to restrain the judgment debtor from selling his goods, notwithstanding a mortgage thereon, not yet due, to another person. Such a bill is sufficient if it alleges that executions upon valid judgments have been levied upon goods in a store; that a sale thereof to satisfy the judgments is sought to be prevented by the holder of a prior mortgage thereon;

212 See Pom Eq Jur., § 1154, Sylvester v. Reed, 3 Edw. Ch. (N. Y) 296, McKaig v James, 66 Md 583, 8 Atl. 663, Davis v. Chapman, 83 Va. 67, 5 Am. St. Rep. 251, 1 S. E. 472, Warfield v. Owens, 4 Gill (Md), 364.

213 Quinn v. Brittain, 3 Edw. Ch. (N. Y.) 314; United States v. Masich, 44 Fed. 10 (the court may issue an injunction in such a case to protect the property and to apply the rents and profits to the satisfaction of the mortgage); Furlong v. Edwards, 3 Md. 79.

214 Freeman v. Stewart, 119 Ala. 158, 24 South. 31.

215 Smith v. Butcher, 28 Gratt. 144; Grantham v. Lucas, 15 W. Va. 425.

that the property is more than sufficient to satisfy the mortgage, and the debtor has no other property; that since the execution of the mortgage, the goods remaining in the possession of the mortgagor, some of them had been sold and other goods substituted in their place, and that if the debtor is allowed to retain the possession of the goods he would so dispose of them that the complainant's claims would be wholly lost.[216]

§ 108. **Same; Nature of the Property as Affecting Appointment—Receiver of Rents.**—The defendant's denial that there is any property to protect is no reason for refusing to appoint a receiver; indeed, the discovery of assets is an important part of the receiver's function.[217]

Where a contest as to the title to real estate is involved in the suit, and a receiver is sought of the rents and profits pending the litigation, the principle which has been mentioned in a previous section comes into play, and the possession of the adverse holder will rarely be disturbed.[218] Thus, where the purpose of the judgment creditor's action is to remove an alleged fraudulent conveyance of real estate, he is not entitled, as against the person claiming the property under the conveyance, to a receiver of the rents and profits *pendente lite,* unless upon a strong case of danger to the property and inability to respond to a decree because of insolvency.[219]

216 Rose v. Bevan, 10 Md 466, 69 Am. Dec. 170.

217 Bloodgood v. Clark, 4 Paige Ch. 574; Fuller v. Taylor, 6 N. J. Eq. 301.

218 See *ante,* § 87.

219 Vause v. Woods, 46 Miss. 120; National Union Bank v. Riger, 38 App Div. 123, 56 N. Y. Supp. 545; Ohlhauser v. Doud, 74 Wis. 400, 43 N. W. 169. In the last case, however, it was held that a receiver was properly appointed for the purpose of taking charge of money substituted for a part of the land by virtue of condemnation proceedings, although the money had been paid to a clerk of court.

Under peculiar circumstances a receiver of rents may be the most effectual means of carrying into effect the decree; as, where a building was erected by the judgment debtor from his individual funds on land occupied by him as a *cestui que trust,* a receiver was appointed to apply the rents on the judgment, and the trustees were enjoined from collecting them.[220]

By the English practice, a receiver of rents of a debtor's real estate might be allowed in the first instance, if the bill claimed satisfaction out of both the personal and real estate of the debtor, and it appeared probable from the defendant's answer that there was no personal estate.[221]

§ 109. **Same; Miscellaneous Cases.**—A receiver has been appointed of a husband's interest in a mercantile business, which he carried on ostensibly as agent for his wife, in order to restrain the disposition of the property, and to subject the property to the payment of a judgment recovered against the husband.[222]

A receiver has been appointed for the purpose of recovering rings and jewelry belonging to the judgment debtor, since these are articles generally worn on the person, and it might be out of the power of the sheriff to levy on, or take possession of them.[223]

It is said that a receiver will not be appointed to take possession of property which, though belonging to the defendant, cannot for any reason be subjected to the complainant's judgment; or for property which, though nominally belonging to defendant, is beneficially owned by third persons, or is encumbered beyond its value. In such a case it can in no sense be said that

220 Johnson v. Woodruff, 8 N. J. Eq. 120.

221 Jones v. Pugh, 8 Ves. 71.

222 Penn v. Whiteheads, 12 Gratt. 74

223 Frazier v. Barnum, 19 N. J. Eq. 316, 97 Am. Dec 666.

such property, or any interest of the defendant therein, is subject to the payment of his debts, or can be reached and applied thereto.[224]

A judgment creditor's bill to reach property or interests unknown to the complainant and perhaps concealed need not point out the specific property sought to be reached.[225]

§ 110. **Receivers in Proceedings Supplementary to Execution.**—Proceedings supplementary to execution being designed to be a substitute for the equity procedure by creditors' bill, receivers are appointed in such proceedings very much as a matter of course, where it appears that the judgment creditor has, or probably has, property that ought to be subjected to the satisfaction of the judgment, after the return of the execution unsatisfied.[226] Probability that the judgment debtor has,

224 McCullough v. Jones, 91 Ala. 186, 8 South. 696.

225 Dutton v. Thomas, 97 Mich 93, 56 N. W. 228.

226 See Hervy v. Gibson, 10 Bosw. (N. Y.) 591, People v Mead, 29 How. Pr. (N Y.) 360; Coates v Wilkes, 92 N. C 376. The last case contains such an excellent statement of the general purpose and character of these proceedings, and of the receivership therein, that I quote at some length: Coates v. Wilkes, 92 N. C. 376, 379-384, per Merrimon, J. "The proceedings supplementary to the execution in an action, as allowed and provided for by the code, §§ 488-500, are mainly, if not altogether, equitable in their nature. While, perhaps, they go beyond in some respects, they are in large part a substitute for, and take the place of the methods of granting relief in equity in favor of a judgment creditor as against his judgment debtor, after he had exhausted his remedy at law by the ordinary process of execution, as these prevailed before the present code system of procedure was adopted: Hasty v. Simpson, 77 N. C. 69; Rand v. Rand, 78 N. C. 12; Hinsdale v. Sinclair, 83 N. C. 338; High on Rec., § 401.

"In the order of procedure, such supplementary proceedings are incident to the action; they extend and enlarge its scope for the purpose of reaching the judgment debtor's property of every kind subject to the payment of his debts, that cannot, for any cause, be successfully reached by the ordinary process of execution, and subjecting or has fraudulently conveyed, such property, is the criterion; certainty or conclusiveness of proof is not

the same, or so much thereof as may be necessary, to the payment of the judgment.

"In effectuating this purpose, it very frequently becomes necessary to grant relief by injunction and the appointment of a receiver, as in other cases. Indeed, a receiver is appointed almost as of course, where it appears that the judgment debtor has, or probably has, property that ought to be so subjected to the satisfaction of the judgment, after the return of the execution unsatisfied. The receivership operates and reaches out in every direction as an equitable execution, and it is the business of the receiver, under the superintendence of the court, to make it effectual by all proper means.

"If it appear that the debtor has funds or property in his own hands, the court may, by proper order, apply the same to the judgment; but if the title to the property alleged or claimed to be that of the debtor, be in dispute, or it be disposed of by the debtor, in fraud of creditors, in such way as that it cannot be promptly reached by execution or the order of the court, then a receiver may be appointed at once. And it is not essential to such appointment that it shall actually appear that the debtor has property; if it appear with reasonable certainty, or that it is probable that he has property that ought to be subjected to the payment of the judgment, a receiver may be appointed: Bloodgood v. Clark, 4 Paige, 574; Osborne v. Hyer, 2 Paige, 342. . . . .

"The judgment debtor cannot complain at the appointment of a receiver. If he has property subject to the payment of his debt, it ought to be applied to it; if he has not such property, this fact ought to appear, with reasonable certainty, to the satisfaction of the creditor. The receiver proceeds to do this, not at the peril of the debtor, but at his own peril, as to costs, if he fails in his action The purpose of the law, in such proceedings, is to afford the largest and most thorough means of scrutiny, legal and equitable, in their character, in reaching such property as the debtor has, that ought justly to go to the discharge of the debt his creditor has against him. . . . .

"It was not necessary, indeed, not proper, under the circumstances of this case, for the court to find *conclusively*, whether or not the defendant had certainly made a disposition of his property, fraudulent as to his creditors. If there was evidence tending strongly to show such a disposition of it, or that he was refusing, covertly or otherwise, to apply his property to the judgment, this was sufficient to warrant the appointment of a receiver, to the end that he might take such steps, and, if need be, bring such actions as would enable him to secure and recover any property of the defendant so required in order to justify the appointment.[227] The defendant's denial of the ownership of property, or his debtor's denial of the existence of an alleged claim, is not conclusive in this matter, but the contrary may be made to appear by other witnesses, and a receiver may be appointed on their testimony.[228] Further, if it appear that the judgment debtor has real estate that is subject to sale under execution, and that there are no obstacles to hinder such sale, a receiver will be refused, in many states, in order that his statutory right of redemption may not be imperiled.[229] Subject to these

conveyed or withheld by him, to be applied to the judgment of the plaintiff. To warrant the appointment of a receiver, it need not appear, certainly or conclusively, that the defendant has property that he ought to apply to the judgment—if there is evidence tending in a reasonable degree to show that he probably has such property, this is sufficient, or if it appears probable that he has made a fraudulent conveyance of his property as to his creditors, this is sufficient."

227 Coate v. Wilkes, 92 N. C. 376, 384. "The discretion to appoint a receiver is legal, not arbitrary. The judge cannot lawfully refuse to appoint a receiver if there be presented to him competent evidence of assets"; Wilkinson v. Market, 65 N. J. L. 518, 47 Atl. 488. On the other hand, when it does not appear probable that the judgment debtor has any property, rights or credits as to which a receiver is required, the appointment will be refused: Rodman v. Harvey, 102 N. C. 1, 8 S. E. 888; Adler v. Turnbull, 57 N. J. L. 62, 30 Atl. 319; Colton v. Bigelow, 41 N. J. L 266 "Mere suspicion or surmise falls far short of what is required to justify the exercise of a power which should be sparingly used": Flint v. Zimmerman, 70 Minn 346, 73 N. W. 175.

228 Seyfert v. Edison, 47 N. J. L. 428, 1 Atl. 502, Colton v. Bigelow, 47 N. J. L. 428, 1 Atl. 502; Knight v. Nash, 22 Minn. 452.

229 Bunn v. Daly, 24 Hun, 526; Second Ward Bank v. Upmann, 12 Wis. 499, but see Bailey v. Lane, 15 Abb. Pr 373, note; and Dilling v. Foster, 21 S. C. 334. In the last case it was held that although the examination disclosed property subject to execution in the debtor's hands, sufficient to satisfy the judgment, a receiver might nevertheless be appointed; that the rule prohibiting the appointment in such cases, in creditor's bills, depended on the fact that equity and law were administered by different tribunals; and as the powers of the court of equity were only invoked in aid of the law

restrictions the appointment is usually spoken of as a matter of sound legal discretion,[230] a power to be exercised only with caution and in the absence of other adequate remedies available to the creditor.[231]

§ 111. **(5) In Suits for Specific Performance, or to Enforce Vendor's Lien.**—A receiver may be appointed in a suit by a vendor to enforce the specific performance of a contract for the sale of land against a vendee who is

court, such powers were not exercised where such aid was not necessary.

230 See Wilkinson v. Markert, 65 N. J. L. 518, 47 Atl 488; Flint v. Webb, 25 Minn. 263; Bean v. Heron, 65 Minn. 64, 67 N W. 805; Flint v. Zimmerman, 70 Minn. 346, 73 N. W. 175; Poppitz v. Rognes, 76 Minn. 109, 78 N. W. 964. "That a receiver may, in the discretion of the court, be appointed immediately upon granting the order for the examination, there can be no doubt, and such, it seems, is the safer and better practice, inasmuch as it effectually secures to the prosecuting creditor that priority upon his debtor's property which his vigilance justly entitles him to"; citing Hervy v. Gibson, 10 Bosw. (N. Y.) 591, and People v. Mead, 29 How. Pr. (N. Y.) 360.

231 "The mere fact that upon a debtor's examination property is disclosed which may be subjected to the satisfaction of the creditor's judgment does not necessarily entitle the latter, as a matter of right, to have a receiver appointed. . . . It is against the general policy of the law to permit a creditor to resort to it [receivership] where he has other adequate remedy": Poppitz v. Rognes, 76 Minn. 109, 78 N. W. 964. "Equitable principles, which are always very flexible, should be taken into account in determining whether a receiver should be appointed. A receivership, the costs of which have to be paid, if any property is reached, out of the debtor's estate, is a very drastic remedy, and is subject to great abuses. At the present day it unfortunately is often more beneficial to the receiver and his attorneys than to the creditor. It should, therefore, be resorted to with great caution, and sparingly. When it clearly appears that a creditor holds mortgage security ample to satisfy his whole debt, his application for a receiver of his debtor's property ought, ordinarily, to be denied. In such a case it would be an abuse of judicial discretion to appoint one, unless, possibly, there were some exceptional circumstances." Such circumstances were held to be present, and the appointment was held not to be an abuse of discretion, although the judgment creditor had not exhausted his mortgage security: Bean v. Heron, 65 Minn. 64, 67 N. W. 805.

in possession, under the same circumstances as in a suit by a mortgagee for foreclosure of his mortgage; viz., when the land is a doubtful or inadequate security, and the vendee is insolvent, or committing waste;[232] and the same rule generally holds true in suits by a vendor who has retained the legal title to foreclose his (so-called) "vendor's lien" by a sale of the property for the unpaid purchase-money.[233] In some states, however, a stronger showing is required, and waste, threatened or committed by the vendee, or bad husbandry, impairing the value of the vendor's security, is essential as a foundation for the relief.[234] In England, a re-

232 Pom. Eq. Jur., § 1334, Phillips v Eiland, 52 Miss. 721; and see Tufts v. Little, 56 Ga. 139; Gunley v. Thompson, 56 Ga. 316; Chappell v. Boyd, 56 Ga. 578; Hall v. Jenkinson, 2 Ves. & B. 125 (vendee insolvent and attempting to convey his estate for the benefit of creditors); Boehm v. Wood, 2 Jacob & W. 236 (receiver pending a reference as to the validity of the plaintiff's title).

233 See Smith v. Kelley, 31 Hun, 387; Belding v. Meloche, 113 Mich. 223, 71 N. W. 592 (relief awarded to a vendor under circumstances where it would be refused to a mortgagee); McCaslin v. State, 44 Ind. 151, 174 (insolvency of vendee, and waste by cutting valuable timber); Cotulla v. American Freehold L. M Co. (Tex. Civ. App.), 86 S. W. 339 (by statute); Hughes v. Hatchett, 55 Ala. 631 (relief refused, where insolvency of vendee not shown, and amount of indebtedness disputed). In Belding v. Meloche, *supra*, it was held that the decision in Wagar v. Stone, 36 Mich. 364, in which a receiver was refused in a suit by a mortgagee, on account of the statute whereby the mortgagor is entitled to possession until after foreclosure, did not apply to the case of foreclosure of a land contract, wherein it was agreed that in case of default the vendor should be entitled to possession.

234 See Columbia Finance etc. Co. v. Morgan, 19 Ky. Law Rep. 1761, 44 S. W. 389, 45 S. W. 65; Collins v. Richart, 14 Bush (Ky), 621. In Georgia, a bill alleging the insolvency of the vendee, and the deterioration in value of the land, but not showing that the vendee is less able to pay when the debt matured than when it was incurred, or that the deterioration is due to the vendee's waste or mismanagement, makes no case for a receiver of the rents and profits of the premises: Turnlin v. Vanhorn, 77 Ga. 315, 3 S. E. 264. As to receiver in foreclosure of the vendor's lien in Tennessee, see Morford v. Hamner, 3 Baxt. 391; Darusmont v. Patton, 4 Lea, 597.

ceiver may be allowed in a suit to enforce a vendor's lien for land sold to an insolvent railway company, after, but not before, a final decree.[235] A receiver to secure the property has occasionally been appointed in a suit for specific performance instituted by the vendee.[236]

§ 112. (6) **In Behalf of Unsecured Creditors Before Judgment.**—It is the almost universal rule that a creditor's bill, whether to set aside a fraudulent transfer or to reach equitable assets, will not lie in behalf of mere general creditors who have not prosecuted their claims to judgment, nor in any other manner acquired a lien upon the debtor's property. The slowness and inadequacy of the legal remedies open to such creditors are not considerations that can move a court of equity, in the absence of statutory authority, to intervene in their behalf with the instrumentality of a receiver, to preserve the debtor's property.[237] An apparent exception

235 Munns v. Isle of Wight R. Co, L. R. 5 Ch. 414; Latimer v. Aylesbury & B. Ry. Co., L R. 9 Ch. D. 385.

236 Where the vendor has fraudulently repossessed himself of the property: Dawson v. Yates, 1 Beav. 301; in an action for the specific performance of a contract to assign a lease giving the right to sink or bore for oil, receiver to operate oil-wells, pending the action, is authorized, where the defendant, a non-resident without property in the state, except the machinery on the land, is operating the wells and selling the product: Galloway v. Campbell, 142 Ind. 324, 41 N. E. 597. See, also, Mead v. Burk, 156 Ind. 577, 60 N. E. 338 But in a suit to enforce an oral contract between father and son, whereby the son was to have the father's land on the death of the latter, in consideration of his agreement to support the father, it was improper to appoint a receiver of the land on the death of the son before full performance on his part: Walters v. Walters, 132 Ill. 467, 23 N. E 1120.

237 Wiggins v. Armstrong, 2 Johns. Ch. 144; Uhl v. Dillon, 10 Md. 500, 69 Am. Dec. 172; Oberholser v. Greenfield, 47 Ga. 530; Kehler v. G. W. Jack Mfg. Co., 55 Ga 639; Johnson v. Farnum, 56 Ga. 144; Mayer v. Wood, 56 Ga. 427, 429; Stillwell v. Savannah Grocery Co.,

to the rule has been established by a series of cases in Georgia, where an insolvent debtor, with fraudulent intent, has bought goods on credit from the plaintiff, and afterwards has made a fraudulent transfer of his

88 Ga. 100, 13 S. E 963; Turnipseed v. Kentucky Wagon Co, 97 Ga. 258, 23 S E. 84; Blondheim v. Moore, 11 Md. 365; Hubbard v. Hubbard, 14 Md. 356; Carter v Hightower, 79 Tex 135, 15 S W 223; Cahn v. Johnson, 12 Tex. Civ. App 304, 33 S. W. 1000; Waples-Platter Co. v. Mitchell, 12 Tex. Civ. App 90, 35 S. W. 200. Uhl v. Dillon, *supra*, was a bill by general creditors for injunction and receiver, alleging that the defendant was indebted to the complainants, that he was disposing of his property, collecting money due him, and secreting his money and property, with the intent, as complainants were informed and believed, to abscond and defraud them. The court says, in part, by Bartol, J.: "Whatever may be the supposed defects of the existing laws of the state, in leaving to the debtor the absolute power of disposing of his property, and leaving the creditor to the slow and very inadequate legal remedies now provided, it is solely in the power of the legislature to correct them. It is not within the province of the chancery courts to stretch their power beyond the limits of the authorities of the law, for the purpose of remedying such defects. Such a course would be productive of great mischief, and make the rights of the citizen depend upon the vague and uncertain discretion of the judges, instead of the safe and well-defined rules of law." Possible exceptions to the rule may be found in Haggarty v. Pittman, 1 Paige, 298, 19 Am. Dec. 434 (fraudulent assignment to an insolvent assignee); Rosenberg v. Moore, 11 Md. 376 (objection that plaintiff had no judgment not urged).

In Aid of Attachment.—A receiver is not warranted in an action on a simple money demand, in which action property has been attached. The fact that a writ of attachment was issued does not change the nature of the action to one for the relief of "subjecting a fund to the plaintiff's claim," within the meaning of the statute authorizing a receiver in an action "by a creditor to subject any property or fund to his claim"; nor do writs of attachment issued by two creditors on simple money demands convert the action into one "between partners or others jointly owning or interested in any property or fund," under another clause of the same statute: State v. Eighth Judicial Dist. Ct., 14 Mont. 577, 37 Pac. 969. But it has been held that the court possesses the power, independently of statute, to appoint a receiver to take charge of property abandoned by a garnishee· Northfield Knife Co. v. Shapleigh, 24 Neb. 635, 8 Am. St. Rep. 224, 39 S. W. 788.

goods to a third person, who is himself insolvent; but the defrauded creditor's right to the equitable relief of a receiver is strictly limited to these circumstances, and is based on the ground that the plaintiff, having a right to rescind the fraudulent sale, had never, in equity, parted with the title to the goods.[238] The right of a creditor without judgment, depending on the general jurisdiction of equity in the administration of the estates of decedents, to come into equity to subject to his demand property fraudulently conveyed by the debtor while in life, there being a deficiency of legal assets, is recognized in some states;[239] and a receiver may be necessary, in such a suit.[240] A further exception has been made in New York, in the case of the creditor, without judgment, of a partnership, suing on behalf of himself and for the benefit of other creditors, where the indebtedness is not disputed, and the firm and its members are insolvent, and have attempted to make a fraudulent assignment of their property.[241] Statutes

238 Cohen v. Meyers, 42 Ga. 46; Johnson v. Farnum, 56 Ga. 144 (relief denied when plaintiff does not claim title to the goods, or right to rescind the sale); Mayer v. Wood, 56 Ga. 427, 429 (same); Wachtel v. Wilde, 58 Ga. 50, Cohen & Co. v. Morris & Co, 70 Ga. 313; Albany etc. Steel Co. v. Southern etc. Works, 76 Ga. 135, 2 Am St. Rep. 26, Wolfe v. Claflin, 81 Ga. 64, 6 S. E. 599; Martin v. Burgyn, 88 Ga. 78, 13 S. E. 958. But the appointment of a receiver is erroneous where it appears that the person to whom the alleged fraudulent transfer was made is solvent and able to respond to a judgment in favor of the plaintiff: Turnipseed v. Kentucky Wagon Co, 97 Ga. 258, 23 S. E. 84; Stillwell v. Savannah Grocery Co., 88 Ga. 100, 13 S. E. 963, and where, under the order of the judge, the plaintiffs had pointed out and separated the goods in question, there should be no receiver appointed except for the purpose of taking charge of the goods so identified; Atlantic Brew. etc. Co. v. Bluthenthal, 101 Ga. 541, 28 S. E. 1003.

239 See Pom. Eq. Jur, § 1154, and note.

240 See Werborn's Admr. v. Kahn, 93 Ala. 201, 9 South. 729.

241 Mott v. Dunn, 10 How Pr. 225; La Claire v. Lord, 10 How. Pr. 461, Levy v. Ely, 15 How. Pr 395; Jackson v Sheldon, 9 Abb. Pr. 127; and see Cohen & Co v. Morris & Co., 70 Ga. 313. Jackson

in several of the states now provide for creditor's bills by general, unsecured creditors in certain exigencies, and the right to receivers in such suits has received much consideration in at least two of these states.[242]

v. Sheldon was a case of limited partnership, and relief was based upon the neglect of the partners to assign to a trustee for the benefit of all the partnership creditors

242 **Alabama.**—Complainants, on filing their bill and service of process, acquire an inchoate lien on the property fraudulently conveyed, and are entitled to a receiver upon showing three things; namely, a reasonable probability of success upon their part in finally subjecting the property to the satisfaction of their lien; a necessity of resorting to the property to make their debts; and a danger that the property will be wasted, disposed of, or gotten out of the reach of the court so that the lien cannot be effectuated: Heard v. Murray, 93 Ala. 127, 9 South. 514; Weis v. Goetter, 72 Ala. 259 A pending suit by creditors for the benefit of all who may join is no bar to a subsequent suit by a simple contract creditor averring the collusive action of parties to the former suit and asking the removal of a receiver appointed thereunder, and that the custody already assumed by the court may be extended to his own case: Alabama etc. Steel Co. v. McKeever, 112 Ala. 134, 20 South. 84. The creditor's remedy by attachment is usually adequate, "it affords as ample redress and protection, in ordinary cases, as a receivership, fully securing the forthcoming of the property to answer any judgment obtained in the attachment suit, if found liable to the attachment": Pearce v. Jennings, 94 Ala. 524, 10 South. 511; hence, when an attachment has been levied on personalty, a receiver will not be appointed in aid of the suit, unless special circumstances are shown rendering the attachment inadequate and inefficacious: Id; and a debtor's threatened removal of his property from the state, while authorizing an attachment by the creditor, does not entitle the latter to the aid of a court of equity, or the appointment of a receiver: Smith-Dimmick Lumber Co. v. Teague, 119 Ala. 385, 24 South. 4. When property of the debtor has been attached, and the statutory claim interposed, it is in the custody of the law, and should not be taken away from such custody and placed in the hands of a receiver, at the suit of another creditor: Dollins v. Lindsay, 89 Ala. 217, 7 South. 234; Williams v. Dismukes, 106 Ala. 402, 17 South. 620, but a receiver may be had of the surplus of the goods over the amount of the prior equitable attachment creditor's claim. Sackhoff v. Vandegrift, 98 Ala. 192, 13 South. 495.

Georgia.—"Insolvent Trader's Law," Stats. 1881, p. 124; Code, § 3297; § 3149, etc. To warrant a receiver at the suit of a general

§ 113. (7) Receiver in Suits for Rescission of Contracts for Sale of Land.—A receiver may be appointed, under special circumstances, in a suit by a vendee of land for

creditor, it must appear that the debtor is insolvent: Collins v. Myers, 68 Ga. 530, and that his effects will not be exhausted by other creditors having liens, before the simple contract creditors will be reached in the order of distribution: Id.; Barnwell v. Wofford, 67 Ga. 50. See, further, as to the right to a receiver under these statutes, Fechheimer v. Baum, 37 Fed. 167, 2 L. R. A. 153; Nussbaum v. Price, 80 Ga. 205, 5 S E. 291; Pendleton v. Johnson, 85 Ga. 840, 11 S. E. 144; Sullivan v McDonald, 86 Ga. 78, 12 S. E. 215; Stillwell v. Savannah Grocery Co., 88 Ga. 100, 13 S. E. 963; Atlanta Brewing Co. v. Bluthental, 101 Ga. 541, 28 S. E. 1003. Receiver in aid of creditors having laborers' liens, before judgment, where the plaintiffs are numerous, the defendants insolvent, and there is "manifest danger of loss" (Code, § 3149) by removal of the property from the state Orton v. Madden, 75 Ga 83.

Michigan.—3 How. Ann Stats., § 8749 (o), providing that a person having a preferred labor claim against an insolvent person or corporation may proceed in chancery for appointment of a receiver, if an assignment for the benefit of creditors has been made. A chattel mortgage is not such an assignment, within the meaning of the statute: Wineman v Fisher Electrical Works, 118 Mich. 636, 77 N. W. 245. An order appointing a receiver of assets of an insolvent debtor, upon a bill by holders of preferred claims, and requiring an attachment creditor to surrender to him property held by virtue of his writ, is improvidently made: Lawton v. Richardson, 115 Mich. 12, 72 N. W 988. See, also, Hall v. Donovan, 111 Mich. 395, 69 N. W. 643.

Minnesota.—Laws 1881, chapter 148, Amend. chap. 30, Laws 1889. As to receivers under the insolvency act of this state, see Hyde v. Weitzner, 45 Minn. 35, 47 N. W. 311 (assignee for benefit of creditors treated as an officer of the court, and receiver refused), Citizens' Nat. Bank v Minge, 49 Minn. 454, 52 N. W. 44 (creditor's claim need not be due, to qualify him to institute proceedings for a receiver); Rollins v. Rice, 60 Minn. 358, 62 N. W. 325.

Rhode Island.—Pub. Laws, c. 723, § 2. Receiver on petition of creditors of insolvent who has made an assignment giving illegal preferences: See Bank of America, Petitioner, 13 R. I. 176.

South Carolina.—Statute authorizing creditors without judgment to attack a voluntary assignment giving preference to creditors. It is error to appoint a receiver when it is not alleged that there was any danger of loss or injury to the property during litigation: Pelzer v. Hughes, 27 S. C. 408, 3 S. E. 781.

rescission of the contract of purchase.[243] It has been held improper to appoint a receiver pending an action to rescind the contract of sale at the instance of the vendor, on the mere ground of the insolvency of the vendee in possession.[244]

§ 114. (8) Receivers in Suits to Enforce Payment of Annuities.—Receivers have sometimes been appointed in suits to enforce payment of the arrears of annuities charged upon land;[245] but in England this relief is given only when the payment cannot be enforced by distress.[246]

§ 115. (9) Receivers in Suits for the Protection of Remainder-men.—If a life tenant neglects or refuses to

Washington.—Code, § 302, allows a receiver at any time for attached property "according to the nature of the property and the exigencies of the case." A receiver is proper when the property "was of such a character that its value would be diminished by mere lapse of time, and that an early sale thereof was desirable": State v. Superior Court of Whatcom County, 14 Wash. 324, 44 Pac. 542.

243 Pom. Eq. Jur., § 1334. The court, in such a suit, has power to appoint a receiver to preserve and retain the purchase money until the rights of the parties are adjudicated· Loaiza v. Superior Court, 85 Cal. 11, 20 Am. St. Rep. 197, 9 L. R. A 376, 24 Pac. 707. A receiver was appointed in an action by the purchasers of a colliery to set aside the sale for fraudulent representations, the ownership being involved in great uncertainty, and it being of great importance that the colliery should be worked, and so worked as to leave as little doubt as possible whether it was properly or improperly worked: Gibbs v. David, L. R. 20 Eq. 373.

244 Jordan v. Beal, 51 Ga. 602. But in England, a receiver has been appointed on the application of the vendor of a leasehold, to preserve the lease from forfeiture for nonpayment of rent by the vendee. Cook v. Andrews, [1897] 1 Ch. 266.

245 Sollory v. Leaver, L. R. 9 Eq. 22; Probasco v. Probasco, 30 N. J. Eq. 108; Abernathy v. Orton, 42 Or. 437, 95 Am. St. Rep. 774, 71 Pac. 327, Pom. Eq. Jur., § 1334. Receiver to enforce agreement to support grantor from the proceeds of propery conveyed: See, *ante*, § 74, note 40; Keister v. Cubine, 101 Va. 768, 45 S. E. 285

246 Sollory v. Leaver, *supra;* Buxton v. Monkhouse, Coop. 41.

keep down the taxes or to make such repairs as he is legally bound to make, a receiver may be appointed, at the instance of the remainder-man, to collect rents sufficient to discharge these liabilities of the life tenant's estate.[247] So, when a life tenant of leasehold premises is allowed by the trustees of the premises to receive the rents, and the houses are not kept in a proper state of repair to prevent a forfeiture according to the covenants of the lease, a receiver may be appointed of the rents, for the purpose of applying them to the proper repair of the houses.[248]

§ 116. (10) Appointment of Receivers of Corporations—The Inherent Jurisdiction of Equity—In General.—The inherent jurisdiction of a court of equity to appoint receivers of corporations, in proper cases, independently of statutory authorization, has been frequently recognized.[249] The cases in which the power is most frequently invoked are as follows:[250] 1. In suits by stock-

247 Cairns v. Chabert, 3 Edw. Ch. 312, Sage v. Gloversville, 43 App. Div. 245, 60 N. Y. Supp. 791; Goodman v. Malcom, 5 Kan. App. 285, 48 Pac. 439; St. Paul Trust Co. v. Mintzer, 65 Minn. 124, 60 Am. St Rep. 444, 67 N. W. 657, 32 L. R. A. 756 (appointed at the instance of executor authorized by the express terms of the will to collect rents and pay taxes); Murch v. Smith Mfg. Co., 47 N. J. Eq. 193, 20 Atl. 213 But in Michigan such appointment is held to be improper under the method of enforcing the payment of unpaid taxes upon real estate and foreclosing liens in that state: Jenks v. Horton, 96 Mich. 13, 55 N. W. 372.

248 In re Fowler, L. R. 16 Ch. D. 723.

249 See Thompson v. Greeley, 107 Mo. 577, criticising the statements on this subject of certain text-books on receivers; Ford v. Kansas City etc. Ry. Co., 52 Mo. App. 439; Matter of Louisiana Savings Bank, 35 La. Ann. 196, criticising Baker v. Louisiana etc. R. R. Co., 34 La. Ann. 754, where a sweeping denial of the existence of the jurisdiction, except in cases of extreme necessity, was made.

250 The supreme court of Louisiana says of the practice in that state that it "had not proceeded further, and should not, without legislative enactment, proceed further, than in making such appointment in cases where the parties litigant agree that it be done, or

holders seeking a remedy for breaches of their fiduciary duty by the directors or officers of the corporation; 2. After dissolution, where no means are provided by statute or otherwise for winding up the affairs of the corporation; 3. When the corporation has no properly constituted governing body, or there are such dissensions in its governing body as to make it impossible for the corporation to carry on its business with advantage; 4. In suits by judgment creditors of the corporation; 5. In suits for the foreclosure of mortgages or other liens upon the corporate property.[251]

Insolvency of the corporation, alone, does not warrant the appointment of a receiver,[252] unless this has been made a ground by statute.

The object of the appointment of a receiver of a corporation is the preservation of its property for the benefit of persons interested, and not the confiscation of the property.[253]

when it is necessary to the execution of a judgment of the court, or in a case where, the property in controversy being under seizure by a writ of the court and in custody, it is necessary as a conservatory process to care for or administer the same, or where the property of a corporation is abandoned, or there are no persons authorized to take charge of and conduct its affairs, or where it is done in aid of proceedings pending before the court for the liquidation of the affairs of a corporation, and rendered necessary for the preservation of the interests of all concerned'': In re Moss Cigar Co., 50 La. Ann. 789, 23 South. 544.

251 That it is improper to appoint a receiver merely for the purpose of representing the corporation in litigation, see Hutchinson v. American Palace-Car Co., 104 Fed. 182.

252 McGeorge v. Big Stone Gap Imp. Co, 57 Fed. 262; Lawrence Iron Works Co. v. Rockbridge Co., 47 Fed. 755; Murray v. Superior Court, 129 Cal. 628, 62 Pac. 191. See, also, Falmouth Bank v. Cape Cod Ship Canal Co., 166 Mass. 550, 44 N. E. 617; Pond v. Framingham & Lowell R. Co., 130 Mass. 194.

253 See Havemeyer v. Superior Court, 84 Cal. 327, 18 Am. St. Rep. 192, 24 Pac. 121. This principle seems clearly to have been disregarded in an Indiana case (Columbia Athletic Club v. State, 143 Ind. 98, 52 Am. St. Rep. 407, 40 N. E. 914, 28 L. R. A. 727), where a

§ 117. **Receivers of Corporations Cautiously Appointed.**—The reasons for the oft-asserted reluctance of the court to assume the responsibilities involved in the appointment of receivers of corporations are well stated in the following extracts: "As a rule of equity practice, the courts are very reluctant to appoint receivers [of the property of corporations], upon the idea that it is a practical displacement of the board of directors. It is an assumption of the function of the directors. It displaces the board of managers placed there by the stockholders, who sustain the relation of trustees for the stockholders, trustees for the corporation, and trustees for its creditors; and before the court will take charge of the corporation and thus displace its chosen directors and managers, it ought to have the clearest evidence of the absolute necessity for such extraordinary action for the protection of the creditors, stockholders, and all parties concerned."[254] "It is no slight matter for a court of chancery to lay its hand upon large business enterprises, take them out of the control of capacity and experience, and charge them with expenses and commissions It should only be done when the court can point to the specific allegation or

receiver was appointed to render more effectual an injunction restraining the continuance of a nuisance—viz., giving exhibitions of prize-fighting—by a corporation. The dissenting opinion of Hackney, J, points out that while the injunction was properly issued, the appointment of a receiver for the purpose merely of staying the commission of crime is entirely without precedent; and that the object sought might have been reached by enlarging the scope of the injunction. However, the fact that the relief was based, in part, on the broad terms of the Indiana statute (Rev. Stats. 1894, § 1236; Rev Stats 1881, § 1222) authorizing a receivership when "in the discretion of the court, it may be necessary to secure ample justice to the parties," probably destroys whatever general value as a precedent this case might possess.

254 Consolidated Tank Line Co. v. Consolidated Varnish Co., 43 Fed. 204.

allegations, sustained by credible evidence, that will justify such action."[255]

The relief cannot be granted on the strength of mere general averments of fraud, when that is the ground

[255] Young v. Rutan, 69 Ill. App. 513. "Courts proceed with extreme caution in the appointment of receivers to take the property of a corporation out of the control of its officers, and are much more readily moved to, by proper orders, restrain the doing of improper acts, and compel the recognition of undoubted rights": Original Vienna Bakery etc. Co. v. Heissler, 50 Ill. App. 406. Before a court "will take the property and business of a liquidating bank from the control of its directors into its own hands, on the application of a stockholder, it must appear that the danger of loss or injury to the rights of the plaintiff is clearly proved, and the necessity and right of appointment of a receiver free from reasonable doubt": Watkins v. National Bank, 51 Kan 254, 32 Pac. 914. "The power is a discretionary one, to be exercised with great circumspection, and only in cases where there is fraud or spoliation, or imminent danger of the loss of the property, if the immediate possession should not be taken by the court; and these facts must be clearly proved But, where these conditions have been fully met, courts do not hesitate to appoint receivers over the property of corporations, for the benefit of all concerned during the controversy": Davis v. United States Electric etc. Co, 77 Md. 35, 25 Atl. 982; Steinberger v. Independent Sav. Assn., 84 Md. 625, 36 Atl. 439. See, also, Thompson v. Greeley, 107 Mo. 577, 17 S. W. 962; People's Investment Co. v Crawford (Tex. Civ. App.), 45 S W. 738. "Cessation of business, alone, does not make a fit case for the appointment of a receiver of the remaining assets of the company; it must be shown, in addition, that the officers have been guilty of mismanagement of its affairs, or that there exists some need to preserve the property, through a receivership, for the benefit of the creditors and stockholders": Clark v. National Linseed Oil Co, 105 Fed. 787, 792, 45 C. C. A. 53. "Undoubtedly, there are cases in which a court of equity may, through its receiver, take possession and control of the business of corporations and individuals But it is a jurisdiction to be sparingly exercised None of the prerogatives of a court of equity have been pushed to such extreme limits as this, and there is none so likely to lead to abuses It is not the province of a court of equity to take possession of the property, and conduct the business of corporations or individuals, except where the exercise of such extraordinary jurisdiction is indispensably necessary to save or protect some clear right of a suitor, which would otherwise be lost or greatly endangered, and which cannot be saved or protected by any other action or mode of proceeding". Overton v. Memphis etc. R. R. Co., 10 Fed. 866, 3 McCrary, 436.

on which the relief is asked. The conduct and facts from which the conclusion is deduced must be averred, so that issue can be formed on the averments.[256]

§ 118. A Receiver is an Ancillary Remedy; not Appointed on the Petition of the Corporation.—Unless authorized by statute, there is no such thing as an action brought distinctively for the mere appointment of a receiver; to justify the appointment it is essential that some proper final relief in equity be asked for in the bill which will justify the court in proceeding with the case.[257] It follows that it is error for the court to appoint a receiver of a corporation on its own petition, alleging its insolvency;[258] and it has been held that such a proceeding is void for want of jurisdiction.[259]

256 Fort Payne Furnace Co. v. Fort Payne Coal etc. Co., 96 Ala. 472, 38 Am. St. Rep. 109, 11 South. 439.

257 Hutchinson v. American Palace Car Co., 104 Fed. 182; Murray v Superior Court, 129 Cal 628, 62 Pac. 191; In re Atlas Iron Construction Co., 2 N. Y. Ann. Cas. 124, 38 N. Y. Supp. 172; Mann v. German-American Inv. Co. (Neb.), 97 N. W. 600.

258 State v. Ross, 122 Mo. 435, 25 S. W. 947, 23 L. R. A. 534; Kimball v Goodburn, 32 Mich. 11; Hugh v. McRae, Chase Dec. 466; Jones v. Bank of Leadville, 10 Colo. 464, 17 Pac. 272, McIlhenny v. Binz, 80 Tex. 1, 26 Am. St. Rep. 705, 13 S. W. 655; In re Moss Cigar Co., 50 La. Ann. 789, 23 South. 544. The notorious "Wabash" case (Wabash etc. R. Co. v. Central Trust Co., 22 Fed. 272), *contra*, appears to have been thoroughly discredited, and does not appear to have been followed, unless Petition of Kittanning Ins. Co., 146 Pa. St. 102, 23 Atl. 336, the report of which is scarcely intelligible, is to be taken as announcing the same doctrine. See the caustic criticism of the Wabash case in State v. Ross, *supra*, and in an article by Gov. D. H. Chamberlain, entitled "New Fashioned Receiverships," in Harvard Law Review. The attempt (in Central Trust Co. v. Wabash, St. L. & P. Ry. Co., 29 Fed. 618) to find support for its doctrine in subsequent *dicta* of the supreme court of the United States, and in the previous case of Brassey v. Railroad Co., 19 Fed. 663 (a suit by a bondholder), is thoroughly exposed in the opinion of Brace, J., in State v. Ross, *supra*.

259 State v. Ross, *supra; contra*, that the appointment, although er-

§ 119. Suit for Dissolution and Receiver; No Inherent Jurisdiction.—It is well settled, with scarcely a dissenting voice, that in the absence of express statutory authority, a court of equity has no power to dissolve a corporation, or to wind up its affairs and sequestrate its property.[260] A few exceptions have, however, been admitted to this rule; as, where the corporation had

roneous, does not render the proceedings of the court consequent thereupon void, so as to be assailable in a collateral proceeding, see McIlhenny v Binz, 80 Tex. 1, 26 Am. St. Rep. 705, 13 S. W. 655.

260 Republican Mountain Silver Mines v. Brown, 7 C. C. A. 412, 24 L. R. A. 776, 58 Fed. 644, 648; Murray v. Superior Court, 129 Cal. 628, 62 Pac. 191; La Societe Francaise v. District Court ("French Bank Case"), 53 Cal. 495; People v. District Court of City and County of Denver (Colo), 80 Pac. 909, People v. Weigley, 155 Ill. 491, 40 N. E. 300; Wheeler v. Pullman Iron etc. Co., 143 Ill. 197, 32 N. E. 420, 17 L. R. A. 818; Baker v. Backus's Admrs., 32 Ill. 79; Belmont v. Erie Ry. Co., 52 Barb. (N. Y.) 637; Howe v. Duel, 43 Barb. 505; Bangs v. McIntosh, 23 Barb. 600; In re The Mart, 22 Abb. N. C. 227, 5 N. Y. Supp. 82; Davis v. Flagstaff etc. Min. Co., 2 Utah, 74, 94; Mason v. Equitable Lodge Supreme Court, 77 Md. 483, 39 Am. St. Rep. 433, 27 Atl. 171; Vila v. Grand Island Electric L. I. & C. S. Co. (Neb.), 94 N. W. 136; Wallace v. Pierce-Wallace Pub. Co., 101 Iowa, 313, 322, 63 Am. St. Rep. 389, 70 N. W. 216, 38 L. R. A. 122; French v. Gifford, 30 Iowa, 153; People's Inv. Co. v. Crawford (Tex. Civ. App.), 45 S. W. 738. Such authority is not to be found in a general statute, not relating to any specific class of cases, such as Code of Iowa, § 2903, declaring that a receiver may be appointed *pendente lite* "on the petition of either party to a civil action or proceeding, wherein he shows that he has a probable right to, or interest in, any property which is the subject of the controversy, and that such property or its rents or profits are in danger of being lost or materially injured or impaired," if the court is "satisfied that the interests of one or both parties will be thereby promoted, and the substantial rights of neither unduly infringed": Wallace v. Pierce-Wallace Pub. Co., and French v. Gifford, *supra*. This section does not warrant the placing of the property of the corporation in the hands of a receiver, when that practically accomplishes the same purpose as a dissolution: Id. That the president of a corporation has no power, without the authority of the directors or stockholders, to consent to the appointment of a receiver to wind up the affairs of a corporation, see Walters v. Anglo-American Mort. & T. Co., 50 Fed. 316.

utterly failed of its purpose because of fraudulent mismanagement and misappropriation of its funds by the president and manager, who owned a majority of its stock, a receiver was appointed to wind up its affairs at the suit of a minority stockholder;[261] and it has been held, even in New York, that a court of equity has inherent power to appoint a receiver on the application of a stockholder for the purpose of the equitable distribution of the assets of an insolvent corporation, without regard to the statutory provisions for the dissolu-

261 In the well-considered case of Miner v. Belle Isle Ice Co., 93 Mich. 97, 53 N. W. 218. The general rule is recognized, but it is pointed out that a strict adherence to the rule, or the attempt to apply any other remedy than a winding up of the business of the corporation through the agency of a receiver would amount to a denial of justice, and violate the fundamental principle of equity that "it is the duty of the court to adapt its practice and course of proceeding to the existing state of society." It appeared that for a number of years the defendant Lorman had controlled the corporation for his own interest and profit, and had appropriated all the profits of the business. The court says, after a discussion of the authorities: "The present case furnishes an instance of gross abuse of trust. Must the *cestui que trust* be committed to the domination of a trustee who for seven years continued to violate the trust? . . . . The trustee has so far absorbed all returns. What is the outlook for the future? This court, in view of the past, can give no assurances. It can make no order that can prevent some other mode of bleeding this corporation, if it is allowed to continue. If Lorman be removed, who shall take his place? He has the absolute power to determine. Once deposed he may elect a dummy to fill his place. . . . . This corporation has utterly failed of its purpose, not because of matters beyond its control, but because of fraudulent mismanagement and misappropriation of its funds. Complainant has a right to insist that it shall not continue as a cloak for a fraud upon him, and shall not longer retain his capital to be used for the sole advantage of the owner of a majority of the stock, and a court of equity will not so far tolerate such a manifest violation of the rules of natural justice as to deny him the relief to which his situation entitles him. I think a court of equity, under the circumstances of this case, in the exercise of its general equity jurisdiction, has the power to grant to this complainant ample relief, even to the dissolution of the trust relations. Complainant is therefore entitled to the relief prayed. A receiver will be appointed, and the affairs of this corporation wound up."

tion of corporations, where the directors refuse to institute statutory proceedings for a voluntary dissolution, and there is danger of the assets being absorbed by judgments that will be recovered, so as to render an application to the attorney-general useless.[262] In a recent case in the United States circuit court for the eastern district of North Carolina the court even went to the length of appointing a receiver for the purpose of the dissolution of a solvent and prosperous corporation, and the sale of its property, for the sole reason, apparently, that this action was desired by a majority of the stockholders, and that a minority stockholder was threatening to procure the passage of a bill by the state legislature forfeiting the charter of the corporation.[263]

262 Porter v. Industrial Information Co., 25 N. Y. Supp. 328, 5 Misc. Rep. 263 The court says. "Whenever, in the course of events, it proves impossible to attain the real objects for which a corporation was formed, or when the failure of the company has become inevitable, it is the duty of the company's agents to put an end to its operations, and to wind up its affairs; and if the majority should attempt to continue its operations, in violation of its charter, or should refuse to make a distribution of the assets, any shareholder feeling aggrieved will be entitled to the assistance of the courts. Mor Corp., § 284; Merchants' etc. Line v. Wagoner, 71 Ala. 581; Cramer v. Bird, L. R. 6 Eq. 143."

263 Arents v. Blackwell's Durham Tobacco Co, 101 Fed. 338, (Simonton, J.). This decision, surely one of the most arbitrary ever rendered by a federal court, even in that circuit, is not cited here, it is hardly necessary to say, for its value as a precedent. No warrant whatever was found, or sought, by the court, in any legislation of the state of North Carolina, and the court expressly recognized the general rule forbidding the interference of a court of equity in the internal management of the affairs of a corporation, and the absence of any jurisdiction in such a court to dissolve a corporation, to wind up its affairs and in that connection to appoint a receiver. The court excuses its action with the vague statement that "a recognized ground of relief in equity is, when the affairs of the corporation are not satisfactory, when it is in the midst of or threatened with disaster, when further prosecution of its business will lead to loss and insolvency." The authorities cited, of course, establish no such

§ 120. Stockholders' Suit for Breach of Fiduciary Duty by Directors.—Cases are to be found which assert that courts of equity, by virtue of their general equitable jurisdiction, will not appoint a receiver of a corporation, and assume control and management of its affairs, at the suit of a stockholder alleging fraud, mismanagement, and collusion on the part of the corporate authorities, or *ultra vires* acts of the directors or of the corporation itself.[264] The denial of the power to grant the relief in such cases is based on one or both of two grounds: First, that such relief, in effect, results in a dissolution of the corporation, and the court should refuse to accomplish indirectly that which it has no power to do directly;[265] second, that an injunction, addressed to the specific wrongs charged, affords a sufficient remedy.[266] But, notwithstanding many *dicta*, and the assertions of the older text-books, the current of recent authority appears to be strongly in favor of the inherent power of the court, in a proper case, to displace the management of guilty or negligent offi-

ground for the dissolution of corporations by courts of equity, but merely concern the right of the majority stockholders themselves to put an end to the business of the corporation under such circumstances.

264 People's Investment Co. v. Crawford (Tex. Civ. App.), 45 S. W. 738; Empire Hotel Co. v. Main, 98 Ga. 176, 25 S. E. 413; Fischer v. Superior Court, 110 Cal. 129, 42 Pac. 561; Neall v. Hill, 16 Cal. 145, 76 Am. Dec. 508; Robison v. Cleveland City R. Co., 7 Ohio Dec. 312; People v. Judge of St. Clair Circuit, 31 Mich. 456; Mason v. Supreme Court of Equitable League, 77 Md. 483, 39 Am. St. Rep. 433, 27 Atl. 171; Goodman v. Jedidjah Lodge, 67 Md. 117, 9 Atl. 13, 13 Atl. 627; Waterbury v. Merchants' Union Express Co., 50 Barb. 157. See, also, High on Receivers, § 288.

265 Fischer v. Superior Court, 110 Cal. 129, 42 Pac. 61.

266 People's Inv. Co. v. Crawford (Tex. Civ. App.), 45 S. W. 738; Empire Hotel Co. v. Main, 98 Ga. 176, 25 S. E. 413; Waterbury v. Merchants' Union Express Co., 50 Barb. 157. And see Laurel Springs Land Co. v. Fougeray, 50 N. J. Eq. 756, 26 Atl. 886.

cials by the instrumentality of its receiver.[267] It has been frequently pointed out that the appointment of a receiver in cases of this character does not necessarily result in the dissolution or extinction of the corporation. "The property and assets of the corporation, which are being dissipated and fraudulently absorbed, will be preserved and rightfully applied under the supervision of the court, and may be restored to the officers of the corporation, when there has been a change of officers, or when it is deemed prudent and safe to restore the property and affairs of the corporation to its duly constituted officers."[268]

§ 121. **Same; Power, When not Exercised.**—In a suit by a stockholder, a receiver will not be appointed to take the property out of the hands of the managers, ex-

267 See Gluck & Becker on Rec of Corp., § 9, and cases cited; Towle v. American Bldg. etc. Soc., 60 Fed. 131; Aiken v. Colorado Riv. Imp. Co., 72 Fed. 591; Wayne Pike Co. v. Hammond, 129 Ind. 368, 27 N. E. 487; Supreme Sitting I. H. v. Baker, 134 Ind. 293, 33 N. E. 1128, 20 L. R. A. 210; In re Lewis, 52 Kan. 660, 35 Pac. 287; Davis v. United States Electrical etc. Co., 77 Md 35, 25 Atl. 982; Miner v. Belle Isle Ice Co., 93 Mich. 97, 53 N. W. 218, 17 L. R. A. 412; State v. Second Judicial District Court, 15 Mont. 324, 48 Am. St Rep. 682, 39 Pac. 316, 27 L. R. A. 392; Ponca Mill Co. v. Mikesell, 55 Neb. 98, 75 N. W. 46; Porter v. Industrial Information Co., 25 N. Y. Supp. 328, 5 Misc. Rep. 262; Line v. Carlisle Mfg. Co., 5 Pa. Dist. R. 642; Cameron v. Groveland Imp. Co., 20 Wash. 169, 72 Am. St. Rep. 26, 54 Pac. 1128; Haywood v. Lincoln Lumber Co., 64 Wis. 639, 26 N. W. 184. In a few of these cases the jurisdiction was aided by the terms of some general statute; but in all of them the inherent power of courts of equity was recognized.

268 In re Lewis, *supra*, Supreme Sitting of the Order of Iron Hall v Baker, 134 Ind. 293, 33 N. E. 1128, 20 L. R. A. 210; State v. Second Judicial District Court, 15 Mont. 324, 48 Am. St. Rep. 682, 27 L. R. A. 392, 39 Pac. 316, Gibbs v. Morgan (Idaho), 72 Pac. 733, and cases cited. That the guilty officers are necessary parties to the suit, see Edwards v. Bay State Gas Co., 91 Fed. 942. That the allegations of fraud must be specific, see Wheeler v. Pullman Iron etc. Co., 43 Ill. App 626; Baker v. Backus's Admr., 32 Ill. 79.

cept as a last resort, and when it is considered absolutely necessary for the preservation of the trust fund.[269] So, when it appears that the appointment of a receiver, with the expenses incident thereto, would probably render the corporation insolvent, the court will endeavor to give relief by enjoining the managers from the further execution of contracts resulting in the diversion of corporate funds, and from committing other acts of mismanagement.[270] Moreover, the principle must be borne in mind that a receivership is a preventive, not a punitive, measure. "Courts do not appoint receivers as a punishment for past dereliction, nor because of past dangers. Receivers are appointed because of present conditions, and well-founded apprehension as to the future."[271] The complaining stockholder must, of course, show that his fears are well grounded.[272] He must himself be free from any partici-

269 United Securities Co. v. Louisiana Electric L. Co., 68 Fed. 673 See, also, Bridgeport Development Co. v. Tritsch, 110 Ala. 274, 20 South. 16; Laurel Springs Land Co. v. Fougeray, 50 N. J. Eq. 756, 26 Atl. 886; Miller v. Kitchen (Neb.), 103 N. W. 297.

270 United Securities Co. v. Louisiana Electric L. Co., 68 Fed. 673.

271 Original Vienna Bak. etc. Co. v. Heissler, 50 Ill. App. 406 "Past conduct and past conditions may be taken into consideration in determining what the present situation is and the future will be, but a receiver will not be appointed because of things done or attempted at a past time, when the present situation and the prospects for the future are not such as to warrant taking the control of the property out of the hands of its owners": Id. See, also, Marcuse v. Gullett Gin Mfg. Co., 52 La. Ann. 1383, 27 South. 846; New Albany Waterworks v. Louisville Banking Co., 122 Fed. 776, 58 C. C. A. 576 (one unauthorized act not ground for appointment; "it cannot be presumed that they will mismanage or act otherwise than in conformity with the order" setting aside an unauthorized act).

272 So, the fears of a complainant that a suit brought by the corporation against an officer will not be diligently prosecuted, owing to the relation of the parties, will not warrant the appointment of a receiver to take charge of the suit, no laches on the part of the corporation being shown: Griffing v. Griffing Iron Co., 96 Fed. 577. That the president of a corporation is in a position where he may betray

pation in the breaches of trust on the part of the ministerial officers of the corporation.[273] His right to the relief must be based on something more than mere irregularities in levying of assessments,[274] or than a denial of the right of the stockholders to inspect the corporate books, as such right may, if necessary, be enforced by other and appropriate orders;[275] or than a refusal by the directors, not shown to be made with corrupt motive, to permit a pledgee of stock to vote it.[276] The appointment of a receiver of a solvent corporation on the application of a minority stockholder is a very drastic remedy, which can be justified only in a very strong case.[277]

its interests will not justify a receivership, when there is no evidence to justify the probability that he will betray them: Young v. Rutan, 69 Ill. App. 513. The appointment of a receiver for a corporation will not be made, the bill containing no allegations of mismanagement, improper application of funds, or other acts of corporate maladministration, merely on the general allegation of the shareholders seeking the appointment that they apprehend exposure in the future, if the corporation is not wound up, to liabilities not contemplated when they became shareholders: Mulqueeney v. Shaw, 50 La. Ann. 1060, 23 South. 915.

273 Hyde Park Gas Co. v. Kerber, 5 Ill. App. 132.

274 Hardee v. Sunset Oil Co., 56 Fed. 51. In this case the directors of a corporation levied an assessment on its stock, and, on failure to pay the same, advertised for sale only the stock of one who held nearly one-third of the entire stock, although other stockholders were also delinquent; it appearing, however, that the other stockholders had promised to pay. At a meeting of the directors at which only the president, secretary and treasurer were present, they voted themselves salaries, which, however, they never collected. It was shown that no actual fraud was intended. *Held*, that the irregularities are not sufficient to justify appointing a receiver for the corporation.

275 Original Vienna Bak. etc. Co. v. Heissler, 50 Ill. App. 406; Alabama Coal & Coke Co. v. Shackelford, 137 Ala. 224, 97 Am. St. Rep. 23, 34 South. 833.

276 Thalmann v. Hoffman House, 27 Misc. Rep. 140, 58 N. Y. Supp. 227.

277 Rothwell v. Robinson, 44 Minn. 538, 47 N. W. 255; Continental Nat. B. & L. Assn. v. Miller, 44 Fla. 757, 33 South. 404. In Rumney v.

§ 122. **Same; Power, When Exercised.**—The following cases may serve to illustrate the circumstances under which receivers have been appointed at the suit of stockholders: Where the officers of a building and loan association have so mismanaged its affairs that its assets amount to less than two-thirds of the capital paid in;[278]

Detroit & M. Cattle Co., 116 Mich 640, 74 N. W. 1043, a receiver was refused on a bill by the owner of one-eighth of the stock of a corporation, alleging that defendant controlled a majority of the stock, loaned the profits in his own name, and refused to declare dividends until threatened with suit, and then withheld dividends coming to complainant, that no meetings of the directors had been held, nor reports of the condition of the company filed, as required by law, and that such condition had not been made known to the stockholders; and that no books of the company were kept, except a private memorandum of the defendant, which was inaccessible to stockholders. It was not shown that other stockholders were dissatisfied with the management, and there was no allegation of insolvency, or that defendant was irresponsible, and it appeared that complainant was in control of most of the property of the corporation, and that a dispute over unsettled claims was the mainspring of the litigation. In Ranger v. Champion Cotton Press Co., 52 Fed. 609, the bill and affidavits charged that the president of the company refused to account for a large sum of money intrusted to him by the company to be used in the promotion of its interests, that he had applied this money to his own use, and obstinately refused to give the complainant an inspection of the books of the company, or any information whatever of its affairs; that he was insolvent, and since the inauguration of the suit had mortgaged all his real estate, with manifest intent to defeat the claim of the company. The bill contained no allegation of fraudulent collusion on the part of the other stockholders, but intimated that the president was sustained by them. The solvency of the company was unquestionable It was held that the allegations were insufficient to warrant the court to appoint a receiver before answer, without the consent of the majority of the stockholders. See, also, Laurel Springs Land Co. v. Fougeray, 50 N. J. Eq. 756, 26 Atl. 886; Baker v. Backus's Admr, 32 Ill. 79, Alabama Coal & Coke Co. v. Shackelford, 137 Ala. 224, 97 Am St. Rep. 23, 34 South. 833 (not because directors hold over in default of election, and refuse to show books, and to disclose facts connected with business).

278 Towle v. American Building, Loan & Investment Society, 60 Fed 131 See, also, Continental Nat. B. & L. Assn. v. Miller, 44 Fla. 757, 33 South. 404.

where the directors of a turnpike company have refused to keep the corporate property in repair, thus rendering it unproductive;[279] where the business and affairs of the corporation have been so mismanaged that it has become insolvent, and it is made to appear that all the officers and directors have conspired together to divert its business to another company, dissipate its funds, and fraudulently absorb and apply its assets to the individual benefit of such officers;[280] where four stockholders get control of the majority of the stock of the corporation, elect their officers, pocket the dividends, keep false books to deceive other stockholders, and buy a worthless franchise for which they mortgage the corporate property for the purpose of having the mortgage foreclosed, and the property of the corporation wiped out, a receiver may be appointed pending an action by minority stockholders to have the mortgage canceled;[281] in a suit to compel an accounting, on allegation that the officers have converted and are continuing to convert the money and property of the corporation to their own use, as pretended salaries and expenses, without any authority therefor, and fraudulently;[282] where the president and secretary of a corporation mortgaged its property, when it was nearly or quite insolvent, to secure their antecedent claims against the

279 Wayne Pike Co. v. Hammons, 129 Ind. 368, 27 N. E. 487. The court relied, in part, on the broad terms of the statute (Ind. Rev. Stats. 1881, § 1222, cl. 7), providing that receivers may be appointed in cases "where, in the discretion of the court, it may be necessary to secure ample justice to the parties."

280 In re Lewis, 52 Kan 660, 35 Pac. 287. The court remarks that "in most cases of this character, no other adequate remedy exists."

281 State v. Second Judicial Dist. Court, 15 Mont. 324, 48 Am. St. Rep. 682, 39 Pac. 316, 27 L. R. A. 392, a vigorous and instructive opinion.

282 Cameron v. Groveland Improvement Co., 20 Wash. 169, 72 Am. St. Rep. 26, 54 Pac. 1128.

corporation in fraud of creditors, and threatened to sell out in gross all the property of the corporation without notice, and in this way to close up the business of the company.[283] "In all such cases the courts should proceed with caution, and carefully avoid having their process made use of for the purpose merely of directing corporate action adversely to the policy of the majority stockholders and that of the regular chosen officers; that is to say, that stockholders must not be permitted to invoke the power of the court, through the appointment of a receiver, simply to enforce their own ideas of the conduct of affairs, against the majority of the duly constituted officers. Matters of corporate policy must be determined by the corporation itself. On the other hand, when it clearly appears that the dispute is not of that character, but arises out of an attempt of the officers or the majority stockholders to abuse their power by misappropriating the corporate property, by using the corporate means for their individual profit, or by so acting as to willfully and wrongfully jeopardize the corporate business, then the courts should not hesitate to afford relief. No one is more helpless, unless aided by the arm of the law, than the holder of a small portion of the stock of a corporation, when the large stockholders combine to advance their private interest at the expense of the corporation."[284]

§ 123. **Receiver After Dissolution.**—"Since it has come to be recognized everywhere that, upon the dissolution of a trading corporation, its property neither reverts to its grantors nor escheats to the state, but belongs,

283 Haywood v. Lincoln Lumber Co., 64 Wis. 639, 26 N. W. 184. For further illustrations, see Elwood v. Bank, 41 Kan. 475, 21 Pac. 673; Du Puy v. Transportation etc. Co., 82 Md. 408, 33 Atl. 889, 34 Atl. 910.

284 Ponca Mill Co. v. Mikesell, 55 Neb. 98, 75 N. W. 46.

after payment of its debts, to those who were stockholders at the date of dissolution, ... some means must be provided for winding up the corporation and distributing its assets according to the equitable rights of those interested. In the absence of any statute regulating the matter, a court of equity would have the undoubted right, in a proper proceeding instituted by a creditor or a stockholder, to appoint a receiver to administer the property."[285] Such statutes exist in a majority of the states, providing, in substance, that upon the dissolution of any corporation, the directors or managers of the affairs of such corporation at the time of its dissolution shall be the trustees of the creditors and stockholders of the corporation dissolved, and shall have full power to settle the affairs of the corporation, collect and pay the outstanding debts, and divide among the stockholders the moneys and other property that shall remain, after the payment of debts and necessary expenses.[286]

285 Havemeyer v. Superior Court, 84 Cal. 327, 362, 18 Am. St. Rep. 192, 24 Pac. 121, 10 L. R. A. 627. See, also, Stark v. Burke, 5 La Ann. 740; United States v. Church of Jesus Christ of L. D. S., 5 Utah, 361, 15 Pac. 473; Olmstead v. Distilling etc. Co., 73 Fed. 44 The last case states the effect of an Illinois statute (Ill. Rev. Stats., c. 32, §§ 10-12), whereby the corporate capacity of corporations whose powers may have expired by limitation or otherwise is continued during the term of two years for the purpose only of collecting the debts due said corporation and selling and conveying the property and effects thereof. It was held that upon a judgment of ouster in *quo warranto* proceedings the corporation itself (not its directors) becomes a trustee for its creditors and, subject to their rights, for its stockholders; and a bill by a stockholder, in behalf of himself and other stockholders who may join with him, showing that the corporation itself, acting through its directors, was unable to execute and carry out the trust, because the affairs of the corporation were involved and its property in danger of being dissipated through executions and attachments, presented a good case for a receiver to administer its assets.

286 See 2 Stimson Am. St. Law, § 8356, enumerating:

Alabama.—Code, 1886, §§ 1691, 1693.

A receiver cannot be appointed to carry on the business of a dissolved corporation, whose assets are in the hands of the statutory trustees, when the corporation is made the sole party defendant to the bill.[287]

In the settlement of the affairs of a dissolved corporation it is not a right of a minority of the stockholders to have a decree for receivers and a sale of assets, especially where they are in the hands of a trustee who admits the existence of the trust and shows his readiness and ability to perform it more effectively and

California.—Civ. Code, § 400.

Colorado.—Gen. Stats. 1883, § 341.

Delaware—Biennial Laws, vol. 17, c. 147, § 32.

Florida.—Digest, 1881, c. 34, § 21 (in cases of voluntary dissolution only).

Idaho.—Rev. Stats. 1887, § 2648.

Kansas.—Kelly's Gen. Stats. 1891, c. 23, § 42.

Maryland.—Public Gen. Laws 1888, c. 23, § 272.

Missouri.—Rev. Stats. 1889, § 2513.

Montana.—Gen. Laws, § 489.

Nebraska.—Comp. Stats. 1885, c. 16, § 62.

Nevada.—Gen. Stats. 1885, § 822.

New Jersey.—Corp. 57.

New Mexico.—Comp. Laws 1884, § 210.

New York.—Laws of 1890, c. 563, § 19.

North Dakota.—Civ. Code, § 420.

Ohio.—Revision of 1890, § 5675. See, also, §§ 5687, 5688.

Oklahoma.—Stats. 1890, § 995.

South Dakota.—Civ. Code, § 420.

Tennessee.—Milliken & Vertrees' Code 1884, §§ 1721, 1723.

Texas.—Rev. Stats. 1879, §§ 606, 607.

Washington.—Code 1881, § 2441.

Wisconsin.—Sanb. & Berr. Stats. 1889, § 1764.

Wyoming.—Rev. Stats. 1887, § 647.

287 Weatherby v. Capital City Water Co., **115 Ala. 156, 22 South. 140.**

more economically than could be done by receivers.[288] And where the charter of a corporation has expired, and its property and assets are in the custody, and its affairs under the management, of the persons designated by statute, the mere fact of dissolution, without more, furnishes no ground for the appointment of a receiver;[289] similarly, when the articles of association provide the manner of winding up the business, and no reason is shown why the mode provided cannot be executed, a receiver cannot be appointed for the corporation on the demand of one of the members who is dissatisfied with the action of the majority.[290]

§ 124. **Dissensions in the Governing Body of the Corporation, and Among the Stockholders.**—"The power of a court of equity to appoint a receiver of a corporation either because it has no properly constituted governing body, or because there are such dissensions in its governing body as to make it impossible for the corporation to carry on its business with advantage to its stockholders, appears to be settled; but it is equally well settled that this power is subject to certain limitations, namely, it must always be exercised with great caution, and only for such time and to such an extent as may be necessary to preserve the property of the corporation, and protect the rights and interests of its stockholders. As soon as a lawfully constituted and competent governing body comes into existence, whether it is brought into existence by an adjustment of the dissensions or

288 Baltimore & O. R. Co. v. Cannon, 72 Md. 493, 20 Atl. 123.

289 Anderson v. Buckley, 126 Ala. 623, 28 South. 729; for facts authorizing appointment, see S. C., on second appeal, Buckley v. Anderson, 137 Ala. 325, 34 South. 238. In support of the text, see, also, Ferrell v. Evans, 25 Mont. 444, 65 Pac. 714.

290 Pringle v. Eltringham Const. Co., 49 La. Ann. 301, 21 South. 515; and see Follett v. Field, 30 La. Ann. 162.

by the election of a new body, and such body is ready to take possession of the property of the corporation, and proceed in the proper discharge of its duties, the court must lift its hand and retire."[291] But mere dis-

291 Edison v. Edison United Phonograph Co., 52 N. J. Eq. 620, 29 Atl. 195, citing Featherstone v. Cooke, L. R. 16 Eq. 298; Trade Auxiliary Co. v. Vickers, L. R. 16 Eq. 303; Einstein v. Rosenfeld, 38 N. J Eq 309; Archer v. Waterworks Co., 50 N. J. Eq. 33, 24 Atl. 508. Also, see Wallace v. Pierce-Wallace Pub Co., 101 Iowa, 313, 329, 63 Am St. Rep. 389, 70 N. W. 216. In the first case it was further said. "Neither of the grounds which this doctrine recognizes as sufficient to warrant the appointment of a receiver exists in this case. The defendant corporation has a lawfully constituted governing body, which is in peaceable possession of all its property, controlling and directing its business, regularly and peacefully, in conformity to the judgment of seven of its nine directors. Two of the nine differ in judgment from the other seven. The two believe that the adoption of a different course of business from that which is now pursued would result in larger gains. Both methods are clearly within the purposes and powers of the corporation. Which method shall be pursued, or whether one or both, is a question which the law commits absolutely and unconditionally to the judgment of a majority of the directors. Though somewhat disguised, the real purpose of the bill in this case appears, when critically examined, to be to induce judicial action which shall substitute the judgment of a minority of the directors of this corporation for that of the majority. That cannot be done. It is beyond judicial power. No rule of law is better settled than that which declares that so long as the directors of a corporation keep within the scope of their powers, and act in good faith and with honest motives, their acts are not subject to judicial control or revision." In Wallace v. Pierce-Wallace Pub. Co., *supra*, a somewhat stronger case, it was held that a receiver will not be appointed on the ground that the corporation has but two stockholders owning an equal number of shares of stock, and owns stock in another corporation, respecting the management of which there is such disagreement between the stockholders in the first-named corporation that they cannot agree in any measures for the voting of such stock, or for the management of the second corporation, nor will a receiver be appointed of such stock alone. Emphasis was laid on the temporary and limited nature of the relief that is permissible in such cases. "Now, a court of equity has no power to make them [the stockholders] agree; and, if their differences are such that it is impossible for them to carry on their business, it is not likely that the appointment of a receiver will bring

satisfaction by a minority of the stockholders of a corporation with its management by the majority, in the

about a reconciliation. . . . . What, then, must result? Either that a court must carry on this business for the interest of the stockholders until the corporation is dissolved by lapse of time, or that one of the parties should sell his stock, or such portion thereof, as will give a majority to one or the other of these litigants.'' See, to the same effect, Little Warrior Coal Co. v. Hooper, 105 Ala. 665, 17 South. 118 In this case one of the grounds of complaint was, that the stock was equally divided between the complainant and the two defendants; that the latter acted and voted in confederation; that the three could not agree as directors in the management of the business, and could not elect directors, and that for this reason a receiver should be appointed to take charge of and operate the business. The bill did not show whether the plaintiff or the defendants were to blame, and charged no fraud. The court says: ''The bill shows a mere disagreement among themselves as to how the business should be operated and managed, and who should control it. No case has been cited, and we have found none, nor any principle of law, which would authorize the appointment of a receiver upon such averments.''

From the brief statement of facts in the last case, it is difficult to distinguish it from Sternberg v. Wolff, 56 N. J. Eq. 389, 67 Am. St Rep. 494, 39 Atl. 397, 39 L R. A. 762, reversing the decision of Vice-Chancellor Pitney in 56 N. J. Eq. 555, 42 Atl. 1078. The importance of this decision justifies a somewhat lengthy quotation from the opinion of Depue, J. ''The two parties to the controversy —Sternberg and his wife, on the one side, and Wolff and his wife, on the other side—are the owners each of one-half of the capital stock These four individuals are directors of the company, and by the by-laws the whole number is necessary to make a quorum for the transaction of business. The dissensions between these two parties—Sternberg and his wife, on one side, and Wolff and his wife, on the other side—have brought the affairs of this company to a deadlock, so far as any corporate action by the board of directors is concerned. It may be assumed that the court of chancery has no jurisdiction to dissolve a solvent corporation, and distribute its assets, on the ground that the business of the corporation is improperly conducted by its board of directors, even though such mismanagement be with the concurrence of a majority of the stockholders; but the jurisdiction of the court of chancery to control the business of a company, especially a trading company, pending a litigation over the management and conduct of its business, must necessarily exist; and we think, pending a litigation such as that which is inaugurated by the proceedings in this case, a receiver may be ap-

absence of fraud or insolvency, is not sufficient to authorize the court to appoint a receiver at the instance

pointed. . . . . No reason appears why in the matter of the control and conduct of its business the corporation and its officers should not be within the control of the court of chancery to an extent corresponding with the control of that court over the business of a mere partnership. The cases seem to establish the power of the court in virtue of its general jurisdiction to preserve the subject of litigation *pendente lite*, though it may relate to the affairs of a trading company in form organized as a corporation. The two cases cited by the vice-chancellor in his second opinion are to that effect Featherstone v. Cooke, L R. 16 Eq. 298, Trade Auxiliary Co. v. Vickers, L. R. 16 Eq. 303. In the first case the complications in the affairs of the company arose out of a division in the board of directors, which made it absolutely impossible that the affairs of the company could be conducted with advantage. Vice-Chancellor Malins, in that case, says 'With regard to private partnerships, nothing is of more frequent occurrence than the quarrels of partners. If partners quarrel, oust each other from the management, or so conduct themselves that the partnership cannot go on with advantage, it is every day's practice for the court to interfere by injunction, and appoint a receiver if necessary. With regard to public companies, I apprehend the same principle is applicable. If a state of things exists in which the governing body are so divided that they cannot act together, and there is the same kind of feeling between the members as there is frequently in the case of private partnerships, it is clearly within the rule of this court to interfere, and it will do so.' The court in that case intervened by injunction and receiver simply to protect the property of the company, to continue, however, no longer than until a governing body was duly appointed. In the latter case the dissension was also in the board of directors, one set of which closed the office doors of the company's building, and the other set, with the aid of some laborers, broke open the doors with crowbars, and forced the office open The prayer of the bill was for the appointment of a receiver until the proper board of directors was constituted. The vice-chancellor placed the affairs of the company in the hands of a receiver *pendente lite* until a new governing body was appointed.'' Mr. Justice Depue also finds warrant for the appointment in certain *dicta* in Einstein v. Rosenfeld, 38 N. J. Eq. 309; in Edison v. Phonograph Co., *supra;* in Fougeray v. Cord, 50 N. J. Eq. 185, 756, 24 Atl. 499, 26 Atl. 866; and in the opinion of Chancellor McGill in Archer v. Waterworks, 50 N. J. Eq 33, 24 Atl. 508. In the last case, a suit by a stockholder, the complainant seemed to have the equitable ownership of certain stock, but the parties in control of the corporation of the minority.[292] "A court of equity has no power to interpose its authority for the purpose of adjusting con-

fraudulently refused to make the transfer of such stock on the corporation's books. This, of course, prevented the complainant from voting. The chancellor said: "I think it is plainly my duty to interfere by injunction, to prevent the perpetration of the wrong here threatened. If the present directors of the company continue their dissensions, so that the affairs of the company are not speedily attended to, upon a proper application I will care for the property, pending the determination of the suit, through the instrumentality of a receiver. Such actions will be supported by precedents and authority [citing the cases from L. R. 16 Eq.]. My interference, however, by injunction and receiver, will be limited to the imperative requirements of the present emergency." Jasper Land Co. v Wallis, 123 Ala. 652, 26 South. 659, was a case of rival boards of directors. "The Jasper Land Company has two boards of directors, or rather there are two sets of men, each claiming to be and constitute its board of directors. Each of these alleged boards is attacking the integrity and existence of the other in divers proceedings at law and in chancery. . . . . It is plain to us that neither set is so in possession and control of the property and affairs of the company as to be able to take the necessary steps to the effectuation of the relief the stockholders are entitled to [viz., relief to minority stockholders against mismanagement and misappropriation of funds of the corporation]. In such case the appointment of a receiver, even though the corporation be solvent, to take charge and control of its effects and concerns, at least until there is a recognized board of directors competent to faithfully and efficiently conserve the interests of all the stockholders, is within the proper exercise of the jurisdiction of the chancery court," citing many of the cases *supra*. For further instances where receivers were appointed because of dissensions, or the existence of rival boards of directors, see Powers v. Blue Grass Building etc. Assn, 86 Fed. 705; Tompkins Co. v. Catawba Mills, 82 Fed. 780 (in suit by creditors); Gibbs v. Morgan (Idaho), 72 Pac. 733; Sheridan Brick Works v. Marion Trust Co., 157 Ind. 292, 87 Am. St. Rep. 207, 61 N. E. 666. As to the appointment of a receiver where there is no governing body of the corporation, see In re Belton, 47 La. Ann 1614, 18 South. 642, 30 L. R. A. 648; Brown v. Union Ins. Co., 3 La. Ann. 177.

The rule of Featherstone v. Cooke and Auxiliary Co. v. Vickers, as stated in the text, thus appears to have met with abundant recognition in this country, save in the case in 105 Ala., where the court's attention was probably not called to these cases, and in the case in 101 Iowa, where they are expressly distinguished

292 Flecker v. Emporia City Ry. Co., 48 Kan. 577, 30 Pac. 18;

troversies that have arisen among the shareholders or directors of a corporation relative to the proper mode of conducting the corporate business, as it may do in case of a similar controversy arising between the members of an ordinary partnership. Corporations are in a certain sense legislative bodies. They have a legislative power when the directors or shareholders are duly convened that is fully adequate to settle all questions affecting their business interests or policy, and they should be left to dispose of all questions of that nature without applying to the courts for relief. A stockholder in a corporation cannot successfully invoke the power of a chancery court to control its officers or board of managers, or to wrest the corporate property from their charge through the agency of a receiver, so long as they neither do nor threaten to do any fraudulent or *ultra vires* acts, and so long as they keep within the limits of by-laws which have been prescribed for their governance."[293]

§ 125. **Receiver on Application of Creditors.**—The question of a general creditor's right to a receiver is practically a question of his right to maintain a creditor's bill, and is, therefore, more appropriately considered in another place.[294] The defendant corporation may lose its right to make the objection that the plaintiff creditors have not exhausted their legal remedy, by ac-

Bridgeport Development Co. v. Tritsch, 110 Ala. 274, 20 South. 16, Hill v. Gould, 129 Mo. 106, 30 S W. 181; Peatman v. Centerville Light etc. Co, 100 Iowa, 245, 69 N. W. 541; Republican Mountain Silver Mines v. Brown, 58 Fed. 647, 7 C. C. A. 412, 24 L. R. A. 776; Hunt v. American Grocery Co., 80 Fed. 70.

293 Republican Mountain Silver Mines v. Brown, 58 Fed. 647, 7 C. C. A. 412, 24 L. R. A. 776.

294 See *post*, vol. II, chapter on "Creditors' Bills"; Hollins v. Brierfield Coal & Iron Co, 150 U. S. 371, 14 Sup. Ct. 127, 37 L. ed. 1113.

quiescence, for a term of several months, in the appointment and possession of a receiver in behalf of general creditors.[295] The general rule is, of course, that a court of equity will not appoint a receiver of a corporation, upon the application of a creditor without a lien who has not reduced his claim to judgment[296]

295 Brown v. Lake Superior Iron Co., 134 U. S 530, 10 Sup Ct. 604, 33 L ed 1021.

296 Texas Consol. etc. Assn. v. Storrow, 92 Fed. 5, 34 C. C. A. 182; Leary v. Colombia etc. Nav. Co., 82 Fed 775; Smith-Dimmick Lumber Co. v. Teague, 119 Ala 385, 24 South. 4, Smith v. Superior Court, 97 Cal. 348, 32 Pac. 322; French Bank Case, 53 Cal 495; International Trust Co. v. United Coal Co., 27 Colo. 246, 83 Am. St. Rep. 59, 60 Pac. 621; Dodge v. Pyrolusite Manganese Co., 69 Ga 665; Klee v. E. H. Steele Co., 60 Minn 355, 62 N W. 399; Mann v. German-American Inv Co. (Neb.), 97 N. W. 600. See, also, Falmouth Nat. Bank v. Cape Cod Ship Canal Co, 166 Mass. 550, 44 N. E. 617. In Nunnally v. Strauss, 94 Va 255, 26 S. E. 580, however, it was held that a simple contract creditor of an insolvent corporation which has ceased to do business and has been abandoned by its officers may sue on behalf of himself and other creditors for a receiver. "In the case of Fainey v. Bennett, 27 Gratt. 365, this court has very aptly likened an insolvent corporation that has ceased to do business to an insolvent decedent's estate, and has argued with much force that, upon the same principle that a court of equity administers a dead man's estate under a bill filed by simple contract creditors for that purpose, it should administer the affairs of a corporation that has ceased to do its life work. That was the case of an insolvent banking institution. Its assets remained in the hands of one or more of the officers last elected by the directors, but no one had been appointed by the directors or stockholders to take charge of its assets and wind up its affairs; and it was held proper, under the circumstances, by analogy to the administration of a dead man's estate, at the suit of simple contract creditors who had no lien, for a court of equity to take charge of the affairs of the abandoned corporation, administer its assets, and apply the same for the benefit of its creditors" See, also, Doe v. Northwest Coal & Transportation Co, 64 Fed. 928, Kentucky Racing & Breeding Assn. v. Galbreaith, 25 Ky. Law Rep. 1212, 77 S. W. 371 (receiver appointed, "where the assets of an insolvent corporation, which a [general] creditor is entitled to have applied in satisfaction of his demands, will probably be lost or fraudulently disposed of by improvident or corrupt officials unless a receiver is

It is held in Ohio that a receiver may properly be appointed, by virtue of the general usages of equity, in the equitable action to enforce payment of the statutory liability of stockholders.[297] A receiver is a means of effectuating the remedy of a judgment creditor of a corporation seeking to enforce, in behalf of himself and other creditors, the application of unpaid stock subscriptions to the discharge of the debts of the corporation.[298]

When the rents and profits of a bridge company for a certain period have been sold under execution to a judgment creditor of the company, the court may cause possession of the bridge to be taken by a receiver to collect the tolls and pay them into court for the purpose of discharging the judgment.[299]

An assignment for the benefit of creditors by a corporation after service of process on it in a suit by a creditor for a receiver does not affect the jurisdiction of the court to appoint a receiver.[300]

If fraud on the part of the corporate management is the ground on which relief is asked, the conduct and

appointed.'' The text-books relied upon by the court hardly warrant so broad a statement); Barber v. International Co. of Mexico, 73 Conn. 587, 48 Atl. 758 (where assets of corporation A were transferred to corporation B, under agreement that B would pay all the liabilities of A, jurisdiction to appoint receiver of A to enforce this agreement for the benefit of A's creditors, two judges dissenting)

In the well-considered case of Darragh v. H. Wetter Mfg. Co., 49 U. S. App. 1, 23 C. C. A. 609, 78 Fed. 7, a suit in the federal court was sustained, by a contract creditor who had not reduced his claim to judgment, under the statutes of Arkansas, for the appointment of a receiver and the sale of the property of an insolvent corporation of that state and the distribution of its assets among its creditors.

297 Zieverink v. Kemper, 50 Ohio St. 208, 34 N. E. 250.

298 See Adler v. Milwaukee etc. Mfg. Co., 13 Wis. 57, 62. See, also, Ogilvie v. Knox Ins. Co., 22 How. 380, 16 L. ed. 349.

299 Covington Drawbridge Co. v. Shepherd, 21 How. 112, 16 L. ed. 38.

300 Belmont Nail Co. v. Columbia Iron etc. Co., 46 Fed. 8.

facts from which the conclusion of fraud is deduced must be averred.[301]

If the case is a proper one for a receiver, the denial by the defendant that the corporation has any property or effects of any kind is no bar to the exercise of the jurisdiction. If the denial in this respect ultimately proves true, the defendant is not injured, and the complainant proceeds at the peril of being obliged to pay costs.[302]

§ 126. In Foreclosure of Mortgages on Corporate Property. The power of a court of chancery to appoint a receiver *pendente lite* in foreclosure cases is a part of its incidental jurisdiction, not depending upon any statute. This jurisdiction is not affected by the character of the mortgagor, whether an individual or a corporation. It rests upon grounds quite independent of the character of the parties to the instrument, or the nature of the mortgaged property.[303] Mere insolvency, arising from no proved fault in the management of private corpora-

301 Fort Payne Furnace Co. v. Fort Payne Coal etc. Co., 96 Ala. 472, 38 Am. St. Rep. 109, 11 South. 439. Thus, a creditors' bill which merely avers that the directors of the defendant corporation, acting in pursuance of a vote of the stockholders, had ordered the issue of bonds, secured by a trust deed on all its property, that a portion of those bonds had been issued and disposed of, that the directors afterwards voted to sell the corporate property at a public sale, that the directors then issued a circular letter appealing to the stockholders to purchase the bonds already disposed of, does not present a case for the appointment of a receiver, there being no allegations that any of the directors had an interest in the bonds or in the sale thereof, or that those bonds were not sold for their value and to *bona fide* purchasers, nor any facts stated which show that the proposed sale was not in strict compliance with the terms of the trust deed: Id.

302 Turnbull v. Prentiss Lumber Co., 55 Mich. 387, 21 N. W. 375

303 United States Trust Co. v. New York, W. S. & B R. Co., 101 N. Y. 478, 5 N. E. 316.

tions, is not a sufficient ground.[304] But where the complainant set up mortgages of realty and personalty, the insolvency of the corporation being averred, and dissensions between the stockholders being alleged, tending to show that the condition of insolvency would continue and the assets of the corporation be exposed to deterioration, and the rights of creditors disregarded, it was held that the jurisdiction of the court was unquestionable, and that the complainant had established its right to the appointment of a receiver.[305]

While it is true, as a general rule, that appointing a receiver is auxiliary to the main purpose of the suit,

304 Trust & Deposit Co. v. Spartanburg Waterworks Co., 91 Fed. 324 (suit for foreclosure by holder of bonds secured by second mortgage). The court further says: "There should be some evidence of waste or mismanagement or carelessness or fraud, or extravagance, wantonness, or collusion; some ground to apprehend that the property will suffer deterioration or serious injury; something to show that there is danger of probable loss, or that some rights may be substantially impaired." In Stewart v. Chesapeake etc. Canal Co., 5 Fed. 149, 4 Hughes, 47, the holder of bonds secured by a first mortgage of the tolls and revenue of a canal applied for a receiver, alleging that the default in payment of the bonds was due to wasteful and corrupt management of the corporation. The mortgage provided that the corporation should remain in possession unless it should be shown that default was from other causes than failure of business. It was held that to justify a receiver to manage for an indefinite time an enterprise attended with such risk and difficulty, it must be shown beyond question that the default was due to mismanagement, or that the safety of the property was threatened by corporate mismanagement, and that a receivership probably would result in effectual relief. See, also, City of Cape May v. Cape May etc. Co., 59 N. J. Eq. 59, 49 Atl. 973.

305 De La Vergne etc. Co. v. Palmetto Brewing etc. Co., 72 Fed. 579, citing Kountze v. Hotel Co., 107 U. S. 378, 2 Sup. Ct. 911, 27 L. ed. 609. For another case where dissensions between the officers of a company, greatly embarrassed by its debts, the value of whose property, franchises, etc., largely depended upon the continuation of its business, rendered a receiver almost a necessity in an action to foreclose a chattel mortgage of the company's property, see State Journal Co. v. Commonwealth Co., 43 Kan. 93, 22 Pac. 982.

and that no suit can be brought until the debt is due, it is held that there is no reason for limiting to rail road companies the doctrine that "where default is imminent and manifestly inevitable, though none has taken place, a receiver of a railroad company may be appointed, on the application of a mortgage bondholder, in order to prevent the breaking up and destruction of its business, and to protect the property against attachments and executions in favor of other creditors."[306]

A formal mortgage is not essential in order to give holders of bonds which are a lien on the property of the corporation standing to apply for a receivership; as in a case where the bonds of a canal company pledged the effects, real and personal, of the company, and contained recitals that they should have preference over all debts to be thereafter contracted, and that in default of the payment of interest the holder of the bonds might enter into possession of the tolls, water rates, and other incomes of the company, and might apply for the appointment of a receiver.[307]

§ 127. **Receivers Authorized by Statutes.**—The statutes of the states that have legislated on the subject of receivers of corporations vary so greatly, not only in de-

306 Thompson v. Natchez Water etc. Co., 68 Miss. 423, 9 South. 821.

307 White Water Valley Canal Co. v. Vallette, 21 How. 414, 16 L. ed. 154.

As to the appointment of receivers and managers on the application of debenture holders, under the liberal terms of the English Judicature Act, see In re Pound, 42 Ch. D. 402; In re Joshua Stubbs, Limited, [1891] 1 Ch. 187, 475; McMahon v. West Kent Iron Works Co., [1891] 2 Ch. 148; Strong v. Carlyle Press, [1893] 1 Ch. 268; British Linen Co. v. South American & Mexican Co., [1894] 1 Ch. 108, Bartlett v. West Metropolitan Tramways Co., [1893] 3 Ch. 437; Marshall v. South Staffordshire Tramways Co., [1895] 2 Ch. 36; and cases cited, *ante*, § 92, note 134.

tails, but in their whole scope and purpose, that no attempt will here be made to classify the many and important cases interpreting this mass of legislation. Perhaps the commonest provision is that allowing the court to appoint a receiver "in the cases where a corporation has been dissolved, or is insolvent, or in imminent danger of insolvency, or has forfeited its corporate rights"; but the courts are by no means unanimous in deciding upon the effect to be given to this statute.[308] The remarks of a very able judge in description of this legislation may be of interest: "In the absence of any statute regulating the matter, a court of equity would have the undoubted right, in a proper proceeding instituted by a creditor or stockholder, to appoint a receiver to administer the property [of a corporation that has ceased to exist]. But in many of the states, statutes have been passed expressly providing for the appointment of receivers, or trustees exercising the same functions, though sometimes called by other names. In all cases it is made their duty to collect the assets, pay the debts, and distribute the surplus *pro rata* to the stockholders. As this is precisely what a court of equity would have done in the absence of a statute, it is to be inferred that the motive of such legislation has been to accomplish some other object,—some object, that is to say, for which express legislation was necessary. This inference is fully justified and amply borne out by reference to the different statutes. They seem to have been enacted with the object, in some instances, of abrogating the old law of forfeiture, and reversion; in others, of committing the administration to other courts than courts of equity; in others, to provide general and uniform rules of procedure, as to giving notice

308 Compare the California cases cited below with those from Idaho, Indiana and Texas.

to creditors, etc., to take the place of rules of court and specific orders to be made by the chancellor in each particular case; in others, to keep the matter out of the courts altogether, as by allowing the dissolved corporation to continue its existence for a term for purposes of liquidation, but for no other purpose. The whole mass of this legislation seems to be pervaded by the one idea of simplifying, expediting, and cheapening the means of accomplishing the one object of transferring to the stockholders of a defunct corporation their full share of its surplus assets. There is, from beginning to end, no suggestion of added penalties or punishment after death."[309]

The more important of these statutes, and the cases interpreting them that appear to be of most general interest, are given at some length in the note.[310]

309 Beatty, C. J., in Havemeyer v. Superior Court, 84 Cal. 327, 363, 18 Am. St. Rep. 192, 24 Pac. 121, 10 L. R. A. 627.

310 Alabama.—The statute relating to proceedings for the voluntary dissolution of corporations provides for the appointment of a receiver upon a decree of dissolution: Code 1886, § 1686; see 2 Stimson's Am. St. Law, §§ 8332, 8335. This statute has no operation upon a corporation dissolved by adversary proceeding, and furnishes no guide for the interpretation of statutory provisions relating thereto. § 1691 (Code 1896, § 1299) provides that trustees shall settle the affairs of a dissolved corporation unless other persons are appointed by a court of competent authority. This section neither enlarges nor restricts the inherent power of the courts to appoint a receiver for a corporation which has been dissolved by *quo warranto* proceedings, except so far as it renders such appointment, in most cases, unnecessary: Weatherly v. Capital City Water Co., 115 Ala. 156, 22 South. 140. "The manifest general purpose of the legislature was to commit the affairs and properties of a corporation so dissolved to the persons who were its managers at the time of the dissolution; but the law-makers recognized that there might be special circumstances or peculiar exigencies in a given case which would breed a necessity to take the corporate affairs and property out of the hands of such managers, and, to exclude any idea that the statutory designation of trustees should have the effect of ousting the ordinary jurisdiction of courts of chancery to appoint receivers

upon such circumstances on exigencies being made to appear, they expressly saved this jurisdiction, though doubtless such reservation was in fact unnecessary. . . . . The rule is created by the act. The exception exists apart from the act, and is merely recognized by it. This mere recognition in and of itself neither adds to nor takes from the powers of the courts It neither confers upon them authority which they had not before, nor takes from them authority which they had before, to appoint receivers, except only that the affirmative provision of the act, committing the estate of the corporation to those who were its managers at the time of dissolution, as trustees for its creditors and bondholders, emasculates the mere fact of dissolution, so far as it might otherwise have been considered as a ground for such intervention of the courts, since the statutory creation of these trustees of the assets and concerns of the defunct corporation supplies the means of settling its affairs, which, in the absence of a statute, could probably be furnished only through the appointment of a receiver. So that under the statute a bill praying the appointment of a receiver must aver facts which, upon general principles of equity jurisprudence and procedure, would call into exercise the power of the court to the end sought. A state of things must be alleged which imports a necessity for the appointment of a receiver. . . . The facts alleged must be of a character to show that the trustees are incompetent or unfaithful, or are mismanaging the property to the injury of the complainant, or are without power and authority to subserve some peculiar interest or right of the party complaining, and that he is being injured thereby, or other like situation''; citing Havemeyer v. Superior Court, 84 Cal. 327, 18 Am. St. Rep. 192, 24 Pac. 121, 10 L. R. A. 627; New Foundland R. R. Construction Co. v. Schack, 40 N. J. Eq. 222, 1 Atl. 23 See, also, Anderson v. Buckley, 126 Ala. 623, 28 South. 729; s. c., on second appeal, Buckley v. Anderson, 137 Ala. 325, 34 South. 238.

California.—The provisions of the Code of Civil Procedure relating to receivers of corporations are:

§ 564. ''A receiver may be appointed by the court in which an action is pending, or by the judge thereof: . . . . 5. In the cases where a corporation has been dissolved, or is insolvent, or in imminent danger of insolvency, or has forfeited its corporate rights.''

§ 565. (Amendment of 1880)· ''Upon the dissolution of any corporation, the superior court of the county in which the corporation carries on its business or has its principal place of business, on application of any creditor of the corporation, or of any stockholder or member thereof, may appoint one or more persons to be receivers or trustees of the corporation, to take charge of the estate and effects thereof, and to collect the debts and property due and belonging to the corporation, and to pay the outstanding debts thereof, and to divide the moneys and other property that shall remain over among the stockholders or members."

In the "French Bank Case" (La Societe Francaise etc. v District Court), 53 Cal. 495, it was held that subd. 5 of § 564, *supra*, did not warrant the appointment of a receiver at the suit of a stockholder or creditor for the purpose of winding up the affairs of an insolvent corporation; that this subdivision created no cause of action for such a purpose. It was pointed out that the New York statute from which this provision was copied (N. Y. Code of Procedure, § 244) read: "A receiver may be appointed. . . . . (4) In the cases *provided in this code and by special statutes*, where a corporation has been dissolved, or is insolvent," etc., that such provision existed in the code and statutes of New York, while, except in § 564, the codes and statutes of California were silent on the subject of the appointment of receivers. The arguments of the eminent counsel engaged in this case are of much interest. See, also, Fischer v. Superior Court, 110 Cal. 129, 141, 42 Pac. 561.

The opinion of Beatty, C. J., in Havemeyer v. Superior Court, 84 Cal. 327, 342-389, 18 Am. St. Rep 192, 24 Pac. 121, 10 L. R. A. 627, is by far the longest and most elaborate to be found in any report on the subject of the appointment of receivers of corporations The proceeding was an application for a writ of prohibition to a court which had appointed a receiver of the property of a corporation in a *quo warranto* proceeding upon judgment of forfeiture of its corporate charter. The following abstract of the opinion, so far as it deals with this subject, follows the order of discussion in the opinion instead of the reporter's syllabus. After conceding the inherent power of a court of equity, in the absence of any statute regulating the matter, in a proper proceeding instituted by a creditor or a stockholder, to appoint a receiver to administer the property of a defunct corporation (p. 362), § 400 of the Civil Code (the usual provision making the directors of the dissolved corporation managers of its affairs and trustees for the creditors and stockholders, with full power of settlement; see *ante*, § 123) is declared to establish the general policy of the state with reference to winding up the affairs of a corporation in all cases of dissolution, whether voluntary or involuntary; and the wisdom of this policy is earnestly defended. (P. 365.) "Under our codes, on the contrary, the rule is not to appoint a receiver, but to leave the whole matter of liquidation and distribution to the exclusive control of the directors of the corporation in office at the date of dissolution. The appointment of a receiver is the exception, not the rule, and is not to be made unless some party interested, either a creditor or a stockholder, can show that for the protection of his rights the appointment of a receiver and the administration of the assets under the control and superintendence of a court of equity is necessary." In reply to the suggestion of absurdity in thus interpreting the legislation so as to leave to directors convicted of violating their duty to the state the trust of administering and distributing the assets of the dissolved corporation, the court uses this vigorous language (p. 369): "We confess there does not appear to us to be any absurdity in this supposition. Because a corporation has violated its duty to the public, it does not follow that its members cannot be trusted to look out for their own interests. Quite the contrary; for it is usually a too exclusive regard for their own interests that constitutes their dereliction to the public. As to creditors, their interests must in most cases be opposed to the appointment of a receiver. They will be paid more quickly and more certainly without a receiver than with one. If there is any one thing more certain than another, it is that the appointment of a receiver implies a material diminution of the fund out of which creditors are to be paid. For, in the first place, the fees of the receiver, his counsel, and assistants, are to be subtracted. Then the estate must, in many cases, as it has been in this case, be condemned to unproductive idleness and disuse, and exposed to danger of loss and dilapidation from rust and decay during the long and tedious progress of the legal proceedings that are necessarily entailed. And all this time the creditors must wait and look on, while the fund upon which they rely for payment is being depleted by the processes above referred to. On the other hand, supposing the affairs of the defunct corporation to be under the control of its late directors as trustees for its creditors and stockholders, the creditors have nothing to do but present their demands and receive payment in the ordinary course of business, or if payment is refused or delayed, they may proceed to enforce their demands. How much better this is for the creditors than to have to wait upon the motions of a receiver and the court, under whose order he acts, everyone knows who has had any experience of the two methods of settling the business of a partnership or a corporation. And then it is, as we have seen, always at the option of a creditor or a stockholder to have a receiver, if they can allege facts showing that a receiver is necessary." The contention that the people of the state have an interest in the appointment of a receiver, whenever the charter of a corporation has been forfeited, was met (p. 374) by a reference to the express enumeration, in § 565 (*supra*), of creditors and stockholders as the persons who are entitled to apply for a receiver in such circumstances, and by the argument (pp. 375 *et seq.*) that a receivership is not designed or prescribed by the legislature as a penalty or part of the punishment to be visited upon the stockholders of the corporation in a proceeding in *quo warranto;* but that the punishment is limited to the forfeiture of the charter, and the fine which the court may in its discretion impose; and that the court cannot further affect the corporate property by its judgment, or confiscate or take it away from the stockholders. (P. 377:) "If it is really true that our laws, as they are written, provide no adequate punishment for corporate transgressions, let the legislature take the matter in hand. It is no part of the function of a court to supply the want of penal legislation." (P. 379:) "What is forfeited to the state, and all that is forfeited, is the charter—the right to be a corporation; and this is resumed solely upon the ground that the condition upon which it was granted has been violated. The doctrine is, that corporate charters are granted upon the implied condition that the privilege conferred will be used for the advantage, or at least not to the disadvantage, of the state. If this condition is broken, the charter which the state has given is taken back by the state; but the property which the corporation has acquired with its own means goes to those who have paid for it, and they have the right to deal with it just as others similarly situated may deal with their property. Whatever the law prevents other natural persons from doing they are prevented from doing,—nothing more." The conclusion is reached (p. 380) that the rendition of the judgment authorized by the statute in *quo warranto* proceedings (viz., exclusion from the franchises, and a fine) ends the proceedings, and that no receiver of the corporate property can be appointed unless a new and distinct proceeding is commenced by a creditor or stockholder of the corporation, under § 565 of the Code of Civil Procedure *(supra)*.

The Havemeyer case has been followed in State Investment and Insurance Co. v. Superior Court, 101 Cal. 135, 35 Pac. 549, holding (p. 148) that "the power of a court to appoint any persons in the place of those who are directors of the corporation at the time of its dissolution is given in § 565 of the Code of Civil Procedure, and the authority given therein is the measure of its power", in Yore v. Superior Court, 108 Cal. 431, 41 Pac. 477, holding that the "dissolution" which is a prerequisite to the appointment means the exclusion of the corporation from the franchise of being a corporation, not merely from the franchise of making certain contracts; and in People v. Union Building & Loan Assn. (Cal.), 58 Pac. 822, holding that a receiver should not be appointed in the absence of any fraud or mismanagement on the part of the directors or officers of the corporation, or any want of competency on their part to liquidate and settle up its affairs economically and in the interest of its creditors and stockholders. See, also, Murray v. American Surety Co., 70 Fed. 341, 17 C. C. A. 138, affirming 59 Fed. 345, and 61 Fed. 273.

Georgia.—For cases construing the "Insolvent Traders' Act," (Code, §§ 3149a *et seq.)*, whereby the assets of an insolvent corporation are subject to seizure under a creditors' bill, see Hale-Berry Co. v. Diamond State Iron Co., 94 Ga. 61, 22 S. E. 217; National Bank of Augusta v. Richmond Factory, 91 Ga 284, 18 S. E 160 (corporation need not be a "trader").

Idaho.—In Security Savings & Trust Co. v. Piper, 40 Pac. 144, it was held that a receiver may be appointed pending proceedings for the voluntary dissolution of a corporation, by virtue of a provision identical with § 564, subd. 5, of the California Code of Civil Procedure, *supra.* The French Bank Case, 53 Cal. 550, was distinguished by the fact that there the suit was by a private individual against the corporation, while in the case at hand the action was by the officers of the corporation, duly authorized by the stockholders. In Gibbs v. Morgan (Idaho), 72 Pac. 733, it was distinctly held that this code provision was not intended as an exhaustive enumeration of the cases in which a receiver of a corporation might be appointed.

Illinois.—Rev. Stats. 1893, c. 32, § 25: "If any corporation or its authorized agents shall do, or refrain from doing, any act which shall subject it to a forfeiture of its charter or corporate powers, or shall allow any execution or decree of any court of record, for a payment of money, after demand made by the officer, to be returned 'No property found,' or to remain unsatisfied for not less than ten days after such demand, or shall dissolve or cease doing business, leaving debts unpaid, suits in equity may be brought against all persons who were stockholders at the time, or liable in any way, for the debts of the corporation, by joining the corporation in such suits, and each stockholder may be required to pay his pro rata share of such debts or liabilities to the extent of the unpaid portion of his stock, after exhausting the assets of such corporation And if any stockholder shall not have property enough to satisfy his portion of such debts or liabilities, then the amount shall be divided equally among all the remaining solvent stockholders. And courts of equity shall have full power, on good cause shown, to dissolve or close up the business of any corporation, to appoint a receiver thereof who shall have authority, by the name of the receiver of such corporation (giving the name), to sue in all courts and do all things necessary to closing up its affairs, as commanded by the decree of such court." It is held that the "good cause" which must be shown to warrant the appointment of a receiver and the dissolution of the corporation means some one or more of the causes mentioned in the first sentence. People v. Weigley, 155 Ill. 491, 40 N. E. 300, Wheeler v. Steel Co., 143 Ill. 197, 32 N. E. 420, 17 L. R. A. 818; Hunt v Skating Rink Co., 143 Ill. 118, 32 N. E. 525 "To justify the appointment of a receiver upon a bill filed under this section, something more is necessary than a mere allegation that it has 'ceased doing business' It must be shown that such cessation has been for such time that the court may infer more than a temporary suspension; or facts must be set forth from which it appears that the suspension is more than an interruption of its usual course by reason of some emergency'': Brabrook Tailoring Co. v. Belding Bros., 40 Ill App. 326.

Indiana.—In § 1236, Rev. Stats. 1894 (§ 1222, Rev. Stats 1881), clause 3, it is provided that a receiver may be appointed where the property in controversy is in danger of being ''materially injured'', in clause 5, where a corporation ''has been dissolved, or is insolvent, or in imminent danger of insolvency, or has forfeited its corporate rights''; and in clause 7, when, in the discretion of the court or the judge in vacation, ''it may be necessary to secure ample justice to the parties.'' Goshen Woolen Mills Co. v City Nat. Bank, 150 Ind. 279, 49 N. E. 154. It is held in this case that a receiver may be appointed on the application of a creditor where the corporation has assigned property for the benefit of certain creditors, although no fraud is shown in such assignment, when the complaint contains allegations as to material injury to the property, and as to the insolvency of the corporation and the want of business capacity and financial responsibility on the part of those left in charge of its affairs by the nominal trustee. In Supreme Sitting of the Order of Iron Hall v. Baker, 134 Ind. 293, 33 N. E. 1128, 20 L. R A. 210, it was held that under clause 5, *supra*, the court had jurisdiction to appoint a receiver of a corporation alleged to be insolvent in a suit to secure an accounting of the officers, and the application of the funds to the proper objects of the corporation. A further statute (Rev Stats. 1881, § 3012; Rev. Stats. 1894, § 3435) authorizes, on the application of any creditor or stockholder, the appointment of a receiver for a corporation whose charter has expired within the three years thereafter allowed by statute for the winding up of its affairs. This statute, it is held, does not require the appointment to be made before the expiration of the three years, if the application is made within the three years: Lime City Bldg., Loan & Sav. Assn. v. Black, 136 Ind. 544, 35 N. E. 829, Hatfield v Cummings, 140 Ind. 547, 40 N. E. 53.

Iowa.—The Code, § 2903, provides: ''On the petition of either party to a civil action or proceeding, wherein he shows that he has a probable right to or interest in any property, which is the subject of the controversy, and that such property or its rents or profits are in danger of being lost or materially injured or impaired, . . . the court, or in vacation, the judge thereof, if satisfied that the interests of one or both parties will be thereby promoted, and the substantial rights of neither unduly injured, may appoint a receiver to take charge of, and control such property under its direction during the pendency of the action.'' In Dickerson v. Cass County Bank, 95 Iowa, 392, 64 N. W. 395, it was held that under this section the court has power to appoint a receiver of a state banking corporation on the application of a stockholder. His statutory liability to the creditors constitutes a "probable right to or interest in" the property, if his petition shows that there will be no surplus for distribution to the stockholders; and a showing that the bank was insolvent and that those in charge of it were continuing the business at a loss, and had allowed the assets to become of such a character, and so scattered, that they could not readily be realized on without great sacrifice, supplies the remaining elements required by this section Statutes providing for ousting corporations from their franchises and winding up their affairs do not exclude any rights given to private individuals under this general statute.

Louisiana.—By act of 1898, No. 159, § 1, par. 2, the "civil district court of the parish of Orleans is empowered to appoint receivers to take charge of the property and business of corporations . . . . at the instance of any stockholder or creditor when the directors or other officers of the corporation are jeopardizing the rights of stockholders or creditors by grossly mismanaging the business, or by committing acts *ultra vires*, or by wasting, misusing, or misapplying the property or funds of the corporation." For facts requiring the appointment of a receiver at the instance of stockholders under this statute, see Sincer v. Alverson, 51 La. Ann. 951, 25 South. 650; for the meaning of "grossly mismanaging," see North American L. & T. Co. v. Watkins, 109 Fed. 101, 48 C. C. A. 254.

Michigan.—How. Stats., c. 281, § 6, provides: "Whenever judgment at law or decree in chancery shall be obtained against any corporation incorporated under the laws of this state, and an execution issued thereon shall have been returned unsatisfied, in part or in whole, upon the petition of the person obtaining such judgment or decree, or his representatives, the circuit court within the proper county may sequestrate the stock, property, things in action, or effects of such corporation, and may appoint a receiver of the same." See this section applied in Turnbull v. Prentiss Lumber Co., 55 Mich. 387, 21 N. W. 375.

Minnesota.—Gen. Stats., c. 76, § 9, gives judgment creditors the right to the appointment of a receiver of the corporate property and effects in aid of their judgments after execution returned unsatisfied. It is held that the return of the execution unsatisfied by the sheriff is conclusive, so long as it remains of record in force, as respects the judgment creditor's right to a receiver, and that the court will not entertain inquiries as to the diligence of the officer in endeavoring to find property upon which to levy. If there is any good ground for setting aside the return of the officer, because of its falsity, the defendant in execution should apply directly to the court on motion. See, further, as to the necessity of exhausting the legal remedies of the creditor, Klee v. E. H. Steele Co., 60 Minn. 355, 62 N. W 399 A receivership in a suit to foreclose a mortgage on property of a corporation will not prevent another receivership, under this same chapter, to sequestrate all the property of the corporation for the benefit of all its creditors. "The powers of the receivers in the two cases are entirely different. There are various classes of property that can be reached by a receiver under chapter 76 which could not be reached by a receiver appointed in a foreclosure suit. The former has substantially all the powers and functions of an assignee in bankruptcy": St. Louis Car Co. v. Stillwater St. Ry. Co., 53 Minn. 129, 54 N. W 1064. And where a creditor has commenced an action under this chapter, an assignment by the corporation under the insolvent law will not defeat or impair his right to a receivership: State v. Bank of New England, 55 Minn. 139, 56 N. W. 575; but where, at the time of commencing such action an assignee in insolvency, previously appointed, has for some time been actively engaged in collecting the assets of the corporation and converting them into cash, the plaintiff creditor is not entitled, as a matter of absolute right, to have a receiver appointed: Walther v. Seven Corners Bank, 58 Minn. 434, 59 N. W. 1077; International Trust Co. v. American Loan etc. Co, 62 Minn. 501, 65 N. W. 78, 632. As to what constitutes "insolvency" of a building and loan association under this chapter, see Sjoberg v. Security Savings and Loan Assn., 73 Minn. 203, 72 Am. St. Rep. 616, 75 N. W. 1116.

New Jersey.—Cases under the New Jersey statute conferring power on the courts of equity to dissolve and wind up an insolvent corporation are of more than local interest. The power "was conferred by a statute passed in 1829 [Act of February 16th], and the language by which it was conferred has remained unchanged from that time to the present [1892]. Elmer, Dig., p. 32, §§ 11, 13; Revision, p 189, §§ 70, 72. This statute empowers the chancellor, on the application of a creditor or stockholder, alleging that the corporation in which he is interested has become insolvent, to proceed in a summary way to inquire into the truth of such allegation, and if, upon such inquiry, it shall be made to appear that the corporation has become insolvent, and shall not be about to resume its business in a short time, with safety to the public and advantage to the stockholders, he may enjoin it from the further exercise of its franchises, and also from the further transaction of business; and he may also, at the same time, or at any subsequent time during the continuance of the injunction, if, in his judgment, the circumstances of the case and the ends of justice require, appoint a receiver to dispose of its assets and distribute the proceeds": Atlantic Trust Co. v. Consolidated Electric Storage Co., 49 N. J Eq. 402, 23 Atl.

934. "The ordering of the statutory injunction which places the corporation under disabilities with reference to the exercise of its franchises, is the jurisdictional fact—the condition precedent—which must occur before any statutory receiver can be appointed": Gallagher v. Asphalt Co of America (N. J. Eq), 58 Atl. 403

It was held in Parsons v. Monroe Manufacturing Co., 4 N. J. Eq. 187, 206, that "the foundation of this whole proceeding [under the act of February 16, 1829] must rest on the question of insolvency; for unless that is satisfactorily made out, the court has no jurisdiction; and when made out, there still resides, and must reside in the chancellor, a discretion as to the ordering of the injunction and the appointment of receivers, to be governed by the facts of the case" The court is authorized by this act to appoint receivers at the time of declaring the company insolvent and ordering an injunction, "if the circumstances of the case and the ends of justice require it." It does not follow, therefore, that because an injunction is granted, receivers should be appointed Oakley v Paterson Bank, 2 N. J. Eq. 178; Rawnsley v. Trenton Mutual Life Ins. Co, 9 N. J. Eq. 347, 350; Nichols v. Perry Patent Arm Co, 11 N. J Eq. 126; Newfoundland R. R Construction Co. v. Schack, 40 N. J. Eq. 222, 1 Atl. 23; and the appointment will not be made where the protection of the public and the interest of the creditors and the stockholders does not require it, where, on the contrary, no one who is a stranger to the extensive business of the company can advantageously wind up its concerns and where the charges of fraud against the directors are not sustained; in such a case the management will be left in the hands of the directors, under the immediate control and direction of the court. Rawnsley v. Trenton Mutual Life Insurance Co. Still, as a general rule, where there is a decree of insolvency, receivers will be appointed, and where it appears that after the insolvency of the company was beyond dispute, and well known to all the directors, unlawful sales of all the company's property were made to various directors, no discretion is left to the court, and the appointment is a matter of duty: Nichols v. Perry Patent Arm Co., 11 N. J. Eq. 126. Where the directors of the insolvent corporation are winding up its affairs, where they are men of property and of experience in business, and there is every reason to believe that their closing of the enterprise will be more advantageous to the stockholders and creditors than the management of a stranger in this respect would be likely to prove, and all the creditors and stockholders of the company, with the single exception of the petitioner, are satisfied with the management, an order appointing a receiver should be reversed: City Pottery Co. v. Yates, 37 N. J. Eq. 543.

On the question of the necessity of showing insolvency, the opinion of Van Fleet, V. C., in Atlantic Trust Co. v. Consolidated Electric

Storage Co., 49 N. J. Eq. 402, 23 Atl. 934, is valuable. "The statute makes insolvency the jurisdictional fact The court can do nothing—neither issue an injunction nor appoint a receiver—until insolvency is first established [citing Oakley v. Bank, *supra*, Parsons v. Manufacturing Co., *supra;* Brendred v. Machine Co., 4 N. J. Eq. 294, 305; and Goodheart v. Mining Co., 8 N. J. Eq. 73, 77]. And Mr Justice Depue, in pronouncing the opinion of the court of errors and appeals in Construction Co. v. Schack, 40 N. J. Eq. 222, 226, 1 Atl. 23, declared, in describing what averments a bill in such a case must contain, that it was not sufficient that the bill should merely allege that the corporation had become insolvent and had suspended its business for want of funds to carry on the same, but that the facts and circumstances on which the complainant relies to prove insolvency must be set out. . . . . The proof in support of a jurisdictional fact must always be clear and convincing, for the court derives its power from the fact; and hence, until the fact is shown to exist, it has no power. To doubt in such a case is to deny. . . . . Nor is it the duty of the court to use its power in all cases where insolvency is shown. Something more is required. The prerequisites prescribed by the statute are that it shall be made to appear that the corporation has become insolvent, and also that it will not be able to resume its business in a short time with safety to the public and advantage to the stockholders. The power is only to be used when the ends of justice require its exercise. The court should strive in such cases to foster and preserve, rather than to strangle or destroy. . . . . The principle which I think should control the court in the exercise of this power is this: never to appoint a receiver unless the proof of insolvency is clear and satisfactory, and unless it also appears that there is no reasonable prospect that the corporation, if let alone, will soon be placed, by the efforts of its managers, in a condition of solvency. To illustrate: Where the corporation attacked is shown to be insolvent, but it also appears that its managers are honest and capable, and that they are striving to the best of their ability, with a fair prospect of success, to relieve the corporation from its embarrassment, and to put it in a condition where it may prosecute its business successfully, and the property of the corporation is free from judgment or other lien under which it may be sold speedily, at a sacrifice, the court should not interfere." See, also, to the same effect, Ft. Wayne Electric Corp. v. Franklin Electric Light Co. (N. J.), 40 Atl. 441, 57 N. J. Eq. 16, 41 Atl. 217. The mere suspension of business by the corporation, even though it does not appear that it is about to resume in a short time, does not afford sufficient warrant for the court to assume jurisdiction, when it is not clearly established that the corporation is insolvent: Cook v. East Trenton Pottery Co., 53 N. J. Eq. 29, 30 Atl. 534. On the other hand, while the statute predicates some interruption of the insolvent's business as an element of insolvency, it does not contemplate an entire suspension of all its workings. An insolvent corporation, therefore, is within the scope of the statute, although its business is continuing, and receipts therefore coming into the treasury: Ft. Wayne El. Corp. v. Franklin Electric Light Co., 57 N. J. Eq. 16, 41 Atl. 217; affirmed, 58 N. J. Eq. 579, 43 Atl. 1098.

The statute authorizing the appointment at suit of any creditor or stockholder when the corporation is insolvent, creates a new equitable right which will be enforced by the federal courts: United States Shipbuilding Co. v. Conklin, 126 Fed. 132, 60 C. C. A. 680.

Where a receiver is sought for a corporation that has been dissolved by proclamation of the governor, under § 56 of the Corporation Act of 1896, the discretionary power of the chancellor is invoked, and should be exercised either to continue the directors as trustees to settle the corporate affairs under said section, or to appoint a receiver for that purpose. Discretion to appoint a receiver should not be disclaimed because of failure of proof of breaches of trust by the directors, since the governor's proclamation; their unfitness to exercise the trust may also be shown by proof of misconduct or breaches of trust previous thereto, or of incapacity to perform the duties of the trust, or of conduct indicating unwillingness to properly perform such duties: American Surety Co. v. Great White Spirit Co., 58 N. J. Eq. 526, 43 Atl. 579.

See Bettle v. Republic Sav. & L. Assn., 63 N. J. Eq. 578, 53 Atl. 11, for an instance of the appointment of a receiver for an insolvent building and loan association under a special statute governing such corporations.

New York.—The provisions of the New York statutes and Code of Procedure relating to receivers of corporations are so numerous, and have been subject to so many changes that any account of them must exceed the limits of an elementary treatise. See, for a statement of these provisions as they existed in 1868, Folger v. Columbian Ins. Co., 99 Mass. 267, 96 Am. Dec. 747; in 1892, 2 Stimson's Am. Stat. Law, §§ 8330-8367, and addenda. See, also, for a history of the legislation, United States Trust Co. v. New York, W. S. & B. R. Co., 101 N. Y. 478, 5 N. E. 316. The case of Bangs v. McIntosh, 23 Barb. 591, has been cited by courts and text-writers as establishing the principle that the prescribed method of obtaining jurisdiction of the person and of the subject-matter under these statutes must be strictly followed; but the published opinion in that case was not concurred in by a majority of the court. That a creditor before judgment is not entitled to a receiver in an action for a dissolution of the corporation on the ground of insolvency, see Galwey v. United States Steam Sugar Refining Co., 13 Abb. Pr. 211; Rodbourn v. Utica, I. & E. R. Co., 28 Hun, 369 (where the creditor's judgment is opened, the order appointing the receiver should be vacated), Lehigh Coal etc. Co. v. Central N. J. R. Co., 43 Hun, 546. That in proceedings by the attorney-general for the dissolution of a corporation and the forfeiture of its franchises the court has no power to appoint a receiver before judgment of forfeiture, see People v. Washington Ice Co., 18 Abb. Pr. 382. That the provision relating to the forfeiture of the corporate charter on the ground of discontinuance of business for a year contemplates proceedings by the attorney-general, not by a stockholder, see Gilman v. Greenpoint Sugar Co., 4 Lans. 483. As to the time when the appointment may be made in proceedings for the voluntary dissolution of a corporation, see Chamberlain v. Rochester S. P. V Co., 7 Hun, 557; Matter of Boynton Saw and File Co, 34 Hun, 369 (no power to appoint a temporary receiver); Re Hitchcock Mfg. Co., 1 App. Div. 164, 37 N. Y. Supp. 834. As to the appointment of a receiver "to carry the judgment into effect," see King v. Barnes, 51 Hun, 550, 4 N. Y. Supp. 247, affirmed 113 N. Y. 655, 21 N. E. 184 (in aid of judgment directing defendants to transfer to plaintiffs certain shares of stock in a corporation, by means of which they had been assuming control of the company in fraud of plaintiffs' rights). It has been held that Code Civ. Proc., § 1810, subd. 3, authorizing the appointment when there is no officer to take charge of the assets, does not apply when officers resign for the purpose of having a receiver appointed: Zeltner v. Zeltner Brewing Co., 174 N. Y. 247, 95 Am. St. Rep. 574, 66 N. E. 810.

Pennsylvania.—In *quo warranto* proceedings against a corporation the court has no jurisdiction, upon motion of the commonwealth, to appoint a receiver: Fraternal Guardian's Estate, 159 Pa. St. 603, 28 Atl. 479; Commonwealth v. Order of Vesta, 156 Pa. St. 531, 27 Atl. 14 (construing act of 1893).

Texas.—The courts of Texas have several times been called upon to interpret a provision of their statutes relating to the appointment of receivers of corporations similar to that of the California code, and have reached a conclusion directly opposite to that reached in Havemeyer v. Superior Court, 84 Cal 327, 18 Am. St. Rep. 192, 24 Pac. 121, 10 L. R. A. 627. In Texas, therefore, under the familiar code provision that receivers may be appointed "in cases where a corporation has been dissolved, or is insolvent, or in imminent danger of insolvency, or has forfeited its corporate rights," a receiver may be appointed on the application of the state after judgment in *quo warranto* proceedings against the corporation. East Line & Red River R. Co. v. State, 75 Tex. 434, 12 S. W. 690; Texas Trunk R. Co. v. State, 83 Tex. 1, 18 S. W. 199; San Antonio Gas Co. v. State, 22 Tex. Civ. App. 118, 54 S. W. 289 In Texas Trunk R. Co. v. State, the court says, in speaking of this section of the statute: "The fact that it does not limit the power to appoint, as do the former sections of the act, to cases in which this is asked by creditors or others having a direct pecuniary interest in the subject matter to which the receivership will relate, evidences an intention to confer upon the courts the power to appoint receivers in all cases to which the law applies, whenever the interest of individuals or public interest may require this to be done. The power of the court, adjudging the forfeiture of a corporate franchise and the dissolution of the corporation, to appoint a receiver is too clear, and although the state may not be a creditor the public has such an interest in the proper management of the property of a dissolved railway company as makes it proper that a receiver should be appointed to manage and control its property, to the end that it shall be faithfully applied to the public purpose for which the corporation was originally created, and that this should be done is the more apparent when the mismanagement or disregard of duty on the part of the governing body of a railway corporation has been such as to require its dissolution." In San Antonio Gas Co. v. State, the court observes: "To place the property again in the hands of the officers of the corporation would be to return it to the custody of those who had failed to perform their trust, and had violated the laws of the state, and the public interests would not be subserved thereby. . . . . That the appointment of a receiver will have the effect of a fine inflicted upon the shareholders in the defunct corporation can have no weight in the decision of a court. The statute plainly confides the authority to the court to make the appointment, and that it will bear heavily upon the shareholders is a matter for legislative, and not judicial, consideration. In this case at least, the violators of the law will be the ones who will suffer from the appointment of a receiver."

This statute, however, does not make insolvency or imminent danger thereof a cause of action, and does not entitle a stockholder or lien creditor of a corporation which is still a going concern to have a receiver appointed on the ground of its insolvency, or imminent danger of insolvency, alone; but such stockholder must show, to entitle himself to such appointment, that he has a cause of action against the corporation, independently of the receivership; that the corporation is insolvent, or in imminent danger thereof; and that his interest as such stockholder requires the appointment to be made People's Investment Co. v. Crawford (Tex. Civ. App.), 45 S. W. 738, Espuela Land etc. Co. v. Bindle, 5 Tex Civ. App. 18, 23 S. W. 819, following French Bank Case, 53 Cal 553; New Birmingham Iron etc Co. v. Blevins, 12 Tex. Civ. App. 410, 34 S. W. 828. A receiver may properly be appointed in a suit to foreclose a deed of trust securing bonds of an insolvent corporation· Childress v. State Trust Co. (Tex. Civ. App.), 32 S. W. 330. The jurisdiction of the court to appoint a receiver in suits by creditors cannot be defeated by a transfer of the property of the insolvent corporation to an assignee: Milam County etc. Alliance v. Tennent-Stribling Shoe Co. (Tex. Civ. App.), 40 S.

W. 331. It is held not to be essential, under the statute, that the claim of the creditor of an insolvent corporation should have become a judgment, or that he should have an express lien upon the property of the corporation· San Antonio & G. S R. Co. v. Davis (Tex. Civ. App), 30 S. W. 693; compare Brenton & McKay v. Peck (Tex Civ. App), 87 S. W. 898.

Washington.—The usual code provision, that a receiver may be appointed "where a corporation has been dissolved or is insolvent, or is in imminent danger of insolvency, or has forfeited its corporate rights," is interpreted as meaning that the court is authorized to appoint such receiver whenever any of these facts is made to appear, at the instance of any party interested. "No other conditions are imposed by the statute, and to import any other would be judicial legislation." A receiver may, therefore, be appointed on the application of any creditor of the corporation, when its insolvency is established to the satisfaction of the court, and this, notwithstanding that the corporation has made a voluntary assignment for the benefit of creditors· Olson v. Bank of Tacoma, 15 Wash 148, 45 Pac. 734 That a receiver can be appointed in an action by the state to exclude defendants from corporate rights and franchises, only after judgment in such action, see State v. Superior Court, 15 Wash. 688, 55 Am. St. Rep. 907, 47 Pac. 31.

Wisconsin.—Rev. Stats., § 3216, provides that an action may be brought against a corporation by a judgment creditor after an execution has been returned unsatisfied in whole or in part, and the court may sequester its stock, property, things in action, and effects, and appoint a receiver. Section 3217 provides for a just and fair distribution of the property among the fair and honest creditors, according to § 3245. § 3221 allows directors and stockholders to be made parties. By § 3226, stockholders may be adjudged to pay what is due on their unpaid stock. By § 3227, an injunction may be issued to restrain proceedings by any other creditor against the defendant corporation. Several other sections provide for making the directors, officers, and stockholders parties, if in any event they may be liable to the creditors. For instances of suits under these sections, see Powers v. C. H. Hamilton Paper Co., 60 Wis. 23, 18 N. W. 20; Ballin v. Loeb, 78 Wis. 404, 47 N. W. 516, 10 L. R. A. 742 (the suit may be founded on a judgment of the federal court in the state); Garden City Bank etc. Co. v. Geilfuss, 86 Wis. 612, 57 N. W. 349; Ford v. Plankinton Bank, 87 Wis. 363, 58 N. W. 766. In the last case it was held that where a banking corporation has made a valid voluntary assignment of all its assets, in the manner and form, and to the effect, prescribed by statute, a receiver cannot be appointed under these sections to supersede the assignment and change the rule for the distribution of the proceeds of the assignment to the rule prescribed by statute in receivership cases. Where, however, such as-

§ 128. Railroad Receivers; in General.—It is not uncommon, in railroad receivership cases, to find strong statements as to the great reluctance of courts to undertake the management of railroads, except in the most urgent cases;[311] but the experience of the last twenty-five years has tended to raise the question in some minds whether these expressions are to be taken very seriously, or whether the magnitude of the interests involved actually does—if, indeed, it should—exercise any strong deterring influence on the action of the courts.[312]

signment is fraudulent, the cause of action under § 3216 is not destroyed, but rather strengthened, by averments in respect thereto Powers v. C H Hamilton Paper Co

311 "The appointment of receivers by a court to manage the affairs of a long line of railroad, continued through five or six years, is one of those judicial powers the exercise of which can only be justified by the presence of an absolute necessity"· Per Miller, J., in Milwaukee & Minnesota R. Co. v. Soutter, 2 Wall. 510. "The appointment of a receiver in a suit for the foreclosure of a mortgage on a railroad is not a matter of right, but rests in the sound discretion of the court, and is a power to be exercised sparingly, and with great caution": Per Caldwell, Cir. J., in Farmers' Loan & Trust Co v. Kansas City, W. & N. W. R. Co., 53 Fed 182, 184. "Whether a receiver shall be appointed is always a matter of discretion, to be exercised sparingly and with great caution in the case of *quasi* public corporations operating a public highway, and always with reference to the special circumstances of each case as it arises": Sage v Railroad Co., 125 U. S. 361, 8 Sup. Ct. 887, 31 L. ed. 694. See, also, Overton v. Memphis etc. R. Co, 10 Fed. 866, 3 McCrary, 436; Kelly v. Alabama etc. R. R., 58 Ala. 489; Merriam v. St. Louis, C. G. & Ft. S. R. Co, 136 Mo. 135, 36 S. W. 630; Stevens v. Davison, 18 Gratt. 819, 98 Am. Dec. 692.

312 "In actions to foreclose railway mortgages, it has come to be the fact that receivers are appointed, especially in the Federal courts, almost as a matter of course; and in these and other cases courts have often shown a discreditable eagerness to possess themselves of so much jurisdiction and power, and a corresponding disinclination to relinquish it when once acquired": 5 Thomp. Corp., § 6833. Allowance should be made, of course, for Judge Thompson's well-known antipathy to the federal courts; but the fact remains that out of the vast multitude of railroad receivership cases that have engaged the attention of these courts in late years, in a very small number

While railroad receivers are usually appointed as an incident of foreclosure proceedings, they are occasionally appointed in other classes of cases; as, at the suit of a judgment creditor[313] or of a shareholder;[314]

only does the court take the trouble to justify its action in appointing the receiver.

313 Sage v. Memphis etc. R. R. Co., 125 U. S. 361, 8 Sup. Ct. 887, 31 L. ed. 694, holding that the suing out of execution was not a prerequisite where it would be useless, and no objection was made on this ground. In Milwaukee & M. R. R. Co. v. Soutter, 2 Wall. 510, 523, 17 L. ed. 860, Mr. Justice Miller remarks: "The idea of appointing or continuing a receiver for the purpose of taking ninety-five miles of railroad from its lawful owners, which is earning a gross revenue of $800,000 per annum, to enforce the payment of a judgment of $16,000, the lien of which is seriously controverted, is so repugnant to all our ideas of judicial proceedings that we cannot argue the question. If the creditor has a valid judgment, the usual modes of enforcing that judgment are open to him, both at law and in chancery; but the extraordinary proceeding of taking millions of dollars' worth of property, of such peculiar character as railroad property is, from its rightful possessors, as one of the usual modes of collecting such a comparatively small debt, can find no countenance in this court." For a special statute in Kentucky authorizing the appointment of a receiver in aid of a judgment creditor whose execution has been returned unsatisfied, see Ball v. Maysville & B. S. R. Co., 102 Ky. 486, 80 Am. St. Rep. 362, 43 S. W. 731.

314 Stevens v. Davison, 18 Gratt. 819, 829, 98 Am. Dec. 692 (receiver appointed in suit by shareholder to set aside an unauthorized lease of the road, until it could be ascertained, by proper inquiry, who are the legitimate stockholders of the company, to whom the custody and management of the railroad should be committed), Union Trust Co. v. Illinois Midland R. Co., 117 U. S. 434, 6 Sup. Ct. 809, 29 L. ed. 963.

In the following special cases a receiver was sought and refused. in aid of an injunction restraining the consolidation of two companies, when it was not shown that the directors of the company intended to transfer its property in violation of such injunction: Cleveland etc. Ry. Co. v. Jewett, 37 Ohio St. 649; in aid of an injunction against the performance of an agreement in restraint of trade. Stockton v. Central R. Co., 50 N. J. Eq. 489, 25 Atl. 942; in aid of an injunction regulating the use of a common easement: Delaware, L. & W. R. Co. v. Erie R. Co., 21 N. J. Eq. 298. As to receivers in aid of judgment creditors of railway companies in England under the Railway Companies Act of 1867, see In re Birmingham & L J. R. Co, 18 Ch. D. 155.

but not on the application of the company itself,[315] nor in aid of an unsecured creditor who has not reduced his claim to judgment.[316]

§ 129. **In Foreclosure of Railroad Mortgages; in General.** Whatever may be thought of the practice, the principle is well settled that a receiver is not to be appointed as a matter of course on the mere ground that the defendant corporation is in default.[317] "The right to foreclose does not carry with it the right to a receiver. There are many considerations that bear upon that question. Every case, of course, stands on its own merits. It is difficult to formulate any rule which, briefly stated, will control in all cases. It should appear that there is some danger to the property; that its protection, its preservation, the interests of the various holders, require possession by the court before a receiver should be appointed. It does not go as a matter of course; and yet it is not a matter that a court can refuse simply because it is an annoyance. If, looking at the situation of the litigating parties, and of the property, with the prospect of the future, it should appear to a court that they would be benefited, that their interests would be subserved by the appointment of a receiver, no court—although a matter resting, as it is

315 See *ante*, § 118.

316 Guilmartin v. Middle Georgia & A. R. Co., 101 Ga. 565, 29 S. E. 189.

317 Williamson v. New Albany etc. R. Co., 1 Biss. 206, Fed. Cas. No. 17,753; Union Trust Co. v. St. Louis, I. M & S. R. Co., 4 Dill. 114, Fed. Cas No. 14,402; Farmers' Loan & Trust Co. v. Chicago & A. R. Co., 27 Fed. 146; American Loan & Trust Co. v. Toledo, C. & G. R Co, 29 Fed. 416; Mercantile Trust Co. v. Missouri, K. & T. R. Co., 36 Fed. 221, 1 L. R. A. 397. See, also, observations in Blair v. St. Louis, H. & K. R. Co., 20 Fed. 348.

A bondholder cannot have the appointment of a receiver as against a lessee in possession under a lease prior in time to the mortgage: Louisville & N. R. Co. v. Eakins, 100 Ky. 745, 39 S. W. 416.

said, in its discretion—could refuse to make the appointment."[318]

The reason why it has become the common practice to appoint receivers for the administration of the mortgaged property of railroads upon default in payment of interest on the bonds is lucidly explained in a recent case, in part as follows: "The fact that so many railroad corporations have issued bonds and mortgaged their property in advance of the construction of their railroads and the acquisition of the property mortgaged, greatly beyond its market value at forced sale, had inclined courts of equity to treat holders of railroad bonds, or the trustees in the mortgages, as the owners of the roads, rather than simply as lienholders, and to charge them as such owners, after default, with the unpaid expenses of operating the property. . . . It is true that such [forced] sales are not a reasonable test of the actual value of such property. It is, however, equally true that the conditions which generally affect such property have been found to render it not practicable to make a sale thereof in any other man-

318 Per Brewer, J., in Mercantile Trust Co. v. Missouri, K. & T. R. Co., 36 Fed. 221, 224, 1 L. R. A. 397. A receiver was appointed in this case under the following circumstances: a railroad, mortgaged to the extent of $28,000 a mile, had made several defaults in the payment of interest, aggregating over $1,000,000; its business was decreasing, and was likely to decrease further from competition by new lines; it was in need of repairs and improvements; its bondholders were not in harmony; and no other way existed for applying the rents and profits of the road to the payment of its debts See, further, as to the discretion of the chancellor in the matter of the appointment, Pullan v. Cincinnati etc. R Co., 4 Biss. 35, Fed. Cas. No 11,461; Pennsylvania Co. for Insurance v. Jacksonville etc. Ry. Co, 55 Fed. 131, 2 U. S. App. 606, 5 C. C. A. 53; Kelly v. Trustees etc., 58 Ala. 489; Farmers' Loan & Trust Co. v. Winona & S. W. Ry. Co., 59 Fed. 960; Sage v. Memphis & L. R. R. Co., 125 U. S. 361, 8 Sup. Ct. 887, 31 L. ed. 694; Tysen v. Wabash Ry. Co., 8 Biss. 247, Fed. Cas. No. 14,315; Williamson v. New Albany etc. R. Co., 1 Biss. 206, Fed. Cas. No. 17,753.

ner to any greater or to an equal advantage to all parties concerned therein. The practical result from these prevalent conditions is that, when a railroad corporation is unable to pay its currently accruing interest, it is actually, as well as technically, insolvent, and its property inadequate security for its mortgage debt. The larger part of the value of the property is dependent upon its continued operation as a public carrier. Its successful operation and ability to earn income are in most cases largely dependent on the railroad's connections, and its friendly relations with other carriers, and on the good will it has secured. And while the appointment of a receiver is not a matter of strict right, and such applications always call for the exercise of judicial discretion, these imminent conditions bearing upon such property, after default by the mortgagor in the payment of interest on the mortgage debt, give to an application for the appointment of a receiver great force, and the practice to grant the prayer therefor in such cases has become settled."[319]

[319] Central Trust Co. v. Chattanooga, R. & G. R. Co., 94 Fed 275, 36 C. C. A. 241. In Farmers' Loan & Trust Co. v. Winona & S. W. Ry. Co., 59 Fed. 957, the allegations of the bill and answer were in conflict as to the solvency of the company, the condition and care of its property, and the wisdom and economy of its methods of operation, but it appeared that the majority of its stock was in the hands of a construction company, which had substantially the same officers, and whose interests were adverse to those of the mortgage bondholders. It was held, by Caldwell, Cir. J., that these facts presented a case for the appointment of a receiver upon default in payment of interest on the bonds. In Kennedy v. St. Paul & Pacific R. Co., 2 Dill. 448, Fed. Cas No. 7706, a ground for the appointment was found in the fact that the financial condition of the company was such as to prevent it from constructing a few miles of road, the completion of which within a given time was necessary to prevent the lapsing of a land-grant which formed an essential part of the bondholders' security. See, also, Allen v. Dallas & W. R. Co, 3 Woods, 316, Fed. Cas. No. 221. In Putnam v. Jacksonville, L. & St. L. Ry. Co, 61 Fed. 440, default in payment of taxes to a large amount was held

§ 130. **Same; at What Stage Appointed.**—A receiver ought not ordinarily to be appointed unless the right of foreclosure is clear and indisputable; the existence of a reasonable dispute as to whether the conditions of the mortgage have been broken is sufficient to cause the court to refuse the appointment.[320]

After the decree of foreclosure has been rendered, but under the laws of the state no sale can be had until the expiration of six months from the date, the bondholders have a right to claim that the net income shall be received by a disinterested trustee.[321]

A receiver to preserve the franchise of a street railroad company from forfeiture was held to be properly

an important circumstance pointing to the propriety of a receivership, in connection with a large indebtedness for wages and supplies, although the company had not yet made default in the payment of interest.

A petition by a minority of bondholders of a street railway company showing that the company had failed to pay accrued interest; that it was allowing claims against it to accumulate; that executions had been levied on the property; that the company was without officers; that the trustees had filed resignations, and had refused to act; and that the franchises were in danger of being repealed because of the mismanagement of the road—shows sufficient grounds for the appointment of a receiver: Ralph v. Shiawassee Circuit Judge, 100 Mich. 164, 58 N. W. 837.

320 American Loan & Trust Co. v. Toledo, C. & S. Ry. Co., 29 Fed. 416. In this case there had been default in the payment of interest coupons, but it appeared that there was a fair and reasonable claim by the defendant company, growing out of contemporaneous contracts, that the time of payment had been extended, or that the plaintiffs were precluded from relying on the default. In Brassey v. New York & N. E. R. Co., 19 Fed. 663, a receiver was appointed by consent before default, when it appeared that the company was insolvent, was unable to pay either its mortgage debt, its floating debts, or the sums due connecting roads; that by virtue of numerous attachments it was in danger of the destruction of its business; and that default in the payment of interest was imminent.

321 Benedict v. St. Joseph & W. R. Co., 19 Fed. 173. In this case hostile bondholders were in possession of the road, which was therefore placed in the hands of a receiver until the sale.

appointed at the prayer of the mortgagee under the following circumstances: the city had power to enforce such forfeiture for failure to make certain repairs; the company confessed its inability to make such repairs; and the mortgagee, a party to the suit between the company and the city, stood ready to advance the necessary funds in case a receiver should be appointed with power to borrow money.[322]

§ 131. **Same; Trustee's Right to Take Possession on Default as Affecting the Question of Appointment.**—A provision frequently found in railway deeds of trust empowers the trustee, on default in payment of principal or interest, to take possession of and manage the property, and apply the net income to the payment of the principal and interest. Such provisions have frequently been passed upon by the courts, with reference to their effect upon the trustee's or bondholders' right to a receiver, with considerable lack of agreement in the results arrived at. In an early case it was held that the trustee may waive his right under this provision and file a bill to foreclose, but that in such a suit the court, in the exercise of its discretion, would refuse to appoint a receiver where no mismanagement or misapplication of the revenue of the road was shown.[323] In a series of cases in one of the circuits the appointment seems to have been looked upon almost as a matter of right on

322 Union St. R. Co. v. Saginaw, 115 Mich. 300, 73 N. W. 243, distinguishing the Michigan cases denying the right to a receiver in foreclosure See *ante*, § 94

323 Williamson v. New Albany etc. R. Co. (1857), 1 Biss. 198, Fed. Cas. No. 17,753. No misapplication was shown where the revenues had been applied to the reduction of a floating debt incurred for the completion and equipment of the road, whereby the security of the bondholders had been improved. The principle of this case furnished a "perfect analogy" in the decision in Union Trust Co. v. St. L. I. M. & S. R. Co., 4 Dill. 114, Fed. Cas No. 14,402, per Miller, J

the mere showing of a default by the company; thus, it was decided that where the trustee has failed to take possession after default and a request by the bondholders, a receiver may be appointed on the ground of such neglect, in their suit to enforce performance of the trust;[324] and that when the deed of trust mortgaged the income and profits, a receiver may be claimed by the trustees on the mere ground of a default, irrespective of any showing as to the insufficiency of the property as a security, or that it is in jeopardy, or that the company is insolvent.[325] A ruling similar to the last has been made by a state court, in a case where the suit was by the trustee to obtain possession, not to foreclose.[326] A distinguished federal judge has held that such a suit for specific enforcement of the mortgagee's right is the proper procedure where the mortgage embraces real, personal and mixed property, which cannot be transferred as a whole by the inflexible form and processes of a court of law; and that a receiver should be appointed during the pendency of the suit, where the mortgaged property is an inadequate security, and the company is insolvent and appropriating its earnings to its own use.[327] A single state court has held, on the contrary, that the legal remedies for the recovery of possession are adequate in such a case, and that no

324 Wilmer v. Atlanta & R. A. R. Co., 2 Woods, 409, Fed. Cas. No. 17,775; Warner v. Rising Fawn Iron Co., 3 Woods, 514, Fed. Cas. No. 17,188.

325 Allen v. Dallas & W. R. Co., 3 Woods, 316, Fed. Cas. No. 321. This case, however, presented the additional grounds that the company was insolvent, and that a land grant was in danger of lapsing and the charter of being forfeited, owing to the inability of the company to complete the road.

326 McLane v. Sacramento & Placerville R. Co, 66 Cal. 606, 6 Pac. 748; Sacramento & Placerville R. Co. v. Superior Court, 55 Cal. 453. The statutory provisions relating to receivers in foreclosure were held not applicable.

327 Dow v. Memphis & L. R. R. Co., 20 Fed. 260.

ground exists for the appointment of a receiver where the trustee has made no attempt to enforce his rights at law.[328]

§ 132. (11) **Receiver in Bankruptcy Proceedings.**—By the Bankruptcy Act of 1898, the courts of bankruptcy have jurisdiction (section 2, clause 3) to "appoint receivers or the marshals, upon application of parties in interest, in case the courts shall find it absolutely necessary, for the preservation of estates, to take charge of the property of bankrupts after the filing of the petition and until it is dismissed, or the trustee is qualified," and to (clause 5) "authorize the business of bankrupts to be conducted for limited periods by receivers, the marshals, or trustees, if necessary in the best interests of the estates."[329]

§ 133 (12) **Alimony and Maintenance—Miscellaneous Cases.**—In a series of recent cases in California, the subject of receivers in suits for divorce or maintenance has been considered. The authority for the appointment of a receiver in a divorce suit is found in the Civil Code

[328] Rice v. St. Paul & P. R. Co., 24 Minn. 464.

[329] See In re Sievers, 91 Fed. 366; In re Etheridge Furniture Co., 92 Fed. 329 (assignee may be appointed); In re Fixen & Co., 96 Fed. 748; In re Reliance Storage & Warehouse Co., 100 Fed. 619; In re Kelly Dry Goods Co., 102 Fed. 747 (as to appointment by referee); In re Floecken, 107 Fed 241 (same), Booneville Nat. Bank v. Blakey, 107 Fed 891, 47 C. C. A. 43 (powers of such receiver limited by terms of the statute); In re Rogers, 125 Fed. 169, 60 C. C. A. 567. For the procedure in obtaining the appointment, and the functions and duties of such receivers, see Loveland, Bankruptcy, 2d ed., § 77a. As to appointment of receivers in connection with bankruptcy proceedings in England, see Riches v. Owen, L. R. 3 Ch. App. 820; Ex parte Jay, L. R. 9 Ch. App. 133; Taylor v. Eckersley, L. R. 5 Ch. D. 740; Ex parte Rylands, L. R. 6 Ch. D. 57; Salt v. Cooper, L. R. 16 Ch. D. 544.

of that state.[330] It is held that the whole object of his appointment is to provide security for the payment of such allowance as is made for the maintenance of the divorced wife, and that this would be accomplished by investing him with the title and control of some productive property of the husband, out of the income of which he could pay such allowance, or by authorizing the sale of property to create a fund, the income of which would be applied to the same purpose.[331] Where a husband has failed to pay alimony pursuant to orders of the court, and has attempted to dispose of his property to prevent his wife from getting any part of it, the lien of the alimony upon the husband's estate may be enforced by appointing a receiver to collect the rents and profits, to sell the property, and pay the sums adjudged to be due.[332] But the court has no jurisdiction to continue the receiver after the entry of a final judgment in the action for permanent alimony in a single sum of money; such judgment must be enforced not by a receiver, but by a writ of execution against the property of the husband.[333] It is also held that the right to a receiver in an equitable action by the wife for maintenance without divorce is not dependent upon

330 Cal. Civ. Code, § 140. "The court may require the husband to give reasonable security for providing maintenance or making any payments required under the provisions of this chapter [concerning Divorce], and may enforce the same by the appointment of a receiver, or by any other remedy applicable to the case."

331 Petaluma Sav. Bank v. Superior Court, 111 Cal. 488, 495, 44 Pac. 177.

332 Huellmantel v. Huellmantel, 124 Cal. 583, 589, 57 Pac. 582.

333 White v. White, 130 Cal. 597, 80 Am. St. Rep. 150, 62 Pac. 1062. The provision of the Code of Civil Procedure, § 564, subd. 3, for a "receiver after judgment, to carry the judgment into effect," applies only to cases where the judgment affects specific property, and not to a simple money judgment, where the writ of execution furnishes an amply sufficient remedy: Id.

this section, but is within the general provision of the code for such an officer in all cases "where receivers have been heretofore appointed by the usages of courts of equity"; and that such a receiver should be appointed, when occasion arises, for reasons like those on which a creditor, seeking to avoid fraudulent conveyances of a debtor, is permitted to employ the same instrumentality.[334]

A statute in Indiana authorizes a receiver in an action of replevin, when the property claimed has a peculiar value that cannot be compensated by damages.[335]

A receiver has been allowed, under peculiar circumstances, for the protection of a trade secret, where the usual remedy by injunction was inadequate. When parties become possessed in a wrongful and fraudulent manner of a knowledge of a secret code or system of letters, figures, and characters, and the key thereto, showing the cost and selling price of wares and merchandise, for use between the plaintiff and its traveling salesmen, and have copied the same into a catalogue of their own, a court of equity should take such marked catalogue into its possession, through a receiver, and retain it pending the action, where, in furtherance of justice and to prevent a fraudulent use of such code or system, such intervention becomes necessary.[336]

334 Murray v. Murray, 115 Cal. 266, 56 Am. St. Rep. 97, 47 Pac. 37, 37 L. R. A. 626; as where the husband has endeavored and is endeavoring to sell or encumber his property in the state, and is a resident of another state, and cannot give personal attention to his properties in the state: Anderson v. Anderson, 124 Cal. 48, 56, 71 Am. St. Rep. 17, 56 Pac 630, 57 Pac. 81.

335 Indiana Rev. Stats. (1881), § 1270; Hellebush v. Blake, 119 Ind. 349, 21 N. E. 976.

336 Simmons Hardware Co. v. Waibel, 1 S. Dak. 488, 36 Am. St Rep. 755, 47 N. W. 814, 11 L. R. A. 267. See, also, as to protection of trade secret by appointment of receiver, Tuttle v. Blow, 176 Mo. 158, 98 Am. St. Rep. 488, 75 S. W. 617.

§ 134. **Fourth Class.**—"This class contains those cases in which a receiver is appointed after judgment for the purpose of carrying the decree into effect. In some instances the receiver appointed on motion pending the action is continued in his office after the decree; in others, he is appointed after the decree, when no appointment would be made before the final hearing. In all instances the object of a receiver is to carry into effect a special decree, which could not otherwise be efficiently executed by ordinary process. Among the most important cases in which a receiver may thus be appointed are creditors' suits and suits to enforce other equitable liens, suits to enforce the contracts of married women against their separate estates, and suits or proceedings generally statutory for the winding up of corporations."[337]

337 4 Pom. Eq. Jur., § 1335. As to receivers in creditor's suits, see *ante*, §§ 106-109; receivers in proceedings for the winding up of corporations, *ante*, § 127, note, in mortgage foreclosure, after the decree, *ante*, § 98; Connelly v. Dickson, 76 Ind. 440; Haas v. Chicago Bldg. Soc., 89 Ill. 498; to carry into effect a decree of alimony, *ante*, § 133. The classification of the preceding paragraphs has been based on the subject of the suit, regardless of the stage in the proceedings at which the appointment of a receiver was requested. A provision of most of the codes expressly authorizes the appointment of a receiver for the purpose of carrying into effect a judgment or decree. See *ante*, § 73. See, also, Covington Drawbridge Co. v. Shepherd, 21 How. (62 U. S.) 112, 16 L ed. 38 (where rents and profits for a given period sold under execution, receiver appointed to collect them); Fox v. Hale & Norcross S. M. Co, 108 Cal. 475, 41 Pac. 328, Stockton v. Central R. Co, 50 N. J. Eq. 489, 25 Atl. 942.

A receiver is not infrequently appointed after decree to preserve the property *during the pendency of an appeal:* See Kreling v. Kreling, 118 Cal. 421, 50 Pac. 549 (pending decision of motion for a new trial, to collect rents and profits of land directed by the judgment to be sold), Corbin v. Thompson, 141 Ind 128, 40 N. E. 533 (not appointed, when question is one of disputed title), Chicago & L. E. R Co. v. St. Clair, 144 Ind. 371, 42 N. E. 225, Mitchell v Roland, 95 Iowa, 314, 63 N. W. 606; Eastman v. Cain, 45 Neb 48, 63 N W. 123, Moran v. Johnston, 26 Gratt. 108 (to collect rents and profits

§ 135. **A Receiver is not Appointed Without Notice to the Defendant.**—The appointment of a receiver, to take property from one who is, *prima facie,* entitled to its possession, before the ultimate rights of the parties can be satisfactorily determined, is such a harsh and extraordinary proceeding that the courts will seldom allow it to be done without notice having been given to the adverse party. The leading case on the subject says: "By the settled practice of the court, in ordinary suits, a receiver cannot be appointed *ex parte,* before the defendant has had an opportunity to be heard in relation to his rights, except in those cases where he is out of the jurisdiction of the court or cannot be found, or where, for some other reason, it becomes absolutely necessary for the court to interfere, before there is time to give notice to the opposite party, to prevent the destruction or loss of the property."[338] This statement has been quoted approvingly and adopted by the courts of nearly every jurisdiction where the opportunity has arisen.[339]

of land directed to be sold for benefit of creditors); Beard v. Arbuckle, 19 W. Va. 145 (same).

338 Verplank v. Mercantile Ins. Co. of N. Y., 2 Paige, 438, citing People v. Norton, 1 Paige, 17. To same effect, see Sanford v. Sinclair, 8 Paige, 372, Simmons v. Wood, 45 How. Pr. 262; Strong v. Epstein, 14 Abb. N. C. 322; Whitney v. N. Y. & A. R. Co., 66 How. Pr. 436; Whitney v. Welch, 2 Abb. N. C. 442; Ramsey v. Erie Ry. Co., 7 Abb. Pr., N. S., 156, Ettlinger v. Persian R. & C. Co., 66 Hun, 94, 20 N. Y. Supp. 772; see as to the effect of a statute, Grace v. Curtiss, 3 Misc. Rep. 558, 28 N. Y. Supp. 321; Henry v. Furbish, 30 Misc. Rep. 822, 62 N. Y. Supp. 247.

339 The following cases uphold, or recognize, the principles stated, many of them in the words of the quoted case:

England.—In re Potts, [1893] 1 Q. B. 648 (holding a receiver should not be appointed *ex parte*).

United States.—Barley v. Gittings, 15 App. D. C. 427, North Am. L. & T. Co. v. Watkins, 109 Fed. 101, 48 C. C. A. 254 ("and to deprive him [the defendant] of the possession of his property, without notice, on the motion of his adversary, is a jurisdiction and a power that should be rarely used, and never except in a clear case of imperious necessity, when the right of the complainant, on the showing made by him, is undoubted, and when such relief and protection can be given in no other way"); Joseph Dry Goods Co. v. Hecht, 57 C. C. A. 64, 120 Fed. 760.

Alabama.—Crowder v. Moone, 52 Ala. 220; Ashurst v. Lehman, 86 Ala. 370, 5 South. 731; Thompson v. Tower Mfg. Co., 87 Ala. 733, 6 South. 928 (citing early cases), Moritz v. Miller, 87 Ala. 331, 6 South. 269, Sims v. Adams, 78 Ala. 395; Peter v. Kahn (Ala.), 9 South. 729; Dallins v. Lindsey, 89 Ala. 217, 7 South. 234; Irwin v. Everson, 95 Ala. 64, 10 South. 320; Bank of Florence v. U. S. Savings & Loan Co., 104 Ala. 297, 16 South. 110; Capital City Waterworks Co v. Weatherly, 108 Ala. 412, 18 South. 841; see Maxwell v. Peters Shoe Co., 109 Ala. 371, 19 South. 412, Smith-Dimmick L. Co. v. Teague, 119 Ala. 385, 24 South. 4; Gilreath v. Trent Co., 121 Ala. 204, 25 South. 581; Meyer v. Thomas (Ala.), 30 South. 89.

California.—Fisher v. Superior Court, 110 Cal. 129, 42 Pac. 561 (it would be a "gross abuse of discretion").

Colorado.—Belknap Sav. Bank v. Lamar Land etc. Co., 28 Colo. 326, 64 Pac. 212.

Florida.—State v. Jacksonville P. & M. R. Co., 15 Fla. 201; Fricker v. Peters etc. Co., 21 Fla. 254, approved in Moyers v. Coiner, 22 Fla. 422; see Jacksonville Ferry v. Stockton, 40 Fla. 141, 23 South. 557; Stockton v. Harmon, 32 Fla. 312, 13 South. 833.

Georgia.—Rogers v. Dougherty, 20 Ga. 271.

Idaho.—Cummings v. Steele, 6 Idaho, 666, 59 Pac. 15.

Illinois.—Gilbert v. Block, 51 Ill. App. 516; Nusbaum v. Locke, 53 Ill. App. 242; Craver & S. Mfg. Co. v. Whitman etc. Mfg. Co., 62 Ill. App. 313; English v. People, 90 Ill. App. 54.

Indiana.—Wabash R. Co. v. Dykeman, 133 Ind. 56, 32 N. E. 823; Chicago & S. E. R. Co. v. Cason, 133 Ind. 49, 32 N. E. 827 (citing many early cases); Sullivan E. L. & P. Co. v. Blue, 142 Ind. 407, 41 N. E. 805; Winchester E. L. Co. v. Gordan, 143 Ind. 681, 42 N. E. 914.

Iowa.—French v. Gifford, 30 Iowa, 148; approved in Bisson v. Curry, 35 Iowa, 72; Howe v. Jones, 57 Iowa, 130, 8 N. W. 451, 10 N. W. 299; see Marsh v. Bird, 59 Iowa, 207, 13 N. W. 298.

Kansas.—Elwood v. First Nat. Bank, 41 Kan. 475, 21 Pac. 673; Guy v. Doak, 47 Kan. 236, 366, 27 Pac. 968.

Louisiana.—State ex rel. Brittin v. New Orleans, 43 La. Ann. 829, 9 South. 643, approved in Mestier v. Chevallier Pav. Co., 51 La. Ann. 142, 24 South. 799 (citing early cases); Martin v. Blanchin, 16 La. Ann 237, Ober v. Excelsior Planting Co., 44 La. Ann. 570, 10 South. 792 (as to construction of a statute in regard to notice). See, also, In re Moss Cigar Co., 50 La. Ann. 789, 23 South. 544.

Maryland.—Thompson v. Diffenderfer, 1 Md. Ch 489; Blondheim v. Moore, 11 Md. 365 (stating, "unless the necessity be of the most stringent character, the court will not appoint a receiver until the defendant is first heard in response to the application"); approved in Triebert v. Burgess, 11 Md. 452; see Voshell v. Heaton, 26 Md. 83; Anderson v. Cecil, 86 Md. 490, 38 Atl. 1074.

Michigan.—People ex rel. Port Huron & G. R. Co. v. St. Clair, 31 Mich. 456; Cook v. Detroit etc. R. Co., 45 Mich. 453, 8 N. W. 74.

Minnesota.—Haugan v. Netland, 51 Minn 552, 53 N. W. 873.

Mississippi.—Mays v. Rose, Freem. Ch. 703; Whitehead v. Wooten, 43 Miss. 523 ("there must be strong and special reasons for the appointment before answer"); Hardy v. McClellan, 53 Miss. 507; Buckley v. Baldwin, 69 Miss. 804, 13 South. 851; Meridian N. & P. Co. v. D. & W. P. Co., 70 Miss. 695, 12 South. 702; Barber v. Manier, 71 Miss. 725, 15 South. 890; Whitney v. Hanover Nat. Bank, 71 Miss. 1009, 15 South. 33, 23 L. R. A. 531; Pearson v. Kendrick, 74 Miss. 235, 21 South. 37.

Missouri.—St. Louis & S. R. Co. v. Wear, 135 Mo. 230, 36 S. W. 357, 658; Merriam v. St. L. C. G. & Ft. S. R. Co., 136 Mo. 145, 36 S. W. 630; Tuttle v. Blow, 176 Mo. 158, 98 Am. St. Rep. 488, 75 S. W. 617.

Montana.—Thornton-Thomas M. Co. v. Second J. D. Ct., 20 Mont. 284, 50 Pac. 852; State v. District Court, 22 Mont. 241, 56 Pac. 281. It should not be made upon affidavit based upon information and belief: Benepe-Owenhouse Co. v. Scheidegger (Mont.), 80 Pac. 1024.

Nebraska.—By express terms of the statute (Code, §§ 267, 274), the appointment is void, and subject to collateral attack, if the notice therein prescribed has not been given: Johnson v. Powers, 21 Neb. 292, 32 N. W. 62; see Farmers & Merchants' Bank v. German Nat. Bank, 59 Neb. 229, 80 N. W. 820.

Nevada.—Maynard v. Railey, 2 Nev. 313.

New York.—See cases *supra*, note 338.

North Carolina.—Corbin v. Berry, 83 N. C. 27.

North Dakota.—Grandin v. Le Bar, 2 N. D. 206, 50 N. W. 151.

Ohio.—Schone v. Consolidated Bldg. & Sav. Co., 4 Ohio N. P. 216; Cleveland C. C. & I. R. Co. v. Jewett, 37 Ohio St. 649 (citing early cases). See, also, Devell v. Hinds, 8 Ohio Dec. 177.

South Carolina.—Dilling B. & Co. v. Foster, 21 S. C. 334; Allen v. Cooley, 53 S. C. 634, 31 S. E. 634.

Texas.—Webb v. Allen, 15 Tex. Civ. App. 605, 40 S. W. 342.

Virginia.—Fredenheim v. Rohr, 87 Va. 764, 13 S. E. 193, 266 (citing cases); Va. Tenn. & C. S. & I. Co. v. Wilder, 88 Va. 942, 14 S. E. 806 (stating that appointment without notice would be "utterly at war with a sound, judicial, discretion"). Underwood v. McVeigh,

§ 136. Notice is Necessary Where Appointment Sought in Pending Suits.—The rule as to appointment without notice extends to a motion for the appointment of a receiver in a pending suit where the defendant has appeared, or for the extension of a receivership;[340] the

23 Gratt 418, has the following to say of *ex parte* appointments: "The authorities on this point are overwhelming, and the decisions of all the tribunals of every country where an enlightened jurisprudence prevails, are all one way. It lies at the very foundation of justice, that every person who is to be affected by an adjudication should have the opportunity of being heard in defense, both in repelling the allegations of fact, and upon matters of law, and no sentence of any court, is entitled to the least respect in any other court, or elsewhere, when it has been pronounced *ex parte* and without opportunity of defense." And again, "A tribunal which decides without hearing the defendant, or giving him an opportunity to be heard, cannot claim for its decrees the weight of a judicial sentence": Bristow v. Home Bldg. Co., 91 Va. 18, 20 S. E. 946, 947.

Washington.—Roberts v Washington Nat. Bank, 9 Wash 12, 37 Pac. 26. See Cole v. Price, 22 Wash. 18, 60 Pac. 153; Larsen v. Winder, 14 Wash. 109, 53 Am. St Rep. 864, 44 Pac. 123. It has been held that an *ex parte* appointment has no force beyond the hearing: State v. Superior Court, 34 Wash. 123, 74 Pac. 1070.

West Virginia.—Ruffner v Mairs, 33 W. Va. 655, 11 S. E. 5. Compare Batson v. Findley, 52 W. Va. 343, 43 S. E. 142.

Wisconsin.—Davelaar v. Blue Mound Inv. Co., 110 Wis. 470, 86 N. W. 185.

Wyoming.—See for notice dispensed with, O'Donnel v. First Nat. Bank, 9 Wyo. 408, 64 Pac. 337.

In addition to these cases, the principle is upheld in many of the cases cited in the following paragraphs, where it is applied to particular classes of cases.

340 Cummings v. Steele, 6 Idaho, 666, 59 Pac. 15 (holding that such appointment is not voidable, but void). See Johnson v. Powers, 21 Neb. 292, 32 N. W 62; State ex rel. Brittin v. City of New Orleans, 43 La. Ann 829, 9 South. 643 ("she is entitled to notice of all proceedings taken in that suit affecting her interest The receivership was originally established, as appears on the order, only on her consent and joinder in the application therefor. It cannot be extended and enlarged without notice to her. The exception that the city was bound to proceed by petition has no merit"). Approved in Mestier v. A. Chevallier Pavement Co., 51 La. Ann. 142, 24 South. 799.

ground being that the defendant's right to show why his property should not be taken from his possession should not be defeated merely because he is already a party to a suit in regard to it.[341] But in such cases the notice need not be as direct and explicit as in those instances where the defendant has had no means of knowing that his right to the possession of his property is contested.[342]

§ 137. **To Whom Notice Must be Given; Waiver; Review of Ex Parte Appointment.**—Not only must notice be given to the defendants generally, but the particular person to be dispossessed must be notified.[343] As the notice is given for the benefit of the defendant, who has possession of the property, the lack of notice, or the expiration of the required time after notice and before

In West Virginia the rules have been laid down as follows: "In every instance, before process served—and the application is thus *ex parte*—such notice must be given, except in cases of emergency, where it is impracticable, else the appointment will be reversible. And even after process served, during the pendency of the suit, if such application is made in vacation, there must likewise be such notice; but there need be no notice when made in term time in a decree on the merits. Where the bill prays for an appointment of a receiver, it may be done any time after process is served, without further notice". Batson v. Findley, 52 W. Va. 343, 43 S. E. 142.

341 And where the code provided that a receiver could be appointed, without further notice, in a pending action, it was so construed as not to include an action pending before a referee, and notice was required: Strong v. Epstein, 14 Abb. N. C. 322.

342 In Clark v. Clark, 11 Abb. N. C. 333, the notice was, "if the present receiver is discharged," motion will be made for the appointment of another one, this was held sufficient notice So, where the defendant had had a hearing that served the purpose of a formal notice Hancock v. American Bonding & Trust Co., 86 Ill. App. 630, citing cases.

343 Gilbert v. Block, 51 Ill. App. 516. It has been held that a defendant who has been notified cannot object that the other defendants have not had notice. Rapp v. Riehling, 122 Ind. 255, 23 N. E. 68. As to what constitutes sufficient service, or notice, see Allen v. Cooley, 53 S. C. 414, 31 S. E. 634; Schleer v. Brock, 124 Ala. 626, 27 South. 473.

hearing, may be waived by the party affected, and it will be considered as waived if there is an appearance, without resisting the appointment for lack of notice.[344]

It has been held that the want of notice of the appointment is reviewable upon appeal only from the order granting the receiver.[345]

§ 138. **Cases Wherein Notice is not Necessary.**—The early and leading cases on the subject of notice recognized exceptions to the general rule, that a receiver cannot be appointed before the defendant has had an opportunity to be heard in relation to his rights;[346] as, where he is out of the jurisdiction of the court or cannot be found; or where there is imminent danger[347] of loss, to some of the parties, if the court does not assume immediate control of the property. Thus, in case of a mortgage, where the mortgagor was insolvent, and refused to give up the possession, claiming the exist-

344 Farmers' and Merchants' Bank v. German Nat. Bank, 59 Neb. 229, 80 N. W. 820.

345 Thus the lack of notice was not inquired into on appeal, though the cause was remanded for further consideration, on other grounds. Voshell v. Heaton, 26 Md. 83. Where the record is silent on the subject, the court will presume that proper proceedings were had: Elwood v. First Nat. Bank, 41 Kan. App. 673, 21 Pac. 673; Miller v. Shriner, 86 Ind. 493. It was held in Cummings v. Steele, 6 Idaho, 666, 59 Pac. 15, that a writ of *certiorari* would lie to annul such appointment: See O'Donnell v. First Nat. Bank, 9 Wyo. 408, 64 Pac. 337, In re Moss Cigar Co., 50 La. Ann. 789, 23 South. 544; State v. Union Nat. Bank, 145 Ind. 537, 57 Am. St Rep. 209, 44 N. E. 585.

346 People v. Norton, 1 Paige, 17; Verplank v. Mercantile Ins. Co., 2 Paige, 438; and see cases cited in preceding paragraph, approving the principle of the text.

347 Ashurst v. Lehman, 86 Ala. 370, 5 South. 731, Moritz v. Miller, 87 Ala. 331, 6 South. 269; Thompson v. Tower Mfg Co, 87 Ala. 733, 6 South 928 ("it should be a strong case of emergency, and peril, well fortified by affidavit"). See, also, Whitehead v. Wootens, 43 Miss. 523; Bristow v. Home Bldg. Co., 91 Va. 18, 20 S. E. 946 (case of mortgage, holding it must be an "obvious necessity").

ence of a prior lien, and the crops were liable to be wasted, it was held that the appointment of a receiver without notice was proper.[348] The requisite in any case seems to be that there must be an urgent necessity for the assumption of control of the property by the court, and this may arise from various circumstances.[349] Where the defendant has acted, or is acting, fraudulently,[350] or is about to remove his property from the jurisdiction, or is himself a non-resident,[351] the courts

348 Ashurst v. Lehman, 86 Ala. 370, 5 South 731 ("considering the nature and character of the subject-matter of the controversy, the facility with which the crops may be disposed of, their liability to waste or destruction, the necessity of their preservation and application to the mortgage debt, the insolvency of the defendant, and his application of a part of the crop in disregard of the rights of the plaintiff, we are of the opinion that the bill makes a good *prima facie* case for the appointment of a receiver, *and shows a good reason for failure to give notice of the application*"). In the following cases, receivers were appointed on *ex parte* application in suits to foreclose chattel mortgages: H. B Claflin Co. v. Furtick, 119 Fed. 429; Haggard v. Sanglin, 31 Wash. 165, 71 Pac. 711.

349 State v. Jacksonville, P. & M. R. Co, 15 Fla. 201, approved in Stockton v. Harman, 32 Fla. 312, 13 South. 833; Frickers v. Peters & Calham Co., 21 Fla. 254, approved in Moyes v. Comer, 22 Fla. 422; Jacksonville Ferry Co. v. Stockton, 40 Fla. 141, 23 South. 557. See, also, Elwood v. First Nat. Bank, 41 Kan. 495, 21 Pac. 673 (insolvent bank); Barley v. Gittings, 15 App. D. C. 427 (holding the existence of the emergency not subject to collateral attack). For further illustration see the cases cited in the following paragraphs, where they are collected, in groups, with reference to the class to which they relate. While the rule of law on the subject is not seriously questioned, in its application to the special circumstances of the individual cases, different courts have arrived at opposite conclusions on what are, *apparently*, identical states of fact.

350 Maxwell v. Peters Shoe Co., 109 Ala. 371, 19 South. 412 (case of fraudulent assignment); Heard v. Murray, 93 Ala. 127, 9 South. 514 (conveyance in fraud of creditors), Sanborn v. Sinclair, 8 Paige, 373 (where the defendant fraudulently withdrew himself from the jurisdiction), May v. Rose, Freem. Ch. 703 See, also, Hutchinson v. First Nat. Bank, 133 Ind. 271, 36 Am. St. Rep. 537, 30 N. E. 952.

351 State v. District Court, 22 Mont. 241, 56 Pac. 281 (imminent danger that property would be removed beyond the jurisdiction); Hendrix v. American Land & Mortgage Co., 95 Ala. 313, 11 South.

have considered the emergency sufficient to warrant the extraordinary relief of appointing a receiver on an *ex parte* application. In such cases the allegations of the bill must be such that the court can satisfy itself that a case of emergency really exists, and is not founded on the mere apprehension, or information and belief of the plaintiff.[352]

§ 139. Same; Tendency to Restriction of Ex Parte Appointments.—The cases of emergency in which the courts have allowed a receiver have, in many instances, become quite well settled, and the frequency of *ex parte* appointments, without a due consideration of the rights of all parties interested, has led to much well-deserved criticism by some of the courts. Thus, it is said: "The right to appoint receivers vested in the court should only be exercised when it is clearly shown to be necessary to prevent the defeat of justice. There has been a tendency in recent years among the courts to appoint receivers almost as a matter of course, if the case as made by the plaintiff's complaint seems to warrant such action. . . . In our opinion, it is the duty of the courts rather to restrict than to extend this grow-

213 (mortgage); Hooper v. Davies, 70 Ill. App. 682 (defendant not in the jurisdiction); People v. Norton, 1 Paige, 17; Alford v. Berkele, 29 Hun, 633 (notice to a non-resident partner not necessary); Grace v. Curtiss, 3 Misc. Rep. 558, 23 N. Y. Supp. 321 (debtor not to be found within the state); Henry v. Furbish, 30 Misc. Rep. 822, 62 N. Y. Supp. 247 (but allegation of search is not equal to "not to be found"), Morgan v. Van Kohnstamm, 60 How Pr. 161, 9 Daly, 335; O'Connor v. Mechanics' Bank, 54 Hun, 272, 7 N. Y. Supp. 380. But see Whitney v. Welch, 2 Abb. N. C. 442, holding that though non-resident, the defendants were entitled to "some" notice, and Smith-Dimmick Lumber Co. v. Teague, 119 Ala. 385, 24 South. 4.

352 Verplank v. Mercantile Ins. Co., 2 Paige, 438. "In every case, where the court is asked to deprive the defendant of his property without a hearing, or an opportunity to oppose the application,

ing tendency."[353] The supreme court of Virginia says:[354] "This court has been emphatic in denunciation of decrees and orders entered *ex parte,* and without hearing the parties interested and affected by such decrees and orders." And the general tendency of the courts at present seems to be in harmony with such criticism.[355]

§ 140. Lack of Notice as Affecting the Appointment in the Various Classes of Cases—In Class I.—In those cases where the party entitled to possession is not competent to hold or manage the property during the litigation, notice of the application for the appointment is held to be necessary. Thus the general rule as to notice applies to the property of infants, so that in a suit by the vendor, a receiver to take charge of land sold to the deceased father of minors cannot be validly appointed upon notice to the minor's attorney.[356]

the particular facts and circumstances which render such a proceeding necessary should be set forth." This would seem to be obvious from the fact that the court, and not the plaintiff, is the one to judge of the sufficient emergency of the case. See Fricker v. Peters, 21 Fla. 254; Moyers v. Coiner, 22 Fla. 422; Jacksonville Ferry v. Stockton, 40 Fla. 141, 23 South. 557; Nusbaum v. Locke, 53 Ill. App. 242.

353 Roberts v. Washington Nat. Bank, 9 Wash. 12, 37 Pac. 26; approved, Larsen v. Winder, 14 Wash. 109, 53 Am. St. Rep. 864, 44 Pac. 123.

354 Fredenhien v. Rohr, 87 Va. 764, 13 S. E. 193, 266, citing Underwood v. McVeigh, 23 Gratt. 418, as a notable illustration of the wisdom of the law in setting its face against such orders.

355 In Illinois it is said (Gilbert v. Block, 51 Ill. App. 516): "Courts of equity are exceedingly averse to the appointment of receivers upon *ex parte* applications." See, also, Craver & S. Mfg. Co. v. Whitman etc. Mfg. Co., 62 Ill. App. 313 (same); Wabash R. Co. v. Dykeman, 133 Ind. 56, 32 N. E. 823; Chicago & S. E. R. Co. v. Cason, 133 Ind. 49, 32 N. E. 827. See Grandin v. Le Bar, 2 N. D. 206, 50 N. W. 151 (stating that to warrant an *ex parte* appointment the case must be such that the plaintiff is reasonably sure to succeed).

356 Hardy v. McClellan, 53 Miss. 507.

§ 141. In Class II—Partnership; Conflicting Claimants of Land.—These are cases where all the parties to the suit are equally entitled to the possession of the disputed property, yet, owing to the controversy, it is not just and proper that either of them should retain possession during the litigation.

On application for a receiver of a partnership it is necessary to give proper notice, unless some case of emergency be shown;[357] thus where the plaintiff partner obtained an *ex parte* receiver against the defendants, who kept the books and managed the partnership finances, the order of appointment was reversed as not being within the authority of the court.[358] But if the case is such that the court would appoint a receiver with notice, the defendant may waive the notice and the appointment will be valid.[359]

In suits between conflicting claimants of land, especially between parties claiming under legal titles, a receiver will not be appointed upon an *ex parte* application. Where an action was brought, in equity, to quiet title to real estate, a receiver was appointed to take

357 Maynard v. Bailey, 2 Nev. 313; Webb v. Allen, 15 Tex. Civ. App. 605, 40 S. W. 542 (stating that in partnership cases the same emergency must be shown as in ordinary cases, in order to warrant appointment without notice); Cole v. Price, 22 Wash. 18, 60 Pac. 153 (stating the rule as generally applied, but the case was one of emergency); or if one of the partners be a non-resident: Alford v. Berkele, 29 Hun, 633. As to what constitutes sufficient notice, see Allen v. Cooley, 53 S. C. 414, 31 S. E. 634.

358 Martin v. Blanchin, 16 La. Ann. 237; and where a partner sued for an accounting it was held that he could not have a receiver, nor an injunction restraining defendant from interfering with the firm property, until notice had been given: Larsen v. Winder, 14 Wash. 109, 53 Am. St. Rep. 864, 44 Pac. 123.

359 Longstaff v. Hurd, 66 Conn. 350, 34 Atl. 91; Veith v. Ress, 60 Neb. 52, 82 N. W. 116. But see Pressley v. Harrison, 102 Ind. 19, 1 N. E. 188, and Pressley v. Lamb, 105 Ind. 171, 4 N. E. 682, to the point that mere consent cannot, in such cases, give the court authority to appoint a receiver.

charge of the growing crops. In reversing this order, the court said: "It was an abuse of discretion to make an *ex parte* order appointing a receiver of the crops sown and planted by defendant, upon land where defendant had long resided. The affidavit upon which the order was made showed no exigency which would justify such an arbitrary, harsh proceeding."[360]

§ 142. **In Class III—Persons in Position of Trust or Quasi Trust.**—Even in those cases where the defendant is holding the property as a trustee or *quasi* trustee, and is violating his fiduciary duties by misusing, misapplying, or wasting the property, and is thereby endangering the rights of the parties beneficially interested, the application for a receiver is not granted without notice unless it be shown that the equitable right, sought to be protected, is in imminent danger of loss, or it is probable that the defendant will dispose of the trust property if he has notice, and thereby thwart the object of the application. Thus, on a bill by an assignor to charge an assignee, as trustee, for an excessive collection on a life insurance policy, the verified affidavit of the assignee's insolvency, and his conversion of the money into other property, showing clear probability of *immediate* loss, was the ground on which the application without notice was sustained.[361] And so, in a suit against an administrator for a contribution as co-surety due from the deceased, the ground supporting the bill was the fact that the administrator was rapidly selling the decedent's assets, and had no property of his own subject to execution, thus making it

360 Grandin v. Le Bar, 2 N. D 206, 50 N W. 151, see Pom Eq. Jur, § 1333. See, also, Miller v. Shriner, 86 Ind. 493.

361 Culver v. Guyer, 129 Ala. 602, 29 South. 779; see Pollard v. Southern Fertilizer Co, 122 Ala 409, 25 South 169, and see Simmons v. Wood, 45 How. Pr 262, for a case showing that the mere fact that the application is in regard to trust property does not

evident that the plaintiff would be damaged by delay; the receiver was therefore allowed, without notice.[362]

§ 143. **In Mortgage Foreclosure.**—As stated in a previous paragraph, the grounds on which a receiver is allowed in the case of mortgaged property, are generally said to be that (1) the security is inadequate, and (2) the mortgagor insolvent, committing acts of waste, or disposing of the property, or its crops or income, so that there is a depreciation of the value of the property, and security. These combined circumstances have, at times, given rise to such extraordinary emergency as justifies an *ex parte* application.[363] Thus where a chattel mortgagor was insolvent, and was squandering the proceeds of the property in riotous living, it was held proper to appoint a receiver without notice.[364] It appears on principle, as well as authority, that mere wasting of the property, insolvency, or inadequacy of security are none of them alone sufficient to justify an *ex parte* appointment, but that they must be combined, so as to present a case where there would be imminent danger of loss if the court did not assume control before notice could be properly given.[365]

give the court power to appoint a receiver, on an *ex parte* application, in cases where a sound discretion would require notice, also, Belknap Sav. Bank v. Lamar Land etc. Co., 28 Colo. 326, 64 Pac. 212.

362 Peter v. Kahn (Ala.), 9 South. 729.

363 See *ante*, §§ 93, 95; Ashurst v. Lehman, 86 Ala 370, 5 South. 731; Hendrix v. American Freehold L. & M. Co., 95 Ala. 313, 11 South. 213 (allowing a receiver without notice), citing early cases See Gilbert v. Block, 51 Ill. App. 516 (citing cases); Maish v. Bird, 59 Iowa, 307, 13 N. W. 298 (allowing receiver without notice).

364 O'Donnell v. First Nat. Bank, 9 Wyo. 408, 64 Pac. 337. For further instances of appointment *ex parte* in suits to foreclose chattel mortgages, see H. B. Claflin Co. v. Furtick, 119 Fed 429, Haggard v. Sanglin, 31 Wash. 165, 71 Pac. 711.

365 Gilbreath v. N. B. & T. Co, 121 Ala. 204, 25 South 581, Moyers v. Coiner, 22 Fla. 422, where insolvency was not alleged,

§ 144. In Creditors' Suits.—In the case of creditors, having a judgment or other lien on the debtor's property, there must be shown some sufficient reason why notice should not be given, in order to warrant an *ex parte* appointment. If the debtor, who is disposing of his property, is still solvent, there seems no reason for an appointment without notice;[366] or if the one to whom the goods are being fraudulently transferred is able to respond to a legal demand, notice should be given.[367] But where an insolvent debtor had fraudulently conveyed all his property, and it was being wasted, it was held that no notice was necessary.[368] If a debtor fraudulently withdraws himself from the jurisdiction, to evade process, no notice is necessary, but, it is held, the mere fact that he is absent does not give the plaintiff a right to seize his property unless there is danger of immediate loss.[369] The rights of creditors,

Hutchison v. First Nat. Bank, 133 Ind. 271, 36 Am St. Rep. 537, 30 N. E. 952, Haugan v. Netland, 51 Minn. 552, 53 N. W. 873; see Pearson v. Kendrix, 74 Miss 235, 21 South. 37, which was affected by statute; Fletcher v. Krupp, 35 App. Div. 586, 55 N Y. Supp. 146; Belknap Sav. Bank v. Lamar Land etc. Co., 28 Colo. 326, 64 Pac. 212.

366 Moritz v Miller, 87 Ala. 331, 6 South. 269 (stating if the insolvency had existed, the appointment would have been made *ex parte*).

367 Thompson v. Tower Mfg. Co., 87 Ala. 733, 6 South. 928.

368 Heard v. Murray, 93 Ala. 127, 9 South. 514. See, also, Peter v. Kahn (Ala.), 9 South. 729 (holding an allegation of deficiency of legal assets sufficient to impart equity to the bill); Bank of Florence v. United States Sav. & Loan Co, 104 Ala. 297, 16 South. 110 (showing that a simple bank creditor cannot, on the insolvency of the bank, obtain a receiver on *ex parte* application and thereby impress the funds with a prior lien), and Smith-Dimmick Lumber Co. v. Teague, 119 Ala. 385, 24 South. 4, that the debtor's insolvency and the fact that he is about to remove his property does not deprive him of the right to notice; see Maxwell v. Peters Shoe Co, 109 Ala. 371, 19 South. 412; State v. Union Nat Bank, 145 Ind. 537, 57 Am. St Rep. 209, 44 N. E. 585; Blondheim v. Moore, 11 Md. 365, one of the leading cases on the subject.

369 Sandford v. Sinclair, 8 Paige, 373; and see, for the effect of

in such cases, are well stated in a leading Mississippi case: "Creditors have rights which should be upheld, so have others, which must not be disregarded," and the appointment of a receiver, in such case, is "never without notice to them (the defendants) and an opportunity to be heard, unless there is a satisfactory showing of the necessity of such emergency."[370]

§ 145. **In Suits by Stockholders Against Corporation**— In a suit against a corporation for the appointment of a receiver, in any of those instances where a receiver is proper, the stockholders must conform to the general practice, and give proper notice of the application unless there is some extremely urgent necessity to justify a departure from the rule. Thus upon a suit by a minority stockholder to obtain a receiver on the ground of unwise management of the property by the corporate directors, the appellate court, in reversing the appointing order, said: "Where notice can be given, it should be given, unless there is imminent danger of loss or great damage, or irreparable injury, or the greatest emergency, or when by the giving of notice the very purpose of the appointment of a receiver would be rendered nugatory."[371] The leading case in regard to

a code provision in such cases, Grace v. Curtiss, 23 N. Y. Supp. 321, 3 Misc. Rep. 558; Henry v. Furbish, 30 Misc. Rep. 822, 62 N. Y. Supp. 247; O'Conner v. Mechanics' Bank, 2 N. Y. Supp. 225, 18 N. Y. St. Rep. 88, 54 Hun, 272; Leggett v. Sloan, 24 How. Pr. 479 (as to what notice is sufficient); Barnett v. Moore, 20 Misc. Rep. 518, 46 N. Y. Supp. 668 (as to waiver of notice on supplementary proceedings); Corbin v. Berry, 83 N. C. 27 (where only part of the defendants appeared, and it was held sufficient). See Ruffner v. Mairs, 33 W. Va. 655, 11 S. E. 5.

370 Buckley v. Baldwin, 69 Miss. 804, 13 South. 851.

371 North American L. & T. Co. v. Watkins, 109 Fed. 101, 48 C. C. A. 254. See, also, Fisher v. Superior Court, 110 Cal. 129, 42 Pac. 561; French v. Gifford, 30 Iowa, 148; State v. Second J. D. Ct., 20 Mont. 284, 50 Pac. 852.

the necessity of notice of an application for a receiver was a stockholders' suit against a corporation.[372]

§ 146. **In Suits by Creditors Against Corporation.**—Even in those instances where a receiver may be properly appointed, in suits against a corporation by its creditors, in order to protect their rights, the courts are extremely averse to making an appointment without notice having been given, and a case of extreme urgency and necessity must be clearly shown in order to obtain an *ex parte* appointment.[373]

In a case where a receiver was appointed without notice, on the ground that the corporation was indebted to various persons, and had equitable interests that could not be reached by execution, and that other creditors had threatened to bring actions, the court, in reversing the order of appointment, said: "The proceeding is drastic. It takes away from the corporation all control of its property, and puts it in the hands of a stranger. . . . . Cases can well be imagined where great interests might be sacrificed by a proceeding without notice."[374]

372 Verplank v. Mercantile Ins. Co., 2 Paige, 438

373 Mestier v. Chevallier Pav. Co, 51 La. Ann. 142, 24 South. 799 (stating, "But we are aware of no authority for the appointment of a receiver *ex parte* in a pending suit against a corporation, as appears to have been done in this case). See Gilbreath v. Trust Co, 121 Ala 204, 25 South. 581; Winchester E. L. Co. v. Gordon, 143 Ind. 681, 42 N. E. 914, approving Sullivan E. L & P. Co. v Blue, 142 Ind 407, 41 N. E. 805 As to creditors of railroad corporations, Whitney v. N. G. & A. R Co, 66 How. Pr. 436. As to a municipal corporation, State *ex rel.* Brittin v. New Orleans, 43 La. Ann 829, 9 South 643.

374 Davelaar v. Blue Mound Inv. Co, 110 Wis. 470, 86 N. W. 185 ("it is not enough to say that the facts stated show the plaintiff would be entitled to such appointment upon notice, and that after a review of the situation the court has decided to allow the appointment to stand").

§ 147. Ex Parte Receivers of Railroads.—The appointment of a receiver to take charge of a railroad and manage it is such an extremely important undertaking, that it will rarely be done without notice having been given to the defendant, and an opportunity of defense offered.[375] The supreme court of Indiana has said: "In passing upon an application for the appointment of a receiver, it is the duty of a court to scrutinize, not only the rights asserted by the moving party, but the injuries that may be suffered by the adverse party and the public at large. This is particularly the case where a line of railroad forming part of a system operated as a unit is thereby detached from the main road. In such cases not only the parties to the suit are affected, but a large number of employees are disturbed in their relation with their employers; and the general public along the line of the road are liable to be greatly inconvenienced by the disturbance of their shipping facilities. . . . . Deprived of possession, the payment of rent on leased lines would cease, and thereby all creditors and stockholders would be affected"; for these reasons the court held that it was error to appoint a receiver *ex parte,* though expressly stating that it ventured no opinion as to the propriety of an appointment, had proper notice been given.[376] After commenting on the

375 Oher v. Excelsior Planting Co., 44 La. Ann. 570, 10 South. 792 (construing a statute so that notice is necessary before a corporation can be deprived of its property); Merriam v. St. Louis, C. G. & F. S. R. Co., 136 Mo. 145, 36 S. W. 630; St. Louis, K. & S. R. Co. v. Wear, 135 Mo. 230, 33 L. R. A. 341, 36 S. W. 357, 658 (a vacation appointment providing for appearance three months hence, controlled by writ of prohibition); Ramsey v. Erie Ry. Co., 7 Abb. Pr., N. S., 156; People ex rel. Port Huron & G. R. Co. v. St. Clair Circuit Judge, 31 Mich 456 (holding an *ex parte* appointment, in case of a railroad, "more than irregular, and absolutely void"); Cook v. Detroit etc. R. R. Co., 45 Mich. 453, 8 N. W. 74.

376 Wabash R. R. Co. v. Dykeman, 133 Ind. 56, 32 N. E. 823; approved, Chicago & S. E. R. Co. v. Cason, 133 Ind. 49, 32 N. E. 827.

gravity of the situation, the supreme court of Florida, in reversing the appointing order, says: "We can hardly imagine a case where it [the appointment] should be done without notice."[377]

§ 148. **Selection and Eligibility of Receiver—In General—Not Disturbed on Appeal.**—In the selection of a person to act as receiver the court acts in the exercise of its judicial discretion, aided by the circumstances of the case and the comparative fitness of the parties proposed, choosing such person as it considers will best subserve the rights and interests of all parties to the controversy.[378] The questions to be considered, generally, are well stated, by a federal case,[379] as follows: "It [the court] places the property in the hands of a receiver, whose duty it is to preserve it, prevent deterioration, and so manage it that the rights of its real owner will be prejudiced as little as possible. The person selected for this duty must possess integrity of character, business experience, a knowledge of affairs, a capacity for the examination into and comprehension of accounts, must not be partisan, and must have no pecuniary interest in any one of the classes of creditors whose claims come before the court."

377 State v. Jacksonville P. & M. R. Co., 15 Fla. 201; approved in Stockton v. Harman, 32 Fla. 312, 13 South. 833.

378 Thomas v. Dawkins, 1 Ves. 452; Morison v. Morison, 4 Mylne & C. 215; Perry v. Oriental Hotel Co., L. R. 5 Ch. 420; People *ex rel.* Gore v. Ill. Bldg. & L. Assn., 56 Ill. App. 642; Robinson v. Dickey, 143 Ind. 214, 42 N. E. 638; Borton v. Brines-Chase Co., 175 Pa. St. 209, 34 Atl. 597 (refusing to appoint a foreign receiver); Shannon v. Hanks, 88 Va. 338, 13 S. E. 437. And thus, where it would "facilitate matters" and be to the "advantage of all parties interested," a foreign receiver was appointed: Taylor v. Life Assn. of America, 3 Fed. 465; also, Bayne v. Brewer Pottery Co., 82 Fed. 391.

379 Farmers' L. & T. Co. v. Cape Fear & G. V. R. Co., 62 Fed. 675 (and these requisites may be present, though the appointed party is not a citizen of the appointing jurisdiction).

The selection of a receiver, being a matter addressed to the discretion of the court, is not generally disturbed on appeal. It is stated that "convincing circumstances, amounting to an overwhelming objection in point of propriety of choice, or something fatal in principle must be shown to secure a reversal by an appellate tribunal."[380]

§ 149. **Appointment of Person Interested in the Suit.**—Accordingly, it is generally stated that a person will not be appointed who is interested in the outcome of the suit, it being considered that such interest will interfere with the proper, impartial management of the entrusted property. Thus, "a receiver should have no personal interest in the controversy, or in the property in his charge, which would prevent the exercise of his duties and powers without favor to either party."[381] While the soundness of this rule is undoubted, there are certain cases in which the receiver, for various reasons, has been selected from among the interested parties; as where the parties consented to such appointment,[382]

380 People ex rel. Gore v. Ill. Bldg. & L. Assn., 56 Ill. App. 642. See, also, Perry v. Oriental Hotel Co., L. R. 5 Ch 420; McGilliard v. Donaldsonville etc. Works, 104 La. Ann. 544, 81 Am. St. Rep. 145, 29 South. 254; Shannon v. Hanks, 88 Va. 338, 13 S. E. 437, as to when the question may be raised, see Rogers v. Rogers (Tenn. Ch. App.), 42 S W. 70.

381 Watson v. Bettman, 88 Fed. 825 (refusing to appoint a person otherwise well qualified). See, also, Cooper v. Leather Mfg. Nat. Bank, 29 Fed. 161; Bayne v. Brewer Pottery Co., 82 Fed. 391; Atkins v. Wabash St. L. & P. R. Co., 29 Fed. 161, In re Lloyd, L R. 12 Ch. D 447; Etowah Min. Co. v. Wills V. M. & M. Co., 106 Ala. 492, 17 South. 522 ("a receiver appointed by the court should be capable, honest, impartial, and without personal interest to serve"); approved in Jordan v. Jordan, 121 Ala. 419, 25 South 855.

382 Tait v. Carey (Ind Ter.), 49 S. W. 50; Iroquois Furnace Co. v. Kimbark, 85 Ill. App 399 (where they had previously agreed as to who should be appointed); Hanover Fire Ins. Co. v. Germania Fire Ins. Co., 33 Hun, 539.

or where a receiver is appointed merely as an aid in the settling of an estate, and it is clear that the defendant's possession can do no harm,[383] or in the case of a temporary appointment.[384] And there are cases in which a receiver has been appointed because of his intimate knowledge of the business to be transacted, regardless of the fact that he was an interested party. It must, indeed, be a strong case to warrant such action, but where a business is extremely complicated, and an experienced manager necessary, from a practical business standpoint, it may be advisable to have it continue in the hands of one acquainted with its management when he can be controlled by the court.[385]

383 Robinson v. Taylor, 42 Fed. 803.

384 Finance Co. v. Charleston C. & C. R. Co, 45 Fed 436

385 Fowler v. Jarvis-Conklin Mtg. Co, 63 Fed. 888, stating, on refusing a motion to discharge a receiver who had been an officer of the corporation: "It was well known to the court where they were appointed, that it was under their management of its affairs that the corporation came to grief, and it would be no surprise to the court to learn that their business judgment had not been sound; that their method of management had not been conservative, that they had been over-sanguine, and improvident in investments But it was apparent to the court then, and it is equally apparent now, that a business of such character, so complicated and intricate, so widely extended, with millions of dollars on small mortgages scattered through several states, requiring prompt attention for collection of interest, maintaining of insurance, and payment of taxes, would be best attended to by receivers who, presumably, were familiar with all its details and with the machinery already established for looking after its interests in hundreds of small towns and hamlets in different states. As receivers there would be no new investments for them to make, calling for the exercise of a discretion which had in the past proved to be not always wise. . . . The mere fact that they had, while officers of the company, been imprudent in investing its money, was no sufficient ground for selecting strangers entirely unfamiliar with its assets or the machinery for their collection." See, to the same effect, People ex rel. Gore v Illinois Bldg. & L. Assn., 56 Ill. App. 642, the court selecting an interested party because of his "fitness for the position by reason of his occupation, experience and character"; Iroquois Furnace Co. v.

§ 150. Appointment of Master in Chancery; of Trustee; of Solicitor.—It is generally true that the court will be slow to appoint one as receiver, whose position will be liable to interfere with the proper exercise of his duties. On these grounds a master in chancery has been held to be improperly appointed, the court saying: "Nor will a man be appointed receiver whose position may cause difficulty in administering justice. A master in chancery, accordingly, was disqualified from being appointed a receiver, because, being an officer whose duty it might be to pass upon the accounts and check the conduct of the receiver, his appointment was open to objection on very obvious grounds."[386] On these grounds, it is generally held that a trustee shall not be appointed to the office; the court saying that the trustee should be the one to check the accounts of the receiver in favor of the beneficiaries.[387] But, as in other cases, if the trustee is the most acceptable person available, he may, in special cases, be appointed without compensation.[388]

One of the grounds on which the court refuses to appoint a solicitor of one of the parties to the office of receiver is, that in the service of his client it may become the duty of the solicitor to call the receiver to

Kimbark, 85 Ill. App. 399; Balles v. Duff, 54 Barb 215, a case where mortgagee of mortgaged premises was appointed. For further instances of interested parties appointed as receivers, see early cases cited in Taylor v. L. Ins. Co. of Am, 3 Fed. 465, and the cases cited *post* in regard to receivers of partnership and corporation property.

386 Ex parte Fletcher, 6 Ves. 427, quoted approvingly in Kilgore v. Hair, 19 S. C. 486, approved in Allen v. Cooley, 60 S. C. 353, 38 S. E. 622, Bemeson v. Bill, 62 Ill. 408 In In re Lloyd, L. R. 12 Ch. D. 447, a solicitor was refused on the same grounds. But this objection does not extend to a clerk of the court, who may be a proper person: Waters v. Melson, 112 N. C. 89, 16 S. E 918.

387 Thomas v. Hawkins, 1 Ves. 452, and note 2, Anon, 3 Ves. 515; —— v. Jolland, 8 Ves. 72; Sutton v. Jones, 15 Ves. 584.

388 Sykes v. Hastings, 11 Ves. 363.

account,[389] and the two characters, being incompatible, cannot be united, as it would result in the receiver supervising his own acts.[390] The interest that a solicitor has, in favor of the client he represents, has also been urged as a valid reason for his non-appointment, or his removal where he was properly appointed as temporary receiver.[391]

§ 151. **Appointment of Partner; of Creditor.**—In the cases where a partnership is placed under the control of the court, one of the partners has, in many instances, been appointed receiver, the fact of his being an interested party not disqualifying him, in the absence of other additional objections. It has been said: "The courts have, therefore, been inclined, where there has been no actual misconduct, to appoint as receiver the managing partner, or the partner most interested."[392] But in such case the partner-receiver is allowed no compensation for his services.[393]

While a creditor is pecuniarily interested in the settlement of the controversy, this fact alone does not appear to affect his eligibility to the position of re-

389 Ex parte Pericke, 2 Mer. 452; Stone v. Wishart, 2 Madd. 67 (where the same principle was applied to the next friend of an infant). Such appointment is prohibited by statute in some jurisdictions: See Cook v. Martin (Ark), 87 S. W. 625.

390 Garland v. Garland, 2 Ves. Jr. 137; Merchants' & Mfg. N Bank of D. v. Kent Cir. J., 43 Mich. 292, 5 N. W. 627 (extending the rule to the partner of the solicitor).

391 Finance Co. of Penn v. Charleston C. & C. R. Co., 45 Fed. 436; State Trust Co. of N. Y. v Nat. L. I. & Mfg. Co., 72 Fed. 575, making him ineligible for permanent appointment: Baker v. Admrs. of Backus, 32 Ill. 79.

392 Todd v. Rich, 2 Tenn. Ch. 107; Blakeney v. Dufour, 15 Beav 40; Wilson v. Greenwood, 1 Swans. 471; Brien v. Harriman, 1 Tenn. Ch. 467, stating "It is an unusual order and can only be sustained by his acting without compensation."

393 Cases cited *supra* in note 392.

ceiver; it is said: "There is no rule of law that a creditor cannot be appointed receiver."[394]

§ 152. **Appointment of Corporation Officer**—In the appointment of a receiver to take charge of the property of a corporation, the general rule is not to appoint those who have been connected with, or responsible for, its unfortunate condition, rendering it necessary for the court to assume its control.[395] The reasons, as generally stated, are two: First, the probable lack of business ability, as explained by a leading federal case in the following language: "But it has been the uniform practice in this circuit to appoint no one receiver of a railroad corporation who has been one of its officers, or who had anything to do with its control prior to its insolvency. It has always been thought that while the insolvency of the company might have been caused by misfortune, and by no default of its direction, nevertheless those who were about to lose their property, or had it placed in jeopardy, were entitled, in all reason and fairness, to a new management, though perhaps not a better one. In the one case, there is some hope; in the other, there can be expected but the former result."[396] The further reason, that they are frequently

394 Chamberlain v. Greenleaf, 4 Abb. N. C. 92. See, also, Barber v. International Co. of Mexico, 73 Conn. 587, 48 Atl 758, Barker v. Wayne Circuit Judge, 117 Mich. 325, 75 N. W 886; Roby v Title G. & T. Co, 166 Ill. 336, 46 N. E. 1110 (where a receiver's becoming a creditor did not disqualify him)

395 See cases cited in notes 396 and 397. But there seems to be no objection to a corporation, as such, being a receiver: Roby v Title G. & T. Co., 166 Ill. 336, 46 N. E. 1110; Barker v. Wayne County Judge, 117 Mich. 325, 75 N. W. 886; Barber v. International Co of Mexico, 73 Conn. 587, 48 Atl. 758.

396 Finance Co. of Penn. v. Charleston C. & C. R. Co, 45 Fed 436 (refusing both a former counsel and an officer as permanent receiver). See, also, Buck v. Piedmont, etc Ins. Co., 4 Fed. 849, 4 Hughes, 415; People v. Third Avenue Sav. Bank, 50 How. Pr 22;

interested parties, while applying particularly to stockholders, is at times a pertinent objection to an officer or manager, especially when he happens to occupy both positions; thus it is said: "Receivers should be impartial between the parties in interest, and stockholders and directors of insolvent corporations should not be appointed, unless the case is exceptional and urgent, and then only on the consent of the parties whose interest is to be intrusted to their charge."[397]

§ 153. Same; Officers or Stockholders Appointed from Necessity.—While the rule as to the non-appointment of officers, directors or stockholders to be receivers over the corporate property is well settled by authority, and founded on practical reasons, the courts are confronted,

Freeholders of Middlesex v. State Bank, 28 N. J. Eq. 166, approved in McCullough v. Merchants' L. & T. Co., 29 N. J. Eq. 217.

397 Atkins v. Wabash St. L. & P. R. R. Co., 29 Fed. 161, removing a receiver because of his interest; Olmstead v. Distilling & Cattle Feeding Co. (Ill.), 69 Fed. 24, stating, when removing a receiver: "I have never felt that an officer of a corporation, whose misfortunes necessitated a receivership, should be ineligible to employment by the court, but this case convinces me that where a corporation is one that covers a vast diversity of conflicting interests, and especially of speculation, a stockholder's appointment to a receivership should be preceded by a most careful and thorough scrutiny into his official and personal antecedents and interests." .... "Indeed, I will knowingly accept no man as a receiver for any corporation who is, or who has been, a speculator in its stock. The private interest of the man is very apt to color, if not to overcome, the duty of the official. .... Especially is it the need of the day that officials who only come in contact with these affairs by virtue of their office should keep clean of any personal intermeddling that might, even remotely, tend to affect their official conduct." See, also, Etowah Min. Co. v. Manufacturing Co., 106 Ala. 492, 17 South. 522 (stockholder); Mercantile Trust & D. Co. v. Water Co., 111 Ala. 119, 19 South. 17 (but the appointment of such interested person is not void); People ex rel. Gore v. Illinois Bldg. & L. Assn., 56 Ill. App. 642 (but the stockholder may remove the objection by a *bona fide* transfer of his stock before appointment); Wiswell v. Starr, 48 Me. 401 (stockholder).

on the other hand, with the fact that in many cases the business of a large corporation is so complicated, and requires such expert and experienced management for its profitable continuance, that it is absolutely necessary to retain, as receiver and manager, one who is thoroughly familiar with the workings of the business[398] Thus it was said: "I concede that, when a court assumes control of an insolvent corporation, it is preferable to take it entirely out of the hands of its managing officers. But there is no inflexible rule rendering such officers ineligible to appointment as receivers." The president of the corporation was, therefore, retained as receiver because of his "good management as president of the company; his knowledge of its requirements, gained by practical experience; his well-known character as a capable, honest, and fair-minded man."[399]

As a receiver is selected with reference to the welfare of the property to be handled, it is not an absolute requisite that he be a resident of the jurisdiction where

398 Fowler v. Jarvis-Conklin M. & F. Co., 63 Fed. 888, 66 Fed. 14 (see, also, for the advisability of appointing one interested, experienced receiver, and one disinterested one); to the same effect, Olmstead v. Distiling etc. Co., 67 Fed. 24, see In re Premier Cycle Mfg. Co., 70 Conn. 473, 39 Atl. 800; People ex rel Gore v. Illinois Bldg. & L. Assn., 56 Ill. App. 642 (stockholder selected); Davis v. Duncan, 19 Fed. 477; Houston v. Redwine, 85 Ga. 130, 11 S E. 662; Moran v. Wayne Circuit Judge, 125 Mich. 6, 83 N. W. 1004, Covert v. Rogers, 38 Mich. 368; Gypsum Plaster & Stucco Co. v. Adsit, 105 Mich. 498, 63 N. W. 518. See, also, Bowling Green Trust Co. v. Virginia Pass. & Power Co., 133 Fed. 186.

399 Ralston v. Washington & C. R. Ry. Co., 65 Fed. 557. See McGilliard v. Donaldsonville etc. Works, 104 La. Ann. 544, 81 Am. St. Rep. 145, 29 South. 254; stating that, "Ordinarily, the fact that a receiver has an interest is a recommendation that he will safeguard the interests of his fellow stockholders as well as his own . . . We will not assume, without testimony, that the one appointed is not a proper person, exclusively because he is a stockholder."

appointed, if he is a thoroughly desirable person on other grounds.[400]

[400] Bayne v. Brewer Pottery Co., 82 Fed. 391 (though the non-residence occasion an additional expense), see Farmers' L. & T. Co. v. Cape Fear & G. V. R. Co., 62 Fed. 675, Phinizy v. Augusta & K. R Co, 56 Fed 273 (for recognition of foreign receiver on the ground of comity); Borton v. Brines-Chase Co., 175 Pa. St. 209, 34 Atl. 597, (but not where it will interfere with the interests of citizens of the state), see Chamberlain v. Greenleaf, 4 Abb. N. C. 92, stating that a non-resident should not be appointed.

See, also, *post*, chapter XI, "Foreign and Ancillary Receivers."

CHAPTER IV.

THE RECEIVER'S POSSESSION; AND CONFLICTING APPOINTMENTS.

ANALYSIS.

§ 154. **Receiver's Possession is that of the Court.**—A receiver is not a mere agent of the complainants, in the suit in which he is appointed. He represents the court for all the parties interested in the property, and acts, instead of the court, for the benefit of all interested parties. He is the "servant of the court." His possession is the possession of the court; and any attempt to interfere with it, without leave of court, is a contempt.[1] It is said: "The appointment of a receiver does not determine any right or affect the title of either party in any manner whatever. He is the officer of the court, and truly the hand of the court. His holding is the holding of the court from him from whom possession was taken. He is appointed on behalf of all parties and not on behalf of the plaintiff or of one defendant only."[2]

It is frequently stated that "the possession of the receiver is the possession of the party ultimately held to be entitled to the property." A federal court, in com-

1 Morrell v. Noyes, 56 Me. 458, 96 Am. Dec. 486. See, also, Chicago Union Nat. Bank v. Bank of K. C., 136 U. S. 223, 10 Sup. Ct. 1013, 34 L. ed. 341, stating: "A receiver derives his authority from the act of the court appointing him, and not from the act of the parties at whose suggestion or by whose consent he is appointed; and the utmost effect of his appointment is to put the property from that time into his custody, as an officer of the court, for the benefit of the party ultimately proved to be entitled, but not to change the title or even the right of possession in the property." See, also, Naumburg v Hyatt, 24 Fed. 898; Southern Granite Co. v. Wadsworth, 115 Ala 570, 22 South. 157, In re Receivership of New Iberia Cotton Mill Co., 109 La. 875, 33 South. 903 (receiver is agent of court, and property is *in custodia legis*); Day v. Postal Tel. Co., 66 Md. 354, 7 Atl. 608, Mays v. Rose, Freem. Ch. (Miss.) 703; Moore v. Mercer Wire Co. (N. J.), 15 Atl. 305, 737, Keeney v. Home Ins. Co., 71 N. Y. 396, 27 Am. Rep. 60; Skinner v. Maxwell, 68 N. C. 400; Robinson v. Atlantic & G. W. Ry. Co., 66 Pa. St. 160.

2 Ellicott v. Warford, 4 Md. 85; quoted approvingly in Howell v. Hough, 46 Kan. 152, 26 Pac. 636. In Bell v. American Protective League, 163 Mass. 558, 47 Am. St. Rep. 481, 40 N E. 857, 28 L. R. A. 452, the court states: "A receiver is merely a ministerial officer of the court, or, as he is sometimes called, the hand of the court. The title to the property does not change; and if he is required to take property into his custody, such custody is that of the court." But it seems there is such "special property" vested in a receiver that an indictment may be properly laid, designating him as the owner, where property in his charge has been the subject of larceny; the court of Iowa has so held: State v. Rivers, 60 Iowa, 381, 13 N. W. 73, 14 N. W. 738.

menting on the expression, says such words are certainly "not intended to be authority for the proposition that the intervention of the court operates to change the rights of any parties to the suit, whether they were originally parties, or made such by subsequent order of the court. The property is taken by the court, and is put into the hands of its officer to hold for the benefit of 'whom it may concern.' He holds and manages it for the benefit of the party to whom the court may ultimately decide it belongs, but it would be a perversion of the whole theory of *custodia legis* if the mere appointment of a receiver were itself determinative of that 'ultimate decision.' "[3]

§ 155. **Receiver's Possession Subject to Existing Liens.**— It is well established that where a court takes possession of the property of a party, and appoints a receiver, to administer the trust for the benefit of all interested parties, the court receives such property impressed with all existing rights and equities, and the relative rank of claims and the standing of liens remain unaffected by the receivership. Every legal and equitable lien upon the property is preserved with the power of enforcing it.[4] "The receivership does not destroy any

3 Central Trust Co. v. Worcester Cycle Mfg. Co., 93 Fed. 712, 35 C. C. A. 547 (citing the following cases in which the form of words discussed was used. Wiswall v Sampson, 14 How. 52, 14 L. ed. 322; Booth v. Clark, 17 How. 322, 15 L. ed. 164; Chicago Union Bank v. Kansas City Bank, 136 U. S. 223, 10 Sup Ct. 1013, 34 L. ed. 341). See, also, Beverley v. Brooke, 4 Gratt 187, 208. That the appointment of a receiver of real property does not so alter possession of the estate in the person who is ultimately found to have been entitled thereto as to prevent the running of the statute of limitations, see Anonymous, 2 Atk. 15.

4 American Trust & Sav. Bank v. McGettigan, 152 Ind. 582, 71 Am St. Rep. 345, 52 N. E. 793. In In re Binghamton General Electric Co., 143 N. Y. 263, 38 N. E. 297, the court says· "It is obvious that every lien upon the property of a corporation resting upon valid

liens that may have been acquired before the appointment."[5] It is said that "it is as much the duty of a receiver, in administering an estate, to protect valid preferences and priorities, as it is to make a just distribution" of the intrusted property.[6]

§ 156. **Same; Instances of Prior Liens Protected.**—The application of the rule is well recognized in the case of liens of creditors of insolvent corporations over which receivers have been appointed.[7] Thus, it is said: "Where the receiver of this court, under authority of statute and under the direction of the court, has as-

agreement or process before the appointment of a receiver, the lienor being lawfully in possession, must be preserved with the right of enforcement, unless courts and legislatures are to override the vested rights of creditors." See, also, In re North American Gutta Percha Co., 17 How. Pr. 549, 9 Abb. Pr. 79, Lowenberg v. Jefferies, 74 Fed. 385 (the proceeds should be paid in the order of priority); Von Roun v. Superior Court, 58 Cal. 358; Smith v. Sioux City Nursery etc. Co., 109 Iowa, 51, 79 N. W. 457; Battery Park Bank v. Western Carolina Bank, 127 N. C. 432, 37 S. E. 461; Hays v. Lycoming Fire Ins. Co., 99 Pa. St. 621. See, *post*, chapter IX, as to "Preferred Claims."

5 Quoted in Garden City Banking & Trust Co. v. Geilfuss, 86 Wis. 612, 57 N. W. 349, from Ellis v. Vernon Ice, Light & Water Co, 86 Tex. Sup. 109, 23 S. W. 858. See, also, Page v. Supreme Lodge, Knights & Ladies of Protection, 161 Mass. 384, 37 N. E. 369.

6 American Trust & Sav. Bank v. McGettigan, 152 Ind. 582, 71 Am. St. Rep. 345, 52 N. E. 793. A receiver cannot claim rents against an assignee thereof under an assignment to secure payment of claim: Brownson v. Roy, 133 Mich 617, 95 N. W. 710.

7 McRae v. Bowers Dredging Co., 86 Fed. 344, states: "Where a court of equity takes control and custody of the assets of an insolvent corporation, it does not assume to destroy existing liens, or to divest the rights of lien creditors. The court assumes the burden of protecting as far as may be the rights of all parties having interests. Therefore, it will not surrender property in its custody, to be disposed of by process under other courts, but will, when necessary to enable creditors to collect their dues, order a sale of the assets, and distribute the funds according to the rights and priorities of the owners and creditors": Risk v. Kansas T. & Bkg. Co., 58 Fed. 45; Talledega Mercantile Co. v. Jenifer Iron Co., 102 Ala. 259, 14 South. 743 (holding that the court may grant leave to the creditor to proceed directly against the receiver).

sumed the possession of all the personal property of the insolvent corporation, this court is bound to give effect to liens which existed as liens on the property when its receiver took possession."[8]

The right of the lienor to protection would seem to be assured from the fact that "the receiver is the hand of the law, and the law conserves and enforces rights—never destroys them."[9] And it is not necessary that the lien be created in any particular manner, so long as there has been a valid right established in favor of the lienor. Thus, the filing of a creditor's bill has been held to create a sufficient lien.[10] In the case of an attachment made before the application for the appointment of a receiver, the court of Massachusetts said: "We are satisfied that under the laws of Massachusetts an attachment is a lien or encumbrance upon the property attached. It fastens itself upon the property, and whoever takes the property takes it *cum onere*, ... and, though the assets pass into the hands of receivers, they take with all the liens thereon, and an existing at-

8 Duryee v. United States Credit System Co., 55 N. J. Eq. 311, 37 Atl. 155; the court cited Doane v. Millville Ins Co., 45 N. J. Eq. 274, 282, 17 Atl. 625, and continued: "And effect is generally given to such statutory liens, in practice, either by providing for their payment by the receiver as preferred claims, or by allowing the claimant, on application to the court, to enforce his lien in the courts, and by the proceedings in which they would clearly be enforceable had no receiver been appointed, and making the receiver a party to such further proceedings, where this is necessary. . . . . And where the property is in the control of the officer of the court, expressly subject to the lien, the fact that the lien cannot be otherwise made effective than by the action of this court is no sufficient reason, as it seems to me, for holding that it is not valid."

9 Von Roun v. Superior Court, 58 Cal. 358.

10 King v. Goodwin, 130 Ill. 102, 17 Am. St. Rep. 277, 22 N. E. 533. But see Battery Park Bank v. Western Carolina Bank, 127 N. C. 432, 37 S. E. 461, stating it does not extend to "tangible personal property"; Davenport v. Kelly, 42 N. Y. 193.

tachment is a lien."[11] And where, after the acquirement of a judgment lien, a receiver was appointed at the suit of creditors, the judgment creditor was allowed to enforce his lien against the receiver, although he might have intervened in the suit in which the receiver was appointed.[12]

It is held that where a sheriff makes a levy under an execution before the appointment of a receiver, the receiver takes the property subject to the lien thus created.[13] It is said: "If the sheriff had made a levy on the property which subsequently came into the hands of the receiver, it is for him to enforce that levy. He is entitled to collect the money and apply it on the execution if the levy was made. It is his duty to do so."[14]

11 Hubbard v. Hamilton Bank, 7 Met. 340; quoted with approval in Arnold v. Weimer, 40 Neb. 216, 58 N. W. 709. See, also, Kittridge v. Osgood, 161 Mass. 384, reported *sub nom* Page v. Supreme Lodge, 37 N E. 369, Lowenberg v. Jefferies, 74 Fed. 385; Roseboom v Whittaker, 132 Ill. 81, 23 N. E. 339, Runner v Scott, 150 Ind. 441, 50 N. E. 479 (partnership receiver); Smith v. Sioux City Nursery etc. Co, 109 Iowa, 51, 79 N. W. 457, Minchin v. Second Nat. Bank, 36 N. J. Eq. 436, Hays v. Lycoming F Ins. Co., 99 Pa. St. 621 (garnishment); Von Roun v. Superior Ct., 58 Cal. 358 (a lien on personal property, which ordinarily depends on the retention of possession is not destroyed by the receiver's taking possession).

12 Talladega Mercantile Co. v. Jenifer Iron Co, 102 Ala. 259, 14 South. 743. See, also, Gere v. Dibble, 17 How. Pr. 31; Battery Park Bank v. Western Carolina Bank, 127 N. C. 432, 37 S. E. 461. But see Doane v. Millville, M, M. & F. Ins. Co, 45 N. J. Eq. 274, 17 Atl. 625, stating, "the mere fact that the debt has been put into a judgment will not secure any preference to the creditor." Approved in Van Steenburgh v. Porsie Button Co. (N. J.), 34 Atl. 135, holding that the delivery of an execution to the sheriff did constitute a lien, though he had made no levy.

13 Van Alstyne v. Cook, 25 N. Y. 489; Becker v. Torrance, 31 N. Y. 631; Davenport v. Kelly, 42 N. Y. 193 (a levy on personalty is not defeated by another creditor's filing a "creditor's bill"); In re Pond, 21 Misc. Rep. 114, 46 N. Y. Supp. 999.

14 In re North American Gutta Percha Co., 17 How. Pr. 549, 9 Abb. Pr. 79 ("if the officer of this court has taken possession of the property thus levied on, and sold the same, he is bound to account to the

It is well settled that an existing lien of a state or municipality for the payment of taxes is neither lost nor impaired by the transfer of the property to the possession of a receiver; "he but takes the property for the benefit of all lienholders and creditors."[15] And while a landlord cannot exercise the right of distraint for rent, because of the manual possession of the goods by the court's appointee, he necessarily has a lien for the payment which attaches to the fund raised by the sale which the court ordered.[16] So a mechanic's lien cannot be impaired by the subsequent appointment of a receiver.[17] As the receiver takes the property subject to all equities good against the one from whom he takes, he is bound by an existing chattel mortgage or conditional sale.[18] It is said a receiver "is trustee for the whole body of general creditors, and takes the property subject, not only to all legal liens, but to all equitable liens as well";[19] he is "affected with all claims, liens

sheriff for the proceeds''); and cases cited, *supra*, in note 13; In re Muehlfeld & Haynes Piano Co, 12 App. Div. 492, 42 N. Y. Supp. 802, 26 Civ. Pr. Rep. 90 (an execution on a judgment where the action was commenced before the appointment of a receiver, is superior to the receiver's right).

15 Union Trust Co. v. Weber, 96 Ill. 346 (''we are wholly at a loss to see any reason for holding that the lien of the state or municipalities for taxes should be lost or defeated. . . . . We apprehend, no one will or can contend that when the state or municipalities have a lien on property for taxes, it is not paramount to all other liens. . . . . The receiver is not a purchaser, but he receives the possession and title, when transferred to him, to hold for all parties in interest''). See, also, Duryee v. United States Credit System Co., 55 N. J. Eq. 311, 37 Atl. 155.

16 Lane v. Washington Hotel Co, 190 Pa. St. 230, 42 Atl. 697. See Woodward v. Winehill, 14 Wash. 394, 44 Pac. 860, holding that *notice to quit*, served on a tenant, is binding on a subsequently appointed receiver.

17 Totten & Hogg I. & S. F. Co. v. Muncie Nail Co., 148 Ind. 372, 47 N. E. 703.

18 Bates v. Wiggin, 37 Kan. 44, 1 Am. St. Rep. 234, 14 Pac. 442.

19 Miller v. Savage, 60 N. J. Eq. 204, 46 Atl. 632; In re Olzendam

and equities which would affect the debtor if he himself were asserting his interest in the property."[20] And a receiver can therefore obtain no title to property where the original vendor reserved his title by a clause in the bill of sale of the chattels;[21] neither can he supersede a prior valid assignment.[22]

§ 157. **Same; Receiver's Right to Possession as Against Prior Lienor.**—The question of the prior lienholder's right to enforce his lien by process is one on which the cases are far from uniform; this question is discussed elsewhere.[23] A number of decisions have been rendered on the analogous subject of the receiver's right to possession, as against the holder of a prior lien, when such lien carries with it the possession of the property. It is held that the receiver cannot replevy goods upon which execution has been levied prior to the appointment, when the defendant's superior right is so clear that the court of chancery would not have ordered the property to be delivered to the receiver;[24] that personal property, possession of which had been taken by the sheriff under attachment from a state court, cannot rightfully be interfered with by a federal receiver while such possession continues, while a prior attachment of

Co., 117 Fed. 179 (subject to equitable lien). See, also, as pertaining to partnership receivers, Hoffman v. Schoyer, 143 Ill. 598, 28 N. E. 823; Chicago Title & Trust Co. v. Smith, 158 Ill. 417, 425, 41 N. E. 1076.

20 Ryder v. Ryder, 19 R. I. 188, 32 Atl. 919 (subject to mortgagee's equity to have a mortgage reformed).

21 Sayles v. Nat. Water Purifying Co., 16 N. Y. Supp. 555, 62 Hun, 618.

22 Garden City Bank etc. Co. v. Geilfuss, 86 Wis. 612, 57 N. W. 349; Chicago Title & Trust Co. v. Smith, 158 Ill. 417, 425, 41 N. E. 1076; Brownson v. Roy, 133 Mich. 617, 95 N. W. 710 (assignment of rents).

23 See *post*, §§ 166, 167.

24 Conley v. Deere, 11 Lea (Tenn.), 274, 279.

real property, not conferring possession, actual or constructive, does not preclude a lawful seizure of such property by a federal receiver;[25] that when personal property is in the custody of a sheriff under a writ of attachment, a court of chancery cannot acquire jurisdiction of the same property, so as to take it from the possession of the sheriff into the custody of its receiver.[26] The subject has received much attention from the supreme court of Washington, which holds that when creditors of a corporation have attached its property, and maintained their lien by the actual possession of the sheriff, a receiver appointed in a suit by a stockholder, to which the attachment creditors were not parties, has no right of possession of the attached property, but the sheriff must keep and dispose of it under his writ.[27] On the other hand, it is held in Wisconsin that proceeds of an execution sale in the hands of the sheriff, though in law the creditor's, may be sequestered, on motion of the other creditors of the debtor corporation, into the hands of a subsequently appointed receiver, on an *ex parte* showing that the confessed judgments on which the executions were issued were intended as a fraudulent and illegal preference.[28]

§ 158. Receiver's Title Vests from Order of Appointment. The general rule is well established that the title and

25 In re Hall & Stilson Co., 73 Fed. 527, citing many cases.

26 Ford v. Judsonia Mercantile Co., 52 Ark. 426, 20 Am. St. Rep. 192, 12 S. W. 876, 6 L. R. A. 714; Pease v. Smith, 63 Ill. App. 411.

27 State v. Superior Court of Chehalis County, 8 Wash. 210, 35 Pac. 1087, 25 L. R. A. 354, 38 Cent. L. J. 341 (but see the strong dissenting opinion of Dunbar, C. J.); State v. Superior Court of Snohomish County, 7 Wash. 77, 34 Pac. 430; State v. Graham, 9 Wash. 528, 36 Pac. 1085; but the doctrine of these cases seems to be materially limited by the later case of State v. Superior Court of King County, 11 Wash. 63, 39 Pac. 244.

28 Ford v. Plankinton Bank, 87 Wis. 363, 58 N. W. 766.

right of a receiver relate to the time of the order appointing him. It is said: "The appointment of a receiver is completed at the farthest by the filing and entering of the order appointing him, although before he proceeds to the discharge of his duties he may be directed to execute and file a proper bond. When that is done, he can take actual manual possession of the property, and his title relates back to the time of his appointment."[29] Accordingly, a levy by an officer, after appointment and before the receiver has filed his bond, will create no lien,[30] and may be enjoined;[31] and a valid judgment, obtained under these circumstances, affords no ground for seizing the property on execution, or creating a lien.[32] A federal court has said: "If the ju-

29 In re Schuyler Steam Towboat Co., 136 N. Y. 169, 32 N. E. 623, 20 L. R. A. 391. See, also, In re Christian Jensen Co, 128 N. Y. 550, 28 N. E. 665 ("the moment he was appointed he became an officer of the court, and from that time the property of the corporation was *in custodia legis*, and the court had the power to preserve and protect it. While the receiver could not interfere with the property of the corporation until he filed his bond, yet after he filed his bond his title related back to the date of his appointment," and the property, therefore, was not subject to replevin); In re Lenox Corporation, 57 App. Div. 515, 68 N. Y. Supp. 103; In re Muehlfeld & Haynes Piano Co, 12 App. Div. 492, 42 N. Y. Supp. 802, 26 Civ. Pr. Rep. 90; Dickey v. Bates, 13 Misc. Rep. 489, 35 N. Y. Supp. 525; Van Alstyne v. Cook, 25 N. Y. 489, Steele v. Sturges, 5 Abb. Pr. 442; Rutter v. Tallis, 5 Sandf. 610; Mosher v. Supreme Sitting of O. T. H., 88 Hun, 394, 34 N. Y. Supp. 816; Maynard v. Bond, 67 Mo. 315; Pope v Ames, 20 Or. 199, 25 Pac. 393; Fogg v. Providence Lumber Co., 15 R. I. 15, 23 Atl. 31; Clinkscales v. Pendleton Mfg. Co., 9 S. C. 318; Regenstein v. Pearlstein, 30 S. C. 192, 8 S. E. 850; Battery Park Bank v. Western Carolina Bank, 127 N. C. 432, 37 S. E. 461.

30 Ex parte Evans, L. R. 13 Ch. D. 252; In re Lenox Corporation, 57 App. Div. 515, 68 N. Y. Supp. 103; Atlas Bank v. Nahant Bank, 23 Pick. 480 (the title relates to the filing of the bill "or at least to the injunction," issued to prevent the transfer of property).

31 In re Schuyler Steam Towboat Co., 136 N. Y. 169, 32 N. E. 623, 20 L. R. A. 391.

32 Connecticut River Banking Co. v. Rockbridge Co., 73 Fed. 709, Temple v. Glasgow, 80 Fed. 441, 42 U. S. App. 417, 25 C. C. A. 540.

risdiction of the court over the property did not attach contemporaneously with the order appointing a receiver, the purpose of the court in appointing a receiver might be defeated by the failure of the person appointed receiver to accept the position, or his inability to give the bond required, or, in the interim between the order appointing a receiver and his giving the required bond, a creditor might obtain an advantage by securing a confession of judgment, and in innumerable other ways."[33]

It is sometimes stated that the title, upon proper bond being given, relates to the date of the filing of the bill; that "the filing of the bill and service of process is an equitable levy on the property, and pending the proceedings such property may properly be held to be *in gremio legis*. . . . . In such cases the commencement of the suit is sufficient to give the court whose jurisdiction is invoked the exclusive right to control the property."[34] In ordinary cases, however, the rule is as

See, also, Battery Park Bank v. Western Carolina Bank, 127 N. C. 432, 37 S. E. 461

33 Connecticut River Banking Co. v. Rockbridge Co, 73 Fed 709; affirmed in Temple v. Glasgow, 80 Fed. 441, 42 U. S. App. 417, 25 C. C. A. 540, stating: "Generally the better rule would seem to be that, when the court has jurisdiction, the order appointing a general receiver for the purpose of liquidation is an adjudication which operates as a sequestration of the property of the corporation, ... and in such cases to hold that the rights of parties are affected by the accident of whether the receiver is able on the instant to proffer his bond for approval is illogical."

34 Illinois Steel Co. v Putnam, 68 Fed. 515, 15 C. C. A. 556, citing Adams v. Trust Co., 66 Fed. 617, 15 C. C. A. 1, and supporting, as not within the principle stated, a transfer of stock made pending a motion for the appointment of a receiver: Merrill v. Commonwealth Mut. Fire Ins. Co., 166 Mass. 238, 44 N. E 144. In Texas the rule appears to be that the title, as against attachments, relates back to the time when the appointing court took jurisdiction of the application, "by acting upon it in such a manner as to indicate that he had determined to investigate the matter and might at some

stated above.[35] The supreme court of Iowa has said: "It is very plain that the commencement of the proceedings for the appointment of the receiver did not subject the property of the gas company to the custody of the law and bring it under the authority of the receiver."[36]

§ 159. Contra; Title Dates from Qualification, or from the Time When He Takes Actual Possession.—The general rule has been expressly departed from in California in the case of a receiver of mortgaged realty;[37] and in Maryland, actual possession by the receiver is demanded before the property is considered under the control of the court. It is said: "Their mere appointment did not, as we think, place the property, as against

future date appoint a receiver": Worden v. Pruter (Tex. Civ. App.), 88 S. W. 434; Rissner v. Railway Co., 89 Tex. 656, 59 Am. St. Rep. 84, 36 S. W. 53, 33 L. R. A. 171.

35 In re Muehlfeld & Haynes Piano Co., 12 App. Div. 492, 42 N. Y. Supp. 802, 26 Civ. Pr. Rep. 90; and cases cited above. In Smith v. Sioux City Nursery & Seed Co., 109 Iowa, 51, 79 N. W. 457, the court says: "The fact that the proceedings were begun for the appointment of a receiver did not suspend the right of creditors to attach, nor that of the company to assign its accounts as security for the payment of its debts, if in doing so it acted in good faith. While there is some conflict in the authorities as to whether property of the debtor passes *in custodia legis* at the time the receiver is appointed, or when he assumes possession, all agree that the *jus disponendi* is not affected by the application, and continues, at least, till the making of the order or appointment." See, also, Cook v. Cole, 55 Iowa, 72, 7 N. W. 419; Van Alstyne v. Cook, 25 N. Y. 489.

36 Cook v. Cole, 55 Iowa, 72, 7 N. W. 419.

37 Bank of Woodland v. Heron, 120 Cal. 614, 52 Pac. 1006 (the court states. "There are, no doubt, authorities—and perhaps a weight of authorities, although there are cases the other way—to the point that the appointment of a receiver operates as a sequestration of the property mentioned in the order of appointment. Still it will be found that the cases in which that principle was declared are mainly cases in which complainants at whose instance the receivers were appointed had some estate in or some right to or lien upon the property involved prior to and independent of the appointment of the receiver").

a stranger to the proceedings, in possession, and claiming the right to retain and sell it, *in custodia legis*. Actual possession was necessary to accomplish this. The authorities speak of the appointment *and possession* by the receivers as necessary in order to place the property in the custody of the court."[38] This is true even though the receiver has given his bond.[39] In New York, it has been held that as the vesting of title by relation is only a legal fiction, such fiction will not be indulged in to permit a wrong against the creditor, when the debtor has, by "frivolous pleading," prevented the creditor from obtaining a prior lien.[40] In Virginia an execution levied after the appointment, and before the giving of the bond, is held to create a valid lien.[41] The court, in the case mentioned, relied principally upon the English case of Edwards v. Edwards,[42] which may be taken to represent the English rule, which is contrary to the general rule in the United States.[43]

38 Everett v. Neff, 28 Md. 176.

39 Farmers' Bank v. Beaston, 7 Gill & J. 421, 28 Am. Dec. 226. See, also, Prentiss Tool & Supply Co. v. Whitman & Barnes Mfg. Co., 88 Md. 240, 41 Atl. 49, where the time of vesting is regulated by statute

40 In re Lewis & Fowler Mfg. Co., 89 Hun, 208, 34 N. Y. Supp. 983 See, also, Chamberlain v. Rochester S. P. V. Co., 7 Hun, 557, where the title of a receiver in the case of voluntary dissolution of a corporation vests on the filing of his bond only.

41 Frayser v. Richmond & A. R. Co., 81 Va. 388.

42 L. R. 2 Ch. D. 291; the court was not unanimous in their reasoning, James, L. J, stating: "It would be very serious to hold that he can take possession before giving security," and Mellish, L. J, maintaining that "if the receiver had really taken possession before the goods were seized, *although he had not been completely appointed receiver*," the case would have been different.

43 The English cases, apparently inconsistent with Edwards v. Edwards, cannot be said to impair its weight as authority on the point decided; thus, in Ex parte Evans, L. R. 13 Ch. D. 252, the court said: "Edwards v. Edwards only decided it was no contempt for creditors to seize property before the bond was given and the case related to

A later Virginia case held that a payment made to a receiver, who had not given bond, was at the peril of the payor, and where the receiver failed to account, the purchaser was bound to pay again, as the receiver's authority dated only from his giving bond.[44]

§ 160. **Vesting of Title in Supplementary Proceedings.**—The statutes in regard to the appointment of receivers in supplemental proceedings and the time when the title to the property, in such cases, vests in the receiver, are not harmonious. In New Jersey, the title relates to the issuing of the execution, as against an assignee with notice of the proceedings.[45] In New York, the code provides that the title is vested in the receiver from the time he files a certified copy of the

chattels, not land.'' In regard to land, the court had the following to say: ''A judgment creditor, not being able to obtain relief at law under the old system, because his debtor had nothing but an equitable interest in the land, came into a court of equity to obtain that relief which he could not obtain at law, and the moment he established the difficulty in his way at law, and the court made the order giving the right to the possession of the lands to the receiver appointed on his behalf, that order giving the right to possession to the creditor through the receiver was as much a delivery in execution of land in which the debtor had only an equitable interest, as was the sheriff's return to the writ of elegit at law, that he had extended the land, a delivery in execution of the land in which the debtor had a legal interest.'' The case of In re Bird, L. R. 22 Ch. D. 604, approving Wickens v. Townshend, 1 Russ. & M. 361, refused to allow a solicitor to retain, on a debt due him, money paid before the receiver's bond was given; but the express ground on which the case was put was the inequitable position of the solicitor who occupied a confidential relation to the case, and it cannot be said that it is opposed to Edwards v. Edwards. See, also, the recent case, Ridout v. Fowler, [1904] 1 Ch. 658 (receiver has no ''title'' to personalty until he has given bond).

44 Woods v. Ellis, 85 Va. 471, 7 S. E. 852 (the case seems open to some question, for apparently the receiver afterwards qualified by giving the required bond).

45 Coleman v. Roff, 16 Vroom, 17, 45 N. J. L. 7; approved in Seyfert v. Edison, 47 N. J. L. 428, 1 Atl. 502.

order of his appointment in the county where the debtor resides;[46] but that, as respects personal property and things in action, it may relate back, for the benefit of the judgment creditor in whose behalf the proceedings were instituted, to the service of the order for the debtor's examination.[47]

§ 161. How the Receiver may Obtain Possession of Property Withheld.—Where possession is withheld from the receiver by persons who are parties to the suit, or by others claiming under such parties, as agents, lessees, and the like, with notice of the appointment of the receiver, the court has authority to enforce its order for the surrender of the property in a summary way by attachment or by a writ of possession.[48] Thus, it has been held that the agents or officers of a corporation or firm, a receiver of which has been appointed, may be ordered to deliver up property belonging to their prin-

46 Nicoll v. Spowers, 105 N. Y. 1, 11 N. E. 138; McCorkle v. Herrman, 117 N. Y. 297, 22 N. E. 948; Webb v. Osborne, 15 Daly, 406, 7 N. Y. Supp. 762 (an order extending the receivership is governed by the same rule).

47 McCorkle v. Herrman, 117 N. Y. 297, 22 N. E. 948; Youngs v. Klunder, 27 N. Y. St. Rep. 32, 7 N. Y. Supp. 498. But in such case the debtor must have been served with notice to attend the examination: In re Sistare's Estate, 27 Abb. N. C. 34, 15 N. Y. Supp. 709.

See, also, Rose v. Baker, 99 N. C. 323, 5 S. E. 919, where the code provides that the title shall vest upon an order restraining the debtor from disposing of his nonexempt property.

48 Thornton v. Washington Savings Bank, 76 Va. 432 (writ of possession against lessee taking a lease from a party, with knowledge of the appointment of a receiver); Ex parte Cohen, 5 Cal. 494; Brandt v. Allen, 76 Iowa, 50, 40 N. W. 82, 1 L. R. A. 653; Ryan v. Kingsbery, 88 Ga. 361, 14 S. E. 596; Delozier v. Bird, 123 N. C. 689, 31 S. E. 834, 125 N. C. 493, 34 S. E. 643; Tolleson v. Green, 83 Ga. 499, 10 S. E. 120; and see Fischer v. Superior Court, 98 Cal. 67, 32 Pac. 875; Miles v. New South Bldg. & L. Assn., 95 Fed. 919; and cases cited in the next note. That the receiver may sometimes attack a fraudulent transfer to a third person, by petition in the cause, see United States v. Late Corporation of Church etc., 5 Utah, 538, 18 Pac. 35.

cipal, although they themselves are not parties to the suit.[49]

[49] Brandt v. Allen, 76 Iowa, 50, 40 N. W. 82, 1 L. R. A. 653; Ex parte Cohen, 5 Cal. 494.

In Tolleson v. People's Savings Bank, 85 Ga. 171, 11 S. E. 599, the receiver appointed by the court applied for an order requiring the president of the insolvent corporation to show cause why he should not be attached for contempt, in not delivering the assets of the corporation to such receiver in obedience to a previous order of the court directed to the corporation. The president appeared as an individual, and responded under oath, and took part in the proceedings. It was held that the court had such jurisdiction of him as would authorize it to deal with him for contempt in not turning over to the receiver the assets of the corporation in his possession. In Ex parte Hollis, 59 Cal. 405, on the other hand, it was held that the president of a corporation against which insolvency proceedings were instituted did not become a party by verifying the pleadings; and that the court could not, by a mere order to show cause why he should not be punished for contempt for not surrendering to the receiver property of the corporation, make him a party and adjudge his adverse claim to the property; and see to the same effect State v. Ball, 5 Wash. 387, 34 Am. St. Rep. 866, 31 Pac. 975.

Refusal of a party to the action to obey an order directing him to deliver certain property of the corporation to the receiver constitutes a contempt, although he claims a lien thereon: Ex parte Tinsley, 37 Tex. Cr. App. 517, 66 Am. St. Rep. 818, 40 S. W. 306; affirmed, 171 U. S. 101, 18 Sup. Ct. 805. Such order must be obeyed, however erroneous it may be, if the court had jurisdiction: Tolman v. Jones, 114 Ill. 148, 28 N. E. 464. And the officers need not be expressly required by the order appointing the receiver to deliver the assets to him, if the receiver is invested "with the usual rights and powers of receivers" and specially with power "to receive into his possession all the effects and choses in action" of the dissolved corporation; and a sale of the assets by the officers in such case may be punished as a contempt: Young v. Rollins, 90 N. C. 125, 131. See, further, American C. Co. v. Jacksonville, T. & K. W. R. Co., 52 Fed. 937.

In Cassilear v. Simons, 8 Paige (N. Y.), 273, the following rule was laid down by Chancellor Walworth: "Where it is referred to a master to appoint a receiver, and the defendant is directed to assign and deliver over his property on oath, under the direction of the master, it is the duty of the party who wishes to have an actual delivery of the property, in addition to the legal assignment thereof, to call upon the master to decide the question as to what property is under the defendant's power and control, and to obtain from the

But the court will not interfere in a summary way as against the possession of a stranger to the action claiming by a paramount title, but will leave the question of title to be tried by a proper action brought by the receiver for that purpose; or the complainant may make such third person a party to the suit, and apply to have the receivership extended to the property in his hands.[50] "The party in possession, who asserts in good faith color and claim of right, is entitled, under the guaranty of due process of law, to his day in court, and a trial according to the customary forms of law."[51] If in such case the receiver attempts by violence to obtain possession of property claimed by third persons, the court will not protect him any further than the law will protect him, but will permit him to be sued as a trespasser by the party aggrieved.[52]

§ 162. Interference with Receiver's Possession; Claimant Must Apply to the Court.—Courts of equity are exceed-

master an order directing the defendant to deliver over the property thus designated by the master, before the complainant can bring such defendant into contempt for disobeying the order of the court." See, also, Parker v. Browning, 8 Paige, 388, 35 Am. Dec. 717.

50 Parker v. Browning, 8 Paige, 388, 35 Am. Dec. 717; Cassilear v. Simons, 8 Paige, 273; Wheaton v. Daily Tel. Co., 59 C. C. A. 427, 124 Fed. 61; Musgrove v. Gray, 123 Ala. 376, 82 Am. St. Rep. 124, 26 South. 643; Havemeyer v. Superior Court, 84 Cal. 327, 387, 18 Am. St. Rep. 192, 24 Pac. 121, 10 L. R. A. 627; Stuparich Mfg. Co. v. Superior Court, 123 Cal. 290, 55 Pac. 985; McCombs v. Merryhew, 40 Mich. 721; Elwell v. Goodnow, 71 Minn. 383, 73 N. W 1092, 1095; In re Muehlfeld, 16 App. Div. 401, 45 N. Y. Supp. 16 (defendant corporation's prior assignee for the benefit of creditors, who is not a party, cannot be compelled on motion to surrender to the receiver); Thornton v. Washington Savings Bank, 76 Va. 432; Andrews v. Paschen, 67 Wis. 413, 30 N. W. 712. But see United States v. Late Corporation of Church etc., 5 Utah, 538, 18 Pac. 35.

51 Musgrove v. Gray, 123 Ala. 376, 82 Am. St. Rep. 124, 26 South. 643.

52 Parker v. Browning, 8 Paige, 388, 35 Am. Dec. 717.

ingly averse to any interference with the possession of their receivers, which is deemed the possession of the court. They jealously and vigilantly guard and maintain against obstruction, under process of another court, their exclusive authority and right to adjudicate upon and distribute the fund in their custody among those entitled.[53] "The court never allows any person to interfere, either with money or property in the hands of its receiver, without its leave; whether it is done by the consent or submission of the receiver, or by compulsory process against him. The court is obliged to keep a strict hand over property in the hands of a receiver, or which, by virtue of the order of the court, may come into his hands, in order to preserve entire jurisdiction over the whole matter, and to do that which is just in the cause between the parties."[54] "When a party is prejudiced by having a receiver put in his way, the course has either been to give him leave to bring an ejectment [or other action], or to permit him to be examined *pro interesse suo*, which may, perhaps, often be the most convenient mode."[55] Where property or funds are in the hands of a receiver, and claimed by persons not parties to the action in which he was appointed, a petition or motion may be presented

53 Ex parte Tillman, 93 Ala. 101, 9 South. 527; Angel v. Smith, 9 Ves. 335; Brooks v Greathed, 1 Jacob & W. 178; Evelyn v Lewis, 3 Hare, 472; Russell v. East Anglian Ry., 3 Macn. & G. 104; Ex parte Cochrane, L. R. 20 Eq. 282; Wiswall v. Sampson, 14 How. 52, 65, 14 L ed. 322; In re Swan, 150 U. S. 637, 14 Sup. Ct. 225, 37 L. ed. 1207; Moore v. Mercer Wire Co. (N. J. Eq.), 15 Atl. 737; Spinning v. Ohio L. I. & T. Co., 2 Disn (Ohio) 336; Vermont & C. R. Co. v. Vermont Central R. Co., 46 Vt. 792.

54 De Winton v. Mayor of Brecon, 28 Beav. 200, per Lord Romilly, M. R.

55 Brooks v. Greathed, 1 Jacob & W. 176. See, also, Ex parte Cochrane, L. R. 20 Eq. 282; Skinner v. Maxwell, 68 N. C. 400.

to the court for an order on the receiver to deliver over the fund or property to the claimant.[56]

§ 163. **Interference with Receiver a Contempt of Court.**—It is well settled that a disturbance of the receiver's possession by any person, whether by force, or by legal proceedings against him, or in any other manner, without the permission of the court by whom the receiver was appointed, constitutes a contempt of that court, since the possession of the receiver is in law the possession of the court itself.[57] And such person may be

[56] Wheeler v. Walton & Wharn Co., 64 Fed. 664, 667, affirmed Winchester v. Davis Pyrites Co., 67 Fed. 45, 14 C. C. A. 300; Kimball v. Gafford, 78 Iowa, 65, 42 N. W. 583, 4 L. R. A. 398; Morrill v Noyes, 56 Me. 458, 96 Am. Dec. 486; Jacobson v. Landolt, 73 Wis. 142, 9 Am. St. Rep. 767, 40 N. W. 636.

[57] Skip v. Harwood, 3 Atk. 564; Russell v East Anglian Ry., 3 Macn. & G. 104; Helmore v. Smith, 35 Ch. D. 449; In re Swan, 150 U S 637, 14 Sup. Ct. 225, 37 L. ed. 1207, Tinsley v. Anderson, 171 U S 101, 18 Sup Ct. 805, 43 L ed 91; In re Doolittle, 23 Fed. 544, and note; United States v. Kane, 23 Fed. 748, In re Wabash R. Co., 24 Fed. 217; In re Higgins, 27 Fed. 443; Beers v. Wabash H L & P. R. Co., 34 Fed. 244; United States v. Murphy, 44 Fed. 39; American C. Co. v. Jacksonville, T. & K. W. R. Co, 52 Fed. 937, Thomas v. Cincinnati, N. O. & T. P. Ry. Co., 62 Fed. 803, United States v. Jose, 63 Fed. 951; In re Acker, 66 Fed. 290; Ex parte Hollis, 59 Cal. 405, Tollison v. Green, 83 Ga. 499, 10 S. E. 120; Tolleson v. People's Sav. Bank, 85 Ga. 171, 11 S. E. 599; Ryan v. Kingsberry, 88 Ga 361, 14 S. E 596; Drakeford v. Adams, 98 Ga. 722, 25 S. E. 833; Richards v. People, 81 Ill. 551; Tolman v. Jones, 114 Ill. 148, 28 N. E. 464; Sercomb v. Catlin, 128 Ill. 556, 15 Am. St. Rep. 147, 21 N. E. 606; In re Lewis, 52 Kan. 660, 35 Pac. 287; Smith v. Hosmer, 84 Mich. 564, 47 N. W. 1092; Moore v. Mercer Wire Co. (N. J. Eq.), 15 Atl. 305; Noe v. Gibson, 7 Paige, 513; Cassilear v. Simons, 8 Paige, 273; Hull v. Thomas, 3 Edw. Ch. 236, Delozier v. Bird, 123 N. C. 689, 31 S. E. 834; on rehearing, 125 N C. 493, 34 S. E. 643; Spinning v. Ohio etc. Tr. Co., 2 Disn. (Ohio) 336; Chafee v. Quidnick Co., 13 R. I. 442; Edrington v. Pridham, 65 Tex. 612; Ex parte Tinsley, 37 Tex. Cr. App. 517, 66 Am. St. Rep. 818, 40 S. W. 306, Vermont etc. R. Co. v. Vermont Cent. R. Co., 46 Vt. 792; State v. Ball, 5 Wash. 387, 34 Am. St. Rep. 866, 31 Pac. 975. As to the degree of proof requisite for punishment for contempt, see United States v.

chargeable with contempt if he has actual knowledge of the granting of the order appointing a receiver, although the order has not been legally served upon him, or even formally drawn up.[58] Further, it is not competent for anyone to interfere with the possession of a receiver on the ground that the appointment was improvident;[59] the order of appointment cannot be assailed as erroneous in contempt proceedings, if the court had jurisdiction of the subject-matter and of the parties in the suit in which the receiver was appointed.[60]

Imprisonment of the defendant by virtue of attachment proceedings, for disobedience in not delivering up a specific sum of money found and adjudged to have

Jose, 63 Fed. 951. That advice of counsel constitutes no defense, see Delozier v. Bird, 123 N. C. 689, 31 S. E. 834; Edrington v. Pridham, 65 Tex. 617. As to punishment for contempt, in the case of rival appointments, of the receivers whose rights are inferior, see People v. Central City Bank, 35 How. Pr. (N. Y.) 428, 53 Barb. 412; Spinning v. Ohio etc. Tr. Co., 2 Disn. 336. That it is not proper, in contempt proceedings, to render a judgment in favor of the receiver to be collected by execution, see Edrington v. Pridham, 65 Tex. 612.

58 Skip v. Harwood, 3 Atk. 564; Hull v. Thomas, 3 Edw. Ch. 236; Drakeford v. Adams, 98 Ga. 722, 25 S. E. 833.

59 Russell v. East Anglian Ry., 3 Macn. & G. 104, per Lord Truro. "The result appears to be this: that it is an established rule of this court that it is not open to any party to question the orders of this court, or any process issued under the authority of this court, by disobedience. I know of no act which this court may do which may not be questioned in a proper form and on a proper application; but I am of opinion that it is not competent for anyone to interfere with the possession of a receiver, or to disobey an injunction, or any other order of the court, on the ground that such orders were improvidently made. . . . . I do not see how the court can expect its officers to do their duty, if they do it under the peril of resistance, and of that resistance being justified on grounds tending to the impeachment of the order under which they are acting."

60 Richards v. People, 81 Ill. 551; Tolleson v. Green, 83 Ga. 499, 10 S. E. 120; Tolman v. Jones, 114 Ill. 148, 28 N. E. 464; In re Lewis, 52 Kan. 660, 35 Pac. 287.

been in his hands or under his control at the time demand was made upon him by the receiver, is not imprisonment for debt, within the meaning of the constitutional prohibition.[61]

A person within the jurisdiction of the appointing court may be held guilty of contempt for acts of interference committed by him against the receiver in a foreign state, as by attaching property of the receivership there situated.[62]

§ 164. **Possession Protected by Injunction.**—It is frequently necessary for a receiver to pray for an injunction to restrain any unauthorized interference with the property in his possession, and the granting of such an injunction in such cases is a necessary incident to the power of appointing receivers.[63] Thus, on the ap-

61 See the able and exhaustive opinion of Lumpkin, J., in Ryan v. Kingsberry, 88 Ga. 361, 14 S. E. 596, reviewing many cases.

62 Chafee v. Quidnick Co., 13 R. I. 442; Sercomb v. Catlin, 128 Ill. 556, 15 Am. St. Rep. 147, 21 N. E. 606; Smith v. Hosmer, 84 Mich. 564, 47 N. W. 1092.

63 Evelyn v. Lewis, 3 Hare, 472; Dixon v. Dixon, [1904] 1 Ch. 161; Davis v. Gray, 16 Wall. 203, 21 L. ed. 447; In re Tyler, 149 U. S. 164, 13 Sup. Ct. 785, 37 L. ed. 689, Fidelity T. & S. V. Co. v. Mobile S R. Co., 53 Fed. 687; Arthur v. Oakes, 63 Fed 310, 11 C. C. A 209, 25 L. R. A. 414; Metropolitan Trust Co. v. Columbia, S. & H. Ry. Co., 95 Fed. 18; Lake Shore & M. S. Ry. Co. v. Felton, 103 Fed. 227, 43 C. C. A. 189; Bibber-White Co. v. White River Valley Electric Ry. Co., 107 Fed. 176; In re Kleinhause, 113 Fed. 107 (receiver in bankruptcy proceedings); Marshall v. Lockett, 76 Ga. 289; Woodburn v. Smith, 96 Ga. 241, 22 S. E 964; Morgan v. New York & A R. Co, 10 Paige, 290, 40 Am. Dec. 244; In re Christian Jensen Co., 128 N. Y. 550, 28 N. E. 665; Woerishoffer v. North River Construction Co., 99 N. Y. 398, 2 N. E. 47. It should be borne in mind that the federal courts are prohibited from granting injunctions to stay proceedings in any court of a state, except as may be authorized by the bankruptcy laws· U. S. Rev. Stats., § 720; Baker v. Ault, 78 Fed. 394. In Davis v. Butters Lumber Co., 132 N. C. 233, 43 S. E. 650, a receiver was allowed an injunction to restrain a resident creditor from suing in another state, it appearing that such action would interfere with the collection of assets.

pointment of a receiver of all the property and effects of a corporation, for the purpose of closing up its affairs, it is proper that the court should make it a part of the order that the directors and officers of the corporation be restrained from collecting any debts or demands due the company, and from paying out, assigning, or delivering any of the property, moneys or effects of the corporation to any other person, and from incumbering the same.[64] The aid of an injunction is frequently invoked in connection with railway receiverships. for instance, in restraint of striking workmen;[65] to protect the right of way from an unwarranted use by another company;[66] to protect the company's right to a joint user of the track of another company;[67] to restrain state officers from disposing of a land grant, under a claim of forfeiture to the state.[68] The parties to a suit concerning real property may be enjoined by the receiver from distraining for rent.[69] And a receiver may apply,

64 Morgan v. New York & A. R. Co., 10 Paige, 290, 40 Am. Dec. 244, per Walworth, C. See, also, In re Christian Jensen Co., 128 N. Y. 550, 28 N. E. 665; Phoenix F. & M. Co v. North River Construction Co., 33 Hun, 156; Woerishoffer v. North River Construction Co., 99 N. Y. 398, 2 N. E. 47, per Finch, J.: "Both parties concede that the possession of the court must not be invaded; that its officers cannot be sued without its permission; and that he cannot be dispossessed except at the peril of a contempt. What then must needs be the effect of the order in this case? It commands nothing which was not already commanded; it forbids nothing which otherwise was permissible; it takes away no right or remedy which the appointment of the receiver had not already taken away. Its sole practical effect was to give notice of that appointment and the right secured by it, and charge the specific creditor with a conscious and willful contempt if he assailed the possession of the court."

65 Arthur v. Oakes, 63 Fed. 310, 11 C. C. A. 209, 25 L. R. A. 414; see *post*, § 169.

66 Fidelity T. & S. V. Co. v. Mobile S. R. Co., 53 Fed. 687.

67 Metropolitan Trust Co. v. Columbus, S. & H. Ry. Co., 95 Fed. 18.

68 Davis v. Gray, 16 Wall. 203, 21 L. ed. 417.

69 Marshall v. Lockett, 76 Ga. 289.

pending confirmation of his sale of property, to protect the possession of his vendee.[70]

Relief for such interference with property belonging to the receiver, by strangers to the suit, may be had either by bill or by petition in the suit, at the discretion of the court.[71]

§ 165. **Attachment Against Receiver.**—Since the possession of the receiver is the possession of the court appointing him, "the property in his hands as such is not subject to attachment,[72] nor is he subject to gar-

70 Woodburn v. Smith, 96 Ga. 241, 22 S E. 964.

71 In re Tyler, 149 U. S. 164, 13 Sup. Ct 785, 37 L. ed. 689; Lake Shore & M. S. R. Co. v. Felton, 103 Fed. 227, 43 C. C. A. 189; Bibber-White Co. v. White R V. E R. Co., 107 Fed. 176; Vermont & C. R. Co. v. Vermont Cent. R. Co., 46 Vt. 792.

72 Ex parte Tillman, 93 Ala. 101, 9 South 527 (refusing to allow a party to obtain possession of attached goods); Atlas Bank v. Nahant Bank, 23 Pick. 480 (attachment after filing of the bill creates no lien on the property); Columbian Book Co. v. De Golyer, 115 Mass 67; Walker v. George Taylor C. Co., 56 Ark. 1, 18 S. W. 1056, 19 S. W. 601; Wadsworth v. Laurie, 164 Ill. 42, 49, 45 N. E. 435; State v. Ellis, 45 La. Ann. 1418, 14 South. 308 ("being [the property] already in the hands of an officer of the court for distribution among creditors, the object to be accomplished by a seizure is attained"); White v. Frankel, 12 Misc. Rep. 271, 33 N. Y. Supp. 1; Mosher v. Supreme Sitting of O. of I. H., 88 Hun, 394, 34 N. Y. Supp. 816; Texas Trunk R. R Co v. Lewis, 81 Tex. 1, 26 Am. St. Rep. 776, 16 S. W. 647; Merrill v. Commonwealth Mut. Fire Ins. Co., 166 Mass. 238, 44 N. E 144 (attachment after proceedings commenced for winding up company is void), Hagedon v. Bank of Wisconsin, 1 Pinn. 61, 39 Am. Dec. 275, Regenstein v. Pearlstein, 30 S. C. 192, 8 S. E. 850 (attachment after appointment, and before bond is given, is ineffectual); but see Naumburg v. Hyatt, 24 Fed. 898, stating: "The fact that a receiver had been appointed with special and limited power to execute the judgment in this case before the levy of the attachment of petitioners does not necessarily avoid the levy and prevent the court from waiving the apparent contempt and recognizing as valid such irregular proceedings. . . . . The possession of the property was in no way disturbed, and there was no hasty interference with the proceedings in the pending cause". Halpern v. Clarendon H. L. Co., 64 Ark. 132, 40 S. W. 784 (vendor's right to lien may be defeated, if not perfected before the appointment).

nishment on account of it,[73] or funds in his hands or subject to his control in that capacity."[74] But in such cases the court "may with propriety permit proceedings in garnishment to be brought,"[75] where, in the discretion of the court, justice requires it.[76] And it has

73 Blum v. Van Vechten, 92 Wis. 378, 66 N. W. 507; Campau v. Detroit Driving Club (Mich.), 98 N. W. 267; Vieth v. Ress, 60 Neb. 52, 82 N. W. 116 ("and he cannot be sued or summoned, as garnishee in respect to property in his possession by virtue of his trust"); Richards v People, 81 Ill. 551 ("the garnishee proceedings were a direct interference with the right of the receiver since they attempted to deprive him of what was his under the order of his appointment"); Missouri Pac. Ry. Co v Love, 61 Kan. 433, 59 Pac. 1072, Commonwealth v. Hide & Leather Ins. Co, 119 Mass. 155, gives the following reason: "The property of the corporation is intrusted to the receivers by the authority of the law, for the purpose of distribution among the creditors of the corporation, not among the creditors of those creditors. To undertake to determine, as incidental to the administration of the estate of the corporation, the validity and equity of the claims of every creditor of a creditor of the corporation, would unreasonably embarrass and delay the distribution of the estate and the settlement of the accounts of the receivers"; Holbrook v. Ford, 153 Ill 633, 46 Am. St. Rep. 917, 39 N. E. 1091, 27 L. R. A. 324, distinguishing Sercomb v. Catlin, 128 Ill. 556, 15 Am. St. Rep. 147, 21 N. E. 606; McGowan v. Myers, 66 Iowa, 99, 23 N. W. 282; Field v. Jones, 11 Ga. 413; Taylor v. Gillean 23 Tex. 508; Kreislee v. Campbell 89 Tex 104, 33 S. W. 853, Blum v. Van Vechten, 92 Wis 378, 66 N. W. 507; but see Central Trust Co. v. Chattanooga R. & C. R. Co., 68 Fed. 685.

74 Blum v. Van Vechten, *supra*. See, also, Ex parte Tillman, 93 Ala. 101, 9 South. 527; People's Bank of Bell v. Calhoun, 102 U. S. 256, 26 L. ed. 101 ("it was for the court having possession to determine how far it would permit any other court to interfere with that possession, and what effect it would give to the attempt of another court to seize the property so under its control").

75 Cohnen v. Sweenie, 105 Mich. 643, 63 N. W. 641 (the assets were shown to be in excess of the debt which the receiver was to satisfy); approved in Citizens' Com. & Sav. Bank v. Bay Circuit Judge, 110 Mich. 633, 68 N. W. 649 (if there is no abuse of discretion in granting the order, it will not be set aside on appeal); Van Bianchi v. Wayne, 124 Mich. 462, 83 N. W. 26 (see for the effect of statute); Yeiser v. Cathers (Neb.), 97 N. W. 840.

76 Ex parte Tillman, 93 Ala. 102, 9 South. 527 ("unquestionably the chancery court had authority to permit the levies of the attach-

been stated that "where the case in which their appointment has been made has been settled, or where they have a fund in their hands over and above the amount necessary to satisfy the judgment," an attachment or garnishment is not an improper interference with the court's possession.[77]

§ 166. **Property in Receiver's Possession not Subject to Sale Under Execution.**—It is a general rule that property in the hands of a receiver is not subject to execution sale without leave of the court.[78] The reason for the rule is thus given: "When a court of equity has under-

ments, and, had they been levied by leave of the court first obtained, the levies would have been legal and valid''). See, also, Wallace v. Wallace, 21 App. Div. 542, 48 N. Y. Supp. 592.

77 Russell v. Millett, 20 Wash. 212, 55 Pac. 44; see, also, Smith v. People, 93 Ill. App. 135. But this is expressly denied by Campbell, J., in People v. Brooks, 40 Mich. 333, 29 Am. Rep. 534.

78 Russell v. East Anglian Ry, 3 Macn. & G. 104; Wiswall v. Sampson, 14 How 52, 65, 14 L. ed. 322; State of Georgia v. Jesup, 106 U. S. 458, 464, 1 Sup. Ct. 363, 27 L. ed. 216; Wheeler v. Walton etc. Co., 65 Fed. 720; In re Hall & Stilson Co., 73 Fed. 527; Dugger v. Collins, 69 Ala. 324; Premier Steel Co. v. McElwaine-Richards Co., 144 Ind. 614, 43 N. E. 876; Gardner v. Caldwell, 16 Mont. 221, 40 Pac. 590, and numerous authorities reviewed; Walling v. Miller, 108 N. Y. 173, 2 Am. St. Rep. 400, 15 N. E. 65; Skinner v. Maxwell, 68 N. C. 400, Pelletier v. Greenville Lumber Co., 123 N. C. 596, 68 Am. St. Rep. 837, 31 S. E. 855, Robinson v. Atlantic & G. W. R. Co., 66 Pa. St. 160; Thompson v. McCleary, 159 Pa. St. 189, 28 Atl. 254; Edwards v. Norton, 55 Tex. 405; Russell v. Texas & P. R Co., 68 Tex. 646, 5 S. W. 686; Ellis v. Vernon etc. Co., 86 Tex. 109, 23 S. W. 858; Hammond v. Tarver, 11 Tex. Civ. App. 48, 31 S. W. 841. For limitations on the rule, see Hickox v. Holladay, 29 Fed. 226, 233 (following Wiswall v. Sampson, but with reluctance); Petaluma Sav. Bk. v. Superior Court, 111 Cal. 488, 44 Pac. 177; Chautauqua Co. Bank v. Risley, 19 N. Y. 369, 75 Am. Dec. 347; In re Loos, 50 Hun, 67, 3 N. Y. Supp. 383; Wilkinson v. Paddock, 57 Hun, 191, 11 N Y. Supp. 442, affirmed on appeal, 125 N. Y. 748, 27 N E. 407; St. Louis etc. R. Co. v. Whitaker, 68 Tex. 630, 5 S. W. 448; Cherry v. Western Washington I. E. Co., 11 Wash. 586, 40 Pac. 136; Case v. Sutherland, 98 Wis. 551, 74 N. W. 337.

taken to adjudicate upon and distribute a fund among the parties entitled to it, it would be inconvenient if a court of law (or any other court) could by its process interrupt the adjudication and create new rights in the property itself."[79] The argument that a sale on execution of land in the possession of a receiver occasions no interference with the possession of the receiver, and hence no contempt of the authority of the court, does not meet the objection.[80] "The end sought by the rule is not only the avoidance of conflict in the jurisdiction of the courts, but the preservation of the interests of creditors and debtor. These interests have been intrusted to the court of equity, which affords a more comprehensive and perfect system of justice than the court of law, in order that all may be guarded and protected, each with reference to every other." Further, sales on execution of property in a receiver's hands would usually be sales at a sacrifice, and redemption from such sales attended with embarrassment.[81]

79 Skinner v. Maxwell, 68 N. C. 404.

80 Wiswall v. Sampson, 14 How. 52, 66, 14 L. ed. 322. "The property is a fund in court, to abide the event of the litigation, and to be applied to the payment of the judgment creditor, who has filed his bill to remove impediments in the way of his execution. If he has succeeded in establishing his right to the application of any portion of the fund, it is the duty of the court to see that such application is made. And, in order to effect this, the court must administer it independently of any rights acquired by third persons, pending the litigation. Otherwise, the whole fund may have passed out of its hands before the final decree, and the litigation become fruitless." See, also, Dugger v. Collins, 69 Ala. 324.

81 Premier Steel Co. v. McElwaine-Richards Co., 144 Ind. 614, 43 N. E. 876, per Hackney, C. J., who continues: "If the right of the lower court was to direct the sale by its own officer, and upon execution, as in other instances, that right would be in utter disregard of the condition of the estate as to the ability of the receiver to realize by certificates, rentals, or other means, permitted by the court in possession, sums sufficient to pay the appellee's claim and extinguish the lien. Any possible right of the receiver to redeem would be embarrassed by additional costs and ultimate losses to the general

The rule is not to be understood as absolutely preventing the acquisition of new rights to the fund in controversy after the commencement of the proceedings. Any person claiming to have acquired such an interest, while he cannot interfere under the process of another court, may, under the old equity practice, apply to the court which has jurisdiction of the fund, *pro interesse suo,* and his claim will be heard.[82] The same result can now be accomplished by a petition and motion in the cause;[83] and in administering the fund, the court will take care that the rights of prior liens or incumbrances shall not be destroyed; and will adopt proper measures, by reference to the master or otherwise, to ascertain them, and bring them before it.[84]

creditors, and a redemption by any creditor would not only meet the same embarrassment, but it would result either in giving such redeeming creditor an advantage over other creditors, or of redeeming to his own inconvenience, that all creditors might be protected. If the whole subject were within the control of the court appointing the receiver, the lienholder's interests could be protected by his right of priority to the proceeds of any sale; the opportunity for competition in selling at private sale would be afforded; the wisdom of the chancellor would be taken upon the prudence and fairness of the sale and the adequacy of the consideration; costs would be spared, and redemption complications avoided " See, also, Gardner v Caldwell, 16 Mont. 221, 40 Pac. 590. In Pelletier v. Greenville Lumber Co, 123 N. C. 596, 68 Am. St. Rep. 837, 31 S. E. 855, Douglas, J, says of the doctrine permitting the sale of real estate, provided it does not interfere with the actual possession of the receiver: "Its practical effect would be either to permit outside parties to stop all further proceedings of a court of equity by disposing of the subject-matter in controversy, or else to put that court in the position of holding simply the naked possession of property and gravely proceeding to determine who would have been entitled to the property if it had not been sold!"

82 Skinner v. Maxwell, 68 N. C. 400, 404; Wiswall v. Sampson, 14 How. 52, 65, 14 L. ed. 322; Dugger v. Collins, 69 Ala. 324.

83 Pelletier v. Greenville Lumber Co., 123 N. C. 596, 31 S. E. 855, 68 Am. St. Rep. 837; and other cases, *supra,* in note 78.

84 Wiswall v. Sampson, 14 How. 52, 66, 67, 14 L. ed. 322; In re Hall & Stillson Co., 73 Fed. 527, 536.

In some cases, where the property in dispute is ample, and the litigation protracted, it may be fit and proper for the court to permit the execution to issue; but such proceedings should be under the control of the discretion of the court, as the condition of the title to the property may frequently be so complicated and embarrassed, that unless the sale is withheld until the title is cleared up by the judgment of the court, great sacrifice must necessarily ensue to the parties interested;[85] and authority to issue an execution on a prior judgment should be withheld, in absence of a satisfactory showing that there is any urgent necessity for a speedy sale, or that the petitioner will be prejudiced by allowing the receiver to administer the estate and to distribute the fund with due regard to priority of claims.[86]

Giving consent to making the receiver a party defendant to an action in another court to establish a lien against the property does not authorize such other court to order a sale of the property on execution.[87]

It is held that the doctrine of non-interference does not extend so far as to prevent a sale, without leave, of property to which the receiver was not entitled under the order of appointment;[88] and it appears to be held

85 Wiswall v. Sampson, 14 How. 52, 68, 14 L. ed. 322; In re Hall & Stillson Co., 73 Fed. 527, 536 (refusing leave to issue execution, where property not ample to meet all claims, and title embarrassed). Leave was granted in Pelletier v. Greenville Lumber Co, 123 N. C. 596, 68 Am St. Rep. 837, 31 S. E. 855, In re Thompson, 10 App. Div. 40, 41 N. Y. Supp. 740; Case v. Sutherland, 98 Wis. 551, 74 N. W 337; and Cohen v. Gold Creek etc. Co., 95 Fed. 580 (receiver showing no diligence in executing the trust).

86 Wheeler v. Walton etc. Co., 65 Fed 720. That the petition should not be determined without notice to the parties in the original suit, see In re Hall & Stillson Co, 69 Fed. 425.

87 Premier Steel Co. v. McElwaine-Richards Co., 144 Ind. 614, 43 N. E. 876.

88 St. Louis etc. R. Co. v. Whitaker, 68 Tex. 630, 5 S. W. 448.

in California that the appointment of a receiver of the separate real estate of the husband in an action for divorce, in order to enforce a decree for alimony awarded to the wife, does not prevent the enforcement of a judgment lien upon such real estate by a judgment creditor of the husband, whether such lien be prior or subsequent to the lien of the decree for alimony, and it is not necessary that there should be an application by such judgment creditor to the court appointing the receiver before proceeding to sell such real estate under execution.[89]

§ 167. **Same; Illustrations; Execution Sales Under Subsequent, and Under Prior Liens.**—When, on a creditor's bill, the judgment debtor has made an assignment of all his property to the receiver, under an order of court, a subsequent judgment against the receiver does not bind the land, since the debtor has no title or interest left to which the judgment could attach; and, therefore, a sale on execution levied under such subsequent judgment is void as against a sale by the receiver.[90] But such an assignment or conveyance to the receiver is not necessary in order to invalidate execution sales upon judgments recovered during the receivership. Thus,

89 Petaluma Savings Bank v. Superior Court, 111 Cal. 488, 44 Pac. 177. It is difficult to determine from the opinion of Beatty, C. J., whether this rule is limited to receivership in this particular class of actions. If intended to be of general application, it is, of course, contrary to the whole current of authority. Wiswall v. Sampson is distinguished (pp. 500, 501) on the ground that there the fund sought to be reached on execution was "the creation of the court appointing the receiver, and was necessarily subject to its disposition." In considering the weight to be attached to this decision it is well to remember that the supreme court of California has, in several cases, taken an extremely narrow view of the receiver's title, in apparent indifference to the consensus of opinion elsewhere.

90 Chautauqua County Bank v. White, 6 N. Y. 236, 57 Am. Dec. 442.

the purchaser at an execution sale of property in the possession of a receiver for the purpose of collecting the rents, on a judgment recovered subsequent to the appointment, takes no title;[91] and the same is true when the judgment was recovered before the appointment, but no lien was acquired by levy upon the land until after the receiver had taken possession.[92] Such levy and sale is not only ineffectual to pass title, but may be restrained on the receiver's petition as an interference with his control; thus, a levy, subsequent to the appointment of a receiver of all the mortgaged property of a company, upon land which was covered by the mortgage, was set aside, and further proceedings under the execution restrained, although the judgment upon which the execution was issued was recovered before the appointment of the receiver;[93] and a receiver having in custody property of a corporation may restrain execution against such property on a subsequent judgment.[94]

Where, on the other hand, the property in the hands of the receiver is subject to a prior lien, the question of the right and power of the holder of such lien to enforce it without the consent of the court which has appointed the receiver is one of much difficulty, and

91 Edwards v. Norton, 55 Tex. 405; see, also, Russell v. Texas P. R. R. Co., 68 Tex. 646, 5 S. W. 686.

92 Dugger v. Collins, 69 Ala. 324.

93 Robinson v. Atlantic & G. W. R. Co., 66 Pa. St. 160. The court says: "If the property might be taken piecemeal from the custody of the receiver, the remedy of the creditors under the mortgage would become worthless, or at least greatly imperiled. . . . . If a creditor believes that the property was not legally mortgaged, or for any good reason should not pass into the hands of the receiver, his duty is to apply to the court having appointed the receiver to ask its discharge out of custody in order that he may proceed against it."

94 Gardner v. Caldwell, 16 Mont. 221, 40 Pac. 590, and cases cited; Thompson v. McCleary, 159 Pa. St. 189, 28 Atl. 254 (decree without prejudice to the defendants' right to apply to the proper court).

has given rise to some conflict of decision. The weight of authority, notwithstanding some vigorous dissent, appears to support the negative of this question. The facts in the leading case[95] have been thus stated (the action was ejectment): "The demanded premises in that action had belonged to Ticknor, who had conveyed them in fraud of creditors to Day prior to December, 1840. At that date plaintiff's lessors recovered a money judgment against Ticknor, execution upon which was returned *nulla bona.* In 1842 another creditor recovered judgment against Ticknor and thereafter commenced a suit in equity to set aside the conveyance to Day. He succeeded in his action, and after the conveyance was set aside a receiver of the property was appointed. While the receiver was in possession plaintiff's lessors, without leave asked or granted, sold it under an *alias* execution issued upon his judgment of 1840. The defendant in the ejectment suit claimed under the receiver, and it was held in his favor that the execution sale passed no title." A few years later the court of appeals of New York reached an opposite conclusion in a case presenting facts very similar.[96] "The opinion in that case lays down the broad doctrine that, if a judgment creditor have a lien upon real estate by virtue of his judgment at the time of the appointment of a receiver, he may be guilty of contempt by the attempt to enforce the collection of his judgment by a

95 Wiswall v. Sampson, 14 How. 52, 14 L. ed. 322 (December term, 1852), opinion by Justice Nelson. The cases holding the affirmative of the question usually attempt to distinguish this case, and limit it to its particular facts. The summary of the facts is taken from the opinion of Beatty, C. J., in Petaluma Sav. Bank v. Superior Court, 111 Cal. 488, 500, 44 Pac. 177.

96 Chautauqua County Bank v. Risley, 19 N. Y. 369, 75 Am. Dec. 347. The summary of this case is taken from the opinion of Gaines, J, in Ellis v. Vernon Ice, Light and Water Co., 86 Tex. 109, 23 S. W. 858.

sale under execution, but that, if the sale be made, it is neither illegal nor void. The facts of the case were that a judgment creditor, where execution had been returned unsatisfied, sued his debtor to set aside a fraudulent assignment of real estate, and had a receiver appointed. He prevailed in his suit, and, by order of the court, the receiver sold the property. A few days after the same property was sold under an execution issued upon a judgment against the same debtor, which was rendered before the appointment of a receiver, and which was a lien upon the property. The court held that the purchaser at the sheriff's sale took a good title. The judgment which was sought to be collected by the suit in which the receiver was appointed was older than the judgment under which the property was sold by the sheriff, and was also a lien upon the property. But the court was of opinion that the defendant, who claimed through the receiver, took only such title as was conveyed to the receiver by the deed of the party over whose property he was appointed, and that this conveyance passed the property subject to the lien of the judgment under which it was sold by the constable, and that, therefore, the purchaser at execution sale took the superior title. It appears that the laws of New York required a conveyance to the receiver, in order to perfect his control over real estate, but that in case of personal property no such conveyance was necessary. Subsequently, in Walling v. Miller, 108 N. Y. 173, 2 Am. St. Rep. 400, 15 N. E. 65, the same court held that where the sheriff had a levy upon personal property, and a receiver was subsequently appointed, a sale by the sheriff after the appointment, without leave of the court, was wholly illegal and void. If these decisions can be reconciled, it must be upon the ground that under the laws of that state the receiver derives his title to real estate only through the conveyance of the defendant in the action, and that, because such conveyance is not necessary as to personal property, a different rule applies. In re Loos, 50 Hun, 67, 3 N. Y. Supp. 383.[97] It would seem, however, that in Walling v. Miller the court intended to overrule the case of Bank v. Risley, although they do not expressly say so. In the later case they rely upon Wiswall v. Sampson," the authority of which was expressly denied in Chatauqua Bank v. Risley. The case from the opinion in which the above extract is taken,[98] was one of an execution of sale of land belonging to a corporation, subsequent to the appointment, under a levy made prior to the appointment of a receiver of the corporation. The court, holding such sale ineffective to pass title, says, with much force: "To permit the control of a receiver to be interfered with by virtue of process from another court would be a practice fraught with injustice, and productive of confusion; and that remark applies with especial force to the receivers of insolvent corporations.

97 The doctrine of Walling v. Miller appears to be limited by a later case, in which it was claimed by a receiver that a sale of the property of the corporation under an execution after his appointment was absolutely void, but the court held that, as the sheriff had seized the property, and had it in his possession at the time of the appointment of the receiver, the sale was not void, but, at most, should be held simply voidable: Varnum v. Hart, 119 N. Y. 101, 23 N. E. 183, as explained in Moore v. Potter, 155 N. Y. 481, 63 Am. St. Rep. 692, 50 N. E. 271. See, also, Smith v. Davis, 63 Hun, 100, 17 N. Y. Supp. 614 (receiver not in possession of the property on which execution was levied, and claimed no right or interest in it).

It was held in an early New York case that the levy and sale by the sheriff of real estate in the receiver's possession, upon a prior judgment which was a lien on the land, did not disturb the receiver's possession, and was not a contempt of court: Albany City Bank v. Schermerhorn, 9 Paige, 372, 38 Am. Dec. 551; 10 Paige, 263; see criticism of this case in Pelletier v. Greenville Lumber Co., 123 N. C. 596, 68 Am. St. Rep. 837, 31 S. E. 855.

98 Ellis v. Vernon Ice, L. & W. Co., 86 Tex. 109, 23 S. W. 858.

After all the assets of a corporation have been taken from its managers, and placed under the control of a receiver, is it just to allow its property to be sold under execution? The court, having deprived the corporation of the power of paying the debt and of avoiding the sale, should, in the interest of all concerned, protect its property from the sacrifice." Further cases to the same effect are cited in the note.[99]

The affirmative of the question under consideration has, however, received vigorous support. Thus, it is held that where the property of an insolvent foreign corporation has been seized by the sheriff under a warrant of attachment issued by a state court in an action which was afterwards prosecuted to judgment, and execution issued and levy made upon the property seized, a receiver appointed subsequent to the attachment by the United States circuit court of the district in which such property is situated cannot obtain a summary order to the sheriff to surrender the seized property.[100] In a series of cases in Washington it is held that where a creditor has attached property, the court has no authority to direct a receiver appointed in an action other than the attachment suit to take possession of the attached property, as the attachment creditor has not only the right to have his debt paid out of the proceeds of such property, but to have the sheriff retain it intact

99 Pelletier v. Greenville Lumber Co., 123 N. C. 596, 68 Am. St Rep. 837, 31 S. E. 855 (holding that land belonging to an insolvent corporation cannot, as a matter of right and without leave of the court, be sold, after the appointment of a receiver, upon a valid judgment obtained before such appointment); State of Georgia v. Jesup, 106 U. S. 458, 1 Sup. Ct. 363, 27 L. ed. 216, as explained in In re Hall & Stillson Co., 73 Fed. 527, 535; Wheeler v. Walton etc. Co., 65 Fed. 720 (execution sale not permitted without urgent reasons); Earle v. Commonwealth, 178 U. S. 449, 20 Sup. Ct. 915, 44 L. ed. 1146.

100 Cole v. Oil-Well Supply Co., 57 Fed. 534. See, also, In re Hall & Stillson Co., 73 Fed. 527.

in the meantime, under ordinary circumstances;[101] and that where a judgment was recovered and execution levied on land prior to the appointment of the receiver of a corporation, the judgment creditor may lawfully proceed to a sale, and the purchaser thereunder is entitled to a deed from the sheriff.[102] A similar view is held in California, at least in relation to the receiver ship of the estate of the husband in an action for divorce.[103]

On the whole, it may be said that the doctrine of Wiswall v. Sampson, in the fifty years of the history of that case, has been generally accepted in the full breadth and scope with which it was laid down. Reasons of convenience are in its favor; and its proper application

101 State v. Superior Court of Snohomish County, 7 Wash. 77, 34 Pac. 430; State v. Superior Court of Chehalis County, 8 Wash. 210, 35 Pac. 1087, 25 L. R. A. 354. In the latter case, Wiswall v. Sampson is distinguished on the ground that the receiver there was in actual possession. See further as to this case, the later case of State v. Superior Court of King County, 11 Wash. 63, 39 Pac. 244, holding that he may be allowed, under some circumstances, to take possession of the property affected by the prior lien.

102 Cherry v. Western Washington I. E. Co., 11 Wash. 586, 40 Pac. 136.

103 Petaluma Savings Bank v. Superior Court, 111 Cal. 488, 44 Pac. 177. Mr. High, in the third edition of his work on Receivers (§ 141, note), gives the weight of his opinion in support of the right of the prior lienholder: "The cases of Walling v. Miller, 108 N. Y. 173, 2 Am. St. Rep. 400, 15 N. E. 65, and Ellis v. Vernon I., L. & W. Co, 86 Tex. 109, 23 S. W. 858, may be regarded as extending the doctrine of non-interference with the receiver's possession to its extreme limits, since the lien of the judgment creditor having been perfected by levying his execution before the appointment of the receiver, it would seem, upon principle, to be the better doctrine that the rights thus acquired are paramount to the receivership, and that the judgment creditor should be permitted to proceed with his levy and sale, without being required to seek relief in the cause in which the receiver is appointed." But, it may be asked, has not the learned author, in thus speaking of these cases as a new departure, overlooked the leading case on the whole subject, Wiswall v. Sampson?

can never result in "the hardship on judgment creditors" which would ensue "if they could be restrained from enforcing collection of a judgment and lien given by the court indefinitely."[104]

§ 168. Property in Receiver's Possession cannot be Seized for Taxes.—The principle that the receiver's possession is exclusive, and will be protected from interference without leave of the court whose hand he is, is strikingly illustrated by the rule, firmly established in the federal courts, that property in the receiver's possession is exempt from levy and sale by state officers in collection of taxes.[105] Such levy and sale may be en-

104 Clark, J, concurring in result in Pelletier v. Greenville Lumber Co., 123 N. C. 596, 68 Am. St. Rep. 837, 31 S. E 855.

105 In In re Tyler, 149 U. S. 164, 13 Sup. Ct. 785, 13 L. ed. 689, the court states: "The general doctrine that property in the possession of a receiver appointed by a court is *in custodia legis*, and that unauthorized interference with such possession is punishable as a contempt, is conceded, but it is contended that this salutary rule has no application to the collection of taxes. Undoubtedly, property so situated is not thereby rendered exempt from the imposition of taxes by the government within whose jurisdiction the property is, and the lien for taxes is superior to all other liens whatsoever except judicial costs, where the property is rightfully in the custody of the law; but this does not justify a physical invasion of such custody, and a wanton disregard of the orders of the court in respect of it. The maintenance of the system of checks and balances characteristic of republican institutions requires the co-ordinate departments of government, whether federal or state, to refrain from any interference with the independence of each other; and the possession of property by the judicial department cannot be arbitrarily encroached upon, save in violation of this fundamental principle.

"The levy of a tax warrant, like the levy of an ordinary *fieri facias*, sequestrates the property to answer the exigency of the writ, but property in the possession of the receiver is already in sequestration, already held in equitable execution, and, while the lien for taxes must be recognized and enforced, the orderly administration of justice requires this to be done by and under the sanction of the court. It is the duty of the court to see to it that this is done, and a seizure of the property against its will can only be predicated upon the as

joined,[106] and the officer making the same may be punished for contempt;[107] and it is held that such sale is void and confers no title upon the purchaser,[108] and that a judgment for the amount of the taxes may be removed as a cloud upon title.[109] This conclusion, says Chief Justice Fuller, "does not involve interruption in the payment of taxes, or the displacement or impairment of the lien therefor; but, on the contrary, it makes it the imperative duty of the court to recognize as paramount, and enforce with promptness and vigor, the just claims of the authorities for the prescribed contributions to state and municipal revenue."[110] The usual

sumption that the court will fail in the discharge of its duty—an assumption carrying a contempt upon its face.'' See King v. Wooten, 2 U. S. App 651, 54 Fed. 612, 4 C. C A. 519; Ex parte Chamberlain, 55 Fed. 706; Oakes v. Myers, 68 Fed. 807; *contra*, Central Trust Co. v. Wabash etc. Co., 26 Fed. 11. For state courts following the same rule, see Cleveland v. McCravy, 46 S C. 252, 24 S. E. 175; Weaver v. Duncan (Tenn. Ch App.), 56 S. W. 39.

106 In re Tyler, *supra;* Ex parte Chamberlain, 55 Fed. 706, Oakes v. Myers, 68 Fed. 807; Burleigh v. Chehalis County, 75 Fed. 873, 34 L. R. A. 393, Clark v. McGhee, 87 Fed. 789, 31 C. C. A. 321; Virginia, T. & C. Co. v. Bristol Land Co., 88 Fed 134 (the receiver may apply for the injunction by petition in the original suit).

107 In re Tyler, *supra.*

108 Virginia, T. & C. Co. v. Bristol Land Co., 88 Fed. 134.

109 Burleigh v. Chehalis County, 75 Fed. 873, 34 L. R. A. 393.

110 In re Tyler, *supra.* See Ex parte Chamberlain, 55 Fed. 704-706, stating: ''There can be no doubt that property in the hands of a receiver of any court, either of a state or of the United States, is as much bound for the payment of taxes, state, county and municipal, as any other property. Persons cannot, by coming into this court, and, for the promotion of their interests, applying for and obtaining the appointment of receivers, obtain exemption from the paramount dnty of a citizen. For this reason, receivers in this district pay all just and lawful taxes without asking or needing the sanction of the court, and in their accounts such payments are passed without question. But, on the other hand, receivers are not bound to pay a tax in their judgment unlawful, without the order of the court, and when they consider the legality of the tax questionable it is their right—their manifest duty—to apply to the court either for instruction or

and proper course pursued by the tax officer is by intervention in the receivership suit.[111]

§ 169. **Other Forms of Interference; Strikes; Arrest; etc.**— Conspiracies by striking workmen to interfere with the operation of railroads in the hands of receivers have been the subject of much adjudication within recent years. While this subject may more appropriately be taken up in another connection, the rule should here be noted that any willful attempt by anyone, with knowledge that the road is in the hands of the court, to prevent or impede the receiver from complying with the order of the court in running the road, when the attempt is unlawful, and as between private individuals would give a right of action for damages, is a contempt of the order of the court.[112]

Immunity from arrest is extended to the receiver for acts done in discharge of the duties imposed upon him by the court, though not for acts done in violation of

protection. Especially is this the case when the question arises between the receiver and persons in the state, county, and municipal government as to the proper construction to be given to the law, upon which individuals may well differ, and it is his right and manifest duty to go to the court, whose creature he is, for instruction. He [the receiver] therefore pursued the proper course when he came in by this petition." See, also, to the same effect, Lamkin v. Baldwin etc. Co., 72 Conn. 59, 43 Atl. 593, 44 L. R. A. 786; Greeley v. Provident Sav. Bank, 98 Mo. 458, 11 S. W. 980.

111 In re Tyler, *supra;* Spalding v. Commonwealth, 88 Ky. 135, 10 S. W. 420 (the court may grant leave to sue the receiver in such case); Weaver v. Duncan (Tenn. Ch. App), 56 S. W. 39 (same).

112 Thomas v. Cincinnati, N. O. & T. P. Ry. Co., 62 Fed. 803, per Taft, Cir. J.; Secor v. Railroad Co., 7 Biss. 513, Fed. Cas. No. 12,605; In re Doolittle, 23 Fed. 544; United States v. Kane, 23 Fed. 748; In re Wabash R. Co., 24 Fed. 217; In re Higgins, 27 Fed. 443; Beers v. Wabash, St. L. & P. R. Co., 34 Fed. 244; In re Acker, 66 Fed. 290. On the general subject of injunctions in strike cases, see *post*, chapter XXVIII.

the ordinary criminal statutes of a state.[113] Distraining for rent upon property in the receiver's possession, without leave;[114] searching premises in his possession without a warrant, and seizing goods therein;[115] and removing a building from the premises[116]—clearly constitute acts of contempt. It is held, in England, that a libel on the business conducted by a receiver and manager amounts to a contempt, in a case where a former clerk of the firm sent around a circular to the customers of the firm, containing an unfair statement of the effect of the order appointing the receiver, and soliciting their custom for his own business.[117]

It has been held, following the analogy of the cases concerning execution sales of lands and other property in the receiver's hands, that the sale of such lands under a power in a trust deed which is a first lien thereon is void, even though it was error for the court not to permit such sale.[118] But those cases do not apply to prevent a sale of property of which the receiver had no possession or right of possession, as where a corporation contracted to purchase certain personal property, and afterwards refused to take and pay for it according to the contract, and the vendor, after the subsequent appointment of a receiver of the corporation, and upon notice to him, elected to sell the property and hold him for the balance.[119]

113 United States v. Murphy, 44 Fed. 39, holding arrest a contempt.

114 Noe v. Gibson, 7 Paige, 513.

115 In re Swan, 150 U. S. 637, 14 Sup. Ct 225, 37 L. ed. 1207.

116 Delozier v. Bird, 123 N. C. 689, 31 S E 834.

117 Helmore v. Smith, 35 Ch. D. 449. Also, tampering with the receiver's employees and inducing them to join a rival business was restrained by injunction in Dixon v. Dixon, [1904] 1 Ch. 161.

118 Scott v. Crawford, 16 Tex. Civ App. 477, 41 S. W. 697.

119 The receiver "had only the right to receive the property purchased by the corporation upon paying the agreed price. No fund or

§ 170. Conflicting Appointments of Receivers.—It often happens that proceedings looking toward the appointment of receivers are instituted in courts having the same territorial jurisdiction, existing side by side. Examples of courts having concurrent territorial jurisdiction are the courts of the state and the courts of the United States within the district; or the courts of different counties or judicial districts in the state whose territorial jurisdiction extends throughout the state. In such cases considerable confusion and diversity of opinion have existed among different courts as to the principles which should control. The following results are probably sustained by the better reasoning and authority: 1. Where, in the first proceeding, the court has actually got possession through its receiver or other process *in rem* of the thing before the second proceedings are begun, that possession will not be disturbed by the second court.[120] 2. Where the first proceeding is an *in rem* proceeding or is in the nature of a proceeding *in rem*, though that court has not yet actually seized the property, the first court will retain exclusive juris-

property that had passed into the hands of the receiver was attempted to be disposed of or sold": Moore v. Potter, 155 N. Y. 481, 63 Am. St. Rep. 692, 50 N. E. 271.

120 Baltimore & O. R. R. v. Wabash R. R Co., 119 Fed. 678; Merritt v. American Steel Barge Co., 79 Fed. 228, 24 C. C. A. 530; Knott v. Evening Post Co, 124 Fed. 342; Gaylord v. Fort Wayne etc. R. R Co., 6 Biss. 286, Fed. Cas. No. 5284, Shields v. Coleman, 157 U. S. 168, 15 Sup. Ct. 570, 39 L. ed. 660; Moran v. Sturgis, 154 U. S. 256, 14 Sup. Ct. 1019, 38 L. ed. 981, citing many authorities; Byers v. McAuley, 149 U. S. 608, 13 Sup. Ct. 906, 37 L. ed. 367; Taylor v. Carryl, 20 How. 583, 15 L. ed. 1028, a leading case; Buck v. Colbath, 3 Wall. 334, 18 L. ed. 257 In Heidritter v. Elizabeth Oil Cloth Co., 112 U. S. 294, 305, 5 Sup. Ct. 135, 28 L. ed. 729, the court says: "Where the object of the action requires the control and dominion of the property involved in the litigation, that court which first acquires possession, or that dominion which is equivalent, draws to itself the exclusive right to dispose of it for the purposes of its jurisdiction." See, also, Pulliam v. Osborne, 17 How. 471, 15 L. ed. 154.

diction.[121] In this connection, however, difficult questions arise as to when the proceeding is or becomes in the nature of an *in rem* proceeding. Thus, take the ordinary case of a foreclosure proceeding, say, of a railroad, where the bill asks the final relief of sale and the intermediate relief of a receiver *pendente lite*. Of course such a proceeding is not strictly an *in rem* proceeding, because the element of notice to all the world is absent, yet it is plain that the ultimate purpose of the suit is a change in title and that as soon at least as possession is rightfully taken, the proceeding begins to assume many of the characteristics of an *in rem* proceeding. At what particular point shall we say the proceeding partakes of this character? Some courts say (a) that the *in rem* character attaches to the proceeding from the time of filing the bill;[122] (b) others, from the time of any order in the proceeding indicating that the court has taken jurisdiction of the case, especially if such order affects possession, as *e. g.*, where the subpoena contains a restraining order;[123] (c) other cases consider that jurisdiction of the *res* attaches at the date of service of subpoena, from which time, under the chancery practice, subsequent purchasers are

121 Farmers' Loan and Trust Co. v. Lake Street Elevated R. R. Co., 177 U. S. 51, 20 Sup. Ct. 564, 44 L. ed. 667; Guaranty T. Co. v. North Chicago St. R. Co., 130 Fed. 801; Knott v. Evening Post Co., 124 Fed. 342, In re Schuyler's Steam Tow-Boat Co., 136 N. Y. 169, 32 N. E. 623, 20 L. R. A. 391, and note; In re Christian Jensen Co., 128 N. Y. 550, 28 N. E. 665; Rogers & Baldwin Co. v. Cleveland Building Co., 132 Mo. 442, 53 Am. St. Rep. 494, 34 S. W. 57, 31 L. R. A. 335; Kurtz v. Phila. etc. R. R. Co., 187 Pa. St. 59, 40 Atl. 988.

122 Gaylord v. Fort Wayne M. & C. R. Co., 6 Biss. 286, Fed. Cas. No. 5284.

123 Appleton Water Co. v. Central T. Co., 93 Fed. 286, 35 C. C. A. 302: "The entry of an order upon filing of the bill for any purpose involved in the action, and especially one tending to the possession by the court of the *res*."

affected with notice;[124] (d) other cases hold that the court making the first appointment of a receiver shall have exclusive jurisdiction of the *res*;[125] (e) while still another view insists on the test of actual seizure in all cases.[126] A final view holds, (f) as between the immediate parties, that the exclusive jurisdiction attaches from the time of filing the bill.[127] It would seem, in

124 Wilmer v. Atlanta etc. R. Co., 2 Wood, 409, Fed. Cas. No. 17,775 (opinion of Woods, C. J.); Adams v. Mercantile Trust Co., 66 Fed. 621, 15 C. C. A. 1; Illinois Steel Co. v. Putnam, 68 Fed. 515, 15 C. C A. 556; Farmers' Loan & Trust Co. v. Lake Street Elev. R. R. Co., 177 U. S. 51, 61, 20 Sup. Ct. 564, 44 L. ed. 667; Haughwout v. Murphy, 22 N. J. Eq. 536, 545; Gluck & Becker on Receivers, 2d ed., 99; Bell v. Ohio L. & T. Co., 1 Biss. 260, Fed. Cas. No. 1260.

125 In re Schuyler's Steam Tow-Boat Co., 136 N. Y. 169, 32 N. E. 623, 20 L. R. A. 391; In re Christian Jensen Co., 128 N. Y. 550, 28 N E. 665.

126 Bradley, C. J., in Wilmer v. Atlanta etc. Co., 2 Wood, 410, Fed. Cas. No. 17,775; Thompson on Corporations, § 6855; East Tenn. etc. R. Co. v. Atlanta etc. R. Co., 49 Fed. 608, 15 L. R. A. 109; Knott v. Evening Post Co., 124 Fed. 342.

127 Farmers' Loan & Trust Co. v. Lake Street Elev. R. R. Co., 177 U. S. 48, 60, 20 Sup. Ct. 564, 44 L. ed. 667. In this case the bill was filed first in the federal court praying foreclosure, but before service, a summons was served in an action in the state court begun by defendant to restrain plaintiff from proceeding to foreclose, alleging conspiracy, etc The court said: "*As between the immediate parties* in a proceeding *in rem*, jurisdiction must be regarded as attaching when the bill is filed and process has been issued." Cf. United States v Supervisors of Johnson Co., 7 Wall 196. It will be noted that in many of the cases, priority is determined by a small fraction of a day: East Tennessee etc. R. Co. v. Atlanta etc. R. Co., 49 Fed. 608, 15 L. R A. 109; North v. Piedmont Bank of Morganton, 121 N. C. 343, 28 S. E. 488. In New York Security & T. Co. v. Saratoga G. & E. L. Co., 159 N. Y. 137, 45 L. R. A. 132, 53 N. E. 758, a receiver in sequestration proceedings and a receiver in foreclosure proceedings were appointed "at the same instant of time." The question involved was which receiver was entitled to certain income of the company, the foreclosure receiver claiming under a clause in the mortgage making such income subject to the lien thereof. The court holds that the lien of the mortgage, so far as concerns future earnings, is consummated only by taking possession, and there can be no retroactive

the absence of authority, that the question should be governed by the principles regarding notice,[128] in which event only those dealing with the property after service of subpoena would have constructive notice of the bill, and this is probably the prevailing rule. 3. Where the first proceeding is not *in rem* in its nature, and the effect of the proceeding will not be to disturb the title of the *res*, a receiver may be appointed of the entire property, notwithstanding the pendency of the prior proceeding. For example, a receiver is sought to manage the affairs of an insolvent corporation until such time as the corporation itself can pay its debts and resume the management of its property; there is no reason why a receiver should not be appointed in proceedings which, though subsequently begun, have as their object the final disposition of the property.[129] This important distinction between proceedings in the nature of proceedings *in rem* and other proceedings has

operation given to his possession so as to defeat the title which the receiver in the sequestration proceedings obtained by the order of appointment.

128 Conner v. Long, 104 U. S. 229, 26 L. ed. 723; Freeman v. Howe, 24 How. 450, 16 L. ed. 749.

129 In Shields v. Coleman, 157 U. S. 168, 15 Sup. Ct. 570, 4 L. ed. 660, Brown, J., says "The mere fact that, in the progress of an attachment or other like action, an exigency may arise, which calls for the appointment of a receiver, does not make the jurisdiction of the court in that respect relate back to the commencement of the action." See, also, Guaranty T. Co. v. North Chicago St. R. Co., 130 Fed. 801, 65 C. C. A. 65; Illinois Steel Co. v. Putnam, 68 Fed. 515, 15 C. C. A 556, holding that the filing of a bill for the appointment of a receiver of an insolvent corporation to take charge of the assets until the corporation shall pay its debts or resume control is not such taking *in gremio legis* as to preclude another court from appointing a receiver. See, also, De la Vergne v. Palmetto Brewing Co., 72 Fed. 579. An instructive discussion of the nature of an *in rem* seizure will be found in First National Bank of Oswego v. Dunn, 97 N. Y. 149, where it is held that property held by the sheriff under a writ of replevin is *in custodia legis*, while property held on execution is not.

often been overlooked, and the determination of the important question arising from different appointments by courts of concurrent jurisdiction has erroneously been made to depend on the test: which court has first obtained jurisdiction of the controversy[130]—and not on the true test: which court has first obtained jurisdiction of the *res*. Many of the courts have founded their decisions, properly yielding jurisdiction to the courts which had first obtained jurisdiction, upon the ground of comity, when in fact they had better have been rested upon the basis that the second court had no jurisdiction of the *res* because some other tribunal already had it.[131] One of the earlier cases in the United States supreme court shows the true extent of the principle, holding a sale made under an execution at law void, where the property was in the custody of a receiver appointed by the state court in a suit in chancery.[132]

130 The test is, for example, incorrectly stated in 23 Am. & Eng. Ency. of Law, 2d ed., p. 1112.

131 That the rule is not a mere rule of comity but a question of jurisdiction, see Dillon v. O. S. L. etc. Ry. Co., 66 Fed. 622; Baltimore & O. R. R Co. v. Wabash R. R Co, 119 Fed. 678, 57 C. C. A 322; Merritt v. American Steel Barge Co., 79 Fed. 226, 24 C. C. A. 530; Covell v. Heyman, 111 U. S. 176, 4 Sup. Ct. 355, 28 L ed. 390. Some authorities say the rule is one of comity: Gaylord v Fort Wayne etc. R. Co, 6 Biss. 286, Fed. Cas. No 5284; De la Vergne v. Palmetto Brewing Co, 72 Fed. 579.

132 Wiswall v. Sampson, 14 How. 52, 14 L. ed. 322. See *ante*, §§ 166, 167.

CHAPTER V.

ACTIONS AGAINST THE RECEIVER.

ANALYSIS.

§ 171. Actions Against Receiver—General Rule; Leave Must be Obtained from Appointing Court.—It is a well-established rule that before suit is brought against a receiver in his official capacity, leave should be obtained from the court by which he was appointed,[1] in the ab-

[1] See the following, among a multitude of cases: Searle v. Choate, 25 Ch. D. 723 (suit to restrain receiver from preventing payment of rents by tenants); Barton v. Barbour, 104 U. S. 126, 26 L. ed. 673; affirming s. c., 3 McAr. 212, 36 Am. Rep. 104; Porter v. Sabin, 149 U. S. 473, 13 Sup. Ct. 1008, 37 L. ed. 815; People's Bank v. Calhoun, 102 U. S. 256, 26 L. ed. 101; Thompson v. Scott, 4 Dill. 508, Fed. Cas. No. 13,975; Werner v. Murphy, 60 Fed. 769; Foreman v. Central Trust Co., 71 Fed. 776, 18 C. C. A. 321; Louisville Trust Co. v. Cincinnati, 76 Fed. 296, 22 C. C. A. 334; Stateler v. California Nat. Bank, 77 Fed. 43; Jones v. Schlapback, 81 Fed. 274; Ross v. Heckman, 84 Fed. 6; Ridge v. Manker (C. C. A.), 132 Fed. 599; Minot v. Mastin, 95 Fed. 734, 37 C. C. A. 234; Talladega Mercantile Co. v. Jenifer Iron Co., 102 Ala. 259, 14 South. 743; Southern Granite Co.

sence of statutes authorizing suits without such leave. It is generally agreed that the rule applies not only to suits the object of which is to take from his possession property which he is holding by order of the court, but also to suits brought against him to recover a money demand or damages.[2] The reasons for the rule have

v. Wadsworth, 115 Ala. 570, 22 South. 157; Montgomery v. Enslen, 126 Ala. 654, 28 South. 626; Links v. Connecticut River Bkg. Co., 66 Conn. 277, 33 Atl. 1003; De Graffenried v. Brunswick etc. R. R Co., 57 Ga. 22; Fort Wayne, M. & C. R. Co. v. Mellett, 92 Ind. 535 (ejectment); Keen v. Breckenridge, 96 Ind. 69; Wayne Pike Co. v. State, 134 Ind. 672, 34 N. E. 440; Meredith Village Sav. Bank v. Simpson, 22 Kan. 414, People ex rel. Tremper v. Brooks, 40 Mich. 333, 29 Am. Rep. 534; Burk v. Muskegon Mach. & F. Co., 98 Mich. 614, 57 N. W. 804; Citizens' Com. & Sav. Bank v. Bay Circuit Judge, 110 Mich. 633, 68 N. W. 649; Wade v. Ringo, 62 Mo. App. 414 (leave of court obtained in vacation); In re Commercial Bank, 35 App. Div. 224, 54 N. Y. Supp. 722 (from what court leave must be obtained, under the New York Code); Payne v. Baxter, 2 Tenn Ch. 517; Melendy v. Barbour, 78 Va. 544; Jones v Browse, 32 W. Va. 444, 9 S. E 873; and other cases in the notes to this and the following sections. See, also, on the general subject, monographic note, Malott v. Shimer, 74 Am. St. Rep. 285-300.

It is held not to be essential to the validity of an order granting leave to bring an action against a receiver, that notice of the application for the order should be given to the parties in the case in which the receiver was appointed. Notice of such application to the receiver is sufficient: Potter v. Bunnell, 20 Ohio St. 150.

The general principle of the text is held not to apply to a suit in a federal court by the owner of a patent to restrain its infringement by a receiver of a state court, since the federal courts have exclusive jurisdiction to determine questions as to the validity and infringement of patents: Hupfeld v. Automaton Piano Co., 66 Fed. 788.

In Ratcliff v. Adler, 71 Ark. 269, 72 S. W. 896, it was held that an appellate court will not reverse a judgment because consent was not obtained, when rendered by the same court and the same judge that has charge of the receivership proceedings.

2 For example, to suits against railroad receivers to recover damages for injuries received at the hands of the receiver's servants, or on other liabilities incurred by the receiver; see Barton v. Barbour, 104 U. S. 126, 26 L. ed. 673, affirming 3 McAr. 212, 36 Am Rep. 104; Thompson v. Scott, 4 Dill. 508, Fed. Cas. No. 13,975 (an in-

been thus stated: "One court having custody of property through its receiver cannot admit that another court, in defiance of its orders, has power to define what are his duties with reference to such property. To admit this is substantially to say that one co-ordinate court can sue another. . . . . Every consideration of economy, of the prevention of vexatious litigation and conflicts of jurisdiction, would indicate the importance of protecting the exclusive possession of the receiver by an inflexible rule of law."[3] It is argued that if judgments in such suits be invalid, no purpose can be effected thereby save the embarrassment of the receiver by expensive and useless litigation; that the judgments, even if repudiated, would cast a cloud upon the title to the property in the receiver's possession and prejudice its sale; while if their validity be recognized, the court of appointment would sit merely to register and pay the judgments and decrees of other courts.[4]

structive opinion); Jones v. Schlapback, 81 Fed. 274; De Graffenried v. Brunswick etc. R. R., 57 Ga. 22; Payne v. Baxter, 2 Tenn. Ch. 517; Melendy v. Barbour, 78 Va. 544. The objections to the doctrine, as applied to suits upon liabilities incurred by railroad receivers, are stated with great force in the dissenting opinion of Miller, J., in Barton v. Barbour, *supra*.

3 Meredith Village Sav. Bank v. Simpson, 22 Kan. 414, per Horton, C. J.

4 Thompson v. Scott, 4 Dill. 508, Fed. Cas. No. 13,975, per Love, D. J. The opinion is so vigorous a presentation of what has come to be the generally accepted rule, that I venture to quote from it at some length: "Such judgment against the receiver would be either valid or invalid. If invalid, it follows that suits against the receiver, resulting in such judgments, would be perfectly futile and useless, and for that reason they ought to be stopped by the receiver's court; for certainly such suits would harass and embarrass the receiver, and expose him to the heavy costs of litigation; and, if they resulted in no benefit to the parties prosecuting them, it would be simply idle, if not absurd, to allow such actions to proceed against the receiver. But, doubtless, if the doctrine of the Iowa court [Allen v. Central R. Co., 42 Iowa, 683] be sound, judgments against the re-

In the leading case upon the subject it is said: "If he [the plaintiff in a suit against the receiver] has the right, in a distinct suit, to prosecute his demand to judgment without leave of the court appointing the receiver, he would have the right to enforce satisfaction of it without leave. By virtue of his judgment he could, unless restrained by injunction, seize upon the property of the trust or attach its credits. If his judgment were recovered outside the territorial jurisdiction of the court by which the receiver was appointed, he could do this, and the court which appointed the receiver and was administering the trust assets would be impotent to restrain him. The effect upon the property of the trust of any attempt to enforce satisfaction of his judgment would be precisely the same as if his suit had been

ceiver would be valid to all intents and purposes, and they must be so treated by all courts in which they should be pleaded. This being the case, what follows? Why, that the court of equity, having control of the fund, would have no alternative but to recognize and pay the judgments and decrees rendered elsewhere against its receiver, and if the fund consisted, in whole or in part, of real estate, the judgments against the receiver would become liens against the property, thus encumbering and casting a cloud upon the title. Under such conditions the sale of the property, under the decree of the court of equity, to satisfy its judgments, would be hopeless and ineffectual. Thus would the whole purpose of the litigation in equity and of the taking possession of property through the receiver, be utterly defeated. The absurdity of such a result requires no explanation. . . . . Again, if any and every body may sue our receiver without our consent, along the line of the road, innumerable suits may be prosecuted against him, and he may be thus exposed to the costs and expenses of ruinous litigation. Now, he is our officer, and suits would be prosecuted against him as such, and not against him as an individual. We have placed him in the breach and exposed him to a deadly fire. Shall we leave him naked to his enemies? Shall the court abandon him to his fate and compel him to pay the costs and charges of a ruinous litigation out of his own pocket? Or, if the court should authorize him to employ counsel and pay the costs of numberless suits out of the trust fund, what then? Why, it would follow that the fund in our hands might be wasted and squandered in useless and fruitless litigation," etc.

brought for the purpose of taking property from the possession of the receiver. A suit, therefore, brought without leave to recover judgment against a receiver for a money demand, is virtually a suit, the purpose of which is, and the effect of which may be, to take the property of the trust from the receiver's hands and apply it to the payment of the plaintiff's claim, without regard to the rights of other creditors, or the order of the court which is administering the trust property. We think, therefore, that it is immaterial whether the suit is brought against the receiver to recover specific property or to obtain judgment for a money demand. In either case leave should be first obtained."[5] The objection that, by leaving all questions relating to the liability of receivers in the hands of the court appointing them, persons having claims against the insolvent corporation or against the receiver will be deprived of their constitutional right to a trial by jury, is thus met, in the same case: "Those who use this argument lose sight of the fundamental principle that the right of trial by jury, considered as an absolute right, does not extend to cases of equity jurisdiction. If it be conceded or clearly shown that a case belongs to this class, the trial of questions involved in it belongs to the court itself, no matter what may be its importance or complexity."[6]

The consequences resulting from the prosecution of a suit against the receiver in his official capacity are, that the plaintiff in such suit may be attached as for a contempt,[7] or restrained by an injunction.[8]

5 Barton v. Barbour, 104 U. S. 126, 26 L. ed. 673, per Woods, J.

6 Barton v. Barbour, 104 U. S 126, 26 L. ed. 673, per Woods, J.

7 Lane v. Capsey, [1891] 3 Ch. 411; Thompson v. Scott, 4 Dill. 508, Fed. Cas. No. 13,975.

8 Evelyn v. Lewis, 3 Hare, 472; Stateler v. California Nat. Bank, 77 Fed. 43; Jones v. Schlapback, 81 Fed. 274; Montgomery v. Enslen, 126 Ala. 654, 28 South. 626.

§ 172. Whether Leave to Sue is a "Jurisdictional Fact." It is the rule of the federal courts, unless changed by statute, and of the courts of many of the states, that leave to prosecute a suit against a receiver, in his official capacity, without the consent of the court of appointment, is a jurisdictional fact; in other words, that want of leave not only subjects the plaintiff to liability to be attached for contempt, or to be enjoined from the prosecution of his suit, but takes away the jurisdiction of the court in which the suit was brought to hear and determine it. Such leave must, therefore, be averred in the complaint.[9] In other courts this rule has received most earnest disapproval, both on the grounds of policy and convenience, and on the ground that it ignores and sets aside well-established principles governing the relations of courts of law to courts of equity. Says Mr. Justice Miller, in his dissenting opinion in the leading case[10] already cited: "I know of no principle nor of

[9] Barton v. Barbour, 104 U. S. 126, 26 L. ed. 673, affirming 3 McAr. 212, 36 Am. Rep. 104; Swope v. Villard, 61 Fed. 417, De Graffenried v. Brunswick etc. R. R., 57 Ga. 22; Martin v. Atchison, 2 Idaho, 624, 33 Pac. 47; Keen v. Breckenridge, 96 Ind. 69, Wayne Pike Co v. State, 134 Ind. 672, 34 N. E. 440; Peirce v. Chism, 23 Ind App. 505, 77 Am. St. Rep. 441, 55 N. E. 795, Peirce v. Jones, 24 Ind. App. 286, 56 N. E. 683; Manker v. Phoenix Loan Assn. (Iowa), 96 N. W. 982; Steel Brick Siding Co. v. Muskegon etc. Co., 98 Mich. 616, 57 N W. 817; Schmidt v. Gayner, 59 Minn 303, 61 N. W 333, 62 N. W. 265; Smith v. St. Louis & S. F. Ry Co., 151 Mo. 391, 52 S W. 378, 48 L R. A. 368; Jones v. Moore, 106 Tenn. 188, 61 S. W 81. In Brown v Rauch, 1 Wash. 497, 20 Pac. 785, a decision by a territorial court, it was held that the question of want of leave may be raised for the first time even upon appeal from a judgment against the receiver, but see Elkhart Car Works v. Ellis, 113 Ind. 215, 15 N. E. 249 (objection not heard upon motion in arrest of judgment) It has been held in a recent federal case that a decree against a receiver will not be held void, in a collateral proceeding, for failure affirmatively to recite that leave to sue was obtained, when the receiver appeared, defended upon the merits, and asked affirmative relief: Ridge v. Manker (C. C. A.), 132 Fed. 599.

[10] Barton v. Barbour, 104 U. S. 126, 26 L. ed. 673. The reasoning

any precedent whereby a court of law, having before it a plaintiff with a cause of action of which that court has jurisdiction, and a defendant charged in regard to his own act also within the jurisdiction, is bound or is even at liberty to deny the party his lawful right to a trial of his cause because the defendant is receiver of some other court, and to leave the suitor to that court for remedy, when it is known that some of the most important guaranties of the trial to which he is entitled and which are appropriate to the nature of his case will be denied him. Whatever courts of equity may have done to protect their receivers, and may do to protect the fund in their hands, it is no part of the duty of courts of law to deny to suitors properly before them the trial of their rights which justice requires and which the constitution and the law guarantee." By many courts, therefore, the rule is laid down "that the question always is, not one of jurisdiction, but of contempt; that the ordinary jurisdiction of other courts is in no manner taken away or affected by the appointment of a receiver; that while the court making the appointment may draw to itself all controversies to which the receiver is a party, it does so by acting directly upon the parties, and not by challenging the jurisdiction of the other tribunals; that while it may so draw to itself all such controversies, it is not compelled to do so, and that not doing so in any particular case, the mere fact of the appointment constitutes no plea to the jurisdiction."[11] The rule as thus defined,

of the learned justice who rendered the opinion of the court in this case is also severely criticised in Lyman v. Central Vermont R. Co., 59 Vt. 167, 10 Atl 346.

11 St. Joseph & D. C. R. R. Co. v. Smith, 19 Kan. 225, 231, per Brewer, J. (now Mr. Justice Brewer of the United States supreme court), Mulcahey v. Strauss, 151 Ill. 70, 37 N. E. 702; Flentham v Stewart, 45 Neb. 640, 63 N. W. 924; Hirshfeld v. Kalisher, 81 Hun,

however, appears to be limited to cases where there is no attempt to interfere with the actual possession of the property held by the receiver; ejectment or garnishment suits against the receiver without leave will not be entertained.[12] It follows from the rule that leave to sue the receiver is not jurisdictional, that the receiver may waive the defense of being sued without leave by a voluntary appearance in the action against him.[13]

§ 173. **Suits Against Federal Receivers; Rule Now Modified by Act of Congress.**—The general rule laid down in the preceding paragraphs was productive of great hardship in those cases where parties were forced to sue receivers whose residence was in a jurisdiction different from that where the cause of action arose. A distinguished and able federal judge has said: "Where property is in the hands of a receiver simply as a custodian, or for sale or distribution, it is proper that all persons having claims against it, or upon the fund arising from its sale, should be required to assert them in the court appointing the receiver. But a very different question is presented where the court assumes the operation of a railroad hundreds of miles in length, and advertises itself to the world as a common carrier. This brings

606, 30 N. Y. Supp. 1027; Le Fevre v. Matthews, 39 App. Div. 232, 57 N. Y. Supp. 128; Blumenthal v. Brainerd, 38 Vt. 402, 91 Am. Dec. 350; Lyman v. Central Vt. R. Co., 59 Vt. 167, 10 Atl. 346; Town of Roxbury v. Central Vt. R. Co., 60 Vt. 121, 14 Atl. 92; Kinney v. Crocker, 18 Wis. 74; Colorado Fuel etc. Co. v. Rio Grande S Ry. Co., 8 Colo. App. 493, 46 Pac. 845; Payson v. Jacobs (Wash.), 80 Pac. 429.

12 St. Louis, A. & S. R. Co. v. Hamilton, 158 Ill. 366, 41 N. E. 777 (ejectment); Blum v. Van Vechten, 92 Wis. 378, 66 N. W. 507 (garnishment).

13 Mulcahey v. Strauss, 151 Ill. 70, 37 N. E. 702; Flentham v. Stewart, 45 Neb 640, 63 N. W. 924; Hubbell v. Dana, 9 How Pr. (N. Y.) 424; Jay's Case, 6 Abb. Pr. (N. Y.) 293, and see Elkhart Car Works Co. v. Ellis, 113 Ind. 215, 15 N. E. 249.

it into constant and extensive business relations with the public. . . . . All the liabilities incident to the operation of a railroad are incurred by a court where it engages in that business; and, when they are incurred, why should the citizen be denied the right to establish the justice and amount of his demand, by the verdict of a jury in a court of the county where the cause of action arose and the witnesses reside? If the road was operated by its owners or its creditors, the citizen would have this right, and when it is operated for their benefit by a receiver, why should the right be denied?"[14] To remedy this condition, and save expense to those suing receivers,[15] section 3 of the act of Congress approved March 3, 1887 (c. 373; 1 U. S. Comp. Stats., p. 582), provides: "That every receiver or man-

14 Dowe v. Memphis & L. R. R. Co., 20 Fed. 260, at 268, by Caldwell, J, who continued: "If the denial of the right to sue can be rested on the ground that it saves money for the corporation and its creditors, why not carry the doctrine one degree further, and declare the receiver shall not be liable to the citizen at all for breaches of contract, or any act of malfeasance or misfeasance in his office as receiver? This would be a great saving to the estate. The difference is one of degree and not of principle. When a court, through its receiver, becomes a common carrier, and enters the lists to compete with other common carriers for the carrying trade of the country, it ought not to claim or exercise any special privilege denied to its competitors, and oppressive on the citizen. The court appointing a receiver of a railroad and those interested in the property, should be content with the same measure of justice that is meted out to all persons and corporations conducting the like business. The court appointing a receiver cannot, of course, permit any other jurisdiction to interfere with its possession of the property, or control its administration of the fund; but, in the case of long lines of railroad, the question of the legal liability of its receiver to the demands of the citizen, growing out of the operation of the road, should be remitted to the tribunals that would have jurisdiction if the controversy had arisen between the citizen and the railroad company; giving to the citizen the option of seeking redress in such tribunals, or in the court appointing the receiver."

15 Gilmore v Herrick, 93 Fed. 525.

ager of any property appointed by any court of the United States may be sued in respect of any act or transaction of his in carrying on the business connected with such property, without the previous leave of court in which such receiver or manager was appointed; but such suit shall be subject to the general equity jurisdiction of the court in which such receiver or manager was appointed, so far as the same shall be necessary to the ends of justice."[16] The statute has been applied in a number of cases,[17] and it is held that the suit may be brought in any court of competent jurisdiction;[18] but the suit must be in regard to some "act or transaction" in connection with the operation of the property, and unless this is strictly true, leave of court should be obtained.[19] Under guise of the statute, a party cannot

16 The act was revised by an act approved August 13, 1888, but was not materially altered.

17 See the following cases as well as those cited in the succeeding notes: Texas & Pac. R. Co. v. Cox, 145 U. S. 593, 12 Sup. Ct. 905, 36 L. ed. 829; Erb v. Morasch, 177 U. S. 584, 20 Sup. Ct 819, 44 L. ed. 897; The St. Nicholas, 49 Fed. 671; Wheeler v. Smith, 81 Fed. 319 (the statute extends to territorial appointments, for the court in making such appointment acts as a federal court); Trumbull v. McKuser, 9 Colo. App. 350, 48 Pac. 825; Louisville Southern Ry. Co. v. Tucker's Admr., 105 Ky. 492, 49 S. W. 314; Southern Pac. R. R. v. Maddox, 75 Tex 300, 12 S. W. 815, Houston & T C. Ry Co. v. State (Tex Civ. App.), 39 S. W 390 (a suit, at the direction of the governor, to determine the title to land in possession of a federal receiver was upheld without leave of court having been obtained, without an express reliance on the statute); Stolze v. Milwaukee & L. W R. Co., 104 Wis. 47, 80 N. W 68.

18 McNulta v. Lochridge, 141 U. S. 327, 12 Sup. Ct. 11, 35 L. ed. 796, Central Trust Co. of N Y. v. East Tenn. V. & G. Ry. Co., 59 Fed 523.

19 Central Trust Co of N Y. v East Tenn, V. & G. Ry. Co., 59 Fed 523; Glover v. Thayer, 101 Ga 824, 29 S. E. 36. Thus, proceedings to condemn property for a grade crossing can be maintained only by leave of court where receivership is pending Coster v. Parkersburg Branch R Co., 131 Fed 115; Buckhannon & N R Co. v. Davis (C C. A), 135 Fed 707. A suit to recover for injuries re-

put in issue the right of the receiver to the possession of the property, or his right to control and manage it under the receivership.[20] It is said that "suits in which it is sought to deal with the property in the custody of the receivers, to subject it to sale or other remedy, can still be brought only by intervening petition, or by independent bill filed by leave of the court."[21] A garnishment proceeding is said not to be a "suit against the receiver, for any act or transaction of his, and such claims must be prosecuted in the manner heretofore settled. . . . . A proceeding for garnishment purposes is an equitable seizure of the funds and property within the custody of the court."[22] But the supreme court of Minnesota has held that money due from a receiver for indebtedness incurred in operating the road, may be garnished in the state court; they say: "But in this case it will be noticed that what is sought to be reached by garnishment is the property, not of the railway company, but of the defendant, viz., a debt due him from the receivers. Moreover, while garnishment of a debt is often called a mode of attachment, yet it does not

ceived before the appointment is not within the statute: Farmers' Loan & Tr. Co. v. Chicago & N. P. R. Co., 118 Fed 204.

20 Swope v. Villard, 61 Fed. 417 (a refusal of the receiver to sue for a cause of action in favor of the corporation, is not an "act or transaction in carrying on the business"); Bennett v. Northern Pac. R. Co., 17 Wash. 534, 50 Pac. 496 (the receiver's wrongful claim to an interest in land is not such act as comes within the statute); Hallifield v. Wrightsville & T. R. Co., 99 Ga. 365, 27 S. E. 715; Glover v. Thayer, 101 Ga. 824, 29 S. E. 36; J. I. Case Plow Works v. Finks, 81 Fed. 529, 26 C. C. A. 46; Dillingham v. Anthony, 73 Tex. 47, 11 S. W. 139, 15 Am. St. Rep. 753, 3 L. R. A. 634 (the statute does not apply to a case where it is sought to establish title to personalty, as against the receiver).

21 Gilmore v. Herrick, 93 Fed. 525.

22 Central Trust Co. v. East Tenn. V. & G. Ry. Co., 59 Fed. 523, Reisner v Gulf etc. R. R. Co, 89 Tex. 656, 36 S. W. 53, 59 Am. St. Rep. 84, 33 L. R. A. 171 (the case did not discuss the statute).

effect a specific lien on any property of the garnishee, such as is acquired by the actual seizure of property. The effect of the judgment is merely to determine the existence and amount of the debt, and to substitute the plaintiff for the defendant as the person to whom it is payable. The judgment against the receivers would not be against them personally, but against them officially. No executory process could be issued on it, for that would interfere with the control of the property in the custody of the federal court."[23] In applying the statute the federal courts have said: "The third section of the judiciary act of March 3, 1887, authorizing suits to be brought against receivers of railroads, without special leave of the court by which they are appointed, was intended, as we think, to place receivers upon the same plane with railway companies, both as respects their liability to be sued for acts done while operating a railroad and as respects the mode of obtaining service."[24] And it is, therefore, generally held that a federal receiver is subject to an action in a state court, without leave of the federal court, for any damage due by reason of the management of the property, when the

23 Irvine v. McKechnie, 58 Minn. 145, 49 Am. St. Rep. 495, 59 N. W. 987, 26 L. R. A. 218. The court continued: "Under the 'removal act' [the act of March 3, 1887, quoted above] the defendant himself could have sued the receivers, and recovered judgment, and we are unable to see why the plaintiff may not, through garnishee proceedings, recover judgment against them for the same claim, or why a judgment in his favor interferes with property in the custody of the federal court any more than would a judgment in favor of the defendant for the same claim."

24 Eddy v. Lafayette, 49 Fed. 807, 1 C. C. A. 441; s. c., 163 U. S. 456, 16 Sup. Ct. 1082, 41 L. ed. 225 (recognizing the receiver's liability for damages for burning hay by fire set by locomotives); Central Trust Co. v. St. Louis, A. & T. R. Co., 40 Fed. 426 (service on an agent of the receiver is binding, though the receiver is not within the jurisdiction).

injury to property or person has resulted from the negligence of the receiver, his agents or employees.[25]

§ 174. Same; Such Suits are "Subject to the General Equity Jurisdiction" of the Court of the Appointment.—But while the act of Congress grants leave to sue in such cases, it expressly provides that "such suits shall be subject to the general equity jurisdiction of the court in which such receiver was appointed so far as the same shall be necessary to the ends of justice." This is construed as "applying only to suits which seek to interfere with the receiver's possession of property, and to process the execution of which would have that effect; any process, whether for the recovery of such property or for the enforcement and collection of a judgment out of it. These shall be subject to the control of the court appointing the receiver, so far as the ends of justice may require. The time when, and the manner in which, a judgment against the receiver shall be paid; the adjustment of equities between all persons having claims against the property in his hands; the just distribution of the funds according to the rights of the several parties interested in it—all must necessarily be under the control of the court having custody of the property by its receiver, and shall be subject to its general equity jurisdiction."[26] But where the state court has juris-

25 Gableman v. Peoria, D. & E. R. R. Co, 179 U. S. 335, 21 Sup. Ct. 171, 45 L. ed. 220; Texas & Pac. R. R. Co v. Cox, 145 U. S. 593, 12 Sup. Ct. 905, 36 L. ed. 829; McNulta v. Lockridge, 137 Ill. 270, 31 Am. St. Rep. 362, 27 N E. 452, 141 U. S. 327, 12 Sup. Ct. 11, 35 L. ed. 796; St. Louis S. W. Ry. Co. v. Holbrook, 73 Fed 112, 19 C. C. A. 385; Ball v. Mabry, 91 Ga. 781, 18 S. E. 64; Malott v. Shiner, 153 Ind. 35, 74 Am. St. Rep. 278, 54 N. E. 101; Fullerton v. Fordyce, 121 Mo. 1, 42 Am. St. Rep. 516, 25 S. W. 587, Robinson v. Mills, 25 Mont. 114, 65 Pac. 114; Meyer v. Harris, 61 N. J L. 83, 38 Atl. 690; Baer v. McCullough, 176 N. Y. 97, 68 N E. 129.

26 Dillingham v. Hawk, 60 Fed. 494, 9 C. C. A. 101, 23 L. R. A. 517. See, also, Dillingham v. Anthony, 73 Tex. 47, 15 Am. St. Rep.

diction of the parties and the subject matter, its judgment against the federal receiver is as final and conclusive as it is against any other suitor. It is said that the right to sue the receiver would be of little utility if its judgment could be annulled or modified at the discretion of the federal court.[27] Since a federal receiver may now be sued in a state court without leave of the appointing court, a receiver cannot have such case removed to the federal court on the ground that it is ancillary to the original suit, unless he shows such additional cause as makes the removal a necessary means

753, 11 S. W. 139, 3 L. R. A 634. In Missouri Pac. Ry. Co. v. Tex. Pac. Ry. Co., 41 Fed. 311, the court states: "The better opinion of the effect of said section is that it merely dispenses with leave of the court appointing the receiver, as a prerequisite to instituting a suit against him in another court, and that a suit brought thereunder has the same *status*, and a judgment rendered therein has the same effect, as if permission to sue had been regularly granted by the court appointing the receiver However this may be, it is clear that when a judgment is so obtained, and is brought to the court of original jurisdiction to be ranked as a lien upon the trust funds, such judgment is subject to the general equity jurisdiction, and the duty of determining the rightfulness of the judgment, including whether the amount is just, is still imposed upon this court, as it would be if it had ordered an issue tried at law; for this court must still, in the language of the statute, exercise a 'general equity jurisdiction, so far as the same shall be necessary to the ends of justice'" The court had held that the district court rendering the judgment did not have jurisdiction of the suit against the receiver under the act of 1887, and the value of the decision would seem to be weakened by that fact. See, also, Reinhart v. Sutton, 58 Kan. 726, 51 Pac. 221, Burke v. Ellis, 105 Tenn. 702, 58 S. W. 855 See particularly, Irwin v. McKechnie, 58 Minn. 145, 49 Am. St. Rep. 495, 59 N. W. 987, 26 L. R. A 218; Rogers v. Chippewa Circuit Judge (Mich.), 97 N. W. 154 (no injunction against enforcing higher telephone rates than city ordinance authorizes).

27 Central Trust Co. v. St. Louis A. & T. R. Co., 41 Fed. 551; and to the same effect, see the cases in note 26. The statute does not require the discontinuance of an action against a federal receiver after his discharge on the ground that the decree of the federal court provided a method for establishing claims against the funds in the hands of the receiver: Baer v. McCullough, 176 N. Y. 97, 68 N. E. 129.

of obtaining justice.[28] But the opposite has been held, and it is stated that an action for damages, growing out of the transactions of the receiver or his employees is ancillary to the suit in which the receiver was appointed, and is within the jurisdiction of that court, regardless of the citizenship of the parties, the nature of the controversy, or the amount involved.[29]

When a receiver is sued without leave of the appointing court, the complaint should contain an allegation that he is a federal receiver, as only such are liable to be sued without leave, and it will not be presumed that he has been appointed by a United States court.[30]

§ 175. **Leave of Court not Necessary When Receiver is a Trespasser.**—"The principle is well settled that the court will not protect a receiver for any acts committed by him outside of the performance of the proper and legitimate duties of his receivership."[31] Therefore, it is

28 Gableman v. Peoria, D. & E. R. R. Co., 179 U. S. 335, 21 Sup. Ct. 171, 45 L. ed. 220, and cases cited, Ray v. Peirce, 81 Fed 881, Pitkin v. Cowen, 91 Fed. 599; Gilmore v. Herrick, 93 Fed. 525, stating: "It is said, however, that a suit against a receiver is ancillary to the suit in which the receiver is appointed, and therefore that, if it is brought in a state court, it may be removed to the federal court in which the principal suit is pending. The power of one court to stop proceedings in a suit lawfully begun and pending in another, and to take such suits within its own jurisdiction for further hearing and final definition, is the exercise of an unusual and high prerogative, and must be based on clear statutory authority. Such a power is not to be presumed or implied. There is no language in any removal statute which justifies removal of a cause from a state court to a federal court on the ground that it is ancillary to a suit in a federal court."

29 Carpenter v. Northern Pac. R. R. Co., 75 Fed. 850, followed in Sullivan v. Barnard, 81 Fed. 886. Both of these cases are expressly departed from in Gilmore v. Herrick, quoted *supra*, note 28

30 Peirce v Chism, 23 Ind. App. 505, 77 Am. St. Rep. 441, 55 N. E. 795; approved in Peirce v. Jones, 24 Ind. App 286, 56 N E. 683

31 In re Young, 7 Fed. 855 (refusing to enjoin an action for trespass, brought without leave of court) In Gutsch v McIlhargey, 69

said, in sustaining a suit in replevin for a locomotive, to which the insolvent corporation had no right: "The decree of a court of chancery appointing a receiver entitles him to its protection only in the possession of property which he is authorized or directed by the decree to take possession of. When he assumes to take or hold possession of property not embraced in the decree appointing him, and to which the debtor never had any title, he is not acting as the officer or representative of the court of chancery, but is a mere trespasser, and the rightful owner of the property may sue him in any appropriate form of action for damages or to recover possession of the property illegally taken or detained."[32]

§ 176. **Leave to Sue Receiver, When Granted.**—The rule is well settled that in ordinary cases the granting or withholding of leave to sue a receiver is within the discretion of the court to which the motion is addressed.[33] The court may, therefore, determine

Mich. 377, 37 N. W. 303, Campbell, J., says: "A receiver may frequently, under color of office, get possession of property which does not belong to him, and his official character ought not to be a defense to his tortious action, or deprive parties of their rights." An action of replevin for a small frame house, of which the receiver had improperly obtained possession, was accordingly sustained, though the plaintiff had not obtained leave to sue.

32 Hills v. Parker, 111 Mass. 508, 15 Am. Rep. 63. See, also, for an instructive case, Curran v Craig, 22 Fed. 101; and to the same effect, Kenney v. Ranney, 96 Mich 617, 55 N. W. 982. See Fallon v. Egbert's Woolen Mills Co., 31 Misc. Rep. 523, 64 N. Y. Supp. 466, 56 App. Div 585, 67 N. Y. Supp. 347, as to when the right to sue a receiver individually may be lost by proceeding against him officially.

That an order directing the receiver to take possession of property not involved in the litigation is void, and that in acting under such order he becomes liable as a trespasser, see Bowman v. Hazen (Kan.), 77 Pac. 589.

33 Walker v. Green, 60 Kan. 20, 55 Pac. 281 (the leave may be given generally, to "all parties"); In re Mackwirth, 15 App. Div. 65, 44

whether it is more desirable to allow the receiver to be sued in some appropriate form of action, or to protect him from the suit entirely.[34] It is said that leave should not be granted to sue a receiver unless the applicant's complaint makes out a *prima facie* case; that "the court should not allow its receiver to be harassed by a suit where, according to his own showing, the plaintiff has no cause of action."[35] But, on the other hand, it is settled that the consent of the court is not to be arbitrarily refused when the plaintiff presents a meritorious case; it is said: "Parties having claims upon the property have a right to prosecute them by suit, which is said to be liable to be abridged, if leave of court must be had for that purpose. The leave is, however, necessary only for the orderly administration of justice, and is not to be denied arbitrarily, but only for legal unfitness for the purposes when and where sought. The right remains, and leave is to be granted according to the right and the proper adaptation of the proceedings."[36] A federal court, after referring to the

N. Y Supp. 80 (refusing leave to a creditor where the receiver was not shown to be lax in his duties in caring for the estate); Shrady v. Van Kirk, 51 App. Div. 504, 64 N Y. Supp. 731 (cannot be given where the receiver is only *pendente lite*); Marshall v. Friend, 68 N. Y Supp 502, 33 Misc. Rep. 443; Pringle v. Woodworth, 90 N. Y. 502; Ludington v. Thompson, 153 N. Y. 499, 47 N. E. 903; Reed v. Axtell, 84 Va. 231, 4 S E. 587.

34 In re Herbst, 63 Hun, 247, 17 N. Y Supp 760 (Van Brunt, P. J., dissented on the ground that the action was not to take from the receiver any property of which he had possession); Taylor v. Hill, 115 Cal. 143, 44 Pac 336, 46 Pac. 922, Mechanics' Nat. Bank v. Landauer, 68 Wis. 44, 31 N W. 160 (and the exercise of the discretion will not be disturbed on appeal unless manifestly abused).

35 Jordan v. Wells, 3 Woods, 527, Fed. Cas. No. 7525.

36 American Loan & Trust Co. v. Central Vt. R. Co., 84 Fed. 917. To the same effect are the English cases of Randfield v. Randfield, 3 De Gex, F. & J. 766; Lane v. Capey, [1891] 3 Ch. 411, 414. See, also, Allan v. Manitoba Ry. Co., 10 Manitoba, 106; Cobb v. Sweet,

general rule, has stated it as follows: "There are other cases, however, where the right of a third party to intervene in a pending case is so imperative, resting, as it does, on grounds of necessity, and the inability of the party to obtain relief by other means, that the right cannot be said to be dependent upon judicial discretion. For example, a court cannot lawfully refuse to permit an intervening petition to be filed when the petitioner shows a title to, or lien upon, property in the custody of a receiver, and a present right to its possession, which is superior to any right or title that is or may be asserted by the parties to the suit in which the intervention is filed, and at whose instance the receiver was appointed."[37]

§ 177. **Practice, Whether by Petition or Independent Action.**—While it is, under some circumstances, proper to direct the prosecution of an action at law against the receiver to determine the amount of compensation or damages to be paid, the better and more commonly recognized practice is to apply for relief to the court in which the receiver is acting.[38] The proper course to

46 App. Div. 375, 61 N. Y. Supp. 545; Citizens' Sav. Bank v. Person, 98 Mich. 173, 57 N. W. 121.

37 Minot v. Mastin, 95 Fed. 734, 37 C. C. A. 234 (but the court approved the general rule indicated by the text in the following words: "In cases of the latter sort, it is usually held to be discretionary with the court or chancellor to whom an application to intervene is addressed, to allow or reject the intervention, and leave to intervene should be obtained").

38 Pacific Ry. Co. v. Wade, 91 Cal. 449, 456, 25 Am. St. Rep 201, 27 Pac. 768, 13 L. R. A. 754 (proceedings to determine compensation for use of tracks of street railway in hands of receiver); Meredith Village Sav. Bank v. Simpson, 22 Kan. 414, 432; Central Trust Co. v. Wabash, St. Louis & P. R. Co., 23 Fed. 858; Citizens' Sav. Bank v. Ingham, Circuit Judge, 98 Mich. 173, 57 N. W 121; Buffum v. Hale, 71 Minn. 190, 73 N W. 856; Goodnough v Gatch, 37 Or. 5, 60 Pac 383; Crutchfield v. Hunter (N. C.), 50 S. E. 557.

be pursued is, for the court to proceed to investigate the matter in a summary way, and if it appears that the case is free from difficulty, and the liability of the receiver plain, or that the dispute involves no question which must necessarily be settled at law, the court should proceed to decide the matter; since the court, in giving leave to sue in such a case, would be authorizing an inexcusable waste of the moneys of the trust.[39] And where the party who has a legal cause of action against a receiver comes voluntarily into court and submits himself to the jurisdiction of the court, offering to do what the court deems equitable, the court is competent to deal with his complaint, notwithstanding the receiver's objection.[40] It has been held that if the proceeding is to assert an equitable right in relation to the property in the receiver's hands, it must be by petition in the cause in which the receiver was appointed, and not by independent suit.[41] A court of law is, however, the more appropriate forum to determine a question of damages for personal injuries.[42]

Since the court of the appointment has power to fix the forum in which suit shall be brought against its receiver, it has also the power to revoke the permission to sue when it is sought to be abused. Thus, where permission was granted to sue the receiver in the court of the appointment, and in no other, and the plaintiff in such action filed his petition and bond for a removal of

39 Lehigh Coal & Navigation Co. v. Central R. R. Co., 38 N. J. Eq. 175, 179

40 Potter v. Spa Spring Brick Co., 47 N. J. Eq. 442, 20 Atl. 852

41 Porter v. Kingman, 126 Mass. 141 (to cancel mortgage); Meeker v Sprague, 5 Wash. 242, 31 Pac. 628 (refusal to allow independent action to foreclose mortgage proper, and not an abuse of discretion); but see Talladega Mercantile Co. v. Jenifer Iron Co., 102 Ala. 259, 14 South 743; Jones v Stewart (Tenn. Ch.), 61 S. W. 105.

42 Palys v. Jewett, 32 N. J. Eq. 302; and see Melendy v. Barbour, 78 Va. 544.

the cause to a federal court, it was not error for the court, of its own motion, to revoke the order granting permission to sue the receiver, and to dismiss the action pending against him.[43]

§ 178. Receiver's Right to Appeal.—It is held that where a judgment is recovered against a receiver, on account of his management of the property, he may properly appeal from the decision; that the court's directions to him to defend do not extend only to the court that hears the trial.[44] But he may not appeal from an order determining the rights of parties, where a payment under the order would be a protection to him,[45] nor can he appeal from an order relative to his rights and duties, without previous authorization from the court.[46] Mr. Justice Brewer, in a recent case,[47] ably summarizes the rules as follows: "First. A receiver may defend, both in the court appointing him and by appeal, the estate in his possession against all claims which are antagonistic to the rights of both parties to the suit.[48] . . . . Second. He may likewise defend the estate against all claims which are antagonistic to the rights of either party to the suit, subject to the limitation that he may not, in such defense, ques-

43 Meredith Village Sav. Bank v. Simpson, 22 Kan. 414, 433.

44 Thorn v. Pittard, 62 Fed. 232, 10 C. C. A. 352.

45 Dorsey v. Sibert, 93 Ala. 312, 9 South. 288, First Nat. Bank v. Bunting & Co., 7 Idaho, 27, 59 Pac. 929, 1106.

46 McKinnon v. Wolfenden, 78 Wis. 237, 47 N. W. 436 ("a receiver is the mere servant or agent of the court to do its bidding, and he cannot be heard to question by appeal the regularity or propriety of the orders of the court in the action, unless the court first authorizes him to do so").

47 Bosworth v. Terminal R. Assn., 174 U. S. 182, 19 Sup. Ct. 625, 43 L. ed. 941, modifying 80 Fed. 969, 26 C. C. A. 279, 53 U. S. App. 302. See, also, Kirkpatrick v. Eastern Milling & Export Co, 135 Fed. 151.

48 For instance, he may thus contest a claim for taxes.

tion any order or decree of the court distributing burdens or apportioning rights between the parties to the suit, or any order or decree resting upon the discretion of the court appointing him. . . . . Third. Neither can he question any subsequent order or decree of the court distributing the estate in his hands between the parties to the suit. It is nothing to him whether all of the property is given to the mortgagee or all returned to the mortgagor. He is to stand indifferent between the parties, and may not be heard, either in the court which appointed him or in the appellate court, as to the rightfulness of any order which is a mere order of distribution between the parties.[49] . . . . Fourth. He may appeal from an order or decree which affects his personal rights, provided it is not an order resting in the discretion of the court.[50] . . . . Fifth. His right to appeal from an allowance of a claim against the estate does not necessarily fail when the receivership is terminated to the extent of surrendering the property in the possession of the receiver. It is a common practice in courts of equity, anxious as they are to be relieved of the care of property, to turn it over to the parties entitled thereto, even before the final settlement of all claims against it, and at the same time to leave to the receiver the further defense of such claims, the party receiving the property giving security to abide by any decree which may finally be entered against the estate."

§ 179. Judgment Against Receiver, How Enforced; as Against Successor in Office; in Case of His Discharge.—As a general rule, actions against the receiver are in law actions against the receivership; his liabilities are offi-

49 Thus, in a foreclosure suit, a receiver may defend the property from an adverse claim, and may appeal.

50 He may not appeal from an order discharging or removing him. He may appeal from an order disallowing him commissions or fees.

cial, not personal;[51] and judgment against him should be so entered as to be enforced only out of the funds properly chargeable to him in the capacity of receiver,[52] leaving the manner of its enforcement to be determined by the court having jurisdiction of the receivership.[53] And an action may be brought against a receiver on a liability incurred by his predecessor in the receivership, since the receivership is continuous and uninterrupted until the court relinquishes its hold upon the property, though its *personnel* may be subject to repeated changes; the position of the receiver in this respect being somewhat analogous to that of a corporation sole.[54] Leave to bring suit against a receiver, therefore, extends to permit suit against his successor in office.[55]

It also follows that no judgment can be rendered against a receiver in his official capacity after he is discharged from the receivership and the property is withdrawn from his custody.[56] The supreme court of

51 McNulta v. Lockridge, 141 U. S 327, 12 Sup Ct 11; affirming 137 Ill. 210, 31 Am. St Rep. 362, 27 N. E. 452; Bonner v. Mayfield, 82 Tex. 234, 18 S. W. 305.

52 McNulta v. Ensch, 134 Ill 46, 24 N. E 631.

53 Brown v. Brown, 71 Tex. 355, 9 S. W. 261. See, also, Painter v. Painter, 138 Cal. 231, 94 Am. St. Rep. 47, 71 Pac. 90 (judgment cannot be enforced on execution, practice is to apply to the court for an order).

54 McNulta v. Lockridge, *supra;* State v. Port Royal & A. R. Co., 84 Fed. 67.

55 Fordyce v. Dixon, 70 Tex. 694, 8 S. W. 504.

56 Farmers' Loan & Trust Co. v. Central R. R Co of Iowa, 7 Fed 537, 2 McCrary, 181; Lehman v. McQuown, 31 Fed. 138; Western N Y. & P. R. Co. v. Penn Refining Co. (C. C. A.), 137 Fed. 343; Archambeau v. Platt, 173 Mass. 249, 53 N. E. 816; Ansley v McLoud (Ind. Ter), 82 S. W. 908, Brawn v. McBean, 54 App. Div. 635, 66 N. Y Supp 785, New York & W W. Tel. Co v. Jewett, 115 N. Y. 166, 21 N. E. 1036, Texas & Pac. R R. Co v. Johnston, 76 Tex. 421, 18 Am. St. Rep. 60, 13 S W. 463; Boggs v Brown, 82 Tex. 41, 17 S W. 830, Fordyce v. Du Bose, 87 Tex. 78, 26 S. W. 1050 (see for the effect of a statute allowing judgment against receiver after his discharge, when

Mississippi says: "The final discharge of the receiver put an end to his official existence, and withdrew from his care and management the road and property of the company. The discharge having terminated the representative character of the receiver, we are at a loss to understand how any judgment could be rendered against him officially that would render liable to its satisfaction any property of the company,—property in his hands when the suit was brought, but now finally withdrawn from him by the extinction of his official character before his plea was filed. . . . It seems plain to us that, with the termination of his representative character, and the withdrawal of the road and its property from his custody by the order discharging him, no judgment could be rendered against him properly, as the representative of the company, whereby to make its property chargeable. His official liability ended with his official existence."[57] But the fact that a re-

suit is pending at the time); Texas & Pac. R. R. Co. v. Watson, 13 Tex. Civ. App. 555, 36 S. W. 290 (a judgment rendered after his discharge binds neither the receiver nor the company represented) But the fact that the property has been sold, and has entirely passed from his control is no bar to an action against him if he has not been finally discharged: Erb v. Popritz, 59 Kan. 264, 68 Am. St. Rep 362, 52 Pac. 871. See, also, Houston City St. Ry Co. v. Storrie (Tex. Civ. App.), 44 S. W. 693; Houston & F C. Ry. Co. v. Stoycharski (Tex. Civ. App.), 35 S. W. 851, 37 S. W. 415; Howe v. Harper, 127 N. C. 356, 37 S. E. 505.

57 Bond v. State, 68 Miss 648, 9 South. 353. See Davis v. Duncan, 19 Fed. 477, stating that the court is aware of no rule by which it can "in any way alter, change, modify, suspend or expand the decree discharging the receiver, and again obtain jurisdiction of the property and funds which it had by its decree ordered the receiver to turn over to the corporation and which it is admitted was done." But that an action against the receiver is not necessarily terminated by the discharge of the receiver and sale of the property under decree of the appointing court, under a section of the New York code allowing a continuance of the action by or against the original party thereto, in case of a transfer of interest or devolution of liability, see Baer v. McCullough, 176 N. Y. 97, 68 N. E. 129.

ceiver has been discharged is no bar to an action against him, where he has sold the property of another with notice of his claim, and no notice of the motion to discharge him was served on the owner;[58] or where he has collected money under a void appointment.[59] And where judgment has been recovered against him in the lower court, and he is discharged pending an appeal, judgment may properly be entered against him if the judgment of the lower court is affirmed.[60]

58 Muller v. Loeb, 64 Barb. 454.

59 Johnston v. Powers, 21 Mo. 292, 32 N. W. 62. But if the receiver has in good faith applied the money in improving the property, and the order was valid on its face, he will be protected to that extent. Edee v Strunk, 35 Neb. 307, 53 N. W. 70.

60 McCarley v. McGhee, 103 Fed. 494; Woodruff v. Jewett, 115 N. Y. 267, 22 N. E. 156.

CHAPTER VI.

SUITS BY THE RECEIVER.

ANALYSIS.

§ 180. Suits by Receivers; Leave of Court Necessary.— In the absence of statute, it is generally held that a receiver can "neither bring nor defend actions except by permission and the direct authority of the court by which he was appointed."[1] It is said: "That rule is a

1 Foster v. Townshend, 68 N. Y. 206. See to the same effect, Phoenix Ins. Co. v. Schultz, 80 Fed. 337, 25 C. C. A. 453 (see for what constitutes leave to sue); First Nat. Bank v. C. B. & Co., 7 Idaho, 27, 59 Pac. 929, 1106 (leave to appeal should be obtained); Herron v. Vance, 17 Ind. 595; Coffin v. Ransdell, 110 Ind 417, 11 N. E. 20; Wayne Pike Co. v. State, 134 Ind. 672, 34 N. E. 440, Hatfield v Cummings, 142 Ind 350, 39 N. E 859; Runner v. Dwiggins, 117 Ind. 238, 36 L. R. A. 645, 46 N. E 580; Vigo Real Estate Co v. Reese, 21 Ind. App. 20, 51 N. E 350; Peirce v. Chism, 23 Ind. App. 505, 77 Am.

necessary result of the nature of the functions of the receiver. He is a mere custodian of the property for the court as one of its officers. His acts are the acts of the court when duly sanctioned, and when not so sanctioned they have no greater effect than the acts of other unauthorized officers or agents."[2] The supreme court of Georgia has stated: "The rule is perhaps an arbitrary one, but it is, nevertheless, well settled, that a receiver has no right to sue without express authority from the chancellor; his general authority to collect and keep the assets is not sufficient to justify him in bringing an action. A receiver is at least only an officer of the court, and the foundation of the rule probably is, that it is always for the court to determine whether it shall be dragged into litigation. At law, the party having the legal right to sue is the proper party, and if one comes suing for the property of another, he must show, as part of his right to recover, the authority he has to come into a court of law asserting another's right."[3]

St. Rep. 441, 55 N. E. 795; Troy Sav. Bank v. Morrison, 27 App. Div. 423, 50 N. Y. Supp. 225; Battle v. Davis, 66 N. C. 262; Davis's Admrs. v. Snead, 33 Gratt. 709; Reynolds's Exr. v. Pettyjohn, 79 Va. 327; McAllister v. Harmon, 97 Va. 543, 34 S. E. 474 (leave of court to sue will not be implied from general order to collect). See the following cases to the effect that the receiver should allege that he has obtained leave of court to sue. Wheat v. Bank of California, 119 Cal. 4, 50 Pac. 842, 51 Pac. 47; Morgan v. Buski, 61 N. Y. Supp. 929, 30 Misc. Rep. 245; Swing v. White River Lumber Co., 91 Wis. 517, 65 N. W. 174; Rhodes v. Hilligoss, 16 Ind. App. 478, 45 N. E. 666, Gainey v. Gilson, 149 Ind. 58, 48 N. E. 633. To the effect that he need not allege that leave of court has been obtained, see Hegewisch v. Silver, 140 N. Y 414, 35 N. E. 658; Hardin v. Sweeney, 14 Wash 129, 44 Pac 138; Compton v. Schwabacher Bros. & Co, 15 Wash. 306, 46 Pac. 338; Howard v. Stephenson, 33 W. Va. 116, 10 S. E. 66; Elliott v. Trahern, 35 W. Va. 634, 14 S. E. 223; Minn. etc. St. Ry. Co. v. Minn. etc. R. Co., 61 Minn. 502, 63 N. W. 1035.

2 Fincke v. Funke, 25 Hun, 616; approved in Ogden v. Arnot, 29 Hun, 146.

3 Screven v. Clark, 48 Ga. 41.

In regard to the case of a receiver *pendente lite,* where leave of court was not obtained, the supreme court of California states: "As a rule, however, the receiver cannot sue to recover property which has not come to his possession, or which, being in the possession of the defendant, ought to have been delivered to him. He cannot maintain trover for property of the insolvent converted before the adjudication, nor to recover property transferred by the debtor in fraud of creditors."[4] There seems to be a lack of harmony in the decisions as to the form in which the consent to sue should be given; some of the courts have held that the order may allow the receiver to prosecute and defend all actions brought against him in his official capacity,[5] while other courts maintain that such general permission is too liberal for judicious management of the property. Such practice is criticised in New York as follows: "It seems to me, however, that that portion of the order which authorizes the receiver to prosecute and defend without the further order of the court all actions brought or about to be brought by or against said co-partners, or any of them, pertaining to said co-partnership business, ... is improper, and its presence in the order was probably overlooked by the justice holding the special term at which the order was made. The rule requiring leave of court to be obtained before the receiver can either sue or be sued is in order to prevent any unnecessary waste of the assets in the receiver's hands in unneces-

4 Tibbets v. Cohn, 116 Cal 365, 48 Pac. 372; quoted with approval in Bishop v. McKillican, 124 Cal. 321, 71 Am St. Rep. 68, 57 Pac. 76, refusing to allow a recovery of personal property of which the receiver had never had possession.

5 Taylor v. Canady, 155 Ind. 671, 57 N. E. 524, 59 N. E 20. See, also, Wason v Frank, 7 Colo. App 541, 44 Pac. 378, Wyman v. Williams, 52 Neb. 833, 73 N. W. 285; Boyd v. Royal Ins. Co., 111 N. C. 372, 16 S. E. 389

sary litigation, and contemplates at least some investigation by the court of the propriety of the commencement of such suits before permission is granted; and to authorize in advance the commencement of suits without any knowledge of what they are for, or of the necessity thereof, is a complete nullification of the rule, and exposes the estate to the very thing that the rule was intended to guard against, and is improper practice."[6] In many states, the rule that the receiver should obtain leave of court, prior to defending or bringing an action, has been changed by statute so that he may sue as freely as the one whom he represents, if it is necessary for the protection of the estate.[7]

§ 181. **Suits by Receiver, in Whose Name.**—While the decisions are not altogether harmonious on the subject, it seems to be generally held that, in the absence of statute, the receiver should sue in the name of the party having the legal title, and over whose property he has been appointed.[8] In Indiana it is stated: "It

6 Witherbee v. Witherbee, 17 App. Div. 181, 45 N. Y. Supp. 297.

7 See Tibbets v. Cohn & Co., 116 Cal. 365, 48 Pac. 372 (refusing to extend the code provision to a sheriff acting as receiver *pendente lite*). In Indiana, a statute providing that "the receiver shall have power, under control of the court, or of the judge thereof in vacation to bring and defend actions," does not authorize a receiver to bring action without leave of court: Rhodes v. Hilligoss, 16 Ind. App. 478, 45 N. E. 666. But see Manlove v. Burger, 38 Ind. 211. In North Carolina, the statute giving "power to prosecute and defend" with no reference to the control of the court, it is held that the receiver may sue without leave having been obtained: Gray v. Lewis, 94 N. C. 392; Weill v. First Nat. Bank, 106 N. C. 1, 11 S. E. 277; Worth v. Wharton, 122 N. C. 376, 29 S. E 370, Everett v. State, 28 Md. 190; Baker v. Cooper, 57 Me. 388; Ueland v. Hangan, 70 Minn. 349, 73 N. W. 169; Boston & M. C. C. & S. M. Co. v. Montana etc. Co., 24 Mont. 142, 60 Pac. 990; Mathis v. Pridham, 1 Tex. Civ. App. 58, 20 S. W. 1015. See, also, McBryan v. Universal Elevator Co., 130 Mich. 111, 97 Am. St. Rep. 453, 89 N. W 683.

8 Dick v. Struthers, 25 Fed. 103; Harland v. Bankers' & M. Tel.

is undoubtedly a correct general proposition that in the absence of authority derived from the statute, or from the court ordering his appointment, a receiver has no power to sue in his own name. . . . . The reason is that the legal title to *choses in action,* or other property which he is authorized to reduce to possession, is ordinarily not transferred to the receiver, but remains in the owner, in whose name suits must be brought, unless the statute or the order of the court authorizes the receiver to proceed in his own name."[9] A leading decision in North Carolina says, "the action must be brought in the name of the legal owner, and he will be compelled to allow the use of his name upon being properly indemnified out of the estate and effects, under the control of the court."[10]

While recognizing the general rule, there are cases holding that in certain instances the receiver may maintain an action in his own name, without the aid of a statute. Thus it is said: "But where the goods have actually come into his possession, it can hardly be contended that he could not maintain this action against one who wrongfully invaded such possession and converted the goods committed to his care. Were such

Co, 32 Fed. 305; Garver v. Kent, 70 Ind 428; Moriarty v. Kent, 71 Ind. 601, Wilson v. Welsh, 157 Mass 77, 31 N. E. 712; Ft. Payne Coal & Iron Co v. Webster, 163 Mass 134, 39 N. E. 786; East Tenn. Land Co. v. Leeson (Mass), 57 N. E. 656; Freeman v. Winchester, 10 Smedes & M. (18 Miss.) 577; Newell v. Fisher, 24 Miss. 392 (the statement of the court would lead to the conclusion that the receiver could sue in his own name if he had the legal title); State v. Gambs, 68 Mo 289; Yeager v. Wallace, 44 Pa. St. 294; Murtey v. Allen, 71 Vt. 377, 76 Am. St. Rep. 779, 45 Atl. 752 (inferring that he could sue at law in his own name if he had the legal title); King v. Cutts, 24 Wis 627.

9 Pouder v. Catterson, 127 Ind. 434, 26 N. E 66

10 Battle v. Davis, 66 N. C. 252 (the rule has since been changed by code).

not the case he would not rise to the dignity and power of the most ordinary bailee. He would be the merest automaton that ever sprang from a legal workshop. In the case in hand, the goods were in the possession of the receiver and were sold by him by virtue of the power conferred upon him by the court for that purpose. The contract of sale was with him; his receipt for the money to the purchaser would have been good to discharge him from the price of the goods; and for them or their price he is responsible. We are of opinion, therefore, that the receiver might maintain this suit in his own name."[11] And where a receiver sought the possession of land to which he as receiver was entitled, the court said: "The object of the suit is to obtain possession of the real estate in question for the receiver and not for the bank. A suit in the name of the bank would not accomplish that purpose; for the execution, or writ of possession, if one was obtained, would require the officer executing it to put the bank, and not the receivers, into possession. As it is the receivers that are seeking the possession, we think the suit is properly brought in their names. It is the direct road to the end in view."[12] It has been said that where an assignee can sue in his own name, a receiver may also where he has analogous rights. The court said, "In the present case the receiver is called by the court in Washington a '*quasi* assignee for creditors.' He is charged with the administration of a trust

11 Singerly v. Fox, 75 Pa. St. 112. See, also, Wason v. Frank, 7 Colo. App. 541, 44 Pac. 378. The statement by Henry, J., in State v. Gambs, 68 Mo. 289, is to the same effect.

12 Baker v. Cooper, 57 Me. 388; Mathis v. Pridham, 1 Tex. Civ. App. 58, 20 S. W. 1015, states that though not authorized by statute or court order to sue in his own name, he may do so when ordered by statute to sue generally. See, also, Evans v. Pease, 21 R. I. 187, 42 Atl. 506.

fund which does not take from nor come into actual existence until after his appointment, and he is the only person who can collect it. By virtue of his official relation to the corporation and its creditors, he is the owner of the legal title to this fund, as a trustee for the creditors. A suit could not have been brought in the name of the corporation, and he is the only person who can now, or who ever could, legally demand and collect the money. We are of opinion that the action is rightly brought in his name."[13]

In those states where the code system prevails and it is provided that suits shall be brought in the name of the real party in interest, a receiver is allowed to sue in his own name on the ground that he is the real party in interest.[14] The supreme court of Minnesota says: "The receiver, as an officer of the court which has taken control of the property, is, for the time being, and for the purpose of the administration of the assets, the real party in interest in the litigation. There is no reason, therefore, why the suit should not be instituted in his own name. . . . . Whatever technical reasons may have existed for refusing to permit common-law receivers to sue in their own names, they exist no longer,

13 Howarth v. Lombard, 175 Mass 570, 56 N. E. 888, 49 L. R. A. 301, Buswell v. Supreme Sitting etc. of Iron Hall, 161 Mass. 224, 36 N. E 1065, 23 L. R. A. 846; Ewing v. King, 169 Mass. 97, 47 N. E. 597 See Wilkinson v. Rutherford, 49 N. J. L. 244, 8 Atl. 507, to the same effect where the statute, authorizing suit, did not provide that it should be in the receiver's name. In Frank v Morrison, 58 Md. 423, the court states the Maryland practice to be to allow suits in the name of the receiver, regardless of statute.

14 Wason v. Frank, 7 Colo. App. 541, 44 Pac. 378 ("but the cases in which it has been held that a receiver could not maintain an action in his own name were, for the most part, cases where the legal right existed in his principal before his appointment. . . . In his representative capacity he was the real party in interest; the suit could be brought and maintained only in his name").

under our code."[15] In many of the states, the code or statute expressly provides that the suit may be in the name of the receiver, or gives such general authority to sue that the courts construe it as giving such power.[16]

§ 182. Appointment cannot be Questioned Collaterally.—The rule is well established that the regularity of the receiver's appointment cannot be attacked collaterally in suits brought by him as receiver.[17] In the case of

15 Henning v. Raymond, 35 Minn. 303, 29 N. W. 132. In Davis v. Ladoga Creamery Co, 128 Ind. 222, 27 N. E. 494, it is said the suit cannot be in the name of the corporation, as long as a receiver has charge.

16 Cockrill v. Abeles, 86 Fed. 505, 30 C. C. A. 223.

See statutes collected, *ante*, note to § 73.

California.—California v Gray (Cal.), 40 Pac. 959; Tibbets v. Cohn & Co., 116 Cal. 365, 48 Pac. 372 (but the code provision was not extended to a receiver *pendente lite*).

Illinois—Chicago Fire Proofing Co. v. Park Nat. Bank, 145 Ill. 481, 32 N. E. 534.

Indiana.—Manlove v. Burgess, 38 Ind. 211; Hatfield v. Cummings, 152 Ind. 280, 50 N. E. 231; Taylor v. Canaday, 155 Ind. 671, 57 N. E. 524, 59 N. E. 20.

Maine.—Hobart v. Bennett, 77 Me. 401.

Minnesota.—Weland v. Hangan, 70 Minn. 349, 73 N. W. 169.

Missouri.—Gill v. Balis, 72 Mo. 424; Alexander v. Relfe, 74 Mo. 516.

Montana.—Boston & M C. C. & S. M. Co. v. Montana etc. Co., 24 Mont. 142, 60 Pac 990.

North Carolina.—Gray v. Lewis, 94 N. C. 392; Weill v. First Nat. Bank, 106 N. C. 1, 11 S. E. 277; Davis v. Industrial Mfg. Co., 114 N. C. 321, 19 S. E. 371, 23 L. R. A. 322.

Texas.—Mathis v. Pridham, 1 Tex. Civ. App. 58, 20 S. W. 1015.

17 Fish v. Smith, 73 Conn. 377, 84 Am. St Rep. 161, 47 Atl. 711 (one who was nominally a party to the appointing suit cannot so attack it), Com. Nat. Bank v. Burch, 141 Ill. 519, 33 Am. St. Rep. 331, 31 N. E. 420, St. Paul Trust Co. v. St. Paul Globe Pub. Co., 60 Minn. 105, 61 N. W. 813 (the order of court, empowering the receiver to sue, is not subject to such attack); Cox v. Volkert, 86 Mo. 505; Block v. Estes, 92 Mo. 318, 4 S. W. 731, Thompson v. Greeley, 107 Mo. 577, 17 S. W. 962; Keokuk N. L P. Co. v. Davidson, 13 Mo. App. 561; Andrew v. Steel City Bank, 57 Neb. 173, 77 N. W. 342,

a corporation receiver, suing to collect unpaid subscriptions, the court said: "The plaintiff's appointment as receiver cannot be attacked collaterally. The regularity, propriety and validity of the appointment of such a receiver can only be questioned in a direct proceeding to test that question;"[18] and "when a judgment debtor appears before a referee and submits to an examination without objection, this will amount to a waiver of any irregularity, and an order for the appointment of a receiver founded on such voluntary appearance and waiver will be valid, and cannot be affected by an objection to the jurisdiction in an action brought by the receiver."[19] The supreme court of Ohio states: "It must be borne in mind that he was an acting receiver. There was at least the form of a legal appointment, and that in a case which certainly invoked the discretion and consideration of the court in the determination of the question whether an appointment could or ought to be made. This was jurisdiction. The court acted. The appointment was made. The receiver proceeded to the discharge of the duties of the trust. This is not a direct proceeding to test the validity or regularity of the appointment. It is not a proceeding in error to review the order of appointment. It is a collateral inquiry. It is not enough that the court erred in its action. Unless it appear manifestly clear to us that the order of appointment was an absolute nullity by reason of the entire absence of jurisdiction in the court that made it, it cannot be assailed in this proceeding."[20]

Capital City Mut Fire Ins. Co. v. Boggs, 172 Pa. St. 91, 33 Atl. 349; Elderkin v. Peterson, 8 Wash. 674, 36 Pac 1089

18 Basting v. Ankeny, 64 Minn. 133, 66 N. W. 266.

19 Quoted in Green v. Bookhart, 19 S C. 466, citing Viburt v. Frost, 3 Abb. Pr. 119; and Bingham v. Disbrow, 37 Barb. 24.

20 Barbour v. Nat Exch. Bank, 45 Ohio St. 133, 12 N. E. 5. See, also, Edee v. Strunk, 35 Neb. 307, 53 N. W. 70.

If the order appointing the receiver is absolutely void, it is held that he cannot protect himself under it, when sued for money collected as rent from the premises in question.[21] It is necessary, in order to constitute a valid appointment, that the appointing court have jurisdiction of the subject matter.[22]

§ 183. Pleading in Suit by Receiver; Must Allege His Authority.—In a suit by a receiver, acting as he does in a purely representative character, it is necessary for him to allege in the complaint the authority and right that entitles him to maintain the action.[23] Thus it has been frequently held that "a receiver, in order to maintain an action, must set out facts showing his appointment, and by what jurisdiction appointed; setting out, also, so much of the proceedings in the cause as will show that his appointment is legal, as the defendant may insist that the facts constituting the appointment as receiver which are set out shall be sufficient to show that an appointment has been made, and that these facts must be so stated, and with such certainty, that they may be traversed."[24] And since it is necessary

21 Johnson v. Powers, 21 Neb. 292, 32 N. W. 62; approved, but distinguished and limited, in Edee v. Strunk, *supra*.

22 See cases cited *supra* in note 19, and Attorney-General v. Guardian M. L. I. Co., 77 N. Y. 272.

23 Daggett v. Gray (Cal.), 4 Pac. 959; Wheat v. Bank of California, 119 Cal. 4, 50 Pac. 842, 51 Pac. 47, Cooper v. Bowers, 42 Barb. 87, 28 How. Pr. 10 (supplementary proceedings); Forker v. Brown, 30 N. Y. Supp. 827, 10 Misc. Rep. 161; Swing v. White River Lumber Co., 91 Wis. 517, 65 N. W. 174; Worth v. Wharton, 122 N. C. 376, 29 S. E. 370

24 Rhorer v. Middlesboro Town and Land Co., 19 Ky. Law Rep. 1788, 44 S W 448. See Rossman v. Mitchell, 73 Minn. 198, 75 N. W. 1053, stating: "But it is now settled by the weight of authority, and on principle, that an allegation in general terms by the plaintiff, suing as receiver, that at such a time, in such an action or proceeding, and by such a court or officer, he was duly appointed receiver of the estate of such a party, is sufficient, and that anything short of this

for the receiver to obtain leave of court to prosecute a suit, it has been held that "a complaint filed by a receiver which fails to allege that leave of the court to institute and prosecute the action has been obtained is fatally defective."[25] So, if the receiver has a right to sue in his own name, it is said he should allege the source of that right; the court states: "The authority from the court to the receiver to sue in his own name lies at the very basis of his right to bring the action"; and the complaint "must show by proper averments that leave of court to institute and prosecute the action has been first obtained."[26]

§ 184. Same; Appointment and Authority, How Alleged. The rule laid down by the cases in the preceding paragraph, as to the particularity with which a receiver should allege his authority, has not been universally followed; in many cases it is held that an allegation that the plaintiff was "duly" appointed may be made in general terms. Thus it is said: "It never was necessary to set out all the proceedings by which a receiver was appointed, but merely that he show the mode of his appointment."[27] It is said that "the insertion of the word 'duly' in the allegation that the plaintiff was appointed receiver, gave him the right to show on the

is not sufficient." See, also, White v. Joy, 13 N. Y. 83; Bangs v. McIntosh, 23 Barb. 591; Lever v. Bailey, 56 N. J. L. 54, 27 Atl. 799.

25 Davis v. Ladoga Creamery Co., 128 Ind. 222, 27 N. E 494, citing Moriarty v. Kent, 71 Ind. 601; approved in Rhodes v. Hilligoss, 16 Ind. App. 478, 45 N. E. 666; Hatfield v. Cummings, 142 Ind. 350, 39 N. E. 859. See, also, Garver v. Kent, 70 Ind. 428; Morgan v. Bucki, 30 Misc. Rep. 245, 61 N. Y. Supp. 929.

26 Hatfield v. Cummings, 142 Ind. 350, 39 N. E. 859. See, also, the cases *supra*, note 25.

27 Stewart v. Beebee, 28 Barb. 34 ("it was sufficient to aver that he was appointed receiver, the court by which the appointment was made, and the date of the order").

trial all the facts conferring jurisdiction."[28] And where the petition alleged that the applicant was appointed receiver in certain proceedings named, it was held a sufficient allegation of the petitioner's title. "He was not bound to plead each step in the proceeding to show his appointment was valid. That could be proven on the hearing, if his appointment was put in issue."[29] It is also maintained that "while it is essential to the complaint that it appear, by clear and express averment, that the receiver was authorized by the court to bring the action, ... it is not necessary that the complaint shall show that the receiver had specific authority from the court to bring this particular action."[30] And it is said that where "it does not appear from the record that he did not have such leave, and, when the plaintiff's authority to bring suit is not denied or disputed, it will be presumed to exist. The plaintiff, in the absence of any denial of his authority to bring such suit, is not required to allege and prove it."[31] This was held to be true in Washington, though the receiver was suing in his own name.[32]

28 Rockwell v. Merwin, 45 N. Y. 166, 8 Abb. Pr., N. S., 330.

29 In re Beecher's Estate, 19 N. Y. Supp. 971, citing the cases, *supra*, in notes 27 and 28. See, also, Morgan v. Bucki, 30 Misc. Rep. 245, 61 N Y. Supp. 929; Daggett v. Gray (Cal.), 40 Pac. 959, Wason v. Frank, 7 Colo. App. 541, 44 Pac. 378; Nelson v. Nugent, 62 Minn. 203, 64 N. W 392.

30 Taylor v. Canaday, 155 Ind. 671, 57 N. E. 524, 59 N. E. 20 The court continued "It is good if it is shown that in the order of appointment authority to sue was sufficiently broad to authorize the receiver to institute and prosecute such suits as become necessary and proper for the collection of the assets and for obtaining possession of the property over which he has charge."

31 Howard v. Stephenson, 33 W. Va. 116, 10 S. E. 66, approved in Elliott v Trahern, 35 W. Va. 634, 14 S E 223. See, also, Boyd v. Royal Ins. Co, 111 N. C. 372, 16 S E. 387, Worth v Wharton, 122 N. C 376, 29 S. E 370.

32 Hardin v. Sweeney, 14 Wash. 129, 44 Pac. 138; approved in Compton v. Schwabacker etc. Co, 15 Wash 306, 46 Pac. 338.

§ 185. **Proof by Receiver of His Appointment and Powers.** When, in a proper proceeding, the authority of a receiver to act is questioned, he should prove his appointment and powers, as any fact would be proved, the proper and general course being to produce a copy of the order appointing him and defining his rights.[33] In the case of a suit by corporation receivers it was said: "Their alleged appointment as receivers is denied by the answer. The only proof that could be made is a certified copy of the order of dissolution and the appointment of receivers. That not having been filed, the court could not recognize their authority to bring this action and invoke the equitable jurisdiction of the court."[34] Such certified copy is generally considered conclusive evidence of the regularity of the proceedings and *prima facie* evidence of the jurisdiction of the court appointing the receiver.[35] And where the jurisdiction of the appointing court was questioned, and the certified copy of the order did not show that an action had been commenced, the court said: "It was necessary to prove the commencement of the action, and that the court obtained jurisdiction over the corporation, ... to sustain the allegation that the plaintiff was duly appointed receiver."[36]

33 Frank v. Morrison, 58 Md. 423; Seymour v. Newman, 77 Mo. App. 578; Potter v. Merchants' Bank, 28 N. Y. 641, 86 Am. Dec. 273 (the pendency of an action resulting in the receivership may be proved by its recitals in the appointing order). See for a case where the defendant was estopped by the fact that the appointment had been declared valid in prior proceedings between the parties, Griffin v. Long Island R. Co., 102 N. Y. 449, 7 N. E. 735. See, also, Scott v. Duncombe, 49 Barb. 73.

34 Pearson v. Leary, 126 N. C. 504, 36 S. E. 35, 127 N. C. 114, 37 S. E. 149.

35 Wright v. Nostrand, 94 N. Y. 32, and cases cited *supra*, in note 33.

36 Spings v. Bowery Nat. Bank, 63 Hun, 505, 18 N. Y. Supp. 574, where the receiver failed to prove that he had filed the bond required

§ 186. Receiver is Subject to the Same Defenses as the One Whom He Represents.—It is generally held that a receiver can occupy no better position than those for whom he acts and is appointed;[37] that he is in the place of the ones he represents, and has only such rights as they had, so that the rights and liabilities of third parties are not increased, diminished or varied by his appointment. There passes to the receiver the property and rights of the one from whom he takes, precisely in the same condition and subject to the same equities as before his appointment,[38] and any defense good against the original party is good against the receiver.[39] This is true in the case of a receiver who

by law, but had been subsequently authorized to sue, the court said: "It is a reasonable inference that the court, when it granted the order to sue, was apprised of the facts affecting the plaintiffs' right to bring the action, and ascertained that he had duly qualified as receiver. . . . . The question is not as to the weight of evidence but whether there was any evidence tending to show that the bond was filed"; Hegewisch v Silven, 140 N. Y. 414, 35 N. E. 658.

37 Bell v. Shibley, 33 Barb. 614 ("it has been repeatedly held that a receiver is subject to all the rights and equities existing against the company"); Cooper v. Bowers, 42 Barb. 87, 28 How. Pr. 10; Falkenbach v. Patterson, 43 Ohio St. 359, 1 N. E. 757; Cox v. Volkert, 68 Mo. 505, 511.

38 Van Wagoner v. Paterson Gas Light Co., 23 N J L. 285.

39 Casey v. La Societe de Credit Mobilier, 2 Woods, 77, Fed. Cas. No. 2496; Tyler v. Hamilton, 62 Fed. 187 (and therefore, in the absence of fraud, he cannot avoid the contracts of the corporation he represents); Mayer v. Thomas, 97 Ga. 772, 25 S. E. 761; Hatch v. Johnson, 79 Fed. 828, 836; Perry v. Godbe, 82 Fed. 141 (thus he may be bound by statements made in a complaint filed by the corporation before his appointment); Bell v. Hanover Nat. Bank, 57 Fed. 822, Security Title & Trust Co. v. Schlender, 170 Ill. 609, 60 N. E. 854, State v. Sullivan, 120 Ind 197, 21 N. E 1095, 22 N E. 325; Wardle v. Hudson, 96 Mich. 432, 55 N. W. 992; Kuser v. Wright, 52 N. J. Eq 825, 31 Atl 397; Little v Garabrant, 90 Hun, 404, 35 N. Y. Supp. 689; Capital City Mut. Fire Ins. Co. v. Boggs, 172 Pa. St. 91, 33 Atl. 349; Shuey v. Holmes, 20 Wash. 13, 54 Pac. 540; State v. Thum, 6 Idaho, 323, 55 Pac 858 (not allowed to recover money held in trust by the bank he represents).

represents a corporation; the court saying: "He is as much bound by a settlement which the company was authorized to make as was the company itself. It would be strange, indeed, if the legal acts of a corporation did not bind the receiver of its effects. If the rule were not so no one would dare venture to deal with a corporation."[40] But in those cases where the receiver is held to represent, not only the corporation, but also the creditors, whose rights he is bound to protect, he may avail himself of any of those rights, and is not subject to defenses that would not be good against the creditors.[41]

§ 187. **Set-off Against the Receiver—In General.**—As stated in a preceding paragraph, the general rule is that a receiver acquires no greater interest in an estate than the one from whom he takes, and it follows that choses in action pass to him subject to any right of set-off existing at the time of his appointment.[42] But the

40 Hyde v. Lynde, 4 N. Y. 387. In McLaren v First Nat Bank of Milwaukee, 76 Wis. 259, 45 N. W. 223, the court states it as follows: "The result is that we must regard the plaintiff [receiver] as standing in the shoes of the carriage company, and as having no more right to recover, as against the bank, than the carriage company would have had." See, also, Ross v. Meehan Brake Shoe Foundry Co. v. Southern M. L. Co., 72 Fed. 957; Moise v. Chapman, 24 Ga. 249.

41 Atwater v. Stromberg, 75 Minn. 277, 77 N. W. 963. In McLaren v. First Nat. Bank of Milwaukee, 76 Wis. 259, 45 N. W 223, it is said: "If the plaintiff [receiver] should make it appear that he in fact represents creditors of the carriage company existing at the time of the misappropriation, then it may be he can make a case entitling him to recover as such receiver." See, also, Appleton v. Turnbull, 84 Me. 72, 24 Atl. 592. See this subject discussed further, *post*, § 190.

42 Fisher v Knight, 61 Fed. 491, 9 C. C. A. 582, 17 U. S. App 502; Wheaton v. Daily Tel. Co. (C. C. A.), 124 Fed. 61, Jefferson v Edrington, 53 Ark. 545, 14 S W 99, 903, Balch v. Wilson, 25 Minn 299, quoted approvingly in Yardley v. Clothier, 49 Fed. at 341; Grant v.

right of set-off must exist before the receiver is appointed, for "when a receiver is appointed, the accounts of the insolvent are closed, and no changes can thereafter be made by any assignments of credits against the estate; as this, if allowed, would injure the trust fund, and defeat the ratable distribution to which each creditor is entitled."[43] The supreme court of Pennsylvania has said: "Now, if each creditor be allowed to purchase goods at the receiver's sale, and pay for them by a set-off, we can readily see how, at least, this part of the proceedings of a court of equity might degenerate from a regular and orderly process to a mere scramble for the debtor's goods."[44]

§ 188. **Set-off by Bank Depositor.**—The principles involved in a set-off against a receiver have received particular application in the case of receivers of insolvent banks, when suing parties who had money on deposit at the bank when it became insolvent. It is said to be well settled that in a suit by a receiver of an insolvent bank upon a note or obligation due the bank, the defendant will be allowed to set off his deposit or certificate of deposit held by him at the time of the sus-

Buckner, 49 La. Ann. 668, 21 South. 580; Mercantile Nat. Bank v. McFarlane, 71 Minn. 497, 70 Am. St. Rep. 352, 74 N. W. 287. The right of set-off is said to be within the statute of 1888 allowing suits against federal receivers without leave of court: Grant v. Buckner, 172 U. S. 232, 19 Sup. Ct. 163, 43 L. ed. 430

43 In re Hamilton, 26 Or. 579, 38 Pac. 1088. See, also, Chicago Arch. Iron Works v McKey, 93 Ill. App. 244 ("a claim of the debtor, accruing before the receiver was appointed, cannot be set off against a claim accruing after the receiver was appointed, and therefore due the receiver and not the insolvent"); Van Dyck v. McQuade, 85 N. Y. 617; U. S. Bung Mfg. Co. v. Armstrong, 34 Fed. 94 (the existence of cross-demands or independent debts which could have been set off at law, had they been asserted at the proper time, cannot be asserted in equity).

44 Singerly v. Fox, 75 Pa. St. 112.

pension of the bank.[45] But in order to avail himself of the right of set-off, the defendant must have acquired his right before the insolvency of the bank, as otherwise the transaction may be void as in fraud of creditors.[46] And it has been held that where a receiver sued a stockholder of an insolvent bank for unpaid subscriptions, the stockholders' deposit could not be set off, the court saying: "They are not in the same right. . . . . To permit him to set off the debt due him would, where the corporation is insolvent, manifestly give him a preference as a creditor. To this he is not entitled. It is the right of the other creditors to have him pay in the money due from him for stock as part of the fund for the payment of debts."[47] There has been some conflict in the decisions as to whether the right of set-off existed when the note on which the receiver was suing did not mature until after his appointment; the right was denied in a federal case, stating: "When the plaintiff was appointed receiver, the defendant was in the list of unsecured depositors, to whom payment, the bank being insolvent, was prohibited. The defendant had thus no right of set-off, nor any equity against its note, not then matured, which passed to the receiver. To

45 Scott v. Armstrong, 146 U. S. 499, 13 Sup. Ct. 148, 36 L. ed. 1059; Snyder v. Armstrong, 37 Fed. 18 (see the case for a discussion of the earlier cases); State v. Brobston, 94 Ga. 95, 47 Am. St. Rep. 138, 21 S. E. 146; Miller v. Receiver of the Franklin Bank, 1 Paige, 444, Davis v. Industrial Mfg. Co., 114 N. C. 321, 19 S. E. 371, 23 L. R. A. 322. See the statement in Hade v. McVay, 31 Ohio St. 231, though the set-off was not allowed by reason of a statute; Armstrong v. Warner, 49 Ohio St. 376, 31 N. E. 877, 17 L. R. A. 466; Clarke v. Hawkins, 5 R. I. 219.

46 Stone v. Dodge, 96 Mich. 514, 56 N. W. 75, 21 L. R. A. 280 (the case contains a full review of the authorities on the subject); Venango Nat. Bank v. Taylor, 56 Pa. St. 14; Smith v. Mosby, 9 Heisk. 501.

47 Williams v. Traphagen, 38 N. J. Eq. 57.

allow the set-off, now that the note has matured, and thereby make payment in full to the defendant in part discharge of its obligation to the bank, would be contrary, not only to the policy of the law, but also to the plain meaning of its provisions."[48] But the decision was reversed by the United States supreme court, and the weight of authority seems to be to the effect that the fact that the claim thus held does not mature until after the receiver's appointment, does not prevent the defendant from using it as a set-off.[49]

48 Armstrong v. Scott, 36 Fed. 63, citing Venango Nat. Bank v. Taylor, 56 Pa. St. 14; the case was followed in Stephen v. Schuckman, 32 Mo. App. 333. It was reversed by the United States supreme court in Scott v Armstrong, 146 U. S. 499, 13 Sup. Ct. 148, 36 L ed. 1059, after having been disapproved by Yardley v. Clothier, 49 Fed 337, which has been favorably received.

49 See Scott v. Armstrong, 146 U. S. 499, 13 Sup. Ct. 148, 36 L ed. 1059. The case of Colton v. Drovers Perpetual Bldg. & Loan Assn. of Baltimore, 90 Md. 85, 78 Am. St. Rep. 431, 45 Atl. 23, 46 L. R. A. 388, contains such a clear presentation of the principles involved that I quote from it at length—Boyd, J.: "But it is said on behalf of the appellants that, inasmuch as the note fell due after the appointment of the first receiver, he took it free from all equities, just as a *bona fide* purchaser would have done, and that a claim in favor of the bank which did not mature until in the hands of the receiver is not subject to a set-off by a claim which existed against the bank before the receiver's rights accrued, in short, that in one case the debt is due by the bank to the customer, and in the other by the customer to the receiver. If that were strictly correct, there would be some ground for the contention, for if, for example, the appellee had purchased some property from the receiver, it would not be permitted to set off its claim against such indebtedness to the receiver, for it would thereby not only obtain an unwarranted preference over other creditors, but it would prevent a proper settlement of the involved estate, and, moreover, they would not be mutual claims. But when the receiver was appointed, he took the assets of the bank, and among those assets was this note. It was a debt already incurred by the appellee and the bank. Although there are some authorities to the contrary, the great weight of authority is to the effect that the fact that the claim thus held by the receiver does not mature until after his appointment does not prevent a defendant from using his claim as a set-off." Among other decisions

§ 189. **Set-off Against Corporation Receiver, in Suit Against Stockholders.**—In the case of a receiver of an insolvent corporation, suing in behalf of its creditors to enforce the liability of the stockholders, the defendant cannot set off a claim that is good against the corporation only.[50] Where the action was for their unpaid subscription the court said: "They are debtors to the full amount subscribed by them, and cannot be allowed to appropriate any part of the fund belonging to the other creditors till their liability has been paid."[51] And where a stockholder was indebted to the corporation for misappropriation of funds, and the receiver had a surplus to divide among the stockholders, he was allowed to set off the amount due the corporation against the distributive share of the stockholder.[52] But where

are Berry v. Brett, 6 Bosw. 627; Scott v. Armstrong, 146 U. S. 499, 13 Sup. Ct. 148, 36 L. ed. 1059; Platt v. Bently, 11 Am. Law Reg., N. S., 171; In re Hatch, 155 N. Y. 401, 50 N. E. 49, 40 L. R. A. 664; Northampton Bank v. Balliet, 8 Watts & S. 311, 42 Am. Dec. 297; Aldrich v. Campbell, 4 Gray, 284; Smith v. Spingler, 83 Mo. 408; McCagg v. Woodman, 28 Ill. 84; Armstrong v. Warner, 49 Ohio St. 376, 31 N. E. 877, 17 L. R. A. 466; Yardley v. Clothier, 2 C. C. A. 349, 51 Fed. 506, 17 L. R. A. 462; Skiles v. Houston, 110 Pa. St. 254, 2 Atl. 30. See, also, Fera v. Wickham, 135 N. Y. 223, 31 N. E. 1028, 17 L. R. A. 456.

The federal courts have not been harmonious on the question of whether the set-off should be allowed in equity, or at law; their conclusion being influenced largely by statute. The case of Yardley v. Clothier, 49 Fed. 337, contains a full discussion of the question. See, also, Scott v. Armstrong, 146 U. S. 499, 13 Sup. Ct. 148, 36 L. ed. 1059, Armstrong v. Scott, 36 Fed. 63; Louis Snyder's Sons v. Armstrong, 37 Fed. 18; Adams v. Spokane Drug Co., 57 Fed. 888, 23 L. R. A. 334; approving Yardley v. Clothier in preference to Armstrong v. Scott, Hale v. McVay, 31 Ohio St. 231.

50 Sheafe v. Larimer, 79 Fed. 921, distinguishing the cases where set-off is allowed on a bank deposit; Wallace v. Hood, 89 Fed. 11 (refusing to allow a cross-petition for false representation upon the sale of the stock to defendant).

51 Bain v. Clinton Loan Assn., 112 N. C. 248, 17 S. E. 154.

52 Merrill v. Cape Ann. Granite Co., 161 Mass. 212, 36 N. E. 797, 23 L. R. A. 313.

the stockholder had actually advanced money to prevent a burdensome assessment on the stockholders, he was allowed to set it off against his unpaid subscription on the ground that the real assets would not be diminished by such payment.[53]

§ 190. **Statutory Receiver of Insolvent Corporation Represents Its Creditors.**—The general rule that a receiver takes the title of the individual or corporation whose receiver he is, and that any defense which would have been good against the former may be asserted against the latter, is subject to two important and well-recognized exceptions. The first of these relates to receivers of insolvent corporations, appointed under the varying terms of the statutes for the purpose of winding up their affairs. Such a receiver, it is almost universally held, "is to be regarded as the representative, not only of the corporation, having power of asserting its rights, taking its title and subject to its liabilities, but occupies a still broader position, for he represents not only the corporation, but also its creditors; and under his duties as representative of the latter class he is invested with powers and may do acts that could not be done by a mere representative of the corporation."[54]

53 Bausman v. Denney, 73 Fed. 69. See, also, Van Wagoner etc. v. Paterson Gas Light Co., 23 N. J. L. 283.

54 Peabody v. New England Waterworks Co., 184 Ill. 625, 75 Am. St. Rep. 195, 56 N. E. 957, reviewing many cases; Hamor v. Engineering Co., 84 Fed. 393; Bayne v. Brewer Pottery Co., 90 Fed. 754; In re Wilcox etc. Co., 70 Conn. 220, 39 Atl. 163; Franklin Nat. Bank v. Whitehead, 149 Ind. 560, 63 Am. St. Rep. 302, 49 N. E. 592, 39 L. R. A. 725; Farmers' Loan v. Trust Co. v. Minneapolis etc. Works, 35 Minn. 543, 29 N. W. 349; Minnesota Thresher Mfg. Co. v. Langdon, 44 Minn. 37, 46 N. W. 310; Alexander v. Relfe, 74 Mo. 516, 9 Mo. App. 133; Werner v. Murphy, 60 Fed. 769, reviewing New Jersey cases; Mechanics' Nat. Bank v. Pennsylvania Steel Co., 57 N. J. L. 336, 30 Atl. 545; Gillett v. Moody, 3 N. Y. 479; Curtis v. Leavitt, 15 N. Y. 45 (a leading case); Pittsburgh Carbon Co. v. McMillan, 119

Since he stands before the court invested with all the rights and equities of the creditors of the insolvent corporation, it is especially his duty to avoid any act of the corporation committed in fraud of those rights and equities.[55] "It is of no importance, so far as the present discussion is concerned, whether such agent of the law takes the technical title to the debtor's property, or takes only the possession of it. In either case he is the sole agent, through whom, and through whom alone, as a general rule, the rights of creditors can be protected and enforced; and, in protecting and enforcing those rights, he is the representative of creditors, and not of the debtor"; and this is especially true where the statute suspends the rights of the creditors to attach or levy upon the corporate property after the appointment of the receiver.[56] Some limitations on these

N. Y. 46, 23 N. E. 530, 7 L. R. A. 46; Bien v. Bixby, 18 Misc. Rep. 415, 41 N. Y. Supp. 433; Cheney v. Maumee Cycle Co., 64 Ohio St. 205, 60 N. E. 207; Cole v. Satsop R. R. Co., 9 Wash. 487, 43 Am. St. Rep. 858, 37 Pac. 700. "The effect of the appointment and the seizure of the property by the receiver was to fasten the claims of creditors upon it, and to give that officer control over it for the benefit of creditors; and in this respect his relation to it was, for all practical purposes, the same as that which an assignee would have had. The property thus sequestered was held by the receiver as effectually as an assignee could have held it, or as creditors could have held it by attachment or levy. In no other way than through him could the right of creditors be worked out, and in this aspect of the case he represented the creditors, rather than the debtor": Cheney v. Maumee Cycle Co., 64 Ohio St. 205, 60 N. E. 207, holding that a mortgage of the corporation's land unrecorded before the appointment of the receiver was not a valid lien as against him. To the effect that for the benefit of creditors a receiver may sue the directors for diverting the assets, see Hays v. Pierson (N. J. Eq.), 58 Atl. 728.

55 Werner v. Murphy, 60 Fed. 769 (creditor of the corporation cannot sue to set aside fraudulent conveyance on the mere refusal of the receiver to do so).

56 In re Wilcox etc. Co., 70 Conn. 220, 39 Atl. 163; Farmers' Loan & T. Co. v. Minneapolis etc. Works, 35 Minn 543, 546, 29 N. W. 349. "The pendency of the proceedings disables the creditors to

broad assertions of the receiver's character as representative of the creditors are noticed hereafter.[57]

go on, each in his own behalf, to enforce his claim by action, judgment, execution, and levy. So that, unless all the rights of the creditors can be enforced in this proceeding, unless their right to avoid transfers can be made available by means of it, then it is, to some extent, an obstruction, rather than a remedy, to them."

57 See *post*, chapter on Creditors' Bills. In Republic Life Ins. Co. v. Swigert, 135 Ill. 150, 167, 177, 25 N. E. 680, 685, 688, 12 L. R. A. 328, it was said: "We understand the rule to be, that where a receiver is appointed for the purpose of taking charge of the property and assets of a corporation, he is, for the purpose of determining the nature and extent of his title, regarded as representing only the corporate body itself, and not its creditors or shareholders, being vested by law with the estate of the corporation, and deriving his own title under and through it; and that for purposes of litigation he takes only the rights of the corporation such as could be asserted in its own name, and that upon that basis only can he litigate for the benefit of either shareholders or creditors. . . . But, so far as his powers are derived from a statute, or from a lawful decree of court, and the powers do not involve rights which, at the time of his appointment, were vested in such owners, he is not merely their representative, but is the instrument of the law, and the agent of the court which appointed him. Such right and authority as the law and the court rightfully give him he possesses, and in respect to such right he is not circumscribed and limited by the right which was vested in and available to the owners." See, also, as supporting or tending to support a similar view, Fairbanks v. Farwell, 141 Ill. 354, 30 N. E. 1056; Gottlieb v. Miller, 154 Ill. 44, 39 N. E. 992; Ray v First Nat. Bank, 111 Ky. 377, 63 S. W. 762; Smith v. Johnson, 57 Ohio St. 486, 49 N. E. 693; McLaren v. First Nat. Bank, 76 Wis. 259, 45 N. W. 223 The doctrine of the Illinois courts seems to have been brought into closer accord with that generally prevailing by the later case of Peabody v. New England Waterworks Co., 184 Ill. 625, 75 Am. St. Rep. 195, 56 N. E. 957, *supra*, note 54.

On the general subject of the representative capacity of the corporation receiver, see, also, Porter v. Sabin, 149 U. S. 473, 13 Sup. Ct. 1008, 37 L. ed. 818; Movius v. Lee, 30 Fed. 298; Crandall v. Lincoln, 52 Conn. 73, 52 Am. Rep. 560; Greene v A. & W. Sprague Mfg. Co., 52 Conn. 330; Davenport v. Lines, 72 Conn. 118, 44 Atl. 17; American T. and Sav. Bank v. McGettigan, 152 Ind. 582, 71 Am. St. Rep. 345, 52 N. E. 793 (action by receiver on behalf of creditors not allowed, when not for the benefit of all the creditors); Holden v. Phelps, 135 Mass. 61; Thompson v. Greeley, 107 Mo. 577, 17 S. W 962; Harrington v. Connor, 51 Neb. 214, 70 N. W. 911; Stokes v. New Jersey

§ 191. **Receiver in Supplementary Proceedings, How Far a Representative of Creditors.**—A receiver in proceedings supplemental to execution is also, in some respects, a representative of and trustee for the creditors at whose instance he was appointed,[58] especially for the purpose of attacking conveyances by the debtor made in fraud of their rights.[59] "For this purpose he represents and stands in place of the creditor, and prosecutes the action in his behalf. The right to maintain the action does not depend upon any succession by the receiver to the title of the debtor, but upon the equitable right of

Pottery Co., 46 N. J. L. 237 (may attack judgment by confession against the corporation); Williams v. Boice, 38 N. J. Eq. 364 (suit to recover improperly paid dividends); Williams v. McKay, 40 N. J. Eq. 189, 53 Am. Rep 775; Graham Button Co v. Spielman, 50 N. J. Eq 120, 24 Atl. 571; Beebe v. George H Beebe Co., 64 N. J. L. 497, 46 Atl. 168; Southard v. Benner, 72 N. Y. 424, Whittlesey v. Delaney, 73 N. Y. 571 (may sue to set aside collusive judgment); Attorney-General v. Guardian M. L Ins Co., 77 N. Y. 272 (is exclusive representative of creditors, and may enjoin their separate actions to avoid the corporation's fraudulent transfers); Stonebridge v. Perkins, 141 N. Y. 1, 35 N. E. 980; Mason v. Henry, 152 N. Y. 529, 46 N. E. 837; Osgood v. Laytin, 3 Keyes, 521 (may recover illegal dividends, and enjoin separate suits of creditors for that purpose); Powers v. C. H. Hamilton Paper Co., 60 Wis. 23, 18 N. W. 20.

58 Bostwick v. Menck, 40 N. Y. 383, Porter v. Williams, 9 N. Y. 142, 59 Am. Dec. 519.

59 See Hill v Western & A. R. Co., 86 Ga. 284, 12 S. E. 635; Farmers' Loan & T. Co. v. Minn. E. & M. Works, 35 Minn. 543, 29 N. W. 349 (may avoid invalid chattel mortgage); Walsh v. Byrnes, 39 Minn. 527, 40 N. W. 831; Miller v. Mackenzie, 29 N. J. Eq. 291; Bergen v. Little, 41 N. J. Eq. 18, 2 Atl. 614; Boid v. Dean, 48 N. J. Eq. 193, 21 Atl. 618; Walsh v. Rosso, 59 N. J. Eq. 123, 44 Atl. 708, Porter v. Williams, 9 N. Y. 142, 59 Am. Dec. 519 (a leading case); Stephens v Perrine, 143 N. Y. 476, 39 N. E. 11 (may avoid invalid chattel mortgage); Stephens v. Meriden Britannia Co., 160 N. Y 178, 73 Am St Rep. 678, 54 N. E. 781 (his right of action is equitable, not legal); Reynolds v. Aetna Life Ins. Co., 160 N. Y. 635, 55 N. E. 305, affirming 28 App. Div. 591, 51 N. Y. Supp. 446 (may reach amounts due on insurance policies, concealed by debtor); Hedges v. Polhemus, 9 Misc. Rep. 680, 30 N. Y. Supp. 556 (may avoid chattel mortgage); Pender v. Mallett, 123 N. C. 57, 31 S. E. 351.

the creditor to have set aside a conveyance which as to him is invalid, but which is effectual as a cloud to prevent the application of the property to the satisfaction of his debt. There is no need that the receiver take possession of the property for this purpose, nor that he be in any way invested with the title."[60] If the property fraudulently transferred has been sold by the transferee, the receiver may, in the right of the creditor, follow the fund or proceeds of the sale into the hands of any person not a *bona fide* owner or holder thereof.[61] But there is no statute and no rule of law which entitles him to sue for anything that does not belong or has not belonged to the debtor; he is not the representative of the creditor to enforce a cause of action to recover damages for a conspiracy between the judgment debtor and others to prevent the collection of the debt;[62] or to enforce a resulting trust created by statute in favor of creditors, in the case where the debtor pays the purchase price of land and causes the title to be conveyed to another.[63] Further, it should be noted that a receiver in supplementary proceedings, like a receiver in a creditor's bill in favor of particular creditors, is not a trustee for the benefit of all the creditors, but only for the benefit of those in whose behalf he is appointed.[64] His primary duty is to apply

60 Dunham v. Byrnes, 36 Minn. 106, 30 N. W. 402; Wright v. Nostrand, 94 N. Y. 32, 43.

61 Mandeville v. Avery, 124 N. Y. 376, 21 Am. St. Rep. 678, 26 N. E. 951.

62 Ward v. Petrie, 57 N. Y. 301, 68 Am. St. Rep. 790, 51 N. E. 1002 (see this case for an instructive summary of the rights and remedies of receivers in supplementary proceedings in New York).

63 Since in such case the trust is construed to result not *through* the debtor to the creditors, but directly to the creditors: Underwood v Sutcliffe, 77 N. Y. 58.

64 Young v. Clapp, 147 Ill. 176, 32 N. E. 187, 35 N. E. 372; Russell v. Chicago T. & S. Bank, 139 Ill 538, 17 L. R. A. 345, 29 N.

the funds which he realizes from the property of the debtor in satisfaction of the judgments which he was appointed to enforce, and no others.[65] He is "clothed with power to set aside transfers fraudulent as against the demands represented by him, only to an extent sufficient to satisfy such demands and costs."[66]

E. 37; Bostwick v. Menck, 40 N. Y. 383; Goddard v. Stiles, 90 N. Y. 199.

65 Young v. Clapp, 147 Ill. 176, 32 N. E. 187, 35 N. E. 372; Bostwick v. Menck, 40 N. Y. 383; Gifford v. Rising, 59 Hun, 42, 12 N. Y. Supp. 428.

66 Bostwick v. Menck, 40 N. Y. 383.

CHAPTER VII.

RECEIVER'S RELATION TO PENDING SUITS; AND WHEN IS HE A NECESSARY PARTY.

ANALYSIS.

§ 192. Substitution of Receiver as Plaintiff in Pending Actions; Effect of His Appointment on Pending Actions.—Authority may be found to the effect that the appointment of a receiver with the right to sue deprives the principal of the right to maintain actions, and therefore that pending proceedings abate by the appointment of a receiver.[1] But the tendency of modern decisions is in favor of the more reasonable rule that the

1 Boston etc. Co v. Montana Ore Purchasing Co, 24 Mont. 142, 60 Pac. 990, where the court says at page 991: "The necessary effect of clothing the receiver with power to sue was to deprive the plaintiff for the time being of like power. We have been cited to no case or text-book announcing the contrary rule, and have been unable to find any." To the same effect are the cases of Idaho Gold Reduction Co. v. Croghan, 6 Idaho, 471, 56 Pac. 164, Kokomo etc. Ry. Co. v. Pittsburg etc. Ry. Co., 25 Ind. App. 335, 58 N. E. 211; Davis v. Ladoga Creamery Co., 128 Ind. 222, 27 N. E. 494. All of these cases rest upon the text authority of Judge Thompson in § 6900 of his Commentaries on the Law of Corporations. The only authority which the learned author cites (Milwaukee Mutual Fire Ins. Co. v. The Sentinel Co., 81 Wis. 207, 51 N. W. 440, 15 L. R. A. 627), was a case holding that a dissolved corporation could not continue an action for libel pending before its dissolution.

appointment of the receiver has no effect upon pending actions, unless indeed the plaintiff in such action has been restrained from prosecuting the action by the court appointing the receiver, or, if a corporation, has been dissolved by a final decree.[2] A general injunctive order, however, will not, under this latter view, be construed as applying to pending actions.[3] Even the facts that a corporation is insolvent and that winding-up proceedings have been instituted in which a receiver has been appointed, do not prevent the action from continuing in the name of the corporation. The name is a mere shell, and the recovery, of course, will be for the benefit of those whom the receiver represents.[4] In cases of pending actions, of course, a receiver who is vested with the *choses in action* of the principal may be substituted as plaintiff, and such is doubtless the better practice. But the failure to substitute him is, at most, only a formal defect, and under the provisions of the codes, notwithstanding a change in interest, the action may be continued in the name of the original party.[5] Of course if the original party ceases to exist, as in case of the final dissolution of a corporation, actions begun by such party perish with it.[6]

§ 193. Substitution of Receiver as Defendant in Pending Actions.—The effect of an appointment of a receiver of

2 Hunt v. Columbia Ins. Co., 55 Me. 290, 92 Am. Dec. 592; Phoenix Warehousing Company v. Badger, 67 N. Y. 294, 299; Sigua Iron Co. v. Brown, 33 Misc. Rep. 50, 68 N. Y. Supp. 141; Warner v. Imbeau, 63 Kan 415, 65 Pac. 648.

3 Sigua Iron Co. v. Brown, 33 Misc. Rep. 50, 68 N. Y. Supp. 141.

4 High on Receivers, § 258; Warner v. Imbeau, 63 Kan. 415, 65 Pac. 648.

5 Warner v. Imbeau, 63 Kan. 415, 65 Pac. 648; Vanderhorst Brewing Co. v. Amrhine, 98 Md. 406, 56 Atl. 833.

6 Milwaukee Mutual Fire Ins. Co. v. The Sentinel Co., 81 Wis. 207, 51 N. W. 440, 15 L. R. A. 627; National Bank v. Colby, 21 Wall. 609, 22 L. ed. 687.

a defendant's property is very different from the effect of the appointment of a receiver of the plaintiff's property. In the case of the plaintiff, it is always proper for the receiver to be substituted where vested with the right to sue, though sometimes, as has been seen, not necessary. But in the case of the receiver appointed for defendants, it is sometimes not proper to substitute the receiver. As the ordinary chancery receiver is not vested with title to the property, there is no change of ownership demanding a substitution in such cases, and as the appointment of such receiver is by no means equivalent to a dissolution, in cases of corporate receivers, there is no abatement of pending actions.[7] Such actions may therefore continue against the original defendant notwithstanding the receiver's appointment. But if the effect of the proceeding disturb the receiver's possession of property, it is clear that he must be made a party under leave of court.[8] Or if the receiver be appointed upon the statutory dissolution of a corporation, it is plain that pending actions abate, and can be con-

7 Decker v. Gardner, 124 N. Y. 334, 26 N. E. 814, 11 L. ed. 480. In this case, an action of trespass was pending against a corporation before the appointment of the receiver *pendente lite;* upon leave of court the receiver was substituted, and afterwards moved for a dismissal of the action on the ground that he was not the proper party, but that the corporation continued to be the proper party defendant. The court dismissed the action, and in a somewhat elaborate opinion discusses the distinction between the receiver *pendente lite* and the receiver on dissolution of the corporation. In Hunt v. Columbia Ins. Co., 55 Me. 290, 296, 92 Am. Dec. 592, Barrows, J., says "Like the apocalyptic church in Sardis, when its existence was recognized and it was addressed in the language of reproof by the apostle, though in some sort it may be said to be dead, 'it has a name to live'; and for the furtherance of justice it is best to 'strengthen the things that are ready to die' ": Griffith v Burlingame, 18 Wash. 429, 51 Pac. 1059; Kelley v. U. P. R. Co., 58 Kan. 161, 48 Pac. 843, with which compare Scannell v. Felton, 57 Kan. 468, 46 Pac 948

8 Calhoun v. Lanoux, 127 U. S. 634, 8 Sup. Ct. 1345, 32 L. ed. 297.

tinued, if at all, only against the receiver, who can be sued, in general, only by leave of court.[9] Nothing short of an actual dissolution, however, abates actions already pending; the mere commencement of winding-up proceedings and the appointment of a receiver *pendente lite* does not have that result.[10] If a corporation be dissolved, actions against it fall, unless expressly reserved by the decree of dissolution, and the plaintiffs in such actions must seek their relief in the administration proceedings in the court granting the order of dissolution.[11] The receiver, by appearing and defending without leave of court, or where he is not a proper

9 Nelson v. Hubbard, 96 Ala. 245, 11 South. 428; Rogers v. Haines, 96 Ala. 586, 11 South. 651; Combes v. Keyes, 89 Wis. 297, 46 Am. St. Rep. 839, 62 N. W. 89, 27 L. R A. 369; Toledo etc. Co. v. Beggs, 85 Ill 80, 28 Am. Rep. 613; People v Knickerbocker Life Ins. Co., 106 N Y. 619, 13 N. E. 447; Morgan v. New York Nat. B. & L. Assn., 73 Conn. 151, 46 Atl. 877; Wilcox v. Continental L. Ins. Co., 56 Conn. 468, 16 Atl. 244; Pendleton v. Russell, 144 U. S. 640, 12 Sup. Ct. 743, 36 L. ed. 574; National Bank v. Colby, 21 Wall. 609, 22 L. ed. 687; Gray v. Taylor (N. J.), 44 Atl. 668. But where in the prior action the court has taken possession of the *res* by its receiver, a subsequent dissolution of the corporation does not hinder the first court from rendering a valid decree: Leadville Coal Co. v. McCreery, 141 U. S. 475, 12 Sup. Ct. 28, 35 L. ed. 824.

10 Page v. Supreme Lodge K. & L. of P., 161 Mass. 584; Warner v Imbeau, 63 Kan. 415, 65 Pac. 648. But the receiver *pendente lite* in winding-up proceedings may have the prosecution of such actions enjoined, for the corporation having no assets and no means of defense, it is proper that the claims should be adjudicated by the court administering its estate: Morton v. Stone Harbor Imp. Co. (N. J.), 44 Atl. 875. A recent writer (Alderson on Receivers, p. 510) suggests that this case is in direct conflict with another decision of the same court in the same volume, Gray v. Taylor (N. J.), 44 Atl. 668. The latter case holds that the dissolution of a foreign corporation by a decree in the court of its domicile abates pending actions everywhere, but holds that the particular action was exempted from the decree of dissolution. In the *Morton* case there was not yet a decree of dissolution, though proceedings looking to that end were instituted. It is not perceived that any inconsistency exists between the two decisions.

11 Gray v. Taylor (N. J.), 44 Atl. 668.

party, cannot bind the fund, and the judgment against him will be without effect.[12]

§ 194. **Intervention by Receivers.**—The receiver's right to intervene in pending actions stands on a different footing both from his right to be substituted as plaintiff and from his right to be substituted as defendant in pending actions. While he may be substituted as plaintiff in every case, and while he may be made a defendant only in cases where the action disturbs his possession or where he has title in trust for creditors and others, the right to intervene stands on a middle ground. Such intervention is allowed where the receiver has an interest in the controversy which it is deemed expedient that he should protect, and is largely a matter for the exercise of the court's discretion.[13]

§ 195. **Effect of Change of Receivers on Pending Actions.** "So long as the property of the corporation remains in the custody of the court and is administered through the agency of a receiver, such receivership is continuous and uninterrupted until the court relinquishes its hold upon the property, although its *personnel* may be subject to repeated changes. Actions against the receiver are, in law, actions against the receivership, and the funds in the hands of the receiver, and his contracts, misfeasances, negligences and liabilities are official and not personal and judgments against him are payable

12 Pendleton v. Russell, 144 U. S. 640, 12 Sup. Ct. 743, 36 L. ed. 574. But compare Smith v. United States Express Co., 135 Ill. 279, 25 N. E 527, Gray v. Taylor (N. J.), 44 Atl. 668.

13 Andrews v. Steel City Bank, 77 Mo. 342, State v. Bank of Ottumwa, 76 Mo. 715; Hedrick v. McElroy (Iowa), 76 N. W. 716, Bowen v. Needles Nat. Bank, 76 Fed. 176. A receiver who is merely a stake-holder cannot intervene. National Park Bank v. Goddard, 65 Hun, 626, 20 N. Y. Supp. 526, 984.

only from the funds in his hands."[14] Accordingly, where successive receivers are appointed, proceedings pending against one should be continued in the name of the successor. The liability continues only so long as the court retains the fund, and therefore the discharge of the receiver, and the turning over of the fund or *res* to the purchaser, terminates the receiver's liability.[15] In case of the termination of the proceedings, it is therefore usual for the court to allow a certain time within which intervening petitions against the receiver may be heard before the fund or *res* is finally surrendered.[16] An interesting extension of equitable principles has made the railroad company to which the property has been surrendered on the termination of the receivership liable for the receiver's wrongs to the extent of the betterments.[17]

§ 196. **When is Receiver a Necessary Party.**—Where the right of action is vested in the receiver by the order of appointment, he is, of course, the only necessary party plaintiff.[18] And where he would be affected directly

14 McNulta v. Lochridge, 141 U. S. 327, 332, 12 Sup. Ct. 11, 35 L. ed. 796; Guaranty Co. of N. D. v. Hanway, 104 Fed. 369, 373, 44 C. C. A. 312; Robinson v. Mills, 25 Mont. 391, 65 Pac. 114. If the second receiver is appointed to control only a portion of the fund controlled by the first, he is not liable for his predecessor's wrongs. Jones v. Schlapback, 81 Fed. 274.

15 Archambeau v. Platt, 173 Mass. 249, 53 N. E. 816; Kansas & G. S. R. R. Co. v. Dorough, 72 Tex. 111, 10 S. W. 711.

16 Such was the decree in Texas & Pacific Ry. v. Johnson, 151 U. S 81, 14 Sup. Ct. 250, 38 L ed. 81; and compare Texas & Pacific Ry. v. Bloom, 164 U. S. 639, 17 Sup. Ct. 216, 41 L. ed. 580; Fidelity Ins. Co. v. Norfolk etc. R. Co., 88 Fed. 815.

17 Texas & Pacific R. Co. v. Bloom, 164 U. S. 636, 17 Sup. Ct. 216, 41 L. ed. 580; Bartlett v. Cicero etc. Co., 177 Ill. 68, 69 Am. St. Rep. 206, 52 N. E. 339.

18 Porter v. Sabin, 149 U. S. 473, 13 Sup. Ct. 1008, 37 L. ed. 815, where a receiver of a manufacturing company has been appointed by a state court, no action can be maintained against its officers for

by the decree he must be made a party defendant. Thus, where a railroad company had its property placed in the hands of a receiver *pendente lite* appointed in foreclosure proceedings, it was held that he was the only necessary party defendant in a bill seeking specific performance of a contract made by the company.[19] So a partnership receiver is a necessary party defendant in an action to foreclose a mortgage given by the partnership.[20] But where the receiver is appointed to hold property in proceedings which do not look toward the ultimate disposition of the property, he is not a necessary party in actions subsequently commenced.[21] And of course where a contract is made by a receiver, say of a partnership, he alone need be sued, and the surviving partner need not be joined.[22] A receiver appointed by the comptroller of the currency to take charge of assets

fraudulent misappropriation of its funds by stockholders. The right of action is in the receiver, and even though the state court has refused to allow him to sue or to be made a party to the bill, his absence is not excused, cf. Brinkerhoff v. Bostwick, 88 N. Y. 52, Ackerman v. Halsey, 37 N. J. Eq. 356; Davis v. Gray, 16 Wall. 203, 21 L. ed. 447.

19 Express Co. v. Railroad Co., 99 U. S. 191, 25 L. ed. 319; Southern Mutual B. & L. Assn. v. Andrews, 122 Ala. 601, 26 South. 113.

20 Kirkpatrick & Corning v. Corning, 38 N. J. Eq. 234, Kirkpatrick v. McElroy, 41 N. J. Eq. 539, 7 Atl. 647; Tyson v. Applegate, 40 N. J. Eq. 305; Comer v Bray, 83 Ala. 217, 3 South. 554

21 Thus, where a receiver was appointed to take charge of mortgaged property and collect the rent thereof, he is not a necessary party to a bill subsequently filed to foreclose a mortgage: Heffron v. Gage, 149 Ill. 182, 36 N. E. 569; Keeney v. Insurance Co., 71 N. Y. 396, 27 Am. Rep. 60; Calhoun v. Lanoux, 127 U. S. 634, 8 Sup. Ct. 1345, 32 L ed. 297. A receiver appointed in an action for an accounting need not be made a party in actions subsequently brought by the creditors: Heath v. Missouri etc. Ry. Co., 83 Mo. 617; Ohio & M. Ry. Co. v. Russell, 115 Ill. 52, 3 N. E. 561; Paddack v. Staley, 13 Colo. App. 363, 58 Pac. 363.

22 Painter v. Painter, 138 Cal. 231, 94 Am. St. Rep. 47, 71 Pac. 90.

of a national bank is not a judicial officer, and is not a proper party, for example, in an action brought for rent due from the bank.[23]

23 Chemical Nat. Bank of Chicago v. Hartford Deposit, 156 Ill. 522, 41 N. E. 225; Bank of Bethel v. Pahquioque Bank, 14 Wall. 383, 20 L. ed. 840

CHAPTER VIII.

RECEIVERS—MANAGEMENT AND DISPOSITION OF PROPERTY.

ANALYSIS.

§ 197. **In General.**—When a receiver is appointed, and property is committed to him, as such, he becomes the officer and custodian of the court. It is his duty to keep and manage the property according to the directions and orders of the court. The court's orders are the measure of his authority, and he must neither exceed nor ignore them. In managing, he must seek instruction on all matters of importance. If he exceeds his authority, he cannot charge the estate for the expenses incurred thereby; and if his wrong has resulted in loss, he must make good the deficiency.[1]

§ 198. **Discretion Allowed to Managing Receiver.**—While the receiver must, in general, confine his action within the scope of the orders of the court, in many matters of administrative detail he is allowed a discretion.[2] Mere mistakes of judgment in regard to such matters will not be charged against him. In many instances it would be impracticable to apply to the court for instructions; and frequently the questions arising are so numerous that the court could not conveniently consider them.[3] Such action by the receiver is at his own risk, and is

1 Henry v. Henry, 103 Ala. 582, 15 South. 916. And see cases cited in subsequent paragraphs.

2 Continental Trust Co. v. Toledo St. L. & K. C. R. Co., 59 Fed. 514; Cowdrey v. Railroad Co., 1 Woods, 336, Fed. Cas. No. 3293; Harrigan v. Gilchrist, 121 Wis. 127, 99 N. W. 909. "Modern practice permits them to exercise their sound discretion in many matters relating to the care and management of property in their custody, subject to the subsequent approval of the court, which will be given when the officer has acted in good faith, and what he has done appears to have been beneficial to the parties interested": State Central Sav. Bank v. Fanning Ball-Bearing Chain Co., 118 Iowa, 698, 92 N. W. 712.

3 "Doubtless the chancellor has power to retain in his hands the administration of such a trust and to personally direct and order each contract into which the receiver should enter. But it would obviously be impracticable to adopt such a course in running a railroad. To select and employ the necessary subordinates; to fix the term of service and the amount of wages; to contract for and purchase materials and supplies; and to anticipate in these respects the future needs of one of the gigantic corporations by express orders in each case,—would require the whole time of the chancellor and could never have been intended by this legislation. . . . . Whether a power to exercise such discretion would not be assumed to exist in every case, without a special order, need not be considered, for it is clear that the chancellor may accord such discretion-

subject to the subsequent approval of the court.[4] In important matters he should first obtain an order, and then keep strictly within its limits. These rules apply with special force to railway receiverships, where the details are many. Mr. Justice Bradley, of the supreme court of the United States, sitting as circuit judge, stated the rule as follows: "All outlays made by the receiver in good faith, in the ordinary course, with a view to advance and promote the business of the road, and to render it profitable and successful, are fairly within the line of discretion which is necessarily allowed to a receiver intrusted with the management and operation of a railroad in his hands. His duties, and the discretion with which he is invested, are very different from those of a passive receiver, appointed merely to collect and hold moneys due on prior transactions, or rents accruing from houses and lands. And to such outlays in ordinary course may properly be referred, not only the keeping of the road, buildings and rolling stock in repair, but also the providing of such additional accommodations, stock and instrumentalities as the necessities of the business may require."[5]

§ 199. **Duty to Obtain Instructions.**—A receiver should, in all matters of importance not covered by the order of the appointing court, apply to the court for instructions. If he does not, he will be held liable in case the court shall subsequently disapprove of his action.[6] Instruc-

ary power to a receiver by a general order, such as was made in this cause": Vanderbilt v. Little, 43 N. J. Eq. 669, 12 Atl. 188, per Magie, J.

4 State Central Sav. Bank v. Fanning Ball-Bearing Chain Co., 118 Iowa, 698, 92 N. W. 712.

5 Cowdrey v. Railroad Co., 1 Woods, 336, Fed. Cas. No. 3293

6 Braman v. Farmers' Loan etc. Co., 114 Fed. 18, 51 C. C. A. 644; In re Angell, 131 Mich. 345, 91 N. W. 611.

tions must be obtained in the receivership action, and frequently they are given on *ex parte* application.[7] In some instances they may be given by the judge in chambers.[8] The better practice is to require notice when any adverse rights are involved, so that the parties may be heard before an order is given. It has been intimated by a federal court that while an *ex parte* order may be binding upon the receiver, it is not conclusive, and may be set aside in the event that the judge changes his mind.[9] Matters of infinite variety may be determined

7 Free Gold Min. Co. v. Spiers, 136 Cal. 484, 69 Pac. 143 (*ex parte* order directing receiver of mining property to purchase a cyanide plant sustained); Weeks v. Weeks, 106 N. Y. 626, 13 N. E. 96 (court may direct receiver to lease the property, upon *ex parte* application; receiver may make such application although original order is silent on question of leasing). An order made in another action is not binding upon the receiver: Merritt v. Sparling, 88 Hun, 491, 34 N. Y. Supp. 882.

8 State v. Port Royal etc. Ry. Co., 45 S. C. 413, 23 S. E. 363 (by virtue of statute authorizing judges, at chambers, and upon reasonable notice, "to make, direct, and award all such process, commissions and interlocutory orders, rules, and other proceedings whenever the same are not grantable of course according to the rules and practice of the court").

9 Missouri Pac. Ry. Co. v. Texas etc. Ry. Co., 31 Fed. 862 ("If there are parties in interest, and they have their day in court, the advice may be decisive. But, if the matter is *ex parte*, the value of the advice depends largely upon the information and ability of the judge, and is probably binding only on the receivers, for the judge may change his mind on hearing full argument"). In Weeks v. Weeks, 106 N. Y. 626, 13 N. E. 96, Finck, J., said: "The general power of a court to modify or vacate its judgments or orders for fraud or irregularity, or where it has acted inadvertently, or imprudently, is well settled. It is true the law protects the title of a third person, being a *bona fide* purchaser on a sale on an execution under a judgment voidable but not void, although the judgment is subsequently reversed for error. This principle does not, we think, preclude the court from modifying or vacating a summary order made improvidently in the course of an action, although the rights of third persons may be affected thereby. . . . . We think the court was authorized to award indemnity out of the fund arising under the judgment in partition, and that nothing else would satisfy the claims of justice."

by the court on such application. It has been held, however, that no instructions as to the disposition of funds will be given until the funds are in court.[10]

§ 200. **Duty to Collect Assets.**—It is generally one of the first duties of a receiver in the performance of his trust to collect the assets. Here, as in all other matters, he must act under the direction of the court. The means by which he may possess himself of the property—by summary proceedings against parties and by action against others—are discussed at length elsewhere.[11]

§ 201. **Right to Continue Business.**—Unless directed by an order of the court, a receiver has no authority to continue a business. If he does, "it is sufficient to show the inventory and appraisement, and the burden is on him to explain and account for the property."[12] In proper cases, where it is for the best interests of all concerned, the court will direct the receiver to continue with the business.[13] Under such circumstances, much must of necessity be left to the discretion of the officer. Such an order impliedly authorizes him to contract debts and incur liabilities on account of the business.

§ 202. **Executory Contracts.**—Where a receiver is authorized by the court to continue the business, he is im-

10 Strauss v. Carolina Interstate B. & L. Assn., 117 N. C. 308, 53 Am. St. Rep 585, 23 S. E. 450, 30 L. R. A. 693, 118 N. C. 556, 24 S. E. 116.

11 See § 161, and chapter VI, *ante*, chapter XI, *post*.

12 Pangburn v. American Vault, Safe & Lock Co., 205 Pa St. 93, 54 Atl 508.

13 For instances where such orders have been given, see Thornton v. Highland Ave. & B. R. Co., 94 Ala. 353, 10 South. 442; Florence Gas, Electric L. & P. Co. v. Hanby, 101 Ala. 15, 13 South. 343; Rochat v. Gee, 137 Cal. 497, 70 Pac 478; Cake v. Woodbury, 3 App. D. C. 60; Dayton v. Wilkes, 17 How. Pr 510, Smith v. New York Con Stage Co, 18 Abb. Pr. 419. And see the very numerous cases of railway receiverships cited in this chapter.

pliedly directed to complete such unfinished contracts as are for the best interests of the trust. He is not bound to complete contracts of which he disapproves;[14] but he is expected to investigate them and either act according to his own judgment or obtain the direction of the court.[15] "The privilege of the receiver in acting for the best interest of the estate and its creditors not only extends to the right to elect what contracts he will adopt, but also to make the election without at least subjecting the fund required for the satisfaction of existing claims of creditors to a charge for damages."[16]

§ 203. **Existing Leases.**—A receiver is not bound by an existing lease, unless he adopts it.[17] The circumstances authorizing such adoption are similar to those which enable him to take advantage of ordinary existing contracts. He is not bound to elect immediately upon his appointment. Instead, he may take and retain possession for such reasonable time as will enable him to intelligently elect whether the interest of his trust will be best subserved by adopting the lease and making it his own, or by returning the property to the lessor.[18] Ac-

14 Dushane v. Beall, 161 U. S. 516, 16 Sup. Ct. 367, 40 L. ed 791 (*dictum*); Central Trust Co. v East Tennessee Land Co., 79 Fed 19; Wells v. Hartford Manilla Co., 76 Conn. 27, 55 Atl 599; Brown v. Warner, 78 Tex. 543, 22 Am. St. Rep. 67, 14 S. W 1032, 11 L R. A. 394. See, however, Elmira Iron & Steel R. M. Co. v. Erie Ry. Co., 26 N. J. Eq. 284, where the court, by its order, directed that "any person or corporation having a contract with the Erie company shall be at liberty to apply by petition in this suit, or by independent bill, for, and obtain relief and injunction, if entitled thereto, to require the company or the receiver to refrain from violating any such contract."

15 Harrigan v. Gilchrist, 121 Wis. 127, 99 N. W. 909

16 Wells v. Hartford Manilla Co., 76 Conn 27, 55' Atl 599.

17 Dayton Hydraulic Co. v. Felsenthall, 116 Fed. 961, 54 C. C. A. 537; Klein v. W. A. Gavenesch Co., 64 N. J. Eq 50, 53 Atl 196.

18 Carswell v. Trust Co, 74 Fed. 88, 20 C. C. A. 282, Dayton Hydraulic Co. v. Felsenthall, 116 Fed. 961, 54 C. C. A. 537. See, also,

cordingly, a railroad receiver may operate a leased line for a reasonable time in order to ascertain the situation of affairs, and such action will not amount to an adoption of the lease.[19] What is a reasonable time for him to so hold must depend largely upon the circumstances of each case.[20] If he holds the premises for a longer time, continues the business, and does nothing to show an election not to adopt, he will be held to the terms of the lease.[21] Payment of rent is a circumstance to be considered as indicating an adoption, although it is not conclusive.[22] If he elects to adopt a lease, he "becomes vested with the title to the leasehold interest, and a privity of estate is thereby created between the lessor and the receiver, by which the latter becomes liable upon the covenant to pay rent."[23]

§ 204. **Right to Make Contracts.**—Receivers can make only such contracts as the court may previously author-

Johnson v. Lehigh Val. Traction Co., 130 Fed. 932; Tradesman Pub. Co. v. Knoxville C. W. Co., 95 Tenn. 634, 49 Am. St. Rep. 943, 32 S. W. 1097, 71 L. R. A. 593. The same principle applies to a lease of rolling stock: Sunflower Oil Co. v. Wilson, 142 U. S. 313, 12 Sup. Ct. 235, 35 L. ed. 1025; Platt v. Railroad Co., 84 Fed. 535, 28 C. C. A. 488.

19 Quincy, M. & P. R. Co. v. Humphreys, 145 U. S. 82, 12 Sup. Ct. 787, 36 L. ed. 632.

20 Ames v. Union Pac. R. Co., 60 Fed. 967 (sixty-five days reasonable, in railroad lease); Carswell v. Farmers' Loan etc. Co., 74 Fed. 88, 20 C. C. A. 282, 43 U. S. App. 300 (ten months reasonable); Smith v. Goodman, 149 Ill. 75, 36 N. E. 621 (four months).

21 Link Belt Machinery Co. v. Hughes, 174 Ill. 155, 51 N. E. 179. Where the receiver completes the term without any act of disaffirmance, he cannot then repudiate and pay only on the basis of a *quantum meruit*. Spencer v. World's Columbian Exposition, 163 Ill. 117, 45 N. E. 250 (affirming 58 Ill. App. 637).

22 Wells v. Higgins, 132 N. Y. 459, 30 N. E. 861; Commonwealth v. Franklin Ins. Co., 115 Mass. 278 (not an adoption when paid as a compromise).

23 See United States Trust Co. v. Wabash W. Ry. Co., 150 U. S. 299, 14 Sup. Ct. 86, 37 L. ed. 1085.

ize or subsequently approve. As we have already seen, the authority may frequently be inferred from the terms of the order, although not expressly given. Thus, where the order directs a receiver to continue the business, he is impliedly authorized to enter into necessary contracts. A party dealing with him, however, is bound to take notice of any want of authority, and cannot complain if the court sets aside the contract as unauthorized.[24] It has been held, on the other hand, that where the contracts are such as the receiver has discretion to make, and there is nothing to show any excess of authority, the court will not repudiate without providing compensation for loss incurred.[25] And where a contract within the discretion of the receiver has been fully performed, the contractor will not be deprived of the agreed compensation merely because the court regards the contract as improvident, injudicious and unreasonable, unless it appears that the contractor had notice of its improper character.[26] The receiver should not deal with and purchase supplies from another company composed of officials under him.[27]

24 Tripp v. Boardman, 49 Iowa, 410. A receiver appointed to conduct the management of a railroad is bound by a transportation contract made by his freight agent Farmers' Loan etc. Co. v. Northern Pac. R. Co., 120 Fed. 873.

25 Vanderbilt v. Central R. Co., 43 N. J. Eq. 669, 12 Atl. 188; Vanderbilt v. Little, 51 N. J. Eq. 289, 26 Atl. 1025. See State Bank of Virginia v. Domestic S M. Co., 99 Va. 411, 86 Am. St. Rep. 891, 39 S. E. 141.

26 Vanderbilt v. Central R. Co., 43 N. J. Eq. 669, 12 Atl. 188.

27 Clarke v. Central R. & B. Co., 66 Fed. 16 ("Parties owing duties to the railroad by reason of their official relations thereto, and connected therewith, could not be permitted to deal, directly or indirectly, through the form of a company with the receiver, in respect to subjects or articles they might have to sell or contract about. Upon well-settled principles, this could not be tolerated by the court. The dual trust relation occupied by parties in such situations would forbid such transactions.")

§ 205. **Rights in Relation to Employees.**—A receiver authorized by the court to continue the business has power to hire necessary employees.[28] In this he is allowed a wide discretion, and the court, which can know much less about the business than the receiver, will not interfere unless an abuse is shown.[29] This principle applies with special force to a receiver appointed to look after the business of a railroad. In recent years the courts have in several instances been required to pass upon disputes between receivers and employees of railroads, and the right of employees to be heard has been expressly affirmed.[30] The court will not countenance an unreasonable reduction of the salaries of railroad employees;[31]

28 Continental Trust Co. v. Toledo, St. L & K. C. R. Co., 59 Fed. 514, Taylor v. Sweet, 40 Mich. 736.

29 Continental Trust Co. v. Toledo, St. L. & K. C. R. Co., 59 Fed. 514, Taylor v. Sweet, 40 Mich 736.

30 Continental Trust Co. v. Toledo, St. L. & K. C. R. Co., 59 Fed. 514.

31 "The first and supreme duty of a court when it engages in the business of operating a railroad is to operate it efficiently and safely. No pains and no reasonable expense are to be spared in the accomplishment of these ends. Passengers and freight must be transported safely. If passengers are killed or freight lost through the slightest negligence to provide all the means of safety commonly found on first-class roads, the court is morally and legally responsible. An essential and indispensable requisite to the safe and successful operation of the road is the employment of sober, intelligent, experienced, and capable men for that purpose. When a road comes under the management of a court on which the employees are conceded to possess all these qualifications—and that concession is made in the fullest manner here—the court will not, upon light or trivial grounds, dispense with their services or reduce their wages, and when the schedule of wages in force at the time the court assumes the management of the road is the result of a mutual agreement between the company and the employees, which has been in force for years, the court will presume the schedule is reasonable and just, and anyone disputing that presumption will be required to overthrow it by satisfactory proof". Ames v. Union Pac. Ry. Co., 62 Fed. 7, per Caldwell, Cir. J. Where the wages are not excessive merely because of inability of the road to pay dividends or interest: United States Trust Co. v. Omaha & St. L. Ry. Co., 63 Fed. 737.

but where the reduction is reasonable, and appears to be necessary, the receiver will be authorized to take such action.[32] It will generally refuse to interfere with the receiver's action in enforcing rules of long standing, or in dealing with strikers.[33] When a faithful employee has been injured in the service of the receiver, without any fault of either party, the court may order that he be paid wages for the time during which he is actually incapacitated.[34]

32 It is said that the employees must show an abuse of the discretion allowed the receiver in order to be given relief. In the following cases the court held the reductions reasonable, under the circumstances: Continental Trust Co. v. Toledo, St. L. & K. C R. Co., 59 Fed. 514; Thomas v. Cincinnati, N. O. & T. P. Ry Co., 62 Fed. 17.

33 Thus, in Platt v. Philadelphia & R. R Co, 65 Fed. 660, the court refused to restrain a receiver from enforcing a rule prohibiting employees from becoming members of labor unions. In Booth v Brown, 62 Fed. 794, the court refused to direct a receiver to re-employ men who had engaged in a sympathetic strike

34 "To pay the intervener for his lost time is a gratuity, of course, there being no legal liability on the part of the receivers. The view of the circuit judge doubtless was that the receivers, as officers of the court, should be required to act toward their employees as persons of ordinary humanity and right feeling would do under similar circumstances toward their employees If an individual acting for himself, or even as head of the corporation, who has a faithful employee who is injured, although without any fault on the part of the employer or the other employees, the injured employee being himself free from fault, the employer, if actuated by proper feeling, would feel disposed to at least allow the injured person compensation for his lost time". Thomas v. East Tennessee, V. & G. Ry. Co, 60 Fed. 7, per Newman, D. J. It is certainly a novelty to rest such a doctrine upon humanity. Officers of corporations, and receivers as well, are not permitted to use funds for merely charitable purposes. It is submitted that the true reason for authorizing such action is that a receiver, as well as a corporation, can obtain better service from all of his employees by treating liberally those injured in his service. Wages were allowed injured employees in Missouri Pac. R. Co. v. Texas & P. R. Co., 33 Fed. 701, and upon another application in the same receivership in 41 Fed. 319. To the effect that only faithful employees are entitled to such consideration, see Thomas v. East Tennessee, V. & G. Ry. Co., 60 Fed. 7.

§ 206. Right to Employ Attorneys.—A receiver has a right to employ counsel to advise him as to the management of the property placed in his hands, and as to his duties in the premises.[35] The compensation of such attorneys is fixed by the court, and is not governed by agreement between the parties.[36] In general, the receiver is allowed to select his own counsel, subject, however, to certain limitations. He is not allowed to select an attorney of one of the parties to the proceeding in which he was appointed, when the interests in-

[35] Hubbard v. Camperdown Mills, 25 S. C. 496, 1 S. E. 5 "First, it is for necessary legal assistance that allowance may be made. A trustee has no authority to employ attorneys, at the expense of the estate, to perform the ordinary duties of the trust or office which any ordinarily competent business man is presumed to be capable of performing. Those are his duties, and he is paid for them. It is for services requiring special legal skill that he will be allowed counsel fees To illustrate: He may have an attorney to obtain for him a necessary order of court to sell a stock of goods, but he can carry out the order as well as the attorney. . . . . His acceptance of the trust presupposes that he is capable of performing all such duties, and, if he employs attorneys to advise and assist him in performing them, he must do so at his own expense. So, also, no legal skill is required in insuring and repairing storehouses, and in renting them out and collecting rents. Any business man, also, can assess and pay taxes. If a demand is made upon the receiver, of questionable legality, he may have legal advice and aid in reference to it. If he has a demand upon another, whose legality is questioned, or which requires legal aid to enforce it, he may have an attorney": Henry v. Henry, 103 Ala. 582, 15 South. 916. See, also, Olson v. State Bank, 72 Minn. 320, 75 N. W. 378.

[36] "It may be very proper for a receiver to have counsel to aid and advise him concerning legal questions arising in his management of the estate, but his contract for a term of employment or a rate of compensation, from the very nature of his office, must be subject to the power of the court to conclude the one or to disallow the other. And questions of this nature belong to the court controlling and settling the receivership. The right of the attorney to charge the property in court with his fee does not arise from the mere contract with the receivers": International & G. N. R. Co. v. Herndon, 11 Tex. Civ. App. 465, 33 S. W. 377. See, also, Hickey v. Parrot Silver & Copper Co. (Mont.), 79 Pac 698.

volved are likely to be conflicting.[37] Where the receiver is not acting adversely to the parties, and there is no conflict, he may select such an attorney.[38] Where a receiver is himself an attorney, he is still entitled to aid of counsel; and if he acts as his own attorney, he is not entitled to any additional compensation therefor.[39]

§ 207. **Right to Make Repairs, Improvements, etc.**—A receiver is appointed to preserve the property pending the litigation, and consequently, he will be authorized to make such repairs as are necessary to keep the property from deterioration.[40] The extent of repairs will depend largely upon the nature of the business, and whether it is being actively carried on by the receiver. In many matters of minor importance he is allowed to

37 Veith v. Ress, 60 Neb. 52, 82 N. W. 116; Blair v. St. Louis, H. & K. R R. Co, 20 Fed. 348. In this last case the court proceeded to say: "It seems that one who accepts the office of receiver under an appointment of this court ought to find some competent attorney of this court, and responsible to it, to aid him with legal advice if needed. If the bar of this circuit is so poor in ability or integrity as to have no member thereof fit for the desired position, then it might be well to seek elsewhere for needed aid. This court is not prepared to make even impliedly such a reflection on the bar of this circuit, nor will it grant a motion which seeks to make one, however able, but who is not a member of this bar, or has just come here with respect to this case mainly, so far as I know, the appointee of this court as attorney and counselor of its officers, nor will it sanction by its appointment the introduction from abroad of anyone, especially a kinsman of the receiver, through the latter's solicitation, under circumstances stated, to fill a position which others long known to the court are, to say the least, equally able to fill."

38 Smith v. New York Con. Stage Co., 18 Abb. Pr. 419; United States v. Late Corp. of Church etc., 6 Utah, 9, 21 Pac. 516.

39 Olson v. State Bank, 72 Minn. 320, 75 N. W. 378.

40 Wallace v. Loomis, 97 U. S. 146, 24 L. ed. 895; Union Trust Co. v. Illinois Midland Ry. Co., 117 U. S. 434, 6 Sup. Ct. 809, 29 L. ed. 963; Hoover v. Montclair & Greenwood Lake Ry. Co., 29 N. J. Eq. 4; Karn v. Rorer Iron Co., 86 Va. 754, 11 S. E. 431.

use his discretion.[41] He is sometimes permitted to make improvements and additions, such as the completion of a new line of railroad already begun;[42] but generally the court hesitates to grant such authority. The principle upon which these are allowed is that they are essential to the profitable enjoyment of the estate and inure to its permanent betterment. If not essential, the court will not speculate upon the probable result.[43] Under circumstances showing the great desirability, the court may authorize the receiver to add to an existing line by leasing another.[44]

§ 208. **Right to Lease Property.**—The court may authorize its receiver to lease certain of the property in

41 Cowdrey v. Railroad Co., 1 Woods, 336, Fed. Cas. No. 3293.

42 Wallace v Loomis, 97 U. S. 146, 24 L. ed. 895; Union Trust Co v. Illinois Midland Ry. Co, 117 U S. 434, 6 Sup. Ct 809, 29 L. ed 963; Kennedy v. St. Paul & P. R. Co, 5 Dill. 519, Fed Cas. No. 7707; Stanton v. Alabama & C R. Co, 2 Woods, 506, Fed. Cas. No. 13,296; Jefferson v Edrington, 53 Ark. 545, 14 S. W. 99 In Wallace v. Loomis, *supra*, a receiver was appointed "with power to put the road and property in repair, and to complete any uncompleted portions thereof, and to procure rolling stock, and to manage and operate the road to the best advantage, so as to prevent the property from further deteriorating, and to save and preserve it for the benefit and interest of the first mortgage bondholders, and all others having an interest therein."

43 Hand v. Savannah & C. R. Co., 10 S. C. 406. See, also, Pueblo Traction & Electric Co. v. Allison, 30 Colo. 337, 70 Pac. 424.

44 "A court of equity having in charge the mortgaged property of a railroad company, is authorized to do all acts that may be necessary within its corporate power to preserve the property, and to give to it additional value, not only for the benefit of the lien creditors, but also for the benefit of the company. . . . . Any act, it would seem, necessary for the protection and preservation of the property, is a legitimate and proper act, and whatever is manifestly appropriate to such preservation and protection, or to the enhancement of the value of the property, not in excess of the powers of the corporation, will always be upheld and enforced by the courts": Gibert v. Washington City, V. M & G. S R. Co, 33 Gratt. 586.

his possession.[45] The court "should act with great circumspection, and see to it that the lease is not given for such a period of time as will needlessly prolong the litigation or endanger the rights of any parties thereto. If need be, clauses should be inserted in such leases reserving to the court the power to cancel them whenever it is deemed expedient to do so."[46] If no such right is reserved, the lessee is entitled to damages upon termination.[47]

§ 209 **Sales—In General.**—When the interests of the parties demand it, or make it desirable, the court may order a receiver to sell the whole or a part of the property What facts are sufficient to induce the court to make such an order must of necessity vary with the circumstances of each particular case. When it appears that affairs are rapidly growing worse under the receiver's management, and a majority of those interested believe a sale to be desirable, it may be ordered.[48] On the other hand, when the condition of the property is such that an immediate sale will result in great loss, and where the purposes of the receivership have not been accomplished, the order will be refused.[49] An order which directs a receiver to sell all the real estate in his hands has been held sufficient to authorize him to sell any particular piece.[50]

45 Mercantile Trust Co. v. Missouri, K. & T. Ry. Co, 41 Fed 8, 11; Farmers' Loan etc. Co. v. Eaton, 114 Fed. 14, 51 C C. A. 640.

46 Farmers' Loan etc. Co. v. Eaton, 114 Fed. 14, 51 C. C. A. 640.

47 Farmers' Loan etc. Co. v. Eaton, 114 Fed. 14, 51 C. C. A. 640. See, also, McAnally v. Glidden, 30 Ind. App. 22, 65 N E. 291.

48 First Nat. Bank v. Shedd, 121 U. S. 74, 7 Sup. Ct. 807, 30 L. ed. 877. A sale may be ordered without a right of redemption: Denny v. Broadway Nat. Bank, 118 Ga. 221, 44 S. E 982.

49 Bibber-White Co. v. White River Val. Electric R. Co., 110 Fed. 473.

50 Barron v. Mullin, 21 Minn. 374.

§ 210. **Sale is Subject to Confirmation.**—A sale by a receiver is a judicial sale, and, as a general rule, is subject to confirmation by the court.[51] In many states the proceedings are regulated entirely by statute, and the validity of the sale depends upon a strict adherence to the statutory provisions. "The rule is almost universal that, at a sale by a master or receiver under an order or decree in equity which contemplates a subsequent report and a confirmation of the sale, a bidder becomes a purchaser when the officer announces the sale to him. Thereafter he may be compelled to complete his purchase, and pay the price which he offered."[52] Mere inadequacy of the price is not, in general, sufficient to authorize a refusal of confirmation, unless it be gross.[53] And where the consideration is fair, it has been held that confirmation will not be refused merely to let in a

51 It has been held that such a sale is impliedly subject to confirmation or rejection: Patterson v. Patterson Dry Goods Co., 207 Pa. St. 252, 56 Atl. 442.

52 Files v. Brown, 124 Fed. 133, 59 C. C. A. 403, per Sanborn, Cir. J.

53 Files v. Brown, 124 Fed. 133, 59 C. C. A. 403. The rule is stated by Grey, V. C, in Porch v. Agnew Co. (N. J. Eq.), 57 Atl. 726, as follows: "The rule is settled that mere inadequacy of price is not of itself sufficient ground for refusing confirmation of a judicial sale. The variance between the bids reported and the fair market value must be so great as to bring the court to the opinion that serious injustice would be done by a confirmation—so great, indeed, that the purchaser himself could not fairly expect the court to ratify the sale, which he was notified it must do, in order that his bid should be finally accepted." In this case the property was shown to be worth probably four times the amount of the bids. This was held to be an inadequacy so gross as to warrant a refusal of confirmation, but the court made a condition that a bond should be filed assuring the presentation of substantially higher bids. In Strickland v. National Salt Co., 88 N. Y. Supp. 323, 43 Misc. Rep. 172, confirmation was refused for a sale at a price amounting to less than one-half of the value. After confirmation, the sale becomes final. Thompson v. Brownlie, 25 Ky. Law Rep. 622, 76 S. W. 172.

higher bid.[54] It has been held that such sales are absolute, and that there is no right of redemption.[55]

§ 211. **Personal Property.**—The same strictness is not required in regard to sales of personal property. As a general rule, an order should be obtained before any sale of importance is made. When the receiver is authorized to continue the business, certain sales are, of course, authorized. In other cases, it is sometimes permissible for the receiver to sell part of the property and obtain subsequent approval from the court. Such sales, when ratified, are as valid as those authorized in the first instance.[56]

§ 212. **Sale is Subject to Existing Liens.**—A receiver's sale is subject to liens of those who are not parties to the receivership proceedings.[57] A lienholder has a right of which he cannot be deprived without an opportunity for a day in court. A purchaser is bound to take such title as an examination of the proceedings shows that he will get.[58] He is bound to examine for himself beforehand to see what title he will obtain by the sale. By statute in New Jersey, sales may be made free from liens in cases where the property is likely to deteriorate and there is a

54 Rogers v. Rogers Locomotive Co., 62 N. J. Eq. 111, 50 Atl. 10 ("the settled policy of our law has been to encourage bidding and purchases at public sales, and that purchasers making *bona fide* bids are to be protected in the advantages of a fair purchase").

55 Watkins v. Minnesota Thresher Mfg Co., 41 Minn 150, 42 N. W. 862. See, also, Mercantile Realty Co. v. Stetson, 120 Iowa, 324, 94 N. W. 859 (holding that the court, by its order, may declare that there shall be no right of redemption).

56 Tobin v. Portland Flouring Mills, 41 Or. 269, 68 Pac. 749, 1108.

57 Lorch v. Aultman, 75 Ind. 162, Snow v. Winslow, 54 Iowa, 200, 6 N. W. 191: In re Coleman, 174 N. Y. 373, 66 N. E. 983.

58 Campbell v. Parker, 59 N. J. Eq. 342, 45 Atl. 116, Fall & Sockeye Fish Co. v. Point Roberts F. & C. Co., 24 Wash. 630, 64 Pac. 792.

contest either as to the validity or as to the relative standing of the liens.[59] In such case the court will hold the proceeds until the rights are determined.

§ 213. Effect of Reversal of Order Appointing Receiver.—Where, upon appeal from an order appointing a receiver, it is determined that the action of the court in making the appointment and in issuing other orders was beyond its jurisdiction, the sale, of necessity, fails. The purchaser becomes entitled to the return of the price paid, and the property sold must be returned by him.[60]

§ 214. Receivers' Certificates—In General.—Receivers of railroad corporations, and perhaps of a few other *quasi* public corporations, may be authorized to borrow money and to incur indebtedness for the general purpose of carrying out the obligation of the corporation to the public.[61] As security, certificates may be issued,

59 Emmons v. Davis & Dowd Pottery Co. (N. J. Ch.), 16 Atl. 158; Randolph v. Larned, 27 N. J. Eq. 557.

60 Lutey v. Clark (Mont.), 77 Pac. 305. ("The decision of this court was to the effect that no sale had been made, in other words, that the pretended sale was without effect, and conveyed no title to the property. Hubbard, having received the money belonging to Lutey Bros. on such void sale, became (on such sale being declared void) an involuntary trustee of Lutey Bros. for the amount of money received from them; and likewise Lutey Bros, having received such goods on such pretended sale, became an involuntary trustee for the mercantile company for the goods which they retained and for the money which they had received from a sale of the portion of the goods disposed of by them.")

61 Wallace v. Loomis, 97 U. S. 146, 24 L. ed. 895; Union Trust Co. v. Illinois Midland Ry. Co., 117 U. S. 434, 6 Sup. Ct. 809, 29 L. ed. 963, Hoover v. Montclair & Greenwood L. R. Co, 29 N. J. Eq. 4. The reasons for the doctrine are well stated in Meyer v. Johnston, 53 Ala. 237: "But the inconvenience and loss which this [the deterioration of the property] would inflict upon the population of large districts, coupled with the benefit to parties who perhaps are

to take priority over the mortgage indebtedness. The reason for the rule is that such corporations owe a peculiar duty to the public to keep their properties in operation. Lienholders take their obligations with that understanding, and when they seek to foreclose, they will not be permitted to interfere with this paramount public duty. This reasoning does not apply to purely private corporations, and consequently it is generally held that in receiverships of such corporations no displacement of the mortgage priority by certificates is allowable.[62] Some cases have extended the doctrine to other *quasi* public corporations owing a similar public duty, but it is in cases of railroads that the doctrine finds its most frequent application.[63]

§ 215. **Nature of Certificates**—Receivers' certificates depend for their validity upon the order of the court au-

powerless to take care of themselves, of preventing the rapid diminution of value, and derangement and disorganization that would otherwise result, seem to require, not for the completion of an unfinished work, or the improvement, beyond what is necessary for its preservation, of an existing one, but to keep it up, to conserve it as a railroad property, if the court has been obliged to take possession of it, that the court should borrow money for that purpose, ... by causing negotiable certificates of indebtedness to be issued, constituting a first lien on the proceeds of the property and redeemable when it is sold or disposed of by the court" We shall see later that the certificates are not negotiable in the sense in which that term is used in the law merchant.

62 Farmers' Loan etc. Co. v. Grape Creek Coal Co., 50 Fed 481 (not allowed in receivership of mining corporation); International Trust Co. v. United Coal Co., 27 Colo. 246, 83 Am. St. Rep. 59, 60 Pac. 621; Standley v. Hendrie & Balthoff Mfg. Co., 27 Colo. 331, 61 Pac. 600; Belknap Sav. Bank v. Lamar Land etc. Co., 28 Colo. 326, 64 Pac. 212; Hooper v. Central Trust Co., 81 Md. 559, 32 Atl. 505, 29 L. R. A. 262.

63 Farmers' Loan etc. Co. v. Bankers & M. Tel. Co., 148 N. Y. 315, 51 Am. St. Rep. 690, 42 N. E. 707, 31 L. R. A. 403 (telegraph company); Ellis v. Vernon Ice, Light & Water Co., 86 Tex. 109, 23 S. W. 858 (water company).

thorizing them, and they are not negotiable instruments.[64] A purchaser is not bound, however, to see to the application of the proceeds.[65] They constitute a lien upon the property prior to the first mortgage bonds.[66] As between certificates, priority has been given to those issued to pay for operating expenses over those issued to pay preferred claims.[67] In order that the priority over the mortgage may be certain, it is necessary that notice of the application for authority be given to the parties interested. "The receiver, and those lending money to him on certificates issued on orders made without prior notice to parties interested, take the risk of the final action of the court in regard to the loans."[68] Receivers' certificates, being merely evidences of indebtedness, can have no higher character than the debts of which they are representatives.[69]

§ 216. **Purposes for Which Certificates may be Issued.**—In general, it may be stated that money may be bor-

64 Union Trust Co. v. Chicago & Lake H. R. Co., 7 Fed. 513; Stanton v. Alabama & C. R. Co., 2 Woods, 506, Fed. Cas. No. 13,296; Turner v. Peoria & S. R. Co., 95 Ill. 134, 35 Am. Rep. 144

65 Union Trust Co. v. Illinois Midland Ry. Co., 117 U. S. 434, 6 Sup. Ct. 809, 29 L. ed. 963; Stanton v. Alabama & C. R. Co., 2 Woods, 506, Fed. Cas. No. 13,296.

66 Wallace v. Loomis, 97 U. S. 146, 24 L. ed. 895; Union Trust Co. v. Illinois Midland Ry. Co., 117 U. S. 434, 6 Sup. Ct. 809, 29 L. ed. 963; Miltenberger v. Logansport R. R. Co., 106 U. S. 287, 1 Sup. Ct. 140, 27 L. ed. 117. Certificates have been held prior to a vendor's lien for rails: Royal Trust Co. v. Washburn, B. & Q. R. Co., 120 Fed. 11, 57 C. C. A. 31.

67 Bank of Commerce v. Central Coal & Coke Co., 53 C. C. A. 354, 115 Fed. 878.

68 Union Trust Co. v. Illinois Midland Ry. Co., 117 U. S. 434, 6 Sup. Ct. 809, 29 L. ed. 963; Raht v. Atrill, 106 N. Y. 423, 60 Am. Rep. 456, 13 N. E. 282.

69 Fidelity I. & S. D. Co. v. Shenandoah Co., 42 Fed. 372. To the effect that such certificates are subject to mechanics' liens, see Gordon v. Newman, 62 Fed. 686, 10 C. C. A. 587.

rowed and certificates issued for purposes of protecting and safely operating the property in the hands of the receiver. In a leading case they were authorized for necessary repairs, for betterments, and for the payment of tax liens.[70] They may be issued to pay for necessary improvements, such as additions to the line or equipment.[71] They have been authorized to enable the receiver to obtain funds with which to prosecute a suit for the collection of rent of a leased line.[72] In a number of instances they have been issued in payment of preferred claims, such as claims for labor, materials and supplies furnished a reasonable time before the receivership.[73] In all cases the issuance depends upon the necessity of the matter for which money is desired. For instance, if it is proper for the court to authorize improvements or repairs, it may direct that money be borrowed to pay for them. If, on the other hand, such work is, under the circumstances, not necessary, the application for an order must fail.

§ 217. **Liability for Fraud, Negligence, etc.**—A receiver is bound to exercise such diligence in the care and man-

70 Union Trust Co. v Illinois Midland Ry. Co., 117 U. S. 434, 6 Sup. Ct. 809, 29 L. ed. 963. In the following cases they were authorized for necessary repairs: Credit Co, Ltd., v. Arkansas Cent. R. Co., 15 Fed. 46, 5 McCrary, 23, Hoover v. Montclair & Greenwood Lake Ry. Co., 29 N. J. Eq 4.

71 Miltenberger v. Logansport R. R. Co., 106 U. S. 287, 1 Sup. Ct. 140, 27 L. ed. 117 (issued for purposes of obtaining rolling stock, and for building six miles of road and a bridge, part of the main line of a road ninety-two miles long). See, however, Bibber-White Co. v. White River Val. E. R. Co., 53 C. C. A. 282, 115 Fed. 786, where an extension of the line would have been speculative and the court held an issuance of certificates for such purpose error

72 Town of Vandalia v. St. Louis, V. & T. H. R. Co., 209 Ill 73, 70 N. E. 662.

73 Union Trust Co. v. Illinois Midland Ry. Co., 117 U. S. 434, 6 Sup. Ct. 809, 29 L. ed. 963; Miltenberger v. Logansport Ry. Co, 106 U. S. 287, 1 Sup. Ct. 140, 27 L. ed. 117.

agement of the property as a prudent man would exercise in closing up his own estate. If, through his neglect, a loss occurs, he is personally liable. Thus, where he neglects to collect certain claims which might have been collected, he is liable and will be held for the amount lost.[74] In order, to charge him, however, it has been held that the loss must be traced directly to his neglect.[75] He is not an insurer of the property, and is not a guarantor that any particular results will be worked out.[76] He must not become interested in any way in the property intrusted to him, and he must not use it for his own advantage. For instance, he must not loan money to himself nor to a firm of which he is a member.[77] And a mortgage taken by him upon property held by him as receiver to secure a debt to him personally, is void as against public policy.[78]

74 In re Angell, 131 Mich. 345, 91 N. W. 611, 9 Detroit Leg. N 380

75 Thus, the fact of allowing animals to remain on a Texas cattle range, where they were lost, and a failure to insure property which afterwards burned, have been held to charge no loss upon the receiver: Hamm v. J. Stone & Sons Livestock Co., 13 Tex. Civ. App. 414, 35 S. W. 427.

76 Ripley v. McGavie, 120 Iowa, 52, 94 N. W. 452.

77 Ryan v. Morrill, 83 Ky. 352, Cook v. Martin (Ark.), 87 S. W 625, quoting Pom. Eq. Jur., § 1075.

78 Thompson v. Holladay, 15 Or. 34, 14 Pac. 725.

CHAPTER IX.

RECEIVERS; CLAIMS AND ALLOWANCES.

ANALYSIS.

§ 218. Duties and Rights of Receiver in Regard to Claims. A receiver is "charged with the duty of carrying into execution the orders of the court, but he is also a custodian of property, and has, by virtue of such custody, certain obligations to the parties owning or interested therein.[1] Accordingly, he may defend, both in the court appointing him and by appeal, the estate in his possession against all claims which are antagonistic to the rights of both parties to the suit. For instance, he may thus contest a claim for taxes, because, if valid, they are superior to the rights of both parties. . . . . He may likewise defend the estate against all claims which are antagonistic to the rights of either party to the suit, subject to the limitation that he may not, in such defense, question any order or decree of the court distributing burdens or apportioning rights between the parties to the suit, or any order or decree resting upon the discretion of the court appointing him. . . . . Neither can he question any subsequent order or decree of the court distributing the estate in his hands between the parties to the suit."[2]

§ 219. Priority of Claims—Taxes.—The appointment of a receiver will not be allowed to defeat the collection of the public revenue. The claim of the state is paramount to all other claims, and therefore the court will order its receiver to pay such taxes as have been legally assessed upon the property.[3] If the receiver believes

1 Bosworth v. Terminal R. Assn., 174 U. S. 182, 19 Sup. Ct. 625, 43 L. ed. 941, per Brewer, J.

2 Id. As to the receiver's right to appeal, see § 178.

3 First Nat. Bank v. Ewing, 103 Fed. 168, 43 C. C. A. 150; George v. St. Louis Cable & W. R. Co., 44 Fed. 117; In re United States Car Co., 60 N. J. Eq. 514, 43 Atl. 673; Central Trust Co. v. New York City & N. R. Co., 110 N. Y. 250, 18 N. E. 92, 1 L. R. A. 260. See, also, City of Los Angeles v. Los Angeles City Water Co., 137 Cal 699, 70 Pac. 770 (applying Pol. Code, § 3647). That the property in the receiver's possession will be protected from seizure for taxes, see *ante*, § 168.

the legality of the tax to be questionable, he may apply to the court for protection.[4]

§ 220. **Expenses of Receivership.**—In general, expenses of the receivership are payable out of the fund in the receiver's hands prior to the payment of a mortgage debt.[5] The reasons for such a rule are apparent. The receiver represents the court and acts for the interests of all concerned. Under such circumstances, it would be inequitable to allow a creditor to obtain the benefit of the receivership before the expenses necessarily incurred are paid. It becomes important, then, to determine what are proper expenses of administration.

§ 221. **What are Proper Expenses.**—As a general principle, it may be laid down that any reasonable expense incurred in the proper care, protection and control of the property should be allowed to the receiver as an expense of administration. What is proper in any given case must depend largely upon the particular circumstances. A receiver is entitled to a reasonable compensation, which, in general, is allowed by the court from the fund in his hands. Such a claim is clearly an expense of administration.[6] We have seen that for many purposes a receiver is authorized to employ an attorney. Compensation for such services is fixed by the court and allowed as a proper expense.[7] Costs of

4 Ex parte Chamberlain, 55 Fed. 704.

5 McLane v. Placerville & S. V. R Co., 66 Cal. 606, 6 Pac. 748, Central Trust Co. v. Thurman, 94 Ga 735, 20 S E. 141; State v. Active Bldg. & Loan Assn., 102 Mo. App. 675, 77 S. W. 171.

6 See *post*, §§ 238-243.

7 See *ante*, § 206. See, also, Petersburg Sav. & Ins. Co. v Dellatorre, 70 Fed. 643, 17 C. C. A. 310, 30 U. S. App. 504; McLane v. Placerville & S. V. R. Co., 66 Cal. 606, 6 Pac. 748, Central Trust Co. v. Thurman, 94 Ga 735, 20 S. E 141; State v. Active Bldg & Loan Assn, 102 Mo. App. 675, 77 S. W. 171; Graham v. Carr, 133 N. C 449,

suits begun or defended by the receiver under the direction or approval of the court are also included.[8]

§ 222. **Expenses of Continuing Business.**—When a receiver is authorized to continue the business, expenses incurred are chargeable upon the fund prior to preexisting liens.[9] As between costs of the litigation itself and the expenses incurred in continuing the business, it would seem that the former should have the priority.[10] Receivers' certificates are allowed a preference over mortgage debts and like claims.[11] Any reasonable expense incured by authority of the court, express or implied, will be allowed. Owners of property used by a receiver are entitled to preferred payment.[12]

45 S. E. 847. It is only for services connected with the proper management or control of the property that compensation will be allowed. Thus, the unsuccessful effort of an attorney to defend his own claim before the master does not entitle him to any additional compensation: In re University Magazine Co., 82 N. Y. Supp. 74, 83 App. Div. 641.

8 Cumberland Lumber Co. v. Clinton Hill L. Co., 64 N. J. Eq. 521, 54 Atl. 452; McLane v. Placerville & S. V. R. Co., 66 Cal. 606, 6 Pac. 748.

9 Clark v. Central R. & B. Co., 66 Fed. 803, 14 C. C. A. 112 (coal), Diamond Match Co. v. Taylor, 83 Md. 394, 34 Atl. 1015; Hoover v. Montclair & G. L. R. Co., 29 N. J. Eq. 4 (repairs); Ellis v. Vernon Ice, Light & Water Co., 86 Tex. 109, 23 S. W. 858. That the expenses are a lien on the *corpus* as well as on the income, see People's Nat Bank v. Virginia Textile Co. (Va.), 51 S. E. 155, and many cases cited; cf. *infra*, § 225, as to "preferred" claims arising before the receivership. Where the receiver continues the business without authority, expenses incurred therein are not entitled to priority United States Inv. Co v. Portland Hospital, 40 Or 523, 67 Pac. 194, 64 Pac. 644, 56 L. R. A. 627.

10 "We consider the allowance as compensation to the receiver and his solicitors as part of the taxable costs in this case, and as such is preferred to the receiver's certificates, and entitled to prior payment" Petersburg Sav. & Ins. Co. v. Dellatorre, 70 Fed. 643, 17 C. C. A. 310, 30 U. S. App. 504.

11 See *ante*, §§ 214-216.

12 See Miltenberger v. Logansport, C. & S. W. R. Co., 106 U. S 286,

No priority is allowed, however, to claims for money loaned without authority of the court, although it was intended that the funds so raised should be used for expenses of operation.[13]

§ 223. **Same—Liability for Torts.**—Receivers who are authorized to continue business and manage property are bound to the same degree of care as the owner would have been under, and are in like manner liable, in their official character, for injuries resulting from the negligence of themselves or their agents and employees.[14] This principle applies strongly to railway receivers, who are held liable for injuries resulting from negligence in the operation of the properties committed to their charge. Claims of this character are treated as expenses of continuing the business, and are allowed priority.[15] Liability for statutory penalties depends largely upon the wording of the statutes themselves. It

1 Sup. Ct. 140, 27 L. ed. 117; Thomas v. Western Car Co., 149 U. S. 95, 13 Sup. Ct. 824, 37 L. ed. 663. Where a lease has not been adopted, the owner can claim only the actual value, not the amount stipulated for in the lease: Lane v. Macon & A. Ry. Co., 96 Ga. 630, 24 S. E 157.

13 Union Trust Co. v. Illinois Midland Ry. Co., 117 U. S. 434, 6 Sup. Ct. 809, 29 L. ed. 963; Maxwell v. Wilmington Dental Mfg. Co., 101 Fed. 852.

14 Fullerton v. Fordyce, 121 Mo. 1, 42 Am. St. Rep. 516, 25 S. W. 587. As to liability, see Missouri Pac. R. Co. v. Texas Pac. R. Co., 30 Fed. 169; Rouse v. Hornsby, 14 C. C. A. 377, 67 Fed. 219; Central Trust Co. v. Denver & Rio Grande R. Co., 97 Fed. 239, 38 C. C. A. 143; Malott v. Shimer, 153 Ind. 35, 74 Am. St. Rep. 278, 54 N. E. 101; Lyman v. Central Vt. R. Co., 59 Vt. 167, 10 Atl. 346. He is not liable for torts committed before the receivership. Northern Pac. R. Co. v. Heflin, 27 C. C. A. 460, 83 Fed. 93; see, also, *post*, § 237.

15 Knickerbocker v. Benes, 195 Ill. 434, 63 N. E. 174; Bartlett v. Cicero Light etc. Co., 177 Ill. 68, 69 Am. St Rep 206, 52 N. E. 339, 42 L. R. A. 715; St. Louis S. W. Ry. Co. v. Holbrook, 73 Fed. 112, 19 C. C. A. 385, 41 U. S. App. 33. To the effect that such a claim should be paid out of the current receipts, see Texas & P. Ry. Co. v. Johnson, 76 Tex. 421, 18 Am. St. Rep. 60, 13 S. W. 463.

has been held that a statute imposing a liability upon a "proprietor, owner, charterer, or hirer" does not affect the receiver.[16] On the other hand, a statute inflicting penalties upon "all lessees or other persons owning or operating," is applicable to the receiver.[17] In some cases liability has been enforced against a corporation in the hands of a receiver, by reason of such statutes.[18]

§ 224. Claims Arising Prior to Receivership—Statement and Rationale of Doctrine.—In cases of railroad receiverships, and perhaps in a few other special instances, priority is allowed to certain claims for operating expenses incurred within a reasonable time before the appointment of a receiver. "The controlling principle appears to be that a railroad, having public duties to discharge, must be kept a going concern while in the hands of the court, and that to that end debts due its employees and other current debts incurred for its ordinary operations, which it is not usually practicable to pay in cash, and which are therefore payable on short terms, should be paid as they would have been paid if the court had not taken away from the corporation the control of the railroad. A cessation of the railroad's operations by failure to pay promptly the operatives or such other debts

16 Such a statute imposing liability for death does not apply to the receiver: Texas & P. R. Co. v. Collins, 84 Tex. 121, 19 S. W. 365, Yoakum v. Selph, 83 Tex. 607, 19 S. W. 145; Turner v. Cross, 83 Tex. 218, 18 S. W. 578; Dillingham v. Blake (Tex. Civ. App.), 32 S. W. 77. A federal statute relating to the transportation of livestock, imposing a penalty upon "any company, owner or custodian of such animals," does not affect the receiver: United States v. Harris, 78 Fed. 290. On the other hand, it has been held that a statute declaring that "every railroad company" shall be liable for injuries to employees, and abolishing the fellow-servant rule, binds the receiver: Rouse v. Harry, 55 Kan. 589, 40 Pac. 1007, Hornsby v. Eddy, 56 Fed. 461, 5 C. C. A. 560.

17 Brockert v. Central Iowa R. Co., 82 Iowa, 369, 47 N. W. 1026.

18 Ohio & Miss. R. Co. v. Russell, 115 Ill. 52, 3 N. E. 561.

as railroads must necessarily incur for their ordinary, current operations, must be prevented."[19] "Every railroad mortgagee in accepting his security impliedly agrees that the current debts made in the ordinary course of business shall be paid from the current receipts before he has any claim upon the income."[20] It is frequently stated that the right to preference depends upon a diversion to the use of the mortgagees of funds which should properly be applied to the payment of current expenses.[21] It is not necessary, however, that the funds be used to pay the mortgage debt, principal or interest.[22] And it would seem that the better rule is that no diversion whatever need be shown.[23] The practical reasons for the rule allowing preferences are as strong in both cases; for it is equally as important to keep the road a going concern where there has, or has not, been such diversion.

19 Parlange, D. J., in Lackawanna Iron & Coal Co v. Farmers' Loan & Tr. Co., 79 Fed. 202, 24 C. C. A. 487 (affirmed, 176 U. S. 298, 20 Sup. Ct. 363, 44 L. ed. 475).

20 Waite, C. J., in Fosdick v. Schall, 99 U. S. 235, 25 L. ed. 339.

21 Quincy, M. & P. R. Co. v. Humphreys, 145 U. S. 82, 12 Sup. Ct. 787, 36 L. ed. 632, Kansas Loan & Tr. Co. v. Electric Ry., L. & P Co, 108 Fed. 702; Rhode Island Locomotive Works v. Continental Trust Co., 108 Fed. 5, 47 C. C. A. 147; Central Trust Co. v. Chattanooga S. R. Co, 69 Fed. 295; Cutting v. Tavares, O. & A R. Co., 61 Fed. 150, 9 C. C. A. 401; Finance Co. of Pa. v. Charleston, C. & C. R Co., 48 Fed. 188; Hammerly v. Mercantile Trust etc. Co, 123 Ala. 596, 26 South. 646. It is said in some cases that the burden of proving such diversion is on the party claiming the preference: Kansas Loan & Tr. Co. v. Electric Ry., L. & P. Co, 108 Fed. 702.

22 Union Trust Co. v. Souther, 107 U. S. 591, 2 Sup. Ct. 295, 27 L. ed. 488.

23 "It is immaterial, in such case, in determining the right to be compensated out of the surplus earnings of the receivership, whether or not during the operation of the railroad by the company there had been a diversion of income for the benefit of the mortgage bondholders, either in payment of interest on mortgage bonds or expenditures for permanent improvements upon the property": Virginia & A. Coal Co. v. Central R. & B. Co., 170 U. S 355, 18 Sup Ct. 657, 42

§ 225. **Growth of the Doctrine.**—Although this doctrine is of comparatively recent origin, it has had a rapid development, and many of the decisions show a resulting conflict. It was originally said that the doctrine rested upon the implied consent of the mortgagees; that when they applied for a receiver they consented to do equity, and accordingly the court would proceed to adjust the claims.[24] Later, however, this theory was abandoned, and the same priority was allowed in a suit instituted neither by the bondholders nor the trustee.[25] It has been held that no preference can be allowed to claims arising prior to the receivership unless the court, at the time of the appointment, makes an order to that effect;[26] but the better rule seems to be that such order is not necessary.[27] By the weight of authority, the preference extends to the income only.[28] By some cases,

L. ed. 1068 (affirming Clark v. Central R. R. & B. Co., 66 Fed. 803, 14 C. C. A. 112). See, also, Burnham v. Bowen, 111 U. S. 776, 4 Sup Ct. 675, 28 L. ed. 596 ("So far as anything appears on the record, the failure of the company to pay the debt to Bowen was due alone to the fact that the expenses of running the road and preserving the security of the bondholders were greater than the receipts from the business. Under these circumstances, we think the debt was a charge in equity on the continuing income, as well that which came into the hands of the court after the receiver was appointed as that before"); Cleveland, C. & S. Ry. Co. v. Knickerbocker Trust Co., 86 Fed. 73; Wood v. New York & N. E. R. Co., 70 Fed. 741; Finance Co. of Pa. v. Charleston, C & C. R. Co., 62 Fed 205, 10 C. C. A. 323, 8 U. S App 547; Farmers' Loan & Tr. Co. v Kansas City, W. & N. W. R. Co., 53 Fed. 182.

24 Fosdick v. Schall, 99 U. S. 235, 25 L. ed. 339.

25 Union Trust Co. v. Illinois & M. R. Co, 117 U. S. 434, 6 Sup Ct. 809, 29 L. ed. 963.

26 Cutting v. Tavares, O. & A. R. Co, 61 Fed. 150, 9 C. C. A. 401; Central Trust Co. v. Chattanooga S. R. Co., 69 Fed. 295.

27 Finance Co. of Pa. v. Charleston, C. & C. R. Co., 62 Fed. 205, 10 C. C. A. 323, 8 U. S. App. 547; Wood v. New York & N. E. R. Co., 70 Fed. 741; Farmers' Loan & Tr. Co. v. Kansas City, W. & N. W. R. Co., 53 Fed. 182.

28 Gregg v. Metropolitan Trust Co., 197 U. S. 183, 25 Sup. Ct. 415;

however, it is held that preferred debts may be paid out of the *corpus* when the income is insufficient.[29]

§ 226. To What Receiverships the Doctrine Applies.—Most of the cases to which the doctrine has been applied have been cases of railroad receiverships, and the courts have been very slow to extend it. In the absence of statute, it cannot apply to receiverships of corporations owing no special obligation to the public.[30] In a few cases preferences have been allowed against mortgage creditors of common carrier corporations,

International Trust Co. v. T. B. Townsend B. & C. Co., 37 C. C A. 396, 95 Fed. 850; Street v. Maryland Cent. R. Co, 59 Fed. 25; Farmers' & Merchants' Nat. Bank v. Waco Electric Ry. & Lt. Co. (Tex. Civ. App.), 36 S. W. 131. See, also, Mersick v. Hartford & W. H. Horse R. Co, 76 Conn. 11, 100 Am. St. Rep. 977, 55 Atl. 664 (does not extend to *corpus* when there has been no diversion of income).

29 Miltenberger v. Logansport, C. & S. W. R. Co., 106 U. S 286, 1 Sup. Ct 140, 27 L ed. 117, Union Trust Co. v. Illinois M. R. Co, 117 U S. 434, 6 Sup. Ct. 809, 29 L. ed. 963 (quoting from the former case); Farmers' Loan & Tr. Co. v. Kansas City, W & N W. R. Co., 53 Fed. 182. See, also, Clark v. Central R. & B. Co, 66 Fed. 803, 14 C. C. A. 112. The very recent case of Gregg v. Metropolitan Trust Co., 197 U. S 183, 25 Sup. Ct. 415, apparently overrules these cases, at least in part. It was there held that a claim for supplies cannot be given preference over the mortgage, out of the *corpus*.

30 Thus, it has been held that there is no right of preference in a receivership of a mining company: Merriam v. Victory Min Co., 37 Or 321, 56 Pac. 75, 58 Pac. 37, 60 Pac. 997, Farmers' Loan & Tr. Co. v. Grape Creek Coal Co., 50 Fed. 481, 16 L R A. 603; nor in a receivership of an iron company Phillips v. Wise (Tex. Civ App.), 31 S. W 428. It has been held that where services are rendered a railroad company in its pursuit of a logging venture, which it undertakes in addition to its railroad, no preference should be allowed. Security Sav. & Tr. Co. v. Goble, N & P. R. Co, 44 Or 370, 74 Pac. 919, 75 Pac. 697. For a preference arising out of statute, see Hicks v. Consolidation Coal Co., 77 Md. 86, 25 Atl 979; Farmers' & Merchants' Nat Bank v. Waco Electric Ry & Lt. Co. (Tex Civ. App), 36 S. W. 131. In Alabama, the doctrine has been extended independently of statute Drennen v. Mercantile Tr. & D. Co., 115 Ala. 592, 67 Am. St. Rep. 72, 23 South 164, 39 L. R. A. 623 (mining company), and in Mississippi: L'Hote v. Boyet (Miss.), 38 South. 1.

such as telephone and telegraph companies;[31] but in at least one case the doctrine was held inapplicable to steamship companies.[32] In one instance priority was allowed to certain creditors of an irrigation company.[33]

§ 227. Time Within Which Debts must have been Contracted.—In order that claims may be allowed a preference under this doctrine, they must have been contracted within a reasonable time before the receivership.[34] It is sometimes stated that six months is the limit.[35] This is not borne out, however, by the weight of authority.[36] What is a reasonable time depends

31 Keelyn v. Carolina etc. Tel. Co., 90 Fed. 29.

32 Bound v. South Carolina Ry. Co., 50 Fed. 312 In discussing the reasons for the distinction, Simonton, D. J., said: "Railroads are of public concern, not simply because they benefit the public; the sovereign power has contributed to their construction in a way to which none but the sovereign can contribute, and they are devoted to a public use. . . . . The public use arises when the sovereign power is essential to the enterprise, and is exercised because of such use. This consideration does not exist in the case of a steamship company, or of any common carrier by water, or of any warehouse company. There are no sovereign, exclusive privileges granted to this navigation company."

33 Atlantic Trust Co. v. Woodbridge Canal Co., 79 Fed. 39.

34 Wood v. New York & N. E. R. Co., 70 Fed. 741; Central Trust Co. v. East Tenn. V. & G. R. Co., 80 Fed. 624, 26 C. C. A. 30; Guaranty Trust Co v. Galveston City R. Co, 107 Fed. 311, 46 C. C. A. 305; Manchester Locomotive Works v. Truesdale, 44 Minn. 115, 46 N. W. 301, 9 L. R. A. 140; Central Trust Co. v. Utah Cent. R. Co., 16 Utah, 12, 50 Pac. 813. See, also, cases cited in note 36, *post.*

35 National Bank of Augusta v. Carolina, K & W. R. Co., 63 Fed. 25 (*dictum*).

36 Burnham v. Bowen, 111 U. S. 776, 4 Sup. Ct 675, 28 L. ed. 596 (claim for coal supplied eleven months before the appointment of a receiver allowed a preference); Northern Pac. R. Co. v. Lamont, 69 Fed. 23, 16 C. C. A 364, 32 U. S App. 480; Farmers' Loan & Trust Co. v. Kansas City, W. & N. W. R. Co., 53 Fed 182; Central Trust Co. v. St. Louis, A & T. Ry. Co., 41 Fed. 551; Wood v. New York & N. E. R. Co., 70 Fed 741; Cleveland C. & S. Ry. Co. v. Knickerbocker Trust Co, 86 Fed 73, New York Guaranty etc. Co. v. Ta-

upon the circumstances of each particular case. The supreme court of the United States has given priority to a claim for materials furnished three years before the appointment of a receiver.[37]

§ 228. **Labor Claims.**—Wherever the doctrine is accepted, claims of employees for labor performed within a reasonable time before the receivership are allowed a preference.[38] All the reasons which exist in favor of allowance in any other case exist here. Without employees the road could not run for a moment.

§ 229. **Extent of this Class.**—It is impossible from the present state of the authorities to define exactly who are included within this class. It is sometimes stated that officers and employees of every grade are included;[39] but this is not warranted by the authorities. The ordinary clerks and employees are clearly entitled to the preference. The question is more difficult when applied to the officials of the company. It has been held, in accord with principle, that a president of a railroad corporation is not entitled to any priority for his salary claim. "If persons who give labor and materials were required in every instance to make careful examination into the condition of the company, so as to as-

coma R. & M. Co, 83 Fed 365, 27 C. C. A. 550; Central Trust Co. v. Utah Cent. R. Co., 16 Utah, 12, 50 Pac. 813.

37 Hale v. Frost, 99 U. S 389, 25 L. ed. 419.

38 Fosdick v. Schall, 99 U. S. 235, 25 L. ed. 339; Miltenberger v. Logansport, C. & S. W. R. Co., 106 U. S. 286, 1 Sup. Ct. 140, 27 L. ed. 117; Wood v. New York & N. E. R. Co., 70 Fed. 741; Finance Co. of Pa. v. Charleston, C. & C. R. Co., 62 Fed 205, 10 C. C. A. 323, 8 U. S. App. 547; Douglass v. Cline, 12 Bush, 608; Litzenberg v. Jarvis-Conklin Trust Co, 8 Utah, 15, 28 Pac. 871; Central Trust Co. v. Utah Cent. R Co., 16 Utah, 12, 50 Pac. 813.

39 Farmers' Loan & Trust Co. v. Vicksburg & M. R. Co., 33 Fed 778.

certain its solvent capacity for paying debts, all of its operations might be brought to a standstill. For this reason, persons dealing with a company are encouraged to do so, with the knowledge that the court will see that all such supplies of labor and material given, and not paid for within a reasonable time before the appointment of a receiver, will be provided for by the court. . . . No case can yet be found which extends the equity to the president of the company. He knows exactly its condition. He has full notice of the liens existing. He is not bound to furnish his services a day after his remuneration seems uncertain. He cannot be included among that class of employees who have no means of ascertaining whether a short credit to the company is safe or not."[40] An attorney whose services result in a recovery which inures to the benefit of the bondholders is entitled to preference for his fee. The party who takes the benefit of such a service ought to pay for it.[41] Likewise, it has been held that where the court orders the receiver to pay wages due, a claim of an attorney regularly employed is entitled to preference.[42] But "claims for legal services rendered a railroad company in the ordinary course of its business under special employment, which do not directly contribute in some way to the advantage of mortgagees, do not stand upon a plane with the labor of operatives, or the claims of those who furnish materials or supplies to maintain it as a going concern."[43]

40 National Bank of Augusta v. Carolina, K. & W. R. Co., 63 Fed. 25.

41 Louisville, E. & St. L. R. Co. v. Wilson, 138 U. S. 501, 11 Sup. Ct. 405, 34 L. ed. 1023.

42 Finance Co. of Pa. v. Charleston, C. & C. R. Co., 52 Fed. 526.

43 Gregg v. Mercantile Trust Co., 109 Fed. 220, 48 C. C. A. 318; Louisville, E. & St. L. R. Co. v. Wilson, 138 U. S. 501, 11 Sup. Ct. 405, 34 L. ed. 1023.

§ 230. **Claims for Supplies.**—Another class of claims entitled to preference includes those arising from the sale of supplies necessary for operating purposes.[44] Such claims clearly come within the reason of the rule. No railroad can run without supplies. Thus, coal being essential to the operation of a railroad, claims for coal are allowed a preference.[45] Some courts are disposed to narrow the class so as to include only claims for supplies which are actually necessary to keep the road in operation.[46] Accordingly, claims for advertis-

44 Union Trust Co. v. Souther, 107 U. S. 591, 2 Sup. Ct. 295, 27 L. ed. 488; Kneeland v. Bass Foundry & Mach. Works, 140 U. S. 592, 11 Sup. Ct. 857, 35 L. ed. 543; Virginia & A. Coal Co. v. Central R. & B. Co., 170 U. S. 355, 18 Sup. Ct. 657, 42 L. ed. 1068; Wood v. New York & N. E. R. Co., 70 Fed. 741, Southern Ry. Co. v. Chapman Jack Co, 54 C. C. A. 598, 117 Fed. 424, Grand Trunk Ry. Co. v Central Vt. R. Co, 88 Fed. 620; Finance Co of Pa. v. Charleston, C. & C. R. Co., 52 Fed. 524. A claim for a gear wheel and pinion, necessary parts of a cable railway, was allowed a preference in Central Trust Co. v. Clark, 81 Fed. 269, 26 C. C. A 397 See, also, New York Guaranty etc Co. v. Tacoma R. & M. Co., 83 Fed. 365, 27 C. C. A. 550. For a statement as to when claims for supplies should be allowed a preference, see Southern Ry. Co. v. Ensign Mfg. Co., 54 C C. A. 591, 117 Fed. 417.

45 "It was thus settled that, where coal is purchased by a railroad company for use in operating lines of railway owned and controlled by it, in order that they may be continued as a going concern, and where it was the expectation of the parties that the coal was to be paid for out of the current earnings, the indebtedness, as between the party furnishing the materials and supplies and the holders of bonds secured by a mortgage upon the property, is a charge in equity on the continuing income, as well that which may come into the hands of a court after a receiver has been appointed as that before": Virginia & A. Coal Co. v. Central R. & B. Co., 170 U. S. 355, 18 Sup. Ct 657, 42 L. ed. 1068 (affirming Clark v. Central R. R & B. Co., 66 Fed 803, 14 C. C. A. 112); Burnham v. Bowen, 111 U S. 776, 4 Sup Ct. 675, 28 L ed. 596, Clark v. Central R. & B. Co., 66 Fed 803, 14 C. C. A. 112.

46 In McCornack v. Salem Consol. St. Ry. Co. 34 Or. 543, 56 Pac. 518, a claim for a heater furnished to a street railway company was refused a preference although it resulted in a saving of fuel, on the ground that it was not necessary in order to keep the company a going concern.

ing matter furnished have been refused priority.[47] Likewise, a claim for locomotives was denied priority when there was no showing that additional engines were necessary.[48]

§ 231. **No Priority When Credit Given.**—Priority is denied to claims for supplies sold on credit.[49] In such a case it must be inferred that interest is to be paid on the mortgage indebtedness during the running of the credit. "The claim is quite different from those ordinary and necessary current expenses of operating a railroad contracted a short time before the receivership, and which, by the sudden action of the court in appointing a receiver, are left unpaid."[50]

§ 232. **Claims for Repairs—Construction—Reconstruction.** In the operation of a railroad, repairs are continually necessary. Hence claims for labor performed and supplies furnished for ordinary and necessary repairs are allowed a preference.[51] It is held, however, that claims for the construction of the road are not such current

47 Central Trust Co. v. East Tenn., V. & G. R. Co., 26 C. C. A. 30, 80 Fed. 624.

48 Gregg v. Mercantile Trust Co., 109 Fed. 220, 48 C. C. A. 318. See, also, Rhode Island Locomotive Works v. Continental Trust Co., 108 Fed. 5, 47 C. C. A. 147.

49 Bound v. South Carolina Ry. Co, 7 C. C. A. 322, 58 Fed. 473; Rhode Island Locomotive Works v. Continental Trust Co., 108 Fed. 5, 47 C. C. A. 147. This principle prevents priority when there is a conditional sale of rolling stock, title being retained until payment. Huidekeper v. Locomotive Works, 99 U. S. 258, 25 L. ed. 344; Fidelity Ins., Trust & S. D. Co. v. Shenandoah Valley R. Co., 86 Va. 1, 19 Am. St. Rep. 858, 9 S. E. 759. See, also, Ruhlender v. Chesapeake, O. & S. W. R. Co., 33 C. C. A. 299, 91 Fed. 5.

50 Bound v. South Carolina Ry. Co., 7 C. C. A. 322, 58 Fed. 473.

51 Southern Ry. Co. v. Carnegie Steel Co., 176 U. S. 257, 20 Sup. Ct. 347, 44 L. ed. 458 (affirming 76 Fed 492, 22 C. C. A. 289); Gregg v. Mercantile Trust Co., 109 Fed. 220, 48 C. C. A. 318, Cleveland, C. & S. Ry. Co. v. Knickerbocker Trust Co., 86 Fed. 73.

debts as are entitled to this preference. An "original construction" is that which is necessary to be done before the road can be opened or used.[52] Such work is clearly not part of the ordinary course of business. Claims for reconstruction are also denied a preference. It is difficult to draw the line between repairs and reconstruction. Each case must depend upon its own facts. The extent of the work is the only criterion.[53]

§ 233. **Miscellaneous Claims.**—Preference has been allowed to claims for providing, furnishing and maintaining waiting-rooms for passengers, office room for ticket agents, and a convenient place for employees to lodge at reduced rates.[54] A like priority has been given to

52 Wood v. Deposit Co, 128 U. S. 421, 9 Sup. Ct. 131, 32 L. ed. 472; Cleveland, C. & S. Ry. Co. v. Knickerbocker Trust Co., 86 Fed. 73; First Nat. Bank v. Ewing, 103 Fed. 168, 43 C. C. A. 150, American L. & T. Co. v. East & West R. Co., 46 Fed. 101, Niles Tool Works Co. v. Louisville, N. A. & C. Ry. Co., 112 Fed. 561, 50 C. C A 390. See, however, McIlhenny v. Binz, 80 Tex. 1, 26 Am. St. Rep. 705, 13 S. W. 655, where the court said: "Ordinarily, when mortgages are issued upon completed roads, it is not contemplated that its income is to be applied to the construction of new road. In such cases, debts incurred for such new construction ought to have no claim against the bondholders either as to the corpus or the increase of the property. But when mortgages are executed upon an unfinished road, and they show upon their face that it was contemplated that the work of construction should be prosecuted to completion, and when the mortgages attach to the new road as fast as it is finished, we are of opinion that the new road should be considered a 'useful improvement,' and that, if the road be put into the hands of a receiver before the work and materials are paid for, the holders of the claims for such work and material should be paid from the net income of the road while under the control of the court, if there be any."

53 Lackawanna Iron & Coal Co v. Farmers' L. & T. Co., 176 U. S. 298, 20 Sup. Ct. 363, 44 L. ed. 475, affirming 79 Fed. 202, 24 C. C. A. 487.

54 Northern Pac. R. Co. v. Lamont, 69 Fed. 23, 16 C. C. A. 364, 32 U. S App. 480 In this case, Caldwell, Cir J., tersely argued: "To defeat the preferential character of this claim, the court would have

claims of other railroads for freight and ticket balances.[55] A claim for the use of terminal property has been held entitled to preference.[56]

§ 234. Money Loaned.—No preference is allowed claims for money loaned. This rule is adhered to although the money may have been used to pay current running expenses, and may have been loaned expressly for that purpose. The fact that the money is loaned to enable the company to pay interest on its mortgage bonds is likewise immaterial.[57]

§ 235. Rental of Leased Lines.—No priority is allowed for claims for rental under a railroad lease accruing before the appointment of a receiver.[58] A distinction

to be satisfied that waiting-rooms for passengers and an office for the ticket agents are not essential or necessary, at a town of several thousand population, on the Northern Pacific Railroad. We are asked, in effect, to hold that passengers on that road, while waiting to take passage on its trains, must endure the rigors of a North Dakota climate without shelter, and that its ticket agent must be content with an office on the public commons, and carry his tickets in his pocket or his hat."

55 Miltenberger v. Logansport, C. & S. W. R. Co., 106 U. S. 286, 1 Sup. Ct. 140, 27 L. ed. 117; Finance Co. of Pa. v. Charleston, C. & C. R. Co., 62 Fed. 205, 10 C. C. A. 323, 8 U. S. App. 547; Gregg v Mercantile Trust Co, 109 Fed. 220, 48 C. C. A. 318; Monsarrat v. Mercantile Trust Co., 109 Fed. 230, 48 C. C. A. 328.

56 Manhattan Trust Co. v. Sioux City & N. R. Co., 102 Fed 710. But see, *contra*, Gregg v. Mercantile Trust Co., 109 Fed. 220, 48 C. C. A. 318

57 Morgan's L & T. R. & S. S. Co. v. Texas Cent. Ry. Co., 137 U S. 171, 11 Sup. Ct. 61, 34 L. ed. 625; Southern Dev. Co. v. Farmers' L. & T Co., 79 Fed. 212, 24 C. C. A. 497; Morgan's La. & T. R. & S. S. Co. v. Farmers' L. & T. Co., 79 Fed. 210, 24 C. C. A. 495; Lackawanna Iron & Coal Co. v. Farmers' L. & T. Co., 79 Fed. 202, 24 C. C. A. 487; Illinois Trust Co. v. Dowd, 105 Fed. 123, 44 C. C. A. 389, 52 L. R A 481; Contracting & Building Co. v. Continental Trust Co., 108 Fed. 1, 47 C. C. A 143; Illinois Trust etc. Bank v. Ottumwa El. Ry., 89 Fed 235.

58 New York, P. & O. R. Co. v. New York, L. E. & W. R. Co., 58 Fed. 268.

has been made, however, between claims for rent and claims arising out of an agreement to divide the earnings. In the latter case, it has been held that an equity arises which entitles the claimant to a preference.[59]

§ 236. **Car Rentals—Track Rentals.**—A claim for car rental that has accrued prior to the receivership is not entitled to preference. "The case of a corporation for the manufacture and sale of cars, dealing with a railroad company, whose road is subject to a mortgage securing outstanding bonds, is very different from that of workmen and employees, or of those who furnish, from day to day, supplies necessary for the maintenance of the railroad. Such a company must be regarded as contracting upon the responsibility of the railroad company, and not in reliance upon the interposition of a court of equity."[60] Priority is also denied to claims for track rentals.[61]

§ 237. **Personal Injuries.**—In accord with the general principle, it is well settled that claims for personal in-

59 Terre Haute & I. R. Co. v. Cox, 102 Fed. 825, 42 C. C. A. 654 The court said: "Two railroad companies, each possessing, and separately operating, a railroad, found it advisable to unify the operation of their roads. They chose, in the execution of their project, that one company should operate, as one line, both roads. The undertaking was, in a certain sense, a joint one; each contributed a part of the means whereby it should be carried out. It certainly was within legal competency, either that the operating company should pay a strict rental for the use of the other's property, or that the earnings of the road, gross or net, as an entirety—the fruit of the joint enterprise—should be divided according to the agreement of the parties."

60 Thomas v. Western Car Co., 149 U. S. 95, 13 Sup. Ct. 824, 37 L ed 663; Grand Trunk Ry. Co. v. Central Vt. R. Co, 90 Fed. 163; Pullman's Palace-Car Co. v. American Loan & Trust Co., 84 Fed. 18, 28 C. C. A. 263 (mileage due under contract for use of Pullman cars)

61 Louisville & N. R. Co. v. Central Trust Co, 87 Fed. 500, 31 C. C. A. 89.

juries arising out of negligence prior to the appointment of a receiver are not entitled to any preference.[62]

62 The reasons are well stated in Farmers' Loan & Trust Co. v. Northern Pac. R. Co, 74 Fed. 431. "But he who has a claim of damages for a negligent act of the railroad company prior to the receivership has no recognized equitable ground for demanding a preferred payment. He has done no act by which either the railroad company or the mortgagee has profited, nor has he surrendered property which has in any way inured to their benefit. Accidents, it is true, are liable to occur, and do occur in the operation of all railroads, and it is impossible to wholly avoid them; but it cannot be said that they are necessary to the road's existence in the same sense that supplies are necessary . . . . He who lends his money on railroad security undoubtedly does so with the contingency that the company may require supplies and equipment, and that, if it become necessary for the protection of the security that a court of chancery shall assume control over the mortgaged property, such claims may intervene between him and the payment of his lien. He incurs also the risk of the negligent conduct of the railroad company, so far as it may directly affect the condition or value of the property. But it cannot be said, and no court has held, that he assumes the risk of the negligence of the railroad company whereby injury results to third persons, and that he, in effect, becomes responsible for the torts which such railroad company may commit against others" In support of the text, see Farmers' Loan & Trust Co. v. Northern Pac. Ry. Co., 79 Fed 227, 24 C. C. A. 511; St. Louis Trust Co. v. Riley, 70 Fed 32, 16 C. C. A. 610, 36 U. S. App. 100, 30 L. R. A. 456; Front St. Cable Ry. Co v. Drake, 84 Fed. 257; Farmers' Loan and Trust Co. v. Nestille, 25 C. C. A. 194, 79 Fed 748; Veatch v. American Loan & Trust Co, 84 Fed. 274, 28 C. C. A. 384; Central Trust Co v. East Tennessee, V. & G. R. Co, 30 Fed 895; Central Trust Co. v Chattanooga etc. R. R. Co., 89 Fed 388; Farmers' Loan & Trust Co. v. Green Bay etc. R. Co, 45 Fed. 664; Farmers' Loan & Trust Co. v Detroit etc. R R. Co, 71 Fed. 29, Davenport v. Alabama & C. R Co, 2 Woods, 519, Fed Cas. No. 3588 A claim for damages for death caused by negligence is not entitled to preference: Veatch v. American L. & T. Co., 79 Fed. 471, 25 C. C A. 39; Farmers' Loan & Trust Co. v. Green Bay etc. R. Co., 45 Fed. 664.

There is a vigorous protest against this line of decisions in Green v. Coast Line R Co., 97 Ga. 15, 54 Am. St. Rep. 379, 24 S. E. 814, 33 L. R. A. 806 The court says "Such corporations incur certain duties and obligations to the public, which adhere firmly to the franchises granted, and cannot be separated from them without legislative consent. These duties and obligations, equally with the franchises them-

§ 238. **Compensation of Receiver—In General.**—A receiver being an officer of the court, provision will be made for his compensation. In cases where the court has jurisdiction to make the appointment, the amount will be fixed by the court and ordered paid out of the fund in the receiver's hands. In the absence of statute, no definite rule governing the allowance can be laid down. Much is left to the sound discretion of the court, and what is reasonable must be determined from a consideration of the particular circumstances of each case. In some states the matter is largely controlled by statute, but even then, provision is frequently made for additional allowances to be determined by the court in the event of special or extraordinary services.[63] In England, the strict rule as to trustees is not applied to receivers.[64]

§ 239. **Discretion as to Amount.**—In the absence of any statutory regulation, the amount of the compensation

selves, are matters of fundamental contract between the corporation and the sovereignty creating it,—a contract which is paramount to all subsequent contracts which the corporation is capable of entering into, with any person or for any purpose. By necessary implication, these latter contracts are always qualified and held in check by the former, and in every conflict they must be subordinated to it. The corporation can grant to others no immunity as to its franchises which it could not claim for itself; nor can it in behalf of its creditors, or any of them, free the franchises from being answerable out of the revenue produced by their exercise, for torts committed in the use of them, whether such torts be committed by the corporation itself or by others using the franchises with its consent or by its permission."

63 For applications of such a statute, see Spears v. Thomas, 24 Ky. Law Rep. 1154, 70 S. W. 1060; Fidelity Nat. Bank's Receiver v. Youtsey, 26 Ky. Law Rep. 340, 81 S. W. 263; United States Trust Co. v. New York, W. S. & B. Ry. Co., 101 N. Y. 478, 5 N. E. 316; Cameron v. Groveland Improvement Co., 72 Am. St. Rep. 77, note.

64 Harris v. Sleep, [1897] 2 Ch. 81.

is left to the discretion of the court.[65] A receiver is entitled to reasonable pay for his services, and such an amount the court will determine and allow. Upon appeal, "the action of the court below is treated as presumptively correct, 'since it has far better means of knowing what is just and reasonable than an appellate court can have.'"[66] This discretion is not absolute, however, and if it can be shown that the amount allowed is unreasonable under all the circumstances, the appellate court will interfere in the interests of justice.[67] Where the receiver is allowed a monthly stipend, the lower court retains the power to change it, and may, in its discretion, reduce the amount.[68]

§ 240. Matters Considered in Determining Amount.—By what means or in what manner the court will arrive at its determination of what is reasonable, no positive rule can be stated. The court is allowed the largest liberty of inquiry and ascertainment. It may, "in connection with the evidence before it, take into consideration its personal knowledge of the general nature and character and value of the services alleged to have been ren-

65 Stuart v. Boulware, 133 U. S. 78, 10 Sup. Ct. 244, 33 L. ed. 568; Cake v. Mohun, 164 U. S. 311, 17 Sup. Ct. 100, 41 L. ed. 447 (amount sustained on appeal, although if question had been an original one, a lower amount would have been fixed); Wilkinson v. Washington Trust Co, 72 C. C. A. 140, 102 Fed. 28; Culver v. H. R. Allen, Sr. Med. & S. Assn., 206 Ill 40, 69 N. E. 53; Heffron v. Rice, 149 Ill. 216, 41 Am St. Rep. 271, 36 N. E. 562; Litchenstein v. Dial, 68 Miss. 54, 8 South. 272; First Nat. Bank v. Oregon Paper Co., 42 Or. 398, 71 Pac. 144, 971.

66 Stuart v. Boulware, 133 U. S. 78, 10 Sup. Ct 244, 33 L. ed. 568, quoting from Trustees v. Greenough, 105 U. S. 527, 537, 26 L. ed. 1157. See, also, Graham v. Carr, 133 N. C. 449, 45 S. E. 847.

67 In Spears v. Thomas, 24 Ky. Law Rep. 1154, 70 S. W. 1060, compensation was reduced from $15,000 to $10,000 See, also, Joralmon v. McPhee, 31 Colo. 40, 76 Pac. 922, Forrester v. Boston & M. Consol. C. & S M. Co., 29 Mont. 397, 76 Pac. 211.

68 In re Angell, 131 Mich. 345, 91 N. W. 611.

dered."[69] But it is only the value of the services as rendered in the particular class of business that will be considered, not the value of the receiver's services in some other line of business.[70] "In receiverships of that character in which the officer is at once receiver and manager of a business, a gross sum may be allowed as specific compensation for services. . . . . In other cases, in which the receiver's duties are confined to the receipt and disbursement of money, the court might wisely refer to the rule and rate of a given percentage in analogous cases, when such percentage is regulated by law, and might properly adopt such rule and rate, if, in its discretion, the same would amount to reasonable compensation."[71] Where the nature of the services is such that the greater part of the work will necessarily have to be done by the receiver's attorney, the court may consider such fact in determining the amount to award.[72]

§ 241. **Effect of Revocation or Reversal of Order Appointing Receiver.**—"If the order appointing a receiver is revoked" for want of jurisdiction, or for such cause is re-

69 Culver v. H R. Allen, Sr. Med. & S. Assn., 206 Ill. 40, 69 N. E. 53. For a good statement of matters which may be considered, see Hickey v. Parrot Silver & Copper Co. (Mont.), 79 Pac. 698.

70 "It is very possible that his time was worth the munificent sum he demands for it, but the court must consider, not the value of his services in larger and more important affairs, but their value to the modest business of which he consented to take charge": Stearns Paint Mfg. Co. v. Comstock, 121 Iowa, 430, 96 N. W. 869.

71 Lichtenstein v. Dial, 68 Miss. 54, 8 South 272. See First Nat. Bank v. Oregon Paper Co., 42 Or. 398, 71 Pac. 144, 971, Tome v. King, 64 Md. 166, 21 Atl. 279 See, also, Jones v. Keen, 115 Mass. 170, where the court intimated that compensation should not be computed upon a percentage basis; Special Bank Commrs. v. Franklin Sav. Inst, 11 R I. 557 (same); Tome v King, 64 Md 166, 21 Atl. 279 (same).

72 Silvers v. Merchants' & M. Sav. Fund & Bldg. Assn. (N. J. Eq.), 56 Atl 294.

versed upon appeal, "and he is directed to return the property to the persons entitled thereto, his compensation, as a general thing, will not be paid out of the funds placed in his hands. When the appointment of the receiver is upon an application adverse to the defendant in the cause, and is without authority of law, the receiver must look for his fees and compensation to the complainant in the suit, upon whose application he was appointed."[73] The amount allowed as compensation in such cases is taxed against the unsuccessful party as costs. In some cases, however, the receiver has been allowed to collect his compensation from the fund, the defendant being protected by being awarded a judgment for costs.[74] It has been held that where a receiver is appointed by the consent of the parties, his compensation may be paid out of the fund in his hands, although it may subsequently develop that the court was without jurisdiction of the subject-matter.[75] And where the appointment was originally valid and within the power of the court, an allowance may be made from the fund, although it may finally be determined that the defendant should prevail.[76]

73 McAnrow v Martin, 183 Ill. 467, 56 N. E. 168. See, also, Link Belt Machinery Co. v. Hughes, 195 Ill. 413, 63 N E. 186 (affirming 95 Ill. App. 323); Highley v. Deane, 168 Ill 266, 48 N. E 50; Ford v. Gilbert, 42 Or. 528, 71 Pac. 971. See St Louis, K. & S. R. Co. v. Wear, 135 Mo. 230, 36 S W. 658, 33 L. R. A. 341, to the effect that when the appointment is in excess of power because the circumstances do not warrant it, compensation should not be deducted from the fund.

74 Cutter v. Pollock, 7 N. D. 631, 76 N. W. 235.

75 Ford v. Gilbert, 42 Or. 528, 71 Pac. 971.

76 Clark v. Brown, 119 Fed. 130, 57 C. C. A. 76; Hopfensack v. Hopfensack, 61 How Pr. 498 ("The receiver's compensation cannot be made to depend upon the result of the litigation. He is the officer of the court who takes the property, the right to which is involved in dispute, and by order of the court holds it for the benefit of the party who shall ultimately be found to be entitled to it.

§ 242. **Effect of Agreement.**—The appointment of a receiver and the fixing of his compensation are judicial acts, and the court is not bound by agreements between individuals as to what it should or should not do.[77] Where, however, one subsequently appointed receiver agrees with a party to serve without compensation in consideration of an agreement of such party not to object to his appointment, the court will not permit him to repudiate his contract. In such case no compensation will be allowed.[78] Nor will compensation be allowed to a receiver who, being interested in the property, represents to the court at the time of his appointment that he will make no such claim.[79] And this has been insisted upon even where it has been shown that the work has proved much greater than was anticipated.[80]

§ 243. **Effect of Adjudication of Bankruptcy.**—The question has arisen as to the source of the receiver's compensation when the debtor goes into bankruptcy subsequently to the appointment of a receiver. It has been

.... The property in the hands of the receiver is the fund from which his fees must be paid'').

77 Lichtenstein v. Dial, 68 Miss. 54, 8 South 272; Polk v. Johnson (Ind. App.), 65 N. E. 536; affirmed, 160 Ind. 292, 98 Am. St. Rep. 274, 66 N. E. 752.

78 Polk v. Johnson (Ind. App.), 65 N. E 536; affirmed, 160 Ind. 292, 98 Am. St. Rep. 274, 66 N. E. 752 (''Beyond question one may waive compensation for any labor performed, both before and after completion; and it is a familiar doctrine that one cannot, after performance, change his mind, and charge for that which he agreed and undertook to do as a gratuity''). It has been held that an agreement with an intervener not to apply for compensation to the detriment of his claim does not entitle the intervener to the allowance of his claim from commissions allowed from funds which would otherwise have been applied in payment of other claims: Broomfield v. Roy, 120 Fed. 502, 56 C. C. A. 652.

79 Steel v. Holladay, 19 Or. 517, 25 Pac. 77.

80 Id.

held that the receiver is entitled to compensation out of the fund before it is turned over to the trustee in bankruptcy. There is no breach of comity between the state and federal courts in such a practice, for the federal court would, if requested, allow such compensation. Ordinarily, the court appointing a receiver can measure more readily and accurately the amount of his services and expenses in the execution of its own decree.[81]

§ 244. Payment of Costs When Fund not Sufficient.—It sometimes happens that the expenses of the receivership are greater than the fund in the hands of the receiver.[82] In such cases the court may ascertain the amount of the deficiency, and it must be borne by the party at whose instance the receiver was appointed. The receiver cannot be justly held to hold and operate the property at his own expense or at that of the court. The party who seeks the aid of the court must see that its officer is protected in his legitimate expenditures.

81 Mauran v. Crown Carpet Lining Co., 23 R. I. 344, 50 Atl. 387; but see *contra*, Bloch v Bloch, 42 Misc. Rep. 278, 86 N. Y. Supp. 1047, holding that where suit was begun and a receiver appointed within four months of the adjudication of bankruptcy, the receiver must look for his compensation to the federal court. The right of the state court to settle the account, allowing payments properly made before the adjudication of bankruptcy was recognized.

82 "If the complainant was not willing to pay the expenses of the receivership it asked for, in the event of the insufficiency of the property to do so, it should not have asked the court to make the appointment, incur the liabilities, and pledge its faith to their payment It was the duty of the complainant to keep informed in respect to the progress of the receivership, the property, and its probable outcome, and, whenever it became unwilling to further stand good for any deficiency, to ask the court to bring to an end the business it undertook and was conducting on complainant's petition": Chapman v. Atlantic Trust Co, 56 C C. A. 61, 119 Fed. 257. See, also, Ephraim v. Pacific Bank, 129 Cal. 589, 62 Pac. 177, Farmers' Nat. Bank v. Backus, 74 Minn. 264, 77 N. W. 142.

The receiver may enforce his right by action after the receivership proceedings are dismissed.[83] In Oregon, however, it is held that employees cannot hold the parties liable for wages due unless terms imposing such liability are made a condition of the appointment or continuance in office of the receiver.[84]

§ 245. **Payment of Costs Where Receivership Proceedings Void.**—Where an order appointing a receiver is beyond the jurisdiction of the court, and is therefore void, the expenses and costs will not be deducted from the fund.[85] In such cases the receiver is left to pursue his remedy against the party at whose instance he was appointed. The same is true when it appears that the property be-

83 Ephraim v. Pacific Bank, 129 Cal. 589, 62 Pac. 177.

84 "The appointment of a receiver in a suit to foreclose a railroad mortgage is not a matter of strict right, but rests in the sound judicial discretion of the court; and it may, as a condition to issuing the necessary order, impose such terms as may, under the circumstances of the particular case, appear to be reasonable, and, if not acceded to, may refuse to make the order. . . . . No court is bound or ought to engage or continue in the operation of a railroad or any other enterprise without the ability to promptly discharge its obligations; and, unless it can do so, it should keep out, or immediately go out, of the business. But, unless such terms are imposed as a condition of the appointment or continuation in office of the receiver, his employees must look to the property in the custody of the court and its income for their compensation . . . . They are the employees and servants of the court, and not of the parties. Their wages are in no sense costs of the litigation; and, although incurred during the progress of the suit, they are not incurred in the suit. They are neither expenses of the plaintiff, nor of the defendant, and are not fees or costs which can be charged against the successful party to the litigation, as is sought to be done in this case": Farmers' Loan & Trust Co. v. Oregon Pac. R Co., 31 Or. 237, 65 Am. St. Rep. 822, 48 Pac. 706, 38 L. R. A. 424, per Bean, J.

85 See § 241, relating to the receiver's compensation in such cases, and authorities there cited. See, also, Sullivan v Gage (Cal.), 79 Pac. 537. Compare Beach v. Macon Grocery Co., 125 Fed. 513, 60 C. C. A. 557; Horn v. Bohn, 96 Md. 8, 53 Atl. 576.

longs to a third person.[86] Where, however, the court has jurisdiction, the fact that the defendant finally prevails will not deprive the receiver of his right to resort to the fund.[87]

86 Howe v. Jones, 66 Iowa, 156, 23 N. W. 376.

87 Clark v. Brown, 119 Fed. 130, 57 C. C. A. 76; Hopfensack v. Hopfensack, 61 How. Pr. 498.

CHAPTER X.

REMOVAL AND DISCHARGE OF RECEIVERS.

ANALYSIS.

§ 246. **Removal of Receiver.**—It is within the discretion of the court to remove a receiver when it appears that for any reason he is not a proper party to remain in charge. If it is shown that he has not accomplished what he should, with due diligence, have succeeded in doing, or if he is incompetent, he may be removed.[1] Any active abuse of trust, such as working for the advancement of private interests at the expense of those of the parties to the proceeding, will warrant such action.[2] Where it appears that his duties as receiver will conflict with his private interests, the court will not hesitate to deprive him of his office.[3] It is his duty to stand neutral between the parties. When, therefore, it appears that there are two hostile parties, both seeking control, the court may remove the representative of one faction and appoint a successor who is not interested with either side.[4]

1 In re Angell, 131 Mich. 345, 91 N. W. 611. To the effect that the receiver cannot appeal from the order removing him, see Ellicott v. Warford, 4 Md. 80, 85; also, § 178, *ante*.

2 Atkins v. Wabash, St. L. & P. Ry. Co., 29 Fed. 161.

3 Eichberg v. Wickham, 21 N. Y. Supp. 647 (duty as assignee to account to receiver).

4 Wood v. Oregon Development Co., 55 Fed. 901 ("The feeling which his appointment creates in the party opposed to those asking his appointment is such that his position will be an embarrassing one, and his usefulness as an officer of the court impaired"); Meier v.

It has been held, however, that the mere fact that the receiver was a director and the treasurer of the defendant corporation is not alone ground for removal.[5] Nor will the fact that he has assisted in promoting a reorganization scheme warrant such action;[6] nor that in the future his private interests may possibly conflict with his duties.[7] The receiver of a large railroad corporation will not be removed on account of fraudulent misconduct of his employees, of which he could know nothing.[8] Mere mistakes in management are not sufficient ground, unless so gross as to show the receiver to be incompetent.[9]

Railway Co., 5 Dill. 478, Fed. Cas. No. 9395 ("It becomes a duty of the court to see that its powers are exercised on principles of strict neutrality as regards the belligerents; and this can be done in this case by removing the representative of these hostile interests, and appointing a receiver who, in feeling and in conduct, will be strictly neutral and strictly honest").

5 Townsend v Oneonta, C. & R. S. Ry Co., 83 N. Y. Supp. 1034, 86 App. Div 604, 13 N. Y. Ann. Cas 402. See *ante*, §§ 152, 153.

6 Clark v. Central R & B Co., 66 Fed. 16; Fowler v. Jarvis-Conklin Mtg Co, 63 Fed. 883. In the former case, Jackson, Cir. J., said: "It is not improper for a receiver in cases like the present, to advise, aid, and encourage reorganization schemes, which offer the prospect of securing the largest measure of protection to the various interests connected with or concerned in the property and assets in the custody of the court, and in the possession of such receiver, for administration and distribution" In the latter case Lacombe, Cir. J., said: "Nor is it any ground for removal that one of the receivers has become a member of a reorganization committee. Several federal courts have approved of such a practice; and although this court entertains a different opinion, and will require absolute neutrality on the part of its officers, as between conflicting plans of reorganization, it will be sufficient if the receiver, now that some conflict over the plan of reorganization is foreshadowed, promptly resign from membership of the committee"

7 Land Title & Trust Co. v. Asphalt Co. of America, 120 Fed. 996.

8 Clarke v Central R. & B. Co., 66 Fed. 16.

9 Clarke v. Central R. & B Co., 66 Fed. 16. In this case the court said "In the management of these extensive properties it is a great deal easier to look back and find faults than it is to guard in advance against mistakes I see things in this case that I disapprove. Some

§ 247. **Discharge of Receiver.**—The removal of a receiver merely changes the personnel; the discharge terminates the receivership.[10] Both of these matters rest largely within the sound discretion of the court.[11] When the object of the appointment has been fulfilled, the receiver should, in general, be discharged.[12] The property should pass, with as little delay as is reasonably practicable, into the possession and control of the owners; and where the parties unduly prolong the proceedings, the court may consider means of ending the matter.[13] It is said that neither entry of judgment in favor of the defendant nor a sale of the property will of itself discharge the receiver. In both cases, however, the court will generally make an order to that effect.[14]

things have been done that were not the best under the circumstances, but, after a careful consideration of the situation, I do not see that the receiver is to be blamed therefor."

10 For a good statement of the distinction between the terms, see Pagett v. Brooks, 140 Ala. 257, 37 South. 263.

11 Hoffman v. Bank of Minot, 4 N. D. 473, 61 N. W. 1031. The order of discharge cannot be collaterally attacked: Ferguson v. Toledo, A. A. & N. M. R. Co., 83 N. Y. Supp. 283, 85 App. Div. 352.

12 Thus, where a receiver is appointed in a stockholder's suit for mismanagement of corporate affairs, the receiver should be discharged when a new set of officers is elected and takes charge. Duncan v. George C. Treadwell Co., 82 Hun, 376, 31 N. Y. Supp. 340. Where the amount of the mortgage debt has been definitely fixed by the court, the defendant has been allowed to pay the sum and have the receiver discharged. Milwaukee & M. R. R. Co. v. Soutter, 69 U. S. 510, 17 L. ed. 900. In general, see Branner v. Webb, 10 Kan. App. 217, 63 Pac. 274

13 Taylor v. Philadelphia & R. R. Co., 9 Fed. 1; Platt v. Philadelphia & R. R. Co, 65 Fed. 872.

14 To the effect that his official character remains until he is discharged by order of the court, see Erb v. Popritz, 59 Kan. 264, 68 Am. St. Rep. 362, 52 Pac. 871. A discharge upon judgment for the defendant is proper, although an appeal may be taken from the judgment: Harris v. Root, 28 Mont. 159, 72 Pac. 429. See, also, Baughman v. Superior Court, 72 Cal 572, 14 Pac. 207. When the order appointing has been vacated, and no property has come into the receiver's hands, he should be discharged. People v. Bushwick

It is said that a receiver should not be discharged upon motion of the complainant upon satisfaction of his claim, against the protest of a non-satisfied creditor, who might be injured thereby.[15] It is held, however, that general creditors are not entitled to notice of the proceedings for discharge.[16] "The effect of a discharge of a receiver, and the surrender of jurisdiction over the trust, without any reservation of existing claims, is to release not only the receiver, but also the property, from further liability."[17]

Chem. Co., 63 Hun, 633, 18 N. Y. Supp. 542; affirmed, 133 N. Y. 694, 31 N. E. 627.

[15] Lenoir v. Linville Imp. Co., 117 N. C. 471, 23 S. E. 442; Fountain v. Mills, 111 Ga. 122, 36 S. E. 428.

[16] New York & W. U. Tel. Co. v. Jewett, 115 N. Y. 166, 21 N. E. 1036; Rockwell v. Portland Sav. Bank, 31 Or. 431, 50 Pac. 566.

[17] Johnson v. Central Trust Co., 159 Ind. 605, 65 N. E. 1028. To the effect that he cannot be sued after discharge, see *ante*, § 179. Where, however, the decree of discharge declares that he may defend suits, a suit commenced at the time may be continued against him: Denver & R. G. R. Co. v. Gunning (Colo.), 80 Pac. 727. For a case holding that the discharge leaves the property subject to all claims and charges, see Texas Pac. R. Co. v. Johnson, 76 Tex. 421, 18 Am. St. Rep. 60, 13 S. W. 463.

CHAPTER XI.

FOREIGN RECEIVERS; ANCILLARY RECEIVERS.

ANALYSIS.

§ 248. **General Tendency Toward Recognition of Rights of Foreign Receiver.**—It has often been said that a receiver appointed by a court of equity has no extra-territorial powers.[1] But while this statement is strictly true, it is apt, under modern conditions, to be misleading. Every reason that would operate, for example, in favor of the recognition of the rights of a foreign corporation would

1 Booth v. Clark, 17 How. 322, 15 L. ed. 164.

operate with equal force in favor of the recognition of the foreign receiver. The latter owes his powers to the order appointing him, which is "the charter of his powers," just as the corporation owes its existence to the charter from the legislature. Both are enabled to act outside of the state of their creation solely by the comity of other states and nations.[2] Those cases which, following *dicta* in the case of Booth v. Clark, broadly lay down the statement that the foreign receiver cannot sue outside of the state of appointment are not in line with the tendency of modern authorities, which is to extend to citizens of or artificial persons created by foreign states the same recognition afforded to the citizens or artificial creatures of the domestic state.[3]

§ 249. **Right of Foreign Receiver to Sue Outside of Jurisdiction of Court of Appointment is Only Recognized Where that Court has Conferred the Power.**—There is no doubt

2 Bank of Augusta v. Earle, 13 Pet. 519, 10 L. ed. 274. The receiver's decree of appointment is called the "charter of his powers" in Schultz v. Phenix Ins. Co., 77 Fed. 375, 387.

3 Gilman v. Ketcham, 84 Wis. 60, 36 Am. St. Rep. 899, 54 N. W. 395, 23 L. R. A. 52, where Pinney, J., says: "The tendency of modern adjudications is in favor of a liberal extension of interstate comity, and against a narrow and provincial policy, which would deny proper effect to judicial proceedings of sister states under their statutes and rights claimed under them, simply because, technically, they are foreign and not domestic"; Boulware v Davis, 90 Ala. 207, 8 South. 84, 9 L. R. A. 601; Hurd v. City of Elizabeth, 41 N. J. L. 1; Tompkins v. Blakey, 70 N. H. 584, 49 Atl. 111. In Lewis v. American Naval Stores Co., 119 Fed. 391, 397, the court says: "The constant tendency of the courts is toward a more enlarged and liberal policy—the recognition of the receiver's right to the possession of the property embraced by the decree appointing him, although situated without the jurisdiction of the court making the appointment. . . . . This tendency is so pronounced and so well sustained by authority that it is probable that the doctrine ultimately to be established will give to receivers the same right of action in all the states of the Union with which they are invested in the jurisdiction in which they are appointed."

that the prevailing rule in America accords the foreign receiver the right to sue outside of the appointing jurisdiction where that right has been conferred upon him in the state of his appointment, when the statutes or public policy of the state do not forbid such suit, and when the rights of domestic creditors, or foreign creditors who have prior attachments are not affected.[4] Of

[4] In Hurd v City of Elizabeth, 41 N. J L. 1, the court, by Beasley, C. J., after quoting the general rule laid down in High on Receivers, § 239, that the foreign receiver cannot sue, says: "There are certainly *dicta* that go even to that exent, so that text-writers seem to have felt themselves warranted in declaring that the powers of an officer of this kind are strictly circumscribed by the jurisdictional limits of the tribunal from which he derives his existence, and that he will not be recognized as a suitor outside of such limits. But I think the more correct definition of the legal rule would be that a receiver cannot sue, or otherwise exercise his functions, in a foreign jurisdiction whenever such acts, if sanctioned, would interfere with the policy established by law in such foreign jurisdiction There seems to be no reason why this should not be the accepted principle .... The question thus raised has nothing to do with that other inquiry that is frequently discussed in the books, whether a receiver at common law is in point of fact clothed with the power to sue in a foreign jurisdiction. .... Conceding that the officer is invested with this fullness of authority, it would appear to be in harmony with those legal principles by which the intercourse of foreign states is regulated, for every government, when its tribunals are appealed to, to render every assistance in its power in furtherance of the execution of such authority, except in those cases when, by so doing, its own policy would be displaced or the rights of its own citizens invaded or impaired. .... To sanction such a plea would be to frustrate, as far as possible, the foreign procedure, simply for the purpose of doing so, the single result being that a court would be baffled, and perhaps prevented from doing justice. Such ought not to be the legal attitude of governments towards each other"; Graydon v Church, 7 Mich. 36, Hale v. Hardon, 95 Fed. 747, 37 C. C. A. 240; Tompkins v. Blakey, 70 N. H 584, 49 Atl. 111; National T. Co. v. Miller, 33 N. J. Eq. 155; Sobernheimer v. Wheeler, 45 N. J. Eq. 614, 18 Atl. 234; Bidlack v Mason, 26 N. J. Eq. 230; Howarth v. Angle, 162 N. Y. 179, 56 N E. 489, 47 L. R. A. 725; Lycoming Ins Co. v. Wright, 55 Vt. 526; Parker v. Stoughton Mill Co, 91 Wis. 174, 51 Am. St. Rep. 881, 64 N. W. 751, Rogers v. Riley, 80 Fed. 759; Barley v. Gittings, 15 App. Dec. 427; and cases cited below in sections on Rights of Attaching Creditors The foreign receiver may

course, a preliminary question in regard to his capacity is always to be answered: Has he been authorized by the appointing jurisdiction to sue? Such power should appear from his pleading; as that he has been expressly authorized to sue,[5] or that he is an assignee vested with

even sue to recover real property, or to foreclose a mortgage on such property Lewis v. Clark, 129 Fed. 570, 64 C. C. A. 138; Small v. Smith, 14 S. D. 621, 86 Am. St. Rep. 808, 86 N. W. 649. Many cases, however, go to the length of denying the foreign receiver the right to sue, even where no rights of creditors or others intervene: Holmes v. Sherwood, 16 Fed. 725, 3 McCrary, 405, Hazard v. Durant, 19 Fed. 471, 476, Commercial Nat. Bank v. Motherwell Iron & Steel Co, 95 Tenn 172, 31 S. W. 1002, 29 L. R. A. 164; Moreau v. Du Bellet (Tex. Civ. App.), 27 S. W. 503; Moseby v. Burrow, 52 Tex. 402. See, also, the recent case, Great Western Min. & Mfg. Co. v. Harris (May 29, 1905), 25 Sup. Ct. 770. These cases all rest on the *dicta* in Booth v. Clark, *supra*, which, it is submitted, decided no such point. The foreign receiver's right rests on a somewhat more substantial ground than "by favor of courtesy" (Boulware v. Davis, 90 Ala. 207, 8 South. 84, 9 L. R. A. 601), nor should it be denied because the court in its "discretion" thinks that the cause of action is inequitable: Wyman v. Eaton, 107 Iowa, 217, 70 Am. St. Rep. 193, 77 N. W. 865, 43 L R. A. 695. "Comity is neither matter of absolute obligation nor of mere courtesy and good-will. It is the recognition which one nation allows within its territory to the legislative, executive, or judicial acts of another nation, having due regard both to international duty and convenience, and to the rights of its own citizens or of other persons who are under the protection of the laws": Hilton v. Guyot, 159 U. S. 113, 16 Sup. Ct. 139, 40 L. ed. 95. It must be remembered that the recognition of the foreign act is made by the political branch of the government, the courts merely declaring the state's mandates. See Wyman v. Kimberly Clark Co., 93 Wis. 554, 67 N. W 932, for a proper conception of "comity." Where the corporation for which the receiver has been appointed has violated the laws of the state, the courts will not allow the receiver appointed in the state of the corporation's domicile to sue: Parker v. Lamb, 99 Iowa, 265, 68 N. W. 686, 34 L. R. A. 704. Compare article on Extra-territorial Jurisdiction of Receivers in 22 Am. L. Reg. 289 (1883), by Adelbert Hamilton, with article on same subject, 58 Cent. L. J. 284 (1903), to illustrate development of law on the subject of rights of foreign receivers.

5 Swing v. White River L. Co., 91 Wis. 517, 65 N. W. 174 (receiver must aver right to sue, unless he is assignee); Castleman v. Templeman, 87 Md. 546, 67 Am. St. Rep. 363, 40 Atl. 275, 41 L. R. A. 367.

an interest which would enable him to maintain an action,[6] or that the defendant has recognized his right.[7] The question is therefore often complicated by local rules of practice and pleading. Thus, in states where the assignee cannot sue at law on an assigned chose in action in his own name, a receiver to whom such chose in action has been assigned by judicial proceedings in the state of his appointment cannot maintain an action at law on such assigned claim.[8] Generally the rules as to capacity of parties depend upon the *lex fori*.[9]

§ 250. **Right of Foreign Receiver to Sue not Dependent on Existence of Cause of Action in State Exercising Comity.**— It is no objection, however, to the right of a foreign receiver to maintain an action in the local courts that the cause of action is unknown to the law administered in those courts. "It is not necessary that the process to enforce the liability in question," says Vann, J., "should be that required by statute in this state in the case of domestic corporations, as that would be frequently impossible and would withhold the right of comity altogether. It is sufficient if the method of procedure in our courts is such that no injustice is done to the de-

6 See *infra*, Action by Receivers not Dependent on Comity; (1) Property Rights, § 255.

7 See *infra*, Actions by Receivers not Dependent on Comity; (2) Rights by Contract, § 256.

8 Murtey v. Allen, 71 Vt. 377, 76 Am. St. Rep. 779, 45 Atl. 752; King v. Cochran, 72 Vt. 107, 47 Atl. 394.

9 Minor on Conflict of Laws, § 206, to the effect that all these matters are determined by the *lex fori*. An ordinary foreign receiver cannot sue in his own name: Wilson v. Welch, 157 Mass. 77, 31 N. E. 712; even though authorized to do so by the court of appointment: Hayward v. Leeson, 176 Mass. 310, 57 N. E. 656, 49 L. R. A. 725. See, also, Rogers v. Haines, 96 Ala. 586, 11 South. 651, 103 Ala. 198, 15 South. 606.

fendant or to any citizen of this state, and the established policy of the state is not interfered with."[10]

§ 251. **Rights of Attaching Creditors Against Foreign Receivers.**—In accordance with these principles it is well settled that courts will permit receivers appointed by tribunals in foreign jurisdictions (in whom, strictly speaking, no *rights* are vested in things outside of the state of appointment) to recover possession of personal property or to enforce the collection of choses in action, even from its own citizens, where no rights of third persons have intervened.[11] Some of the cases seem to place this right of the foreign receiver to sue for choses in action upon the ground that the situs of the chose in action is at the domicile of the creditor, and therefore he becomes vested with the property by assignment at the domicile,[12] but this principle could not explain his right to sue for tangible and immovable things in the second jurisdiction, and it is submitted that the better ground upon which these decisions rest is the right of comity. The real reason is, as was said by the New Hampshire court: "The question is not strictly one of law. It is, rather, one of courteous treatment of an officer of a sister state."[13]

§ 252. **Right of Attaching Creditors with Reference to Citizenship or Residence.**—Where the rights of third persons, citizens of the state in which the foreign receiver sues, have attached to property, or to a fund, before the

10 Howarth v. Angle, 162 N. Y. 179, 56 N. E. 489, 47 L. R. A. 725, 730.

11 See cases cited in note 4, *supra.*

12 Gilbert v. Hewetson, 79 Minn. 326, 79 Am. St Rep 486, 82 N. W. 655; Parker v. Stoughton Mill Co., 91 Wis. 174, 51 Am. St. Rep. 881, 64 N. W. 751.

13 Tompkins v. Blakey, 70 N. H. 584, 49 Atl. 111.

foreign receiver has been appointed, it is generally held that such rights will prevail, and that the rule of comity does not extend to aiding the foreign receiver in collecting the fund or property so as to impair such vested rights.[14] The cases have usually had to deal with the rights of attaching creditors who were also citizens or residents of the state in which the attachment was levied, but where the question has been raised it has been held that a *bona fide* attaching creditor, even though he be not a citizen of the state, will be protected in his lien or possession as against a foreign receiver subsequently appointed.[15] It is submitted that this doctrine is not only equitable, but also that no distinction can be permitted between citizens and other

14 Catlin v. Wilcox Silver Plate Co., 123 Ind. 477, 18 Am. St. Rep. 338, 24 N. E. 250, 8 L. R. A. 62; Solis v. Blank, 199 Pa. St. 600, 49 Atl. 302; Frowert v. Blank, 205 Pa. St. 299, 54 Atl. 1000; Southern B & L. Assn. v. Price, 88 Md. 155, 41 Atl. 53, 42 L. R. A. 206; Taylor v. Columbian Ins. Co., 14 Allen, 353; Ward v. Connecticut Pipe Mfg. Co., 71 Conn. 345, 71 Am St. Rep. 207, 41 Atl. 1057, 42 L. R. A. 706; Ward v. Pacific Mut. Life Ins. Co., 135 Cal. 235, 67 Pac. 124; Zacher v. Fidelity T. & S. V. Co., 106 Fed. 593, 45 C. C. A. 480; Hunt v. Columbian Ins. Co., 55 Me. 290, 92 Am. Dec. 592; Booth v. Clark, 17 How. 322, 15 L. ed. 164 Even where no rights by way of lien appear courts will not exercise comity to the prejudice of other creditors: Olney v. Tanner, 10 Fed. 101; Baldwin v. Hosmer, 101 Mich. 119, 59 N. W. 432, 25 L. R. A. 739; Holbrook v. Ford, 153 Ill. 633, 46 Am. St. Rep. 917, 39 N. E. 109, 27 L. R. A. 324. In the case of Falk v. Janes, 49 N. J. Eq. 484, 23 Atl. 813, a foreign receiver appointed on a creditor's bill was held entitled to maintain the action even to the prejudice of a citizen of New Jersey, where he prosecuted the action solely for the benefit of another citizen of New Jersey.

15 Ward v. Connecticut Pipe Mfg. Co, 71 Conn. 345, 41 Atl. 1057, 71 Am. St. Rep. 207, 42 L. R. A. 706; Linville v. Hadden, 88 Md. 594, 41 Atl. 1097, 43 L. R. A. 222; Solis v. Blank, 199 Pa. St. 600, 49 Atl. 302; Catlin v. Wilcox Silver Plate Co., 123 Ind. 477, 24 N. E. 250, 18 Am. St. Rep. 338, 8 L. R. A. 62. That the same protection is often extended to such creditors, attaching *after* the appointment of the foreign receiver, see Gerding v. East Tennessee L. Co., 185 Mass. 380, 70 N. E. 206, and cases cited; cf. next section.

persons under the equal protection of the law clause in the federal constitution. Even where the attaching creditor is a resident or citizen of the state where the receiver is appointed, there would seem to be no reason on principle why he should not be allowed to retain his preference by the courts of the state of the attachment,[16] unless he has been enjoined by the state of his citizenship in the order appointing a receiver from maintaining the attachment proceeding. If such injunction has been issued—and it is well settled that the appointing court may enjoin those subject to its jurisdiction from prosecuting attachments in foreign states—the court of the state in which the attachment was issued would doubtless have power to suspend proceedings until the court in which the receiver was appointed could enforce its orders, and, in a spirit of comity, such would probably be the procedure.[17]

§ 253. Rights of Foreign Receiver Against Subsequent Attaching Creditors.—Difficult questions often arise where the attaching creditors in the local state have attached after the appointment of the receiver in the domiciliary state. If the receiver has obtained possession, his possession should be protected. His possession is in the nature of a property right, and is held so to be almost universally.[18] But where the receiver has not yet col-

16 Hibernia National Bank v. Lacombe, 84 N. Y. 367, 38 Am. Rep. 518.

17 Avery v. Boston Safe Deposit & T. Co, 72 Fed. 700. In American Waterworks Co. v. Farmers' L. & T. Co., 20 Colo. 203, 46 Am. St. Rep 285, 37 Pac. 269, 25 L. R. A. 338, the court, on motion of a foreign receiver, granted a motion to dismiss a writ of error brought by the corporation's officers, where the court of appointment had enjoined them from taking such proceedings.

18 Chicago etc. Ry. v. Keokuk etc. Packet Co., 108 Ill. 317, 48 Am. Rep 557, where the receiver appointed in the foreign state brought into Illinois a vessel which was attached by local creditors.

lected the fund or taken the property into his possession, and creditors or others have obtained rights or liens upon the property or fund in the state where it is situated, some distinctions must be observed. If the appointment of the receiver is involuntary, especially in aid of a statutory judicial proceeding, the prevailing doctrine seems to be that, where the rights of domestic creditors are involved, the assignment will not be recognized outside of the jurisdiction of appointment.[19] But if the appointment be by voluntary act, as on the dissolution of a corporation on its own petition, or if a common-law assignment be made to the receiver, the assignment will be recognized elsewhere.[20] In the latter case, therefore, if the foreign receiver's title be rec-

The foreign receiver was allowed to replevy the vessel: Robertson v Staed, 135 Mo. 135, 58 Am St. Rep. 569, 36 S. W. 610, 33 L. R. A 203, where the receiver was appointed in Mexico; Osgood v. Maguire, 61 N Y. 524; Merchants' etc. Bank v. McLeod, 38 Ohio St. 174; Bagby v. Atlantic etc. R R. Co., 86 Pa. St. 291; Pond v. Cooke, 45 Conn. 126, 29 Am. Rep. 668, Merchants' Nat. Bank v. Penn. Steel Co., 57 N. J. L. 336, 30 Atl. 545. The case of Humphreys v. Hopkins, 81 Cal. 551, 15 Am. St. Rep. 176, 22 Pac. 892, 6 L. R. A. 792, is out of the line of authority.

19 Security Trust Co. v. Dodd, Mead & Co., 173 U. S. 624, 19 Sup. Ct. 545, 43 L. ed. 835; Cole v. Cunningham, 133 U. S. 107, 129, 10 Sup. Ct 269, 33 L ed. 538; Catlin v. Wilcox Silver Plate Co., 123 Ind. 477, 18 Am. St. Rep. 338, 24 N. E. 250, 8 L R. A. 62; Gray v. Covert, 25 Ind. App. 561, 81 Am. St. Rep. 117, 58 N. E. 731; Ward v. Connecticut Pipe Co., 71 Conn. 345, 71 Am. St. Rep. 207, 41 Atl. 1057, 42 L. R. A. 706; Gilbert v. Howetson, 79 Minn. 326, 79 Am. St. Rep. 486, 82 N. W. 655. In Reynolds v. Adden, 136 U. S. 348, 354, 10 Sup Ct. 843, 34 L. ed. 360, the supreme court of the United States says: "When the transfer of a debtor's property is the result of a judicial proceeding, there is no provision of the constitution which requires the courts of another state to carry it into effect, and as a general rule no state court will do this to the prejudice of the citizens of its own state." See, also, Zacher v. Fidelity Trust etc. Co., 109 Ky. 441, 59 S. W. 493, Zacher v. Fidelity Trust etc. Co., 106 Fed 593, 45 C. C. A. 480.

20 In addition to cases cited in last note, see note in 23 L. R. A. 33.

ognized, those who attach after such assignment have nothing to levy upon, and the receiver's title will prevail over the attaching creditor's.[21] This is almost uniformly held to be the law in cases where the attaching creditors are not domestic creditors, but many states protect the domestic creditor, though his lien be subsequent to the assignment, without recognizing the distinction between voluntary and involuntary assignments.[22] If the assignment and appointment were involuntary, it is uniformly held that the rights of the attaching creditors will prevail.[23]

§ 254. Same; As Affected by Questions of Citizenship or Residence.—In some of the cases the attaching creditor has been a citizen of the state in which the foreign receiver was appointed, and notwithstanding the appointment of the receiver in the creditor's home state, has attached property in a foreign state. If he had been enjoined from so proceeding, or had been a party to the

21 "A voluntary conveyance of goods made by the owner at his domicile in a form which is sufficient there and also at common law, is effectual to transfer the title, although they may be at the time in another state, unless the statutes or the local policy of that state forbid": Ward v. Connecticut Pipe Mfg. Co., 71 Conn 345, 71 Am. St. Rep. 207, 41 Atl. 1057, 42 L. R. A. 706; Weller v J. B. Pace Tobacco Co., 2 N. Y. Supp. 292, in which a foreign receiver was given preference over a subsequent domestic attaching creditor.

22 Lackmann v. Supreme Council (1904), 142 Cal. 22.

23 Gray v. Covert, 25 Ind. App. 561, 81 Am. St. Rep. 117, 58 N E. 731; Ward v. Connecticut Pipe Mfg. Co., 71 Conn. 345, 71 Am. St. Rep. 207, 41 Atl 1057, 42 L. R A. 706; Barth v. Backus, 140 N. Y. 230, 37 Am. St. Rep. 545, 35 N. E. 425, 23 L. R. A. 47; Catlin v. Wilcox Silver Plate Co., 123 Ind. 477, 18 Am. St. Rep. 338, 24 N. E. 250, 8 L. R. A. 62; Thum v. Pingree, 21 Utah, 348, 61 Pac. 18, The Willamette Valley, 66 Fed. 565, 13 C. C. A. 635; Hibernia Nat. Bank v. Lacombe, 84 N. Y. 367, 38 Am. Rep. 518, Gilman v. Ketcham, 84 Wis. 60, 36 Am. St. Rep. 899, 54 N. W. 395, 23 L. R A. 52; Choctaw Coal & M. Co. v. Williams-Echols Dry Goods Co. (Ark.), 87 S. W. 632, Gerding v. East Tenn. L. Co., 185 Mass. 380, 70 N. E. 206.

proceeding in which the receiver was appointed—in this case even though not a citizen of the state of appointment—and has attempted to gain a priority by attaching before the receiver could get possession, he will not only be adjudged guilty of a contempt by the court of appointment, but his attachments will not be allowed to prevail in the other jurisdiction.[24] If no injunction had been issued, however, even though the attaching creditor was not only subject to the jurisdiction of the appointing court as a citizen or resident, but also had actual notice of the appointment of the receiver, some courts permit him to enter into a race with the receiver to get possession and reward his diligence by holding that while he is on the same footing with other persons, the receiver appointed in involuntary proceedings will not be recognized so as to prejudice the diligent creditor's rights. It is submitted that the better rule is with those courts which deny priority to a creditor attaching under such circumstances.[25]

§ 255. **Actions by Foreign Receiver not Dependent on Comity; (1) Property Rights.**—Some confusion has arisen from the failure on the part of certain courts to recog-

24 Gilman v. Ketcham, 84 Wis 60, 36 Am St. Rep. 899, 54 N. W. 395, 23 L. R. A. 52; Cole v. Cunningham, 133 U. S. 107, 129, 10 Sup. Ct. 269, 33 L ed. 538, Farmers' L. & T. Co. v. Bankers' Tel. Co., 148 N. Y. 315, 51 Am. St. Rep. 690, 42 N. E. 707, 31 L. R. A. 403; Hibernia Nat. Bank v. Lacombe, 84 N. Y. 367, 38 Am. Rep. 518; Bacon v. Horne, 123 Pa. St. 452, 16 Atl 794, 2 L. R. A. 355; Schindelholz v. Cullum, 55 Fed. 885, 5 C. C. A. 293; Barth v. Backus, 140 N. Y. 230, 37 Am. St. Rep. 545, 35 N. E. 425, 23 L. R. A. 47; Rhawn v. Pierce, 110 Ill. 350, 51 Am. Rep. 691; Faulkner v. Hyman, 142 Mass. 53; Castleman v. Templeman, 87 Md. 546, 67 Am. St. Rep. 363, 40 Atl. 275, 41 L. R. A. 367.

25 Hibernia Nat. Bank v. Lacombe, 84 N. Y. 367, 38 Am. Rep. 518; Barth v. Backus, 140 N. Y. 230, 37 Am. St. Rep. 545, 35 N. E. 425, 23 L. R. A. 47, Gilman v. Ketcham, 84 Wis. 60, 36 Am. St. Rep. 899, 54 N. W. 395, 23 L. R. A. 52; and cases cited in last note.

nize the difference between acts of the receiver which are permitted by comity and acts which give rise to rights in the receiver. Of the latter class are the assignments already mentioned where the receiver is clothed with the legal title to the assets of the corporation or person whom he represents. In such cases he sues in the foreign jurisdiction not by reason of the comity of the state, but as a matter of right. It matters not whether the thing was in possession or a chose in action; the assignee or receiver who has been invested with the title should, on principle, have the right, aside from comity, to sue on his legal title in any state of the Union. The owner of the thing has a right to transfer it, and such transfer passes title. Not so with a judicial transfer which owes its force to a statute, the effect of which can only be carried out by foreign states through the exercise of comity. The modern cases recognize the difference and hold that a receiver who is in effect a trustee or assignee may sue in his own name. "The effect of such a transfer on goods in another state is not to be determined simply by the rule of comity which is applicable to extra-territorial assignments by operation of law, but rests on the general principles of jurisprudence as to the right of every one to dispose of what he owns."[26]

[26] Baldwin, J., in Ward v. Connecticut Pipe Mfg. Co., 71 Conn. 345, 71 Am. St. Rep. 207, 41 Atl. 1057, 42 L. R. A. 706. Where the receiver is practically an assignee or trustee he may sue in his own name: Howarth v. Lombard, 175 Mass. 570, 56 N. E. 888, 49 L. R. A. 301, Cushing v. Perot, 175 Pa. St. 66, 52 Am. St. Rep. 835, 34 Atl. 447, 34 L. R. A 737; Merchants' National Bank v. Northwestern Mfg. etc. Co, 48 Minn 349, 51 N. W. 117; American Nat. Bank v. National Ben etc. Co., 70 Fed. 420; Failey v. Talbee, 55 Fed. 892; Avery v. Boston S. D. & T. Co., 72 Fed. 700, Homer v. Barr Pumping Engine Co., 180 Mass. 163, 91 Am. St. Rep. 269, 61 N. E. 883, Buswell v. Order of Iron Hall, 161 Mass. 224, 36 N. E. 1065, 23 L. R. A. 846; Howarth v. Angle, 162 N. Y. 179, 56 N. E. 489, 47 L. R. A. 725.

§ 256. **Same; (2) Rights by Contract.**—Another case in which the receiver maintains the action not on principles of comity, but on grounds of right is where the defendant has by contract assented to the appointment of the receiver, in the event of dissolution of a corporation, *e. g.,* of which he is a stockholder, or the winding up of an insurance company in which he is a policy holder. In such cases the right of the receiver to sue depends upon the promise of the subscriber or policy holder "to pay the sum in question to any receiver properly appointed." The action is "founded not on the right of a foreign receiver to sue upon demands in favor of the party he may represent, but on the right of a substituted promisee to sue a promisor whose contract provided for such substitution."[27]

§ 257. **Power of Court of Appointment Over Receiver and Other Parties.**—Several cases are reported where a court of equity has appointed a receiver of land situated in a foreign state. There is no doubt in such cases but that the court can enforce its orders against those who are subject to its jurisdiction, either territorially or by having submitted themselves to the court in the proceeding in which the receiver has been appointed. The court, of course, has control of its receiver wherever he may act, and in the same manner it can control the parties to the action and interveners. The court often enjoins parties from proceeding with actions pending in a foreign court. In such case, the foreign state

27 Baldwin, J., in Fish v. Smith, 73 Conn. 377, 84 Am. St. Rep. 161, 47 Atl. 711, 713; Wheeler v. Dime Savings Bank, 116 Mich. 271, 72 Am. St. Rep. 521, 74 N. W. 496; Relfe v. Rundle, 103 U. S. 222, 26 L. ed. 337; Rundle v. Life Assn. of America, 10 Fed. 720, 4 Woods, 94; Taylor v. Life Assn. of America, 13 Fed. 493, Fry v. Charter Oak L. Ins. Co., 31 Fed. 197; Weingartner v. Insurance Co, 32 Fed. 314; Hale v. Hardon, 95 Fed. 747, 37 C. C. A. 240.

should enforce the injunction issued in the domiciliary state by refusing to proceed with the litigation or ordering proceedings dismissed.[28] In a case in Michigan, the supreme court of that state gave effect to a sale by a receiver appointed in a foreign state of land lying in Michigan.[29] The decision seems conformable with the spirit of comity that prevails among the American states. No rights of creditors or others being involved, the court properly recognized the act of the foreign receiver in selling the land under order of court.

28 In Schindelholz v. Cullum, 54 Fed. 885, 5 C. C. A. 293, Thayer, J., says. "Courts which have appointed receivers over property situated in a foreign jurisdiction may either restrain or punish persons who interfere with the receiver's possession of such property; even though the interference consists in attaching it under process obtained from some court in the foreign state. . . . . In all these cases, however, the person proceeded against for interfering with the receiver's constructive possession of property located in a foreign jurisdiction was either a party to the litigation in which the receiver had been appointed, or in privity with a party, or was otherwise subject to the jurisdiction of the court by virtue of his residence or citizenship." See, also, Mercantile Ins. Co. v. River Plate etc. Agency Co, [1892] 2 Ch. 303; Lord Cranstown v. Johnston, 3 Ves. 170, Cole v. Cunningham, 133 U. S. 107, 129, 10 Sup. Ct. 269, 33 L. ed 538; Chesapeake etc. Ry. Co. v. Swayze, 60 N. J. Eq. 417, 47 Atl. 28; Chafee v. Quidnick Co., 13 R. I. 442; Sercomb v. Catlin, 128 Ill. 556, 15 Am. St. Rep. 147, 21 N. E. 606, Holbrook v. Ford, 153 Ill. 633, 46 Am. St. Rep. 917, 39 N. E. 1091, 27 L. R. A. 324. A receiver acting beyond the territorial jurisdiction of the court is still subject to its orders: Guarantee T. & S. D. Co. v. P. R. & N. E R. R., 69 Conn. 709, 38 Atl. 792, 38 L R. A 804. A receiver may be appointed in a creditor's bill or in proceedings supplementary to execution, and the debtor who is within the jurisdiction of the court may be required to convey land outside of the state to such receiver: Mitchell v. Bunch, 2 Paige, 606, 22 Am. Dec. 669; Bailey v. Ryder, 10 N. Y. 363, Towne v. Campbell, 35 Minn 231, 28 N. W. 254; Tomlinson etc. Co. v. Shatto, 34 Fed. 380. In American Waterworks Co. v. Farmers' L. & T. Co., 20 Colo. 203, 46 Am. St. Rep. 285, 37 Pac. 269, 25 L. R. A. 338, a writ of error was dismissed where the corporation prosecuting the writ had been enjoined in a foreign court appointing a receiver of the corporation, from prosecuting the action.

29 Dunlap v. Byers, 110 Mich. 109, 67 N. W. 1067.

§ 258. **Ancillary Receivers; Appointment.**—Instead of delivering to the foreign receiver the property or fund, the courts of the state may appoint an ancillary receiver for the purpose of taking charge of such fund or property.[30] This will be done where it is necessary to protect the rights of resident creditors, or of nonresidents who have attached the property or fund.[31] But it is entirely discretionary with the court whether an ancillary receiver will be appointed or not.[32] Although certain courts have permitted such appointment on an *ex parte* application,[33] the proper practice is to file an independent bill showing grounds for the appointment of such receiver. Where the property is situated in several states, as a railroad, the federal courts have adopted the rule *ex comitate* that the primary receiver will be appointed ancillary receiver in the several districts through which the railroad passes, in this way artificially providing for a harmony which could as well be preserved on the general principles of comity without the creation of ancillary receivership.[34]

30 Williams v. Hintermeister, 26 Fed. 889; Mabon v. Ongley Electric Co., 156 N. Y. 196, 50 N. E. 805; Holbrook v. Ford, 153 Ill. 633, 46 Am. St. Rep. 917, 39 N. E. 1091, 27 L. R. A. 324; Evans v. Pease, 21 R. I. 187, 42 Atl. 506; Irwin v. Granite State Prov. Assn., 56 N J. Eq. 244, 38 Atl. 680; Lewis v. American Naval Stores Co., 119 Fed 391. The court of domicile in all such cases is the primary court: Southern B. & L. Assn. v. Miller, 118 Fed 369, 55 C. C. A. 195; and the ancillary courts must follow the courts of primary jurisdiction, except so far as the purposes of the ancillary receivership are concerned: Farmers' L. & T. Co. v. Northern Pac. R. R., 72 Fed. 26.

31 Mabon v. Ongley Electric Co, 156 N. Y. 196, 50 N. E. 805.

32 See the cases cited in the last two notes.

33 Mercantile Trust Co. v. Kanawha etc. Ry. Co., 39 Fed. 337, to the effect that independent bill should be filed. In Platt v. Philadelphia etc. Ry. Co., 54 Fed. 569, the appointment was granted *ex parte*. In Mabon v. Ongley Electric Co, 156 N. Y 196, 50 N. E. 805, it is held that the court will not appoint an ancillary receiver on the mere petition of the primary receiver.

34 Dillon v. Oregon S. L. etc Co, 66 Fed 622; Central Trust Com-

§ 259. Ancillary Receivers; Administration of the Fund.—A broad distinction exists between the powers of ancillary receivers and those of primary receivers. So far as the court of their appointment is concerned, the latter are absolutely amenable to its process, and, as we have seen, the administration of the entire fund, wherever it may lie, can by means of the injunctive process of the appointing court, aided by the comity of the courts of sister states, be conducted by the primary tribunal. But in the case of an ancillary receiver, *ex vi termini,* there can be no administration of any fund lying outside of the territorial jurisdiction of the appointing court. The very word "ancillary" implies a principal, in whom is vested the general administration. Accordingly, we find it determined that the court of ancillary appointment cannot exercise any control over assets in another state by means of injunction against its citizens or against the parties,[35] and that a judgment rendered against an ancillary receiver binds only property in the jurisdiction of appointment.[36] So, also, because the entire fund is being administered elsewhere, claims which more properly exist against the general estate have been referred to the

pany v. Wabash etc. Ry. Co., 29 Fed. 620; Jennings v. Philadelphia etc. R. R. Co., 23 Fed. 569; Young v. Montgomery R. R. Co., 2 Woods, 618, Fed. Cas. No. 18,166; New York P. & O R. v. New York L. E. etc. R. Co., 58 Fed. 268; Coltrane v. Templeton, 106 Fed. 370, 45 C. C. A. 328; Central R. Co. v. Farmers' L. & T. Co, 125 Fed. 1001, 60 C. C. A. 400. In two cases this rule was not followed, by Judge Gresham in Atkins v. Wabash Ry. Co., 29 Fed. 162, and by Judge Simonton in Phinzy v. Augusta R. R. Co., 56 Fed 273. The same rule was followed in Port Royal etc. Ry. Co. v. King, 93 Ga. 63, 19 S. E. 809, 24 L. R. A. 730, as between state courts.

35 Holbrook v. Ford, 153 Ill. 633, 46 Am. St. Rep. 917, 39 N. E. 1091, 27 L. R. A. 324

36 Reynolds v. Stockton, 140 U. S. 254, 11 Sup. Ct. 773, 35 L. ed. 464.

original court.[37] Of course, the ancillary receiver in managing the estate in his possession may do acts in other jurisdictions, such as making contracts to carry on the branch of the business under his management, or the carrying of cars belonging to the division of a railroad of which he is receiver, giving rise to jural relations. Where such relations arise they will be respected, and the ancillary receiver may have proper remedies even outside the state of his appointment to protect him in doing said acts, in accordance with the principle that his possession and vested rights will be protected everywhere as property rights, just as any bailee's possession or promisee's right is protected.[38]

§ 260. **Ancillary Receivers; Administration of the Fund; How Far Conclusive on Primary Receiver.**—"Where a receiver or administrator or other custodian of an estate is appointed by the courts of one state, the courts of that state reserve to themselves full and exclusive jurisdiction over the assets of the estate within the limits of the state. Whatever orders, judgments or decrees may be rendered by the courts of another state in respect of so much of the estate as is within its limits, must be accepted as conclusive in the courts of primary jurisdiction; and whatever matters are permitted by the courts of primary jurisdiction to be litigated in the courts of another state come within the same rule of conclusiveness. Beyond this, the proceedings of the courts of a state in which ancillary administration is held are not conclusive upon the administration in the courts of the state in which primary administration is

37 Central Trust Co. v. East Tenn. etc. R. Co., 30 Fed. 895; Clyde v. Richmond etc. R. R. Co., 56 Fed. 539.

38 Guarantee T. & S. D. Co. v. P. R. & N. E. R. R., 69 Conn. 709, 38 L. R. A. 804, 38 Atl. 792; and cases cited *supra*, § 255.

had."[39] Neither the party whose estate is being administered, nor the primary receiver who submits to the foreign court without leave from the court of appointment, can confer a jurisdiction on the ancillary court, by voluntary appearance, because the jurisdiction over the subject matter is absent.[40] The determination of the ancillary court on questions of local law, *e. g.*, taxation, are, of course, binding on the primary court.[41]

§ 261. **Ancillary Receivers; Surrender of Fund.**—Although it has been held that the court of ancillary administration will provide that the citizens of its state be paid in full, before the balance is transmitted to the primary receiver,[42] it is submitted that no rule can be supported which does not put other persons on an equality in regard to the administration.[43] But the requirement that all shall have the equal protection of the law does not prevent the court of ancillary administration from demanding security from the primary receiver for the equal treatment of its own citizens in the final distribution, as a condition of the surrender of the funds in its possession.[44] And it is proper that the court of ancillary jurisdiction should provide for the retention of a fund required by the laws of the state as a condition precedent to an insurance com-

39 Brewer, J., in Reynolds v. Stockton, 140 U. S. 254, 272, 11 Sup. Ct. 773, 35 L. ed. 464.

40 Reynolds v. Stockton, *supra*.

41 Fletcher v. Harney Peak Tin Min. Co., 84 Fed. 555.

42 Sands v. Greeley, 83 Fed. 772.

43 Blake v. McClung, 172 U. S. 239, 19 Sup. Ct. 165, 43 L. ed. 432; People v. Granite State Provident Assn., 161 N. Y. 492, 55 N. E. 1053.

44 People v. Granite State Provident Assn., 161 N. Y. 492, 55 N. E. 1053; Baldwin v. Hosmer, 101 Mich. 119, 59 N. W. 432, 25 L. R. A. 739; Buswell v. Order of Iron Hall, 161 Mass. 224, 36 N. E. 1065, 23 L. R. A. 846.

pany's transacting business in the state, until all domestic creditors and policy-holders should be paid in full—the fund being primarily devoted to that purpose.[45] In general, it may be said that the court of ancillary jurisdiction will not surrender possession of the funds in its control to the primary receiver until satisfied that those for whom the ancillary administration was had—the citizens and residents of the state, and creditors invoking its laws—will be fully protected if the fund is surrendered.[46] It may, if it prefers, retain the fund and pay its citizens a proportionate amount of their debts, when such proportion is determined.[47]

45 People v. Granite State Provident Assn., 161 N. Y. 492, 55 N. E. 1053.

46 Hunt v. Columbian Ins. Co. (Me.), 92 Am. Dec 592; Fawcett v. Order of Iron Hall, 64 Conn. 170, 29 Atl. 614, 24 L. R. A. 815; and cases cited in preceding notes.

47 Fawcett v. Order of Iron Hall, *supra;* Failey v. Fee, 83 Md. 83, 55 Am. St. Rep. 326, 34 Atl. 839, 32 L. ed. 311; Frowert v. Blank, 205 Pa. St. 299, 54 Atl. 1000.

CHAPTER XII.

INJUNCTIONS; GENERAL PRINCIPLES—INJUNCTION TO PROTECT EQUITABLE ESTATES AND INTERESTS.

ANALYSIS.

§ 262. General Nature and Object—Abstract of Statutes. "The remedy of injunction was undoubtedly borrowed by the chancellors from the 'interdicts' of the Roman law.[1] An injunction may be either a final remedy ob-

1 "As to 'interdicts,' see Gaius' Inst., lib 4, §§ 138-170; Poste's ed, 492-520; Just. Inst, lib. 4, tit. 15, §§ 1-8; Sandars' ed, 1st Am ed, 58, 570-580. The general definition as given by Gaius (Id., § 139) is as follows 'Under certain circumstances, chiefly when possession or *quasi* possession [i e, possession of a servitude] is in dispute, the first step in the legal proceedings is the interposition of the praetor or pro-consul, who commands some performance or forbearance; which commands, formulated in solemn terms, are called interdicts' The most general formula was '*vim fieri veto, exhibeas, restituas,*' 'I forbid you to use violence, you must produce, you must restore.' There were thus three distinct species of interdicts. 1. The prohibitory, where the defendant was commanded to refrain or desist from some act, answering to our ordinary injunction; 2. The exhibitory, where the defendant was commanded to produce and exhibit something in his possession—*exhibeas*, which does not answer to any kind of injunction, but has some analogies with certain common-law writs; 3. The restorative, where the defendant was commanded to restore something to its original position, clearly resembling in its effect our manda-

tained by a suit, or a preliminary and interlocutory relief granted while the suit is pending. In the first case it is a decree, in the second, an order or writ. Whatever be its form, decree or order, the remedy by ordinary injunction is wholly preventive, prohibitory, or protective. The same is true in theory and in form of a mandatory injunction, which always by its language prohibits the continuance of an act or of a structure, although in effect and in its essential nature it is wholly restorative, and compels the defendant to restore the thing to its original situation. While injunctions may thus be final, or preliminary and ancillary to other final relief, they all depend upon the same *general* principles, doctrines, and rules which determine and regulate the exercise of the jurisdiction to award them. In the states adopting the reformed procedure, the codes contain general provisions describing the cases in which an injunction may be issued, but these provisions do not materially alter the settled equitable jurisdiction, except in reference to injunctions against actions or judgments at law."[2]

tory injunction. Interdicts were granted where some danger was apprehended, or some injury was being done, to something of a *quasi* public character, as the stopping up of a highway, or to some private interest or right. One of the most common occasions of the interdict was to protect the plaintiff in his possession of a thing, in which case the interdict *uti possidetis* was used to protect possession of land and buildings, and the interdict *utrubi* for movables. In the interdict *uti possidetis*, the defendant was forbidden to interfere with the possession '*nec vi, nec clam, nec precario.*' The granting of interdicts belonged wholly to the 'extraordinary' or equitable jurisdiction of the magistrate.''

2 Pom. Eq Jur., § 1337. In the following abstract of statutes the general code provisions are given in full, for the purpose of exhibiting their divergencies in details; and reference is also made to the most important legislation authorizing injunction in special cases. In some states injunctions for an enormous variety of purposes are authorized by statute. For a tabulation of the contents of these statutes mentioned below, see the index to this work.

Alabama.—Civ. Code, 1896, §§ 784-798. Chiefly matters of practice.

§ 2580: May issue to restrain insolvent insurance companies from doing business.

§ 838: An injunction *pendente lite* may issue to restrain waste of property by intemperate person.

§ 2537: In cases of voluntary separation of husband and wife where application is made for custody of children, court may grant injunction *pendente lite* to insure safety and well-being of wife and children.

Arizona.—Rev. Stats. 1901, §§ 2742-2763.

§ 2742: "Judges of the district courts may, either in term time or vacation, grant writs of injunction, returnable to said courts, in the following cases:

"1. Where it shall appear that the party applying for such writ is entitled to the relief demanded, and such relief or any part thereof requires the restraint of some act prejudicial to the applicant.

"2. Where, pending litigation, it shall be made to appear that a party is doing some act respecting the subject of litigation, or threatens, or is about to do some act, or is procuring or suffering the same to be done in violation of the rights of the applicant, which act would tend to render the judgment ineffectual.

"3. In all other cases where the applicant for such writ may show himself entitled thereto under the principles of equity."

§ 2743: No injunction against judgments, etc., except to so much as complainant may show himself equitably entitled to be relieved against, and costs.

§ 2744: No injunction to stay execution on valid judgment after one year.

§ 2745: May be granted on complaint or on affidavits.

§ 2746: Notice of application.

§ 2750: To stay proceedings, must be returnable and tried in court where proceedings pending or judgment rendered.

§ 2751: Bond of complainant.

§§ 2755, 2756: Dissolution of injunctions.

§ 2759: "An injunction to suspend the general and ordinary business of a corporation shall not be granted except by the court or judge."

§ 2763: General principles of equity apply to, except where conflict with statute.

§ 3120: In suit for divorce, wife may obtain injunction restraining husband from disposing of community property, and of her separate property in his possession.

Arkansas.—Sandel's & Hill's Stats. 1894, §§ 3774-3813.

"§ 3774: The writ of injunction is abolished."

"§ 3775: An injunction is a command to refrain from a particular act."

"§ 3776: It may be the final judgment in an action, or may be allowed as a provisional remedy, and where so allowed it shall be by order."

"§ 3777: Where it appears by the complaint that the plaintiff is entitled to the relief demanded, and such relief, or any part thereof, consists in restraining the commission or continuance of some act which could produce great or irreparable injury to the plaintiff, or where, during the litigation, it appears that the defendant is doing, or threatens, or is about to do, or is procuring or suffering to be done, some act in violation of the plaintiff's rights, respecting the subject of the action and tending to render the judgment ineffectual, a temporary injunction may be granted to restrain such act. It may also be granted in any case where it is specially authorized by statute."

"§ 3778: The judge of the circuit court may grant injunctions and restraining orders in all cases of illegal or unauthorized taxes and assessments by county, city or other local tribunals, boards or officers." . . . .

"§ 3798: An injunction to stay proceedings on a judgment or final order of a court shall not be granted in an action brought by a party seeking the injunction in any other court than that in which the judgment or order was rendered or made."

Against illegal municipal taxation and payments:

"§ 5169. Any person owning property and having taxes to pay in any city or town may, upon application to any judge or court having authority to grant injunctions, enjoin the collection of any tax levied in such city or town, without authority of law, and may also enjoin the issue or the payment by such city or town of any warrants, certificates or other form or evidence of indebtedness against such city or town issued or contracted without authority of law."

Injunction suspending proceedings on a judgment or order:

"§ 4202: The party seeking to vacate or modify a judgment or order may obtain an injunction suspending proceedings on the whole or part thereof, which injunction may be granted by the court, or any officer authorized to grant injunctions, upon its being rendered probable, by affidavit or by exhibition of the record, that the party is entitled to have such judgment or order vacated or modified."

§ 4203: Concerns the case where the judgment is rendered prematurely, before the action stood for trial; it may be suspended although no valid defense to the action is shown.

California.—Code Civ. Proc., §§ 525-533.

§ 525: "An injunction is a writ or order requiring a person to refrain from a particular act."

§ 526· "An injunction may be granted in the following cases:

"1. When it appears by the complaint that the plaintiff is entitled to the relief demanded, and such relief, or any part thereof, consists in restraining the commission or continuance of the act complained of, either for a limited period or perpetually.

"2. When it appears by the complaint or affidavit that the commission or continuance of some act during the litigation would produce waste, great or irreparable injury to the plaintiff.

"3. When it appears during the litigation that the defendant is doing, or threatens, or is about to do, or is procuring or suffering to be done, some act in violation of the plaintiff's rights, respecting the subject of the action, and tending to render the judgment ineffectual."

Nuisance may be enjoined, Code Civ. Proc., § 731: "Anything which is injurious to health, or indecent or offensive to the senses, or an obstruction to the free use of property, so as to interfere with the comfortable enjoyment of life or property, is a nuisance, and the subject of an action Such action may be brought by any person whose property is injuriously affected, or whose personal enjoyment is lessened by the nuisance; and by the judgment, the nuisance may be enjoined or abated, as well as damages recovered."

Waste during foreclosure or after execution sale, Code Civ. Proc., § 745· "The court may by injunction, on good cause shown, restrain the party in possession from doing any act to the injury of real property during the foreclosure of a mortgage thereon; or, after a sale on execution, before a conveyance."

No injunction to enforce a penal law, a penalty or a forfeiture, Civ. Code, § 3369. "Neither specific nor preventive relief can be granted to enforce a penal law, except in a case of nuisance, nor to enforce a penalty or forfeiture in any case."

"Preventive relief," Civ. Code, §§ 3420-3423.

§ 3420: "Preventive relief is granted by injunction, provisional or final."

§ 3421: "Provisional injunctions are regulated by the Code of Civil Procedure."

§ 3422: "Except where otherwise provided by this title, a final injunction may be granted to prevent the breach of an obligation* existing in favor of the applicant:

"1. Where pecuniary compensation would not afford adequate relief;

"2 Where it would be extremely difficult to ascertain the amount of compensation which would afford adequate relief;

* "Obligation" is elsewhere defined as a "legal duty": Civ. Code, § 1427.

"3. Where the restraint is necessary to prevent a multiplicity of judicial proceedings; or,

"4. Where the obligation arises from a trust."

§ 3423: "An injunction cannot be granted:

"1. To stay a judicial proceeding pending at the commencement of the action in which the injunction is demanded, unless such restraint is necessary to prevent a multiplicity of such proceedings;

"2. To stay proceedings in a court of the United States;

"3. To stay proceedings in another state upon a judgment of a court of that state;

"4. To prevent the execution of a public statute, by officers of the law, for the public benefit,

"5. To prevent a breach of a contract, the performance of which would not be specifically enforced;

"6. To prevent the exercise of a public or private office, in a lawful manner, by the person in possession;

"7. To prevent a legislative act by a municipal corporation."

Injunction against the infringement of trade-marks is provided for in Political Code, § 3199.

Colorado.—Rice's Code of Procedure (1890), §§ 142-161.

§ 142: "An injunction is generally an order requiring a person to refrain from doing a particular act, but where simply refraining from doing a particular act will not effectuate the relief to which the plaintiff is entitled, the injunction may be made mandatory, and require such acts to be done as will give the plaintiff the full protection which he may be entitled to."

§ 143: When an injunction may be granted: substantially the same grounds as in California Code of Civil Procedure (*supra*), § 526, with the addition, "and in such other cases as courts of equity have hitherto granted relief by injunction, or which may be specially provided for in this act."

§ 145: Venue of injunctions to stay proceedings at law.

§ 158: Injunction for defendant on his cross-complaint or affidavit.

§ 159: Injunction having effect of writ of restitution of mining property. See, also, as to injunctions relating to mines and mining, Mills' Statutes (1891), §§ 1057, 3159, 3191, 3214, 3238-3241.

Connecticut.—Gen. Stats. (1888), §§ 1273-1293.

§ 1273: May be granted "according to the course of proceedings in equity, in all actions for equitable relief where such relief is properly demandable."

§ 1277: Injunction may be granted "against the malicious erection . . . . of any structure upon 'land' intended to annoy and injure any owner or lessee of adjacent land in respect to his use or disposition of the same."

§§ 1278-1282: Public or private nuisance by a manufacturer; any persons aggrieved may unite in a complaint for its abatement or discontinuance.

See, also, § 525 (against insolvent debtor's disposing of his property); § 1830 (against bank, savings bank, or trust company when its charter is forfeited); § 2656 (against building injuring source of municipal water supply); § 2668 (against bridges obstructing navigable streams); § 2811 (concerning custody of minor children in divorce proceedings); §§ 2822, 2823, 2836 (concerning the business of insurance companies); § 3429 (on application of railroad commissioners, to restrain any person from exercising the duties of any officer in such company).

Delaware.—Rev. Stats. 1852, as am. 1893, p. 666, c. 88 § 11.

"Upon the petition of a person holding any lien upon real estate, whether by judgment, recognizance, mortgage, or otherwise, the chancellor may, in a proper case, award an injunction, or the Superior Court of the county, wherein such real estate is, may award a writ of estrepement, for the purpose of restraining waste upon the premises subject to the lien."

Florida.—Rev. Stats. 1892, §§ 1463-1472.

§ 1468. Injunction may issue against sale of real property of third person under a writ of *fieri facias*.

§ 1469: Injunctions may issue to restrain trespasses on timber lands, by cutting trees, etc.

§ 1472: Injunction may issue to restrain the removal of mortgaged personal property from the state.

§ 800: Injunction may issue at suit of a board of health to restrain the violation of rules adopted by it for the protection of the public health.

§ 2006 "The circuit courts shall have equity jurisdiction to enjoin the sale of all property, real and personal, that is exempt from forced sale"

§ 2007: Injunction may issue to restrain officer from setting apart nonexempt property as exempt.

Georgia.—Code, 1895, §§ 4913-4928.

"§ 4913 (3210): *For what purpose granted.*—Equity, by a writ of injunction, may restrain proceedings in another or the same court, or a threatened or existing tort, or any other act of a private individual or corporation which is illegal or contrary to equity and good conscience, and for which no adequate remedy is provided at law."

"§ 4914: *Administration of criminal laws, no interference by equity.*—A court of equity will take no part in the administration of the criminal law. It will neither aid criminal courts in the exercise of their jurisdiction, nor will it restrain or obstruct them."

"§ 4915 (3218): *Enjoining a court of law.*—Equity will not enjoin the proceedings and processes of a court of law, unless there is some intervening equity, or other proper defense, of which the party, without fault on his part, cannot avail himself at law. Writs of injunction may be issued by judges of the superior court to enjoin sales by sheriffs, at any time before the sale takes place, in any proper case made by the bill or application for injunction." (As to setting aside judgments, see §§ 3987, 3988)

§ 4916 (3219): *To restrain a trespass*—Equity will not interfere to restrain a trespass, unless the injury is irreparable in damages, or the trespasser is insolvent, or there exist other circumstances which, in the discretion of court, render the interposition of this writ necessary and proper, among which shall be the avoidance of circuity and multiplicity of actions.

§ 4917: *Waste not enjoined when title in dispute*—Equity will not interfere by injunction to restrain waste when petitioner's title is not clear Such relief is granted only when the title is free from dispute.

§ 4918: *Creditors without lien.*—Creditors without lien cannot, as a general rule, enjoin their debtors from disposing of property, nor obtain injunction or other extraordinary relief in equity.

§ 4919: *Injunction to restrain breach of contract for personal services*—Generally, an injunction will not issue to restrain the breach of a contract for personal services, unless they are of a peculiar merit or character, and cannot be performed by others.

§ 4920 (3220). *In sound discretion of judge.*—The granting and continuing of injunctions must always rest in the sound discretion of the judge, according to the circumstances of each case.

See, also, the following sections:

§ 3863 (3002): *Nuisance.*—Where the consequences of a nuisance about to be erected or commenced will be irreparable in damages, and such consequences are not merely possible, but to a reasonable degree certain, a court of equity may interfere to arrest a nuisance before it is completed.

§ 4902: "The power of appointing receivers and ordering injunctions should be prudently and cautiously exercised, and except in clear and urgent cases should not be resorted to."

Idaho.—Code Civ. Proc, §§ 3283-3293, 3373.

Same as California, with some additions. § 3284 (6) provides for injunction having force and effect of a writ of restitution, in case of ouster by force, etc.

Illinois.—Hurd's Rev. Stats. (1889), c. 69. Concerns chiefly matters of practice. § 1: *What part of judgment may be enjoined*—"Only so much of any judgment at law shall be enjoined as the complainant shall show himself equitably not bound to pay, and so much as shall be sufficient to cover costs."

Indiana.—Burns' Rev. Stats. 1894, §§ 1161-1180 (1147-1166); Code Civ. Proc., §§ 177-196.

"§ 1162 (1148). *Proceedings to obtain.*—178. When it appears by the complaint that the plaintiff is entitled to the relief demanded, and the relief, or any part thereof, consists in restraining the commission or continuance of some act, the commission or continuance of which, during the litigation, would produce great injury to the plaintiff, or when, during the litigation, it appears that the defendant is doing, or threatens, or is about to do, or is procuring or suffering some act to be done, in violation of the plaintiff's rights, respecting the subject of the action, and tending to render the judgment ineffectual; or when such relief, or any part of it, consists in restraining proceedings upon any order or judgment,—an injunction may be granted to restrain such act or proceedings until the further order of the court; which may, afterward, be modified upon motion. And when it appears in the complaint at the commencement of the action, or during the pendency thereof by affidavit, that the defendant threatens or is about to remove or dispose of his property, with intent to defraud his creditors, a temporary injunction may be granted to restrain the removal or disposition of his property."

"§ 292 (291). *Nuisance—Remedy.*—711 Where a proper case is made, the nuisance may be enjoined or abated, and damages recovered therefor."

Iowa.—McClain's Code (1888), §§ 4622-4643 (3386-3407).

"§ 4622 *Grounds for.*—3386. An injunction may be obtained as an independent remedy in an action by equitable proceedings, in all cases where such relief would have been granted in equity previous to the adoption of this code; and in all cases of breach of contract or other injury, where the party injured is entitled to maintain, and has brought an action by ordinary proceedings, he may, in the same cause, pray and have a writ of injunction against the repetition or continuance of such breach of contract or other injury, or the committal of any breach of contract or injury of a like kind, arising out of the same contract, or relating to the same property or right, and he may also, in the same action, include a claim for damages or other redress.

"§ 4623. *Temporary or permanent.*—3387. In any of the cases mentioned in the preceding section, the injunction may either be a part of the judgment rendered in the action or it may, if proper grounds therefor are shown, be granted by order at any stage of the case before judgment, and shall then be known as a temporary injunction."

§ 4624: *Temporary, when allowed.*—Similar to first two clauses of the Indiana section, *supra.*

See, also, § 1746 (against insolvent life insurance companies); § 2047 (to enforce rulings, orders and regulations of the board of railroad commissioners); § 2384 (to enjoin nuisance committed by the sale, etc., of intoxicating liquors; at the suit of any citizen of the county. See, also, §§ 2386, 2387, 2397); § 4390 (suspending proceedings on a judgment sought to be vacated or modified); § 4553 (to procure transfer of proceeding for foreclosure of chattel mortgage); § 4567 (nuisance defined; same as California code).

Kansas.—Gen. Stats. 1901, §§ 4684-4700; Code, §§ 237-253.

Code, § 237: "The injunction provided by this code is a command to refrain from a particular act. It may be the final judgment in an action, or may be allowed as a provisional remedy, and, when so allowed, it shall be by order. The writ of injunction is abolished."

Code, § 238: *Grounds for injunction.*—Similar to Arkansas, although wording varies slightly, and adding the following: "And when, during the pendency of an action, it shall appear, by affidavit, that the defendant threatens or is about to remove or dispose of his property with intent to defraud his creditors, or to render the judgment ineffectual, a temporary injunction may be granted to restrain such removal or disposition. It may also be granted in any case where it is specially authorized by statute."

Code, § 239: May be granted at time of commencement of action, or afterward, upon affidavit.

Code, § 240: Court may direct reasonable notice to be given, but may restrain action until hearing.

Code, § 241: "An injunction shall not be granted against a party who has answered, unless upon notice; but such party may be restrained until the decision of the application for an injunction."

Code, § 242: Bond.

Code, § 252: "A defendant may obtain an injunction upon an answer in the nature of a counterclaim. He shall proceed in the manner hereinbefore described."

Code, § 253: "An injunction may be granted to enjoin the illegal levy of any tax, charge or assessment, or the collection of any illegal tax, charge or assessment, or any proceeding to enforce the same; and any number of persons whose property is affected by a tax or assessment so levied may unite in the petition filed to obtain such injunction. An injunction may be granted in the name of the state to enjoin and suppress the keeping and maintaining of a common nuisance. The petition therefor shall be verified by the county attorney of the proper county, or by the attorney-general, upon information and belief, and no bond shall be required."

Gen Stats. 1901, §§ 7656, 7658: Duty of treasurer upon dissolution of injunction restraining collection of tax.

§ 3176: Injunction may issue against collection of special assessment when officers are interested in contract.

§ 2450· Declares places used for unlawful purposes, such as for bucket shops, to be nuisances. "The attorney-general, county attorney or any citizen of the county where such nuisance exists or is kept and maintained may maintain an action in the name of the state to abate and perpetually enjoin the same The injunction may be granted at the commencement of the action, and no bond shall be required."

§ 2231: Declares places where gaming, etc., is carried on to be nuisances, and authorizes injunction as in § 2450.

§ 2686: Electors may maintain action for injunction to restrain removal of county offices and to determine validity of county seat election.

§ 7855: Injunction may issue to restrain wrongful use of labels, trade-marks, etc., of any association or union of workingmen.

Kentucky.—Code (1888), §§ 271-297.

§ 272: Defines causes for temporary injunction in language similar to that of the Iowa Code, § 4624.

§ 285: Judgment can be enjoined only in the court rendering it.

§ 17. "A judgment obtained in an ordinary action shall not be annulled nor modified by any order in an equitable action, except for a defense which arises or is discovered after rendition of the judgment."

§ 523 [584]: Injunction suspending proceedings on a judgment may be obtained by a party seeking to vacate or modify it.

§ 436: Injunction, in action in equity for settlement of decedent's estate, against prosecution of actions by creditors against the representatives of the decedent.

§ 467· In forcible entry and detainer proceedings, to restrain waste and destruction of the premises.

§ 476: In mandamus or prohibition proceedings, to prevent damage or injury to the applicant.

"§ 378: *When Collection of Judgment may be Enjoined.*—During the pendency of an action, the judgment in which when recovered could be used as a set-off against a judgment in favor of the defendants or either of them, the court, to prevent loss by insolvency, non-residence, or otherwise, may enjoin the collection of the judgment in favor of such defendants."

Maine.—Rev. Stats. 1903.

Page 447: Upon dissolution of corporation, injunction may be granted.

Page 396: Injunction may issue to restrain infringement of trade marks.

Page 952: The attorney-general may have an injunction to restrain a lottery.

Page 76: Injunction may issue at suit of ten or more taxable citizens to restrain any action in which municipal officers are privately interested.

Page 678: "When counties, cities, towns, school districts, village or other public corporations, for a purpose not authorized by law, vote to pledge their credit or to raise money by taxation or to exempt property therefrom, or to pay money from their treasury, or if any of their officers or agents attempt to pay out such money for such purpose, the court shall have equity jurisdiction on petition or application of not less than ten taxable inhabitants thereof, briefly setting forth the cause of complaint."

Page 269: "All places used as houses of ill-fame, or for the illegal sale or keeping of intoxicating liquors, or resorted to for lewdness or gambling; all houses, shops or places where intoxicating liquors are sold for tippling purposes, and all places of resort where intoxicating liquors are kept, sold, given away, drank or dispensed in any manner not provided for by law, are common nuisances. The supreme judicial court shall have jurisdiction in equity, upon information filed by the county attorney or upon petition of not less than twenty legal voters of such town or city, setting forth any of the facts contained herein, to restrain, enjoin or abate the same, and an injunction for such purpose may be issued by said court or any justice thereof."

Pages 517, 518: Injunction to prevent taking of property by eminent domain until compensation made.

Page 827: Injunction against waste by defendant in action to recover possession of land.

Maryland.—Pub. Gen. Laws, 1904.

Page 400, art. 16, § 80: "No court shall refuse to issue a mandamus or injunction on the mere ground that the party asking for the same has an adequate remedy in damages, unless the party against whom the same is asked shall show to the court's satisfaction that he has property from which the damages can be made, or shall give a bond in a penalty to be fixed by the court, and with a surety or sureties approved by the court, to answer all damages and costs that he may be adjudged by any court of competent jurisdiction to pay to the party asking such mandamus or injunction by reason of his not doing the act or acts sought to be commanded, or by reason of his doing the act or acts sought to be enjoined, as the case may be."

Page 437, art. 16, § 190: Court has power to issue mandatory injunctions.

Page 1548, art. 66, § 16: No injunction to stay sale or proceedings after mortgage sale, except at suit of party to mortgage, or of one claiming under him, and upon oath that debt has been fully paid, or that mortgagee refuses to give credit for part paid, or that there has been fraud.

Massachusetts.—Pub. Stats. 1882. Among other provisions, see Chapter 27, § 129: *Abuse of corporate power by towns*, providing for suit by not less than ten taxable inhabitants, and injunction therein, "when a town votes to raise by taxation or pledge of its credit, or to pay from its treasury, any money for a purpose other than those for which it has the legal right and power." On the subject of this section, see Babbitt v. Selectmen of Savoy, 3 Cush. 530; Tash v. Adams, 10 Cush. 252, Hood v. Lynn, 1 Allen, 103; Fuller v. Melrose, 1 Allen, 166; Frost v. Belmont, 6 Allen, 152; Allen v. Marion, 11 Allen, 108; Copeland v. Huntington, 99 Mass. 525; Carlton v. Salem, 103 Mass. 141; Fisk v. Springfield, 116 Mass. 88, 89; Mead v. Acton, 139 Mass. 341, 345, 1 N. E. 413; Prince v. Boston, 148 Mass. 285, 19 N. E. 218.

Chapter 76, § 7: To restrain the illegal use of trade-marks or names See Ames v. King, 2 Gray, 379; Bowman v. Floyd, 3 Allen, 76, 80 Am. Dec. 55; Magee Furnace Co. v. Le Barron, 127 Mass. 115; Connell v. Reed, 128 Mass. 477, 35 Am. Rep. 397; Lawrence Mfg. Co. v. Lowell etc. Mills, 129 Mass. 325, 37 Am. Rep. 362; Russia Cement Co. v. Le Page, 147 Mass. 206, 9 Am. St. Rep. 685, 17 N. E. 304.

Chapter 80, § 26: To restrain a nuisance affecting the public health.

§ 26: To prevent offensive trades: See Watertown v. Mayo, 109 Mass. 315, 12 Am. Rep. 694.

§§ 98, 99. To prevent pollution of sources of water supply. See Harris v. Mackintosh, 133 Mass. 228, 230.

Chapter 112, § 104: Against taking of land by railroad.

Chapter 179, §§ 12-14. To stay waste by person whose land is attached, etc.

Chapter 180, §§ 5, 6, 7: Nuisance; injunction either in a suit in equity or in an action of tort.

Provisions in the statutes since 1882 for injunctions in special cases are exceedingly numerous.

Michigan.—Comp. Laws, 1897.

§§ 502-514: Courts have jurisdiction to stay proceedings at law, but security must be given.

§ 3937: "No injunction shall issue to stay proceedings for the assessment or collection of taxes under this act."

§ 3938: Holder of certificate of tax sale is entitled to injunction to restrain waste on timber land.

§§ 4363, 4364: No injunction against collection of drain taxes.

§ 8687. Husband may be enjoined from disposing of property pending suit by wife for maintenance.

§ 11132: "The circuit court for each county shall have equity jurisdiction of all matters concerning waste, in which there is not a plain, adequate and complete remedy at law; and may grant injunctions to stay or prevent waste; and whenever it shall be necessary or proper to have any fact tried by a jury, such court may award a feigned issue for that purpose, as in other cases."

Minnesota.—Stats. (1894), §§ 5343-5350.

§ 5344. Relating to the granting of temporary injunctions, resembles, in general, the first two clauses and the last clause of the Indiana statutes, § 1162.

See, also, §§ 393 (c), 399 (injunction to enforce order of railroad and warehouse commission), §§ 432, 1496 (to enforce orders of state board of health relating to pollution of water supply, or to noxious trades); § 2261 (against orders of factory inspectors); § 2911 (by judgment creditor of co-operative association to restrain alienation of property and doing business).

§ 5434 (Acts of 1877, c. 131, § 1): *Actions to set aside judgment for fraud*, etc.—"That in all cases where judgment heretofore has been or hereafter may be obtained in any court of record by means of the perjury, subornation of perjury, or any fraudulent act, practice or representation of the prevailing party, an action may be brought by the party aggrieved to set aside said judgment, at any time within three years after the discovery by him of such perjury," etc. . . . . "In such action the court shall have and possess the same powers heretofore exercised by courts of equity in like proceedings, and may perpetually enjoin the enforcement of such judgment, or command the satisfaction thereof, and may also compel the prevailing party to make restitution of any money or other property received by virtue thereof, and may also make such other or further order or judgment as may be just or equitable, provided" that rights of innocent third parties under the judgment shall not be affected. See this statute interpreted in Wieland v. Shillock, 24 Minn. 345; Baker v. Sheehan, 29 Minn. 235, 12 N. W. 704; Spooner v. Spooner, 26 Minn. 138, 1 N. W. 838; Bornsta v. Johnson, 38 Minn. 230, 36 N. W. 341; Stewart v. Duncan, 40 Minn. 410, 42 N. W. 89; Hass v. Billings, 42 Minn. 63, 43 N. W. 797; Wilkins v. Sherwood, 55 Minn. 154, 56 N. W. 591; Clark v. Lee, 58 Minn. 410, 59 N. W. 970.

See, also, § 5893 (injunction, at suit of attorney-general, against usurpation of corporate powers), §§ 5900, 5901 (against insolvent banking and insurance companies); § 5972 (against corporation, after judgment of exclusion from corporate rights); §§ 6921, 6922 (against counterfeiting the labels, trade-marks, etc., of labor unions; § 6928 (against counterfeiting of trade-marks in general); § 7715 (against operating warehouses without a license).

Mississippi.—Annotated Code, 1892.

§ 558: An injunction to stay proceedings at law shall not be issued until the party shall enter into a bond conditioned to pay the judgment at law in case the injunction is dissolved.

§ 559: Bond in other cases.

§ 561: No injunction shall issue to restrain collection of taxes unless bond is filed conditioned for payment of tax if injunction dissolved.

§ 483: "The chancery court shall have jurisdiction of suits by one or more tax-payers of any county, city, town, or village, to restrain the collection of any taxes levied or attempted to be collected without authority of law."

§ 484. If such an injunction is dissolved, the court shall enter decree against the complainant and his sureties for the amount of taxes enjoined and ten per cent thereon, and costs of suit.

Missouri.—Rev. Stats. 1889, §§ 3627-3649.

§ 3630: Granting of temporary injunction; same as Indiana, first two clauses.

"§ 3635: *Extent of judgment to stay proceedings.*—No injunction shall be granted to stay any judgment or proceeding, except so much of the recovery or cause of action as the plaintiff shall show himself equitably entitled to be relieved against, and so much as will cover costs."

§ 3648: To protect property of married woman from waste by husband.

"§ 3649. The remedy by writ of injunction or prohibition shall exist in all cases where a cloud would be put on the title of real estate being sold under an execution against a person, partnership or corporation having no interest in such real estate subject to execution at the time of sale, or an irreparable injury to real or personal property is threatened, and to prevent the doing of any legal wrong whatever, whenever in the opinion of the court an adequate remedy cannot be afforded by an action for damages."

See, also, § 1023 (injunction against corporation for failure to maintain a general office within the state); § 1031 (against corporation failing to restore grants in certain cases); § 1043 (railroad may be enjoined from running trains in certain cases); § 1150 (against common carriers); § 1059 (against consolidation of railroads); § 1306 (against bank or trust company, when not to issue); § 1421 (fraternal beneficiary association enjoined from doing business, when); § 3074 (to stay plaintiff in ejectment from taking possession of the land until the value of improvements is ascertained); § 8025 (against insolvent insurance company).

Montana.—Code Civ. Proc., §§ 870-881.

§ 871: When injunction may be granted: substantially the same as California Code Civ. Proc., § 526, with this addition: "4. When it appears, by affidavit, that the defendant, during the pendency of the action, threatens, or is about to remove, or to dispose of his property, with intent to defraud the plaintiff, an injunction order may be granted, to restrain the removal or disposition"

Civ Code, §§ 4460-4463: Same as California Civ. Code, §§ 3420-3423

Nebraska.—Code Civ. Proc, §§ 250-265

§ 251. Cause for allowance of temporary injunction, the usual code provision.

Taxation.—Comp. Stats. 1899, c. 77, § 144: "No injunction shall be granted by any court or judge in this state, to restrain the collection of any tax, or any part thereof, hereafter levied, nor to restrain the sale of any property for the non-payment of any such tax, except such tax, or the part thereof enjoined, be levied or assessed for an illegal or unauthorized purpose." See, also, as to drainage assessments, c. 89, art. 1, § 28

Against common carrier disobeying order of board of transportation, c. 72, art. 8, § 16.

Suspending proceedings on judgment; injunction allowed in favor of party seeking to vacate or modify a judgment or order: Code Civ. Proc, §§ 607, 608.

New Hampshire—Pub. Stats. (1891), c. 205, § 1.

"The supreme court . . . . may grant writs of injunction whenever the same are necessary to prevent fraud or injustice." See, also, c. 162, § 13 (prohibiting transaction by bank, on application of bank commissioners); § 19 (restraining proceedings at law by creditors of insolvent bank); c. 171, § 10 (against life insurance companies, etc, failing to make statements to insurance commission); c 175, § 12 (in divorce proceedings, prohibiting the husband from imposing any restraint upon the personal liberty of the wife, or from entering the tenement where she resides during the pendency of the libel); c. 176, § 12 (to protect divorced wife's custody of minor child); c. 205, § 5 (enjoining certain nuisances).

New Jersey.—Gen. Stats. 1895

Pages 387, 388: No injunction against proceedings at law after verdict or judgment, unless bond filed conditioned to abide such order as the chancellor may make.

New York.—Code Civ. Proc. (1896), §§ 602-630.

§ 602 (being part of Code of Procedure, § 218): "*Writ of injunction abolished and order substituted.*—The writ of injunction has been abolished. A temporary injunction may be granted by order, as prescribed in this article."

§ 603 (Code Proc., § 219, first clause): *Injunction, when the right thereto depends upon the nature of the action.*—"Where it appears, from the complaint, that the plaintiff demands and is entitled to a judgment against the defendant, restraining the commission or continuance of an act, the commission or continuance of which, during the pendency of the action, would produce injury to the plaintiff, an injunction order may be granted to restrain it."

§ 604 (amended, 1877; Code Civ. Proc., § 219): *Injunction, when the right thereto depends upon extrinsic facts.*—"In either of the following cases, an injunction order may also be granted in an action

"1. Where it appears, by affidavit, that the defendant, during the pendency of the action, is doing, or procuring, or suffering to be done, or threatened, or is about to do, or to procure, or suffer to be done, an act, in violation of the plaintiff's rights, respecting the subject of the action, and tending to render the judgment ineffectual, an injunction order may be granted to restrain him therefrom.

"2. Where it appears, by affidavit, that the defendant, during the pendency of the action, threatens, or is about to remove, or to dispose of his property, with intent to defraud the plaintiff, an injunction order may be granted, to restrain the removal or disposition."

See, also, § 719 (Code Proc., § 401), plaintiff asking for order of arrest, injunction, and warrant of attachment, or two of them, may be required to elect between them.

§ 1806 (2 Rev. Stats., 466, § 56): In certain actions prescribed by the title on "Actions Relating to Corporations," creditors may be enjoined from bringing or prosecuting actions against the defendants.

North Carolina.—Clark's Code of Civ. Proc.

§ 334 Injunction as a provisional remedy is abolished, and temporary injunction by order is substituted therefor.

Page 285. "No injunction shall be granted by any court or judge in this state to restrain the collection of any tax, or any part thereof, hereafter levied, nor to restrain the sale of any property for the non-payment of any such tax, except such tax, or the part thereof enjoined, be levied or assessed for an illegal or unauthorized purpose, or be illegal or invalid, or the assessment be illegal or invalid"

§ 338: "(1) When it shall appear by the complaint that the plaintiff is entitled to the relief demanded, and such relief or any part thereof consists in restraining the commission or continuance of some act, the commission or continuance of which, during the litigation, would produce injury to the plaintiff; or,

("In an application for an injunction to enjoin a trespass on land, it shall not be necessary to allege the insolvency of the defendant when the trespass complained of is continuous in its nature, or is the cutting or destruction of timber trees";)

"(2) When, during the litigation, it shall appear by affidavit of plaintiff, or any other person, that the defendant is doing, or threatens, or is about to do, or procuring or suffering some act to be done in violation of the plaintiff's rights respecting the subject of the action and tending to render the judgment ineffectual, a temporary injunction may be granted to restrain him therefrom;

"(3) And where, during the pendency of the action, it shall appear by affidavit of plaintiff or any other person, that the defendant threatens, or is about to remove or dispose of his property, with intent to defraud the plaintiff, a temporary injunction may be granted to restrain such removal or disposition."

§ 339: May be granted at time of commencement of action, or at any time afterwards, before judgment.

§ 341: Undertaking on injunction.

North Dakota.—Revised Code, 1899.

§ 5343: "The writ of injunction as a provisional remedy is abolished, and an injunction by order is substituted therefor."

§ 5344: When temporary injunctions issued.—Practically the same as North Carolina.

§ 5045: "Except when otherwise provided by this chapter, a final injunction may be granted to prevent the breach of an obligation existing in favor of the applicant:

"1. When pecuniary compensation would not afford adequate relief.

"2. When it would be extremely difficult to ascertain the amount of compensation which would afford adequate relief.

"3. When the restraint is necessary to prevent a multiplicity of judicial proceedings, or,

"4. When the obligation arises from a trust."

§ 5046: "An injunction cannot be granted:

"1. To stay a judicial proceeding pending at the commencement of the action in which the injunction is demanded, unless such restraint is necessary to prevent a multiplicity of such proceedings.

"2. To stay proceedings in a court of the United States.

"3. To stay proceedings in a state upon a judgment of a court of that state.

"4. To prevent the execution of a public statute by officers of the law for the public benefit.

"5. To prevent the breach of a contract, the performance of which would not be specifically enforced.

"6. To prevent the exercise of a public or private office in a lawful manner by the person in possession.

"7. To prevent a legislative act by a municipal corporation"

§ 5347: Undertaking on injunction.

§ 5349: Not issued to suspend business of corporation, without notice, unless state is a party.

Ohio—Rev. Stats. (1897), §§ 5571-5586.

§ 5572: *Causes for an injunction* (the usual code provisions).

§ 1277: "The prosecuting attorneys of the several counties of the state, upon being satisfied that the funds of the county, or any public moneys in the hands of the county treasurer are about to be misapplied, or that a contract in contravention of the laws of this state is about to be entered into, or is being executed, or that a contract was procured by fraud or corruption, shall apply by civil action in the name of the state to a court of competent jurisdiction, to restrain such contemplated misapplication of funds, and to restrain the completion or execution of such contract."

§ 1278: "In case the prosecuting attorney fails, upon the written request of any of the tax-payers of the county, to make the application contemplated in the preceding section, such tax-payer may institute such civil action in the name of the state," etc.

§§ 1777, 1778: Similar provisions as to the duty of corporation counsel of cities to apply for injunction, and right of tax-payers to sue on his refusal.

§§ 3231-3233: To enforce labor liens on railroads, public structures, etc.

§ 3371: To prevent discrimination, etc., by railroads.

§ 4490: Assessments for county ditches not to be enjoined for error.

§ 5361: Suspending proceedings on judgment or order, in favor of party seeking to vacate or modify the same (usual provision).

§ 5701: In divorce proceedings, to prevent disposal or incumbrance of property to defeat right of alimony.

§ 5705: To protect married woman's property from conversion or waste by husband.

§§ 5848-5851: Provides for actions to enjoin the illegal levy of taxes and assessments, or the collection of either; parties to such actions, plaintiff in action to enjoin collection, who admits a part to have been legally levied, must first pay or tender the sum admitted to be due.

§§ 6786-6788. Injunction ancillary to proceedings in *quo warranto* against banking association.

Oklahoma—Rev. Stats. 1903.

§ 4424. "The injunction provided by this code is a command to refrain from a particular act. It may be the final judgment in an action, or may be allowed as a provisional remedy. The writ of injunction is abolished."

§ 4425 Temporary injunctions Same as North Carolina, adding· "It may, also, be granted in any case where it is specially authorized by statute."

§ 4427: "If the court or judge deem it proper that the defendant, or any party to the suit, should be heard before granting the injunction, it may direct a reasonable notice to be given to such party to attend for such purpose, at a specified time and place, and may, in the meantime, restrain such party."

§§ 4429, 4435: Bond for injunction.

§ 4440: "An injunction may be granted to enjoin the illegal levy of any tax, charge or assessment, or the collection of any illegal tax, charge or assessment, or any proceeding to enforce the same; and any number of persons whose property is affected by a tax or assessment so levied may unite in the petition filed to obtain such injunction. An injunction may be granted in the name of the territory to enjoin and suppress the keeping and maintaining of a common nuisance The petition therefor shall be verified by the county attorney of the proper county, or by the attorney general, upon information and belief, and no bond shall be required."

Oregon.—Bellinger & Cotton's Codes and Stats.

§ 417: "An injunction is an order requiring a defendant in a suit to refrain from a particular act, it is only allowed as a provisional remedy, and when a decree is given enjoining a defendant, such decree shall be effectual and binding on such defendant without other proceeding or process, and may be enforced if necessary as provided in section 415."

§ 418. Undertaking on injunction.

§ 343: Individual may enjoin private nuisance when legal remedy inadequate.

Pennsylvania.—Pepper & Lewis' Digest (1894).

Page 3887, § 14: Judgment of ouster and exclusion in *quo warranto* proceedings to be enforced by injunction.

Supplement, 1894-97.

Page 614, § 4: Injunction to prevent counterfeiting of trades union labels.

Rhode Island.—Gen. Laws, 1896.

Chapter 161, § 2: To prevent discrimination by common carriers.

Chapter 178, §§ 42, 43, 46, 47, 49, 67, 70, 73. Against banks and institutions for savings.

Chapter 181, §§ 5-9: Against domestic insurance companies.

Chapter 195, § 16: Temporary injunctions in divorce proceedings.

Chapter 274, §§ 19, 20: To restrain insolvents from leaving the state, etc.

South Carolina.—Code Civ. Proc., § 240 (usual threefold code provision).

South Dakota.—Civ. Code, §§ 5850-5853 (same as California Civil Code).

Code Civ. Proc., §§ 6190-6198.

§ 6191 (usual threefold code provision).

In aid of mortgagees—§ 6679: "The court may, by injunction, on good cause shown, restrain the party in possession from doing any act to the injury of real property during the existence of the lien or foreclosure of a mortgage thereon and until the expiration of the time allowed for redemption."

Pol. Code, § 2673: Injunction to restore possession of mining property taken by force, fraud or threats.

Tennessee.—Code, 1896.

§ 5161: Injunction against waste.

§ 1004: "No injunction or petition for mandamus shall be granted by any judge or court in this state, or any bill or petition for mandamus, alleging the illegality or unconstitutionality of any of the revenue laws of this state, restraining any officer or officers charged with the collection of the public taxes of this state, except upon a final hearing of any cause in the court of last resort, if an appeal should be taken to that court."

§ 6256. Bond for injunction.

Texas—Sayles' Rev. Stats. (1888), arts. 2873-2898.

"Art. 2873. *Writs of, granted, when.*—Judges of the district and county courts may, either in term time or vacation, grant writs of injunction, returnable to said courts, in the following cases:

"1. Where it shall appear that the party applying for such writ is entitled to the relief demanded, and such relief or any part thereof requires the restraint of some act prejudicial to the applicant.

"2. Where, pending litigation, it shall be made to appear that a party is doing some act respecting the subject of litigation, or threatens, or is about to do some act, or is procuring or suffering the same to be done in violation of the rights of the applicant, which act would tend to render judgment ineffectual.

"3. In all other cases where the applicant for such writ may show himself entitled thereto under the principles of equity."

"Art. 2874 *None, against a judgment, except, etc.*—No injunction shall be granted to stay any judgment or proceedings at law, except so much of the recovery or cause of action as the complainant shall in his petition show himself equitably entitled to be relieved against, and so much as will cover the costs."

"Art. 2875. *Injunction to stay execution within twelve months, unless, etc.*—No injunction to stay an execution upon any valid and subsisting judgment shall be granted after the expiration of one year from the rendition of such judgment, unless it be made to appear that an application for such injunction has been delayed in consequence of the fraud or false promises of the plaintiff in the judgment, or unless for some equitable matter or defense arising after the rendition of such judgment If it be made to appear that the applicant was absent from the state at the time such judgment was rendered, and was unable to apply for such writ within the time aforesaid, such injunction may be granted at any time within two years from the date of the rendition of the judgment."

"Art. 2898. *Principles of equity applicable.*—The principles, practice and procedure governing courts of equity shall govern proceedings in injunctions when the same are not in conflict with the provisions of this title or other law."

See, also, art 2868 (injunction pending divorce suit, restraining husband from disposing of property).

Act of May 12, Aug. 14, 1888 (Supplement to Sayles' Civ. Stat., art. 2873a), is important. "The full right, power, and remedy of injunction may be resorted to and invoked by the state at the instance of the county or district attorney or attorney-general, to prevent, prohibit, or restrain the violation of any revenue or penal law of this state."

Utah.—Rev. Stats. (1888), §§ 3057-3063: Taken from the California Code of Civil Procedure, §§ 525-533, with some changes.

See, also, § 153 (taken from North Dakota (1895), § 5584) as to restraining foreclosure by advertisement of chattel mortgage, when the mortgagor "has a legal counterclaim or any other valid defense against the collection of the whole or any part of the amount claimed to be due on such mortgage."

§ 1219. Injunction in statutory action by wife for separate maintenance restraining husband from disposing of or incumbering real estate.

§ 2683. "*Injunction to restrain collection of tax*—No injunction shall be granted by any court or judge to restrain the collection of any tax or any part thereof, nor to restrain the sale of any property for the non-payment of the tax, except where the tax, or some part thereof sought to be enjoined, is illegal, or is not authorized by law, or the property is exempt from taxation. If the payment of a part of a tax is sought to be enjoined, the other part must be paid or tendered before action can be commenced."

§ 3266 (Cal. Code Civ. Proc., § 706): To restrain waste during period of redemption from execution.

§ 3281: Injunction in connection with receiver, in proceedings supplementary to execution.

§ 3518 (Cal. Code Civ. Proc., § 745): Injunction to restrain waste pending foreclosure of a mortgage, or after a sale on execution, before a conveyance.

Vermont.—Stats. (1894), §§ 954-961 (relating to injunction bonds): § 2688 (in suits for divorce, restraining husband from conveying such portion of his property as is necessary to secure the alimony. See Foster v. Foster, 56 Vt. 540; Curtis v. Gordon, 62 Vt. 340, 495, 20 Atl. 820; Noyes v. Hubbard, 64 Vt. 302, 35 Am. St. Rep. 928, 23 Atl. 727, 15 L. R. A. 394; Stearns v. Stearns, 66 Vt. 187, 44 Am. St. Rep. 836, 28 Atl. 875); § 3893 (against abandoning or discontinuing railroad stations); §§ 4208, 4209 (on application of insurance commissioners); §§ 4522 *et seq.* (to abate liquor nuisances).

Virginia.—Code (1887), §§ 3434-3446; Supplement (1898), § 3438a. "§ 3434. *Injunction to protect plaintiff in suit for specific property.*—An injunction may be awarded to protect any plaintiff in a suit for specific property, pending either at law or in equity, against injury from the sale, removal, or concealment of such property."

See, also, § 1081 (to stay proceedings in condemnation of land for internal improvements); § 2495 (to protect lien for advance on crops); § 3656 (to restrain sale of exempt property, or garnishment of wages, of a "householder").

Washington.—Ballinger's Codes and Statutes (1897), §§ 5431-5452.

§ 5432: Injunction, when granted. Taken from Indiana, § 1148.

"§ 5433. Injunction for malicious erection of structures. An injunction may be granted to restrain the malicious erection, by any owner or lessee of land, of any structure intended to spite, injure or annoy an adjoining proprietor. And where any owner or lessee of land has maliciously erected such a structure with such intent, a mandatory injunction will lie to compel its abatement and removal."

§ 5661: Injunction in action for nuisance, when the remedy of warrant to abate the nuisance is inadequate.

"§ 5658. Injunction to prevent waste. When any two or more persons are opposing claimants under the laws of the United States to any land in this state, and one is threatening to commit upon such land waste which tends materially to lessen the value of the inheritance, and which cannot be compensated by damages, and there is imminent danger that unless restrained such waste will be committed, the party, on filing his complaint and satisfying the court or judge of the existence of the facts, may have an injunction to restrain the adverse party." See Arment v. Hensel, 5 Wash. 152, 154, 31 Pac. 464; McBride v. Board of Commrs., 44 Fed. 17.

Injunction in proceedings supplemental to execution: See § 5323.

Injunction in favor of party seeking to vacate or modify a judgment or order, suspending proceedings or the whole or part thereof: See § 5160.

§ 6119: Restraining order against executor or administrator, pending application to prove a lost or destroyed will.

"§ 5678. Tender condition precedent to action to enjoin tax collection. Hereafter no action or proceeding shall be commenced or instituted in any court of this state to enjoin the sale of any property for taxes, or to enjoin the collection of any taxes, or for the recovery of any property sold for taxes, unless the person or corporation desiring to commence or institute such action or proceeding shall first pay, or cause to be paid, or shall tender to the officer entitled under the law to receive the same, all taxes, penalties, interest and costs justly due and unpaid from such person or corporation on the property sought to be sold or recovered."

"§ 5679. What complaint must state. In all actions to enjoin the collection of any tax, and in all actions for the recovery of any property sold for taxes, the complainant must state and set forth specially in his complaint the tax that is justly due, with penalties, interest and costs, the tax alleged to be illegal, and point out the illegality thereof, that the taxes for that and previous years have been paid." . . . .

"§ 5680. Construction. The provisions of sections 5678 and 5679 shall be construed as imposing additional conditions upon the power of the court or judge in granting injunctions to those already imposed."

§ 3714: Mandatory injunction authorized in proceedings to establish diking districts; § 3754, in proceedings to establish drainage districts.

West Virginia.—Code 1899, c. CXXXIII.

Page 889: "An injunction may be awarded to enjoin the sale of property set apart as exempt in the case of a husband or parent, under chapter forty-one, or to protect any plaintiff in a suit for specific property, pending either at law or in equity, against injury from the sale, removal or concealment of such property."

Page 890: Injunction bond.

Chapter XCVI, p. 762: Injunction may issue to prevent sale of property for usurious debt.

Page 1134: Injunctions against waste of natural gas.

Wisconsin.—Stats. 1898.

§ 2773: Writ of injunction is abolished. "The injunction provided by law is a command to refrain from a particular act."

§ 2774: "Where it shall appear by the complaint that the plaintiff is entitled to the judgment demanded and such judgment, or any part thereof, consists in restraining the commission or continuance of some act the commission or continuance of which, during the litigation, would produce injury to the plaintiff; or when, during the litigation, it shall appear that the defendant is doing, or threatens, or is about to do, or is procuring or suffering some act to be done in violation of plaintiff's rights respecting the subject of the action and tending to render the judgment ineffectual, a temporary injunction may be granted to restrain such act. And when, during the pendency of an action, it shall appear by affidavit that the defendant threatens or is about to remove or dispose of his property with intent to defraud his creditors, a temporary injunction may be granted to restrain such removal or disposition."

§ 2775: When granted to defendant.

§ 2778: Bond for injunction.

§ 2780: Not granted to suspend ordinary business of corporation without notice.

§ 3170: "The circuit courts have jurisdiction of actions for waste and may grant injunctions to stay or prevent waste."

§ 3180: "The circuit courts shall have jurisdiction of actions to recover damages for and to abate private nuisances or a public nuisance from which any person suffers a private or special injury peculiar to himself, so far as necessary to protect the rights of such person, and to grant injunctions to prevent the same; and in case such nuisance may work an irreparable injury, interminable litigation, a multiplicity of actions, or either, or the injury is continuous or constantly recurring, or there is not an adequate remedy at law, or the injury is not susceptible of adequate compensation in damages at law, then an action in equity may be maintained and an injunction issued therein, and an equitable action may be brought before the nuisance or the infringement of plaintiff's right is established at law."

Wyoming —Rev. Stats. 1899.

§ 4038: "The injunction provided by this chapter is a command to refrain from a particular act; it may be the final judgment in an action or may be allowed as a provisional remedy; and when so allowed it shall be by order."

§ 4039: "When it appears by the petition that the plaintiff is entitled to the relief demanded, and such relief, or any part thereof, consists in restraining the commission or continuance of some act, the commission or continuance of which, during the litigation, would produce great or irreparable injury to the plaintiff, or when, during the litigation, it appears that the defendant is doing, or threatens or is about to do, or is procuring or suffering to be done, some act in violation of the plaintiff's rights, respecting the subject of the action, and tending to render the judgment ineffectual, a temporary order may be granted restraining such act; and such order may also be granted in any case where it is specially authorized by statute."

§ 4041: Court may require notice of application.

§ 4043: Undertaking on injunction.

§ 4053: "A defendant may obtain an injunction upon an answer in the nature of a counterclaim, and he shall proceed in the manner prescribed in this chapter."

§ 4172: "District courts shall have jurisdiction to enjoin the illegal levy of taxes and assessments, or the collection of either, and of actions to recover back such taxes or assessments as have been collected, without regard to the amount thereof, but no recovery shall be had unless the action be brought within one year after the taxes or assessments are collected."

§ 4175: "If the plaintiff, in an action to enjoin the collection of taxes or assessments admit a part thereof to have been legally levied, he must first pay or tender the sum admitted to be due; if an order of injunction be allowed, an undertaking must be given as in other cases; and the injunction shall be a justification of the officer charged with the collection of such taxes or assessments for not collecting the same."

§ 3802: "The party seeking to vacate or modify a judgment or order may obtain an injunction suspending proceedings on the whole or a part thereof, which injunction may be granted by the court or any judge thereof when it is rendered probable by affidavit or by exhibition of the record that the party is entitled to have such judgment or order vacated or modified."

§ 263. **Fundamental Principle.** — "In determining whether an injunction will be issued to protect any right of property, to enforce any obligation, or to prevent any wrong, there is one fundamental principle of the utmost importance, which furnishes the answer to any questions, the solution to any difficulties which may arise. This principle is both affirmative and negative, and the affirmative aspect of it should never be lost sight of, any more than the negative side.[3] The general principle may be stated as follows: Wherever a right exists or is created, by contract, by the ownership of property or otherwise, cognizable by law, *a violation of that right will be prohibited,* unless there are other considerations of policy or expediency which forbid a resort to this prohibitive remedy. *The restraining power of equity extends, therefore, through the whole range of rights and duties which are recognized by the law, and would be applied to every case of intended violation, were it not for certain reasons of expediency and policy which control and limit its exercise.*[4] This jurisdiction of equity to prevent the commission of wrong is, however, modified and restricted by considerations of expediency and of convenience which confine its application to those cases in which the legal remedy is not full and adequate. Equity will not interfere to restrain the breach of a contract, or

3 "A comparison of the English and American reports will show that our courts have dwelt too much on the negative side of this principle, and have almost ignored its affirmative aspect. While the English judges have gradually but steadily enlarged the scope of the injunction, the tendency of the American decisions has been to narrow it even within the well-established limits of the jurisdiction. If 'an ounce of prevention is worth a pound of cure,' this tendency is clearly opposed to the best interests of society": Pom. Eq. Jur., § 1338, and note.

4 Quoted in Tuchman v. Welch, 42 Fed. 548, 559.

the commission of a tort, or the violation of any right, when the legal remedy of compensatory damages would be complete and adequate. The incompleteness and inadequacy of the legal remedy is the criterion which, under the settled doctrine, determines the right to the equitable remedy of injunction."[5]

§ 264. **Preliminary or Interlocutory Injunctions.**—Preliminary or interlocutory injunctions are granted to preserve the property *in statu quo* pending the determination of the suit.[6] The right to such relief depends upon a showing of irreparable injury, and rests within the sound discretion of the court.[7] It is not necessary that the

5 Pom. Eq. Jur., § 1338. See, also, Watson v. Sutherland, 5 Wall. 74, 18 L. ed. 580; North v. Peters, 138 U. S. 271, 11 Sup. Ct. 346, 34 L. ed. 936; Johnson v. Conn. Bank, 21 Conn. 148; Powell v. Foster, 59 Ga. 790; Mayor & Aldermen of Jersey City v. Gardner, 33 N. J. Eq. 622.

"The general effect produced by some text-books and judicial opinions might lead the reader to suppose that the main object of the writers or the judges was to show when injunctions could *not* be granted. The full force and effect of this most beneficial remedy, and the freedom with which it is granted by courts of the highest authority, can only be ascertained by an actual examination of the decided cases" Pom. Eq. Jur., § 1338, note.

6 "The controlling reason for the existence of the right to issue a preliminary injunction is that the court may thereby prevent such a change of the conditions and relations of persons and property during the litigation as may result in irremediable injury to some of the parties before their claims can be investigated and adjudicated": City of Newton v. Levis, 79 Fed. 715, 25 C. C. A. 561, 49 U. S. App. 266, per Sanborn, Cir. J. See, also, Blount v. Societe Anonyme du Filtre, 53 Fed. 98, 6 U. S. App. 335, 3 C. C. A. 455.

7 Southern Pac Co. v. Earl, 82 Fed. 691, 27 C. C. A. 185; Sanitary Reduction Works v. California Reduction Co, 94 Fed. 693; Strasser v. Moonelis, 108 N. Y. 611, 15 N. E. 730 (not reviewable unless complaint fails to state grounds for final relief); Ward v. Sweeney, 106 Wis 44, 82 N. W. 169 ("That discretion is of the broadest, and is seldom interfered with"); Reddall v Bryan, 14 Md. 444, 74 Am. Dec. 550, North Carolina R. Co. v. Drew, 3 Woods, 674, Fed. Cas. No. 17,433.

court be satisfied that the plaintiff will certainly prevail on the final hearing; "a probable right, and a probable danger that such right will be defeated, without the special interposition of the court," is all that need be shown.[8] When there is grave doubt, however, as to the complainant's right, preliminary relief will generally be denied.[9] It should not, save in exceptional circumstances, be used for the purpose of taking property out of the possession of one party and giving it to another.[10]

"The final injunction is in many cases matter of strict right, and granted as a necessary consequence of the decree made in the cause. On the contrary, the preliminary injunction, before answer, is a matter resting altogether in the discretion of the court, and ought not to be granted unless the injury is pressing and the delay dangerous": New York Printing & Dyeing Establishment v. Fitch, 1 Paige, 97.

8 Georgia v. Brailsford, 2 Dall. 402, 1 L. ed. 433; Southern Pac. Co. v. Earl, 82 Fed. 691, 27 C. C. A. 185; Sanitary Reduction Works v. California Reduction Co., 94 Fed. 693; Great Western Ry. Co v. Birmingham Ry. Co., 2 Phill. Ch. 602. "The rule is well settled that evidence sufficient to authorize a granting of a preliminary injunction or to warrant the refusal thereof may not be sufficient to maintain a like decision upon a final trial of the action on its merits": Colusa Parrot Min. & S. Co. v. Barnard, 28 Mont. 11, 72 Pac. 45. Of course a preliminary injunction should be denied when the bill or complaint states no ground for final relief: McHenry v. Jewett, 90 N. Y. 58.

9 Home Ins. Co. v. Nobles, 63 Fed. 642; Mitchell v. Colorado Fuel & Iron Co., 117 Fed. 723; Huntington v. City of New York, 118 Fed. 683 (complainant must show reasonable probability of ultimate success); Newark Aqueduct Board v. Passaic, 46 N. J. Eq. 552, 20 Atl. 54, 22 Atl. 55 (doubtful whether nuisance existed); Atlantic C W. W. Co. v. Consumers' W. Co., 44 N. J. Eq. 527, 15 Atl. 581; Roberts v. Scull, 58 N. J. Eq. 396, 43 Atl. 583; Hicks v. American Natural Gas Co., 207 Pa. St. 570, 57 Atl. 55. See, also, Connolly v. Van Wyck, 35 Misc. Rep. 746, 72 N. Y. Supp. 382; McHenry v. Jewett, 90 N. Y. 58.

10 "Possession is *prima facie* evidence of rightful title, because it is one of the elements of title, is sacred, and no court can in any form of proceeding take it from a man without a hearing, without overthrowing the maxim that no man shall be condemned in person

In the exercise of its discretion, the court may consider the injury to be done the adverse parties by its action; and if the questions involved are grave and difficult, and the injury to the moving party will be immediate, certain, and great if relief is denied, while the loss or inconvenience to the opposing party will be comparatively small if it is granted, a preliminary injunction may issue.[11] On the other hand, where the injury to the complainant will not be irreparable from a refusal, while the defendants might suffer great injury for which they will be without adequate remedy from the granting of the writ, it will be refused.[12]

A distinction is made in some jurisdictions between a restraining order issued on *ex parte* application, and a preliminary injunction issued upon an order to show cause. It is said that the former should not issue "except on a moral certainty of an irreparable injury if it be refused."[13] In many of the states the right to preliminary relief is governed by statute.

or deprived of property without a day in court and due process": Bettman v. Harness, 42 W. Va. 433, 26 S. E. 271, 36 L. R. A. 566, per Brannon, J. See, also, Cosmos Exploration Co. v. Gray Eagle Oil Co., 104 Fed. 20; State v. Graves, 66 Neb. 17, 92 N. W. 144; Forman v. Healey, 11 N. D. 563, 93 N. W. 866; Farmers' R. Co. v. Reno O. C. & P. Ry. Co., 53 Pa. St. 224.

11 Allison v. Corson, 88 Fed. 581, 32 C. C. A. 12; City of Newton v. Levis, 79 Fed. 715, 49 U. S. App. 266, 25 C. C. A. 161; Cohen v. Delavina, 104 Fed. 946; Denver & R. G. R. Co. v. United States, 124 Fed. 156, 59 C. C. A. 579; Packard v. Thiel College (Pa.), 56 Atl. 869.

12 New York Printing & Dyeing Establishment v. Fitch, 1 Paige, 97; Ogden v. Kip, 6 Johns. Ch. 160. See, also, Booraem v. North Hudson Co. R. Co., 40 N. J. Eq. 557, 5 Atl. 106 (no urgent necessity). For specific rules as to the use of preliminary injunctions, see the chapters following, *passim;* especially the chapters on Trespass, Nuisance, Patent Rights, Mandatory Injunctions, etc.

13 Ryan v. Seaboard & R. R. Co., 89 Fed. 385 ("a restraining order in anticipation of the hearing on a motion for an injunction is a serious exercise of power. It should not be granted except upon the moral certainty of an irreparable injury, if it be refused. It

§ 265. Injunctions to Protect Purely Equitable Estates or Interests, and in Aid of Purely Equitable Remedies.—"The jurisdiction to grant injunctions restraining acts in violation of trusts and fiduciary obligations, or in violation of any other purely equitable estates, interests, or claims in and to specific property, is really commensurate with the equitable remedies given to enforce trusts and fiduciary duties, or to establish and enforce any other equitable estates, interests, or claims, with respect to specific things, whether lands, chattels, securities, or funds of money, or to relieve against mistake, or fraud done or contemplated with respect to such things. In all such cases the question whether the remedy at law is adequate cannot arise; much less can it be the criterion by which to determine whether an injunction can be granted; for there is no remedy at law. Since the estate, interest, or claim of the complainant is purely equitable, it is exclusively cognizable by equity; and if its existence is shown, a court of equity not only has the jurisdiction, but is bound to grant every kind of remedy necessary to its complete establishment, protection, and enforcement according to its essential nature. Many breaches of trust are of such a nature that, if accomplished, they would completely defeat the right of the beneficiary to the specific trust property. The equitable reliefs against mistake or fraud with respect to specific equitable property, and the equitable remedies of all kinds to enforce trusts, express or by operation of law, and fiduciary duties concerning specific property, and to enforce any other equitable estate, interest, lien, or right in or over specific property, would be of comparatively little practical value, unless

should not be continued when it be made to appear that such a result is not imminent.") For a statement of the distinction, see Wetzstein v Boston & M. Consol. C. & S. M. Co., 25 Mont. 135, 63 Pac. 1043, 1044.

the court could by injunction restrain the alienation, transfer, or encumbrance of such property, and all other modes of dealing with it which would prejudice the rights of the complainant, and prevent him from acquiring the title, or from enjoying his estate, or from enforcing his claim, or from receiving the full benefits of his final relief.[14] It may therefore be stated as a general proposition, that whenever the equitable relief against mistake or fraud with respect to specific property, or the equitable remedy of enforcing trusts or fiduciary duties concerning specific property, or of enforcing any other equitable estates, interests, or claims in or to specific property, *requires the aid of an injunction*, a court of equity has jurisdiction, and will exercise that jurisdiction, to grant an injunction, either pending the suit or as a part of the final decree, to restrain a breach of trust or of fiduciary duty, or to restrain an alienation, transfer, assignment, encumbrance, or other kind of dealing with the property, which would be in violation of the trust or fiduciary duty, or in fraud of the complainant's rights, and which would therefore interfere with and prejudice the ultimate remedies to which he may be entitled with respect to such property. The particular instances to which this doctrine is applied are almost numberless, and extend through the entire range of equitable remedies against mistake and fraud, or to enforce trusts and fiduciary

14 "It is true that in suits concerning land, the statute authorizing a notice of *lis pendens* to be filed affords some security to the complainant against transfers and encumbrances pending suit. But this statute does not affect the truth nor generality of the proposition contained in the text. *At the utmost*, it only shows that in such cases '*the aid of an injunction is not required.*' But the notice of *lis pendens* is, at best, only a partial relief; it does not prevent a transfer; it does not even obviate the necessity of an injunction in many suits concerning land; and it does not generally extend to other suits at all": Pom. Eq. Jur., § 1339, and note.

duties, or to establish and enforce other equitable estates, interests, liens, and primary rights in and to specific property of any kind or form."[15]

§ 266. **Instances; to Restrain Breaches of Trust.**—In suits by a beneficiary against his trustee, an injunction, if needed, will be granted as a matter of course.[16] Thus, a wrongful alienation or encumbrance of land which is the subject-matter of the trust,[17] or a payment of money in violation of the trust,[18] or a sale in violation of conditions imposed by the instrument creating the trust,[19] or a sale with conditions attached by the trustee which are unreasonable and tend to depreciate the property,[20] or waste and mismanagement,[21] may be en-

15 Pom. Eq. Jur., § 1339.

16 Pom. Eq. Jur , § 1340, and note. See Williams v. Tozer, 185 Pa. St. 302, 64 Am. St. Rep. 650 (restraining acts in excess of his powers).

17 McCreary v. Gewinner, 103 Ga. 528, 29 S. E. 960; Lee v. Simpson, 37 Fed. 12, 2 L. R. A. 659 (threatened conveyance to state; preliminary injunction). To restrain sale of trust property on execution against the trustee. Hawkins v. Willard (Tex. Civ. App.), 38 S. W. 365, citing Pom. Eq. Jur., §§ 1339, 1340.

18 Reeve v. Perkins, 2 Jacob & W. 390; State v. Maury, 2 Del. Ch. 141; Drake v. Wild, 65 Vt. 611, 27 Atl. 427 (against payment of legacies to the detriment of the trust estate commingled by the executor with other moneys); Coleman v. McGrew (Neb.), 99 N. W. 663 But when the defendants, to whom money has been paid in alleged breach of trust, do not admit the trust, and its existence is the question to be decided at the hearing, an interlocutory injunction is not proper: Bank of Turkey v. Ottoman Co., L. R. 2 Eq. 366.

19 Pool v. Potter, 63 Ill. 533 (sale without giving the bond required by the deed of trust).

20 Dance v. Goldingham, L. R. 8 Ch. 902 (whether such effect is actually produced or not).

21 Cohn v. Morris, 70 Ga. 313 (assignee for benefit of creditors) In such cases a receiver is often appointed: Id.; *ante*, §§ 89, 90. An injunction will be continued until the hearing to retain control of a trust fund in dispute, where the plaintiff in the action seeks to have a judgment reformed and the validity of an assignment determined,

joined. The creator of the trust, at least of a charitable trust, may sometimes be entitled to the relief; thus, it is held that the founder of a charity may restrain the diversion of the property donated from the charitable uses for which it was given.[22]

§ 267. **To Restrain Violations of Confidence.**—Analogous to the jurisdiction to restrain breaches of trust is the jurisdiction, well established but somewhat undetermined in its limits, to restrain a person from the disclosure or unfair use of knowledge which has come to him in the course of a confidential employment by another. A common instance in England is where a solicitor is restrained from communicating to a party who is suing a former client, documents or matters of evidence which have come to his possession or knowledge in the course of his employment for such client.[23] So, a confidential clerk or agent, who uses the information which he obtained in the course of his employment

alleging that the same was procured by fraud which was denied in the answer, and where the testimony bearing upon the question is conflicting: Morris v. Willard, 84 N. C 293.

22 Mills v. Davison, 54 N. J Eq. 659, 55 Am. St. Rep. 594, 35 Atl. 1072, 35 L. R. A. 113.

23 Lewis v. Smith, 1 Macn. & G. 417 (the subsequent client also restrained from making use of such documents or evidence); Davis v. Clough, 8 Sim. 262; Little v. Kingswood Colliery Co., L. R. 20 Ch. D 733 (the jurisdiction "is founded upon the principle that a man ought to be restrained from doing any act contrary to the duty which he owes to another"; and "will be exercised at the instance of the former client irrespective of the question whether the solicitor was discharged by him or discharged himself, whenever the transaction in reference to which the injunction is sought so flows out of or is connected with that in which the solicitor was formerly retained that the same matter of dispute will probably arise"). On the same principle, it was held that a plaintiff who obtained information from the production of documents by his adversary was not at liberty to make it public, and an injunction would, if necessary, be granted to restrain him: Williams v. Prince of Wales Life etc. Co., 23 Beav. 340.

for the purpose of securing, for himself, without his employer's knowledge, the renewal of the lease of his employer's business premises, which is about to expire, and for which his employer is negotiating, may be enjoined from proceeding to recover the premises.[24] Partly on the ground of breach of confidence was rested the decision in a striking recent English case, where a photographer was restrained from exhibiting and selling to the public copies of the photographs of a woman which he had taken for her own use.[25]

§ 268. **Same; Disclosure of Trade Secrets.**—An important application of the principle of the last section is seen in the well-established jurisdiction[26] to enjoin the disclosure or use of secrets of trade, such as secret processes of manufacture, communicated to one in the course of a confidential employment. Different grounds have, indeed, been assigned for the exercise of the jurisdiction;[27] in some cases it has been referred to a

24 Gower v. Andrew, 59 Cal. 119, 43 Am. Rep. 242. On a familiar principle, the agent is a constructive trustee for the principal in such a case, and may be ordered to convey. See Pom. Eq. Jur., § 1050.

25 Pollard v. Photographic Co., 40 Ch. D. 345. The decision was based partly on the ground of breach of an implied contract not to use the photographic negative for such purposes. There is nothing in the case to support the so-called "right of privacy"; as to which see *post*, c. 29.

26 In the earliest reported case on the subject, Newbery v. James, 2 Mer. 446, Lord Eldon refused to enjoin a breach of an agreement not to impart a secret, unpatented process of manufacture, on the ground that the court could not, without having it disclosed, ascertain whether it had been infringed; but the same chancellor in a later case unhesitatingly granted an injunction against one who had obtained a knowledge of such a secret by a breach of trust: Yovatt v. Winyard, 1 Jacob & W. 394; and see Williams v. Williams, 3 Mer. 157; and the jurisdiction has since been undoubted in England, and in the United States, save for the case of Denning v. Chapman, 11 How. Pr. (N. Y.) 383.

27 Morrison v. Moat, 9 Hare, 241.

right of property in the secret unpatented process—not an exclusive right to it as against the public, or against those who in good faith acquire knowledge of it, but a property "which a court of chancery will protect against one who in violation of contract and breach of confidence undertakes to apply it to his own use, or to disclose it to third parties."[28] In other cases the jurisdiction has been referred to breach of an implied contract inferred from the nature of the employment;[29] in others it has been treated as founded upon trust or confidence;[30] more often it is spoken of as resting on both of the last two grounds combined.[31] Not only the

28 Peabody v. Norfolk, 98 Mass. 452, 96 Am. Dec. 664. See, also, Tabor v. Hoffman, 118 N. Y. 30, 16 Am St. Rep. 740, 23 N. E. 12.

29 The following *dictum* of Wigram, V. C, in Tipping v. Clarke, 2 Hare, 393, has often been referred to with approval: "It is clear, that every clerk employed in a merchant's counting house is under an implied contract that he will not make public that which he learns in the execution of his duty as clerk." The secret may, of course, be protected by express agreement; such an agreement is not in general restraint of trade See *post*, § 297.

30 Yovatt v. Wingard, 1 Jacob & W. 394. See a clever argument in favor of this theory in 11 Harvard Law Review, 262.

31 "Perhaps the real solution is that the confidence postulates an implied contract; that, when the court is satisfied of the existence of the confidential relation, then it at once infers or implies the contract arising from that confidential relation": Merryweather v. Moore, [1892] 2 Ch. 518, 522, *per* Kekewich, J. In addition to the cases already cited, see the following recent cases, all concerning the disclosure or unfair use of secret processes: C. F. Simmons Medicine Co v. Simmons, 81 Fed. 163, Stewart v. Hook, 118 Ga. 445, 45 S. E. 369; Westervelt v. National Paper etc. Co., 154 Ind. 673, 57 N. E. 552 (reviewing many cases); O. & W. Thum Co. v. Tloczynski, 114 Mich. 149, 68 Am. St. Rep. 469, 72 N. W. 140, 38 L. R. A. 200, 45 Cent. L. J. 348 (reviewing many cases), Salomon v. Hertz, 40 N. J. Eq. 400, 2 Atl. 379; Stone v. Goss, 65 N. J. Eq. 756, 55 Atl. 736; Chaplin v. Stoddart, 30 Hun, 300, Eastman Co. v. Reichenbach, 20 N. Y. Supp. 110, 36 Cent. L. J. 433, 47 N. Y. St. Rep. 435; Little v. Gallus, 38 N. Y. Supp. 487, dissenting opinion, Id. 1014, 4 App. Div. 569. See, also, Simmons Hardware Co. v Waibel, 1 S. D. 488, 36 Am. St. Rep. 755, 47 N. W. 814, 11

person acquiring the knowledge by breach of contract or of confidence will be enjoined, but also all persons to whom he has disclosed the secret.[32] The protection of an injunction is, of course, extended only to that which is really the plaintiff's secret, and not to knowledge or information which is accessible to all the world.[33]

§ 269. **Other Instances.**—Among other instances in which equity will grant an injunction, preliminary or final, to protect purely equitable estates or interests, or in aid of purely equitable remedies, the following

L. R. A. 267 (receiver appointed of a secret code). The jurisdiction is thus described in Westervelt v. National Paper etc. Co., *supra:* "It is evident from the authorities cited that if a person employs another to work for him in a business in which he makes use of a secret process or of machinery invented by himself, or by others for him, but the nature and particulars of which he desires to keep a secret, and of which desire on the part of the employer the employee has notice at the time of his employment, even if there is no express contract on the part of the employee not to divulge said secret process or machinery, the law will imply a promise to keep the employer's secret thus intrusted to him; and any attempt on his part to use the secret process or machinery, or to construct the machinery for his own use, as against the master, or to communicate said secret to others, or in any manner to aid others in using the same or in constructing the machinery, will not only be a breach of his contract with his employer, but a breach of confidence and violation of duty which will be enjoined by a court of equity."

To the effect that an assignee of the secret may enjoin former employees of the assignor, see Vulcan Detinning Co. v. American Can Co. (N. J. Eq.), 58 Atl. 290. In Pressed Steel Car Co. v. Standard Steel Car Co. (Pa.), 60 Atl. 4, blue-prints were delivered by the complainant to certain railroad companies, to be used in ordering parts of cars, etc., from complainant. One company delivered the prints to a rival. It was held that this was a breach of confidence, and that an injunction should issue.

32 See nearly all the cases cited in the preceding notes.

33 See Reuter's Telegram Co. v. Byron, 43 L. J. (Ch.) 661, opinion of Jessel, M. R.; Williams v. Williams, 3 Mer. 15.

may be enumerated: In aid or in place of cancellation, to prevent the transfer of negotiable instruments, at the suit of the defrauded maker or acceptor, or of the party claiming to be the true owner, or to have an interest in them;[34] or the transfer, under like circumstances, of stocks or other securities not strictly negotiable;[35] to prevent the transfer or injury of chattels of a special nature and value,[36] or of other chattels wrongfully detained by an agent in violation of his trust,[37] in connection with a suit for their delivery up; in aid of the rights of an equitable assignee against interference by his assignor;[38] to protect the estate of a supposed insane person during the pendency of lunacy proceedings;[39] in connection with creditors' bills;[40] to prevent a defendant from affecting or encumbering the property in litigation by contract, conveyance, mortgage, or any other act;[41] and, in general, in all suits to enforce an equitable right against specific property,—as to enforce an equitable estate and compel the conveyance of

34 Pom. Eq. Jur., § 1340. See *post*, chapter on Cancellation.

35 Pom. Eq Jur., § 1340. See *post*, chapter on Cancellation.

36 Lloyd v. Loaring, 6 Ves. 773 (Masonic regalia); Church v. Haeger (Com. Pl. S T.), 33 N. Y. Supp. 47 (wedding presents). See *post*, chapter on Specific Performance.

37 Wood v. Rowcliffe, 3 Hare, 304, 308. See *post*, chapter on Specific Performance.

38 Dulaney v. Scudder, 94 Fed. 6, 36 C. C. A. 52 (and the court may retain jurisdiction for the purpose of assessing damages, but not in aid of a legal assignee, whose right has been acknowledged by the debtor, to prevent execution on a judgment recovered by the assignor against the debtor, since the assignee's right is not prejudiced thereby, and his remedy at law against the debtor is complete); Perry v. Thompson, 108 Ala. 586, 18 South. 524.

39 In re Harris, 7 Del. Ch. 42, 28 Atl. 329.

40 See *post*, chapter on Creditors' Suits For instance of injunction to preserve the fund belonging to the debtor until judgment at law is obtained, see Hawks v. Hawks (Vt.), 54 Atl. 959.

41 Pom Eq Jur, § 1340, Daly v. Kelly, 4 Dow, 417, 440. See *ante*, § 262, note 2, § 264, as to preliminary or interlocutory injunction.

the legal title, to enforce a trust, or an equitable lien,[42] to compel the specific performance of a contract;[43] and the like,—the court will grant an injunction to restrain a threatened transfer of the property, whether land, chattels, or securities, during the pendency of the action.[44]

42 See Williams v. Harlan, 88 Md. 1, 71 Am. St. Rep. 394, 41 Atl. 51 (lien of tenant in common for improvements benefiting the estate, or of one subrogated to his rights, protected from an unfair partition); Pensacola & G. R. Co. v. Spratt, 12 Fla. 26, 91 Am. Dec. 747 (holder of equitable lien may have relief on ground of waste only when defendant's use of the property impairs the security); Robinson v. Pickering, L. R. 16 Ch. D. 371, 660 (in suit to enforce married woman's contract against her separate estate, an injunction restraining her from alienating her property will not be granted before the plaintiff establishes his right by obtaining a judgment, because her contract, by the English doctrine, creates no lien or charge on her estate).

43 See *post*, chapters on Injunction to Prevent Breach of Contract, and on Specific Performance.

44 Pom. Eq. Jur., § 1340.

"To prevent a *cloud upon title*. The use of the injunction to prevent acts which would create a cloud upon title is governed by the same rules which control the remedy of removing a cloud from title": 4 Pom. Eq. Jur., § 1345; cited, McConnaughy v. Pennoyer, 43 Fed. 342. See *post*, chapters on Injunction Against Taxation, *passim*, and (in Vol. II) on Cloud on Title.

"To protect *married women's property*. An injunction may be needed for this purpose; as, for example, to restrain the sale of her property for her husband's debts when her title is clear, but not unless it *is* clear: Allen v. Benners, 10 Phila. 10; Simson v. Bates, 10 Phila. 66; to prevent the collection of a mortgage assigned by a wife, when the assignment was void: French v. Snell, 29 N. J. Eq. 95"; 4 Pom. Eq. Jur., § 1345, and note 6; cited, Filler v. Tyler, 91 Va. 458, 22 S. E. 235. See, also, Kirkpatrick v. Buford, 21 Ark. 268, 76 Am. Dec. 363 (to protect separate property from husband's creditors); Pritchett v. Davis, 101 Ga. 236, 65 Am. St. Rep. 298, 28 S. E. 666 (to protect homestead); Hulett v. Inlow, 57 Ind. 412, 26 Am. Rep. 64; Wagoner v. Wagoner, 77 Md. 189, 26 Atl. 284 (to protect legal separate estate; case of probable irreparable injury must be shown); Dority v. Dority (Tex.), 71 S. W. 950 (husband's interference with statutory separate estate enjoined). Injunction is often authorized by statute as an incident to a suit for divorce, to prevent alienation

of the husband's property to defeat the right to alimony· See In re White, 113 Cal. 282, 45 Pac 323; Uhl v. Irwin, 3 Okla. 388, 41 Pac. 376; cf. Smith v. Smith (S. C.), 29 S E. 227; or to prevent his interference with the wife's property: See Robinson v. Robinson, 123 N. C. 136, 31 S. E. 371; Lyon v. Lyon, 102 Ga. 453, 66 Am. St. Rep. 189, 31 S. E. 34, 42 L. R. A. 194; Symonds v. Hallett, L. R. 24 Ch. D. 346.

CHAPTER XIII.

INJUNCTIONS TO PREVENT THE VIOLATION OF CONTRACTS.

ANALYSIS.

§ 270. Injunctions to Prevent the Violation of Contracts—In General.—"An injunction restraining the breach of a contract is a negative specific enforcement of that contract. The jurisdiction of equity to grant such injunction is substantially coincident with its jurisdiction to compel a specific performance. Both are governed by the same doctrines and rules; and it may be stated as a general proposition that wherever the contract is one of a class which will be affirmatively specifically enforced, a court of equity will restrain its breach by injunction, if this is the only practical mode of enforcement which its terms permit.[1] Where the agreement stipulates that certain acts shall not be done, an injunction preventing the commission of those acts is evidently the only mode of enforcement; but the remedy of injunction is not confined to contracts whose stipulations are negative; it often extends to those which are affirmative in their provisions, where the affirmative stipulation implies or includes a negative. The universal test of the jurisdiction, admitted alike by the courts of England and of the United States, is the inadequacy of the legal remedy of damages in the class of contracts to which the particular instance belongs."[2]

§ 271. Principles Regulating Specific Performance Apply. Since restraining the breach of a contract by injunction

1 Quoted in Chicago Municipal G. L. & C. Co. v. Town of Lake, 130 Ill. 42, 22 N. E. 616; South Chicago City R. Co. v. Calumet El. St. R. Co., 171 Ill. 391, 49 N. E. 576; Welty v. Jacobs, 171 Ill. 624, 49 N. E. 723, 40 L. R. A. 98.

2 4 Pom. Eq. Jur, § 1341. The author adds in the note: "The modern English decisions have been much more liberal than the American cases in applying this test, and the English courts have more freely used the injunction to prevent the violation of contracts than the majority of the American judges have been willing to go. The *tendency* of the American courts has been to limit, rather than to enlarge, the jurisdiction in cases of contracts. English courts will

is merely a mode of specifically enforcing the contract, it follows that the discretion of the court in awarding the injunction is guided by the same equitable principles and doctrines as those which regulate the remedy

enjoin the violation of some contracts, even though they cannot be specifically enforced. The American decisions, with few exceptions, refuse to adopt this doctrine.'' These remarks have hardly the force, at the present day, that they possessed at the time when they were written (1883). Indeed, the English and American courts appear to have changed places in respect to their attitude towards one important class of contracts—those for personal services: See *post*, §§ 288, 289.

Injunction refused because contract one of a class which, because of the adequacy of the legal remedy, will not be affirmatively specifically enforced: Fothergill v. Rowland, L. R. 17 Eq. 132, a contract for the sale of chattels, viz., of all the coal which defendants should get from a certain mine; Harlow v. Oregonian Pub. Co. (Or.), 78 Pac. 737. See, also, *infra*, § 271, and *post*, Vol. II., chapters on Specific Performance.

For instances of injunction granted, although there was no express negative stipulation, if such negative can reasonably be implied. Montague v. Flockton, L. R. 16 Eq 189; Manchester Canal Co. v. Manchester Racecourse Co., [1901] 2 Ch. 37; Singer Sewing Machine Co. v. Union B & E. Co., 1 Holmes, 253, Fed. Cas. No. 12,904; Chicago & A. R. Co v. New York, L. E. & W. R. Co., 24 Fed. 516; Beatty v Coble, 142 Ind. 329, 41 N. E. 590; Dwight v. Hamilton, 113 Mass. 175; Duff v. Russell, 60 N. Y. Super. Ct. (28 Jones & S) 80, 39 N. Y. St. Rep 266, 14 N. Y. Supp. 134, affirmed without opinion, 133 N. Y. 678, 31 N. E. 622 (contract for personal services); Hoyt v. Fuller, 19 N. Y. Supp. 962 (same); Cort v. Lassard, 18 Or. 221, 17 Am. St. Rep. 726, 22 Pac. 1054, 6 L. R. A. 653 So far as contracts for personal services are concerned, it is now generally taken to be settled in England that an express negative clause in the contract is necessary to warrant an injunction Whitwood Chemical Co. v. Hardman, [1891] 2 Ch. 416; and the stipulation must be negative in substance as well as in form: Davis v. Foreman, [1894] 3 Ch. 654. See, also, Burton v. Marshall, 4 Gill (Md.), 487, 45 Am. Dec. 171.

For instances of injunction granted, notwithstanding that some parts of the contract were incapable of specific enforcement, see Whittaker v. Howe, 3 Beav. 383; Rolfe v. Rolfe, 15 Sim. 88, Dietrichsen v. Cabburn, 2 Phill. Ch 52, per Lord Cottenham, C. (''the of specific performance. Thus, the breach of a contract will not be enjoined unless the terms of the contract are certain and definite;[3] if the injunction will work a "hardship" to the defendant or innocent third parties, within the meaning of that term in equity;[4] if the con-

equitable jurisdiction to restrain by injunction an act which the defendant by contract or duty was bound to abstain from, cannot be confined to cases in which the court has jurisdiction over the acts of the plaintiff"); Lumley v. Wagner, 1 De Gex, M. & G. 604 (the leading case, decided in 1852, reviewing all prior authorities); Donnell v. Bennett, L. R. 22 Ch. D. 835 (immaterial whether the negative clause is a separable part of the whole contract); Singer Sewing Machine Co. v. Union Button Hole etc. Co, 1 Holmes, 253, Fed. Cas. No. 12,904, per Lowell, J, reviewing many English cases ("I think the fair result of the later cases may be thus expressed: If the case is one in which the negative remedy of injunction will do substantial justice between the parties, by obliging the defendant either to carry out his contract or lose all benefit of the breach, and the remedy at law is inadequate, and there is no reason of policy against it, the court will interfere to restrain conduct which is contrary to the contract, although it may be unable to enforce a specific performance of it"); Western Union Tel. Co. v. Union Pac. R. Co, 1 McCrary, 558, 3 Fed. 423, Western Union Tel. Co. v. St. Joseph & W. R. Co., 1 McCrary, 565, 3 Fed. 430; Chicago & A. R. Co. v. New York, L. E. & W. R. Co, 24 Fed. 516 (enjoining diversion of traffic from a railroad); Xenia Real Estate Co v. Macy, 147 Ind. 568, 47 N. E. 147 (contract to supply natural gas); Standard Fashion Co. v Siegel-Cooper Co, 157 N. Y. 60, 68 Am. St. Rep 749, 51 N. E. 408, 43 L. R. A. 854, affirming 30 App. Div. 564, 52 N. Y. Supp. 433, and reversing 22 Misc Rep. 624, 50 N. Y. Supp. 1056 (see *post*, § 295); Peabody v. Norfolk, 98 Mass 452, 96 Am. Dec. 664, House v. Clemens, 24 Abb. N. C. 381, 9 N Y. Supp. 484 (agreement by defendant, an author, to permit plaintiff to dramatize a novel written by the former). But see Welty v. Jacobs, 171 Ill 624, 49 N. E. 723, 40 L. R A. 98; Iron Age Publishing Co. v. Western Union Tel Co., 83 Ala. 498, 3 Am. St. Rep. 758, 3 South. 449, Strang v. Richmond, P. & C. R. Co, 93 Fed. 71; Hills v. Croll, 2 Phill. Ch. 60.

3 See Gaslight & E Co. of New Albany v. City of New Albany, 139 Ind. 660, 39 N. E. 462; Xenia Real Estate Co. v. Macy, 147 Ind. 568, 47 N. E. 147, Giles v. Dunbar, 181 Mass. 22, 62 N. E. 985; Strang v. Richmond, T. & C. R. Co., 93 Fed. 71.

4 Goddard v. American Queen, 27 Misc Rep. 482, 59 N. Y. Supp.

tract is tainted with illegality;[5] if there has been no performance by the plaintiff of that which, under the terms of the contract, he was obliged first to perform;[6] or when the decree of injunction would be nugatory,[7] etc.

§ 272. **Restrictive Covenants—Equitable Easements.**—Injunctions are frequently allowed to restrain the violation of covenants restricting the use of the land. "When the owner of land enters into a covenant concerning it, when in a deed the grantor or the grantee covenants, or in a lease the lessor or the lessee covenants, concerning the land, concerning its use, restricting certain specified uses, stipulating for certain specified uses, subjecting it to easements or servitudes, and the like, and the land is afterwards conveyed, or sold, or passes to one who has actual or constructive notice of the covenant, the grantee or purchaser will take the premises bound by the covenant, and will be compelled in equity either to specifically execute it, or will be restrained from violating it, at the suit of the original covenantee or of any other person who has a sufficient equitable interest, although perhaps without any legal interest,

46. Nor will a contract inequitable and unconscionable, which defendant probably did not understand, be enforced by injunction Pope Mfg. Co. v. Gormully, 144 U. S. 224, 12 Sup. Ct. 632, 36 L. ed. 414.

5 See Pacific Postal Tel. Co. v. Western Union Tel. Co., 50 Fed. 493; South Chicago City R. Co. v. Calumet E. St. R. Co., 171 Ill. 391, 49 N. E. 576; Olin v. Bale, 98 Ill. 53, 38 Am. Rep. 78 (contract of doubtful propriety); Fullington v. Kyle Lumber Co., 139 Ala. 242, 35 South 852.

6 See Chicago M. G. L. & F. Co. v. Town of Lake, 130 Ill. 42, 22 N. E 616; New York Chemical Co v Halleck (Com. P S. T.), 15 N. Y. Supp. 517. As to *mutuality*, see *supra*, § 271, last paragraph of note 2.

7 See Brett v. East India & L. S. Co, 2 Hem & M. 404. See, generally, on all these subjects, *post*, Vol. II, chapters on Specific Performance.

in such performance."[8] The application of this doctrine is wholly independent of the question whether the covenant is of such a character as to run with the land.[9] It is a creation of equity and can be enforced by an equitable remedy.[10]

8 Pom. Eq. Jur., § 1295.

9 Tulk v. Moxhay, 2 Phill. 774. "The question is not whether the covenant runs with the land, but whether a party shall be permitted to use the land in a manner inconsistent with the contract entered into by his vendor, and with notice of which he purchased." See, also, Morris v. Tuskaloosa Mfg. Co., 83 Ala. 565, 3 South. 690; Willoughby v. Lawrence, 116 Ill. 11, 4 N. E. 356, 56 Am. Rep. 758, citing Pom. Eq. Jur., §§ 1295, 1342.

It is questionable whether affirmative covenants of similar nature will be enforced in equity. Professor Pomeroy in Pom. Eq. Jur., § 1295, says: "I have, as it will be seen, continued to state the doctrine in its most general form as applying to affirmative as well as to restrictive covenants, and as rendering the owner liable to the affirmative duty of specifically performing the covenant, as well as to the negative remedy of restraint from violating it, notwithstanding the very recent decisions by the English court of appeal holding that the doctrine applies only to restrictive covenants, and does not extend to those which stipulate for affirmative acts." See London etc. Ry. v. Gomm, L. R. 8 Q. B. D. 562; Haywood v. Brunswick Bldg. Soc., L. R. 8 Q. B. D. 403. In Morland v. Cook L. R. 6 Eq. 252, an affirmative covenant was enforced. In Stevens v. Annex Realty Co., 173 Mo. 511, 73 S. W. 505, an affirmative covenant to pay assessments for improvements was enforced.

10 "The most frequent condition of facts to which the doctrine has been applied in the United States is the following: A, the owner of a block of land, divides it into lots for sale, and sells all these lots to different grantees. In the deed of lot No 1 are covenants of the grantee not to build nearer the street than a certain line, or not to build certain kinds of buildings, or not to use the lots for certain purposes, or not to build so as to cut off a certain prospect, or other negative or affirmative covenants. The deeds of all the other lots contain similar covenants. Finally, the whole land is sold, so that A retains no interest whatever. The lots are afterwards conveyed to subsequent grantees. Each subsequent grantee would be charged with constructive notice of the covenants in the original deed under which he claimed title. If the subsequent grantee of any lot—say No. 1—should violate the covenants in the deed of his lot, then plainly there would be no right of action at law against him in favor

§ 273. **Questions Stated.**—"Every owner of real property has the right so to deal with it as to restrain its uses by his grantees within such limits as to prevent its appropriation to purposes which will impair the value or diminish the pleasure of the enjoyment of the land which he retains. The only restriction on this right is, that it shall be exercised reasonably, with due regard to public policy, and without creating any unlawful restraint of trade."[11] When a restriction has once been

of the owner of any other lot, for there would be no legal privity whatsoever between them." "The following cases also illustrate the doctrine: In Clark v. Martin, 49 Pa. St. 289, each grantee of adjoining lots covenanted not to build on the rear portion of his premises above a certain height, and this was enforced; Schwoerer v. Boylston Market Assn., 99 Mass. 285 (a covenant that a strip of land should not be subject to fences, and should be used as a way, was enforced by the subsequent grantee of other land benefited thereby); Peck v. Conway, 119 Mass. 546 (a covenant not to erect a building on the land conveyed was enforced against a subsequent grantee of the covenantor by a subsequent grantee of the original covenantee; the defendant had constructive notice from his title deeds), Whitney v. Union etc. Ry. Co., 11 Gray, 359, 71 Am. Dec. 715 (a covenant not to use the land in a certain manner enforced against a subsequent grantee charged with notice); Parker v. Nightingale, 6 Allen, 341, 83 Am. Dec. 632 (in conveyances of adjoining lots by same grantor, each grantee covenanted that the lot should only be used for dwelling-houses; held binding on all subsequent grantees, and enforceable by any subsequent grantee against another"): Pom. Eq. Jur., § 1295, note.

This doctrine is known by various names in the different jurisdictions. Most of the cases have arisen in England, New York, Massachusetts, New Jersey, or Pennsylvania. In some jurisdictions such covenants are called covenants running with the land. Elsewhere they are said to be in the nature of easements. And in still other jurisdictions they are simply called restrictive covenants Under whatever name, the principles applied are practically the same, so that for the purpose of this treatment we may disregard the diversity. Even where they are called covenants running with the land it is held that they are covenants enforceable only in equity. It would seem that the most accurate designation is "equitable easements," for these terms describe the particular covenants, to the exclusion of all others.

11 Whitney v. Union Ry. Co., 11 Gray, 359, 71 Am Dec. 715.

placed upon the use of land, questions arise as to who is bound and who may enforce.

§ 274. **Action by Grantor.**—When the action is brought by the grantor, the case is simple. If, in such a case, the defendant is the original grantee, an action can be maintained at law, and in a proper case an injunction will be awarded. If he is a grantee of a grantee, an injunction will be allowed upon the principle that a party shall not be permitted to use land in a manner inconsistent with the contract entered into by his vendor, with notice of which he purchased.[12] This is subject to the limitation in some jurisdictions that the restriction must "touch or concern," or "extend to the support" of the land.[13]

12 Tulk v. Moxhay, 2 Phill. Ch. 774; Wilson v. Hart, 2 Hem & M 551, 11 Jur., N S., 735, L R. 1 Ch. 463; Fielden v. Slater, L. R 7 Eq 523; Sullivan v. Kohlenberg, 31 Ind. App. 215, 67 N E. 511 (recorded contract not to sell liquor enforced against purchaser), Hayes v Waverly & P. R Co, 51 N. J. Eq. 348, 27 Atl 649, Cornish v. Wiessman, 56 N. J Eq. 610, 35 Atl. 408; Walker v. McNulty, 19 Misc. Rep. 701, 45 N. Y Supp. 42 In Jenks v. Pawlowski, 98 Mich 110, 39 Am St. Rep 522, 56 N. W. 1105, 22 L. R. A. 863, it was held that if the grantor sells his remaining land without inserting restrictions, he waives them as to his prior grantee. In Los Angeles University v. Swarth, 107 Fed. 798, 46 C. C. A. 647, 54 L R. A. 262, it was held that a grantor who has disposed of all his land in the vicinity cannot obtain an injunction. The argument is that he suffers no injury by the breach. That, where the grantor sells the *whole* of his land, to one purchaser, with a restrictive covenant by the vendee, such covenant is personal, and the vendor's executor cannot enjoin an assign of the purchaser in respect of a breach committed after the vendor's death, see Formby v. Barker, [1903] 2 Ch. 539, reviewing many cases. It has been held that where several grantors unite in a deed to a city and covenant therein that no buildings shall be built on a certain strip, one grantor may enjoin another from violating the covenant· Evans v. New Auditorium Pier Co. (N. J. Eq), 58 Atl 191.

13 Norcross v. James, 140 Mass. 188, 2 N. E 946. See, also, Los Angeles Terminal Land Co. v. Muir, 136 Cal. 36, 68 Pac 308.

§ 275. Action by Purchaser of Other Land.—When it clearly appears that such restrictions are intended to inure to the benefit of other land, at the time of conveyance or formerly belonging to the grantor, a subsequent grantee of such other parcel may enforce the restriction by injunction. The principal question to be determined in such cases is whether the intent is sufficiently clear to warrant the court in giving relief. It is a matter for construction of the words of the covenant, in connection with the surrounding circumstances. If the language is explicit in stating the intent, the grantee's right is admitted[14] The difficulty arises when the covenant merely restrains the use without indicating the beneficiary.

Where an owner of a tract of land lays it out in building lots, makes a plan showing a general building scheme, and sells in accordance therewith to various purchasers, inserting restrictions in all the deeds, the intent will be inferred. The purpose of the restrictions is clearly to benefit all the land in the tract and to make an inducement for purchase Accordingly, one grantee may enjoin a breach by another, or by one who takes with notice.[15] Some courts have intimated that either

14 Lattimer v. Livermore, 72 N. Y 174; Schwoerer v Boylston Market Assn, 99 Mass 285, Ragen v Hasegood, [1900] 2 Ch. 388.

15 In the following cases there was a general scheme of improvement which was held sufficient to show an intent to give a grantee a right to enforce: Collins v. Castle, L R 36 Ch D 243; Child v. Douglas, Kay, 560, Spicer v. Martin, L. R. 14 App Cas. 12; Parker v. Nightingale, 88 Mass (6 Allen) 341, 83 Am Dec. 632, Hamlen v. Werner, 144 Mass. 397, 11 N. E 684; Hano v. Bigelow, 155 Mass. 341, 29 N. E 628, Winfield v. Henning, 21 N J. Eq. 188, Tallmadge v. East River Bank, 26 N Y 105, Bimson v. Bultman, 3 App. Div 198, 38 N. Y. Supp 209; Barrow v Richard, 8 Paige, 351 35 Am. Dec. 713; Summers v. Beeler, 90 Md 474, 78 Am St. Rep 446, 45 Atl. 19, 48 L. R. A. 54; Whatman v. Gibson, 9 Sim. 196, Schreiber v. Creed, 10 Sim. 196, Pellard v. Gore, [1901] 1 Ch 834, Fisk v. Ley, 76 Conn. 295, 56 Atl. 559. For a collection of authorities see note, 21 Am. St. Rep. 489.

a general building scheme or an express declaration in the covenant is essential; but the better view seems to be that the intent may be otherwise determined.[16]

16 The rules are summed up in De Gray v. Monmouth Beach Clubhouse Co., 50 N. J. Eq. 329, 24 Atl. 388, as follows: "The action is held not to be maintainable between purchasers not parties to the original covenant, in cases in which—(1) It does not appear that the covenant was entered into to carry out some general scheme or plan for the improvement or development of the property which the act of defendant disregards in some particular. (2) It does not appear that the covenant was entered into for the benefit of the land of which complainant has become the owner. (3) It appears that the covenant was not entered into for the benefit of subsequent purchasers, but only for the benefit of the original covenantee and his next of kin. (4) It appears that the covenant has not entered into the consideration of the complainant's purchase. (5) It appears that the original plan has been abandoned without dissent, or the character of the neighborhood has so changed as to defeat the purpose of the covenant, and to thus render its enforcement unreasonable." All of the statements seem fully supported by authority, with the exception of the first. In probably the majority of the cases where injunctions have been granted there has been a general building scheme. But it will be seen that such relief has been granted where there has been no such scheme.

In Beals v. Case, 138 Mass. 138, the rule was laid down as follows: "But it is always a question of intention of the parties; and, in order to make this rule applicable, it must appear from the terms of the grant, or from the situation and surrounding circumstances, that it was the intention of the grantor in inserting the restriction to create a servitude or right which should inure to the benefit of the plaintiff's land, and should be annexed to it as an appurtenance."

In the following cases the court found sufficient evidence of the intention: Tobey v. Moore, 130 Mass. 448; Peck v. Conway, 119 Mass. 546; Bauer v. Gribbel, 2 App. Div. 80, 37 N. Y. Supp. 609; Electric City Land & Imp. Co. v. West Ridge Coal Co., 187 Pa. St. 500, 41 Atl. 458, Muzzarelli v. Hulshizer, 163 Pa. St. 643, 30 Atl. 291; St. Andrew's Church's Appeal, 67 Pa. St. (17 P. F. Smith), 512; Clark v. Martin, 49 Pa St. 289; Duncan v. Central Passenger Ry. Co., 85 Ky. 425, 4 S W. 228, Morris v. Tuskaloosa Mfg. Co, 83 Ala. 565, 3 South. 689, Greene v. Creighton, 7 R. I. 1; Phoenix Ins. Co. v. Continental Ins. Co., 14 Abb. Pr., N. S, 266; Hills v. Metzenroth; 173 Mass. 423, 53 N. E. 890, Linzee v Mixer, 101 Mass. 512; Coughlin v. Barker, 46 Mo. App. 54; Moxhay v. Inderwick, 1 De Gex & S. 708 (not an injunction case); In re Birmingham & D. L. Co., [1893] 1 Ch. 343;

§ 276. **Restrictions as to Use of Property.**—These rules are not confined to mere restrictions as to the character or situation of buildings, but apply as well to restrictions as to their use. Very frequently it is stipulated that no intoxicating liquors shall be sold on the premises. These restrictions are sustained on the ground that a party has the right, in disposing of his property, to prevent such a use by the grantee as might diminish the value of remaining land or impair its eligibility for other uses.[17] Restrictions prohibiting the carrying on of

Nottingham Patent Brick & Tile Co. v. Butler, L. R. 15 Q. B. D 268 (not an injunction case); Meriwether v. Joy, 85 Mo. App. 634.

In the following cases it was held that the evidence of intention was not sufficiently clear to warrant an injunction. Lowell Inst. for Sav. v. City of Lowell, 153 Mass. 530, 27 N. E. 518; Dana v Wentworth, 111 Mass. 291; Jewell v. Lee, 14 Allen, 145, 92 Am. Dec 744; Sharp v. Ropes, 110 Mass. 381, Nottingham Patent Brick & Tile Co. v. Butler, L. R. 16 Q. B. D. 778 (not an injunction case), Badger v. Boardman, 16 Gray, 559 (not an injunction case), Renals v. Cowlishaw, L. R. 9 Ch. D. 125; Knapp v. Hall, 63 Hun, 624, 17 N Y. Supp. 487; Keates v. Lyon, L. R. 4 Ch. App. 218 (not an injunction case); Master v. Hansard, L. R. 4 Ch. D. 718. The use of the word "heirs" in a covenant not to build without the consent of the "grantor or her heirs" has been held to indicate an intention to make the covenant personal: Hemsley v. Marlborough Hotel Co, 65 N. J. Eq. 167, 55 Atl. 994. It is held that when a party whose land is subject to a restrictive covenant sells part of it without any restriction, he cannot enjoin the purchaser, although the other land owners can. The restriction on the part sold was not intended to inure to the benefit of the part retained by the plaintiff: King v. Dickeson, L. R. 40 Ch D. 596. In the following cases the injunction was denied because of special facts arising in the cases· Davis v. Corporation of Liecester, [1894] 2 Ch 208; Kirby v. School Board, [1896] Ch. 437. In Guardian of Tendring Union v Dawton, [1891] 3 Ch. 265, the plaintiff had a charge against land for street improvements The land was subject to a restriction against building The court held that the plaintiff could not sell the land free from the restriction. In Welch v. Austin (Mass), 72 N. E. 972, a restriction was construed so as to limit its effect to the first house built upon the lot

17 Jenks v. Pawlowski, 98 Mich. 110, 39 Am. St Rep 522, 56 N W 1105, 22 L. R. A. 863; Stees v. Kranz, 32 Minn 313, 20 N W. 241,

any obnoxious business on the premises will be sustained upon the same ground.[18] Of course, to enable anyone but the original covenantee to sue, it must appear that the restrictions were intended for the benefit of the plaintiff's land. Strong evidence of this is shown when similar restrictions are put into all the deeds given by the grantor and the benefit is made part of the inducement to the purchase.

§ 277. **Restrictions Which are Enforceable.**—The courts are divided on the question of what restrictions may be attached to land. It is held that a personal, as distinguished from a real, obligation, insisted upon by a grantor and assumed by a grantee, restricting the use of land, may be enforced against the grantee and subsequent purchasers with notice. Thus, in New York an injunction will issue to restrain a purchaser with notice from violating an agreement not to sell sand from the land conveyed.[19] In Massachusetts, however, it has been held that where a grantor covenants not to open a quarry on his remaining land, an injunction will not issue against a purchaser of such remaining land.[20]

Watrous v. Allen, 57 Mich. 362, 58 Am. Rep 363, 24 N. W. 104; Wilson v. Hart, L. R. 1 Ch. App 463; Sutton v. Head, 86 Ky. 156, 9 Am. St. Rep. 274, 5 S. W. 410; Carter v Williams, L R. 9 Eq. 678, Hall v. Solomon, 61 Conn 476, 29 Am. St. Rep 218, 23 Atl 876; Atlantic Dock Co. v. Leavitt, 54 N. Y. 35, 13 Am. Rep 556; Star Brewing Co v Primas, 163 Ill. 652, 45 N. E. 145; Anderson v. Rowland, 18 Tex. Civ. App 460, 44 S. W 911. See, also, Gilmer v Mobile & M R. Co, 79 Ala 569, 58 Am. Rep. 623 (citing Pom. Eq. Jur, § 1342).

18 Haskell v. Wright, 23 N. J. Eq 389; Brouwer v Jones, 23 Barb. 153.

19 Hodge v. Sloan, 107 N. Y. 244, 1 Am. St Rep 816, 17 N. E 335.

20 Norcross v. James, 140 Mass. 188, 2 N. E. 946. In this case the court said: "If it be asked what is the difference in principle between an easement to have land unbuilt upon, and an easement to have a quarry left unopened, the answer is, that, whether a difference of degree or of kind, the distinction is plain between a grant or cove-

Where such a stipulation creates an invalid restraint upon trade, equitable relief will be denied.[21] In Pennsylvania it is held that where a railroad company contributes money for the development of ore land and the owners agree to give all the traffic to and from the land to such company, a party acquiring title by foreclosure and taking all the benefits of the contract will be enjoined from shipping over other lines.[22] In Minnesota, however, it is held that an agreement to give a railroad the exclusive transportation of the products of the land does not impose an obligation which attaches to or concerns the land or its use or mode of enjoyment, and that therefore it will not be enforced in equity.[23]

§ 278. **Liability of Grantor.**—Where a *grantor* upon conveyance agrees with the grantee not to use his remaining land for certain specified purposes, the covenant will generally be held to be for the benefit of the land, and an injunction will be granted to restrain a breach. Thus, a covenant not to build on a common facing the land conveyed, or to fix a certain building line upon his remaining land will be enforced.[24] It has been held that, in case of doubt, a clause creating an

nant that looks to direct physical advantage in the occupation of the dominant estate, such as light and air, and one which only concerns it in the indirect way we have mentioned."

21 West Va. Trans. Co. v. Ohio River Pipe Line Co., 22 W. Va. 626, 46 Am. Rep. 527; Brewer v. Marshall, 19 N. J. Eq. 537.

22 Bald Eagle Val. R. Co. v. Nittany Val. R. Co., 171 Pa. St. 284, 50 Am. St. Rep. 807, 33 Atl. 239, 29 L. R. A. 423.

23 Kettle River R. Co. v. Eastern R. Co., 41 Minn. 461, 43 N. W. 469, 6 L. R. A. 111. To same effect see Keppell v. Bayley, 2 Mylne & K. 517.

24 Trustees etc. v. Cowen, 4 Paige, 510, 27 Am. Dec. 80; Hills v. Miller, 3 Paige, 254, 24 Am. Dec. 218; Kilpatrick v. Peshine, 24 N. J. Eq (9 C. E. Green) 206; Halls v. Newbold, 69 Md. 265, 14 Atl. 662. This last is not an injunction case, however.

equitable restriction is to be construed against the grantor.[25]

§ 279. **Effect of Change of Character of Neighborhood.**—The purpose of all these restrictions is to benefit certain land. When, therefore, the character of the neighborhood has so changed that the restriction is of no value to the land intended to be benefited, an injunction will be refused.[26] For instance, if the use of land is restricted to residence purposes, it would be inequitable to enforce the covenant after the neighborhood has so changed that the adjoining property is used exclusively for business purposes. To enforce it would simply lessen the value of the property without ac-

25 American Unitarian Assn. v. Minot, 185 Mass. 589, 71 N. E. 551, and cases cited.

26 Ewertsen v. Gerstenberg, 186 Ill. 344, 57 N. E. 1051, 51 L. R. A. 310; Jackson v. Stevenson, 156 Mass. 496, 32 Am. St. Rep. 476, 31 N. E. 691; Page v. Murray, 46 N. J. Eq. 325, 19 Atl. 11; Amerman v. Deane, 132 N. Y. 355, 28 Am. St. Rep. 584, 30 N. E. 741; Landell v. Hamilton, 175 Pa. St. 327, 34 Atl. 663, 34 L. R. A. 227. See, also, Trustees etc. v. Thacher, 87 N. Y. 311 (not an injunction case). In the case first cited the court laid down the rule as follows: "Equity will not, as a rule, enforce a restriction, where, by the acts of the grantor who imposed it, or of those who derived title under him, the property, and that in the vicinage, has so changed in its character and environment and in the uses to which it may be put as to make it unfit or unprofitable for use if the restriction be enforced, or where to grant the relief would be a great hardship on the owner and of no benefit to the complainant, or where the complainant has waived or abandoned the restriction; or, in short, it may be said that where, from all of the evidence, it appears that it would be against equity to enforce the restriction by injunction, relief will be denied, and the party seeking its enforcement will be left to whatever remedy he may have at law." In England it is held that change in the character of the neighborhood is ground for refusal of an injunction only where the alteration takes place through the acts or permission of the plaintiff or those under whom he claims, so that his enforcing his covenant becomes unreasonable: Sayers v. Collyer, L. R. 28 Ch. D 103; Duke of Bedford v Trustees British Museum, 2 Mylne & K. 552; Osborne v. Bradley, [1903] 2 Ch. 446.

complishing the purpose for which the restriction was made. Where, however, the restriction, notwithstanding the change of use of the land and buildings, is still of substantial value to the dominant lot, equity will restrain its violation.[27] It has been held that where an injunction would work a great hardship, damages may be awarded in lieu thereof.[28]

§ 280. Complainant Must Come into Court with Clean Hands—Acquiescence.—An injunction will not be granted if the plaintiff has acted so as to make its issuance inequitable. A person who seeks to enforce such a covenant must permit no such breach of the stipulation as will frustrate all the benefit that would otherwise accrue to the other parties to the agreement. One who stands by and acquiesces in repeated violations by the defendant and others cannot be heard to deny the right.[29] And where a party has violated the restric-

27 Landell v. Hamilton, 175 Pa. St. 327, 34 Atl. 663, 34 L. R. A. 227; Zipp v. Barker, 55 N. Y. Supp. 246.

28 Equitable Life Assur. Soc v. Brennan, 30 Abb N. C 260, 24 N Y. Supp. 784. In Langmaid v. Reed, 159 Mass. 409, 34 N. E. 593, it was held that where the restriction expires by lapse of time during the pendency of injunction proceedings, damages may be awarded.

29 Peek v. Matthews, L. R. 3 Eq. 515; Knight v. Simmonds, [1896] 2 Ch. 294; Ewertsen v Gerstenberg, 186 Ill. 344, 57 N. E. 1051, 51 L. R A. 310; Hemsley v. Marlborough Hotel Co., 62 N. J Eq 164, 50 Atl. 14; Trout v. Lucas, 54 N. J. Eq. 361, 35 Atl. 153; Flint v. Charman, 6 App. Div. 121, 39 N. Y. Supp. 892; Moore v. Murphy, 89 Hun, 175, 34 N. Y. Supp. 1130; Aldrich v. Billings, 14 R. I. 233. But where the restriction is as to the use of buildings, the right is not lost by failure to interfere with their construction: Trustees etc. v. Lynch, 70 N Y. 440, 26 Am. Rep. 615. It has been held that even a grantor who sells off an estate in lots with restrictions will lose his right in equity if he permits other grantees to violate the same restrictions. The rule "rests upon the equitable ground that, if anyone who has a right to enforce the covenant, and so preserve the conditions which the covenant was designed to keep unaltered, shall acquiesce in material alterations of those conditions, he cannot thereafter ask a

tions in his own deed, he cannot enjoin violations by others, even though the covenant violated by the plaintiff is entirely different from that disregarded by the defendant[30] But where the violations by plaintiff are not substantial, and violations by other parties have been in places remote from plaintiff's lot, an injunction will not be denied.[31] Of course the injured party must make prompt application for relief, and must not knowingly permit money to be expended without taking any action.[32]

§ 281. **Remedy Independent of Amount of Injury.**—"The injunction in this class of cases is granted almost as a matter of course upon a breach of the covenant. The amount of damages, and even the fact that the plaintiff has sustained any pecuniary damages, are wholly im-

court of equity to assist him in preserving them. The complainant may be in privity with the defendant, and have his action at law for breach of covenant, but nevertheless in this situation a court of equity will not assist him": Ocean City Assn v. Chalfant, 65 N. J. Eq. 156, 55 Atl. 801. The same court has held, however, that where no general scheme of improvement is shown, it is no answer to a suit to enforce restrictions on defendant's lot to say that he has waived like restrictions elsewhere· Haines v. Einwachter (N. J. Eq), 55 Atl. 38. It has been held that where there is a general building scheme, a failure to insert restrictions in a few of the deeds does not prevent relief by others against those who do take subject to restrictions: Frink v. Hughes, 133 Mich 63, 94 N. W. 601.

30 Alvord v. Fletcher, 28 App Div 493, 51 N. Y. Supp 117; Page v. Murray, 46 N. J. Eq. 325, 19 Atl. 11.

31 McGuire v. Caskey, 62 Ohio St 419, 57 N. E. 53; German v. Chapman, L. R. 7 Ch. D. 271; Richards v. Revitt, L. R 7 Ch. D. 224, Lloyd v. London etc. R. Co, 2 De Gex, J. & S. 568; Western v. Macdermott, L. R. 2 Ch. App 72.

32 Hemsley v. Marlborough Hotel Co., 62 N. J Eq. 164, 50 Atl. 14; Trout v. Lucas, 54 N J Eq. 361, 35 Atl. 153, Ocean City Assn v. Schurch, 57 N. J. Eq. 268, 41 Atl 914. In Coles v. Sims, 5 De Gex. M & G 1, it was held that it is not necessary to bring suit as soon as the work is started. It is sufficient if notice of the right is given and suit is brought within a reasonable time.

material. In the words of one of the ablest of modern equity judges: 'It is clearly established by authority that there is sufficient to justify the court interfering, if there has been a breach of the covenant. It is not for the court, but for the plaintiffs, to estimate the amount of damages that arises from the injury inflicted upon them. The moment the court finds that there has been a breach of the covenant, that is an injury, and the court has no right to measure it, and no right to refuse to the plaintiff the specific performance of his contract, although his remedy is that which I have described,' namely an injunction."[33]

§ 282. **Actual Notice not Necessary.**—It is not necessary that a party, to be bound by such restrictions, should have actual notice. Constructive notice is sufficient, and the ordinary rules as to that subject apply.[34] It is sufficient if the notice is contained in the chain of title. It has been held that the notice consisting of knowledge that all buildings erected on certain property have been placed on a certain line is sufficient.[35] The covenants are not binding, however, on one who takes without notice[36]

§ 283. **Mandatory Injunctions.**—Where a party knowingly, and against remonstrances, builds in violation of

33 See Pom. Eq. Jur., § 1342, and note, quoting Sir George Jessel, M. R., in Leech v. Schweder, L. R. 9 Ch. 463. To the same effect, see Kilpatrick v. Peshine, 24 N J. Eq. (9 C. E Green) 206; St. Andrew's Church's Appeal, 67 Pa. St. (17 P. F. Smith) 512, Walker v. McNulty, 19 Misc. Rep. 701, 45 N. Y. Supp. 42; Osborne v. Bradley, [1903] 2 Ch. 446.

34 Whitney v Union Ry. Co, 11 Gray, 359, 71 Am. Dec. 715; Cornish v. Wiessman, 56 N. J. Eq 610, 35 Atl. 408. See 2 Pom. Eq. Jur., § 689.

35 Tallmadge v. East River Bank, 26 N. Y 105.

36 Atlantic City v. New Auditorium Pier Co. (N. J. Eq.), 59 Atl. 159.

restrictive covenants, a mandatory injunction may issue to compel the removal of such portions of the building as are in violation thereof. And in such a case it is no answer that the violation is slight.[37] If such relief were not allowed, something not much short of a right would be gained by stoutly asserting an invalid claim. But a mandatory injunction will not issue if the plaintiff's rights are not clear or if it is not clear that the building violates the restriction.[38]

§ 284. **Extension of the Doctrine—Application to Personal Property.**—An interesting extension of the doctrine is found in the case of Lewis v. Gollner.[39] Gollner, who owned a city lot upon which he intended to build flats, sold to neighbors and agreed not to erect such buildings in the vicinity. He then purchased a lot across the street, commenced to build a flat, and conveyed to his wife when suit was threatened. It was held that the restriction applied as soon as the land was purchased by the covenantor, and that the wife would be enjoined from violating because she took with notice. It will be observed that the restriction was applied to after-acquired property.

In New York, in at least one case, the doctrine of restrictive covenants has been extended to personal property. A press company agreed with plaintiff's predecessor that it would not sell to anyone else a press upon which strip tickets could be printed. The company, in violation of its agreement, sold such a press to the defendant, who had full notice. It was held that an in-

37 Attorney-General v. Algonquin Club, 153 Mass. 447, 27 N. E. 2, 11 L. R. A. 500.

38 Gatzmer v. German Roman Catholic etc. Asylum, 147 Pa. St. 313, 23 Atl. 452; Bowes v. Law, L. R. 9 Eq. 636.

39 Lewis v. Gollner, 129 N. Y. 227, 26 Am. St. Rep. 516, 29 N. E. 81.

junction should issue against user of the press by the defendant, but that the press company should be made a party defendant. The party purchasing under such circumstances takes the property burdened with the contracts made by its owner in reference thereto and which he had the power to make.[40]

§ 285. **Injunctions Against Breaches of Covenants Between Landlord and Tenant.**—Injunctions are granted with great freedom to restrain breaches of covenants between landlord and tenant. Where a lease stipulates that the premises are not to be used for certain purposes, or are to be used only for certain purposes, or are to be subject to certain restrictions, an injunction will issue at suit of the lessor to restrain a breach.[41] This jurisdiction is based upon the covenant, and is entirely independent of the question whether the acts complained of amount to waste. It will be observed, also, that the courts do not confine the relief strictly to negative covenants.[42]

40 New York Bank Note Co. v. Hamilton Bank Note Co., 83 Hun, 593, 31 N. Y. Supp. 1060.

41 De Wilton v. Saxon, 6 Ves. 106; Drury v. Molins, 6 Ves. 328; Gillian v. Norton, 33 How. Pr. 373; Maddox v. White, 4 Md. 72, 59 Am. Dec. 67 (see note to this case in 59 Am. Dec.); Linwood Park Co. v. Van Dusen, 63 Ohio St. 183, 58 N. E. 576; Kraft v. Welch, 112 Iowa, 695, 84 N. W. 908; Mander v. Falke, [1891] 2 Ch. 554, Steward v. Winters, 4 Sandf. Ch. 628; Bryden v. Northrup, 58 Ill. App. 233; Dodge v. Lambert, 2 Bosw. 570; Frank v. Brunneman, 8 W. Va. 462 In this last case the court held that a court of equity will, in a proper case, grant an injunction to restrain the tenant from doing a certain act, whether it amounts to waste or not, provided it be directly contrary to the tenant's own covenant, or even in contravention of an agreement which may be inferred from the course of dealing between the parties. See, also, Nicholson v. Rose, 4 De Gex & J. 10; Clements v. Welles, L. R. 1 Eq. 200. To the effect that the right to relief may be lost by laches, see Barret v. Blagrave, 6 Ves. 104.

42 Kraft v. Welch, 112 Iowa, 695, 84 N. W. 908. But that injunction is not a matter of course, by the English rule, where the cove-

If the agreement is necessarily exclusive the injunction will issue. The grounds upon which the jurisdiction rests are the inadequacy of the legal remedy and the prevention of multiplicity of suits. If the lessor were obliged to depend upon his remedy at law, he would have difficulty in securing a proper estimate of damages, and besides, he would be obliged to bring suits every few days. It is not necessary that substantial damages be proved.[43] The lessor is entitled to have the covenant performed, and he must be the one to decide if he is damaged. It has been held, however, that an injunction will not issue to restrain a lessee from subletting in violation of covenant, where the lease provides for re-entry, for the remedy at law is said to be adequate.[44]

The lessor is allowed an injunction when the lessee fails to keep open a private gangway, in violation of covenant, or where the lessee interferes with the lessor's rights under the lease to enter upon or use the demised premises.[45] Thus, relief will be granted when the lessee

nant is not negative in form, see Harris v. Boots, etc, Ltd, [1904] 2 Ch. 376 (covenant by assignee of lease to perform and observe the negative covenants in the lease, is not itself negative, within the rule.)

43 In Consolidated Coal Co. v. Schmisseur, 135 Ill. 371, 25 N. E. 795, it was held that no damage need be shown if the covenant is express. Where it is implied, substantial injury must be shown. "The party not having seen fit to expressly stipulate against the act in his contract, a court of equity will not by implication insert it, and then enforce it, unless substantial injury is thereby to be prevented." See, also, McEacharn v. Colton, [1902] App. Cas. (Priv. Coun.) 104, citing Doherty v. Allman, 3 App. Cas. 719 (covenant by lessee not to assign lease without consent of lessor).

44 Gillian v. Norton, 33 How. Pr. 373. In Brown v. Niles, 165 Mass. 276, 43 N. E. 90, it was intimated that where there is a right to terminate the lease for breach of a covenant, an injunction will be refused.

45 Beckwith v. Howard, 6 R. I 1; State Bank of Nebraska v. Rohren, 55 Neb 223, 75 N. W. 543; United States Trust Co v. O'Brien, 61 N. Y. Super. Ct. (29 Jones & S.) 1, 18 N. Y. Supp 798.

refuses to allow the lessor to enter to plow the land, or to post "to let" signs, when the lease expressly permits.[46] It is also held that the lessor may enjoin a lessee who has covenanted not to sell any beer on the premises except that furnished by the plaintiff.[47] And it is held that such a covenant may be enforced at the suit of a brewing company, not a party to the contract, but its beneficiary.[48] In some states an insolvent lessee will be restrained from disposing of property subject to a landlord's lien.[49] In England it is held that where a lessee builds in violation of a covenant, the lessor may have a mandatory injunction.[50]

§ 286. **Same—Rights of Lessee.**—On the other hand, the lessee is frequently allowed an injunction against his lessor. If the lessor covenants as to the use of his remaining land, the lessee may enjoin him from committing a breach.[51] He may also enjoin any act by the

46 State Bank of Nebraska v. Rohren, 55 Neb. 223, 75 N. W. 543, United States Trust Co. v. O'Brien, 61 N. Y. Super. Ct. (29 Jones & S.) 1, 18 N. Y. Supp. 798.

47 Star Brewery Co. v. Primas, 163 Ill. 652, 45 N. E. 145. In Luker v. Dennis, L. R. 7 Ch. D 227, the lessee was restrained from selling beer at another public house owned by a different landlord, in violation of a covenant with the first landlord. See, also, Clegg v. Hands, L. R. 44 Ch. D. 503; Stees v. Kranz, 32 Minn. 313, 20 N. W. 341; Manchester Brewing Co. v. Coombs, [1901] 2 Ch. 608 (covenant by lessee to purchase all his beer of the lessor or "his successors in business," enforced by the latter).

48 Ferris v. American Brewing Co., 58 N. E. 701, 155 Ind. 539, 52 L. R. A. 305.

49 Gray v. Bremer & Strother, 122 Iowa, 110, 97 N W. 991; Wallin v. Murphy, 117 Iowa, 640, 91 N. W. 930.

50 Wood v. Cooper, [1894] 3 Ch 671.

51 Neiman v. Butler, 46 N. Y. St. Rep. 928, 19 N. Y Supp. 403; Rankin v. Huskisson, 4 Sim. 13; Hovnanian v Bedessern, 63 Ill. App 353 But that a covenant not to "let" other parts of a building for a business similar to lessee's does not include an agreement not to "use" for such purpose, see Brigg v. Thornton, [1904] 1 Ch. 386 (lessor enjoined, but not the rival lessee), citing Kemp v. Bird, L. R. 5 Ch. D 974.

lessor which will make the lease useless or of less value. Thus, where the lessor has agreed to furnish water or power, he may be enjoined from cutting it off.[52] Likewise, he may be enjoined from pulling down the building for the purpose of erecting a new one or of adding to the old.[53] In these cases the courts will not consider the relative inconvenience to the parties. Although the construction of an expensive building may be indefinitely postponed as the result of an injunction issued at the suit of a party renting only a few rooms, still, if the suit is brought before the building is completed or substantially started, relief will not be denied. The principle is that a wrong-doer should not be allowed to compel an innocent party to sell at a valuation. After the completion, however, a mandatory injunction will not issue to compel removal.[54] Where a party has leased a building to be constructed according to certain plans, he may enjoin a construction under other plans which will deprive him of the benefit for which he has contracted.[55] It is held that where a large building is rented, according to a general scheme, for residence purposes, a lessee may enjoin the lessor from using it for other purposes.[56] A lessee who is to take possession

52 Hendricks v. Hughes, 117 Ala. 591, 23 South. 637, Brauns v. Glesige, 130 Ind. 167, 29 N. E. 1061; Traitel Marble Co. v. Chase, 35 Misc. Rep. 233, 71 N. Y. Supp. 628. For instances of relief against interference in general, see Ingle v. Bottoms, 160 Ind. 73, 66 N. E. 160; Foster v. Roseberry (Tex. Civ. App.), 78 S. W. 701 (against insolvent landlord).

53 Brande v. Grace, 154 Mass. 210, 31 N. E. 633; Lynch v. Union Inst. for Savings, 158 Mass. 394, 33 N. E. 603, Proskey v. Cumberland Realty Co., 35 Misc. Rep. 50, 70 N. Y. Supp. 1125.

54 Brande v. Grace, 154 Mass. 210, 31 N. E. 633; Hessler v. Schafer, 20 Misc. Rep. 645, 46 N. Y. Supp. 1076.

55 Backes v. Curran, 69 App. Div. 188, 74 N. Y. Supp. 723.

56 Hudson v. Cripps, [1896] 1 Ch. 265. And where a covenant, against carrying on a trade, purports to bind the lessor, his heirs, executors and administrators, it may be enforced against his other

in the future cannot, however, enjoin future interference by one who purchases with notice.[57]

§ 287. **Same—Rights of Sub-tenant.**—Where a lessee has contracted with third persons in regard to the use of the premises, as where the lessee of a trotting park gives a sign privilege, or where a hotel lessee gives an exclusive right to a telegraph company, such person may enjoin a breach.[58] In such cases it is immaterial that the lease prohibits the acts.

§ 288. **Contracts for Personal Services of Special Character.**—"Where a contract stipulates for special, unique or extraordinary personal services or acts, or for such services or acts to be rendered or done by a party having special, unique, and extraordinary qualifications,—as, for example, by an eminent actor, singer, artist, and the like,—it is plain that the remedy at law of damages for its breach might be wholly inadequate, since no amount of money recovered by the plaintiff might enable him to obtain the same or the same kind of services or acts elsewhere, or by employing any other person. It is, however, a familiar doctrine that a court of equity will not exercise its jurisdiction to grant the remedy of an *affirmative* specific performance, however inadequate may be the remedy of damages, whenever the contract is of such a nature that the decree for its specific performance cannot be enforced and its obedience compelled by the ordinary processes of the court. A specific performance in such cases is said to be im-

lessees: Holloway Bros, Ltd., v. Hill, [1902] 2 Ch 612, citing Johnstone v. Hall, 2 Kay & J. 414, Wilson v. Hart, L. R. 1 Ch. 463, and Feilden v Slater, L. R. 7 Eq. 523.

57 Forbes v. Carl (Iowa), 101 N. W. 100.

58 Willoughby v. Lawrence, 116 Ill. 11, 56 Am. Rep. 758, 4 N. E. 356, Western Union Tel. Co. v. Rogers, 42 N. J. Eq. 311, 11 Atl. 13.

possible; and contracts stipulating for personal acts have been regarded as the most familiar illustrations of this doctrine, since the court cannot in any direct manner compel an actor to act, a singer to sing, or an artist to paint. Applying the same course of reasoning, the English courts formerly held that they could not *negatively* enforce the specific performance of such contracts by means of an injunction restraining their violation.[59] Those courts have, however, entirely receded from this latter conclusion. The rule, [as late as 1891, appeared to be] firmly established in England that the violation of such contracts may be restrained by injunction, whenever the legal remedy of damages would be inadequate, and the contract is of such a nature that its negative specific enforcement is possible";[60] and as so formulated, the rule is now generally accepted and applied in this country.

§ 289. Same; Lumley v. Wagner—Whether Stipulation Must be Expressly Negative in Form.—The leading case on the subject is Lumley v. Wagner (1852).[61] In that case a famous "prima donna" agreed to sing in the com-

59 4 Pom. Eq. Jur., § 1343; citing Kemble v. Kean, 6 Sim. 333; Kimberley v. Jennings, 6 Sim. 340. These cases were expressly overruled by Lumley v. Wagner, but have a considerable following in the earlier American cases; see, for example, Sanquirico v. Benedetti, 1 Barb. 315.

60 4 Pom. Eq. Jur., § 1343. For the recent restriction of the rule in England, see the next section. The stipulation on the defendant's part, express or, it may be, implied, not to engage in an employment inconsistent with his contract obligation to the defendant, is freely enforced by injunction, notwithstanding that the complainant's obligation is frequently of a character incapable of enforcement by the processes of a court of equity: See *ante*, § 270, notes. For the bearing of these cases on the doctrine as to mutuality of remedy, in the law of specific performance, see *post*, Vol. II, chapter on Specific Performance

61 1 De Gex, M. & G. 604.

plainant's opera-house for a certain time and not to sing for anyone else during that time. The court held that the services were of such a character that damages would be inadequate, and that therefore an injunction was proper to restrain the defendant from singing elsewhere. The opinion of Lord Chancellor St. Leonards fully reviews the previous authorities, and has been generally accepted, both in England and in this country, upon a similar state of facts. The most frequent application has been in cases of actors and actresses of established reputation.[62] Contracts for their services often stipulate that they shall not perform elsewhere during their engagement with a particular manager. Their services being extraordinary and special, an injunction is generally granted against the breach of such a stipulation. It will likewise be granted when an artist agrees to work for the complainant and for no one else.[63] Miscellaneous cases will be found in the note. Upon the question whether the negative covenant must be express in order to warrant an injunction, there is now a direct conflict of opinion. In England it was formerly (1873) held that a negative would be implied in cases of this kind, and that the implied covenant would be enforced by injunction.[64] Later (1891) it was held that a negative will not be implied even where the

62 Daly v. Smith, 38 N. Y. Super. Ct. 158; Hayes v. Willis, 11 Abb. Pr., N. S, 167, McCaull v. Braham, 16 Fed. 37; Canary v. Russell, 9 Misc. Rep. 558, 30 N. Y. Supp. 122. See *contra*, Sanquirico v. Benedetti, 1 Barb. 315.

63 Fredericks v. Mayer, 13 How. Pr. 566 (*dictum*).

Miscellaneous.—In Morris v. Colman, 18 Ves. 436, a playwright was enjoined from writing for another theater in violation of contract. In Philadelphia Ball Club v. Lajoie, 202 Pa. St. 210, 90 Am. St. Rep. 627, 51 Atl. 973, 58 L. R. A. 227, a professional baseball player was enjoined from playing with any other club.

64 Montague v. Flockton, L. R. 16 Eq 189. See, also, De Mattos v. Gibson, [1859] 4 De Gex & J 276 (*semble*, injunction proper to enforce a charter-party containing no express negative stipulation).

defendant has agreed to give the "whole of his time" to the complainant's business; and the case last referred to was expressly overruled.[65] This late restriction of the rule in England appears to have had little influence in the United States.[66] In New York, where this class of contracts has most frequently come before the courts, it seems to be established that where a contract is intended "to give the plaintiffs, not the divided, but exclusive, services of the defendant . . . . a negative clause is unnecessary."[67]

§ 290. **Same—No Relief upon Contracts for Ordinary Services.**—Where the services contracted for are neither special, extraordinary nor unique, the courts generally refuse equitable relief. "It may sometimes be difficult to say just what is a special, unique and extraordinary

65 Whitwood Chemical Co. v. Hardman, [1891] L. R. 2 Ch. 416; Lindley, L. J., took strong ground against the policy of enjoining breaches of negative contracts, and spoke of Lumley v. Wagner as an "anomaly." In Clarke v. Price, [1819] 2 Wils. Ch. 157, Lord Eldon had refused to enjoin the defendant from writing law books for another firm There was no express negative stipulation It should be observed that this restrictive rule of Whitwood Chemical Co. v. Hardman, *supra*, applies to contracts for personal services only, in other kinds of contracts a negative may still be implied, so explained in the recent case, Metropolitan Electric Supply Co., Ltd, v. Gender, [1901] 2 Ch. 799.

66 Holding an express negative necessary, see the early case, Burton v Marshall, 4 Gill, 487, 45 Am. Dec 171, *contra*, Cort v. Lassard, 18 Or. 221, 17 Am. St. Rep. 726, 22 Pac. 1054, 6 L. R. A. 653. In this case the court said· "The agreement to perform at a particular theater for a particular time of necessity involves an agreement not to perform at any other during that time. According to the true spirit of such an agreement, the implication precluding the defendant from acting at any other theater during the period for which he has agreed to act for the plaintiff follows as inevitably and logically as if it was expressed"

67 Hoyt v. Fuller, 19 N. Y Supp 962, Duff v. Russell, 133 N. Y. 678, 31 N. E. 622, affirming 41 N. Y. St. Rep. 955, 16 N Y. Supp. 958, and 60 N Y. Super. Ct 80, 14 N. Y. Supp. 134, on opinion in latter case, Daly v. Smith, 38 N. Y. Sup. Ct. 158 (*dictum*).

service, or whether the employee possesses special, unique or extraordinary qualifications. The solution may generally be reached by an inquiry as to whether a substitute for the employee can readily be obtained, and whether such substitute will substantially answer the purpose of the contract; in other words, whether the individual service specially contracted for is essential to prevent irreparable injury."[68] Accordingly, when it appears that the plaintiff has himself substituted another in place of the defendant, an injunction has been refused.[69] In the note will be found a number of instances where it has been held that the employment is not so special as to warrant an injunction.[70]

§ 291. **Limitations.**—It is held that an employee cannot restrain his employer from discharging him.[71] In

68 Strobridge Lithographing Co. v. Crane, 12 N. Y. Supp. 898.

69 W. J. Johnston Co. v. Hunt, 66 Hun, 504, 21 N. Y. Supp. 314, affirmed, 142 N. Y. 621, 37 N. E. 564.

70 Lithographer—Strobridge Lith. Co. v. Crane, 58 Hun, 611, 12 N. Y. Supp. 898. Solicitor—Burney v. Ryle, 91 Ga. 701, 17 S. E. 986. Miscellaneous—Rogers Mfg. Co. v. Rogers, 58 Conn. 356, 20 Atl. 467, 18 Am. St. Rep. 278, 7 L. R. A. 779; Universal Talking Mach. Co. v. English, 34 Misc. Rep. 342, 69 N. Y. Supp. 813, Carter v. Ferguson, 58 Hun, 569, 12 N. Y. Supp. 580 (actor of no extraordinary qualifications; quoting Pom. Eq. Jur., § 1343); Cort v. Lassard, 18 Or. 221, 17 Am. St. Rep. 726, 22 Pac. 1054, 6 L. R. A. 653 (acrobat); Kimberly v. Jennings, 6 Sim. 340; Chain Belt Co. v. Von Spreckelsen, 117 Wis. 106, 94 N. W. 78. See, also, Eberman v Bartholomew, [1898] 1 Ch. 671 (agreement of traveling agent of wine merchants "not to engage in any other business" during the ten years' term of employment contracted for; injunction refused, on the ground that the stipulation was unreasonable).

71 Davis v. Foreman, [1894] 3 Ch. 654; Miller v. Warner, 42 App Div. 208, 59 N. Y. Supp. 956; Stewart v. Pierce, 116 Iowa, 733, 89 N. W. 234. See, also, Welty v. Jacobs, 171 Ill. 624, 49 N. E. 723, 40 L. R. A. 98; Stocker v. Brockelbank, 3 Macn. & G. 250. But see Jones v. Williams, 139 Mo. 1, 61 Am. St. Rep. 436, 39 S. W. 486, 40 S. W. 353, 37 L. R. A. 682, where such relief was allowed on special facts.

general, in applying the remedy the courts will be bound by the equitable principles which govern the remedy of specific performance. The rights of third persons will be considered; and if the granting of equitable relief will work an injustice to innocent third parties who have contractual rights with the employee, it will be refused.[72] Nor will an injunction be granted when the agreement is uncertain or where it would work a hardship on the defendant.[73] By hardship must be understood such hardship as would be a defense to a bill for specific performance.

§ 292. Other Agreements, Generally Negative in Their Nature.—"In all these agreements, where the stipulations are expressly negative in form, and where they belong to a class of which the specific performance would be enforced if they were affirmative in form, an injunction to restrain their violation will be granted as a general rule, and almost as a matter of course. The inadequacy of the legal remedy is the criterion; but the fact that the agreements belong to a class which would be specifically enforced necessarily shows that the legal remedy is inadequate."[74] Among the commonest of such agreements are those (1) not to carry on a trade or (2) not to compete; and (3) agreements giving an exclusive right.

§ 293. Agreements not to Carry on a Trade, Express or Implied—Sale of Good-will.—A class of cases where injunction is held to be a proper remedy to restrain the

72 Roosen v. Carlson, 46 App. Div. 233, 47 App. Div. 638, 62 N. Y. Supp. 157.

73 Arena Athletic Club v. McPartland, 41 App. Div. 352, 58 N. Y. Supp. 477; Metropolitan Exhibition Co. v Ewing, 42 Fed. 198, 7 L. R. A. 381; Rice v. D'Arville, 162 Mass. 559, 39 N. E. 180.

74 Pom. Eq. Jur., § 1344.

breach of contract is where there is an agreement not to engage in a particular profession or trade. A discussion of the rules as to the validity of contracts in restraint of trade belongs properly to a treatise on the law of contracts. Where such a contract is illegal, of course equity will not enjoin a breach;[75] the questions to be here considered, therefore, concern the remedy by injunction against violations of valid contracts of this character.

It is very common, when a tradesman sells his business to another or retires from a partnership, to insert a stipulation in the agreement that the selling party shall not engage in a similar business within certain prescribed limits. These agreements are usually upheld as reasonable restraints of trade. Equity courts will grant injunctive relief against violations because generally the remedy of damages is inadequate.[76] The

75 See, also, 2 Pom. Eq. Jur., § 934.

76 Rolfe v. Rolfe, 15 Sim. 88; Williams v. Williams, 2 Swans. 253; Nordenfelt v. Maxim-Nordenfelt G. & A. Co., Ltd., [1894] App. Cas. 535; Davis v. A. Booth & Co., 131 Fed. 31, 65 C. C. A. 269 (affirming 127 Fed. 875); American Fisheries Co. v. Lennen, 118 Fed. 869; Moore etc. Hardware Co. v. Towers Hardware Co., 87 Ala. 206, 13 Am. St. Rep. 23, 6 South. 41; Brown v. Kling, 101 Cal. 295, 35 Pac. 995; Mullis v. Nichols, 105 Ga. 465, 30 S. E. 654; W. F. Markert & Co. v. Jefferson (Ga.), 50 S. E. 398; Frazer v. Frazer Lubricator Co., 121 Ill. 147, 2 Am. St. Rep. 73, 13 N. E. 639, Beard v. Dennis, 6 Ind. 200, 63 Am. Dec. 380; Baker v. Pottmeyer, 75 Ind. 451; Eisel v. Hayes, 141 Ind. 41, 40 N. E. 119; Swigert v. Tilden, 121 Iowa, 650, 100 Am. St. Rep. 374, 97 N. W. 82; Pohlman v. Dawson, 63 Kan. 471, 88 Am. St Rep. 249, 65 Pac. 689, 54 L. R. A. 913, Guerand v. Dandelet, 32 Md. 561, 3 Am. Rep. 164, Anchor Elect. Co. v. Hawkes, 171 Mass. 101, 68 Am. St. Rep. 403, 50 N. E. 509, 41 L. R. A. 189; Ropes v. Upton, 125 Mass. 258; Angier v. Webber, 96 Mass. (14 Allen) 211, 92 Am. Dec. 748; Up River Ice Co. v. Denler, 114 Mich. 296, 68 Am. St. Rep. 480, 72 N. W. 157; Beal v. Chase, 31 Mich. 490, Grow v. Seligman, 47 Mich. 607, 41 Am. Rep. 737, 11 N. W. 404; Hubbard v. Miller, 27 Mich. 15, 15 Am. Rep. 153, Downing v. Lewis, 56 Neb. 386, 76 N W. 900; Bailey v. Collins, 59 N. H. 459; Richardson v. Peacock, 26 N. J. Eq. 40, 28 N. J. Eq 151, 33 N. J.

relief is not confined to contracts between parties engaged in trade, but applies equally to contracts between professional men, such as physicians, lawyers and the like.[77] It must be certain that there has been a violation before the court will interfere.[78] The bene-

Eq. 597, Scudder v. Kilfoil, 57 N. J. Eq. 171, 40 Atl. 602, 43 L. R. A. 86, Fleckenstein Bros. Co. v. Fleckenstein (N. J. Eq.), 53 Atl. 1043; Jarvis v. Peck, 10 Paige, 118; A. Booth & Co. v. Seibold, 37 Misc. Rep. 101, 74 N. Y. Supp. 776; Zimmerman v. Gerzog, 13 App. Div. 210, 43 N. Y. Supp. 339; United States Cordage Co. v. Wm. Wall's Sons Rope Co, 90 Hun, 429, 35 N. Y. Supp. 978; Diamond Match Co. v. Roeber, 106 N. Y. 473, 60 Am. Rep. 464, 13 N. E. 419; Francisco v. Smith, 143 N. Y. 488, 38 N. E. 980; Baumgartner v. Broadway, 77 N. C. 8; Kramer v. Old, 119 N. C. 1, 25 S. E. 813, 56 Am. St. Rep. 650, 34 L. R. A. 389; Cowan v. Fairbrother, 118 N. C. 406, 54 Am. St. Rep. 733, 24 S. E. 212, 32 L. R. A. 829; Morgan v. Perhamus, 36 Ohio St. 517, 38 Am. Rep. 607; Patterson v. Glassmire, 166 Pa. St. 230, 31 Atl. 40; Stofflet v. Stofflet, 160 Pa. St. 529, 28 Atl. 857; Monongahela River Consol. Coal & Coke Co. v. Jutte (Pa.), 59 Atl. 1088; Oakdale Mfg. Co. v. Garst, 18 R. I. 484, 49 Am. St. Rep. 784, 28 Atl. 973, 23 L. R. A. 639; Jackson v. Byrnes, 103 Tenn. 698, 54 S. W. 984 (*dictum*). See, also, Turner v. Evans, 2 De Gex, M. & G. 740. In O'Neal v. Hines, 145 Ind. 32, 43 N. E. 946, the court laid down the rule as follows "It is a general rule that when one has made a valid contract with another that he will not engage in a certain business or occupation, and it is shown by the other party to the contract that the same is being violated to his injury, he is entitled to an injunction restraining the offending party. This is upon the ground that from the nature of the case just and adequate damages cannot be estimated for a breach of the contract"

77 In the following cases the rule was laid down in contracts between physicians: McCurry v Gibson, 108 Ala. 451, 51 Am. St. Rep. 177, 18 South 806, Beatty v Coble, 142 Ind 329, 41 N E. 590; Cole v. Edwards, 93 Iowa, 477, 61 N. W. 940; Doty v. Martin, 32 Mich. 462, Timmerman v. Dever, 52 Mich. 34, 50 Am. Rep. 240, 17 N. W. 230, McClurg's Appeal, 58 Pa. St. 51, Wilkinson v. Colley, 164 Pa. St. 35, 30 Atl. 286, 35 Week. Not Cas. 177, 26 L. R. A. 114; French v. Parker, 16 R. I. 219, 27 Am. St. Rep 733, 14 Atl. 870, Butler v. Burleson, 16 Vt. 176; Hulen v. Earel, 13 Okla 246, 73 Pac 927 (*dictum*); Ryan v. Hamilton, 203 Ill. 191, 68 N. E. 781. Lawyer—Whittaker v. Howe, 3 Beav. 383. Dentist—Niles v. Fenn, 12 Misc. Rep 470, 33 N Y. Supp. 857 Playwright—Moris v Coleman, 18 Ves. 436

78 Caswell v Gibbs, 33 Mich. 331; Bowers v. Whittle, 63 N. H. 147, 56 Am. Rep. 499.

fit of the covenant may be assigned with the business, and the assignee's rights will be protected by injunction.[79] What amounts to a breach is a question of substantive law; but the courts of equity will not allow a violation under color of compliance with the letter of the contract. Thus, an injunction will not be denied because the promisor has taken in a partner or has formed a corporation to compete with the plaintiff, or has put the business in his wife's name.[80] Where it appears that the parties engaging in business with the party violating the agreement had notice of its terms, they may be enjoined from carrying it on in connection with him.[81] Third parties, however, will not be enjoined from receiving business aid from such person, nor from purchasing goods from him.[82] As the injury is difficult to measure in all these cases, only nominal damage need be shown.[83] The injured party need not

79 Cowan v. Fairbrother, 118 N. C. 406, 54 Am. St. Rep. 733, 24 S. E. 212, 32 L. R. A. 829; Francisco v. Smith, 143 N. Y. 488, 38 N. E. 980; Fleckenstein Bros. Co. v. Fleckenstein (N. J. Eq.), 53 Atl. 1043.

80 Beard v. Dennis, 6 Ind. 200, 63 Am. Dec. 380; Kramer v. Old, 119 N. C. 1, 56 Am. St. Rep. 650, 25 S. E. 813, 34 L. R. A. 389; Up River Ice Co. v. Denler, 114 Mich. 296, 68 Am. St. Rep. 480, 72 N. W. 157; Pittsburg Stove & Range Co. v. Pennsylvania Stove Co., 208 Pa. St. 37, 57 Atl. 77. When the business belongs to the wife, however, and not to the husband, she is not bound by the covenant: Smith v. Hancock, [1894] 2 Ch. 377, Fleckenstein Bros. Co. v. Fleckenstein (N. J. Eq.), 57 Atl. 1025. In Gophir Diamond Co. v. Wood, [1902] 1 Ch. 950, it was held that a covenant not to become directly or indirectly "interested" in a similar business to that of the covenantee does not prevent the covenantor from becoming a servant at a fixed salary in a similar business.

81 A. Booth & Co. v. Seibold, 37 Misc. Rep. 101, 74 N. Y. Supp. 776.

82 Appeal of Harkinson, 78 Pa. (28 P. F. Smith) 196, 21 Am. Rep. 9; Reeves v. Sprague, 114 N. C. 647, 19 S. E. 707.

83 Brown v. King, 101 Cal. 295, 35 Pac. 995; Andrews v. Kingsbury (Ill.), 72 N. E. 11.

establish his right at law.[84] In Pennsylvania, it is held that damages will be awarded in connection with the equitable relief.[85]

It is questionable whether an express negative covenant is necessary, the same conflict of opinion existing here as in regard to injunctions against the violation of contracts of personal service. In some jurisdictions it is held as a matter of substantive law that no covenant not to engage in business can be implied from a sale of good-will, and of course an injunction is denied.[86] In a late case it is said that "where the good-will of a business is sold, without further provision, the vendor may set up a rival business, but he is not entitled to canvass the customers of the old firm, and may be restrained by injunction from soliciting any person who was a customer of the old firm prior to the sale to continue to deal with the vendor or not to deal with the purchaser."[87] It has been held that where a physician sells the good-will of his practice or agrees to retire, an injunction will issue to restrain him from continuing in practice.[88] And an

84 Carll v. Snyder (N. J. Eq.), 26 Atl. 977.

85 Stofflet v. Stofflet, 160 Pa. St. 529, 28 Atl. 857; Patterson v. Glassmire, 166 Pa. St. 230, 31 Atl. 40.

86 Jackson v. Byrnes, 54 S. W. 984, 103 Tenn. 698; Newark Coal Co. v. Spangler, 54 N. J. Eq. 354, 34 Atl. 932; Close v. Flesher, 8 Misc Rep. 299, 28 N. Y. Supp. 737; MacMartin v. Stevens (Wash), 79 Pac. 1099. For a definition of "good-will," see 4 Pom. Eq. Jur., § 1355.

87 Althen v. Vreeland (N. J. Eq.), 36 Atl. 479. See similar statements in Zantierjian v. Boornazian (R. I.), 55 Atl. 199; Trego v. Hunt, [1896] App. Cas. 7; Gillingham v. Beddow, [1900] 2 Ch. 242; Curl Brothers, Ltd., v. Webster, [1904] 1 Ch. 685; Rauft v. Reimers (Ill.), 65 N. E. 720. The vendor will not be restrained from merely dealing with former customers. Leggott v. Barrett, 15 Ch. D. 306 It has been held that this rule does not apply as against a bankrupt whose good-will has been sold by his trustees in bankruptcy Walker v. Moltram, 19 Ch D 355

88 Dwight v Hamilton, 113 Mass. 175; Beatty v. Coble, 142 Ind. 329, 41 N E. 590.

injunction has been granted to restrain parties who have sold good-will from using a firm name similar to that of the firm from which they have retired.[89]

An injunction will not issue when it would be inequitable. Thus, when a party signs an agreement without reading it and plaintiff makes no objection until the defendant has expended a large sum in fitting up his place of business, an injunction will be refused.[90] Likewise, it will not issue against mere nominal members of a firm, the active members of which have agreed for the firm not to engage in certain business.[91]

In some jurisdictions it is held that these agreements are valid and will be enforced only when the promisor sells out his business or retires from the firm.[92]

§ 294. **Same—Injunctions Against Employees.**—Where an employee stipulates that he will not engage in similar business within a certain territory for a certain period after the termination of his employment, an injunction will issue to restrain a breach.[93] But where the restraint is unreasonable and extends beyond any-

89 Myers v. Kalamazoo Buggy Co., 54 Mich. 215, 52 Am. Rep. 811, 19 N. W. 961, 20 N. W. 545

90 Smith v. Brown, 164 Mass. 584, 42 N. E. 101.

91 United States Cordage Co. v. Wm. Wall's Sons Rope Co, 90 Hun, 429, 35 N. Y. Supp. 978.

92 Chapin v. Brown, 83 Iowa, 156, 32 Am. St. Rep. 297, 48 N W. 1074, 12 L. R. A. 428. Thus, in California, an agreement by a vendor of stock in a corporation not to engage in the same business cannot be enforced: Dodge Stationery Co. v. Dodge, 145 Cal. 380, 78 Pac 879.

93 Davies v. Racer, 72 Hun, 43, 25 N. Y. Supp. 293, A L. & J J. Reynolds Co. v. Dreyer, 12 Misc. Rep. 368, 33 N. Y. Supp. 649, Hayes v. Doncan, [1899] 2 Ch. 13. See, also, Robinson v. Heuer, 67 L. J Ch. 644, [1898] 2 Ch. 451, 79 L. J, N S., 281, 47 Week Rep 31 (not to compete during term of employment); Dubowski v. Goldstein, [1896] 1 Q. B 478.

thing apparently necessary for the protection of the employer, an injunction will be refused.[94]

§ 295. **Agreements not to Compete.**—Instances of such agreements enforced by injunction are: An agreement by a rival quarry not to supply stone to a municipal corporation during a certain period;[95] an agreement by a city with a water company not to build rival waterworks;[96] a contract between plaintiff, a manufacturer of patterns, and defendant, a dealer, whereby the latter was appointed agent of the former for the sale of its patterns, defendant covenanting not to sell, or allow to be sold, on his premises any other make of patterns; specific performance was refused of the contract in its entirety, but defendant enjoined from selling patterns of another make.[97] It has been held, however, that a vendor cannot restrain his vendee from selling a patented article at less than a fixed price, in violation of contract.[98]

94 Herreshoff v. Boutineau, 17 R. I. 3, 33 Am. St. Rep. 850, 19 Atl. 712, 8 L. R. A. 469, Stanley v. Pollard, 5 Misc. Rep. 490, 25 N. Y. Supp. 766. See, also, Ehrmann v. Bartholomew, 67 L. J. Ch. 319, [1898] 1 Ch. 671, 78 L. J., N. S., 646, 46 Week. Rep. 509.

95 Jones v. North, L. R. 19 Eq. 426.

96 City of Walla Walla v. Walla Walla Water Co., 172 U. S. 1, 19 Sup. Ct. 77; the remedy at law by recovery of damages held to be inadequate. Columbia Ave. etc. Co. v. City of Dawson, 130 Fed. 152; Farmers' Loan & Trust Co. v. City of Sioux Falls, 131 Fed. 890. See *post*, § 299.

97 Standard Fashion Co. v. Siegel-Cooper Co., 157 N. Y. 66, 68 Am. St. Rep. 749, 51 N. E. 408, affirming 30 App. Div. 564, 52 N. Y. Supp. 433, and reversing 22 Misc. Rep. 624, 50 N. Y. Supp. 1056. It is observed that "the court should extend its remedy as far as it is able, and thus prevent the principal defendant not only from making money by breaking its agreement, but from inflicting a double wrong upon the plaintiff by depriving it of the right to sell, and conferring that right on a business competitor." For further instances of such contracts, see Royer Wheel Co. v. Miller, 20 Ky. Law Rep. 1831, 50 S. W. 62.

98 National Phonograph Co. v. Schlegel, 117 Fed. 624.

§ 296. **Contracts Conferring an Exclusive Right.**—Where a contract confers on one party an exclusive right or privilege, a breach of the contract through conduct of the other party inconsistent with the exclusiveness of the right or privilege may be enjoined, subject to the general principle as to the inadequacy of the legal remedy for the breach. It is immaterial that such inconsistent conduct is not prohibited by the express terms of the contract. Contracts giving to one party an exclusive right to the personal services of another are a common species of agreements of this general class, and have already been discussed.[99] Contracts giving the plaintiff the exclusive right to buy articles manufactured or produced by the defendant, or constituting the plaintiff the sole agent for their sale, have frequently been enforced by enjoining the sale of the articles by the defendant to third parties, if the article is of such a character that an agreement for its sale would be specifically enforced.[100] Other instances of

99 See *ante*, §§ 288-291. For injunction to protect exclusive *franchises*, see chapter XXVII.

100 Dietrichsen v. Cabburn, 2 Phill. Ch. 52, where defendant, having agreed to employ plaintiff as agent and supply him with oil at forty per cent discount, and not to allow more than twenty-five per cent discount to others, was enjoined from committing a breach of the latter stipulation; Donnell v. Bennett, L. R. 22 Ch. D. 835, injunction against breach of express negative covenant not to sell fish to manufacturers other than the plaintiff; Singer Sewing Machine Co v. Union Button Hole Co., 1 Holmes, 253, Fed. Cas. No 12,904, contract making plaintiff sole agent for a patented article; Lowenbein v. Fuldner, 2 Misc. Rep. 176, 21 N. Y. Supp. 615, contract to manufacture for plaintiff, and no one else, furniture of a special and unique design furnished by plaintiff; Valley Iron Works Mfg. Co. v. Goodwick, 103 Wis. 436, 78 N. W. 1096, specific performance of agreement to transfer patent, and injunction against disposing of it to other parties; Manhattan Mfg. etc. Co. v. New Jersey etc. Co., 23 N. J. Eq. 161, contract by stock-yards company giving complainant, a fertilizer company, sole right to remove offal from its premises enforced by injunction against its lessee with notice; injunc-

exclusive rights protected by injunction are enumerated in the note.[101]

§ 297. Miscellaneous Agreements, Expressly Negative.— The following contracts, enforced by injunction, are given as illustrations merely: An agreement not to ring

tion to avoid multiplicity of suits, and because of impossibility of computing damages, Myers v. Steele Mach. Co. (N. J. Eq.), 57 Atl. 1080 On the other hand, a breach of a contract to sell to plaintiff all the coal defendants should get from a certain mine will not be enjoined, since coal is not an article a contract for the sale of which will be specifically enforced: Fothergill v. Rowland, L. R. 17 Eq. 132. So, in case of a contract to sell a certain amount of wood to the plaintiff every year for a period of years, and not to sell to anyone else so as to prevent fulfillment of the contract, injunction was refused: St. Regis Paper Co. v. Santa Clara Lumber Co, 55 App. Div. 225, 67 N. Y. Supp. 149, reversing 31 Misc. Rep. 695, 66 N. Y. Supp. 59

101 Exclusive right of removing garbage, or dead animals, under contract with a city: National Fertilizer Co. v. Lambert, 48 Fed. 458, Sanitary Reduction Works of San Francisco v. California Reduction Co., 94 Fed. 693. Contract allowing plaintiff exclusive right for one year to display an advertising curtain in front of the stage of defendant's theater: Beer v. Canary, 2 App. Div. 518, 38 N. Y Supp 23 (defendant insolvent, plaintiff had a number of advertising contracts; and damages could not be ascertained). A contract to purchase from plaintiff exclusively all of a certain article which defendant should need Petrolia Mfg. Co. v. Jenkins, 29 App Div. 403, 51 N. Y. Supp. 1028 (injunction to avoid multiplicity of suits for breaches of the contract). But in James T. Hair Co. v. Huckins, 56 Fed. 366, 5 C. C A 522, 12 U. S. App. 359, it was held, without discussion, that for breach of defendant's contract to use plaintiff's hotel register in his business, and no others, the remedy at law was adequate

In the recent case of Manchester Ship Canal Co. v. Manchester R. Co., [1901] 2 Ch 37, affirming [1900] 2 Ch. 352, the contract was, to give the plaintiff the "first refusal" of certain land. It was held that a negative was involved, and an injunction was granted against the owner and an intending purchaser. In Metropolitan El Supply Co, Ltd, v. Gender, [1901] 2 Ch. 799, there was a contract by a consumer to take the whole of the electric energy required for certain premises, from the company; held, in substance, an agreement not to take such energy from another source, and injunction awarded.

a certain bell;[102] agreements not to disclose trade secrets;[103] by subscribers to news associations, not to publish the information received or furnish it to others;[104] by the vendor of the plates of a book, not to publish the book except under certain conditions;[105] ante-nuptial contract by woman, not to apply for dower;[106] mutual covenants of persons owning two sides of a building that no change shall be made in the front without mutual consent.[107] Other illustrations are given in the note.[108]

102 Martin v. Nutkin, 2 P. Wms. 266, the leading case. Ringing the bell was an injury to one of the complainants, who was an invalid.

103 Peabody v. Norfolk, 98 Mass. 452, 96 Dec. 664; S. Jarvis Adams Co. v Knapp, 121 Fed. 34; Murjahn v. Hall, 119 Fed. 186; Stone v. Goss, 65 N. J. Eq. 756, 55 Atl. 736; Fralich v. Despar, 165 Pa. St. 24, 30 Atl. 521; Salomon v. Hertz, 40 N. J. Eq. 400, 2 Atl 379; National Gum & M. Co. v. Braendly, 27 App. Div. 219, 51 N Y. Supp. 93. See *ante*, § 268.

104 Gold & Stock Tel. Co. v. Todd, 17 Hun (N. Y.), 548; Board of Trade v. Christie Grain & Stock Co. (U. S.), 25 Sup. Ct. 637 (against divulging board of trade quotations, although they may concern illegal acts). See, also, F. W. Dodge Co. v. Construction Information Co., 183 Mass. 62, 97 Am. St. Rep. 412, 66 N. E. 204, 60 L. R. A. 810 (agreement apparently not expressly negative).

105 Standard Am. Pub. Co. v. Methodist Book Concern, 33 App. Div. 409, 54 N. Y. Supp. 55.

106 Cummings v. Cummings (R. I.), 57 Atl. 302.

107 First Nat. Bank v. Portsmouth Sav. Bank, 71 N. H. 547, 53 Atl. 1017.

108 Thus, one who procures a retailer to violate an agreement not to sell goods of a manufacturer at less than a certain price, may himself be enjoined from so selling: Garst v. Charles (Mass.), 72 N E. 839. See, also, for an application of the same principle, Exchange Tel. Co., Ltd., v. Central News, Ltd., [1897] 2 Ch. 48. In general, see Dickenson v. Grand Junction Canal Co., 15 Beav. 260, 2 Keener's Cas on Eq. Jur. 312 (injunction against diverting water). In the following cases injunctions were issued to restrain a railroad from running trains past a station without stopping, in violation of contract: Rigby v. Great West. Ry., 2 Phill. Ch. 44; Hood v. North East Ry., L. R. 8 Eq. 666, 5 Ch. 525; Phillips v. Great Western Ry. Co., L. R. 7 Ch. 409.

§ 298. Miscellaneous Agreements, not Expressly Negative. Threatened breaches of the contracts of gas and water companies, by shutting off the supply of gas or water from the consumer, have frequently been restrained by injunction. It is plain that in such cases the damages which will be suffered by the consumer may either be irreparable, or not readily capable of ascertainment, and that the recovery of damages may involve a multiplicity of actions at law. Moreover, there is usually no other source of supply of which the plaintiff may avail himself.[109] It has also been held that a municipality may enjoin a gas company from charging rates

[109] Gallagher v. Equitable Gaslight Co., 141 Cal. 699, 75 Pac. 329; Edwards v. Milledgeville Water Co, 116 Ga. 201, 42 S. E. 417; Xenia Real Est. Co. v. Macy, 147 Ind. 568, 47 N. E. 147; Simpson v. Pittsburgh Plate Glass Co., 28 Ind. App. 343, 62 N. E. 753; Graves v. Key City Gas Co., 83 Iowa, 714, 50 N. W. 283; Wood v. City of Auburn, 87 Me. 287, 32 Atl. 906, 29 L. R. A 376; Horsky v. Helena Cons. Water Co., 13 Mont. 229, 33 Pac. 689 (breach would ruin plaintiff's business); Sickles v. Manhattan Gas-Light Co., 64 How. Pr. 33; Whiteman v. Fayette Fuel Gas Co., 139 Pa. St. 492, 20 Atl. 1062 (mandatory preliminary injunction); School District of Borough of Sewickley v. Ohio Val. Gas Co., 154 Pa. St. 539, 25 Atl. 868. *Contra*, in Loy v. Madison etc. Gas Co., 156 Ind. 332, 58 N. E. 844, plaintiffs were held not entitled to enjoin a gas company from shutting off their supply of gas on the ground of irreparable injury, as there was no evidence that they had no other means of heating and lighting their houses. In Bienville W. S. Co. v. Mobile, 112 Ala. 260, 57 Am. St. Rep. 28, 20 South. 742, 33 L R. A. 59, the injunction was granted against shutting off the water supply of a city on the ground of a breach of public duty, in the nature of a public nuisance.

A telephone company may be enjoined from removing its instrument from plaintiff's residence: Anderson v. Mt. Sterling Telephone Co. (Ky.), 86 S. W. 1119.

Of course one who refuses to pay reasonable rates demanded is not entitled to an injunction: Mulrooney v. Obear, 171 Mo. 613, 71 S. W. 1019. It is held that a purchaser of water rights from a water company may enjoin the company from destroying his headgates and ditches: Hargrave v. Hall, 3 Ariz. 252, 73 Pac. 400.

to individuals in excess of the maximum fixed, in violation of contract with the city.[110]

Further illustrations of the use of injunction to restrain the breach of contracts, although such breach was not forbidden by an express negative, are found in the following cases: Contract by a railroad to maintain and keep open a passageway for stock under its road;[111] lease of a railroad enforced against the lessee by an injunction against abandoning the operation of the road;[112] many other contracts relating to the operation of railroads;[113] contract by a street railroad with a city to change its tracks from the side to the center of the street.[114] A publisher agreed with an author to publish his book and pay him a royalty; pending suit for accounting against the publisher, who was insolvent and unable to pay, the defendant was restrained from publishing the book, notwithstanding that the author's interest therein was not protected by copyright.[115] Defendant, a novelist, agreed to permit plaintiff, a playwright, to dramatize a novel written by the former;

110 Muncie Nat. Gas Co. v. City of Muncie, 160 Ind. 97, 66 N. E. 436.

111 Rock Island & P. R. Co. v. Dimick, 144 Ill. 628, 32 N. E. 291, 19 L. R. A. 105; Moore v. Chicago, R. I. & P. Ry. Co., 7 Kan. App. 242, 53 Pac. 775.

112 Southern R. Co. v. Franklin & P. R. Co., 96 Va. 693, 32 S. E. 485, 44 L. R. A. 297. Suit at law would not afford an adequate remedy, since the damages to the lessor from loss of traffic, decay of buildings and structures, and possible forfeiture of its franchises could not be estimated, or if such injuries were reparable in damages, it would require a multiplicity of actions for the daily breach of the agreement.

113 See *post*, Vol II, chapters on Specific Performance: Brooklyn El. R. Co. v. Brooklyn, B. & W. E. R. Co., 23 App. Div. 29, 48 N. Y. Supp 665.

114 City of Gloversville v. Johnstown, G. & H. Horse R. Co., 66 Hun, 627, 21 N. Y. Supp. 146.

115 Saltus v. Belford Co, 133 N. Y. 499, 31 N. E. 518, affirming 64 Hun, 632, 18 N. Y. Supp. 619.

the novelist having subsequently authorized a dramatization of the novel by the other defendants, its performance on the stage was enjoined, although the court could not have enforced a performance of the contract as an entirety by compelling the defendant to put plaintiff's dramatization on the stage.[116] An agreement among the merchants of a town to close their stores at a certain hour in the evening was repudiated by one of the parties; injunction was held to be the proper remedy, to avoid a multiplicity of actions, by numerous plaintiffs, for recurring breaches of the contract.[117] Where the proprietor of a water-power leases the use of a specific quantity of water, and the lessee persistently uses water in excess of the amount covered by the lease, and threatens to continue in so doing, and where the extent of such use is contingent, and its value difficult of ascertainment and of doubtful estimation, such proprietor may enjoin the lessee from using such excess, without alleging or proving that such excess is essential to the operation of other mills, or is diverted therefrom.[118]

§ 299. **Adequate Remedy at Law.**—In all these cases, if the breach of the contract, committed or threatened, can be adequately redressed by the recovery of dam-

116 House v. Clemens, 24 Abb. N. C. 381, 9 N. Y. Supp. 484.

117 Stovall v. McCutchen, 107 Ky. 577, 92 Am. St. Rep. 373, 54 S. W. 969, 47 L. R. A. 287.

118 Lawson v. Menasha Wooden-Ware Co, 59 Wis. 393, 48 Am. Rep 528, 18 N. W. 440. The decision rests on the ground not only of the impossibility of proving the amount of the excess used, but also of avoiding a multiplicity of suits for recurring breaches of the contract. Compare Saltsburg Gas Co. v. Borough of Saltsburg, 138 Pa. St. 250, 20 Atl. 844, 10 L. R. A. 193, where it seems to be held that a gas company cannot enjoin a town from using more gas than it is entitled to under its contract, since the company may sue at law for the excess.

ages in a single suit at law, injunction will not issue to restrain the breach.[119] Thus an injunction has been refused against retaining money belonging to the plaintiff under the contract;[120] against a turnpike company collecting toll from one who claimed exemption from payment by virtue of an agreement with the company;[121] against a board of education substituting another text-book for use in schools in violation of contract with publishers.[122] Likewise, an injunction to restrain breach of an agreement not to use any other trading stamp than plaintiff's[123] has been denied. It has been held that a toll-road company has an adequate remedy at law for unnecessary encroachments by an electric railway company which has a contract authorizing necessary encroachments.[124]

§ 300. **Effect of Provisions for Penalties and Liquidated Damages.**—It frequently happens in cases of negative covenants that stipulations for penalties or liquidated damages are inserted. The question which arises in these cases is whether such provisions furnish an adequate remedy at law so as to oust equity of its jurisdiction to

119 See cases *passim* in preceding sections, also Gaslight etc. Co. of New Albany v. City of New Albany, 139 Ind. 660, 39 N. E. 462; Glassbrenner v. Groulik, 110 Wis. 402, 85 N. W. 962, Wabaska Electric Co. v City of Wymore, 60 Neb. 199, 82 N. W. 626; World's Columbian Exposition v. United States, 56 Fed. 654, 6 C. C. A. 58, 18 U. S. App. 42; Gallagher v Fayette Co. R R., 38 Pa. St. 102.

120 Chicago & A. R. Co. v. New York, L. E. & W. R. Co., 24 Fed 516.

121 Kellett v. Clayton, 99 Cal. 210, 33 Pac. 885. The court were of the opinion that a multiplicity of actions by plaintiff to recover the tolls paid was not probable, but that one such action would end the dispute.

122 Attorney-General v. Board of Education, 133 Mich. 681, 95 N. W. 746.

123 Sperry & Hutchinson Co. v. Vine (N. J. Eq.), 57 Atl 1036.

124 Detroit & B. Plank Road Co. v. Oakland Ry. Co., 131 Mich. 663, 92 N. W 346.

grant an injunction. It seems to be generally conceded that if the stipulation is to be construed as a penalty, equity does not lose its jurisdiction.[125] A penalty is merely a security for the performance of the contract, and is not the price for doing what a man has expressly agreed not to do. "In determining the question whether in a given case the sum named is a penalty or liquidated damages, courts give but little weight to the mere form of words, but gather the intent from the general scope and purport of the contract."[126] Where the stipulation is construed as one for liquidated damages, the courts are not agreed as to the remedy. The better rule seems to be that it is a question of intention. "It is, of course, competent for parties to a covenant to agree that a fixed sum shall be paid in case of a breach by the party in default, and that this should be the exclusive remedy. The intention in that case would be manifest that the payment of the penalty should be the price of non-performance. But the taking of a bond in connection with a covenant does not exclude the jurisdiction of equity in a case otherwise cognizable therein, and the fact that the damages in the bond are liquidated does not change the rule. It is a question of intention, to be deduced from the whole instrument and the circumstances; and if it appear that the performance of the covenant was intended, and not merely the payment of damages in case of a breach, the covenant will be enforced."[127] All

125 Dills v. Doebler, 62 Conn. 366, 36 Am. St. Rep 345, 26 Atl 398, 20 L. R. A. 432, Wilkinson v. Colley, 164 Pa. St. 35, 30 Atl. 286, 26 L. R. A. 114; Ropes v. Upton, 125 Mass. 258; Robinson v. Heuer, 67 L. J. Ch. 644, [1898] 2 Ch. 451, 79 L. T., N. S., 281, 47 Week. Rep. 34. See, also, 1 Pom. Eq. Jur., § 446.

126 Dills v. Doebler, 62 Conn. 366, 36 Am. St. Rep. 345, 26 Atl. 398, 20 L. R. A. 432.

127 Diamond Match Co. v. Roeber, 106 N. Y. 473, 60 Am. Rep 469, 13 N. E. 419; Zimmerman v Gerzog, 13 App. Div. 210, 43 N. Y. Supp.

that is settled by the insertion of an agreement for liquidated damages is that if an action is brought for damages, the recovery shall be for the amount named, neither more nor less.[128] On the other hand, there is a line of cases holding that where liquidated damages are stipulated for, injunctive relief must be denied, the argument being that the ground of the jurisdiction is the inadequacy of the legal remedy. When parties have stipulated as to the amount of damage, the difficulty is removed. Accordingly, the legal remedy is held to be exclusive.[129]

339; A. L. & J. J. Reynolds Co. v. Dreyer, 12 Misc. Rep. 368, 33 N. Y. Supp. 649, Ropes v. Upton, 125 Mass. 258; McCurry v. Gibson, 108 Ala. 451, 54 Am. St. Rep. 177, 18 South. 806. See, also, Howard v. Woodward, 10 Jur, N. S., 1123. Where it appears that performance and payment are made alternative, relief will be refused: Sainter v. Ferguson, 1 Macn. & G. 286.

128 McCurry v. Gibson, 108 Ala. 451, 54 Am. St. Rep. 177, 18 South 806.

129 Dills v. Doebler, 62 Conn. 366, 36 Am. St. Rep. 345, 26 Atl. 398, 20 L. R. A. 432; O'Neal v. Hines, 145 Ind. 32, 43 N. E. 946, Martin v. Murphy, 129 Ind. 464, 28 N. E. 1118; Hahn v. Concordia Soc., 42 Md. 460. Compare 1 Pom. Eq. Jur., 3d ed., § 447, and note (a).

CHAPTER XIV.

INJUNCTIONS AGAINST CORPORATIONS AND THEIR OFFICERS.

ANALYSIS.

§ 301. **Ultra Vires Acts—Questions Stated.**—The principles governing the jurisdiction of equity to restrain *ultra vires* acts of private corporations vary with the character of the parties plaintiff. It is obvious that actions for such injunctions may be brought by three different classes of plaintiffs, viz.: (1) the attorney-general on behalf of the state; (2) a stockholder, and (3) a third party, having no connection with the corporation. In each of these cases the right to an injunction rests upon a theory of its own; therefore, each must be considered separately.

§ 302. **Suits by the Attorney-General.**—It is now well settled that where a corporate excess of power or misuse of franchise "tends to the public injury or to defeat public policy," it may be restrained at the suit of the attorney-general.[1] This jurisdiction is somewhat

[1] Stockton v. Central R. Co., 50 N. J. Eq. 52, 24 Atl. 964, 17 L. R. A. 97; State v. American etc. Assn., 64 Minn. 349, 67 N. W. 1;

similar to that of equity to restrain a public nuisance.[2] The question which arises in many of the cases, therefore, is simply whether the acts tend to the public injury. Thus, where a railroad company violates a penal statute by charging excessive fares, the injury to the public is such as will warrant an injunction.[3] Likewise, an injunction is proper when the abuse tends to foster a monopoly, as where, in violation of the constitution or statutes of a state, one railroad is about to purchase a parallel line,[4] or, under circumstances tending to stifle competition, is about to lease its lines to,[5] or buy shares in,[6] another railroad. The reason is well laid down in a leading English case, as follows:[7] "Now, why has the rule been established, that railway companies must not carry on any business other than that for which they were constituted? It is because these companies, being armed with the power of raising large sums of money, if they were allowed to apply their funds to purposes other than those for which they were constituted, might acquire such a preponderating influence and command over some particular branch of trade or commerce, as would enable them to drive the ordinary private traders out of the field, and create

Louisville & N. R. Co. v. Com., 97 Ky. 675, 31 S. W. 476, Attorney-General v. Chicago etc. R. R. Companies, 35 Wis 530; Attorney-General v. Great North. Ry. Co., 1 Drew & S. 154; Trust Co. of Ga. v. State, 109 Ga. 736, 35 S. E. 323, 48 L. R. A. 520.

2 Attorney-General v. Chicago etc. R. R. Companies, 35 Wis. 530. This case contains a good statement of the principles and an exhaustive citation of authority.

3 Attorney-General v. Chicago etc. R. R. Companies, 35 Wis. 530.

4 Louisville & N. R. Co. v Commonwealth, 97 Ky. 675, 31 S. W. 476.

5 Stockton v. Central R. Co., 50 N. J. Eq 52, 24 Atl. 964, 17 L. R. A. 97

6 Trust Co. of Ga. v. State, 109 Ga. 736, 35 S. E. 323, 48 L. R. A. 520.

7 Attorney-General v. Great North. Ry., 1 Drew & S. 154.

in their own favor a practical monopoly, whereby the interests of the public would be most seriously injured."

There is a tendency in some jurisdictions to extend the remedy, and to allow the attorney-general an injunction against every abuse of corporate power by a *quasi* public corporation.[8] The argument is that every excess of corporate power is a violation of the charter contract with the government, and is therefore an invasion of public rights which equity should protect. Thus, it has been held that a railroad company will be enjoined at the suit of the attorney-general from unlawfully laying its tracks in a highway, even though no public injury results.[9] This expansion of the rule, however, has not been applied to purely private business corporations,[10] the theory being that as equity protects only substantial rights, the jurisdiction must be confined to enjoining acts which tend to substantial public injury.

The adequacy of the legal remedy by *quo warranto* is no defense to an action by the attorney-general. In many cases he is allowed a discretion to choose either remedy.[11] It is often better for the public interest to restrain such violations than to enforce a forfeiture, and this is especially true in regard to *quasi* public corporations.[12] Moreover, as stated in a *quo warranto*

8 Attorney-General v. London & N. W. R. Co., [1900] 1 Q. B. 78; Attorney-General v. Birmingham & O. T. Co., 3 Macn. & G. 453, 461

9 Attorney-General v. Greenville & H. Ry. Co., 59 N. J. Eq. 372, 46 Atl. 638; Grey v. Greenville & H. Ry. Co., 60 N. J. Eq. 153, 46 Atl. 636.

10 Attorney-General v. Tudor Ice Co., 104 Mass 239, 6 Am. Rep. 227; Attorney-General v. Bank of Niagara, Hopk. Ch. 354; Attorney-General v. Utica Ins. Co., 2 Johns. Ch. 371.

11 Stockton v Central R. Co., 50 N. J. Eq. 52, 24 Atl. 964, 974, 17 L. R A. 97.

12 Louisville & N. R. Co. v. Commonwealth, 97 Ky. 675, 31 S. W. 476.

case, "acts *ultra vires* may justify interference on the part of the state by injunction to prohibit a continuance of the excess of powers which would not be a sufficient ground for a forfeiture in proceedings in *quo warranto*."[13]

§ 303. **Suits by Stockholders.**—As a general rule, it may be stated that a stockholder may obtain an injunction against *ultra vires* acts. This is based on the principle that there is a contract relation between the stockholders and the corporation which is a subject of equitable protection. "The directors are their trustees to employ the joint capital in the management, ... to the end that from the investment the stockholders have chosen they may reap the contemplated profits. And this is the agreement of the stockholders among themselves. They each contract with the other that their money shall be so employed. What the majority determine within the scope of this mutual contract, they agree to abide by, but there their mutual contract ends, and no majority, however large, has a right to divert one cent of the joint capital to any purpose not consistent with, and growing out of this original fundamental joint intention."[14] Thus, a minority stockholder is entitled to an injunction to restrain a corporation from selling, leasing, or transferring all of its property,[15] or from consolidating, *ultra vires*, with an-

13 State v. Minnesota Thresher Mfg. Co., 40 Minn. 213, 41 N. W. 1020, 3 L. R. A. 510.

14 Kean v. Johnson, 9 N. J. Eq 401, 409. See, also, on the subject of this section, 3 Pom. Eq. Jur., § 1093.

15 Kean v. Johnson, 9 N. J. Eq. 401; Abbott v. American Hard Rubber Co., 33 Barb. 578; Small v. Minneapolis Electro-Matrix Co., 45 Minn. 264, 47 N. W. 797; Black v. Delaware & R. C. Co, 24 N. J. Eq 455; Forrester v. Boston & M. Cons. C. & S. M. Co, 21 Mont. 544, 55 Pac. 229, 353; New Albany Waterworks v. Louisville Banking Co, 122 Fed. 776.

other corporation,[16] or from issuing paper to circulate as money,[17] or from guaranteeing bonds of another corporation.[18] Likewise, such a stockholder may obtain an injunction to restrain the appropriation of corporate funds for any object not warranted by the charter,[19] or to prevent the fraudulent payment of private debts with corporate funds.[20] Upon the same principle, he is entitled to an injunction to restrain the *ultra vires* purchase of land;[21] to restrain such a change in the certificate of incorporation as will reduce the dividend on preferred shares;[22] and to restrain an increase of capital stock to be given for property worth less than the face value of the stock.[23] Likewise, a stockholder may enjoin a bank from discounting notes at usurious rates, in violation of its charter.[24] The fact that such contracts may be beneficial both to the corporation and to the stockholder is no ground for refusing the relief, for the stockholder has a contract right which he is en-

16 Botts v. Simpsonville & B. C. Turnpike Road Co., 88 Ky. 54, 10 S. W. 134, 2 L. R. A. 594; Langan v. Francklyn, 29 Abb. N. C. 102, 20 N. Y. Supp. 404.

17 Bliss v. Anderson, 31 Ala. 612, 70 Am. Dec. 511.

18 Zabriskie v. Cleveland, C. & C. R. Co., 23 How. (64 U. S.) 381, 16 L. ed. 488.

19 Platteville v. Galena etc. R. R., 43 Wis. 493; Stevens v. Erie R. Co., 29 Vt. 545; Cohen v. Wilkinson, 1 Macn. & G. 481; Hodgson v. Earl of Powis, 1 De Gex, M. & G. 6; Kernaghan v. Williams, L. R. 6 Eq. 228; Pickering v. Stephenson, L. R. 14 Eq. 322; Alexander v. Atlanta & W. P. R. Co., 113 Ga. 193, 38 S. E. 772, 54 L. R. A. 305; Bagshaw v. Eastern Union Ry., 7 Hare, 114, 130, 131; Bernan v. Rufford, 6 Eng. L. & Eq. 106, 1 Sim. (N. S.) 550; Simpson v. Denison, 10 Hare, 51; Colman v. Eastern Counties Ry., 10 Beav. 1; Central Ry. Co. v. Collins, 40 Ga. 582; Stewart v. Erie & W. T. Co., 17 Minn. 372; Salomons v. Laing, 12 Beav. 377.

20 Sears v. Hotchkiss, 25 Conn. 171, 65 Am. Dec. 557.

21 Hough v. Cook County Land Co., 73 Ill. 23, 24 Am. Rep. 230.

22 Pronick v. Spirits Dist. Co., 58 N. J. Eq. 97, 42 Atl. 586.

23 Donald v. American S. & R. Co., 62 N. J. Eq. 729, 48 Atl. 771, 1116.

24 Manderson v. Commercial Bank, 28 Pa. St. 379.

titled to have protected.[25] But until this contract is fully made there is no ground for action. Therefore, a subscriber for stock who has not fulfilled the conditions of his subscription, has no standing in court.[26] It has sometimes been held that relief will be granted only to a *bona fide* stockholder,[*] and accordingly the injunction has been refused when the plaintiff has been in reality acting in the interest of another corporation.[27] It is said that a stockholder cannot restrain payment for benefits received under an *ultra vires* contract, where the other party had no notice of the excess of power.[28]

While a stockholder may thus obtain final relief, he is often denied a preliminary injunction. Such an injunction is granted ordinarily only where a clear case can be made out in the complaint. Questions of *ultra vires* depend largely upon the construction and constitutionality of laws and charters, and consequently are frequently of too difficult a nature to be determined upon a preliminary application.[29] And in order to obtain any relief whatever, he must act promptly.[30] "Shareholders cannot lie by, sanctioning, or by their silence at least acquiescing in, an arrangement which is *ultra vires* of the company to which they belong,

25 Byrne v. Schuyler Elect. Mfg. Co, 65 Conn. 336, 31 Atl. 833, 28 L. R. A. 304.

26 Busey v. Hooper, 35 Md. 15, 6 Am. Rep. 350.

27 Jenkins v. Auburn City Ry. Co., 27 App. Div. 553, 50 N. Y. Supp. 852; Filder v. London etc. R. R. Co., 1 Hem. & M. 489. Cf. *post*, § 305, at note 59.

28 Rankin v. Southwestern Brewery & Ice Co. (N. M.), 73 Pac. 612.

29 Stevens v. Missouri, K. & T. Ry. Co., 106 Fed. 771, 45 C. C. A. 611; Smith v. Reading City Pass. Ry. Co., 156 Pa. St. 5, 26 Atl. 779.

30 Black v. Delaware & R. C. Co., 22 N. J. Eq. 415; Great Western Ry. Co. v. Oxford, W. & W. Ry. Co, 3 De Gex, M. & G. 341; Tanner v. Lindell Ry. Co., 180 Mo. 1, 103 Am. St. Rep. 534, 79 S. W. 155.

watching the result—if it be favorable and profitable to themselves, to abide by it and insist on its validity; but if it prove unfavorable and disastrous, then to institute proceedings to set it aside."[31] Thus, where a corporation issued preferred stock *ultra vires*, a stockholder was refused an injunction to restrain payment of privileged dividends, after the stock had reached the hands of a *bona fide* purchaser.[32]

§ 304. **Suits by Third Parties.**—A private individual who is not a stockholder is not entitled to an injunction to restrain an act merely *ultra vires*. He has no relation of a contractual nature which gives him any rights, nor is he entitled to sue on behalf of the state.[33] Where, however, the *ultra vires* act amounts to a private nuisance, or is a public nuisance which specially injures the individual, or where it interferes with some vested right and is otherwise a subject of equitable jurisdiction, an injunction will be granted. In accordance with these principles relief has been denied where a railroad track, although a public nuisance, would not specially injure the plaintiff;[34] where a railroad moved its station and abandoned part of its track;[35] and where a road corporation was using material not authorized by its charter.[36] Likewise, a simple contract creditor

31 Gregory v. Patchett, 33 Beav. 595, 602; Rabe v. Dunlap, 51 N. J. Eq. 40, 25 Atl. 959.

32 Kent v. Quicksilver Min. Co., 78 N. Y. 159.

33 Henry v. Ann Arbor Ry. Co., 116 Mich. 314, 75 N. W. 886. See Packard v. Thiel College (Pa.), 56 Atl. 869, where the question was left undecided, whether subscribers to a fund to build a college at a certain place were sufficiently interested to enjoin the *ultra vires* act of its removal to another location.

34 Philadelphia W. & B. R. Co. v. Wilmington City Ry. Co (Del.), 38 Atl. 1067.

35 Moore v. Brooklyn City R. Co., 108 N. Y. 103, 15 N. E. 191.

36 Erin Tp. v. Detroit & E. Plank Road Co., 115 Mich. 465, 73 N. W. 556.

has been denied an injunction to restrain the corporation from dealing with assets *ultra vires*, upon an allegation that thereby the funds available for paying debts would be diminished.[37] On the other hand, the injunction has been granted when a street railroad was laying its tracks *ultra vires* on the street, to plaintiff's injury;[38] where a street railroad was changing its tracks in violation of the rights of a borough, which was plaintiff;[39] where a gas company was laying its pipes in a country highway which passed plaintiff's premises;[40] where a railroad company was about to build over plaintiff's land without authority;[41] and where a turnpike company was attempting to charge tolls to persons exempted by its charter, on the ground of a vested right in the plaintiffs.[42] The injunction, however, will not be granted where the injury is slight,[43] or where it will result in public inconvenience.[44]

§ 305. Suits by Stockholders Against Directors for Wrongful Dealing with Corporate Property.—It is not within the scope of this chapter to attempt any general discussion of the great variety of cases in which equitable relief

37 Mitts v. Northern Ry., L. R. 5 Ch. 621.

38 Bonaparte v. Baltimore etc. Ry. Co, 75 Md 340, 23 Atl. 784

39 Borough of Shamokin v. Shamokin & M. C. Elect. Ry. Co., 196 Pa. St. 166, 46 Atl. 382.

40 Sterling's Appeal, 111 Pa. St. 35, 56 Am. Rep. 246, 2 Atl. 105; and the same rule may apply when a gas company, in excess of charter powers, attempts to lay gaspipes in the street of a city, whereby plaintiff will suffer special injury; Seattle Gas & Electric Co. v. Citizens' Light & Power Co, 123 Fed. 588.

41 Western Md. R. R. Co. v. Owings, 15 Md. 204, 74 Am. Dec. 563.

42 Louisville & T. Turnpike Co. v. Ross, 19 Ky. Law Rep. 1954, 44 S. W. 981.

43 Becker v. Lebanon & M. Ry. Co., 188 Pa. St. 484, 41 Atl. 612, 43 Wkly. Not. Cas 229.

44 Ware v. Regents' Canal Co., 3 De Gex & J. 212.

is sought by stockholders against wrongful dealing with corporate property. Such a discussion should be looked for in treatises on substantive equity,[45] or on the law of corporations. Suits of this character, so far as the form of the remedy is concerned, are usually suits for an accounting. Where, however, the nature of the facts calls for preventive relief, it is usually granted with great freedom.

In this class of suits, since the cause of action exists primarily in behalf of the corporation, the stockholder is not permitted to sue unless he shows, either that the corporation actually refuses to bring the suit, or that a refusal of the managing body, if it had been requested to bring the suit, might be inferred with reasonable certainty.[46] Further, the right of the stockholder to sue in cases where the corporation is the proper party to bring the suit is limited to cases where the acts of the directors or stockholders complained of are either fraudulent, illegal or in breach of trust; in other cases than these a court of equity has no jurisdiction to interfere in the internal management of the affairs of corporations.[47] Subject to these fundamental rules, a stock-

45 See 3 Pom. Eq. Jur., §§ 1094, 1095.

46 Id.; in addition to the cases there cited, see the following cases, in which an injunction was sought. Putnam v. Ruch, 54 Fed. 216, Ball v. Rutland R. Co, 93 Fed. 513 (sufficient demand on the corporation); Memphis & C R. Co. v. Woods, 88 Ala. 630, 16 Am. St Rep 81, 7 South. 108, 7 L. R. A. 605; Mack v. De Bardeleben Coal & I. Co, 90 Ala. 396, 8 South. 150, 9 L. R A. 650 (demand excused), Harding v American Glucose Co., 182 Ill 551, 74 Am. St. Rep. 189, 55 N. E 577; Lewisohn v. Anaconda Copper Min. Co., 26 Misc. Rep. 613, 56 N. Y Supp 807; Fitchett v. Murphy, 61 N. Y. Supp. 182, 46 App Div. 181

47 Hawes v. Oakland, 104 U. S. 450, 26 L. ed 827; MacDougall v. Gardiner, L. R 1 Ch. D. 14; Shaw v. Davis, 78 Md. 314, 28 Atl. 619, 23 L R A. 294, Leslie v Lorillard, 110 N. Y. 519, 18 N. E 363, 1 L. R A. 456, Burden v Burden, 159 N Y 287, 54 N. E 17; Lewisohn v. Anaconda Copper Min Co., 26 Misc. Rep. 613, 56 N. Y

holder's right to enjoin *infra vires* acts on the part of the corporate authorities has been recognized in an almost unlimited variety of instances, of which the following may serve as illustrations: he may enjoin misappropriation of corporate funds;[48] fraudulent prosecution of suits against the company by the directors;[49] but not, it seems, the auditing of a fraudulent account, since the allowance of the account would not conclude anyone, and no irreparable injury would result;[50] he may enjoin a wrongful lease of the corporate property, amounting to a breach of trust;[51] the payment of illegal dividends, but not of dividends already declared, unless all the shareholders are before the court;[52] the payment of an illegal tax;[53] the fixing of a particular date for holding the general meeting of the company for the purpose of preventing shareholders from exercising their voting powers;[54] the voting of the majority of

Supp. 807; Peabody v. Westerly Waterworks, 20 R. I. 176, 37 Atl. 807; Phillips v. Providence Steam Engine Co, 21 R. I. 302, 43 Atl 598, 45 L. R. A. 560.

48 People's Sav. Bank v. Colorado Min. etc. Co., 8 Colo. App. 354. 46 Pac. 620.

49 Birmingham Min. etc. Co. v. Mutual Loan & Trust Co., 96 Ala 364, 11 South. 368.

50 Rogers v. Lafayette Agricultural Works, 52 Ind. 296. The correctness of this decision may well be doubted.

51 Pond v. Vermont etc. R. R. Co., 12 Blatchf. 280, Fed. Cas. No. 11,265.

52 Since each shareholder has a right of action to recover a dividend that has been declared: Carlisle v. South Eastern Ry., 1 Macn. & G. 689.

53 Dodge v. Woolsey, 18 How. (59 U. S.) 331, 15 L. ed. 401; Mechanics' & Traders' Bank v. Debolt, 18 How. (59 U. S.) 380, 15 L. ed. 458; Pollock v. Farmers' Loan & Trust Co., 157 U. S. 429, 15 Sup. Ct. 673, 39 L. ed. 759 (the question of the adequacy of the legal remedy was waived); but see Corbus v. Treadwell Gold Min. Co., 99 Fed. 334.

54 Cannon v. Trask, L R. 20 Eq 669 But that the directors will not be restrained from holding an irregular meeting, when all the

the stock in the corporation, held by a rival corporation whose interests are in conflict with those of the former;[55] the voting of shares of stock fraudulently transferred or acquired, under various circumstances;[56] winding up the affairs of the corporation and disposing of its assets in a manner inconsistent with good faith toward the minority stockholders,[57] or at variance with the statutes on the subject.[58]

It has been held that a *bona fide* minority stockholder in a substantial amount is not precluded from enjoining the majority stockholders from voting to make a certain disposition of the corporate property merely because his principal motive is to protect another corporation and his interest therein.[59]

In a very important recent case it was held that a dissenting stockholder may sue in behalf of himself and other stockholders to prevent the corporation and its officers from carrying out an agreement to convey its property to another corporation whose purpose was to

acts of such meeting will be void for want of a quorum, see Sullivan v. Venner, 63 Hun, 634, 18 N. Y. Supp. 398.

55 Memphis & C. R. Co. v. Woods, 88 Ala. 630, 16 Am. St. Rep. 81, 7 South. 108, 7 L. R. A. 605, and cases cited; George v. Central R. R. & B. Co., 101 Ala. 607, 14 South. 752.

56 Campbell v. Poultney, 6 Gill & J. (Md.) 94, 26 Am. Dec. 559; Webb v. Ridgely, 38 Md. 364; Hilles v. Parrish, 14 N. J. Eq. 380. But one who was induced to subscribe for stock of a corporation upon the assurance of a stockholder that a particular business would not be engaged in, cannot enjoin such stockholder from voting to take up such business: Converse v. Hood, 149 Mass. 471, 21 N. E 878, 4 L. R. A. 521

57 Hayden v. Official Hotel etc. Co., 42 Fed. 875 (preliminary injunction refused), Treadwell v. United Verde Copper Co., 62 N. Y. Supp. 708, 47 App. Div. 613 (preliminary injunction granted; a history of outrageous fraud by a notorious public character).

58 Hunt v. American Grocery Co., 81 Fed. 532.

59 Lewisohn v. Anaconda Copper Min. Co., 26 Misc. Rep. 613, 56 N. Y. Supp 807, 50 N. Y. Supp. 253, 23 Misc. Rep. 31. Compare *ante*, § 303, at note 27.

create a monopoly prohibited by statute; the stockholder's right to sue was maintained, not on the ground of protecting the public interests, but because the creation of the monopoly would expose the corporation to a forfeiture of its charter rights, and the value of the complainant's stock would thereby be destroyed.[60]

§ 306. **Other Suits by Stockholders.**—Injunction is sometimes an appropriate remedy where the stockholder's individual rights, as distinguished from those of the corporation, are invaded.[61] Thus, an injunction is allowed in some cases to restrain the enforcement, by sale of the complainant's stock, of the corporation's lien thereon for a debt or liability incurred to the corporation by the stockholder;[62] or to restrain the forfeiture and sale by the company of non-assessable shares, when there would probably be no way of accurately estimating their market value, and irreparable injury might result;[63] against assessing stock beyond its par value;[64] but not to restrain an action to recover dues imposed under a by-law, on the ground of its invalidity, when that would constitute a perfect defense at law.[65]

60 Harding v. American Glucose Co., 182 Ill 551, 74 Am. St. Rep 189, 55 N. E. 577; distinguishing Coquard v. Oil Co., 171 Ill. 480, 49 N. E. 563, where the stockholder sought the forfeiture of the corporation's charter for injury to the public rights, a relief that could only be enforced by the state; and also distinguishing Cops v. District Fair Assn., 99 Ill. 489, 39 Am. Rep. 30, where no pecuniary injury to the company or the complainants from the alleged illegal acts was shown

61 For injunction in connection with suits to procure the transfer of stock upon the company's books, see *post*, Vol. II.

62 See Elliott v Sibley, 101 Ala. 344, 13 South 500, for requisite pleading in such cases.

63 San Antonio St. Ry. Co. v. Adams (Tex. Civ. App.), 25 S. W. 639.

64 Redkey v. Citizens' Natural Gas etc. Co., 27 Ind. App. 1, 60 N. E. 716.

65 Kinnan v. Sullivan County Club, 26 App. Div. 213, 50 N. Y. Supp. 95.

It is well settled that a suit will lie by a holder of common stock to enjoin any unlawful or unauthorized issue of preferred stock, to the prejudice of the stockholder's vested individual right in his proportionate share of the corporate property and of the profits of the business.[66]

In Ohio, injunction is held to be the proper remedy to enforce the stockholder's right to inspect the books and records of the corporation, although in other states the remedy is usually by *mandamus;*[67] and the latter, and not injunction, is the proper remedy to compel the corporation to post for the public benefit a copy of their by-laws and financial statement.[68]

§ 307. **No Injunction to Determine Title to Corporate Office.**—A court of equity will not primarily take jurisdiction to determine the legality of an election of directors, or to remove a director who is in possession of the office. The court will inquire into the regularity of the election, or the right of the person to the office, only when the question arises incidentally and collaterally, in a suit of which the court has rightful jurisdiction on other grounds,[69] such as fraud and breach of

66 Ernst v. Elmira Municipal Improvement Co., 24 Misc. Rep. 583, 54 N. Y. Supp 116; Kent v. Quicksilver Min. Co., 78 N. Y. 159, Campbell v. Zylonite Co., 122 N. Y. 455, 25 N. E. 853, 11 L. R. A. 596.

67 The Ohio rule depends on the wording of the statute defining the writ of *mandamus:* Cincinnati Volksblatt Co. v. Hoffneister, 62 Ohio St. 189, 78 Am. St. Rep. 707, 56 N. E. 1033, 48 L. R. A. 732.

68 Boardman v. Marshalltown Grocery Co., 105 Iowa, 445, 75 N. W. 343.

69 Perry v. Oil Mill Co., 93 Ala. 364, 9 South. 217; Elliott v. Sibley, 101 Ala. 344, 13 South. 500; Carmel Natural Gas etc. Co. v. Small, 150 Ind. 427, 47 N. E. 11, 50 N. E. 476; Sherman v. Clark, 4 Nev. 138, 97 Am Dec. 516; Kean v. Union Water Co., 52 N. J. Eq. 813, 46 Am. St. Rep. 538, 31 Atl. 282, reversing 52 N. J. Eq. 111, 27 Atl. 1015; Owen v. Whitaker, 20 N. J. Eq. 122; Mickles v. Rochester City

trust.[70] The remedy to determine the right to corporate office is by *quo warranto* or special statutory proceeding, and these are at least as adequate as the remedy by injunction would be.[71] When a court of equity takes jurisdiction on other grounds, and the title to corporate office is incidentally involved, its judgment cannot go to the extent of ousting a *de facto* officer.[72] The court may protect by injunction the possession of *de facto* trustees against rival claimants of their office, until their title can be properly adjudicated upon in a legal proceeding, for the purpose of preventing an unseemly struggle for possession between the rival boards of trustees.[73]

§ 308. Existence of a Corporation cannot be Challenged by Injunction—Injunction in Connection with Receivership. A court of equity has no inherent jurisdiction, either at the suit of the state or of a private person, to challenge or question the legal existence of a *de facto* corporation, or to take away its chartered privileges, even though the purpose for which it was organized may have been unlawful; the remedy is by *quo warranto.*[74]

Bank, 11 Paige (N. Y.), 118, 42 Am. Dec. 103; Ciancimino v. Man, 48 N. Y. St. Rep 697, 20 N. Y. Supp. 702; Model Building & L. Assn v. Patterson, 34 N. Y. Supp. 241, 12 Misc. Rep 400; Mozley v. Alston, 1 Phill. Ch. 790; Bedford Springs Co v. McMeen, 161 Pa. St. 639, 29 Atl. 99. But see Haskell v. Read (Neb.), 93 N. W. 997.

70 Johnston v Jones, 23 N. J. Eq. 216.

71 Carmel Natural Gas etc. Co. v. Small, 150 Ind. 427, 47 N. E. 11, 50 N. E. 476, Kean v. Union Water Co., 52 N. J. Eq. 813, 46 Am St. Rep. 538, 31 Atl 282; Mickles v. Rochester City Bank, 11 Paige (N. Y.), 118, 42 Am. Dec. 103; Ciancimino v. Man, 48 N Y. St. Rep. 697, 20 N. Y. Supp. 702.

72 Ciancimino v. Man, 48 N. Y. St. Rep. 697, 20 N. Y. Supp. 702, and cases cited.

73 Model Building & L. Assn. v. Patterson, 12 Misc. Rep. 400, 34 N Y. Supp. 241.

74 Stockton v American Tobacco Co, 55 N J Eq 352, 36 Atl. 971; affirmed *sub nom.* Miller v. American Tobacco Co., 42 Atl. 1117;

There is a clear distinction between an injunction directed against acts outside the scope of the charter privileges of a corporation, and an injunction against *infra vires* acts, resting upon the conduct of the incorporators preceding and leading up to the incorporation of the company.[75] An injunction cannot be allowed which would strike at the authority of the corporation to act at all as a corporation; and a decree restraining the officers and agents of a corporation from executing corporate acts is the same as a decree enjoining the corporation itself.[76] Nor does the rule laid down in the last paragraph, that the legality of an election of corporate officers may be questioned when the matter arises incidentally in connection with some recognized ground for equitable jurisdiction, apply by analogy, so as to enable a court of equity to determine collaterally a question of corporate existence.[77]

When a receiver is appointed under the statutes providing for the dissolution of corporations, an injunction depriving the officers of the corporation of control over the corporate property is appropriate and customary; such injunction is frequently authorized by the terms of the statute.[78]

National Docks R. Co v. Central Ry. Co., 32 N. J. Eq 755; Elizabethtown Gas-Light Co. v. Green, 46 N. J. Eq. 117, 18 Atl. 844; affirmed 49 N. J. Eq 329, 24 Atl. 560; Harrison v. Hebbard, 101 Cal. 152; Bayless v. Orne, 1 Freem. Ch. (Miss.) 173.

75 Stockton v. American Tobacco Co., *supra.*

76 Stockton v. American Tobacco Co, *supra.*

77 Stockton v. American Tobacco Co., *supra.*

78 See Morgan v. New York & A. R. R. Co, 10 Paige, 290, 40 Am. Dec. 244. As to injunction restraining creditors from enforcing their demands against the corporation, when proceedings have been begun for its voluntary dissolution, see In re Binghamton General Electric Co, 143 N. Y. 261, 38 N. E. 297; In re French Mfg. Co., 12 Hun, 488.

CHAPTER XV.

INJUNCTIONS RELATING TO VOLUNTARY ASSOCIATIONS AND NON-STOCK CORPORATIONS.

ANALYSIS.

§ 309. **In General.**—The jurisdiction of equity over voluntary associations and corporations not organized for profit is of a very limited character. So long as the organization acts in accordance with its valid rules, equity will not interfere at the suit of members;[1] nor will relief be given when proper redress can be obtained within the body itself.[2] But when powers are exceeded and rules are disregarded, equity may enjoin at the suit of injured members.[3] The ground of the jurisdiction is that there is a contract between the organization and its members, for a violation of which an injunction is a proper remedy.

§ 310. **Expulsion of Members.**—Courts of equity have often been called upon of late to enjoin the illegal ex-

[1] Bateman v. Hollinger (N. J. Eq.), 30 Atl. 1107; Francis v. Taylor, 31 Misc. Rep. 187, 65 N. Y. Supp. 28.

[2] Grand Castle of the Golden Eagles v. Bridgeton Castle (N. J. Eq.), 40 Atl. 849.

[3] Supreme Lodge, Order of Golden Chain v. Simering, 88 Md. 276, 71 Am. St. Rep. 409, 40 Atl. 723, 41 L. R. 720; State v. Bankers'

pulsion of members of unincorporated associations and benevolent corporations. Persons becoming members of these organizations usually subscribe to and are bound by certain by-laws; and so long as the association keeps strictly within its rules, the court will not generally interfere. The cases calling for the aid of equity arise when the rules are exceeded, and in rare cases, when the rules are themselves illegal.

It is generally asserted to be a fundamental principle of equity that only substantial property rights will be protected. Therefore, it would seem that an injunction should be granted in cases of this kind only where some such right is involved. In cases of social clubs, however, the courts have sometimes gone further. "In all these cases the suit in law or equity has been sustained upon the ground that the relations of a member to such society were contractual, and, if the relation had been severed in violation of the law regulating membership enacted by themselves, that there was a breach of contract."[4] Thus, it has been said that "in every proceeding before a club, society, or association, having for its object the expulsion of a member, the member is entitled to be fully and fairly informed of the charge, and to be fully and fairly heard"; and if such hearing is not allowed, he is entitled to an injunction.[5] "In the absence of defined regulations as

Union of the World (Neb.), 99 N. W. 531; German Mut. Fire Ins Co. v. Schwarzwalder (N. J. Eq.), 44 Atl. 769, Kalbitzer v. Goodhue, 52 W. Va. 435, 44 S. E. 264; Flaherty v. Portland etc. Benev. Assn. (Me.), 58 Atl. 58 (unwarranted use of funds of mutual benefit society).

4 Nance v. Busby, 91 Tenn. 303, 18 S. W. 874, 15 L. R. A. 801.

5 Fisher v. Keane, L. R. 11 Ch. D. 353; Labouchere v. Earl of Wharncliffe, 13 Ch. D. 346. In Harington v. Sendall, [1903] 1 Ch 921, expulsion was enjoined, of a member who had violated a resolution raising the annual dues, which resolution was not authorized by the rules governing the club.

to the causes for expulsion, the ordinary principles of justice govern. Offenses against the tenets of the order justify action. Caprice and malice do not."[6] Accordingly, it has been held that an injunction may issue when no just cause for expulsion is shown, even though the outward forms of procedure have been followed.[7] Before resorting to equity, however, the injured party should first exhaust his remedy within the organization, especially where no property right is directly involved.[8]

§ 311. **Same—Injury to Property.**—Where an illegal expulsion works a direct injury to property rights, the jurisdiction of equity is clear, and the injunction will be granted without question. The only inquiry in such cases is whether the expulsion is illegal; and when that is determined, the injunction follows as a matter of course. Thus, when a suspension will necessarily re-

6 Heaton v. Hull, 28 Misc. Rep. 97, 59 N. Y. Supp. 281.

7 Id. In this case the court said: "I should therefore hold that, even if the outward forms of the society had been observed in degrading this chapter and its members, still such a blow was struck to the vital principles of the order and the rights of its members that no formalities could justify such destructive action, and any one aggrieved could appeal to the only resource left,—the benign, yet powerful, protection of the law. And it is a mistake to rest upon the assertion that law recognizes only material property injuries, and has no care for wounded emotions or character. Even in the cruder days of the common law, it gave to the lost service of a daughter or wife pence, while it gave to the hurt sensibilities of the father or husband hundreds of pounds. It atoned for injury to character and wounded feeling by exemplary damages. And courts of equity, such as the one now appealed to, grasp jurisdiction of other than property injuries, where equitable considerations require action to prevent hurt to standing or character which damages may not compensate."

8 Mead v. Stirling, 62 Conn. 586, 27 Atl. 591, 23 L. R. A 227; Thomas v. Musical Mut. Pro. Union, 121 N. Y 45, 24 N. E. 24, 8 L. R. A. 175 (reversing 49 Hun, 171, 2 N. Y Supp. 195); O'Brien v. Musical Mut. P. & B. Union, 64 N. J. Eq. 525, 54 Atl. 150.

sult in affecting a member's financial standing, as well as deprive him of the use of property that is common to the whole association, the court will enjoin action under an illegal by-law.[9] In the case just cited in the note, the plaintiff was a member of a local Board of Fire Underwriters, and was threatened with suspension for employing more agents than the rules allowed. The court held that the rules were void because in restraint of trade, and that therefore a suspension would be invalid. The injury consisted in loss of business and inconvenience resulting from denial of a membership right to consult fire maps. Likewise, a suspension from a Merchants' Exchange for violating a rule which does not warrant suspension,[10] or an expulsion from a Board of Trade without opportunity to make a defense which the by-laws permit members to make,[11] will be enjoined at the suit of the injured party. It has been held, however, in a similar case that there can be no injunction after the expulsion has taken place.[12] The reason given is that the writ of injunction is preventive only, and will not issue to redress past wrongs. It would seem that a sufficient answer to this line of argument is that where the proceedings are illegal there is not an expulsion which the courts will recognize. Hence, the injunction should issue to

9 Huston v. Rentlinger, 91 Ky. 333, 34 Am. St. Rep 225, 15 S. W. 867.

10 Albers v. Merchants' Exchange, 39 Mo. App. 583.

11 Ryan v. Cudahy, 157 Ill. 108, 48 Am. St. Rep. 305, 41 N. E. 760, 49 L. R. A. 353; Bartlett v. L. Bartlett & Son Co., 116 Wis. 450, 93 N. W. 473. An injunction has been allowed to restrain the expulsion of a member from a news association: Inter-Ocean Pub. Co. v. Associated Press, 184 Ill. 438, 75 Am. St. Rep 184, 56 N. E. 822, 48 L R. A. 568.

12 Fisher v. Board of Trade, 80 Ill. 85 ("If appellant has been improperly expelled by proceedings contrary to the constitution and by-laws or rules of the board, a court of chancery cannot restore him").

protect the plaintiff's present right of membership. The injunction will not be granted, in the absence of any other ground, when the property injury is conjectural only, as, for instance, where the punishment is a fine which may lead to suspension if not paid, or if the offense is repeated;[13] nor will relief be awarded on the ground that due notice of the hearing has not been given, when, as a matter of fact, the member has known of the proceeding and is therefore not injured;[14] nor when the association itself is an illegal one.[15]

In determining whether or not the expulsion is wrong, the court will generally inquire only into the regularity of the proceedings, and sometimes, as stated above, into the legality of the rules. "Proceedings for expulsion from a beneficiary association must be in accordance with its constitution and by-laws, to the extent that the member expelled shall have notice and shall be tried on a charge within the jurisdiction of the tribunal trying him."[16]

§ 312. Expulsion from Religious Organizations.—An injunction will not ordinarily issue to restrain expulsion from a church or religious organization, for generally there is no property right involved. "Church relationship stands upon an altogether higher plane, and church membership is not to be compared to that resulting from connection with mere human associations for profit, pleasure or culture. The church undertakes to

13 Thomas v. Musical Mut. Pr. Union, 121 N. Y. 45, 24 N. E. 24, 8 L. R. A. 175 (reversing 49 Hun, 171, 2 N. Y. Supp. 195).

14 Grand Com. of Mass. United Order of the Golden Cross v. Stewart, 177 Mass. 235, 58 N. E. 689.

15 Greer v. Payne, 4 Kan. App. 153, 46 Pac. 190.

16 Women's Catholic Order of Foresters v. Haley, 86 Ill. App. 330. Gregg v. Massachusetts Med. Soc., 111 Mass. 185, 15 Am. Rep. 24, is apparently *contra*.

deal only with the spiritual state of man. It does not appeal to his purely human and temporal interests. . . . . No property rights of a personal kind depend upon membership. No pecuniary right, or civil right of any character" is affected by expulsion.[17] Therefore, a minister cannot be enjoined from striking plaintiff's name from the roll of church communicants.[18] In the case cited, the court said: "All questions of faith, doctrines, and discipline belong exclusively to the church and its spiritual officers; and the courts will neither review their determination on the facts, nor their decision on the question of jurisdiction." "The question of church membership is purely ecclesiastical." Likewise, it is held that a minister cannot enjoin a church court from proceeding with a trial against him[19] It was urged that a minister has a vested right in his office and the salary and emoluments attached to it; but in answer it was held that the right to salary depended upon the continued performance of duties as rector, and that the contract must be construed and enforced by reference to the canons. Whether an exemption from taxation and performance of certain civil duties are such property rights as would give the court jurisdiction is more of a question; but granting that they are, the court will determine only whether the tribunal had power to act.[20] It cannot inquire into the truth of the charges.

A distinction is made in at least one case between expulsion of a member by a properly organized tribunal and by one not authorized. The "court will

17 Nance v. Busby, 91 Tenn. 303, 18 S. W. 874. And a court of equity will not in an action for an injunction try title to a church office· Dayton v. Carter, 206 Pa. St. 491, 56 Atl. 30.

18 Waller v. Howell, 23 Misc. Rep. 236, 45 N Y. Supp. 790.

19 Chase v Cheney, 58 Ill. 509, 11 Am Rep. 95.

20 Walker v. Wainwright, 16 Barb. 486.

have nothing to do with the charge of a spiritual offense. That is an ecclesiastical question purely. But the inquiry whether or not the tribunal has been organized in conformity with the constitution of the church is not ecclesiastical. It is the same question, and that only, that may arise with respect to any voluntary association, such as fraternal orders and social clubs. The assertion of jurisdiction in such a case is not an interference with the control of the society over its own members; but, on the contrary, it assumes that the constitution was intended to be mutually binding upon all, and it protects the society in fact by recalling it to a recognition of its own organic law."[21] There apparently is no property right here, and consequently the case seems difficult to reconcile with the doctrines laid down above.

§ 313. **Expulsion from Other Societies**.—Because there is no property right involved, it has been held that an injunction will not issue to restrain expulsion from a temperance society,[22] nor from a purely political organization.[23] In both of these cases the right of membership is entirely distinct from any right of property.

§ 314. **Protection of Church Property Rights.**—While equity is not concerned with matters purely ecclesiastical, it will interfere by injunction to protect the illegal impairment of vested rights in church property.

21 Hatfield v. De Long, 156 Ind. 207, 83 Am. St. Rep. 194, 59 N. E. 483, 51 L. R. A. 751; s. c., 31 Ind. App. 210, 67 N. E 551. In Bonacum v. Murphy (Neb.), 98 N. W. 1030, an injunction was said to be proper pending an appeal to a higher church tribunal; but see s. c, 104 N. W. 180.

22 Hussey v. Gallagher, 61 Ga. 86.

23 Kearns v. Howley, 188 Pa. St. 116, 68 Am. St. Rep. 852, 41 Atl. 273, 42 L R. A. 235; McKane v. Adams, 123 N. Y. 609, 20 Am. St. Rep. 785, 25 N. E. 1057.

In a leading case on the subject, the questions which may arise were divided into three groups, viz.:

"1. The first of these is when the property which is the subject of controversy has been, by the deed or will of the donor, or other instrument by which property is held, by the express terms of the instrument devoted to the teaching, support or spread of some specific form of religious doctrine or belief.

"2. The second is when the property is held by a religious congregation which, by the nature of its organization, is strictly independent of other ecclesiastical associations, and so far as church government is concerned, owes no fealty or obligation to any higher authority.

"3. The third is where the religious congregation or ecclesiastical body holding the property is but a subordinate member of some general church organization in which there are superior ecclesiastical tribunals with a general and ultimate power of control more or less complete in some supreme judicatory over the whole membership of that general organization."[24] The cases will nearly all fall into this classification, and therefore will be discussed according to it.

(1) The rule in regard to the first class is so well expressed in the same case that it is unnecessary to add to it. "In regard to the first of these classes it seems hardly to admit of a rational doubt that an individual or an association of individuals may dedicate property by way of trust to the purpose of sustaining, supporting and propagating definite religious doctrines or principles, provided that in doing so they violate no law of morality, and give to the instrument by which their purpose is evidenced, the formalities which the laws

24 Watson v. Jones, 13 Wall. 679, 20 L. ed. 666.

require. And it would seem also to be the obvious duty of the court, in a case properly made, to see that the property so dedicated is not diverted from the trust which is thus attached to its use. So long as there are persons qualified within the meaning of the original dedication, and who are also willing to teach the doctrines or principles prescribed in the act of dedication, and so long as there is anyone so interested in the execution of the trust as to have a standing in court, it must be that they can prevent the diversion of the property or fund to other and different uses. This is the general doctrine of courts of equity as to charities, and it seems equally applicable to ecclesiastical matters."[25]

(2) In the second class, the ordinary rules as to voluntary associations apply. The property must be managed and controlled according to the rules of the organization. As a general rule, the majority may deal with the property as it sees fit, subject only to the restriction that the regular method of procedure must be followed. Therefore, the majority may enjoin the minority from unlawful interference with the church property where the ordinary equitable rules permit such a remedy.[26] But if the majority attempts to act without regard to the rights of the minority, as where it attempts without authority to make a change in the customs of the church by installing an organ in the house of worship,[27] an injunction will issue upon the petition of the minority. Where the majority decides upon a course of action at a meeting of which due notice

25 Watson v. Jones, 13 Wall. 679, 20 L. ed. 666. See, also, Cape v. Plymouth Congregational Church, 117 Wis. 150, 93 N. W. 449

26 Trustees etc. German Evangelical Cong. v. Hoessli, 13 Wis. 388. A deposed pastor may be enjoined from using the church property: Morris St. Baptist Church v. Dart, 67 S. C. 338, 100 Am. St. Rep. 727, 45 S. E. 753.

27 Hackney v. Vawter, 39 Kan. 615, 18 Pac. 699.

is not given, it cannot enjoin interference with such plans.[28] The majority may determine the rules of discipline, and may expel members for violations thereof. After such expulsion, the rights of the former member as to the church property have ceased, and, therefore, he can be enjoined from interfering.[29] But, of course, the minority cannot expel the majority, and if such a thing is attempted, the rights of the majority in the property will be protected by injunction.[30]

§ 315. **Same—When Rights Depend upon Decision of Superior Church Tribunal.**—(3) In the third class, where the congregation is but a subordinate member of some general church organization, the rights of any faction to the control of the property depend upon the decision of the church tribunals. "Whenever the questions of discipline or of faith, or ecclesiastical rule, custom or law have been decided by the highest of these church judicatories to which the matter has been carried, the legal tribunals must accept such decisions as final, and as binding on them, in their application to the case before them."[31] Therefore, the trustees of every local church must hold the property for the use of the party decided by such judicatory to be the real representative of the denomination. In the leading case from which the foregoing abstract is taken, the question arose as to the respective rights of two factions of the Presbyterian Church. The General Assembly, the highest court of the church, expressed views

28 Long v. Harvey, 177 Pa. St. 473, 55 Am. St. Rep. 733, 35 Atl. 869, 34 L. R. A. 169.

29 Shannon v. Frost, 42 Ky. (3 B. Mon.) 253. Likewise an excommunicated member cannot enjoin diversion of property: Nance v. Busby, 91 Tenn. 303, 18 S. W. 874.

30 Bouldin v. Alexander, 15 Wall. 131, 21 L. ed. 69.

31 Watson v. Jones, 13 Wall. 679, 20 L. ed. 666.

on the subject of slavery, which led to the secession of a large number of members from the Southern churches. The result was a dispute as to the rights to the property. The court held that the questions of discipline and of slavery, under the circumstances, were matters of ecclesiastical cognizance alone; that the decision of the General Assembly was final; that therefore the party acceding to its decision was entitled to the property, and could enjoin interference therewith by the other faction.[32]

32 Watson v. Jones, 13 Wall. 679, 20 L. ed. 666. Similar questions arose in a line of decisions which for convenience may be called the United Brethren cases. The constitution of this religious organization provided: "There shall be no alteration of the foregoing constitution unless by request of two-thirds of the whole society." "No rule or ordinance shall at any time be passed to change or do away with the confession of faith as it now stands, nor to destroy the itinerant plan." At a general conference it was decided to amend the constitution in such a way as to add to the clearness of expression without a change of meaning. The proposition was submitted to the members and was carried by a vote of more than two-thirds of those voting, but not by two-thirds of all the members. Thereupon a minority withdrew, set up a claim to be the true church, alleged that the majority, by its action, had withdrawn, and claimed the right to control the different congregations. The result was a number of injunction suits to determine the rights of different congregations in the several states. In some instances it was held that the question whether the old confession of faith had been superseded was ecclesiastical, that the courts would not inquire into it, and that therefore the majority was entitled to the aid of the court: Kuns v. Robertson, 154 Ill. 394, 40 N. E. 343; Brundage v. Deardorf, 92 Fed. 214, 34 C. C. A. 304; Lamb v. Cain, 129 Ind. 486, 29 N. E. 13, 14 L. R. A. 518 (not an injunction case). In one case it was held that the change was valid, and that therefore the majority was entitled to an injunction: Schlichter v. Keiter, 156 Pa. St. 119, 27 Atl. 45, 22 L. R. A. 161. And in another it was held that the action of the conference was legislative rather than judicial; that it was subject to review; that while the change was illegal, it was not so great as to change the identity, and that therefore the majority was entitled to control: Philomath College v. Wyatt, 27 Or. 390, 37 Pac. 1022, 26 L. R. A. 68 (see, also, 31 Pac. 206). See as to the general proposition, Bonacum v. Harrington, 65 Neb. 831, 91 N. W. 886.

The action of the supreme judicatory being final on all such matters, it follows that a determination by such a body of the validity of the appointment of a pastor cannot be questioned in an injunction suit.[33] It is for the church court to determine upon the validity of such proceedings.[34] And it would seem the better rule to refuse an injunction to restrain a party from preaching, for that is a mere naked trespass;[35] but there is authority for such relief.[36]

[33] Gross v. Wieand, 151 Pa. St. 639, 25 Atl. 50.

[34] Wehmer v. Fokenga, 57 Neb. 510, 78 N. W. 28.

[35] German Evangelical Luth. Church v. Maschop, 10 N. J. Eq. 57.

[36] Perry v. Shipway, 4 De Gex & J. 353; Cooper v. Gordon, L. R. 8 Eq. 249.

CHAPTER XVI.

INJUNCTIONS BETWEEN MORTGAGOR AND MORTGAGEE.

ANALYSIS.

§ 316. **Injunction Against Sale Under Power in Mortgage or Trust Deed.**—A court of equity will enjoin the execution of a power of sale in a mortgage when it appears that the mortgagee is proceeding in an improper or oppressive manner, or is perverting the power from its legitimate purpose;[1] as where, having refused repeated tender, he files a bill to foreclose, dismisses it without prejudice when the cause is ready for hearing, and advertises the land for sale under a power in the mortgage with the avowed purpose of compelling the payment of another claim which is disputed.[2] And in a suit for cancellation[3] or redemption[4] of a mortgage, a motion for a temporary injunction restraining the exercise of a power of sale may be granted, when it appears that less inconvenience and injustice will

1 McCalley v. Otey, 99 Ala. 584, 42 Am. St. Rep. 87, 12 South. 406; s. c., 90 Ala. 302, 8 South. 157; Struve v. Childs, 63 Ala. 473.

2 McCalley v. Otey, *supra*.

3 New England Mortg. Sec. Co. v. Powell, 97 Ala. 483, 12 South. 55. See, also, Hodge v. McMahon, 137 Ala. 171, 34 South. 185 (chattel mortgage).

4 Whitley v. Lumber Co., 89 Ala. 493, 7 South. 810.

thereby be caused to the defendant than would result to the complainant from refusing the motion. A sale under a mortgage given by a married woman may be enjoined until a hearing is had on the question of her power to execute the mortgage.[5] But a sale under a power in a mortgage cannot be enjoined upon the mere ground that the time of the sale is unpropitious, if there is no fraud or collusion on the part of the mortgagee.[6]

Sales under trust deeds in the nature of mortgages come under the general jurisdiction of equity to compel trustees to perform their duties, and to interfere by injunction to restrain the improper exercise of their powers. The trustee, in such cases, is the agent of both parties, bound to act impartially between them, and ought of his own motion to apply to the court to remove an impediment to a proper execution of the trust; and if he should fail to do this, the party injured by his default has a right to make such application, and to enjoin the sale under the trust until such impediment is removed.[7]

5 Strom v. American Freehold Land Mort. Co., 42 S. C. 97, 20 S. E. 16.

6 Warner v. Jacob, L. R. 20 Ch. D. 220.

Injunction for the purpose of obtaining a set-off.—"Without averment of insolvency, or other special equity, a power of sale will not be enjoined for the purpose of enabling the mortgagor to have ascertained and set off against the mortgage debt an uncertain balance that may be due him on a settlement of partnership accounts, or other claim in controversy between him and the mortgagee, though the cross-demands may be mutual. Such is not a case where the great and irreparable injury will result, which authorizes the court to exercise its extraordinary jurisdiction": Glover v. Hembree, 82 Ala. 324, 8 South. 251. See, also, Sidney Land & Colony Co. v. Milner, Caldwell & F. L. Co., 138 Ala. 185, 35 South. 48, where an injunction to prevent the sale for a debt of $35,000 on account of a claim of $10, was denied.

7 Hartman v. Evans, 38 W. Va. 669, 18 S. E. 810, and cases cited;

§ 317. Same; in Case of Usury.—Relief by injunction is freely granted to restrain the sale under power in a mortgage or trust deed of land mortgaged to secure a usurious debt, until an accounting is had of the amount legally due.[8] It is a familiar application, in such cases, of the maxim, "He who seeks equity must do equity," that relief will be refused when the mortgagor has not paid or offered to pay the amount of the

Hudson v. Barham, 101 Va. 63, 99 Am. St. Rep. 849, 43 S. E. 189. Thus, where a trust deed was given to secure the payment of the purchase-money of land, and an adverse claim to the land was afterward discovered, a sale under the trust deed was enjoined until such adverse claim should be regularly decided: Gay v. Hancock, 1 Rand. (Va.) 72; Miller v. Argyle's Exr., 5 Leigh (Va.), 460; but see Morgan v. Glendy, 92 Va. 86, 22 S. E. 854, where the defendant offered to correct the defect in the title. See, also, George v. Derby Lumber Co., 81 Miss. 725, 33 South. 496.

An injunction should not issue on account of defects in advertising, etc., when it appears that the complainant could prevent a sale by paying the amount admitted to be due Meetz v. Mohr, 141 Cal. 667, 75 Pac 298. In Smith v. Parker, 131 N. C. 470, 42 S. E. 910, a temporary injunction was issued to restrain a sale under a deed of trust given by sureties, who claimed that they had been released by an extension of time given to the principal. In Dunnaway v. O'Reilly (Mo. App.), 79 S. W. 1004, an injunction was issued on the ground that the time had been extended and that the sum secured was therefore not due.

8 Alston v. Morris, 113 Ala. 506, 20 South. 950; Edmund's Exrs. v. Bruce, 88 Va. 1007, 14 S. E. 840; Marks v. Morris, 2 Munf. (Va.) 407, 5 Am. Dec 481; Hartman v Evans, 38 W. Va. 669, 18 S. E. 810; Smith v. McMillan, 46 W. Va. 577, 33 S. E 283. Statutes in some states expressly provide for an injunction to prevent such sale, pending suit to determine the existence of the usury: Code W. Va. (1891), c. 96, p. 713. Where the court, by its final decree, ascertains the amount legally due, after deducting the usurious interest, and orders a foreclosure under direction of the court unless payment is made, it is error to dissolve a preliminary injunction which had been granted restraining a sale under the power: Alston v. Morris, *supra*. In Rorer v. Holston Nat. B. & L. Assn. (W. Va.), 46 S E. 1018, relief was granted at suit of a grantor in a trust deed who had sold his interest in the land.

principal and legal interest that is due.[9] When, however, the complaint leaves the mortgage unimpeached, to stand for the full balance of the principal lent upon it, and legal interest, and seeks only to restrain the sale of the mortgaged premises for a greater amount, no tender is necessary of the principal and interest admitted to be equitably due on the mortgage.[10] It is held that the defense of failure to make tender of the legal amount, if not taken advantage of by answer, will be deemed to be waived.[11]

§ 318. **Same; Payment by the Mortgagor, or Necessity for an Accounting.**—Payment of the mortgage indebtedness is a sufficient ground for restraining a sale under the power in the mortgage or trust deed;[12] or a tender of the amount to the trustee, followed by his refusal to execute a release in proper form, and a payment of the amount into court.[13]

Where there is a controversy as to the amount due on the mortgage, arising out of numerous transactions between the parties, and an accounting is therefore

9 Stanley v. Gadsby, 10 Pet. (35 U. S.) 521, 9 L. ed. 518; Ward v. Bank of Abbeville, 130 Ala. 597, 30 South. 341. By statutes in some states all interest is forfeited, and payment of the principal only can be made a condition of relief: Southern Home B. & L. Assn. v. Toney, 78 Miss. 916, 29 South. 825. See Pom. Eq. Jur., § 391.

10 Haggerson v. Phillips, 37 Wis. 364.

11 Price v. Empire Loan Assn., 75 Mo. App. 551.

12 Dockery v. French, 69 N. C. 308, under a statute (Maryland, Code, art. 66, § 16), providing that no injunction to stay a sale of mortgaged property shall be granted unless the party praying the injunction shall on oath allege payment in whole or in part, and that the mortgagee refuses to credit the same, the court has jurisdiction, on a bill to enjoin such sale, to determine not only that the mortgage debt was unpaid, but that the persons named in the mortgage had power to make the sale: Barrick v. Horner, 78 Md. 253, 44 Am. St. Rep. 283, 27 Atl. 1111.

13 Chappell v. Clarke, 92 Md. 98, 48 Atl. 36.

necessary to ascertain the sum still due, a proper case is presented for an injunction to suspend the proposed sale under the power until the balance due is ascertained and declared by a decree of the court.[14] When it is found that the debt due is less than the amount called for by the deed of trust, the court may, in its discretion, either dissolve the injunction as to the amount due, and dismiss the bill, or may retain the case, and have the trust executed under its own supervision.[15]

§ 319. **Injunction on Behalf of the Mortgagee.**—The jurisdiction to restrain waste of mortgaged premises is treated elsewhere.[16] Injunction is sometimes sought to restrain a sale of the mortgaged property under subsequent liens. It is held that a mortgagee in possession, whose mortgage is duly recorded, cannot enjoin a sale under execution issued upon a junior judgment against the mortgagor, simply because his mortgage is

14 Bridgers v. Morris, 90 N. C. 32; Capehart v. Biggs, 77 N. C. 261; Purnell v. Vaughan, 77 N. C. 268; Harrison v. Bray, 92 N. C. 488; Faison v. Hardy, 114 N. C. 58, 19 S. E. 91; Farmers' Savings & B. & L. Assn. v. Kent, 117 Ala. 624, 23 South. 757; Henson v. Brooks, 67 Ala. 491, Martin v. Kester, 46 W. Va. 438, 33 S. E. 238; Sandusky v. Faris, 49 W. Va. 150, 38 S. E. 563 In the last case it is said: "When, from any cause, the amount due and to be raised from a sale is uncertain, such uncertainty is an impediment to the proper execution of the trust, and application may be made by the trustee, the grantor, or any of the beneficiaries of the trust, to a court of equity to have it removed But, to sustain an injunction upon the ground of such uncertainty, the complainant must sufficiently allege it, and, if it be denied in the answer, he must prove it." In this case the deed of trust amounted to a general assignment for the benefit of creditors, and the grantee was not permitted to enjoin a sale thereunder, because of uncertainty as to the amounts of his debts, etc.

15 Fry v. Old Dominion B. & L. Assn., 48 W. Va. 61, 35 S. E. 842; Crenshaw v. Seigfried, 24 Gratt. 272.

16 See chapter XXII. That a mortgagee in possession under the mortgage may enjoin the removal of crops by one claiming under the mortgagor, see Bagnall v. Villar, L. R. 12 Ch. D. 812.

a prior lien upon the property; since any sale under the execution can only pass the title to the mortgaged property subject to the mortgage if valid.[17] Whether a prior mortgagee whose mortgage has been canceled of record by mistake is entitled to the same relief against a junior lienholder is a question which, upon the authorities, is open to doubt.[18]

§ 320. Injunctions Relating to Chattel Mortgages.—In suits to restrain the foreclosure of chattel mortgages the question usually arises of the adequacy of the legal remedy or defense. It has been held that a chattel mortgagor, having both the title to and possession of the mortgaged property, may have a temporary injunction to restrain its sale, without seizure, by the mortgagee, on a complaint showing a tender rendering the mortgage null and void (under the terms of a statute); in such case the plaintiff, obviously, could neither bring an action of replevin nor an action for damages for

17 American Freehold Land & M. Co. v. Maxwell, 39 Fla. 489, 22 South. 751. "If the real estate is sold, it cannot be removed, nor is it rendered less valuable by a rule under execution. If a prior mortgagee were allowed to enjoin sales by subsequent lienholders, it would, at his election, as against the demands of other creditors, place in his hands a perpetual shield, and incase the mortgaged property in impenetrable armor."

18 Compare Merchants' & Mechanics' Bank v. Tillman, 106 Ga. 55, 31 S. E. 794, with Wiedner v. Thompson, 66 Iowa, 283, 23 N. W. 670.

Temporary injunction against enforcement of a subsequent tax lien. In Allison v. Corson, 88 Fed. 581, 32 C. C. A. 12, a first mortgagee brought an action to enjoin the assignee of a tax certificate from taking a deed to the mortgaged premises, alleging that the taxes, a part of which were illegal, were levied after his mortgage was made; that until after the hearing in a suit to foreclose his mortgage, to which the second mortgagee was a party, the certificate was held by the second mortgagee, and then assigned. It was held that, it not being clear that the complainant might not succeed upon the merits, a temporary injunction should issue pending the final hearing.

an unlawful seizure of the property.[19] On the other hand, one who has obtained the legal title to the mortgaged chattels cannot enjoin a sale on foreclosure by a mortgagee who is in possession of them, for the purpose of testing the validity of the mortgage, since the complainant has a full remedy by action of replevin or tort;[20] and a mortgagor who is sued in replevin for the recovery of mortgaged property for the purpose of foreclosure may in such action interpose any defense to the mortgage debt, such as usury, and cannot, therefore, maintain an independent suit to enjoin the foreclosure.[21] Where a chattel mortgage gives the mortgagee the right to take possession and sell the property at any time when he feels insecure, such sale will not be enjoined.[22]

Where the chattel mortgage does not transfer the right to the immediate possession of the mortgaged property, the mortgagee, pending foreclosure,[23] or even before the mortgage debt is due, may, as against the mortgagor or purchasers from him with notice or without consideration, restrain by injunction the destruction or disposal of the mortgaged chattels, their removal from the jurisdiction, and other acts done, with a view to defeating his lien.[24] The mortgagor, how-

19 Seabrook v. Mostowitz, 51 S. C. 433, 29 S. E. 202. See, also, that a chattel mortgagor in possession, on a complaint alleging that nothing is due on the mortgage, may have an injunction against foreclosure by extra-judicial proceedings: Badgett v. Frick, 28 S. C. 176, 6 S. E. 355; Mayrant v. Dickerson, Rich. Eq. Cas. (S. C.) 201.

20 Jersey City Milling Co. v. Blackwell, 58 N. J. Eq. 122, 44 Atl. 153, 49 Cent. L. J. 441.

21 Treanor v. Sheldon Bank, 90 Iowa, 575, 58 N. W. 914.

22 Cline v. Libby, 46 Wis. 123, 32 Am. Rep. 700, 49 N. W. 832.

23 Schoonover v. Condon, 12 Wash. 475, 41 Pac. 195.

24 Walker v. Radford, 67 Ala. 446; Clagett v. Salmon, 5 Gill & J. (Md.) 314; Bank of Ukiah v. Moore, 106 Cal. 673, 39 Pac. 1071; McCormick v. Hartley, 107 Ind. 248, 6 N. E. 357 (to restrain foreclosure

ever, is not to be thus hindered in the legitimate use of the property; and a mere temporary removal of the property out of the state, accompanied by an honest intention to return it before the law day of the mortgage, and without any intention to affect, embarrass, or impair the rights of the mortgagee, will not authorize an injunction to prevent the removal of the property.[25] In Iowa it is held that one chattel mortgagee cannot enjoin the foreclosure of another chattel mortgage, whether prior or subsequent, as the legal remedies are adequate.[26]

of mortgage subsequent to plaintiff's, executed in fraud of mortgagor's creditors), citing Pom. Eq. Jur., § 1345.

25 Walker v. Radford, *supra*.

26 McCormick Harvesting Machine Co. v. De La Mater, 114 Iowa, 382, 86 N. W. 365; Rankin v. Rankin, 67 Iowa, 322, 25 N. W. 263.

CHAPTER XVII.

INJUNCTIONS AGAINST PUBLIC OFFICERS.

ANALYSIS.

§ 321. Public Officers—In General.—In general, a public officer may be restrained, in a case coming under some recognized head of equity jurisdiction, from acting illegally to the injury of individuals. The mere fact that he is an officer and is acting illegally, is not sufficient to warrant equitable interference.[1] There must,

1 This rule is well stated in People v. Canal Board, 55 N. Y. 390: "A court of equity exercises its peculiar jurisdiction over public officers to control their action only to prevent a breach of trust affecting public franchises, or some illegal act under color or claim of right affecting injuriously the property rights of individuals. A court of equity has, as such, no supervisory power or jurisdiction over public officials or public bodies, and only takes cognizance of actions against or concerning them when a case is made coming

in addition, be an injury to a property right of the party applying for relief. Equity does not concern itself with political affairs, as such.

§ 322. **Same—When Relief Granted.**—When a violation of a plain official duty, requiring no exercise of discretion, is threatened, one who will sustain injury thereby, for which adequate compensation cannot be had at law, may have an injunction to prevent it.[2] Therefore, when, in such a case, there is irreparable injury and no adequate remedy at law, an injunction is proper. Thus, it will issue to restrain a board of pilot commissioners from revoking a license for an act which the statute does not make cause for forfeiture;[3] or to restrain an insurance commissioner from illegally refusing a license to do business in the state, when the statute does

within one of the acknowledged heads of equity jurisdiction. To entitle plaintiff to prohibition by injunction from a court of equity, either provisional or perpetual, he must not only show a clear legal and equitable right to the relief demanded or to some part of it, and to which the injunction is essential, but also that some act is being done by the defendant, or is threatened and imminent, which will be destructive of such right, or cause material injury to him." In La Chapelle v. Bubb, 69 Fed. 481, however, a contrary doctrine seems to be laid down. The court in that case said. "Under ordinary circumstances this court would not grant an injunction to prevent a trespass; but the defendant Bubb justifies his proposed action on the ground that he is an officer of the United States government, acting only in obedience to orders from his superior officers in the Indian department, and for that reason, I deem it entirely proper to restrain him from committing a tort while assuming to act in his official capacity."

2 Louisiana Board of Liquidation v. McComb, 92 U. S. 531, 23 L. ed. 623; Mizner v. School District (Neb.), 96 N. W. 128; Trustees of Burroughs School Dist. v. Board of Control, 62 S C. 68, 39 S. E. 793. In School Township v. Wiggins, 122 Iowa, 602, 98 N. W. 490, a school township was allowed to maintain the action. See, also, School Dist. No. 44 v. Turner, 13 Okla. 71, 73 Pac. 952.

3 Morris v. Board of Pilot Commissioners, 7 Del. Ch. 136, 30 Atl. 667.

not give an absolute discretion;[4] or to restrain a state board of health from interfering with one in the practice of his profession as an osteopath, when such board has no jurisdiction.[5] Likewise, it is proper where health officers impose unlawful quarantine regulations, the property right in such a case being the right to travel to different parts of the state;[6] or where a postmaster improperly refuses to deliver mail to the complainant;[7] or where the Secretary of the Interior attempts without authority to annul the action of his predecessor in approving the location of a railroad's right of way over the public lands;[8] or where a state official attempts to deprive an individual of his real property without due process of law under an unconstitutional enactment.[9] And in general, whenever such acts will do great harm to the plaintiff's business,[10] or make him liable to heavy penalties, he is entitled to this relief.[11]

An injunction is the proper remedy when wrongful acts, involving no discretion, amount to a trespass which is either continuous in its nature or of such a character as to be a permanent injury to the freehold.[12]

4 Mutual Life Ins Co. v. Boyle, 82 Fed. 705. It may likewise issue to restrain him from compelling the use of a uniform policy, in excess of authority: Phenix Ins. Co. v. Perkins (S. D.), 101 N. W. 1110.

5 Nelson v. State Board of Health, 108 Ky. 769, 22 Ky. Law Rep. 438, 57 S. W. 501, 50 L. R. A. 383.

6 Wong Wai v. Williamson, 103 Fed. 1.

7 Fairfield Floral Co. v. Bradbury, 87 Fed. 415.

8 Noble v. Union River Logging R. Co., 147 U. S. 165, 13 Sup. Ct. 271.

9 Davis v. Gray, 16 Wall. 203, 21 L. ed. 447.

10 Cotting v. Kansas City Stock Yards Co., 82 Fed. 850; Union Terminal R. Co. v. Board of R R. Commrs., 54 Kan. 352, 38 Pac. 290.

11 Briggs v Buckingham, 6 Del. Ch. 267, 23 Atl. 858; Van Lear v. Eisele, 126 Fed. 823; Buster v. Wright (Ind. Ter.), 69 S. W 882.

12 Ryan v. Brown, 18 Mich. 196, 100 Am. Dec 154, Raleigh v. Goshens, [1898] 1 Ch. 73.

Thus, where inspectors acting under a claim of right exceed their powers in providing for the drainage of swamp lands,[13] or where canal commissioners threaten to make an illegal appropriation of land for canal purposes, an injunction will issue.[14] It will also issue when the illegal acts amount to a nuisance,[15] cast a cloud upon the title to real estate[16] or will necessitate a multiplicity of suits.[17] Thus, where a failure to obey an order unauthorized and void would subject a plaintiff in his daily business to large numbers of individual actions and heavy penalties, an injunction is the only efficacious remedy.[18] Likewise, it has been held in the federal courts that when a state insurance commissioner by an unauthorized act attempts to keep a great number of companies out of the state, an injunction is proper because of the great number of suits which would be necessary at law.[19]

§ 323. **Same—When not Granted.**—An injunction will not be granted, however, where the case is not brought under some recognized head of equity jurisdiction,[20] nor where there is a complete and adequate remedy at law.[21] Thus, it will be refused where there is an ade-

13 Belknap v. Belknap, 2 Johns. Ch. 463, 7 Am. Dec. 548.

14 McArthur v. Kelly, 5 Ohio, 139.

15 Sels v. Greene, 88 Fed. 129.

16 Kirwan v. Murphy, 83 Fed. 275, 28 C. C. A. 348.

17 Kirwan v. Murphy, 83 Fed. 275, 28 C. C. A. 348; Pacific Express Co. v. Cornell, 59 Neb. 364, 81 N. W. 377.

18 Dinsmore v. Southern Express Co., 92 Fed. 714.

19 Liverpool & London & Globe Ins. Co. v. Clunie, 88 Fed. 160.

20 Balogh v. Lyman, 6 App. Div. 271, 39 N. Y. Supp. 780.

21 It is believed that this statement is borne out by the cases cited in illustration. However, it has been held that an injunction will issue to restrain a trespass by a public officer acting under a claim of right in cases where it will not issue against individuals: La Chapelle v. Bubb, 69 Fed. 481; Ryan v. Brown, 18 Mich. 196, 100 Am. Dec. 154 (*dictum*).

quate remedy by mandamus,[22] as where a county clerk denies a searcher of records access to the records of a particular title.[23] Likewise, it will be refused where full relief can be obtained by certiorari.[24] And in many cases ample satisfaction can be obtained in a suit to recover damages.[25] Thus, where an inspector, acting under an unconstitutional law, threatens to sell oyster grounds for non-payment of rent,[26] or where a commissioner of highways unlawfully threatens to remove a house encroaching on a highway,[27] there is said to be an adequate remedy at law, and equitable relief will be refused. Mere unconstitutionality affords no ground for such relief.[28] Again, an injunction will not issue to prevent the misappropriation of money by an officer of another court, for ordinarily there is an adequate remedy there.[29]

It is necessary to show irreparable injury to a substantial property right, and if such injury is not clearly made out, relief will be refused.[30] Therefore, when it is not apparent that irreparable injury will result

22 Nassau Electric R. Co. v. White, 12 Misc. Rep. 631, 34 N. Y. Supp 960; Barber v. West Jersey Title & Guar. Co, 53 N. J. Eq 158, 32 Atl. 222, 371; Coquard v. Indian Grave Drainage Dist., 69 Fed. 867, 16 C. C. A. 530, 34 U. S. App. 169.

23 Barber v. West Jersey Title & Guar. Co., 53 N. J. Eq 158, 32 Atl. 222, 371.

24 Pennsylvania R. Co. v. N. D. & N. J. J. C. Ry. Co., 56 Fed. 697.

25 Coquard v. Indian Grave Drainage Dist., 69 Fed. 867, 16 C. C. A. 530, 34 U. S. App. 169.

26 Thomas v. Rowe (Va.), 22 S. E. 157.

27 Flood v. Van Wormer, 147 N. Y. 284, 41 N. E. 569, affirming 70 Hun, 415, 24 N. Y. Supp. 460.

28 State ex rel. Kenamore v. Wood, 155 Mo. 425, 56 S. W. 474, 48 L. R. A. 596, People v. District Court, 29 Colo. 182, 68 Pac. 242.

29 Johnson v. Gilmer, 113 Ga. 1146, 39 S. E 469.

30 Seccomb v. Wurster, 83 Fed. 856; Business Men's League v. Waddill, 143 Mo. 495, 45 S. W. 262, 40 L. R. A. 501.

therefrom, an injunction will not issue to restrain a board from taking testimony preparatory to fixing telephone rates,[31] nor to restrain a board of arbitration from hearing a dispute when its jurisdiction is questioned,[32] nor to prevent the enforcement of a statute regulating street-car fares.[33] Again, where it is doubtful whether any injury whatever will result, no relief will be granted.[34]

Where the legality of the officer's action is doubtful, but it is not clearly illegal, a court of equity will not interfere.[35] Therefore, an injunction will not issue to prevent interference with Sunday baseball games, when the legality of such games is in doubt.[36] And even though the officer may be exceeding his authority, a party who does not come into court with clean hands will be refused relief.[37] When an injunction against an officer will be really against another individual, it will not be granted until such other party is brought into court.[38] It is also held that an injunction will be denied when the injury to the people in general from its issuance will overshadow the benefit to the complainants.[39]

§ 324. **Political Acts.**—As equity deals with property rights alone, an injunction will not issue to restrain

31 Nebraska Tel Co. v. Cornell, 58 Neb 823, 80 N. W. 43.

32 N O. City & L. R. Co. v. State Board of Arbitration, 47 La. Ann 874, 17 South. 418.

33 Ahern v Newton & B. St. Ry. Co., 105 Fed. 702.

34 New York Cent. & H. R. R. Co. v. Haffen, 90 Hun, 260, 35 N. Y. Supp. 806.

35 Glaze v. Bogle, 97 Ga. 340, 22 S. E. 969.

36 Capital City v. Police Commissioners, 9 Misc. Rep. 189, 29 N. Y. Supp 804.

37 Weiss v. Herlihy, 23 App. Div. 608, 49 N. Y. Supp. 81.

38 Union Terminal R. Co. v. Board of R. R. Commrs., 52 Kan. 680, 35 Pac. 224.

39 People v. District Court, 29 Colo. 182, 68 Pac 242.

political acts of public officers. Thus, the Secretary of War will not be enjoined from taking action which might destroy the government of a state, for only a political question is involved.[40] Likewise, a Secretary of State will not be enjoined from issuing a city charter;[41] nor will an injunction issue in that class of cases, considered later, where title to office or questions relating to elections are involved.[42] This rule prevails although a state by its election law deprives a person of rights to vote guaranteed by the fifteenth amendment.[43]

§ 325. **Federal Officers.**—An injunction cannot be issued by a state court to restrain a federal officer or any subordinate in the discharge of his duties as a government officer.[44] To allow such a jurisdiction would result in conflict between the state and federal authorities. It might result in an army officer, for instance, being dismissed from the service if he refused to obey the commands of his superiors, or being thrown into a county jail for contempt if he did obey.

§ 326. **State Officers—Tax-payers' Suits.**—The right of a tax-payer to enjoin acts of an officer of a municipal corporation which involve waste and improper expenditure

40 Georgia v. Stanton, 6 Wall. 50, 18 L. ed. 721.

41 Larcom v. Olin, 160 Mass. 102, 35 N. E. 113.

42 Tupper v. Dart, 104 Ga. 179, 30 S. E. 624; State v. Gibbs, 13 Fla. 55, 7 Am. Rep 233, Hardesty v. Taft, 23 Md. 513, 87 Am. Dec. 584; Melody v. Goodrich, 70 N. Y. Supp. 568, 35 Misc Rep. 138.

43 Green v. Mills, 69 Fed. 852, 16 C. C. A. 516, 30 L. R. A. 90, Gowdy v. Green, 69 Fed. 865. And equity will not compel an officer to place an applicant's name upon the polling list: Giles v. Harris, 189 U S. 475, 23 Sup. Ct. 639, 47 L. ed. 909.

44 In re Turner, 119 Fed 231, applying the principle laid down in In re Neagle, 135 U. S. 1, 10 Sup. Ct. 658, 34 L ed 55, and in Ohio v. Thomas, 173 U. S. 276, 19 Sup. Ct. 453, 43 L. ed. 699. See, also, Sheriff v. Turner, 119 Fed. 782.

of public funds is considered in the chapter on Municipal Corporations. A different question arises, however, when a tax-payer seeks to enjoin a state officer. "The principle upon which the doctrine in regard to municipal, or *quasi* municipal, corporations is based, flows from its analogy to a well-settled doctrine in equity governing private corporations, where each stockholder has an interest in the property of the corporation, and may interfere to protect the corporate funds from the illegal or fraudulent acts of its officers. But this reasoning cannot apply to a state government. The county is a *quasi* corporation; the state is a sovereignty. The county only possesses such powers as the legislature of the state confers upon it. Its revenues, its property, its very existence, depend upon statutory enactment. It can be enlarged, dismembered, or annihilated, at the will of the state. The state, on the contrary, has all the powers not relinquished to the general government by the articles of federation and, subject to these relinquishments, its sovereignty is supreme. One of the necessary attributes of sovereignty is the protection of the sovereign power and the maintenance of the state organization."[45] Hence it would seem that an injunction should not issue against a state officer unless some special and direct injury to the plaintiff is shown.[46] It is clear that it should not issue to

45 Jones v. Reed, 3 Wash. 57, 27 Pac. 1067.

46 Gibbs v. Green, 54 Miss. 592; Thompson v. Canal Fund Commrs., 2 Abb. Pr. 248; City of Tacoma v. Bridges, 25 Wash. 221, 65 Pac. 186. See, also, Taylor v. Montreal Harbor Commrs., 17 Rap. Jud. Que. C. S. 275. In Commissioners of Barber Co. v. Smith, 48 Kan. 331, 29 Pac. 565, the rule as to county officers is laid down as follows: "This court has always held that, before a private citizen can be allowed to maintain an action of this character, he must allege and show some interest, personal and peculiar to himself, that is not shared by or does not affect the general public; and it is not enough that his damages are greater than those sustained by the

restrain state officers from erecting a public building at a place other than that prescribed by law, where no special injury is shown and the burden of taxation is not increased;[47] nor to restrain a state grain inspector from employing deputies under an unconstitutional law, when this is not shown to cause any injury to the plaintiff.[48] As in the case of purely municipal corporations, however, the rules are not in harmony. In Pennsylvania, for instance, it is held that the governor may be enjoined from enforcing a law exempting a railroad from taxation and thus increasing the burden upon other tax-payers.[49]

§ 327. **No Relief When, in Effect, Against State.**—The eleventh amendment to the federal constitution denies to individuals the right to sue a state. Consequently, when a bill for an injunction against a public officer is in effect a suit against a state, and no statute authorizes such suit, relief will be denied. In determining whether the state is a party, the courts will look beyond the parties to the record and decide according to the real effect.[50] "Where it is manifest upon the face of the

general public, thus differing only in degree, but they must be different in kind.''

Under the New York statute, it is held that a tax-payer's suit cannot be maintained against a state officer: Hutchinson v. Skinner, 21 Misc. Rep. 729, 49 N. Y. Supp. 360.

47 Sherman v. Bellows, 24 Or. 553, 34 Pac. 549; State v. Lord, 28 Or. 498, 43 Pac. 471, 31 L. R. A. 473; State v. Pennoyer, 23 Or. 205, 37 Pac. 906, 41 Pac. 1104, 25 L. R. A. 862.

48 Birmingham v. Cheetham, 19 Wash 657, 54 Pac. 37.

49 Mott v. Pennsylvania R. Co., 30 Pa. St. (6 Casey) 9, 72 Am. Dec. 664. And apparently a tax-payer's suit against a state officer may be maintained in Illinois: Burke v. Snively, 208 Ill. 328, 70 N. E. 327.

50 See Manchester Fire Ins Co. v. Herriott, 91 Fed 711. A good illustration is found in suits to enjoin state officers from prosecuting violators of state statutes. The state is said to be the real party

record, that the defendants have no individual interest in the controversy, and that the relief sought against them is only in their official capacity as representatives of the state, which alone is to be affected by the judgment or decree, the question then arising whether the suit is not substantially a suit against the state, is one of jurisdiction."[51] "It is not enough that the state should have a mere interest in the vindication of her laws, or in their enforcement as affecting the public at large, or as they affect the rights of individuals or corporations, but it must be an interest of value to herself as a distinct entity,—of value in a material sense."[52] In case of contracts, moreover, the acts of the officers are wrongful only as they are considered to be the acts of the state. As individuals, the officers are not capable of committing a breach, for they are not parties to the contract.[53] The state, therefore, is clearly the real party in interest.

In accordance with these principles, it has been held that an injunction will not issue against the executive officer of a state in order to give relief to bondholders who claim that the state has not lived up to its agreement;[54] nor to restrain a state officer from carrying out a contract made in the name of the state.[55] But, on the other hand, where officers acting under an unconstitutional law will injure substantial property rights, an injunction will not be refused merely because

in interest· Union Trust Co v. Stearns, 119 Fed. 790; Arbuckle v. Blackburn, 113 Fed. 616, 51 C. C. A. 122.

51 Ex parte Ayers, 123 U. S. 443, 8 Sup. Ct. 164, 31 L. ed. 216.

52 McWhorter v. Pensacola & A. R. R. Co., 24 Fla. 417, 12 Am. St. Rep. 220, 3 South. 129, 2 L. R A. 508.

53 Ex parte Ayers, 123 U. S. 443, 8 Sup. Ct. 164, 31 L. ed. 216.

54 Louisiana v. Jumel, 107 U. S. 711, 2 Sup. Ct. 128, 27 L. ed. 448.

55 Peeples v. Byrd, 98 Ga. 688, 25 S. E. 677.

they are state officers;[56] and the same is true when they threaten to act in excess of authority.[57]

§ 328. **Injunctions Against Executive Officers.**—An injunction will not issue against an executive officer of the government, nor against one acting under him, to restrain the performance or execution of administrative acts and orders within the scope of his authority. This is based upon the principle which governs also the legal remedy of mandamus. It would be contrary to our theory of government for the judicial department to interfere with the reasonable discretion of the executive. Hence, courts of law and of equity refuse the remedies of mandamus and injunction when they will have the effect of controlling a reasonable discretion. Where no question of discretion is involved, both law and equity will interfere without hesitation. It is generally stated that mandamus may issue in a proper case to compel the performance of a ministerial act. The corresponding statement as to injunction is that it may issue in a proper case to restrain an act in excess of the officer's authority.

In accordance with these principles, it is held that an injunction will not issue to restrain the Secretary of the Interior or the Register of the Land Office from canceling entries for land, receiving and acting upon applications and making surveys.[58] Likewise, no injunc-

56 Scott v. Donald, 165 U. S. 107, 17 Sup. Ct. 262, 41 L. ed 648; Pabst Brewing Co v. Crenshaw, 120 Fed. 144 (state beer inspector restrained from interfering with interstate commerce under authority of state statute), Union Pac. R. Co. v. Alexander, 113 Fed. 347; Starr v. Chicago R. I. & P. Ry. Co., 110 Fed. 3; Cobb v. Clough, 83 Fed 604; President etc. of Yale College v. Sanger, 62 Fed. 177. And see Simpson v. Union Stockyards Co., 110 Fed. 799.

57 Metropolitan Life Ins. Co v. McNall, 81 Fed. 888.

58 Gaines v. Thompson, 74 U. S (7 Wall) 347, 19 L. ed 62; City of New Orleans v. Paine, 147 U. S. 261, 13 Sup. Ct. 303, 37 L. ed.

tion will issue against the execution of an authorized discretionary order of the Postmaster General in excluding certain matter from the mails.[59] The same principle applies to the executive officers of a state.[60]

On the other hand, where officers of the Interior Department are about to make a resurvey or to do other acts which under the circumstances do not rest in discretion, and some ground for equity jurisdiction appears, an injunction is proper.[61] Likewise, it is proper to enjoin the enforcement of an order of the Postmaster General excluding from the mails matter not authorized to be excluded;[62] and to restrain a state railroad commission from fixing railroad rates for interstate commerce, in excess of authority.[63]

§ 329. **Discretionary Acts.**—When a public officer is vested with discretion, an injunction will not issue to restrain acts coming within the discretionary power unless fraud or corruption is shown, or it is clear that

162; Litchfield v. Richards, 9 Wall. 577, 19 L. ed. 681; Kirwan v. Murphy, 189 U. S. 35, 23 Sup. Ct. 599, 47 L. ed. 698.

59 Public Clearing-House v. Coyne, 194 U. S. 497, 24 Sup. Ct. 789, 48 L. ed. 1092; Enterprise Sav. Assn. v. Zumstein, 67 Fed. 1000, 15 C. C. A. 153, 37 U. S. App. 71.

60 Frost v. Thomas, 26 Colo. 222, 77 Am. St Rep. 259, 56 Pac. 899; Coleman v. Glenn, 103 Ga. 458, 68 Am. St. Rep. 108, 30 S. E. 297; Mott v. Pennsylvania R. Co., 30 Pa. St. (6 Casey) 9, 92 Am. Dec. 664 See, also, Delaware Surety Co. v. Layton (Del. Ch.), 50 Atl. 378 As to the power of federal courts to enjoin the governor of a state, see Davis v. Gray, 16 Wall. 203, 21 L. ed. 447.

61 Caldwell v. Robinson, 59 Fed. 658, Noble v. Union River Logging Co, 147 U S. 165, 13 Sup. Ct. 271, 37 L. ed. 123; Smith v. Reynolds, 9 App. D. C 261.

62 American School of Magnetic Healing v. McAnnulty, 187 U. S. 94, 23 Sup. Ct. 33, 47 L. ed. 90.

63 Hanley v. Kansas City Southern R. Co, 187 U. S. 617, 23 Sup. Ct. 214, 47 L. ed. 333 And it will likewise issue to prevent other interference with interstate commerce by such a board: Southern Ry. Co. v Greensboro Ice & Coal Co., 134 Fed. 82.

the discretion has been abused. The distinction between discretionary and ministerial acts should be carefully noted, however, for if the act is of a ministerial nature it may be freely enjoined. This distinction has been explained in the preceding section.

According to the principle as stated, an injunction will not issue to restrain a railroad or arbitration commission from taking testimony as to rates and earnings;[64] nor to restrain commissioners appointed to appraise and sell Indian lands from carrying out their powers;[65] nor to regulate the discretion of canal commissioners as to the amount of water to be used,[66] nor of commissioners appointed to condemn rights of way as to the land to be taken,[67] nor of prison commissioners as to the letting of contracts.[68] Likewise, it will not be granted to restrain the exercise of a ferry franchise on the ground that the officers erred in judgment in granting it.[69]

Where, however, there is a clear abuse of discretion, the court may interfere.[70] Cases of this sort frequently arise when state commissions attempt to lower the rates of *quasi* public corporations. The officers are bound to act within reason, and in such a manner that their ac-

64 New Orleans City & L. R. Co. v. State Board of Arbitration, 47 La. Ann. 874, 17 South. 418; Higginson v. Chicago, B & I. R. Co., 102 Fed. 197, 42 C. C. A. 254. See, also, McChord v. Cincinnati etc. R. Co., 183 U. S. 483, 22 Sup. Ct. 165, 46 L. ed. 289.

65 Lane v. Anderson, 67 Fed. 563.

66 Cooper v. Williams, 4 Ohio (4 Ham.) 253, 22 Am. Dec. 745.

67 Pennsylvania R. Co. v. National Docks & N. J. J. C. Ry. Co., 56 Fed. 697.

68 Southern Min. Co. v. Lowe, 105 Ga. 352, 31 S. E 191.

69 Hudspeth v. Hall, 113 Ga. 4, 84 Am. St. Rep. 200, 38 S E. 358. See the following miscellaneous cases where relief was denied: Scofield v. Perkerson, 46 Ga. 350; Henkel v. Millard, 97 Md. 24, 54 Atl. 657; Union Transp. Co. v. Bassett, 118 Cal. 604, 50 Pac. 754.

70 In general, see Shanks v. Pearson, 66 Kan 168, 71 Pac. 252.

tion will not amount to confiscation. Therefore, when state commissioners fix rates which are so unreasonable that the property of the corporation is made of little value, or which are so low that expenses and dividends cannot be earned, courts of equity will interfere by injunction.[71] A private individual, however, cannot enjoin the enforcement of the rates on the ground that they discriminate against him.[72]

§ 330. **Suits by Officers Against Other Officers.**—When the state as plaintiff invokes the aid of a court of equity, it is not exempt from the rules applicable to ordinary suitors; that is, it must establish a case of equitable cognizance, and a right to the particular relief demanded.[73] In some jurisdictions, however, local or state officers are allowed injunctive relief in order to restrain inferior or other officers from failing to properly perform the duties of their offices.[74] And a county has been allowed an injunction to restrain a commissioner of the general land office from re-establishing its boundary.[75]

71 Smyth v. Ames, 169 U. S. 466, 18 Sup. Ct. 418, 42 L. ed. 819; Prout v. Starr, 188 U. S. 537, 23 Sup. Ct. 398, 47 L. ed. 584; Southern Pac. R. Co. v. Board of R. R. Commrs., 78 Fed. 236; Chicago & N. W. R. Co. v. Dey, 35 Fed. 866, 1 L. R. A. 744; Louisville & N. R. Co. v. Brown, 123 Fed. 946, Western Union Tel. Co v. Myatt, 98 Fed. 335; San Joaquin etc. Co. v. Stanislaus County, 90 Fed. 516, Cotting v. Kansas City Stockyards Co., 79 Fed. 679

72 Board of R. R. Commrs. v. Symns Grocer Co, 53 Kan. 207, 35 Pac. 217.

73 People v. Canal Board, 55 N. Y. 390; State v. Pennoyer, 23 Or. 205, 37 Pac. 906, 41 Pac. 1104, 25 L. R. A. 862; State v. Lord, 28 Or. 498, 43 Pac. 471, 31 L. R. A. 473.

74 Hornaday v. State, 62 Kan. 822, 62 Pac. 329; Catlin v. Christie, 15 Colo. App. 291, 63 Pac. 328.

75 Kaufman Co. v. McGaughey, 3 Tex. Civ. App. 655, 21 S. W. 261. An opposite result was reached in Commrs. of Chatham Co. v. Thorne, 117 N C. 211, 23 S. E. 184, on the ground that it was within the power of the legislature to change the boundary.

§ 331. **Elections.**—An injunction will not issue, as a general rule, for the purpose of restraining the holding of an election, or of directing or controlling the mode in which, or of determining the rules of law in pursuance of which, an election shall be held.[76] An election is a political matter, with which courts of equity have nothing to do. Moreover, the effect of interference in such matters might often result in the destruction of the government. This is especially so when the relief is sought to prevent the holding of an election. "The attempt to check the free expression of opinion—to forbid the peaceable assemblage of the people—to obstruct the freedom of elections—if successful, would result in the overthrow of all liberty regulated by law. The mere effort to assume such power is dangerous to the rights of the citizen. If the courts can dictate to the officers of the people that they shall not hold an election from fear of some imaginary wrong, then people and officers are entirely subservient to the courts, and the consequences are too fearful to contemplate."[77] Thus, an injunction will not issue to restrain

[76] Fletcher v. Tuttle, 151 Ill. 41, 42 Am. St. Rep. 220, 37 N. E. 683, 25 L. R. A. 143; Morgan v. Wetzel County Court, 53 W. Va. 372, 44 S. E. 182. Nor will equity interfere to control a political party in its management of a primary election: Winnett v. Adams (Neb.), 99 N. W. 681.

[77] Walton v. Develing, 61 Ill. 201. In some jurisdictions, however, these considerations are not controlling In Wisconsin, an injunction will issue to restrain the Secretary of State from calling an election when the apportionment act is illegal: State v. Cunningham, 81 Wis. 440, 51 N. W. 724, 15 L. R. A. 561; State v. Cunningham, 83 Wis. 90, 35 Am. St. Rep. 27, 53 N. W. 35, 17 L. R. A. 145. In England, under the Judicature Act, authorizing the issuance of injunctions to protect any right which could be asserted either at law or in equity, an injunction will issue to restrain an election to office: Richardson v Michby School Board, [1893] 3 Ch. 510; Aslatt v. Corporation of Southampton, 16 Ch. D. 143, North London Ry. Co. v. Great Northern Ry. Co., 11 Q B. D. 30. In the following cases injunctions were granted to restrain the calling of county seat elections: Solomon v.

the holding of an election although it is alleged that it is without authority of law,[78] or that the act authorizing it or providing for apportionment is unconstitutional.[79] And the mere fact that the cost of the election will have to be borne by the state and indirectly by the tax-payers, is no ground for an injunction at the relation of a tax-payer, for the injury is too trifling.[80]

§ 332. Same—Continued.—Likewise, an injunction will not be issued to forbid any of the steps in the proceedings.[81] Thus, it is not proper to restrain officers from returning a list of voters on the ground that it is illegal;[82] nor to restrain the county clerk from putting on the ballot the candidates of one faction under the party designation;[83] nor to compel election officers to

Fleming, 34 Neb. 40, 51 N. W. 304; Streissguth v. Geib, 67 Minn. 360, 69 N. W. 1097. For other instances of relief granted, see Cascaden v. City of Waterloo, 106 Iowa, 673, 77 N. W. 333; City of Macon v. Hughes, 110 Ga. 795, 36 S. E. 247; Layton v. City of Monroe, 23 South. 99, 50 La. Ann. 121.

78 Walton v. Develing, 61 Ill. 201; Darst v. People, 62 Ill. 306; Harris v. Schryock, 82 Ill. 119; Kerr v. Riddle (Tex. Civ. App.), 31 S. W. 328.

79 Fletcher v. Tuttle, 151 Ill. 41, 42 Am. St. Rep. 220, 37 N. E. 683, 25 L. R. A. 143; Fesler v. Brayton, 145 Ind. 71, 44 N. E. 37, 32 L. R. A. 578. But see *contra*, State v. Cunningham, 81 Wis. 440, 51 N. W. 724, 15 L. R. A. 561, State v. Cunningham, 83 Wis. 90, 35 Am. St Rep. 27, 53 N. W. 35, 17 L. R. A. 145; Gile v. Stegner (Minn.), 100 N. W 101.

80 State v. Thorson, 9 S. D. 149, 68 N. W. 202, 33 L. R. A. 582.

81 In general, see People v. Barfett, 203 Ill. 99, 96 Am. St Rep. 297, 67 N. E 742; Anthony v. Burrow, 129 Fed. 783

82 Hardesty v. Taft, 23 Md. 513, 87 Am. Dec. 584; Ex parte Lumsden, 41 S. C. 553, 19 S. E. 749.

83 State v. Johnson, 18 Mont. 556, 46 Pac. 440. See, also, Mayor etc. of Annapolis v. Gadd (Md), 57 Atl. 941. But it is held in Montana, following the Wisconsin cases, that an injunction will issue to restrain the county clerk from printing an unauthorized ticket on the ballot. Thus, an injunction has been awarded against printing names of candidates nominated by petition under a party

admit certain representatives to the polling places;[84] nor to prevent the publication of the result as required by law,[85] nor the canvassing of the vote,[86] nor the certification of the result to the governor,[87] nor the delivery of the sealed returns to the speaker of the lower house of the legislature.[88] And a Secretary of State will not be enjoined from publishing proposed amendments to the state constitution, although such amendments, if adopted, might be invalid.[89]

§ 333. **Title to Public Office.**—It is a principle of universal application that an injunction will not issue when its object is to try title to public office.[90] The reasons for this rule are that such cases involve political rights, with which equity has nothing to do, and that generally there is an adequate remedy at law. In case of contested elections this legal remedy is often of

designation: State v. Moran, 24 Mont. 433, 63 Pac. 390; State v. Reek, 18 Mont. 557, 46 Pac. 438; State v. Rotwitt, 18 Mont. 502, 46 Pac. 370; State v. Tooker, 18 Mont. 540, 46 Pac. 530, 34 L. R. A. 315; State v. Johnson, 18 Mont. 548, 46 Pac. 533; State v. Bailey, 18 Mont. 554, 46 Pac. 1116; State v. Fisher, 18 Mont. 560, 46 Pac. 1117.

84 Weaver v. Toney, 107 Ky. 419, 54 S. W. 732, 50 L. R. A. 105.

85 Robinson v. Wingate (Tex. Civ. App.), 80 S. W. 1067; Ex parte Mayes (Tex.), 44 S. W. 831; Ogburn v. Elmore (Ga.), 48 S. E. 702. But see *dictum* in Sweeney v. Webb (Tex. Civ. App.), 76 S. W. 766. Compare L. Epstein & Son v. Webb (Tex. Civ. App.), 75 S. W. 337.

86 Willeford v. State, 43 Ark. 63; Weil v. Calhoun, 25 Fed. 865; State v. Carlson (Neb.), 101 N. W. 1004; Mendenhall v. Denham, 35 Fla. 250, 17 South. 561.

87 Alderson v. Commissioners, 32 W. Va. 640, 25 Am. St. Rep. 840, 9 S. E. 868, 5 L. R. A. 334.

88 Fleming v. Guthrie, 32 W. Va. 1, 25 Am. St. Rep. 792, 9 S. E. 23, 3 L. R. A. 53; Smith v. Myers, 109 Ind. 1, 58 Am. Rep. 375, 9 N. E. 692.

89 People v. Mills, 30 Colo. 262, 70 Pac. 322.

90 In general, see Beebe v. Robinson, 52 Ala. 66; Moulton v. Reid, 54 Ala. 320.

statutory origin, but in most cases the relief by the common-law writ of *quo warranto* is ample.

It may be laid down as a general rule that a claimant out of possession will not be awarded an injunction against the party in possession of a public office.[91] In such a case the only question involved is the title to the office; and often the effect of an injunction would be to render an office vacant, to the injury of the public. Likewise, it will not be issued when both parties are out of possession;[92] nor when the suit is brought against the appointing body and in effect is for reinstatement.[93] And the same result is reached although the application for relief is made in the name of the state at the relation of the claimant.[94]

§ 334. **Same—Continued.**—For the same reasons an injunction will not issue at the suit of a member of the appointing body, to restrain a person alleged to have

91 Cochran v. McCleary, 22 Iowa, 75, Neeland v. State, 39 Kan. 154, 18 Pac 165; State v. Rost, 47 La. 53, 16 South. 776, Washington Co. Commrs v. Board of County School Commrs., 77 Md. 283, 26 Atl. 115, Arnold v. Henry, 155 Mo. 48, 78 Am St Rep 556, 55 S. W. 1089; People v. Draper, 24 Barb. 265; Patterson v. Hubbs, 65 N. C. 119, State v. Wolfenden, 74 N C 103; Harding v. Eichinger, 57 Ohio St. 371, 49 N. E. 306, Hagner v. Heyberger, 7 Watts & S. 104, 42 Am Dec. 220; Gilroy's Appeal, 100 Pa. St. 5; Kilpatrick v. Smith, 77 Va 347, Mullen v. City of Tacoma, 16 Wash. 82, 47 Pac. 215, Huels v. Hahn, 75 Wis. 468, 44 N. W. 507, State v Rice, 67 S. C. 236, 45 S. E. 153; Brower v. Kantner, 190 Pa. St. 182, 43 Atl. 7; McAllen v. Rhodes, 65 Tex. 348. But see Ehlinger v. Rankin, 9 Tex. Civ. App. 424, 29 S. W. 240.

92 State v. Rost, 47 La. Ann. 53, 16 South. 663; People v. District Court of Lake County, 29 Colo. 277, 93 Am. St. Rep. 61, 68 Pac. 224.

93 Callan v. Fire Dept. Commrs., 45 La. Ann 673, 12 South. 834; McNiece v. Sohmer, 29 Misc. Rep. 238, 61 N. Y. Supp. 193.

94 State v Herreid, 10 S. D. 16, 71 N. W 319, State v. Alexander, 107 Iowa, 177, 77 N. W 841, State v. Wolfenden, 74 N. C. 103; State v. Duffel, 32 La. Ann 649.

been illegally appointed;[95] nor at the suit of a tax-payer or elector;[96] nor at the suit of a local body or muncipal corporation.[97]

Again, it will not issue in aid of an election contest to restrain canvassing of the votes,[98] the issuance of a certificate of election,[99] nor to determine which party is entitled to the office.[100] Nor will it issue to restrain the issuance of a commission to a person alleged to be illegally appointed.[101] And the fact that an election authorizing the change of a township organization is illegal is not sufficient to warrant an injunction against the appointment of commissioners, for the remedy by *quo warranto* after the office is assumed will be adequate.[102]

§ 335. **Possession of Office Protected.**—While the title to public office will not be determined in an injunction proceeding the possession of a *de facto* officer will be protected against interference of an adverse claimant whose title is in dispute, until the latter shall establish

95 Goldsworthy v. Boyle, 175 Pa. St. 246, 34 Atl. 630; Updegraf v. Crans, 47 Pa. St. 103.

96 State v. Aloe, 152 Mo. 466, 54 S. W. 494; State v. Van Beek, 87 Iowa, 569, 43 Am. St. Rep. 397, 54 N. W. 525; Fahy v. Johnstone, 21 App. Div. 154, 47 N. Y. Supp. 402; Brumley v. Boyd, 28 Tex. Civ. App. 164, 66 S. W. 874.

97 State v. Withrow, 154 Mo. 397, 55 S. W. 460; District Tp v. Barrett, 47 Iowa, 110, District Tp. v. Myles, 109 Iowa, 541, 80 N. W. 544.

98 Ex parte Wimberley, 57 Miss. 437; Wilder v. Underwood, 60 Kan. 859, 57 Pac. 965.

99 Coleman v. Glenn, 103 Ga. 458, 68 Am. St. Rep. 108, 30 S E. 297; Ward v. Sweeney, 106 Wis. 44, 82 N. W. 169, People v. McClees, 20 Colo. 403, 38 Pac. 468, 26 L. R. A. 646.

100 Dickey v. Reed, 78 Ill. 261; Updegraf v. Crans, 47 Pa. St. 103.

101 Coleman v. Glenn, 103 Ga 458, 68 Am. St. Rep 108, 30 S. E. 297.

102 Fort v. Thompson, 49 Neb. 772, 69 N. W. 110.

his title at law.[103] In such a case the right to the office is not considered. "The welfare and good order of society and government require that those engaged in the discharge of public duties should not be disturbed by claimants whose right to discharge their functions is as yet uncertain. Equity will protect the possession of the incumbents from any unlawful intrusion. The public welfare requires that such protection should not be left to the totally inadequate remedy of an action for trespass."[104] But in order to warrant this relief it must appear that there has been some act or threat indicating an intent to interfere with possession. If this is not present the injunction will be refused, for only the title to office is involved.[105] For the same reason, a party in possession cannot enjoin the appointing power from naming his successor on the ground that the incumbent fears that the new appointee may interfere with his possession.[106] And in all cases the

103 Rhodes v. Driver, 69 Ark. 606, 86 Am. St. Rep. 215, 65 S. W. 106; State v. Superior Court of Snohomish County, 17 Wash. 12, 61 Am. St. Rep. 893, 48 Pac. 741; Appeal of Town Council (Pa.), 15 Atl. 730; Parsons v. Durand, 150 Ind. 203, 49 N. E. 1047; City of Huntington v. Cast, 149 Ind. 255, 48 N. E. 1025; Guillotte v. Poincy, 41 La. Ann 333, 6 South. 507, 5 L. R. A. 403; Poyntz v. Shackelford, 107 Ky. 546, 54 S. W. 855; Hopkins v. Swift, 100 Ky. 14, 37 S. W. 155; Brady v. Sweetland, 13 Kan. 41; Palmer v. Foley, 45 How. Pr. 110, Kerr v. Trego, 47 Pa. St. 292; Reemelin v. Mosby, 47 Ohio St. 570, 26 N. E. 717; Wheeler v. Fire Commrs., 46 La. Ann. 731, 15 South. 179; Stenglein v. Beach, 128 Mich. 440, 8 Detroit Leg. N. 721, 87 N. W. 449. But see Osgood v. Jones, 60 N. H. 543. In such an action the title to the office cannot be tried: Scott v. Sheehan, 145 Cal. 691, 79 Pac. 353.

104 City of Huntington v. Cast, 149 Ind. 255, 48 N. E. 1025.

105 Jones v. Commissioners of Granville, 77 N. C. 280; State v. Judge, 48 La. Ann. 1501, 21 South. 94.

106 Reemelin v. Mosby, 47 Ohio St. 570, 26 N. E. 717; Delahanty v. Warner, 75 Ill. 185, 20 Am. Rep. 237.

court should require the strongest showing before interfering.[107]

It has been held that while it is proper for the court to take cognizance of a case where the facts upon which the title to the office depends are disputed and uncertain, "it would seem anomalous for a court of equity to exercise its preventive jurisdiction in favor of one who, upon the undisputed facts had no right to retain possession of an office against one who, upon the equally undisputed facts, was entitled to it."[108]

§ 336. **Payment of Salaries.**—An injunction will not issue to restrain the payment of salary or fees to a *de facto* officer whose title is questioned.[109] "The public welfare demands that a public office be filled by some person; and if compensation is withheld from the incumbent pending litigation over his right thereto, much of the inducement to an efficient discharge of the duties of the position is withdrawn, and in many cases the ability to continue the discharge of such duties prevented. Equity, therefore, will not jeopardize the due performance of an important public trust in order merely to secure to one of the claimants the fees and emoluments pertaining to it, in the event he should finally succeed in establishing his claim."[110] And this rule prevails although it may be perfectly apparent that the incumbent is not legally entitled to the position.[111]

107 Goldman v. Gillespie, 43 La. Ann. 83, 8 South. 880; Ward v. Sweeney, 106 Wis. 44, 82 N. W. 169.

108 School District v. Waseca Co., 77 Minn. 167, 79 N. W. 668.

109 Greene v. Knox, 175 N. Y. 432, 67 N. E. 910; Tappan v. Gray, 9 Paige, 507; Stone v. Wetmore, 42 Ga. 601; McAllen v. Rhodes, 65 Tex. 348; Lawrence v. Leidigh, 58 Kan. 676, 50 Pac. 889; Burgess v. Davis, 138 Ill. 578, 28 N. E. 817. See, also, Colton v. Price, 50 Ala. 424.

110 Lawrence v. Leidigh, 58 Kan. 676, 50 Pac. 889.

111 Tappan v. Gray, 9 Paige, 507.

In case the claimant succeeds at law, he may recover from the incumbent the amount of the salary or fees collected; but the mere fact that the incumbent is insolvent and cannot therefore respond at law is not sufficient to warrant equitable relief.[112]

§ 337. **Removal of Officers.**—An officer in possession cannot, however, enjoin other officers from removing him.[113] The right to an office is said not to be a property right. An action to enjoin removal raises a political question as to the title to the office, for only by determining the right can the court decide the question. Hence this line of cases is distinguishable from

112 Lawrence v. Leidigh, 58 Kan. 676, 50 Pac. 889.

113 In re Sawyer, 124 U. S. 200, 8 Sup. Ct. 482, 31 L. ed. 402; White v Berry, 171 U. S. 366, 18 Sup. Ct. 917, 43 L. ed. 199; Page v. Moffett, 85 Fed. 38, Couper v. Smyth, 84 Fed. 757, Morgan v. Nunn, 84 Fed. 551; Dudley v. James, 83 Fed. 345; Carr v. Gordon, 82 Fed. 373; Taylor v. Kercheval, 82 Fed. 497; Palmer v. Board of Education, 47 App. Div. 547, 62 N. Y. Supp. 485; Muhler v. Hedekin, 119 Ind. 481, 20 N. E. 700, Heffran v. Hutchins, 160 Ill. 550, 52 Am. St. Rep. 353, 43 N. E. 709 (affirming 56 Ill. App. 581); Marshall v. Board of Managers, 201 Ill. 9, 66 N. E. 314; Cozart v. Fleming, 123 N. C. 547, 31 S. E. 822; Howe v. Dunlap, 12 Okla. 467, 72 Pac. 365, Riggins v. Thompson, 30 Tex. Civ. App. 242, 70 S. W. 578.

And it follows that a mandatory injunction will not issue to compel reinstatement McNiece v. Sohmer, 29 Misc. Rep. 238, 61 N. Y. Supp 193. It has been held that an injunction will not issue to restrain city officers from recognizing the new appointee: Howe v. Dunlap, 12 Okla. 467, 72 Pac. 365, 895.

There is a slight dissent from the rule of the text. In Armatage v. Fisher, 74 Hun, 167, 26 N. Y. Supp. 364 (affirming 4 Misc. Rep. 315, 24 N. Y. Supp. 650), it was held that a president of a city council might enjoin his colleagues from removing him without authority from his position as president; and in Stahlhut v. Bauer, 51 Neb. 64, 70 N. W. 496, it was held that an injunction will issue to restrain a city council from removing a mayor when it has absolutely no jurisdiction in the matter. And in Aslatt v. Corporation of Southampton, L. R 16 Ch D. 143, the relief was granted under the "just and convenient" section of the Judicature Act.

that in which the injunction is granted to prevent intrusion pending dispute. Moreover, the courts hesitate to interfere with the executive branch of the government in matters affecting the performance of its functions.

In recent years the federal courts have been called upon frequently to restrain the removal of officers whose tenure is supposed to be protected by civil service rules. But it has been held, with one or two exceptions, that such relief is not proper.[114] In some instances the decisions are rested on the ground that the regulations as to removal are mere rules of the executive, and that therefore there is no vested right to protect. But generally, the judges have come back to the fundamental principle, and have placed their decisions squarely upon the ground that equity has no jurisdiction over political matters.

Since the court will not enjoin the executive from removing an officer, it follows as a matter of course that

114 White v Berry, 171 U. S. 366, 18 Sup. Ct. 917, 43 L. ed. 199; Page v. Moffett, 85 Fed. 38; Couper v. Smyth, 84 Fed. 757; Morgan v. Nunn, 84 Fed. 551; Carr v. Gordon, 82 Fed. 373; Taylor v. Kercheval, 82 Fed. 497. In Priddie v. Thompson, 82 Fed. 186, and Butler v. White, 83 Fed. 578, the opposite conclusion was reached. Speaking of an officer as entitled to the protection of equity, Jackson, J., in the latter case said: "Has not a person who holds and is in possession of an office to which there is a fair salary attached, to remunerate him for his services, a right to the protection of the law to prevent an injury to him by the doubtful assertion of the rights of another as to his office? Has he not a material interest in the possession of the office and the salary attached to it? If he has such an interest in the office and emoluments, is there not a right which should be recognized and protected by the law in the employment of it? The fact that another party desires and seeks the office is evidence of its value to him, and, if it is valuable to the one seeking it, surely it must be to the one holding it." "Equity alone furnishes that remedy, and, if this remedy does not exist, then there is a case of an alleged wrong without a remedy."

it will not enjoin a trial on charges preferred.[115] And this rule will be adhered to although it is alleged that the body of triers is prejudiced and will abuse its discretion.[116]

Upon the same principle, the enforcement of a municipal ordinance will not be enjoined merely on the ground that it will deprive the complainant of his office.[117]

§ 338. **Action of De Facto Officers.**—An injunction will not issue to restrain *de facto* public officers from performing certain acts on the ground that they are powerless because not legally qualified.[118] Where, however, a legislative body, by the vote of persons not legally entitled, directs an officer to do an act which will be valid only if the authorization is proper, an injunction will issue against the performance. Thus, where a board of supervisors, by a vote in which a person not legally entitled to office had the deciding voice, ordered the clerk to submit the question of changing a county seat to the electors, an injunction was allowed.[119]

115 White v. Wahlenberg, 113 Iowa, 236, 84 N. W. 1026; Cox v. Moores, 55 Neb. 34, 75 N. W. 35.

116 Cox v. Moores, 55 Neb. 34, 75 N. W. 35.

117 Sheridan v. Colvin, 78 Ill. 237.

118 Graeff v. Felix, 200 Pa. St. 137, 49 Atl. 758; Hardesty v. Taft, 23 Md. 513, 87 Am. Dec. 584.

119 Williams v. Boynton, 147 N. Y. 426, 42 N. E. 184; Buck v. Fitzgerald, 21 Mont. 482, 54 Pac. 942.

CHAPTER XVIII.

INJUNCTIONS AGAINST MUNICIPAL CORPORATIONS AND THEIR OFFICERS.

ANALYSIS.

§ 339. **Limitations on the Exercise of the Remedy—Injunctions Against Legislative Acts; Cases Examined.**[1]—"Has equity the power to enjoin the passage of ordinances,

1 The opinion of Magruder, J., in Stevens v. St. Mary's Training School, 144 Ill. 336, 36 Am. St. Rep. 438, 32 N E. 962, 18 L. R. A. 832, 36 Cent. L. J. 275, 27 Am. Law Rev. 618, contains by far

by-laws, resolutions, and orders by municipal corporations, or is its power confined to the issuance of injunctions against the enforcement and execution of such ordinances, by-laws, resolutions, and orders, after the same have been passed? . . . . There are cases which hold, or seem to hold, that where a municipal corporation is about to pass a resolution or ordinance which is void, as being *ultra vires,* a court of chancery will enjoin it from so doing.[2] In none of the cases [just] cited, except the first four, was the question now under consideration expressly passed upon, but the facts stated in the opinions seem to warrant the conclusion that injunctions were sustained against the corporate action of the municipalities, as distinguished from the action of agents or officers proceeding under their orders. In the New York cases it was held that a court of chancery could enjoin the board of aldermen of a city from passing an ordinance to construct a railway in one of the streets; that municipal corporations are creatures of limited powers in the appropriation of the

the most thorough examination of this question on the authorities, that has come to the present writer's attention; I have, therefore, made it the basis of this and the two following sections.

2 "Among such cases may be mentioned the following: Davis v. Mayor etc., 1 Duer (N. Y.), 451; People v. Sturtevant, 9 N Y. 263, 59 Am. Dec. 536; Davis v. Mayor, 14 N. Y. 506, 67 Am. Dec. 186, Spring Valley Waterworks v. Bartlett, 16 Fed. 615; Town of Jacksonport v. Watson, 33 Ark. 704; State v. Commissioners, 39 Ohio St. 58; Page v Allen, 58 Pa. St. 338, 98 Am. Dec. 272; Follmer v Nuckolls Co, 6 Neb. 204; Peter v. Prettyman, 62 Md. 566; Patton v. Stephens, 14 Bush, 324; Board of Education v. Arnold, 112 Ill. 11; Spilman v. City of Parkersburg, 35 W. Va. 605, 14 S. E. 279; City of Valparaiso v. Gardner, 97 Ind. 1, 49 Am. Rep. 416; City of Springfield v. Edwards, 84 Ill. 626; Howell v. City of Peoria, 90 Ill. 104." See, also, People v. Dwyer, 90 N. Y. 402, holding that "whether the act enjoined was or was not legislative or discretionary, and if so, whether other facts still justified the interposition of equity, were proper subjects for the consideration of the trial court whose error, if any, could only be corrected by appeal."

funds of the people; that when they attempt to appropriate such funds to purposes not authorized by their charters or by positive law, whether it be done by resolution, ordinance, or under the form of legislation, their acts are void and that, while courts will not attempt to control their discretion, yet if, under pretence of exercising such discretion, they threaten or are about to do what amounts to a gross abuse of power, to the injury and in fraud of the rights of individuals and the public, the courts will interfere to prevent the threatened injury. But later decisions in New York, some of which are referred to hereafter, have taken a different view, refusing to follow the earlier cases above mentioned, as going too far in the direction of subjecting the legislative and political powers of municipal bodies to the control of the courts.[3] In Spring Valley Waterworks v. Bartlett, *supra* [in note 2], an injunction against the mayor and supervisors of San Francisco, restraining them from passing an ordinance to fix the price of water furnished to the city, was sustained, over the objection that the defendants were a legislative body, endowed with legislative powers, to be exercised with absolute discretion; and it was held that the board of supervisors of a municipal corporation will be enjoined from passing an ordinance which is not within the scope of their powers, when its passage will work an irreparable injury. The Bartlett case, however, seems to have been overruled by the later case of Alpers v. San Francisco, *supra* [in note 3].[4] The last

3 "Alpers v. San Francisco, 12 Saw. 631, 32 Fed. 503."

4 It is hardly accurate to say that the Bartlett case was overruled by the Alpers case. Sawyer, J., who delivered the opinion in the Bartlett case, concurred in Mr Justice Field's opinion delivered in the Alpers case, with the understanding that the decision in the prior case was not thereby overruled. "I am not prepared to say," remarks Judge Sawyer (32 Fed. 510), "that the court can, in no in-

four cases above cited [in note 2] . . . . are cases where cities were enjoined from incurring indebtedness in excess of the constitutional limit, or from entering into contracts which would involve such excess of indebtedness. But in these cases the point to which attention was more especially directed was the meaning of the word 'indebtedness,' and what constitutes a 'debt' within the meaning of the constitution; and it is not altogether clear that 'incurring indebtedness' does not refer as well to the enforcement as to the passage of corporate resolutions.

"A large number of the decisions which uphold the right of equity to interfere with the action of municipal corporations when such action is in excess of their legal powers will be found, on examination, to be based upon facts which show that the injunctions were issued against the officers or agents attempting to execute or enforce corporate resolutions, ordinances, by-laws, or orders."[5] . . . .

stance, or under no circumstances, enjoin the legislative department of a municipal corporation from passing an ordinance, which is wholly without its constitutional, or lawful power to enact. . . . . I do not understand, that the limitation in the opinion of the circuit justice is broader in its scope, than the principle herein stated." "In what we have said of the want of authority in courts of equity over the action of a municipal corporation," says Mr. Justice Field (32 Fed. 507), "we confine ourselves strictly to such action as is purely legislative, upon a matter which is, by its charter or law, made subject to its legislative discretion."

5 Citing New London v. Brainard, 22 Conn. 553; Webster v. Town of Harwinton, 32 Conn. 131; The Liberty Bell, 23 Fed. 843; Harney v. Indianapolis etc. Railroad Co., 32 Ind. 244; Davenport v. Kleinschmidt, 6 Mont. 502, 13 Pac. 249; Willard v. Comstock, 58 Wis. 565, 46 Am. Rep. 657, 17 N. W. 401; Lynch v. Eastern Ry. Co., 57 Wis. 430, 15 N. W. 743, 825; Place v. City of Providence, 12 R. I. 1; Austin v. Coggeshall, 12 R. I. 329, 34 Am. Rep. 648; Sherman v. Carr, 8 R. I. 431; Newmeyer v. Missouri etc. Ry. Co., 52 Mo. 81, 14 Am. Rep. 394; Osterhout v. Hyland, 27 Hun, 167; Mayor etc. of Baltimore v. Gill, 31 Md. 375, Merrill v. Plainfield, 45 N. H. 126; Hospers v. Wyatt, 63 Iowa,

§ 340. Same; Injunction Generally Refused.—"But we are not limited, in the investigation of this subject, to an examination of the facts of the cases which, while sustaining the general power of equity to restrain the action of municipal bodies, do not make any special reference to the mode of exercising such power. There are many decisions which hold, in express and definite terms, that 'the courts will not enjoin the passage of unauthorized ordinances, and will ordinarily act only when steps are taken to make them available.'[6] . . . . The weight of authority, and the tendency of the more recent decisions, are in favor of the position, that the restraining power of the courts should be directed against the enforcement, rather than the passage, of unauthorized orders and resolutions or ordinances by municipal corporations.[7] In Alpers v. San Francisco,

264, 19 N. W. 204; Roberts v. Mayor etc. of New York, 5 Abb. Pr. 41, Schumm v. Seymour, 24 N. J. Eq. 143; List v. Wheeling, 7 W. Va 501, Rutz v. Calhoun, 100 Ill. 392, McCord v. Pike, 121 Ill. 288, 2 Am. St. Rep. 85, 12 N. E. 259; English v. Smock, 34 Ind. 115, 7 Am. Rep. 215, City of Madison v. Smith, 83 Ind. 502; Sackett v. City of New Albany, 88 Ind. 473, 45 Am. Rep. 467; Wright v. Bishop, 88 Ill. 302, Sherlock v. Village of Winnetka, 59 Ill. 389; Crampton v. Zabriskie, 101 U. S. 601, 25 L ed. 1070. The learned justice then proceeded to examine in some detail the facts in the leading case of Crampton v. Zabriskie, *supra*, in Sherlock v. Village of Winnetka, and in Colton v. Hanchett, 13 Ill. 615, Perry v. Kinnear, 42 Ill. 160, Beauchamp v. Kankakee Co, 45 Ill. 274, and Carter v. City of Chicago, 57 Ill. 283, and to show that in each case the injunction was directed against the enforcement of, or acts done in pursuance of, the illegal legislation, not against its passage or enactment.

6 1 Dill. Mun. Corp., 4th ed., § 308, note on page 387.

7 "To this effect are the following authorities: Des Moines Gas Co. v. City of Des Moines, 44 Iowa, 505, 24 Am. Rep. 756; Linden v Case, 46 Cal. 171; Merriam v. Board of Supervisors, 72 Cal. 517, 14 Pac. 137; City of Chicago v. Evans, 24 Ill. 52; Whitney v. Mayor etc, 28 Barb. 233; People v. Mayor, 32 Barb. 35; People v. Mayor, 9 Abb. Pr. 253; Cincinnati etc. R. R Co. v. Smith, 29 Ohio St. 291, Harrison v. City of New Orleans, 33 La. Ann. 222, 39 Am. Rep. 272; Alpers v.

supra [in note 3], Mr. Justice Field, who wrote the opinion in Crampton v. Zabriskie, *supra* [in note 16,

San Francisco, 12 Saw. 631, 32 Fed. 503; 2 High, Inj. (3d ed.), sec. 1243.'' See, in addition, the following cases: New Orleans Waterworks Co. v. City of New Orleans, 164 U. S. 471, 17 Sup. Ct. 161, 41 L. ed 518; Murphy v. East Portland, 42 Fed. 308; Lewis v. Denver City Waterworks Co., 19 Colo. 236, 41 Am. St. Rep. 248, 34 Pac. 993; Belington & N. R. Co. v. Town of Alston, 54 W. Va. 597, 46 S. E. 612 (no relief against repeal of order granting permission to use streets), State v. Sup. Ct. of Milwaukee Co., 105 Wis. 651, 81 N. W 1086, 48 L. R. A. 819; Barto v. Board of Supervisors, 135 Cal. 494, 67 Pac. 758; Dailey v. Nassau County R. Co., 65 N. Y. Supp. 396, 52 App. Div. 272; McBride v. Newlin, 129 Cal. 36, 61 Pac. 577 (board acting in a *judicial* capacity, in allowing a claim, not enjoined); Roby v. City of Chicago (Ill), 74 N. E. 768 (ordinance granting franchise to street railway); Glide v. Superior Court (Cal.), 81 Pac. 225 (ordinance relating to formation of reclamation district).

The importance of the subject may justify some further quotation from well-considered recent cases ''It is a general principle in the governmental system of this country that the judicial department has no direct control over the legislative department. . . . The same principle, with perhaps some exceptions, or seeming exceptions, extends to the local legislative bodies of municipal corporations. A court of equity cannot properly interpose any obstacle to the exercise of their legislative discretion upon a subject within the scope of their delegated powers. A municipal ordinance passed in pursuance of valid authority emanating from the state legislature has the same force and effect, within proper limits, as if passed by the legislature itself. . . . It is true, the municipal legislative body may adopt an illegal ordinance So the state legislature may enact an unconstitutional statute. The remedy is the same in either case. By proper and timely application to the courts the enforcement of the unconstitutional statute, as well as the enforcement of the illegal ordinance, may be restrained or corrected. In such case, however, the judicial process is executed against some ministerial or administrative officer, or against some individual or corporation, and thus all substantial injury is averted without direct interference with legislative action or discretion.'' Per Elliott, J., in Lewis v. Denver City Waterworks Co, 19 Colo 236, 41 Am. St Rep. 248, 74 Pac. 993.

Of course, an injunction will be denied when the proposed ordinance is merely inexpedient: Wright v People, 31 Colo. 461, 73 Pac. 869; and also where *infra vires*, but consequences may be injurious: Rico v. Snider, 134 Fed. 953.

§ 344, and note 5, § 339], says: 'If by either body—the legislature or the board of supervisors—an unconstitutional act be passed, its enforcement may be arrested. The parties seeking to execute the invalid act can be reached by the courts, while the legislative body of the state or of the municipality, in the exercise of its legislative discretion, is beyond their jurisdiction. The fact that in either case the legislative action threatened may be in disregard of constitutional restraint, and impair the obligation of a contract . . . . does not affect the question. It is legislative discretion which is exercised, and that discretion, whether rightfully or wrongfully exercised, is not subject to interference by the judiciary. . . . . The principle that the exercise of legislative power by a municipal body is beyond control is too important, in our institutions, to be weakened by occasional decisions in disregard of it.' In Des Moines Gas Co. v. City of Des Moines, *supra* [in note 7], where the city of Des Moines had chartered a gas company, with certain exclusive privileges, and attempted by a subsequent ordinance to repeal said charter, and grant the same privileges to another company, it was sought to enjoin the passage of the repealing ordinance on the ground that it would be a violation of the contract created by the charter, and therefore unconstitutional, but it was held that the court had no power to issue the injunction, under the circumstances; and it was there said: 'The general assembly is a co-ordinate branch of the state government, and so is the law-making power of public municipal corporations, within the prescribed limits. It is no more competent for the judiciary to interfere with the legislative acts of the one than the other. But the unconstitutional acts of either may be annulled. Certainly, the passage of an unconstitutional law by the general assembly could not be enjoined. If so, under the pretense that any proposed law was of that character, the judiciary could arrest the wheels of legislation. . . . . After its passage the judiciary may declare the law unconstitutional. But previous to that time judicial powers cannot be invoked. . . . . A void law is no law, and this, without doubt, is true as to an ordinance. . . . . While it is not the province of the judiciary to interfere and arrest the passage of the ordinance, yet the doors are open for the purpose of testing its legality.' "

§ 341. Same; Exceptions to the General Rule.—"There may be instances when this restriction upon the power of the courts will sometimes be disregarded, as where municipal corporations are exercising mere business or ministerial, rather than legislative, powers,[8] or are wrongfully disposing of property held by them as trustees for the public,[9] or are attempting to act upon mat-

8 Citing City of Valparaiso v. Gardner, 97 Ind. 1, 49 Am. Rep. 416; Dill Mun. Corp (4th ed.), §§ 473, 474, 927, 1048. See, also, Board of Commissioners of Henry County v. Gillies, 138 Ind. 667, 38 N E. 40 (letting contract a ministerial act).

9 Citing Milhau v. Sharp, 15 Barb. 193; Sherlock v. Village of Winnetka, 59 Ill. 389. See, especially, Roberts v. City of Louisville, 92 Ky. 95, 36 Am. St. Rep. 449, note, 17 S. W. 216, where an injunction was sustained against a city and its officials, at the suit of a tax-payer, to prevent the passage of an ordinance by the city council, authorizing the mayor to convey certain real property acquired and held by the city under an act of the legislature. The court says in part: "A municipal corporation is created for a double purpose, and consequently has a dual character,—one governmental or public, the other private or proprietary. . . . . A municipal corporation, when holding, in its private or proprietary character, property or funds in trust for tax-payers and inhabitants within its limits, occupies towards them a relation like that of a purely private corporation to its cestuis que trustent, who are its shareholders. . . . . In our opinion, the general proposition, a court of equity may not enjoin passage of a municipal ordinance, must be confined in its application to subjects over which the corporation, in its governmental or public character, has discre-

ters not, by their charters or by the law, subject to their jurisdiction,[10] or when it appears that the mere voting on, and formal passage of, a resolution or ordinance, will instantly, without any action or attempt to enforce any right or privilege under it, effect an irremediable private injury."[11] It can hardly be claimed, however, that the foregoing exceptions have met with universal recognition.

tionary authority; and, if it be conceded taxable inhabitants have a right to resort to equity at all to restrain a municipal corporation and its officers from making an illegal or wrongful disposition of public property, whereby the plaintiffs will be injuriously affected, it reasonably follows the power exists to enjoin passage of the ordinance authorizing the act whenever irreparable injury will be done to the plaintiffs, and they have no adequate remedy at law. . . . . The plain legal duty is imposed upon the general council to hold, control, and manage the wharf property for use of the public, which cannot be evaded by transfer of it, or otherwise," etc. See, also, People v. Dwyer, 90 N. Y. 402.

10 Citing Alpers v. San Francisco, 12 Saw. 631, 32 Fed. 503. See, also, Wabaska Electric Co. v City of Wymore, 60 Neb. 199, 82 N. W. 626 (the injunction should be directed to the mayor and city council, and not to the city, since in attempting to legislate upon matters beyond its jurisdiction the governing body of a city does not represent the city, and does not act as its agent, nor by color of its authority), International Trading Stamp Co. v. City of Memphis, 101 Tenn 181, 47 S. W. 136. In Poppleton v. Moores, 62 Neb. 851, 88 N. W. 128, it was held that "where the proposed action on the city's part involves the entering into, or, rather, continuing in, contractual relations materially affecting the interests of citizens, and is an extension of a franchise not only unauthorized, but forbidden, by the city charter, it would seem to warrant the trial court's interposing by injunction," citing People v. Sturtevant, 9 N. Y. 263, 59 Am. Dec. 536. But the court is without jurisdiction to enjoin the passage of an ordinance granting a franchise to a street railway, when the power of granting such franchise is, by statute, confided to the discretion of the governing body of the city: State v. Superior Court of Milwaukee County, 105 Wis. 651, 81 N. W. 1046, 48 L. R. A. 819.

11 Citing Whitney v. Mayor etc., 28 Barb. 233 See, also, the *dictum* in Lewis v. Denver City Waterworks Co., 10 Colo. 236, 41 Am. St Rep. 248, 34 Pac. 993, conceding an exception to the doctrine of non-interference, "if it should be made to appear that the legislative

§ 342. **Second Limitation; Acts Within Discretionary Powers not Interfered with.**—A second limitation is found in the well-settled principle that where municipal authorities are acting within their well-recognized powers, or are exercising a discretionary power, a court of equity has no jurisdiction to interfere, unless their action is tainted with fraud, or the power or discretion is being manifestly abused to the oppression of the citizen.[12] "The court will not interfere to see whether they

body of a municipality was about to pass some ordinance, resolution, or order, and that its mere passage would immediately occasion or be immediately followed by, some irreparable loss or injury beyond the power of redress by subsequent judicial proceedings, a court of equity might, perhaps, extend its strong arm to prevent such loss or injury,'' citing Spring Valley Water Co. v. Bartlett, 16 Fed. 615, 8 Saw. 555. In International Trading Stamp Co. v. City of Memphis, 101 Tenn. 181, 47 S. W. 136, injunction was allowed before the passage of an illegal ordinance taxing the use of trading stamps, because after its passage a multiplicity of suits would be necessary.

12 McCarmel v. Shaw, 155 Ill. 37, 46 Am. St. Rep. 311, 39 N. E. 584, 27 L. R. A. 580; Fitzgerald v. Harms, 92 Ill. 372, Brush v. City of Carbondale, 78 Ill. 76; Andrews v. Board of Supervisors, 70 Ill. 65, Mutual Electric Light Co. v. Ashworth, 118 Cal 1, 50 Pac. 10; Dailey v. City of New Haven, 60 Conn 314, 22 Atl. 945, 14 L. R A. 69 (no injunction against a city refusing to accept a certain trust); Whitney v City of New Haven, 58 Conn. 450, 20 Atl. 666 (demolition of public building not enjoined), Mayor v. Camak, 75 Ga. 429 (sale of stock owned by city not enjoined); Downing v. Ross, 1 App. D. C. 251 (letting contracts for public improvements); Board of Commissioners of Perry County v. Gardner, 155 Ind. 165, 57 N. E. 908, Soden v. City of Emporia, 7 Kan. App. 583, 52 Pac 461 (manner of constructing sewerage system is within discretionary power); Sullivan v. Phillips, 110 Ind. 320, 11 N E. 300 (same), Trustees of Hazelgreen v. McNabb, 23 Ky. Law Rep. 811, 64 S. W 431 (necessity of street improvements is a question of discretion); Kelly v. Mayor of Baltimore, 53 Md 134 (discretion in awarding contract); Glasgow v. City of St. Louis, 107 Mo. 198, 17 S. W 743 (expediency of vacating a street is a question of discretion); Atkinson v. Wykoff, 58 Mo. App. 86 (same); Lane v. Morrill, 51 N. H. 422, Morgan v. Binghampton, 102 N. Y. 500, 7 N. E. 424 (construction of sewer); Black v. Commissioners of Buncombe County, 129 N. C. 121, 39 S E. 818 (discretion in issuing bonds); Delaware County's Appeal, 119 Pa. St. 159, 13

are acting wisely or judiciously."[13] "Where legislative power is conferred upon [an incorporated city] by the state, it is necessary that a degree of freedom should be allowed in its exercise; otherwise, the city would be so hampered in the government of its people as would defeat the very ends of its incorporation. Hence it is that the state courts will never interfere with the free exercise of such rights as are left to the discretion of a corporate authority, unless such authority should go beyond the scope of power delegated, or unless the discretion given should be abused by an arbitrary exercise thereof, and by a plain and unwarranted violation of private rights."[14]

§ 343. No Injunction to Test the Validity of Municipal Organization.—It is a well-established doctrine that *quo warranto,* and not injunction, is the proper remedy to

Atl. 62; Linden Land Co. v. Milwaukee Electric Ry. & Lighting Co., 117 Wis. 493, 83 N. W. 851 (granting of franchise); Kendall v. Frey, 74 Wis 26, 17 Am. St. Rep. 118, 42 N. W. 466 (suitableness of site for public building). But gross abuse of discretion, as in the purchase for $28,000 of waterworks worth only $10,000, and inadequate and unsuited to the purpose, may be enjoined at the suit of a taxpayer. Avery v. Job, 25 Or. 512, 36 Pac. 293. See People v. Dwyer, 90 N. Y. 402.

13 Western Union Tel. Co. v. City of New York, 38 Fed. 552, 3 L R. A. 449.

14 Burckhardt v. City of Atlanta, 103 Ga. 302, 30 S. E. 32, *per* Lewis, J. (question of necessity of repairs to street). In a leading English case Lord Chancellor Cottenham said, speaking of acts of poor-law commissioners: "The court will not interfere to see whether any alteration or regulation which they may direct is good or bad, but, if they are departing from that power which the law has vested in them, if they are assuming to themselves a power over property which the law does not give them, this court no longer considers them as acting under the authority of their commission, but treats them, whether they be a corporation or individuals, merely as persons dealing with property without legal authority": Frewin v. Lewis, 4 Mylne & C 254. See, also, Lord Auckland v. Westminster Board, L. R 7 Ch. 597.

inquire whether a municipal corporation was legally created, as well as to oust persons exercising the privileges and powers of corporate officers when the municipal corporation has no legal existence.[15]

§ 344. **Tax-payers' Suits; General Principle.**—The prevailing doctrine as to equitable relief against the abuse of power by officers of municipal corporations was formulated in an often-quoted opinion of the supreme court of the United States, speaking by Mr. Justice Field: "Of the right of resident tax-payers to invoke the interposition of a court of equity to prevent an illegal disposition of the moneys of the county [or other municipality], or the illegal creation of a debt which they, in common with other property-holders of the county, may otherwise be compelled to pay, there is at this day no serious question. The right has been recognized by the state courts in numerous cases; and from the nature of the powers exercised by municipal corporations, the great danger of their abuse, and the necessity of prompt action to prevent irremediable injuries, it would seem eminently proper for courts of equity to interfere, upon the application of the tax-payers of a county, to prevent the consummation of a wrong, when the officers of these corporations assume, in excess of their powers, to create burdens upon property-holders. Certainly, in the absence of legislation restricting the right to interfere in such cases to public officers of the state or county, there would seem to be no substantial reason why a bill

15 Osborn v. Village of Oakland, 49 Neb. 340, 68 N. W. 506, and cases cited (no injunction to prevent the election of officers to manage the affairs of the municipality on the ground that it has no corporate existence); MacDonald v. Rehrer, 22 Fla. 198, and cases cited; People v. Clark, 70 N. Y. 518, Hughes v. Dobbs, 84 Tex. 502, 19 S. W. 684. As to injunctions relating to municipal elections and the title to municipal offices, see *ante*, §§ 331-338.

by or on behalf of individual tax-payers should not be entertained to prevent the misuse of corporate power. The courts may be safely trusted to prevent the abuse of their process in such cases."[16]

16 Crampton v. Zabriskie (1879), 101 U. S. 601, 25 L. ed. 1070. Of innumerable cases affirming the doctrine, the following may be consulted with advantage for their statement of the doctrine and its reasons:

Alabama.—New Orleans, M. & C. R. R. Co. v. Dunn, 51 Ala. 128 ("the remedy is simple, expeditious, and preventive of the abuse of corporate powers").

Arkansas.—Town of Jacksonport v. Watson, 33 Ark. 704; Russell v. Tate, 52 Ark. 541, 20 Am. St. Rep. 193, 13 S. W. 130, 7 L. R. A. 180.

California.—Winn v. Shaw, 87 Cal. 631, 636, 25 Pac. 968, distinguishing earlier cases; Bradford v. City and County of San Francisco, 112 Cal. 537, 44 Pac. 912.

Colorado.—McIntyre v. Board of Commissioners of El Paso County, 15 Colo. App. 78, 61 Pac. 237.

Connecticut.—Scofield v. Eighth School District, 27 Conn. 499.

Florida.—Chamberlain v. City of Tampa, 40 Fla. 74, 23 South. 572.

Georgia.—City of Macon v. Hughes, 110 Ga. 795, 36 S. E. 247.

Illinois.—The Illinois reports abound in well considered cases applying the general principle of the text. The rule is thus formulated: "A tax-payer of a city has a right to enjoin any intended misappropriation of public money by the council or officers of the city, or payment of such money on an illegal contract or without authority of law, or the execution of such contracts, or the incurring of illegal indebtedness." See Holden v. City of Alton, 179 Ill. 318, 53 N. E. 556, and cases cited; Adams v. Brenan, 177 Ill. 194, 69 Am. St. Rep 222, 52 N. E. 314, 42 L. R. A. 418, and cases cited, City of Chicago v. Nichols, 177 Ill. 97, 52 N. E. 359; Stevens v. St. Mary's Training School, 144 Ill. 336, 36 Am. St. Rep. 438, 32 N. E 962, 18 L. R. A. 832, 36 Cent. L. J. 275, 27 Am. Law Rev. 618; McCord v. Pike, 121 Ill. 288, 2 Am. St. Rep. 85, 12 N E. 259, and cases in monographic note; Wright v. Bishop, 88 Ill. 302, City of Springfield v. Edwards, 84 Ill. 626; Sherlock v. Village of Winnetka, 59 Ill. 389, 68 Ill. 530; Perry v. Kinnear, 42 Ill. 160; Colton v. Hanchett, 13 Ill. 615; Scott v. Allen, 53 Ill. App. 341; Gorman v. Tidholm, 94 Ill. App. 371.

Indiana.—Harney v. Indianapolis etc. R. Co., 32 Ind. 244; English v. Smock, 34 Ind. 115, 7 Am. Rep. 215; Board of Commissioners of Henry County v. Gillies, 138 Ind. 667, 38 N. E. 40.

Iowa.—Hospers v. Wyatt, 63 Iowa, 264, 19 N. W. 204; Anderson v. Orient Fire Ins Co., 88 Iowa, 579, 55 N. W. 348; Hanson v. Hunter etc. Co., 86 Iowa, 722, 48 N. W. 1005, 53 N. W. 84; Snyder v. Foster, 77 Iowa, 638, 42 N. W. 506; Brockman v. City of Creston, 79 Iowa, 587, 44 N. W. 822.

Kentucky.—Patton v. Stephens, 14 Bush, 324; Roberts v. City of Louisville, 92 Ky. 95, 36 Am. St. Rep 449, 17 S. W. 216.

Louisiana —State v. City of New Orleans, 50 La Ann. 880, 24 South. 666.

Maryland.—Mayor etc. of Baltimore v Gill, 31 Md. 375; Peter v. Prettyman, 62 Md. 566; Mayor of Baltimore v. Keyser, 72 Md. 107, 19 Atl. 706.

Michigan —Savidge v. Village of Spring Lake, 112 Mich. 91, 70 N. W. 425; Black v. Common Council of City of Detroit, 119 Mich. 571, 78 N. W. 660; Curtenius v. Hoyt, 37 Mich. 583.

Minnesota.—Hodgman v. Chicago & St. P. R. Co, 20 Minn. 48, 20 Gil. 36 (the tax-payer's "damages" are *special*, affecting his private property and private rights); Sinclair v. Commissioners of Winona County, 23 Minn. 404, 23 Am. Rep. 694 (tax-payer has a "special interest distinct from the public"); Flynn v. Little Falls E. & W. Co., 74 Minn. 180, 77 N. W. 38, 78 N. W. 106, Grannis v. Board of Commissioners of Blue Earth County, 81 Minn. 55, 83 N. W. 495.

Missouri —Newmeyer v. Missouri & M. R. Co., 52 Mo. 81, 14 Am. Rep. 394; Wagner v. Meetz 69 Mo. 151

Montana.—Davenport v. Kleinschmidt, 6 Mont. 502, 13 Pac. 249.

Nebraska.—Tukey v. City of Omaha, 54 Neb. 370, 69 Am. St Rep. 711, 74 N. W. 613, Ackerman v. Thummel, 40 Neb. 95, 58 N. W. 738; City of South Omaha v. Tax-payers' League, 42 Neb. 671, 60 N. W. 957.

New Hampshire.—Blood v. Manchester Elect. Lt. Co., 68 N. H. 340, 39 Atl. 335. See Brown v. Reding, 50 N. H. 336.

North Carolina —Vaughn v. Board of Commissioners, 118 N. C. 636, 24 S. E. 425.

North Dakota.—Roberts v. City of Fargo, 10 N. D. 230, 86 N. W. 726.

Ohio —Hays v. Jones, 27 Ohio St. 218.

Oregon —Brownfield v. Houser, 30 Or. 534, 49 Pac 843.

Pennsylvania.—Page v. Allen, 58 Pa. St. 338, 98 Am. Dec. 272.

Rhode Island —Ecroyd v. Coggeshall, 21 R. I. 1, 71 Am. St. Rep. 241, 41 Atl. 260.

South Carolina —Mauldin v. City Council of Greenville, 33 S. C. 1, 11 S. E. 434, 8 L. R. A. 291.

South Dakota.—Graves v. Jasper School Township, 2 S. D 414, 50 N. W. 904.

Texas.—Wood v. City of Victoria, 18 Tex. Civ App 573, 46 S W. 284 (no injunction against *ultra vires* municipal act when plaintiff not injured and burden of taxation not increased).

Virginia.—Lynchburg & R. St. Ry. Co. v. Dameron, 95 Va. 545, 28 S. E. 951.

Washington.—Times Publishing Co. v. City of Everett, 9 Wash. 518, 43 Am. St. Rep. 865, 37 Pac. 695.

Wisconsin.—Willard v. Comstock, 58 Wis 565, 46 Am. Rep. 657, 17 N. W 401; Webster v. Douglas County, 102 Wis. 181, 72 Am. St. Rep. 870, 77 N. W. 885; and see Linden Land Co. v. Milwaukee Electric Ry. & L. Co., 107 Wis. 493, 83 N. W. 851.

United States.—Davenport v. Buffington, 97 Fed. 234, 38 C. C. A. 453, 46 L. R. A. 377, Downing v. Ross, 1 App. D. C. 251; Roberts v. Bradfield, 12 App. D. C. 453; Dewey Hotel Co. v. United States Elect. Lighting Co., 17 App. D. C. 356.

The plaintiff's capacity to sue depends on his character as a tax-payer, not on his residence within the municipality: Brockman v. City of Creston, 79 Iowa, 587, 44 N W. 822. The fact that the value of his property is inconsiderable, and his taxes therefor are trifling, is immaterial; Id.; see, also, Scofield v. Eighth School District, 27 Conn. 499, where injunction was awarded against an illegal use of school property for religious purposes, although the injury to the property was not serious.

The tax-payer's right to an injunction denied when an adequate legal remedy provided by statute: Taylor v. Davey, 55 Neb. 153, 75 N. W 553; Manly Mfg. Co. v. Broaddus, 94 Va. 547, 27 S. E. 438; Wahl v. School Directors, 78 Ill. App. 403; or by *certiorari:* Jackson v. City of Newark, 53 N. J. Eq. 322, 31 Atl. 233.

The mere fact that an act is illegal does not warrant an injunction at suit of tax-payer, when public funds will not be affected: Strickland v. Knight (Fla.), 36 South. 363 (not against illegal licensing of saloon); Clark v. Interstate Ind. Tel. Co. (Neb.), 101 N. W. 977 (not against granting franchise).

The conclusions arrived at by Judge Dillon in his discussion of the subject have been generally accepted by the courts: Dillon Mun. Corp. (4th ed.), § 922. "Upon a survey of the decisions in Great Britain and the United States, while they exhibit some diversity of opinion, it seems to us, in view of the nature of municipal powers, the danger of abuse, the necessity for prompt remedy on the part of those most interested in the proper administration of municipal affairs,—to wit, the taxable inhabitants,—that the following conclusions rest upon sound reason, and have also the support of the decided preponderance of judicial authority.

The suit by the tax-payer has practically superseded, in this country, the remedy of information in chancery by the attorney-general to restrain *ultra vires* acts of public corporations; still, the right of the state, by the proper officer, to maintain proceedings by injunction to restrain municipal corporations from doing acts in violation of the constitution and laws of the state has met with abundant recognition in our reports.[17]

It seems that the motive which actuates the tax-payer in bringing suit to enjoin illegal expenditures of public

"1 The proper parties may resort to equity, and equity will, in the absence of restrictive legislation, entertain jurisdiction of their suit against municipal corporations when these are acting *ultra vires*, or assuming or exercising a power over the property of the citizen, or over corporate property or funds, which the law does not confer upon them, and where such acts affect injuriously the property owner or the taxable inhabitant. But if in these cases the property owners or the taxable inhabitants can have full and adequate remedy at law, equity will not interfere, but leave them to their legal remedy.

"2. That, in the absence of special controlling legislative provision, the proper public officer of the commonwealth, which created the corporation and prescribed and limited its powers, may, in his own name, or in the name of the state, on behalf of residents and voters of the municipality, exercise the authority, in proper cases, of filing an information or bill in equity to prevent the misuse of corporate powers, or to set aside or correct illegal corporate acts.

"3. That the existence of such a power in the state, or its proper public law officer, is not inconsistent with the right of any taxable inhabitant to bring a bill to prevent the corporate authorities from transcending their lawful powers where the effect will be to impose upon *him* an unlawful tax, or to increase *his* burden of taxation. Much more clearly may this be done when the right of the public officer of the state to interfere is not admitted, or does not exist; and in such case it would seem that a bill might properly be brought in the name of one or more of the taxable inhabitants for themselves and all others similarly situated, and that the court should then regard it in the nature of a public proceeding to test the validity of the corporate acts sought to be impeached, and deal with and control it accordingly."

17 See State v. County Court of Saline County, 51 Mo. 350, 11 Am Rep. 454, and the exhaustive examination of the authorities in the opinions of Shipley, J., and Bliss, J.; Board of Education v. Territory, 12 Okla. 286, 70 Pac. 792.

moneys—the fact, for example, that he is interested in preventing the awarding to a business rival of an illegal contract whose execution is sought to be enjoined—is immaterial, if he sues in his representative character as tax-payer.[18]

§ 345. **Rationale of the Doctrine.**—"The grounds upon which such suits by tax-payers have been held unmaintainable are, that it requires some individual interest distinct from that which belongs to every inhabitant of the town or county to give the party complaining a standing in court, where it is an alleged delinquency in the administration of public affairs which is called in question; and that the ownership of taxable property is not such a peculiarity as to take the case out of the rule; and that the only remedies against an abuse of administrative power tending to taxation is furnished by the elective franchise or a proceeding on behalf of

18 Packard v. Hayes, 94 Md. 233, 51 Atl. 32: Board of Commissioners of Henry County v. Gillies, 138 Ind. 699, 38 N. E. 40; Times Publishing Co. v. City of Everett, 9 Wash. 518, 43 Am. St. Rep. 865, 37 Pac. 95; Keen v. City of Waycross, 101 Ga. 588, 29 S. E. 42; Brockman v. City of Creston, 79 Iowa, 587, 44 N. W. 822; Engstad v. Dinnie, 8 N. D. 1, 76 N. W. 292; but see Highway Commissioners v. Deboe, 43 Ill. App. 25, that relief will be refused if it appears that the tax-payer is merely a colorable plaintiff, suing in behalf of other parties in interest. Compare Kelly v. Mayor etc. of Baltimore, 53 Md. 134, where relief was refused because the plaintiff did not sue in a representative capacity; Commissioners' Court of Perry County v. Medical Society of Perry County, 128 Ala. 257, 29 South. 586 The fact that the plaintiff, as an individual, is injured in his business by the competition of the municipality engaging in such business *ultra vires*, does not entitle him to maintain the suit: Keen v. City of Waycross, *supra;* Pudsey Gas Co. v. Corporation of Bradford, L. R. 15 Eq. 167.

It has been said that if the matter is fully presented to the court and is decided upon the merits, a subsequent tax-payer's suit upon the same subject-matter is barred; but where the matter is not fully presented, as where the suit is dismissed by consent, there is no bar: Lindsay v. Allen (Tenn.), 82 S. W. 171.

the state, or, in the case of an act without jurisdiction, in treating the attempt to enforce the illegal tax as an act of trespass."[19] In other words, the courts which have taken a view adverse to the maintenance of such suits by the tax-payer have followed the analogy of the familiar rule as to parties plaintiff in suits to enjoin a public nuisance. It cannot be claimed that there is perfect agreement in the reasons assigned by the courts which uphold the doctrine. Most of the earlier cases are content to rest it upon the ground of urgent public necessity, and of the ultimate injury to tax-payers as a special class, distinct from the general public. "It is certainly well settled that public wrongs cannot be redressed at the suit of individuals, who have no other interest in the matter than the rest of the public. Thus an individual cannot maintain a bill of injunction to prevent a public nuisance, unless he suffered thereby some special damage; and the principle governing cases of that kind has been supposed to be applicable to the present case. But it appears from the averments of the bill, that these complainants, as tax-payers of the city, and others similarly situated, in whose behalf as well as their own the bill is filed, constitute a class specially damaged by the alleged unlawful act of the corporation, in the alleged increase of the burden of taxation upon their property situated within the city. The complainants have therefore a special interest in the subject-matter of the suit, distinct from that of the general public. The people of the state outside of the city of Baltimore, who are not liable to city taxation, can suffer no damage from the illegal act of the corporation complained of in the bill. Why, then,

19 Newmeyer v. Missouri & M. R. Co. (1873), 52 Mo. 81, 85, 14 Am. Rep. 394, reviewing the earlier cases *pro* and *con*. See, among other cases, Craft v. Jackson County, 5 Kan. 518.

is it necessary that the state, by the attorney-general, should be a party to the cause?"[20] "The injury charged [illegal issue of county bonds] as the result of the acts complained of is a private injury in which the tax-payers of the county are the individual sufferers, rather than the public. The people out of the county bear no part of the burden; nor do the people within the county, except the tax-payers, bear any part of it."[21] "The jurisdiction is sustained on the ground that the injury would be irreparable. The misappropriation of corporate funds would not render the tax levied to repair the waste or supply the deficiency illegal."[22] "The citizen may not be able to protect himself in any other way. If this is not his remedy, he has none. The money drawn from him by taxation may be squandered by unlawful donations to forward all manner of visionary schemes; other contributions may be wrung from him from year to year, and wasted in the same way, in defiance of laws carefully framed for his protection, and he would nevertheless be helpless. A more proper case for injunction cannot well be conceived than that in which a tax-payer seeks to protect from lawless waste a public fund, which, when dissipated thus, the law will with strong hand compel him to replenish."[23] Judge

20 Mayor etc. of Baltimore v. Gill (1869), 31 Md. 375, 394.

21 Newmeyer v. Missouri & M. R. Co., 52 Mo. 81, 14 Am. Rep. 394.

22 Willard v. Comstock, 58 Wis. 565, 46 Am. Rep 657, 17 N. W. 401.

23 Harney v. Indianapolis etc. R. R. Co, 32 Ind. 244. "The foundation of the doctrine is the interference with the rights of the tax-payer in the increase of the burden of taxation, or the liability thereto, by misappropriating the property of the city, which may demand the levy of taxes to acquire other property in its place; or, the property having been acquired through taxation, it's disposition would be in effect a misappropriation of taxes which may occasion levies to take the place of the misapplied tax": Brockman v. City of Creston, 79 Iowa, 587, 44 N. W. 822.

Dillon finds sufficient support for the doctrine in the analogy presented by the familiar rules of equity relating to suits by stockholders of private corporations to prevent or redress malfeasance or *ultra vires* acts on the part of their governing bodies.[24] This explanation has met with much favor from the courts,[25] but it is obvious that the analogy is not a perfect one.

24 Dillon, Mun. Corp. (4th ed.), § 915. Professor Pomeroy (Equity Jurisprudence, §§ 259-270) classes these cases among those in which jurisdiction is assumed by equity for the purpose of avoiding a multiplicity of suits, where numerous persons are injured by the same unlawful act. He lays aside, as obviously not pertinent to a discussion of the doctrine relating to multiplicity of suits, the cases where it has been decided that the citizen indirectly sustaining an injury from an illegal official act has no cause of action whatever. It is the impression of the present writer that precisely this question, viz., the reasons for the existence or non-existence of any cause of action whatever in the tax-payer because of his ultimately having to bear an increased burden of taxation, is the crucial one in the theory of "tax-payers' suits," and that it has not received a thoroughly convincing answer. It is to be noticed that Judge Dillon advances his suggestion on the subject in a tentative manner, and does not attempt to support it by any earlier authority. The propriety of the remedy of injunction, on the other hand, is clear enough, if it be assumed or proved that the wrong to the tax-payer is not a "*damnum absque injuria.*" The question is, of course, chiefly of theoretical interest, the rule itself is established by an overwhelming weight of authority.

25 See Russell v. Tate, 52 Ark. 541, 20 Am St. Rep. 193, 13 S. W. 130, 7 L. R. A. 180; McIntyre v. Board of Commissioners of El Paso County, 15 Colo. App. 78, 61 Pac. 237; Hospers v. Wyatt, 63 Iowa, 264; Tukey v. City of Omaha, 54 Neb 370, 69 Am. St. Rep. 711, 74 N. W. 613, Blood v. Manchester Elect. Lt. Co., 68 N. H. 340, 39 Atl. 335; Linden Land Co. v. Milwaukee Elect. Ry. & Lighting Co., 83 N. W. 851, 107 Wis. 493; Roberts v. City of Louisville, 92 Ky. 95, 36 Am. St. Rep. 449, 17 S W. 216, 13 L. R. A. 844; Scofield v. Eighth School District, 27 Conn. 499; New Orleans, M. & C. R. R. Co. v. Dunn, 51 Ala 128.

As an outgrowth of this analogy, it has been held that the taxpayer may not only sue to enjoin an illegal diversion of funds, but also "to compel the restitution of public funds which have been illegally diverted and lodged in the hands of persons not entitled to

§ 346. **New York Rule.**—The rule in New York, although now settled by statute, has gone through various changes. In the early cases in the inferior courts the right of the tax-payer to obtain relief was clearly recognized. It was laid down that "when an act is clearly illegal, and when the necessary effect of such act will be to injure, or impose a burden upon the property of any corporation, there is enough, according to every principle which has regulated the action of courts of equity, to warrant the interference of the court." This right of the tax-payers was supported on the ground that "the necessary effect of the act complained of will be to impose a burthen upon their real estate. Their interest, then, is as certain and direct as that of a stockholder in a moneyed or other corporation."[26] The illegal disposition of public money or property amounts to a breach of trust; therefore, an injunction was held proper.[27] Somewhat later a narrower rule was adopted, and it was held that a tax-payer in his character as such, whose position was not different from that of the whole body of tax-payers, had no such interest as entitled him to resort to a court of equity, to revise, restrain, or set aside the ac-

the same, who have taken them with notice of the wrongful diversion, and the governing body of the subordinate or local government will not act or take the necessary steps to have such funds restored'': Johnson v. Black (Va.), 49 S. E. 633, and cases cited. In strict accordance with this principle is the decision in a recent case (Reed v. Cunningham (Iowa), 101 N. W. 1055), where it was held that a taxpayer cannot sue to recover money illegally paid by a municipality, unless he shows a demand upon the officers to sue or that such demand would be unavailing.

26 Christopher v. Mayor, 13 Barb. 567.

27 Christopher v. Mayor, 13 Barb. 567; Milhau v. Sharp, 15 Barb. 193, Stuyvesant v. Pearsall, 15 Barb. 244. But to sustain an injunction it must appear that the appropriation was beyond the power of the corporate authorities by whom it was passed: Roberts v. Mayor, 5 Abb. Pr. 41.

tion of town or municipal authorities, upon an allegation that their acts were unauthorized and illegal, or that unless arrested they would subject the plaintiff to unjust or illegal taxation.[28] This, as we have seen, is an application of the rules relating to public nuisance. The reasoning upon which it was supported is similar to that applied to nuisance cases. "Every person may legally question the constitutional validity of an act of the legislature which affects his private rights; but if a citizen may maintain an action for such a purpose in respect to his rights as a voter and tax-payer, the courts may regularly be called upon to revise all laws which may be passed."[29]

The rule was finally embodied in a series of statutes familiarly known as the Tax-payers' Acts.[30] These statutes authorize actions to be maintained by tax-payers against officers, agents, commissioners, or other persons acting in behalf of any county, town, village, or municipal corporation "to prevent any illegal official act on the part of any such officers, agents, commissioners or other persons, or to prevent waste or injury to any property, funds or estate of such county, town, village or municipal corporation." It will be observed that these provisions contemplate two classes of public acts, viz.: Acts in and of themselves illegal and acts illegal because involving a waste of public funds. This distinction must be kept in mind, for otherwise the decisions will seem in hopeless conflict.

In the first class of cases, the injunction is freely granted whenever it clearly appears that the action is

28 Doolittle v. Supervisors, 18 N. Y. 155; Roosevelt v. Draper, 23 N. Y. 318; Kilbourne v. St. John, 59 N. Y. 21, 17 Am. Rep. 291.

29 Doolittle v. Supervisors, 18 N Y. 155.

30 Laws of 1872, c. 161; Laws of 1881, c. 531; Laws of 1891, c. 276, § 8, Code Civ. Proc., § 1925.

illegal.[31] Thus, it has issued to restrain the appointment of officers under an unconstitutional law,[32] to restrain the employment or payment of persons who have not passed civil service examinations,[33] and to prevent the payment of a salary out of a trust fund without audit.[34] Likewise, it is proper when municipal funds are about to be expended under authority of an unconstitutional law,[35] or when a board of supervisors illegally threatens to submit the question of removal of the county seat to the electors[36] or to allow the illegal assignment of a right to construct a railway in a highway,[37] or to restrain a village from contracting debts in excess of the charter limit.[38]

In the second class of cases, however, the right to relief is much narrower. "The terms 'waste' and 'injury' used in this statute comprehended only illegal, wrongful or dishonest official acts, and were not intended to subject the official action of boards, officers, or municipal bodies acting within the limits of their jurisdiction and discretion, but which some tax-payer might conceive to be unwise, improvident, or based on errors of judgment, to the supervision of the judicial tribunals."[39] Accordingly, it may be laid down as a general principle that an injunction will not issue to restrain waste or injury of public property by officers acting un-

31 Evans v. City of Hudson St. Commrs., 84 Hun, 206, 32 N. Y. Supp. 547; West v. City of Utica, 71 Hun, 540, 24 N. Y. Supp. 1075; Beebe v. Board of Supervisors, 64 Hun, 377, 19 N. Y. Supp. 629; Bush v. O'Brien, 164 N. Y. 205, 58 N. E. 106.

32 Rathbone v. Wirth, 150 N. Y. 459, 45 N. E. 15, 34 L. R. A. 408.

33 Peck v. Belknap, 130 N. Y. 394, 29 N. E. 977; Rogers v. Common Council, 123 N. Y. 173, 25 N. E. 274, 9 L. R. A. 579.

34 Warrin v. Baldwin, 105 N. Y. 534, 12 N. E. 49.

35 Mercer v. Floyd, 24 Misc. Rep. 164, 53 N. Y. Supp. 433.

36 Williams v. Boynton, 147 N. Y. 426, 42 N. E. 184.

37 Case v. Cayuga Co., 88 Hun, 59, 34 N. Y. Supp. 595.

38 Gerlach v. Brandreth, 34 App Div. 197, 54 N. Y. Supp. 479.

39 Talcott v. City of Buffalo, 125 N. Y. 280, 26 N. E. 263.

der their discretionary powers unless fraud, collusion, corruption or bad faith can be shown.[40] For instance, where a statute provides that all contracts for public work shall be let to the lowest and best bidder, a strong case of abuse of discretion must be shown before a court will interfere with a contract let to a higher bidder.[41] Thus, it has been held that where a telephone franchise has been granted to a corporation for nothing when a private individual has offered fifteen thousand dollars, no injunction should be granted in the absence of an additional showing, for it might be to the public interest to have the privilege awarded to the corporation, and it therefore might be the best bidder.[42] Where, however, a clear case of fraud or abuse of discretion is

[40] Talcott v. City of Buffalo, 125 N. Y. 280, 26 N. E. 263; Ziegler v. Chapin, 126 N. Y. 342, 27 N. E. 471; Boon v. City of Utica, 5 Misc. Rep. 391, 26 N. Y. Supp. 932; Rogers v. O'Brien, 1 App. Div. 397, 37 N. Y. Supp. 358; Chittenden v. Wurster, 152 N. Y. 345, 46 N. E. 857, 37 L. R. A. 809; Abraham v. Meyers, 29 Abb. N. C. 384, 23 N. Y. Supp. 226; New York Central & H. R R. Co. v. Maine, 71 Hun, 417, 24 N. Y. Supp. 962; Bell v. City of Rochester, 61 N. Y. St. Rep. 721, 30 N. Y. Supp 365; Wilkins v. Mayor etc. of City of New York, 9 Misc. Rep. 610, 30 N. Y. Supp. 424, Adamson v. Nassau R. R. Co., 89 Hun, 261, 34 N. Y. Supp 1073; Sheehy v. McMillan, 26 App. Div. 140, 49 N. Y. Supp. 1088; Kittinger v. Buffalo Traction Co., 25 App. Div. 329, 49 N. Y. Supp. 329, Holtz v. Diehl, 26 Misc. Rep. 224, 56 N. Y. Supp. 841; Rockefeller v. Taylor, 28 Misc. Rep. 460, 59 N. Y. Supp. 1038; Press Pub. Co. v. Holahan, 29 Misc. Rep. 684, 62 N. Y. Supp. 872; Keator v. Dalton, 29 Misc. Rep. 692, 62 N. Y. Supp. 878; Basselin v. Pate, 30 Misc. Rep. 368, 63 N. Y. Supp. 653; Norris v. Wurster, 23 App. Div. 124, 48 N. Y. Supp. 656; Gusthal v. Board of Aldermen, 23 App. Div. 315, 48 N. Y. Supp. 652.

[41] Berghoffen v. City of New York, 31 Misc. Rep. 205, 64 N Y. Supp. 1082; Kingsley v. Bowman, 33 App. Div. 1, 53 N. Y. Supp. 426, Terrell v. Strong, 14 Misc. Rep. 258, 35 N. Y. Supp. 1000. Where, however, it is clearly illegal to let the contract according to certain requirements, as where one bidder is discriminated against because he employs non-union labor, an injunction is proper: Meyers v. City of N. Y., 58 App. Div. 534, 69 N. Y. Supp. 529; Davenport v. Walker, 57 App. Div. 221, 68 N. Y. Supp. 161.

[42] Barhite v. Home Tel. Co., 50 App. Div. 25, 63 N. Y. Supp. 659.

made out, and the result will be a waste of public funds, an injunction will be granted.

§ 347. **The Rule in Massachusetts.**—The general equity jurisdiction in Massachusetts is narrow and closely confined by statute. Consequently, it is held that in the absence of a statute, a court has not jurisdiction to entertain a suit by individual tax-payers to restrain a municipality from doing an illegal act.[43] It is provided by statute, however, that "when a town votes to raise by taxation or pledge of its credit, or to pay from its treasury, any money for a purpose other than those for which it has the legal right and power, the supreme judicial court may, upon the suit or petition of not less than ten taxable inhabitants thereof, briefly setting forth the cause of complaint, hear and determine the same in equity."[44] This statute is confined in its application to cases coming within its terms; and although such a case is made out, relief will be refused if it appears that the tax-payers have been guilty of laches.[45]

§ 348. **The Rule in Ohio.**—In Ohio the tax-payer is authorized to sue only when it is made the duty of the solicitor of the corporation to commence an action and he, on demand, refuses to do so. The statute provides that the solicitor "shall apply in the name of the corporation to a court of competent jurisdiction for an order or injunction to restrain the misapplication of funds of the corporation or the abuse of its corporate powers, or the execution or performance of any contract

43 Baldwin v. Inhab. of Wilbraham, 140 Mass. 459, 4 N. E. 829; Steele v. Municipal Signal Co., 160 Mass. 36, 35 N. E 105; Prince v. Crocker, 166 Mass. 347, 44 N. E. 446, 32 L. R. A. 610.

44 Pub. Stats. Mass., c. 27, § 129. See, also, Stats. 1847, c. 37, § 1.

45 Tash v. Adams, 10 Cush. 252; Fuller v. Inhab. of Melrose, 1 Allen, 166; Parsons v. City of Northampton, 154 Mass. 410, 28 N. E. 350.

made in behalf of the corporation in contravention of the laws or ordinance governing the same, which was procured by fraud or corruption."[46] In construing this, the supreme court of the state has held that where proceedings of a municipal corporation are unauthorized and void, either from the want of power or from its unlawful exercise, and are designed to raise a fund by taxation to be applied to the object contemplated by such proceedings, an injunction will issue.[47]

§ 349. **Illustrations of the General Principle; Municipal Aid Bonds.**—Abundant illustration of the principles discussed in the preceding sections has been afforded by tax-payers' suits to restrain the unauthorized issue of bonds by municipalities in aid of the construction of railways or other *quasi* public works.[48] A strong ground for equitable interference in such cases is found in the facts that such bonds are usually negotiable and valid in the hands of any *bona fide* purchaser, and the tax-payer is consequently remediless unless the issuance of the bonds can be arrested.[49] It is not within the

46 Rev Stats. Ohio, § 1777.

47 Elyria Gas & Water Co. v. City of Elyria, 49 N. E. 335, 57 Ohio St. 374.

48 Wright v. Bishop, 88 Ill. 302 (railway aid subscriptions prohibited by present constitution of Illinois); Chestnutwood v. Hood, 68 Ill. 132; City of Madison v. Smith, 83 Ind. 502; City of Alma v. Loehr, 42 Kan. 368, 22 Pac. 424 (no injunction when the bonds already negotiated); Menard v. Hood, 68 Ill 121 (same); Curtenius v. Hoyt, 37 Mich. 583; Wagner v. Meety, 69 Mo 150; State v. Saline County Court, 51 Mo 350, 11 Am. Rep. 454; Newmeyer v. Missouri & M. R. Co., 52 Mo. 81, 14 Am. Rep. 394; North v. Platte County, 29 Neb. 447, 26 L. R. A. 395, 45 N. W. 692 (relief defeated by laches); List v. City of Wheeling, 7 W. Va. 501, Lynch v. Eastern, L. F. & M. R. Co., 57 Wis. 430, 15 N. W. 743, 825; Whiting v. Sheboygan etc R. Co., 25 Wis. 167, 3 Am Rep. 30; and cases cited in the following notes.

49 Hodgman v. Chicago & St. P. Ry. Co., 20 Minn. 48 (Gil. 36); Harrington v. Town of Plainview, 27 Minn. 224, 6 N. W. 777; Hamilton v. Village of Detroit, 85 Minn. 83, 88 N. W. 419. "It can re-

scope of this work to discuss the grounds on which various attempted issues of railway aid bonds have been held invalid. Any failure to comply substantially with the terms of the constitution or statute authorizing their issuance and regulating the manner thereof will warrant the exercise of the restraining power of a court of equity.[50] Injunction is also properly granted if the terms and conditions prescribed by the voters of the town in making their grant of aid have not been complied with by the recipient.[51]

main no longer a question whether the restraining power of equity should be exercised to prevent abuses of, and deviations from, the special power conferred upon the municipal officers in the execution and delivery of such negotiable bonds. If the tax-payers and real parties in interest have not the remedy by injunction, then there exists none whatever for the wrong. It becomes an evil wholly without prevention or redress by any process known to the law. The court is therefore of the opinion that the writ of injunction will issue in such a case, not only to give effect to the safeguards and restraints imposed by the legislature or the constitution of the state, but also to enforce the terms and conditions prescribed by the voters of the town": Lawson v. Schnellen, 33 Wis. 288, 294. If the bonds are void in the hands of innocent holders, the question whether the existence of the defense in suits at law upon the bonds affords an adequate remedy so as to preclude equitable relief is one on which the authorities are at variance See *post*, chapter on Cancellation of Instruments. The better opinion seems to be, that this fact "is no sufficient reason why the tax-payers of the corporation should not have the right to call upon a court of equity to prevent them [the securities] from being issued, and thus avoid the threatened wrong, and provide a remedy which will at once reach the whole mischief, secure the rights of all, both for the present and the future, and thus avoid a *multiplicity of suits* " Lynchburg & R. St. Ry. Co. v. Dameron, 95 Va. 545, 28 S. E. 951. To the effect that tax-payers may be estopped by acquiescence to question such bonds, see Schmitz v. Zeh, 91 Minn 290, 97 N. W. 1049

50 See Hodgman v. Chicago & St. P. R Co., 20 Minn. 48, 20 Gil. 36; English v. Smock, 34 Ind. 115, 7 Am Rep 215; Town of Clarksdale v. Broadlus, 77 Miss 667, 28 South. 954 (insufficient notice); Wullenwaber v. Dunigan, 30 Neb. 877, 47 N. W. 420, 13 L. R. A. 811; Chestnutwood v. Hood, 68 Ill. 132.

51 Lawson v. Schnellen, 33 Wis. 288, 294; Wagner v Meety, 69 Mo. 150; Wullenwaber v. Dunigan, 30 Neb. 877, 47 N. W. 420, 13

§ 350. Injunctions Against Exceeding Constitutional or Statutory Limits of Indebtedness.—In many of the states it is provided in the constitution, statutes or city charters that no municipal corporation shall incur indebtedness in excess of certain limits. Tax-payers have often called upon the courts to prevent a violation of such provisions. As a general rule, when it can be shown that action is to be taken in disregard of such limits, injunctive relief will be readily granted. Accordingly, under the provisions as they exist in many states, when it appears that contracts have been let which will entail an excessive expenditure, an injunction will issue.[52] A like principle often applies to the issuance of bonds, the courts holding that an injunction is proper when the amount of the issue exceeds the limit, and sometimes when the issue is for the purpose of taking up an excessive debt.[53] One form of statute prohibits the in-

L. R. A. 811; Township of Midland v. County Board of Gage County, 37 Neb. 582, 56 N. W. 317 (the railroad to which aid was voted assigned to another company; the county board was enjoined from delivering the bonds to the vendee. "The electors of the township are entitled to stand on the very letter of their promise. If they promised a donation to A if he would build a certain improvement, it does not follow that B is entitled to the donation, though he builds the improvement"); Nash v. Baker, 37 Neb. 713, 56 N. W. 376 (same point)

52 Dorothy v. Pierce, 27 Or. 373, 41 Pac. 668; Wormington v. Pierce, 22 Or. 606, 30 Pac. 450; O'Malley v. Borough of Olyphant, 198 Pa. St. 525, 48 Atl. 483; Honaker v. Board of Education, 42 W. Va. 170, 57 Am. St. Rep. 847, 24 S. E. 544, 32 L. R. A. 413; City of Springfield v. Edwards, 84 Ill. 626; Scott v. City of Goshen, 162 Ind. 204, 70 N. E. 79. For an admirable discussion of the statutes, see Dillon, Municipal Corporations, § 130ff.

53 Rogers v. Leseur Co., 57 Minn 434, 59 N. W. 488, Rice v. City of Milwaukee, 100 Wis. 516, 76 N. W. 341; Town of Winamac v. Huddleston, 132 Ind. 217, 31 N. E. 561, Fowler v. City of Superior, 85 Wis. 411, 54 N. W. 800; Anderson v. Orient Fire Ins. Co., 88 Iowa, 579, 55 N W. 348, City of Council Bluffs v. Stewart, 51 Iowa, 385, 1 N. W. 628; Dunbar v. Board of Commissioners, 5 Idaho, 407, 49 Pac. 409, Crampton v. Zabriskie, 101 U. S. 601, 25 L. R. A. 1070;

curring of indebtedness for one year in anticipation of the revenues of future years.[54] Under such provision, however, it is not necessary to wait until the revenues for the current year are collected before incurring the debt.[55] In granting relief in all of these cases the courts will look to the real nature of the transaction, and if the statute is really violated, a shallow expedient for evasion will not bar an injunction.[56]

§ 351. Awarding Contracts—"Lowest Bidder"—Discriminating in Favor of Union Labor.—Another class of cases where the remedy is awarded freely is where a contract, although within the general powers of the municipality, is improperly let because of some abuse of discretion

City of Ottumwa v. City Water Supply Co., 56 C. C. A. 219, 119 Fed. 315; Purcell v. City of East Grand Forks, 91 Minn. 486, 98 N. W. 351. In Kyes v. St. Croix Co., 108 Wis. 136, 83 N. W. 637, an injunction was issued because the ordinance authorizing the bonds violated a statute in that no provision was made for providing funds for paying the interest.

54 Webster v. Douglas Co., 102 Wis. 181, 72 Am. St. Rep. 870, 77 N. W. 885, 78 N. W. 451; Shinn v. Board of Education, 39 W. Va. 497, 20 S. E. 604; Davenport v. Kleinschmidt, 6 Mont. 502, 13 Pac. 249; Bradford v. City and County of San Francisco, 112 Cal. 537, 44 Pac. 912. And the rule holds, although the money be needed for necessary current expenses: Sackett v. City of New Albany, 88 Ind. 473, 45 Am. Rep. 467.

55 Hanley v. Randolph Co. Court, 50 W. Va. 439, 40 S. E. 389; City of Alpena v. Kelley, 97 Mich. 550, 56 N. W. 941. Sometimes it is held proper for a city to contract for necessities for a period covering a number of years, provided the amount to be paid annually does not exceed the limit. City of Valparaiso v. Gardner, 97 Ind. 1, 49 Am. Rep. 416. But see Putnam v. City of Grand Rapids, 58 Mich. 416, 25 N. W. 330.

56 Hoffman v. Board of Commissioners, 18 Mont. 224, 44 Pac. 973; Reynolds v. City of Waterville, 92 Me. 292, 42 Atl. 553. In Ramsey v. City of Shelbyville, 26 Ky. Law Rep. 1102, 83 S. W. 116, an injunction was issued restraining the enforcement of an ordinance accepting a library building and agreeing to pay $1,000 per year for the support thereof.

or non-compliance with law. Such questions often arise under constitutional or other provisions requiring contracts to be let to the lowest bidder. These provisions are of two kinds, and the distinction must be carefully observed. Where it is declared that contracts must be let to the "lowest bidder," no discretion is left to the governing body, and if it appears that a higher bidder has been allowed the preference, an injunction will issue at the instance of the tax-payer.[57] On the other hand, under a frequent form of the statute declaring that contracts shall be let to the "lowest responsible bidder" or to the "lowest and best bidder," a large discretion is given, and an injunction will be allowed only in a clear case of abuse.[58] A result of these provisions is that if certain described public work is about to be done without a call for bids, or if a proper advertisement is not made giving a description of the work and what will be required, or if the contract is let before the expiration of the time designated in the call for bids, an injunction will issue.[59] This is

[57] Mueller v. Eau Claire County, 108 Wis. 304, 84 N. W. 430; Holden v. City of Alton, 179 Ill. 318, 53 N. E. 556 (*dictum*)

[58] Inge v. Board of Public Works, 135 Ala. 187, 93 Am. St Rep. 20, 33 South. 678; Diamond v. City of Mankato, 89 Minn. 48, 93 N. W. 911; Downing v Ross, 1 App. D. C. 251, Keith v. Johnson, 22 Ky. Law Rep. 947, 59 S. W. 487 (a case of awarding a franchise which was required to be given to the highest and best bidder; the principle is the same). In Times Pub. Co. v. City of Everett, 9 Wash. 518, 43 Am. St. Rep. 865, 37 Pac. 695, it was held that when the contract is let to other than the lowest bidder, the contracting agent should judicially find the facts which, in its judgment, render the apparently lowest bid not the lowest in fact.

[59] Follmer v. Nuckolls Co., 6 Neb. 204; Littler v. Jayne, 124 Ill. 123, 16 N. E. 374; Manly Bldg. Co. v. Newton, 114 Ga 245, 40 S E. 274; Schumm v. Seymour, 24 N. J. Eq. 143; Jones Bros. Hardware Co. v. Erb, 54 Ark. 645, 17 S. W. 7, 13 L. R. A. 353; Mazet v. City of Pittsburg, 137 Pa. St. 548, 20 Atl. 693; Mayor etc. v. Keyser, 72 Md. 106, 19 Atl. 706, Woodruff v. Welton (Neb.), 97 N. W. 1037. See, also, Diamond v. City of Mankato, 89 Minn. 48, 93 N. W. 911;

a necessary consequence, for otherwise the statutes could be easily evaded. The motive of the tax-payer in bringing the suit is immaterial, provided he can show a case of injury to himself as a tax-payer. Consequently, an unsuccessful bidder may be and often is the plaintiff.[60]

Cases involving the same or similar principles, arise when a town or city, by ordinance or otherwise, attempts to discriminate in favor of union labor. Where there is a provision requiring contracts to be let absolutely to the lowest bidder, the principle stated above of course controls.[61] Where discretion is given, proof of the fact that discrimination has been made for that reason will be sufficient to show abuse of discretion and to warrant an injunction.[62] And even when there is no provision as to bidders, if a contract is let under an ordinance declaring that contracts shall be let only with union labor provisions, injunctive relief will be awarded.[63] The theory is that the ordinance being void, any contract made under it must also of necessity be void. The reasons for holding the ordinance void, and which are additional to those which apply to tax-payers' suits in general, are that an unlawful discrimination results, and that a monopoly is fostered; both of these results are contrary to the policy of the law.

Le Tourney v. Hugo, 90 Minn. 420, 97 N. W. 115; City of Chicago v. Mohr (Ill.), 74 N. E. 1056 (permitting changes to be made after bids were opened).

60 Times Pub. Co. v City of Everett, 9 Wash. 518, 43 Am. St. Rep. 865, 37 Pac. 695; Holden v. City of Alton, 179 Ill. 318, 53 N. E. 556; Chippewa Bridge Co. v. City of Durand (Wis.), 99 N. W. 603.

61 Holden v. City of Alton, 179 Ill. 318, 53 N. E. 556 (*dictum*).

62 Holden v. City of Alton, 179 Ill. 318, 53 N. E. 556, Adams v. Brenan, 177 Ill. 194, 69 Am. St. Rep. 222, 52 N. E 314, 42 L. R. A. 718.

63 City of Atlanta v. Stein, 111 Ga. 789, 36 S. E. 932, 51 L. R A. 335.

§ 352. Injunctions Against Removal of County Seats.— Tax-payers frequently have sought to invoke the aid of equity to prevent the removal of a county seat. In a sense, this is a political matter, but on the other hand, it may involve a waste of a large sum of money and thus be a great and direct injury to the tax-payers. The tendency of the modern authorities, therefore, is to allow an injunction when it appears that the illegal removal will result in a waste of public funds.[64] Applying this principle, injunctions are allowed when the election authorizing the removal is void because of failure to take the proper preliminary steps or because not authorized by statute.[65] For the same reason, when the removal is legal, an injunction will issue to

64 In Stuart v. Bair, 8 Baxt. 141, this principle is laid down. In Lanier v. Padgett, 18 Fla. 842, the tax-payers were allowed relief because the "proceeding might involve them and the whole people of the county in great expense and confusion, and jeopardize the titles to property." See, also, Rickey v. Williams, 8 Wash. 479, 36 Pac. 480; Way v. Fox, 80 N. W. 405, 109 Iowa, 340; Board of Supervisors v. Buckley (Miss.), 38 South. 104; Lindsay v. Allen (Tenn.), 82 S. W. 178; Mitchell v. Lasseter, 114 Ga. 275, 40 S. E. 287.

65 Rickey v. Williams, 8 Wash. 479, 36 Pac. 480; Todd v. Rustad, 43 Minn. 500, 46 N. W. 73. In some jurisdictions it is held, contrary to the general rule as to elections, that an injunction will issue to prevent the calling or holding of an unauthorized county seat election: Solomon v. Fleming, 34 Neb. 40, 51 N. W. 304; Streissguth v. Geib, 67 Minn. 360, 69 N. W. 1097. The better rule would seem to be that the equity court should not interfere with the election. When the court takes jurisdiction in such matters it is asserting a right to hear election contests, which are not a subject of equitable cognizance: People v. Board of Supervisors, 75 Cal. 179, 16 Pac. 776; Caruthers v. Harnett, 67 Tex. 127, 2 S. W. 523. See chapter on Public Officers, *ante*, § 331. In Washington it is held that an injunction will issue to prevent removal when there has been fraud in counting the votes: Krieschel v. Board of Snohomish County Commissioners, 12 Wash. 428, 41 Pac. 186; but mere errors in counting will not be sufficient to warrant the relief: Parmeter v. Bourne, 8 Wash. 45, 35 Pac. 586, 757.

prevent the erection of an expensive county building at the old site.[66]

§ 353. Miscellaneous Illustrations.—Whenever a city's money is about to be paid or used for a purpose not authorized by law or under a contract *ultra vires* for any reason, or is to be paid wrongfully, a tax-payer will be allowed an injunction.[67] As a common example, such relief will be granted when public funds are to be used *ultra vires* for purposes of entertainment of vis-

66 Wells v. Ragsdale, 102 Ga. 53, 29 S. E. 165.

67 A tax-payer has been allowed an injunction in the following cases, the purposes for which the money was intended being held to be improper: Against paying an attorney under an illegal contract for the collection of taxes: Storey v. Murphy, 9 N. D. 115, 81 N. W. 23; Grannis v. Board of Commissioners, 81 Minn. 55, 83 N. W. 495; Frederick v Douglas Co., 96 Wis. 411, 71 N. W. 798; but not to annul the contract: Board of Commissioners of Wayne Co. v. Dickinson, 153 Ind. 682, 53 N. E. 929. Against spending money *ultra vires* for a dispensary for the sale of liquor: Leesburg v. Putnam, 103 Ga. 110, 68 Am St Rep. 80, 29 S. E. 602; McCullough v. Brown, 41 S. C. 220, 19 S. E. 458, 23 L. R. A. 410. Against paying a water company, under an illegal contract extending over a number of years· Flynn v. Little Falls E. & W. Co, 74 Minn. 180, 77 N. W. 38, 78 N. W. 106. Against paying a reward, *ultra vires*, for the arrest of a defaulting official: Patton v. Stephens, 14 Bush, 324. Against illegally using highway fund for waterworks. Savidge v Village of Spring Lake, 112 Mich. 91, 70 N. W. 425. Against paying a collusive judgment: Beyer v. Town of Crandon, 98 Wis. 306, 73 N. W. 771; Nevill v. Clifford, 55 Wis 161, 12 N. W 419. Against contract making an illegal exemption from taxation: Altgelt v. City of San Antonio, 81 Tex. 447, 17 S. W. 75, 13 L. R. A. 383. Against publishing delinquent tax list in paper not a newspaper: Sinclair v. Commrs of Winona Co., 23 Minn. 404, 23 Am. Rep. 694. See Dillon on Municipal Corporations, § 914ff. But see Normand v. Otoe Co., 8 Neb. 18. In general, see Daviess Co. v. Goodwin, 25 Ky. Law Rep. 1081, 77 S. W. 185. For an instance of the remedy of cancellation granted at suit of a tax-payer, see Bowman v Frith (Ark.), 54 S. W. 709. By statute in Wisconsin, a tax-payer has been allowed to maintain suit to recover money paid by a county without authority Estell v Knight, 117 Wis. 540, 94 N. W. 290 See, also, *ante*, end of note 25.

itors or to aid charitable associations.[68] Frequently, statutes declare that public officers shall not be interested in public contracts, and under such provisions, an injunction will be granted if a violation is shown[69] Likewise, where the object is illegal, an injunction will issue to prevent the issuance or payment of warrants,[70] or the execution of a mortgage or bonds.[71]

Upon the same principle, a tax-payer may enjoin the improper use of public property.[72] Such use involves both a breach of trust and a direct pecuniary injury. Often it results in more—in a direct inconvenience to the tax-payer.

68 Black v. Common Council of City of Detroit, 119 Mich. 571, 78 N. W. 660; Austin v. Coggeshall, 12 R. I. 329, 34 Am Rep 648, State v. City of New Orleans, 50 La. Ann. 880, 24 South. 666.

69 McElhinney v. City of Superior, 32 Neb 744, 49 N. W. 705; Weitz v. Independent Dist. of Des Moines, 87 Iowa, 81, 54 N. W. 70; Alexander v. Johnson, 144 Ind. 82, 41 N. E. 811; Miller v. Sullivan, 32 Wash. 115, 72 Pac. 1022; Nuckols v. Lyle, 8 Idaho, 589, 70 Pac. 401.

70 Ackerman v. Thummel, 40 Neb. 95, 58 N. W. 738; Russell v. Tate, 52 Ark. 541, 20 Am. St. Rep. 193, 13 S. W. 130, 7 L. R. A 180.

71 Vaughn v. Board of Commissioners of Forsyth Co., 118 N. C. 636, 24 S. E. 425, Bolton v. City of Antonio (Tex. Civ. App.), 21 S. W. 64; Mayor etc. v. Gill, 31 Md. 375.

72 Thus, it has been held that a tax-payer may enjoin the use of a school building for religious or other private purposes· Scofield v. Eighth School Dist., 27 Conn. 499; Lewis v. Bateman, 26 Utah, 434, 73 Pac. 509, Spencer v. School Dist., 15 Kan. 259, 22 Am Rep 268 In the first case the court said. "It is quite obvious that more or less injury must arise, not merely from the use of the building and its furniture, but from deranging the furniture, books and stationery belonging to the school, and by materially increasing the risk of destroying the house by fire" "But the value of the right . . . . cannot be measured by the mere pecuniary injury. . . . . It is more correct to estimate it by the value of the building, if it was to be rented for the purposes for which it is used gratuitously." "And we know of no principle that will justify the misappropriation of trust property for any purpose whatever." See, also, Nerlien v. Village of Brooten (Minn.), 102 N. W. 867 (use of town hall for commercial purposes enjoined). Likewise, an injunction will issue

In some jurisdictions the courts have refused to enjoin an act manifestly illegal when it has seemed more inequitable to grant than to refuse an injunction.[73] Such cases are of rare occurrence, and must depend upon their own facts. Occasionally the doctrine of laches is applied to these suits;[74] but it would seem that

to prevent the unlawful removal of a school-house· McLain v. Maricle, 60 Neb. 353, 83 N. W. 85. But see Parody v. School Dist, 15 Neb. 514, 19 N. W. 633. A tax-payer may enjoin a county from building a court-house on a city lot dedicated to park purposes, although the city consents: McIntyre v. Board of Commissioners of El Paso Co., 15 Colo. App. 78, 61 Pac. 237. He may also enjoin the illegal sale of public property: Willard v. Comstock, 58 Wis. 565, 46 Am Rep. 657, 17 N. W. 401. See Davenport v. Buffington, 97 Fed. 234, 38 C. C. A. 453. In Sherburne v. City of Portsmouth (N. H.), 58 Atl. 38, a tax-payer was allowed an injunction to restrain a common council from granting the use of a public common to individuals for a baseball park See, however, Davidson v. Mayor etc of Baltimore, 96 Md. 509, 53 Atl. 1121, where it was held that a tax-payer cannot enjoin officers from changing use of a school building from an English-German school to a colored high school, without showing special damage See, also, Amusement Syndicate Co v. City of Topeka, 68 Kan 801, 74 Pac. 606; Bryant v. Logan (W. Va.), 49 S. E. 21 (tax-payer cannot enjoin unless specially injured); Village of Riverside v. MacLean, 210 Ill. 308, 102 Am. St. Rep. 164, 71 N. E. 408 (owners of lots adjoining a tract dedicated for a public park may enjoin the municipality from constructing a highway through the park, without showing special damage), citing many cases.

73 Ebert v. Langlade Co., 107 Wis. 569, 83 N. W. 942; Brasher v. Miller, 114 Ala. 485, 21 South. 467; Farmer v. City of St. Paul, 65 Minn. 176, 67 N. W. 990, 33 L. R. A. 199. In this case the court said: "While it is true that, upon grounds of sound public policy, the doctrine of *ultra vires* is applied with greater strictness to municipal than to private corporations, and that in this state a tax-payer may enjoin an unauthorized appropriation of public money, yet in cases where the proposed appropriation is only technically illegal, and it would be more inequitable to grant the injunction than to refuse it, it may be refused." In Appleton Water Works Co. v. City of Appleton, 116 Wis. 363, 93 N. W. 262, it was said that this principle should be considered only in cases of extreme doubt.

74 Tash v. Adams, 10 Cush 252; Mahon v. City of New Orleans, 52 La. Ann. 1226, 27 South. 650.

generally the doctrine is inapplicable, especially if the tax-payer acts promptly upon receiving information.[75]

An injunction, it has been held, will not be granted to a tax-payer to restrain the enforcement of a void municipal ordinance, when the case is not brought within the principles laid down above.[76]

§ 354. Relief Against Ordinances Injuring the Individual in a Capacity Other than that of Tax-payer.—The principle is generally, but not universally, accepted, that the enforcement of a void municipal ordinance may be enjoined, where an injunction is necessary for the purpose of avoiding a multiplicity of suits,[77] or of prevent-

75 Storey v. Murphy, 9 N. D. 115, 81 N. W. 23; Black v. Common Council of City of Detroit, 119 Mich. 571, 78 N. W. 660; Austin v. Coggeshall, 12 R. I. 329, 34 Am. Rep. 648.

76 Field v. Village of Western Springs, 181 Ill. 186, 54 N. E. 929.

77 Davis v. Fasig, 128 Ind. 271, 27 N. E. 726; City of Rushville v. Rushville Natural Gas Co., 132 Ind. 575, 28 N. E. 853, 15 L. R. A. 321; Brown v. Catlettsburg, 11 Bush (Ky.), 435; Shinkle v. City of Covington, 83 Ky. 420; City of Newport v. Newport & C. Bridge Co., 90 Ky. 193, 13 S. W. 720, 8 L. R. A. 484; South Covington etc. Ry. Co. v. Berry, 93 Ky. 43, 40 Am. St. Rep. 161, 18 S. W. 1026, 15 L. R. A. 604; Sylvester Coal Co. v. City of St. Louis, 130 Mo. 323, 51 Am. St. Rep. 566, 32 S. W. 649; Third Ave. R. R. Co. v. Mayor, 54 N. Y. 159; United Traction Co. v. City of Watervliet, 35 Misc Rep. 392, 71 N. Y. Supp. 977.

In these cases the multiplicity of suits sought to be avoided consisted in numerous prosecutions of the single complainant or his servants for numerous violations of the invalid ordinance. It was once held in New York (West v. Mayor, 10 Paige, 539) that equity would not assume jurisdiction in this class of cases until the complainant had established his right by a successful defense in at least one of the actions at law. See 1 Pom. Eq. Jur., § 254, note, where it is shown that this case is irreconcilable with the later case of Third Ave. R. R. Co. v. Mayor, 54 N. Y. 159. It is held elsewhere that the rule in West v. Mayor cannot apply under the blending of law and equity in the code system: Sylvester Coal Co. v. City of St. Louis, 130 Mo. 323, 51 Am. St. Rep. 566, 32 S. W. 649. It is followed, however, in Illinois: Chicago, B. & Q. R. Co. v. City of

ing irreparable injury to private rights.[78] Multiplicity of suits may be a ground for the injunction either when a large group of persons are threatened with prosecution for violation of the invalid ordinance,[79] or numerous prosecutions are begun or threatened against a single person.[80] Some cases, however, deny the right to equitable interference, on the ground that the com-

Ottawa, 148 Ill. 397, 36 N. E. 80, Poyer v. Village of Des Plaines, 123 Ill. 111, 5 Am. St. Rep. 494, 13 N. E. 819.

It seems that when the question is not of the validity of the ordinance, but of its application to the complainant, injunction will not be granted unless, perhaps, to avoid a multiplicity of prosecutions: Ludlow & C. Coal Co. v. City of Ludlow, 102 Ky. 354, 43 S. W. 435.

78 Des Moines City R. Co. v. City of Des Moines, 90 Iowa, 770, 58 N. W. 906, 26 L. R. A. 767; McFarlain v. Town of Jennings, 106 La. 541, 31 South. 62; Coast Co. v. Borough of Spring Lake (N. J.), 36 Atl. 21; United Traction Co. v. City of Watervliet, 35 Misc. Rep. 392, 71 N. Y. Supp. 977; City of Austin v. Austin City Cemetery Assn., 87 Tex. 330, 47 Am. St. Rep. 114, 28 S. W. 528; Bristol Door & Lumber Co. v. Bristol, 97 Va. 304, 75 Am. St. Rep. 783, 33 S. E. 588, City of Atlanta v. Gate City Gaslight Co., 71 Ga. 106; Cicero Lumber Co. v. Town of Cicero, 176 Ill. 9, 68 Am. St. Rep. 155, 51 N. E. 758, 42 L. R. A. 696; City of Roanoke v. Bolling, 101 Va. 182, 43 S. E. 343, Old Colony Trust Co. v. City of Wichita, 123 Fed. 762; Glucose Refining Co. v. City of Chicago (Ill.), 138 Fed. 209. In Maryland, any party whose interests are injuriously affected by a void ordinance may enjoin its enforcement: City of Baltimore v. Radecke, 49 Md 217, 33 Am. Rep. 239 (ordinance within general grant of power, but clearly unreasonable and oppressive); Deems v. City of Baltimore, 80 Md. 164, 45 Am. St. Rep. 339, 30 Atl. 648, 26 L R. A. 54 (milk inspection ordinance). An injunction will not issue when the enforcement will amount to a mere trespass for which there is an adequate remedy at law: Town of Orange City v. Thayer (Fla.), 34 South 573.

79 City of Chicago v. Collins, 175 Ill. 445, 67 Am St. Rep. 224, 51 N. E. 907, 49 L. R. A. 408; Wilkie v. City of Chicago, 188 Ill. 444, 80 Am. St. Rep. 182, 58 N. E. 1004; Glucose Refining Co. v. City of Chicago, 138 Fed. 209, Spiegler v. City of Chicago (Ill), 74 N. E. 718. See Pom. Eq. Jur., § 254 *et seq.*, where the subject is examined at large.

80 See cases *supra*, note 77.

plainant's defense to the prosecution affords him an adequate remedy at law.[81]

Relief has been more frequently denied against the enforcement of penal ordinances on the ground that the proceedings for their enforcement were of a criminal or *quasi* criminal nature, and that equity declines to interfere with the administration of the criminal laws.[82]

81 See Devron v. First Municipality, 4 La Ann. 11; Levy v. City of Shreveport, 27 La. Ann. 620, Cohen v. Commissioners of Goldsboro, 77 N. C. 2; Wardens v. Washington, 109 N. C. 21, 13 S. E. 700; Scott v. Smith, 121 N. C. 94, 28 S. E. 64. See, also, the Illinois cases *supra*, in note 77.

Reasons for this view are stated with some fullness in the opinion from which the following extract is taken: "If the ordinance is invalid, we cannot assume that the court in which appellee may be tried for its violation will not so hold, if this question is presented; nor can we presume that, if he is acquitted on this ground, the officer of the city will continue to harass him with further arrests; so that, if his own contention is true, he is in no danger of suffering the irreparable injury of which he complains; nor would he, under such circumstances, be subjected to a multiplicity of suits. It would doubtless be convenient for appellee to have the judgment of the court upon the validity of the ordinance before submitting himself to liability for accumulated penalties; but, if arrested and convicted, and he chooses to take the chances of ultimately defeating the ordinance upon the ground of its invalidity, that is no ground for equitable interference". City of Denver v. Beede, 25 Colo. 172, 54 Pac. 624 To the present writer, the logic of the last sentence seems as faulty as its grammar. At all events, deliverance from this too common form of persecution is often much more than a matter of "convenience" to its victim, as the facts of reported cases abundantly show.

82 Poulk v. City of Sycamore, 104 Ga. 24, 30 S. E. 417, 41 L. R. A. 772 (ordinance penalizing sale of intoxicating liquors); Phillips v. Mayor, 61 Ga. 386 (same); Garrison v. City of Atlanta, 68 Ga 64, Mayor etc. of City of Moultrie v. Patterson, 109 Ga 370, 34 S. E. 600; Coykendall v. Hood, 36 App. Div. 558, 55 N. Y. Supp. 718; Wade v. Nunnelly, 19 Tex. Civ. App. 256, 46 S. W. 668. See, however, Sylvester Coal Co. v. City of St. Louis, 130 Mo. 323, 51 Am. St. Rep. 566, 32 S. W. 649, holding that "the doctrine that criminal statutes cannot be tested or their enforcement restrained in the civil courts has no application to the case. Municipal ordinances,

It is believed, however, that in applying this rule the courts have sometimes lost sight of its qualification, which is as well settled as the rule itself, that a court of equity may in a proper case interfere by injunction to restrain any act or proceeding, whether connected with crime or not, which tends to the destruction or impairment of property or property rights.[83]

The general principle stated at the beginning of this section has found a frequent application, of late years, in the cases where an injunction has been sought against the enforcement or passage of ordinances fixing the rates of gas companies, water companies, or other "public utilities," or other municipal legislation impairing the obligation of the contract contained or implied

though penal, are not criminal statutes. They are *quasi* criminal in form, but not so regarded in procedure." See, also, *post*, chapter XXI.

83 Glucose Refining Co. v. City of Chicago (Ill.), 138 Fed. 209 (smoke ordinance); United Traction Co. v. City of Watervliet, 35 Misc. Rep. 392, 71 N. Y. Supp. 977 (against enforcement of ordinance limiting speed of street-cars to six miles an hour); Dobbins v. City of Los Angeles, 195 U. S. 223, 25 Sup. Ct. 18; City of Atlanta v. Gate City Gaslight Co., 71 Ga. 106 (against enforcement of ordinance tending to the destruction of a franchise for the use of streets by a gas company); City of Austin v. Austin City Cemetery Assn., 87 Tex. 330, 47 Am. St. Rep. 114, 28 S. W. 528. In the last case an injunction was sought by a cemetery association against the enforcement of an ordinance making it a "misdemeanor" for anyone to bury human bodies in certain territory comprising the plaintiff's burial ground. The court says in part in its able opinion: "It is clear to us . . . . that the effect of the ordinance is such that, if its enforcement be not restrained, it may result in a total destruction of the value of appellee's property for the purpose for which it was acquired. . . . . No one, we apprehend, without some considerable inducement, will do an act which may cause him to be arrested and prosecuted, however clear he might be in his own mind that the act constituted no violation of the criminal law. . . . . As long as the ordinance remains undisturbed, it acts *in terrorem*, and practically accomplishes a prohibition against the burial of the dead within the limits of the city of Austin, save in the excepted localities," etc.

in the complainant's franchise, or conflicting with other constitutional guaranties. These cases chiefly have to do with questions of constitutional law; but the appropriateness of the remedy by injunction seems to have been conceded in most of them,[84] and has been expressly decided in many.[85]

84 See Capital City Gaslight Co. v. City of Des Moines, 72 Fed. 829; Cleveland City Ry. Co. v. City of Cleveland, 94 Fed. 385; Los Angeles City Water Co. v. City of Los Angeles, 103 Fed. 711, 738, etc.; Penn Mutual Life Ins. Co. v. City of Austin, 168 U. S. 685, 18 Sup. Ct. 223 (right to injunction lost by five years' laches); Spring Valley Water Works v. San Francisco, 82 Cal. 286, 16 Am. St. Rep 116, 22 Pac. 910, 1046, 6 L. R. A. 756; and cases cited in Los Angeles City Water Co. v. City of Los Angeles, 103 Fed. 711, 716. See, also, Little Falls Elect. & Water Co. v. City of Little Falls, 102 Fed 663; Spring Valley Water Works v. City and County of San Francisco, 124 Fed. 575; Palatka Water Works v. City of Palatka, 127 Fed 161; City of Chicago v. Rogers Park Water Co., 214 Ill. 212, 73 N. E. 375 And the same result has been reached where the municipal body has no power to fix rates: Mills v. City of Chicago, 127 Fed. 731.

85 In City of Walla Walla v. Walla Walla Water Co., 172 U. S. 1, 19 Sup. Ct. 77, 82, 43 L. ed. 341, injunction was sought against the erection of competing waterworks by the city, in violation of complainant's contract and franchise. The court, speaking of the remedy at law for the threatened breach of the contract, says: "In the meantime great—perhaps irreparable—damage would have been done to the plaintiff. What the measure of such damages was would be exceedingly difficult of ascertainment, and would depend largely upon the question of whether the value of plaintiff's plant was destroyed or merely impaired. It would be impossible to say what would be the damage incurred at any particular moment, since such damage might be more or less dependent upon whether the competition of the city should ultimately destroy, or only interfere with, the business of the complainant." The case of Southwest Missouri Light Co. v. City of Joplin, 101 Fed. 23, 33, was similar. In Los Angeles City Water Co. v. City of Los Angeles, 88 Fed. 720, 748, the court says in regard to an ordinance fixing water rates, when the state laws and constitution impose severe penalties for charging more than the legal rates: "The ordinance, by reason of the severe pains and penalties which apparently fortify it, is daily, hourly, and momentarily enforcing itself. The defendants must either submit to the terms of the ordinance,

§ 355. Injunctions Against Wrongful Acts in General.—Where municipal corporations, or their officers, threaten to do some wrongful act which will directly injure an individual, such a party may, if the case comes within some recognized head of equity jurisdiction, restrain such action. Thus, where municipal authorities wrongfully threaten to remove certain shade trees from a street, the abutting owner may obtain an injunction, his injury being irreparable.[86] Likewise, abutting owners have been allowed to enjoin the change of a park into a highway, where the park had been dedicated in conformity with a general building plan.[87] A few miscellaneous illustrations are appended in the note.[88]

or incur unusually onerous expenditures. It is reasonably certain that if, with the ordinance standing, they were to undertake the collection of rates in excess of those prescribed in the ordinance, they would be resisted at every point by the consumers of water, and thus be driven to innumerable actions at law. Besides, should they, in any instance, succeed in collecting without an action a higher rate than the ordinance prescribes, it is equally certain that they would thereby bring upon themselves protracted and heavy litigation, having for its object forfeiture of their entire system of works. Surely these injuries are irreparable, and actions at law, so far from being adequate to the exigencies of the situation, are, as complainants, in their brief, forcibly put it, mere mockeries of a remedy.'' See, also, Los Angeles City Water Co. v. City of Los Angeles, 103 Fed. 711, 738 (city threatens to enforce constitutional provision for forfeiture of complainant's works if ordinance is disobeyed); New Memphis Gas & Light Co. v. City of Memphis, 72 Fed. 952 (where injunction *pendente lite* granted against ordinance fixing rates); Riverside & A. Ry. Co. v. City of Riverside, 118 Fed. 736.

86 Mayor etc. of City of Frostburg v. Wineland, 98 Md. 239, 103 Am. St. Rep. 399, 56 Atl. 811. See, also, Burget v. Incorporated Town of Greenfield, 102 Iowa, 432, 94 N. W. 933.

87 Village of Riverside v. Maclean, 210 Ill. 308, 102 Am. St. Rep 164, 71 N. E. 408.

88 See Lerch v. City of Duluth, 88 Minn. 295, 92 N. W 1116; Nebraska Telephone Co. v. City of Fremont (Neb.), 99 N. W.

811 (interference with telephone poles and wires enjoined); West Jersey & S. R. Co. v. Waterford Tp., 64 N. J. Eq. 157, 55 Atl. 157, Rochester & L. O. Water Co. v. City of Rochester, 176 N. Y. 36, 68 N. E. 117; Schooling v. City of Harrisburg, 42 Or. 494, 71 Pac. 605, Belington & N. R. Co. v. Town of Alston, 54 W. Va. 597, 46 S. E. 612 (injunction against tearing up railroad tracks).

CHAPTER XIX.

INJUNCTION AGAINST TAXATION; AND AGAINST SPECIAL OR LOCAL ASSESSMENTS.

ANALYSIS.

§ 356. **In General—Two Classes of States.**—The rules governing the issuance of injunctions to restrain the collection of invalid taxes are far from uniform. In general, the states may be divided into two classes, although in but few of the states will all the rules be found to agree. In states of the first type the jurisdiction depends upon the existence of some recognized ground for general equitable relief, such as the prevention of a multitude of suits, the removal of a cloud upon title, and the like. In states of the second type the jurisdiction rests upon the illegality or invalidity of the tax, and is independent of the existence of any generally recognized ground for equitable relief. Owing to this great diversity and to the importance of the subject, the rules in all of the several states will be examined separately.

§ 357. **Principles of General Application—Irregularities—Tender.**—It is a principle of general application that mere irregularities in the assessment are not sufficient to warrant the interference of equity.[1] The collection of public revenue will not be prevented unless there is some substantial defect which renders the tax invalid as to the complainant. Public policy demands that no needless restriction be placed upon the securing of the necessary means for conducting the government. It is also generally the rule that where a tax is valid in part and invalid in part, no relief will be awarded unless a payment or tender is made of the portion admitted to be valid.[2] This is an application of the maxim that "he who seeks equity must do equity." In some states it is held that such payment or tender is merely a condition of relief, and that it need not be made before suit.[3] In others it is said that a mere aver-

1 It has been so held, *e. g.*, in the federal courts, and in Arizona, Arkansas, California, Illinois, Indiana, Kansas, Kentucky, Maryland, Michigan, Missouri, Nebraska, Oklahoma, Oregon, Pennsylvania and Texas. See cases cited in notes to sections discussing the rules in these jurisdictions

2 It has been so held, *e. g.*, in the federal courts, and in Alabama, Arizona, Arkansas, California, Colorado, Florida, Indiana, Kansas, Kentucky, Michigan, Mississippi, Montana, Nebraska, North Dakota, Oklahoma, Oregon, Utah, Washington and Wisconsin. See cases cited in notes to sections discussing the rules in these jurisdictions.

3 It is so held, *e. g.*, in Florida, and it is probably the rule in Missouri. See cases cited in notes to sections discussing the rules in these states.

ment of readiness and willingness to pay is not sufficient; that the amount must be either paid or tendered before suit.[4]

§ 358. **First Type.**—In states of the first type the mere illegality of the tax is not ground for equitable relief. "It must appear that the enforcement of the tax would lead to a multiplicity of suits, or produce irreparable injury; or if the property is real estate, throw a cloud upon the title of the complainant, or there must be some allegation of fraud, before the aid of a court of equity can be invoked. There must in every case be some special circumstance attending a threatened injury of this kind, which distinguishes it from a common trespass, and brings the case under some recognized head of equity jurisdiction before the extraordinary and preventive remedy of injunction can be invoked."[5]

§ 359. **Same; Inadequacy of the Legal Remedy—Taxes on Personal Property.**—The inadequacy of the legal remedy is a fundamental ground of jurisdiction. In tax cases this test is frequently applied to assessments upon personal property. Ordinarily, in states of this class, it is held that there is an adequate remedy at law for injuries to personalty. If the officers of the law seize it for non-payment of an invalid tax, they are liable in trover or trespass, and damages are presumed to fully compensate for any loss. Consequently it is stated that in general an injunction will not issue to prevent

4 It has been so held in the federal courts and in Kansas. See cases cited in notes to sections discussing the rules in these jurisdictions

5 Wells, Fargo & Co. v. Dayton, 11 Nev. 161. The leading case of this type is Dows v. City of Chicago, 11 Wall. 108, 20 L. ed. 65.

the collection of an invalid tax on personal property.[6] Cases may arise, however, where the unauthorized interference of the tax officer will work irreparable injury, and in such cases injunctive relief is proper. Thus, the unlawful seizure of railroad cars for non-payment of an invalid tax may work such an injury to the company as to warrant the interposition of equity.[7] Where the business of the owner will be seriously interfered with or ruined by the enforcement of the tax, equity may enjoin its collection; and such relief is authorized where the destruction of a corporate franchise is imminent.[8] The application of the test of inadequacy of the legal remedy is not confined to cases of personal property. It applies to cases of realty as well.[9]

§ 360. **Same; Fraud.**—In some of the states of this class fraud appears to be a ground for relief.[10] Accordingly, when officers, by a systematic, intentional and illegal

6 It has been so held, *e. g.*, in the federal courts, and in California, Colorado, Florida, Michigan, Minnesota, Nevada, North Carolina, North Dakota, West Virginia and Wisconsin. See cases cited in notes to sections discussing the rules in these jurisdictions.

7 Southern Ry. Co. v. City of Asheville, 69 Fed. 359; City of Detroit v. Wayne Circuit Judge, 127 Mich. 604, 8 Detroit Leg. N. 465, 86 N. W. 1032.

8 Osborn v. Bank of the United States, 9 Wheat. 738, 6 L. ed. 204. In some jurisdictions no recovery of invalid taxes paid is allowed unless payment is made under duress. Where such a statute, in connection with another imposing a penalty of fifty dollars per day for non-payment, threatens injury to one upon whom an invalid tax has been assessed, injunctive relief has been allowed: Stone v. Bank of Kentucky, 174 U. S. 799, 19 Sup. Ct. 881, 43 L. ed. 1177, First Nat. Bank v. City of Covington, 103 Fed. 523.

9 For an application to realty, see United States v. Rickert, 188 U. S. 432, 23 Sup. Ct. 478, 47 L. ed. 532.

10 Such seems to be the rule in the federal courts, and in California, Michigan, Oregon and Wisconsin. See cases cited in notes to sections discussing the rules in these jurisdictions.

under-valuation of other property, make an unjust discrimination against the complainant, an injunction may issue.[11] The same relief is allowed when an assessment is so excessive as to give rise to a presumption of fraud.[12] Proof of discrimination must be clear and convincing to warrant interference.[13] An assessment is not fraudulent merely because of being excessive. If the assessor has acted from proper motives, an injunction is not the proper remedy; but when he purposely, or in reckless disregard of duty levies a tax which discriminates against a tax-payer, equity may grant relief.[14]

§ 361. **Same: Multiplicity of Suits.**—The avoidance of a multiplicity of suits as a ground for equitable jurisdiction in tax cases has been so fully discussed elsewhere[15] that a brief summary only is here called for. The propriety of exercising this jurisdiction is seldom denied in the cases belonging to Professor Pomeroy's "Second Class"—where the complainant, in the absence of equitable interference, is exposed to repeated

11 Louisville Trust Co. v. Stone, 107 Fed. 305, 46 C. C. A. 299, Southern Ry. Co. v. North Carolina Corp. Com., 104 Fed. 700, Nashville, C. & St L. R. Co v. Taylor, 86 Fed. 168; Walsh v. King, 74 Mich 350, 41 N. W. 1080. The fraudulent omission of mortgages from the assessment has been held to be ground for relief: Hamblin Real Estate Co. v. City of Astoria, 26 Or. 599, 40 Pac. 230; Smith v. Kelly, 24 Or. 464, 33 Pac. 642. A tax based upon an assessment "fraudulently and corruptly made, with the intention of discriminating" against a party, may be enjoined: Pacific Postal etc. Cable Co. v. Dalton, 119 Cal. 604, 51 Pac. 1072.

12 Oregon & C. R. Co. v. Jackson County, 38 Or. 589, 64 Pac. 307, 65 Pac. 369.

13 Louisville Trust Co. v. Stone, 46 C. C. A. 299, 107 Fed. 305; and see § 371, *infra*.

14 Pioneer Iron Co. v. City of Negaunee, 116 Mich. 430, 74 N. W. 700.

15 See 1 Pom. Eq. Jur. (3d ed.), §§ 258-260, 265, 266, 270, and notes.

litigation with the same defendant[16]—or in those of the "Fourth Class,"—where the single complainant would be compelled to bring or defend numerous suits against different parties, all involving the same questions of fact or law.[17] The exercise of the jurisdiction

16 Suits to enjoin collection of a tax, the invalidity of which had been established at law, were upheld on this ground in Paterson etc. R. R. Co. v. Jersey City, 9 N. J. Eq. 434; Bank of Kentucky v. Stone, 88 Fed. 383; Union & Planters' Bank v Memphis, 111 Fed. 561, 49 C C. A. 455; see 1 Pom. Eq. Jur., § 253, notes 2 and (b).

But it has been held that the plaintiff must show that the danger of repeated suits by the state is "a probable, and not possible danger. . . . . Whatever the rule may be in the case of natural persons, the court will presume that a state is incapable of such a vulgar passion, and, until the fact is shown to be otherwise, will act on the assumption that a state will not bring any more suits than are fairly necessary to establish and maintain its rights" Pacific Exp. Co. v. Seibert, 44 Fed. 310; see 1 Pom. Eq. Jur. (3d ed), § 251¾, note (b).

17 See 1 Pom. Eq Jur. (3d ed.), § 261, note (b), "Class Fourth," pp. 417, 418. A common instance is where a railroad or telegraph company is exposed to tax suits in different counties, all involving a common question; especially where such companies are assessed by a state board on all of their property within the state, and proportionate parts of this assessment are certified for collection to the tax officials of the various counties in which the company operates. Union Pac. R. R. Co. v. McShane, 3 Dill. 303, Fed. Cas. No. 14,382, affirmed, 22 Wall. 444, 22 L ed. 747; Union Pac. R. R. Co. v Cheyenne, 113 U. S. 516, 5 Sup. Ct 601, 28 L. ed. 1098, Northern Pac. R R. Co v. Walker, 47 Fed 681; Western Union Tel. Co. v. Poe, 61 Fed. 449, 453; Sanford v Poe, 69 Fed. 546, 548, 16 C. C A. 305, 60 L. R. A. 641, Western Union Tel. Co. v. Norman, 77 Fed. 13, 21, Railroad & Telephone Cos. v. Board of Equalizers, 85 Fed. 302; Taylor v. Louisville & N. R R Co, 88 Fed. 350, 31 C. C. A. 537, Coulter v. Weir, 62 C. C. A. 429, 127 Fed. 897; Philadelphia, W. & B. R Co. v. Neary, 5 Del. Ch. 600; Mobile & O. R. R. Co. v. Moseley, 52 Miss. 127, 137; Chesapeake & O. R R. Co. v. Miller, 19 W. Va. 408. Again, where a bank or other corporation is required by law to pay the taxes assessed on all of its shares, and reimburse itself by withholding proportionate parts of the dividends from its shareholders, it may enjoin an illegal tax, since its payment thereof would subject it to a suit by each shareholder Cummings v. Merchants' Nat. Bank, 101 U S. 153, 25 L. ed. 903, and

in the "Third Class" of Professor Pomeroy's analysis is a question on which the cases are more evenly divided. In this class, it will be remembered, "a number of persons have separate and individual claims and rights of action against the same party, but all arise from some common cause, are governed by the same legal rule, and involve similar facts, and the whole matter might be settled in a single suit brought by all these persons uniting as co-plaintiffs, or one of the persons suing on behalf of the others, or even by one person suing for himself alone."[18] The equity in this class of cases arises from two considerations: first, the public convenience and economy in determining, in a single equitable issue, a question that, without such determination, might lead to innumerable trials of the same question in separate suits at law; and secondly, the practical failure of justice that must result from leav-

other cases cited; 1 Pom. Eq Jur. (3d ed.), § 261, p. 418. *Contra*, see Equitable Guarantee & T Co. v. Donahoe (Del.), 45 Atl. 583, in 1 Pom. Eq Jur, § 266, note (a).

18 1 Pom Eq Jur., § 245. Among the cases of this class supporting, the jurisdiction are, Greedup v. Franklin County, 30 Ark. 101, Keese v. City of Denver, 10 Colo. 113, 15 Pac. 825 (special assessment); Dumars v. City of Denver, 16 Colo. App. 375, 65 Pac. 580 (special assessment); Bode v. New England Inv. Co., 6 Dak 499, 42 N. W. 658, 45 N. W. 197, Carlton v. Newman, 77 Me. 408, 1 Atl. 194; Sherman v. Benford, 10 R. I. 559, McTwiggan v. Hunter, 18 R. I. 776, 30 Atl. 962, 2 Ames Cas. Eq Jur, 71, 73, and notes, Quimby v. Wood, 19 R. I. 571, 35 Atl. 149; McMickle v. Hardin, 25 Tex Civ. App 222, 61 S. W. 322 (but no injunction after suits have already been begun for the collection of taxes), McClung v Livesay, 7 W. Va. 329; Doonan v. Board of Education, 9 W. Va. 246; Corrothers v Board of Education, 16 W. Va. 527; Williams v. Grant County Court, 26 W. Va. 488, 53 Am Rep. 94 (an exhaustive discussion of the subject); Blue Jacket Co. v. Scherr, 50 W Va. 533, 40 S. E. 514. In states of the second type, also, where the mere illegality of the tax is a ground for its injunction at the suit of the single plaintiff, the avoidance of a multiplicity of suits is recognized as a further ground. See *infra*, Illinois and Missouri. See, also, cases collected in 1 Pom. Eq. Jur., § 260.

ing each member of the community to obtain redress at law for his small share of the injury suffered by all alike. To the vast majority of tax-payers, a suit to recover back illegal taxes paid is, of course, an adequate remedy in theory only; the amount recovered is not worth the expense of litigation.[19] In the view of many courts, however, these considerations of economy and convenience, both to the community as a body and to all its individuals, do not outweigh the "other reasons of policy, founded on the necessity of speedy collection of taxes, which ought to prevent a court of chancery from suspending these [tax] proceedings, except upon the clearest grounds."[20] It is to be observed that the jurisdiction arises, in cases of this class, only "when the illegality extends to the whole tax, so that the question involved is the validity of the whole tax and its assessment on every person taxed";[21] where, for example, the question is one of the exemption from taxation of the separate property of several owners, no "multiplicity of suits" is avoided by the attempt to consolidate the various issues in a single case in equity, since "each complainant must make his own case upon the facts" peculiar to him.[22]

19 See, especially, the passages from the opinions in Greedup v. Franklin County, 30 Ark. 109; Ranney v. Bader, 67 Mo. 476, 480; Carlton v. Newman, 77 Me. 408, 1 Atl 194; and Knopf v. First Nat. Bank, 173 Ill. 331, 50 N. E. 660, quoted in 1 Pom. Eq. Jur. (3d ed.), § 260, note (d).

20 Dodd v. City of Hartford, 25 Conn. 232 See cases cited in 1 Pom. Eq. Jur., §§ 265, 266. This view appears to obtain in Connecticut, Delaware, District of Columbia, Idaho, Michigan, Mississippi, New York, Wisconsin, and possibly in other states.

21 McTwiggan v. Hunter, 18 R. I. 776, 30 Atl. 962.

22 Schulenberg-Boeckeler Lumber Co. v. Town of Hayward, 20 Fed. 422, 424; see 1 Pom Eq. Jur. (3d ed.), § 251½, note (d). Of course, in many states the fact that property is by law exempt from taxation is an independent ground for injunction See *post*, § 363.

§ 362. Same; Cloud on Title.—Taxes on realty, and sometimes those on personalty as well, are generally made a lien upon real estate. Accordingly, if the proceedings are valid on their face, every such tax will cast a cloud upon the title to land. The prevention and removal of such clouds on title are well established and familiar grounds of equitable jurisdiction. Consequently, equity will interfere by injunction to prevent and remove the cloud cast by such an illegal or invalid tax.[23] Where the proceedings are defective upon their face, it is generally held that there is no cloud to remove, the argument being that no injury can result from an instrument which, upon its face, confers no valid right. While the reasoning appears faulty, the decided weight of authority is on its side; and accordingly it is held that an injunction will not issue.[24] In New York, it is held that to warrant relief it must not only be shown that the proceedings are regular on their face and invalid only because of defects *dehors* the record, but also that the defect will not necessarily appear in proceedings to enforce the lien.[25] In some states, a tax deed is made *prima facie* evidence of the validity of the proceedings; and if it is valid upon its face, though invalid in fact, an injunction may issue.[26]

23 The prevention of a cloud on title is probably a ground for the issuance of an injunction against an invalid tax in all jurisdictions save Connecticut, Massachusetts, and Rhode Island.

24 See *e. g.*, cases in the federal courts, and in California, Colorado, Delaware, Idaho, and Minnesota. For a full discussion of these principles, see Vol. II, chapter on Cloud on Title

25 See cases cited in notes to section discussing rules in New York, *post.*

26 See cases cited in notes to sections discussing rules in Wisconsin; but in Minnesota the injunction will not issue when the defect is apparent on the face of the proceedings unless the issuance of such a deed is threatened.

§ 363. **Second Type.**—In states of this type, the mere illegality of a tax is (subject to some limitations) a ground of jurisdiction for its injunction, apart from any question of irreparable injury, of multiplicity of suits, or of cloud on title. No distinction, in principle, is made between taxes on real and on personal property. As might be expected, the tax litigation in many of these states is very extensive. As a result of this litigation, several of the states have worked out a large body of special rules on the subject of equitable relief against taxation, wholly unaided by reference to the development of the subject in sister states; thus rendering any generalizations drawn from a comparison of these rules somewhat difficult, if not unprofitable. In a few of these states, moreover, injunction of illegal taxation is expressly authorized and, to some extent, regulated by statute.[27] Injunction is usually a matter of right when property exempt by law from taxation is sought to be taxed; on the other hand, where the question is one of an oppressive overvaluation, the complainant must, as a general rule, first pursue the statutory remedy of appeal to the board of review or equalization. As to what constitutes a substantial illegality in the assessment or levy of a tax, as distinguished from a mere irregularity that is not a matter for injunctive relief, the decisions are numerous and varying. Where the tax as a whole is illegal, any number of tax-payers may join in the suit, or one may sue on behalf of all others similarly affected.[28] The states clearly belonging in this group are: Georgia, Illinois, Indiana, Iowa, Kansas, Kentucky, Mississippi, Mis-

27 See *infra*, Kansas, Mississippi, Montana, Nebraska, North Carolina, Ohio, Oklahoma, Utah, Wyoming.

28 For further details, see index to this treatise. The numerous and able decisions of the Illinois courts, *infra*, may be consulted with profit as representative of this type of states.

souri (by recent decisions), Montana, Nebraska, North Carolina, Ohio, Oklahoma, Pennsylvania, South Dakota, Tennessee, Utah, Washington, and Wyoming

§ 364. **Special or Local Assessments.**—Special or local assessments, for the purpose of defraying the expense of local improvements, such as the opening, paving, or repairing of streets, and levied by municipal authority upon the property owners embraced within a limited district, are a form of taxation, subject to equitable control upon the same principles which regulate the injunction of general taxation. The "recognized head of equity jurisdiction" under which these cases are nearly always brought is, the prevention of a cloud on the title to real property. The proceedings, therefore, against which relief is sought, must not be invalid upon their face, since otherwise, according to the usual definition, no "cloud" will be cast upon the complainant's title.[29] As in the case of general taxation, mere irregularities in the proceedings do not warrant an injunction, where sufficient has been done, in compliance with statutory directions, to give the municipal authorities jurisdiction of the subject.[30] Of the substantial defects which, when not apparent upon the face of the proceedings, furnish grounds for equitable relief, perhaps the most frequent are: the lack of a consent of the majority of the property-holders to be affected, when that is a statutory prerequisite;[31] that the ordinance,

29 See cases, *infra*, *e. g.*, in the United States courts, California, New York, Vermont, Wisconsin. In Massachusetts, as in cases of general taxation in that state, a threatened cloud upon title does not render the legal remedy inadequate, and is not a ground for injunction.

30 See cases, *infra*, *e. g.*, in the United States courts, Indiana, Michigan, Nebraska, Wisconsin.

31 See cases, *infra*, *e. g.*, in the United States courts, Colorado,

or notice of resolution, was not published as required by statute;[32] that the assessment is apportioned among the owners by a plan or method that involves no consideration of the benefits to be received by them from the improvement or public work.[33] The equitable doctrines of estoppel and acquiescence have a frequent application in cases of this class, either when the owner benefited by the improvement has joined in the petition,[34] or, with full knowledge of the proceedings, has stood by and allowed the work to be prosecuted to completion without objection.[35] The complainant, also, must do equity, in a suit to enjoin an assessment partly valid and partly invalid, by making payment or tender of the sum justly due;[36] but where the assessment is wholly unauthorized and void, no tender or payment for benefits received from the improvement is prerequisite to relief.[37]

§ 365. United States Courts—Federal Taxes.—Under federal statutes no injunction can issue to restrain the collection of taxes levied by the federal government.[38]

Maryland, Nebraska; but see cases in Indiana where the legal remedy provided by statute was adequate.

32 See cases, *infra*, *e. g.*, in Arkansas, California, Nebraska, Oregon.

33 See cases, *infra*, *e. g.*, in the United States courts, Michigan, Missouri, New York, Ohio, Oregon, Washington, Wisconsin.

34 See cases *infra*, *e. g.*, in Kansas and Michigan.

35 See cases *infra*, *e. g.*, in Indiana, Kansas, Michigan, Nebraska, Ohio, Oregon. But where the proceedings are wholly void and unauthorized, it has frequently been held that such silence on the owner's part does not estop him from attacking the assessment even after the completion of the work; compare cases, *infra*, in Colorado, Iowa, Missouri, Oregon.

36 See cases *infra*, *e. g.*, in Indiana, Missouri, Nebraska, and especially in Wisconsin.

37 See cases *infra*, *e. g.*, in the United States courts, California (but decisions appear to conflict), New York, Oregon, Wisconsin.

38 U. S. Rev. Stats., § 3224; Snyder v. Marks, 109 U. S 189, 3 Sup. Ct 157, 27 L. ed. 901; Burgdorf v. District of Columbia, 7 App. D. C. 405.

The only remedy of the tax-payer is to pay the money and then sue to recover it back. The only cases where federal courts can enjoin taxation are those where state taxes are involved. Therefore, an injunction requiring a collector of internal revenue to accept an export bond and to allow the withdrawal of goods without payment of a tax thereon, will not issue, for it in effect would restrain the collection of internal revenue taxes.[39]

§ 366. **State Taxes; Federal Jurisdiction.**—Of course the federal courts will not interfere with state taxation unless the case presents some features which make it of federal cognizance. So long as a state, by its laws prescribing the mode and subject of taxation does not intrench upon the legitimate authority of the Union, nor violate any right secured by the Constitution of the United States, the federal court, as between the state and its citizen, can afford no relief, no matter how unjust, oppressive or onerous the tax may be.[40]

If the claim to relief clearly within the federal jurisdiction is fair and colorable, not fictitious and fraudulent, jurisdiction attaches, although the ultimate decision may be against the right claimed. When the jurisdiction has properly attached, it extends to the whole case, and to all the issues involved, whether of a federal or non-federal character, and the court has power to decide upon all questions involved. Therefore, when the court has obtained jurisdiction on some ground, it may go ahead and examine into the legality of a state tax, whether or not it involves a federal question, and if it finds there is not an adequate remedy at law in the state courts, it may grant an injunction.[41]

39 Miles v. Johnson, 59 Fed. 38.
40 Kirkland v. Hotchkiss, 100 U. S. 497, 25 L. ed. 558.
41 Louisville Trust Co. v. Stone, 107 Fed. 305, 46 C. C. A. 299.

Thus, it has been held that the statutes of Kentucky do not afford an adequate remedy when capital stock of a corporation is illegally assessed, and therefore an injunction may issue.[42]

A suit to enjoin the collection of a tax imposed by a state is not a suit against a state within the meaning of the Eleventh Amendment of the federal constitution. It is rather a suit against individuals, seeking to enjoin them from doing certain acts which they assert to be by the authority of the state, but which the complainant avers to be without lawful authority.[43]

§ 367. **Adequate Remedy in State Courts.**—The federal courts are not ousted of their jurisdiction to grant injunctions in tax cases, where federal questions are involved, because a state furnishes an adequate statutory remedy in its own courts.[44] And this is true, even though the state statute provides that its remedy shall be exclusive and forbids injunctions.[45]

Where a valid state statute gives a right of appeal to the courts from an assessment, and no federal question is involved, it is an adequate remedy for any error or illegality. Therefore, a tax-payer who does not avail himself of such remedy cannot maintain a suit in the United States courts to enjoin the collection of a tax

42 Id.

43 Taylor v. Louisville & N. R. Co., 88 Fed 350, 31 C. C. A. 537, Gregg v. Sanford, 65 Fed. 151, 12 C. C. A. 525, Ex parte Tyler, 149 U. S. 164, 13 Sup. Ct. 785, 39 L. ed. 689, Ex parte Ayers, 123 U. S. 443, 8 Sup. Ct. 164, 31 L. ed. 216. This decision distinguishes between this class of cases and those where breach of contract by the state is involved. See, also, Union Pac. R. Co. v Alexander, 113 Fed. 347

44 Brown v. French, 80 Fed. 166; Ex parte Tyler, 149 U. S 164, 13 Sup. Ct. 785, 39 L. ed. 689; Cummings v. Merchants' Nat. Bank, 101 U. S. 153, 25 L. ed. 903.

45 Taylor v. Louisville & N. R. Co., 88 Fed. 350, 31 C. C. A. 537.

illegally assessed.[46] Likewise, where state laws provide for an appeal to a board of equalization for redress against an excessive tax, a party who fails to resort to such a tribunal cannot obtain relief in the federal courts.[47] And it is for the state court to determine whether or not the statutory remedy is exclusive.[48]

§ 368. **Grounds of the Equitable Jurisdiction.**—A federal court of equity will not enjoin the collection of a state tax, "except where it may be necessary to protect the rights of the citizen whose property is taxed, and he has no adequate remedy by the ordinary processes of law. It must appear that the enforcement of the tax would lead to a multiplicity of suits, or produce irreparable injury, or where the property is real estate, throw a cloud upon the title of the complainant, before the aid of a court of equity can be invoked." "The illegality of the tax and the threatened sale . . . . for its payment constitute of themselves alone no ground for such interposition. There must be some special circumstances attending a threatened injury of this kind, distinguishing it from a common trespass, and bringing the case under some recognized head of equity jurisdiction."[49] Thus, the mere fact that a tax is unconsti-

46 Pittsburgh, C., C. & St. L. Ry. Co. v. Board of Pub. Works, 172 U. S. 32, 19 Sup. Ct. 90, 43 L. ed. 354.

47 Altschul v. Gittings, 86 Fed. 200; Dundee Mortgage Trust Inv. Co. v. Charlton, 13 Saw. 25, 32 Fed. 192.

48 Northern Pac. Railroad Co. v. Patterson, 154 U. S. 130, 14 Sup. Ct. 977, 38 L. ed. 934

49 Dows v. City of Chicago, 11 Wall. 108, 20 L. ed. 65; Arkansas B & L Assn. v. Madden, 175 U. S. 269, 20 Sup. Ct 119, 44 L. ed. 159, Pittsburgh, C., C. & St. L. Ry. Co v. Board of Pub. Works of W. Va., 172 U. S. 32, 19 Sup. Ct. 90, 43 L. ed. 354, Pacific Express Co. v. Seibert, 142 U. S. 339, 12 Sup. Ct. 250, 30 L. ed. 1035; Shelton v. Platt, 139 U. S. 596, 11 Sup. Ct. 646, 35 L. ed. 276; Union Pac. Ry. Co. v. Cheyenne, 113 U. S. 516, 5 Sup. Ct 601, 28 L ed. 1098, State Railroad Tax Cases, 92 U. S. 616, 23 L. ed 663; Hannewinkle

tutional is no ground for an injunction.[50] And an injunction will not be granted when full relief can be obtained by an action at law to recover the amount paid;[51] nor where there is a mere irregularity in the assessment,[52] as where shares of stock are listed to the corporation instead of to the stockholders;[53] or where the tax-roll is completed after the statutory time;[54] nor because of a mere error in judgment on the part of the assessing officers. Fraud or misconduct must be proved, as well as facts bringing the case under some recognized head of equity jurisdiction.[55]

§ 369. **Personal Property.**—A federal court will not, except under very special circumstances, enjoin the collection of a tax which is only a personal charge against the party taxed or a charge against his personal property. Presumptively, the remedy at law is adequate in

v. City of Georgetown, 15 Wall. 547, 21 L. ed. 231, Bank of Kentucky v. Stone, 88 Fed. 383; Taylor v. Louisville & N. R. Co., 88 Fed. 350, 31 C. C. A 537; Robinson v. City of Wilmington, 25 U. S. App. 144, 65 Fed. 856, 13 C. C. A. 177; Tilton v. Oregon C. M. R. Co., 3 Saw. 22, Fed. Cas. No. 14,055; Union & Planters' Bank v. City of Memphis, 111 Fed. 561, 49 C. C. A. 455

50 Pacific Exp. Co. v. Seibert, 142 U. S 339, 12 Sup. Ct. 250, 30 L. ed. 1035; Allen v. Pullman's Palace Car Co., 139 U. S. 661, 11 Sup. Ct. 682, 35 L. ed. 304; Shelton v. Platt, 139 U. S. 596, 11 Sup. Ct. 646, 35 L. ed. 276.

51 Arkansas B. & L. Assn. v. Madden, 175 U. S. 269, 20 Sup Ct 119, 44 L. ed. 159; Robinson v. City of Wilmington, 65 Fed. 856, 25 U. S. App. 144, 13 C. C. A. 177; Shelton v. Platt, 139 U. S. 596, 11 Sup. Ct. 646, 35 L. ed. 276; State Railroad Tax Cases, 92 U. S. 616, 23 L ed. 663; Dows v. City of Chicago, 11 Wall. 108, 20 L. ed 65.

52 State Railroad Tax Cases, 92 U. S. 616, 23 L. ed. 663; Douglas County v. Stone, 110 Fed. 812.

53 Robinson v. City of Wilmington, 25 U. S. App. 144, 65 Fed. 856, 13 C. C. A. 177.

54 Woodman v. Ely, 2 Fed. 839.

55 Maish v. Arizona, 164 U. S. 599, 17 Sup. Ct 193, 41 L. ed 567; Albuquerque Nat. Bank v. Perea, 147 U. S. 87, 13 Sup. Ct. 194, 37 L. ed. 91; Woodman v. Ely, 2 Fed 839.

such cases. And the mere fact that the property is used in interstate commerce is not sufficient to warrant an injunction;[56] nor will it issue even though the complainant is a non-resident and the tax is therefore absolutely illegal.[57] Where, however, the collection of a tax on personal property involves a threat of irreparable injury and inconvenience to the public, an injunction may issue. Thus, where the business and traffic of a railroad company will be stopped by a seizure of its cars, an injunction is proper.[58]

§ 370. **Irreparable Injury.**—When the remedy at law for an illegal tax is inadequate in the state courts, a federal court may, after acquiring jurisdiction, interfere by injunction to prevent irreparable injury. Thus, under the Kentucky law, an action to recover illegal taxes paid will not lie unless they are paid under duress, and yet in certain cases a penalty of fifty dollars per day is provided where payment is delayed. The legal remedy, therefore, of defending a tax suit is attended with a great and oppressive burden of risk, and is entirely inadequate. Hence, an injunction may issue.[59] Upon the same principle an injunction will

56 Linehan Ry. & Transfer Co. v. Pendergrass, 70 Fed. 1, 16 C. C. A. 585, Nye, Jenks & Co. v. Town of Washburn, 125 Fed 817; Shelton v. Platt, 139 U. S. 596, 11 Sup Ct. 646, 35 L. ed. 276; Union Pac. R. Co. v. Lincoln Co., 2 Dill. 279, Fed. Cas. No. 14,379. In Hazzard v. O'Bannon (Cir Ct, E. D. Mo.), 36 Fed. 854, it was held, however, that an injunction will issue to restrain the collection of an illegal excess on personal property when the writ is not absolutely void, and would therefore protect the sheriff in an action of trespass.

57 City of Milwaukee v. Koeffler, 116 U. S. 219, 6 Sup. Ct. 372, 29 L. ed. 612.

58 Southern Ry. Co. v. City of Asheville, 69 Fed. 359.

59 Bank of Kentucky v. Stone, 88 Fed 383. Affirmed, Stone v. Bank of Kentucky, 174 U. S. 799, 19 Sup. Ct. 881, 43 L. ed. 1177; First Nat. Bank v. City of Covington, 103 Fed. 523.

issue when the collection of an illegal tax will destroy a corporate franchise. This rule was laid down by Chief Justice Marshall in the case of Osborn v. Bank of the United States[60] In that case, the state of Ohio had imposed an illegal tax upon the Bank of the United States with the avowed intention of driving it from the state. The agent whose duty it was to collect could not properly respond in damages. Consequently, the franchise of the bank would have been of no effect so far as it authorized the transaction of business in Ohio unless the injunction had been granted. Therefore, the injunction was allowed, to prevent irreparable injury. The United States may enjoin the enforcement of a state tax on lands allotted in severalty, and which it holds in trust for Indians, for the legal remedy is inadequate.[61]

§ 371. Valuation Resulting in Unjust Discrimination.— To the general rule there seems to be one exception. "When the overvaluation of property has arisen from the adoption of a rule of appraisement which conflicts with a constitutional or statutory direction, and operates unequally, not merely on a single individual, but on a large class of individuals or corporations, a party aggrieved may resort to equity to restrain the exaction of the excess, upon payment or tender of what is admitted to be due."[62] So, where a standard of valuation results in discrimination, the parties injured may obtain an injunction.[63] Likewise, an injunction will

60 9 Wheat. 738, 6 L. ed. 204.

61 United States v. Rickert, 188 U. S. 432, 23 Sup. Ct. 478, 47 L. ed 532.

62 Stanley v. Supervisors, 121 U. S. 535, 7 Sup. Ct. 1234, 30 L. ed. 1000; Cummings v. Merchants' Nat. Bank, 101 U. S. 153, 25 L. ed. 903; Pelton v Commercial Nat. Bank, 101 U. S. 143, 25 L. ed. 901; German Nat. Bank v Kimball, 103 U. S. 732, 26 L. ed. 469.

63 Trustees Cincinnati Southern Ry. v. Guenther, 19 Fed. 395.

be issued when state officers, by a systematic, intentional and illegal under-valuation of other property, make an unjust discrimination against the plaintiff, the federal jurisdiction arising because of the equal protection of the laws guaranteed by the Fourteenth Amendment.[64] But the proof of discrimination must be clear and convincing before the injunction will issue.[65] If it appears, however, that the assessing officers intentionally and habitually violate the law in this regard, it need not affirmatively appear that they do so with intent to injure the complainant and his class of tax-payers.[66]

§ 372. **Multiplicity of Suits.**—This ground of jurisdiction has met with abundant recognition in cases of the "Second Class" and of the "Fourth Class";[67] but appears to have been rejected in one case of the "Third Class,"[68] where the equity arises from the fact that the burden of an illegal tax falls on numerous individuals in the same way. This class is, at any rate, confined to cases where the tax as a whole is invalid;[69] and in any event the jurisdiction is asserted to prevent a probable, not a possible, multiplicity of suits.[70]

§ 373. **Cloud on Title.**—Where an invalid tax, valid on its face, casts a cloud on the title of the plaintiff's

64 Louisville Trust Co. v. Stone, 107 Fed. 305, 46 C C. A. 299; Southern Ry. Co. v. North Carolina Corp. Com., 104 Fed. 700; Nashville, C. & St. L. Ry. Co. v. Taylor, 86 Fed. 168.

65 Coulter v. Louisville & N. R. Co., 196 U. S. 599, 25 Sup Ct. 342, 49 L. ed. ——; Michigan Railroad Tax Cases, 138 Fed. 223, 244-248; Louisville Trust Co. v. Stone, 107 Fed. 305, 46 C. C. A. 299.

66 Taylor v. Louisville & N. R. Co., 88 Fed. 350, 31 C. C. A. 537.

67 See *ante*, § 361, notes 16, 17.

68 People's Nat. Bank v. Marye, 107 Fed. 570.

69 See *ante*, § 361, note 22.

70 See *ante*, § 361, note 16.

real estate, an injunction will issue.[71] Thus, where an illegal tax on the stock of a national bank is made a lien on its real estate, its collection or enforcement may be enjoined.[72] And where an illegal tax against a common carrier is made a lien on its realty, although personalty is to be resorted to first, equitable relief will be allowed.[73] Likewise, it will be allowed where a settlement of illegal back taxes will, when the proper steps are taken, constitute a lien on real estate;[74] or where an assessment willfully made in disregard of a statute is made a lien on realty,[75] although a Board of Equalization has refused relief.

There is no cloud upon the title, however, which justifies the interference of a court of equity, where the proceedings are void upon their face; that is, where the same record which must be introduced to establish the title claimed will show that there is no title.[76]

§ 374. **State Tax in Violation of Contract.**—Where a state imposes a tax on a corporation in violation of the terms of its charter, a federal court may issue an injunction because of the violation of contract.[77] And where the corporation itself refuses to sue, the suit

71 Tilton v. Oregon C. M. R. Co., 3 Saw. 22, Fed. Cas. No. 14,055; Taylor v. Louisville & N. R. Co., 31 C. C. A. 537, 88 Fed. 350; Ogden City v. Armstrong, 168 U. S. 224, 18 Sup. Ct. 98; Kansas City, Ft. S. & M. R Co. v. King, 120 Fed. 615; People's Sav. Bank v. Layman, 134 Fed. 635; Gregg v. Sanford, 65 Fed. 151, 12 C. C. A. 525; Union Pac. Ry. Co. v. Cheyenne, 113 U. S. 516, 5 Sup. Ct. 601, 28 L. ed. 1098.

72 Brown v. French, 80 Fed. 166.

73 Southern Ry. Co. v. Asheville, 69 Fed. 359.

74 Sanford v. Gregg, 58 Fed. 620.

75 California & O. Land Co. v. Gowen, 48 Fed. 771.

76 Hannewinkle v. City of Georgetown, 15 Wall. 547, 21 L. ed. 231.

77 Dodge v. Woolsey, 18 How. 331, 15 L. ed. 401; Detroit, G. H. & M. R. Co. v. Powers, 138 Fed. 264.

may be brought by a stockholder, the corporation being made a party defendant.[78]

§ 375. **Injunction Warranted by State Laws.**—Where the federal court acquires jurisdiction of the case and facts are shown which, under the state law, warrant the issuance of an injunction, such relief may be awarded, whether the facts are such as ordinarily warrant such relief in federal courts, or not. Thus, under section 5848 of the Ohio statutes providing that the illegal levy of taxes and assessments, or either, may be enjoined, a federal court may enjoin an increase in the assessment of a national bank, illegal because made by a board of equalization without notice.[79] Under the same statute, the federal court may enjoin the collection of any tax found to be illegal,[80] such, for instance, as a tax on federal bonds which are exempt from taxation.[81] Likewise, where, under the decisions of the supreme court of Kansas an injunction will issue when one class of property is intentionally assessed in greater proportion than another, federal courts, in like cases coming from that state, will grant an injunction.[82] And, following the supreme court of Washington, an injunction will be granted where there has been an unjust discrimination.[83]

§ 376. **Tender.**—The collection of a tax valid in part cannot be enjoined unless the party seeking the in-

78 Dodge v. Woolsey, 18 How 331, 15 L. ed. 401.

79 Mercantile Nat. Bank v. Hubbard, 105 Fed. 809, 45 C. C. A. 66.

80 Cummings v. Merchants' Nat. Bank, 101 U. S. 153, 25 L. ed. 903; Brinckerhoff v. Brumfield, 94 Fed. 422.

81 Grether v. Wright, 75 Fed. 742, 23 C. C. A. 498.

82 Chicago, B. & Q. R. Co. v. Board of Commissioners of Republic Co, 67 Fed. 411, 14 C. C. A. 456

83 First Nat. Bank v. Hungate, 62 Fed. 548.

junction has paid or tendered, unconditionally, so much of the tax as it is certain he should pay.[84] An averment of readiness to pay, or a tender made in the bill, is not sufficient.[85] If it appears that a sufficient sum has not been tendered, the complainant must actually tender the true amount before he can obtain relief.[86] And upon application of the defendant, he may be compelled to pay into court.[87]

When a tax is wholly void, it is not necessary to make a tender as a prerequisite to an injunction;[88] nor is it necessary when county officers have declared in advance that they will not accept less than the full amount.[89]

§ 377. Property in Hands of Federal Receiver.—When property is in the hands of a receiver appointed by a federal court, an injunction may issue *pendente lite* forbidding state taxing officers to collect disputed taxes

84 Northern Pac. R. Co. v. Clark, 153 U. S. 252, 14 Sup Ct. 809, 38 L. ed. 706; Albuquerque Nat. Bank v. Perea, 147 U. S. 87, 13 Sup. Ct. 194, 37 L. ed. 91; Dundee Mortgage Trust Inv. Co. v. Parrish, 24 Fed. 197; German National Bank v. Kimball, 103 U. S. 732, 26 L. ed. 469; State Railroad Tax Cases, 92 U. S. 616, 23 L. ed. 674, Parmley v. Railroad Companies, 3 Dill. C. C. 25, Fed. Cas. No. 10,768; Morenci Copper Co. v. Freer, 127 Fed. 199; People's Nat. Bank v. Marye, 191 U. S. 272, 24 Sup. Ct. 68, 48 L. ed. 180.

85 Chicago, B. & Q. R. Co. v. Board of Commissioners of Norton Co., 67 Fed. 413, 14 C. C. A. 458; Huntington v. Palmer, 7 Saw. 355, 8 Fed. 449, State Railroad Tax Cases, 92 U. S. 616, 23 L. ed. 674

86 Chicago, B. & Q. R. Co. v Board of Commissioners of Norton Co., 67 Fed. 413, 14 C. C. A. 458.

87 Richmond & D R. Co. v. Blake, 49 Fed. 904.

88 Fargo v. Hart, 193 U. S. 490, 24 Sup. Ct. 498, 48 L. ed 761; First Nat. Bank v. City of Covington, 103 Fed 523, Albany City Nat. Bank v. Maher, 19 Blatchf. 175, 9 Fed. 884. And this rule holds, although a state law requires that the amount of the tax must be deposited before suit. Northern etc. R. R. Co. v. Kurtzman, 82 Fed. 241.

89 First Nat. Bank v. Hungate, 62 Fed. 548.

levied against it.[90] The property being in custody of the court, any charge against it, even for taxes, can be enforced against it only through the orders of the court. Therefore the court may well insist that the hands of the executive officers be tied until the issue can be determined.

§ 378. **Special Assessments.**—The rules as to local assessments are similar to those relating to general taxation. An injunction will not ordinarily be granted unless the case is brought within some recognized head of equity jurisdiction, other than mere illegality.[91] An injunction will not issue because of a mere irregularity in the proceedings.[92] Where a state statute provides for an appeal from an assessment on questions of law alone, it is an adequate remedy for errors and irregularities occurring subsequent to the adoption of the ordinance and the making of the contract under which the improvement was constructed, and therefore no injunction will issue to restrain the collection of an assessment on the ground of such irregularities.[93]

Where an invalid local assessment casts a cloud upon the title to real estate, and the defect is not apparent upon the face of the proceedings, an injunction is the proper remedy. Thus, where statute makes the consent of a majority of the property owners essential to the validity of an assessment which is a lien on land, an injunction may be obtained if the assessment is lev-

90 Clark v. McGhee, 87 Fed. 789; Ex parte Chamberlain, 55 Fed. 704, Ex parte Tyler, 149 U. S. 164, 13 Sup Ct. 785, 37 L. ed. 689. See, also, *ante*, chapter IV, § 168.

91 Ogden City v. Armstrong, 168 U. S. 224, 18 Sup. Ct. 98, 42 L. ed. 444.

92 Ogden City v. Armstrong, 168 U. S. 224, 18 Sup. Ct. 98, 42 L. ed. 444.

93 Rickcords v. City of Hammond, 67 Fed. 380.

ied without such consent, for the defect is not apparent on the face of the proceedings.[94] A federal court may enjoin the enforcement of a special assessment made under a rule or system in violation of the Constitution of the United States.[95] Thus, an injunction is proper when the assessment is rested upon a basis which excludes any consideration of benefits.[96]

Where an owner of land subject to a mortgage joins in a petition for the improvement, a subsequent owner who acquires title by foreclosure is not estopped from attacking the assessment.[97] When the complainant has been guilty of laches, injunctive relief will be denied. Thus, after an assessment has been levied for seven years it is too late to enjoin a threatened sale thereunder.[98]

Where the assessment is wholly void, it is not necessary to make any tender for the benefits conferred as a prerequisite to relief.[99]

§ 379. **Alabama.**—In Alabama, "in addition to illegality, hardship, or irregularity, the case must be brought within some of the recognized foundations of equitable jurisdiction, and . . . . mere errors of excess in valuation, or hardships, or injustice of the law, or any grievance which can be redressed by a suit at law, either before or after payment of the taxes, will not

94 Ogden City v. Armstrong, 168 U. S. 224, 18 Sup. Ct. 98, 42 L. ed. 444

95 Village of Norwood v. Baker, 172 U. S. 269, 19 Sup Ct. 187, 43 L ed 443; Craighill v. Lambert, 168 U. S. 611, 18 Sup. Ct. 217, 42 L. ed. 599. See, also, Charles v. City of Marion, 98 Fed 166

96 Village of Norwood v. Baker, 172 U. S. 269, 19 Sup Ct. 187, 43 L ed. 443, Zehnder v. Barber Asphalt Co, 106 Fed 103, Bidwell v. Huff, 103 Fed 362; Lyon v. Town of Tonawanda, 98 Fed. 361.

97 Lyon v. Town of Tonawanda, 98 Fed. 361.

98 Ross v. City of Portland, 105 Fed. 682.

99 Village of Norwood v. Baker, 172 U. S. 269, 19 Sup. Ct 187, 43 L. ed 443

justify a court of equity to interfere by injunction to stay collection of the tax." Thus, even though an illegal tax will cast a cloud on title, it will not be enjoined where there is an adequate remedy at law.[100]

The tax-payer is not entitled to any relief whatever unless the legal part of the tax is either tendered or paid.[101]

§ 380. **Arizona.**—In Arizona, an injunction will issue to restrain the collection of a tax on property exempt from taxation. Thus, shares of stock in a corporation being a class of property which takes the situs of its owner, an injunction will be granted to restrain the collection of a tax on such property elsewhere.[102] Mere errors in the assessment, however, are not sufficient to warrant relief.[103]

In order to obtain relief it is usually necessary for the plaintiff to tender or pay the part of the tax which is legal. A tender may possibly be excused after sale when the purchaser is a party who was in duty bound to pay the tax.[104]

§ 381. **Arkansas.**—Where the assessment is committed by law to certain commissioners, a mere allegation of excess is not sufficient to warrant an injunction. "In the absence of fraud, intentional wrong, or error in the method of assessment, the finding by the board cannot

100 Boyd v. City of Selma, 96 Ala. 144, 11 South. 393, 16 L. R. A. 729.

101 Nashville, C. & St. L. Ry. Co v. City of Attalla, 118 Ala 262, 24 South. 450; Tallahassee Mfg. Co. v. Spigener, 49 Ala. 262.

102 National Bank of Arizona v. Long (Ariz.), 57 Pac. 639.

103 County of Cochise v. Copper Queen Consol. Min Co. (Ariz.), 71 Pac 946.

104 Murray v. Evans (Ariz.), 64 Pac. 412.

be overturned by evidence going only to show an error of judgment."[105]

An injunction will issue to restrain the collection of a tax on exempt property, provided irreparable injury would follow refusal. Thus, an injunction has been granted against a sale of exempt railroad property for non-payment of a tax, the court saying:—"The illegality of the taxes alone could not give the court jurisdiction to restrain the sale, but the sale of the road would most probably, if not necessarily, result in the stoppage of its trains and the suspension of its business for an indefinite time, and until the company could regain possession; an injury which, because the actual damages by reason of their uncertain nature, could not be ascertained, would be irreparable, and to prevent which it was the duty of the court to interpose by injunction."[106]

An injunction will issue to restrain the collection of an illegal tax which is a lien on land when extrinsic evidence is necessary to show its invalidity.[107] In such a case, it seems, a tax-payer may sue on behalf of himself and all other tax-payers in the county, the court taking jurisdiction to prevent multiplicity of suits.[108]

An injunction will not issue against the collection of an excessive tax good in part unless the amount admitted to be legally due is paid or tendered before suit.[109]

105 Wells, Fargo & Co.'s Express v. Crawford County, 63 Ark. 576, 40 S. W. 710, 37 L. R. A. 371.

106 Oliver v. Memphis etc. R. R. Co, 30 Ark. 128.

107 Greedup et al. v. Franklin County, 30 Ark. 101.

108 Id. See quotation from the opinion in this case, in 1 Pom. Eq. Jur. (3d ed.), § 260, note (d). The jurisdiction on this ground is now expressly conferred by the constitution, 1874, art 16, § 13· Little Rock v. Prather, 46 Ark. 471; Taylor v. Pine Bluff, 34 Ark. 603; Little Rock v. Barton, 33 Ark. 436.

109 Wells, Fargo & Co.'s Express v. Crawford County, 63 Ark. 576, 40 S. W. 710, 37 L. R. A. 371.

This is upon the principle that "he who seeks equity must do equity." Upon the same principle, an injunction will not be granted against the issuance of a tax deed after sale for excessive taxes, unless the amount really due is tendered or paid.[110]

§ 382. **Special Assessments.**—When a special assessment is levied on land without authority, an injunction will issue. Thus, where a statute requires publication of the ordinance creating the district within five days, no jurisdiction to make the levy attaches unless such publication is made. Therefore an injunction will issue to restrain the collection of an assessment when the proper publication has not been made.[111]

§ 383. **California.**—In California, it is held that an injunction will not issue to restrain the collection of a tax, unless the case is brought under some recognized head of equity jurisdiction. It must appear that enforcement would lead to a multiplicity of suits, or produce irreparable injury, or where the property is real estate, throw a cloud upon the title of the complainant.[112]

An injunction will not issue to restrain the collection of a tax on personal property, unless the injury is irreparable; and where the tax-collector is able to respond in damages, the injury is not irreparable;[113] nor to restrain the collection of a tax because of irregularities which could have been corrected by an appeal to the board of equalization, when such appeal has not been made.[114] Likewise, it will not issue against col-

110 Worthen v. Badgett, 32 Ark. 496.

111 Crane v. City of Siloam Springs, 67 Ark. 30, 55 S. W. 955.

112 Savings & Loan Soc. v. Austin, 46 Cal. 417.

113 Ritter v. Patch, 12 Cal. 298.

114 Merrill v. Gorham, 6 Cal. 41.

lection of a tax levied by an irrigation district, because of mere irregularities, unless the tax-payer shows an injury to himself. Thus, a complaint which alleges that a board of equalization has raised assessments after it has lost jurisdiction, does not state a cause of action unless it shows that plaintiff's assessment has been raised, or that other assessments have been lowered, so as to increase plaintiff's proportionate liability.[115]

"A tax-payer may enjoin the collection of a tax founded upon an assessment fraudulently and corruptly made with the intention of discriminating against him, and for the purpose of causing him to pay more than his share of public taxes."[116] "But in appealing to a court of equity for relief by way of injunction against such fraudulent assessment, the plaintiff must show by his complaint that he has paid or tendered the amount of taxes which would have been due from him if his property had been assessed at what he concedes would have been a fair valuation, and he must in addition offer to pay what the court shall find to be equitable and just."[117]

Cloud on Title.—An injunction will issue against the collection of an illegal tax when the invalidity of the assessment will not appear upon the face of a deed given to a purchaser at a tax sale. Thus, where an

115 Lahman v. Hatch, 124 Cal. 1, 56 Pac. 621. Section 71 of the act providing for irrigation districts (Stats. 1897, p. 534) provides. "The court hearing any of the contests herein provided for, in inquiring into the regularity, legality or correctness of such proceedings, must disregard any error, irregularity or omission which does not affect the substantial rights of the parties to such action or proceeding."

116 Pacific Postal etc. Cable Co. v. Dalton, 119 Cal. 604, 51 Pac. 1072, County of Los Angeles v. Ballerino, 99 Cal. 597, 32 Pac. 581, 34 Pac. 329 (*dictum*)

117 County of Los Angeles v. Ballerino, 99 Cal. 597, 32 Pac. 581, 34 Pac. 329 (*dictum*).

assessment is void because not authorized by the electors of a district, as required by statute, an injunction will issue because the fact will not appear on the face of the tax deed.[118] Where, however, the irregularity will appear upon the face of the deed, as where the assessment is levied under a repealed law, there is no cloud on title, and no injunction will issue.[119]

§ 384. **Special Assessments.**—It has been stated by the supreme court that an injunction will not issue to restrain the collection of a special assessment when it does not appear that the complainant would sustain irreparable injury, or that a sale would cast a cloud upon title to real estate.[120] It may be laid down as a general principle that an injunction will not be allowed where the proceedings are void on their face, for in such a case there is no cloud on title.[121] Hence, when it appears on the face of the proceedings that they are taken under the general law when they should be according to the provisions of a city charter, an injunction will not issue.[122] Where, however, the assessment is void, constitutes a lien on real estate, and the defect is not apparent on the face of the proceedings, an injunction will issue. Thus, it has been held where the publication of the notice of passage of a resolution of intention was made in a newspaper not designated by the city council, that no jurisdiction attached; that the defect was not apparent on the face of the proceedings; and that therefore an injunction was the proper remedy.[123]

118 Woodruff v. Perry, 103 Cal. 611, 37 Pac. 526.

119 Burr v. Hunt, 18 Cal. 303.

120 Dean v. Davis, 51 Cal. 406.

121 Bucknall v. Story, 36 Cal. 67.

122 Byrne v. Drain, 127 Cal. 663, 60 Pac 433.

123 Chase v. City Treasurer, 122 Cal. 540, 55 Pac. 414.

Payment or Tender.—As to whether it is necessary to pay the amount of the benefit as a prerequisite to relief there is a direct conflict of authority. The later decision holds that where the defect is such as to prevent the council from acquiring jurisdiction (and it is generally held that no jurisdiction attaches unless the statute is strictly complied with), no tender or payment is necessary.[124] On the other hand, it was held in a case five years earlier that so long as a moral obligation to pay any portion exists, a court of equity will not lend its aid to prevent a cloud on title.[125]

§ 385. **Colorado.**—In Colorado "it is well settled that courts of equity will not enjoin the collection of a tax solely on the ground of its illegality, or the threatened sale of property to satisfy it. Additional facts must be alleged, and plainly appear, to bring a case within some recognized head of equity jurisdiction. It must be shown that not only would the plaintiff be without an adequate remedy at law, but that the enforcement of the tax would produce irreparable injury, or lead to a multiplicity of suits, or bring a cloud upon his title."[126] Thus, an injunction will not be granted to restrain the collection of a tax on personal property when the tax collector is able to respond in damages, for there is an adequate remedy at law.[127]

124 Chase v. City Treasurer, 122 Cal. 540, 55 Pac 414.

125 Esterbrook v. O'Brien, 98 Cal. 671, 33 Pac. 765. This case was cited with approval in Hellman v. Shoulters, 114 Cal. 136, 44 Pac. 915, 45 Pac. 1057. In an early case, Weber v. City of San Francisco, 1 Cal. 455, it was held that the validity of the ordinance would not be inquired into after the completion of the work.

126 Wason v. Major, 10 Colo. App. 181, 50 Pac. 741; City of Highlands v. Johnson, 24 Colo. 371, 51 Pac. 1004; Dumars v. City of Denver, 16 Colo. App 375, 65 Pac. 580.

127 Insurance Co of North America v. Bonner, 24 Colo. 220, 49 Pac. 366, Id., 7 Colo. App. 97, 42 Pac. 681.

Cloud on Title and Multiplicity of Suits.—Where an invalid tax casts a cloud on title, an injunction will issue to restrain its collection.[128] The illegality, as a general rule, must not appear on the face of the proceedings. Thus, where the tax is assessed under an unconstitutional law, no injunction will be granted, for the illegality is said to be apparent.[129] But where some other ground of equity jurisdiction appears, the mere fact that the proceedings are void on their face will not warrant a refusal of relief. "While void proceedings cast no cloud upon title to real estate, and a single individual, moving only in his own behalf, and for his own purposes, to restrain such proceedings, will be remitted to his remedy at law, yet where a number of persons are similarly affected, and the rights of all may be adjusted in one proceeding, a court of equity will assume jurisdiction, notwithstanding there is no cloud to remove, and the ground of its jurisdiction is the prevention of a multiplicity of suits."[130] In order to be entitled to an injunction against an invalid assessment, plaintiff must make his objection before the board of equalization first.[131]

Tender.—Where part of a tax is valid and part invalid, no injunction will issue until the valid part is either tendered or paid.[132] Where, however, the entire

128 Dumars v. City of Denver, 16 Colo. App. 375, 65 Pac. 580.

129 Wason v. Major, 10 Colo. App. 181, 50 Pac. 741.

130 Dumars v. City of Denver, 16 Colo. App 375, 65 Pac. 580. "Class Third" is thus distinctly recognized: See 1 Pom. Eq. Jur. (3d ed), § 260, note (b).

131 American Refrigerator Transit Co. v. Adams, 28 Colo 119, 63 Pac. 410.

132 Insurance Co. of North America v. Bonner, 24 Colo. 220, 49 Pac. 366; American Refrigerator Transit Co. v. Thomas, 28 Colo. 119, 63 Pac. 410; Wason v. Major, 10 Colo. App. 181, 50 Pac. 741; People v. Henderson, 12 Colo. 379, 21 Pac. 144.

tax fails by reason of an illegal assessment, the injunction will be granted without a tender.[133]

§ 386. **Special Assessments.**—An injunction will issue to restrain the collection of a special assessment when there is a jurisdictional defect in the proceedings. Thus, when a majority do not petition for the improvement, as required by statute, the city council has no authority to order it, and an injunction will issue even though the resolution states that a majority have petitioned.[134] And in such a case the owners are not estopped by acquiescence because they make no objection until the work is completed.[135] A mere irregularity, however, such as the fact that the city engineer has made the assessment instead of the assessor, when it is based upon an arithmetical calculation, is not sufficient to warrant an injunction.[136]

§ 387. **Connecticut.**—In Connecticut, it is held that the prevention of a multiplicity of suits is no ground for enjoining the collection of a tax, when each individual will have an adequate remedy at law.[137] And even a threatened cloud upon the title to real property is not recognized as a ground for enjoining proceedings to collect an illegal tax.[138] Indeed, it is laid down in the most sweeping terms that "the extraordinary remedy by injunction cannot be invoked to hinder or interfere

133 Dumars v City of Denver, 16 Colo. App. 375, 65 Pac. 580.

134 Keese v. City of Denver, 10 Colo. 112, 15 Pac. 825.

135 Id.

136 Id.

137 Sheldon v. Centre School District, 25 Conn. 224; Dodd v. City of Hartford, 25 Conn. 232.

138 Rowland v. School District, 42 Conn. 30; Waterbury Savings Bank v. Lawler, 46 Conn. 243, 246.

with a collector of taxes in the discharge of his public duty."[139]

§ 388. **Delaware.**—In Delaware, equity will not "enjoin the collection of a tax alleged to be illegal, where there is an adequate remedy at law. It will not interfere by its preventive process, on account of mere irregularities, hardship, and injustice in the assessment, or errors or excess in valuation." "The ordinary remedies in the case of taxes illegally assessed and levied are an action at law after a compulsory payment, either of trespass against the collecting officer, or of assumpsit against such officer or the public corporation to which the amount has been paid."[140]

The prevention of a multitude of suits is not ground for enjoining the collection of a state tax, where the multiplicity results merely from the fact that plaintiff is guardian of a large number of estates and will be obliged to maintain a separate action at law for each one.[141] But it is a ground, in a case where a railroad, exempt by law from taxation, is threatened with tax proceedings in the several tax districts in which its property lies.[142] Multiplicity of suits in cases of the "Third Class," however, is not recognized as a ground for equitable interference in this state.[143]

In order to warrant an injunction against the collection of a tax alleged to be a cloud on title of real estate, the proceedings must be valid on their face. Ev-

139 Waterbury Savings Bank v. Lawler, 46 Conn. 243, 246; Arnold v. Middleton, 39 Conn. 406.

140 Philadelphia, W. & B. R. Co. v. Neary, 5 Del. Ch 600; Equitable Guarantee & Trust Co. v. Donahoe (Del), 45 Atl. 583.

141 Equitable Guarantee & Trust Co. v. Donahoe (Del.), 45 Atl. 583.

142 Philadelphia, W. & B. R. Co. v. Neary, 5 Del. Ch. 600.

143 Murphy v. City of Wilmington, 6 Houst. 108, 139, 140, 22 Am. St. Rep. 345; see *ante*, § 361

eryone is presumed to know the law, and therefore if the proceedings themselves show that they are defective, or if the act under which the tax is levied is unconstitutional, the injunction will be denied.[144]

§ 389. **Florida.**—In Florida, an injunction against collection of a tax will be granted only when the tax is illegal, or is being illegally collected.[145] The injunction will not issue merely because the collector might adopt a mode more equitable and fair.[146]

Collection of a tax will be enjoined when the illegal proceedings for the levy, assessment and collection will cast a cloud over the title to complainant's real estate.[147] An injunction, however, will not be granted where there is an adequate remedy at law, and, therefore, equity will not interfere when the tax is to be collected out of personal property unless it has some peculiar, intrinsic value to the owner that cannot be compensated in money.[148]

Tender.—The constitution of Florida provides that "no person or corporation shall be relieved from the payment of any tax that may be illegal, or illegally or irregularly assessed, until he or it shall have paid such portion of his or its taxes as may be legal, and legally and regularly assessed."[149] In construing this, the supreme court of Florida has held that payment is not a

144 Murphy v. City of Wilmington, 6 Houst. 108, 22 Am. St Rep. 345

145 Bloxham v. Consumers' etc. R. R. Co., 36 Fla. 519, 51 Am. St. Rep 44, 18 South 444, 29 L. R. A. 507.

146 Id.

147 Pickett v. Russell, 42 Fla. 116, 634, 28 South. 764; Smith v. Longe, 20 Fla. 697

148 Odlin v. Woodruff, 31 Fla. 160, 12 South. 227; City of Jacksonville v Massey Business College (Fla.), 36 South. 432; Florida Packing & Ice Co v. Carney (Fla.), 38 South. 602.

149 Const 1885, art IX, § 8.

prerequisite to beginning proceedings, "but that such payment must be made before the applicant is relieved from the illegal tax."[150]

§ 390. **Georgia.**—The Political Code of Georgia provides: "No replevin shall lie, nor any judicial interference be had, in any levy or distress for taxes under the provisions of this code; but the party injured shall be left to his proper remedy in a court of law having jurisdiction thereof."[151] In construing this section the supreme court of Georgia has held that "for an officer to exact money, under the name of a tax, where there is no law to warrant the exaction, is not an attempt to collect taxes, but an attempt to collect something else; and the rule which excludes interference in the collection of taxes does not apply."[152] Following this interpretation, it has been held that an injunction will issue to restrain a tax-collector who is attempting to collect an amount claimed to be due for taxes upon property which is not required by law to be returned for taxation in the county in which he holds his office;[153] or to restrain the collection of an unconstitutional tax.[154] A party claiming an injunction because of the unconstitutionality of the taxing act or because of an exemption, must make the invalidity as to him clearly and unequivocally appear.[155]

§ 391. **Special Assessments.**—Where the statute authorizes certain street work whenever "in the judgment

150 Pickett v. Russell, 42 Fla. 116, 634, 28 South. 764.

151 Pol Code, § 903.

152 Decker et al. v. McGowan, 59 Ga. 805.

153 Penick v. High Shoals Mfg. Co, 113 Ga. 592, 38 S. E. 973. See, also, Linton v. Lucy Cobb Institute, 117 Ga. 678, 45 S. E. 53

154 Wright v S. W. R. Co., 64 Ga. 783.

155 L B Price Co v City of Atlanta, 105 Ga. 358, 31 S. E. 619.

of the city council of said city, the pavement has become worn out," a court of equity will not interfere with the exercise of the discretion of the municipal authorities. And the mere fact that the assessment levied accordingly is excessive is no ground for an injunction where the statute provides an adequate remedy.[156]

§ 392. **Idaho.**—In Idaho, an injunction will issue to restrain the collection of a tax which casts a cloud on the title to land. The rule that there is no cloud where the proceedings are void on their face seems to have been adopted.[157]

The injunction will not issue after the tax sale; nor will it be granted without notice to the municipality.[158]

§ 393. **Illinois—In General.**—The grounds of the jurisdiction to enjoin the collection of taxes were at an early date formulated in a definite rule, to which the courts of Illinois have consistently adhered. "A court of equity will not entertain a bill to enjoin the collection of a tax, except where the tax is unauthorized by law, or when it is assessed upon property which is exempt from taxation, or when property has been fraudulently assessed at too high a rate,"[159] or according to a few cases, when the injunction is necessary to pre-

156 Regenstein v. City of Atlanta, 98 Ga. 167, 25 S. E. 428; Rice v. Mayor etc. of City of Macon, 117 Ga 401, 43 S. E. 773.

157 Bramwell v. Guheen, 3 Idaho, 347, 29 Pac. 110.

158 Wilson v. City of Boise City, 7 Idaho, 69, 60 Pac. 84.

159 Siegfried v. Raymond, 190 Ill. 424, 60 N. E. 868; Coxe Bros v. Salomon, 188 Ill. 571, 59 N. E. 422; White v. Raymond, 188 Ill 298, 58 N. E. 976; Earl v. Raymond, 188 Ill. 15, 59 N. E. 19; Kochersperger v Larned, 172 Ill 86, 49 N. E. 988; Illinois Central R. R. Co. v. Hodges, 113 Ill. 323; Porter v. Rockford etc. R. Co., 76 Ill. 561 (596) (a leading case); Chicago, B. & Q. R. Co. v. Cole, 75 Ill. 591, McConkey v. Smith, 73 Ill. 313; Vieley v. Thompson, 44 Ill. 9; Munson v. Miller, 66 Ill. 380; Union Trust Co. v. Weber, 96 Ill. 346, 357.

vent irreparable injury.[160] In Illinois, collection of taxes on personal property may be enjoined, in the cases enumerated above, notwithstanding the existence of the legal remedy to recover back the amount of the tax paid, and notwithstanding that the proceedings for collection of the tax may constitute only a case of ordinary trespass.[161]

That the statute under which the assessor made an analysis of the assessment is unconstitutional is not a ground for injunction, where the taxes are authorized and there is no irreparable injury to complainant; a court of law is as competent as a court of equity to try the question of constitutionality.[162]

The court will not enjoin the collection of taxes for mere irregularities in the assessment, levying, or collection.[163]

Where the tax-collector levied upon property of one for the taxes of another, and the collector was insolvent, and replevin would not lie, and the use of the article levied upon was indispensable to the complainant's business, an injunction was held proper.[164]

§ 394. **Illegality.**—The courts of Illinois have gone further than most courts in restraining the collection of taxes alleged to be illegal, but have always professed to recognize the universal rule that relief of that kind cannot be granted except upon some ground of equity

160 Deming v. James, 72 Ill. 78; Vieley v. Thompson, 44 Ill. 9.

161 Searing v. Heavysides, 106 Ill. 85.

162 Ayers v. Widmayer, 188 Ill. 121, 58 N. E. 956.

163 Chicago, B. & Q. R. Co. v. Frary, 22 Ill. 34; see the forcible statement of the reasons for the rule in the opinion of Caton, C. J.; Huck v. Chicago & A. R. Co., 86 Ill. 360; Union Trust Co. v. Weber, 96 Ill. 346, 351, 357.

164 Deming v. James, 72 Ill. 78. The decision appears to rest upon the general ground that the injury is irreparable.

jurisdiction.[165] The rule is laid down that "when the law has conferred no power to levy a tax, or in case a person or officer not authorized by law to exercise such a power, shall levy a tax, or when the proper persons shall make the levy for purposes on the face of the levy, not authorized, or for fraudulent purposes, a court of equity may stay its collection by injunction."[166]

If the tax is levied for a lawful purpose, and without fraud, a mere erroneous determination as to the place of the complainant's residence does not constitute such illegality as will be relieved against in equity.[167]

As to the stage of the tax proceedings at which the court may interfere, it is held that a court of equity will never restrain the extension of a tax unless it is wholly unauthorized and void in all its parts. If any portion of the tax is valid, then the court will never interpose until the taxes have been extended on the collector's books.[168]

The statute providing that the township board of review is authorized to raise complainant's assessment only after giving notice in writing, the collection of the increase of tax based on an increased assessment made without such notice will be enjoined on the ground that the assessment is void as to the increase, and this without reference to the fairness or unfairness of the valuation.[169]

165 Williams v. Dutton, 184 Ill. 608, 56 N. E 868.

166 Town of Ottawa v. Walker, 21 Ill. 605, 610, 71 Am. Dec. 121, approved in Knopf v. First Nat. Bank, 173 Ill. 331, 50 N. E 660. See, also, Chicago & M. Electric Ry. Co. v. Vollman, 213 Ill. 609, 73 N. E. 360.

167 Williams v. Dutton, 184 Ill. 608, 56 N. E. 868.

168 Ottawa Glass Co. v. McCaleb, 81 Ill. 562.

169 Huling v. Ehrich, 183 Ill. 315, 55 N. E. 636, and cases cited; and see First Nat Bank of Shawneetown v. Cook, 77 Ill. 622, Darling v. Gunn, 50 Ill. 424.

A tax levied wholly without authority of law may be enjoined; as when an assessor, in assessing a party's personal property and credits, went back three years, and raised the amount of his credits for those years seven thousand dollars, which was entered on the books, and assessed against the party as for such prior years;[170] or where the assessor assesses personal property against one who was not the owner of the same, and had no possession or control over the same, and no interest therein, and the boards of review refuse to give relief;[171] or where a county board of review, in equalizing the valuation between the different towns, makes a material increase in the aggregate amount of all the towns, beyond what is actually necessary or incidental,[172] or where taxes for several years previous are extended upon the assessment of the current year, instead of upon the assessments for the several years for which the levies were made, in violation of the constitutional provision that all taxes shall be levied by valuation.[173]

§ 395. **Illegal Municipal Taxes**.—Where bonds have been issued by a township to a railroad company, under a vote at an election held without authority of law, both state and local officers may be enjoined from attempting to cause a tax to be levied for the payment of the principal or interest of such bonds.[174]

A municipality may be enjoined at the suit of a taxpayer, from the levy and collection of a tax for the pur-

170 Allwood v. Cowen, 111 Ill. 481. See, also, Cox v. Hawkins, 199 Ill. 68, 64 N. E. 1093 (illegal increase of assessment on personal property enjoined).

171 Searing v. Heavysides, 106 Ill. 85.

172 Kimball v. Merchants' S. L. & T. Co, 89 Ill 611.

173 Town of Lebanon v. Ohio & M. Ry. Co., 77 Ill. 539.

174 Rutz v. Calhoun, 100 Ill 392.

pose of paying an indebtedness incurred in excess of the constitutional limit of five per cent of the valuation of taxable property;[175] or for the payment of indebtedness incurred in the purchase of land for a private purpose;[176] or for the payment of bounties to volunteer soldiers, etc., where the terms of the statute authorizing a special tax for such a purpose have not been complied with in essential particulars,[177] or the tax is unauthorized by statute.[178]

When a bill is filed to stay the collection of a tax levied to pay county orders issued for bounties, a portion of which are authorized, and a portion unauthorized by law, the court should ascertain the amount the unauthorized bear to those authorized, and reduce the levy by the proportion the former bears to the latter, and require the remainder to be collected and applied to the payment of those legally issued.[179] But the general rule prevails in Illinois, that when a bill is filed to enjoin the collection of taxes, on the ground that they are in part illegal, the bill must show to what extent they are, in order that the court may enjoin only the illegal portion, or must show that they are so levied that it is impossible to discriminate between the legal and illegal portions.[180]

§ 396. **Illegal Taxes; Parties Plaintiff.**—It is held that the illegal tax, as an entirety, may be enjoined either where the suit is by a number of tax-payers on behalf

175 Howell v. City of Peoria, 90 Ill. 104; City of Springfield v. Edwards, 84 Ill. 626; Dollahon v. Whittaker, 187 Ill. 84, 58 N. E. 301.

176 Sherlock v. Village of Winnetka, 59 Ill. 389, 68 Ill. 530.

177 Vieley v. Thompson, 44 Ill. 9.

178 Drake v. Phillips, 40 Ill. 388.

179 Briscoe v. Allison, 43 Ill. 291.

180 Taylor v. Thompson, 42 Ill 9.

of themselves and others similarly situated, or by one suing on behalf of all others, or even where the suit is by one suing for himself alone, where the effect would be to settle the rights of all;[181] and this for the purpose of avoiding a multiplicity of actions by different tax-payers, although there is no privity or legal relation of common property or common right as between the tax-payers, and the only common interest between them is in the question of the legality of the tax, and in the fact that all are injured by the same wrongful and illegal act of levying the tax.[182] But the right of a single tax-payer should be limited to himself, and he should not be permitted to enjoin the entire tax, in a case where it could not be presumed that the other tax-payers desired to stop the administration of the government, and where such disastrous consequence would surely result.[183]

§ 397. **Exempt Property.**—A court of equity will grant relief, by way of injunction, against the imposition of a tax upon property exempt from taxation.[184] In cases where a tax is assessed upon property, some of which is exempt, equity will enjoin the collection of that

181 Knopf v. First Nat. Bank, 173 Ill. 331, 50 N. E. 660, reviewing the Illinois cases. In this case the suit was by a single tax-payer, "but the necessary effect is to determine the right of every tax-payer in the district, and it would be an irrelevant distinction that the bill does not, in set phrase, purport to be on behalf of all others having individual and separate interests of the same character." See German Alliance Ins. Co. v. Van Cleve, 191 Ill. 410, 61 N. E. 94 (action by forty-two complainants).

182 Knopf v. First Nat. Bank, 173 Ill. 331, 50 N. E. 660.

183 Board of Supervisors of Du Page County v. Jenks, 65 Ill. 275, as explained in Knopf v. First Nat. Bank, 173 Ill. 331, 50 N. E. 660.

184 Siegfried v. Raymond, 190 Ill. 424, 60 N. E. 868, and cases cited; Rosehill Cemetery Co. v. Kern, 147 Ill. 483, 35 N. E. 240; Illinois Central R. R. Co. v. Hodges, 113 Ill. 323; Huck v. Chicago & A. R. Co., 86 Ill. 360.

part of the tax which is assessed upon the exempt property, if it is possible to ascertain what part of the tax assessed upon the whole property is assessed upon the property which is exempt from taxation;[185] but the complainant must show that the property claimed to be exempt was included in the assessment.[186]

The owner has a right to assume that the exemption will be respected, and is not required to take notice of its illegal assessment and valuation, nor to appear before the local tribunals in that regard.[187] He must, however, be prepared to maintain his claimed right of exemption by clear and satisfactory proof.[188] If he has elected to pursue his statutory remedy by application to the board of review, and their decision is adverse, his further remedy is by appeal from that decision, not by bill in chancery to enjoin the collection of the tax.[189]

§ 398. **Fraudulent Increase of Assessment.**—The complainant should first seek a hearing from the board of review. If that board refuses a hearing, or fails to consider the objections, mandamus to compel it to perform its duty in that respect will lie, is an adequate remedy, and should be resorted to.[190] "The valuation

185 Siegfried v Raymond, 190 Ill. 424, 60 N. E. 868, and cases cited. The court will not enjoin the collection of the whole tax because in determining the valuation of an aggregate property exempt property may have been included as a factor; it is incumbent on the plaintiff to show that it is injured, and to what extent, by the fact of such inclusion, as the exempt property may be of no value, or of a purely nominal value: Huck v. Chicago & A. R. Co, 86 Ill. 360.

186 Siegfried v. Raymond, 190 Ill. 424, 60 N. E 868.

187 Rosehill Cemetery Co. v. Kern, 147 Ill. 483, 35 N E 240; Illinois Central R. R. Co v. Hodges, 113 Ill. 323.

188 Rosehill Cemetery Co. v. Kern, 147 Ill. 483, 35 N E. 240.

189 Preston v. Johnson, 104 Ill. 625.

190 Standard Oil Co. v Magee, 191 Ill. 84, 60 N E. 802, and cases cited; Coxe Bros. v. Salomon, 188 Ill 571, 59 N. E. 422 (postponement of hearing by board until too late for *mandamus*, not a ground for

is not [like an assessment of exempt property] an act without jurisdiction or authority, and, if it is excessive, the law intends that application shall be made to the board. . . . . Fraud is a familiar ground of equity jurisdiction, and, if an assessment is fraudulent, equity should relieve against it, where the tax-payer has been diligent in seeking the remedy which the statute affords. In matters of revenue it is important that all questions should be speedily settled, and the tax-payer should first seek the remedy given by the statute, which it is presumed will be sufficient. If he fails to do so, it is his own neglect or folly."[191]

When the board of review have jurisdiction of the person and of the subject-matter, the court has no power to restrain the collection of the tax, in the absence of fraud either in the procedure of the board or in the conclusion reached by them.[192] Fraudulent conduct on the part of the assessor is purged by the hearing, review, and action of the board of review, if the latter is not charged with having itself been guilty of fraud.[193]

The determination of the value to be fixed on property liable to be assessed is not, in the absence of fraud, subject to the supervision of the judicial department

injunction afterwards); White v. Raymond, 188 Ill. 298, 58 N E 976, and cases cited; Kinley Mfg. Co. v. Kochersperger, 174 Ill. 379, 51 N. E. 648; New Haven Clock Co. v. Kochersperger, 175 Ill. 383, 51 N. E. 629 (an important case); Kochersperger v. Larned, 172 Ill. 86, 49 N. E. 988; Beidler v. Kochersperger, 171 Ill. 563, 49 N. E. 716; Camp v. Simpson, 118 Ill. 224, 8 N. E. 308; Felsenthal v. Johnson, 104 Ill. 21.

191 New Haven Clock Co v. Kochersperger, 175 Ill 383, 51 N. E. 629.

192 Earl v. Raymond, 188 Ill. 15, 59 N. E. 19, American Express Co. v. Raymond, 189 Ill. 232, 59 N. E. 528; Sterling Gas Co. v. Higby, 134 Ill 557, 25 N E. 660.

193 Burton Stock-car Co. v. Traeger, 187 Ill. 9, 58 N. E. 418, and cases cited.

of the state, under a provision of the constitution of Illinois.[194] Where, however, the valuation is so grossly out of the way as to show that the assessor could not have been honest in his valuation, and must have known of its excessive character, such valuation will be accepted as proof of a fraud upon his part against the tax-payer, and in such case a court of equity will grant relief; but the excessive valuation by itself does not establish fraud, the question depending largely upon the attending circumstances.[195] Thus, where the property of the complainant was assessed at two and a half times its cash value, as part of a general plan of dishonest spoliation, by which complainant and others were selected as victims from whom bribes might be obtained, the assessment should be set aside, unless the complainant is barred of relief in equity by submitting to be sent away from the statutory board of review without a hearing and decision.[196] And where the assessor, after he had accepted from the owner a list and valuation of his property, arbitrarily and without notice materially increased the valuation, and this increase did not come to the owner's knowledge until after the time allowed for legal redress, an injunction

194 Burton Stock-Car Co. v. Traeger, 187 Ill. 9, 58 N. E. 418, and cases cited, New Haven Clock Co. v. Kochersperger, 175 Ill. 383, 51 N. E. 629, and cases cited ("value is largely a matter of opinion, and the opinion of these officers, when honestly exercised and applied upon a basis authorized by the law, cannot be reviewed or revised by the courts"); Kochersperger v. Larned, 172 Ill. 86, 49 N. E. 988; Pacific Hotel Co. v. Lieb, 83 Ill. 602 (bill must state facts distinctly showing fraud); Porter v. Rockford etc. R. Co, 76 Ill 561, 595; Chicago, B. & Q. R. R. Co. v. Cole, 75 Ill. 591; Ottawa Glove Co. v. McCaleb, 81 Ill. 556; Union Trust Co. v. Weber, 96 Ill. 346, 352.

195 Burton Stock-Car Co. v. Traeger, 187 Ill. 9, 58 N. E. 418, New Haven Clock Co. v. Kochersperger, 175 Ill 383, 51 N. E. 629.

196 New Haven Clock Co. v. Kochersperger, 175 Ill. 383, 51 N. E. 629.

was proper.[197] Where the state board of equalization, in assessing the property and franchises of a railroad, undertakes to fix valuations through prejudice or a reckless disregard of duty, in opposition to what must necessarily be the judgment of all persons of reflection, it is the duty of the courts to interfere.[198]

§ 399. **Special or Local Assessments.**—The question of the necessity of a local improvement is, by the law, committed to the city council, and courts have no right to interfere to prevent such improvement except in cases where it clearly appears that such discretion has been abused. The ground on which the courts interfere is that the ordinance is so unreasonable, unjust, and oppressive, as to render it void.[199] Courts of equity will interfere to restrain any substantial departure from the terms of an ordinance in the performance of work thereunder, if applied to in apt time, while the work is in progress.[200] If the work, as performed by the contractor, is accepted by the city, and the contractor settled with and paid, the remedy to be invoked by the property-holder, if the work is not done in substantial compliance with the provisions of the ordinance, is the writ of mandamus to compel the city authorities to complete the work as contemplated by the ordinance. An injunction will not be awarded in such case to restrain the collection of a special assessment.[201]

197 First Nat. Bank of Shawneetown v. Cook, 77 Ill. 622; McConkey v. Smith, 73 Ill. 313; Cleghorn v. Postlewaite, 43 Ill. 428.

198 Chicago, B. & Q. R. Co. v. Cole, 75 Ill. 591.

199 Field v Village of Western Springs, 181 Ill. 186, 54 N. E. 929 (adequate remedy at law); Walker v. Village of Morgan Park, 175 Ill. 570, 51 N. E. 636.

200 A deviation causing no injury to complainant is not ground for enjoining the collection of the assessment: Rossiter v. City of Lake Forest, 151 Ill 489, 38 N. E. 359.

201 Callister v. Kochersperger, 168 Ill. 334, 48 N. E. 156, Heinroth

§ 400. **Indiana.**—An injunction will not be granted at the suit of a tax-payer because of irregularities in the proceedings of the county officers, where there was authority to levy the tax.[202] It is only in cases where the record shows a clear invasion of the rights of the citizens by void acts, and they have no remedy by the ordinary processes of the law, that the court will interfere by injunction.[203]

A court of equity will not interfere to protect a person from the payment of a just tax,[204] nor will it give relief where he is not prejudiced in a substantial right.[205]

There can be no injunction when the acts alleged amount to no more than a simple threat to commit a trespass; as where the complaint does not aver that the tax duplicate is in the hands of the treasurer, without which, having no power to levy, the act of leying would be a mere trespass.[206]

Where an attempt to annex territory to a city is in-

v Kochersperger, 173 Ill. 205, 50 N. E. 171; Smith v. Kochersperger, 180 Ill 527, 54 N. E. 614.

202 Ricketts v. Spraker, 77 Ind. 371; Yocum v. First Nat. Bank (Ind), 38 N. E. 599, Hendricks v. Gilchrist, 76 Ind 369, City of Delphi v. Bowen, 61 Ind 33; Center & W. Gravel Road Co. v. Black, 32 Ind. 468; Cleveland, C. C. & St. L. Ry. Co. v. Town of Waynetown, 153 Ind. 550, 55 N. E 451; Crowder v. Riggs, 153 Ind. 158, 53 N. E. 1019, Morton C. Hunter Stone Co. v Woodard, 152 Ind. 474, 53 N E 947; McCrory v. O'Keefe, 162 Ind. 534, 70 N. E 812

203 Yocum v. First Nat. Bank (Ind.), 38 N E. 599 See notes below for instances of illegal taxes enjoined; also, Knight v. Turnpike Co., 45 Ind. 134 (illegal tax for benefit of a turnpike company which had not been incorporated); Toledo etc. R. Co. v. City of Lafayette, 22 Ind. 262.

204 Reynolds v. Bowen, 138 Ind. 434, 36 N E 756, 37 N. E 962

205 Miller v. Vollmer, 153 Ind. 26, 53 N. E. 949.

206 Anthony v Sturgis, 86 Ind. 479. See, also, Smith v. Smith, 159 Ind 388, 65 N. E. 183, where suit before threat to levy was held premature.

valid, a municipal tax on property situated in such district may be enjoined.[207]

Where a person resides in a town in Indiana, and his personal property belongs elsewhere, such town has no authority to assess taxes upon such property, and the collection of the same will be enjoined.[208]

The sale of lands, for the payment of delinquent taxes thereon, where the owner has leviable personal property within the county sufficient to pay the taxes assessed against him, may be enjoined.[209]

A tax unauthorized by law, against the capital stock of a foreign corporation, may be enjoined.[210]

A reason for the free exercise of the remedy of injunction to restrain the collection of an illegal and void tax, regardless of whether the case presents some peculiar ground for equity jurisdiction, as the prevention of a multiplicity of suits, or the removal of a cloud upon title, or the inadequacy of an action at law, is found in the abolishment of the distinctions between actions at law and suits in equity.[211]

Courts will not give relief against erroneous assessments by the state board of equalization, except on the ground of fraud[212]

Where the statute gives persons aggrieved by the acts of the board of county commissioners the right to appeal, an injunction will not be granted to prevent the

207 City of Logansport v. La Rose, 99 Ind 117, Windman v City of Vincennes, 58 Ind 480; City of Peru v. Bearss, 55 Ind. 576.

208 Eversole v. Cook, 92 Ind. 222; and see Luke v. Sheridan, 26 Ind App. 529, 60 N. E. 359; Stephens v. Smith, 30 Ind. 120, 65 N. E. 546.

209 Abbott v. Edgerton, 53 Ind 196.

210 Riley v. Western Union Tel. Co., 47 Ind 511.

211 City of Delphi v Bowen, 61 Ind 29, 37.

212 Cleveland, C. C. & St. L. R. Co. v. Backus, 133 Ind. 513, 33 N. E. 421, 18 L. R A 729.

collection of a tax levied by such board;[213] this has been frequently held of acts of such boards in passing upon a petition for county aid in the construction of railroads.[214] But when a tax in aid of railroads is levied in excess of the amount authorized by statute, the collection of the excess may be enjoined by one who has paid the part of the tax legally due.[215]

The right to enjoin an illegal tax may be lost by laches.[216]

§ 401. **Tender of Legal Tax.**—While injunction is the proper remedy against the collection of taxes where the assessment is wholly void,[217] yet the burden is upon the plaintiff to allege and prove facts necessary to show that the whole of the property in question was not subject to assessment for taxation.[218] If any of the taxes against which the injunction is sought were legally

213 Jones v. Cullen, 142 Ind. 335, 40 N. E. 124; Senour v. Matchett, 140 Ind. 636, 40 N. E. 122; Pittsburgh, C. C. & St. L. R. Co. v Harden, 137 Ind. 486, 37 N. E. 324; otherwise, where the order levying a special tax is an administrative one, from which there is no appeal: Board of Commissioners of Owens Co. v. Spangler, 159 Ind. 575, 65 N. E. 743.

214 See cases in last note; Faris v. Reynolds, 70 Ind. 359; s. c. *sub nom* Reynolds v Faris, 80 Ind 14; Board of Commissioners v. Hall, 70 Ind. 469; Goddard v. Stockman, 74 Ind. 400; Hill v. Probst, 120 Ind 528, 22 N. E. 664; Bell v. Maish, 137 Ind. 226, 36 N. E. 358, 1118.

215 Miles v. Ray, 100 Ind. 166.

216 Jones v. Cullen, 142 Ind. 335, 40 N. E. 124; Vickery v. Blair, 134 Ind. 554, 32 N. E. 880; Montgomery v Wasem, 116 Ind. 343, 15 N. E. 795, 19 N. E. 184 (drainage assessment).

217 Buck v. Miller, 147 Ind. 586, 62 Am. St. Rep. 436, 45 N E. 647, 47 N. E. 8, 37 L. R. A. 384; Senour v. Ruth, 140 Ind. 318, 39 N E. 946, Yocum v. First Nat. Bank, 144 Ind. 272, 43 N. E. 231, and cases cited; Hobbs v Board of Commissioners, 103 Ind. 575, 3 N. E. 263; and notes *supra*.

218 Buck v. Miller, *supra;* Saint v. Welsh, 141 Ind. 382, 40 N E. 903.

assessed, then, in the absence of a showing of payment or tender, no relief can be granted.[219] The tender must be kept good by a payment into court.[220]

Where the complaint is not to enjoin the collection of taxes, part of which are legal and part illegal, but to set aside a particular order alleged to be void, whereby a specific sum was illegally added to the assessed value of the plaintiff's property, the averment of payment or tender of payment of the legal taxes need not be made;[221] so, where plaintiff seeks to prevent the levy of an assessment upon property not subject to taxation.[222]

§ 402. **Special Assessments.**—An injunction will issue to restrain the collection of a special assessment by a municipal body in cases where, through some defect in the proceedings or otherwise, there is a want of jurisdiction to make the levy, or the assessment is absolutely void.[223] Thus, it is proper where an assessment is levied for the purpose of improving a public market

219 Buck v. Miller, *supra;* Shepardson v. Gillette, 133 Ind. 125, 31 N. E. 788, Bundy v. Summerland, 142 Ind. 92, 41 N. E. 322, Smith v. Union County Nat. Bank, 131 Ind 201, 30 N. E. 948, Smith v. Rude Bros. Mfg. Co., 131 Ind 150, 30 N. E 947, Hyland v. Central I. & S. Co., 129 Ind. 68, 28 N. E. 308, 13 L. R. A. 515, City of Logansport v. McConnell, 121 Ind. 419, 23 N. E. 264, Montgomery v. Wassem, 116 Ind. 343, 15 N. E. 795, 19 N. E. 184 (drainage assessment); Board of Commissioners v. Dailey, 115 Ind. 360, 17 N. E. 619; Morrison v. Jacoby, 114 Ind. 84, 14 N. E. 546, 15 N E. 806 (a leading case); Ricketts v. Spraker, 77 Ind. 371; Mesker v. Koch, 76 Ind. 68; City of Delphi v. Bowen, 61 Ind. 33.

220 Bundy v. Summerland, 142 Ind. 92, 41 N. E. 322, Hewett v. Fenstamaker, 128 Ind. 315, 27 N. E. 621; City of Logansport v. Case, 124 Ind. 254, 24 N E. 88 (enjoining execution of tax deed), Morrison v. Jacoby, 114 Ind. 84, 14 N E. 546, 15 N. E. 806

221 Yocum v. First Nat. Bank, 144 Ind 272, 43 N. E. 231.

222 Hyland v. Brazil Block Coal Co., 128 Ind. 335, 26 N E. 672.

223 Studabaker v. Studabaker, 152 Ind. 89, 51 N. E. 933; De Puy v. City of Wabash, 133 Ind 336, 32 N E. 1016.

although the statute authorizes such assessments only for streets and highways;[224] or where the engineer improperly assesses property not abutting on the street improved;[225] or where the preliminary estimate which is a requisite of jurisdiction is omitted;[226] or where the work is of absolutely no benefit to plaintiff's land;[227] or where the municipal body intends to assess the total cost, irrespective of benefits, against the abutting owner.[228]

Where the local board has jurisdiction of the general subject, the assessment cannot be collaterally attacked by injunction.[229] An injunction will not be granted because of mere irregularities in the proceedings which do not deprive the assessing body of jurisdiction or make the assessment void.[230] Thus, it will not be granted because the boards of commissioners of two counties sat separately and not conjointly, nor because viewers obtained an extension of time in which to make their report;[231] nor because the work is not completed according to plans and specifications.[232]

Equitable relief will not be granted when there is an adequate remedy at law. Thus, an injunction will not issue because an assessment will be greater than the actual benefits, when the statute provides an adequate remedy by hearing before a special tribunal,[233] nor be-

224 City of Fort Wayne v. Shoaf, 106 Ind. 66, 5 N. E. 403.

225 City of Terre Haute v. Mack, 139 Ind. 99, 38 N. E. 468.

226 Goring v. McTaggart, 92 Ind. 200.

227 Millikan v. Wool, 133 Ind. 51, 32 N. E. 828.

228 McKee v. Town of Pendleton, 154 Ind. 652, 57 N. E. 532.

229 Tucker v. Sellers, 130 Ind. 514, 30 N. E. 531.

230 Florer v. McAfee, 135 Ind. 540, 35 N. E. 277.

231 Sarber v. Rankin, 145 Ind 236, 56 N. E. 225.

232 Studabaker v. Studabaker, 152 Ind 89, 51 N. E 933; Muncey v. Joest, 74 Ind. 409.

233 Taylor v. City of Crawfordsville, 155 Ind. 403, 58 N. E. 490; McKee v. Town of Pendleton, 162 Ind. 667, 69 N. E. 997.

cause the requisite petition with the signatures of the owners of a majority of the frontage has not been filed when no appeal has been taken as provided by statute.[234] In such a case it is held that the fact that others have appealed and have succeeded in having the assessment declared void will not avail. Likewise, an injunction will not issue against the collection of an amount spent for drainage purposes upon the ground that the requisite petition was not filed, for the statute provides an adequate remedy in all cases where the preliminary notice has been given.[235] And the relief will of course be denied when the owner has unsuccessfully prosecuted his legal remedy.[236]

A landowner who stands by in silence, with full knowledge, and allows the work to be completed, is estopped by acquiescence from attacking the proceedings in a collateral action for an injunction.[237]

Where part of an assessment is valid and part invalid, a tender of the valid part is a prerequisite to an injunction against the invalid part.[238]

§ 403. **Iowa.**—In Iowa, an injunction will issue against the collection of a tax which is illegal, and not merely irregular.[239] Thus, an injunction will be granted to restrain the collection of an increase made by a county board of equalization without authority.[240]

234 Cason v. Harrison, 135 Ind. 330, 35 N. E 268.

235 Zimmerman v. Savage, 145 Ind. 124, 44 N. E. 252.

236 Du Puy v. City of Wabash, 133 Ind. 336, 32 N. E. 1016.

237 Montgomery v. Wasem, 116 Ind. 343, 15 N. E. 795, 19 N. E. 184; Muncey v. Joest, 74 Ind. 409.

238 Studabaker v. Studabaker, 152 Ind. 89, 51 N. E. 933; Montgomery v. Wasem, 116 Ind. 343, 15 N. E. 795, 19 N. E. 184, Florer v. McAfee, 135 Ind. 540, 35 N E. 277.

239 Montis v. McQuiston, 107 Iowa, 651, 78 N. W. 704; Chicago, M. & St. P. Ry. Co. v. Phillips, 111 Iowa, 377, 82 N. W. 787.

240 Brandirf v. Harrison Co., 50 Iowa, 164, Montis v. McQuiston, 107 Iowa, 651, 78 N. W. 704.

Likewise, an injunction will issue to restrain the collection of a tax levied by virtue of a mistaken certificate as to the result of an election;[241] and when the tax was voted by the electors as the result of misrepresentation.[242]

An injunction will not issue to restrain the collection of a tax when there is an adequate remedy at law by appeal. Thus, an injunction will not be granted because of corruption in levying the tax, because an adequate legal remedy is provided.[243] Nor will such relief be granted when there is an adequate remedy by application to the board of equalization, and no such application is made.[244]

In order to obtain an injunction to restrain a sale for taxes, the plaintiff must show that he is the owner of the land about to be sold. When there is grave doubt as to the ownership, the injunction will be refused.[245]

§ 404. **Special Assessments.**—An injunction will issue against the collection of a special assessment when there is a jurisdictional defect in the proceedings. Thus, where the city council neglects to determine in advance of the publication of notice the kind of material to be used, as required by statute, an injunction will issue.[246] And in such a case the owner is not estopped because some of the work has been done.[247] If a city

241 Cattell v. Lowry, 45 Iowa, 478.

242 Sinnett v. Moles, 38 Iowa, 25.

243 Bogaard v. Independent School Dist., 93 Iowa, 269, 61 N. W. 859.

244 Collins v. City of Keokuk, 118 Iowa, 30, 91 N. W. 791.

245 Broderick v. Allamakee County, 104 Iowa, 750, 73 N. W. 884

246 Coggeshall v. Des Moines, 78 Iowa, 235, 41 N. W. 617. Rehearing denied, 42 N. W. 650.

247 Id.

council has no authority whatever to assess the property of the plaintiff for an improvement, he may enjoin the enforcement of the assessment without resorting to the appeal to the district court provided for in Code of 1897, section 839.[248] Where the entire proceedings for a street improvement are void, a sale of his property thereunder may be enjoined, though he did not appear before the council and object to the assessment.[249]

§ 405. **Kansas.**—The Kansas code provides that "an injunction may be granted to enjoin the illegal levy of any tax, charge, or assessment, or the collection of any illegal tax, charge or assessment, or any proceeding to enforce the same; and any number of persons whose property is affected by a tax or assessment so levied may unite in the petition filed to obtain such injunction."[250] The supreme court of the state has held that this gives an enlarged or additional remedy to the taxpayer, but that the jurisdiction is to be exercised upon equitable principles.[251] An injunction will therefore issue at the suit of interested parties to restrain the collection of an illegal tax as against themselves. Thus, where an assessor illegally raises an assessment on personal property after a proper return has been made, an injunction will issue.[252] Likewise, where a railroad is assessed at its full value while other property is rated at only twenty-five per cent, the company may obtain an injunction against the collection of the illegal

248 Ft. Dodge Electric L. & P. Co. v City of Ft. Dodge, 115 Iowa, 568, 89 N. W. 7, and cases cited.

249 Gallagher v. Garland (Iowa), 101 N. W. 867.

250 Code, § 253.

251 Stewart v. Commissioners of Wyandotte Co., 45 Kan. 708, 23 Am. St. Rep. 746, 26 Pac. 683.

252 Gibbins v. Adamson, 44 Kan. 203, 24 Pac. 51.

excess upon tendering the amount legally due.[253] Again, where a state board of equalization orders an increase in assessments upon all except railroad property, and the local officers fail to make the increase, the railroad company is injured and may obtain an injunction.[254] And an injunction will also issue when a bank is illegally assessed on its capital stock.[255] But the injunction will not issue merely because plaintiff fears that an illegal tax may be levied.[256]

Where, however, the property is not exempt from taxation, and in justice the tax ought to be paid, an injunction will not issue to restrain its collection because of errors or irregularities in the proceedings of the taxing officers.[257] Thus, an injunction will not issue when a tax legally voted is illegally reduced;[258] nor where assessments are based upon only twenty-five per cent of the actual cash value although a statute requires that they be levied at the actual value;[259] nor when the assessment is set out in detail on the books when a statute provides that it be grouped under one head.[260] Likewise, it has been held that the assessment

253 Chicago, B & Q. R. Co. v. Board of Commissioners, 54 Kan. 781, 39 Pac. 1039.

254 Missouri, K. & T. Ry Co. v. Board of Commissioners, 9 Kan. App. 350, 58 Pac. 121.

255 First Nat. Bank v. Fisher, 45 Kan 726, 26 Pac. 482.

256 Wyandotte & K. C. Bridge Co. v. Board of Commissioners, 10 Kan. 326.

257 Kansas Mut. Life Assn. v. Hill, 51 Kan. 636, 33 Pac. 300; Missouri River F. S. & G. R. Co. v. Morris, 7 Kan. 210, Challiss v. Commrs. of Atchison County, 15 Kan. 49; Chicago, B. & Q. R. Co. v. Clerk of Norton County, 55 Kan 386, 40 Pac. 654; Parker v. Challiss, 9 Kan. 155; Dutton v. Citizens' Nat. Bank, 53 Kan. 440, 36 Pac. 719; Ryan v. Board of Commissioners, 30 Kan 185, 2 Pac. 156; City of Lawrence v. Killam, 11 Kan. 499.

258 Seward v. Rheiner, 2 Kan. App. 95, 43 Pac. 423.

259 Challiss v. Rigg, 49 Kan. 119, 30 Pac. 190.

260 Kansas City, Ft. S. & G. R. R. Co. v. Scammon, 45 Kan. 481, 25 Pac. 858.

of some at the full cash value while others are assessed at much less,[261] or the failure of township assessors to meet and agree upon an equal basis of valuation,[262] or the levying of a slight excess,[263] are all mere irregularities which do not warrant the issuance of an injunction. For the same reason, an injunction will not issue when an assessment is excessive merely as an error of judgment, unless the excess is so great as to raise a presumption of fraud.[264] And it is well settled that it will not issue when an error in assessment is induced by the action of the tax-payer himself.[265]

§ 406. **Parties.**—Under the statute any one or more of a number of persons, whose property is affected by an illegal tax or assessment, may maintain an action to enjoin the collection of such tax or assessment so far as it affects his or their property, without joining others as plaintiffs whose property may also be affected.[266] This does not authorize, however, one to maintain an action for the benefit of all.[267] And where the plaintiff is a municipal corporation it will not be allowed to maintain the action for the benefit of its citizens.[268] In such a case there is a double reason for refusing relief, for the corporation has no such direct interest as to give it a standing in court to enjoin any part of the tax, for it is not a tax-payer. The statute

261 Adams v. Beman, 10 Kan. 37.

262 Smith v. Commrs. of Leavenworth Co., 9 Kan. 296.

263 Id.

264 Board of Commissioners of Lincoln Co. v. Bryant, 7 Kan. App. 252, 53 Pac. 775.

265 Bank of Santa Fe v. Buster, 50 Kan. 356, 31 Pac. 1094; Winfield Bank v. Nipp, 47 Kan. 744, 28 Pac. 1015.

266 Code, § 253; Gilmore v. Fox, 10 Kan. 509.

267 Wyandotte & K. C. Bridge Co. v. Board of Commissioners, 10 Kan. 326.

268 Center Township v. Hunt, 16 Kan. 430.

does not give the right to two or more persons to unite in an action to enjoin two illegal taxes severally assessed against each of them. When the tax is illegal in itself, then as many as have property within the district may join. But when a tax is valid, and becomes illegal only as applied to particular persons or property, or to particular cases, then each person severally interested must sue alone.[269]

In actions to restrain the collection of municipal taxes, it is generally held that the taxing corporation is a necessary party defendant.[270] The reason for the rule is that such corporation is interested in the outcome, and should not be deprived of its rights without a hearing. Where, however, the suit is to enjoin the sale of property under a tax warrant, and the only question is whether the property is subject to levy, the sheriff may be made sole defendant.[271]

§ 407. **Tender.**—When a tax is valid in part and void in part, an injunction will be refused, upon the principle that he who seeks equity must do equity, unless a tender is made of the amount legally due.[272] Thus, where a tax is attacked as being excessive,[273] or as discriminating against the plaintiff,[274] a tender is a condition of relief.[275] And a mere averment of readiness

269 Missouri River, F. S. & G. R Co. v. Morris, 7 Kan. 210.

270 Gilmore v. Fox, 10 Kan. 509; Jeffries-Ba Som v. Nation, 63 Kan. 247, 65 Pac. 226.

271 Cook v. Condon, 6 Kan. App. 574, 51 Pac. 587.

272 City of Lawrence v. Killam, 11 Kan. 499; Bank of Garnett v. Ferris, 55 Kan. 120, 39 Pac. 1042, City of Ottawa v. Barney, 10 Kan. 270; Gibbins v. Adamson, 44 Kan. 203, 24 Pac. 51; Wilson v. Longendyke, 32 Kan. 267, 4 Pac. 361.

273 City of Ottawa v. Barney, 10 Kan. 270.

274 Bank of Garnett v Ferris, 55 Kan. 120, 39 Pac. 1042.

275 Hagaman v. Commissioners of Cloud County, 19 Kan. 394.

and willingness to pay is not sufficient.[276] Where, however, the tax is wholly void, a tender is obviously unnecessary.

§ 408. **Special Assessments.**—When a special assessment is illegal and void, and the action is brought within the statutory time, an injunction will issue against its collection.[277] Thus, where a city council inserts in a contract a provision that the contractor shall keep the streets in repair for a term of years, the assessment levied is void and an injunction will issue.[278]

A property owner, however, who lives in the neighborhood, who signs the petition for the improvement, and whose property is greatly benefited, is not entitled to an injunction to restrain the collection of an assessment levied therefor, although the improvement is made without any authority whatever.[279] This rule is based upon the doctrine of estoppel.

By statute it is provided that no suit to enjoin the making of a special assessment shall be brought after the expiration of thirty days from the time the amount due on each lot is ascertained.[280] Under this statute, it is held that an injunction will not issue when the suit is brought after the expiration of this time, especially if the proceedings are valid on their face.[281]

276 First Nat. Bank v. Fisher, 45 Kan. 726, 26 Pac. 482.

277 Andrews v. Love, 50 Kan. 701, 31 Pac. 1094.

278 City of Kansas City v. Hanson, 8 Kan. App 290, 55 Pac. 513.

279 Downs v. Wyandotte Co. Commissioners, 48 Kan. 640, 29 Pac. 1077; Stewart v. Commissioners, 45 Kan. 708, 23 Am. St. Rep. 746, 26 Pac. 683; Commissioners v. Hoag, 48 Kan. 413, 29 Pac. 758.

280 Gen Stats. 1897, c. 32, § 212.

281 City of Kansas City v. Gray, 62 Kan. 198, 61 Pac. 746; Wahlgreen v. City of Kansas City, 42 Kan. 243, 21 Pac. 1068, City of Topeka v. Gage, 44 Kan. 87, 24 Pac. 82; Doran v. Barnes, 54 Kan. 238, 38 Pac. 300; City of Leavenworth v. Jones, 69 Kan. 857, 77 Pac. 273.

Until an appraisement is made and the amount to be charged against each lot or parcel of land is ascertained, no cause of action accrues. Before that time the danger of injury to the plaintiffs is too remote and problematical to warrant the granting of an injunction.[282]

An injunction to restrain the building of curbing and the levying and assessing of taxes therefor will not issue when all the things sought to be prevented have actually been done.[283]

§ 409. **Kentucky.**—In Kentucky, an injunction will issue to restrain the collection of an illegal and void tax upon the ground of the inadequacy of the remedy at law. "The officer, acting in good faith and under the color of right, is justified by his process, and is not liable as a trespasser; and, as suit would not lie against the state directly, the only complete remedy is by injunction."[284] Thus, an injunction will be granted to restrain the collection of a tax based on an assessment which has been illegally raised without notice to the tax-payer.[285] Likewise, the injunction will issue to restrain the collection of a municipal tax based on an assessment void because the assessor acts under the instruction of the local legislative body and copies the assessment from the county roll instead of making one himself.[286] And the mere fact that the assessment includes a valid poll-tax is no ground for refusing the in-

282 Mason v. City of Independence, 61 Kan. 88, 59 Pac. 272, City of Kansas City v. Smiley, 62 Kan. 718, 64 Pac. 613; Dever v. City of Junction City, 45 Kan. 417, 25 Pac. 861.

283 McCurdy v. City of Lawrence, 9 Kan. 883, 57 Pac. 1057.

284 Gates v Barrett, 79 Ky. 295; Negley v. Henderson Bridge Co., 107 Ky. 414, 54 S. W. 171.

285 Negley v. Henderson Bridge Co., 107 Ky. 414, 54 S. W. 171.

286 Turner v. Town of Pewee Valley, 100 Ky. 288, 38 S. W. 143, 688.

junction when it appears that the tax-payer has sufficient personal property out of which it might be satisfied.[287] But the injunction will not be granted merely because the plaintiff thinks the assessment excessive;[288] nor will it be granted merely because there have been irregularities in the procedure. Thus, an injunction will not be granted merely because the city has failed to tax certain personalty not exempt from taxation;[289] nor because property belonging to a mother and her son has been assessed in the name of the father, it having been so listed by the son.[290] And it is no ground for an injunction that the taxing officer, who is an officer *de facto,* may not be the legal official because of certain irregularities in the election.[291] The court will not, at the suit of an individual tax-payer, inquire into the necessity for the levy.[292]

Personal Property.—The rule as laid down above is broad enough to warrant the issuance of an injunction to restrain the collection of an illegal tax on personal property, for the court holds that there is not an adequate remedy at law.[293]

An injunction will not issue, however, to restrain the collection of a tax on the ground that property not taxable has been assessed, unless the statutory mode of correction has been tried first.[294] In such a case there is an adequate remedy at law.

287 Id.

288 Royer Wheel Co. v. Taylor County, 104 Ky. 741, 47 S. W. 876.

289 Levi v. City of Louisville, 97 Ky. 394, 30 S. W. 973, 28 L R. A. 480.

290 Ryan v. City of Central City, 21 Ky. Law Rep. 1070, 54 S. W. 2.

291 Chambers v. Adair, 23 Ky. Law Rep. 373, 62 S. W. 1128.

292 McInerney v. Huelefeld, 116 Ky. 28, 25 Ky. Law Rep. 272, 75 S W 237.

293 Gates v. Barrett, 79 Ky. 295.

294 Bell County Coke & Imp. Co. v. Board of Trustees etc., 19 Ky. Law Rep. 789, 42 S. W. 92.

Not only will the injunction issue against the collection of an illegal tax, but where the county judge is proceeding to assess property for taxation to which it is not legally liable, he may be restrained from so assessing, because his action is final.[295] Where, however, the assessment is being made by an ordinary taxing officer from whom an appeal may be taken, an injunction will not issue to restrain the mere making of the assessment.

A *quasi* public corporation, such as a water company which supplies a municipality, may enjoin the seizure of its property for taxes, where such seizure would deprive the public of the benefits to be derived from it. Such a corporation, however, is not entitled to escape taxation, and therefore the court will require it to pay the money into court, or to place the management in the hands of a receiver, in order that the burden may be discharged.[296]

In an action to enjoin the collection of a tax the presumption is in favor of its legality, and therefore the burden of proof is upon the plaintiff to show its illegality.[297]

If the tax-payer is unsuccessful in his application for an injunction, judgment will be entered against him for the amount of the tax.[298]

Tender.—Where part of a tax is legal and part illegal, the tax-payer is entitled to an injunction only upon paying the legal part.[299]

295 Baldwin v. Shine, 84 Ky. 510, 2 S. W. 164.

296 Louisville Water Co. v. Hamilton, 81 Ky. 517.

297 Board of Councilmen of City of Frankfort v. Mason & Foard Co., 100 Ky 48, 37 S W. 290.

298 Town of Central Covington v. Park, 21 Ky. Law Rep. 1847, 56 S W. 650.

299 Thompson v. City of Lexington, 104 Ky. 165, 46 S. W. 481.

§ 410. **Louisiana.**—In Louisiana, "it is well settled that where an officer is proceeding to collect a state tax illegally, either on account of a void assessment or irregularity in the mode of collecting, or for other cause, though the state is interested in such proceeding and the officer is acting under the direct authority from the state, that the proceedings may be arrested by injunction in a suit against the officer alone."[300] Where, however, the tax is apparently valid on its face, and the tax roll has been placed in the hands of the tax collector, the legality cannot be tested by an injunction suit against the collector alone.[301]

An injunction will not be granted to restrain the collection of an excessive tax, unless the tax-payer has first appealed to the board of reviewers;[302] nor will it be granted at the suit of a municipal corporation suing in the interests of its tax-payers;[303] nor to prevent the holding of an election to vote a tax.[304]

An injunction may be granted to restrain a sale for taxes which have been paid.[305]

§ 411. **Maine.**—The mere illegality of a tax is no ground for the injunction; but the prevention of a multiplicity of suits is very distinctly recognized as a ground, where the entire tax is illegal because assessed without authority of law.[306]

300 Budd et al. v. Tax Collector, 36 La. Ann. 959.

301 Gaither v. Green, 40 La. 362, 4 South. 210; Kansas City S. & G. Ry. Co. v. Davis, 50 La. 1054, 23 South 946.

302 Liquidating Commissioners of N. O. Warehouse Co. v. Marrero, 106 La. 130, 30 South. 305.

303 Town of Donaldsonville v. Police Jury, 113 La. 16, 36 South. 873.

304 Roudanez v. New Orleans, 29 La. Ann. 271.

305 Kock v. Triche, 52 La. 825, 27 South. 354.

306 Carlton v. Newman, 77 Me. 408, 1 Atl. 194; see passage quoted in 1 Pom. Eq. Jur. (3d ed.), § 260, note (d).

§ 412. **Maryland.**—In Maryland, "the collection of taxes will not be interferéd with or restrained by a court of equity for mere irregularities in their proceedings, or for any hardship that may result from their collection. It is only when the tax itself is clearly illegal, or the tribunal imposing it has clearly exceeded its powers, or the rights of the tax-payers have been violated, that the interposition of the special remedy by injunction can be successfully invoked, and only then when no appellate tribunal has been created with power to remedy the wrong."[307] In accordance with the rule as thus laid down, an injunction has been granted to restrain the collection of a tax on exempt property.[308] Likewise, an injunction has been granted to restrain the collection of a tax on property improperly returned by the registrar of wills as being in the hands of an administrator, when it has really been distributed.[309]

Ordinarily, no relief by injunction will be granted unless the tax-payer applies first to the county commissioners for correction of the tax.[310] But this application is unnecessary when the tax is void for a jurisdictional defect.[311]

307 County Commissioners of Allegany Co. v. Union M. Co., 61 Md. 545. In general, see Mayor etc. of Baltimore v. Porter, 18 Md. 284, 79 Am. Dec. 686.

308 Sindall v. Mayor etc. of Baltimore, 93 Md. 526, 49 Atl. 645; Valentine v. City of Hagerstown, 86 Md. 486, 38 Atl. 931. In Joesting v. Mayor, 97 Md. 589, 55 Atl. 456, an injunction was granted restraining the collection of an assessment on property not subject thereto.

309 Nicodemus v. Hull, 93 Md. 364, 48 Atl. 1094.

310 Baldwin v. Commissioners of Washington Co., 85 Md. 145, 36 Atl 764; O'Neal v. Va. & Md. Bridge Co., 18 Md. 1, 79 Am Dec. 669; Methodist Protestant Church v. City of Baltimore, 6 Gill, 391, 48 Am. Dec. 540.

311 Mayor etc. of Baltimore v. Poole, 97 Md 67, 54 Atl. 681.

A mere error in the assessment is not ground for relief.[312]

Under a code provision that courts of equity have no jurisdiction of suits where the original debt or damage does not amount to twenty dollars,[313] it has been held that an injunction will not issue to restrain the collection of a tax of seven dollars and thirty-two cents.[314]

§ 413. **Special Assessments.**—Equity will enjoin the collection of special assessments levied without authority, in order to prevent multiplicity of suits or cloud on title. Thus, an injunction will issue to prevent the sale of land to satisfy a street assessment levied without the assent of the owners of a majority of feet fronting on the street, when the statute requires such assent.[315]

§ 414. **Massachusetts.**—The collection of illegal taxes, whether on real or on personal property, is not subject to injunction in this state. A tax-payer who has been illegally assessed has an adequate and complete remedy at law by paying the tax and suing to recover it back.[316] "The legislature has evidently regarded this remedy as adequate and complete, having regard to a prompt and unembarrassed assessment and collection of taxes for the maintenance of the government."[317]

312 Moffatt v. Calvert Co. Commissioners, 97 Md. 266, 54 Atl 960

313 Code of Pub. Gen. Laws, art. 16, § 91.

314 Kuenzel v. Mayor etc. of Baltimore, 93 Md. 750, 49 Atl 649.

315 Holland v. Mayor etc. of Baltimore, 11 Md. 186, 69 Am. Dec. 195.

316 Brewer v. City of Springfield, 97 Mass. 152; Loud v. City of Charlestown, 99 Mass. 208; Macy v. Nantucket, 121 Mass. 351 (interpleader not maintainable to determine in which town plaintiff is liable to be taxed; but the objection may be waived: Forest River Lead Co. v. Salem, 165 Mass. 193, 202, 42 N. E. 802); Kelley v. Barton, 174 Mass. 396, 54 N. E. 860.

317 Loud v. City of Charlestown, 99 Mass. 208.

Illegal special assessments stand upon the same ground as general taxes, with respect to the adequacy of the legal remedy by paying the assessment and suit to recover back.[318] An injunction will not issue to restrain the collection of an illegal assessment for local improvement when there is no threat to collect;[319] but where the property has been sold for non-payment and the recitals would in a short time become *prima facie* evidence of the facts stated in the deed, equity may interfere to remove the cloud on the title.[320] Danger of multiplicity of suits to collect installments of the assessment is not ground for relief, when these may be avoided by payment of the whole and a single suit to recover back.[321]

§ 415. **Michigan.**—In Michigan, the rule has been laid down by Judge Cooley "that equity will not interfere to restrain the collection of the public revenue for mere irregularities. Either it should appear that the property is exempt from taxation, or that the levy is without legal power, or that the persons imposing it were unauthorized, or that they have proceeded fraudulently."[322] Accordingly, an injunction will not issue against the collection of a general tax on the ground that the money is needed only to replace money unlawfully expended from the public treasury.[323] On the other hand, it will issue when the tax is fraudulently levied.[324] Therefore a tax founded on a fraudulent assessment will be enjoined. "An assessment is not

318 Hunnewell v. City of Charlestown, 106 Mass. 350

319 Clark v. City of Worcester, 167 Mass. 81, 44 N. E. 1082.

320 White v. Gove, 183 Mass. 333, 67 N. E. 359.

321 Greenhood v. MacDonald, 183 Mass. 342, 67 N. E. 336.

322 Albany & Boston Min. Co. v. Auditor-General, 37 Mich. 391.

323 Clee v. Village of Trenton, 108 Mich. 293, 66 N. W. 48.

324 Merrill v. Humphrey, 24 Mich. 170.

fraudulent merely because of being excessive, if the assessors have not acted from improper motives; but if it is purposely made too high, through prejudice or a reckless disregard of duty, in opposition to what must necessarily be the judgment of all competent persons, or through the adoption of a rule which is designed to operate unequally upon a class, and to violate the constitutional rule of uniformity, the case is a plain one for the equitable remedy of injunction."[325] Likewise, such relief is proper where the assessing officers have purposely, in violation of law, exempted property from taxation, so that the burden rests unequally.[326] But in the absence of fraud, the mere fact that the assessment is unequal is no ground for an injunction, for the courts will not revise the action of a board of equalization.[327]

Personal Tax.—Ordinarily, an injunction will not issue against the collection of a purely personal tax which is not a charge upon land;[328] nor will it be granted to restrain the collection of a tax upon land when sufficient personal property has already been levied upon to satisfy the tax.[329] But there are exceptions when the personal property is of peculiar value to the owner, or where a valuable franchise would be interfered with, and in such cases the injunction will be allowed.[330] Thus, an injunction has issued against the

325 Pioneer Iron Co. v. City of Negaunee, 116 Mich. 430, 74 N. W. 700, quoting from Cooley, Taxation, p. 784.

326 Walsh v. King, 74 Mich. 350, 41 N. W. 1080.

327 McDonald v. City of Escanaba, 62 Mich. 555, 29 N. W. 93.

328 Henry v. Gregory, 29 Mich. 68; Youngblood v. Sexton, 32 Mich. 408, 20 Am. Rep. 654.

329 Id.

330 City of Detroit v. Donovan, 127 Mich. 604, 8 Detroit Leg. N. 465, 86 N. W. 1032.

collection of an illegal personal tax by seizure of railroad cars.[331]

Multiplicity of Suits.—Parties severally taxed, and having no common interest except in the question of law which is involved, cannot unite to have the tax enjoined on the ground of preventing a multiplicity of suits, when their cases severally present no ground for equitable interference.[332]

Tender.—When a tax is valid in part, the tax-payer must, as a condition of relief, tender the amount legally due.[333] This is upon the principle that he who seeks equity must do equity.

§ 416. **Special Assessments.**—An injunction will issue when a special assessment levied under an unconstitutional act is made a lien on real estate.[334] Thus, an assessment levied according to superficial area without regard to benefits will be enjoined. Relief will be granted where the assessment is made without jurisdiction.[335] But an injunction will not issue on account of mere irregularities in the assessment.[336]

Where a contract for a public improvement is regularly let and the work is accepted by the proper board, an injunction will not issue to restrain the levying of an assessment to pay therefor on the ground that the work has been improperly done.[337] Such questions are for the legislative body to decide in the exercise of its discretion.

331 Id.

332 Youngblood v. Sexton, 32 Mich. 406, 20 Am. Rep. 654.

333 Albany & Boston Min Co. v. Auditor-General, 37 Mich. 391; Merrill v. Humphrey, 24 Mich. 170.

334 Thomas v. Gain, 35 Mich 156, 24 Am. Rep. 535

335 Wreford v City of Detroit, 132 Mich. 348, 93 N. W. 876.

336 Township of Flynn v. Woolman, 133 Mich. 508, 95 N. W. 567.

337 Dixon v. City of Detroit, 86 Mich. 516, 49 N. W. 628; Motz v City of Detroit, 18 Mich 495.

An injunction will not be granted when the complainants, upon the principle of equitable estoppel, have lost their right to equitable relief. Thus, where a street is paved as a result of a petition signed by complainants and no objection is made until the work is completed, an injunction against the assessment will be refused.[338] Likewise, it will be refused where the property owners, although they may not have petitioned for the improvement, stand by and make no objection until the work is completed.[339]

§ 417. **Minnesota.**—In Minnesota, "the general rule appears to be that equity will not interfere, merely because the tax is illegal and void, but there must be some special circumstances attending the threatened injury, to distinguish it from a mere trespass, and thus bring the case within some recognized head of equity jurisprudence."[340] To bring the case within the rule it must appear that there will be irreparable injury, or that a multiplicity of suits will result, or that a cloud will be cast upon title to real estate.[341]

Personal Property Tax.—As there is generally an adequate remedy at law in case of a tax on personal property, it is held that an injunction will not be granted to restrain its collection.[342] In order to bring the case within the jurisdiction it must appear that

338 Motz v. City of Detroit, 18 Mich. 495.

339 Walker Township v. Thomas, 123 Mich. 290, 82 N. W. 48; Lundbom v. City of Manistee, 93 Mich. 170, 53 N. W. 161; Byram v. City of Detroit, 50 Mich. 56, 12 N. W. 912, 14 N. W 698; Farr v. City of Detroit (Mich.), 99 N. W. 19; Gates v. City of Grand Rapids, 134 Mich. 96, 95 N W. 998.

340 Clarke v. Ganz, 21 Minn. 387.

341 Scribner v. Allen, 12 Minn. 148 (Gil. 85).

342 Clarke v. Ganz, 21 Minn. 387; Laird, Norton & Co. v. Pine County, 72 Minn. 409, 75 N. W. 723; Bradish v. Lucken, 38 Minn. 186, 36 N. W. 454.

there is no adequate remedy at law or that such remedy will be practically valueless, as where the collector is insolvent, or where a multiplicity of suits will be necessary.[343] The mere fact that there are numerous tax-payers in the same position as the plaintiff does not give jurisdiction on the ground of multiplicity of suits, at least in the absence of any claim that the suit was brought in pursuance of a common understanding, and by the authority of such tax-payers.[344]

Cloud upon Title—Where the tax proceedings are void on their face they do not cast a cloud upon the title of real estate, and consequently in such a case an injunction will not ordinarily be granted.[345] And even where a tax deed is *prima facie* evidence of a valid title in the grantee, the injunction will not issue unless the issuance of such a deed is threatened. The mere levying of a tax for which the land might be sold and such a deed given, is not a sufficient threat to warrant an injunction.[346]

§ 418. **Special Assessments**—An injunction will be refused when a local assessment cannot be enforced without giving the property owner a full and adequate opportunity to be heard in court;[347] but the relief may be granted if the city does not object to the matter being presented in such a proceeding.[348]

343 Clarke v. Ganz, 21 Minn. 387.

344 Bradish v. Lucken, 38 Minn. 186, 36 N. W. 454.

345 Scribner v. Allen, 12 Minn. 148 (Gil 85).

346 Id.

347 Kelly v City of Minneapolis, 57 Minn 294, 47 Am St. Rep. 605, 59 N. W. 304, 26 L. R. A 92; Albrecht v City of St Paul, 47 Minn. 531, 50 N. W. 608; Fajder v Village of Aitkin, 87 Minn. 445, 92 N. W 332, 934.

348 Albrecht v. City of St. Paul, 47 Minn. 531, 50 N W. 608.

§ 419. **Mississippi.**—The Mississippi code provides that "the chancery court shall have jurisdiction of suits by one or more tax-payers in any county, city, town or village, to restrain the collection of any taxes levied, or attempted to be collected without authority of law."[349] Before the issuance of the injunction the plaintiff must enter into a bond conditioned for the prompt payment of the taxes enjoined, and damages and costs, in case the injunction be dissolved.[350] Upon dissolution, a decree must be entered against the plaintiff and his bondsmen for the amount of the taxes, ten per cent penalty, and costs.[351] These sections have been construed as allowing the injunction whenever the tax is without authority of law.[352] The injunction will not be granted, however, until the proceedings have gone far enough to enable the court to tell the amount for which a decree against the plaintiff must be entered in case of dissolution, and therefore an injunction will not issue to restrain the mere assessment of an *ad valorem* tax.[353]

Apart from statutory authorization, an injunction will not ordinarily issue to restrain the collection of a tax on personal property, because in such a case there is a complete and adequate remedy at law.[354] And the mere fact that there are a great many tax-payers similarly situated, will not give the court jurisdiction.[355] But the insolvency of the tax-collector renders the legal remedy inadequate, within the meaning of the rule.[356]

349 Code, § 483.

350 Code, § 561.

351 Code, § 484.

352 Yazoo & M. V. R. Co. v. Adams, 73 Miss. 648, 19 South. 91.

353 Yazoo & M. V. R. Co. v. Adams, 73 Miss. 648, 19 South. 91.

354 Coulson v. Harris, 43 Miss. 728.

355 Id.

356 Richardson v. Scott, 47 Miss. 236.

Where a tax levy is in excess of the legal limit, only the excess will be enjoined.[357] Tender of the valid part of the tax is a prerequisite to injunctive relief.[358]

§ 420. **Missouri.**—The supreme court of Missouri has stated that it would be difficult to reconcile the authorities, either in that state or elsewhere; but that of late years the court has been disposed to regard with favor proceedings which are preventive in their character, rather than compel the injured party to seek redress after the damage is accomplished.[359]

The court should require the payment of taxes confessedly due, before granting the injunction.[360]

Irregularities.—Equity will not relieve by injunction against mere informality of tax procedure, where no substantial right of the complaining party has been infringed. Equity deals with the substance of transactions, and treats their form as of secondary importance, unless the positive law (which it is bound to follow) otherwise ordains.[361]

Void Tax.—Where property has been levied on to enforce the payment of a void tax, injunction is the proper remedy, according to the later authorities.[362] Thus,

357 Lewis v. Village of Bogue Chitto, 76 Miss 356, 24 South. 875.

358 Lewis v. Village of Bogue Chitto, 76 Miss. 356, 24 South. 875; Mobile & O. R. R. Co. v. Mosely, 52 Miss. 127.

359 Overall v. Ruenzi (1877), 67 Mo. 203.

360 Overall v. Ruenzi, 67 Mo. 203. See Burnham v. Rogers, 167 Mo. 17, 66 S. W. 970.

361 St. Louis & S. F. Ry. Co. v. Gracy, 126 Mo. 472, 29 S. W. 579.

362 St. Louis & S. F. Ry. Co. v. Apperson, 97 Mo. 301, 10 S. W 478, Noll v. Morgan, 82 Mo. App 112. See, however, McPike v. Pew, 48 Mo. 525, holding that an officer seizing property under a void tax levy would be a mere trespasser, and that the injured party would have an ample remedy at law, to the same effect with the last case, Barrow v. Davis, 46 Mo. 394, and Sayre v. Tompkins, 23 Mo. 443, distinguishing between void taxes on real and on personal property.

Multiplicity of suits is emphatically recognized as a ground of jur-the property owner may have relief by injunction as to city or county taxes which are levied in excess of the constitutional limit.[363]

Property not Subject to Taxation.—Injunction is an appropriate remedy to prevent the collection of taxes against property not the subject of taxation.[364]

Excessive Assessment.—The right of appeal to the county board of equalization, provided by statute, is an adequate remedy, and excludes any remedy in equity.[365]

Cloud on Title.—A tax sale of real property exempt by law from taxation, may be enjoined, to prevent a cloud on the title;[366] and in general, the sale of lands for the payment of an illegal tax will be enjoined, for the same reason.[367]

§ 421. **Special Assessments.**—An injunction will issue to restrain the collection of a void special assessment which casts a cloud upon the title of real estate. It is not necessary to constitute a cloud which will warrant the interposition of a court of equity that the defect should not be apparent on the face of the proceedings.

isdiction, where one tax-payer sues for all the tax-payers of a township or county, in Ransey v. Bader, 67 Mo. 476, 480, see 1 Pom. Eq. Jur. (3d ed), § 260, note (d).

363 Arnold v. Hawkins, 95 Mo. 569, 8 S. W. 718; Overall v. Ruenzi, 67 Mo. 203

364 Valle v. Zeigler, 84 Mo. 214 (bonds kept out of the state, and shares of stock in manufacturing companies), Mechanics' Bank v. City of Kansas, 73 Mo. 555 (exempt real property).

365 National Bank of Unionville v. Staats, 155 Mo 55, 55 S. W. 626; Meyer v. Rosenblatt, 78 Mo. 495; Deane v. Todd, 22 Mo. 90.

366 Mechanics' Bank v. City of Kansas, 73 Mo. 555.

367 McPike v. Pen, 51 Mo. 63, holding that failure to give notice of municipal aid election rendered the tax based thereon illegal, Leslie v. City of St. Louis, 47 Mo. 474 (street assessment); Fowler v. City of St. Joseph, 37 Mo. 229 (street assessment); Lockwood v. City of St. Louis, 24 Mo. 20.

If the defect is such as to require legal acumen to discover it, whether it appears on the deed or proceedings, or is to be proven *aliunde,* equity will take jurisdiction.[368] Thus, where an ordinance for street improvements provides for an unauthorized maintenance of the street, and the assessment levied is a lien on realty, an injunction is a proper remedy.[369] Likewise, it is proper when a hearing is denied to the property owners;[370] or where the assessment is to pay for property condemned when the condemnation proceedings are invalid;[371] or where the ordinance providing for the improvement is fraudulent and oppressive, and imposes a burden without any corresponding benefit.[372]

One property owner may maintain a suit, on behalf of himself and others similarly situated, to restrain the execution of an ordinance, illegally passed, for the improvement of a street at the expense of the property owners, in order to prevent a multiplicity of suits [373]

An injunction will not issue to restrain the collection of an assessment to pay for land acquired for street purposes by condemnation on the ground that the city already had title, when the property owners were duly notified of the assessment proceedings.[374] Nor will it be granted on the ground that the city has made a contract that such property should be exempt from such assessments, for such a contract is invalid.[375] Again,

368 Verdin v. City of St. Louis, 131 Mo. 106, 33 S. W. 480, 36 S. W. 52.

369 Verdin v. City of St. Louis, 131 Mo. 106, 33 S. W 480, 36 S. W. 52.

370 Dennison v. City of Kansas, 95 Mo. 430, 8 S. W. 429.

371 Leslie v. City of St. Louis, 47 Mo. 474.

372 Skinker v. Heman, 148 Mo. 349, 49 S. W. 1026.

373 Dennison v. City of Kansas, 95 Mo. 430, 8 S. W. 429.

374 Michael v. City of St. Louis, 112 Mo. 610, 20 S. W. 666; Buddecke v. Ziegenhein, 122 Mo. 239, 26 S. W. 696.

375 Verna v. City of St. Louis, 164 Mo. 146, 64 S. W. 180.

it is not authorized merely because other property is exempted from the assessment, especially when it does not appear that the complainant is assessed more than his share.[376]

An injunction will not issue when there is an adequate remedy at law.[377] But the mere right to interpose an equitable defense to any action of ejectment which might be brought on the strength of a sheriff's deed is not an adequate remedy, for such action might not be brought promptly; and in such event, the title to plaintiff's land would be so clouded as to prevent a sale.[378]

Where the work is done without authority, as under a void ordinance or contract, the abutting owner is not estopped by his failure to object before the work is completed.[379]

Where there is some irregularity in doing the work, or invalidity of some part of the contract for street improvements, an abutting owner will be required, as a condition precedent to an order enjoining the collection of a general tax, to make payment or tender of the sum justly due.[380] Thus, where the illegality results from a construction of the work under a valid ordinance and contract and the mistake consists in pointing out the lines of the street by the city authorities, the abutting owner will be compelled to do equity.[381]

376 Page v. City of St. Louis, 20 Mo. 137.

377 Michael v. City of St. Louis, 112 Mo. 610, 20 S. W. 666.

378 Verdin v. City of St. Louis, 131 Mo. 106, 33 S. W. 480, 36 S. W. 52; Skinker v. Heman, 148 Mo. 349, 49 S. W. 1026.

379 Verdin v. City of St. Louis, 131 Mo. 106, 33 S. W. 480, 36 S. W. 52.

380 Verdin v. City of St. Louis, 131 Mo. 106, 33 S. W. 480, 36 S. W. 52.

381 Johnson v. Duer, 115 Mo. 366, 21 S. W. 800.

§ 422. **Montana.**—The Political Code of Montana prohibits injunctions to restrain the collection of a tax or the sale of property for non-payment of a tax, except where the tax is illegal, or not authorized by law, or where the property is exempt from taxation.[382] A board of equalization is provided to correct all irregularities. Therefore an injunction will not be granted when relief can be obtained, or could have been, before the board.[383] But where the tax is absolutely void, as where a school tax is levied upon a party whose place of business is not within the district, the injunction will be granted.[384] Relief will likewise be granted to prevent the sale of personal property against which the tax is not a lien.[385]

Tender.—If the tax is valid in part and void in part, no relief can be obtained unless tender is made of the valid part[386]

§ 423. **Nebraska**—In Nebraska, it is provided by statute that "no injunction shall be granted by any court or judge in this state to restrain the collection of any tax or any part thereof, hereafter levied, nor to restrain the sale of any property for the non-payment of any such tax except such tax, or the part thereof enjoined, be levied or assessed for an illegal or unauthorized purpose."[387] Hence, a tax-payer may obtain an

[382] Mont. Pol. Code., §§ 4023-4026, incl.

[383] Cobban v. Hinds, 23 Mont. 338, 59 Pac. 1; Deloughrey v. Hinds, 23 Mont. 260, 58 Pac. 709; First Nat. Bank v. Bailey, 15 Mont. 301, 39 Pac. 83; Northern Pac. R. R. Co. v. Patterson, 10 Mont. 93, 24 Pac. 704; Ward v. Board of Commissioners, 12 Mont. 23, 29 Pac. 658.

[384] Green Mountain Stock Ranch Co. v. Savage, 15 Mont. 189, 38 Pac. 940.

[385] Walsh v. Croft, 27 Mont. 407, 71 Pac. 409.

[386] Ward v. Board of Commissioners, 12 Mont. 23, 29 Pac. 658.

[387] Comp. Stats., art. 1, c. 77, § 144. See construction in Philadelphia Mtg. & Tr. Co. v. City of Omaha, 63 Neb. 280, 93 Am. St. Rep.

injunction to restrain the levying of a tax to pay the principal or interest on void bonds.[388]

The courts have construed this and similar statutes, however, in such a manner as to make the rule really broader. It is held that the section has no reference to taxes wholly void, that a void tax is no tax, and that, therefore, it would be beyond the power of the legislature to take away the equitable remedy in such a case; for such an act would be in conflict with the constitutional provision giving the courts general equity jurisdiction.[389] Another theory upon which the broader rule has been supported is that a tax levied without authority of law is levied for an unauthorized purpose.[390] At any rate, it may be safely laid down as a general rule that an injunction will be granted when a void tax or assessment is sought to be collected.[391] Thus, where a tax is levied on property without the jurisdiction of the taxing district,[392] or where the property is situated in territory which the taxing municipality has ineffectually tried to annex,[393] the injunction will issue. Likewise, where a statute authorizes a tax of nine mills and the taxing body levies a tax of twelve mills,[394] and where a board of equalization

442, 56 L. R. A. 150, 88 N. W. 523, 65 Neb. 93, 90 N. W. 1005; Union Pac. Ry. Co. v. Cheyenne County, 64 Neb. 777, 90 N. W. 917.

388 Morton v. Carlin, 51 Neb 202, 70 N. W. 966.

389 Touzalin v. City of Omaha, 25 Neb. 817, 41 N. W. 796; Chicago, B. & Q. R. Co. v. Cass County, 51 Neb. 369, 70 N. W. 955; Rothwell v. Knox County, 62 Neb. 50, 86 N. W. 903; Grand Island & M. C. R. Co. v. Dawes County, 62 Neb. 44, 86 N. W. 834.

390 Earl v. Duras, 13 Neb. 234, 13 N. W. 206.

391 Morris v. Merrell, 44 Neb. 423, 62 N. W. 865.

392 Sioux City Bridge Co. v Dakota County, 61 Neb. 75, 84 N. W. 607.

393 Chicago, B. & W. R. Co. v City of Nebraska City, 53 Neb. 453, 73 N. W. 952.

394 Grand Island & W. C. R. Co. v. Dawes County, 62 Neb. 44, 86 N. W. 834.

fraudulently and without notice raises an assessment to an excessive amount,[395] equitable relief is proper, especially where it is necessary to prevent a cloud on title. It is also proper when no tax whatever is due.[396]

An injunction will issue to restrain the collection of a valid tax in an unlawful manner. Thus, an injunction will be granted to restrain the sale of realty for non-payment of a tax when there is sufficient personalty belonging to the owner and subject to the levy, to satisfy it.[397]

Personal Property Tax.—The remedy is not confined to cases of void taxation of real property, but will be granted equally to restrain the collection of a void tax on personal property.[398] The reason for this rule is that taxes on any specific personal property are a lien on all of the owner's personalty. Hence, the court argues, there is just as much reason for an injunction in this case as in the case of realty. "It would be a vain thing for the law to require a tax to be paid, the payment of which would immediately give rise to an action for its recovery."[399]

Irregularities.—An injunction will not issue to restrain the collection of a tax because of mere irregularities in the proceedings, unless enforcement would be inequitable and unconscionable.[400] In cases of ir-

395 South Platte Land Co. v. Commissioners of Buffalo Co., 7 Neb. 253.

396 Earl v. Duras, 13 Neb. 234, 13 S. W. 206.

397 Johnson v. Hahn, 4 Neb. 139.

398 Rothwell v. Knox County, 62 Neb. 50, 86 N. W. 903; Chicago, B. & Q. R. Co. v. Cass County, 51 Neb. 369, 70 N. W. 955.

399 Rothwell v. Knox County, 62 Neb. 50, 86 N. W. 903.

400 Spargur v. Romine, 38 Neb. 736, 57 N. W. 523, Chicago, B. & W. R. Co. v. City of Nebraska City, 53 Neb. 453, 73 N. W. 952; Wilson v. City of Auburn, 27 Neb 435, 43 N. W. 257; Bellevue Imp. Co. v. Village of Bellevue, 39 Neb. 876, 58 N. W. 446.

regularity an adequate remedy is provided at law. And especially where the irregularity is the result of the plaintiff's own act, as where an officer of a corporation made a return of its property in his own name and was assessed for it in consequence, there is no ground for equitable interference.[401] An error of a tax-collector in marking an assessment paid does not entitle one who purchases in reliance upon the record to equitable relief.[402]

Laches.—A suit to restrain the collection of a tax need not be brought within any fixed time. Therefore the question as to whether the right to relief is barred by laches depends upon the facts in each particular case.[403] Mere delay does not amount to laches, especially where the record fails to show that the plaintiff had notice of the levy.[404]

Proof.—In actions to restrain the collection of taxes, the burden is upon the plaintiff to allege and prove the invalidity.[405]

Tender.—Where any part of a tax or assessment is legal, no injunction will issue to restrain the collection of the void part unless the legal part has been paid or tendered.[406] Where, however, a tax is wholly void, no tender is necessary.[407]

401 McGillin v. Chase County, 39 Neb. 422, 58 N. W. 138.

402 Philadelphia Mtg. & Tr. Co. v. City of Omaha, 63 Neb. 280, 93 Am. St. Rep. 442, 88 N. W. 523, 57 L. R. A. 150.

403 Richards v. Hatfield, 40 Neb 879, 59 N. W. 777.

404 Casey v. Burt County, 59 Neb. 624, 81 N. W. 851.

405 Webster v. City of Lincoln, 50 Neb. 1, 69 N. W. 394; Parrotte v. City of Omaha, 61 Neb. 96, 84 N. W. 602.

406 Burlington & M. R. R. v. Commissioners of York County, 7 Neb. 487.

407 Sioux City Bridge Co. v. Dakota County, 61 Neb. 75, 84 N. W. 607.

§ 424. **Special Assessments.**—Although the statute prohibits injunctions against taxation, general or local, unless levied for an illegal or unauthorized purpose, an injunction will issue to restrain the collection of an assessment which is levied without authority.[408] The statute authorizing local improvements must be strictly complied with, and if any of the substantial requirements, such as the petition of the owners of a majority of the frontage,[409] or the publication of the ordinance[410] are not fulfilled, the assessment is beyond the authority of the legislative body, and an injunction will issue. But where jurisdiction is acquired, an injunction will not issue because of mere irregularities in the proceedings.[411]

An injunction will not be refused because the abutting owner has allowed the work to be completed unless it appears, (1) that he knew the improvement was being made, (2) that he knew that an assessment was contemplated, (3) that he knew of the infirmity or defect, and (4) that some special benefit has accrued to his property.[412] Where these concur, the owner must pay what is justly due before he can obtain relief.[413] Relief will not be granted to one who, by covenants in his deed, has assumed the payment of the assessment.[414]

408 Morris v. Merrel, 44 Neb. 423, 62 N. W. 865.

409 Harmon v. City of Omaha, 53 Neb. 164, 73 N. W. 671; Morse v. City of Omaha (Neb.), 93 N. W. 734.

410 Ives v. Irey, 51 Neb. 136, 70 N. W. 961.

411 Darst v. Griffin, 31 Neb. 668, 48 N. W. 819; Bemis v. McCloud (Neb.), 97 N. W. 828 (no injunction unless some jurisdictional fact is wanting on face of record).

412 Harmon v. City of Omaha, 53 Neb. 164, 73 N. W. 671. For a case where it was held that the property owner was barred by his acquiescence, see Redick v. City of Omaha, 35 Neb. 125, 52 N. W. 847.

413 Darst v. Griffin, 31 Neb. 668, 48 N. W. 819.

414 Eddy v. City of Omaha (Neb.), 101 N. W. 25.

§ 425. **Nevada.**—In Nevada it is held "that no court of equity will ever allow its injunction to issue to restrain the collection of a tax, except where it is actually necessary to protect the rights of citizens who have no plain, speedy and adequate remedy at law. It must . . . . appear that the enforcement of the tax would lead to a multiplicity of suits, or produce irreparable injury; or if the property is real estate, throw a cloud upon the title of the complainant, or there must be some allegation of fraud, before the aid of a court of equity can be invoked. There must in every case be some special circumstances attending a threatened injury of this kind, which distinguishes it from a common trespass, and brings the case under some recognized head of equity jurisdiction before the extraordinary and preventive remedy of injunction can be invoked."[415] Therefore, the collection of a tax on personal property will not be enjoined even though the tax has been once paid.[416]

§ 426. **New Hampshire.**—In New Hampshire, an application for abatement is the proper remedy, not only when the assessment is made upon an overvaluation, but also when the whole assessment is illegal. There being this adequate remedy at law, an injunction will not ordinarily be granted to restrain the collection of a tax.[417]

§ 427. **New Jersey.**—The prevention of a multiplicity of suits is a ground for the injunction, in a case where

415 Wells, Fargo & Co. v. Dayton, 11 Nev. 161.

416 Conley v. Chedic, 6 Nev. 223.

417 Rockingham Ten Cent Savings Bank v. Portsmouth, 52 N. H. 17; Brown v. Concord, 56 N. H. 375.

the invalidity of a similar tax as against the plaintiff has already been established at law.[418]

Special Assessments.—The abutting owner is entitled to an injunction to restrain the city council from voluntarily paying a contractor for imperfect street work, when such owner's property will be assessed for part of the cost of the work.[419]

§ 428. **New Mexico.**—In New Mexico, the collection of a tax unauthorized by law will be restrained, especially when it casts a cloud on title to real estate. Tax deeds are *prima facie* evidence of regularity of proceedings, and therefore cast a cloud on title.[420] The courts will "arrest any attempt to enforce the collection of a tax when it is apparent that the power to do so was not originally and clearly vested in the taxing power."[421]

§ 429. **New York.**—In New York, public policy forbids the granting of injunctions in tax cases, unless facts are shown clearly bringing the case under some acknowledged head of equity jurisdiction, as the necessity for the intervention of the court to prevent a multiplicity of suits or irreparable damage, where there is no adequate remedy at law, or to remove a cloud on title.[422] It is sometimes stated that the injunction will

418 Paterson etc. R. R. v. Jersey City, 9 N. J. Eq. 434; see 1 Pom. Eq. Jur., § 253, note.

419 Lodor v. McGovern, 48 N. J. Eq. 275, 27 Am. St. Rep. 446, 22 Atl. 199 That a slight and harmless variance in the performance from the precise terms of the contract is not a ground for restraining such payment, see McCartan v. Inhabitants of City of Trenton, 57 N. J. Eq. 571, 41 Atl. 830.

420 Town of Albuquerque v. Zeiger, 5 N. M. 674, 27 Pac. 315.

421 Poe v. Howell (N. M.), 67 Pac. 62.

422 Mercantile Nat. Bank v. City of New York, 27 Misc. Rep. 32, 57 N. Y. Supp. 254; Susquehanna Bank v. Supervisors of Broome Co., 25 N. Y. 312; Western R. R. Co. v. Nolan, 48 N. Y. 514; Mutual Ben.

be granted only under circumstances of great necessity to prevent irreparable damage.[423] The courts have adhered strictly to this rule, and accordingly there are few cases where the injunction will be granted. It will not be granted on the ground of mere unconstitutionality or illegality, unless the case is brought under some recognized head of equity.[424] Ordinarily, when a statute is unconstitutional, the sheriff is a mere trespasser when he attempts to levy upon the tax-payer's property, and hence the remedy at law is amply sufficient. And the fact that the remedy at law has been lost by laches gives the court no jurisdiction.[425] Generally, when an assessment is excessive or illegal, there is an adequate remedy at law, and hence injunctive relief will be refused.[426] Thus, a national bank cannot enjoin the collection of a tax on the ground that its property is assessed at a higher rate than other property within the state, in violation of the federal statute, for an ample remedy is provided by the state statute.[427] And a remainder-man, for the same reason, cannot enjoin a sale for taxes left unpaid by the life tenant.[428] A broader rule has been laid down in one

Life Ins. Co. v. Supervisors, 2 Abb. Pr., N. S., 233; Mayor etc. v. Meserole, 26 Wend. 132; Heywood v. City of Buffalo, 14 N. Y. 534.

423 Rome W. & O. R. R. Co. v. Smith, 39 Hun, 332, Brass v. Rathbone, 8 App. Div. 78, 40 N. Y. Supp. 466.

424 United Lines Tel. Co. v. Grant, 137 N. Y. 7, 32 N. E. 1005; Postal Tel. Cable Co. v. Grant, 11 N. Y. Supp. 323, 33 N. Y. St. Rep. 997.

425 United Lines Tel. Co. v. Grant, 68 Hun, 634, 18 N. Y. Supp 534; Mercantile Nat. Bank v. City of New York, 27 Misc. Rep. 32, 57 N. Y. Supp. 254.

426 Mercantile Nat. Bank v. Mayor etc. of New York, 172 N. Y. 35, 64 N. E. 756.

427 Mercantile Nat. Bank v. City of New York, 27 Misc. Rep. 32, 57 N Y. Supp. 254.

428 Sage v. City of Gloversville, 43 App. Div. 245, 60 N. Y. Supp. 791.

recent lower court case, but it is at least doubtful if it will be followed. The plaintiff was assessed upon the same personal property in two boroughs, in one of which the property had never been. The court held that equity had jurisdiction to correct a mistake by which double liability is incurred where such mistake depends upon proof of facts outside the record, and where, in consequence of such mistake, an obligation that has already been paid and discharged still appears of record as a valid claim. The case is brought within the general rule by a holding that it is within the jurisdiction of equity to restrain the enforcement of unconscionable demands.[429] It would seem that this rule is too broad, and that if adhered to it would open the door to injunctive relief in almost every case.

§ 430. **Cloud on Title.**—It is one of the recognized principles of equity jurisdiction that relief will be granted to prevent a cloud on title to real estate. Therefore, whenever an illegal tax casts such a cloud, the court will interfere by injunction.[430] Not every tax which is declared a lien on real estate casts such a cloud, however. In order to warrant relief, it must appear that the proceedings are regular on their face and invalid only because of defects *dehors* the record, and also that the defect will not necessarily appear in proceedings to enforce the lien.[431] An assessment levied without authority is held not to be even an apparent lien.[432]

429 Jackson v. City of New York, 62 App. Div. 46, 70 N. Y. Supp. 877.

430 Mutual Ben. Life Ins. Co. v. Supervisors, 2 Abb. Pr., N. S., 233.

431 Alvord v. City of Syracuse, 163 N. Y. 158, 57 N. E. 310; Trowbridge v. Horan, 78 N. Y. 439; Van Rensselaer v. Kidd, 4 Barb. 17; Van Doren v. Mayor, 9 Paige, 388.

432 Heywood v. City of Buffalo, 14 N. Y. 534.

But where a cloud is cast, the courts will interfere, as in case of a threatened sale for non-payment of an illegal tax regular on its face.[433]

§ 431. **Special Assessments.**—As a general rule, an injunction will issue when an illegal special assessment, valid on its face, casts a cloud on the title of real estate. Thus, it is proper where the assessment is invalid because the assessors adopt the wrong rule in apportionment;[434] or when land benefited by an improvement is excluded from the assessment district, for there is an illegality not apparent on the face which creates a cloud on title;[435] but it will be presumed that the assessment is apportioned according to benefits until the contrary is shown.[436] The mere fact that the assessment is in excess of benefits, where there is no claim that any land benefited is not assessed nor that there was any fraud in making the assessment, will not warrant an injunction.[437]

Where, however, the proceedings are void on their face, an injunction will be refused.[438] Thus, where a resolution fails to specify which of two plans on file is to be followed, the illegality is apparent and no injunction will issue.[439]

433 Litchfield v. City of Brooklyn, 13 Misc. Rep. 693, 34 N. Y. Supp. 1090.

434 Clark v. Village of Dunkirk, 12 Hun, 181; affirmed, 75 N. Y. 612.

435 Copcutt v. City of Yonkers, 83 Hun, 178, 31 N. Y. Supp. 659; Providence Retreat v. City of Buffalo, 29 App. Div. 160, 51 N. Y. Supp. 654; affirmed, 31 App. Div. 635, 53 N. Y. Supp. 1113; Hassan v. City of Rochester, 67 N. Y. 528.

436 Denise v. Village of Fairport, 11 Misc. Rep. 199, 32 N. Y. Supp. 97.

437 Hoffield v. City of Buffalo, 130 N. Y. 387, 29 N. E 747.

438 Mayor etc. of Brooklyn v. Meserole, 26 Wend. 132; Van Doren v. Mayor, 9 Paige Ch. 388.

439 Copcutt v. City of Yonkers, 83 Hun, 178, 31 N. Y Supp. 659.

Where statute provides an adequate remedy at law for an illegal assessment, an injunction will be refused.[440] By section 897 of the Consolidation Act (New York City) it is provided: "No suit or action in the nature of a bill in equity or otherwise shall be commenced for the vacation of any assessment in said city, or to remove a cloud upon title, but owners of property shall be confined to their remedies in such cases to the proceedings under this title."[441] Where this applies, it has been held that no injunction can issue to prevent the sale of property for a void assessment, for to allow it would in substance be to vacate the assessment.[442]

When an assessment is void, it is not necessary to make any tender as a condition to injunctive relief.[443]

§ 432. **North Carolina.**—It is provided by statute in North Carolina that injunctions shall not be issued to restrain the collection of any tax or the sale of any property for the non-payment of any tax, except such tax as has been levied or assessed for an illegal or unauthorized purpose, or except the tax be illegal or invalid, or the assessment be illegal and invalid.[444] Thus, an injunction will not be granted merely because the defendant was not the lawful tax-collector for the year.[445] On the other hand, when the tax is illegally levied, the injunction will issue.[446] In such a case,

440 Schulz v. City of Albany, 42 App. Div. 437, 59 N. Y. Supp. 235, affirming 27 Misc. Rep. 51, 57 N. Y. Supp. 963.

441 Laws 1882, c. 410.

442 Scudder v. Mayor etc. of New York, 146 N. Y. 245, 40 N. E. 734; affirming, 79 Hun, 613, 29 N. Y. Supp. 422; Sixth Ave. R. Co. v. City of New York, 63 Hun, 271, 17 N. Y. Supp. 903.

443 Hassan v. City of Rochester, 67 N. Y. 528.

444 Acts of 1895, c. 119, § 76.

445 McDonald v. Teague, 119 N. C. 604, 26 S. E. 158.

446 Graves v. Moore Co. Commissioners, 135 N. C. 49, 47 S. E. 134;

any tax-payer may bring the suit in his own behalf only, or on behalf of all others similarly situated.[447]

The injunction will not be granted when there is an adequate remedy at law. The statute provides that if any person claiming that any tax is illegal or excessive pays the same, and, within thirty days after payment, makes a written demand for a repayment thereof, and the same is not refunded within ninety days thereafter, he may sue to recover it.[448] This provides an adequate remedy at law for an illegal or excessive personal tax, at least, and hence in such a case an injunction will be refused.[449]

Tender.—An injunction will issue to restrain the collection of an illegal excess of tax, but as a preliminary condition of relief the plaintiff must tender the amount legally due.[450]

§ 433. **Special Assessments.**—An injunction will not issue to restrain the collection of a special assessment when the act provides an adequate remedy at law by suit to recover back after payment.[451]

§ 434. **North Dakota.**—In North Dakota, it is held that courts of equity should interfere to restrain the collection of a tax, only where the property sought to be taxed is exempt, or where the tax itself is not warranted by law, or the persons assuming to assess and

Purnell v. Page, 133 N. C. 125, 45 S. E. 534; Moore v. Sugg, 112 N. C. 233, 17 S. E. 72.

447 Moore v. Sugg, 112 N. C. 233, 17 S. E. 72.

448 Laws 1887, c. 137, § 84.

449 Hall v. City of Fayetteville, 115 N. C. 281, 20 S. E. 373. The same has been held as to a tax fraudulently assessed on realty: Wilson v. Green, 135 N. C. 343, 47 S. E. 469.

450 London v. City of Wilmington, 78 N. C. 109.

451 Hilliard v. City of Asheville, 118 N. C. 845, 24 S. E. 738.

levy the same are without authority to do so, or where the proper taxing officials have acted fraudulently; and in addition, plaintiff must bring himself within some recognized head of equity jurisdiction. As a condition to relief, the applicant must pay or tender the amount of taxes properly chargeable against his property.[452] An injunction will not issue against the collection of taxes on personal property unless plaintiff can by proof of special circumstances show that the remedy at law is inadequate.[453] A tax-payer cannot enjoin a tax levy on the ground that it is to be used in part in the payment of an illegal claim.[454]

§ 435. **Ohio.**—The Revised Statutes of Ohio are very explicit as to injunctions in tax cases. "Courts of common pleas and superior courts shall have jurisdiction to enjoin the illegal levy of taxes and assessments, or the collection of either . . . . without regard to the amount thereof, but no recovery shall be had unless the action be brought within one year after the taxes or assessments are collected."[455] "Actions to enjoin the illegal levy of taxes and assessments must be brought against the corporation or person for whose use or benefit the levy is made; and if the levy would go upon the county duplicate the county auditor must be joined in the action."[456] "Actions to enjoin the collection of taxes and assessments must be brought against the of-

452 Farrington v. New England Investment Co., 1 N. D. 102, 45 N. W. 191, Douglas v. City of Fargo (N. D.), 101 N. W. 919.

453 Schaffner v. Young, 10 N. D. 245, 86 N. W. 733; Minneapolis St. P. & S. S. M. R. Co. v. Dickey County, 11 N. D. 107, 90 N. W. 260.

454 Torgrinson v. Norwich School Dist. No. 31 (N. D.), 103 N. W. 414.

455 Ohio Rev. Stats., § 5848.

456 Ohio Rev. Stats., § 5849.

ficer whose duty it is to collect the same."[457] "If the plaintiff in an action to enjoin the collection of taxes or assessments admit a part thereof to have been legally levied, he must first pay or tender the sum admitted to be due; if an order of injunction be allowed, an undertaking must be given as in other cases; and the injunction shall be a justification of the officer charged with the collection of such taxes or assessments for not collecting the same."[458]

"When the power to tax in any particular case is challenged, the citizen has the right to be heard in court as to the legality of the tax; but when the power to tax is conceded, and the complaint is only as to the valuation, a valuation made in good faith, and according to the best judgment of the taxing officer, will not be disturbed by the courts in the absence of gross mistake."[459] Thus, an injunction will be granted at suit of a tax-payer when the tax is levied without authority of law,[460] as where levied for an illegal object. It will also be granted to restrain the sale of realty for an illegal tax, when such sale would cast a cloud on title.[461] It has been held that an injunction will not issue to restrain the collection of a tax when the action of the collecting officer amounts to a mere trespass for which there is an adequate remedy at law; and the mere fact that a number of persons are in the same condition as the plaintiff is not sufficient to warrant the relief[462]

An injunction against the collection of a tax will be granted only at the suit of a tax-payer. The same de-

457 Ohio Rev. Stats., § 5850

458 Ohio Rev. Stats., § 5851.

459 Hagerty v. Huddleston, 60 Ohio St. 149, 53 N E. 960.

460 Moss v. Board of Education, 58 Ohio St. 354, 50 N. E. 921; Jones v. Davis, 35 Ohio St. 474.

461 Burnet v. Cincinnati, 3 Ohio, 73, 17 Am. Dec. 582.

462 McCoy v. Chillicothe, 3 Ohio, 370, 17 Am. Dec. 607.

gree of interest is requisite as in all other cases where the extraordinary aid of equity is invoked. Thus, the collection of a school tax cannot be enjoined at the suit of a board of education, because the board, as such, is not a tax-payer.[463]

The plaintiff seeking the aid of a court of equity must come with clean hands; therefore an injunction will be refused to one who, for the purpose of evading taxation upon certain securities at the place of his residence, has made a pretended transfer thereof by an instrument in writing, but retains the full and actual control of the property.[464]

§ 436. **Special Assessments.**—An injunction will issue to restrain the collection of a special assessment levied without authority of law.[465] Thus, it will issue when the statute authorizing the work is unconstitutional;[466] or when some jurisdictional requirement is omitted.[467]

It is no ground for an injunction that the improvement has not been constructed according to plans and specifications;[468] nor that the proceedings do not show affirmatively that benefits were considered, when the land, as a matter of fact, has been benefited.[469]

A petition for an injunction is premature when filed before steps have been taken to make the assess-

463 Board of Education v. Guy, 64 Ohio St. 434, 60 N. E. 573.

464 Sisler v. Foster (Ohio), 74 N. E. 639.

465 Jonas v. Cincinnati, 18 Ohio, 318.

466 Lewis v. Symmes, 61 Ohio St. 471, 76 Am. St. Rep. 428, 56 N. E. 194.

467 Joyce v. Baron, 67 Ohio St. 264, 65 N. E. 1001.

468 Putnam Co. Commissioners v. Krauss, 53 Ohio St. 628, 42 N E. 831.

469 Schroder v. Overman, 61 Ohio St. 1, 55 N. E. 158, 47 L. R. A. 156.

ment;[470] on the other hand, it is too late when not filed until after the assessment has been paid voluntarily.[471]

In the earlier cases it was held that an injunction will be refused, although the proceedings are void, when the landowner knowingly stands by and allows the improvement to be made without objection;[472] but the rule does not apply when he has no actual notice of the improvement and is not guilty of any want of diligence in asserting his rights.[473] It has been held in a recent case that it is not necessary to take effective measures to prevent the expenditure; that the landowner is not obliged to take any steps whatever until an attempt is made to assess his property.[474]

§ 437. **Oklahoma.**—In Oklahoma it is provided by statute that "an injunction may be granted to enjoin the illegal levy of any tax, charge or assessment, or the collection of any illegal tax, charge or assessment, or any proceeding to enforce the same, and any number of persons, whose property is affected by a tax or assessment so levied may unite in the petition filed to obtain such injunction."[475] In construing this provision, the supreme court of the territory has held that it enlarges the remedy by injunction in tax cases, and clearly gives the complaining party a right to injunction in every case when the tax or assessment levied against him is

470 Lutman v. Lake Shore & M. S. Ry. Co., 56 Ohio St. 433, 47 N. E. 248.

471 State v. Bader, 56 Ohio St. 718, 47 N. E. 564.

472 Kellogg v. Ely, 15 Ohio St. 64; Commissioners of Putnam Co. v. Krauss, 53 Ohio St. 628, 42 N. E. 831.

473 Teegarden v. Davis, 36 Ohio St. 601.

474 Lewis v. Symmes, 61 Ohio St. 471, 76 Am. St. Rep. 428, 56 N. E. 194.

475 Okla. Stats. 1893, § 4143.

illegal.[476] Thus the question to be decided in most of the cases is simply whether the tax is illegal.

Under the provision of the statute that any proceeding to enforce an illegal tax may be enjoined, it has been held that an injunction will issue to restrain a county treasurer from issuing a warrant to the sheriff to levy on the tax-payer's property to satisfy an illegal tax.[477]

Taxes have also been held illegal when the rate is higher than necessary for the purposes for which the tax is levied;[478] and where a township assessor has attempted to assess property within the limits of an incorporated town.[479] Hence in such cases an injunction will be granted.

An injunction will not be granted, however, upon a mere allegation that municipal authorities intend to misapply the funds;[480] nor where a party who claims his property is exempt because assessed in another state fails to make oath to the fact as required by law.[481]

476 Bardrick v. Dillon, 7 Okla. 535, 54 Pac. 785. It is difficult to reconcile this statement with language used by the same court in a decision filed the same day. Thus, in Wilson v. Wiggins, 7 Okla 517, 54 Pac 716, the court says expressly that the statute does not substantially enlarge the remedy, and that such relief cannot be invoked unless the party brings himself within the general principles of equitable relief, in addition to establishing the illegality complained of. Apparently the only effect of this holding is that an injunction will not be granted because of a mere irregularity not making the tax illegal, unless the case is brought under some equitable head, and it will be noticed that such a case does not come within the terms of the statute The rule as embodied in the text seems to be the true one. Wallace v. Bullen, 6 Okla. 17, 52 Pac. 954, tends to sustain the text

477 Gray v. Stiles, 6 Okla. 455, 49 Pac. 1083.

478 Atchison, T. & S. F. Ry Co. v. Wiggins, 5 Okla. 477, 49 Pac. 1019.

479 Durham v. Linderman, 10 Okla. 570, 64 Pac. 15.

480 Bardrick v Dillon, 7 Okla. 535, 54 Pac 785.

481 Wilson v Wiggins, 7 Okla. 517, 54 Pac. 716.

Irregularities.—While the injunction will be granted with great freedom when the tax is illegal, it will not be granted because of mere irregularities in the proceedings which do not injure the substantial rights of the citizen or tax-payer.[482] Thus, an injunction will not be granted merely because a tax is levied a few days too late.[483]

Parties Plaintiff.—It will be noticed that the statute provides that any number of persons whose property is affected by an illegal assessment may join in an action for an injunction. This statute, however, does not authorize one tax-payer to maintain the action for the benefit of all.[484] It applies only where a tax is illegal in the abstract, illegal in and of itself, illegal as applied to every owner of taxable property in the county or district.[485] But when the tax, as a tax, is valid, but becomes illegal only as applied to particular persons or property, or to particular cases, as where there is an over-assessment, then each person severally interested must sue alone.[486]

§ 438. **Increase of Assessment.**—Many of the cases have grown out of the action of boards of equalization in raising assessments. It has been held that the territorial board of equalization has no power to raise all of the assessments in the territory, that if it attempts to do so its action is illegal, and that therefore an in-

482 Sweet v. Boyd, 6 Okla. 699, 52 Pac. 939; Boyd v. Wiggins, 7 Okla. 85, 54 Pac. 411.

483 Sharpe v. Engle, 2 Okla. 624, 39 Pac. 384.

484 Stiles v. City of Guthrie, 3 Okla. 26, 41 Pac. 383; Caffrey v. Overholser, 8 Okla. 202, 57 Pac. 206; Martin v. Clay, 8 Okla. 46, 56 Pac. 715.

485 Bardrick v. Dillon, 7 Okla. 535, 54 Pac. 785.

486 Bardrick v Dillon, 7 Okla. 535, 54 Pac. 785, Weber v. Dillon, 7 Okla. 568, 54 Pac. 894.

junction will issue.[487] And when the tax-payer makes a return of his property at the true cash value, as required by statute, he may enjoin the collection of any increase ordered by a board of equalization.[488] It is held that such a board is not vested with judicial powers, and that therefore when property is over-valued to such an extent as to raise the presumption that it was over-estimated from design, a court of equity will determine the true valuation, and will enjoin the collection of the illegal excess.[489] And the injunction will be granted whether or not the tax-payer appeared before the board to protest against its action.[490] But the injunction will not be granted unless it appears that the increased assessment is greater than the actual cash value, for unless it is, the assessment is not illegal;[491] nor will it be granted unless the plaintiff has listed and returned the property to the assessor at its actual cash value, as required by statute.[492]

§ 439. **Tender.**—It is provided by statute that in all actions to enjoin the collection of a tax, "the true and just amount of taxes due upon such property or by such person if in dispute, must be ascertained and paid before the judgment prayed for."[493] But further than this, it is held that before the plaintiffs can be heard to question in a court of equity the legality of any portion of the taxes, they must pay, or offer to pay, that

487 Gray v. Stiles, 6 Okla. 455, 49 Pac. 1083, overruling Wallace v. Bullen, 6 Okla. 17, 52 Pac. 954.

488 Caffrey v. Overholser, 8 Okla. 202, 57 Pac. 206; Cranmer v. Williamson, 8 Okla. 683, 59 Pac. 249.

489 Bardrick v. Dillon, 7 Okla. 535, 54 Pac. 785.

490 Wiggins v. A. T. &. S. F. R. Co., 9 Okla. 118, 59 Pac. 248

491 Streight v. Durham, 10 Okla. 361, 61 Pac. 1096; Rose v. Durham, 10 Okla. 373, 61 Pac. 1100.

492 Alva State Bank v. Renfrew, 10 Okla. 26, 62 Pac. 285.

493 Okla. Stats 1893, § 5671.

part over which there is no dispute, if any there be, and at least offer in their petition to pay such portion as the court may determine to be legal and just.[494] It is suggested in one case that the reason for this latter requirement is that as the court cannot otherwise compel the payment of the tax found to be legal the offer in the petition to pay whatever is found to be due must be made, so that full justice may be done.[495] But where it is clear that a part of the tax is legal, an actual tender must be made before suit. An averment of readiness and willingness to pay is not sufficient.[496] Thus, where an injunction is sought on the ground of excess, tender must be made of the amount legally due.[497]

§ 440. **Oregon.**—In Oregon, the considerations which influence a court of equity to restrain the collection of a tax are confined to cases where the tax itself is not authorized, or, if it is, where the tax is assessed upon property not subject to taxation, or where the persons imposing it are without authority, or are acting fraudulently. In addition, the plaintiff must bring his case within some of the recognized principles of equity.[498]

An injunction will not be granted because of a mere irregularity in the assessment. Thus, it is no ground for an injunction that the property is assessed in the

494 Collins v. Green, 10 Okla. 244, 62 Pac. 813; Halff v. Green, 10 Okla. 338, 62 Pac. 816; Russell v. Green, 10 Okla. 340, 62 Pac. 817; McIntyre v. Williamson (Okla.), 54 Pac. 928.

495 Lasater v. Green, 10 Okla. 335, 62 Pac. 816.

496 State Nat. Bank v. Carson (Okla.), 50 Pac. 990.

497 McIntyre v. Williamson (Okla.), 54 Pac. 928.

498 Welch v. Clatsop County, 24 Or. 452, 33 Pac. 934; Southern Or. Co. v. Coos County, 39 Or. 185, 64 Pac. 646; Goodnough v. Powell, 23 Or. 525, 32 Pac. 396; Portland Hibernian Ben. Soc. v. Kelly, 28 Or. 173, 42 Pac. 3, 52 Am. St. Rep. 769; Alliance Trust Co. v. Multnomah County, 38 Or. 433, 63 Pac. 498, 30 L. R. A. 167.

wrong name.[499] And the mere illegality of an order of a county court in directing penalties to be added to unpaid taxes is no ground for such relief when the sheriff has no authority to enforce collection and has made no attempt to do so.[500] For the same reason that it is denied in this case, it will be denied when it is sought to restrain an extension of a tax on the tax-books, unless it is wholly unauthorized and void in all its parts.[501] In none of these actions, however, will the motives of the plaintiff be inquired into.[502]

Fraud.—When an assessment is fraudulent and oppressive equity will relieve by injunction. Thus, where the assessor and the board of equalization fraudulently combine to put an excessive valuation on plaintiff's property,[503] or when mortgages are fraudulently omitted from taxation,[504] the injunction will be granted; but plaintiff must first do equity by tendering the amount legally due. The mere fact that the assessment is excessive or illegal is not alone sufficient to warrant an injunction, unless the amount is so grossly excessive as to imply fraud.[505] The reason for this is that the assessor and the board of equalization act in a judicial capacity in making assessments, and therefore where the assessment is the result of honest judgment fairly

499 Portland Hibernian Ben. Soc. v. Kelly, 28 Or. 173, 52 Am. St. Rep. 769, 42 Pac. 3.

500 Oregon Real Estate Co. v. Multnomah County, 35 Or. 285, 58 Pac. 106.

501 Goodnough v. Powell, 23 Or. 525, 32 Pac. 396.

502 Vaughn v. School District, 27 Or. 57, 39 Pac. 393.

503 Oregon & C. R. Co. v. Jackson County, 38 Or. 589, 64 Pac 307, 65 Pac 369.

504 Hamblin Real Estate Co v. City of Astoria, 26 Or. 599, 40 Pac. 230, Smith v. Kelley, 24 Or. 464, 33 Pac. 642.

505 Southern Oregon Co. v. Coos County, 39 Or. 185, 64 Pac. 646, Oregon & C. R. Co. v. Jackson County, 38 Or. 589, 64 Pac. 307, 65 Pac. 369.

applied, no injunction will issue.[506] And as there is an appeal provided for from the action of the assessor, this must be taken before the injunction is sought.[507] For this reason an allegation of fraud of the assessor alone in a bill to enjoin the collection of a tax is not sufficient to warrant the court in granting an injunction. In addition, fraudulent action by the board of equalization must be alleged.[508]

Cloud on Title.—The injunction will be more freely granted when it is sought to prevent a cloud on title by a sale of real property for delinquent taxes under void process. Proceedings for the collection of taxes are summary and *ex parte,* and therefore it must appear that all statutory requirements have been strictly complied with before a sale is authorized.[509] Thus, where a sheriff fails to attach to the warrant an affidavit required by statute, the sale will be void, and may be enjoined; and it is not necessary as a prerequisite to relief that the legal tax be tendered or paid.[510]

Tender.—Upon the principle that he who seeks equity must do equity, a party seeking to enjoin the collection of a tax valid in part must tender the legal amount before obtaining an injunction against the illegal part.[511] Thus, where there is a fraudulent excess in the assessment, the tax-payer must tender the amount rightfully due.[512] And in order to make the tender effectual, the

506 Southern Oregon Co. v. Coos County, 39 Or. 185, 64 Pac. 646; West Portland Park Assn. v. Kelly, 29 Or. 412, 45 Pac. 901.

507 West Portland Park Assn. v. Kelly, 29 Or. 412, 45 Pac. 901

508 Southern Oregon Co. v. Coos County, 39 Or. 185, 64 Pac. 646.

509 Hughes v. Linn County, 37 Or. 111, 60 Pac. 843.

510 Id.

511 Dayton v. Multnomah County, 34 Or 239, 55 Pac 23, Alliance Trust Co. v. Multnomah County, 38 Or. 433, 63 Pac. 498; Goodnough v. Powell, 23 Or. 525, 32 Pac. 396; Welch v. Clatsop County, 24 Or. 452, 33 Pac. 934

512 Welch v. Clatsop County, 24 Or. 452, 33 Pac. 934.

money, if refused by the tax-collector, must be paid into court.[513]

§ 441. **Special Assessments.**—An injunction will issue to restrain the collection of a special assessment which is invalid by reason of some defect preventing the local body from acquiring jurisdiction to make it. The statutory procedure must be strictly followed. Therefore, where proper publication is not made, an injunction will issue;[514] and if no encouragement has been given so as to raise an equitable estoppel, it is not necessary to make any tender for benefits received.

Where property has received any benefit from a local improvement, courts will not measure the amount, and hence an injunction will not issue merely because the assessment is in excess of benefits. Where, however, the property is so situated that it could not possibly derive any benefit, the court will interfere and grant an injunction.[515]

Where the proceedings for the improvement of a street are regular, the fact that independent proceedings for fixing the grade are irregular or invalid, will not warrant an injunction against the collection of an assessment.[516]

It is no ground for an injunction that the statute does not provide for notice, when notice has in fact been given.[517]

Where the municipal authorities have jurisdiction to improve a street, a property owner, who, with knowl-

513 Welch v. Astoria, 26 Or. 89, 37 Pac. 66.

514 Ladd v. Spencer, 23 Or. 193, 31 Pac. 474.

515 Oregon & C. R. Co. v. City of Portland, 35 Or. 229, 35 Pac. 452, 22 L. R. A. 713.

516 Wingate v. City of Astoria, 39 Or. 603, 65 Pac. 982.

517 Shannon v. City of Portland, 38 Or. 382, 62 Pac. 50.

edge of such improvement, makes no objection until after the work has been completed, cannot enjoin the collection of the assessment on the ground that the proceedings have not been regular.[518] Where, however, there is no jurisdiction, as where the requisite petition is not filed, there is no estoppel, and the injunction will issue although no objection has been made until after completion.[519]

§ 442. **Pennsylvania.**—In Pennsylvania, where the matters complained of are mere irregularities in the valuation or assessment and the tax is lawfully assessed, an injunction will not issue, but the complainant will be remanded to his remedy at law. Where, however, there is either a want of power to tax or a disregard of the constitution in the mode of assessment, an injunction will issue.[520] Thus, such relief may be obtained to restrain the collection of a tax on exempt property.[521] Likewise, an injunction will issue when an illegal excess is imposed and when the tax is levied without authority.[522]

§ 443. **Rhode Island.**—In Rhode Island, equity will not enjoin the collection of a tax at the suit of an individual tax-payer on the ground of illegality, when the illegality affects him alone, unless special equities

518 Wingate v. City of Astoria, 39 Or. 603, 65 Pac. 982; Wilson v. City of Salem, 24 Or. 504, 34 Pac. 9, 691.

519 Strout v. City of Portland, 26 Or. 294, 38 Pac. 126.

520 St. Mary's Gas Co. v. Elk County, 191 Pa. St. 458, 43 Atl. 321; Banger's Appeal, 109 Pa. St. 79, 16 Wkly. Not. Cas. 289; Arthur v. School Dist., 164 Pa. St. 410, 30 Atl. 299, 35 Wkly. Not. Cas. 289; Moore v. Taylor, 147 Pa. St. 481, 23 Atl. 768.

521 St. Mary's Gas Co. v. Elk County, 191 Pa. St. 458, 43 Atl. 321; Lehigh Coal & Nav. Co., v. Miller, 155 Pa. St. 542, 26 Atl. 660.

522 Appeal of Conners, 103 Pa. St. 356.

are shown.[523] And it has been held that the cloud upon title to land cast by a sale under a void tax is too easily dispelled to warrant the court in taking jurisdiction on that ground.[524] But when the illegality extends to the whole tax, so that the question involved is the validity of the whole tax and its assessment on every person taxed, equity will take jurisdiction at the suit of one or more tax-payers, suing in behalf of all the tax-payers as well as in his or their own behalf for the purpose of preventing a multiplicity of suits.[525]

An injunction will not lie against a tax-collector to prevent a mode of levy authorized by statute because some other mode may be more equitable.[526]

§ 444. South Carolina.—In South Carolina an injunction will issue to restrain the collection of a tax on exempt property which casts a cloud on title.[527]

§ 445. South Dakota.—In South Dakota injunctions are readily granted to restrain the collection of illegal taxes. Just where the limitations are is hard to determine. The injunction will be granted to restrain the collection of an illegal excess, provided the amount legally due is tendered.[528] It will also be granted to enjoin the collection of a tax on personal property, regu-

523 Greene v. Mumford, 5 R. I. 472, 73 Am. Dec. 79.

524 Id , Sherman v. Leonard, 10 R. I. 469.

525 McTwiggan v Hunter, 18 R. I 776, 30 Atl. 962; Tefft v. Lewis (R I), 60 Atl. 243; Sherman v. Benford, 10 R. I. 559; Quimby v. Wood, 19 R. I. 571, 35 Atl. 149.

526 People's Sav. Bank v. Tripp, 13 R. I. 621.

527 Vesta Mills v. City Council of Charleston, 60 S. C. 1, 38 S. E. 226. But by Code 1902, § 412, Rev. Stats. 1893, § 339, "collection of taxes shall not be stayed or prevented by any injunction, writ or order": Western Union Tel Co. v. Town of Winnsboro (S. C.), 50 S E. 870.

528 Dakota Loan & Trust Co. v. County of Coddington, 9 S. D. 159, 68 N. W. 314.

lar on its face, which is made a lien on land, especially when there is a possibility of a multiplicity of actions.[529] Thus, a public sale to numerous purchasers of shares in a corporation for illegal personal taxes, constituting a lien on real property, suggests a multitude of suits and irreparable injury, to avoid which the aid of a court of equity may be invoked.[530] But the courts, in at least one instance, have gone further, and have held that an injunction will issue to restrain the sale of personal property for an illegal tax, irrespective of whether it constitutes a lien on land or not. Thus, an injunction will issue to prevent the seizure and sale of personal property in satisfaction of a tax wrongfully and unlawfully levied thereon, in a county in which the plaintiff is not a resident, and in which the property is presumed not to have been when the assessment was made.[531] Inconsistent as it may seem with some of their other holdings, the courts have held that no injunction will issue to restrain the collection of an illegal tax when there is an adequate remedy at law. Thus, the collection of a state inspection tax will not be restrained simply because the act authorizing it may be unconstitutional, for if such prove to be the case, the officer enforcing it will be a mere trespasser, and accordingly the plaintiff will have an adequate remedy at law.[532]

Where a tax deed is set aside for defects not affecting the validity of the tax, a decree that the party attacking shall reimburse the purchaser is within the equitable powers of the court.[533]

529 Macomb v. Lake County, 9 S D. 466, 70 N. W. 652.

530 Id.

531 Knapp v. Charles Mix County, 7 S. D. 399, 64 N. W. 187.

532 Franklin v. Appel, 10 S. D. 391, 73 N. W. 259.

533 McKinney v. Minnehaha County (S. D.), 97 N. W. 15.

§ 446. **Special Assessments.**—There is a presumption that the proceedings of municipal officers in imposing special assessments are regular. Therefore, a party seeking an injunction must set up in his complaint some substantial requirement of the statute which has not been complied with.[534]

§ 447. **Tennessee.**—In Tennessee tax-books are process equivalent to an execution in the hands of an officer. An injunction will issue to restrain the collection of a tax, even on personal property, under void process, although there is a concurrent remedy by *certiorari*.[535] An injunction, however, will not issue to restrain the collection of a void tax when the complainant waits until the greater part has been paid.[536]

§ 448. **Texas.**—In Texas an injunction will issue to restrain the collection of an illegal or fraudulent tax. Thus, where the property of an individual is about to be sold to satisfy a tax levied against him on property which he does not own,[537] as, for instance, where a bank is assessed upon its own stock which is the property of its stockholders,[538] or where real property is about to be sold for an illegal tax on personal property,[539] an injunction will issue to prevent the wrong. Any illegality not apparent on the face of the proceedings,[540] such as a case of double taxation,[541] is sufficient

534 Phillips v. City of Sioux Falls, 5 S. D. 524, 59 N. W. 881.

535 Alexander v. Henderson, 105 Tenn. 431, 58 S. W. 648; National Bank of Chattanooga v. Mayor & Aldermen of Chattanooga, 8 Heisk. 816.

536 Kennedy v. Montgomery, 98 Tenn. 165, 38 S. W. 1075.

537 Davis v. Burnett, 77 Tex. 3, 13 S. W. 613.

538 Waco National Bank v. Rogers, 51 Tex. 606.

539 Court v. O'Connor, 65 Tex. 339.

540 Cook v. Galveston, H. & S. A. R. Co., 5 Tex. Civ. App. 644, 24 S. W. 544; Blessing v. City of Galveston, 42 Tex. 641.

541 Schmidt v. Galveston, H. & S. A. R. Co. (Tex. Civ. App.), 24 S. W. 547.

to warrant the court in granting the relief. And where an illegal tax affecting numerous persons is sought to be enforced, any one or more of the parties sought to be subjected to the imposition may, in the same suit, restrain its collection.[542] Thus, any number of tax-payers may join in an action to restrain the collection of an illegal poll-tax.[543] In cases where the whole tax is illegal, it is not necessary to apply to the board of equalization.[544] The function of that board is to correct errors in the valuation of property which has been properly assessed. It has no power to add to the rolls property not previously assessed, nor to take from them property which they embrace. Hence such an appeal would be useless.

Where, however, it is only an excess in the assessment that is complained of, the tax-payer must resort to the board of equalization, because of the familiar doctrine that in matters of this kind equity will not take jurisdiction when there is an adequate remedy at law.[545] And no trifling excuse, such as the illness of a corporation's agent, will be sufficient to give the court jurisdiction.[546] Where the board errs in honest judgment, there is no appeal from its decision, and no injunction will issue; but when, in raising or fixing the value of property, it acts from corrupt or fraudulent motives, and in violation of the laws of the state, whether constitutional or statutory, its acts are voidable at the suit

542 Morris v. Cummings, 91 Tex. 618, 45 S. W. 383.

543 Id. But injunction does not lie after suits have already been begun for the collection of the taxes: McMickle v. Hardin, 25 Tex. Civ. App. 222, 61 S. W. 322

544 Court v. O'Connor, 65 Tex. 339; Davis v. Burnett, 77 Tex. 3, 13 S. W. 613.

545 Duck v. Peeler, 74 Tex 272, 11 S. W. 1111

546 Clawson Lumber Co. v. Jones, 20 Tex. Civ. App. 208, 49 S. W. 909.

of the party aggrieved, and an injunction will issue to restrain the collection of the excess.[547] And in an action to restrain the collection of an illegal excess, the plaintiff must allege the definite amount of excess. Thus, an allegation that plaintiff's assessment had been illegally increased because the city had illegally exempted certain property from taxation, is not sufficient unless the amount of such increase is alleged.[548] And in all of these cases the plaintiff must do equity before obtaining the injunction by making a tender of the amount legally due.[549]

Where property is subject to taxation, a tax levied upon it will not be enjoined because of mere irregularities in the assessment. Thus, where there is a misdescription of the property by the assessor, or an irregularity in his entering it upon the assessment list or roll, no ground for an injunction is presented[550]

An injunction will not issue to restrain the collection of a municipal tax on the ground of the invalidity of the municipal incorporation, although both the corporation and its officers are insolvent.[551]

§ 449. **Special Assessments.**—The statute providing a procedure for local improvements must be strictly followed, and if not, an injunction will issue to restrain the collection of the assessment. Thus, an injunction will issue when an estimate of the cost is not first made by the city authorities, as required by statute.[552]

547 Johnson v. Holland, 17 Tex 210, 43 S. W. 71.

548 Altgelt v. City of San Antonio, 81 Tex 436, 17 S. W. 75, 13 L. R. A. 383.

549 George v. Dean, 47 Tex. 73.

550 George v. Dean, 47 Tex. 73.

551 Troutman v. McCleskey, 7 Tex. Civ. App. 561, 27 S. W. 173.

552 Kerr v. City of Corsicana (Tex. Civ. App.), 35 S. W. 694

§ 450. **Utah.**—In Utah it is provided by statute that "no injunction shall be granted by any court or judge to restrain the collection of any tax or any part thereof, nor to restrain the sale of any property for the non-payment of the tax, except, first, where the tax, or any part thereof sought to be enjoined is illegal, or is not authorized by law. If the payment of a part of a tax is sought to be enjoined, the other part must be paid or tendered before action can be commenced."[553] In construing this, the supreme court has held that the remedy should not be invoked, except in clear cases, based upon unquestionable facts, coming within the clear terms, letter, and spirit of the statute[554]

Before the enactment of the statute quoted above, it was held that an injunction will not issue to restrain the collection of an illegal tax on the ground that it casts a cloud on title to real estate, when personal property has already been levied upon to satisfy it[555] The presumption is that the levy is sufficient to satisfy the tax, and hence the cloud is removed.

§ 451. **Vermont.**—An injunction will not be granted to restrain the collection of a tax on the ground of fraud, where there has been an adverse decision by a board of listers.[556]

§ 452. **Special Assessments.**—An assessment void upon its face does not create a cloud on title which the court will remove;[557] so held of an assessment which did not affirmatively show, as required by the city charter, that

553 Laws 1896, p. 465, § 179

554 Mercur Gold M & M. Co. v. Spry, 16 Utah, 222, 52 Pac. 382.

555 Mercur Gold M. & M. Co. v. Spry, 16 Utah, 222, 52 Pac. 382.

556 Phillips v. Bancroft, 75 Vt 357, 56 Atl. 9.

557 Blanchard v. City of Barre Vt), 60 Atl. 970.

it was made "according to special benefits" to the property assessed.[558]

§ 453. **Virginia.**—In Virginia, an injunction has been granted to restrain a county clerk from conveying lands sold to the state for illegal taxes to an applicant for purchase, on the ground that such conveyance would cast a cloud on title.[559] And the enforcement of a tax on exempt property will be enjoined.[560] Unconstitutionality alone is no ground for injunction.[561] When a municipal assessment has been corrected by the tribunal provided by law and yet the municipal authorities proceed to levy the tax upon the original assessment, an injunction against the collection of such a tax will issue.[562]

§ 454. **Washington.**—In Washington, an injunction will issue to restrain the collection of a tax when it is illegal or fraudulent, and in certain cases where it is excessive. Where the tax is illegal, it is immaterial whether the subject matter is real or personal property. Thus, an injunction will issue to restrain the sale of personal property under a tax beyond the jurisdiction of the assessor to assess;[563] and to restrain the sale of corporate stock to satisfy an illegal assessment.[564] And in case of personal property, at least, it will issue to restrain an illegal sale, even though the original tax

558 Id.

559 Baker v. Briggs, 99 Va. 360, 3 Va. Sup. Ct. Rep. 252.

560 City of Staunton v. Mary Baldwin Seminary, 99 Va. 653, 3 Va. Sup Ct. Rep. 468, 39 S. E. 596.

561 Thomas v. Rowe (Va.), 22 S. E. 157.

562 City of Richmond v. Crenshaw, 76 Va. 936.

563 Northwestern Lumber Co. v. Chehalis County, 24 Wash. 626, 64 Pac. 787.

564 Lewiston Water & Power Co. v. Asotin County, 24 Wash. 371, 64 Pac. 544.

was valid. Thus, where personal property is purchased in good faith by a person who has no notice of any lien upon it for taxes, such person may enjoin a sale to satisfy such lien.[565]

Where a tax is fraudulently levied, it is also held that an injunction will issue. Thus, it will be granted where the tax-payer, relying upon a statement by the assessor that the assessment will be the same as in the previous year, fails to go before the board of equalization to protest against an increase.[566]

The rules as to excessive valuation are slightly different for real and personal property. While the court will not interfere "to correct mere mistakes or inadvertences, or to contravene or set aside the judgments of assessors or boards of equalization in relation to values, it will interfere when the officers fraudulently, capriciously, or tyrannically refuse to exercise their judgment by adopting a rule or system of valuation designed to operate unequally and to violate a fundamental principle of the constitution."[567] Thus, where the assessment of real property is arbitrary and made without regard to the true value, as where a mortgage is assessed at thirty thousand dollars while the land itself is assessed at only two thousand, an injunction will issue, although the board of equalization refuses relief.[568] And the injunction will issue notwithstanding that a statutory remedy is provided by allowing objections to the rendition of a judgment, for the plaintiff is entitled to such relief in order to remove the

565 Phelan v. Smith, 22 Wash. 397, 61 Pac. 31.

566 Landers' Estate Co. v. Clallam County, 19 Wash. 569, 53 Pac. 670.

567 Andrews v. King County, 1 Wash. 46, 22 Am. St. Rep. 136, 23 Pac. 409.

568 Knapp v. King County, 17 Wash. 567, 50 Pac. 480.

cloud from his title.[569] In cases of personal property the rule is said to be not quite so broad. Thus, in such cases, it has been held that no injunction will issue when the sole question is whether or not the board of equalization acted under an honest belief in placing a value on the property.[570] The case of Andrews v. King County, cited *supra,* is distinguished as an exceptional case.

An injunction will not issue because of a slight irregularity It has been held accordingly that a statute requiring the rate to be fixed within thirty days after the filing of the assessment-roll is not so mandatory that a slight delay will invalidate the levy; and consequently an injunction will not issue.[571]

Tender.—When a tax is valid in part and void in part, a tender must be made of the valid part before the other can be enjoined.[572] If the tender is *bona fide,* the finding of the court that a larger amount is due affects only the question of costs. The bill should allege the amount justly due, a tender of it, and an offer to pay such further sum as should be found to be due.[573] Where the tax is wholly void, however, no tender is necessary.[574]

§ 455. **Special Assessments.**—Where the assessment is manifestly unequal, an injunction is proper. Thus, where the value of the abutting property is made the basis for the assessment and it appears that plaintiff's property is taken for a distance of a thousand feet back

569 Benn v. Chehalis County, 11 Wash. 134, 39 Pac. 365.

570 Olympia Water Works v. Gelbach, 16 Wash. 482, 48 Pac. 251.

571 Wingate v. Ketner, 8 Wash. 94, 35 Pac. 591.

572 2 Ballinger's Ann. Codes & Stats., § 5678.

573 Landes's Estate Co. v. Clallam County, 19 Wash. 569, 53 Pac. 670.

574 Lewiston Water & Power Co. v. Asotin County, 24 Wash. 371, 64 Pac. 544.

from the street for purpose of assessment while other property is assessed for a much less distance, an injunction is proper.[575] And in such a case it is immaterial that the plaintiff has petitioned for the improvement. An injunction is also proper when the work has been done in such a manner that it is a detriment rather than a benefit to the property. Where this appears it is immaterial whether or not the work has been accepted by the proper board.[576]

§ 456. **West Virginia.**—In West Virginia an injunction will not issue to restrain the collection of a tax on the mere ground of illegality. There must exist in addition circumstances bringing the case within some recognized head of equity jurisdiction, such as the prevention of multiplicity of suits, irreparable injury or cloud on title.[577] Likewise, an injunction will not issue when a tax is merely irregular, as where property subject to taxation is erroneously assessed.[578] In such cases the tax-payer is left to his remedy at law.

A statute giving a remedy at law for an illegal tax which does not by its terms take away the equitable jurisdiction will be construed as creating an additional remedy, and will not oust the court of equity of its jurisdiction.[579]

575 Howell v. City of Tacoma, 3 Wash. 711, 28 Am. St. Rep. 83, 24 Pac. 449.

576 Hasch v. City of Seattle, 10 Wash. 435, 38 Pac. 1131.

577 Douglass v. Town of Harrisville, 9 W. Va. 162, 27 Am. Rep. 548, Winifrede Coal Co. v. Board of Education, 47 W. Va. 132, 34 S. E. 776; Christie v. Melden, 23 W. Va. 667, Riddle v. Town of Charlestown, 43 W. Va. 796, 28 S. E. 831, Williams v. County Court, 26 W. Va. 488, 53 Am. Rep. 94, Blue Jacket Consol. Copper Co. v. Scherr, 50 W. Va. 533, 40 S. E 514.

578 Tygart's Val. Bank v. Town of Philippi, 38 W. Va. 219, 18 S. E. 489; Christie v. Melden, 23 W. Va. 667.

579 Winifrede Coal Co. v. Board of Education, 47 W. Va. 132, 34 S. E. 776.

Personal Property.—The sale of personal property for unpaid taxes will not be restrained unless it is of peculiar value to the owner, and it is manifest that great injury would result from the sale.[580] The rule is laid down more broadly when purely municipal taxation is in question. Thus, it has been held that if municipal authorities tax persons or property not legally taxable, or if they exceed the limit prescribed by the statute conferring their power to tax, their action is *ultra vires* and void, and equity has power to grant relief.[581]

Multiplicity of Suits.—Where all the tax-payers of a county are affected by an illegal tax, one or more tax-payers, in behalf of himself or themselves and all other tax-payers of the county subject thereto, may obtain an injunction to prevent the collection of such tax, in order to prevent a multiplicity of suits.[582]

Cloud on Title.—Taxes assessed on real property without lawful authority cast a cloud on title, and therefore their collection will be enjoined.[583]

§ 457. Special Assessments.—An injunction will not issue to restrain the collection of a special assessment on the ground of illegality unless facts exist bringing the case under some other recognized head of equity

580 White v. Stender, 24 W. Va. 615, 49 Am. Rep 283.

581 Christie v. Melden, 23 W. Va. 667; Crim v. Town of Philippi, 38 W. Va. 122, 18 S. E. 466.

582 Williams v. County Court, 26 W. Va. 488, 53 Am. Rep. 94 (a leading case); Winifrede Coal Co. v. Board of Education, 47 W. Va. 132, 34 S. E. 776; McClung v. Livesay, 7 W. Va 329; Doonan v. Board of Education, 9 W. Va. 246; Corrothers v. Board of Education, 16 W. Va. 527, Blue Jacket Co. v. Scherr, 50 W. Va. 533, 40 S E. 514. But the suit must be brought expressly on behalf of all the tax-payers. See cases cited.

583 Powell v. City of Parkersburg, 28 W. Va. 698; Tygart's Val. Bank v. Town of Philippi, 38 W. Va. 219, 18 S E. 489.

jurisdiction.[584] And the mere fact that the assessment is a lien on real estate is not sufficient to confer jurisdiction when there is an adequate remedy at law by suit to recover back the amount paid under protest.[585] In a recent case, however, the rule is laid down broadly, that equity has jurisdiction to enjoin the collection of an *ultra vires* assessment.[586]

§ 458. **Wisconsin—In General.**—It is the settled doctrine in Wisconsin that it is not enough to avoid a tax in equity to show that the proceedings were irregular, or even void, but, in addition, it must be shown that the taxes were inequitable, and that it will be against conscience to let them go on.[587]

From the general principle that equity possesses no power to revise, control, or correct the action of public, political or executive officers, at the suit of a private person, except as incidental and subsidiary to the protection of some private right, or the prevention of some private wrong, the mere fact that the voters of a town have voted an illegal tax is not sufficient ground for an in-

584 Wilson v. Town of Philippi, 39 W. Va. 75, 19 S. E. 553; Douglass v. Town of Harrisville, 9 W. Va. 162, 27 Am. Rep. 548.

585 Wilson v. Town of Philippi, 39 W. Va. 75, 19 S. E. 553.

586 Cain v. City of Elkins (W. Va.), 49 S. E. 898

587 Wells v. Western Paving etc. Co., 96 Wis. 116, 70 N. W. 1071; Chicago & N. W. R. Co. v. Forest County, 95 Wis. 80, 70 N. W. 77; Hayes v. Douglas County, 92 Wis. 429, 53 Am. St. Rep. 926, 65 N. W. 482, 31 L. R. A. 213; Hixon v. Oneida County, 82 Wis. 531, 52 N. W. 445; Bond v. City of Kenosha, 17 Wis. 286 (no injunction where the irregularity diminished rather than increased plaintiff's taxes); Warden v. Board of Supervisors of Fond du Lac County, 14 Wis 618 (same; a leading case). Marsh v. Supervisors of Clark County, 42 Wis. 502, Goff v. Supervisors of Outagamie County, 43 Wis. 55, and Schettler v. City of Fort Howard, 43 Wis 48, so far as they may be considered as having departed from this principle, have since been overruled: See Hixon v. Oneida County, *supra*.

junction, in advance of any invasion of the legal rights of the plaintiff.[588]

A court of equity has no jurisdiction to restrain the collection of taxes illegally or improperly assessed upon personal property, inasmuch as the party injured has an ample remedy by action against the municipal corporation to which the money is paid or for which it is collected.[589]

§ 459. **Defects Going to the Validity of the Assessment.**— The doctrine was laid down by the supreme court of Wisconsin at an early day, that a court of equity will not interfere to declare a tax invalid and restrain its collection, unless the objections to the proceedings are such as go to the very groundwork of the tax, and necessarily affect materially its principle, and show that it must necessarily be unjust and unequal.[590] When the objection is a mere non-compliance with some direction of the statute, notwithstanding which the tax may have been entirely just or equal, it ought not to have the effect of rendering the whole tax invalid.

Where the assessment-roll was unverified, and all the rules established by law to govern the assessment of property had been violated, and one of the assessors testified that he could not make the oath required by law without being guilty of perjury, the assessment

588 Judd v. Town of Fox Lake, 28 Wis. 583.

589 Van Cott v. Board of Supervisors of Milwaukee County, 18 Wis. 259.

590 Hixon v. Oneida County, 82 Wis. 531, 52 N. W. 445, and cases cited; Wisconsin Central R. Co. v Ashland County, 81 Wis. 10, 50 N. W. 937; Canfield v. Bayfield County, 74 Wis. 60, 64, 41 N W. 437, 42 N. W. 100, Hart v. Smith, 44 Wis. 217, Kaehler v. Dobberpuhl, 56 Wis. 480, 14 N. W. 644; Marsh v. Supervisors of Clark County, 42 Wis. 502, 512; Mills v. Johnson, 17 Wis. 598, 602; Warden v. Supervisors of Fond du Lac County, 14 Wis. 618; Mills v. Gleason, 11 Wis. 470, 497, 78 Am. Dec 721.

was held to be necessarily unequal and the whole tax vitiated;[591] so, where there was an arbitrary classification of lands by rules that disregarded the principles laid down by statute to guide the assessor in making valuations.[592] A complaint alleging a corrupt and fraudulent assessment, to the great injury of the plaintiff, in that the assessors, in violation of law, intentionally assessed vacant lands at a much greater sum in proportion to their value than improved lands, states a defect going to the validity of the assessment and affecting the groundwork of the tax.[593] The intentional omission, as exempt property, of property not exempt, goes to the groundwork of the whole tax.[594] It has been held that where the assessor adopted a rule of valuation based on what he thought the lands would bring at a forced sale, in violation of the statutory rule that lands should be assessed at the value which could ordinarily be obtained therefor at private sale, the whole tax is vitiated, and an injunction is proper;[595] so, where the assessment was made on a basis of one-third of the real value.[596]

§ 460. **Defects not Going to the Validity of the Assessment.**—A complaint alleging that in making the levy one

591 Marsh v. Supervisors of Clark County, 42 Wis. 502, as explained in Fifield v. Marinette County, 62 Wis. 532, 538, 22 N. W. 705.

592 Hersey v. Board of Supervisors of Barron County, 37 Wis. 75.

593 Anderson v. Douglas County, 98 Wis. 393, 74 N. W. 109

594 Green Bay & M. Canal Co. v Outagamie County, 76 Wis. 587, 45 N. W. 536; Hersey v. Board of Supervisors of Milwaukee County, 16 Wis. 186, 82 Am. Dec. 713; Weeks v. City of Milwaukee, 10 Wis. 242.

595 Goff v. Supervisors of Outagamie County, 43 Wis. 55.

596 Schettler v. City of Fort Howard, 43 Wis 48 Doubt has been cast upon these two cases, however, by later decisions: See Hixon v. Oneida County, 82 Wis. 531, 52 N. W. 445.

item was for a certain sum for "the general fund," and that the city had no authority to levy for such a fund, does not state a defect going to the validity of the assessment.[597] The fact that the resolution of a town for raising taxes fails to designate the specific purposes for which the taxes were to be raised does not "go to the groundwork" of the tax, and necessarily affect materially its principle, so as to be available in a court of equity to enjoin or restrain its collection.[598] The honest opinion and judgment of the assessor and of the board of review must be conclusive, unless the inequalities or overvaluations are shown to be so gross as to be evidence of bad faith or arbitrary judgment.[599] The mere failure of the assessor to verify the assessment-roll as required by law, does not necessarily render the taxes apportioned upon such assessment unequal or unjust.[600] All reasonable presumptions must be made in favor of the regularity of proceedings of the board of review; and a complaint which merely states that the plaintiff testified before the board as to the value of the land, and that the board refused to reduce the valuation in accordance with his testimony, without stating that this was the only evidence presented on the subject, does not show that the board acted arbitrarily, in disregard of all the evidence before it, so as to sustain an injunction.[601]

597 Anderson v. Douglas County, 98 Wis. 393, 74 N. W. 109.

598 Chicago & N. W. Ry. Co. v. Forest County, 95 Wis. 80, 70 N. W. 77.

599 Green Bay & M. Canal Co. v. Outagamie County, 76 Wis. 587, 45 N. W 536.

600 Fifield v. Marinette County, 62 Wis. 532, 22 N. W. 705, criticising language used in Marsh v. Supervisors of Clark County, 42 Wis. 502.

601 Tainter v. Lucas, 29 Wis. 375.

§ 461. **Cloud on Title.**—Under the Wisconsin statutes, a tax upon lands, where the proceedings are not void upon their face, is a lien thereon from the time of the assessment; and, if illegal, it constitutes a cloud upon the title, before as well as after the tax sale. Equity will therefore interfere, not only after the sale to cancel the certificate, but before a sale, to declare the assessment void and restrain the collection.[602] The statute making the tax deed *prima facie* evidence of the regularity of all the proceedings, illegalities that would probably not appear on the face of the tax deed, and could only be shown by proof *dehors* the deed, render the deed a cloud on title, and its issuance should be enjoined.[603]

It is not an abuse of discretion to refuse to restrain by preliminary injunction a sale of lands for taxes pending the determination of a controversy as to their validity, when the controversy can be finally concluded before plaintiff's title can be disturbed or injuriously clouded by a tax deed.[604]

Where jurisdiction has attached for the purpose of canceling a tax certificate as a cloud on title, the court may go on and give complete relief by restraining the sale of personal property which had been seized for the tax, although for the latter purpose alone a court of equity would not have interfered by injunction.[605]

But one person cannot maintain an action to set aside any tax upon real estate, except upon such as he owns, or has some interest in; and two persons cannot

602 Milwaukee Iron Co. v. Town of Hubbard, 29 Wis 51.

603 Jenkins v. Board of Supervisors of Rock County, 15 Wis. 11; and see Dean v. City of Madison, 9 Wis. 402.

604 Chicago & N. W. R. Co. v. Langlade County, 104 Wis. 373, 80 N. W. 598.

605 Hamilton v. City of Fond du La[illegible] Wis. 490.

properly be joined as plaintiffs in the same action to set aside taxes which are a lien upon their separate property only.[606]

§ 462. **Payment or Tender.**—Following the familiar principle of equity jurisprudence that he who seeks equity must do equity, it is well established that a court of equity will not grant relief to restrain a tax sale, cancel a tax certificate, or restrain the issue of a tax deed thereon, except upon terms that the taxes be first paid to which there are no objections, or which, in justice and equity, the property owner ought to pay.[607] This doctrine, though supposed, for a time, to have been somewhat discredited,[608] has since been repeatedly affirmed, and stands now unassailable.[609] Where taxes are legal, or, whether strictly legal or not, are just and equitable, and are joined with such as are illegal and inequitable, the illegal excess, if it can be separated, is only conditionally voidable in equity, the condition being payment of the balance of the taxes.[610] A complaint which does not allege in direct terms the injustice and inequality of the tax, and further alleges a state of facts which, if proved on the trial, would establish the truth of the general allegation of its injustice, does not state a cause of action for equitable relief, unless

606 Gilkey v. City of Merrill, 67 Wis. 459, 30 N. W. 733; Newcomb v. Horton, 18 Wis. 566; Barnes v. Beloit, 19 Wis. 93.

607 Wells v. Western Paving etc. Co., 96 Wis. 116, 70 N. W. 1071, and cases cited; Fifield v. Marinette County, 62 Wis. 532, 537, 22 N. W. 705.

608 See Marsh v Supervisors of Clark County, 42 Wis. 502.

609 Wells v. Western Paving etc. Co., 96 Wis. 116, 70 N. W. 1071, and cases cited.

610 Wells v. Western Paving etc. Co., 96 Wis. 116, 70 N. W. 1071; Mills v. Johnson, 17 Wis. 598, 603; Bond v. City of Kenosha, 17 Wis. 286; Hersey v. Board of Supervisors of Milwaukee County, 16 Wis. 186, 82 Am. Dec. 713.

there be a further allegation of an offer to pay the taxes justly chargeable to the property of the plaintiff on account of which he seeks relief.[611]

In an action to restrain the issue of a tax deed, on the ground of a fraudulent assessment, where it was impossible for the plaintiff to determine, by computation or otherwise, what amount of the taxes was justly chargeable against his lands, an allegation of payment or tender is dispensed with; and there is no good reason for requiring an averment of willingness to pay, as that would be an allegation of mere mental condition, of no benefit to the defendant, and incapable of disproof.[612] And the rule requiring payment of the legal taxes as a condition of relief against the illegal cannot be applied in a case where two lots are assessed together as the property of a person who did not own and never had owned one of them.[613]

§ 463. **Special Assessments.**—It has been repeatedly held that where legal authority exists to make local assessments for street improvements, and sufficient has been done in an attempt to comply therewith to give the municipality jurisdiction of the subject in the given case, subsequent irregularities, where no injustice is shown, are immaterial in equity as against the duty of the property owner to bear his just share of the expense of such improvement.[614] Where there has been a substantial compliance with statutory requisites in

611 Fifield v. Marinette County, 62 Wis. 532, 22 N. W. 705; Wisconsin Central R Co. v. Ashland County, 81 Wis 10, 50 N. W. 937; Kaehler v. Dobberpuhl, 56 Wis. 480, 14 N. W. 644.

612 Anderson v. Douglas County, 98 Wis. 393, 74 N. W. 109.

613 Crane v. City of Janesville, 20 Wis. 305.

614 Gleason v. Waukesha County, 103 Wis. 225, 79 N. W 249; Hennessy v. Douglas County, 99 Wis. 129, 74 N. W 983; Wells v. Western Paving etc. Co., 96 Wis. 116, 70 N. W. 1071.

regard to the imposition and collection of special taxes or legal assessments, and the complainant is unable to show that any injustice has been done to him, equity will afford him no relief against such taxes or assessments.[615]

Cloud on title is the ground of equitable jurisdiction, as in cases of general taxation. A court of equity will interfere to prevent a cloud on the plaintiff's title, where his lands are threatened to be sold on a void tax or assessment, whenever the defect complained of is not merely formal, but is substantial and important, and would not appear on the face of the tax deed.[616] Equity will restrain a sale of land under a special assessment that is void for want of authority in the city council to make it. It is not necessary to show, as in the case of general taxes, in order to obtain equitable relief, that the assessment was not only invalid, but inequitable.[617]

There is a plain ground of equity jurisdiction to set aside the sale of lots made to enforce a void assessment for the purpose of changing the grade of a street, when it is found that the lots are greatly injured and ren-

615 Gleason v. Waukesha County, 103 Wis. 225, 79 N. W. 249; Hennessy v. Douglas County, 99 Wis. 129, 74 N. W. 983; Wells v. Western Paving etc. Co., 96 Wis. 116, 70 N. W. 1071.

616 Mitchell v. City of Milwaukee, 18 Wis. 92, 97; Myrick v. City of La Crosse, 17 Wis. 442; Jenkins v. Board of Supervisors of Rock County, 15 Wis. 11.

617 Dietz v. City of Neenah, 91 Wis. 422, 64 N. W. 299, 65 N. W. 500, distinguishing Hixon v. Oneida County, 82 Wis. 515, 52 N. W. 445. In the one case there is an antecedent duty or equitable burden against all property liable to taxation, and the power to raise money to meet public necessities and obligations; while in the case of the special assessment "the proceeding here initiated was to create such a charge or duty, and the law under which the common council acted was unconstitutional and void; so no duty or charge whatever was created."

dered less valuable by the change of grade.[618] And a void assessment may be canceled, and proceedings to collect it enjoined, although the proceedings have not been carried so far as to make the tax a lien on the plaintiff's lots; since the proceedings will necessarily create a cloud on the plaintiff's title.[619]

Payment or Tender.—Special taxes levied for local improvements are to be regarded as one of the constitutional methods of taxing the citizen for the benefit of the public, and any equitable rule which applies to other constitutional methods must, with equal propriety, be applied to it.[620] When the statutory requisites to the assessment of a tax for a street improvement upon abutting property are all complied with up to the time of filing the estimates or specifications for letting the work,—that is, when the assessment of benefits has been in all respects legally made, so as to determine a proper basis upon which to apportion the cost of the improvement properly chargeable to abutting property,—and the subsequent proceedings result in charging such property an excessive amount for any cause, the owner cannot wait until the improvement is completed, and his property has received the full benefit thereof, and then screen himself from the entire tax because of the illegal excess. If such excess can be determined by mere computation, or without proof, failure to tender or offer to pay the balance before suit will be fatal to any claim for costs, and failure to plead an offer to pay fatal to the cause of action. If

618 Liebermann v. City of Milwaukee, 89 Wis. 336, 61 N. W. 1112.

619 Beaser v. City of Ashland, 89 Wis. 28, 61 N. W. 77. So, the issue of a certificate to the contractor for work done may be restrained, the assessment being wholly invalid: Johnson v. City of Milwaukee, 40 Wis. 315, 327.

620 Mills v. Charleton, 29 Wis. 400, 418, Wels v. Western Paving etc. Co, 96 Wis. 116, 70 N. W. 1071.

such excess cannot be determined by computation, and without proof, the court should determine the same, as near as practicable, to a reasonable certainty, from the evidence produced on the trial, and require the payment of the balance as terms of granting relief against such excess.[621] The rule is not applied when the assessment of benefits requisite to jurisdiction to impose any tax on the abutting property for the improvement was not made,[622] as when the cost of the improvement is assessed on the abutting property in proportion to the front footage, without regard to the benefit secured thereby, as required by statute; since the defect goes to the very foundation of the assessment, and makes it necessarily unequal.[623]

§ 464. **Wyoming.**—The statutes in this state provide for the remedy of injunction to restrain the illegal levy or collection of taxes.[624] This relief "will not be allowed on account of the mere failure of the taxing officers to fulfill the requirements of the statute in the levy and assessment, but it must appear that the tax itself is inequitable for the reason that the property

621 Wells v. Western Paving etc. Co, 96 Wis. 116, 70 N. W. 1071. See, also, Yates v. City of Milwaukee, 92 Wis. 352, 66 N. W. 248; Meggett v. City of Eau Claire, 81 Wis 326, 51 N. W 566; Cook v. City of Racine, 49 Wis. 243, 5 N. W. 352 (the sum which plaintiff ought to pay being definitely ascertained by the proofs, judgment directed restraining collection of the assessment in case plaintiff, within a specified time, shall pay the proper amount, with interest); Mills v. Charleton, 29 Wis. 400, 418, 9 Am. Rep. 578 (excess being clearly ascertainable by computation, its collection restrained only on condition that the proper amount is paid).

622 See Hayes v. Douglas County, 92 Wis. 429, 53 Am. St. Rep. 926, 65 N. W. 482, 31 L. R. A. 213.

623 Hayes v. Douglas County, *supra*.

624 Rev. Stats. 1899, § 4172.

was not taxable, or that it was not the property of the complainant, or the like."[625]

A mere excessive assessment and overvaluation by a board of equalization will not be revised by the court, in the absence of a showing of fraud,[626] and such errors as assessment of land in the wrong district, or mistakes in description or levy *en masse* on separate parcels, are not a ground for injunction, when the owner made no effort to have them corrected by the board of equalization.[627]

625 Horton v. Driskell (Wyo.), 77 Pac. 354.
626 Ricketts v. Crewdson (Wyo.), 79 Pac. 1042.
627 Id.

CHAPTER XX.

INJUNCTION AGAINST EXERCISE OF THE POWER OF EMINENT DOMAIN.

ANALYSIS.

§ 465. **General Principle.**—It has come to be generally recognized that injunction against the unlawful or improper exercise of the power of eminent domain constitutes an independent head of equity jurisdiction, uncontrolled in its exercise by the principles which regulate injunctive relief against trespass. The constitutional guaranty that "property shall not be taken for public use without just compensation" by agents of the state to whom this power is delegated, is deemed to establish a right of so high and sacred a character that any threatened infringement of the right should be restrained, without consideration of the inadequacy of the legal remedy. Injunction, in this class of cases, is a matter of strict right, not of equitable discretion; although it is true that special equities, such as acquiescence or estoppel, may constitute a defense. It is eminently true, in this connection, that "judges have been brought to see, and to acknowledge, contrary to the opinion of Chancellor Kent, that the common-law theory of not interfering with persons until they shall have actually committed a wrong is fundamentally erroneous; and that a remedy which prevents a threatened wrong is, in its essential nature, better than a remedy which permits a wrong to be done, and then attempts to pay for it by the pecuniary damages which a jury may assess."[1] The fundamental principle now generally accepted is well expounded in the following extract from the opinion of a most able court, and is further elucidated in the excerpts in the following note: "The principle upon which a court of equity proceeds, in interfering to prevent bodies corporate having compulsory power to enter upon, take, and appropriate for their own uses the lands of others, differs materially from the principle upon which it intervenes to prevent the commission or continuance of waste, or of nuisances, or of trespasses, when only private rights, or the acts of persons, natural or artificial, not having such powers, are involved. In the latter class of cases, if the right be strictly legal, and there is no relation of privity between the parties, it is of the essence of the jurisdiction of the court that a case of irreparable injury should be shown—a case for which the courts of law do not furnish an adequate remedy. . . . It is most essential to the preservation of the rights of private property, to the protection of the citizen, and to the preservation of the best interests of the community, that all who are invested with the right of eminent domain, with the extraordinary power of depriving persons, natural or artificial, without their consent, of their property, and its possession and enjoyment,

1 3 Pom. Eq. Jur, § 1357, quoted and applied in a case of this character, Payne v. Kansas & A. Val. R. Co., 46 Fed. 546, 553.

should be kept in the strict line of the authority with which they are clothed, and compelled to implicit obedience to the mandates of the constitution. A court of equity will intervene to keep them within the line of authority, and to compel obedience to the constitution, because of the necessity that they should be kept within control, and in subjection to the law, rather than upon the theory that they are trespassers, or that the injury which they are inflicting is irreparable. The owner of the land has the right to say that, unless they keep within the strict limits prescribed by law, they shall not disturb him in the possession and enjoyment of his property. The power is so capable of abuse, and those who are invested with it are often so prone to its arbitrary and oppressive exercise, that a court of equity, without inquiring whether there is irreparable injury, or injury not susceptible of adequate redress by legal remedies, will intervene for the protection of the owner."[2]

[2] East & West R. Co. of Alabama v. East Tennessee, V. & G. R. Co, 75 Ala. 280, by Brickell, C. J; Birmingham Traction Co v. Birmingham Ry. & Elec. Co., 119 Ala. 129, 24 South. 368; City Council of Montgomery v. Lemle, 121 Ala. 609, 25 South. 919; Mobile & M. Ry. Co. v. Alabama Midland Ry. Co., 123 Ala. 145, 26 South 324, Western R. of Alabama v. Alabama G. T. R. Co., 96 Ala. 272, 11 South. 483, 17 L. R. A. 474. "Whenever the power of eminent domain is about to be exercised without compliance with the conditions upon which the authority for its exercise depends, courts of equity are not curious in analyzing the grounds upon which they rest their interposition. Equitable jurisdiction may be invoked in view of the inadequacy of the legal remedy where the injury is destructive or of a continuous character, or irreparable in its nature; and the appropriation of private property to public use, under color of law, but in fact without authority, is such an invasion of private rights as may be assumed to be essentially irremediable, if, indeed, relief may not be awarded *ex debito justitiae*": Fuller, C. J., in D. M Osborne & Co. v. Missouri Pac. R. Co., 147 U. S. 248, 13 Sup. Ct. 299, 37 L. ed. 155. "There are numerous cases in this court wherein equity has interfered by injunction to restrain road

While the above seems the sounder principle on which to base injunctive relief in this class of cases, many courts are content to rest it on the general doctrines

supervisors and others from removing or interfering with fences, hedges, watercourses, and the like, in the discharge of their official duty. Relief in these cases was not based upon the grounds of the irreparable character of the injury and the insolvency of the defendants [citing Bills v. Belknap, 36 Iowa, 583; Grant v. Crow, 47 Iowa, 632; McCord v. High, 24 Iowa, 336, Quinton v. Burton, 61 Iowa, 471, 16 N. W. 569]. . . . . Justice and sound public policy demand that for the protection of both the landowner and the supervisor the question of the legality of the supervisor's proposed act should be determined before the injury should be done to the farm, and the liability of the latter should be incurred The law provides a remedy for the settlement of the controversy between the parties, in advance of the injury to the one and the liability incurred by the other, by an action in chancery, wherein an injunction will suspend the act of the supervisor until the question of law and facts involved in the controversy are judicially settled'': Bolton v. McShane, 67 Iowa, 207, 25 N. W. 135, by Beck, Ch. J. ''It is not disputed that injunction is the proper remedy against the appropriation of land for the use of a public corporation which has not acquired a right to the proposed use either by purchase or by condemnation, and, contrary to the general rule that equitable relief is granted only when equitable considerations require it, the injunction in such cases may be, and perhaps more frequently than otherwise is, sought in vindication of a purely legal right, and, if the technical right and a threatened infraction of it be established, the relief will be granted without inquiry into the general equities of the case. By this we do not mean that a specific equity, like an estoppel, may not be a defense to such a suit; but, if a complete defense be not shown, the court will not refuse the relief on grounds of equitable discretion, as it might do in a suit for specific performance or rescission or other cause involving no special constitutional or statutory right of such a nature as to be capable of vindication only by injunction'': Bass v. Metropolitan West Side El. R. Co., 82 Fed. 857, 27 C. C. A. 147, 39 L. R. A. 711, by Woods, Cir. J. ''In cases of this character courts of equity have acted on broader principles [than in ordinary cases], and have adopted as a rule that an injunction will be granted to prevent a railway company from exceeding the power granted in their charter. . . . . The courts do not require when the effort is manifested by a railway company to wrongfully appropriate private property, or force their structures to places not authorized, that there should be a want of concerning irreparable injury of a permanent character, going to the destruction of the inheritance.[3] On whichever ground the jurisdiction is based, the rule is now

remedy at law": Cobb v. Illinois & St. L. R. & C. Co., 68 Ill. 233. See, also, in support of the view that the question of irreparable injury is not involved, but that injunction is a matter of right: Eidemiller v. Wyandotte City, 2 Dill. 376, Fed. Cas. No. 4313, by Dillon, Cir. J., as reported in the Federal Cases; observations of Brewer, J., in McElroy v. Kansas City, 21 Fed. 257, quoted *post*, § 471; Sidener v. Norristown Turnpike Co., 23 Ind. 623; Western Maryland Ry. Co. v. Owings, 15 Md. 199, 74 Am. Dec. 563 ("the nature of the damage complained of, whether irreparable or not, has nothing to do with the question"); Commonwealth v. Pittsburgh & C. R. Co., 24 Pa. St. 159, 62 Am. Dec 342; Bird v. Wilmington & M. R. Co., 8 Rich. Eq. (S C.) 46, 64 Am. Dec. 739; Searle v. City of Lead, 10 S. D. 312, 73 N. W. 101, 39 L. R. A. 345; Travis County v. Trogdon (Tex. Civ. App.), 29 S. W. 46; Hodges v. Seaboard & R. R. Co., 88 Va. 653, 14 S. E. 380; Manchester Cotton Mills v. Town of Manchester, 25 Gratt. 828; Foley v. Doddridge County Court, 54 W. Va. 16, 46 S. E 246; Brown v. City of Seattle, 5 Wash. 35, 31 Pac. 313, 32 Pac. 214, 18 L. R. A. 161, Bohlman v. Green Bay & M. R. Co, 40 Wis. 157, Stolze v. Milwaukee & L. W. R. Co., 104 Wis. 47, 80 N. W. 68, Lewis, Eminent Domain, § 632.

Where, as is usual in recent state constitutions, the provision is that "property shall not be taken for public use, unless compensation is *first* made or tendered," it is obvious that injunction is the only remedy by which the provision can be enforced according to its terms: See Searle v. City of Lead, 10 S. D. 312, 73 N. W. 101, 39 L. R. A. 345, Travis County v. Trogdon (Tex. Civ. App.), 29 S. W. 46; Brown v. City of Seattle, 5 Wash. 35, 31 Pac. 313, 32 Pac. 214, 18 L. R. A. 161.

3 See Bonaparte v. Camden & A R. Co., 1 Baldw. 218, Fed. Cas. No. 1617; Eidemiller v. Wyandotte City, 2 Dill 376, Fed. Cas. No. 4313 (as reported in Dillon's Reports); Payne v. Kansas & A. Val. R. Co, 46 Fed. 546; Ex parte Martin, 13 Ark. (8 Eng) 198, 58 Am. Dec. 321; Commissioners v Durham, 43 Ill. 86; City of Peoria v. Johnston, 56 Ill. 45; Lowery v. City of Pekin, 186 Ill. 387, 57 N. E. 1062, 51 L. R A 301; Erwin v. Fulk, 94 Ind. 235; City of New Albany v. White, 100 Ind. 206; Kern v. Isgrigg, 132 Ind. 4, 31 N. E. 455 (contempt proceedings not an adequate remedy); Welton v. Dickson, 38 Neb 767, 41 Am. St. Rep. 771, 57 N. W. 559, 22 L. R. A. 496, Bigler's Exr. v. Penn Canal Co, 177 Pa. St. 28, 35 Atl. 112; *post*, chapter XXIII, "Trespass," §§ 495, 499. "The injury complained of as impending over his property is, its permanent occupation and appropriation to a

almost universal that "an entry upon private property under color of the eminent domain power will be enjoined until the right to make such entry has been perfected by a full compliance with the constitution and the laws," whether such compliance is lacking either through failure to pay, tender, or deposit just compensation as required by law, or through invalidity of the condemnation proceedings, or of the statute under which the right to enter is claimed.[4]

continuing public use, which requires the divestiture of his whole right, its transfer to the company in full property, and his inheritance to be destroyed as effectively as if he had never been its proprietor. No damages can restore him to his former condition, its value to him is not money which money can replace, nor can there be any specific compensation or equivalent; his damages are not pecuniary (*vide*, 7 Johns. 731), his objects in making his establishment were not profit, but repose, seclusion, and a resting place for himself and family. If these objects are about to be defeated, if his rights of property are about to be destroyed, without the authority of law; or if lawless danger impends over them by persons acting under color of law, when the law gives them no power, or when it is abused, misapplied, exceeded, or not strictly pursued, and the act impending would subject the party committing it to damages in a court of equity for a trespass, a court of equity will enjoin its commission": Bonaparte v Camden & A. R. Co., 1 Baldw. 218, Fed. Cas. No. 1617, per Baldwin, J.

4 Lewis, Eminent Domain, § 632, and cases cited. In addition to the cases cited in the preceding notes, see St. Louis & S. F. R. Co. v. Southwestern T. & T. Co., 121 Fed. 276, 58 C. C. A. 198; Midland Ry. Co. v. Smith, 113 Ind. 233, 15 N. E. 256; Hudson v. Voreis, 134 Ind. 602, 34 N. E. 503 (proceedings for laying out highway invalid); Town of Hardinsburg v. Cravens, 148 Ind. 1, 47 N. E. 153 (taking land for street without compensation or notice); City of Fort Wayne v. Fort Wayne & T. R. Co. (Ind.), 48 N. E. 342 (same); State ex rel. Cotting v. Sommerville, 104 La. 74, 28 South. 977 (injunction not dissolved upon giving bond); Spurlock v. Dorman, 182 Mo. 242, 81 S. W. 412; Mayor of Frederick v. Groshon, 30 Md. 436, 96 Am. Dec. 591; Kime v. Cass County (Neb.), 99 N. W. 546 (taking land for street); Folley v. Passaic, 26 N. J. Eq. 216; Stratford v. City of Greenboro, 124 N. C. 127, 32 S. E. 394 (appropriating property for private use by municipality); Ft. Worth & R. G. R. Co. v. Jennings, 76 Tex. 373, 13 S. W. 270, 8 L. R. A. 180;

Cummings v. Kendall County, 7 Tex. Civ. App. 164, 26 S. W. 439 (opening road; no notice, and no order allowing damages); City of San Antonio v. Sullivan, 23 Tex. Civ. App. 658, 57 S. W. 45 (unauthorized changes in location of street after damages assessed); Olson v. City of Seattle, 30 Wash 687, 71 Pac. 201 *(dictum);* Boughner v. Town of Clarksburg, 15 W. Va. 394; Wenger v. Fisher (W. Va.), 46 S. E. 695; Baier v. Hosmer, 107 Wis. 380, 83 N. W. 645.

A few cases appear to be *contra* to the weight of authority or depend on special facts: Atchison, T. & S. F. R. Co. v. Meyer, 62 Kan 696, 64 Pac. 597 (no injunction against improvement of roadbed of railroad, when injury slight and capable of compensation); Jersey City v. Gardner, 33 N. J. Eq. 622 (no injunction against use for street of land condemned for street purposes, after damages assessed; remedy at law adequate); Thomas v. Grand View Beach R Co., 76 Hun, 601, 28 N. Y. Supp. 201 (operation of railroad already constructed not restrained, when ejectment an adequate remedy); Raleigh & W. Ry. Co. v. Glendon etc. Co, 112 N. C. 661, 17 S. E. 77, Wellington & P. R. Co. v. Cashie & C. R. & L. Co., 116 N. C. 924, 20 S. E. 964; Cherry v. Matthews, 25 Or. 484, 36 Pac. 529 (no injunction where constitution does not require prepayment of damages); Delaware County's Appeal, 119 Pa. St. 159, 13 Atl. 62 (power of taxation is sufficient security when property is taken or damaged by a municipal corporation); Colby v. City of Spokane, 12 Wash. 690, 42 Pac. 112, Rockwell v. Bowers, 88 Iowa, 88, 55 N. W. 1 (adequate remedy by *certiorari* to review proceedings for condemnation of street). That injunction will not issue where the defendant's title is uncertain or in dispute, see Troy & B. R. Co. v. Boston, H. T. & W. Ry. Co, 86 N. Y. 107; Kanawha G. T. & E. R. Co. v. Glen Jean, L. L. & D. W. R. Co., 45 W. Va. 119, 30 S. E. 86; but that mere denial of plaintiff's title is not sufficient to prevent relief, see Birmingham Traction Co. v. Birmingham R. & E. Co., 119 Ala. 129, 24 South. 368; Mobile & M Ry. Co. v. Alabama Midland Ry. Co., 123 Ala. 145, 26 South. 324; Lewis, Eminent Domain, § 633. The last four cases concern the condemnation of a right of way across the property of a rival railroad. That the owner of an easement for the use of water for mill purposes cannot restrain the taking of water by a municipality from the mill pond, if he is not the owner of the land covered by the pond, unless his easement is materially impaired, see Bass v. City of Fort Wayne, 121 Ind. 389, 23 N. E. 259.

The giving of a sufficient bond to pay damages has been held to dispense with the necessity of a preliminary injunction: Davis v. Port Arthur Channel & Dock Co, 87 Fed. 512, 31 C. C. A. 99

That the purchase of the land, pending condemnation proceedings, by the president of a rival railroad, for the purpose of delay and obstruction, may defeat the right to an injunction, see Piedmont

It appears that the entry may be enjoined pending appeal from the condemnation proceedings,[5] unless the statute declares that the right to enter is not suspended by appeal, in which case the constitutional guaranty is sufficiently satisfied by the award of damages by the inferior tribunal, and the payment, tender, or deposit of the same.[6]

The above cases illustrate the principle as applied to railways, streets and highways. Illustrations of its application to takings for other public uses are appended in the note.[7]

& C. Ry. Co. v. Speelman, 67 Md. 260, 10 Atl. 77, 293; Ocean City R. Co. v. Bray, 55 N. J. Eq. 101, 35 Atl. 839; Kanawha, G. T. & E. R. Co. v. Glen Jean, L. L. & D. W. R. Co., 45 W. Va. 119, 30 S. E. 86

The eminent domain power should be distinguished from the *police power;* the exercise of the latter by a city in keeping open a street which had been used by the public for many years does not present a proper case for an injunction at the suit of one claiming to own the land comprised within the street: City of Chicago v. Wright, 69 Ill. 318.

5 Eidemiller v. Wyandotte City, 2 Dill. 376, Fed. Cas. No. 4313; City of Terra Haute v. Farmers' Loan & T. Co., 99 Fed. 838, 40 C. C. A. 117 (where fraud or failure to comply with statutory requirements); City of Kansas v. Kansas Pac. Ry. Co., 18 Kan. 331; Travis County v. Tragdon (Tex. Civ. App.), 29 S. W. 46.

6 Bauchman v. Heinselman, 180 Ill. 251, 54 N. E. 313; Central Branch U. P. R. Co. v. Atchison T. & S. F. R. Co., 28 Kan. 463; Chicago & A. R. Co. v. Maddox, 92 Mo. 469, 4 S. W. 417; Shoppert v. Martin, 137 Mo. 455, 38 S W. 967 (no injunction where owner refuses to prosecute appeal); Lionberger v. Pelton, 62 Neb. 252, 86 N. W. 1067.

7 An injunction will issue when private property is about to be taken without compensation for the following purposes: For a ditch—McGhee Irr. Ditch Co. v Hudson, 85 Tex. 587, 22 S. W. 398; for a reservoir—Gardner v. Village of Newburgh, 2 Johns. Ch. 162, 7 Am. Dec. 526; for a school-house—Church v. Joint School District, 55 Wis. 399, 13 N. W. 272 It is proper when an attempt is made, without compensation, to flood land—Wilmington Water Power Co. v. Evans, 166 Ill. 548, 46 N. E. 1083; or to build a pier in a mill-race—McMillian v. Lauer (Sup. Ct.), 24 N. Y. Supp. 951. Likewise, it will issue where a city, without compensation, discharges surface

§ 466. No Injunction Against Prosecution of Condemnation Proceedings.—It is to be observed that where injunction is granted against the exercise of the power of eminent domain, the entry upon or appropriation of the plaintiff's land is the specific act enjoined. No injunction lies against the prosecution of condemnation proceedings when the matter which is set up as a ground for injunction may be urged as a defense in such proceedings.[8]

water at a certain point in such a manner as to make a channel through plaintiff's land: Miller v. Morristown, 47 N. J. Eq. 62, 20 Atl. 61. When property has once been taken for public use, it cannot be taken again, unless there is an express authorization A preliminary injunction will issue to prevent a city from taking railroad property for street purposes until it can be determined whether the two uses can exist together: City Council of Augusta v. Georgia R & B. Co, 98 Ga. 161, 26 S. E. 499 An injunction will issue against a taking for an unauthorized use: Bigler's Exr. v. Penn. Coal Co., 177 Pa. St. 28, 35 Atl. 112, 38 Wkly. Not. Cas. 408.

8 See Lewis, Eminent Domain, § 646, and cases cited; Eureka & K. R. R. Co. v. Cal. & N. Ry. Co., 103 Fed. 897, 902 (proceedings by two rival railroads to condemn the same land; procedure provided by statute); Black Hills & N. W. R. Co. v. Tacoma Mill Co., 129 Fed. 312, 63 C. C. A. 544; St. Louis & S. F. R. Co. v. Southwestern T. & T. Co., 121 Fed. 276, 58 C C. A. 198; Birmingham Ry. & Elec. Co. v. Birmingham Traction Co., 121 Ala. 475, 25 South. 777 (no injunction, though the court in which the proceedings are pending has no jurisdiction; adequate remedy by appeal or prohibition, etc.); Winkler v Winkler, 40 Ill. 179; East St. Louis Connecting R Co. v. East St. Louis Union R. Co., 108 Ill. 265 (no injunction against rival railroad condemning tracks for crossing); Chicago & N. W. Ry. Co. v. City of Chicago, 151 Ill. 348, 37 N. E. 842 (question of condemning for street property already taken for public use); Smith v. Goodknight, 121 Ind. 312, 23 N. E. 148; Boyd v. Logansport, R. & N. T Co., 161 Ind. 587, 69 N. E. 398, Waterloo Water Co v. Hoxie, 89 Iowa, 317, 56 N. W 499 (question of condemning property already appropriated to public use); Western Maryland R. Co. v. Patterson, 37 Md. 125, Detroit, G. H. & M. Ry. Co. v. City of Detroit, 91 Mich. 444, 52 N. W. 52; National Docks R. Co. v. Central R. Co., 32 N. J. Eq. 755, 767; Kip v. New York & H R. Co, 6 Hun (N. Y.), 24 (question of constitutionality of statute authorizing con-

§ 467. **Railroads in Streets and Highways.**—In approaching a consideration of the vexed subject of the abutting owner's remedy in equity against railroads of various kinds in streets, it is necessary first to lay to one side two classes of cases: (1) Those holding that a railroad of some particular sort is a legitimate and proper use of the street or highway, and does not create an additional burden or servitude. This is generally held of horse and electric railroads, while the contrary, at the present day, is generally held of steam railroads. If the particular use is held to be a proper and legitimate one, the abutting owner has no substantive right to be protected by an injunction.[9] (2) Cases where the rail-

demnation), Grafton & B R Co. v. Buckhannon & N. R. Co. (W. Va.), 49 S E 32. See, also, Morris & E R. Co. v. Hoboken & M. R. Co. (N. J. Eq.), 59 Atl 332. See, however, Colby v. Village of La Grange, 65 Fed. 554, where it seems to be held that the proceedings may be enjoined when they are brought for a wholly unauthorized purpose. See, also, Riley v. Charleston Union Station Co., 67 S. C. 84, 45 S. E. 149; Chestatee Pyrites Co. v. Cavenders Creek G. M. Co., 119 Ga. 354, 100 Am St Rep. 174, 46 S. E. 422.

In Schneider v. City of Rochester, 160 N. Y. 165, 54 N. E. 721, reversing 33 App. Div. 458, 53 N. Y. Supp. 931, the city, being dissatisfied with the award of commissioners in proceedings to open a street, sought to apply for the appointment of new commissioners; this was enjoined, at the suit of the property owner. The latter had no remedy by appeal from the order of appointment, and thus might be subjected to all the expense and trouble of defending her title or securing her rights before numerous commissioners successively appointed.

9 Cases holding steam railroad not an "additional servitude": Moses v. Pittsburgh, Ft. Wayne & C. R. Co., 21 Ill. 516 (since overruled); Lexington & O. R. R. Co. v. Applegate, 8 Dana (Ky.), 289, 33 Am. Dec. 497; Henry Gaus & Sons Mfg. Co. v. St. Louis, K. & N. W. Ry. Co., 113 Mo. 308, 20 S. W. 658, 18 L. R. A. 339, Decker v. Evansville Suburban & N Ry. Co., 133 Ind. 493, 33 N. E. 349. See Dillon, Mun. Corp. (4th ed.), § 725 (576)

Cases holding horse or electric railway constructed in the usual manner not an additional servitude: Chicago, B. & Q. R Co. v. West Chicago St. R. Co., 156 Ill. 255, 40 N. E. 1008, 29 L. R. A. 485; Snyder road is constructed without proper authority, and the question, therefore, is one, not of restraining the exercise of the eminent domain power, but of the remedy of the abutting owner, as one specially injured, to restrain a public nuisance.[10]

Granting that the railroad whose construction or operation is sought to be enjoined creates an "additional servitude" in the street, it is found that the abutting owner's remedial right to an injunction, or even his right to any remedy whatever, is, in many jurisdictions, made to depend upon the fact of his ownership of the fee of the land included in the street. If the fee is in the abutting owner, affected only by an easement in the public for legitimate street purposes, a permanent diversion of the street to other purposes, authorized by the proper public authority, constitutes a "taking" of such owner's property which will readily be enjoined if just compensation is not provided. The case is otherwise if the ownership of the street is in the municipality. This rule has been most strongly reprobated

v. Ft. Madison St Ry. Co., 105 Iowa, 284, 75 N. W. 179, 41 L. R. A. 345, Louisville Bagging Mfg. Co. v. Central Pass. Ry. Co., 95 Ky. 50, 44 Am. St. Rep. 203, 23 S. W. 592; Green v. City & Suburban Ry. Co, 78 Md. 294, 44 Am. St. Rep. 288, 28 Atl. 626; Poole v. Falls Road Elec. Ry. Co, 88 Md. 533, 41 Atl. 1069, Nagel v. Lindell Ry. Co., 167 Mo. 89, 66 S. W. 1090; Hinchman v Paterson Horse R. Co, 17 N. J. Eq. (2 C. E. Greene) 75, 86 Am. Dec. 252; Morris & E. R. Co. v. Newark Pass Ry. Co., 51 N. J. Eq. 379, 29 Atl. 184; West Jersey R. Co. v. Camden, G. & W. Ry. Co., 52 N. J Eq. 1, 29 Atl. 423; Budd v. Camden Horse R. Co., 61 N. J. Eq. 543, 48 Atl. 1028; Aycock v. San Antonio Brewing Assn., 26 Tex. Civ. App. 341, 63 S. W. 953 (street railway for transporting freight); Birmingham Traction Co v Birmingham Ry. & Elec. Co., 119 Ala 137, 24 South. 502, 43 L R. A. 233, and exhaustive citation of authorities; Dillon, Mun. Corp (4th ed), §§ 722, 723.

10 See, for example, Garnet v. Jacksonville, St. A. & H. R. R. Co., 20 Fla. 889; Birmingham Traction Co. v. Birmingham Ry & Elec Co., 119 Ala. 137, 24 South. 502, 43 L. R. A. 233. *Post,* chapter XXIV, *Public Nuisance.*

by eminent writers, as making the owner's remedial or substantive rights depend on the merest technicality; and it was thought that the departure from the rule by the courts of New York in the Elevated Railroad cases marked a period of transition, and pointed to the eventual overthrow of the rule. It can hardly be said that that result has yet been reached.

§ 468. Same; Fee of Street in Abutting Owner.—It is the almost universal rule, that the owner of land abutting upon a public street, who owns the fee in such street subject to the public easement, can enjoin the laying of tracks, and the use and occupation of such street by a steam railroad company under authority of a municipal ordinance, in such manner as to create an additional servitude upon the street, where no compensation to such owner has been ascertained or made.[11]

11 Bond v. Pennsylvania Co., 171 Ill. 508, 49 N. E. 545, reversing 69 Ill. App. 507; O'Connell v. Chicago Terminal Transfer Co., 184 Ill. 308, 56 N. E. 355; Rock Island & P. R. Co. v. Johnson, 204 Ill. 488, 68 N. E. 549 (injunction against laying second track); O'Connor v. Southern Pac. R. Co., 122 Cal. 681, 55 Pac. 688, Schurmeier v. St. Paul & P. R. Co., 10 Minn. 82 (Gil 59), 88 Am. Dec. 59; Lewis v. Pennsylvania R. Co. (N. J. Eq.), 33 Atl. 932; Williams v. New York Cent. R. Co., 16 N. Y. 97, 69 Am. Dec 651; Henderson v. New York Central R. Co., 78 N. Y. 423; Hodges v. Seaboard & R. R. Co., 88 Va. 653, 14 S. E. 380; Ford v. Chicago & N. W. R. Co., 14 Wis. 609, 80 Am. Dec 791; Coatsworth v. Lehigh Val. R. Co., 156 N. Y. 451, 51 N. E. 301; Mattlage v. New York El. R Co., 35 N. Y. Supp. 704, 14 Misc. Rep. 291, affirmed without opinion, 157 N. Y. 708, 52 N. E. 1124; and see cases cited in Lewis, Eminent Domain, § 635, note 2. In the few cases, chiefly in New York, where a horse or electric railway, or a structure used in operating the latter, is held to be an additional servitude, injunction at the suit of the abutting owner in whom was the fee of the street or highway was held to be a proper remedy. See Canastota Knife Co. v. Newington Tramway Co, 69 Conn. 146, 36 Atl. 1107, able concurring opinion of Hamersley, J.; Snyder v. Fort Madison St. Ry. Co., 105 Iowa, 284, 75 N. W. 179, 41 L. R. A. 345 (injunction against unnecessary electric railway pole placed in front of plaintiff's residence to annoy); Craig v. Rochester etc. R.

In most of the cases no distinction appears to be made between the owner's remedial right to an injunction against a taking without compensation, when his land is thus affected with a public easement, and when he has the full beneficial use of the land. In others, the question of injunction is treated as one addressed to the discretion of the court, which should balance the relative inconvenience and injury to the parties and the public likely to result from granting or withholding the writ.[12] In a few jurisdictions the courts refuse

R. Co., 39 N. Y. 404; Spofford v. R. R. Co., 15 Daly, 162, 4 N. Y. Supp. 388; Peck v. Schenectady R. Co., 170 N. Y. 298, 63 N. E. 357 (subject re-examined in light of all the authorities, and the Craig case followed, with much reluctance, by a divided court); Dempster v. United Traction Co., 205 Pa. St. 70, 54 Atl. 501; Lange v. La Crosse & E. R. Co., 118 Wis. 558, 95 N. W. 952.

It has been held that an abutting owner who owns the fee to the center of the street cannot enjoin the construction of a railroad on the opposite side of the street, because none of his property is taken: North Pennsylvania R. Co. v. Inland Traction Co., 205 Pa. St. 579, 55 Atl. 774.

Where telephone and telegraph poles are held to impose an additional servitude, an abutting owner who owns the fee in the street may enjoin their erection until compensation is made: Donovan v. Allert, 11 N. D. 289, 95 Am. St. Rep. 720, 91 N. W. 441, 58 L. R. A. 775.

12 In an instructive series of cases in Alabama, all the more noteworthy for the stringency of the general rule as to injunctions in eminent domain cases in that state (see *ante*, § 465). In Columbus & W. Ry. Co. v. Witherow, 82 Ala 190, 3 South. 23, an injunction granted restraining the defendant from the further construction, without compensation to complainant, of its embankment in a street the fee of which was owned by complainant, was dissolved upon the defendant's furnishing security deemed adequate for the damage it might do in the erection of the embankment. The court said: "The proceeding is one in restraint of a public work of great utility—the construction of a railroad—thus presenting a case in which injunctions are granted with great caution Delay in the construction of the work may operate very oppressively against the defendant, as well as result in great injury to the public. Courts very often, in such cases, balance the question of damages to the one party, and that of benefit to the other, resulting from the maintenance of the in

to recognize any distinction as to the abutting owner's rights based on his ownership of the fee in the street, holding that there is no taking of his property, but only of the public easement in the street; and the same courts refuse to enforce by injunction the constitutional provision against "damaging" property without just compensation, unless the damaging amounts to a virtual destruction.[13]

junction, on the one hand, and its dissolution on the other, and refuse to take any action which will cause great injury to one party, and probably be of serious detriment at the same time to the public, without corresponding advantage to the other party." In Western Railway of Alabama v. Alabama G. T. R. Co., 96 Ala. 272, 11 South. 483, 17 L. R. A. 474, a temporary injunction was dissolved, it appearing that the construction of defendant's railway would not interfere with the tracks of complainant, nor with any track it had the right to construct, that the damage to complainant would be nominal; that the defendant was not shown to be insolvent, and that to stop the work under the circumstances would probably result in grievous disaster to its enterprise, which was of a public nature, without any advantages to accrue to the complainant. See, also, Mobile & M. Ry. Co. v. Alabama M. Ry. Co., 116 Ala. 51, 23 South. 57, reviewing prior cases; Hinnershitz v. United Traction Co., 199 Pa. St. 3, 48 Atl. 874.

13 Spencer v. Point Pleasant & O. R. R. Co., 23 W. Va. 406, 420 ff, reviewing the then existing cases at great length, and holding that there was no "taking" of the abutting owner's fee, but only of the public easement in the street, and criticising with great force any distinction based on ownership of the fee in the street, and holding that "damaging of property for public use without just compensation" gave no right to an injunction, but only to recover damages in an action at law; unless under peculiar circumstances, as where the property is entirely destroyed in value as effectively as if it had actually been taken by the railroad company in constructing its road. All damages of a permanent character may be recovered in a single suit at law, and an injunction is therefore not necessary to avoid repeated suits at law: Smith v. Point Pleasant & O. R. R. Co., 23 W. Va. 451. The Spencer case was followed in Arbenz v. Wheeling & H R Co, 33 W. Va. 1, 10 S. E. 14, 5 L R. A. 371; Watson v. Fairmount & S. Ry. Co, 49 W. Va. 528, 39 S. E. 193. See, also, Planet Property etc. Co. v. St. Louis etc Ry Co, 115 Mo 613, 22 S. W 616; Rische v. Texas Transportation Co., 27 Tex. Civ. App. 33, 66 S. W. 324.

§ 469. Same; Fee of Street in the Municipality.—Where the abutting owner has not retained the fee in the street, but that is vested in the municipality in trust for the public, it is probably the rule still generally held that the injury to his easements of light, air, and access caused by the authorized construction or operation of a railroad in the street constitutes no "taking" of "property" within the meaning of the constitutional inhibition, and therefore no ground for an injunction.[14] To remedy the gross injustice and hardship of this rule, nearly all recent state constitutions have prohibited the "damaging" or "injuring" of property for public use without just compensation. This constitutional provision, however, has not, like the former, generally been construed by the courts as requiring the aid of an injunction for its enforcement.[15] A reason for mak-

14 O'Brien v. Baltimore Belt R. R. Co., 74 Md. 369, 22 Atl. 141, 13 L. R. A. 126 (statute authorizes recovery of damages for all injury), Garrett v. Lake Roland El. Ry. Co, 79 Md. 280, 29 Atl. 830, 24 L. R. A. 396, and many cases cited. See, also, cases in following notes.

15 Illinois.—Doane v. Lake St. El. R. Co., 165 Ill. 510, 56 Am. St. Rep. 265, 46 N E 520, 36 L. R. A. 97, and cases cited; Stetson v. Chicago & E. R. Co., 75 Ill 74; Peoria & R I. R. Co. v. Schertz, 84 Ill. 135, Truesdale v. Peoria Grape Sugar Co, 101 Ill 561, Corcoran v. Chicago, M. & N. R. Co., 149 Ill. 291, 37 N. E. 68; Stewart v. Chicago General St Ry. Co., 166 Ill. 61, 46 N. E. 765; General Elec. Ry. Co. v. Chicago & W. I. R Co, 184 Ill. 588, 56 N. E. 963, Blodgett v. Northwestern El. R. Co., 80 Fed. 601, 26 C. C. A. 21; Coffeen v. Chicago, M. & St. P. Ry. Co., 84 Fed 46, 28 C. C. A. 274; but see Beeson v. City of Chicago, 75 Fed. 880.

Missouri.—Clemens v. Connecticut Mut. Life Ins. Co. (Mo.), 82 S. W. 1.

Colorado.—Denver & S. F. R. Co. v. Domke, 11 Colo. 247, 17 Pac. 777; Denver, U. & P. Ry. Co. v. Barsaloux, 15 Colo. 290, 25 Pac. 165, 10 L. R. A. 89; Haskell v. Denver Tramway Co, 23 Colo. 60, 46 Pac. 121.

Georgia.—See Brown v. Atlanta R. & P. Co., 113 Ga. 462, 39 S. E. 71.

Nebraska.—Bronson v. Albion Tel. Co. (Neb.), 93 N. W. 201.

ing this distinction is found in the difficulty of ascertaining, before the railroad is actually in operation, the amount of damage that will be caused to abutting premises; also in the fact, sometimes referred to, that legislatures have not seen fit to provide a procedure for condemning the easements of abutting owners or appraising the damage to their property. They are therefore left to pursue their remedies at law for the recovery of such damage as they may suffer; unless, indeed, some incident such as the insolvency of the railroad company renders the collection of the damages recovered impossible, and the intervention of a court of equity essential.[16]

In a number of states, while the abutting owner is usually left to his legal remedy, if the operation of the railroad amounts to a total obstruction of the street or of plaintiff's access to his premises,[17] or causes a

16 *Dictum* in Peoria & R. I. R. Co. v. Schertz, 84 Ill. 135.

17 Missouri.—Lockwood v. Wabash R. R. Co., 122 Mo 86, 43 Am. St. Rep. 547, 26 S. W 698 (street so narrow that use by railroad necessarily destroys it as a public thoroughfare, and deprives abutting owners of access to their property); Knapp, Stout & Co. v. St. Louis Transfer Ry. Co., 126 Mo. 26, 28 S W. 627 (track so close to plaintiff's building as to practically obstruct access); Schulenberg & Borckeler Lumber Co. v. St. Louis, K. & N. W. Ry. Co., 129 Mo. 455, 31 S. W. 796; Sherlock v. Kansas City Belt Ry. Co., 142 Mo. 172, 64 Am. St. Rep. 551, 43 S. W. 629 (railroad in alley; injunction before running of cars has begun). In D. M. Osborne & Co. v. Missouri P. R. Co., 147 U. S. 248, 13 Sup. Ct. 299, 37 L. ed. 155, Fuller, C. J., after reviewing the Missouri decisions and stating the general principle as to equitable relief against the exercise of the eminent domain power, makes the following general statement, which has been often quoted: "But where there is no direct taking of the estate itself, in whole or in part, and the injury complained of is the infliction of damages in respect to the complete enjoyment thereof, a court of equity must be satisfied that the threatened damage is substantial, and the remedy at law in fact inadequate, before restraint will be laid upon the progress of a public work, and if the case made discloses only a legal right to recover damages rather than to demand compensation, the court will decline to interfere."

destruction of his property for the purposes for which it was used, equivalent in effect to a physical appropriation of the land, he may resort to equity for an injunction.[18]

§ 470. Same; New York Rule; Elevated Railroad Cases— The New York doctrine as laid down in the "Elevated Railroad cases" appears to have, as yet, but a slight following in other states; but these cases are so notable from their vast number, the eminence of the counsel engaged in many of them, and the thoroughness with which the fundamental principles are discussed and subsidiary rules worked out, that a somewhat full statement of the chief conclusions arrived at seems called for even in a work of an elementary character. It is important to notice, however, that these conclusions are held not to apply to a steam railroad on the surface of the street, operated in such a manner as not to obstruct public traffic.

The doctrine was thus summed up in one of the leading cases of the series: "The decisions of this court have settled the rights of abutting property owners to an easement in the street occupied by the defendants' structure, for free egress and ingress, and for the free admission of light and circulation of air. That easement is property, and constitutes an interest in real estate; and because the defendants' railroad was a use of the street not originally designed, and was an appropriation to themselves of property rights, it cannot be maintained without compensation being made to the abutting owners for the injury inflicted upon their property and rights; and, for the annoyance caused through the operation of the road to the abutting owners, in their enjoyment of the use of their property, they are en-

18 See cases cited *ante*, last section, note 13.

titled to recover such damages as may be shown to be the result of the defendants' acts: Story v. New York etc. R. R. Co., 90 N. Y. 122, 43 Am. Rep. 146; Lahr v. New York etc. Railroad Co., 104 N. Y. 268, 10 N. E. 528. Although property owners have a remedy at law for the intrusion upon their rights, yet, as the trespass is continuous in its nature, they can invoke the restraining power of a court of equity in their behalf, in order to prevent a multiplicity of suits, and they can recover the damages they have sustained, as incidental to the granting of the equitable relief: Williams v. New York Cent. R. R. Co., 16 N. Y. 97, 69 Am. Dec. 651; Henderson v. New York Central R. R. Co., 78 N. Y. 423. The violation of the property rights of abutting owners being adjudged in such an action, the awarding of damages sustained in the past from the defendants follows; they being, on equitable principles, deemed incidental to the main relief sought."[19]

19 Shepard v. Manhattan Ry. Co., 117 N Y. 442, 23 N. E. 30, per Gray, J. The decisions in the Story case and other elevated railroad cases are based upon the character of the structure and do not apply to a steam surface railroad operated in a reasonable way. Forbes v. Rome, W. & O. R. Co., 121 N. Y. 505, 24 N. E 921, 8 L R. A. 453; Drake v. Hudson R. R. Co., 7 Barb. 508. The principles of the Story and Lahr cases were again announced and explained in Abendroth v. New York El. R. Co., 122 N. Y. 1, 25 N. E. 496, 19 Am. St. Rep. 461, 11 L. R A. 634; Kane v. Metropolitan El. R. Co, 125 N. Y 164, 26 N. E. 278, 11 L. R. A. 640, explaining the legal basis for the doctrine of the abutter's easements in the street; Kernochan v. New York El. R Co., 128 N. Y 568, 29 N. E 65, Hughes v New York El. R. Co, 130 N. Y. 14, 28 N. E. 765, O'Reilly v. New York El. R Co, 148 N. Y. 347, 42 N. E. 1063, 31 L R. A. 407. See, also, Knox v. Metropolitan El. R. Co., 36 N. Y. St. Rep. 2, 12 N. Y. Supp. 848. The doctrine of the elevated railroad cases was followed in Willamette Iron Works v. Oregon R. & N. Co., 26 Or. 224, 46 Am St. Rep. 620, 37 Pac. 1016, 29 L. R. A. 88; and appears to have been anticipated, in substance, in Scioto Val. R. Co. v. Lawrence, 38 Ohio St. 41, 43 Am. Rep. 419. In Iowa a statute provides that railroad tracks shall not be constructed in streets, etc., until damages to abutters are ascertained and com

In a common-law, as distinguished from an equitable, action, the abutter can only recover such temporary damages as have been sustained up to the time of the commencement of the action, and is not entitled to damages measured by the permanent diminution in the value of his property.[20] "But the owner may resort to equity for the purpose of enjoining the continuance of the trespass, and to thus prevent a multiplicity of actions at law to recover damages; and in such an action the court may determine the amount of damage which the owner would sustain if the trespass were permanently continued, and it may provide that upon payment of that sum, the plaintiff shall give a deed or convey the right to the defendant, and it will refuse an injunction when the defendant is willing to pay upon the receipt of a conveyance. The court does not adjudge that the defendant shall pay such sum and that the plaintiff shall so convey. It provides that if the conveyance is made and the money paid, no injunction shall issue. If defendant refuses to pay, the injunction issues."[21] The award of damages for past injuries

pensated. The abutter may have an injunction under this statute to prevent its violation: See Harbach v. Des Moines & K. C. R. Co., 80 Iowa, 593, 44 N. W. 348, 11 L. R. A. 113.

20 Pond v. Metropolitan El. R. Co., 112 N. Y. 186, 8 Am. St Rep. 734, 19 N. E. 487, Uline v. New York etc. R. R. Co., 101 N. Y. 98, 54 Am. Rep. 661, 4 N. E. 536.

21 Pappenheim v. Metropolitan El. R. Co., 128 N. Y. 436, 26 Am. St. Rep 486, 28 N. E. 518, 13 L. R. A. 401. See, also, McGean v. Metropolitan El. R. Co., 133 N. Y. 9, 30 N. E. 647; Van Allen v. New York El R. Co., 144 N. Y. 174, 38 N. E. 997, Pegram v. New York El. R. Co, 147 N. Y. 135, 41 N. E. 424. See, also, Woodworth v. Brooklyn El R. Co., 29 App. Div. 1, 51 N. Y. Supp. 323 (when railroad in hands of receiver); Siegel v. New York & H. R. Co., 62 App. Div. 290, 70 N. Y. Supp. 1088, Larney v. New York & H R. Co, 62 App. Div. 311, 71 N. Y. Supp. 27; Auchincloss v. Metropolitan El. R Co. 69 App. Div 63, 74 N. Y. Supp. 534, reversing 60 N. Y. Supp. 792; Lane v. Metropolitan El. R. Co., 69 App. Div. 231, 74 N. Y. Supp.

sustained being incidental to the equitable relief, the defendant is not entitled to a jury trial of such claim for damages.[22]

Actual damage suffered by the abutting property is of the gist of the equitable action. A court of equity is at liberty to disregard the mere technical trespass upon the abutter's rights, and to refuse an injunction, "in a case where the plaintiffs are unable to show any actual damage to their property, or loss suffered, by reason of the defendants' acts, and in the face of the fact that, by reason of the presence and operation of the elevated railroad in the street, the value of their property has greatly increased, and that it has shared equally with all the property in the vicinity in the general increase of values which has taken place."[23]

595. See, also, Muhlker v. New York & H. R. Co., 197 U. S. 455, 25 Sup. Ct. 522.

22 Lynch v. Metropolitan El. R. Co., 129 N. Y. 274, 26 Am. St. Rep. 523, 29 N. E. 315, 15 L. R. A. 287, ably discussing the general subject of damages as incidental to relief in equity; Shepard v. Manhattan Ry. Co., 131 N. Y. 215, 30 N. E. 187; Hunter v. Manhattan R. Co., 141 N. Y. 281, 36 N. E. 400.

23 O'Reilly v. New York El. R. Co, 148 N Y. 347, 42 N E 1063, 31 L. R. A. 407, citing Jerome v. Ross, 7 Johns. Ch. 315, 11 Am Dec. 484; Kerlin v. West, 4 N. J. Eq. 449; Troy & B. R. Co. v. Boston, H. T. & W. R. Co., 86 N. Y. 123; Gray v. Railway Co, 128 N. Y. 499, 28 N. E. 498; Shepard v. Railway Co., 131 N. Y. 215, 30 N. E. 187; Hunter v. Railway Co., 141 N. Y. 281, 36 N. E. 400; Doyle v. Railway Co., 136 N. Y. 505, 32 N. E. 1008; Bookman v. Railroad Co., 147 N. Y. 298, 49 Am. St. Rep. 664, 41 N. E. 705. See, also, Purdy v. Manhattan El. R. Co., 36 N. Y. St. Rep. 43, 13 N. Y. Supp. 295; Brush v. Manhattan El. R. Co. (Com. P.), 17 N. Y. Supp. 540, Steinmetz v. Metropolitan El. R. Co. (Sup. Ct.), 18 N. Y. Supp. 209; Pratt v. New York C. & H. R. R. Co, 90 Hun, 83, 35 N. Y. Supp. 557; Rorke v Kings Co. El. R. Co., 22 App. Div. 511, 48 N. Y. Supp. 42, Tillson v. Manhattan R. Co., 24 App. Div 623, 48 N. Y. Supp. 224; Marsh v. Kings Co. El R. Co., 86 Fed. 189, 29 C. C. A. 655. Compare Maitland v. Manhattan R. Co., 9 Misc. Rep. 616, 30 N Y. Supp 428. The opinion of Gray, J., in the O'Reilly case, is one of the most instructive in the whole course of the elevated railroad litigation. He says,

in part: "Therefore, the only ground for the claim of the plaintiffs, that they are entitled to equitable relief, is in the mere fact that the defendants have invaded their rights in the public street, without their consent, and without having first condemned the same by an exercise of the right of eminent domain. . . . . But it seems to me to be perfectly clear that the court, when appealed to by the property owners to enjoin the operation by the corporation of its franchises, upon the ground that certain easements have been invaded, will consider the fact that the corporation is there for the public convenience, and is executing a *quasi* public work; and, if it finds that no injury is in truth inflicted, and that the property owner has suffered no actual damage, it may and should refuse to grant the relief prayed for. . . . . The court recognizes the fact that the defendants had the right to appropriate the street easements by condemnation proceedings, and hence, when appealed to to enjoin them from operating their franchises, it looks into the question of the substantial nature of the damage alleged to have been done to the property, or of the loss suffered by the owner. If it is found to be such, then the court proceeds in the matter as though the proceeding was one to condemn to the defendants' uses the property appropriated, and, having ascertained the value of the property, it suspends the decree, which it finds the plaintiffs are entitled to to restrain the continuance of the defendants' acts, for a sufficient period within which to permit the defendants to acquire the right to appropriate the easements through a conveyance, as a condition of avoiding the enforcement of the decree The proceedings by which the court ascertains and fixes the damages done to the abutting property in the deprivation of easements are, in fact, but a substitute for condemnation proceedings," etc.

Parties Plaintiff; Title, etc.: See Shepard v. Manhattan R. Co, 117 N. Y. 442, 23 N. E. 30 (joinder); Kernochan v. New York El. R Co., 128 N. Y. 568, 29 N. E. 65 (lessor a proper plaintiff; right of action accruing after death vests in heirs, not in administrator); Hughes v. New York El. R. Co., 130 N. Y. 14, 28 N. E. 765 (evidence of plaintiff's title); McGean v. Metropolitan El. Ry. Co., 133 N. Y. 9, 30 N. E. 647 (effect of transfer of plaintiff's title *pendente lite*); Mitchell v. Metropolitan El. R. Co., 56 Hun, 543, 9 N. Y. Supp. 829, 134 N. Y. 11, 31 N. E. 260 (permanent damages should be paid to heirs, not to executors, of deceased owner); Hunter v. Manhattan R Co., 141 N. Y. 281, 36 N. E. 400 (a part of the claim for damages rests on assignment); Van Allen v. New York El. Ry. Co., 144 N. Y. 174, 38 N. E. 997 (effect of conveyance *pendente lite* on jurisdiction of the court of equity to award damages); Pegram v. New York El. R. Co., 147 N. Y. 135, 41 N. E. 424 (same question); Domschke v. Metropolitan El. R. Co, 148 N. Y. 343, 42 N E. 804 (conveyance *pendente lite);* Koeler v. New York El. R Co, 159 N. Y. 218, 53 N. E. 1114 (*pendente lite* grantee may be joined as plaintiff or defendant); Mooney v. New York El. R. Co, 163 N. Y. 242, 57 N. E. 496. See, also, Welsh v. New York El. R. Co. (Com. Pl.), 12 N. Y. Supp 545 (where plaintiff has leasehold interest, injunction only during continuance of his interest), Odell v. Metropolitan El. R. Co., 3 Misc. Rep. 335, 22 N. Y. Supp. 737, Wright v. New York El. R. Co, 78 Hun, 450, 29 N. Y. Supp. 223 (where conveyance from plaintiffs is impossible, decree should be for injunction unless defendant pay a certain sum upon conveyance, and if that could not be made, unless defendant condemn the easements): McKee v. New York El. R. Co., 79 Hun, 366, 29 N. Y. Supp. 457 (same question); Skelly v. Metropolitan El. R. Co, 1 App. Div. 51, 37 N. Y. Supp 7, affirmed without opinion, 158 N. Y. 677, 52 N. E 1126 (same question); Jacobson v. Brooklyn El R. Co, 22 Misc Rep. 281, 48 N. Y. Supp. 1072 (such claim for damages as passes to executors of owner is merely basis for common-law action).

Measure of Damages in Equity: See Drucker v. Manhattan R. Co., 106 N. Y. 157, 60 Am. Rep. 437, 12 N. E. 568; Newman v. Metropolitan El. R. Co., 118 N Y 618, 23 N. E. 901, 7 L. R. A 289, Kane v. Metropolitan El. R. Co, 125 N Y. 164, 26 N. E. 278, 11 L. R. A. 640; Pappenheim v. Metropolitan El. R. Co., 128 N. Y. 436, 26 Am. St. Rep. 486, 28 N. E. 518, 13 L. R. A. 401, Roberts v. New York El. R. Co., 128 N. Y. 455, 28 N. E. 486, 13 L. R. A. 499 (as to opinion evidence and testimony of experts), Gray v Manhattan R. Co., 128 N. Y. 499, 28 N. E. 498 (same); Bohm v. Metropolitan El. R. Co, 129 N. Y. 576, 29 N. E. 802, 14 L. R. A. 344; Hughes v. New York El. R Co, 130 N. Y. 14, 28 N. E. 765; Storck v. Metropolitan El. R. Co., 131 N. Y. 514, 30 N. E 497; Becker v. Metropolitan El. R. Co, 131 N. Y. 509, 30 N. E 499, Woolsey v New York El. R Co, 134 N Y. 323, 30 N. E. 387; affirmed on rehearing, 31 N E 891, Sperb v. Metropolitan El. R. Co., 137 N. Y. 155, 32 N. E. 1050, 20 L. R. A. 752, reviewing prior cases ("the principle which should guide an award of damages to be paid by the railroad company in order to obviate the injunction is the same as in proceedings under the statute to condemn property for the railroad use"); Hunter v. Manhattan R. Co., 141 N. Y. 281, 36 N E. 400 (what expert testimony is admissible); Bookman v. New York El. R. Co, 147 N Y. 298, 49 Am. St. Rep. 664, 41 N. E. 705; Jamieson v. Kings Co. El. R. Co., 147 N. Y 322, 41 N. E. 693; Roberts v. New York El. R. Co., 155 N. Y. 31, 49 N. E. 262. See, also, Emigrant Mission Com. v. Brooklyn El. R. Co., 20 App. Div. 596, 47 N. Y. Supp. 344.

Statute of Limitations —Since the trespass is a continuing one, the action for injunction may be maintained so long as a legal claim for the trespass exists; and no lapse of time or inaction merely on the

§ 471. Changing Grade of Street; Other Uses of Streets; Vacating Streets.—Here, again, it is necessary to segregate the cases which hold that the injury caused to the abutting owner by the action of a municipal or other authority, acting within the limits of its power, in raising or lowering the grade of a street, confers no right of action whatever upon the abutter;[24] and cases holding that such structures as electric light poles,[25] telegraph or telephone poles, and the like, create no "additional servitude" in the street. If the abutter owns the fee in the street, and such structures are held to create an additional servitude, and are shown to

part of the plaintiff, unless it has continued for the length of time necessary to effect a change of title in the property claimed to have been injured, is sufficient to defeat the right of the owner to damages, and, consequently, to equitable relief: Galway v. Metropolitan Elev. R. Co, 128 N. Y. 145, 28 N. E. 479.

Laches, Acquiescence and Estoppel.—Conduct not amounting to: Galway v. Metropolitan El. R. Co., 128 N. Y. 145, 28 N. E. 479, 13 L. R. A 788, Brush v. Manhattan El. R. Co., 26 Abb. N. C. 73, 13 N. Y. Supp. 908.

Abandonment of Easements, evidenced by written *consent* to the building of the railroad. White v. Manhattan R. Co., 139 N. Y. 19, 34 N. E. 887; Heimburg v Manhattan R. Co., 162 N Y. 352, 56 N. E. 899, 19 App. Div. 179, 45 N. Y. Supp. 999; see, also, Bellew v New York, W. & C. Traction Co., 47 App. Div. 447, 62 N. Y Supp. 242, or where plaintiff purchased from city, which had given consent Herzog v. New York El. R. Co., 76 Hun, 486, 27 N Y. Supp. 1034, affirmed without opinion, 151 N. Y. 665, 46 N E. 1148. As to the effect of consent conditional on compensation, see Kornder v. Kings Co El R. Co., 41 App. Div. 357, 58 N. Y. Supp 518.

24 See, for example, Fellowes v. City of New Haven, 44 Conn 240, 26 Am. Rep. 447, Churchill v. Beethe, 48 Neb. 87, 66 N. W. 992, 35 L. R. A. 442 (change of grade diverting surface water on to plaintiff's land); Talbot v. New York & H. R. Co., 151 N. Y. 155, 45 N. E. 382 (change of street grade in constructing bridge over railroad); and see Lewis, Eminent Domain, §§ 92-109. For further cases holding, in general, that the exercise of discretionary powers by municipal authorities will not be enjoined, see *ante*, § 342.

25 Loeber v. Butte General Elec. Co., 16 Mont. 1, 50 Am St. Rep. 468, 39 Pac. 912. See monographic note, 28 Am. St. Rep. 229.

abridge the right of the abutter to the use of the street as a means of ingress and egress, or otherwise, a proper case is made for an injunction until compensation is made.[26]

In the limited class of cases where the injury caused by a change of grade is held to constitute a "taking" of the abutter's property, it seems that an injunction may issue in accordance with the general principles governing injunction against the exercise of the eminent domain power.[27]

Where, under the modern constitutional provision, "damaging" property for public use without compensation is prohibited, and paying or securing the compensation is treated as a condition precedent to doing the work which causes the damage, an injunction will usually be granted until the condition is complied with. The considerations which should guide the court in granting or refusing the injunction at the suit of the

26 Chesapeake & P. Tel. Co. v. Mackenzie, 74 Md. 36, 28 Am. St. Rep. 219, 21 Atl. 690. See, also, Donovan v. Allert, 11 N. D. 289, 95 Am. St. Rep. 720, 91 N. W. 441, 58 L. R. A. 775. Where the abutter's cause of action is dependent upon his ownership of the fee in the street, a bill by him to enjoin a telephone company from laying conduits under the sidewalk is demurrable, when it does not allege that the plaintiff owned the fee in the walk or street, or that the walk or street was dedicated to the public by one who at the time owned the fee. Erwin v. Central Union Tel. Co, 148 Ind. 365, 46 N. E. 667, 47 N. E. 663.

27 See Vanderlip v. City of Grand Rapids, 73 Mich. 522, 16 Am. St. Rep. 597, 41 N. W. 677, 3 L. R. A. 247, where the injury was done by raising the grade, thereby burying a portion of the dwelling-house and barn of the abutting owner. In those jurisdictions, like New York, where the plaintiff's right of action with reference to an additional servitude is not dependent upon his ownership of the fee, it seems that he cannot enjoin such a structure as a telephone conduit, authorized to be laid in the street, in the absence of a showing of substantial pecuniary damage to his property: Castle v. Bell Tel. Co. of Buffalo, 30 Misc. Rep. 38, 61 N Y Supp. 743, following the principle of O'Reilly v. Railroad Co., *ante*, § 470, at note 23.

abutting owner in such cases are thus stated in a most instructive opinion by Judge Brewer:

"*First.* A chancellor, in determining an application for an injunction, must regard not only the rights of the complainant which are sought to be protected, but the injuries which may result to the defendant or to others from the granting of the injunction. If the complainant's rights are of a trifling character, if the injury which he would sustain from the act sought to be enjoined can be fully and easily compensated, while, on the other hand, the defendant would suffer great damage, and especially if the public would suffer a large inconvenience if the contemplated act was restrained, the lesser right must yield to the larger benefit; the injunction should be refused, and the complainant remitted to his action for damages. This rule has been enforced in a multitude of cases, and under a variety of circumstances, and is one of such evident justice as needs no citation of authorities for its support.

"*Second.* When the defendant has an ultimate right to do the act sought to be restrained, but only upon some condition precedent, and compliance with the condition is within the power of the defendant, injunction will almost universally be granted until the condition is complied with. This principle lies at the foundation of the multitude of cases which have restrained the taking of property until after the payment of compensation, for in all those cases the legislature has placed at the command of the defendant means for ascertaining the value of the property. In those cases the courts have seldom stopped to inquire whether the value of the property sought to be taken was little or great, whether the injury to the complainant was large or small, but have contented themselves with holding that as the defendant had full means for ascertaining such compensation, it was his first duty to use such means, determine and pay the compensation, and until he did so the taking of the property would be enjoined.

"*Third.* Where the defendant has an ultimate right to do the act sought to be enjoined upon certain conditions, and the means of complying with such conditions are not at his command, the courts will endeavor to adjust their orders so on the one hand as to give to the complainant the substantial benefit of such conditions, while not restraining the defendant from the exercise of his ultimate rights. Thus, in the case at bar, the defendant has of course the ultimate right to grade this street. As a condition of such right is a payment of damages, but it has no means of ascertaining those damages; no tribunal has been created, no provision of law made, for their ascertainment. Hence, if possible, the court should provide for securing to the defendant this ultimate right, and at the same time give to the complainant the substantial benefit of the prior conditions." It was further held that in applying the rule first stated to a case like the one at bar, the court should have principal regard to three matters, viz.: the amount of injury to the complainant, the solvency of the defendant, and the importance to the public of the proposed improvement.[28]

28 McElroy v. Kansas City, 21 Fed. 257, 261, et seq., per Brewer, Cir. J.; approved in D. M. Osborne & Co. v. Missouri Pac. R. Co., 147 U. S. 248, 13 Sup. Ct. 299, 37 L. ed. 155 It was found that the injury to the complainant's lot would be serious; that the defendant was unquestionably solvent; and that the improvement was not one of pressing public necessity. A restraining order was issued, with a provision for the appointment of commissioners by the court to ascertain and report the complainant's damages, and for vacating the injunction on payment of such damages. See, also, in support of the plaintiff's right to an injunction under the "damaged" clause of the constitution, Brown v. City of S[illegible]e, 5 Wash.

The courts are not in accord on the question, what right to compensation, if any, is given to owners of property abutting on a street by the constitutional provisions cited in this chapter, consequent on the authorized vacating of the street by the proper authorities[29] Granting that such right to compensation exists, in a given case, the owner's right to an injunction until damages are paid or secured would seem to depend on the usual principles regulating injunction against the exercise of the eminent domain power, where the abutter's easements in the street are taken or impaired.[30]

§ 472. **Acquiescence.**—The equitable doctrine of acquiescence is freely applied to cases involving eminent do-

35, 31 Pac. 313, 32 Pac. 214, 18 L. R. A. 161; Searle v. City of Lead, 10 S. D. 312, 73 N. W. 101, 39 L R. A. 345. *Contra*, Moore v. City of Atlanta, 70 Ga. 611; compare Hurt v. City of Atlanta, 100 Ga. 280, 28 S. E. 65 (no injunction against bridge in street where no actual damage shown). In the well-considered case of Geurkink v. City of Petaluma, 112 Cal. 306, 44 Pac. 570, it was held that a city should be enjoined from so changing a natural watercourse as to damage an abutting owner's property by preventing a free access to and use thereof, unless compensation for such damage should be first made, or paid into court, for him.

Where it is held that the payment of consequential damages is not a condition precedent, no injunction will issue to prevent a change of grade: Clemens v. Connecticut Mut. Life Ins. Co. (Mo.), 82 S. W. 1.

29 See Lewis, Eminent Domain, § 134.

30 That injunction will issue at the suit of owner whose property abuts on the part vacated, or whose access to his property is destroyed by the vacating, but not where other means of access remain to the owner, see McQuigg v. Cullins, 56 Ohio St. 649, 47 N. E. 595; Kinnear v. Beatty, 65 Ohio St. 264, 87 Am. St. Rep. 600, 62 N. E. 341; Glasgow v. City of St. Louis, 107 Mo. 198, 17 S. W. 743; Wooters v. City of Crockett, 11 Tex. Civ. App. 474, 33 S. W 391. See, also, Parker v. Catholic Bishop of Chicago, 146 Ill. 158, 34 N. E. 473 (where property is merely injured, tender of compensation is not a condition precedent to exercise of eminent domain power); McLachlan v. Incorporated Town of Gray, 105 Iowa, 259, 74 N. W. 773 (when *certiorari* an adequate remedy); Prince v. McCoy, 40 Iowa, 533 (no injunction where plaintiff not injured).

main rights. The underlying principle of the constitutional provisions allowing the taking of private property is that it is to be devoted to public use. Hence, when a landowner stands by until the public has acquired an interest in the use, there is a strong reason for applying the doctrine, in addition to the familiar grounds governing its application to other cases. The United States supreme court in a recent case[31] has laid down the rule in no uncertain language. "If one, aware of the situation, believes he has certain legal rights, and desires to insist upon them, he should do so promptly. If by his declarations or conduct he leads the other party to believe that he does not propose to rest upon such rights but is willing to waive them for a just compensation, and the other party proceeds to great expense in the expectation that payment of a fair compensation will be accepted and the right waived—especially if it is in respect to a matter which will largely affect the public convenience and welfare—a court of equity may properly refuse to enforce those rights, and, in the absence of an agreement for compensation, compel him to submit the determination of the amount thereof to an impartial tribunal." Accordingly, when a landowner stands by and makes no attempt to enjoin a railroad company from building over his land until large expenditures have been made, or the road has been completed, injunctive relief will be denied, and the party will be left to his remedy at law for damages.[32] The same principle applies to the lay-

31 City of New York v. Pine, 185 U. S. 93, 22 Sup. Ct 592, 46 L. ed. 820, quoting Pom. Eq. Jur, § 418, and many cases. See, also, Goodin v. Cincinnati & W. Canal Co., 18 Ohio St. 169, 98 Am. Dec 95; Bravard v. Cincinnati, H. & I. R. Co., 115 Ind. 1, 17 N. E. 183, Midland Ry. Co. v. Smith, 135 Ind. 348, 35 N. E. 284; Midland Ry. Co. v. Smith, 113 Ind. 233, 15 N. E. 256.

32 Midland Ry. Co. v. Smith, 135 Ind. 348, 35 N. E. 284; Louis-

ing of pipes or to a taking for any other public use.[33] And although permission is granted to take upon the distinct understanding that compensation is to be made, an injunction will not issue, after the work has been done, for the purpose of enforcing payment.[34] The doctrine also applies to cases involving the rights of railroads in streets.[35]

§ 473. Assessment of Damages by the Court, with Injunction as Alternative to Their Payment.—"Where a corporation which has the right to acquire property by an ex-

ville, N. A. & C. Ry. Co. v. Beck, 119 Ind. 124, 21 N. E 471; Ross v. Elizabeth R. R. Co., 2 N. J. Eq. 422; Erie Ry. Co. v. Delaware, L. & W. R. Co., 21 N. J. Eq. 283. And the rule, of course, applies when the road is built at the owner's instigation: Pettibone v. La Crosse & M. R. Co., 14 Wis. 443.

33 Biddler v. Wayne Waterworks Co., 190 Pa. St 94, 42 Atl. 380; Kincaid v. Indianapolis N. G. Co., 124 Ind. 577, 19 Am. St. Rep. 113, 24 N. E. 1066, 8 L. R A. 602.

34 Florida Southern R. Co. v. Hill, 40 Fla. 1, 74 Am. St. Rep. 124, 23 South. 566.

35 Hinnershitz v. United Traction Co., 199 Pa. St. 3, 48 Atl. 874; Baltimore & O. R. Co v. Strauss, 37 Md. 237; Ferguson v. Covington & C. El. R. & T. & B. Co., 108 Ky. 662, 57 S. W. 460; Byron v Louisville & N. R. Co., 22 Ky. Law Rep. 1007, 59 S. W. 519; Heilman v. Lebanon & A. St. Ry. Co., 175 Pa. St. 188, 34 Atl. 647, 180 Pa St. 627, 37 Atl. 119. In the New York Elevated Railroad cases the doctrine of *laches*, as distinguished from estoppel, is held inapplicable upon this principle: "It must be regarded as settled in this state that the doctrine of acquiescence or laches as a defense to an equity action is limited to actions of an equitable nature exclusively, or to those where the legal right has expired, or the party has lost his right of property by prescription or adverse possession; and that, where a legal right is involved, and upon grounds of equity jurisdiction the courts have been called upon to sustain the legal right, the mere laches of a party, unaccompanied by circumstances amounting to an estoppel, constitute no defense": Syracuse Solar Salt Co. v. Rome, W. & O. R. Co., 67 Hun, 153, 22 N. Y. Supp. 321 See, also, Galway v. Metropolitan El. R. Co., 128 N. Y. 145, 28 N. E. 479, 13 L. R. A. 788; Brush v. Manhattan El. R. Co., 13 N. Y. Supp. 908. In the latter case relief was allowed ten years after the construction of the road.

ercise of the power of eminent domain has taken possession of property, and has erected or is engaged in the erection of structures thereon, but has not complied with some condition precedent necessary to render its acts in all respects lawful (such, for instance, as a failure on its part to pay some person the damages necessarily incident to the maintenance of the structure), and such person appeals to a court of equity for an injunction to restrain the maintenance or to compel the removal of the structure, the court to which such appeal is made has the power to determine the amount of unpaid damages, and to withhold an injunction, and direct that the structure be permitted to remain and be operated, provided the assessed damages are paid. Courts of equity will, as it seems, the more readily pursue such a course when important public interests are at stake, and a contrary course would be productive of much public inconvenience and annoyance."[36] This rule applies with special force when the complainant, by making no objection, acquiesces in the work. It finds frequent application in the New York Elevated Railroad cases, which are discussed elsewhere in this chapter.[37]

36 St. Paul, M. & M. Ry. Co. v. Western Union Tel. Co., 118 Fed. 497, 55 C. C. A. 263, *per* Thayer, Cir. J. See, also, City of New York v. Pine, 185 U. S. 93, 22 Sup. Ct. 592, 46 L. ed. 820; McElroy v. Kansas City, 21 Fed. 257; Cowan v. Southern Ry. Co, 118 Ala. 554, 23 South. 754; Benjamin v. Brooklyn Union El. R. Co., 120 Fed. 428.

37 See *ante*, § 470.

CHAPTER XXI.

INJUNCTIONS TO PREVENT OR RESTRAIN THE COMMISSION OF TORTS IN GENERAL; TO RESTRAIN CRIMINAL ACTS.

ANALYSIS.

§ 474. **The Estates and Interests Generally Legal.**—"The estates, interests, and primary rights to be secured by injunctions of this kind are in most instances legal; and the injunctions themselves, as a class, are frequently described as those for the protection of legal rights and interests. So far as they do thus sustain and enforce legal rights, they are, of course, supplementary to or in lieu of the legal remedies which courts of common law originally gave, and perhaps now give, by action, under the same circumstances. For this reason, the general test as stated in a former paragraph applies with special force. The inadequacy of the legal remedies is the criterion which determines the exercise of this preventive jurisdiction; and the criterion is enforced, especially by the American courts, with great strictness."[1]

1 Pom. Eq. Jur., § 1346.

§ 475. **Kinds and Classes of Torts Restrained.**—"The legal remedy is ordinarily considered as adequate in cases of torts to the person, and to property held by a legal title, and equity does not interfere. There are, however, certain species of torts, in respect to each of which, as a class, it is settled that the legal remedy is generally inadequate, so that equity will generally interfere to prevent the wrong by injunction. There are other species of torts, in respect to each of which, as a class, the legal remedy is adequate, but may become inadequate, in individual instances, from their particular circumstances, so that in those instances an injunction will be granted. In the kind of torts for which the legal remedy is generally inadequate, so that an injunction is a proper remedy, the title of the injured party must be clear, the injury real, and not merely temporary or transient. They are waste, nuisance, including interference with easements, servitudes, and similar rights, infringements of patent rights, of copyrights, of trade-marks, and of other intangible property rights, the pecuniary value of which cannot be certainly estimated, such as literary property in manuscript writings and good-will. In ordinary trespasses the injured party is left to his remedy of damages, but the circumstances of a trespass to property—especially to real property—may be such that the compensatory remedy is inadequate, and a court of equity will prevent the wrong by injunction."[2]

§ 476. **Criminal Acts—In General.**—A court of equity is in no sense a court of criminal jurisdiction. Its primary province is the protection of property rights.

2 Pom. Eq. Jur., § 1347. This section is cited, to the point that the plaintiff must show a clear title, in Perkins Lumber Co. v. Wilkinson (Ga.), 43 S. E. 696.

Hence, an injunction will not be granted to restrain an act merely criminal, where no property right is directly endangered thereby.[3] Thus, an act morally wrong, such as gambling, will not be enjoined at the suit of an individual;[4] nor will a violation of a Sunday law;[5] nor a violation of a statute, where no property rights are involved.[6] But where property rights are endangered, the fact that the acts are criminal will not prevent the court from exercising its jurisdiction. The United States supreme court, in a leading case, has laid down the rule as follows: "Something more than the threatened commission of an offense against the laws of the land is necessary to call into exercise the injunctive powers of the court. There must be some interferences, actual or threatened, with property or rights of a pecuniary nature; but when such interferences appear the jurisdiction of a court of equity arises, and is not destroyed by the fact that they are accompanied by or are themselves violations of the criminal law."[7]

§ 477. **Applications of the Principle.**—The instances of the exercise of this jurisdiction are many and various. All that is necessary is a state of fact which ordinarily gives rise to a right for injunctive relief. Thus, an injunction has been granted to restrain a criminal tres-

3 Hamilton-Brown Shoe Co. v. Saxey, 131 Mo. 212, 52 Am. St. Rep. 622, 32 S. W. 1106; Cope v. District Fair Assn., 99 Ill. 489, 39 Am. Rep. 30; Ocean City Assn. v. Schurch, 57 N. J. Eq. 268, 41 Atl. 914; People ex rel. L'Abbe v. District Court of Lake Co., 26 Colo. 386, 58 Pac. 604, 46 L. R. A. 850; Tiede v. Schneidt, 99 Wis. 201, 74 N. W. 798.

4 Cope v. District Fair Assn., 99 Ill. 489, 39 Am. Rep. 30; People ex rel. L'Abbe v. District Court of Lake Co., 26 Colo. 382, 58 Pac. 604, 46 L R. A. 850.

5 Ocean City Assn. v Schurch, 57 N. J. Eq. 268, 41 Atl. 914; York v. Yzaguairre, 31 Tex. Civ. App. 26, 71 S. W. 563.

6 Tiede v. Schneidt, 99 Wis. 201, 74 N W. 798.

7 In re Debs, 158 U. S. 564, 15 Sup. Ct. 900, 39 L. ed. 1092.

pass on oyster beds;[8] and to restrain so-called "ticket scalpers" from disposing of "round-trip" tickets in violation of a penal statute.[9] Recently the courts have entertained many applications for injunctive relief against criminal acts by labor leaders and organizations; and the same principle has been applied. Thus, it is now clearly settled that a court of equity will enjoin the criminal intimidation of workingmen, in order to protect the property interests of their employers.[10] Similarly, the court will enjoin strikers from committing criminal acts of violence.[11] And likewise, it will restrain a criminal conspiracy of any number of people to injure property.[12] These applications of the rule, while recent, are still in accordance with well-established equitable principles, and will be discussed fully and in detail in a later chapter.

§ 478. **Same—Public Nuisance—Suits by Individuals.**— One of the most frequent applications of the principle is to suits by individuals to restrain public nuisances. It is a familiar principle of law that an individual cannot maintain a suit to abate or to recover damages for a public nuisance unless he suffers some special dam-

8 Jones v. Oemler, 110 Ga. 202, 35 S. E. 375.

9 Nashville & St. L. Ry. Co. v. McConnell, 82 Fed. 65 (*dictum*). See *post*, chapter XXIX.

10 Cons. Steel & Wire Co. v. Murray, 80 Fed. 811; Vegelahn v. Guntner, 167 Mass. 92, 57 Am. St. Rep. 443, 44 N. E. 1077, 35 L. R. A. 722; Hamilton-Brown Shoe Co. v. Saxey, 131 Mo 212, 52 Am. St. Rep. 622, 32 S. W. 1106. See *post*, chapter XXVIII.

11 Cumberland Glass Mfg. Co. v. Glass Bottle Blowers' Assn., 59 N. J. Eq. 49, 46 Atl. 208; Coeur d'Alene Cons. & Min. Co. v. Miners' Union of Wardner, 51 Fed. 260, 19 L. R. A. 382. See *post*, chapter XXVIII.

12 Arthur v. Oakes, 63 Fed. 310, 11 C. C. A. 209, 25 L. R. A. 414; Elder v. Whitesides, 72 Fed. 724; Davis v. Zimmerman, 91 Hun, 489, 36 N. Y. Supp. 303; Longshore Printing Co. v. Howell, 26 Or. 527, 46 Am. St. Rep. 640, 38 Pac. 547, 28 L. R. A. 464.

age different and other from that suffered by the rest of the community. Hence it follows that equity will not enjoin a public nuisance at the suit of an individual unless he has suffered or is likely to suffer such damage as would entitle him to maintain an action at law. "Where the injury resulting from the nuisance is, in its nature, irreparable, as when loss of health, loss of trade or destruction of the means of subsistence, or permanent ruin to property will ensue from the wrongful act or erection, courts of equity will interfere by injunction, in furtherance of justice and the violated rights of property."[13] Thus, a party specially injured may enjoin the maintenance of a house of ill-fame, although it be a crime to use property for such a purpose.[14] Likewise, a person who would suffer a special injury by an explosion may obtain an injunction to restrain the criminal storage of nitroglycerin within the limits of a city.[15] Again, an injunction will be granted to a person specially injured to prevent the removal of a wooden building from outside to within the fire limits of a town in violation of an ordinance,[16] or to restrain the erection of such a building within the fire limits,[17] where the act if carried out would amount to a nuisance; but the mere violation of the ordinance is no ground for relief unless the acts themselves actually constitute a nuisance.[18] Again, an individual

13 Wahle v. Reinback, 76 Ill. 322; Barrett v. Mt. Greenwood Cemetery Assn, 159 Ill. 385, 50 Am. St. Rep. 168, 42 N. E. 891, 31 L. R. A. 109. See *post*, chapter XXIV.

14 Cranford v. Tyrrel, 128 N. Y 341, 28 N. E. 514. But see Neaf v. Palmer, 103 Ky. 496, 45 S. W. 506, 41 L. R. A. 219.

15 People's Gas Co. v. Tyner, 131 Ind. 277, 31 Am. St. Rep. 433, 31 N. E. 59, 16 L. R. A. 443.

16 Kaufman v. Stein, 138 Ind. 49, 46 Am. St Rep. 368, 37 N. E. 333.

17 Village of St John v McFarlan, 33 Mich 72, 20 Am. Rep. 671

18 Village of New Rochelle v. Lang, 75 Hun, 608, 27 N. Y. Supp.

may obtain an injunction to restrain the criminal sale of liquor when he is specially injured thereby. In such a case a clear injury to property greater than that suffered by the general public must be shown.[19]

While, independently of statute, a private individual cannot maintain an action to restrain a public nuisance unless he has suffered special, pecuniary or property injury, it seems that there is no objection to such an action without such injury when a statute authorizes it. "It is surely within the power of the legislature to designate the persons at whose suit a nuisance may be enjoined and abated. The reason for the rule which formerly obtained, that a private action will not lie for a public nuisance without special damages, was that to authorize private actions would create a multiplicity of suits, one being as well entitled to bring an action as another. But because the enforcement of a statute may create a multiplicity of actions is no ground for declaring it unconstitutional. . . . There can be no doubt that it is within the power of the legislature to designate the person or class of persons who may maintain actions to restrain and abate public nuisances, and when that is done the action is for all purposes an action instituted in behalf of the public, the same as though brought by the attorney general or public prosecutor."[20] Under such a statute, the plaintiff in the case cited was granted an injunction to restrain defendant from criminally selling liquor, although the plaintiff could show no special damage.

600; Waupun v. Moore, 34 Wis. 450, 17 Am. Rep. 446; Inc. Town of Rochester v. Walters, 27 Ind. App. 194, 60 N. E. 1101.

19 O'Brien v. Harris, 105 Ga. 732, 31 S. E. 745.

20 Littleton v. Fritz, 65 Iowa, 488, 54 Am. Rep. 19, 22 N. W. 641.

§ 479. **Same—Same—Suit by Government.**—As a public nuisance concerns the public generally, it is the duty of the government to take measures to abate or enjoin it. Hence it follows that the government can obtain an injunction to restrain a public nuisance, without showing any property right in itself. The duty of protecting the property rights of all its citizens is sufficient to warrant issuing the injunction. Therefore, wherever a public nuisance is shown, equity must enjoin it at the suit of the government. "Every place where a public statute is openly, publicly, repeatedly, continuously, persistently and intentionally violated, is a public nuisance."[21] This definition does not include all public nuisances, by any means; but it includes a class particularly covered by the principle under discussion. Injunctions obtained by the state to restrain the criminal sale of intoxicating liquors are among the most numerous of this class. Writs of this kind have been granted to restrain violations of prohibition laws,[22] and to restrain the maintenance of gambling-houses.[23] Where

21 State v. Crawford, 28 Kan. 726, 42 Am. Rep. 182.

22 State v. Crawford, 28 Kan. 726, 42 Am. Rep 182; State v. Greenway, 92 Iowa, 472, 61 N. W. 239; State v. Marston, 64 N. H. 603, 15 Atl. 222 The case of Manor Casino v. State (Tex.), 34 S. W. 769, seems *contra* to the proposition laid down in the text The court there held that in the absence of statute equity will not enjoin the criminal sale of liquor at the suit of the state, unless property rights are involved. It is possible that the cases may be reconciled on the theory that the sale of liquor is not of itself a nuisance. While the legislature cannot declare every act a nuisance (State v. Saunders, 66 N. H. 39, 25 Atl. 588, 18 L. R. A. 646), it can declare such an act as selling liquor to be a nuisance. When an act is a nuisance it *prima facie* affects property rights, and hence it can clearly be enjoined. Thus, where criminally selling liquor is a public nuisance, as it apparently is in Kansas, Iowa and New Hampshire, equity will interfere; where it is not, equity will not interfere.

23 State v. Noyes, 30 N. H. 279. The case of State v. Patterson, 14 Tex. Civ. App. 465, 37 S. W. 478, which seems *contra*, may be

prizefighting is regarded as a public nuisance, the state may enjoin individuals from taking any part in such contests, and from in any way aiding therein.[24] Of course, cases involving purprestures[25] or in which the defendant is emptying refuse into a public stream,[26] are clearly within the general principle.

§ 480. Same—Right of Government to Enjoin Act Analogous to Nuisance.—While the right of the government to obtain an injunction to restrain criminal acts is not confined strictly to cases of nuisance, it would seem that it should be limited to cases closely analogous. Such relief, if applied to criminal acts in general, would supersede the criminal law and deprive parties of the right to a jury trial. Where the property rights of many citizens are involved, it is proper for the government, on their behalf, to invoke the powers of equity; and it would seem that only in such a case should the jurisdiction be assumed.[27] By statute, it is provided

supported on the theory that gambling is not a public nuisance in Texas.

24 Columbian Athletic Club v. State, 143 Ind. 98, 52 Am. St. Rep. 407, 40 N. E. 914, 28 L. R. A. 727.

25 Attorney-General v. Cohoes Co., 6 Paige Ch. 133, 29 Am. Dec. 755.

26 People v. Truckee Lumber Co., 116 Cal. 397, 58 Am. St. Rep. 183, 48 Pac. 374, 39 L. R. A. 581.

27 In the case of In re Debs, 158 U. S. 564, 15 Sup. Ct. 900, 39 L. ed. 1092, the court said: "Every government, intrusted by the very terms of its being with powers and duties to be exercised and discharged for the general welfare, has a right to apply to its own courts for any proper assistance in the exercise of the one and the discharge of the other, and it is no sufficient answer to its appeal to one of those courts that it has no pecuniary interest in the matter. The obligations which it is under to promote the interest of all and to prevent the wrongdoing of one, resulting in injury to the general welfare, is often of itself sufficient to give it a standing in court." While this language is broad, it will be observed upon examination of the case that property rights both of the government

that violations of the interstate commerce act may be restrained at suit of the United States.[28]

§ 481. **Exception—Libel.**—An exception to the general rule that equity will restrain a crime at suit of an individual when property rights are involved, exists in cases of libel. The early English cases laid down the rule as stated, and held that equity has no jurisdiction to restrain libels.[29] It will be noticed, however, that in most cases of libel property rights are only indirectly, if at all, involved. But in cases where a man is directly libeled in his business, there is a question of property right. Realizing this, the later English cases, aided somewhat by statute, have receded from their former view, and will now restrain a libel when it directly affects business.[30] The American states, however, have generally refused to adopt the later rule. The rule was established in cases in which no property right was directly involved,[31] and is now so firmly settled, that it has been expressly held that libels will not be enjoined even for the protection of property.[32] This outcome is

and of many of its citizens were involved. It is believed that the jurisdiction will not be extended to crimes which, while injurious to society, do not directly affect any property right.

28 See United States v Elliott, 62 Fed. 801; Toledo, A. A. & N. M. R. Co. v. Penn. Co., 54 Fed. 730, 19 L R. A. 387; and see *post*, chapter XXVIII.

29 Prudential Assur. Co. v. Knott, L R. 10 Ch. App. 142.

30 Thorley's Cattle-food Co. v. Massam, 14 Ch. D. 763, Thomas v. Williams, 14 Ch. D. 864, Loog v. Bean, 26 Ch. D 306

31 Brandreth v. Lance, 8 Paige Ch. 24, 34 Am. Dec. 368; Boston Diatite Co. v. Florence Mfg. Co., 114 Mass. 69, 19 Am. Rep. 310.

32 De Wick v. Dobson, 18 App. Div. 399, 46 N. Y. Supp. 390; Kidd v. Horry, 28 Fed. 773. A compromise between the English and the American views was reached in Beck v. Railway Teamsters' Protective Union, 118 Mich. 497, 74 Am. St. Rep. 421, 77 N. W. 13, 42 L. R. A. 407. It was there held that a court of equity will restrain the publication of a libel consisting of a boycotting circular,

in part the result of a desire not to place any more restrictions upon the exercise of free speech than are absolutely necessary.

when the acts are accompanied by threats, express or covert, or intimidation and coercion, and the accomplishment of the purpose will result in irreparable injury to property. See, further, on this subject, *post*, chapter XXIX.

CHAPTER XXII.

INJUNCTION AGAINST WASTE.

ANALYSIS.

§ 482. **Origin and Nature of the Jurisdiction.**—"Waste is the destruction or improper deterioration or material alteration of things forming an essential part of the inheritance, done or suffered by a person rightfully in possession by virtue of a temporary or partial estate,—as, for example, a tenant for life or for years. The rightful possession of the wrongdoer is essential, and constitutes a material distinction between waste and trespass."[1] The jurisdiction of the common law over waste was curiously defective. Originally an action at common law for waste lay only against a defendant whose estate was created by law, on the theory that as to estates created by the owner of the fee, provision against waste should be made against it by himself or else it was his own default. This narrow jurisdiction was

1 4 Pom. Eq. Jur, § 1348. For the substance of this and the four succeeding chapters the author is indebted to Mr. J. T. Burcham formerly instructor in Equity in Stanford University.

early enlarged by statutes,[2] which, however, gave a remedy only in favor of one having an immediate estate of inheritance, so that a person holding any estate less than a fee, or one whose estate in fee was preceded by a smaller estate, had still no remedy at law.[3] It is evident that in such a situation there was a twofold reason for the interposition of equity to prevent waste. In the first place, from its very nature waste was a wrong such that the legal remedy of damages was inadequate. It involved as its chief characteristic a serious injury to real property, and, on this ground alone, a preventive remedy was necessary. It is true that the writ of *estrepement* was a preventive remedy, but at best it was only an auxiliary to real actions to preserve property *pendente lite*,[4] and hence had no application to the ordinary case of waste in which no question was made as to the tenant's right to possession. In the second place, the fact that there was in a large class of cases no remedy at all at law, furnished a sufficient ground for the jurisdiction of equity—at least in those cases.[5] Of the two reasons, the first was the controlling one, however, and the second was apparently often regarded as requiring some explanation to prove that it was not an obstacle to, rather than a ground of, equity jurisdiction.[6]

2 Statutes of Marlebridge (52 Hen. III, c. 23) and Gloucester (6 Edw. I, c 5).

3 2 Black. Com., 282, 283; 3 Id. 227.

4 3 Black. Com., 225-227.

5 See suggestion of counsel in Castlemain v. Craven, 22 Vin. Abr. 523; Skelton v. Skelton, 2 Swanst. 170.

6 Farrant v. Lovell, 3 Atk. 723; Perrot v. Perrot, 3 Atk. 94; Kane v. Vanderburgh, 1 Johns. Ch. 11 The explanation of this attitude of the chancery courts doubtless lay in the fact that equity jurisdiction over torts was primarily to furnish a better remedy for a *legal* wrong. Hence in determining the existence of the wrong, and from that inferring the right to a remedy, the equity judges were accustomed to follow the rule of law. Consequently they felt

The fact that waste is nearly always an irreparable injury has resulted in the full establishment of the remedy by injunction, whether in a case where there is or is not a legal remedy; and because prevention is of greater efficacy than damages after the event, the equitable remedy has not only virtually superseded the old common-law "action of waste," but has to a great extent taken the place of the "action on the case" for damages,[7] which might have supplied the lack of a remedy at law to those remainder-men who could not comply with the strict requisite of the statute of Gloucester.[8]

§ 483. **Extent of Equity Jurisdiction—Legal Waste.**—In entering upon a fuller discussion of the jurisdiction of equity over waste it will be convenient to follow the lines of old and familiar classification, and treat, first of *Legal Waste,* which is the waste that courts of law always recognized (though they did not in all cases give a remedy for it), and, next, of *Equitable Waste,* which is the waste that, by the rules of the common law, is permitted to a tenant in possession, but which courts of equity nevertheless do not allow. It has already been pointed out that from its very definition waste generally falls within that class of injuries which courts of equity deem irreparable and therefore not to be adequately remedied at law.[9] Hence injunctions against

the need of explaining why they gave a remedy where the courts of law did not. So, Lord Hardwicke, in Perrot v. Perrot, *supra,* said it was an "accident" that there was no legal remedy in the class of cases under discussion, and Lord Nottingham, in Skelton v. Skelton, 2 Swanst. 170, took the distinction that the tenant who committed waste in such cases had "only *impunitatem*" and not "a right in the thing itself."

7 4 Pom. Eq. Jur., § 1348.

8 See cases collected in 1 Ames, Cases in Eq. Juris., 467, note 1, 468, note 1.

9 In Vandemark v. Schoonmaker, 9 Hun, 11, the court used the

legal waste have always been common, and the jurisdiction extensive. Illustrations are injunctions against cutting timber,[10] changing, destroying or removing buildings, or the erection of new buildings,[11] taking minerals, gas or stone,[12] changing the character of land,[13] taking away crops, or manure,[14] and improper modes of tillage.[15] It should be noted in this connec-

following language: "Waste has always been a subject of chancery jurisdiction. It is generally irreparable in its results, and hence especially within the restraining power of that court. And it has been well remarked that courts of equity will exercise a liberal jurisdiction in respect to waste, and in its restraint."

10 Duvall v. Waters, 1 Bland (Md.), 569, 18 Am. Dec. 350; Sarles v. Sarles, 3 Sandf. Ch. 601; Kerlin v. West, 4 N. J. Eq. 449; Kane v. Vanderburgh, 1 Johns. Ch. 11; Hawley v. Clowes, 2 Johns. Ch. 122; Kyle v. Rhodes, 71 Miss. 487, 15 South. 40; State v. Judge, 52 La. Ann. 1037, 26 South. 769; Jones v. Britton, 102 N. C. 166, 9 S. E. 554, 4 L. R. A. 178; Elliott v. Boyd, 40 Or. 326, 67 Pac. 202.

11 Jungerman v. Bovee, 19 Cal. 354; Palmer v. Young, 108 Ill. App. 252; Maddox v. White, 4 Md. 72, 59 Am. Dec. 67; Snyder v. Hopkins, 31 Kan. 557, 3 Pac. 367; Woods v. Early, 95 Va. 307, 28 S. E. 374, Tate v. Field, 57 N. J. Eq. 53, 40 Atl. 206; Brock v. Dole, 66 Wis 142, 28 N. W. 334; Davenport v. Magoon, 13 Or. 1, 57 Am. Rep. 1.

12 Whitfield v Bewit, 2 P. Wms. 240, Gerkins v. Kentucky Salt Co., 100 Ky. 734, 66 Am. St Rep. 370, 39 S. W. 444; Smith v. City Council of Rome, 19 Ga. 89, 83 Am. Dec. 298; Chambers v. Alabama Iron Co., 67 Ala. 353; Binswanger v. Henninger, 1 Alaska, 509; Williamson v. Jones, 43 W. Va. 562, 64 Am. St. Rep. 891, 27 S. E. 411, 38 L. R A. 694.

13 Pulteney v. Shelton, 5 Ves. 259, note; Onslow v. ———, 16 Ves 173; Snyder v. Hopkins, 31 Kan. 557, 3 Pac. 367.

14 Pulteney v. Shelton, 5 Ves. 259, note, Onslow v. ———, 16 Ves. 173; Manning v. Ogden, 70 Hun, 399, 24 N. Y. Supp. 70; Baker v. National Biscuit Co., 96 Ill. App. 228; Ashby v. Ashby (N. J.), 40 Atl. 118.

15 Wilds v. Layton, 1 Del. Ch. 226, 12 Am. Dec. 91. Miscellaneous cases which may be added to those given above are, Bathurst v. Burden, 2 Bro. C. C. 84 (damaging fish-ponds); Pratt v. Brett, 2 Madd. 62 (sowing mustard seed, and other waste of common character); West Ham etc. Board v. East London Water Works Co., 69 L. J. Ch. 257, [1900] 1 Ch. 624, 84 L. T., N. S., 85, 48 Week. Rep. 284 (covering land with rubbish); Clagon v. Veasey, 7 Ired.

tion, however, that American courts frequently refuse to enjoin acts which the English courts would enjoin almost as a matter of course, not because the jurisdiction of equity is narrower in scope in this country, but because the substantive law of waste is different and more liberal. Courts of equity in denying injunctions have often had occasion to point out the differences. As said by the court in one case: "The law of waste, as understood in England, would have made it impossible for tenants to cultivate the wild lands of this country";[16] and in another: "To apply the ancient doctrines of waste to modern tenancies, even for short terms, would in some of our cities and villages put an entire stop to the progress of improvement, and would deprive the tenant of those benefits which both parties contemplated at the time of the demise, without any possible advantage to the owner of the reversion."[17] In the spirit of this language, knowing that conditions in this country often made acts really beneficial which, according to the strict definition of waste, fell easily within its scope, American judges have refused to enjoin the cutting of timber according to the rules of good husbandry,[18]

Eq. 173 (removal of a slave to parts unknown); Lehman v. Logan, 7 Ired. Eq. 296 (same as preceding case); Du Pre v. Williams, 5 Jones Eq. 96 (same as preceding case). Additional cases of the same kinds as given above are collected in 1 Ames, Cases in Eq Juris., 461, note

16 Crowe v. Wilson, 65 Md. 479, 57 Am. Rep. 343, 5 Atl. 427 See, also, 4 Pom. Eq. Jur., § 1348, note 1.

17 Winship v. Pitts, 3 Paige, 259.

18 Board of Supervisors of Warren Co. v. Gans, 80 Miss. 76, 31 South. 539; McLeod v. Dial, 63 Ark. 10, 37 S. W. 306; McCullough v. Irvine's Exrs., 13 Pa. St. 438; Lynn's Appeal, 31 Pa St. 44, 72 Am. Dec 721; Morris v. Knight, 14 Pa. Super. Ct. 324; Kidd v. Dennison, 6 Barb. 10; Alexander v. Fisher, 7 Ala. 514; Shine v Wilcox, 1 Dev & B. Eq. 631, Crowley v. Timberlake, 2 Ired. Eq. 460. See Disher v. Disher, 45 Neb. 100, 63 N. W. 368.

or the erection of new[19] or the destruction of old buildings.[20]

§ 484. **Waste must be Threatened.**—The purpose of this jurisdiction is, to prevent future acts of waste, and also, though rarely, to restore things to their former condition.[21] Hence, in general, an injunction will not be granted after the acts complained of are finished,[22] nor to prevent the removal of the personalty produced by acts of waste, such as timber cut.[23] In determining the propriety of granting its preventive remedy, equity requires a plaintiff to show a need of its protection. He must establish that the defendant has been guilty of acts or words which justify a reasonable apprehension on his part of future waste. "The court never grants injunctions on the principle that they will do no harm to the defendant, if he does not intend to commit the act in question—but if there be no ground for the injunction, it will not support it."[24] And a plaintiff who does not show a sufficient case of threatened waste will have his bill dismissed with costs.[25] This is not saying that the courts make a plaintiff's way hard or impose on him a heavy burden. For a single act of waste is considered a sufficient threat of further acts of the same kind;[26] or mere uttered threats, or acts

19 Winship v. Pitts, 3 Paige, 259

20 Crowe v. Wilson, 65 Md. 479, 57 Am. Rep. 343, 5 Atl. 427; Melms v. Pabst Brewing Co., 104 Wis. 7, 46 L. R. A. 478, 79 N. W. 738.

21 See *infra*, § 491.

22 Owen v. Ford, 49 Mo. 436; Southard v. Morris Canal Co., 1 N. J. Eq. 519.

23 Bishop of London v. Webb, 1 P. Wms. 527; Watson v. Hunter, 5 Johns. Ch. 169, 9 Am. Dec. 295.

24 Lord Elden in Coffin v. Coffin, Jacob, 70.

25 Clement v. Wheeler, 25 N H. 361.

26 Barry v. Barry, 1 Jacob & W. 651; Sarles v. Sarles, 3 Sandf. Ch. 601.

which, though not themselves waste, yet signify an intention to commit waste, will support an injunction.[27] And it is no defense to a bill for an injunction for a defendant who has been guilty of waste to say that he does not intend to do so again,[28] or that he has committed no waste since the filing of the bill,[29] or for one who has threatened waste to say that he does not mean to carry out his threat.[30] Such declarations do not, under the circumstances, overturn the case which the plaintiff has made, and the injunction will issue in spite of them.

§ 485. Legal Waste Which is not Subject to Injunction. In view of the extensive jurisdiction of equity over waste it is sometimes said that, in general, an injunction may be obtained to stay waste in all cases where an action of waste would lie at common law.[31] The qualifications to this statement of the scope of equity's jurisdiction over waste should be made at this point. They are three in number: First, equity will not enjoin permissive waste.[32] The reason for this holding is not made clear in the cases. In one of them[33] counsel argued, that to grant such injunctions "would tend to

27 Jackson v. Cator, 5 Ves. 688; Coffin v. Coffin, Jacob, 70; London v. Warfield, 5 J. J. Marsh. (Ky.) 196; Sheridan v. McMullen, 12 Or. 150, 6 Pac. 497; Duvall v. Waters, 1 Bland Ch. (Md.) 569, 18 Am. Dec. 350, 357; Palmer v. Young, 108 Ill. App. 252, citing Pom. Eq. Jur., §§ 237, 1348.

28 Packington v. Packington, Dick. 101; Sowerby v. Fryer, L R. 8 Eq. 417.

29 Attorney-General v. Burrows, Dick. 128.

30 Packington v. Packington, *supra.*

31 Duvall v. Waters, 1 Bland Ch (Md.) 569, 18 Am. Dec 350, 357.

32 Castlemain v. Craven, 22 Vin. Abr 523; Powys v. Blagrave, 4 De Gex, M. & G. 448, 458; Wood v. Gaynon, Amb. 395; Cannon v. Barry, 59 Miss. 289, 303. But see Bathurst v Burden, 2 Bro. C C 64, Caldwall v. Baylis, 2 Mer. 408; Williams v. Peabody, 8 Hun, 271; 2 Story, Eq Jur., § 917.

33 Wood v. Gaynon, *supra.*

harass tenants for life, and jointresses, and suits of this kind would be attended with great expense in depositions about the repairs." A more satisfactory reason would seem to be the same one which leads to the refusal to decree specific performance of contracts to make repairs, viz., the practical difficulty of giving adequate supervision to the performance of the decree. Second, equity will not enjoin ameliorating waste, which is any act that though technically waste, yet in fact improves the inheritance.[34] The reason for refusing the injunction in such cases is obvious. And, third, equity will not enjoin trivial acts of waste, but will require that substantial damage be shown.[35]

§ 486. **Must the Injury be Irreparable?**—The last preceding statement immediately suggests the inquiry whether a showing of even substantial damage is enough to justify an injunction against waste. Does not the usual rule that a legal wrong will be enjoined only when the legal remedy is inadequate apply here, and must not the injury therefore be irreparable? It would seem that in assuming jurisdiction over waste the courts have not always had this fundamental inquiry in mind; or else have considered it not the test of jurisdiction. Hence injunctions have been granted when, tested by the above rule, it would seem they should have been denied, as when the waste consisted in carrying away personal property not possessing any peculiar qualities or special value.[36] And in such cases

34 Doherty v Allman, L. R. 3 App. Cas. 709; Meux v. Cobley, [1892] 2 Ch. 253; Mollineux v. Powell, 3 P. Wms 268n (F).

35 Mollineux v. Powell, 3 P. Wms. 268n (F); Barry v. Barry, 1 Jacob & W. 651; Doherty v. Allman, L. R. 3 App. Cas. 709; Birch-Wolfe v. Birch, L. R 9 Eq. 683.

36 Pulteney v. Shelton, 5 Ves. 259, note; Onslow v. ——, 16 Ves. 173; Georges Creek etc. Co. v. Detmold, 1 Md. Ch. 371.

some American courts have taken the contrary view.[37] If prohibited by a covenant in a lease, it seems that the fair weight of authority holds in favor of granting the injunction against any waste, whether causing irreparable injury or not.[38]

§ 487. **Plaintiff's Title.**—A great deal has always been said in the cases about the title which a plaintiff who is seeking an injunction against waste must show, and of the effect on plaintiff's right to the injunction of a dispute as to title between him and the defendant. It is to be noted that there are here two distinct questions, which have not always been kept clearly apart. The first is as to the showing of title which a plaintiff must make in his bill to entitle him to relief, assuming his allegations of title to be admitted; it is the question of title which is raised by a demurrer to the bill as being insufficient in the allegations of title. The second is raised when the plaintiff's allegations of title, sufficient in themselves, are disputed by the defendant. In answer to the first question it can be said that the courts

37 Gregory v. Hay, 3 Cal. 332; Greathouse v. Greathouse, 46 W. Va. 21, 32 S. E. 994. The question does not seem to have arisen often, doubtless because of the fact (already suggested) that waste is generally, from its very nature, a serious injury to realty, and hence obviously within the class of acts called irreparable. It is interesting to note in this connection and in view of the difference of holdings of modern courts on the point in trespass cases, that so long ago as 1792 Lord Thurlow, in Smallman v. Onions, 3 Brown Ch 621, held the insolvency of the defendant a sufficient ground for enjoining waste.

38 Tipping v. Eckersley, 2 Kay & J. 264; Steward v. Winters, 4 Sandf. Ch. 587; Frank & Co. v. Bounneman, 8 W. Va. 462; Barret v. Blagrave, 5 Ves. 555; and see note to Maddox v. White, 4 Md 72, in 59 Am. Dec. 67, 70. The ground of the jurisdiction in such cases is probably to avoid multiplicity of suits for a continuing breach of covenant. This reason may reconcile Gregory v. Hay, 3 Cal 332, in which case an injunction against violation of a lease was refused.

require the plaintiff to set out his chain of title fully and to support it by positive evidence.[39] Hence Lord Thurlow in an early case refused to grant a temporary injunction because the plaintiff made affidavit generally that he was entitled to a fee simple and did not set out a particular title. And shortly afterwards Lord Eldon refused a motion for injunction because, though the plaintiff alleged his title sufficiently, yet his affidavits supported it only as a matter of belief on plaintiff's part, the court saying there ought to be "positive evidence of an actual title." The reason for this rule is stated in a recent American case as follows: "This rule is a simple recognition of the general principle that one is not entitled to invoke the extraordinary powers of a court of equity unless he can establish in a manner satisfactory to the law the fact that he will[40] suffer an irreparable injury in his estate. Unless the estate be his, he can suffer no injury, and unless the title be in him there is no estate."[41] In other words, for a plaintiff to obtain standing in a court of equity to enjoin waste, he must make a *prima facie* showing of title in himself. It is sometimes said that a plaintiff must show a "clear title" upon "unquestionable evi-

39 Whitelegg v. Whitelegg, 1 Bro. C C. 57, by Lord Thurlow, Davis v. Leo, 6 Ves. 784, by Lord Eldon, Wearin v. Munson, 62 Iowa, 466, 17 N. W. 746, Denning v. Corwin, 4 Wend. 208. In the last case cited a part of the reason for refusing a temporary injunction was that it was consistent with plaintiff's allegation of title that the defendants were tenants in common with him and therefore not wrong-doers. See also, Field v. Jackson, Dick. 599.

40 The word "may," it is submitted, would be a better one here.

41 Flannery v. Hightower, 97 Ga. 592, 25 S E. 371. It should be said that the language quoted was used in support of the holding that a mere dispute as to title between plaintiff and defendant *per se* precludes the granting of a temporary injunction—a proposition which, it will be shown, is not supported by the sound weight of authority.

dence"[42]—a requirement which seems more strict than is demanded either on principle or on authority, and the application of which would prevent the granting of an injunction in any case whenever there is a substantial dispute as to title between plaintiff and defendant.

§ 488. **Title in Dispute.**—And this is the state of facts which raises the second question above mentioned. In the definition of waste at the beginning of this chapter it is pointed out that the material distinction between waste and trespass in equity lies in the fact that waste is committed by one rightfully in possession, trespass, by one wrongfully in possession or not in possession at all. This is a purely technical distinction, and hence identical acts will in one case be waste, in another, trespass. Influenced by this identity of substance, it has been an inveterate habit of equity judges and lawyers since the time of Lord Eldon[43] to speak of acts as "waste" when with strict observance of the technical distinction they would have called them trespass It is clear that in cases of waste, strictly, since it involves privity of title and rightful possession of defendant, disputes as to title will not often be present. And a scrutiny of the cases shows this to be true, most of those in which there have been decision or *dictum* as to the effect of a dispute concerning title on the granting of an injunction to stay "waste" being really cases of trespass. A fuller discussion of the subject is therefore reserved for the chapter on Trespass. It may be sufficient to point out here that, if there is really a substantial dispute as to title, the injunction prayed, and the only

42 See Flannery v. Hightower, *supra*, and cases collected in notes to Whitelegg v. Whitelegg, *supra*, and Davis v. Leo, *supra;* High on Injunctions, § 651.

43 Pillsworth v. Hopton, 6 Ves. 51.

one proper to grant, generally, is a temporary injunction pending the settlement of the dispute; that a stronger case of apprehended injury must be shown to entitle a plaintiff to a temporary than to a permanent injunction, because of the injury which the injunction will have done the defendant if he eventually prove title in himself;[44] and, finally, that if the above conditions are complied with, though the authorities are not uniform, the injunction will issue.[45]

§ 489. **Equitable Waste—Definition.**—Equitable waste arose out of the different effect given in law and in equity to the phrase "without impeachment of waste," or equivalent words, in a lease, or the settlement or devise creating an estate less than a fee. Courts of law held that such a phrase gave to the tenant the same absolute power of changing or destroying the inheritance that a tenant in fee would have. Courts of equity early "set up a superior equity"[46] and began to restrain acts

44 See Lusting v. Conn, 1 Ir. Ch. 273.

45 Case cited in Mogg v. Mogg, Dick. 670; Duvall v. Waters, 1 Bland (Md.), 569, 18 Am. Dec 350; Woods v. Riley, 72 Miss. 73, 18 South. 384; Baker v. National Biscuit Co., 96 Ill. App. 228; Meadow Valley Mining Co. v. Dodds, 6 Nev. 261; Littlejohn v Leffingwell, 40 App. Div. 13, 57 N. Y. Supp. 839; Dooley v. Stringham, 4 Utah, 107, 7 Pac. 405 (a case of real waste, dispute being as to extent of plaintiff's estate), citing 2 Pom. Eq Jur., §§ 917, 919; 4 Pom. Eq. Jur., 1348. *Contra*, Nevitt v. Gillespie, 1 How. (Miss.) 108, 26 Am. Dec. 696; Poindexter v. Henderson, 1 Miss. (Walk.) 176, 12 Am. Dec. 550, Lewis v. Christian, 40 Ga. 187; Flannery v. Hightower, 97 Ga. 592, 25 S. E. 371; Blackwood v. Van Vleet, 11 Mich. 252. See further cases cited *infra* under same subject in chapter on Trespass. It should be added that the holding of an early case (Lathropp v. Marsh, 5 Ves. 259) that a landlord cannot enjoin waste by a tenant unless he has brought ejectment is discredited: Note 2 to the case, 5 Ves. 261; Kane v. Vanderburgh, 1 Johns. Ch. 11; Eden on Injunctions, 237, note (b).

46 Per Lord Hardwicke, in Rolt v. Lord Somerville, 2 Eq. Cas. Abr. 759. See, also, opinion of Lord Turner in Micklethwait v. Micklethwait, 1 De Gex & J. 504, 524.

by the tenant that were really destructive, and after more or less diversity of opinion[47] finally adopted as the equitable waste which would not be allowed even to a tenant without impeachment of waste, "that which a prudent man would not do in the management of his own property."[48] This definition makes the phrase "without impeachment of waste" nothing more than a corrective of the close restrictions which the common law put on the rights of a tenant who held impeachable of waste, and is strikingly similar to the definitions of legal waste often given by American courts.[49]

§ 490. Extent of Jurisdiction.—The cases of equitable waste are almost, if not exclusively, confined to destruction or removal of buildings,[50] carrying away of the soil,[51] cutting ornamental or sheltering trees or

47 See opinion of Lord Nottingham in Skelton v. Skelton, 2 Swanst. 170; of Lord Parker in Bishop of London v. Web, 1 P. Wms 527; of Lord Hardwicke in Aston v. Aston, 1 Ves Sr. 264; and of Lord Eldon in Smythe v. Smythe, 2 Swanst. 251.

48 Per Lord Campbell in Turner v. Wright, 3 De Gex, F. & J 234, 243. For substantially similar descriptions of equitable waste, see Baker v. Sebright, L. R. 13 Ch. D. 179, 186, Stevens v. Rose, 69 Mich. 259, 37 N. W. 205, 210; Duncombe v. Felt, 81 Mich. 332, 45 N. W. 1004, 1006. In this last case the defendants had conveyed land, taking back a lease for life which contained the following clause. "And it is expressly understood that the second parties are to have as full and complete control of said premises . . . . as though such conveyance had not been made." Yet they were enjoined from stripping the land of timber. Lord Campbell also pointed out in Turner v. Wright, *supra*, that no sensible distinction in waste can be based upon the malice of the defendant, though it is often said that equity will enjoin a tenant from committing malicious waste

49 See cases cited, *ante*, § 483.

50 Vane v. Barnard, 2 Vern 738; Rolt v Somerville, 2 Eq Cas. Abr 759, Anonymous, Mos. 237; Williams v. Day, 2 Cas in Ch. 32; Stevens v. Rose, 69 Mich. 259, 37 N. W 205 (action on the case for damages under statute [How. St. Mich., c. 271, § 1], but decided according to principles of equitable waste).

51 Bishop of London v. Web, 1 P. Wms. 527.

shrubs,[52] cutting saplings,[53] and stripping the land of timber.[54] Of these various classes the first two need no special mention, the cases in them being very few and founded on obvious reasons "Ornamental" as applied to trees and shrubs in matters of equitable waste is a technical term. "The question is not, whether the timber is or is not ornamental; but the fact to be determined is that it was planted for ornament; or, if not originally planted for ornament, was, as we express it, left standing for ornament by some person having the absolute power of disposition."[55] It is also held that cutting trees planted to exclude certain objects from view will be enjoined, on the same principle;[56] and that the owner of the fee may change ornamental timber into non-ornamental timber.[57] The principle would, therefore, seem to be, that whatever trees or shrubbery the last owner of the fee manifests an intention to have left standing, is within the rule as to equitable waste. The cutting of saplings is enjoined on the ground that as they are not fit for timber it is despoiling the estate as a prudent owner would not do.[58]

52 Packington's Case, 3 Atk 215; Coffin v. Coffin, Jacob, 70; Wombwell v. Belasyse, 6 Ves. (2d ed.) 110a, note; Morris v. Morris, 15 Sim. 505 (injunction granted, though house about which the trees had formerly stood had been removed; cf. Micklethwait v. Micklethwait, 1 De Gex & J. 504); Wellesley v. Wellesley, 6 Sim. 497; Stevens v. Rose, 69 Mich 259, 37 N. W. 205. And see other cases collected in 1 Ames, Cases in Eq Juris., 469, note 2

53 Aston v. Aston, 1 Ves. Sr. 264; O'Brien v. O'Brien, Amb. 107; Chamberlayn v. Dummer, 1 Bro. C. C. 166; Strathmore v. Bowes, 2 Bro. C. C. 88; Allard v. Jones, 15 Ves. 605.

54 Bishop of Winchester's Case, 1 Rolle Abr. 380 (J, 3); Duncombe v. Felt, 81 Mich. 332, 45 N. W. 1004.

55 Per Lord Eldon in Wombwell v. Belasyse, 6 Ves. (2d ed.) 110a, note See, also, Downshire v. Sandys, 6 Ves. 107; Burges v. Lamb, 16 Ves. 174, 185.

56 Day v. Merry, 16 Ves 375.

57 Micklethwait v. Micklethwait, 1 De Gex & J 504.

58 This was admitted to be equitable waste by Lord Eldon, who

Stripping the land of timber is likewise enjoined because fair husbandry forbids it.[59]

§ 491. **Relief Against Waste in Equity.**—The only relief against legal waste for which one is entitled to come into equity is an injunction. This injunction is almost always prohibitive, but in a proper case it may be mandatory for the restoration of the thing destroyed.[60] But though one can secure standing in equity with reference to legal waste only because of his right to an injunction, he is also in addition given an accounting for the waste already done. This further relief is given on the broad general principle of equity that when once it has acquired jurisdiction of a case it will give complete relief, even though part of such relief be purely legal in its nature, rather than to compel a plaintiff to bring another suit at law in order to obtain the full remedy to which he is entitled.[61] This accounting is given only as an incident to the injunction, which is the basis of plaintiff's right in equity, and therefore it cannot be prayed alone; and if the injunction is refused the right to the accounting falls with it.[62] The proceeds of such waste to go to the remainder-man in fee, though there be intermediate remainder-men for life or years, following

was inclined to restrict cases of equitable waste more than later judges: Smythe v. Smythe, 2 Swanst. 251.

59 Duncombe v. Felt, 81 Mich. 332, 45 N. W. 1004.

60 Vane v. Lord Barnard, 2 Vern. 738, Prec. Ch. 454; Rolt v. Lord Somerville, 2 Eq. Cas. Abr. 759, Bass v. Metropolitan etc. Co., 82 Fed. 857, 27 C. C. A. 147, 39 L. R. A. 711; Klie v. Von Broock, 56 N. J. Eq. 18, 37 Atl. 469.

61 Jesus College v. Bloom, Amb. 54, 3 Atk. 262; Castleman v. Craven, 22 Vin. Abr. 523; Jungerman v. Vovee, 19 Cal. 354; Williamson v. Jones, 43 W. Va. 562, 64 Am. St Rep. 891, 27 S. E. 411, 38 L. R. A. 694.

62 Jesus College v. Bloom, Amb. 54, 3 Atk. 262; Smith v. Cooke, 3 Atk. 378; Watson v. Hunter, 5 Johns. Ch. 169, 9 Am. Dec. 295; Lippincott v. Barton, 42 N. J. Eq. 272, 10 Atl. 884.

the legal rule that the person in whom is the fee has title to, and may bring trover for, the personalty which results from acts of waste.[63] The accounting for equitable waste differs from that given for legal waste in one particular. Since equitable waste is wholly a creation of the courts of equity, there is no legal remedy for it whether it is past or future. Hence, one may file his bill for an accounting for equitable waste without praying, or being entitled to, an injunction.[64] The accounting which equity gives for waste, both legal and equitable, differs from the damages a court of law gives for the former in that it is estimated according to the profits which the wrong-doer has received, and not according to the damage done to the estate nor the value of the personalty produced by the acts of waste;[65] and no allowance is made for the defendant's labor or expense.[66]

§ 492. **Parties for and Against Whom Injunction will Issue.**—It remains to note the estates of parties for and against whom injunctions to prevent waste will issue. No citations will be needed to show that a reversioner or remainder-man in fee may enjoin waste. So may a contingent remainder-man,[67] a trustee to preserve contin-

63 Whitfield v. Bewit, 2 P. Wms. 240; Rolt v. Somerville, 2 Eq. Cas. Abr. 759; Castlemain v. Craven, 22 Vin. Abr. 523; Gent v. Harrison, Johns. 517; Birchwolfe v. Birch, L. R. 9 Eq. 683.

64 Whitfield v. Bewit, 2 P. Wms. 240, Lansdowne v. Lansdowne, 1 Madd. 116; Lushington v. Boldero, 15 Beav. 1; Gent v. Harrison, Johns 517.

65 Lee v. Alton, 1 Ves. 78, 82; Morris v. Morris, 2 De Gex & J. 323, Tate v. Field, 57 N. J. Eq. 53, 40 Atl. 206.

66 Sweeney v. Hanley, 126 Fed. 97.

67 Brashear v. Macey, 3 J. J. Marsh. 89; University v. Tucker, 31 W. Va. 621, 8 S. E. 410; Cannon v. Barry, 59 Miss. 289; Peterson v. Ferrell, 127 N. C. 169, 37 S. E. 189; Kallock v. Webb, 113 Ga. 762, 39 S. E. 339.

gent remainders,[68] or a tenant for life whether with or without impeachment of waste.[69] A mortgagee or a purchaser at a foreclosure sale may also enjoin waste by a mortgagor in possession who threatens to do acts which impair his security.[70] The injunction will not issue, however, unless the sufficiency of the security is threatened.[71] But in determining this point, the courts aim to protect the mortgaged property up to "the value which was the basis of the contract between the parties at the time it was entered into."[72] Equity jurisdiction over mortgaged property rests on a broader ground than in most cases of waste, since courts of equity have very fully taken the entire subject of mortgages into their hands. Hence mortgages of personal property are given the same protection as those of realty.[73] On the same principle of protecting a secur-

68 Garth v. Cotton, 1 Ves. 524, 556, Dick. 183, 1 Lead. Cas. Eq. (4th Am. ed.) 955; Perrot v. Perrot, 3 Atk. 94.

69 Perrot v. Perrot, 3 Atk. 94; Rolt v. Somerville, 2 Eq. Cas. Abr. 759, Davis v. Leo, 6 Ves. 784; Halstead v. Coen, 31 Ind. App. 302, 67 N. E. 757.

70 Parsons v. Hughes, 12 Md. 1; Bunker v. Locke, 15 Wis. 635; Humphreys v. Harrison, 1 Jacob & W. 581; Usborne v. Usborne, Dick. 75; Brady v. Waldron, 2 Johns. Ch. 148, Phoenix v. Clark, 6 N. J. Eq. 447; Taylor v. Collins, 51 Wis. 123, 8 N. W. 22; Moses v. Johnson, 88 Ala. 517, 16 Am. St. Rep. 58, 7 South. 146, Robinson v. Russell, 24 Cal. 467; Mitchell v. Amador etc. Co., 75 Cal. 464, 17 Pac. 246; Lavenson v. Standard Soap Co., 80 Cal. 245, 13 Am. St. Rep. 147, 22 Pac. 184; Minneapolis Trust Co. v. Veshulst, 74 Ill. App 350; Life Ins. Co. v. Bigler, 79 N. Y. 568; Beaver Lumber Co. v. Eccles, 43 Or. 400, 99 Am. St. Rep. 759, 73 Pac. 201; Terry v. Robbins, 122 Fed. 725.

71 Fairbank v. Cudworth, 33 Wis 358; Smith v. Frio County (Tex. Civ. App.), 50 S. W. 958; Moriarty v. Ashworth, 43 Minn. 1, 19 Am. St. Rep. 203, 44 N. W. 531; Beaver etc. Co. v. Eccles, 43 Or. 400, 99 Am. St. Rep. 759, 73 Pac. 201; Robinson v. Russell, 24 Cal. 467.

72 King v. Smith, 2 Hare, 239, 243, Moriarty v. Ashworth, 43 Minn 1, 19 Am. St. Rep. 203, 44 N. W. 531.

73 McCormick v Hartley, 107 Ind. 248, 6 N. E. 357; Brown v. Stewart, 1 Md. Ch. Dec. 87, Clagett v. Salmon, 5 Gill & J. 314; Bagnall

ity, a vendor of land who retains title may enjoin waste by a vendee in possession,[74] and a vendee, because of his equitable estate, may enjoin a vendor in possession.[75] So, also, the security of an attachment creditor[76] or judgment creditor,[77] or the lien which a landlord has for rent[78] will be protected by injunction. It was formerly thought that, because of the nature of their legal rights, an injunction would not issue between tenants in common for any ordinary acts of waste either legal or equitable, but that acts of waste so destructive as to go beyond the requisites of either of these might be enjoined.[79] But the cases show that the exercise of equity jurisdiction is now more liberal, and any acts of waste by one tenant in common that are inconsistent with prudent management of the estate or that jeopardize the interest of his co-tenants will be enjoined.[80] An underlessee will be enjoined from

v. Villar, L. R. 12 Ch. D. 812; Parsons v. Hughes, 12 Md 1, State v. Northern Cent. Ry. Co., 18 Md. 193, Walker v. Radford, 67 Ala. 446.

74 Moses Brothers v. Johnson, 88 Ala. 517, 16 Am. St. Rep. 58, 7 South. 146; Taylor v. Collins, 51 Wis. 123, 8 N. W. 22, May v. Williams, 22 Ky. Law Rep. 1328, 60 S. W. 525, Shickell v. Berryville etc. Co., 3 Va. Sup. Ct. 45; Miller v. Waddingham, 91 Cal 377, 27 Pac. 750, 13 L. R A. 680 And see cases collected in 1 Ames, Cases in Eq Juris, 222, note 2, 483, note 1

75 Smith & Fleek's Appeal, 69 Pa. St. 474; Chambers v. Alabama Iron Co, 67 Ala. 353.

76 Camp v. Bates, 11 Conn 51, 27 Am Dec. 707; People v. Van Buren, 136 N. Y. 252, 32 N. E. 775, 33 N. E. 743, 20 L. R. A. 446; Moritz v. Kaliske, 31 Abb. N. C. 49, 28 N. Y. Supp. 380.

77 Jones v. Britton, 102 N. C 166, 9 S. E. 554, 4 L. R. A. 178; Hughlett v. Harris, 1 Del. Ch. 349, 12 Am. Dec. 104; Vandemark v. Schoonmaker, 9 Hun, 16; Tessier v. Wyse, 3 Bland Ch. (Md.) 28.

78 Garner v. Cutting, 32 Iowa, 547, Carson v. Electric etc. Co., 85 Iowa, 44, 51 N W. 1144.

79 Smallman v. Onions, 3 Bro. C. C. 621; Hale v. Thomas, 7 Ves. 589; Twort v. Twort, 16 Ves. 128.

80 Hawley v. Clowes, 2 Johns. Ch. 122; Woods v. Early, 95 Va. 307, 28 S E. 374, Arthur v. Lamb, 2 Drew. & S 430; Southworth v.

waste at suit of the ground landlord.[81] A tenant in tail will not be restrained from waste, because he may at any time bar the entail and give himself a fee;[82] but tenant in tail after possibility of issue extinct is subject to be restrained from committing equitable waste[83] And the owner in fee of an estate subject to an executory devise will also be enjoined from committing equitable waste.[84] Tenant by the curtesy is subject to injunction against all waste.[85] The injunction against waste may include anyone who is colluding with the tenant in committing it.[86]

Smith, 27 Conn. 355, 71 Am. Dec. 72; Connole v. Boston etc. Co., 20 Mont. 523, 52 Pac. 263; Morrison v. Morrison, 122 N. C. 598, 29 S. E. 901; Williamson v. Jones, 43 W. Va. 562, 64 Am. St. Rep. 891, 27 S. E. 411, 38 L. R. A. 694, State v. Judge, 52 La. Ann. 103, 26 South. 769; Mott v. Underwood, 148 N. Y. 463, 51 Am. St. Rep. 711, 42 N. E. 1048; Ashby v. Ashby (N. J.), 40 Atl. 118, Binswanger v. Henninger, 1 Alaska, 509.

81 Farrant v. Lovel, 3 Atk. 723, Maddox v. White, 4 Md. 72, 59 Am. Dec. 67.

82 Turner v. Wright, 2 De Gex, F. & J. 234; Savile's Case, Cases *temp.* Talbot, 16 (cited), Attorney-General v. Marlborough, 3 Madd. 498. *Contra*, Wallington v. Taylor, 1 N. J. Eq. 314, 318

83 Williams v. Day, 2 Cas. in Ch. 32; Attorney-General v. Marlborough, 3 Madd. 498.

84 Turner v. Wright, 2 De Gex, F. & J. 234; Wallington v. Taylor, 1 N. J. Eq. 314, 318; Gannon v. Peterson, 193 Ill. 372, 62 N. E. 210, 55 L. R. A. 701. *Contra*, Matthews v. Hudson, 81 Ga. 120, 12 Am. St. Rep. 305, 7 S. E. 286.

85 Ware v. Ware, 6 N. J. Eq. 117.

86 Rodgers v. Rodgers, 11 Barb. 595.

CHAPTER XXIII.

INJUNCTIONS AGAINST TRESPASS.

ANALYSIS.

§ 493. **Nature of the Jurisdiction.**—The term "trespass" as used in equity differs from waste in respect to the privity of title between the plaintiff and the defendant, and in respect to the rightfulness of the defendant's possession of the land, which two facts constitute the technical requisites of waste. It differs from trespass in law in that it does not require that plaintiff be either entitled to, or actually in, possession, but includes also cases in which plaintiff's action at law would be on the case or in ejectment. At an early day the court of chancery refused to interfere and restrain any trespasser. Lord Thurlow broke through this rule, and began to use the preventive relief against such wrongs. He was followed by Lord Eldon,[1] and the jurisdiction is now firmly established in its principles, although there is no little disagreement among the courts—and especially the American courts—in applying these principles.[2] The ultimate criterion by which the jurisdiction is determined is the inadequacy of the legal remedy, but this the cases prove to be a somewhat flexible standard. The ideal remedy in any perfect system of administering justice would be that which absolutely precludes the commission of a wrong, not that which awards punishment or satisfaction for a wrong after it is committed.[3] Tried by this test all legal remedies are inadequate, and if "adequacy of legal remedy" were used in this sense by courts of equity they would enjoin any and all threatened trespasses, however trivial, whether to realty or to personalty—a length, it is hardly necessary to say, to which they have never gone

§ 494. **Extent of the Jurisdiction.**—Instead, the equity courts have marked the limits of their jurisdiction far short of this. Trespasses to personalty are not enjoined at all, in general, on the ground that for a trespass, even one so serious as to amount to complete destruction, the damages which a jury will award are an

1 Hamilton v. Worsefold, 10 Ves. 290, note (3). See opinions of Lord Eldon in Hanson v. Gardiner, 7 Ves. 305; Thomas v. Oakley, 18 Ves. 184; Mitchell v. Dors, 6 Ves. 147.

2 4 Pom. Eq. Jur., § 1356. The subject of injunctions against trespass is treated in the monographic note to Moore v. Halliday, 43 Or. 243, 99 Am. St. Rep. 724, 72 Pac. 801.

3 Pom. Eq. Jur., § 1357. This section of Pom. Eq. Jur. is quoted to this effect in Xenia Real Estate Co. v. Macy, 147 Ind. 568, 47 N. E. 147.

adequate remedy.[4] And the same thing is true of trespasses to realty when they consist of single acts or of occasional acts which are temporary in their nature and effect, and which are of such nature that damages as estimated by a jury will be adequate reparation.[5] On the other side, speaking now affirmatively of the many cases in which trespasses to realty are enjoined, they can be divided into the following four classes: 1. The legal remedy is inadequate because the injury is irreparable in its nature. 2. The legal remedy is inadequate because the trespass is continuous, or because repeated acts of wrong are done or threatened, although each of these acts, taken by itself, is not destructive. 3. The legal remedy is inadequate because the defendant is insolvent. 4. The legal remedy is inadequate in a miscellaneous class of cases because the courts of law for one reason or another cannot give any or, at best, not accurately estimated or sufficient damages, though damages would be a perfectly adequate *kind* of remedy. The four classes will be discussed in order.

4 This familiar rule does not require extensive citation of cases to support it; see however, Kistler v. Weaver, 135 N. C. 388, 47 S. E. 478; Gannon v. Denney (Neb.), 97 N. W. 959. It is subject to an exception in the case of chattels of unique or peculiar qualities such that damages for their injury or destruction would be an inadequate remedy: Arundell v. Phipps, 10 Ves. 139. See cases collected in 1 Ames, Eq. Juris., 532, note 2.

5 Indian Land & Trust Co. v. Shoenfelt (C. C. A.), 135 Fed. 484; Kredo v. Phelps, 145 Cal. 526, 78 Pac. 1044; Griffith v. Hilliard, 64 Vt. 643, 25 Atl. 427; Smith v. Pettingill, 15 Vt. 82, 40 Am. Dec. 667; Hunting v. Hartford St. Ry. Co., 73 Conn. 179, 46 Atl. 824; Peterson v. Orr, 12 Ga. 466, 58 Am. Dec. 484; Putney v. Bright, 106 Ga 199, 32 S E. 107; Fort Clark etc. Co. v. Anderson, 108 Ill. 643, 48 Am. Rep 545; Bridges v. Sargent, 1 Kan. App. 442, 40 Pac. 823; Sims v. City of Frankfort, 79 Ind. 446; Miller v. Burket, 132 Ind. 470, 32 N. E. 309; Cross v Morristown, 18 N. J. Eq. 305; Worthington v. Moon, 53 N. J. Eq 46, 30 Atl 251; Hart & Hoy v. Mayor etc. Albany, 9 Wend. 571, 24 Am Dec. 165, Gates v. Johnstown Lumber Co, 172 Mass. 495, 52 N. E. 736; Garrett v. Bishop, 27 Or. 349, 41 Pac. 10;

§ 495. **Irreparable Injury.**—The term "irreparable" has been often defined by the courts in varying language.[6] It is believed that the characteristics which

Cresap v. Kemble, 26 W. Va. 603; Le Roy v. Wright, 4 Saw. 530, Fed. Cas. No. 8273; Kennedy v. Elliott, 85 Fed. 832; Thorn v. Sweeney, 12 Nev. 251; Birmingham etc. Co. v. Birmingham etc. Co., 119 Ala. 137, 24 South. 502, 43 L. R. A. 233, Washington etc. Co. v. Cœur d'Alene etc. Co., 2 Idaho, 580, 21 Pac. 562; Moore v. Halliday, 43 Or. 243, 97 Am. St. Rep. 724, 72 Pac. 801; O'Neil v. City of McKeesport, 201 Pa. St 386, 50 Atl. 920.

6 The following are examples of the more carefully worded definitions: "Irreparable, as being beyond any method of pecuniary estimation": Per Van Fleet, J., in Kellogg v. King, 114 Cal. 378, 55 Am. St. Rep. 74, 46 Pac. 166. "An injury is irreparable when it is of such nature that the injured party cannot be adequately compensated therefor in damages, or when the damages which may result therefrom cannot be measured by any certain pecuniary standard": Per Lyon, J., in Wilson v. City of Mineral Point, 39 Wis. 160. "The word 'irreparable' means that which cannot be repaired, restored or adequately compensated for in money, or where the compensation cannot be safely measured": Per Brannon, J., in Bettman v. Horness, 42 W. Va. 433, 26 S. E. 271, 36 L. R. A. 566.

"In the application of this restriction much difficulty occurs in defining what injury is irreparable. The word means that which cannot be repaired, put back again, atoned for. The most absolute and positive instance of it is the cutting down 'ornamental trees,' such as the noble oaks in our State-House grove. 'A tree that is cut down cannot be made to grow again.' But the meaning of the word 'irreparable' pointed out by this example, is not that which has been adopted by the courts either in England or in this state. Grass that is cut down cannot be made to grow again, but the injury can be adequately atoned for in money. The result of the cases fixes this to be the rule: The injury must be of a peculiar nature, so that compensation in money cannot atone for it; where from its nature it may be thus atoned for, if in the particular case the party be insolvent, and on that account unable to atone for it, it will be irreparable": Per Pearson, J., in Gause v. Perkins, 56 N. C. (3 Jones Eq.) 177, 69 Am. Dec. 728, 730. In the leading case of Jerome v. Ross, 7 Johns. Ch. 315, 332, 11 Am. Dec. 484, 487, 488, Chancellor Kent defined "irreparable" as the "great and irremediable mischief, which damages could not compensate, because the mischief reaches to the very substance and value of the estate, and goes to the destruction of it in the character in which it is enjoyed" But that this definition of Chancellor Kent is far too narrow, in the light of modern decisions, see 4 Pom. Eq. Jur., § 1357, and note 1.

the courts should seek as certainly marking an injury as irreparable, and which the majority of the decisions show to be its essential features, are: (1) That the injury is an act which is a serious change of, or is destructive to, the property it affects either physically or in the character in which it has been held and enjoyed. (2) That the property must have some peculiar quality or use such that its pecuniary value, as estimated by a jury, will not fairly recompense the owner for the loss of it.[7] In the application of this test, however, there are many conflicting decisions. Thus, some courts treat land as *per se* property of peculiar value and will enjoin destructive trespasses to its substance without regard to the question whether, in the particular case, it really does have any peculiar value or not. By these courts it is made a subject for protection by injunction, just as in cases of contract it is a subject for specific performance without reference to its quality, use or value.[8] Other courts, however, in similar

7 It will be observed that this definition is largely drawn from those of Chancellor Kent in Jerome v. Ross, and Pearson, Ch. J., in Gause v. Perkins, quoted in the previous note. It attempts to describe those trespasses which are from their nature beyond reparation in money payment, such as a jury would give, and to exclude other cases for which the legal remedy may, indeed, be inadequate, but for other reasons than this. There is sometimes a tendency to make the term "irreparable" virtually extensive enough to include all cases for which the legal remedy is inadequate, as, for example, the statement of Pearson, Ch. J., *supra*, that the insolvency of the defendant will make trespass irreparable. See, also, Camp v. Dixon, 112 Ga 872, 876-877, 38 S. E. 71, 52 L. R. A 755. Cf. Elliott on Roads and Streets (2d ed.), § 665, and Wood on Nuisance (3d ed.), § 778 The meaning of "irreparable" does not preclude all possibility of money compensation, such, for instance, as the plaintiff himself might fix. See this point discussed in Dent v. Auction Mart Co., L. R. 2 Eq. 238.

8 See Thomas v. Oakley, 18 Ves. 184; Hexo v. Gill, L. R. 7 Ch. App. 699; Richards v. Dower, 64 Cal. 62, 28 Pac 113. And see, also, Walker v. Emerson, 89 Cal 456, 26 Pac. 968, in which the court en-

cases, have taken the attitude that the question, whether an injury is irreparable or not, is an open matter of fact to be inquired into in every case, and have refused injunctions against destructive trespasses because the value of the land injured was small, and it had no peculiar use or quality for the owner.[9] So, too, in the case of mining, the courts have sometimes applied the test of irreparability to the particular case, and finding that the owner had no use for the land beyond getting its value from it in the shape of minerals, have refused to grant the injunction when the defendant was

joined the taking of water from plaintiff's land by a ditch which defendant dug on plaintiff's land for the purpose, saying: "Such an act is an injury to the *right*, and if threatened to be continued should be enjoined, whatever opinion persons other than the owner may have about the extent of the damage that may result." In Richards v. Dower, *supra*, the bill was to enjoin the digging of a tunnel through the plaintiff's land. The lower court found that the tunnel would not cause irreparable injury, and refused the injunction. On appeal this holding was reversed, the court, per Sharpstein, J., saying: "The finding that the injury is not irreparable is inconsistent with the findings which describe the character of the work which it is sought to have enjoined."

9 Jerome v. Ross, 7 Johns Ch. 315, 11 Am. Dec. 484; Bassett v Salisbury etc. Mills, 47 N. H. 426, Ocean City R. Co. v. Bray, 55 N. J. Eq. 101, 35 Atl. 839; Crescent Min. Co v. Silver King Min Co., 17 Utah, 444, 17 Am. St. Rep. 810, 54 Pac. 244; Schuster v. Myers, 148 Mo. 422, 50 S. W. 103; King v. Mullins, 27 Mont. 364, 71 Pac 155; Harley v. Montana Ore Purchasing Co., 27 Mont. 388, 71 Pac. 407. These cases are not to be reconciled with those cited in the previous note. In Crescent Min. Co. v. Silver King Min. Co, *supra*, the trespass complained of was the laying and keeping of water pipes in land of the plaintiff. Because the land was barren and rocky, and of small value, the court held that the injury was not irreparable, and refused the injunction, McCarty, J., dissenting, and citing Richards v. Dower, *supra*, as indistinguishable. In King v. Mullins, *supra*, the trespass complained of was the sinking of a shaft in a mining claim. In both of these cases stress is laid on the fact that the worthless soil dug up was not carried away, but left on the owner's premises But in Jerome v. Ross, *supra*, the thing complained of was the digging and carrying away of stone from the plaintiff's land.

solvent, and thus was able to give the legal relief of damages,[10] although in England, and generally in America, mining is a form of trespass that is generally considered as irreparable, and, as such, is enjoined.[11] And the same thing may be said of the cutting of or destruction of timber.[12] These conflicts in

10 Rice v. Looney, 81 Ill. App. 537; Erskine v. Forest Oil Co., 80 Fed. 583; Deep River Co. v. Fox, 4 Ired. Eq. (39 N. C.) 61; Kellar v. Bullington, 101 Ala. 267, 14 South. 466. No English court has acted on this view, though in a comparatively early case (Haight v. Jaggar, 2 Coll. 231, decided in 1845), Bruce, V. C., said: "The defendants . . . . are, it is true, by working the coal, taking away the very substance of the property; which may, in a sense, be perhaps called in this case, and might in others most certainly be, waste or destruction; but, on the other hand, it is the only mode in which the property in question can be usefully enjoyed or made available, and may therefore, in a sense, perhaps, be deemed not more than taking the ordinary usufruct of the thing in dispute."

11 Mitchell v. Dors, 6 Ves. 147; Anderson v. Harvey's Heirs, 10 Gratt. 386; Merced Mining etc. Co. v. Fremont, 7 Cal. 317, 68 Am. Dec. 262; Hammond v. Winchester, 82 Ala. 470, 2 South. 892; Bettman v. Harness, 42 W. Va. 433, 26 S. E. 271, 36 L. R A. 566; Moore v. Jennings, 47 W. Va. 181, 34 S. E. 793, Erhardt v. Boaro, 113 U. S. 537, 5 Sup. Ct. 565, 28 L. ed. 1116. In Erhardt v. Boaro, *supra*, there was an application for a temporary injunction pending the settlement of a dispute over a mining claim, the bill alleging that about one hundred and fifty tons of ore containing gold and silver to the value of $25,000 had been extracted, and that about one hundred tons of it were still on the premises. In granting a temporary injunction against further digging or removing the ore already dug, the court, per Field, J., said: "It is now a common practice in cases where irremediable mischief is being done or threatened, going to the destruction of the substance of the estate, such as the extracting of ores from a mine, or the cutting down of timber, or the removal of coal, to issue an injunction, though the title to the premises be in litigation."

12 In Musch v Burkhart, 83 Iowa, 301, 32 Am St. Rep. 305, 48 N. W. 1025, 12 L R. A. 484, plaintiff sought to enjoin the setting of boundary trees, alleging he would be damaged to the extent of $200. In commenting on this allegation as to damages, the court said. "But it does not follow that the damages would not be irreparable within the meaning of the law. The trees cannot be replaced, nor can their benefit to plaintiff and the comfort and satisfaction which

the cases thus result, not so much from different views of what constitutes an irreparable injury, as an original question, as from a different practice with reference to distributing certain cases of the same general character in subject-matter, into fixed groups that shall be

he derives from them be accurately measured by a pecuniary standard. . . . . A person is not obliged to suffer his property to be destroyed at the will of another, even though he may be able to recover ample pecuniary compensation therefor. This is especially true of property like trees, planted for and adapted to a certain use, and serving a special purpose. Their owner has an interest in them which he may protect, and to be deprived of it without his consent would be to suffer irreparable injury, within the meaning of the law" Injunctions against cutting timber were granted in the following cases. Courthope v. Mapplesden, 10 Ves. 290; Kinder v. Jones, 17 Ves. 110; Neale v. Cripps, 4 Kay & J. 472; Lowndes v. Bettle, 3 New Rep. 409, 33 L. J Ch. 451, 10 Jur., N. S., 226; Stanford v. Hurlestone, L. R. 9 Ch. App. 116; United States v. Guylard, 79 Fed 21; King v. Stuart, 84 Fed. 546; King v. Campbell, 85 Fed 814, Shipley v. Ritter, 7 Md. 408, 61 Am. Dec. 371; Smith v Rock, 59 Vt. 232, 9 Atl. 551, Griffith v. Hilliard, 64 Vt. 643, 25 Atl 427; Crane v. Davis (Miss), 21 South. 17; Daubenspeck v. Grear, 18 Cal 443, Sapp v. Roberts, 18 Neb. 299, 25 N. W. 96; Markham v. Howell, 33 Ga. 508; Powell v. Cheshire, 70 Ga. 357, 48 Am. Rep. 572; Fluharty v. Mills, 49 W. Va. 446, 38 S E. 521; Camp v. Dixon, 112 Ga 872, 38 S E. 71, 52 L. R. A. 757, citing 4 Pom Eq. Jur., § 1357; Ramey v. Counts (Va.), 47 S. E. 1006; Newton v. Brown, 134 N. C. 439, 46 S E. 994; Scars v. Ackerman, 138 Cal. 583, 72 Pac. 171; Louisville etc. Co. v. Gibson, 43 Fla. 315, 31 South. 230 (statutory); Heuck v Patty, 100 Mo. App. 389, 73 S. W. 389. Injunctions against cutting timber were refused in the following cases: Wilcox Lumber Co v. Bullock, 109 Ga. 532, 35 S. E. 52; Schoonover v. Bright, 24 W. Va. 698; Watson v. Ferrell, 34 W Va 406, 12 S. E. 724, Curtin v. Stout (W. Va.), 50 S. E. 810; Gause v. Perkins, 56 N. C. (3 Jones Eq) 177, 69 Am. Dec. 728; Sharpe v. Loane, 124 N. C. 1, 32 S. E. 318; Myers v. Hawkins, 67 Ark. 413, 56 S. W. 640; Woodford v. Alexander, 35 Fla. 333, 17 South. 658 (disapproved in Brown v Selary, 37 Fla. 102, 19 South. 161); Cainey v. Hadley, 32 Fla 344, 37 Am. St. Rep. 101, 14 South. 4, 22 L R. A. 233; Thatcher v. Humble, 67 Ind. 444. Observe that Georgia and West Virginia have some decisions in which the injunctions were granted and others in which they were refused, the special circumstances of the cases distinguishing them. In Gause v. Perkins, *supra*, Pearson, J., said: "In the considered as *per se* cases of irreparable injury. As a further source of conflict, there are a number of cases which, when dealing with trespasses to real property, tend to give to the term "irreparable" an enlarged signification, and make it virtually synonymous with

present condition of our country, does the cultivation of pine trees for turpentine, or the cutting down of oak trees for staves, or cypress trees for shingles, cause an irreparable injury—one which cannot be compensated for in damages? The very purpose for which these trees are used by the owners of land is to get from them turpentine, staves and shingles for sale. It follows, therefore, as a matter of course, that if the owner of the land recovers from a trespasser the value of the trees that are used for those purposes, he thereby receives compensation for the injury, and it cannot in any sense of the word be deemed irreparable.'' In Camp v. Dixon, *supra,* the plaintiffs owned large bodies of timber and had invested large sums of money in mills and other equipment. The defendants threatened to denude the land of its timber, and as this would be the ruin of the plaintiff's business, the court held that the facts of the case showed irreparable injury, stronger than the ordinary one of cutting timber. The case was also rested on the ground of preventing multiplicity of suits, and on the fact that a jury's estimate of damages would be conjectural. In Fluharty v. Mills, *supra,* the bill alleged that the timber which the defendant was threatening to destroy was especially valuable to the land, and that the taking away of the timber would permanently injure the land; this the court thought was a sufficient showing of irreparable injury. But the same court, in Watson v. Ferrell, *supra,* refused an injunction against cutting timber, on the ground that irreparable injury was not shown, saying as to this: ''When we look further at the allegations of the bill we find that he alleges that the greater portion of the land is in a state of nature, and covered by a valuable growing timber, etc., which timber is very valuable, and makes such land much more valuable than it would be without said growing timber, *non constat,* that the land is not filled with coal, iron, and other minerals, or that the timber constitutes its chief value; and there are no facts stated on the face of the bill that would show that the plaintiff would suffer irreparable injury by the cutting and removal of seventy-five or any number of trees from said land when it is not alleged that the defendants are insolvent.'' In Brown v. Solary, 37 Fla. 102, 19 South. 161, the court, per Mabry, C. J., said: ''When the value of land consists chiefly, if not entirely, in the timber thereon, its destruction amounts to irreparable injury, within the rule on the subject.''

"serious injury."[13] There are, of course, no particular classes of cases to which irreparable injuries are confined. Other illustrations are collected in the note.[14]

13 In a recent case the court, after quoting the definition of Pearson J., in Gause v Perkins, which has been given *ante*, note 6, said: "This definition is fairly deducible from the earlier cases, but it is entirely too narrow to meet the decisions of more modern times. . . . . In the light of modern decisions, an irreparable injury may be said to be one which, either from its nature, or from the circumstances surrounding the person injured, or the financial condition of the person committing the injury, cannot be readily, adequately, and completely compensated with money": Per Cobb, J., in Camp v. Dixon, 112 Ga. 872, 38 S. E. 71, 73, 52 L. R. A. 757. See, also, Champ v. Kendrick, 130 Ind. 549, 30 N. E. 787, citing Pom. Eq. Jur., § 1357, and Lemmon v. Guthrie Center, 113 Iowa, 36, 86 Am. St. Rep. 361, 84 Mo. 986. In this last case the court enjoined town authorities from moving a building of the plaintiff, saying: "An examination of all the cases indicates a strong tendency to grant equitable relief whenever the trespass permanently diminishes the substance of the estate in that which constitutes its chief value, without reference to the fact that the value may be measured in money, on the ground that the plaintiff is entitled to have the identity and integrity of his estate preserved."

14 Injury to or removal of buildings: Patton v. Moore, 16 W. Va. 428, 37 Am. Rep 789, De Veney v. Gallagher, 20 N. J. Eq. 33, Echelkamp v. Schroder, 45 Mo. 505; Everett v. City of Marquette, 53 Mich 450, 19 N. W. 140; Lemmon v. Town of Guthrie Center, 113 Iowa, 36, 86 Am. St. Rep. 361, 84 N. W. 986; Auckland v. Westminster Board, L. R. 7 Ch. App. 597; District Tp. of Lodomillo v. Dist. Tp. of Cass, 54 Iowa, 115, 6 N. W. 163; Lewis v. Town of North Kingstown, 16 R. I 15, 27 Am. St. Rep. 724, 11 Atl. 173. Laying out public roads over plaintiff's land: Erwin v. Fulk, 94 Ind 235, citing 4 Pom. Eq Jur, § 1357, Grigsby v. Burtnett, 31 Cal. 406 (cf. Leach v. Day, 27 Cal. 643); Ballentine v. Town of Harrison, 37 N. J. Eq. (10 Stew.) 560, 45 Am. Rep. 667. Grazing sheep on plaintiff's land: Northern Pac. R. R. Co. v. Cunningham, 89 Fed. 594; Martin v. Platte Valley Sheep Co. (Wyo.), 76 Pac. 571; Strawberry etc. Co. v. Chipman, 13 Utah, 454, 45 Pac. 348; Dastervignes v. United States, 122 Fed. 30. Interference with graves: First Evangelical Church v. Walsh, 57 Ill. 363, 11 Am. Rep 21; Choppin v. Dauplin, 48 La. Ann. 1217, 55 Am. St. Rep. 313, 20 South 681, 33 L. R. A. 133; Beatty v. Kurtz, 2 Pet. 566, 7 L. ed. 521; Davidson v. Reed, 111 Ill. 167, 53 Am. Rep. 613; Wormley v Wormley, 207 Ill. 411, 69 N E. 865. Removal and defacing of landmarks: Preston v. Preston, 85 Ky. 16, 2

§ 496. **Continuous or Repeated Trespasses.**—The jurisdiction of equity to restrain continuous or repeated trespasses rests on the ground of avoiding a repetition of similar actions.[15] It is a basis of jurisdiction that is frequently found in cases where the injury is also irreparable. Very often, indeed, the injury is irreparable only because it is continuous or repeated, when it would not be if temporary, and in such cases the injunction will issue as a matter of course.[16] For the further discussion of this subject, it will be convenient to consider, first, the cases in which the injury is the result of a single act, or set of acts, of the defendant, which afterwards operate by virtue of natural laws to produce the injury; and, second, the cases in which there are several or many acts of the defendant or de-

S. W. 501. Removal of a fence: Bolton v. McShane, 67 Iowa, 207, 25 N. W. 135; Gilfillan v. Shattuck, 142 Cal. 27, 75 Pac. 646; Wolf etc. Co. v. Lonyo, 132 Mich. 162, 102 Am. St. Rep. 412, 93 N. W. 251. Beatty v. Kurtz, *supra*, is an excellent example of one of the clearest kinds of irreparable injury. The bill was to enjoin the defendants from removing tombstones and graves and dispossessing the plaintiffs of the burying-ground. In granting the injunction, Story, J., said: "This is not a case of a mere private trespass; but a public nuisance, going to the irreparable injury of the Georgetown congregation of Lutherans. The property consecrated to their use by a perpetual servitude or easement, is to be taken from them, the sepulchres of the dead are to be violated, the feelings of religion, and the sentiments of natural affection of the kindred and friends of the deceased are to be wounded; and the memorials erected by piety or love, to the memory of the good are to be removed, so as to leave no trace of the last home of their ancestry to those who may visit the spot in future generations." An injury falling far short of this may, of course, be irreparable.

15 4 Pom. Eq. Jur., § 1357. This entire class of cases is comprehended in the broader jurisdiction of equity to prevent multiplicity of suits, for a consideration of which see 1 Pom. Eq. Jur., §§ 243-275.

16 See, *e. g.*, Griffith v. Hilliard, 64 Vt. 643, 25 Atl. 427; Kellogg v. King, 114 Cal. 378, 55 Am. St. Rep. 74, 46 Pac. 166; Ellis v Blue Mountain Forest Assn., 69 N. H. 385, 41 Atl. 856, 42 L. R. A. 570.

fendants which give rise to as many different causes of actions. The distinction is roughly that between continuing and repeated trespasses, and is based on the distinctions made in the cases themselves. If a trespass is of the first class and produces substantial damage to the plaintiff, the authorities are well agreed that a proper case for an injunction is presented.[17] If, however, the injury is little or nothing more than the technical invasion of plaintiff's legal right without substantial damage, there is a division among the courts, though a majority of the decisions show that the foundation principle of this branch of the jurisdiction fairly includes all such cases, whether the damage is substantial or not.[18] If plaintiff's legal remedy may be vexatious, harassing, and hence inadequate when he recovers substantial damages, still more would it

17 Fitzgerald v. Urton, 5 Cal. 308, Mohawk etc. Co. v. Artcher, 6 Paige, 83; Henderson v. New York Cent. R. R. Co., 78 N. Y. 423; Birmingham Traction Co. v. Southern Bell etc. Co., 119 Ala. 144, 24 South. 731, Davis v. Frankenlust Tp., 118 Mich. 494, 76 N W. 1045; Calmelet v. Sichl, 48 Neb. 505, 58 Am. St. Rep. 700, 67 N. W. 467; Gobeille v. Meunier, 21 R. I. 103, 41 Atl. 1001; Barbee v. Shannon, 1 Ind. Ter. 199, 40 S. W. 584; McCloskey v. Doherty, 97 Ky. 200, 30 S. W. 649.

18 That an injunction should issue in such a case: Goodson v. Richardson, L. R. 9 Ch. App. 221; Powell v. Aiken, 4 Kay & J. 343; Allen v. Martin, L. R. 20 Eq. 462; Delaware etc. Co. v. Breckenridge, 57 N. J. Eq. 154, 41 Atl. 966, affirmed in 58 N. J. Eq. 581, 43 Atl 1097, and the language of the courts in most of the cases in which in fact there is substantial damage shown, indicates that this question is of no moment. Injunctions were refused in McCullough v. Denver, 39 Fed. 307; Nicodemus v. Nicodemus, 41 Md. 529; Hoy v. Sweetman, 19 Nev. 376, 12 Pac. 504; Fisher v. Carpenter, 67 N. H. 569, 39 Atl. 1018; Crescent etc. Co. v. Silver etc. Co., 17 Utah, 444, 70 Am. St. Rep. 810, 54 Pac. 244; Savannah etc. Co. v. Suburban etc. Co., 93 Ga. 240, 18 S. E. 824; Whitlock v. Consumers' etc. Co., 127 Ind 62, 26 N. E. 570; Christman v. Howe (Ind.), 70 N. E. 809 If the plaintiff is a reversioner, however, it is proper to require that he show substantial damage, because otherwise he shows no legal cause of action in himself: Cooper v. Crabtree, L. R. 20 Ch. D. 589; Coney v.

seem to be so when his recovery is only nominal.[19] When the trespasses complained of are caused by the separate acts of individuals, a multiplicity of suits may be caused to plaintiff either because the defendants are numerous or because a single defendant does the same or similar acts repeatedly. The principle involved in all such cases is the same, and injunctions should issue. And when the basis of the multiplicity of suits which plaintiff fears is that the defendants are numerous, all authorities agree in granting the injunctions.[20] But when it is the case of a

Brunswick etc. Co., 116 Ga. 222, 42 S. E. 498. The following are additional cases in which continuing trespasses were enjoined: Dosoris Pond Co. v. Campbell, 164 N. Y. 596, 58 N. E. 1087, affirming 25 App Div. 179, 50 N. Y. Supp. 819; Cobb v. Mass. Chem. Co., 179 Mass. 423, 60 N. E. 790; Rhodes v. McNamara (Mich.), 98 N. W. 392; Simpson v. Moorhead, 65 N. J. Eq. 623, 56 Atl. 887; McClellan v Taylor, 54 S. C. 430, 32 S. E. 527; Hall v. Nester, 122 Mich. 141, 80 N. W. 982; Ragsdale v. Southern Ry. Co., 60 S. C. 381, 38 S. E. 609; Olivella v. New York etc. Co., 31 Misc. Rep. 203, 64 N. Y. Supp. 1086; Hahl v. Sugo, 46 App. Div. 632, 61 N. Y. Supp. 770, affirming 27 Misc. Rep. 1, 57 N. Y. Supp. 920; Providence etc. Co. v. City of Fall River, 183 Mass. 535, 67 N. E. 647; Miller v. Hoeschler, 121 Wis. 558, 99 N. W. 228 (citing 4 Pom. Eq. Jur., § 1347).

19 It is often given as an additional reason for enjoining repeated or continuing trespasses to land that otherwise there is danger lest they "ripen into an easement." Apart from the remoteness of any such danger, which alone would seem enough to defeat the injunction, the reason would appear to be unsound because of the fact that plaintiff, by bringing suit, or interfering with the trespasses once in every period necessary for the ripening of an easement, would prevent that danger: See McGregor v. Silver King Min Co, 14 Utah, 47, 60 Am. St. Rep. 883, 45 Pac. 1091, Hart v. Hilderbrandt, 30 Ind. App. 415, 66 N. E. 173.

20 This statement is, of course, subject to the qualifications which the questions of "community of interest" or "identity of issues" have made in the decisions with reference to the proper joinder of the defendants in one suit. For a full discussion of this point and collection of the authorities, see 1 Pom. Eq. Jur., §§ 243-275 Typical cases illustrating this group are, Smith v. Bivens, 56 Fed 352; United States Freehold Land etc. Co. v. Gallegos, 89 Fed. 769, 32

single defendant who, by repeating his acts of trespass, makes it necessary for plaintiff to pursue his legal remedy only by a succession of actions, the decisions are curiously diverse. It is held, in a small group of cases, that this is not the kind of multiplicity of suits which equity enjoins, but that instead an injunction is proper only when different persons assail plaintiff's right.[21] The other view, and the one sustained alike by the weight of authority and by principle, is that if a defendant manifests a purpose to persist in perpetrating his unlawful acts, the vexation, expense and trouble of prosecuting the actions at law make the legal remedy inadequate, and justify a plaintiff in coming into equity for an injunction.[22] None of the cases show

C. C. A. 470; New York Cent. etc. Co. v. Warren, 31 Misc. Rep. 571, 64 N. Y. Supp. 781; Boston etc. Co. v. Sullivan, 177 Mass. 230, 83 Am. St. Rep. 275, 58 N. E. 689, Palmer v. Israel, 13 Mont. 209, 33 Pac. 134.

21 Best v. Drake, 11 Hare, 369; Smith v. Gardner, 12 Or. 221, 53 Am. Rep. 342, 6 Pac. 771; Jerome v. Ross, 7 Johns. Ch. 315, 11 Am. Dec. 484; Carney v. Hadley, 32 Fla. 344, 37 Am. St. Rep. 101, 14 South. 4, 22 L. R. A. 233; Roebling Sons' Co. v. First Nat. Bank, 30 Fed. 744; Deegan v. Neville, 127 Ala. 471, 85 Am. St. Rep. 137, 29 South. 173, Taylor v. Pearce, 71 Ill. App. 525.

22 Musselman v. Marquis, 1 Bush (Ky.), 463, 89 Am. Dec 637; Ladd v. Osborne, 79 Iowa, 93, 44 N. W. 235; Gray Lumber Co. v. Gaskin (Ga.), 50 S. E. 164, quoting Pom. Eq. Jur., § 1357; Mendelson v. McCabe, 144 Cal. 230, 103 Am. St Rep. 78, 77 Pac. 915; Boglino v. Giorgetta (Colo. App.), 78 Pac. 612; Heman v. Wade, 74 Mo App. 339, citing 4 Pom. Eq Jur., § 1357; McClellan v. Taylor, 54 S. C. 430, 32 S. E. 527; Allen v. Martin, L. R. 20 Eq. 462; Lembeck v Nye, 47 Ohio St. 336, 21 Am. St. Rep. 828, 24 N. E. 686, 8 L. R. A. 578; New York etc. Co. v. Scovill, 71 Conn. 136, 71 Am. St. Rep. 159, 41 Atl. 246, 42 L. R. A. 157; Owens v. Crossett, 105 Ill. 354; Valentine v. Schreiber, 3 App. Div 235, 38 N. Y Supp 417; Sills v. Goodyear, 80 Mo. App. 128; Pohlman v. Lohmeyer, 60 Neb 364, 83 N. W. 201; Garrett v. Bishop, 27 Or. 349, 41 Pac. 10, Barbee v. Shannon, 1 Ind. Ter 199, 40 S. W. 584, citing 1 Pom Eq Jur , § 264, Lynch v. Egan (Neb.), 93 N. W. 775; Atchison etc Co v. Spaulding, 69 Kan. 431, 77 Pac. 106; Blondell v. Consolidated Gas Co., 89 Md. 732,

any tendency to make the seriousness of the damage the criterion,[23] and the jurisdiction attaches as well to trespasses to personalty as to realty.[24]

§ 497. **Insolvency of Defendant.**—The inadequacy of legal remedies, ordinarily, against an insolvent trespasser is obvious, and the reason for equity's intervention in such cases is clear. The number of cases in which the defendant's insolvency is made a material part of the court's reason for granting an injunction is very great.[25] The number of cases in which the question has arisen whether insolvency alone is enough to support an injunction is not so large, but is suffi-

43 Atl. 817, 46 L R. A. 187, Thomas v. Robinson (Iowa), 92 N. W. 70; Hayoie v. Salt River etc Co. (Ariz), 71 Pac. 944; Lake Shore etc. Co. v. Felton, 103 Fed. 227, 43 C. C. A. 189; Gulf, C. & S. F. Ry. Co. v. Puckett (Tex. Civ. App.), 82 S. W. 662 (using railway velocipede on railroad track repeatedly). In Musselman v Marquis, *supra*, the bill was to enjoin the defendant from throwing down and removing fencing. The facts were that the defendant had already repeatedly thrown down the fencing, and had declared his intention of continuing the commission of similar trespasses. In allowing the injunction the court, per Hardin, J, said· "Indeed, without regard to the alleged insolvency of the defendant, as the other facts alleged disclose a determined purpose on his part to persist in perpetrating the unlawful acts complained of, thus rendering redress at law only obtainable by a multiplicity of suits, and probably without any sufficient compensation for the vexation, expense, and trouble attending their prosecution, we are of the opinion that the chancellor had power to enjoin the mischief, in order to prevent oppressive litigation, the principle of equitable jurisdiction being, that where there is no adequate remedy at law, the chancellor must take jurisdiction, or otherwise the damage is irreparable."

23 See Ellis v. Wren, 84 Ky. 254, 1 S. W. 440.

24 Warren Mills v. New Orleans Seed Co., 65 Miss. 391, 7 Am. St. Rep. 671, 4 South. 298.

25 See *e. g*, Musselman v. Marquis, 1 Bush (64 Ky.), 463, 89 Am. Dec. 637; Milan Steam Mills v. Hickey, 59 N. H. 241; Bensley v. Mountain etc. Co, 13 Cal. 306, 73 Am. Dec. 575; Owens v. Crossett, 105 Ill. 354; McKay v. Chapin, 120 N. C. 159, 26 S. E. 701; Clark v. Wall (Mont.), 79 Pac. 1052.

cient to show the general recognition by the courts of the glaring insufficiency of a judgment for damages against an insolvent.[26] When, however, the legal remedy is not rendered inadequate because of the defendant's insolvency, as when the desired relief is possession of the land which may be procured by the ordinary possessory action at law, the injunction will be refused.[27]

§ 498. **Miscellaneous Cases.**—Besides the three classes of cases just discussed, there are other cases which permit of no definite classification, but which, largely for that reason, show most clearly the comprehensive nature of equity jurisdiction to restrain trespasses. In one of the leading cases of this kind the supreme court of the United States quoted as the criterion of the jurisdiction: "It is not enough that there is a remedy at law; it must be plain and adequate, or, in other words, as practical and efficient to the ends of justice, and its prompt administration, as the remedy in equity."[28] Cases which illustrate this broad rule are collected in the note.[29]

26 West v. Walker, 3 N. J. Eq. 279, note B; Wilson v. Hill, 46 N. J. Eq. 369, 19 Atl. 1097; Paige v Akins, 112 Cal. 401, 44 Pac. 666, Harms v. Jacobs, 158 Ill. 505, 41 N. E. 1071; Ryan v. Fulghum, 96 Ga. 234, 22 S. E. 940; Champ v. Kendrick, 130 Ind. 549, 30 N. E. 787, Leach v Harbough (Neb.), 91 N. W. 521; Hanley v. Waterson, 39 W. Va. 214, 19 S. E. 536. And see further cases collected in 1 Ames, Cases in Eq. Juris. 524, note 2. *Contra*, Pensacola etc. Co. v. Spratt, 12 Fla. 26, 91 Am. Dec. 747; Parker v. Furlong (Or.), 62 Pac. 490; Moore v. Halliday, 43 Or. 243, 99 Am. St. Rep. 724, 72 Pac. 801; Loyd v. Blackburn (W. Va.), 50 S. E. 740; Heilman v. Union Canal Co, 37 Pa. St. 100; Puryear v. Sanford, 124 N. C. 276, 32 S. E. 685.

27 Warlier v. Williams, 53 Neb. 143, 73 N. W. 539.

28 Watson v. Sutherland, 5 Wall. 74, 18 L. ed. 580.

29 Watson v. Sutherland, 5 Wall. 74, 18 L ed. 580 (seizure of stock of goods on execution enjoined because law of damages would allow plaintiff to recover only value of the goods and not the loss

§ 499. **Eminent Domain.**—There is one class of cases in which an injunction will issue against a trespass without regard to the character of the act, viz., when property is taken or used by a defendant under the right of eminent domain without first complying with the prescribed formalities for ascertaining and making compensation. In such cases, the courts do not stop to inquire whether the value of the property to be taken was little or great, whether the injury to the complainant was great or small, but grant the injunction first, on the ground that the constitutional provision makes the payment of a properly ascertained compensation a condition precedent to the right to take, and that injunction is the only way to enforce this provision.[30]

to his business); North v. Peters, 138 U. S. 271, 34 L. ed. 936 (same as preceding case). Other cases of the same sort are collected in 1 Ames, Cases in Eq. Juris., 532, note 3. But see Tomlinson v. Rubio, 16 Cal. 202, disapproved by Currey, J., in Tevis v. Ellis, 25 Cal. 518; Thomas v. James, 32 Ala. 723 (bill by a *cestui que trust*, who would maintain no action at law); and see Lytle v. James, 98 Mo. App. 337, 73 S. W. 287 (licensee plaintiff); Payne v. Kansas etc. Co, 46 Fed. 546 (damages would be conjectural); London etc. Co. v. Lancashire etc. Co, L. R. 4 Eq. 174 (same), Westmoreland etc. Gas Co. v. De Witt, 130 Pa. St. 235, 18 Atl. 724, 5 L. R A. 731 (same); Poughkeepsie Gas Co. v. Citizens' Gas Co., 89 N. Y. 493 (same); Phillips v. Winslow, 57 Ky. (18 B. Mon) 431, 68 Am. Dec. 729 (seizure and sale of cars under wrongful execution enjoined because it would stop business of a railroad); Barbee v. Shannon, 1 Ind. Ter. 199, 40 S. W. 584 (damages which plaintiff, a lessor, could recover, might be less than he would be liable for to his lessee for breach of covenant); Miller v. Wills, 95 Va. 337, 28 S. E. 337 (non-residence of defendant of weight in determining propriety of granting an injunction); Morgan v. Baxter, 113 Ga. 144, 38 S. E. 411 (same, but non-residence alone not enough). See Pokegama etc. Co. v. Klamath River etc. Co., 96 Fed. 34; Allen Coal Co. v. Challis, 103 Ill. App. 52; City of Los Angeles v. Los Angeles etc. Co., 124 Cal. 368, 5 Pac. 210.

30 McElroy v. Kansas City, 21 Fed. 257; Searle v. City of Lead, 10 S. D. 405, 73 N. W. 913, Donovan v. Allert, 11 N. D. 289, 95 Am. St. Rep. 720, 91 N. W. 441, 58 L. R. A. 775; Birmingham Trac-

The injunction granted in such cases may be an absolute one which forbids defendant further to trespass till after proper condemnation proceedings,[31] or it may be so framed as to reach the same end as such proceedings would, and thus save a second legal action.[32]

§ 500. **What Plaintiff Must Allege.**—A plaintiff who asks for the aid of equity against trespass, must, of course, show a case to justify the extraordinary relief he seeks. Hence, he must show in his bill not only a legal wrong,[33] but, further, why the legal remedy is not adequate.[34] And it is not sufficient for this purpose

tion Co v Birmingham Ry. etc. Co. (Ala.), 24 South. 368; Village of Itasca v. Schroeder, 182 Ill. 192, 55 N. E. 50; Yates v. Milwaukee, 10 Wall. 479, 19 L. ed. 984. This subject is treated at length, *ante*, chapter XX. See the following cases for instances of relief granted when no attempt has been made to condemn the property: Baya v. Town of Lake City, 44 Fla. 491, 33 South. 400; Shipley v. Western Md. Tidewater R. Co., 99 Md. 115, 56 Atl. 968, Freud v Detroit & P. Ry. Co., 133 Mich. 413, 95 N. W. 559. See, also, Atlantic & B. R. Co. v. Seaboard Air Line Ry., 116 Ga. 412, 42 S. E. 761.

31 Gilman v. Sheboygan etc. Co., 40 Wis. 653; Rosenberger v. Miller, 1 Mo. App. 640, 61 Mo. App. 422; Bensley v. Mountain etc. Co., 13 Cal. 306, 73 Am. Dec. 575; Central etc. Co. v. Philadelphia etc. Co., 95 Md. 428, 52 Atl. 752, Folley v. City of Passaic, 26 N. J. Eq. 216; Peck v. Schenectady Ry. Co., 170 N. Y. 298, 63 N. E. 357, modifying 67 App. Div. 359, 73 N. Y. Supp. 794.

32 Henderson v New York Cent. etc. Co., 78 N. Y. 423; Pappenheim v. Metropolitan etc. Co, 128 N Y. 436, 26 Am. St. Rep. 486, 28 N. E. 518, 13 L R. A. 401. See *ante*, §§ 473, 470.

33 State v. Rost, 59 La. Ann. 995, 23 South. 978; Flannery v Hightower, 97 Ga. 592, 25 S. E. 371; Kellogg v. King, 114 Cal. 378, 55 Am. St. Rep. 74, 46 Pac. 166. And so if a plaintiff's bill fails to show he has title to the property in question, he will be refused relief: Amos v. Norcross, 58 N J. Eq. 256, 43 Atl. 195; Perkins v. Mason, 105 Mo. App. 315, 79 S. W. 987, Powell v. Brinson, 120 Ga. 36, 47 S. E. 499; Tiernan v. Miller (Neb.), 96 N. W. 661.

34 Collins v. Sutton, 94 Va. 127, 26 S E. 415; Smith v. Schlink, 15 Colo. App. 325, 62 Pac. 1044. *Contra*, Kaufman v. Wiener, 169 Ill. 596, 48 N. E. 479, affirming 68 Ill. App. 250, Murphy v. Lincoln, 63 Vt. 278, 22 Atl. 418.

that he merely allege an "irreparable" or a "continuing" trespass. He must set forth the facts from which the court may draw the inference that the legal remedy is not sufficient.[35] Nor is it necessary that he should allege that the injury will be irreparable;[36] the same reason which makes it necessary for him to set out the facts, makes it unnecessary for him to do more.

§ 501. **Threatened Trespass.**—In the subject of trespass as elsewhere the main function of an injunction is to preserve property from future injury. Courts will not, however, enjoin against a mere speculative or possible injury. Instead, a reasonable probability of the injury resulting must be shown.[37] Hence, if defendant has neither done nor threatened any wrongful acts, and denies his intention to do the acts against which an injunction is sought, it will be refused.[38] On the other hand, if plaintiff shows that defendant has threatened to do acts of the kind which equity enjoins, that is enough to rest his case upon.[39] And threats may be

35 Waldron v. Marsh, 5 Cal. 119; Carlisle v. Stevenson, 3 Md. Ch. 504; Kesner v. Miesch, 90 Ill. App. 437; Thorn v. Sweeney, 12 Nev. 251; Wiggins v. Middleton, 117 Ga. 162, 43 S. E. 433.

36 Boston etc. R. R. v. Sullivan, 177 Mass. 230, 83 Am. St. Rep. 275, 58 N. E. 689; Kaufman v. Wiener, 169 Ill. 596, 48 N. E. 479, reversing, 68 Ill. App. 250; Chappell v. Jasper County etc. Co., 31 Ind. App. 170, 66 N. E. 515.

37 Haupt v. Independent etc. Co., 25 Mont. 122, 63 Pac. 1033; Lorenz v. Waldron, 96 Cal. 243, 31 Pac. 54; Montana Ore etc. Co. v. Boston & M. etc. Co., 22 Mont. 159, 56 Pac. 120.

38 Hagemeyer v. Village of St. Michael, 70 Minn. 482, 73 N. W. 412; Chicago etc. Co. v. Brandan, 81 Mo. App. 1; Kerlin v. West, 4 N. J. Eq 449.

39 New York etc. Co. v. Seovill, 71 Conn. 136, 71 Am. St. Rep. 159, 41 Atl. 246, 42 L. R. A. 157; Union Mill etc. Co. v. Warren, 82 Fed. 522; Negaunee etc. Co. v. Ironcliffs Co. (Mich.), 96 N. W. 468, More v. Massini, 32 Cal. 590.

purely verbal without any acts,[40] or they may consist of acts from which the inference as to defendant's intention may be made.[41] If, however, the wrongful act is done, and it is not accompanied by threats of repetition, and does not itself constitute a threat, the injunction will not issue, since, in such case, it is needless.[42]

§ 502. **Dispute as to Title; General Principles.**—The effect of a dispute as to title on the propriety of granting an injunction to a plaintiff who seeks to enjoin destructive acts of a defendant who, in turn, justifies on the ground that he is the owner of the land affected, has been much discussed by the courts, and a considerable difference of judicial opinion has resulted. The source of the difficulty was a *dictum*[43] and a decision[44] of Lord Eldon that when a plaintiff stated that the defendant claimed by an adverse title, he stated himself out of court,—a statement of the law which, when taken absolutely, Lord Eldon himself disapproved, and which, after repeated expressions of disapproval,[45] the English courts finally modified a half century later.[46] As will appear below, the great weight of American authority is also opposed to the rule thus unqualifiedly formulated. The reason that a dispute as to title should

40 Union Mill etc. Co. v. Warren, 82 Fed. 522; Lyon v. Hunt, 11 Ala. 295, 46 Am. Dec. 216.

41 Bonaparte v. Camden etc. Co., Baldw. (C. C.) 205, 231, 232, Fed. Cas. No. 1617; McMinn v. Karter, 123 Ala. 502, 26 South. 649.

42 Ocmulgee Lumber Co. v. Mitchell, 112 Ga. 528, 37 S. E. 749, Ketchum v. Depew, 81 Hun, 278, 30 N. Y. Supp. 794.

43 Pillsworth v. Hopton, [1801] 6 Ves. 51.

44 Smith v. Collyer, [1803] 8 Ves. 89.

45 See Jones v. Jones, 3 Mer. 160; Haigh v. Jaggar, 2 Coll. C. C. 231; Davenport v. Davenport, 7 Hare, 217.

46 Commissioners v. Blackett, [1848] 12 Jur. 151; Neale v. Cripps, 4 Kay & J. 472; Lowndes v. Bettle, 3 New Rep. 409, 33 L. J. Ch. 451, 10 Jur., N. S., 226. The point is now covered by statute in England (36 & 37 Vict., c. 66, § 25, subsec. 8).

preclude the granting of an injunction permanently is that under such circumstances "it is possible that title may be in the defendant. . . . . If he has the title, then he has a right to possession, and ought not to be precluded from acquiring it. But if the injunction stands, he is under a permanent judicial inhibition from in 'any wise' meddling with the property. His right to litigate the title in an action at law should be preserved to him."[47] In brief, one should not be finally enjoined from acts which may be wholly rightful and lawful. But on the other hand, it does not follow from this that the injunction should be wholly refused. There being a substantial dispute over the title, it is clear that the plaintiff may prove to be the owner, and his possible interest should be protected at once, because otherwise "the injury may be committed before trial."[48] Hence, a true regard for the interests of both parties requires that a temporary injunction should issue to preserve the property in its present condition till the ownership is decided. Such temporary injunction is of course subject to the usual governing principles of temporary injunctions, which are discussed elsewhere. Some of the more important of these principles in this connection are that, since the action of the court may wrong one party, whether it grant or refuse the injunction,—the defendant is wronged by granting the injunction if he is the rightful owner, the plaintiff is wronged by refusing it if he proves title,—the courts are largely guided in forming their conclusion by balancing these possible wrongs against each other, and acting unfavorably toward whichever party will be least injured by unfavorable action;[49] a small degree of

47 Echelkamp v. Schrader, 45 Mo. 505.

48 Gause v Perkins, 3 Jones Eq 177, 69 Am. Dec. 728

49 Mabel Mining Co. v. Pearson etc. Co, 121 Ala. 567, 25 South.

laches will lose plaintiff his right to it;[50] its purpose is almost always to preserve the *status quo;*[51] the prospective injury on which plaintiff must rest his case is that which will occur before he can have time to establish his right, not the full and entire injury on which his right to a permanent injunction may rest, and the injury to occur in this interval must be sufficient to support an injunction;[52] and, finally, its continuance or dissolution is dependent upon the outcome of the dispute as to title.[53] It follows that when the sole basis of equity's jurisdiction is to prevent a multiplicity of suits caused by a continuing trespass or by repeated trespasses of a single individual, a temporary injunction will rarely, if ever, be appropriate.[54] For

754; Hicks v. Compton, 18 Cal. 206; City of Terre Haute v. Farmers' etc. Co., 99 Fed. 838, 40 C. C. A. 117, Brower v. Williams, 44 App. Div. 337, 60 N. Y. Supp. 716; Ehrenreich v. Froment, 54 App. Div. 196, 66 N. Y. Supp 597; Rogers v. Ashbridge, 23 Pa. Co. Ct. 492, 9 Pa. Dist. 195; McGregor v. Silver King etc. Co., 14 Utah, 47, 60 Am. St. Rep. 883, 45 Pac. 1091; Crescent etc. Co. v. Silver King etc. Co., 17 Utah, 444, 70 Am. St. Rep. 810, 54 Pac. 244, New York etc. Establishment v. Fitch, 1 Paige, 97; Lownsdale v. Grays Harbor, 117 Fed. 983, New Jersey etc. Co. v. Gardner etc. Co., 113 Fed. 395.

50 Field v. Beaumont, 1 Swanst 204; Jones v. Jones, 3 Mer 163; Real Del Monte etc. Co. v. Pond Co., 23 Cal. 82; Higgins v. Woodward, Hopk. 342, remark of Bruce, L. J., in Attorney-General v. Sheffield etc. Co., 3 De Gex, M. & G. 304, 328.

51 Blakemore v. Glamorganshire etc. Co., 1 Mylne & K. 154, Mammoth etc. Co.'s Appeal, 54 Pa. St. 183.

52 New York etc. Establishment v. Fitch, 1 Paige, 97.

53 Hill v. Bowie, 1 Bland (Md.), 593.

54 New York etc. Establishment v. Fitch, 1 Paige, 97. In this case the plaintiff sought an injunction against the defendant using its dock from day to day for landing and taking on freight and passengers A preliminary injunction having been granted, a motion to dissolve was made on the matter of the bill only. In granting the motion, Walworth, C., said: "Whether the facts stated by the counsel on the argument, in relation to the controversy in this cause, would be sufficient to sustain the jurisdiction of this court on the principle of quieting them in the enjoyment of their property, and

it is the plaintiff's own fault if, during the interval while he is establishing his right, he brings a number of suits. He can afford to wait till the right is determined in his favor at least better than the defendant can afford to give up even temporarily the right to use the property, if it be his.

§ 503. **Defendant in Possession Enjoined from Destructive Acts.**—In the leading English case which discusses the effect of a dispute as to title on the granting of an injunction against trespass, the court, after an exhaustive review of the cases, made the following distinction: "Where a defendant is in possession, and a plaintiff claiming possession seeks to restrain him from committing acts similar to those here complained of [cutting timber, ornamental trees and shrubs, and sods], the court will not interfere unless, indeed (as in Neale v. Cripps), the acts amount to such flagrant instances of spoliation as to justify the court in departing from the general principle. . . . . But where the person in possession seeks to restrain one who claims by an adverse title, the tendency of the court will be to grant

preventing the necessity of a perpetual litigation, it is not necessary to decide at this time.

"It is sufficient for the decision of the question immediately before the court, that it does not appear that any serious damage or irreparable injury will take place, if the defendants continue to run their boat and land their passengers, as they have heretofore done, until the complainants' rights are admitted by the answer or settled on the hearing. On the other hand, I can readily see that retaining the preliminary injunction may produce great injury to the defendants, and for which they would be entirely without remedy, if it should finally appear that they were only in the exercise of their legal rights." And see, also, to the same effect, Carney v. Hadley, 32 Fla. 344, 37 Am St. Rep. 101, 14 South 4, 22 L. R. A. 233; Nevitt v. Gillespie, 2 Miss. (1 How) 108, 26 Am. Dec. 696; Delaware etc. Co. v. Breckinridge, 55 N. J. Eq. 141, 35 Atl. 756; Smith v. Gardner, 12 Or. 221, 53 Am. Rep. 346, 6 Pac. 771.

the injunction, at least when the acts either do or may tend to the destruction of the estate."[55] A close analysis of the above passage may perhaps lead to the conclusion that the class of acts which will lead to an injunction in the one case usually will have the same effect in the other. Nevertheless the distinction is one which cannot be disregarded in view of the state of authority, nor is it without reason. That reason, as given in the same case, is as follows: "If a man claims to be owner of an estate of which he either is in possession, or in a position tantamount to that, the court will be very slow to interfere to restrain such an apparent owner from doing those acts which an owner so situated may properly do. There is a wide difference between such a case and that of a person claiming to be owner (whatever the ground of his claim), not taking proceedings at law to recover, but coming on the owner's estate, and doing acts injurious to it."[56] In other words, the fact of possession in the defendant is regarded as strong evidence of title in him, and the plaintiff must therefore make a stronger case to justify an interference with him. The logical effect of this reasoning is, that the plaintiff should be granted an injunction either if he produce stronger evidence of title than would otherwise be required of him, in order to offset the inference of title which defendant's possession raises, or if (as is suggested in the passage above cited), he show that defendant is committing "flagrant instances of spoliation"—that is, more than ordinarily destructive acts. The actual effect is that some courts either grant the injunction only in the latter case, or

55 Lowndes v. Bettle, 33 L. J. Ch. 451, 457, 3 New Rep. 409, 10 Jur., N. S., 226.

56 33 L. J. Ch. 451, 453; Leininger's Appeal, 106 Pa. St. 398; see for another reason, Talbot v. Scott, 4 Kay & J. 96.

else lay down the hard-and-fast rule that no injunction will issue when the defendant is in possession under claim of title, till the plaintiff has established his ownership in an action brought for that purpose.[57] The weight of authority, however, has now come to be that even in this case a temporary injunction will issue if, pending litigation, there will otherwise be such serious acts of trespass that damages will not be an adequate remedy.[58] The reason which sustains this holding has never been more forcibly and clearly stated than in Duvall v. Waters,[59] one of the earliest American cases in which the question was considered, in which Chancellor Bland said: "Should it turn out that the defendant had an unquestionable title, then the granting of

57 Storm v. Mann, 4 Johns. Ch. (N. Y.) 21; Perry v. Parker, 1 Wood. & M. 280, Fed. Cas. No. 11,010; Leininger's Appeal, 106 Pa. St. 398; Schoonover v. Bright, 24 W. Va. 698; Munyon v Filmore (Ind. Ter.), 76 S. W. 257; Cresap v. Kemble, 26 W. Va. 603, Carpenter v. Gwynn, 35 Barb. 395; Nevitt v. Gillespie, 2 Miss (1 How.) 108, 26 Am. Dec. 696 (overruled in Woods v. Riley, 72 Miss. 73, 18 South. 384); Taylor v. Clark, 89 Fed 7; Graham v. Womack, 82 Mo. App. 618; Gildersleeve v. Overstolz, 97 Mo. App. 303, 71 S. W. 371.

58 Shubrick v. Guerard, 2 Desaus. 616; Neale v. Cripps, 4 Kay & J. 472; Duvall v. Waters, 1 Bland Ch. 569, 18 Am. Dec 350; Harris v. Thomas, 1 Hen. & M. (Va.) 18; Erhardt v. Boaro, 113 U. S. 537, 5 Sup. Ct. 565, 28 L. ed. 1116, affirming 8 Fed. 692, 2 McCrary, 141; Buskirk v. King, 25 U. S. App. 607, 72 Fed. 22, 18 C. C. A. 418; Hicks v. Michael, 15 Cal. 107; Williams v. Long, 129 Cal. 229, 61 Pac. 1087; Heman v. Wade, 74 Mo. App. 339; Snyder v. Hopkins, 31 Kan. 557, 3 Pac. 367; Hamilton v. Brent Lumber Co., 127 Ala 78, 28 South. 698; Bettman v. Harness, 42 W. Va. 433, 26 S. E. 271, 36 L. R. A. 566; Gaines v. Leslie, 1 Ind. Ter. 546, 37 S. W. 947; Woods v. Riley, 72 Miss. 73, 18 South. 384 (overruling earlier Mississippi cases, *contra*); Lanier v. Alison, 31 Fed. 100; Waterloo Co. v. Doe, 82 Fed. 45, 27 C. C. A. 50; King v. Campbell, 85 Fed. 814; Northern Pac Co. v. Soderberg, 86 Fed. 49; Wadsworth v Goree, 96 Ala. 227, 10 South. 848; Heinze v. Butte etc. Co., 20 Mont. 528, 52 Pac. 273; McBrayer v. Hardin, 7 Ired. Eq. 1, 53 Am. Dec. 389; Bishop v. Baisley, 28 Or. 120, 41 Pac. 936

59 Duvall v. Waters, 1 Bland Ch. (Md.) 569, 18 Am. Dec. 350, 361.

such an injunction could only operate temporarily and partially to the prejudice of the free exercise of his right of property. But on the other hand, if it should be eventually shown that the plaintiff had the title, then, as the injunction turns no one out of possession nor displaces anything, it must necessarily leave to the defendant the advantage of fighting the plaintiff with his own property. Upon which, had not the injunction been granted, the most irretrievable destruction might have been perpetrated; acts of waste might have been committed which would deprive the plaintiff of the very substance of his inheritance, mischief might have been done which it would require years to repair; and things might have been torn away or destroyed which it would be difficult or impossible to restore in kind, such as the building, fixtures, trees, or other peculiarities about the estate, which a multitude of associated recollections had rendered precious to their owner; but as compensation for the loss of which, a jury would not give one cent beyond their mere value."

§ 504. **Defendant not Enjoined from Mere Use.**—It is not to be inferred from the above that the courts which have gone thus far are at all hasty, or even ready, to enjoin one in possession claiming title. It has already been pointed out that the injunction granted is a temporary one, subject to all the restraints which the courts always throw about this exercise of "the strong arm of equity." It is only acts for which there is no adequate legal remedy that will be thus enjoined. Hence, the courts never enjoin a defendant in possession from mere use of the premises.[60] "Pending an action for the possession, while the title is disputed and

[60] Bodwell v. Crawford, 26 Kan. 292, 40 Am. Rep. 306; Snyder v Hopkins, 31 Kan 557, 3 Pac. 367; Booher v. Browning, 169 Pa St. 18, 32 Atl 85, Waddingham v Robledo, 6 N. Mex. 347, 28 Pac. 663,

undetermined by a judgment at law, equity ought not to interfere to restrain the defendant from continuing the possession, from the ordinary and natural use of the premises, and the enjoyment of all benefits which flow from possession. If the premises be a farm, the defendant should not be restrained from cultivating the land and enjoying all the benefits which flow from the natural and ordinary use of a farm as a farm. To this end he should be permitted to sow and gather any ordinary crop upon the cultivated ground. He should be permitted to put up any temporary sheds or other buildings necessary for the protection of his stock or the preservation of his crops. He should be permitted to use all the usual agricultural implements in the cultivation of the broken land, not merely in the harvesting of crops as seems to be indicated by the restraining order, but also in planting and cultivation. He should be at liberty to pasture his stock on the grass lands, providing, at least, he has no more stock than is ordinarily raised and kept on such a farm. In short, he should be permitted to use the farm in any ordinary way, as such a farm is used, with the single limitation that he commit no waste, and make no substantial and injurious change in its condition."[61] And in the determination of what is such use, the courts of a particular jurisdiction will, of course, act consistently with their own holding as to what constitutes irreparable injury; hence, acts may in one jurisdiction be permitted as mere ordinary use which, in others, would be enjoined as destruction.[62]

Duvall v. Waters, 1 Bland Ch. (Md.) 569, 18 Am. Dec. 350; Gause v. Perkins, 3 Jones Eq. (56 N. C.) 177, 69 Am. Dec. 728, Carney v. Hadley, 32 Fla. 344, 37 Am. St. Rep. 101, 14 South. 4, 22 L. R. A. 233.

61 Snyder v. Hopkins, 31 Kan 557, 3 Pac 367, *per* Brewer, J.

62 See Gause v Perkins, 3 Jones Eq (56 N C) 177, 69 Am. Dec. 728; Sharpe v. Loane, 124 N. C. 1, 32 S E. 318.

§ 505. **Plaintiff in Possession.**—In view of what has been said above, and of the state of authority on the question of granting a temporary injunction against a defendant in possession claiming title, no argument or discussion will be necessary to show that when the plaintiff is in possession claiming title, he should be granted a temporary injunction, pending the litigation over title, against all trespasses, such that, from their nature or the surrounding circumstances (as, for example, the defendant's insolvency) he cannot have an adequate legal remedy for them. And this is the almost unanimous holding of the courts,[63] though there is an occasional intimation that the mere existence of a dispute as to title is of itself, regardless of the state of possession, enough to preclude the granting of any injunction, temporary or permanent.[64]

63 Santee etc. Co. v. James, 50 Fed. 360; Chapman v. Toy Long, 4 Saw. 28, Fed Cas. No. 2610; Thomas v. Nantahala etc. Co., 8 U. S. App 429, 58 Fed. 485, 7 C. C. A. 330; Pittsburg etc. Co. v. Fiske, 123 Fed. 760; Lyon v. Hunt, 11 Ala 295, 46 Am. Dec. 216; More v. Massini, 32 Cal. 590; Merced Min. Co. v Fremont, 7 Cal. 317, 68 Am. Dec. 262; Thigpen v. Aldridge, 92 Ga. 563, 17 S. E. 860; English v. James, 108 Ga. 123, 34 S. E. 122, Staples v. Rossi, 7 Idaho, 618, 65 Pac. 67, Long v. Casebeer, 28 Kan 226, Peak v. Hayden, 3 Bush (Ky.), 125; Scully v. Rose, 61 Md. 408; Clayton v. Shoemaker, 67 Md. 216, 9 Atl. 635; Butman v. James, 34 Minn. 547, 27 N. W 66; Kyle v. Rhodes, 71 Miss. 487, 15 South. 40; Echelkamp v. Schrader, 45 Mo 505; Lee v Watson, 15 Mont. 228, 38 Pac. 1077; Southmayd v. McLaughlin, 24 N. J. Eq. 181; Piper v. Piper, 38 N. J. Eq. 81, Manning v. Ogden, 70 Hun, 399, 24 N. Y. Supp. 70, Mendenhall v. Harrisburgh etc Co, 27 Or. 38, 39 Pac. 399; Allen v. Dunlap, 24 Or. 229, 33 Pac. 675; Westmoreland etc. Co. v. De Witt, 130 Pa. St 235, 18 Atl. 724, 5 L. R. A. 731.

64 Wilson v. City of Mineral Point, 39 Wis. 160; Woodford v. Alexander, 35 Fla. 333, 17 South. 658; Brown v. Solary, 37 Fla. 102, 19 South. 161; Citizens' etc. Co. v. Camden etc. Co., 29 N. J. Eq. (2 Stew.) 299; National etc. Co. v. Central etc. Co. of N. J., 32 N. J. Eq. 755, 767; Hacker v. Barton, 84 Ill. 313. It should be noticed in this connection that the question here presented is different from that involved in cases in which the sole basis of equity's intervention

§ 506. **Establishment of Title.**—The following language of the court in a leading American case[65] is often quoted: "Two conditions must concur to give [equity] jurisdiction [over trespasses]—the plaintiff's title must be admitted, or be established by a legal adjudication, and the threatened injury must be of such a nature as will cause irreparable damage." This language was used by the court in speaking of the granting of a permanent injunction (a fact not always noticed in quoting it) and from what has been said it follows that in this connection only is it true, and that it is to be so confined in its application.[66] The suggestion of the court that the establishment of plaintiff's title must take place at law is not necessarily true, however. The general principle of equity, that having taken jurisdiction of a cause for one purpose it will retain it and give complete relief, makes it a proper proceeding for courts of equity, if they see fit, to investigate the title themselves at the hearing of the same suit in which the temporary injunction is granted, and then make permanent or dissolve the temporary injunction according to the

is the prevention of multiplicity of suits caused by one defendant's repeated or continuing trespass. In such cases, as has been already pointed out (*ante*, § 496, at note 54), a temporary injunction should not be granted; what plaintiff seeks, and all he is entitled to, is a permanent injunction to save him the annoyance and expense of frequent suits at law. Hence it is very proper, if his title is in doubt, to require that he establish it before he is given an injunction, although it would seem, on principle, to be a matter of discretion, even in that class of cases, whether to require that the disputed title be settled at law or by the court of equity itself. See 1 Pom. Eq. Jur., § 252; Wheelock v. Noonan, 108 N. Y. 179, 2 Am. St. Rep. 405, 15 N. E. 67, affirming 53 N. Y. Super. Ct. (21 Jones & S.) 286.

65 Gause v. Perkins, 3 Jones Eq. (56 N. C.) 177, 69 Am. Dec. 728, *per* Pearson, J.

66 For a statement which makes this limitation see Norton v. Elwert, 29 Or. 583, 41 Pac. 926.

result of the inquiry.[67] Courts of equity, however, more usually send the question to be tried at law, but this is from reasons of policy rather than of jurisdiction.[68] If the plaintiff's title is clear, though denied by the defendant, a permanent injunction may issue at once.[69] If the court decides to have the question tried at law it may procure diligence in the prosecution of the ejectment suit by framing an issue as an incident to its own proceedings and sending the parties to law with it;[70] or by granting the temporary injunction to a plaintiff out of possession on terms that the injunction shall continue only if he begins and prosecutes his action of ejectment with diligence;[71] or, if the defendant is the party out of possession, and therefore the proper person to bring ejectment, by a provision that the injunc-

67 "When there is irreparable damage, injunction lies, though there be conflicting title. . . . . And equity, having once taken jurisdiction, will go on to do complete justice, though in so doing it have to try title, and administer remedies which properly pertain to courts of law": Bettman v Harness, 42 W. Va. 433, 26 S. E. 271, 36 L. R. A. 566. Other cases to the same effect are, City of Peoria v Johnston, 56 Ill. 45; Griffith v. Hilliard, 64 Vt. 643, 25 Atl. 427; Stetson v. Stevens, 64 Vt. 649, 25 Atl. 429; Coppage v. Griffith, 19 Ky. Law Rep. 459, 40 S. W. 908, Shirley v. Hicks, 110 Ga. 516, 35 S. E. 782; West etc Co. v. Reymert, 45 N. Y. 703; Broiestedt v. South Side Co., 55 N. Y. 220; McLaughlin v. Kelly, 22 Cal. 212; Jennings etc. Co. v. Beale, 158 Pa. St 283, 27 Atl. 948; Haskell v. Sutton, 53 W. Va. 206, 44 S. E. 533. *Contra*, Freer v. Davis, 52 W. Va. 1, 94 Am. St. Rep. 895, 43 S. E. 164, 59 L. R. A 556. For an analytical note with further cases, see 1 Ames, Cases in Eq. Juris., 515.

68 Pom. Eq. Jur., § 252. These reasons seem to be two: 1. The desire to preserve to the parties the right to a jury trial; 2. The traditional reluctance of equity courts to extend their jurisdiction over the field already occupied by the law courts.

69 Carpenter v. Grisham, 59 Mo. 247; Miller v. Lynch, 149 Pa. St. 460, 24 Atl. 80.

70 Harris v. Thomas, 1 Hen. & M. (Va.) 18; Santee etc. Co. v. James, 50 Fed. 360.

71 Johnson v. Hughes, 58 N. J. Eq. 406, 43 Atl. 901.

tion shall be made permanent if he fail to do this within a reasonable time.[72]

§ 507. **Possession, When Given by Injunction.**—The question has not infrequently come before the courts just how much relief, if any, is to be given a plaintiff out of possession against a defendant in possession. It has been shown that if the defendant is engaged in acts of a kind proper to invoke equity's preventive power against, he will be enjoined even when he claims title; *a fortiori* it is clear that the same thing should be true if he is admittedly a trespasser, and such is the law.[73] But in general this is the only relief that equity will give in such a case. The further relief which the plaintiff may desire is usually possession of the land. If this is asked for as part of the prayer of a bill for an injunction, it would be consistent with the general equitable rule of giving complete relief to award possession to the plaintiff in such a case. This course seems to be almost never followed,[74] but instead the plaintiff must bring his action of ejectment at law. If possession alone is what plaintiff desires, he can get no relief in equity, because the legal remedy afforded by an action of ejectment or of forcible entry and detainer is adequate for the specific relief desired.[75] And this is no

72 Echelkamp v. Schrader, 45 Mo. 505.

73 Brown v. Solary, 37 Fla. 102, 19 South. 161; Hall v. Nester, 122 Mich. 141, 80 N. W. 982; Webster v. Cooke, 23 Kan. 637; Turner v. Stewart, 78 Mo 480.

74 It was adopted in Bussier v. Weekey, 11 Pa. Super. Ct. 463, citing McGowin v. Remington, 12 Pa. St. 56, 51 Am. Dec. 584, and Nutbrown v. Thornton, 10 Ves 159. See Lattin v. McCarty, 41 N. Y. 107, in which possession was awarded in the same suit in which a deed was vacated.

75 Tawas B. etc. R. R. Co. v Tosco Cir. Judge, 44 Mich. 479, 7 N. W. 65; Calvert v. State, 34 Neb. 616, 52 N. W. 687; Coalter v. Hunter, 4 Rand. (Va.) 58, 15 Am. Dec 726, Brocken v. Preston, 1 Pinn.

less true, though the defendant is insolvent,[76] or though plaintiff, if he had brought his bill sooner, might have secured an injunction against the destructive acts which accompanied the taking of possession by the defendant.[77] Beyond the fact that the legal remedy is adequate, a further reason against transferring possession by injunction, when that is the only relief given, in this country is that it deprives the defendant of jury trial, and so is unconstitutional;[78] and if the transfer is sought by a temporary injunction, an additional reason against it is that this is an attempt to use a temporary injunction for the purpose of changing the *status quo*, whereas its more usual and proper function is to preserve the *status quo*.[79]

But though the rule is general that possession will not be granted by injunction, it is subject to exceptions which exist because legal remedies in the particular cases fail or become insufficient. So, if the plaintiff's estate is purely equitable, and thus legal remedies are not open to him, he may be put in possession by a mandatory injunction.[80] It has also been frequently held

(Wis.) 584, 44 Am. Dec. 412; Fredericks v. Huber, 180 Pa. St 572, 37 Atl. 90; Lowenthal v. New Music Hall Co., 100 Ill. App. 274, Lockhart v. Leeds, 10 N. Mex. 568, 63 Pac. 48, In re Black Point Syndicate, 79 L. T., N. S, 658, Catholic etc. Co. v. Ferguson, 7 S. D 503, 64 N. W. 539, Wehmer v. Fokenga, 57 Neb 510, 78 N. W. 28.

76 Warlier v. Williams, 53 Neb. 143, 73 N. W. 539; Gillick v. Williams, 53 Neb. 146, 73 N. W. 540.

77 Deere v. Guest, 1 Mylne & C 516.

78 Trustees etc of Florida v Gleason, 39 Fla. 771, 23 South. 539, State ex rel. Reynolds v. Graves, 66 Neb. 17, 92 N. W. 144, Forman v Healey, 11 N. D. 563, 93 N. W. 866

79 Dickson v. Dows, 11 N. D. 404, 92 N. W. 797, San Antonio etc. Co. v. Bodenhamer etc Co, 133 Cal. 248, 65 Pac. 471. This reason is not conclusive, however, as shown by the fact that mandatory temporary injunctions are not at all unknown to the law See "Temporary Injunctions," *infra*, in chapters on Nuisance and Easements.

80 Pokegama etc Co v. Klamath River etc. Co., 86 Fed. 528; s. c., 96 Fed. 34, 55, 56; Richter v. Kabat, 114 Mich. 575, 72 N. W. 600.

that one who has begun the process of acquiring title to public land according to the prescribed rules, but who has not yet acquired a title such that he can adequately enforce and protect his right to possession by legal remedies, may procure the possession to which he is entitled by injunction;[81] but his right to get an injunction ceases as soon as he has progressed far enough in acquiring title so that he can maintain ejectment.[82] Another class of cases which has frequently led to a restoration of possession by injunction is that in which the defendant has erected a building which encroaches on the plaintiff's land. In such a case, three remedies are open to him. First, he may remove the building as far as it encroaches over the line, and then sue the defendant for the expense incurred, a remedy which is inadequate because it compels him to undo the wrong of another, because it compels him to advance the cost of men and machinery to effect the removal and take the risk of securing reimbursement from the defendant,[83] and because it burdens him with the risk of injury to other portions of defendant's building not included within the encroaching part.[84] Second, he may submit to the trespass and seek relief by actions for damages at intervals of time, a remedy the inadequacy

81 Sproat v. Durland, 2 Okla. 24, 35 Pac. 682, 886; Woodruff v. Wallace, 3 Okla. 355, 41 Pac. 357; Laughlin v. Fariss, 7 Okla. 1, 50 Pac. 254, 256, West Coast Imp Co. v. Winsor, 8 Wash. 490, 36 Pac. 441; Lee v. Watson, 15 Mont. 228, 38 Pac. 1077; Jackson v. Jackson, 17 Or. 110, 19 Pac. 847.

82 Laughlin v. Fariss, 7 Okla. 1, 50 Pac. 254, Black v. Jackson, 177 U. S 349, 20 Sup. Ct. 648, 44 L. ed. 801, reversing 6 Okla. 751, 52 Pac. 406; Potts v. Hollen, 177 U. S. 365, 20 Sup. Ct. 654, 44 L. ed. 808, reversing 6 Okla. 696, 52 Pac. 917, Harris v. McClung, 10 Okla. 701, 64 Pac. 4.

83 Wheelock v. Noonan, 108 N. Y. 179, 2 Am. St. Rep. 405, 15 N. E 67, affirming 53 N Y Super. Ct. (21 Jones & S) 286.

84 See Baron v. Korn, 127 N. Y. 224, 27 N. E. 804.

of which is attested by the whole doctrine of injunction to prevent multiplicity of suits. Third, he may bring an action of ejectment, the judgment in which puts upon the sheriff in executing it the risk of injuring more of the building than is trespassing, so that this remedy, too, is an impracticable one.[85] On the other hand, the remedy by injunction places the obligation to remove directly on the one who caused the structure to be erected. Hence, equity usually grants an injunction in such cases, and thus as a part of its relief restores possession of land to the owner.[86]

§ 508. **The Balance of Injury.**—The state of facts which has just been considered often occurs in such form as to raise another question which courts of equity have had some difficulty in answering. If a defendant's building encroaches slightly on the plaintiff's land and the plaintiff's damage is small, while the cost to the defendant of removing it is great, should a court of equity disregard wholly the injury which granting relief to the plaintiff will cause the defendant, and issue the injunction? Or, should it balance the injury which its course will cause in granting or in withholding relief, and be influenced by this consideration in its decision? A further element is sometimes introduced into the case by the fact that the defendant is engaged in a busi-

85 Hahl v. Sugo, 27 Misc. Rep. 1, 57 N. Y. Supp. 920, affirmed in 46 App. Div. 632, 61 N. Y. Supp. 770.

86 Baron v. Korn, 127 N. Y. 224; Norton v. Elwert, 29 Or. 583, 41 Pac. 926; Long v. Ragan, 94 Md. 462, 51 Atl. 181; Pile v. Pedrick, 167 Pa. St. 296, 46 Am St. Rep 677, 31 Atl. 646, 36 Wkly Not. Cas. 224; Harrington v. McCarthy, 169 Mass. 492, 48 N. E. 278; Proprietors etc. Wharf v Proprietors etc. Wharf, 85 Me 175 27 Atl. 93; Ryan v. Schwartz, 94 Wis. 403, 69 N. W. 178. *Contra*, Botsford v. Wallace, 72 Conn. 195, 44 Atl. 10; Coast Co. v. Mayor etc. Spring Lake, 56 N. J. Eq. 615, 51 L. R. A. 657, 36 Atl. 21; Schuster v Myers, 148 Mo. 422, 50 S. W. 103.

ness which serves public convenience, and thus can plead not only the injury to himself, but also to the public, as a reason for not granting the injunction. It should be premised in the beginning that the question cannot arise except in a case in which some sufficient reason for equity jurisdiction, such as irreparable injury or the prevention of a multiplicity of suits, exists; in other cases, the injunction will be refused on the simple ground that the legal remedy is adequate. It is believed, too, that the question of the convenience of the public should be treated as immaterial, though it must be said that courts have sometimes allowed their decision to be influenced by this consideration.[87] In answer to the suggestion that the convenience of the public should be taken account of in determining the propriety of granting an injunction, Lord Selborne, L. C., replied: "It is said that the objection of the plaintiff to the laying of these pipes is an unneighborly thing, and that his right is one of little or no value, and one which Parliament, if it were to deal with the question, might possibly disregard. What Parliament might do if it were to deal with the question, is, I apprehend, not a matter for our consideration now, as Parliament has not dealt with the question. Parliament is, no doubt, at liberty to take a higher view upon a balance struck between private interests and public interests than this court can take."[88] In other words, so far as

87 McElroy v. Kansas City, 21 Fed. 261, Rouse v. Martin, 75 Ala 510, 51 Am. Rep. 463; Fogarty v. City of Cincinnati, 7 Ohio N. P. 100, 9 Ohio St. & C. P. Dec. 753. That this is not a proper consideration in such cases, see Goodson v. Richardson, L. R. 9 Ch. App. 221; Attorney-General v. Council etc. of Birmingham, 4 Kay & J. 528, 538, 539; Hinchman v. Horse R. R. Co., 2 C. E. Green (N. J.), 75, 86 Am. Dec. 252; Canastota Knife Co. v. Newington Tramway Co., 69 Conn. 146, 36 Atl. 1107; Sammons v. City of Gloversville, 17 N. Y. Supp. 284, 286 (citing authorities).

88 Goodson v. Richardson, L. R. 9 Ch. App. 221.

the utility to the public is made the basis of an argument, it would seem to be simply urging the propriety of taking private property for public use without the requisite condemnation proceedings[89]—the unwise policy of which cannot be doubted.

Assuming, then, that the only question before the court is the propriety of balancing the injury that may be caused to the parties by the decree, and remembering that the question does not arise except when equity has jurisdiction of the case because the plaintiff's legal remedy is inadequate, it should be noted that to deny the injunction is (1) "to allow the wrong-doer to compel innocent persons to sell their right at a valuation,"[90] and (2) to refuse him altogether any equitable relief in a case where, on the ground of avoiding multiplicity of suits at least, he is clearly within one of the most frequently given reasons for assuming jurisdiction, and where, also, his injury may be irreparable. In view of this situation it is clear that the plaintiff's prayer will not readily be denied, and it can safely be said that the argument based on the balance of injury to the defendant will be availing only in a limited class of cases. On the other hand, it is a general rule of equity not to exercise its extraordinary jurisdiction when it will operate inequitably and oppressively.[91] The problem presented is, therefore, to strike a medium rule between these principles that, as fairly as may be, will do justice. The courts of Massachusetts and New York have considered the question, upon various states of facts, oftener than the courts of any other jurisdiction; and acting independently, have arrived at

89 Hinchman v. Horse R. R. Co., 2 C. E. Green (N. J.), 75, 86 Am. Dec. 252.

90 Tucker v. Howard, 128 Mass. 361.

91 Starkie v. Richmond, 155 Mass. 188, 29 N. E. 770.

substantially the same result. That result, in the words of the Massachusetts court, is as follows:[92] "Where, by an innocent mistake, erections have been placed a little upon the plaintiff's land, and the damage caused to the defendant by the removal of them would be greatly disproportionate to the injury of which the plaintiff complains, the court will not order their removal, but will leave the plaintiff to his remedy at law." The language of the New York court is:[93] "It must be remembered that a willful trespasser cannot in this way acquire an inch of land, because the mandatory injunction must issue as to him; that in other cases where the injury to the plaintiff is irreparable the mandatory injunction will issue, and permanent damages will not be awarded; that where the granting of an injunction would work greater damage to an innocent defendant than the injury from which the plaintiff prays relief, the injunction could be refused absolutely, and the plaintiff compelled to seek his remedy at law." In practice these rules are probably almost the same,[94]

92 Lynch v. Union Institution for Savings, 159 Mass. 306, 34 N. E. 364, 20 L. R. A. 842. Other Massachusetts cases which show the development and working of the rule are Tucker v. Howard, 128 Mass. 361; Brande v. Grace, 154 Mass. 210, 31 N. E. 633; Starkie v. Richmond, 155 Mass. 188, 29 N. E. 770; Lynch v. Union Institution for Savings, 158 Mass. 394, 33 N. E. 603; Boland v. St. John's Schools, 163 Mass. 129, 39 N. E. 1035; Methodist etc. Society v. Akers, 167 Mass. 560, 46 N. E. 381; Harrington v. McCarthy, 169 Mass. 492, 48 N. E. 278; Cobb v. Massachusetts Chem. Co., 179 Mass. 423, 60 N. E. 790.

93 Goldbacher v. Eggers, 38 Misc. Rep. 36, 76 N. Y. Supp 881, 886, affirmed in 84 N. Y. Supp. 1127. See, also, Crocker v. Manhattan Life Ins. Co., 61 App Div. 226, 70 N. Y. Supp. 492, modifying 31 Misc. Rep. 687, 66 N. Y. Supp. 84; Proskey v. Cumberland Realty Co., 35 Misc. Rep. 50, 70 N. Y. Supp 1125.

94 The difference between the two rules, if any, is in the amount of damage to the plaintiff which the court will balance against the greater damage to the defendant. From the language of the Massachusetts court, "erections have been placed *a little* upon the plain-

and they perhaps represent as nearly a fair resultant of the arguments on the side of both parties as can be arrived at. Both rules protect the plaintiff from very serious injury, both deny any protection to a willful wrong-doer, and both, as far as possible, refuse to apply the remedy of mandatory injunction when to do so would be oppressive to the defendant. Doubtless they will be followed, though cases can be found which, not including the elements making necessary carefully qualified statements, contain broad *dicta* that the balance of injury will or will not be considered.[95] It

tiff's land,'' it would seem a fair inference that the rule would not be applied against a plaintiff whose damage was at all serious, and the cases that so far have arisen bear out the inference. The New York rule has no such limitations short of ''irreparable'' injury to the plaintiff; and in the two principal New York cases above cited the permanent damages awarded to the plaintiff were $600 and $5,000 respectively. The explanation of this difference, if it exists, lies in the fact that the Massachusetts courts seem to adopt the traditional view of equity courts that land is *per se* within the protection of equity, and therefore any trespass on it which amounts to a confiscation of ever so small a portion of it is ''irreparable'' injury, hence the rule under discussion is to be confined within the narrowest compass. On the other hand, it is evident not only from the statement of the rule above quoted but also from other portions of the opinion, and from the opinion in Crocker v. Manhattan Life Ins. Co., *supra*, that the New York courts do not regard the plaintiff as entitled to come into equity in this class of cases on the ground of irreparable injury at all, but solely on the ground of preventing multiplicity of suits; hence even when his damages are large it does not follow that he is ''irreparably'' injured, and therefore the question is simply one of balancing two injuries, neither of which is irreparable, between two innocent parties The ideal consideration that it is an irreparable injury to the plaintiff to be deprived of his property without his consent is, of course, not admitted.

95 That the balance of the injury is to be given weight. McElroy v. Kansas City, 21 Fed. 257, 261; Fullenwider v. Supreme Council etc. League, 73 Ill App. 321, Wilcox v. Wheeler, 47 N. H. 488; Scharr v. City of Camden (N. J. Ch.), 49 Atl. 817; Fisher v. Carpenter, 67 N. H. 569, 39 Atl 1018, Edwards v. Allouez Min. Co., 38 Mich 46, 31 Am. Rep. 301. That the balance of injury is not to be

should be added by way of caution that the foregoing discussion applies only to the granting of permanent injunctions; it has already been pointed out that on an application for a temporary injunction, when the rights of the parties are undecided, the balance of injury is a controlling consideration.[96]

§ 509. **Personal Remedy Open to Plaintiff.**—In a number of cases a plaintiff has sought injunctions against trespasses when it would be possible for him by his own personal efforts to put an end to the trespass, and thus render the legal remedy adequate. In the leading case in which the question was considered, the defendant had covered a lot belonging to the plaintiff with large rocks, and in reply to the argument of counsel the court said:[97] "It is now said that the remedy was at law; that the owner could have removed the stone and then recovered of the defendant for the expense incurred. But to what locality could the owner remove them? He could not put them in the street; the defendant presumably had no vacant lands of his own on which to throw the burden; and it would follow that the owner would be obliged to hire some vacant lot or place of deposit, become responsible for the rent, and advance the cost of men and machinery to effect the removal. If any adjudication can be found throwing such burden upon the owner, compelling him to do in advance for the owner what the latter is bound to do, I should very much doubt its authority. On the contrary, the law

considered: Norton v. Elwert, 29 Or. 583, 41 Pac. 926; Hennessy v. Carmony, 50 N. J. Eq. 616, 25 Atl. 374 (case of nuisance, but the argument is none the less in point here).

96 *Ante*, § 502.

97 Per Finch, J., in Wheelock v. Noonan, 108 N. Y. 179, 2 Am. St. Rep. 405, 15 N. E. 67, affirming 53 N. Y. Super. Ct. (21 Jones & S.) 286.

is the other way. And all the cases which give to the injured party successive actions for the continuance of the wrong are inconsistent with the idea that the injured party must once for all remove it." These arguments are not easy to meet, and there are cases in accord with its suggestion;[98] on the other hand, there are cases in which the burden thrown upon the plaintiff in putting an end to the trespass himself would not be heavy, and in which, therefore, the injunction has been denied.[99] If, however, the party whose land is trespassed upon wishes by his own efforts to remove the trespassing object, he may of course do so, and equity will not interfere with him.[100]

§ 510. **Relief Given.**—A brief paragraph may perhaps properly be given to noting the relief which equity gives in such cases of trespass as fall within its jurisdiction It is, of course, clear that the only ground on which a case of trespass can be brought into equity is the plaintiff's right to an injunction, and this is therefore the primary relief given him. It is usually prohibitory, but only because prohibitory relief is more often desired. Despite occasional *dicta* to the contrary,[101] the use of mandatory injunctions is well established. The

98 Sylvester v. Jerome, 19 Colo. 128, 34 Pac. 760; Kern v. Field, 68 Minn. 317, 64 Am. St. Rep. 479, 71 N. W. 393. See Beach v. Crane, 2 N. Y. 86, 97, 49 Am. Dec. 369.

99 Indianapolis Rolling Mill Co. v. City of Indianapolis, 29 Ind. 245; Boyden v. Bragaw, 53 N. J. Eq. (8 Dick.) 26, 30 Atl. 330; Mechanics' Foundry of San Francisco v. Ryall, 75 Cal. 601, 17 Pac. 703; cf. De Groot v. Peters, 124 Cal. 406, 71 Am. St. Rep. 91, 57 Pac. 209. And see Rankin v. Charless, 19 Mo. 551, 61 Am. Dec. 574; Avery v. Empire Woolen Co, 82 N. Y. 582.

100 Lyle v. Little, 83 Hun, 532, 33 N. Y. Supp. 8; Windfall etc. Co. v. Terwilliger, 152 Ind. 364, 53 N. E. 284; De Sale v. Millard, 108 Mich. 581, 66 N. W. 481.

101 Way Cross etc. Co. v. Southern Pine Co., 111 Ga. 233, 36 S. E. 641; Newlin v. Prevo, 81 Ill. App. 75.

discussion of the questions when equity will put a plaintiff in possession, and the effect of the balance of injury which will be caused by granting or withholding its relief, have made necessary previous citation in this chapter of numerous cases in which mandatory injunctions were issued. A few others are collected in the note,[102] in some of which the court went the length of decreeing not only the *undoing* of wrongful acts, but also the *doing* of rightful ones—not merely destructive, but constructive acts.[103] Further, the general principle of equity to give full relief in a cause in which it has jurisdiction for any purpose applies in case of trespass as well as elsewhere. That it is under this rule that equity acts in passing on disputed titles has already been seen.[104] On the same principle equity gives damages for past trespassing in addition to an injunction,[105] but not when the injunction is refused for want of jurisdiction.[106] Or damages only may be given when the court has jurisdiction of the cause, but finds it necessary to refuse the injunction for some other reason than want of jurisdiction, as, for example, because an injunction would be futile.[107] The flexibility of in-

102 Crocker v. Manhattan etc. Co., 61 App. Div. 226, 70 N. Y. Supp. 492, modifying 31 Misc. Rep. 687, 66 N Y. Supp. 84, Norton v. Elwert, 29 Or. 583, 41 Pac. 926; United States v. Brighton Ranche Co, 26 Fed. 218; Creely v. Bay State etc. Co., 103 Mass. 514; Wilmarth v. Woodcock, 66 Mich. 331, 33 N. W. 400; Norwalk Heating etc. Co. v. Vernam, 75 Conn. 662, 96 Am. St. Rep. 246, 55 Atl. 168.

103 Lake Shore etc. Co. v. Wiley, 193 Pa. St. 496, 44 Atl. 583; Bussier v. Weekey, 11 Pa. Super. Ct. 463.

104 *Ante*, § 506. See, also, Kilgore v. Norman, 119 Fed. 1006.

105 Morris v. Bean, 123 Fed. 618; Bird v. Wilmington etc Co, 8 Rich. Eq (S. C.) 46, 64 Am. Dec. 739; Downing v Dinwiddie, 132 Mo. 92, 33 S. W 470; Bishop v. Baisley, 28 Or. 119, 41 Pac. 936.

106 Pres. etc. Baltimore etc. Road v. United etc. Co., 93 Md. 138, 48 Atl. 723.

107 Lewis v. Town of N. Kingston, 16 R I. 15, 27 Am. St. Rep. 724, 11 Atl. 173, Lane v. Michigan Traction Co., 10 Det. Leg. News, 685, 97 N. W. 354.

junctions in the hands of the courts also enables them, by simply framing the decree in the alternative, to accomplish the purpose of condemnation proceedings in cases in which the defendant has the right of eminent domain,[108] or to give permanent damages to the plaintiff in cases in which at law he could recover only the damages caused him up to the date of the suit.[109]

§ 511. **Estoppel, Laches, Acquiescence.**—The general equitable rules as to estoppel, laches and acquiescence also apply in the subject of this chapter. No discussion of these rules will be undertaken here, as they are treated elsewhere; a few cases illustrating their application in cases of trespass are collected in the note.[110]

108 Henderson v. New York Cent. etc. Co., 78 N. Y. 423, Pappenheim v. Metropolitan etc. Co., 128 N. Y. 436, 26 Am. St. Rep. 486, 28 N. E. 518, 13 L. R. A. 401. See *ante*, §§ 473, 470.

109 Crocker v. Manhattan Ins. Co., 61 App. Div. 226, 70 N. Y. Supp. 492, affirming 31 Misc Rep. 687, 66 N. Y. Supp. 84, Goldbacher v. Eggers, 38 Misc. Rep. 36, 76 N. Y. Supp 881; affirmed in 84 N. Y. Supp. 1127.

110 Estoppel.—City of New York v. Pine, 185 U S. 93, 22 Sup. Ct. 592, 46 L. ed. 820, reversing 50 C. C. A. 145, 112 Fed 98, 103 Fed. 337, Pennsylvania R. Co. v. Glenwood etc. Co., 184 Pa. St. 227, 41 Wkly. Not. Cas. 441, 39 Atl. 80, Bright v. Allan, 203 Pa. St 394, 93 Am. St. Rep. 769, 53 Atl. 251.

Laches.—Southard v. Morris Canal Co, 1 N. J. Eq. 519; Scudder v. Trenton etc. Co., 1 N. J. Eq. 694, 23 Am. Dec. 756; Becker v. Lebanon etc Co., 188 Pa. St. 484, 43 Wkly. Not. Cas. (Pa) 229, 41 Atl. 612. See, also, *ante*, chapter I.

Acquiescence.—Bassett v Salisbury etc. Mills, 47 N. H. 426; Blanchard v. Doering, 23 Wis. 200.

CHAPTER XXIV.

INJUNCTION AGAINST NUISANCE.

ANALYSIS.

§ 512. **Nature and Extent of the Jurisdiction.**—The term "nuisance" has in equity no different signification from that given it in law. Anything which is a nuisance in law is also a nuisance in equity, and, on the other hand, "it is true that equity will only interfere, in case of nuisance, where the thing complained of is a nuisance at law: there is no such thing as an equitable nuisance."[1] This is not saying that the jurisdiction of law and that of equity are co-extensive; it is simply pointing out that equity in the determination of what constitutes a nuisance follows the law.[2] Whether, assuming a nuisance to exist, equity will take jurisdiction to enjoin it, is another question, a question which is answered in every particular case by determining whether there is a need of equity interposing; whether, in the usual phrase, the legal remedy is adequate. No special attention need, therefore, be given here to a definition of nuisance, though such of its characteristics as affect the equitable remedy will be spoken of in connection with those features of the equitable remedy to which they are related.

§ 513. **When the Legal Remedy is Adequate.**—While the jurisdiction of law over nuisance and that of equity are not co-extensive, much more nearly than in cases of trespass it is true that every person injured by a nuisance may come into law or equity, whichever he prefers, for his remedy. The reason for this is, that from their nature and effect, most nuisances cannot be satis-

1 Per Kindersley, V. C., in Soltau v. De Held, 2 Sim., N. S., 133 151.

2 Baines v Baker, 1 Amb. 158; Wolcott v. Melick, 11 N. J. Eq. 204, 66 Am. Dec 790, Mississippi etc. Co. v. Ward, 67 U. S. (2 Black) 485, 17 L. ed. 311; Brady v. Weeks, 3 Barb. 157; Watson v. City of Columbia, 77 Mo. App. 267; Northern Pac. R. R. Co. v. Whalen, 149 U. S 157, 13 Sup Ct. 822, 37 L. ed. 686.

factorily remedied at law. The grounds on which equity enjoins nuisances are chiefly two, viz., irreparable injury to plaintiff, and the prevention of multiplicity of suits. Those which will not be enjoined, therefore, are such nuisances only as do not fall within either of the above classes. But this necessarily means a comparatively small number of cases, for it is characteristic of nuisances in general that they are either continuous or recurring, or else they cause irreparable injury, and in many cases, indeed, they are of a character to bring them within both of the reasons for equity's intervention. It is said in one case: "It is not in every case of nuisance that this court should interfere. I think that it ought not to do so in cases in which the injury is merely temporary and trifling; but I think that it ought to do so in cases in which the injury is permanent and serious."[3] The language of another court is that nuisances which are "temporary and occasional only, are not grounds for the interference of this court by injunction, except in extreme cases."[4] These two extracts taken together probably contain a complete statement of the kinds of nuisances for which the legal remedy is considered adequate. They are: (1) Nuisances which are temporary and single and which do not cause irreparable injury. (2) Nuisances which, not doing irreparable injury, are yet repeated, but only occasionally, not so often that the suits at law to redress them cause a vexatious or oppressive amount of litigation.[5]

3 Goldsmid v. Tunbridge etc. Commrs., L. R. 1 Ch. App. 349, 354, 355.

4 Swaine v. Great Northern Ry. Co., 4 De Gex, J & S. 211, 216. "The present or threatened injury must be real, not trifling, transient, or temporary": 4 Pom. Eq. Jur., § 1350; cited, McLaughlin v. Sandusky, 17 Neb. 110, 22 N. W. 241

5 For cases of this kind, see Attorney-General v Sheffield Gas etc.

§ 514. **Extent of the Jurisdiction; Irreparable and Continuing or Recurring Nuisances.**—In the preceding paragraph it is said that the chief forms in which the inadequacy of the common law—the fundamental basis of all equity jurisdiction over torts—manifests itself, are cases of irreparable injury, and cases of continuous or repeated nuisances involving a multiplicity of suits at law.[6] These two grounds of jurisdiction do not readily, if at all, admit of separate treatment, however. The definitions of nuisance very generally agree in including as one of its elements that it is something which interferes with one's comfort in, or enjoyment of, his property, and it is the loss of this comfort and enjoyment in the use of his property which gives the right of action. Now "comfort" and "enjoyment" are almost

Co., 3 De Gex, M. & G. 304; Blain v. Brady, 64 Md. 373, 1 Atl. 609, Bartlett v. Moyers, 88 Md. 715, 42 Atl. 204; Harrison v. Southwark etc. Co., [1891] 2 Ch. D. 409, Peterson v. City of Santa Rosa, 119 Cal. 387, 51 Pac. 557; Hagge v. Kansas etc. Co., 104 Fed. 391; Nelson v. Milligan, 151 Ill. 462, 38 N. W. 239; Cooke v. Forbes, L. R. 5 Eq. 166; Mayor etc. Canton v. Canton etc. Warehouse (Miss.), 36 South. 266. See, also, Dennis v. Mobile etc. Co., 139 Ala. 109, 35 South. 651; Penn. etc. Co. v. City of Chicago, 181 Ill. 289, 54 N. E. 825, 53 L. R. A. 223.

6 "Whenever this court interferes by way of injunction in the shape of prevention rather than allow an injury to be inflicted, it does so in cases where the act complained of is one in respect of which there is also a legal remedy, upon two grounds (they being of a totally distinct character)—first, where the injury is irreparable in the eye of this court, as the cutting down of a tree, although its value may be paid for; and secondly, where the act is continuous, and so continuous that this court acting on the same principle as it acted on in olden times with reference to bills of peace by restraining actions after repeated trials, so now will restrain repeated acts which can only end in incessant actions being brought, will restrain them at once on account of the continuous character of the wrong, which continuous character in itself makes the injury to be grievous, and so far in the eye of this court, irreparable": Per Wood, L J, in Attorney-General v. Cambridge etc. Gas Co., 17 Week. Rep. 145, L. R 4 Ch. App. 71.

ideal illustrations of the sort of thing for the permanent loss of which damages will not be a fair or just compensation. They are not to be paid for in money. They are in this respect essentially of the same character as the *pretium affectionis* which the courts sometimes have made the basis for decreeing specific performance of contracts to sell chattels, or for injunctions against trespasses to chattels. Hence it follows that most nuisances when permanent, or when continuing for any considerable length of time, or when frequently repeated, are properly to be classed as irreparable in their nature. Besides this feature of nuisance (which pertains only to its effect on the person injured) it is to be remembered that the property affected is usually land, which is regarded as peculiarly within the protection of equity; and so far as one's enjoyment of his land is destroyed, it is a destruction, if not physical, yet at least in the character in which it has been held and enjoyed, of what is generally regarded in equity as property so peculiar as not properly to be made a subject of compensation by a jury. In brief, then, a continuing nuisance is in general an irreparable injury, for two distinct reasons: (1) From its effect on the person injured. (2) From the destructive nature of the injury to the use of property of a peculiar character.[7]

[7] The argument of the text is well illustrated by the facts and the language of the court in Campbell v. Seaman, 63 N. Y. 568, 20 Am. Rep. 567, as the following quotation from the decision, per Earl, J., will show: "The plaintiffs had built a costly mansion and had laid out their grounds and planted them with ornamental and useful trees and vines, for their comfort and enjoyment How can one be compensated in damages for the destruction of his ornamental trees, and the flowers and vines which surround his home? How can a jury estimate their value in dollars and cents? The fact that trees and vines are for ornament or luxury entitles them no less to the protection of the law. Every one has the right to surround himself with articles of luxury, and he will be no less protected than one who pro-

But in both the above reasons the fact that the nuisance is permanent or continuous or repeated is a very important, if not essential, element, and, as most nuisances are permanent or continuous, or repeated, this fact alone is enough to bring them into equity. Hence it has not been necessary for the courts to attempt careful definitions of irreparable injury in nuisance cases, as a more obvious and simple ground of jurisdiction is usually ready at hand. And the fact that the studied care of the meaning of the term, which is common in the cases on trespass, is largely wanting in the cases on nuisance, may be perhaps thus explained.[8] This may also ex-

vides himself only with articles of necessity. The law will protect a flower or a vine as well as an oak. These damages are irreparable, too, because the trees and vines cannot be replaced, and the law will not compel a person to take money rather than the objects of beauty and utility which he places around his dwelling to gratify his taste or to promote his comfort and his health.

"Here the injunction also prevents a multiplicity of suits. The injury is a recurring one, and every time the poisonous breath from defendant's brick-kiln sweeps over plaintiff's land they have a cause of action. Unless the nuisance be restrained the litigation would be interminable. The policy of the law favors, and the peace and good order of society are best promoted by the termination of such litigations by a single suit.

"The fact that this nuisance is not continual, and that the injury is only occasional, furnishes no answer to the claim for an injunction. The nuisance has occurred often enough within two years to do the plaintiffs large damage. Every time a kiln is burned some injury may be expected, unless the wind should blow the poisonous gas away from the plaintiffs' land. Nuisances causing damage less frequently have been restrained."

8 The following are illustrations of the rather cursory treatment given to the definition of the word in the cases on nuisance: "The foundation of this jurisdiction, interfering by injunction, is that head of mischief, alluded to by Lord Hardwicke (1 Dick. 164), that sort of material injury to the comfort of the existence of those who dwell in the neighboring house, requiring the application of a power to prevent, as well as remedy, an evil, for which damages, more or less, would be given in an action at law". Per Lord Eldon in Attorney-General v. Nichol, 16 Ves. 338, 342. "The familiar ground on which

plain the frequent practice of the equity courts in nuisance cases to confine their attention to the question of fact whether a nuisance exists or not, and to assume jurisdiction as a matter of course.[9] Both of the above

the extraordinary power of the court is invoked in such cases is that it is inequitable and unjust that the injured party should be compelled to resort to repeated actions at law to recover damages for his injury, which, after all, in this class of cases, are incapable of measurement'': Per Pitney, V. C., in Hennessy v. Carmony, 50 N. J. Eq. 616, 25 Atl. 374, 377, 378. ''There are many injuries which in the very nature of things cannot be repaired by any money consideration—such, for instance, as result from acts which outrage the feelings and wound the sensibilities, or deprive us of objects of affection, and of things, perhaps trivial in themselves, but of inestimable value by reason solely of being associated with some precious memory or touching incident of our lives; or it may be that the maintenance of the writ was required to preserve to us our homes, and to establish us in a state or condition which, lost for the moment, can never be recovered nor the loss atoned for by money'': Crescent City etc. Co. v. Police Jury, 32 La. Ann. 1194, quoted with approval in State ex rel. Violett v. King, 46 La. Ann. 78, 14 South. 423, 425.

9 Crump v. Lambert, L. R. 3 Eq. 409; Proprietors etc. Wharf v. Proprietors etc. Wharf, 85 Me. 175, 27 Atl. 93; Hennessy v. Carmony, 50 N. J. Eq. 616, 25 Atl. 374. In Crump v. Lambert, Lord Romilly, M. R., said: ''With respect to the question of law, I consider it to be established by numerous decisions that smoke, unaccompanied with noise or noxious vapors, that noise alone, that offensive vapors alone, although not injurious to health, may severally constitute an injury to the owner of adjoining or neighboring property; that if they do so, substantial damages may be recovered at law, and that this court, if applied to, will restrain the continuance of the nuisance by injunction in all cases where substantial damages could be recovered at law. . . . The law on this subject is, I apprehend, the same, whether it be enforced by action at law or by bill in equity. In any case where a plaintiff could obtain substantial damages at law, he is entitled to an injunction to restrain the nuisance in this court. . . . The real question in all the cases is the question of fact, viz., whether the annoyance is such as materially to interfere with the ordinary comfort of human existence'' In Hennessy v. Carmony, the court, per Pitney, V. C., said: ''The result of a careful review of the evidence upon my mind is to lead me to the conclusion that the degree of injury is such as to entitle the complainant to damages in an action at law, with the result that he is entitled to an injunction in this court.''

suggestions are borne out by the following language of the court in a well-considered American case: "The next position taken in behalf of the defendant is, that even if the subtraction of this water is to be held to be wrongful with respect to the complainant, still a court of equity will not give relief by way of injunction, but will leave the parties injured to their remedy at law. If this were an application for a preliminary injunction it is clear that an objection of this kind should prevail, for the act which the defendant threatens to do is obviously not of a character to inflict any irreparable injury. But after a court of equity has entertained a bill, and, instead of sending the case to a trial at law, has itself tried the questions of fact involved, and settled the legal right in favor of the complainant, it certainly would be a result much to be deprecated, if, at such a stage of the controversy, it was the law that the chancellor were required to say to such a complainant, 'Your right is clear; if you sue at law you must inevitably recover, and after several recoveries it will then be the duty of this court, on the ground of avoiding a multiplicity of suits, to enjoin the continuance of this nuisance; still you must go through the form of bringing such suits, before this court of equity can or will interfere.' In those cases in which to the mind of the chancellor, the right of the complainant is clear, and the damage sustained by him is substantial, so that his right to recover damages at law is indisputable, and the chancellor has considered and established his right, I think it not possible that any authority can be produced which sustains the doctrine contended for by the counsel of the defendant."[10]

10 Per Beasley, C. J., in Higgins v. Flemington Water Co., 36 N. J. Eq. 538, 544.

§ 515. **Illustrations.**—The cases in which nuisances were enjoined were not frequent before the middle of the last century, but since that time they have become very numerous, covering a wide variety of states of fact. Illustrations are injunctions against the pollution,[11] diversion,[12] obstruction,[13] or abstraction[14] of running water; the pollution, taking, or waste of percolating water;[15] noises of various kinds;[16] vibration from

11 Crossley v. Lightowler, L. R. 2 Ch. App. 478; Holt v. Corporation of Rochdale, L. R. 10 Eq. 354; McIntyre Bros. v. McGavin, [1893] App. Cas. 268; Platt v. Waterbury, 72 Conn. 531, 77 Am. St. Rep. 335, 45 Atl. 154, 48 L. R. A. 691; Chapman v. City of Rochester, 110 N. Y. 273, 6 Am. St. Rep. 366, 18 N. E. 88; Strobel v. Kerr Salt Co., 164 N. Y. 303, 79 Am. St. Rep. 643, 58 N. E. 142, 51 L R. A. 687; Fuller v. Swan etc. Co., 12 Colo. 12, 19 Pac. 836; Village of Dwight v. Hayes, 150 Ill. 273, 41 Am. St. Rep. 360, 37 N. E. 218; Valparaiso v. Hagen, 153 Ind. 337, 74 Am. St. Rep. 305, 54 N. E. 1062, 48 L. R. A. 707; Barton v. Union Cattle Co., 28 Neb. 350, 26 Am. St. Rep. 340, 44 N. W. 454, 7 L. R. A. 457.

12 Pugh v. Golden etc. Ry. Co., L. R. 15 Ch. D. 330; Gardner v. Village of Newburgh, 2 Johns. Ch. 162, 7 Am. Dec. 526; Smith v. City of Rochester, 92 N. Y. 463, 44 Am. Rep. 393; Pine v. Mayor etc. N. Y., 103 Fed. 337; Rupley v. Welch, 23 Cal. 452; Ferrea v. Knipe, 28 Cal. 340, 87 Am. Dec. 128; Moore v. Clear Lake Water Works, 68 Cal. 146, 8 Pac. 816; Saint v. Guerrerio, 17 Colo. 448, 31 Am. St. Rep. 320, 30 Pac. 335; Watson v. New Milford etc. Co., 71 Conn. 442, 42 Atl. 265; Kay v. Kirk, 76 Md. 41, 35 Am. St. Rep. 408, 24 Atl. 326; Raymond v. Winsette, 12 Mont. 551, 33 Am. St. Rep. 604, 31 Pac 537.

13 McKee v. Delaware etc. Co., 125 N. Y. 353, 21 Am. St. Rep. 740, 26 N. E. 305; Belknap v. Trimble, 3 Paige, 577.

14 Mostyn v. Atherton, [1899] 2 Ch. 360; Arthur v. Case, 1 Paige, 447. For a fuller discussion of nuisances to running water, see *post*, Vol. II, chapter on Injunctions for Protection of Water Rights.

15 Ballard v. Tomlinson, L. R. 29 Ch. D. 115; Proprietors etc. River v. Braintree etc. Co., 149 Mass. 480, 21 N. E. 761, 4 L. R. A. 272; Barclay v. Abraham, 121 Iowa, 619, 100 Am St. Rep. 365, 96 N. W. 1080. See Trinidad Asphalt Co. v. Abard, 68 L. J. P. C. 114, [1899] App. Cas. 594, 81 L. J., N. S., 132, 48 Week. Rep 116.

16 Soltau v. De Held, 2 Sim., N. S., 133 (ringing of bells in a chapel and a church at frequent intervals every day); Walker v. Brewster, L. R 5 Eq. 25 (brass band which played twice a week from two or three o'clock in the afternoon until eleven o'clock at night);

machinery or from pounding;[17] unpleasant odors from urinals, privies, horses, stables, slaughter-houses, and the like;[18] noxious vapors, gases or smoke from brick-kilns, factories, blacksmith-shops and the like;[19] objects or acts which are dangerous to those in their vicinity, such as powder magazines,[20] hospitals for contag-

Bellamy v. Wells, 60 L. J. Ch. D. 156 (sporting club, patrons of which annoyed the plaintiffs by whistling for cabs after midnight), Ball v. Ray, L. R. 8 Ch. App. 467 (noise made by horses in a stable adjoining the plaintiff's hotel); Bishop v. Banks, 33 Conn. 118, 87 Am. Dec. 197 (bleating of calves during the night-time in the defendant's slaughter-house pens); Hill v. McBurney, 112 Ga. 788, 38 S. E 42, 52 L. R. A. 398 (blowing of a factory whistle at unseasonable hours); Trom v. Lewis, 31 Ind. App. 178, 66 N. E. 490 (beer-garden); Snyder v. Cabell, 29 W. Va. 48, 1 S. E. 241 (skating-rink); Stevenson v. Pucci, 32 Misc. Rep. 464, 66 N. Y. Supp. 712 (blasting near plaintiff's house before seven o'clock in the morning or after six o'clock in the evening); Sturges v. Bridgman, L. R. 11 Ch. D. 852 (vibration from mortar and pestle); Rogers v. John Week etc. Co., 117 Wis. 5, 93 N. W. 821.

17 Hennessy v. Carmony, 50 N. J. Eq. (5 Dick) 616, 25 Atl 374; Sturgis v. Bridgman, L. R 11 Ch. D. 852; English v. Progress etc. Co., 95 Ala. 259, 10 South. 134 (injunction refused, because fact that nuisance existed was not established); Colwell v. St. Pancras etc. Council, [1904] L. R. 1 Ch. 707.

18 Vernon v. Vestry etc. Westminster, L. R. 16 Ch D. 449; Radican v. Buckley, 138 Ind. 582, 38 N. E. 53; Perrine v. Taylor, 43 N. J. Eq. 128, 12 Atl. 769; Lippincott v. Leslie, 44 N. J. Eq. 120, 14 Atl. 103; Rapier v. London etc. Co., [1893] 2 Ch. 589; Pruner v. Pendleton, 75 Va. 516, 40 Am Rep. 738; Reichert v. Geers, 98 Ind. 73, 49 Am Rep. 736; Shroyer v. Campbell, 31 Ind. App. 83, 67 N. E. 193.

19 Campbell v. Seaman, 63 N. Y. 568, 20 Am. Rep. 567; Pollock v Lester, 11 Hare, 266; Crump v. Lambert, L. R. 3 Eq. 409; Ross v Butler, 19 N. J. Eq. 294, 97 Am. Dec. 654; McMorran v. Fitzgerald, 106 Mich 649, 58 Am. St. Rep 511, 64 N. W. 569; Peacock v. Spitzelberger, 16 Ky. Law Rep. 803, 29 S. W. 877; Daugherty etc. Co v Kittanning etc Mfg. Co., 178 Pa. St. 215, 35 Atl. 1111. See, also, St. Louis Safe Deposit & Sav. Bank v Kennett Estate, 101 Mo. App 370, 74 S. W. 474 (heat from smoke-stack adjoining plaintiff's building).

20 Heeg v. Licht, 80 N. Y. 579, 36 Am. Rep. 654; Wier's Appeal, 74 Pa St. 230; Tyner v. People's Gas Co., 131 Ind. 408, 31 N. E. 61 (keeping nitroglycerin near plaintiff's dwelling); Blanc v. Murray, 36 La. Ann. 162, 51 Am. Rep. 7 (inflammable building); Kaufman v. Stein, 138

ious diseases,[21] blasting[22] and similar dangers; things which offend the moral sense, such as brothels;[23] ob-

Ind. 49, 46 Am. St. Rep. 368, 37 N. E. 33 (same as preceding case). In Heeg v Licht, *supra*, the injunction was sought to restrain the defendant from manufacturing and storing upon his premises fireworks or other explosive substances. In pointing out that the existence of a nuisance does not depend at all upon any negligence of the defendant, the court, per Miller, J, said: "Most of the cases cited rest upon the maxim '*sic utere tuo*,' etc, and where the right to the undisturbed possession and enjoyment of property comes in conflict with the rights of others, that it is better, as a matter of public policy, that a single individual should surrender the use of his land for especial purposes injurious to his neighbors or to others, than that the latter should be deprived of the use of their property altogether or be subjected to great danger, loss and injury, which might result if the rights of the former were without any restriction or restraint. The keeping of gunpowder or other materials in a place, or under circumstances, where it would be liable, in case of explosion, to injure the dwelling-houses or the persons of those residing in close proximity, we think rests upon the same principle, and is governed by the same rules. An individual has no more right to keep a magazine of powder upon his premises, which is dangerous, to the detriment of his neighbor, than he is authorized to engage in any other business which may occasion serious consequences." With Blanc v. Murray and Kaufman v. Stein, *supra*, compare Rhodes v. Dunbar, 57 Pa. St. (7 P. F. Smith) 274, 98 Am. Dec. 221, Duncan v. Hayes, 22 N. J. Eq 25, Chambers v. Cramer, 49 W. Va. 395, 38 S. E. 691, 54 L R A. 545; English v. Progress etc. Co., 95 Ala. 259, 10 South. 134—which cases hold that mere increased risk from fire and consequent rise of insurance rates do not constitute a nuisance and will not be enjoined.

21 Metropolitan Asylum v. Hill, L. R. 6 App Cas 196; Gilford v. Babies' Hospital etc. N. Y., 21 Abb. N. C. 159, 1 N Y. Supp 448.

22 Hill v. Schneider, 4 N. Y. Ann. Cas. 70, 13 App. Div. 299, 43 N. Y. Supp. 1, Stevenson v. Pucci, 32 Misc. Rep. 464, 66 N. Y. Supp 712.

23 Cranford v. Tyrrell, 128 N. Y. 341, 28 N. E 514; Hamilton v. Whitridge, 11 Md. 128, 69 Am. Dec. 184, Weakley v. Page, 102 Tenn. 178, 53 S. W. 551, 46 L R. A. 552; Farrell v. Cook, 16 Neb. 483, 49 Am. Rep. 721, 20 N. W. 720 (standing of jacks and stallions in sight of plaintiff's dwelling); Ingersoll v. Rousseau, 35 Wash. 92, 76 Pac. 513, Dempsie v. Darling (Wash.), 81 Pac. 152. These cases do not, of course, hold that immorality is *per se* a basis for an injunction; such further characteristics as will bring it within the usual definitions of nuisance must be shown. In Craw-

struction of highways[24] or navigation;[25] removal of support to land;[26] acts which cause a physical invasion of the plaintiff's land, such as overflowing it,[27] or casting

ford v. Tyrrell, *supra*, Gray, J., said on this point· "The rule of law requires of him who complains of his neighbor's use of his property, and seeks for redress and to restrain him from such use, that he should show that a substantive injury to property is committed. The mere fact of a business being carried on, which may be shown to be immoral and, therefore, prejudicial to the character of the neighborhood, furnishes, of itself, no ground for equitable interference at the suit of a private person."

24 Cabbell v. Williams, 127 Ala. 320, 28 South. 405, Green v. Oaks, 17 Ill. 249, Martin v. Marks, 154 Ind. 549, 57 N E 249; Newcome v. Crews, 98 Ky. 339, 32 S. W. 947; Streeter v. Stainaker, 61 Neb. 205, 85 N. W. 47; Morris etc. Co. v. Greenville etc. Co. (N. J), 46 Atl. 638, De Witt v. Van Schoyk, 110 N. Y. 7 (affirming 35 Hun, 103), 17 N. E. 425, 6 Am. St. Rep. 342, Hill v. Hoffman (Tenn. Ch. App.), 58 S. W. 929; Callanan v. Gilman, 107 N. Y. 360, 1 Am. St. Rep 828, 14 S. E. 264; Mayor etc. Columbus v. Jaques, 30 Ga. 506, Winsor v. German Sav. & L. Soc., 31 Wash. 365, 72 Pac. 66 (obstructing common hallway). An unauthorized railroad track in a street may be such a nuisance: Holst v. Savannah Electric Co., 131 Fed. 931; Lake Shore & M. S. Ry. Co. v. City of Elyria, 69 Ohio, 414, 69 N. E. 738; Tennessee Brewing Co. v. Union Ry. Co. (Tenn.), 85 S. W. 864. See, also, Zook v. Pennsylvania R. Co., 206 Pa. St. 603, 56 Atl. 82.

25 Pennsylvania v. Wheeling etc. Co., 13 How. (U. S.) 518, 14 L. ed. 249, Attorney-General v. Eau Claire, 37 Wis. 400. See, also, Monroe Mill Co v. Menzel, 35 Wash. 487, 102 Am. St. Rep. 905, 77 Pac. 813 (floating timber); Reyburn v. Sawyer, 135 N. C. 328, 102 Am. St. Rep. 555, 47 S. E. 761.

26 Trowbridge v. True, 52 Conn. 190, 52 Am. Rep. 579; Finegan v. Eckerson, 32 App. Div. 233, 52 N. Y. Supp. 993; Hunt v. Peske, Johns. 705, 6 Jur., N. S., 1071; Morrison v. Latimer, 51 Ga. 519.

27 Dayton v. Drainage Commrs., 128 Ill. 271, 21 N. E. 198; Pence v. Garrison, 93 Ind. 345; Jacobsen v. Van Boening, 48 Neb. 80, 48 Am. St. Rep. 684, 66 N. W. 993, 32 L. R. A. 229, Lake Erie etc. Co. v. Young, 135 Ind. 426, 41 Am. St. Rep. 430, 35 N. E. 177; Patoka Tp. v. Hopkins, 131 Ind. 142, 31 Am St. Rep. 417, 30 N. E. 896; Pettigrew v. Village of Evansville, 25 Wis. 223, 3 Am. Rep. 50; Lamborn v. Covington Co., 2 Md. Ch. 409; Moore v. Chicago etc Co, 75 Iowa, 263, 39 N. W. 390; Baker v. Weaver, 104 Ga. 228, 30 S. E. 726; Davis v. Londgreen, 8 Neb. 43, Noyes v. Cosselman, 29 Wash. 635, 92 Am. St. Rep. 937, 70 Pac 61; Sullivan v. Dooley, 31 Tex. Civ. App. 589, 73 S. W. 82; Starr v. Woodberry etc. Works

refuse matter upon it.[28] This list[29] is not designed to be an exhaustive classification,—from the nature of nuisance no list could be exhaustive—but it will serve to show the more common forms of nuisances which have been enjoined and something of the extent of equity jurisdiction of the subject.

§ 516. Injunctions on Sole Ground of Preventing Multiplicity of Suits.—In the cases in which the only reason of equity's intervention to enjoin has been to prevent the necessity of a multiplicity of suits at law because of a continuing or recurring nuisance, the courts have shown the same lack of unanimity that is always common to this ground of jurisdiction, whether it arises from a trespass, nuisance or other tort. Consonant to principle, the weight of authority holds that the mere existence of a continuing or recurring nuisance, however trivial, provided only it is sufficient to sustain an action at law for damages, will support a bill for an injunction.[30] There are authorities, however, which hold that this is not enough to base an injunction upon,

(N. J. Ch.), 48 Atl. 911; Abbott v. Pond, 142 Cal 393, 76 Pac 60, Carley v. Jennings, 131 Mich. 385, 91 N. W. 634.

28 Logan v. Driscoll, 19 Cal. 623, 81 Am. Dec. 90 (mining debris washed upon the plaintiff's land); Haugh's Appeal, 102 Pa. St. 42, 48 Am. Rep. 193 (privy from which fluid percolated into the plaintiff's well).

29 In the making of the above list, the collection and arrangement of the cases in 1 Ames's Cases in Equity Jurisdiction, pages 611-614, has been of material assistance

30 Whitfield v. Rogers, 26 Miss. (4 Cush) 84, 59 Am. Dec. 244; Baltimore etc. R. R. Co. v. Baptist Church, 108 U S. 317, 329, 2 Sup Ct. 719, 27 L. ed. 739; City of Demopolis v. Webb, 87 Ala. 659, 6 South. 408, Lux v. Haggin, 69 Cal. 256, 10 Pac. 674; Koopman v. Blodgett, 70 Mich. 610, 14 Am St Rep 527, 38 N. W. 649; Stevens v. Stevens, 52 Mass. (11 Met.) 251, 45 Am Dec. 203; Fleischner v. Citizens' etc Co, 25 Or. 119, 35 Pac. 174; Corning & Winslow v. Troy etc Factory, 40 N. Y. 191, 39 Barb. 311, 34 Barb. 485, 6 How Pr. 89; Sullivan v. Jones etc. Co, 208 Pa St. 540, 57 Atl 1065; Har-

and that the only multiplicity of suits which equity will interfere to prevent is that in which there are a number of parties to the controversy on one side or the other.[31] It may be added further, though the matter calls for no discussion in this place, that the subject of nuisance is the most fruitful field in furnishing the questions of greatest difficulty under the head of bills of peace, viz., questions as to the propriety of joining as plaintiffs or defendants parties between whom there is no "community of interest in the subject-matter of the suit."[32]

per etc. Co. v. Mountain etc. Co., 65 N. J. Eq. 479, 56 Atl. 297; Carpenter v. Capital etc. Co., 178 Ill 29, 69 Am. St. Rep. 286, 52 N. E. 973, 43 L R. A. 645, Sherry v. Perkins, 147 Mass. 212, 9 Am. St. Rep. 689, 17 N. E. 307; Campbell v. Seaman, 63 N. Y. 568, 20 Am. Rep. 567; Hennessy v. Carmony, 50 N. J. Eq. (5 Dick) 616, 25 Atl 374. In Whitfield v. Rogers, *supra,* the bill was to enjoin the erection of a mill-dam which would cause the plaintiff's land to be overflowed. In affirming the issuance of an injunction by the lower court, Handy, J., said: "It is insisted, in the first place, on the part of the appellant, that the complainant was not entitled to relief in equity on the ground of the private nuisance; because relief in equity will only be granted in such cases where the mischief is irreparable and cannot be compensated in damages. Authorities are to be found holding this doctrine, but the modern and more approved cases extend the relief much further. . . . . The inundations occasioned by the erection of the dam, the injuries thereby caused to the complainant's lands, and the periodical destruction of his timber, did not constitute a single trespass, but, from their nature, must have been 'constantly recurring grievances ' It would have been unreasonable and oppressive to force the complainant into a court of law to redress each repetition of the injury as it might recur from time to time; and therefore, on the very principle of 'suppressing interminable litigation,' and of 'preventing multiplicity of suits,' courts of equity alone can give just and adequate relief in such cases."

31 See Cherry v. Stein, 11 Md 1, and General Electric Ry Co v. Chicago etc. Co., 184 Ill. 588, 56 N. E. 963, which in effect hold that the fact of a nuisance being continuous is not enough to allow a plaintiff to come into equity, though there is no discussion of the point in either case.

32 See the discussion of this subject in 1 Pom. Eq. Jur., §§ 255-270.

§ 517. **Miscellaneous Grounds of Jurisdiction.**—It has already been pointed out in these pages that the fundamental reason for equity's enjoining nuisances is the lack of an adequate legal remedy. It has also been seen that the most common illustrations of inadequacy are the cases in which the injury is irreparable or of a continuing or recurring nature, and that these two grounds of jurisdiction are usually found together in the same cases. This is so largely true that almost all of the cases are rested on one or both of these grounds. The few cases that remain are, perhaps, on this account, the more significant in demonstrating that the fundamental reason—the inadequacy of the legal remedy—is not to be reduced to a few or any specific number of forms of manifestation. It is an open inquiry in every case whether the plaintiff can get adequate relief at law; if not, for any reason, he may come into equity. Here, as elsewhere, "it is not enough that there is a remedy at law; it must be plain and adequate, or, in other words, as practical and efficient to the ends of justice and its prompt administration as the remedy in equity."[33] Hence inadequacy has been found in the fact that independent acts of several defendants combine to produce the injury to the plaintiff so that the particular share of damage done by each one is incapable of ascertainment.[34] This reason may apply

33 Quoted in Lockwood v. Lawrence, 77 Me. 297, 312, 52 Am. Rep. 763, from Boyce's Exrs. v. Grundy, 3 Pet. 210, 215, 7 L. ed. 655.

34 Woodruff v. North Bloomfield Gravel Min. Co., 8 Saw. (U. S. C. C.) 628, 16 Fed. 25; Lockwood v. Lawrence, 77 Me. 297, 52 Am. Rep. 763; Woodyear v. Schaefer, 57 Md. 1, 40 Am. Rep 419; Madison v. Ducktown, S., C. & I. Co. (Tenn.), 83 S. W. 658. In the first cited of these cases the court said: "There is a very great difference between seeking to recover damages at law for an injury already inflicted by several parties acting independently of each other, and restraining parties from committing a nuisance in the future. In equity the court is not tied down to one particular form

equally to different states of facts whenever, for any cause, the amount of damage is unascertainable. Its substance is simply the obvious proposition that whenever the estimate of damages recoverable at law must be based largely, or to any considerable degree, upon conjecture, the legal remedy cannot be adequate.[35]

of judgment. It can adapt its decrees to the circumstances in each case, and give the proper relief as against each party, without reference to the action of others, and without injury to either. Each is dealt with, with respect to his own acts, either as affected or as unaffected by the acts of the others. It is not necessary for the prevention of future injury, to ascertain what particular share of the damages each defendant has inflicted in the past, or is about to inflict in the future. It is enough to know he has contributed and is continuing to contribute to a nuisance, without ascertaining to what extent, and to restrain him from contributing at all."

35 In Heilbron v. Fowler Switch Canal Co., 75 Cal. 426, 7 Am. St. Rep. 183, 17 Pac. 535, the facts were that the defendant proposed to divert fifteen hundred cubic feet of water per second from Kings river, which formed the boundary of the plaintiff's farm for thirty miles and flowed through it for ten miles. In affirming a judgment granting an injunction the court, per Temple, J., said: "It does not follow because the injury is incapable of ascertainment, or of being computed in damages, and therefore only nominal damages can be recovered, that it is trifling or inconsiderable. It is doubtful if it can be said that there is any evidence in the case which tends to show, or if that which was offered would have tended to show, that the injury to plaintiffs was inconsiderable, that it was unascertainable, and in that sense inappreciable; may be a good reason why an injunction should issue. . . . . It is obvious that in a climate like that where this land is situated, the benefit derived from a flow of water for thirty miles along its boundary, and ten miles through it, cannot be inconsiderable, but yet the extent of benefit must ever be an unknown quantity." In Lockwood v. Lawrence, *supra*, the court, per Foster, J., said: "The very difficulty of obtaining substantial damages was stated to be a ground for relief by injunction in Clowes v. Staffordshire Potteries Co., 8 L. R. Ch. App. 125. With still greater force does this apply where the injury is caused by so many, and in such a way, that it would be difficult if not impossible to apportion the damage, or say how far anyone may have contributed to the result, and so damages would be but nominal, and repeated actions, without any substantial benefit, might be the result." See, to the same effect, Lyon v. McLaughlin, 32 Vt. 423. See, also, Gilbert v.

Other unusual reasons for granting injunctions have been: in a bill to enjoin the obstruction of a public street by municipal officers, that the social standing, and character and reputation, of the defendants would make indictment ineffectual, while abatement would not be an adequate remedy because the expense of abating would fall on the tax-payers;[36] and, in a bill by a tenant to have a bridge, which obstructed the entrance to the building he occupied, removed, that the plaintiff's legal remedy was inadequate because he, being a tenant and not owner of the fee, could not maintain an action for abatement but could sue only in case for damages.[37] No case has been found so holding, but it would seem clear that the insolvency of a defendant might well be a basis of injunction here just as, by the weight of authority, it is in trespass.[38] As in trespass, too, the basis of an injunction is sometimes said to be that otherwise the defendant would acquire a prescriptive right to do the wrongful act.[39]

Mickle, 4 Sandf. Ch. 357. It is not meant to be said that the only ground on which the cases cited in connection with this paragraph of the text might have been, or even were, placed is that to which, in each case, attention is directed here; the present purpose is simply to point out the readiness of the equity courts to make the inadequacy of the legal remedy, in whatever form it may appear, the criterion of their jurisdiction.

36 Mayor etc. of Columbus v. Jaques, 30 Ga. 506. See, also, Le frois v. Monroe County, 24 App. Div. 421, 48 N. Y. Supp. 519.

37 Knox v. Mayor etc. of New York, 55 Barb 404.

38 See Wilson v. Featherstone, 120 N. C. 449, 27 S. E. 121, Walker v. Walker, 51 Ga. 22; Porter v. Armstrong, 132 N. C. 66, 43 S. E. 542; Reyburn v. Sawyer, 135 N. C. 328, 102 Am. St. Rep. 555, 47 S. E 761.

39 Meyer v. Phillips, 97 N. Y. 485, 49 Am. Rep. 538. The criticism of this reason made in the chapter on trespass—viz., that an action at law or an interference with the defendant's wrongful act once in every prescriptive period, will prevent any right from arising by prescription—applies here also: See Hart v. Hildebrandt, 30 Ind. App. 415, 66 N. E. 173.

§ 518. **What the Plaintiff Must Allege.**—A plaintiff who seeks an injunction against a nuisance must allege his own right clearly and definitely in order that the court's order for the protection of it may be certain and without ambiguity; otherwise the decree will, of course, be impossible of intelligent enforcement.[40] He must also, for obvious reasons, allege that the defendant is doing or threatening to do the acts complained of.[41] It is not necessary for the plaintiff to allege that his injury will be irreparable or that the legal remedy is otherwise inadequate, as that is a mere conclusion of law; he must, however, allege facts which will show the injury to himself[42] and the inadequacy of his legal remedy.[43] And in the courts of the United States, at least, this inadequacy is regarded as so important, that it may be insisted on by the court *sua sponte,* though not raised by the pleadings, nor suggested by counsel.[44]

§ 519. **Previous Trial at Law.**—Since the rights that are involved in cases of nuisance are purely legal, equity taking jurisdiction in particular cases only to furnish a more perfect remedy than the law affords, and following the legal rules in the determination of all questions save the adequacy of the legal remedy, it follows that a problem of procedure may be presented to the equity courts when an injunction is sought by a plaintiff in whose favor the legal right, or the fact that a nuisance

40 Fisk v. Wilber, 7 Barb. 395; Peterson v. Beha, 161 Mo. 513, 62 S. W. 462.

41 Ploughe v. Boyer, 38 Ind. 115; Chastey v. Ackland, [1895] L. R. 2 Ch. D. 389.

42 Spooner v. McConnell, 1 McLean, 337, Fed. Cas. No. 13,245.

43 Sprague v. Rhodes, 4 R. I. 301; Burrus v. City of Columbus, 105 Ga. 42, 31 S. E. 124.

44 Parker v. Winnipisiogee etc. Co., 67 U. S. (2 Black) 545, 17 L. ed. 333. And see Burnham v. Kempton, 44 N. H. 78, 92.

exists, has never been determined. In such case, should the court of equity pass on the questions of law or fact raised? or should it refuse its extraordinary relief until the plaintiff has procured a judgment of a court of law in his favor?

§ 520. **Not Necessary to Granting of Temporary Injunctions.**—The scope of the inquiry may be narrowed by first pointing out the classes of cases in which, though there has been no trial at law, the above problem is not raised. Chief among these is that class of cases in which only a temporary injunction is sought. The purpose of a temporary injunction generally is to keep matters *in statu quo* while some disputed question of law or fact is being settled. Obviously, granting or refusing it cannot turn upon the settlement of the question, either in law or equity. It has its own rules, which will be considered later,[45] but this is not one of them. The supreme court of the United States in a comparatively early case on this subject said: "The true distinction in this class of cases is that, in prospect of irremediable injury by what is apparently a nuisance, a temporary or preliminary injunction may at once issue. . . . But not a permanent or perpetual one till the title, if disputed, is settled at law."[46] And the law is clearly in accord with so much of this distinction as pertains to the granting of temporary injunctions.[47]

§ 521. **Nor in all Cases of Permanent Injunctions.**—There are, also, some cases in which a permanent injunction

45 See *infra*, § 535.

46 Irwin v. Dixion, 50 U. S. (9 How.) 10, 28, 29, 13 L. ed. 25, per Woodbury, J.

47 Sutton v. Lord Montfort, 4 Sim. 565; Kennerty v. Etiwan Phosphate Co., 17 S. C. 411, 43 Am. Rep. 607; Cronin v. Bloemecke, 58 N. J. Eq. 313, 43 Atl. 605; Rochester v. Erickson, 46 Barb. 92; Burnham v. Kempton, 44 N. H. 78.

is sought, where the objection that the plaintiff has not obtained a judgment at law should be disregarded wholly by a court of equity. The first of these is the case in which the defendant does not dispute either the plaintiff's right or the fact that a nuisance exists; to insist on a trial at law in such case would be to impose needless hardship on both parties to the suit. "The only object in establishing title at law, is to show that the right is in the plaintiff. The suit at law is only a means to accomplish a given end. When the end is already obtained, there could be no reason for doing an idle thing. This, the law, as a rational system, never requires to be done. If the title of the plaintiff be conceded, then there can be no need of a trial at law to establish that which is already admitted,"[48] and the reasoning is, of course, the same as to an admission that a nuisance exists. Hence the courts are agreed that no judgment or verdict at law is necessary in such cases.[49] On the same reasoning it is held that a plaintiff's bill is not demurrable for failing to state a previous trial at law; by demurring the defendant admits the plaintiff's right and the fact of an existing nuisance.[50] In the next place, a trial at law will not be

48 Tuolumne Water Co. v. Chapman, 8 Cal. 392, 397.

49 Duncan v. Hayes and Greenwood, 22 N. J. Eq. 25; Ross v. Butler, 19 N. J. Eq. (4 C. E. Green.) 294, 97 Am. Dec. 654; and the cases cited in the next two notes, are *a fortiori* authorities on this point, also.

50 Tuolumne Water Co. v. Chapman, 8 Cal. 392; Aldrich v. Howard, 7 R. I. 87, 80 Am. Dec. 636, Smitzer v. McCulloch, 76 Va. 777, Texas etc. Ry. Co. v. Interstate Transp. Co., 155 U. S. 585, 15 Sup Ct. 228, 39 L. ed. 271; Soltau v. De Held, 2 Sim., N. S., 133; Appeal of Bitting, 105 Pa. St. 517. But see Eastman v. Amoskeag etc Co, 47 N. H. 71; Weller v. Smeaton, 1 Cox, 102, 1 Brown Ch. 572. In Aldrich v. Howard, *supra*, the bill was to enjoin the defendant from erecting a large livery-stable in close proximity to the complainant's dwelling-house Defendant demurred to the bill because, among other reasons, it did not allege a previous trial at law. In

required when, from the evidence at the hearing, the controverted questions are clear in favor of one or the other party to the suit. Here, too, a trial at law would be superfluous.[51] It is on this ground that courts proceed when they hold that a "mere denial of the complainant's rights by the defendant in his answer will not oust the court of its jurisdiction by injunction";[52] or that a party who has been for a long time in the undisputed possession of the property or enjoyment of the right with respect to which he complains, may procure an injunction in spite of such denial.[53] And, finally, if both parties consent[54] or request that the equity court

passing on this point of the demurrer the court, per Ames, C. J, said "Nor is it true, that a bill to enjoin such nuisance is demurrable, because it does not state that the rights of the parties, in support of the bill, have been settled by a judgment at law. It may be very proper that they should be, if uncertain, before the court affords its specific relief; but the title of the plaintiff to the relief he asks may be admitted by the answer, as it is by this demurrer, and, then, why should it be further ascertained, to induce the action of the court?"

51 Inchbald v. Barrington, L. R. 4 Ch. 388; Reid v. Gifford, Hopk. Ch. 416; Learned v. Hunt, 63 Miss. 373; Appeal of Pennsylvania Lead. Co., 96 Pa. St. 116, 42 Am. Rep. 534; City of Newcastle v. Raney, 130 Pa. St. 546, 18 Atl. 1066, 6 L. R. A 737; Deaconess etc. Hospital v. Bontjes, 104 Ill App 484; Village of Dwight v. Hayes, 150 Ill. 273, 41 Am St. Rep. 367, 37 N. E. 218, affirming 49 Ill. App. 530; Shields v. Arndt, 4 N. J. Eq. (3 Green's Ch.) 234; Wood v. McGrath, 150 Pa. St. 451, 24 Atl. 682, 16 L. R. A. 715; Harelson v Kansas City etc. Co, 151 Mo. 483, 52 S. W 368.

52 Carlisle v. Cooper, 21 N. J. Eq (6 C. E. Green) 576, 580; Shields v. Arndt, 4 N. J. Eq. (3 Green Ch) 234.

53 Gardner v. Trustees etc. Newburgh, 2 Johns. Ch. 162; Finch v. Resbridger, 2 Vern. 390; Falls Village etc. Co. v. Tibbetts, 31 Conn 165; Burnham v. Kempton, 44 N. H. 78.

54 Mayor of Cardiff v. Cardiff etc. Co, 4 De Gex & J. 596; Ladd v Granite State Brick Co., 68 N. H 185, 37 Atl. 1041. As to cases in which the disputed question is one of law, and not of fact, see Rigby v. Great Western Ry Co., 2 Phill Ch. 49, 51; Harmon v Jones, Craig & P 299, 301, in which a distinction is taken that would have

try the merits of the disputed question, it will do so;[55] and it has been held that an objection to this course of proceeding cannot be taken if it has not been raised by the answer.[56]

§ 522. **Cases in Which It is Important.**—The class of cases not yet discussed is that in which on application for a permanent injunction, the plaintiff's right, or the fact that a nuisance exists, is doubtful on the evidence before the court, and the parties do not consent to have the controversy settled by the court of equity. In this situation the general doctrine is that "either party is entitled to insist that the questions on which the legal rights depend should be tried at law."[57] Satisfactory grounds to support this rule as a matter of reason are not to be found in the cases. Doubtless the explanation of it is largely the fact that in early days the courts of equity were reluctant to undertake the decision of purely legal rights, or questions of fact which ordinarily were tried by a jury.[58] It was "a rule of expedi-

great force in a jurisdiction in which the courts of law and equity are distinct.

55 Walter v. Selfe, 4 De Gex & S. 315.

56 Lambert v. Huber, 22 Misc. Rep. 462, 50 N Y Supp. 793.

57 Mayor of Cardiff v. Cardiff etc. Co., 4 De Gex & J. 596.

58 Potts v. Levy, 2 Drew. 272, 277; Harman v. Jones, Craig & P. 299, 301, Walts v. Foster, 12 Or. 247, 7 Pac. 24; Roath v. Driscoll, 20 Conn. 533, 538, 52 Am. Dec. 352. In Roath v. Driscoll, *supra*, Ellsworth, J., said "The court doubtless possesses the necessary power, but it is not to be exercised as a matter of course, even when the plaintiff suffers some injury to his real estate. Whenever the right is doubtful, or needs the investigation of a jury, a court of equity is always reluctant to interpose its summary authority, for it is rather the duty of the court to protect acknowledged rights than to establish new and doubtful ones.'' In Harman v. Jones, *supra*, an injunction had been granted forbidding the defendant from taking land which plaintiff claimed. No legal proceedings were directed On appeal Lord Cottenham said: ''It is said the omission of such a direction was owing to its not having been asked in the

ency and policy, rather than an essential condition and basis of the equitable jurisdiction."[59] As such, the grounds on which it arose have largely, if not quite, disappeared with the decay of all hostility of the courts of law against the equity courts and the general merging of both law and equity functions in the same courts. The rule, however, still persists in most jurisdictions in which it has not been abrogated by statute.[60] It has

court below; but it is the duty of the court to give such direction, whether it be asked for or not. The proper office of the court, upon an application of this kind, is not to ascertain the existence of a legal right, but solely to protect the property, until that right can be determined by the jurisdiction to which it properly belongs It is the duty of this court to confine itself within the limits of its own jurisdiction; and, therefore, it is a fundamental error in an order of this kind to assume finally to dispose of legal rights, and not to confine itself to protecting the property pending the adjudication of those rights by a court of law.'' This extract shows clearly the ground on which the rule is based.

59 1 Pom. Eq. Jur., § 252.

60 Earl of Ripon v. Hobart, 3 Mylne & K. 169; Mayor of Cardiff v. Cardiff etc. Co, 4 De Gex & J. 596; Elmhurst v. Spencer, 2 Macn. & G. 45; Van Bergen v. Van Bergen, 3 Johns. Ch. 282, 8 Am. Dec. 511; Irwin v. Dixion, 50 U. S. (9 How.) 10, 13 L. ed. 25; Kingsbury v. Flowers, 65 Ala. 479, 39 Am. Rep 14; Tracy v. Le Blanc, 89 Me. 304, 36 Atl. 399; Green v. Lake, 54 Miss. 540, 28 Am. Rep. 378; Burnham v. Kempton, 44 N. H. 78; Hinchman v. Paterson, 17 N. J. Eq 75, 86 Am. Dec. 252; Walts v. Foster, 12 Or. 247, 7 Pac. 24; Rhea v. Forsyth, 37 Pa. St. 503, 78 Am. Dec. 441; Wood v. Mc Grath, 150 Pa. St. 451, 24 Atl. 682, 16 L. R. A. 715; Roath v. Driscoll, 20 Conn. 538, 52 Am. Dec. 352; Kennerty v. Etiman Phosphate Co., 17 S. C. 411, 43 Am. Rep 607; Sterling v. Littlefield, 97 Me. 479, 54 Atl. 1108; Sullivan v. Browning (N. J.), 58 Atl. 302; Harrelson v. Kansas City etc. Co, 151 Mo. 482, 52 S. W. 368. See, however, Olmsted v. Loomis, 9 N. Y. 423, and Minke v. Hopeman, 87 Ill. 450, 29 Am. Rep. 63, in which the court of equity decided the question of fact for itself, without putting the case on any of the usual grounds for taking it out of the rule. In England the rule is abolished by statute, Rolt's Act, 25 & 26 Vict., c 42 [1862], for a discussion of which see Eaden v. Firth, 1 Hen. & M. 573. The Reformed Procedure has accomplished the same result in New York and California: Corning & Winslow v. Troy etc. Factory, 40 N. Y. 191, 39 Barb. 311, 34 Barb.

never gone so far, however, as to require the plaintiff's bill to be dismissed because the legal questions had not been determined; the court may retain the bill and procure their ascertainment by directing an issue, or an action, or a case stated, at law; basing its final decree upon the results thus reached.[61] In leaving the subject it should be noted that when the bill is to enjoin a threatened, as distinguished from an existing, nuisance, from the nature of the case the requirement of a previous trial at law cannot be applied. "No such question in this case can be tried at law, no nuisance exists—the object of the bill is to enjoin the defendant from creating one."[62] From the foregoing discussion it would appear that the following is an accurate summary of the general rules of equity with respect to the requirement of a previous establishment of the plaintiff's right at law. The requirement does not apply at all to applications for temporary injunctions; nor to bills for permanent injunctions on account of irreparable injury, when the defendant admits the plaintiff's right, or when the right is clear in favor of one of the parties, though disputed, or when both parties consent to a trial of the merits by the equity court; nor to bills for permanent injunctions against threatened, as distinguished from existing, nuisances; it does apply to all other bills for permanent injunctions, but

485, 6 How. Pr. 89; Pollitt v Long 58 Barb. 20; Lux v. Haggin, 69 Cal. 255, 284, 285, 10 Pac. 674. And in Michigan also this has been done by statute: Comp. Laws 1871, § 6377; Robinson v. Baugh, 31 Mich. 290, 292.

61 Attorney-General v Cleaver, 18 Ves. 211, 219; Rigby v. Great Western Ry. Co., 2 Phill. Ch 49, 51; Davidson v. Isham, 9 N. J. Eq. 186; Clark v. Lawrence, 59 N. C. 83, 78 Am. Dec. 241.

62 Bell v. Blount, 11 N. C. 384, 15 Am Dec. 526; Porter v. Whitham, 17 Me. 294; Varney v. Pope, 60 Me 192; Tracy v Le Blanc, 89 Me. 304, 36 Atl. 399. See, also, Sterling v. Little, 97 Me. 497, 54 Atl. 1108.

there is a tendency to do away with the requirement by statute or judicial innovation.

§ 523. **Threatened Nuisances; Imminent Danger.**—In one sense all injunctions against nuisances are injunctions against threatened nuisances. The only purpose of giving equitable relief at all is the prevention of future harm; but this harm, being future, cannot be a matter of absolute certainty and therefore is only threatened. If, however, at the time the bill is filed a nuisance is actually being committed, there will, in general, be no question that the threatened danger is sufficiently made out to justify an injunction, if the case, in its other aspects, is sufficient. But when the nuisance has not yet come into existence and the plaintiff, therefore, must make out his case of apprehended danger by other means than by pointing to an existing nuisance, a question may be raised concerning the rules by which the court is to be guided. What is believed to be a proper statement of these rules was thus formulated in a leading English case: "There must, if no actual damage is proved, be proof of imminent danger, and there must also be proof that the apprehended statement will, if it comes, be very substantial. I should almost say, it must be proved that it will be irreparable, because, if the danger is not proved to be so imminent that no one can doubt that, if the remedy is delayed, the damage will be suffered, I think it must be shown that, if the damage does occur at any time, it will come in such a way and under such circumstances that it will be impossible for the plaintiff to protect himself against it if relief is denied to him in a *quia timet* action."[63] In

63 Fletcher v. Bealey, L. R. 28 Ch. D. 688, per Pearson, J. The facts of this case were that: The defendants proposed to deposit refuse matter from their alkali mills on the bank of a stream about

a word, the threatened danger must be imminent, and of a character to do irreparable injury. In a bill to enjoin the erection of an engine to pump water into a river which the plaintiffs were cleansing and improv-

a mile and a half above the plaintiff's paper-mills, in which the water from the river was largely used. It was admitted that after a time there would flow from this "vat waste" a greenish liquid of such noxious character, that any considerable amount of it in the water of the river would be very destructive to the plaintiff's manufacture, and the court thought this liquid, in the natural course of events, might begin to flow into the river in the course of ten years. The plaintiff also contended that the bank where the refuse matter was to be deposited was in danger of slipping into the river. The defendants insisted that they were going to take precautions to provide against both dangers. The court refused the injunction. On the first ground the court said: "I have no doubt that at the end of ten years the water would be sufficiently polluted to do a great amount of injury to the plaintiff. . . . . I think that in ten years' time it is highly probable that science (which is now at work on the subject) may have discovered some means for rendering this green liquid innocuous But, even if no such discovery should be made in that time, I cannot help seeing that there are contrivances, such as tanks and pumps, and other things of that kind, by which the liquid may, as the defendants say, be kept out of the river altogether. Therefore, upon that ground alone, I do not think the action can be supported. . . . . I think the danger is not imminent, because it must be some years before any such quantity of the liquid will be found issuing from the heap as would pollute the Irwell to the detriment of the plaintiff" On the claim that the bank was in danger of slipping the court said· "I think that, if any slip does take place, there will be some premonitory symptoms which will warn the plaintiff and the defendants, and give the defendants time to do whatever may be necessary to prevent the heap from slipping into the river, and at the same time enable the plaintiff, if he should think it right to do so, to bring an action against the defendants on the ground of positive and imminent danger at that time." On similar reasoning an injunction against a sewer was refused when the allegation was that it would become noxious in three years· Morgan v. Binghamton, 102 N. Y. 500, 7 N. E. 424; so, an injunction was denied against the erection of a pest-house by city authorities when the latter had taken no official action looking to its erection, the danger in such case being too remote to be considered imminent: City of Kansas City v. Hobbs, 62 Kan. 866, 62 Pac 324.

ing, the court discussed the nature of an imminent danger as follows: "If, indeed, this be a work which not only gives the power of doing mischief, but cannot be used or can hardly, in the common course of things, be used without working mischief, if, in short, it be a thing which can hardly be used without being abused, the case comes to be very different. For, in matters of this description, the law cannot make over-nice distinctions, and refuse the relief merely because there is a bare possibility that the evil may be avoided. Proceeding upon practical views of human affairs, the law will guard against risks which are so imminent that no prudent person would incur them, although they do not amount to absolute certainty of damage. Nay, it will go further, according to the same practical and rational view, and, balancing the magnitude of the evil against the chances of its occurrence, it will even provide against a somewhat less imminent probability in cases where the mischief, should it be done, would be vast and overwhelming. Accordingly, if it appeared that the works in question could hardly be used without damage to the inferior districts, I might hold that erecting them was, in itself, a beginning of injury, though there might be a possibility of otherwise using them; and if the damage, should it happen at all, were the destruction and the subjecting of the lower districts to a deluge, I might scrutinize less narrowly the probability of the engines being injuriously worked."[64] This

64 Earl of Ripon v. Hobart, 3 Mylne & K. 169, 176. The injunction was refused, the court saying as its conclusion on the score of imminence of the danger: "But upon carefully examining the evidence, and indeed it might be enough to say, upon attentively considering the nature of the case, the kind of works and of working in question, and the sort of mischief apprehended, there is no reason for holding that the danger is either certain or very imminent, or that mischief of a very overwhelming nature is likely to be suddenly done; or, in-

passage states and illustrates clearly the principles which guide the courts in this matter. On the one hand, a mere possibility of a future nuisance will not support an injunction; it must be probable. On the other hand, the plaintiff—who, of course, has the burden of proof[65]—does not need to establish this probability by proof amounting to virtual certainty that the nuisance will occur, nor even proof which establishes it beyond a reasonable doubt;[66] it is sufficient if he show that the *risk* of its happening is greater than a reasonable man would incur. And the balance between these two rules will be affected by the seriousness of the nuisance feared, the strength required for the plaintiff's proof diminishing somewhat as the greatness of the apprehended damage increases.

§ 524. **Illustrations.**—In accordance with these rules it is held that a thing which may or may not be a nuisance, according to the way it is managed or controlled when in use, will not be enjoined. The plaintiff, by showing only the intended construction or use of the thing complained of, does not meet the burden of proof that is on him, "the presumption being that a person entering into a legitimate business will conduct it in a proper way so that it will not constitute a nuisance."[67] Hence injunctions have been refused against the erection of a

deed, that any serious injury can be done, without time being afforded for coming to the court with a case free from the present defects." See, also, Mohawk Bridge Co. v. Utica etc. Co., 6 Paige, 554, 563.

65 Columbia Ave. etc. Co. v. Prison Commission of Ga., 92 Fed. 801; Maysville etc. Co. v Beyersdorfer, 19 Ky. Law Rep. 1212, 43 S W. 254, Lambert v. Alcorn, 144 Ill. 313, 331, 33 N. E 53, 21 L. R. A. 611.

66 Owen v. Phillips, 73 Ind. 284.

67 Pope v Bridgewater, 52 W. Va 252, 43 S. E. 87. Compare West v. Ponca City Milling Co. (Okla.), 79 Pac. 100.

stable,[68] or a planing-mill,[69] or a cotton-gin,[70] or a jail,[71] or a coal-chute;[72] the building of a dam,[73] or an embankment;[74] the opening of a gas-well;[75] the establishment of a private burial ground;[76] the operation of a business, as of a slaughter-house,[77] or a dairy;[78] the discharge of sewage on the plaintiff's land;[79] or the sale of water for purposes of hydraulic mining when the defendant does not know the mining is to be done in a wrongful manner;[80] or the laying of railroad

68 Kirkman v. Handy, 30 Tenn. (11 Hump.) 406, 54 Am. Dec. 45 (livery-stable); Shiras v. Ollinger, 50 Iowa, 571, 32 Am. Rep. 138 (livery-stable); St. James's Church v. Arrington, 36 Ala. 546, 76 Am. Dec. 332 (private stable); Rounsaville v. Kohlheim, 68 Ga. 668, 45 Am. Rep. 505 (private stable); Keiser v. Lovett, 85 Ind. 240, 44 Am. Rep. 10 (private stable). In Kirkman v. Handy, the court said: "A livery-stable in a town is not necessarily a nuisance in itself," and therefore a court of equity has no jurisdiction to restrain by injunction, either the completion, because intended for that purpose, or its appropriation to the purpose intended.

69 Dorsey v. Allen, 85 N. C. 358, 39 Am. Rep. 704.

70 Rouse v. Martin, 75 Ala. 510, 51 Am. Rep. 463.

71 Burwell v. Vance County Commrs., 93 N. C. 73, 53 Am. Rep. 454.

72 Dalton v. Cleveland etc. Ry. Co., 144 Ind. 121, 43 N. E. 130

73 Hoke v. Perdue, 62 Cal. 545; Blair v. Boswell, 37 Or. 168, 61 Pac. 341.

74 Lake Erie etc. Co. v. City of Fremont, 92 Fed. 721.

75 Pope v. Bridgewater Gas Co., 52 W. Va. 252, 43 S. E. 87; Windfall Mfg. Co. v. Patterson, 148 Ind. 414, 62 Am. St. Rep. 532, 47 N. E. 2, 37 L R. A 381.

76 Kingsbury v. Flowers, 65 Ala. 479, 39 Am. Rep. 14 (private burial ground); Ellison v. Commissioners of Washington, 58 N. C. 57, 75 Am. Dec. 430 (public cemetery); Elliott v. Ferguson (Tex. Civ. App.), 83 S. W. 56 (same).

77 Beckhan v. Brown, 19 Ky. Law Rep. 519, 40 S. W 684. The court in this case said: "A business of itself legitimate should not be enjoined upon the sole ground that it may contingently or eventually become a nuisance."

78 McDonough v. Robbens, 1 Mo. App. Rep 78, 60 Mo. App. 156.

79 Vicker v. City of Durham, 132 N. C. 880, 44 S. E. 685.

80 County of Yuba v. Cloke, 79 Cal. 239, 21 Pac. 740.

tracks in front of the plaintiff's land;[81] in every case the thing complained of may be done in a manner that will cause no harm to the plaintiff, and the mere fact that it is to be done is no proof that it will be done wrongfully. But if the plaintiff can show that the thing complained of will probably be a nuisance to him, he is entitled to an injunction appropriately framed to protect his right that is threatened. Thus, if a structure is being erected, and the plaintiff can show that it is to be used in such a way as will probably be a nuisance to him, he may have this use enjoined, although he may not be able to enjoin the erection of the structure;[82] while if the structure itself, without regard to any use of it, will cause a nuisance, the injunction will forbid its erection at all.[83] And if this distinction is

81 Drake v. Hudson River etc. Co., 7 Barb. 508.

82 Cleveland v. Citizens' etc. Co, 20 N. J. Eq (5 C. E. Green) 201, Attorney General v. Steward, 20 N. J. Eq. (5 C. E. Green) 415, Ross v. Butler, 19 N. J. Eq (4 C. E. Green) 294, 97 Am. Dec. 654; Lake Erie etc. Co. v. Young, 135 Ind 426, 41 Am. St Rep. 430, 35 N. E 177. In Cleveland v. Citizens' etc. Co., *supra*, the bill was brought to enjoin the erection of a gas plant near the plaintiffs' homes. On the facts the court thought the manufacturing of gas might, or might not, be a nuisance, according to the way in which it was conducted, except as to a process of purifying by lime, which the court was satisfied would be a nuisance to the plaintiffs, if used. The injunction was therefore refused as to the building and the manufacturing of gas as a whole, but granted against the particular process of purifying by lime. In Attorney-General v. Steward, *supra*, the bill was for an injunction against erecting a slaughter-house. Here, too, the court was of the opinion that the business might be so carried on as not to be a nuisance. The defendants admitted, however, that they might discharge the blood from one hundred slaughtered hogs daily into a creek which flowed past plaintiffs' land below, contending that this would not pollute the stream. The court thought it would pollute the stream; hence the injunction was refused as to the erection of the building, and the slaughtering, but was granted to restrain the defendants from permitting the blood to flow into the creek

83 Rochester v. Erickson, 46 Barb. 92 (projecting wall into a navigable river); Bell v. Blount, 11 N. C. 384, 15 Am. Dec. 526 (mill-

sometimes disregarded and the structure as well as the wrongful use of it enjoined, it is doubtless because of the fact that the erection will be useless for any other purpose than the wrongful one; hence a strict limitation of the scope of the injunction is not very closely observed.[84] Thus the courts have enjoined the erection of a privy near plaintiff's house;[85] of a toll-gate;[86] and of a powder magazine.[87] So, too, threatened acts which if done would cause a nuisance, as the diversion of water,[88] or discharge of sewage on the plaintiff's land,[89] or the use of an artificial pond as a place for dumping mining debris,[90] have been enjoined. In a

dam, when the pond collected by it would very probably render the community unhealthy).

84 On this point the court in Cleveland v. Citizens' etc. Co, *supra*, said. "The application is to restrain putting up the building, and also manufacturing gas. As to the building itself, it can be of no injury to anyone if no gas is ever made in it. But it is usual and proper, where a building or works are being erected that can only be used for a purpose that is unlawful, to restrain the erection. The works, if erected, might tempt the owner to use them, and it seems like trifling to permit anyone to go on with a building which he can never be permitted to use." This reasoning could not apply, of course, in any case in which the defendant wished to go on with the building for some other purpose, if rightful, than the prohibited one, nor would it seem to make any difference that this other purpose was formed after the defendant learned he would be enjoined from carrying out his original plan.

85 Miley v. O'Hearn, 13 Ky. Law Rep. 834, 18 S. W 529 (erection of a privy ten feet from the plaintiff's well and thirteen feet from her dining and bed rooms. But, in the same jurisdiction, the erection of a privy one hundred and fifty feet from the plaintiff's well and dwelling was not enjoined: Davis v Atkins, 18 Ky. Law Rep. 73, 35 S. W. 271).

86 President etc. Road Co v. Anderson, 22 Ky. Law Rep 1626, 61 S. W. 13.

87 Wier's Appeal, 74 Pa. St. 230.

88 Kimberly v Hewitt, 75 Wis 371, 44 N. W. 303.

89 New York Cent. etc. Co. v. City of Rochester, 127 N. Y. 591, 28 N E. 416.

90 United States v Lawrence, 53 Fed. 632. Compare with United

majority of the cases of bills to enjoin threatened nuisances, however, the injunction has been refused. The explanation of this is that most nuisances consist in doing in a wrongful manner something which is not wrongful in itself; hence till it is actually being done in a wrongful way, the plaintiff has so heavy a task in proving the probability of its being so done, that, in general, he cannot meet it. The courts will not grant the injunction simply because it will do no harm to the defendant;[91] the plaintiff must show clearly that he stands in need of it.[92]

§ 525. **Must Threatened Injury be Irreparable?**—On the second branch of the rule quoted above concerning injunctions against threatened nuisances, viz., that the injury must be irreparable, little needs to be said. The significance of it is, of course, that it excludes wholly from the class of cases in which an injunction may be granted against a purely threatened, as distinguished from an existing, nuisance, all those in which the basis of the intervention of equity is solely to prevent a multiplicity of suits. In favor of the rule thus limited, it can be said that there is little, if any, reason for granting relief *quia timet* with the lack of certainty that any wrong will ever be done which is in-

States v. North Bloomfield etc. Co., 53 Fed. 625. See further City of St. Louis v. Knopp etc. Co., 104 U. S. 658, 26 L. ed. 883, and Crompton v. Lea, L R. 19 Eq. 115, 121, which show that lack of imminence of the threatened nuisance cannot, in general, be taken by demurrer.

91 Otaheite Gold etc. Co. v. Dean, 102 Fed. 929.

92 Adams v. Michael, 38 Md. 123, 17 Am. Rep. 516; Branch Turnpike Co. v. Yuba, 13 Cal. 190; Sayre v. Mayor etc. Newark, 58 N. J. Eq (13 Dick.) 136, 148, 42 Atl. 1068. In Gallagher v. Flury, 99 Md. 181, 57 Atl. 672, it is said that threatened nuisances only of things nuisances *per se* will be enjoined, but this is clearly an erroneous view, both in reason and by the authorities.

herent in such cases, except when there is strong ground for believing that, unless *quia timet* relief is given, an adequate remedy will be impossible should the anticipated wrong occur. Negatively, the fact, that almost all the cases of bills for injunction against threatened nuisances conform to the restricted rule, supports this reasoning. There is, however, some American authority the other way.[93]

§ 526. **Damage Necessary to Justify an Injunction.**—The question what amount or character of damage is necessary to sustain an injunction will require only brief treatment, as, in the main, the question, when it arises, is settled by simply applying the rule which is applied on the same point in an action at law. If the injury is irreparable, or such that the damages given by a jury would be conjectural, it is clear, of course, that the question of the extent of damage will not need to be gone into. The class of cases, then, in which it will arise is chiefly, if not exclusively, that in which the reason for coming into equity is to put an end to a permanent or continuing nuisance in order to avoid multiplicity of suits. In this situation the courts generally require no more, but just the same, damage that will sustain an action at law. "The result of a careful review of the evidence upon my mind," said the court in a leading American case,[94] "is to lead me to the con-

93 Whitfield v. Rogers, 26 Miss. (4 Cush.) 84, 59 Am. Dec. 244. See, also, Lake Erie etc Co. v. Young, 135 Ind. 426, 41 Am. St. Rep. 430, 35 N. E. 177.

94 Per Pitney, V. C., in Hennessy v. Carmony, 50 N. J. Eq. 616, 25 Atl. 374. To the same effect are Salvin v. North Brancepeth Coal Co., L. R. 9 Ch. App. 705, in which the court applied the rule given to the jury in St. Helen's Smelting Co. v. Tipping, 11 H. L. Cas. 642, which was an action at law for damages; Bostock v. North Staffordshire Ry., 5 De Gex & S. 584; Broder v. Saillard, L. R. 2 Ch. D. 692; Proprietors of Me. Wharf v. Proprietors etc. Wharf, 85 Me. 175, 27

clusion that the degree of injury is such as to entitle the complainant to damages in an action at law, with the result that he is entitled to an injunction in this court." This is the only logical result of the rule that to prevent multiplicity of suits is a head of equity jurisdiction; to hold otherwise would be to say that equity will prevent multiplicity of suits only when the damages are according to some standard of the equity courts, and this would be to do away with just so much of the salutary result of the rule as was affected by applying this different standard. It follows equally that in the class of nuisances in which an action at law may be maintained without showing any damages, because a legal right is invaded, as the interference with water rights, or the right to lateral support, or overflowing the plaintiff's land, and the like, that equity should also enjoin on the same showing; and such is the rule.[95]

Atl 93, Pach v. Geoffrey, 67 Hun, 401, 22 N. Y. Supp. 275, affirmed in 143 N. Y. 661, 39 N. E. 21; Crump v Lambert, L. R. 3 Eq. 409 Conversely, an injunction was refused in Farrell v. New York Steam Co., 23 Misc. Rep. 726, 53 N. Y. Supp. 55, because the plaintiff did not show that the acts would amount to sufficient to maintain an action at law. The bill was to enjoin the operation of a steam plant. The injunction was refused, the court saying: "The evidence does not show that the acts of the defendant have materially lessened the plaintiff's enjoyment of his property. By this I mean those acts of the defendant of which the plaintiff has the legal right to complain" But see Smith v Ingersoll-Sergeant etc. Co., 12 Misc. Rep 5, 33 N. Y. Supp. 70, reversing 7 Misc Rep. 374, 27 N. Y. Supp 907, in which the language of the court is not consistent with the above cases.

95 Union etc. Co. v. Dangberg, 81 Fed. 73 (diversion of water); Potter v. Howe, 141 Mass 357, 6 N E. 233 (flowing land); Learned v Castle, 78 Cal. 454, 18 Pac. 872, 21 Pac. 11 (flowing land; cf. Jacob v. Day, 111 Cal. 571, 44 Pac. 243); Trowbridge v. True, 52 Conn 190, 52 Am. Rep 579 (interference with lateral support enjoined, though damages trifling). *Contra,* McMaugh v. Burke, 12 R. I. 499. For further cases on injunction to prevent interference with water rights, see *post,* chapter XXVI.

§ 527. **Criminal and Statutory Nuisances.**—The jurisdiction of equity over nuisance is essentially a civil jurisdiction. "The plaintiff insisted that it was illegal for Roman Catholics to ring and toll bells in a steeple annexed to their place of worship," said the court in Soltau v. De Held.[96] "It appears to me that whether that be so or not, is perfectly immaterial in this case; because, if it be illegal, I am not to grant an injunction to restrain an illegal act merely because it is illegal. I could not grant an injunction to restrain a man from smuggling, which is an illegal act. If it be illegal, the illegality of it is no ground for my interfering." In accordance with this language the law is settled that an act will not be enjoined as a nuisance merely because it is criminal, even though prohibited by statutes, whether at the suit of a private person[97] or of the pub-

96 Per Cranworth, V. C., 2 Sim., N. S., 133.

97 Sparhawk v. Union etc. Ry. Co, 54 Pa. St. 401; Finegan v. Allen, 46 Ill. App. 553; Sheldon v. Weeks, 51 Ill. App. 314, Rice v. Jefferson, 50 Mo. App. 464; Smith v. Lockwood, 13 Barb. 209; Tiede v. Schneidt, 99 Wis. 201, 74 N. W. 798; City of Utica v. Utica Tel. Co., 24 App. Div. 361, 48 N. Y. Supp. 916. See, however, First Nat. Bank of Mt. Vernon v. Sarlls, 129 Ind. 201, 28 Am. St. Rep. 185, 28 N. E. 434, 13 L. R A. 481 (removal of wooden building within fire limits, against city ordinance); Kaufman v. Stein, 138 Ind. 49, 46 Am. St. Rep. 368, 37 N. E. 333 (same as preceding case); Schulze v Corporation of Galasheils, [1895] App. Cas. 656; Dubos v. Dreyfous, 52 La. Ann 1117, 27 South 663 (failure to ventilate stables, as required by ordinance); State v. Crawford, 28 Kan. 726, 42 Am Rep 182. In this last case the court uttered the following *dictum*: "We would think that every place where a public statute is openly, publicly, repeatedly, continuously, persistently and intentionally violated, is a public nuisance." In the two Indiana cases, also, the court seemed to think that the effect of the statute was to make the prohibited act a nuisance. In Griswold v. Brega, 160 Ill. 490, 52 Am. St. Rep. 350, 43 N. E. 864, affirming 57 Ill App. 554, the required statutory consent of property owners to allow a wooden building to be brought within the fire limits was procured by fraud on some of them, and on this account the court enjoined the defendant from bringing in the building.

lic.[98] The converse of this is not true; indeed it is well established that it is no defense to a bill to enjoin that which is a nuisance to show that it is also a crime;[99] if the law were otherwise, public nuisances which at common law are public offenses, could never be enjoined.[100] A more difficult question is raised when the legislature makes an act a nuisance which was not such at common law, and provides that it shall be subject to injunction in equity. Is such legislation consistent with the provision of the federal, and most of the state, constitutions that the right of trial by jury shall be preserved inviolate? It is held generally, if not universally, that there is nothing unconstitutional in such statutes The jury trial guarded by the constitutional provision is that which was required by the principles of the common law. Jurisdiction to enjoin future acts in the nature of nuisances has always been a matter for the equity courts, and as such has never required a jury trial; hence an enlargement of this jurisdiction does not

98 Village of St. John v McFarlan, 33 Mich. 72, 20 Am. Rep. 671 (erection of wooden building contrary to a village ordinance); Inc Town of Rochester v. Walters, 27 Ind. App. 194, 60 N E. 1101 (same as preceding case), Village of New Rochelle v. Lang, 75 Hun, 608, 27 N. Y. Supp. 600 (same as preceding case); Pres. etc. Village of Waupun v. Moore, 34 Wis. 450, 17 Am. Rep. 446 (same as preceding case); Manor Casino v. State (Tex. Civ. App.), 34 S. W. 769 (sale of intoxicating liquor in violation of statute); Borough of Cambridge Springs v. Moses, 22 Pa. Co. Ct Rep. 637.

99 United States v. Debs, 64 Fed. 724, 753; People v. Truckee Lumber Co., 116 Cal. 397, 58 Am. St. Rep. 183, 48 Pac 374; Barrett v Mt. Greenwood etc. Assn., 159 Ill. 385, 50 Am. St Rep 168, 42 N E 891, 31 L. R. A. 109; People's Gas Co. v. Tyner, 131 Ind. 277, 31 Am. St. Rep. 433, 31 N. E 59, 16 L. R. A. 443; Columbian Athletic Club v. State, 143 Ind. 98, 52 Am St. Rep. 407, 40 N. E. 915, 28 L. R. A. 727; Hamilton v. Whitridge, 11 Md 128, 69 Am. Dec. 184, State v. Saunders, 66 N. H. 39, 25 Atl. 588, 18 L. R. A. 646; North Bloomfield etc. Co. v. United States, 88 Fed. 664, 32 C. C. A. 84, affirming 81 Fed. 243.

100 State v. Crawford, 28 Kan. 726, 42 Am. Rep 182.

trench on the requirement for preserving jury trial.[101] If it could be shown that the purpose of the act were to punish or make compensation for past acts in equity without jury trial, the decision might be different.[102]

§ 528. **The Defendant's Motive.**—How far the defendant's motive may be of importance in cases of nuisance

101 Littleton v. Fritz, 65 Iowa, 488, 54 Am. Rep. 19, 22 N. W. 641 (keeping a saloon); State v. Saunders, 66 N H. 39, 25 Atl. 588, 18 L. R A 646 (same as preceding case); Davis v. Auld, 96 Me. 559, 53 Atl. 118; Eilenbecker v. Dist. Ct. of Plymouth Co., 134 U. S. 31, 10 Sup. Ct. 424, 33 L. ed. 801. In the last case cited the plaintiff having been enjoined from violating the liquor law, was afterwards found guilty of contempt for disobeying the injunction and sentenced to pay $500 or go to prison for three months. He carried the case to the supreme court, because, among other things, the equity court had imposed this punishment upon him without trial by jury. In affirming the decision of the state court it was said: "If the objection is that it authorizes a proceeding in the nature of a suit in equity to suppress the manufacture and sale of intoxicating liquors, which are by law prohibited, and to abate the nuisance which the statute declares such acts to be, wherever carried on, we respond that, so far as at present advised, it appears to us that all the powers of a court, whether at common law or in chancery, may be called into operation by a legislative body for the purpose of suppressing the objectionable traffic And we know of no hindrance in the constitution of the United States to the form of proceedings, or to the court in which this remedy shall be had. Certainly it seems to us to be quite as wise to use the processes of the law and the powers of the court to prevent the evil as to punish the offense as a crime after it has been committed." A city sheltering itself under authority of law from liability for acts which between private individuals would be a nuisance must show an express or clearly implied authority to do such acts Hill v. Mayor etc. N. Y., 139 N. Y. 495, 34 N. E. 1090, reversing 63 Hun, 633, 18 N. Y. Supp. 399; Spring v. Delaware, L. & W. R. Co., 88 Hun, 385, 34 N. Y. Supp. 810.

102 State v Saunders, 66 N H. 39, 25 Atl 588, 594, 18 L. R A. 646. It is not a violation of such statutes for an officer to sell intoxicating liquors under execution, if the sale is an honest one for the benefit of the plaintiff in execution under proper process; it is a violation, subject to injunction, if the sale by the officer is a collusive attempt to evade the statute: Fears v State, 102 Ga 274, 29 S. E. 463. On the subject of this section, see also, *ante*, chapter XXI.

is, strictly, a matter of substantive law, and not of the equitable remedy. But, inasmuch as, in a narrow range of cases, the question has, of late years, received considerable attention, largely in applications for injunctions, and as it is likely to arise in the future in similar applications, rather than in actions at law, because the equitable remedy is the only one to afford adequate redress, it may be well briefly to treat of it here. If one draws off percolating water and thus dries up his neighbor's well; or erects a high fence on his own land which shuts off the light from the house of his neighbor (who has no easement of light and air), in both cases acting from a malevolent motive to injure the neighbor, and not otherwise to benefit himself than by causing the injury, has the neighbor any legal cause for complaint? In this form, and almost exclusively on the above facts, the question has arisen. In cases of percolating water there are *dicta* from the earliest cases down, that such water cannot be drawn off for the sole and malicious purpose of injuring one's neighbor.[103] The cases in which the courts have actually decided the question have been mainly on application for injunctions, which have been granted.[104] The

103 Chasemore v. Richards, 7 H L. Cas. 349, 387; Greenleaf v Francis, 18 Pick. 117; Wheatley v. Baugh, 25 Pa. St. 528, 64 Am. Dec. 721; Chesley v. King, 74 Me. 164, 43 Am. Rep. 569, Roath v Driscoll, 20 Conn 538, 52 Am. Dec. 352. *Contra*, Frazier v. Brown, 12 Ohio St. 294.

104 Forbell v. City of New York, 164 N. Y. 522, 79 Am. St. Rep 666, 58 N E. 644, 51 L. R. A. 695, Stillwater Water Co. v. Farmer, 89 Minn. 58, 99 Am. St. Rep. 541, 93 N. W. 907, 60 L. R. A. 875, Barclay v Abraham, 121 Iowa, 619, 100 Am. St. Rep. 365, 96 N W. 1080. *Contra*, Huber v. Merkel, 117 Wis. 355, 98 Am. St. Rep. 355, 94 N W 354. In actions at law the same thing has been held in Bassett v. Salisbury Mfg. Co., 43 N. H. 569, 82 Am. Dec. 179; Swett v. Cutts, 50 N. H 439, 9 Am. Rep. 276. *Contra*, Phelps v Nowlan, 72 N. Y 39, 28 Am Rep. 93. In Forbell v. City of New York, *supra*, it was held that the owner of land could not draw the percolating

ground of decision, however, is narrower than the mere impropriety of the defendant's motive; instead it takes the form of a rule of property that one may collect and consume percolating water only for beneficial use on the land on which it is collected; collection of it for any other purpose may be enjoined by any person affected injuriously. Thus expressed it, is no more drastic a limitation of property rights than are all the rules

water into wells for the purpose of selling it for consumption off the land. .In Barclay v. Abraham, *supra*, and Stillwater Co. v. Farmer, *supra*, it was held that one could not collect percolating water on his own land and waste it to the injury of others In the latter of these cases the court, per Collins, J., said: "In holding as we do, and in laying down a rule which confessedly is something of a departure from the general doctrine found in the books, and is an advanced position, we are not really discarding the maxim, *cujus est solum ejus est usque ad coelum*, or doing violence to any of the reasons which have been given for it We are not involving any set of legal rules in hopeless uncertainty, and therefore rendering their application practically impossible, for the rule which we adopt is not only just, but is exceeding plain, certain, practical, and easy to apply to real conditions. Nor will our recognition of the doctrine of correlative rights interfere in any manner with material improvements, to the detriment of the state. On the contrary, it will tend to promote the prosperity and general welfare of all citizens whose necessities bring them within its influence. Nor are we entirely without authority for such a doctrine. We therefore formulate and announce the rule governing the facts here to be that, except for the benefit and improvement of his own premises, or for his beneficial use, the owner of land has no right to drain, collect, or divert percolating waters thereon, when such acts will destroy or materially injure the spring of another person, the waters of which spring are used by the general public for domestic purposes." In Barclay v. Abraham, *supra*, the court, per Ladd, J., said: "The prevention of carrying the water from the land of the owner for the purposes of commerce or waste cannot retard the improvement of the land itself, and there is no just ground for tolerating such diversion when the direct result is to deprive the adjoining land owners by the incidental drainage of their land of a supply of water from the same natural reservoir. This would be extracting the subterranean water from the adjoining land to its injury, without any counter benefit to the land through which taken."

which ordinarily define a nuisance; indeed, it is doubtful if it goes so far, while the beneficial results to flow from it are obvious. In dealing with the cases of "spite fences" and similar erections, the courts have made them turn on the malevolent motive of the defendant in erecting the structure. The objections which have been made to such a criterion of legal rights and liabilities have been expressed as follows: "To permit a man to cause a certain injurious effect upon the premises of his neighbor by the erection of a structure on his premises if such structure is beneficial or ornamental, and to prohibit him from causing the same effect in case the structure is neither beneficial nor ornamental, but erected from motives of pure malice, is not protecting a legal right, but is controlling his moral conduct."[105] It would seem clear, however, there is neither justice nor expediency in allowing such things as the building of a spite fence to be done, unless the preservation of property rights demands it. "It is plain that the right to use one's property for the sole purpose of injuring others is not one of the immediate rights of ownership; it is not a right for the sake of which property is recognized by law, but is only a more or less necessary incident of rights which are established for very different ends."[106] And, however forcible the objections may be to founding relief upon the defendant's immoral motive alone, it seems clear that here the actual interference with the defendant in the use of his property would be less radical than in most cases of nuisance. There he is not allowed to make a use of his premises which is generally beneficial both to himself

105 Letts v. Kessler, 54 Ohio St. 73, 42 N. E. 765, 40 L. R. A. 177, overruling 7 Ohio Cir. Rep. 108.

106 Per Holmes, J., in Rideout v. Knox, 148 Mass. 368, 12 Am. St. Rep. 560, 19 N. E. 390, 2 L. R. A. 81.

and to society; here the use he is making is beneficial to neither and may be equally harmful with recognized nuisances to the plaintiff. As a result of the antagonistic influences that bear on the case in this form, the authorities are divided. Partly by judicial declaration,[107] but more largely by virtue of statutes,[108] the weight of authority is that structures of the kind under discussion are unlawful and their maintenance may be enjoined. But the malevolent motive must in such cases be the dominant one, such that even if no other were present it would induce the act complained of; it will not do if it is simply present together with other motives which are worthy.[109] Some courts, however, have declined to adopt even this restricted doc-

107 Burke v. Smith, 69 Mich. 380, 37 N. W 838; Flaherty v. Moran, 81 Mich. 52, 2 Am. St. Rep. 510, 45 N. W. 381, 8 L. R. A. 183; Kirkwood v. Finegan, 95 Mich. 543, 55 N. W. 457; Peck v. Roe, 110 Mich. 52, 67 N. W. 1080.

108 **Connecticut.**—Gen. Stats, ed 1902, §§ 1013, 1107. Injunctions allowed in Harbison v. White, 46 Conn. 106; Whitlock v. Uhle, 75 Conn. 423, 53 Atl. 891.

Maine.—Freeman's Supplement, c. 17, § 5. Construed in Lord v. Langdon, 91 Me. 221, 39 Atl. 552.

Massachusetts.—Acts and Resolves, 1887, c. 348. Actions for damages allowed in Rideout v. Knox, 148 Mass. 368, 12 Am. St. Rep. 560, 19 N E. 390, 2 L. R A. 81; Smith v. Morse, 148 Mass. 407, 19 N. E. 393; not allowed in Spaulding v. Smith, 162 Mass. 543, 39 N. E. 189.

New Hampshire.—Stats., ed. 1902, c. 143, §§ 28, 29, 30. Construed in Hunt v. Coggin, 66 N. H. 140, 20 Atl. 250.

Vermont.—Laws of Vermont, 1886, No. 84.

Washington.—2 Hill's Ann. Stats. & Codes, § 268; Ballinger's Ann. Codes, § 5433. Injunction allowed in Karasek v. Peier, 22 Wash. 419, 61 Pac. 33, 50 L. R. A. 345.

109 Kuzniak v. Kozminski, 107 Mich. 444, 61 Am. St. Rep. 344, 65 N. W. 275; Ladd v. Flynn, 90 Mich. 181, 51 N. W. 203; Rideout v. Knox, 148 Mass. 368, 12 Am. St. Rep. 560, 19 N. E. 390, 2 L. R. A. 81, Gallegher v. Dodge, 48 Conn. 387, 40 Am. Rep. 182, Lord v. Langdon, 91 Me. 221, 39 Atl. 552; see Hunt v. Coggin, 66 N. H. 140, 20 Atl. 250.

trine, and, preferring the hardship of individual cases to a ground of jurisdiction considered to be so fallible as the defendant's immoral motive, have refused relief.[110] It may be permissible to suggest that if the lead of the cases on percolating water were followed, and the decisions based on the reasoning that a man's property right in the passage of light and air over his land is not an absolute right to interfere with it arbitrarily as he chooses, but only for purposes useful and beneficial to him in connection with the land itself, the unfortunate criterion of bad motive would be removed, no harmful restriction of property rights would be created, and the ends of justice would be furthered.

110 Mahan v. Brown, 13 Wend. 261, 28 Am. Dec. 461; Letts v Kessler, 54 Ohio St. 73, 42 N. E. 765, 40 L. R. A. 177, overruling Kessler v. Letts, 7 Ohio Cir. Rep. 108; Metzker v. Hochrein, 107 Wis 267, 81 Am St. Rep. 841, 83 N. W. 308, 50 L. R. A. 305; Bordeaux v. Greene, 22 Mont 254, 74 Am. St. Rep. 600, 56 Pac. 218; Falloon v. Schilling, 29 Kan. 292, 44 Am Rep. 642 See, also, Guest v. Reynolds, 68 Ill 478, 18 Am. Rep. 570; Housel v. Conant, 12 Ill. App 259. In Burke v. Smith, 69 Mich. 380, 37 N. W. 838, Mahan v. Brown, *supra*, was distinguished on the ground that the existence of the doctrine of ancient lights in New York made the holding necessary in order that a land owner may be able to prevent an easement of light over his land from arising

The question of allowing natural gas to escape on one's land has given rise to a similar discussion to that concerning air and percolating water. See Ohio Oil Co. v. State of Indiana, 150 Ind. 698, 50 N. E. 1124, affirmed in 177 U. S. 190, 20 Sup. Ct. 576, 44 L ed. 729; Hague v. Wheeler, 157 Pa. St. 324, 37 Am. St. Rep. 736, 27 Atl. 714, 22 L. R. A. 141.

In the following cases there are intimations that the court will consider the parties' motive in ordinary cases of nuisance: Christie v. Davie, [1893] 1 Ch 316 (motive of defendant in making a noise), Medford v. Levy, 31 W Va. 649, 13 Am. St. Rep. 887, 8 S E 302, 2 L. R. A. 368 (quarrel between neighbors); Bassett v. Salisbury, 47 N. H. 426 (plaintiff bought land flooded by defendant's dam in order to compel defendant to buy other land from him); Edwards v. Allouez Mining Co., 38 Mich. 46, 31 Am. Rep 301 (similar to preceding case).

§ 529. **The Balance of Injury.**—The question how far courts of equity, in dealing with cases of admitted or established nuisances, should be influenced, in their determination whether to grant an injunction or to turn the plaintiff over to his remedy at law, by the balance between the injury to the plaintiff from refusing, and to the defendant from granting the injunction, has received considerable attention from the courts, and has met with conflicting answers—often from courts within the same jurisdiction. It is to be noted that the question as here raised excludes certain situations in which its consideration is, beyond all doubt, proper and even necessary. The first of these is on application for temporary injunctions, in which, the questions in dispute being undetermined, the courts must take account of the possibilities of injury in a course of action which the hearing may prove to be the wrong one.[111] The second, is in the determination of the wrongfulness of the defendant's act—the fact of nuisance or no nuisance—in that large class of cases in which there is no invasion of a clearly defined right of the plaintiff—such as, say, the right to have water flow in its accustomed channel—but, rather, of a right which is determined by all the circumstances of the case, place, time, degree, and the like—nuisances such as noise, vibration and pollution of air. In cases of this sort a balancing of injury—the plaintiff's comfort and enjoyment against the public benefit from the prosecution of the business complained of, the defendant's advantage in carrying on his offending business against the plaintiff's welfare—is, of course, an essential factor in the decision whether any nuisance exists or not. But this point having been determined in the plaintiff's favor, the question now to be discussed is, whether, on

[111] See *infra*, § 535.

an application for a permanent injunction against an admitted or proved nuisance, the courts of equity should carry this balancing of injury admittedly further than the courts of law carry it, and make it a test for the granting or withholding of their peculiar relief.

§ 530. **Balance Between Private Parties.**—The balance of injury which may determine the granting or refusing of an injunction arises in two forms, which, however, may appear together in the same case. In the first of these the balance is between the injuries to the plaintiff, a private individual, and to another private individual; in the second, between the injuries to the plaintiff, a private individual, and to the public, which benefits from the defendant's wrongful enterprise. On the first of these questions, curiously enough, the same jurisdiction furnishes as strong statements on both sides as may be found. In Richard's Appeal,[112] an injunction was sought against the use of bituminous coal in the defendant's iron-works, which materially injured the plaintiff's dwelling-house and his cotton factory. In refusing the injunction the court said: "An error seems somewhat prevalent in portions, at least, of this commonwealth in regard to proceedings in equity to restrain the commission of nuisances. It seems to be supposed that, as at law, whenever a case is made out of wrongful acts on the one side and consequent injury on the other, a decree to restrain the act complained of must as certainly follow as a judgment would follow a verdict in a common-law court. This is a mistake. It is elementary law that in equity a decree is never of right, as a judgment at law is, but of grace. Hence, the chancellor will consider whether he would not do a

112 57 Pa. St. 105, 98 Am. Dec. 202.

greater injury by enjoining than would result from refusing, and leaving the party to his redress at the hands of a court and jury. If in conscience the former should appear, he will refuse to enjoin." In Evans v. Reading etc. Fertilizing Co.[113] the bill was to enjoin the operation of a fertilizer factory, the stench from which rendered the plaintiff's house almost uninhabitable. After remarking that the proper application of the "balance of injury notion" was to motions for preliminary injunctions, the court continued: "But where, upon final hearing, the mind of the chancellor is satisfied that the complainant's right is clear, and the injury sustained by him substantial, so that his claim to damages at law is indisputable, and where, moreover, such damages could not give him adequate redress except by an endless repetition of suits, a refusal of an injunction upon the ground that plaintiff cannot suffer as great a loss from the continuance of the nuisance as defendant would from its interdiction, would be as far from equity as can be. There is, to my mind, no more offensive plea than that by which one seeks to justify an act injurious to his neighbor on the ground of its advantage to himself." The court, in another jurisdiction, replying to the argument for a balancing of the injury said: "If the injuries to the plaintiffs were of a trivial character, they should, perhaps, be considered *damnum absque injuria;* but a comparison of the value of the conflicting rights would be a novel mode of determining their legal superiority."[114] The suggestion of these last two quotations that a balancing of injury is given effect to once in the determination of the fact of nuisance and, hence, does not need to be made a second time in determining the proper remedy,

[113] 160 Pa. St. 209, 20 Atl. 702.

[114] Weaver v. Eureka Lake Co., 15 Cal. 271.

and that it is anomalous to deny the equitable relief in a case where the legal wrong and the inadequacy of the legal remedy are established, is very hard to meet. Denying the injunction puts the hardship on the party in whose favor the legal right exists instead of on the wrong-doer. If relief intermediate between the radical remedy of injunction and the insufficient one of repeated actions at law for damages as they accrue is desirable, it would seem that a legislative provision is necessary to supply it. The weight of authority is against allowing a balancing of injury as a means of determining the propriety of issuing an injunction.[115]

115 Higgins v. Flemington Co., 36 N. J. Eq. (9 Stew.) 538; Hennessy v. Carmony, 50 N. J. Eq. (5 Dick.) 616, 25 Atl. 374; Evans v. Reading etc. Fertilizing Co., 160 Pa. St. 209, 28 Atl. 702; Weaver v. Eureka Lake Co., 15 Cal. 271; Corning v. Troy etc. Factory, 40 N. Y. 191, 39 Barb. 311, 34 Barb. 485, 6 How. Pr. 89; Amsterdam etc. Co. v. Dean, 13 App. Div. 42, 43 N. Y. Supp 29; Banks v. Frazier, 23 Ky. Law Rep 1197, 64 S. W. 983; Suffolk etc. Co. v. San Miguel etc. Co., 9 Colo. App. 407, 48 Pac. 828; Clowes v Staffordshire etc. Co., L. R. 8 Ch App. 125; Pennington v. Brinsop etc. Co., L. R. 5 Ch D 769; Young v. Banker etc. Co., [1893] App. Cas. 691, 702; Hobbs v. Amador Co, 66 Cal. 161, 4 Pac. 1147; Chestatee Co. v. Cavenders Co., 118 Ga 255, 45 S. E. 267; Weston Paper Co. v Pope, 155 Ind. 394, 57 N. E. 719, 56 L. R. A. 899; Townsend v. Bell, 62 Hun, 306, 17 N. Y. Supp. 210; Brown v. Ontario etc. Co., 31 App. Div. 273, 80 N. Y. Supp. 837; Beckwith v. Howard, 6 R. I. 1. See, also, 14 Harv. Law Rev, p. 458. In Weston Paper Co. v. Pope, *supra*, the court, per Hadley, J., said: "The fact that the appellant has expended a large sum of money in the construction of its plant and that it conducts its business in a careful manner and without malice can make no difference in its rights to the stream Before locating the plant the owners were bound to know that every riparian proprietor is entitled to have the waters of the stream that washes his land come to it without obstruction, diversion, or corruption, subject only to the reasonable use of the water, by those similarly entitled, for such domestic purposes as are inseparable from and necessary for the free use of their land, and they were bound also to know the character of their proposed business, and to take notice of the size, course and capacity of the stream, and to determine for themselves and at their own peril whether they should be able to conduct their business upon a stream

§ 531. **Balance Between the Plaintiff and the Public.**— When the defendant's business which constitutes the nuisance complained of is one from which the public benefits directly or in an unusually marked degree, the balance of injury presents itself in a different form. Shall the plaintiff by procuring an injunction put an end to a business from which the public receives large benefit, and from the stopping of which public hardship would ensue? The extreme case which will fully test

of the size and character of Brandywine creek without injury to their neighbors; and the magnitude of their investment and their freedom from malice furnish no reason why they should escape the consequences of their own folly.'' In the following cases there are statements of the courts that the balance of injury between the plaintiff and defendant is to be considered in determining whether to issue an injunction. In almost every case, however, the statement has been repudiated by the court making it, or is a *dictum*, or is a part only of the ground of decision: Davis v. Sawyer, 133 Mass 289, 43 Am. Rep. 519 *(dictum)*; Wood v. Sutcliffe, 2 Sim., N. S., 163 (part only of ground of decision, and clearly not the doctrine ot the English courts; see cases cited, *supra)*; Richards' Appeal, 57 Pa. St. (7 P. F. Smith) 105, 98 Am. Dec. 202 (overruled in Evans v. Reading etc. Fertilizing Co., *supra*); Herr v. Central etc. Asylum, 22 Ky. Law Rep. 1722, 61 S. W. 283 (acquiescence of defendant also shown), Hawley v. Beardsley, 47 Conn. 571 (but injury was such that the legal remedy was adequate); Robinson v. Clapp, 67 Conn. 538, 52 Am. St. Rep. 298, 35 Atl. 504 (it was doubtful if thing threatened—cutting away projecting trunk of a boundary tree—was a legal wrong at all); Tuttle v. Church, 53 Fed. 422 (but no nuisance was established in fact); Fox v. Holcomb, 32 Mich. 494; Turner v Hart, 71 Mich. 128, 15 Am. St. Rep. 243, 38 N. W. 890; City of Big Rapids v. Comstock, 65 Mich. 78, 31 N. W. 811 *(dictum)*; Potter v. Saginaw etc. Ry. Co., 83 Mich. 285, 47 N. W. 217, 10 L. R. A. 176 *(dictum)*; cf. Stock v. Jefferson Tp., 114 Mich. 357, 72 N. W. 132, 38 L. R. A. 355; Dana v. Craddock, 66 N. H. 593, 32 Atl. 757 *(dictum)*; Goodall v. Crofton, 33 Ohio St. 271, 31 Am. Rep. 535 *(dictum)*; Wahl v. Cemetery Assn., 197 Pa. St. 197, 46 Atl. 913 *(dictum)*; Becker v. Lebanon etc. Co., 188 Pa. St. 484, 41 Atl. 612 (but laches also present in the case; cf. Pennsylvania cases cited, *supra)*; Morris etc. Co. v. Prudden, 20 N. J Eq. 530 (cf. New Jersey cases cited, *supra)*; Madison v. Ducktown S, C. & I. Co. (Tenn.), 83 S. W. 658 (but decision is influenced by a statute).

the rule is that in which the defendant is a *quasi*-public corporation engaged in supplying a city with water or other necessity. In such a case the nuisance complained of was the smoke from the defendant's waterworks, which, in a material degree, deprived the plaintiffs of the enjoyment of their property. In denying an injunction the court said: "If the defendant were enjoined even for a time, the result might be disastrous; for the water supplied by it is the only efficient means of extinguishing conflagrations at the command of the city or its citizens. Besides this, a daily and hourly supply of water used for many purposes would be cut off. We think it may be safely assumed that the rule in equity is, that where the damages can be admeasured and compensated, equity will not interfere where the public benefit greatly outweighs private and individual inconvenience."[116] On the other side, it has been said by an able chancellor on substantially similar facts: "If it should turn out that the company had no right so to manufacture gas as to damage the plaintiff's market garden, I have come to the conclusion, that I cannot enter into any question of how far it might be con-

116 Per Seevers, J., in Daniels v. Keokuk Water-works, 61 Iowa, 549, 16 N. W. 705. To the same effect are statements in the following cases: Miller v. City of Webster City, 94 Iowa, 162, 62 N. W. 648; Rouse v. Martin, 75 Ala. 510, 51 Am. Rep. 463; Clifton Iron Co v. Dye, 87 Ala. 468, 6 South. 192 (acquiescence on plaintiff's part also found); Stewart Wire Co. v. Lehigh Coal etc. Co., 203 Pa. St. 474, 53 Atl. 352 (plaintiff guilty of acquiescence, however); Riedeman v. Mt. Morris etc. Co., 56 App Div. 23, 67 N. Y. Supp 391 (but there was doubt whether plaintiff was substantially damaged by the thing complained of); Atchison etc. Co. v. Meyer, 62 Kan. 696, 64 Pac 597 (but the legal remedy was adequate); Grey v. City of Paterson (N. J), 45 Atl. 995, 48 L. R. A. 717 (but plaintiffs were guilty of acquiescence); Fisk v. City of Hartford, 70 Conn. 720, 66 Am. St. Rep. 147, 40 Atl. 906 (but the legal remedy was adequate, and plaintiff had been guilty of laches); Wees v. Coal etc Co., 54 W. Va. 421, 46 S. E. 166, Lillywhite v. Trimmer, 36 L. J. Ch. 525.

venient for the public that the gas manufacture should go on. That might be a good ground for the legislature to declare that the company might make gas if they indemnified the plaintiff; but, unless the company had such a right I think the present is not a case in which this court can go into the question of convenience or inconvenience, and say where a party is substantially damaged, that he can only be compensated by bringing an action *toties quoties.* That would be a disgraceful state of the law; and I quite agree with the vice-chancellor, in holding that in such a case this court must issue an injunction, whatever may be the consequences with regard to the lighting of the parishes and district which this company supplies with gas."[117]

[117] Lord Cranworth in Broadbent v. Imperial Gas Co, 7 De Gex, M. & G. 436, 462, affirmed in 7 H. L. Cas. 600. To the same effect are Attorney-General v. Council etc Birmingham, 4 Kay & J. 528, 538; Attorney-General v. Colney etc. Asylum, L. R. 4 Ch App. 146; Attorney-General v. Terry, L R. 9 Ch. App. 423, Sammons v. City of Gloversville, 34 Misc Rep. 459, 70 N. Y. Supp 284; Stock v. Jefferson Township, 114 Mich 357, 72 N. W. 132, 38 L. R. A. 355; Ex parte Martin, 13 Ark. 198, 58 Am. Dec 321, Village of Dwight v. Hayes, 150 Ill. 273, 41 Am. St Rep. 367, 37 N E. 218, affirming 49 Ill. App. 530; Hinchman v. Paterson etc. Co, 17 N J. Eq. (2 C. E. Green) 75, 86 Am. Dec. 252 (*dictum*); Aquackanock etc. Co. v Watson, 29 N J. Eq. 366, Harper etc. Co v. Mountain Water Co, 65 N. J. Eq. 479, 56 Atl. 297; Smith v. City of Rochester, 38 Hun, 612, affirmed in 104 N. Y. 674; Duesler v. City of Johnstown, 24 App. Div. 608, 48 N. Y. Supp. 683. In Attorney-General v. Council etc. Birmingham, *supra,* Wood, V. C., said: "It has been urged upon me more than once during the argument by the counsel for the defendants, that there are 250,000 inhabitants in the town of Birmingham, and that this circumstance must be taken into consideration in determining the question of the plaintiff's right to an injunction. . . . . Now, with regard to the question of the plaintiff's right to an injunction, it appears to me, that, so far as this court is concerned, it is a matter of almost absolute indifference whether the decision will affect a population of 250,000 or a single individual carrying on a manufactory for his own benefit. The rights of the plaintiff must be measured precisely as they have been left by the legislature. I am not sitting here as a

On its merits, as well as on authority, the superiority of this latter view seems hardly to admit of doubt. The refusal of the injunction, in the first place, leaves the plaintiff to suffer an admitted legal wrong and to obtain his only redress by an admittedly inadequate remedy. And, in the second place, so far as the interests of the public are considered, that case is not to be distinguished in principle from the taking of property for public purposes which the federal constitution forbids; true, the damage from a nuisance may not always be a "taking" as defined by the authorities, but it would seem within the same reasoning;[118] and, if the public need requires it, the plaintiff's property can be taken or legislative provision made for the payment of permanent damages to him. The objection that temporary hardship to the public may result from granting the injunction at once can be obviated by allowing time for the necessary readjustment, before putting it into effect.[119]

§ 532. **Nuisance Easily Avoided by the Plaintiff.**—Closely related to the question discussed in the preceding paragraphs is another which is raised when there is offered as a defense to a bill for an injunction against a nuisance, the fact that the plaintiff could prevent the nuisance by a comparatively small outlay of labor or expense. In most of the cases in which the question has arisen, the defense has been rejected, sometimes with vigor. "Neither does it make any difference,"

committee for public safety, armed with arbitrary power to prevent what, it is said, will be a great injury, not to Birmingham only, but to the whole of England,—that is not my function.''

118 See Pennsylvania R. R. Co. v Angel, 41 N. J. Eq. (14 Stew.) 316, 56 Am. Rep. 1, 7 Atl 432; Baltimore etc. Co. v. Fifth Baptist Church, 108 U. S. 317, 2 Sup. Ct. 719.

119 See the form of decree in Harding v. Stamford Water Co., 41 Conn. 87, and the remarks of Selwyn, L. J, in Attorney-General v. Colney etc. Asylum, 4 Ch. App. 146, 165, 166.

said the court in Paddock v. Somes,[120] "or in any measure operate as an excuse that the nuisance cannot be obviated without great expense, or that the plaintiff himself could obviate the injury at a trifling expense. It is the duty of every person or public body to prevent a nuisance, and the fact that the person injured could, but does not, prevent damages to his property therefrom is no defense either to an action at law or in equity. A party is not bound to expend a dollar, or to do any act to secure for himself the exercise or enjoyment of a legal right of which he is deprived by reason of the wrongful acts of another." In a comparatively early case the same question was raised on the following facts: The plaintiff's spring was overflowed and sediment deposited in it as a result of the working of the defendant's mill. It appeared that the spring could be protected by digging a ditch two hundred and fifty yards long. On these facts it was clear that a small expenditure of labor would give the plaintiff protection equal to that of an injunction and at the same time leave the defendant undisturbed in the exercise of his lawful business. Hence the injunction was refused.[121] The unqualified refusal of the injunction may perhaps be open to criticism in that it leaves the plaintiff to incur the risk of recovering from the defendant compensation for whatever labor or expense he should be put to in doing away with the nuisance. But it seems that a very simple and not uncommon exercise of the court's power to mold decrees according to the needs of the case would, in all such cases, meet this criticism and yet save to the defendant the right to continue his business. A decree so framed as

120 102 Mo. 226, 238, 14 S. W. 746, 10 L. R. A. 254, per Sherwood, J., quoting Wood on Nuisances, 2d ed., 506

121 Rosser v. Randolph, 7 Port. (Ala.) 238, 31 Am. Dec. 712.

to grant the injunction unless the defendant would either himself do the acts necessary to avoid the nuisance or give sufficient undertaking to protect the plaintiff in doing them, and requiring the plaintiff either to allow the defendant to do the acts or to accept the undertaking, as the case might be, on pain of losing all equitable relief, would do full justice to both parties without hardship to either.[122] It must be said, however, that this form of decree has not been adopted by any court in this particular class of cases, although the situation would seem an eminently appropriate one for it. The clear weight of authority is with the first case cited above, granting the injunction unqualifiedly.[123]

§ 533. Relief Given; Mandatory Injunctions.—The relief sought in equity against nuisance is, of course, preventive, either to prohibit the creation of a nuisance or to prevent an existing one from continuing in the fu

122 For illustration of this form of decree, see Henderson v. New York Cent. etc. Co., 78 N. Y. 423; Pappenheim v. Metropolitan etc. Co., 128 N. Y. 436, 26 Am. St. Rep. 486, 28 N E. 518, 13 L R. A. 401.

123 Paddock v. Somes, 102 Mo 226, 14 S. W. 746, 10 L R. A. 254; Boston Ferrule Co. v. Hills, 159 Mass. 147, 34 N. E. 85, 20 L R. A. 844; Masonic etc. Assn. v Banks, 94 Va. 695, 27 S. E. 490; Richmond Mfg Co. v Atlantic etc. Co, 10 R. I. 106, 14 Am. Rep 658; Middlestadt v. Waupaca etc. Co., 93 Wis. 1, 66 N W. 713; Suffolk etc Co v San Miguel etc. Co, 9 Colo App. 407, 48 Pac. 828; Clowes v. Staffordshire etc. Co., 8 Ch. App 125; Town of Burlington v. Schwarzman, 52 Conn. 181, 52 Am. Rep. 571; Martin v. Marks, 154 Ind. 549, 57 N. E. 249. *Contra,* Rosser v Randolph, 7 Port. (Ala) 238, 31 Am. Dec. 712; English v Progress etc. Co., 95 Ala. 259, 10 South 134; Kingsbury v Flowers, 65 Ala. 479, 39 Am. Rep 14; Porter v. Armstrong, 132 N. C. 66, 43 S. E. 542. The suggestion of the text would, of course, apply only where the nuisance arose out of the application of the doctrine of correlative rights, not where the defendant's acts which cause the nuisance are wrongful *per se;* nor would it apply when the acts by which the nuisance was obviated would cause substantial or permanent damage to the plaintiff.

ture. Ordinarily, this end is achieved by a mere prohibitive injunction. When, as is not uncommonly the case, however, the nuisance is one which exists, and will continue to exist, because of acts already done—as, for example, the building of a dam—without further acting on the defendant's part, mere prohibition will not serve to accomplish the desired result; mandatory relief is necessary to end the wrong. In such a case it was said by the court: "It is not to correct a wrong of the past, in the sense of redress for the injury already sustained, but to prevent further injury. The injury consists in the overflow of the lands of the plaintiff. It was not alone the building of the dam that caused the injury, but its maintenance, or continuance, which is a part of the act complained of; and its maintenance can only be estopped so as to prevent its injury by its removal. The removal of the dam, wrongfully constructed, is necessary for and incidentally involved in the preventive redress which the law authorizes."[124] On this ground the use of mandatory injunctions is resorted to whenever necessary to give the full relief to which the plaintiff is entitled. In such cases it is generally destructive acts requiring no supervision that are required, as the removal of an object that is, or causes, a nuisance.[125] Occasionally, however, it may be con-

124 Troe v. Larson, 84 Iowa, 649, 35 Am. St. Rep. 336, 51 N. W. 179.

125 Troe v. Larson, *supra;* Holmes v. Calhoun Co., 97 Iowa, 360, 66 N. W. 145; Middlesex Co. v. City of Lowell, 149 Mass. 509, 21 N. E. 872; Crocker v. Manhattan etc. Co., 61 App. Div. 226, 70 N. Y. Supp. 492; Rothery v. New York Rubber Co, 90 N. Y 30; Hammond v. Fuller, 1 Paige, 197; City of Mt. Clemens v. Mt. Clemens etc. Co, 127 Mich. 115, 86 N. W 537, 8 Det. Leg. N. 282; Atchison etc. Co. v. Lang, 46 Kan. 701, 26 Am. St. Rep. 165, 27 Pac. 182; Shroyer v. Campbell, 31 Ind. App 83, 67 N. E. 193; Martin v. Marks, 154 Ind. 549, 57 N. E. 249; Lake Erie etc. Co. v Essington, 27 Ind. App. 291, 60 N. E. 457; City of Eau Claire v. Matzke, 86 Wis. 291,

structive or continuing acts that are directed.[126] Subject to the reluctance of equity courts to order the doing of acts that will require supervision,[127] it is no distinction between prohibitory and mandatory injunctions or between different kinds of mandatory relief that guides the court in the form of injunction issued, but rather the nature of the relief demanded in order to give the plaintiff the protection to which he is entitled.

§ 534. **Form of Injunction.**—The forms of injunction used against nuisances illustrate to an unusual degree both the flexibility of equitable procedure and also the relative nature of nuisances. In a great many cases a thing is a nuisance not because it is in itself deemed wrongful in law, but because the manner in which it is done, or the extent to which it is carried, causes it to cross the line beyond which the law will not allow one

56 N. W. 874; City of Wauwatosa v. Dreutzer, 116 Wis. 117, 92 N. W. 551; McHugh v. Louisville Bridge Co., 23 Ky. Law Rep 1546, 65 S. W. 456; Great Northern etc. Co. v. Clarence Ry., 1 Coll. C. C 507; Laybourn v. Gridley, [1892] 2 Ch. 53; Attorney-General v. Heatley, [1897] 1 Ch. 560; Goodrich v. Georgia etc. Co., 115 Ga. 340, 41 S. E. 659; Broome v. New York etc. Co., 42 N. J. Eq. 141, 7 Atl 851, Clifton v. Town of Weston, 54 W. Va. 250, 46 S. E. 360; Baumgartner v Bradt, 207 Ill 345, 69 N. E. 912, Norwalk etc. Co v. Vernam, 75 Conn 662, 96 Am. St. Rep. 246, 55 Atl. 168; Ackerman v. True, 175 N. Y. 353, 67 N. E. 629, Village of Oxford v. Willoughby (N. Y.), 73 N. E. 677; Allen v. Stowell, 145 Cal. 666, 104 Am. St Rep. 80, 79 Pac. 371.

126 City of Moundsville v. Ohio etc. Co., 37 W. Va. 92, 16 S. E 514, 20 L. R. A 161; City of Kankakee v. Trustees etc. Hospital, 66 Ill. App. 112; Manchester etc. Co. v. Worksop Board of Health, 23 Beav 198; Kaspar v. Dawson, 71 Conn 405, 42 Atl. 78; Corning v. Troy etc Factory, 40 N. Y. 191, 39 Barb. 311, 34 Barb. 485, 61 How Pr 39, Bucholz v. New York etc. Co, 148 N. Y. 640, 43 N. E. 76, reversing 66 Hun, 377, 21 N. Y. Supp. 503.

127 See Bradfield v. Dewell, 48 Mich 9, 11 N. W. 760; Wende v Socialer Turn Verein, 66 Ill. App. 591; cf Kaspar v. Dawson, *supra*.

to go, even in the strict conduct of his own business. This situation is recognized by equity courts in granting injunctions, with the result that they are generally so framed as to prohibit only that part of the thing complained of which is injurious, saving to the defendant the right to continue his business if it can be conducted in a harmless way. "Injunctions against carrying on a legitimate and lawful business should go no further than is absolutely necessary to protect the lawful rights of the parties seeking such injunction. When a person is engaged in carrying on such business, he should not be absolutely prohibited from doing so, unless it appears that the carrying on of such business will necessarily produce the injury complained of. If it can be conducted in such a way as not to constitute a nuisance, then it should be permitted to be continued in that manner."[128] This result is sometimes reached by inserting in the prohibition such qualifying words as "to the injury or damage of the plaintiff,"[129] or others of similar nature;[130] sometimes by

128 Chamberlain v. Douglas, 24 App. Div. 582, 48 N. Y. Supp. 710.

129 Lingwood v. Stowmarket Co., L. R. 1 Eq 77, 336; Ulbricht v. Eufaula Water Co., 86 Ala. 587, 11 Am. St. Rep. 72, 6 South. 78, 4 L. R. A. 572; Sullivan v. Royer, 72 Cal. 248, 1 Am. St. Rep. 51, 13 Pac. 655; Snow v. Williams, 16 Hun, 468. See, also, McNenomy v. Baud, 87 Cal. 134, 26 Pac. 795; cf. Earl of Ripon v Hobart, Cooper *temp.* Brougham, 333, 343; Miller v. Edison etc. Co. of N. Y., 33 Misc. Rep. 664, 68 N. Y. Supp 900; Schaub v. Perkinson Bros. Const. Co., 108 Mo. App. 122, 82 S. W. 1094.

130 Winchell v City of Waukesha, 110 Wis. 101, 84 Am. St. Rep. 902, 85 N. W. 668 (injunction against discharging sewage into a river, "unless the same shall have first been so deodorized and purified as not to contain foul, offensive, or noxious matter capable of injuring the plaintiff or her property or causing nuisance thereto"); York v Davidson, 39 Or. 81, 65 Pac. 819 (allowing defendants to impound mining debris only "when they shall have adopted and constructed an efficient and durable system or device for the purpose, such as will meet with the advice and approval of persons skilled in such matters and the court"); cf City of Grand Rapids v. Weiden

giving the defendant leave to apply for a modification of the injunction upon giving satisfactory proof that he can and will conduct his business so as not to amount to a nuisance.[131] Or the court may make a tentative specific order, subject to be modified if experience shows it does not satisfactorily accomplish its purpose.[132] In accordance with the same principle injunctions will not be issued, it is said, against a business which is a nuisance, when the nuisance can be remedied by the use of scientific appliances; instead the court will direct the introduction of such appliances,[133] and whenever necessary to prevent hardship a reasonable amount of time, in which the defendant may conform to the injunction, will be allowed.[134]

§ 535. **Temporary Injunctions.**—The granting of a temporary injunction in cases of alleged nuisances does not proceed on different principles from those common to this particular exercise of equity jurisdiction in other cases. Its function is to preserve property until disputed questions concerning it are settled. A plaintiff

97 Mich. 82, 56 N. W. 233, in which the court granted an absolute injunction, saying: "A change of method would probably involve large expense in plant, and while it might reduce the evil, would not entirely remove the cause of complaint. An order directing such change would but invite outlay, and leave defendant subject to other proceedings, probably in the near future, to the same end."

131 Chamberlain v. Douglas, 24 App. Div. 582, 48 N. Y. Supp. 710.

132 Babcock v. New Jersey Stock Yard Co., 20 N. J. Eq. 296 (injunction against keeping hogs in a stockyard more than three hours a day, this time to be further shortened if plaintiff was not adequately protected by the first order); Northwood v. Barber etc. Co, 126 Mich. 284, 8 Det. Leg. N. 1, 85 N. W. 724, 54 L. R. A. 54.

133 Green v. Lake, 54 Miss. 540, 28 Am. Rep. 378; English v. Progress etc. Co, 95 Ala. 259, 10 South. 134.

134 Winchell v. City of Waukesha, 110 Wis. 101, 84 Am. St. Rep. 902, 85 N W. 668; Sammons v. City of Gloversville, 34 Misc. Rep. 459, 70 N. Y. Supp. 284; Bailey v. City of New York, 38 Misc. Rep. 641, 78 N. Y. Supp. 210.

who moves for such protection must show a *prima facie* case of right in himself;[135] otherwise he makes no title in himself to relief of any kind. And, further, since the time for which the injunction is sought is limited to the period necessary for deciding the disputed questions—that is, till the judgment at law or the decree in equity, as the case may be,—it is clear he must show danger of injury occurring within that interval such that the damages recoverable at law would not be an adequate remedy; which means, generally, that he must show danger of irreparable injury.[136] It is probably because of this that one may lose his right to a temporary injunction by delay in a shorter time than will bar him from procuring a permanent injunction;[137] by his delay he shows that he himself did not consider his damage so serious as to require emergency protection. For the same reason, the injunction is denied if the defendant denies all intention to do the acts which the plaintiff alleges will constitute the nuisance

135 Hilton v. Earl of Granville, 1 Craig & P. 283, 292; Catlin v. Valentine, 9 Paige, 575, 38 Am. Dec. 567; Peck v. Elder, 3 Sandf. 126.

136 Earl of Ripon v. Hobart, 3 Mylne & K. 169, Cooper *temp.* Brougham, 333, 343; Reyburn v. Sawyer, 128 N. C. 8, 37 S. E. 954; Chalk v. Wyott, 3 Mer. 688; Mohawk Bridge Co. v. Utica etc. R. R., 6 Paige, 554; Manhattan etc. Co. v. Barker, 7 Rob. (N. Y.) 523; Wilson v. Eagleson (Idaho), 71 Pac. 613; Eden v. Firth, 1 H. & M. 673; Dana v. Valentine, 5 Met. 8. Although no case has been found repudiating or stating any different principle than this, there is, perhaps, a tendency not to inquire strictly whether the injury likely to happen before the trial or hearing will be irreparable or not. See the following cases: Attorney-General v. Steward, 20 N. J. Eq. 415; Wilsey v. Callanan, 66 Hun, 629, 21 N. Y. Supp. 165; Dimon v. Shewan, 34 Misc. Rep. 72, 69 N. Y. Supp. 402; City of Wilmington v. Addicks (Del. Ch.), 47 Atl. 366.

137 Attorney-General v. Sheffield etc. Co., 3 De Gex, M. & G 304; Hilton v. Earl of Granville, 1 Craig & P. 283, 292, 293; Turner v. Mirfield, 34 Beav. 390; Carlisle v. Cooper, 21 N. J. Eq. 576, 591.

complained of,[138] though it does not apply if he simply denies that they will amount to a nuisance, that being simply his opinion.[139] It has already been suggested that since temporary injunctions must be granted while the rights of the parties are yet undetermined, and hence, whichever course the court may pursue, a wrong may result,—from granting an injunction against a defendant whose defense may prove good, or from refusing it to a plaintiff who may prove to be entitled to it,—therefore the courts should take into account, on applications for such injunctions, the balance of injury likely to result from the one or the other of the two courses open, and act accordingly. In the language of a case from which quotation has been made before: "So far as the 'balance of injury' notion refers to the parties to the litigation . . . . its legitimate application is to motions for preliminary injunctions, not to final decrees. Where the question before the court is as to the propriety of stopping a business by preliminary injunction upon an *ex parte* showing, which may or may not be substantiated by further examination of the case in due course, it is very well for the chancellor to take into account the magnitude of the defendant's investment, and compare it with the character of the plaintiff's alleged injury; and if the latter appears trifling beside that which would result from the impairment of the former, he may well refuse to exercise his power until more fully advised,"[140] and although, as has been seen, all the courts do not agree in limiting

138 Levy v. Rosenstein, 66 N. Y. Supp. 101; affirmed in 56 App. Div 618, 67 N. Y. Supp 630, Manhattan etc. Co. v. Barker (N. Y.), 7 Rob. 523. But see Coker v. Birge, 9 Ga. 425, 54 Am. Dec 347; s. c., 10 Ga 326

139 Attorney-General v. Cohoes, 6 Paige, 133, 29 Am. Dec. 755; Attorney-General v. Steward, 21 N. J. 340.

140 Evans v. Reading etc. Co., 160 Pa. St. 209, 28 Atl. 702.

the application of the doctrine as narrowly as this, yet they are all agreed that its application here is a proper one.[141] It is perhaps nothing more than the effect of this rule that occasions the frequent expressions of caution and reluctance in granting mandatory temporary injunctions.[142] To order the removal or destruction of an object which is alleged to be or to cause a nuisance is to compel the defendant generally to lose its value, and whatever labor and expense is necessary to obey the order as well. This is often obviously more than it would be merely to order him not to do something, to refrain, by the injunction; hence the balance in his favor against granting the injunction is by so much increased. This is apparently what Lord Thurlow had in mind in an early case in which he refused to order a ditch filled up on motion saying: "I do not like granting these injunctions on motion. The ditch may be a mile long."[143] Yet if the plaintiff's case is strong enough to make the balance of injury favorable to him, the courts have from the time of Lord Thurlow himself granted mandatory temporary injunctions in his behalf; the test for granting or refusing it is the same as for prohibitory injunctions, the difference is in the facts.[144]

141 Hilton v. Earl of Granville, 1 Craig & P. 283, 297, Wynstanley v Lee, 2 Swanst. 333, 335; Eden v. Firth, 1 H. & M. 573; Copper King v. Wabash Min Co., 114 Fed. 991, Daugherty etc. Co. v. Kittanning etc. Co , 178 Pa. St. 215, 35 Atl. 1111; Toyalack Township v. Monoursville etc. Ry. Co., 7 Pa. Dist. Rep. 291; Coe v. Winnipisiogee etc. Co , 37 N. H. 254; Duncan v. Hayes, 22 N. J Eq. 25; Department of Buildings, City of N. Y. v. Jones, 24 Misc. Rep. 490, 53 N. Y. Supp. 836; Amelia etc. Co. v. Tenn. etc. Co., 123 Fed. 811.

142 See Blakemore v. Glamorganshire Canal Navigation, 1 Mylne & K. 154, 185, Lord's Exrs. v Carbon etc. Co., 38 N. J. Eq. 452, 459; Herbert v. Pennsylvania R. R. Co , 43 N. J. Eq. 21, 10 Atl. 872.

143 Anon., 1 Ves. 140.

144 Mandatory temporary injunctions were allowed in the following cases of nuisance: Robinson v. Lord Byron, 1 Brown C. C. 588,

§ 536. Complete Relief.—While the only ground for coming into equity in cases of nuisance is the right to an injunction, yet a party who has established this jurisdictional right will be given all the relief, both equitable and legal in nature, to which his case entitles him. The principle on which this is done is the same that always controls the action of courts of equity, viz., to prevent the obvious hardship of compelling a party to seek relief from a single wrong in two suits prosecuted in different courts. Hence, in addition to an injunction, damages for the past nuisance will be awarded.[145] And if, after suit is brought and the jurisdiction in equity has attached, the defendant ceases to commit the nuisance, none the less the equity court will give the plaintiff damages and not turn him out of court and compel him to bring another action at law;[146] and it is

Hepburn v. Gordon, 2 Hen. & M. 345; Westminster Co. v. Clayton, 36 L. J. Ch. 476; Johnson v. Superior Court of Tulare Co, 65 Cal. 567, 4 Pac. 575; New Rice Milling Co. v. Romero, 105 La. Ann. 439, 29 South. 876. They were refused in Hagen v. Beth, 118 Cal. 330, 50 Pac 425; Village of Keeseville v. Keeseville etc. Co., 59 App. Div. 381, 69 N. Y. Supp. 249; People v. People's etc. Co., 32 Misc. Rep. 478, 66 N. Y. Supp. 529, Anon., 1 Ves. 140; Blakemore v. Glamorganshire Canal Navigation, 1 Mylne & K. 154. See, further, on the subject of preliminary mandatory injunction, *post*, Vol. II, chapter XXX.

145 Roberts v. Vest, 126 Ala. 355, 28 South. 412; Platt v. City of Waterbury, 72 Conn. 531, 77 Am. St. Rep. 335, 45 Atl. 154, 48 L. R. A. 691; Coe v. Winnipisiogee etc Co., 37 N. H. 254; Lonsdale v. City of Woonsocket, 25 R. I. 428, 56 Atl. 448; Keppel v. Lehigh etc. Co., 9 Pa. Dist. Rep. 219; Richi v. Chattanooga etc. Co., 105 Tenn. 651, 58 S. W. 646; Davis v. Lambertson, 56 Barb. 480; Seaman v Lee, 10 Hun, 607; Rothery v. New York Rubber Co., 24 Hun, 172; Baker v. McDaniel, 178 Mo. 447, 77 S. W. 531. *Contra,* Miner v. Nichols, 24 R. I. 199, 52 Atl. 893. See, also, Pom. Eq Jur., § 237.

146 Smith v. Ingersoll etc. Co., 7 Misc. Rep. 374, 27 N. Y. Supp. 907; Moon v. Nat. etc Co. of Am., 31 Misc. Rep. 631, 66 N. Y Supp. 33; Whaley v. City of New York, 83 App. Div. 6, 81 N. Y Supp 1043, McCarthy v. Gaston Ridge Mill & M Co., 144 Cal 542, 78 Pac. 7. Of course damages will not be allowed if the plaintiff's right to an injunction at the time of filing his bill is not established.

sometimes held that the injunction also will issue even in this case.[147]

§ 537. **Estoppel, Acquiescence, Laches.**—These subjects require no special treatment here, being adequately discussed elsewhere.[148] An important distinction common to all cases in which an injunction is sought in aid of a legal right is well brought out in the following quotation from a case in which the maintenance and operation of an elevated street railroad adjacent to the plaintiff's property was sought to be enjoined: "The defendants, failing to establish the bar of the statute of limitations, still insist that the affiliated principle of acquiescence constitutes a defense to the action. There is no foundation in the case for a claim that the plaintiff's conduct amounted to an estoppel, and, indeed, the claim is not seriously urged by the appellants. It is obvious that such conduct has never led the defendants into a line of action which they would not otherwise have pursued, or encouraged them to expend money or make improvements by reason of their reliance upon the alleged inaction or acquiescence of the plaintiff. They inaugurated their enterprise in the face of persistent opposition by the plaintiff and other abutting owners, and carried it to completion while earnest efforts were being made to prevent them. The

Rosenheimer v. Standard etc. Co., 39 App. Div. 482, 57 N. Y. Supp. 330.

147 Dean etc. Chester v. Smelting Corp, 85 L T. 67. But see Barber v. Penley, [1893] 2 Ch. 447; Carlin v. Wolff (Mo.), 51 S. W. 679. See *contra*, Perry v. Howe Co-op. Creamery Co. (Iowa), 101 N. W. 150 (citing Pom. Eq. Jur., § 1357) In Carlisle v. Cooper, 21 N. J. Eq. 576, the defendant partially abated the nuisance after the bill was filed and then insisted that the injunction should be refused because the legal remedy was now adequate, but the point was not allowed.

148 See 2 Pom. Eq Jur., §§ 816-821; *ante*, chapter I.

case is entirely destitute of proof showing the existence of any elements of estoppel, and the defendants are, therefore, driven to rely, in this respect upon the mere inaction of the plaintiff to prosecute his claim. But this question, we also think, is governed by authority equally conclusive with that relating to the statute of limitations. The doctrine of acquiescence as a defense to an equity action has been generally limited here to those of an equitable nature exclusively, or to cases where the legal right has expired, or the party has lost his right of property by prescription or adverse possession. Whatever may be the rule in other states, it can be said that here no period of inaction merely has been held sufficient to justify a nuisance or trespass, unless it has continued for such length of time as will authorize the presumption of a grant. The principle that so long as the legal right exists the owner is entitled to maintain his action in equity to restrain violations of this right has been uniformly applied in this court."[149]

149 Per Ruger, Ch. J., in Galway v. Metropolitan etc. Co., 128 N. Y. 132, 28 N. E 479, 13 L. R. A. 788. To the same effect are Campbell v. Seaman, 63 N. Y. 568, 20 Am. Rep. 567, affirming 2 Thomp. & C. 231; Burden v. Stein, 27 Ala. 104, 62 Am. Dec. 758; Carlisle v. Cooper, 21 N. J. Eq. 576; 2 Pom. Eq. Jur., § 817, at note 2. See Beekman v. Third Ave. etc. Co., 13 App. Div. 279, 43 N. Y. Supp 174; Heilman v. Lebanon etc. Co., 175 Pa. St. 188, 34 Atl. 647. The following cases contain discussions of such estoppel and acquiescence as will bar a plaintiff's right to enjoin nuisances: Priewe v. Wisconsin etc. Co., 103 Wis. 537, 74 Am. St Rep. 904, 79 N. W. 780; Herr v. Kentucky etc. Asylum, 22 Ky. Law Rep. 1722; Fisk v. City of Hartford, 70 Conn. 720, 66 Am. St. Rep. 147, 40 Atl. 906; Clifton Iron Co. v. Dye, 87 Ala. 468, 6 South. 192, Sheldon v. Rockwell, 9 Wis. 166, 76 Am. Dec. 265; Townsend v. Epstein, 93 Md. 537, 86 Am St. Rep. 441, 49 Atl. 629, 52 L. R. A. 409; Stowell v. Tucker, 7 Idaho, 312, 62 Pac. 1033; City of Leavenworth v. Douglass, 59 Kan. 416, 53 Pac. 123; Pennsylvania etc. Co. v. Montgomery etc Ry., 167 Pa. St. 62, 46 Am. St. Rep. 659, 31 Atl. 468, 36 Wkly. Not. Cas. 153, 27 L. R. A. 766; McKee v. City of Grand Rapids (Mich.), 100 N. W. 580.

§ 538. **Parties.**—The parties who have a sufficient interest to enjoin a nuisance are, in general, those who sustain legal injury. A landlord may do so if the nuisance is one which will permanently damage the reversion;[150] not if it is one that will not do so, and is likely to terminate before the tenancy ends.[151] A tenant may also procure an injunction even when his tenancy is very brief or shortly to end,[152] though there are intimations that he must join the reversioner as a co-plaintiff.[153] A town has been held entitled to maintain suit against an obstruction of a highway because of its liability to an action for damages by any person injured by the obstruction.[154] On the other hand, a

150 Peck v. Elder, 3 Sandf. 126; Faulkenbury v. Wells, 28 Tex. Civ. App. 621, 68 S. W. 327; Shelfer v. London etc. Co., [1895] L. R. 1 Ch. D. 287. But see Goodall v. Crofton, 33 Ohio St. 271, 31 Am. Rep. 535.

151 Jones v. Chappel, L. R. 20 Eq. 539; Broder v. Saillard, L. R. 2 Ch. D. 692; Cooper v. Crabtree, L. R. 20 Ch. D. 589; Matt v. Shoolbred, L. R. 20 Eq 22.

152 Boston Ferrule Co. v. Hills, 159 Mass 147, 34 N. E. 85, 20 L. R. A. 844; Hill v. Schneider, 13 App. Div. 299, 4 N. Y. Ann. Cas. 70, 43 N. Y. Supp. 1 (tenancy to expire in less than a year); Broder v. Saillard, L. R. 2 Ch. D. 692; Shelfer v. London etc. Co., [1895] 1 Ch. D. 287; Inchbald v. Robinson, L. R. 4 Ch. 388 (tenant from year to year); Jones v. Chappel, L. R. 20 Eq. 539 (tenant from week to week may enjoin—*dictum*); Bly v. Edison etc. Co., 172 N. Y. 1, 64 N. E. 745, 58 L. R. A. 500. See McNulty v. Mt. Morris etc. Co, 172 N. Y. 410, 65 N. E. 196, in which a tenant whose term expired pending suit was denied an injunction.

153 Broder v. Saillard, L. R. 2 Ch. D. 692; Jones v. Chappel, L. R. 20 Eq. 539.

154 Town of Burlington v. Schwarzman, 52 Conn. 181, 52 Am. Rep. 571; Waukesha v. Village of Waukesha, 83 Wis. 475, 53 N W. 675; Pittsburgh v. Epping etc. Co., 194 Pa. St. 318, 45 Atl. 129. See, also, Needham v. New York etc. R. R., 152 Mass. 61, 25 N. E. 20; Coast etc. Co. v. Borough of Spring Lake, 56 N. J. Eq 615, 51 L. R. A. 657, 36 Atl. 21; Webb v. City of Demopolis (Ala.), 13 South. 289; Tp. of Plymouth v. Chestnut Hill etc. Co., 168 Pa. St. 181, 32 Atl. 19; Woodbridge Tp. v. Raritan etc. Co., 64 N. J. Eq. 169, 53 Atl. 175.

county has been enjoined from allowing a nuisance to continue because the remedy by mandamus was inadequate;[155] and a landowner from permitting a public nuisance to continue on his land, though he did not cause it himself.[156] It has also been held that a grantee of one who has been enjoined from a nuisance connected with the use of the land, is bound by the injunction, though not a party to the suit.[157] That the person committing the nuisance is a tenant, is, of course, no answer to a bill against him,[158] and the lessor may also in such case be enjoined if he threatens to continue the nuisance after the termination of the tenancy.[159]

§ 539. **Reasonable Use not a Defense.**—In this and the two succeeding paragraphs the questions involved are purely legal, having to do with the substantive law of nuisance rather than the equitable remedy. They will require, therefore, no more than a bare statement of the law, with a citation of a few cases in which it has been applied in suits for injunction. It is no defense to an action at law or a bill for an injunction against a nuisance for the defendant to say he is conducting himself reasonably in doing the thing which is complained of. "The application of principle governing the jurisdiction of the court in cases of nuisance does not depend on the question whether the defendant is using his own reasonably or otherwise. The real ques-

155 Lefrois v. Monroe County, 24 App. Div. 421, 48 N. Y. Supp. 519.

156 Attorney-General v. Tod Headley, [1897] 1 Ch. 560.

157 Ahlers v. Thomas, 24 Nev. 407, 77 Am. St. Rep. 820, 56 Pac. 93.

158 Broder v. Saillard, L. R. 2 Ch. D. 692; Attorney-General v. Props. etc. Canal, L. R. 2 Eq. 71.

159 Attorney-General v. Props. etc. Canal, L. R. 2 Eq. 71.

tion is, does he injure his neighbor?'"[160] It is perhaps accurate to say, therefore, that there can be no such thing as a nuisance resulting from reasonable conduct. Nuisance is not based on any rule of negligent or willfully wrongful conduct, but rather on rules of policy which do not allow a person to do those acts which constitute nuisances. If he does so, he is not acting reasonably.[161]

§ 540. **Nor the Fact that Other Causes Contribute.**—Nor is it a defense that other persons or other causes than the defendant's wrongful acts contribute to the nuisance. If the plaintiff wishes to submit to certain nuisances, that is no reason for allowing the defendant to impose one on him against his will.[162] And if the nuisance results from the combined effect of separate acts of the defendant and others, that also is no defense to a bill for an injunction.[163]

160 Reinhardt v. Mentasti, L. R. 42 Ch. D. 685.

161 Attorney-General v. Cole, [1901] 1 Ch. D 205; Broder v. Saillard, L. R. 2 Ch. D. 692; Callanan v. Gilman, 107 N. Y. 360, 1 Am. St. Rep. 831, 14 N. E. 264; Filson v. Crawford, 23 N. Y. St. Rep 355, 5 N. Y. Supp. 882; Susquehanna etc. Co. v. Malone, 73 Md. 268, 25 Am. St. Rep. 595, 20 Atl. 900, 9 L. R. A. 737 (action at law). *Contra*, Sanders-Clark v. Grosvenor etc., [1900] 2 Ch. D. 373

162 Richards v. Daugherty, 133 Ala. 569, 31 South. 934; Stone v. Roscommon etc. Co., 59 Mich. 24, 26 N. W. 216; Weston Paper Co. v. Pope, 155 Ind. 394, 57 N. E. 719, 56 L. R A. 899; Butler v. Village of White Plains, 59 App. Div. 30, 69 N. Y. Supp. 193; Indianapolis etc. Co. v. American etc. Co., 57 Fed. 1000, affirming 53 Fed. 970; Richmond etc. Co. v. Atlantic etc. Co., 10 R. I. 106, 14 Am. Rep. 658; Jacobson v. Van Boening, 48 Neb. 80, 48 Am. St. Rep. 684, 66 N W. 993, 32 L. R. A. 229; Pittsburg etc. Co. v. Town of Crothersville, 159 Ind. 330, 64 N. E. 914. But see Mackey-Smith v. Crawford, 56 App. Div. 136, 67 N. Y. Supp. 541.

163 Lamberton v. Mellish, [1894] L. R. 3 Ch. D. 163; People v. Gold Run etc. Co , 66 Cal. 138, 56 Am. Rep. 80, 4 Pac. 1152. *Contra*, West etc. Co. v. Moroni etc. Co., 21 Utah, 229, 61 Pac. 16. See Hillman v. Newington, 57 Cal. 56.

§ 541. **Legalized Nuisances.**—Acts which at common law are nuisances may be legalized by statute, if such legislation does not amount to the taking or damaging of property forbidden by constitutional provisions.[164] The effect of such statutes is to take away the wrongful character of the acts legalized; they are no longer torts. and hence, the remedy by injunction against them, of course, ceases.[165]

§ 542. **Public Nuisances.**—Public nuisances, as a subject of equity jurisdiction, require only a brief discussion in this place, because the equitable doctrines applicable are essentially the same as those applied to private nuisances; and cases to support the text of this chapter have been drawn from both classes without distinction. "It is on the ground of injury to property that the jurisdiction of this court must rest; and taking it to rest upon that ground, the only distinction which seems to me to exist between cases of public nuisance and private nuisance is this,—that in cases of private nuisance the injury is to individual property, and in cases of public nuisance the injury is to the property of mankind. I think, therefore, that the same principle must govern the question as to the interference of the court, whether the case be one of public or of private nuisance. What, then, is the principle by which the court ought to be governed? I take it to be this: whether the extent of the damage and injury be

164 See Woodruff v. N. Bloomfield etc. Co., 9 Saw. 441, 18 Fed. 753; Le Clercq v. Trustees of Gallipolis, 7 Ohio, 217, 28 Am. Dec. 641.

165 Jordeson v. Sutton etc. Co., [1898] 2 Ch. D. 614, [1899] 2 Ch. 218; Davis v. Mayor of New York, 14 N. Y. (4 Kern) 506, 67 Am. Dec 186; Hoey v. Gilroy, 129 N. Y. 132, 29 N. E. 85; Sayre v. Mayor etc. of Newark, 60 N. J. Eq. 361, 83 Am. St. Rep. 629, 45 Atl. 985; Grey (Attorney-General) v. Mayor etc. of Patterson, 60 N. J. Eq 385, 83 Am. St. Rep. 642, 45 Atl. 994; McWethy v. Aurora etc. Co., 202 Ill. 218, 67 N. E. 9.

such that the law will not afford an adequate remedy."[166] Here, too, as in cases of private nuisance, the chief causes of inadequacy lie in the fact that the injury is irreparable or will occasion a multiplicity of suits.[167] If there is a substantial dispute as to fact or law, and the question is in doubt, a trial at law will be required before equity will intervene.[168] A purely threatened public nuisance may be enjoined, if it is shown to be imminent and serious.[169] Damage will be required or not according as it is, or is not, necessary to

166 Per Turner, L. J., in Attorney-General v. Sheffield etc. Co., 3 De Gex, M. & G. 304.

167 Suits on behalf of the public: Attorney-General v. Sheffield etc. Co., *supra;* Attorney-General v. Cambridge etc. Co., 17 Week. Rep. 145, 4 Ch. App. 71; Attorney-General v. Gee, L. R. 10 Eq. 131; Town of Newcastle v. Haywood, 67 N. H. 178, 37 Atl. 1040; State v. Paterson, 14 Tex. Civ. App. 465, 37 S. W. 478; State v. Mayor etc. of Mobile, 5 Port. (Ala) 279, 30 Am. Dec. 564. Suits by private individuals: Kenney v. Consumers' etc Co., 142 Mass. 417, 8 N. E. 138; Attorney-General v Sheffield etc. Co., 3 De Gex, M. & G. 304; Allen v. Board of Freeholders, 13 N. J. Eq. 68; Whaley v Wilson, 112 Ala. 627, 20 South. 922, citing 4 Pom. Eq. Jur. § 1349; Milhau v. Sharp, 27 N. Y. 611, 84 Am. Dec. 314, Georgia Chemical etc. Co. v. Colquitt, 72 Ga. 172; Bigelow v. Hartford Bridge Co., 14 Conn. 565, 579, 36 Am. Dec. 502; Harlan etc. Co v. Paschall, 5 Del. Ch. 435; Van Wegenen v. Cooney, 45 N. J. Eq. 24, 16 Atl. 689. In Milhau v. Sharp, *supra,* the court said: "To entitle a plaintiff to relief by injunction who is sustaining, or about to sustain a peculiar injury from a public nuisance, it is also necessary that the injury should be such as cannot be well or adequately compensated in damages at law or such as from its continuance or permanent mischief must occasion a constantly recurring grievance which cannot be otherwise prevented, but by injunction." For a fuller discussion of the grounds of equity jurisdiction, see *ante,* §§ 514ff.

168 Mohawk etc. Co. v. Utica etc. Co., 6 Paige, 554; Attorney-General v. Cleaver, 18 Ves. 217; Earl of Ripon v. Hobart, 3 Mylne & K. 169; Attorney-General v. Hunter, 1 Dev. Eq. (16 N. C) 12. See *ante,* §§ 519-522.

169 Attorney-General v. Steward, 20 N. J. Eq. (5 C. E. Green) 415; County of Yuba v. Cloke, 79 Cal. 239, 21 Pac. 740; City of Rochester v. Erickson, 46 Barb. 92. See *ante,* §§ 523-525.

maintain an action at law.[170] All public nuisances are crimes, and so, as before pointed out, the entire jurisdiction of equity over them is a denial of the contention that the mere criminality of an act precludes equitable intervention.[171] Public nuisances may be created by statute,[172] and, conversely, common-law public nuisances may be legalized by statute.[173] The balance of injury doctrine is subject to the same differences of holding as in cases of private nuisance.[174] It is gen-

170 This statement is subject to the qualifications suggested *ante*, § 526. In accordance with it are the holdings that purprestures may be enjoined, though there is no damage shown, since the state or crown has the right that its property should not be encroached upon: People v. Vanderbilt, 28 N. Y. 396, 84 Am. Dec. 351, affirming 38 Barb. 282, Attorney-General v. Cohoes Co., 6 Paige, 133, 29 Am. Dec. 755; Attorney-General v Eau Claire, 37 Wis 400; Revell v. People, 177 Ill. 468, 69 Am. St. Rep. 257, 52 N. E. 1052, 43 L. R A. 790. See Wood on Nuisances (3d ed), pp. 107-125. But for a public nuisance generally, actual damage must be proved: See People v. Mould, 37 App. Div 35, 55 N Y. Supp. 453, reversing 24 Misc. Rep. 287, 52 N. Y. Supp. 1032, and cases cited: Town of Newcastle v. Haywood, 67 N. H. 178, 37 Atl. 1040. See, however, Attorney-General v. Shrewsbury etc. Co., L R. 21 Ch. D. 752.

171 See *ante*, § 527, and note 9. On the general subject, see *ante*, chapter XXI.

172 Carleton v. Rugg, 149 Mass. 550, 14 Am. St. Rep. 446, 22 N. E 55, 5 L. R A. 193 (saloon); State v. Crawford, 28 Kan. 726, 42 Am. Rep. 182 (saloon); State v. Noyes, 30 N. H. 279 (bowling-alley); State v. Marston, 64 N. H. 603, 15 Atl. 222 (saloon); State v. Saunders, 66 N. H. 39, 25 Atl. 588, 18 L. R. A. 646 (saloon); State v. Lawler, 85 Iowa, 564, 52 N. W. 490 (saloon); State v. Seeverson, 88 Iowa, 714, 54 N. W. 347 (saloon); State v. Greenway, 92 Iowa, 472, 61 N. W. 239 (saloon), State v. Van Vliet, 92 Iowa, 476, 61 N. W. 241 (saloon); Carter v. Steyer, 93 Iowa, 533, 61 N. W. 956; Detroit etc. Co. v. Eldredge, 109 Mich. 371, 67 N. W. 531 (construction of road from other material than that required by statute) See *ante*, § 527, and note 101.

173 Davis v. Mayor etc. N. Y ,14 N. Y. (4 Kern.) 506, 67 Am. Dec. 186; Hocy v. Gilroy, 129 N. Y. 132, 29 N E. 85; Grey, Attorney-General, v. City of Paterson, 60 N. J. Eq. 385, 83 Am. St. Rep. 642, 45 Atl. 995, 48 L. R. A. 717. See *ante*, § 541.

174 That it will be applied: Grey, Attorney-General, v. City of

erally held that a plaintiff may enjoin a nuisance even though he himself easily could avoid or remove it.[175] The relief given is adjusted to the needs of the particular case; though usually prohibitive, it may be by mandatory injunction;[176] it will save to the defendant the right to continue the act complained of in a harmless way if such thing is possible;[177] temporary injunctions are applied here as elsewhere, subject to the general rules governing their use;[178] and complete relief, legal as well as equitable, will be given.[179] Inasmuch as a prescriptive right to commit a nuisance as against the public cannot arise, the public cannot be precluded by laches at all from procuring an injunction.[180] The parties who may enjoin a public nuisance are, first, the public, through the proper public offi-

Paterson, 60 N. J. Eq. 385, 83 Am. St. Rep. 642, 45 Atl. 995, 48 L. R. A. 717. That it will not be applied, see the cases cited, *ante*, § 531, note 117.

175 Town of Burlington v. Schwarzman, 52 Conn. 181, 52 Am. Rep. 571; Martin v. Marks, 154 Ind. 549, 57 N E. 249.

176 Pascagoula etc Co. v. Dixon, 77 Miss. 587 78 Am St. Rep. 537, 28 South. 724. See, also, cases cited *ante*, § 543, note 125.

177 Earl of Ripon v. Hobart, 3 Mylne & K. 169; Winchell v. City of Waukesha, 110 Wis. 101, 84 Am. St Rep. 902, 85 N. W. 668.

178 Earl of Ripon v. Hobart, 3 Mylne & K 169, Cooper *temp.* Brougham, 333; Attorney-General v. Steward, 20 N. J. Eq. 415; City of Wilmington v. Addicks (Del. Ch.), 47 Atl. 366; Attorney-General v. Sheffield etc. Co., 3 De Gex, M. & G. 304, Attorney-General v. Cohoes, 6 Paige, 133, 29 Am. Dec. 755, Attorney-General v. Steward, 21 N. J. Eq. 340. See *ante*, § 535

179 Richi v. Chattanooga etc. Co., 105 Tenn. 651, 58 S. W. 646.

180 People v. Gold Run etc Co, 66 Cal 138, 56 Am Rep. 80, 4 Pac. 1152. And it is held that the same doctrine applies to suits by private individuals who are specially damaged: Mills v. Hall, 9 Wend 315, 24 Am. Dec. 160; Woodruff v N Bloomfield etc. Co., 9 Saw. 513, 18 Fed 753; Bowen v. Wendt, 103 Cal 236, 37 Pac. 149. See Clerk & Lindsell, *The Law of Torts*, pp. 349, 350.

cial;[181] second, private parties. While the public which acts is generally the state, yet by virtue of legislative delegation, often implied, it may be a municipality that files the information.[182] Public nuisances may also be enjoined by private individuals who suffer a special damage.[183]

181 "In the case of a public nuisance, the remedy at law is indictment; the remedy in equity, is information at the suit of the attorney-general": Per Cranworth, V. C., in Soltau v. De Held, 2 Sim, N. S., 133. No citation of cases is necessary to sustain so familiar a rule.

182 Town of Neshkoro v. Nest, 85 Wis. 126, 55 N. W. 176; Clayton County v. Herwig, 100 Iowa, 631, 69 N. W. 1035, Village of Buffalo v Harling, 50 Minn. 551, 52 N. W. 931; City of Huron v. Bank of Volga, 8 S. Dak. 449, 66 N. W. 815; City of Mt Clemens v. Mt. Clemens etc. Co., 8 Det. Leg. N. 282, 127 Mich. 115, 86 N. W 537; People v. Equity etc. Co, 141 N. Y. 232, 36 N. E. 194; Village of Pewaukee v. Savoy, 103 Wis 271, 79 N. W. 436, 50 L. R A. 836 In Village of Oxford v. Willoughby (N. Y.), 73 N. E. 677, a village was allowed to maintain the action. The right of towns to enjoin public nuisances is sometimes put upon the ground that their special interest entitles them to maintain action because of special damage to them. See *supra*, § 538, note 154. Other cases of injunction against public nuisances at the suit of the public are: Pennsylvania v. Wheeling etc. Co, 13 How 518, 14 L. ed. 249; Attorney-General v. Brighton, [1900] 1 Ch 276, Morris etc. Co. v. Greenville (N. J.), 46 Atl. 638; Streeter v. Stalnaker, 61 Neb. 205, 85 N. W. 47, People v. Third Ave. R. R, 45 Barb. 68; United States v. Debs, 64 Fed. 724; State v. Meek, 112 Iowa, 338, 84 Am St. Rep. 342, 84 N. W. 3, 51 L. R. A. 414; Coosaw Min. Co. v. South Carolina, 144 U. S. 564, 12 Sup. Ct. 689, 36 L. ed. 537, United States v. N. Bloomfield etc. Co, 53 Fed. 625, Berks County v. Reading City etc. Co., 167 Pa. St. 102, 31 Atl. 474, 36 Wkly. Not. Cas. 173, City of Detroit v. Detroit City etc. Co., 56 Fed. 867; Grey v. New York etc. Co., 56 N. J. Eq. 463, 40 Atl. 21; Allegheny City v. Millville etc. Co., 159 Pa. St 411, 28 Atl. 202.

183 Injunctions were allowed on this ground in the following cases:

For obstruction of streets and highways: Savannah etc. Co. v. Shiels, 33 Ga. 601; Hill v. Hoffman (Tenn. Ch. App.), 58 S. W. 929, Pettibone v. Hamilton, 40 Wis. 402; Martin v. Marks, 154 Ind. 549, 57 N. E 249; Green v. Oakes, 17 Ill. 249; Ewell v. Greenwood, 26 Iowa, 377; Smith v. Mitchell, 21 Wash. 586, 75 Am. St. Rep 858, 58 Pac. 667; Flynn v. Taylor, 127 N. Y. 596, 28 N. E. 418, 14 L. R. A. 556;

De Witt v. Van Schoyk, 110 N. Y. 7, 6 Am. St. Rep. 342, 17 N. E 425, affirming 35 Hun, 103; Stevenson v. Pucci, 32 Misc. Rep. 464, 66 N. Y. Supp. 712, Cabbell v. Williams, 127 Ala. 320, 28 South. 405; Newcome v Crews, 98 Ky. 339, 32 S. W. 947, Brauer v. Baltimore etc. Co., 99 Md 367, 58 Atl. 21, Thompson v. Maloney, 199 Ill. 276, 93 Am St. Rep 183, 65 N. E 237; Cereghino v. Or. etc. Co., 26 Utah, 467, 99 Am. St. Rep. 843, 73 Pac. 634; Pence v. Bryant, 54 W. Va. 263, 46 S. E. 275, Illinois Cent. etc Co v. Thomas, 75 Miss. 54, 21 South. 601, Central etc. Co. v. Metropolitan etc. Co, 16 App. Div. 229, 44 N. Y. Supp. 752; Haunum v. Media etc. Co., 200 Pa. St. 44, 49 Atl. 789; Irvine v. Atlantic etc Co., 42 N. Y. Supp. 1103, City etc. of Montgomery v. Parker, 114 Ala. 118, 62 Am. St. Rep. 95, 21 South. 452; Longworth v. Sedevic, 165 Mo. 221, 65 S. W. 260, Sherlock v. Kansas etc. Co, 142 Mo. 172, 64 Am. St. Rep. 551, 43 S W. 629; Kalteyer v. Sullivan, 18 Tex Civ. App. 488, 46 S W. 288, Pittsburgh etc. Co. v. Point Bridge Co, 165 Pa. St. 37, 30 Atl. 511, 35 Wkly. Not. Cas. 393, 26 L R. A. 323. See, also, Dean v. Ann Arbor R. R. (Mich.), 100 N. W. 773; Forbes v. City of Detroit (Mich.), 102 N. W. 740 (encroachment on street).

For obstruction of navigable waters: Milnor v. N. G. R. Co., 70 U. S (3 Wall) 782, 16 L. ed 1; Morris v Graham, 16 Wash. 343, 58 Am St. Rep. 33, 47 Pac 752; Mayor etc of New York v. Baumberger, 7 Rob. (N. Y.) 219, Walker v. Sheperdson, 2 Wis. 384, 60 Am. Dec 423; Reyburn v. Sawyer, 135 N C. 328, 102 Am. St. Rep. 555, 47 S. E. 761.

For pollution of water: Green v. Nunnemacher, 36 Wis. 50.

For flowage of land: Whitfield v. Rogers, 26 Miss. 84, 59 Am. Dec. 244.

For keeping a bawdy-house; Cranford v. Tyrrell, 128 N. Y. 341, 28 N. E. 514, affirming 59 Hun, 618, 13 N. Y. Supp. 951; Dempsie v. Darling (Wash.), 81 Pac. 152.

For interference with common right of fishery. Cherry Point Fish Co. v. Nelson, 25 Wash. 558, 7 Pac. 55

For creating a stench: Sayre v. Mayor etc of Newark, 58 N. J Eq. 136, 42 Atl. 1068, Wilcox v. Henry (Wash.), 77 Pac. 1055 (odors from slaughter-house).

Statutory nuisance: Kaufman v. Stein, 138 Ind. 49, 46 Am. St. Rep. 368, 37 N. E. 333 (wooden building within fire limits). Compare Lang v. Merwin (Me.), 59 Atl. 1021 (injunction against gambling place, at suit of twenty voters, under statute).

Beer garden: Tron v. Lewis, 31 Ind. App. 178, 66 N. E. 490.

Sunday ball games: Gilbaugh v. West etc. Co., 64 N. J. Eq. 27, 53 Atl. 289; Seastream v. New Jersey Exhibition Co. (N. J. Eq.), 58 Atl 532.

In the following cases injunctions were refused because the plaintiff failed to show special damage: Taylor v. Portsmouth etc. Co., 91 Me. 193, 64 Am. St. Rep. 216, 39 Atl. 560, Buck etc. Co. v. Lehigh etc. Co., 50 Pa. St. 91, 88 Am. Dec. 534; Pearson v. Allen, 151 Mass. 79, 21 Am. St. Rep 426, 23 N E. 731; Schall v. Nusbaum, 56 Md. 512; Osborne v. Brooklyn etc Co., 5 Blatchf. 366, Currier v. Davis, 68 N. H. 596, 41 Atl. 239, Gulick v. Fisher, 92 Md. 353, 48 Atl 375, Van Wegenen v. Cooney, 45 N. J. Eq. 24, 16 Atl. 689; Black v. Philadelphia etc. Co., 58 Pa St 249; Bosworth v. Normon, 14 R I. 521, Georgetown v. Alexandria etc. Co., 12 Pet. 91, 9 L. ed. 1012, Bigelow v. Hartford etc. Co., 14 Conn 565, 36 Am. Dec. 502, O'Brien v. Harris, 105 Ga. 732, 31 S. E. 745; Coast Line R. R. v. Cohen, 50 Ga. 451; Hay v. Weber, 79 Wis 587, 24 Am. St. Rep. 737, 48 N. W. 859; Hartshorn v. South Reading, 3 Allen, 501, Pittsburg etc. Co v. Cheevers, 149 Ill. 430, 37 N E. 49, 24 L. R. A. 156; Manufacturers etc. Co. v. Indiana etc. Co, 155 Ind. 566, 58 N. E. 851; Rhymer v. Fretz, 206 Pa. St. 230, 98 Am. St. Rep. 777, 55 Atl 959; Parsons v. Hunt (Tex. Civ. App.), 81 S. W. 120. See, also, Dennis v. Mobile & M. R. Co, 137 Ala. 649, 97 Am. St. Rep. 69, 35 South. 30 (citing Pom. Eq. Jur., §§ 1347, 1349, 1350); George v. Peckham (Neb.), 103 N. W. 664.

In Whitfield v. Rogers, 26 Miss. (4 Cush.) 84, 59 Am. Dec. 244, it is said that one who suffers from a public nuisance in common with others may enjoin it without showing special damage And the same thing was held under statutes in Milhiser v. Willard, 96 Iowa, 327, 65 N. W. 325; Carleton v. Rugg, 149 Mass. 550, 14 Am. St. Rep. 446, 22 N. E 55, 5 L. R. A. 193.

On the general subject of public nuisances, see, also, *ante*, chapter XXI.

CPSIA information can be obtained
at www.ICGtesting.com
Printed in the USA
LVHW052221281220
675217LV00041B/664

9 780342 608614